4th Edition

Business Statistics

Norean R. Sharpe
St. John's University

Richard D. De Veaux
Williams College

Paul F. Velleman
Cornell University

*With Contributions by David Bock
and Special Contributor Eric M. Eisenstein*

 Pearson

Director, Portfolio Management: Deirdre Lynch
Senior Portfolio Management Analyst: Patrick Barbera
Editorial Assistant: Morgan Danna
Managing Producer: Scott Disanno
Content Producer: Peggy McMahon
Senior Publishing Services Analyst: Joe Vetere
Manager, Quality Control: Mary Durnwald
Manager, Content Development: Robert Carroll
Senior Producer: Aimee Thorne

Product Marketing Analyst: Kaylee Carlson
Marketing Support Assistant: Shannon McCormack
Manager, Rights/Permissions Gina Cheselka
Project Management, Rights & Permissions Editing: SPi Global
Text and Cover Design, Illustrations, Composition: Cenveo® Publisher Services
Cover Images: (Mobile Phone and Tablet Computer Screens) © Can Yesil/ Shutterstock; (Business people meeting in modern office) © Johnny-Greig/E+/Getty Images

Credits and acknowledgments borrowed from other sources and reproduced, with permission, in this textbook appear on the appropriate page within text or in Appendix C, which is hereby made part of this copyright page.

Library of Congress Cataloging-in-Publication Data

Names: Sharpe, Norean Radke, author. | De Veaux, Richard D., author. | Velleman, Paul F., 1949- author.
Title: Business statistics / Norean R. Sharpe, Georgetown University, Richard D. De Veaux, Williams College, Paul F. Velleman, Cornell University; with Contributions by David Bock and Eric Eisenstein.
Description: 4th Edition. | Boston, MA: Pearson, [2018] | Revised edition of the authors' Business statistics, [2015] | Includes index.
Identifiers: LCCN 2018019089 | ISBN 9780134705217 (student edition) | ISBN 0134705211
Subjects: LCSH: Commercial statistics.
Classification: LCC HF1017 .S467 2018 | DDC 650.01/5195—dc23 LC record available at https://lccn.loc.gov/2018019089

ISBN-10: 0-134-70521-1
ISBN-13: 978-0-134-70521-7

To my loving family for their patience and support
—Norean

To my father, whose daily stories informed me how the world
of business really worked, and to my family, for giving me
the love and support that made this book possible
—Dick

To my father, who taught me about ethical business practice by
his constant example as a small businessman and parent
—Paul

Meet the Authors

Norean R. Sharpe, Ph.D., is Dean and the Joseph H. and Maria C. Schwartz Distinguished Chair at The Peter J. Tobin College of Business at St. John's University. As the chief academic officer of the Tobin College of Business, she is responsible for the curriculum for 2500 undergraduate business majors and 600 graduate students in one of seven M.S./M.B.A. programs, all supported by more than 150 faculty and staff on the Manhattan, Queens, Staten Island, and Rome, Italy, campuses. Within the Tobin College is the Center for Enterprise Risk Management, the Applied Finance Institute, and the Global Business Stewardship Center, as well as the acclaimed School of Risk Management, Insurance, and Actuarial Science.

Dr. Sharpe is an accomplished scholar, with 30 years of teaching experience at Yale University, Bowdoin College, Babson College, and Georgetown University—and with more than 30 scholarly publications in analytics and statistics education. Her research interests include time series analysis, forecasting, analytics, and women's roles in entrepreneurship in the Middle East. Dr. Sharpe earned her B.A. from Mt. Holyoke College, her M.S. from the University of North Carolina, and her Ph.D. in Systems Engineering from the University of Virginia.

Richard D. De Veaux (Ph.D. Stanford University) is an internationally known educator, consultant, and lecturer. Dick has taught statistics at a business school (Wharton), an engineering school (Princeton), and a liberal arts college (Williams). While at Princeton, he won a Lifetime Award for Dedication and Excellence in Teaching. Since 1994, he has taught at Williams College, although he returned to Princeton for the academic year 2006–2007 as the William R. Kenan Jr. Visiting Professor of Distinguished Teaching. He is currently the C. Carlisle and Margaret Tippit Professor of Statistics at Williams College. Dick holds degrees from Princeton University in Civil Engineering and Mathematics and from Stanford University where he studied statistics with Persi Diaconis and dance with Inga Weiss. His research focuses on the analysis of large datasets and data mining in science and industry. Dick has won both the Wilcoxon and Shewell awards from the American Society for Quality. He is an elected member of the International Statistics Institute (ISI) and a Fellow of the American Statistical Association (ASA). Dick was elected Vice President of the ASA in 2018 and will serve from 2019 to 2021. Dick is also well known in industry, having consulted for such *Fortune* 500 companies as American Express, Hewlett-Packard, Alcoa, DuPont, Pillsbury, General Electric, and Chemical Bank. He was named the "Statistician of the Year" for 2008 by the Boston Chapter of the American Statistical Association. In his spare time he is an avid cyclist and swimmer, and is a frequent singer and soloist with various local choirs, including the Choeur Vittoria of Paris, France. Dick is the father of four children.

Paul F. Velleman (Ph.D. Princeton University) has an international reputation for innovative statistics education. He designed the Data Desk® software package and is also the author and designer of the award-winning ActivStats® multimedia software, for which he received the EDUCOM Medal for innovative uses of computers in teaching statistics and the ICTCM Award for Innovation in Using Technology in College Mathematics. He is the founder and CEO of Data Description, Inc. (**www.datadesk.com**), which supports both of these programs. Data Description also developed and maintains the Internet site *Data and Story Library* (DASL; **dasl.datadescription.com**), which provides all of the datasets used in this text as well as many others useful for teaching statistics, and the statistics conceptual tools at **astools.datadesk.com**. Paul coauthored (with David Hoaglin) the book *ABCs of Exploratory Data Analysis*. Paul is Emeritus Professor of Statistical Sciences, at Cornell University where he was awarded the MacIntyre Prize for Exemplary Teaching. Paul earned his M.S. and Ph.D. from Princeton University, where he studied with John Tukey. His research often focuses on statistical graphics and data analysis methods. Paul is a Fellow of the American Statistical Association and of the American Association for the Advancement of Science. He was a member of the working group that developed the GAISE 2016 guidelines for teaching statistics. Paul's experience as a professor, entrepreneur, and business leader brings a unique perspective to the book.

Richard De Veaux and Paul Velleman have authored successful books in the introductory college and AP High School market with David Bock, including *Intro Stats*, Fifth Edition (Pearson, 2018); *Stats: Modeling the World*, Fifth Edition (Pearson, 2019); and *Stats: Data and Models*, Fourth Edition (Pearson, 2016).

Special Contributor

Eric M. Eisenstein (Ph.D. Wharton School of Business) is an internationally known educator, researcher, and consultant. Eric has taught at multiple business schools, including Wharton, Cornell's Johnson School, ESADE, and Temple University's Fox School of Business. At Fox, he serves as the Director of the MS in Business Analytics in the department of Statistical Science, Director of Graduate Programs in the department of Marketing and Supply Chain Management, and Chair of the Undergraduate Program (curriculum) Committee. Eric teaches data analytics, quantitative strategy, and marketing. His research focuses on the psychology of expertise, how to improve decision making, and strategic analytics. Prior to becoming an academic, Eric worked at Mercer Management Consulting (now Oliver Wyman) where he focused on management of technology and marketing research in the financial services and telecommunications industries. His teams won the outstanding team award three times consecutively; clients invested over $30 million based on the recommendations of his teams, and the teams' strategic recommendations affected more than $10 billion in revenue and $2 billion in profits. He continues to consult and serve on the board of numerous companies and charities. Eric earned his Ph.D. in Applied Economics and an M.A. in Statistics at the Wharton School of Business, University of Pennsylvania and graduated from the Management and Technology dual degree program at the University of Pennsylvania, where he concurrently earned a B.S. in Economics from Wharton and a B.S. in Computer Systems Engineering from the School of Engineering and Applied Science. He is the proud father to three children.

Contents

Preface

The question that should motivate a business student's study of statistics should be "Even without perfect information, how can I make better decisions?"[1] As entrepreneurs and consultants, we know that in today's data-rich environment, knowledge of statistics is essential to survive and thrive in the business world. But, as educators, we've seen a disconnect between the way business statistics is traditionally taught and the way it should be used in making business decisions. In *Business Statistics*, we try to narrow the gap between theory and practice by presenting relevant statistical methods that will empower business students to make effective, data-informed decisions.

Of course, students should come away from their statistics course knowing how to think statistically and how to apply statistics methods with modern technology. But they must also be able to communicate their analyses effectively to others. When asked about statistics education, a group of CEOs from *Fortune* 500 companies recently said that although they were satisfied with the technical competence of students who had studied statistics, they found the students' ability to communicate their findings to be woefully inadequate.

Our Plan, Do, Report rubric provides a structure for solving business problems that mimics the correct application of statistics to solving real business problems. Unlike many other authors, we emphasize the often neglected thinking (Plan) and communication (Report) steps in problem solving in addition to the methodology (Do). This approach requires up-to-date, real-world examples and data. So we constantly strive to illustrate our lessons with current business issues and examples.

What's New in This Edition?

We've been delighted with the reaction to previous editions of *Business Statistics*. We've made some changes to the organization of the fourth edition to help students focus on the essentials and think about the data-rich world they will find in the workplace. And, of course, we continue to update examples and exercises so that the story we tell is always tied to the ways statistics informs modern business practice.

- **Recent data.** We teach with real data whenever possible, so we've updated data throughout the book. New examples reflect current stories in the news and recent economic and business events. When a historical dataset is especially good at illuminating a pedagogical point, we have, from time to time, chosen pedagogy over recency.

- **Improved organization.** We have retained our "data first" presentation of topics because we find that it provides students with both motivation and a foundation in real business decisions on which to build an understanding.

  - Chapters 1–4 have been streamlined to cover collecting, displaying, summarizing, and understanding data in four chapters. We find that this provides students with a solid foundation to launch their study of probability and statistics.
  - Chapters 5–7 introduce students to randomness and probability models. We've moved the discussion of probability trees and Bayes' rule into these chapters.
  - Chapters 8 and 9 cover data collection by survey and by designed experiments. New discussions here address technology-enabled sampling, online data, and Big Data. We've moved the discussion of experiments up front because of the increased importance of online testing, but we've

---

[1]Unfortunately, not the question most students are asking themselves on the first day of the course.

moved the analysis of such designs (ANOVA), which many instructors find difficult to cover in a first course, to the online Chapter 25.

- Chapters 10–15 cover inference for both proportions and means. We introduce inference by discussing proportions because most students are better acquainted with proportions reported in surveys and news stories. However, this edition ties in the discussion of means immediately so students can appreciate that the reasoning of inference is the same in a variety of contexts. We've added an optional discussion of bootstrapping. This may help students' intuition about inference as well as providing a relatively new modern method.
- Chapters 16–19 cover regression-based models for decision making.
- Chapter 20 discusses time series methods.
- Chapter 21 is a newly expanded discussion of data mining and Big Data.
- Chapters 22–24 discuss special topics that can be selected according to the needs of the course and the preferences of the instructor.

- **Streamlined design.** Our goal has always been a readable text. This edition sports a new design that clarifies the purpose of each text element. The major theme of each chapter is linear and easy to follow without distraction. Supporting material is clearly boxed and shaded, so students know where to focus their study efforts.

- **Enhanced Technology Help.** We've updated Technology Help (now called Tech Support) in almost every chapter.

- **Updated examples to reflect the changing world.** The time since our last revision has seen marked changes in the U.S. and world economies. This has required us to update many of our examples. Our selection of course content reflects the wisdom of the GAISE2016 report adopted by the American Statistical Association as a standard for introductory statistics teaching. Our "In Practice" elements have all been re-structured to reflect real-world business challenges. The result is a text that is realistic and useful.

- **Increased focus on core material.** Statistics in practice means making smart decisions based on data. Students need to know the methods, how to apply them, and the assumptions and conditions that make them work. We've tightened our discussions to get students there as quickly as possible, focusing increasingly on the central ideas and core material.

Our Approach

Statistical Thinking

For all of our improvements, examples, and updates in this edition of *Business Statistics* we haven't lost sight of our original mission—writing a modern business statistics text that addresses the importance of *statistical thinking* in making business decisions and that acknowledges how Statistics is actually used in business.

Statistics is practiced with technology, and this insight informs everything from our choice of forms for equations (favoring intuitive forms over calculation forms) to our extensive use of real data. But most important, understanding the value of technology allows us to focus on teaching statistical thinking rather than calculation. The questions that motivate each of our hundreds of examples are not "How do you find the answer?" but "How do you think about the answer?"; "How does it help you make a better decision?"; and "How can you best communicate your decision?" Our redesigned "In Practice" elements in each chapter have been recast as conversations between managers and analysts to emphasize the business relevance of each method and its importance in making good business decisions.

Our focus on statistical thinking ties the chapters of the book together. An introductory Business Statistics course covers an overwhelming number of new terms, concepts, and methods, and it is vital that students see their central core: how we can understand more about the world and make better decisions by understanding what the data tell us. From this perspective, it is easy to see that the patterns we look for in graphs are the same as those we think about when we prepare to make inferences. And it is easy to see that the many ways to draw inferences from data are several applications of the same core concepts. It follows naturally that when we extend these basic ideas into more complex (and even more realistic) situations, the same basic reasoning is still at the core of our analyses.

Our Goal: Read This Book!

The best textbook in the world is of little value if it isn't read. Here are some of the ways we made *Business Statistics* more approachable:

- *Readability.* We strive for a conversational, approachable style, and we introduce anecdotes to maintain interest. Instructors report (to their amazement) that their students read ahead of their assignments voluntarily. Students tell us (to *their* amazement) that they actually enjoy the book. In this edition, we've focused our discussions even more clearly on the central ideas we want to convey.

- *Focus on assumptions and conditions.* More than any other textbook, *Business Statistics* emphasizes the need to verify assumptions when using statistical procedures. We reiterate this focus throughout the examples and exercises. We make every effort to provide templates that reinforce the practice of checking these assumptions and conditions, rather than rushing through the computations. Business decisions have consequences. Blind calculations open the door to errors that could easily be avoided by taking the time to graph the data, check assumptions and conditions, and then check again that the results and residuals make sense.

- *Emphasis on graphing and exploring data.* Our consistent emphasis on the importance of displaying data is evident from the first chapters on understanding data to the sophisticated model-building chapters at the end. Examples often illustrate the value of examining data graphically, and the exercises reinforce this. Good graphics reveal structures, patterns, and occasional anomalies that could otherwise go unnoticed. These patterns often raise new questions and inform both the path of a resulting statistical analysis and the business decisions. Hundreds of new graphics found throughout the book demonstrate that the simple structures that underlie even the most sophisticated statistical inferences are the same ones we look for in the simplest examples. This helps tie the concepts of the book together to tell a coherent story.

- *Consistency.* We work hard to avoid the "do what we say, not what we do" trap. Having taught the importance of plotting data and checking assumptions and conditions, we are careful to model that behavior throughout the book. (Check the exercises in the chapters on multiple regression or time series and you'll find us still requiring and demonstrating the plots and checks that were introduced in the early chapters.) This consistency helps reinforce these fundamental principles and provides a familiar foundation for the more sophisticated topics.

- *The need to read.* In this book, important concepts, definitions, and sample solutions are not always set aside in boxes. The book needs to be read, so we've tried to make the reading experience enjoyable. The common approach of skimming for definitions or starting with the exercises and looking up examples just won't work here. (It never did work as a way to learn about and understand statistics.)

Coverage

The topics covered in a Business Statistics course are generally mandated by our students' needs in their studies and in their future professions. But the *order* of these topics and the relative emphasis given to each is not well established. *Business Statistics* presents some topics sooner or later than other texts. Although many chapters can be taught in a different order, we urge you to consider the order we have chosen.

We've been guided in the order of topics by the fundamental goal of designing a coherent course in which concepts and methods fit together to provide a new understanding of how reasoning with data can uncover new and important truths. Each new topic should fit into the growing structure of understanding that students develop throughout the course. For example, we teach inference concepts with proportions first and then with means. Most people have a wider experience with proportions, seeing them in polls and advertising. And by starting with proportions, we can teach inference with the Normal model and then introduce inference for means with the Student's *t*-distribution.

We introduce the concepts of association, correlation, and regression early in *Business Statistics*. Our experience in the classroom shows that introducing these fundamental ideas early makes statistics useful and relevant even at the beginning of the course. By Chapter 4, students can discuss relationships among variables in a meaningful way. Later in the semester, when we discuss inference, it is natural and relatively easy to build on the fundamental concepts learned earlier and enhance them with inferential methods.

GAISE Report

We've been guided in our choice of what to emphasize by the GAISE 2016 (Guidelines for Assessment and Instruction in Statistics Education) Report, which emerged from extensive studies of how students best learn Statistics (**www.amstat .org/asa/files/pdfs/GAISE/GaiseCollege_Full.pdf**). The GAISE Report was extensively revised in 2016 to reflect the evolution of technology and new wisdom about teaching statistics. The new recommendations have been officially adopted and recommended by the American Statistical Association and urge (among other detailed suggestions) that statistics education should:

1. Teach statistical thinking.
2. Focus on conceptual understanding.
3. Integrate real data with a context and a purpose.
4. Foster active learning.
5. Use technology to explore concepts and analyze data.
6. Use assessments to improve and evaluate student learning.

In this sense, this book is thoroughly modern.

Syllabus Flexibility

To be effective, a course must fit comfortably with the instructor's preferences. The early chapters—Chapters 1–15—cover core material that will be part of most introductory courses. Chapters 16–20—multiple regression, model building, and time series. Analysis of Variance—may be included in an introductory course, but our organization provides flexibility in the order and choice of specific topics. Chapters 21–25 may be viewed as "special topics" and selected and sequenced to suit the instructor or the course requirements.

Here are some specific notes:

- Chapter 4, Correlation and Linear Regression, may be postponed until just before covering regression inference in Chapter 16. (But we urge you to teach it where it appears.) Chapter 4 now includes an early glimpse of multiple regression (as advised by GAISE 2016). We urge you not to skip that discussion.
- Chapter 19, Building Multiple Regression Models, must follow the introductory material on multiple regression in Chapter 18.
- Chapters 20 and 25, Time Series Analysis and ANOVA, require material on multiple regression from Chapter 18.

The following topics can be introduced in any order (or omitted) after basic inference has been covered:

- Chapter 15, Inference for Counts: Chi-Square Tests
- Chapter 21, Introduction to Big Data and Data Mining
- Chapter 22, Quality Control
- Chapter 23, Nonparametric Methods
- Chapter 24, Decision Making and Risk

Continuing Features

A textbook isn't just words on a page. A textbook is many elements that come together to form a big picture. The features in *Business Statistics* provide a real-world context for concepts, help students apply these concepts, promote problem solving, and integrate technology—all of which help students understand and see the big picture of Business Statistics.

Providing Real-World Context

Motivating Vignettes. Each chapter opens with a motivating vignette, often taken from the authors' consulting experiences. Companies featured include Amazon.com, Zillow.com, Keen Inc., and Whole Foods Market. We analyze data from or about the companies in the motivating vignettes throughout the chapter.

Brief Cases. Each chapter includes one or more Brief Cases that use real data and ask students to investigate a question or make a decision. Students define the objective, plan the process, complete the analysis, and report a conclusion. Data for the Brief Cases are available on the website, formatted for various technologies.

Case Studies. Throughout the book we present Case Studies. Students are given realistically large datasets and challenged to respond to open-ended business questions using the data. Students can bring together methods they have learned throughout the book to address the issues raised. Students will have to use a computer to work with the large datasets that accompany these Case Studies.

What Can Go Wrong? In each chapter, What Can Go Wrong? highlights the most common statistical errors and the misconceptions about statistics. The most common mistakes for the new user of statistics often involve misusing a method—not miscalculating a statistic. One of our goals is to arm students with the tools to detect statistical errors and to offer practice in debunking misuses of Statistics, whether intentional or not.

Applying Concepts

In Practice. Almost every section of every chapter includes focused examples that illustrate and apply the concepts or methods of that section to a real-world business context. Each one now ends with a specific written report. They are now structured as conversations between a manager and an analyst or employee with the requirement that a report be made to the manager. This format helps to frame the issues in a practical way.

Step-by-Step Guided Examples. The answer to a statistical question is almost never just a number. Statistics is about understanding the world and making better decisions with data. Guided Examples model a thorough solution in the right column with commentary in the left column. The overall analysis follows our innovative **Plan, Do, Report** template. Each analysis begins with a clear question about a business decision and an examination of the data (**Plan**), moves to calculating the selected statistics (**Do**), and finally concludes with a **Report** that specifically addresses the question. To emphasize that our goal is to address the motivating question, we present the **Report** step as a business memo that summarizes the results in the context of the example and states a recommendation if the data are able to support one. To preserve the realism of the example, whenever it is appropriate, we include limitations of the analysis or models in the concluding memo, as one should in making such a report.

By Hand. Even though we encourage the use of technology to calculate statistical quantities, we recognize the pedagogical benefits of occasionally doing a calculation by hand. The By Hand boxes break apart the calculation of some of the simpler formulas and help the student through the calculation of a worked example.

Reality Check. We regularly offer reminders that statistics is about understanding the world and making decisions with data. Results that make no sense are probably wrong, no matter how carefully we think we did the calculations. Mistakes are often easy to spot with a little thought, so we ask students to stop for a reality check before interpreting results.

Notation Alert. Throughout this book, we emphasize the importance of clear communication. Proper notation is part of the vocabulary of statistics, but it can be daunting. We've found that it helps students when we are clear about the letters and symbols statisticians use to mean very specific things, so we've included Notation Alerts whenever we introduce a special notation that students will see again.

Math Boxes. When we present the mathematical underpinnings of the statistical methods and concepts, we set proofs, derivations, and justifications apart from the narrative. In this way, the underlying mathematics is there for those who want greater depth, but the text itself presents the logical development of the topic at hand without distractions.

From Learning to Earning. Each chapter ends with a From Learning to Earning summary that includes learning objectives and definitions of terms introduced in the chapter. Students should use these as study guides. We encourage them to take this opportunity to see the "big picture" of the chapter and see how it applies to making business decisions.

Promoting Problem Solving

Just Checking. Throughout each chapter we pose short questions to help students check their understanding. The answers are at the end of the exercise sets in each chapter to make them easy to check. The questions can also be used to motivate class discussion.

Ethics in Action. Statistics is not just plugging numbers into formulas; most statistical analyses require a fair amount of judgment. Ethics in Action vignettes—updated for this edition—in each chapter provide a context for some of the judgments needed in statistical analyses. Possible errors, a link to the American Statistical Association's Ethical Guidelines, and ethically and statistically sound alternative approaches are presented in the Instructor's Solutions Manual.

Section Exercises. The exercises for each chapter begin with straightforward exercises targeted at the topics in each section. These are designed to check understanding of specific topics. Because they are labeled by section, it is easy to turn back to the chapter to clarify a concept or review a method.

Chapter Exercises. These exercises are designed to be more realistic than section exercises and to lead to conclusions about the real world. They may combine concepts and methods from different sections, and they contain relevant, modern, and real-world questions. Many come from news stories; some come from recent research articles. The exercises marked with a **T** indicate that the data are available on the book's companion website, in a variety of formats. We pair the exercises so that each odd-numbered exercise (with answer in the back of the book) is followed by an even-numbered exercise on the same statistics topic. Exercises are roughly ordered within each chapter by both topic and level of difficulty.

Integrating Technology

Data and Sources. Most of the data used in examples and exercises are from real-world sources and whenever we can, we include URLs for Internet data sources. The data we use, are usually available at the online Data and Story Library (DASL) at **dasl.datadescription.com** and on the companion website, **www.pearsonhighered.com/sharpe**.

Videos with Optional Captioning. Videos, featuring the *Business Statistics* authors, review the high points of each chapter. The presentations feature the same student-friendly style and emphasis on critical thinking as the textbook. In addition, 10 *Business Insight Videos* feature Deckers, Southwest Airlines, Starwood, and other companies and focus on statistical concepts as they pertain to the real world. Videos are available with captioning. They can also be viewed from within the online MyLab Statistics course.

Tech Support. In business, statistics is practiced with computers using a variety of statistics packages. In Business-school statistics classes, however, Excel is the software most often used. In the Tech Support sections at the end of each chapter, we summarize what students can find in the most common software, often with annotated output. In updating for this edition, we offer extended guidance for Excel 2016, and start-up pointers for Minitab, SPSS, JMP, StatCrunch, R, and XLStat, formatted in easy-to-read bulleted lists. This advice is not intended to replace the documentation for any of the software, but rather to point the way and provide start-up assistance.

Get the Most Out of
MyLab Statistics

MyLab™ Statistics is the leading online homework, tutorial, and assessment program for teaching and learning statistics, built around Pearson's best-selling content. MyLab Stats helps students and instructors improve results; it provides engaging experiences and personalized learning for each student so learning can happen in any environment. Plus, it offers flexible and time-saving course management features to allow instructors to easily manage their classes while remaining in complete control, regardless of course format.

Preparedness

One of the biggest challenges in many mathematics and statistics courses is making sure students are adequately prepared with the prerequisite skills needed to successfully complete their course work. Pearson offers a variety of content and course options to support students with just-in-time remediation and key-concept review.

- Build homework assignments, quizzes, and tests to support your course learning outcomes. From Getting Ready (GR) questions to the Conceptual Question Library (CQL), we have your assessment needs covered from the mechanics to the critical understanding of Statistics. The exercise libraries include technology-led instruction, including new Excel-based exercises, and learning aids to reinforce your students' success.

- Using proven, field-tested technology, auto-graded Excel Projects allow instructors to seamlessly integrate Microsoft® Excel® content into their course without having to manually grade spreadsheets. Students have the opportunity to practice important statistical skills in Excel, helping them to master key concepts and gain proficiency with the program.

pearson.com/mylab/statistics

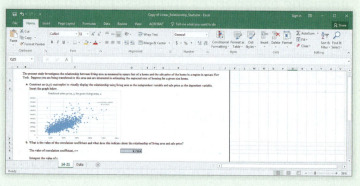
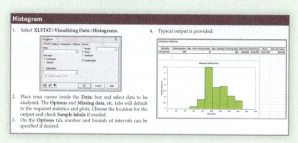

Resources for Success

Pearson
MyLab

Instructor Supplements

Instructor's Edition contains answers to all exercises. (ISBN-13: 978-0-13-468758-2; ISBN-10: 0-13-468758-2)

Instructor's Resource Guide (download only), written by the authors, contains chapter-by-chapter comments on the major concepts, tips on presenting topics (and what to avoid), teaching examples, suggested assignments, basic exercises, and web links and lists of other resources. Available to qualified instructors through Pearson's online catalog at **www.pearson.com/us/higher-education** or within MyLab Statistics.

Online Test Bank (download only), by Dirk Tempelaar, Maastricht University, includes chapter quizzes and part-level tests. Available to qualified instructors through Pearson's online catalog at **www.pearson.com/us/higher-education** or within MyLab Statistics.

Instructor's Solutions Manual (download only), by Linda Dawson, University of Washington, contains detailed solutions to all of the exercises. The Instructor's Solutions Manual is available to qualified instructors through Pearson's online catalog at **www.pearson.com/us/higher-education** or within MyLab Statistics.

TestGen® Computerized Test Bank (**www.pearsoned .com/testgen**) enables instructors to build, edit, print, and administer tests using a computerized bank of questions developed to cover all the objectives of the text. TestGen is algorithmically based, allowing instructors to create multiple but equivalent versions of the same question or test with the click of a button. Instructors can also modify test bank questions or add new questions. The software and test bank are available for download from Pearson's online catalog at **www.pearson.com/ us/higher-education**. Test Forms (download only) are also available from the online catalog.

PowerPoint Lecture Slides: Free to qualified adopters, this classroom lecture presentation software is geared specifically to the sequence and philosophy of *Business Statistics*. Key graphics from the book are included to help bring the statistical concepts alive in the classroom. These files are available to qualified instructors through Pearson's online catalog at **www.pearson.com/us/higher-education** or within MyLab Statistics.

Learning Catalytics™ is a web-based engagement and assessment tool. As a "bring-your-own-device" direct response system, Learning Catalytics offers a diverse library of dynamic question types that allow students to interact with and think critically about statistical concepts. As a real-time resource, instructors can take advantage of critical teaching moments both in the classroom and through assignable and gradable homework.

Student Resources

Business Statistics, for-sale student edition. (ISBN-13: 978-0-13-470521-7; ISBN-10: 0-13-470521-1)

Student's Solutions Manual, by Linda Dawson, University of Washington, provides detailed, worked-out solutions to odd-numbered exercises. (ISBN-13: 978-0-13-470548-4; ISBN-10: 0-13-470548-3)

Study Cards for Business Statistics Software: This series of study cards, available for Excel 2016 with DAT: 0-13-457679-9; Excel 2016 with XLSTAT: 0-13-457683-7; StatCrunch: 0-13-397513-4, R: 0-13-522870-0; and R Studio: 0-13-522869-7 provides students with easy step-by-step guides to the most common business statistics software.

pearson.com/mylab/statistics

Resources for Success

Technology Resources

MyLab Statistics Online Course (access code required) MyLab™ Statistics is the teaching and learning platform that empowers you to reach *every* student. By combining trusted author content with digital tools and a flexible platform, MyLab Statistics personalizes the learning experience and improves results for each student. With MyLab Statistics and StatCrunch®, an integrated web-based statistical software program, students learn the skills they need to interact with data in the real world. Learn more about MyLab Statistics at **pearson.com/mylab/statistics**.

Used by nearly one million students a year, MyLab Statistics is the world's leading online program for teaching and learning statistics. MyLab Statistics delivers assessment, tutorials, and multimedia resources that provide engaging and personalized experiences for each student, so learning can happen in any environment. Each course is developed to accompany Pearson's best-selling content, authored by thought leaders across the statistics curriculum, and can be easily customized to fit any course format.

Methods for teaching statistics are continuously evolving to provide today's students with the skills they need to interact with data in the real world. In addition, statistics students are coming to the classroom with a wide range of backgrounds and learner styles. The flexibility to build a course that fits instructors' individual course formats and every student's needs—with a variety of content options and multimedia resources all in one place—has made MyLab Statistics the market-leading solution for teaching and learning statistics since its inception.

Thanks to feedback from instructors and students from more than 10,000 institutions, MyLab Statistics continues to transform—delivering new content, innovative learning resources, and platform updates to support students and instructors, today and in the future.

Deliver Trusted Content

You deserve teaching materials that meet your own high standards for your course. That's why Pearson partners with highly respected authors to develop interactive content and course-specific resources that you can trust—and that keep your students engaged.

Tutorial Exercises with Multimedia Learning Aids: The homework and practice exercises in MyLab Statistics align with the exercises in the textbook, and they regenerate algorithmically to give students unlimited opportunity for practice and mastery. Exercises offer immediate helpful feedback, guided solutions, sample problems, animations, videos, and eText clips for extra help at point-of-use.

Auto-Graded Excel Projects: Using proven, field-tested technology, auto-graded Excel Projects let you seamlessly integrate Microsoft® Excel® content into your course without having to manually grade spreadsheets. Students can practice important statistical skills in Excel, helping them master key concepts and gain proficiency with the program. They simply download a spreadsheet, work live on a statistics problem in Excel, and then upload that file back into the MyLab. Within minutes, they receive a report that provides personalized, detailed feedback to pinpoint where they went wrong in the problem.

StatCrunch: MyLab Statistics integrates the web-based statistical software, StatCrunch, within the online assessment platform so that students can easily analyze datasets from exercises and the text. In addition, MyLab Statistics includes access to **www.StatCrunch.com**, a website where users can access tens of thousands of shared datasets, conduct online surveys, perform complex analyses using the powerful statistical software, and generate compelling reports.

Business Insight Videos: Ten engaging videos show managers at top companies using statistics in their everyday work. Assignable questions encourage debate and discussion.

StatTalk Videos: Fun-loving statistician Andrew Vickers takes to the streets of Brooklyn, New York, to demonstrate important statistical concepts through interesting stories and real-life events. This series of 24 videos includes available assessment questions and an instructor's guide.

Empower Each Learner

Each student learns at a different pace. Personalized learning pinpoints the precise areas where each student needs practice, giving all students the support they need—when and where they need it—to be successful.

■ **Study Plan:** Acts as a tutor, providing personalized recommendations for each of your students based on his or her ability to master the learning objectives in your course. This allows students to focus their study time by pinpointing the precise areas they need to review, and allowing them to use customized practice and learning aids—such as videos, eText, tutorials, and more—to get them back on track. Using the report available in the Gradebook, you can tailor course lectures to prioritize the content where students need the most support, offering you better insight into classroom and individual performance.

■ With the **Companion Study Plan Assignments** you can now assign the Study Plan as a prerequisite to a test or quiz, guiding students through the concepts they need to master.

■ **Getting Ready for Statistics:** A library of questions now appears within each MyLab Statistics course to offer the developmental math topics students need for the course. These can be assigned as a prerequisite to other assignments, if desired.

Conceptual Question Library: In addition to algorithmically regenerated questions that are aligned with your textbook, there is a library of 1,000 Conceptual Questions available in the assessment manager that require students to apply their statistical understanding.

Teach the Course Your Way

Your course is unique. So whether you'd like to build your own assignments, teach multiple sections, or set prerequisites, MyLab gives you the flexibility to easily create *your* course to fit *your* needs.

■ **Learning Catalytics:** Generate class discussion, guide your lecture, and promote peer-to-peer learning with real-time analytics. MyLab Statistics now provides Learning Catalytics™—an interactive student response tool that uses students' smartphones, tablets, or laptops to engage them in more sophisticated tasks and thinking.

■ **LMS Integration:** You can now link Blackboard Learn™, Brightspace® by D2L®, Canvas™, or Moodle® to the MyLabs. Access assignments, rosters, and resources, and synchronize grades with your LMS gradebook. For students, single

sign-on provides access to all the personalized learning resources that make studying more efficient and effective.

Improve Student Results

When you teach with MyLab, student performance improves. That's why instructors have chosen MyLab for over 15 years, touching the lives of more than 50 million students.

MathXL Online Course (access code required)

Part of the world's leading collection of online homework, tutorial, and assessment products, MathXL® delivers assessment and tutorial resources that provide engaging and personalized experiences for each student. Each course is developed to accompany Pearson's best-selling content, authored by thought leaders across the math curriculum, and can be easily customized to fit any course format.

With MathXL, instructors can:

■ Create, edit, and assign online homework and tests using algorithmically generated exercises correlated at the objective level to the textbook.

■ Create and assign their own online exercises and import TestGen tests for added flexibility.

■ Maintain records of all student work tracked in MathXL's online gradebook.

With MathXL, students can:

■ Take chapter tests in MathXL and receive personalized study plans and/or personalized homework assignments based on their test results.

■ Use the study plan and/or the homework to link directly to tutorial exercises for the objectives they need to study.

■ Access supplemental animations and video clips directly from selected exercises.

MathXL is available to qualified adopters. For more information, visit our web site at **www.mathxl.com** or contact your Pearson representative.

StatCrunch

Integrated directly into MyLab Statistics, StatCrunch® is powerful web-based statistical software that allows users to perform complex analyses, share data-sets, and generate compelling reports of their data.

pearson.com/mylab/statistics

The vibrant online community offers tens of thousands of shared datasets for students to analyze.

- **Collect.** Users can upload their own data to StatCrunch or search a large library of publicly shared datasets, spanning almost any topic of interest. Datasets from the text and from online homework exercises can also be accessed and analyzed in StatCrunch. An online survey tool allows users to quickly collect data via web-based surveys.

- **Crunch.** A full range of numerical and graphical methods allows users to analyze and gain insights from any dataset. Interactive graphics help users understand statistical concepts, and are available for export to enrich reports with visual representations of data.

- **Communicate.** Reporting options help users create a wide variety of visually appealing representations of their data.

StatCrunch is also available by itself to qualified adopters. It can be accessed on your laptop, smartphone, or tablet when you visit the StatCrunch website from your device's browser. For more information, visit the StatCrunch website at **www.StatCrunch.com** or contact your Pearson representative.

TestGen

TestGen® (**www.pearsoned.com/testgen**) enables instructors to build, edit, print, and administer tests using a computerized bank of questions developed to cover all the objectives of the text. TestGen is algorithmically based, allowing instructors to create multiple but equivalent versions of the same question or test with the click of a button. Instructors can also modify test bank questions or add new questions. The software and test bank are available for download from Pearson's Instructor Resource Center at **www.pearsonhighered.com/irc**.

PowerPoint Lecture Slides

PowerPoint® Lecture Slides provide an outline to use in a lecture setting, presenting definitions, key concepts, and figures from the text. These slides are available within MyLab Statistics and in the Instructor Resource Center at **www.pearsonhighered.com/irc**.

Foster student engagement and peer-to-peer learning

Generate class discussion, guide your lecture, and promote peer-to-peer learning with real-time analytics.

MyLab™ Math and MyLab Statistics now provide Learning Catalytics™—an interactive student response tool that uses students' smartphones, tablets, or laptops to engage them in more sophisticated tasks and thinking.

Instructors, you can:

- Pose a variety of open-ended questions that help your students develop critical thinking skills.

- Monitor responses to find out where students are struggling.

- Use real-time data to adjust your instructional strategy and try other ways of engaging your students during class.

- Manage student interactions by automatically grouping students for discussion, teamwork, and peer-to-peer learning.

XLSTAT™ for Pearson

Used by leading businesses and universities, XLSTAT is an Excel® add-in that offers a wide variety of functions to enhance the analytical capabilities of Microsoft Excel, making it the ideal tool for your everyday data analysis and statistics requirements. XLSTAT is compatible with all Excel versions. Available for bundling with the text as ISBN-13: 978-0-321-75940-5; ISBN-10: 0-321-75940-0. Standalone: ISBN-13: 978-0-321-75932-0; ISBN-10: 0-321-75932-X

Minitab and Minitab Express™

Minitab and Minitab Express™ make learning statistics easy and provide students with a skill set that's in demand in today's data-driven workforce. Bundling Minitab software with educational materials ensures students have access to the software they need in the classroom, around campus, and at home. And having the latest version of Minitab ensures that students can use the software for the duration of their course. Access Card only; not sold as standalone: ISBN 13: 978-0-13-445640-9; ISBN 10: 0-13-445640-8.

JMP Student Edition

JMP Student Edition is an easy-to-use, streamlined version of JMP desktop statistical discovery software from SAS Institute, Inc., and is available for bundling with the text. Access Card only; not sold as standalone: ISBN-13: 978-0-13-467979-2; ISBN-10: 0-13-467979-2.

pearson.com/mylab/statistics

Acknowledgments

This book would not have been possible without many contributions from David Bock, our coauthor on several other texts. Many of the explanations and exercises in this book benefit from Dave's pedagogical flair and expertise. We are honored to have him as a colleague and friend.

Many people have contributed to this book from the first day of its conception to its publication. *Business Statistics* would have never seen the light of day without the assistance of the incredible team at Pearson. The Director of Portfolio Management, Deirdre Lynch, was central to the support, development, and realization of the book from day one. Patrick Barbera, Senior Portfolio Management Analyst; Morgan Danna, Editorial Assistant; Kaylee Karlson, Product Marketing Manager; and Shannon McCormack, Marketing Support Assistant, were essential in managing all of the behind-the-scenes work that needed to be done. Peggy McMahon, Content Producer, and Chere Bemelmans, Project Manager at SPi Global, worked miracles to get the book out the door. We are indebted to them. Aimee Thorne, Senior Producer, put together a top-notch media package for this book. Designer Jerilyn Bokorick and Cenveo® Publisher Services are responsible for the wonderful way the book looks.

We'd also like to thank our accuracy checker, whose monumental task was to make sure we said what we thought we were saying: Dirk Tempelaar, Maastricht University.

We also thank those who provided feedback through focus groups, class tests, and reviews:

Hope M. Baker, Kennesaw State University

John F. Beyers, University of Maryland—University College

Scott Callan, Bentley College

Laurel Chiappetta, University of Pittsburgh

Anne Davey, Northeastern State University

Joan Donohue, The University of South Carolina

Robert Emrich, Pepperdine University

Michael Ernst, St. Cloud State

Mark Gebert, University of Kentucky

Kim Gilbert, University of Georgia

Nicholas Gorgievski, Nichols College

Clifford Hawley, West Virginia University

Kathleen Iacocca, University of Scranton

Chun Jin, Central Connecticut State University

Austin Lampros, Colorado State University

Roger Lee, Salt Lake Community College

Monnie McGee, Southern Methodist University

Richard McGowan, Boston College

Mihail Motzev, Walla Walla University

Robert Potter, University of Central Florida

Eugene Round, Embry-Riddle Aeronautical University

Sunil Sapra, California State University—Los Angeles

Dmitry Shishkin, Georgia Gwinnett College

Courtenay Stone, Ball State University

Gordon Stringer, University of Colorado—Colorado Springs

Arnold J. Stromberg, University of Kentucky

Joe H. Sullivan, Mississippi State University

Timothy Sullivan, Towson University

Minghe Sun, University of Texas—San Antonio

Patrick Thompson, University of Florida

Jackie Wroughton, Northern Kentucky University

Ye Zhang, Indiana University—Purdue Indianapolis

Finally, we want to thank our families. This has been a long project, and it has required many nights and weekends. Our families have sacrificed so that we could write the book we envisioned.

Norean Sharpe
Richard De Veaux
Paul Velleman
Eric Eisenstein

Index of Applications

Note: Page numbers followed by n indicate footnotes.

Data and Decisions

H&M

Even if you haven't bought something from H&M recently, chances are good that you've passed by one of their stores. With over 4000 stores in 64 markets worldwide, they are one of the largest and fastest-growing clothing retailers in the world. Over the past decade, H&M has built new stores at an astounding rate of over 10% a year. Thanks to this growth, the CEO, Karl-Johan Persson, grandson of the founder, is now the richest person in Sweden.

Like most companies, H&M's online presence has been increasing as well. Of their 64 worldwide markets, 35 offer e-commerce where customers can shop 24 hours a day, 7 days a week, with just the click of a mouse. H&M now reaches their customers in ways no one could even imagine just a generation ago. But what of the future? Will the company be better off continuing to grow brick and mortar stores at the same pace, or should they devote more resources into the digital space?[1]

---

[1]We developed this hypothetical example in late 2017 based on our business and consulting experience. As we were going to press, the news caught up with us. It turns out that indeed H&M had been struggling with their balance of online sales vs. brick and mortar inventory. Perhaps if this book had been published a year earlier, they could have solved the problem: www.nytimes.com/2018/03/27/business/hm-clothes-stock-sales.html

A few generations ago, many store owners knew their customers and their business well. With that knowledge, they could forecast growth, see trends, and even personalize their suggestions to customers, guessing which items that particular customers might like. Businesses today rely on similar information to make decisions, but most never meet their customers. With 4000 different stores and thousands of online customers, H&M has to obtain and analyze their data in other ways.

The key to turning data into information and knowledge is Statistics—the collection of tools that extract information from data. These tools that you will learn also provide the foundation for more advanced methods like data mining and analytics. According to CEO Karl-Johan Persson, "advanced analytics provide an important support for our operations. The algorithms we have started to use will contribute to improvements within everything from assortment planning and logistics to sales."[2] Using statistical methods to turn data into information, information into knowledge, and knowledge into smart business decisions is the key to all successful modern business enterprises.

And it all starts . . . with data.

Thomasine has just landed her first job out of school as a marketing and strategy analyst working for H&M. Her team's first assignment is to decide whether to build more brick and mortar stores or invest more in online operations. To help make the decision, they investigate store sales data over the past ten years and display them in the following graph:

FIGURE 1.1 H&M's store growth has remained steady at just over 10% a year, but operating profit growth seems to be coming down.

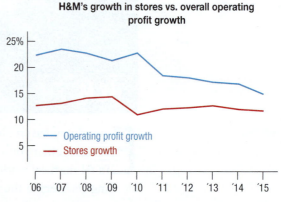

H&M's growth in stores vs. overall operating profit growth

Thomasine wonders if the decline she sees in the stores' profit growth (the blue line in Figure 1.1) means she should recommend putting more resources into online sales instead of just building more stores.

Displays like this, called *data visualizations*, can summarize large amounts of data in a concise way that helps make good business decisions, and can often reveal things that weren't expected.

IN PRACTICE 1.1   Business insights from visualizations

One of the authors was consulting for a large multinational firm and was given access to their sales data. Management wondered if there might be sales opportunities around the world and where they might be. Because the company sold many consumer items to individuals, the consultant decided that rather than focus on the total sales

---

[2]2016 H&M Group annual report, about.hm.com/en/media/news/financial-reports/2017/1/2441626.html

(in dollars) in each country he should divide the total sales in each country by the population size, creating the new variable *Sales per Capita*. When he displayed this variable on a map, management was shocked:[3]

MANAGER We know that we sell more in the United States than anywhere else in the world, but why are some countries redder than the U.S.?

CONSULTANT In this color scheme, low *Sales per Capita* ($ spent per customer) is indicated by dark blue, average by white (grey) and higher than average by red. The countries in the brightest red are the ones with the highest sales per person.

MANAGER You mean we sell more per person in Norway, Finland, and even Australia than in the U.S.?

CONSULTANT Exactly. Norway has the highest sales at more than $600 per person, compared with the U.S. at $364.

MANAGER Wow! I had no idea. I never would have guessed that. Thank you for the insight!

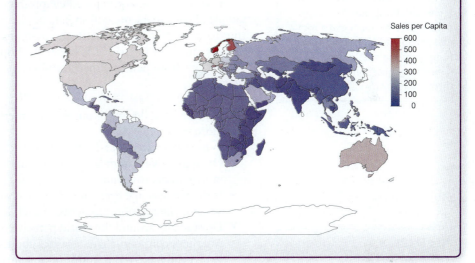

We will be using visualizations, summaries, and models of data to understand, explain, and predict throughout the course. Along the way we will encounter many types of data and corresponding ways to visualize, model, and analyze the data we collect. And because it all starts with data, we'll spend the rest of this chapter getting to know more about the nature of data.

1.1 Data

> Data is king at Amazon. Clickstream and purchase data are the crown jewels at Amazon. They help us build features to personalize the website experience.
> —Ronny Kohavi, former director of data mining and personalization, amazon.com

Every time you make an online purchase, more information is captured than just the details of the purchase itself. What pages did you search to get to your purchase? How much time did you spend looking at each? These recorded values, whether numbers or labels, together with their context are called **data**. They are recorded and stored electronically, in vast digital repositories called **data warehouses**. Businesses have always relied on data to make good decisions, but today, more than ever before, companies use data to make decisions about virtually all aspects of their business, from inventory to advertising to website design.

---

[3]This is based on a true story. We can't reveal the name of the company due to a non-disclosure agreement.

Every swipe of your credit card and every click of your mouse has helped these data warehouses grow. The challenges of collecting, managing, storing, and curating all of this information collectively fall under the term **Big Data**.

But data alone can't make good decisions. To start the process of turning data into useful information, you first need to know what decisions you want to make. Without a question, you have no idea what might be interesting about the data. Should you look at the time of transactions, their location, their price, which products were bought, or something else? Your knowledge of the business issues and the questions you want to answer will help guide your search for insights from the data, and help you harness data to make better decisions.

Once you have data and a clear vision of the problem, the statistics techniques in this book can empower your decision making. They will help you in two ways: You'll learn how to estimate the likely values needed for your decisions and—possibly more important—you'll learn how to quantify the *uncertainty* of those estimates.

Before H&M introduces a new product they usually test market it to a small sample of customers and collect data on the product's performance before committing to it worldwide. Statistics helps them make the leap from a sample to an understanding of the world at large. We hope this text will empower you to draw conclusions from data and make valid business decisions in response to such questions as:

- Will the new design of our website increase click-through rates and result in more sales?
- What is the effect of advertising on sales?
- Do aggressive, "high-growth" mutual funds really have higher returns than more conservative funds?
- Is there a seasonal cycle in your firm's profits?
- What is the relationship between shelf location and cereal sales?
- Do students around the world perceive issues in business ethics differently?
- Are there common characteristics about your customers and why they choose your products?—and, more importantly, are those characteristics the same among those who aren't your customers?

Your ability to answer questions such as these and make sound business decisions with data depends largely on your ability to take a business problem, *translate* it into a question that data can answer, and *communicate* that answer to others. The steps to follow are shown in the box in the margin. The **Plan**, **Do**, and **Report** strategy is found throughout the book. The main headings will stay the same although the specific subparts will vary slightly depending on the topic we're learning.

Rarely does the journey from problem definition to solution proceed straight from Step 1 to Step 7. As you learn more about your data you'll probably want to rethink earlier steps, possibly even modifying the original question itself. Or you may decide to collect different data after you see the limitations of your current model. But bearing this process in mind will help you to strategize your data analytics process and keep you on the road toward the goal of delivering good decisions.

Why are you taking this course?
The typical answer is "because it's required." But why is it required? Because these are the tools that will help you leverage your business domain knowledge with data.

Albert Einstein is credited with saying "If I had one hour to save the world, I'd spend 55 minutes defining the problem and 5 minutes solving it."[4] The wisdom of using your business acumen to define your question will be clear throughout this book.

Plan (1–2)
1. **Define** the problem.
2. **Collect** and/or find data and **identify** the variables.

Do (3–6)
3. **Prepare** and wrangle data.
4. **Characterize** the data.
5. **Explore** the data.
   Summarize
   Visualize
6. **Model** (if appropriate).
   Check conditions and assumptions for modeling.
   Fit the model and make the necessary calculations.

Report (7)
7. Communicate and **present**.

---

[4]According to quoteinvestigator.com there is "no substantive evidence that Einstein ever made a remark of this type." It appeared in a paper by William H. Markle, who credited an unnamed Yale professor. But many people, including those at goodreads.com, still give the credit to Einstein.

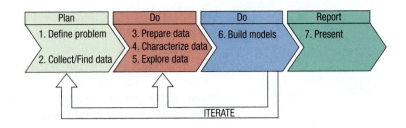

1.2 The Role of Data in Decision Making

Q: What is analytics?

A: Analytics is the term for extracting information from data.

Q: Is there really a difference between statistics and analytics?

A: Essentially no. We'll use the terms interchangeably. Some use the term "advanced analytics" to include modern machine learning methods not traditionally found in statistics. (See Chapter 21)

THE W'S:

WHO

WHAT

WHEN

WHERE

WHY

When companies try to obtain actionable information from data that may have been collected in the course of doing business (such as records of transactions or a customer database) it is usually called **data mining**. Sometimes the analysis is called **predictive analytics** if it focuses on future performance. The more general term, **business analytics** (or sometimes simply analytics), refers to any use of data and statistical analysis to inform business decisions. Leading companies are embracing analytics to extract value from their data. As Clive Humby, author of *The Loyalty Myth*, said, "data is the new oil." For example, Zillow recently offered $1,200,000 to improve the prediction of home sale prices from publicly available data. As of June 2017, 791 teams were competing for the prize.

Companies use data to make decisions about nearly every aspect of their business. By studying the past behavior of customers and predicting their responses, they hope to better serve their customers and to compete more effectively.

eBay collected data and used analytics to examine its own use of computer resources. Although not obvious to its own technical people, once they crunched the data they found huge inefficiencies. According to Forbes, eBay was able to "save millions in capital expenditures within the first year."

Data come in many forms. Some are numerical (consisting only of numbers), others are alphabetic (consisting only of letters), and yet others are alphanumerical (mixed numbers and letters). But data are useless unless we know their **context**. Newspaper journalists know that the lead paragraph of a good story should establish the "Five W's": *who, what, when, where,* and (if possible) *why.* Often, we add *how* to the list as well. Answering these questions connects the data to the business problem at hand. The answers to the first two questions are essential. If we don't know *who* and *what*, we don't have any useful information.

We can make the meaning clear if we add the context of *who* the data are about and *what* was measured and organize the values into a **data table**. Table 1.1 shows part of a data table of purchase records from an online music retailer. Each row represents a purchase of a music album. The most general term for a row of a data table is **case** or **record**. Each column of the table records some characteristic

Order Number	Name	State/Country	Price	Area Code	Album Download	Gift?	Stock ID	Artist
105-2686834-3759466	Katherine H.	Ohio	5.99	440	Identity	N	B00000I5Y6	James Fortune & Flya
105-9318443-4200264	Samuel P.	Illinois	9.99	312	Port of Morrow	Y	B000002BK9	The Shins
105-1872500-0198646	Chris G.	Massachusetts	9.99	413	Up All Night	N	B000068ZVQ	Syco Music UK
103-2628345-9238664	Monique D.	Canada	10.99	902	Fallen Empires	N	B000001OAA	Snow Patrol
002-1663369-6638649	Katherine H.	Ohio	11.99	440	Sees the Light	N	B002MXA7Q0	La Sera

TABLE 1.1 Example of a data table. The variable names are in the top row. Typically, the *Who* of the table are found in the leftmost column.

of the cases. The columns are called **variables**. You'll usually find the name of the variable at the top of the column as in Table 1.1.

We call cases by different names, depending on the situation. Individuals who answer a survey are referred to as **respondents**. People on whom we experiment are **subjects** or (in an attempt to acknowledge the importance of their role in the experiment) **participants**, but animals, plants, websites, and other inanimate subjects are often called **experimental units**. Often we call cases just what they are: for example, *customers, economic quarters*, or *companies*. When referring to a transaction, rows are often called *records*. In Table 1.1, the rows are the individual orders, or purchase records. A common place to find the *who* of the table is the leftmost column. It's often an identifying variable for the cases, in this example, the order number.

JUST CHECKING

1 What is the "*who*" of Table 1.1? That is, does each row refer to a) a person or b) an order? How can you tell?

If you collect the data yourself, you'll know what the cases are and how the variables are defined. But, often, you'll be looking at data that someone else collected. The information about the data, called the metadata, might have to come from the company's database administrator or from the information technology department of a company. **Metadata** typically contains information about *how*, *when*, and *where* (and possibly *why*) the data were collected; *who* each case represents; and the definitions of all the variables.

A general term for a data table like the one shown in Table 1.1 is a **spreadsheet**, a name that comes from bookkeeping ledgers of financial information. The data were typically spread across facing pages of a bound ledger, the book used by an accountant for keeping records of expenditures and sources of income. For the accountant, the columns were the types of expenses and income, and the rows were transactions, typically invoices or receipts. These days, it is common to keep modest-size datasets in a spreadsheet even if no accounting is involved. It is usually easy to move a data table from a spreadsheet program to a program designed for statistical graphics and analysis, either directly or by copying the data table and pasting it into the statistics program.

Although data tables and spreadsheets are great for relatively small data sets, they are cumbersome for the complex data sets that companies must maintain on a day-to-day basis. Try to imagine a spreadsheet from a company the size of Amazon with customers in the rows and products in the columns. Amazon has hundreds of millions of customers and millions of products. But very few customers have purchased more than a few dozen items, so almost all the entries in the spreadsheet would be blank—not a very efficient way to store information. For that reason, various other database architectures are used to store data. The most common is a relational database.

In a **relational database**, two or more separate data tables are linked together so that information can be merged across them. Each data table is a *relation* because it is about a specific set of cases with information about each of these cases for all (or at least most) of the variables ("fields" in database terminology). For example, a table of H&M customers, along with demographic information on each, is such a relation. A data table of all the items sold by the company, including information on price, inventory, and past history, is another relation. Transactions may be held in a third "relation" that references each of the other two relations. Table 1.2 shows a small example.

In statistics, analyses are typically performed on a single relation because all variables must refer to the same cases. But often the data must be retrieved from a relational database. Retrieving data from these databases may require specific expertise with that software. In the rest of the book, we'll assume that the data have been retrieved and placed in a data table or spreadsheet with variables listed as columns and cases as the rows.

Customers						
Customer Number	**Name**	**City**	**State**	**ZIP Code**	**Customer since**	**Gold Member?**
473859	R. De Veaux	Williamstown	MA	01267	2007	No
127389	N. Sharpe	New York City	NY	10021	2000	Yes
335682	P. Velleman	Ithaca	NY	14580	2003	No
...						

Items			
Product ID	**Name**	**Price**	**Currently in Stock?**
42-8719	Resort Shirt	24.99	Yes
73-2671	Lace Dress	69.99	No
35-0518	Cashmere Sweater	129.00	Yes
72-9665	Leather Derby Shoes	69.00	Yes

Transactions						
Transaction Number	**Date**	**Customer Number**	**Product ID**	**Quantity**	**Shipping Method**	**Free Ship?**
T23478923	9/15/17	473859	42-8719	1	UPS 2nd Day	N
T23478924	9/15/17	473859	35-0518	1	UPS 2nd Day	N
T63928934	10/20/17	335682	73-2671	3	UPS Ground	N
T72348299	12/22/17	127389	72-9665	1	Fed Ex Ovnt	Y

TABLE 1.2 A relational database shows all the relevant information for three separate relations linked together by customer and product numbers.

IN PRACTICE 1.2   Gaining insight from data by identifying variables and the W's

Carly is an analyst at a credit card issuer. Her manager wants to know if an offer mailed 3 months ago has affected customers' use of their cards. To answer, Carly asks the IT department to assemble some data on recent customer spending. The IT department sends her a spreadsheet. The first six rows look like this:

Account ID	Pre Spending	Spending	Age	Segment	Enroll?	Offer	Segment Spend
393371	$2,698.12	$6,261.40	25–34	Travel/Ent	NO	None	$887.36
462715	$2,707.92	$3,397.22	45–54	Retail	NO	Gift Card	$5,062.55
433469	$800.51	$4,196.77	65+	Retail	NO	None	$673.80
462716	$3,459.52	$3,335.00	25–34	Services	YES	Double Miles	$800.75
420605	$2,106.48	$5,576.83	35–44	Leisure	YES	Double Miles	$3,064.81
473703	$2,603.92	$7,397.50	<25	Travel/Ent	YES	Double Miles	$491.29

(continued)

> **MANAGER**   Thanks for the information. I'm not quite sure about the structure. Can you tell me what each row represents and what was measured on each?
>
> **ANALYST (CARLY)**   The cases are individual customers. The data are from our internal records for the past 6 months (3 months before and 3 months after an offer was sent to the customers). The variables include the account ID of the customer (*Account ID*), and the amounts charged on the card before (*Pre Spending*) and after (*Post Spending*) the offer was sent out. We also have the customer's *Age*, marketing *Segment*, whether they enrolled on the website (*Enroll?*), what offer they were sent (*Offer*), and how much they charged on the card in their marketing segment (*Segment Spend*). (The marketing *Segment* classifies cardholders based on their spending patterns.)

1.3   Variable Types

When the values of a variable are simply the names of categories we call it a **categorical**, or **qualitative**, **variable**. When the values of a variable are measured numerical quantities, we call it a **quantitative variable**.

Descriptive responses to questions are often categories. For example, the responses to the questions "What type of mutual fund do you invest in?" or "What kind of advertising does your firm use?" yield categorical values. An important special case of categorical variables is one that has only two possible responses (usually "yes" or "no"), which arise naturally from questions like "Do you invest in the stock market?" or "Do you make online purchases from this website?"

Question	Categories or Responses
Do you invest in the stock market?	__ Yes __ No
What kind of advertising do you use?	__ Newspapers __ Internet __ Direct mailings
What is your class at school?	__ Freshman __ Sophomore __ Junior __ Senior
I would recommend this course to another student.	__ Strongly Disagree __ Slightly Disagree __ Slightly Agree __ Strongly Agree
How satisfied are you with this product?	__ Very Unsatisfied __ Unsatisfied __ Satisfied __ Very Satisfied

TABLE 1.3   Some examples of categorical variables.

Categorical or Quantitative?

Dates can be confusing. Depending on how a date is used, it may be categorical or quantitative. For example, *Day of the Week* has no units, and is categorical. What about a date such as October 31, 2017 (which is a string of characters)? Most software will treat this as categorical. However, many statistics programs can add and subtract dates to determine that there are 60 days between 10/30/17 and 12/30/17, and that 11/30/17 falls exactly in the middle of this date range. Most programs can convert any date into the number of seconds, minutes or hours past a given starting date. If this is the case, then dates may be treated as a quantitative variable, but be sure to specify the units.

Many measurements are quantitative. In a purchase record, price, quantity, and time spent on the website are all quantitative values with **units** (dollars, count, and seconds). For quantitative variables, the units tell how each value has been measured. Even more important, units such as yen, cubits, carats, angstroms, nanoseconds, miles per hour, or degrees Celsius tell us the *scale* of measurement, so we know how far apart two values are. Without units, the values of a measured variable have no clear meaning. It does little good to be promised a raise of 5000 a year if you don't know whether it will be paid in euros, dollars, yen, or Estonian krooni. An essential part of a quantitative variable is its units. Some quantitative variables, however, don't have obvious units. The Dow Jones Industrial "Average" has units (points?) but no one talks about them. Percentages are ratios of two quantities and so the units "cancel out," but they are still percentages of something. So, although it isn't imperative that a quantitative variable have explicit units, when they are not explicit, be careful to think about whether adding their values, averaging them, or otherwise treating them as numerical, makes sense.

The distinction between categorical and quantitative variables seems clear, but there are reasons to be careful. First, some variables can be considered as either categorical or quantitative, depending on the kind of questions we ask about them. For example, the variable *Age* would be considered quantitative if the responses were numerical and they had units. A doctor would certainly consider *Age* to be

Area Codes?

When area codes were first introduced all phones had dials. To reduce wear and tear on the dials and to speed calls, the lowest-digit codes (the fastest to dial—those for which the dial spun the least) were assigned to the largest cities. So, New York City was given 212, Chicago 312, LA 213, and Philadelphia 215, but rural upstate New York was 607, Joliet was 815, and San Diego 619. Back then, the numerical value of an area code could be used to guess something about the population of its region. But after dials gave way to push buttons, new area codes were assigned without regard to population and area codes are now just categories, with no quantitative information.

Variable Names That Make Sense

A tradition still hangs on in some places to name variables with cryptic abbreviations in uppercase letters. This can be traced back to the 1960s, when computer programs were controlled with instructions punched on cards. The earliest punch card equipment used only uppercase letters, and statistics programs limited variable names to six or eight characters, so variables had names like PRSRF3. Modern programs don't have such restrictive limits, so there is no reason not to use names that make sense.

quantitative. The units could be years, or for infants, the doctor would want even more precise units, like months, or even days. On the other hand, a retailer might lump together the values into categories like "Child (12 years or less)," "Teen (13 to 19)," "Adult (20 to 64)," or "Senior (65 or over)." For many purposes, like knowing which song download coupon to send you, that might be all the information needed. Then *Age* would be a categorical variable.

How to classify some variables as categorical or quantitative may seem obvious. But be careful. Area codes may look quantitative, but are really categories. What about ZIP codes? They are categories too, but the numbers do contain information. If you look at a map of the United States with ZIP codes, you'll see that as you move West, the first digit of ZIP codes increases, so treating them as quantitative might make sense for some questions. Area codes present a similar set of issues; see the sidebar.

Another reason to be careful about classifying variables comes from the analysis of Big Data. When analysts want to decide what advertisement to send to the web page you're looking at, or what the probability is that you'll renew your phone contract, they use automatic methods involving dozens or even hundreds of variables. Usually the software used to do the analysis has to guess the type of variable from its values. When the variable contains symbols other than numbers, the software will correctly type the variable as categorical, but just because a variable has numbers doesn't mean it is quantitative. We've seen examples (area code, order number) where that's just not the case. Data miners spend much of their time going back through data sets to correctly retype variables as categorical or quantitative to avoid silly mistakes of misuse.

Identifiers

A special kind of categorical variable is worth mentioning. **Identifier variables** are categorical variables whose only purpose is to assign a unique identifier code to each individual in the data set. Your student ID number, social security number, and phone number are all identifiers.

Identifier variables are crucial in this era of Big Data because, by uniquely identifying the cases, they make it possible to combine data from different sources and provide unique labels. Your school's grade transcripts and your bursar bill records are kept separately, but both refer to you. Your student ID is what links them. Most companies keep such relational databases. The identifier is crucial to linking one data table to another in a relational database. The identifiers in Table 1.2 are the *Customer Number*, *Product ID*, and *Transaction Number*. Variables like *UPS Tracking Number* and *Social Security Number* are other examples of identifiers.

Other Data Types

AirBnB, like many travel sites, uses stars to rate their listings. But are star ratings categorical or quantitative? There is certainly an *order* of perceived worth; more stars indicate higher perceived worth. An AirBnB property whose customer responses average around 4 stars is better than one whose average is around 2, but is it *twice* as good? These values are not quantitative, so we can't really answer that question. When the values of a categorical variable have an intrinsic order, we can say that the variable is **ordinal**. By contrast, a categorical variable with unordered categories is sometimes called **nominal**. Values can be individually ordered (e.g., the ranks of employees based on the number of days they've worked for the company) or ordered in classes (e.g., Freshman, Sophomore, Junior, Senior). Ordering is not absolute; how the values are ordered depends on the purpose of the ordering. For example, are the categories Infant, Youth, Teen, Adult, and Senior ordinal?

Well, if we are ordering on age, they surely are and how to order the categories is clear. But if we are ordering on purchase volume, it is likely that either Teen or Adult will be the top group.[5]

Cross-Sectional and Time Series Data

The quantitative variable *Total Revenue* in Table 1.4 is an example of a time series. A **time series** is an ordered sequence of values of a single quantitative variable measured at regular intervals over time. Time series are common in business. Typical measuring points are months, quarters, or years, but virtually any consistently spaced time interval is possible. Variables collected over time hold special challenges for statistical analysis, and Chapter 20 discusses these in more detail.

By contrast, most of the methods in this book are better suited for **cross-sectional data**, where several variables are measured at the same time point. If we collect data on sales revenue, number of customers, and expenses for last month at *each* Starbucks (more than 25,000 locations as of 2017) at one point in time, these would be cross-sectional data. Cross-sectional data may contain some time information (such as dates), but they aren't a time series because they aren't measured at regular intervals. Because different methods are used to analyze these different types of data, it is important to be able to identify both time series and cross-sectional data sets.

Year	Total Revenue (in $B)
2007	9.44
2008	10.38
2009	9.77
2010	10.71
2011	11.70
2012	13.30
2013	14.79
2014	16.44
2015	19.16
2016	21.31

TABLE 1.4 Starbucks's total revenue (in $B) for the years 2007 to 2016.

IN PRACTICE 1.3   Identifying the types of variables

MANAGER I want to understand the data we've collected. How should we begin?

ANALYST (CARLY) First we must classify each variable. Here is a list of the variables and their descriptions.

Account ID – categorical (nominal, identifier)

Pre Spending – quantitative (units $)

Post Spending – quantitative (units $)

Age – categorical (ordinal). Could be quantitative if we had more precise information

Segment – categorical (nominal)

Enroll? – categorical (nominal)

Offer – categorical (nominal)

Segment Spend – quantitative (units $)

All these data are cross-sectional. We do not have successive values over time.

1.4   Data Sources: Where, How, and When

We must know *who*, *what*, and *why* to analyze data. Without knowing these three, we don't have enough to start. Of course, we'd always like to know more because the more we know, the more we'll understand and the better our decisions will be. If possible, we'd like to know the *where*, *how*, and *when* of data as well.

---

[5]Some people differentiate quantitative variables according to whether their measured values have a defined value for zero. This is a technical distinction and usually not one we'll need to make. (For example, it isn't correct to say that a temperature of 80°F is twice as hot as 40°F because 0° is an arbitrary value. On the Celsius scale those temperatures are 26.67°C and 4.44°C—a ratio of 6.) The term *interval scale* is sometimes applied to quantitative variables that lack a defined zero, and the term *ratio scale* is applied to measurements for which such ratios are appropriate.

Values recorded in 1947 may mean something different than similar values recorded last year. Values measured in Abu Dhabi may differ in meaning from similar measurements made in Mexico. Conclusions drawn about data collected from a store in Singapore last spring may not apply to other locations, or other seasons. Knowing *how*, *when*, *where*, and *why* the data were collected can mean the difference between valid and spurious conclusions.

How the data are collected can make the difference between insight and non-sense. As we'll see later, data that come from a voluntary survey on the Internet are almost always worthless. In a recent Internet poll, 84% of respondents said "no" to the question of whether subprime borrowers should be bailed out. While it may be true that 84% of those 23,418 respondents did say that, it's dangerous to assume that that group is representative of any larger group. To make inferences from the data you have at hand to the world at large, you need to ensure that the data you have are representative of the larger group. Chapter 8 discusses sound methods for *designing* a *survey* or poll to help ensure that the inferences you make are valid.

Another way to collect valid data is by performing an experiment in which you actively manipulate variables (called factors) to see what happens. Most of the "junk mail" credit card offers that you receive are actually experiments done by marketing groups in those companies. They may make different versions of an offer to selected groups of customers to see which one works best before rolling out the winning idea to the entire customer base. Chapter 9 discusses both the design and the analysis of experiments like these.

Sometimes, the answer to a question you may have can be found in data that someone or some organization has already collected. Internally, companies may analyze data from their own databases or data warehouse. They may also supplement or rely entirely on data collected by others. Many companies, nonprofit organizations, and government agencies collect vast amounts of data via the Internet. Some organizations may charge you a fee for accessing or downloading their data. The U.S. government collects information on nearly every aspect of life in the United States, both social and economic (see, for example, www.census.gov, or more generally, www.usa.gov), as the European Union does for Europe (see ec.europa.eu/eurostat). International organizations such as the World Health Organization (www.who.org) and polling agencies such as Pew Research (www.pewresearch.org) offer information on a variety of current social and demographic trends. Data like these are usually collected for different purposes than to answer your particular business question. So you should be cautious when generalizing from data like these. Unless the data were collected in a way that ensures that they are representative of the population in which you are interested, you may be misled. Chapter 21 discusses data mining, which attempts to use Big Data to make hypotheses and draw insights.

There's a World of Data on the Internet

These days, one of the richest sources of data is the Internet. With a bit of practice, you can learn to find data on almost any subject. We found many of the data sets used in this book by searching on the Internet. The Internet has both advantages and disadvantages as a source of data. Among the advantages are the fact that often you'll be able to find even more current data than we present. One disadvantage is that references to Internet addresses can "break" as sites evolve, move, and die. Another disadvantage is that important metadata—information about the collection, quality, and intent of the data—may be missing.

Our solution to these challenges is to offer the best advice we can to help you search for the data, wherever they may be residing. We usually point you to a website. We'll sometimes suggest search terms and offer other guidance.

Some words of caution, though: Data found on Internet sites may not be formatted in the best way for use in statistics software. Although you may see a data table in standard form, an attempt to copy the data may leave you with a single column of values. You may have to work in your favorite statistics or spreadsheet program to reformat the data into variables. You will also probably want to remove commas from large numbers and such extra symbols as money indicators ($, ¥, £, €); few statistics packages can handle these.

Throughout this book, we often provide a margin note for a new dataset listing some of the W's of the data. When we can, we also offer a reference for the source of the data. It's a habit we recommend. The first step of any data analysis is to know why you are examining the data (what you want to know), whom each row of your data table refers to, and what the variables (the columns of the table) record. These are the *Why*, the *Who*, and the *What*. Identifying them is a key part of the *Plan* step of any analysis. Make sure you know all three before you spend time analyzing the data.

IN PRACTICE 1.4 Identifying data sources

On the basis of her initial analysis, Carly asks her colleague Ying Mei to e-mail a sample of customers from the Travel and Entertainment segment and ask about their card use and household demographics. Carly asks another colleague, Gregg, to design a study about their double miles offer. In this study, a random sample of customers receives one of three offers: the standard double miles offer; a double miles offer good on any airline; or no offer.

MANAGER It looks like we have three sources of data for our customer spending analysis. How are they different and will you analyze them all the same way?

ANALYST (CARLY) My data set was derived from routine data that we collect on each customer transaction. The data were not part of a survey or experiment. I will need to be careful in drawing conclusions, but my initial exploration of the data helped me decide that we needed more information. Ying Mei's data come from a designed survey, so it should be representative of our customers. Gregg's data come from a designed experiment, which may allow us to decide which of these offers will work the best.

JUST CHECKING

An insurance company that specializes in commercial property insurance has a separate database for their policies that involve churches and schools. Here is a small portion of that database.

2 List as many of the W's as you can for this data set.

3 Classify each variable as to whether you think it should be treated as categorical or quantitative (or both); if quantitative, identify the units.

Policy Number	Years Claim Free	Net Property Premium ($)	Net Liability Premium ($)	Total Property Value ($000)	Median Age in ZIP Code	School?	Territory	Coverage
4000174699	1	3107	503	1036	40	FALSE	AL580	BLANKET
8000571997	2	1036	261	748	42	FALSE	PA192	SPECIFIC
8000623296	1	438	353	344	30	FALSE	ID60	BLANKET
3000495296	1	582	339	270	35	TRUE	NC340	BLANKET
5000291199	4	993	357	218	43	FALSE	OK590	BLANKET
8000470297	2	433	622	108	31	FALSE	NV140	BLANKET
1000042399	4	2461	1016	1544	41	TRUE	NJ20	BLANKET
4000554596	0	7340	1782	5121	44	FALSE	FL530	BLANKET
3000260397	0	1458	261	1037	42	FALSE	NC560	BLANKET
8000333297	2	392	351	177	40	FALSE	OR190	BLANKET
4000174699	1	3107	503	1036	40	FALSE	AL580	BLANKET

⊘ WHAT CAN GO WRONG?

- **Don't label a variable as categorical or quantitative without thinking about the data and what they represent.** The same variable can sometimes take on different roles.

- **Don't assume that a variable is quantitative just because its values are numbers.** Categories are often given numerical labels. Don't let that fool you into thinking they have quantitative meaning. Look at the context.

- **Always be skeptical.** One reason to analyze data is to discover the truth. Even when you are told a context for the data, it may turn out that the truth is a bit (or even a lot) different. The context colors our interpretation of the data, so those who want to influence what you think may slant the context. A survey that seems to be about all students may in fact report just the opinions of those who visited a fan website. The question that respondents answered may be posed in a way that influences responses.

ETHICS IN ACTION

Sarah Potterman, a doctoral student in educational psychology, is researching the effectiveness of various interventions recommended to help children with learning disabilities improve their reading skills. One particularly intriguing approach is an interactive software system that uses analogy-based phonics.

Sarah contacted the company that developed this software, RSPT Inc., to obtain the system free of charge for use in her research. RSPT Inc. expressed interest in having her compare its product with other intervention strategies and was quite confident that its approach would be the most effective. Not only did the company provide Sarah with free software, but RSPT Inc. also generously offered to fund her research with a grant to cover her data collection and analysis costs.

- **Identify the ethical dilemma in this scenario.**

- **What are the undesirable consequences?**

- **Propose an ethical solution that considers the welfare of all stakeholders.**

Jim Hopler is operations manager for a local office of a top-ranked full-service brokerage firm. With increasing competition from both discount and online brokers, Jim's firm has redirected attention to attaining exceptional customer service through its client-facing staff, namely brokers. In particular, management wished to emphasize the excellent advisory services provided by its brokers.

Results from surveying clients about the advice received from brokers at the local office revealed that 20% rated it poor, 5% rated it *below average*, 15% rated it *average*, 10% rated it *above average*, and 50% rated it *outstanding*. With corporate approval, Jim and his management team instituted several changes in an effort to provide the best possible advisory services at the local office. Their goal was to increase the percentage of clients who viewed their advisory services as *outstanding*.

Surveys conducted after the changes were implemented showed the following results: 5% *poor*, 5% *below average*, 20% *average*, 40% *above average*, and 30% *outstanding*. In discussing these results, the management team expressed concern that the percentage of clients who considered their advisory services *outstanding* fell from 50% to 30%.

One member of the team suggested an alternative way of summarizing the data. By coding the categories on a scale from 1 = poor to 5 = outstanding and computing the average, they found that the average rating increased from 3.65 to 3.85 as a result of the changes implemented. Jim was delighted to see that their changes were successful in improving the level of advisory services offered at the local office. In his report to corporate, he only included average ratings for the client surveys.

- **Identify the ethical dilemma in this scenario.**

- **What are the undesirable consequences?**

- **Propose an ethical solution that considers the welfare of all stakeholders.**

1

FROM LEARNING TO EARNING

**LEARNING
OBJECTIVES**

Understand the business context of the data and the problem you are trying to solve to be successful when making decisions from data.

- *Who, what, why, where, when* (and *how*)—the W's—help nail down the context of the data.
- We must know *who, what,* and *why* to be able to say anything useful based on the data. The *who* are the cases (or records or rows). The *what* are the variables. A variable gives information about each of the cases. The *why* helps us decide which way to treat the variables.
- Stop and identify the W's whenever you have data, and be sure you can identify the cases and the variables.

Identify whether a variable is being used as categorical or quantitative.

- Categorical variables identify a category for each case. Usually we think about the counts of cases that fall in each category. (An exception is an identifier variable that just names each case.)
- Quantitative variables record measurements or amounts of something; they must have units.
- Sometimes we may treat the same variable as categorical or quantitative depending on what we want to learn from it, which means some variables can't be pigeonholed as one type or the other.

Consider the source of your data and the reasons the data were collected. That can help you understand what you might be able to learn from the data.

TERMS

Big Data	The collection and analysis of data sets so large and complex that traditional methods typically brought to bear on the problem would be overwhelmed.
Business analytics	The process of using statistical analysis and modeling to drive business decisions.
Case	A case is an individual about whom or which we have data. Also called a record or row.
Categorical (or qualitative) variable	A variable that names categories (whether with words or numerals) is called categorical or qualitative.
Context	The context ideally tells *who* was measured, *what* was measured, *how* the data were collected, *where* the data were collected, and *when* and *why* the study was performed.
Cross-sectional data	Data taken from situations that vary over time but measured at a single time instant are said to be a cross-section of the time series.
Data	Recorded values, whether numbers or labels, together with their context.
Data mining (or predictive analytics)	The process of using a variety of statistical tools to analyze large databases or data warehouses.
Data table	An arrangement of data in which each row represents a case and each column represents a variable.
Data warehouse	A large database of information collected by a company or other organization usually to record transactions that the organization makes, but also used for analysis via data mining.
Experimental unit	An individual in a study for which or for whom data values are recorded. Human experimental units are usually called subjects or participants.
Identifier variable	A categorical variable that records a unique value for each case, used to name or identify it.
Metadata	Auxiliary information about variables in a database, typically including *how, when,* and *where* (and possibly *why*) the data were collected; *who* each case represents; and the definitions of all the variables.
Nominal variable	The term "nominal" can be applied to a variable whose values are used only to name categories.

Ordinal variable	The term "ordinal" can be applied to a variable whose categorical values possess some kind of order.
Participant	A human experimental unit. Also called a subject.
Quantitative variable	A variable in which the numbers are values of measured quantities with units.
Record	Information about an individual in a database.
Relational database	A relational database stores and retrieves information. Within the database, information is kept in data tables that can be "related" to each other.
Respondent	Someone who answers, or responds to, a survey.
Spreadsheet	A spreadsheet is a layout designed for accounting that is often used to store and manage data tables. Excel is a common example of a spreadsheet program.
Subject	A human experimental unit. Also called a participant.
Time series	Data measured over time. Usually the time intervals are equally spaced or regularly spaced (e.g., every week, every quarter, or every year).
Units	A quantity or amount adopted as a standard of measurement, such as dollars, hours, or grams.
Variable	A variable holds information about the same characteristic for many cases.

TECH SUPPORT   Entering Data

These days, nobody does statistics by hand. We use technology: a programmable calculator or a statistics program on a computer. Professionals all use a *statistics package* designed for the purpose. We will provide many examples of results from a statistics package throughout the book. Rather than choosing one in particular, we'll offer generic results that look like those produced by all the major statistics packages but don't exactly match any of them. Then, in the Tech Support section at the end of each chapter, we'll provide hints for getting started on several of the major packages.

If you understand what the computer needs to know to do what you want and what it needs to show you in return, you can figure out the specific details of most packages pretty easily.

For example, to get your data into a computer statistics package, you need to tell the computer:

- Where to find the data. This usually means directing the computer to a file stored on your computer's disk or to data on a database. Or it might just mean that you have copied the data from a spreadsheet program or Internet site and it is currently on your computer's clipboard. Usually, the data should be in the form of a data table with cases in the rows and variables in the columns. Most computer statistics packages prefer the *delimiter* that marks the division between elements of a data table to be a tab character (comma is another common delimiter) and the delimiter that marks the end of a case to be a *return* character.
- Where to put the data. (Usually this is handled automatically.)
- What to call the variables. Some data tables have variable names as the first row of the data, and often statistics packages can take the variable names from the first row automatically.
- Excel is often used to help organize, manipulate, and prepare data for other software packages. Many of the other packages take Excel files as inputs. Alternatively, you can copy a data table from Excel and Paste it into many packages, or export Excel spreadsheets as tab delimited (.txt) or comma delimited files (.csv), which can be easily shared and imported into other programs. All data files provided with this text are in tab-delimited text (.txt) format.

EXCEL

To open a file containing data in Excel:

- Choose **File > Open**.
- Browse to find the file to open. Excel supports many file formats.
- Other programs can import data from a variety of file formats, but all can read both tab delimited (.txt) and comma delimited (.csv) text files.
- You can also copy tables of data from other sources, such as Internet sites, and paste them into an Excel spreadsheet. Excel can recognize the format of many tables copied this way, but this method may not work for some tables.
- Excel may not recognize the format of the data. If data include dates or other special formats ($, €, ¥, etc.), identify the desired format. Select the cells or columns to reformat and in the **Home** menu choose **Home > Format > Format Cells** (found under Cells). Often, the General format is the best option for data you plan to move to a statistics package.

JMP

To import a text file:

- Choose **File > Open** and select the file from the dialog. At the bottom of the dialog screen you'll see **Open As:**—be sure to change to **Data with Preview**. This will allow you to specify the delimiter and make sure the variable names are correct. (JMP also allows various formats to be imported directly, including .xls files.)

You can also paste a data set in directly (with or without variable names) by selecting:

- **File > New > Data Table** and then **Edit > Paste** (or **Paste with Column Names** if you copied the names of the variables as well).

Finally, you can import a data set from a URL directly by selecting:

- **File > Internet Open** and pasting in the address of the website. JMP will attempt to find data on the page. It may take a few tries and some edits to get the data set in correctly.

MINITAB

To import a text or Excel file:

- Choose **File > Open**. From **Files of type**, choose **Text (*.txt)** or **Excel (*.xls; *xlsx)**.
- Browse to find and select the file.
- In the lower right corner of the dialog, choose **Open** to open the data file.
- Click **Open**.

R

R can import many types of files, but text files (tab or comma delimited) are easiest. If the file is tab delimited and contains the variable names in the first row, then:

> $>$ mydata = read.delim(file.choose())

will give a dialog where you can pick the file you want to import. It will then be in a data frame called mydata. If the file is comma delimited, use:

> $>$ mydata = read.csv(file.choose())

COMMENTS

RStudio provides an interactive dialog that may be easier to use. For other options, including the case that the file does not contain variable names, consult **R** help.

SPSS

To import a text file:

- Choose **File > Open > Data**. Under "Files of type," choose **Text (*.txt,*.dat)**. Select the file you want to import. Click **Open**.
- A window will open called Text Import Wizard. Follow the steps, depending on the type of file you want to import.

STATCRUNCH

StatCrunch offers several ways to enter data. Click **MyStatCrunch > My Data**. Click a dataset to analyze the data or edit its properties.

Click a data set link to analyze the data or edit its properties to import a new data set.

- Choose **Select a file on my computer**,
- Enter the URL of a file,
- Paste data into a form, or
- Type or paste data into a blank data table.

For the "select a file on my computer" option, StatCrunch offers a choice of space, comma, tab, or semicolon delimiters. You may also choose to use the first line as the names of the variables.

After making your choices, select the **Load File** button at the bottom of the screen.

BRIEF CASE

Credit Card Bank

Like all credit and charge card companies, this company makes money on each of its cardholders' transactions. Thus, its profitability is directly linked to card usage. To increase customer spending on its cards, the company sends many different offers to its cardholders, and market researchers analyze the results to see which offers yield the largest increases in the average amount charged.

The dataset (**Credit Card Bank**) is part of a much larger database actually used by the researchers. For each customer, it contains several variables in a spreadsheet. Information on the variables is found in the file **Credit Card Bank Info**.

Examine the data in the data file. List as many of the W's as you can for these data and classify each variable as categorical or quantitative. If quantitative, identify the units.

SECTION 1.2

1. A real estate major collected information on some recent local home sales. The first 6 lines of the database appear below. The columns correspond to the house identification number, the community name, the ZIP code, the number of acres of the property, the year the house was built, the market value, and the size of the living area (in square feet).

a) What does a row correspond to in this data table? How would you best describe its role: as a participant, subject, case, respondent, experimental unit, or something else?

b) How many variables are measured for each case?

House_ID	Neighborhood	Mail_ZIP	Acres	Yr_Built	Full_Market_Value	Size
413400536	Greenfield Manor	12859	1.00	1967	$1,00,400	960
4128001474	Fort Amherst	12801	0.09	1961	$1,32,500	906
412800344	Dublin	12309	1.65	1993	$1,40,000	1620
4128001552	Granite Springs	10598	0.33	1969	$67,100	900
412800352	Arcady	10562	2.29	1955	$1,90,000	1224
413400322	Ormsbee	12859	9.13	1997	$1,26,900	1056

2. A local bookstore is keeping a database of its customers to find out more about their spending habits so that the store can start to make personal recommendations based on past purchases. Here are the first five rows of their database:

a) What does a row correspond to in this data table? How would you best describe its role: as a participant, subject, case, respondent, or experimental unit?

b) How many variables are measured for each case?

Transaction ID	Customer ID	Date	ISBN Number of Purchase	Price	Coupon?	Gift?	Quantity
29784320912	4J438	11/12/2009	345-23-2355	$29.95	N	N	1
26483589001	3K729	9/30/2009	983-83-2739	$16.99	N	N	1
26483589002	3K729	9/30/2009	102-65-2332	$9.95	Y	N	1
36429489305	3U034	12/5/2009	295-39-5884	$35.00	N	Y	1
36429489306	3U034	12/5/2009	183-38-2957	$79.95	N	Y	1

SECTION 1.3

3. Referring to the real estate data table of Exercise 1,

a) For each variable, would you describe it as primarily categorical, or quantitative? If quantitative, what are the units? If categorical, is it ordinal or simply nominal?

b) Are these data a time series, or are these cross-sectional? Explain briefly.

4. Referring to the bookstore data table of Exercise 2,

a) For each variable, would you describe it as primarily categorical, or quantitative? If quantitative, what are the units? If categorical, is it ordinal or simply nominal?

b) Are these data a time series, or are these cross-sectional? Explain briefly.

SECTION 1.4

5. For the real estate data of Exercise 1, do the data appear to have come from a designed survey or experiment? What concerns might you have about drawing conclusions from this data set?

6. A student finds data on an Internet site that contains financial information about selected companies. He plans to analyze the data and use the results to develop a stock investment strategy. What kind of data source is he using? What concerns might you have about drawing conclusions from this data set?

CHAPTER EXERCISES

For each description of data in Exercises 7 to 26, identify the W's, name the variables, specify for each variable whether its use indicates it should be treated as categorical or quantitative, and for any quantitative variable identify the units in which it was measured (if they are not provided, give some possible units in which they might be measured). Specify whether the data come from a designed survey or experiment. Are the variables time series or cross-sectional? Report any concerns you have as well.

7. The news. Find a newspaper or magazine article in which some data are reported (e.g., see *The Wall Street Journal, Financial Times, Business Week,* or *Fortune*). For the data discussed in the article, answer the questions above. Include a copy of the article with your report.

8. The Internet. Find an Internet site on which some data are reported. For the data found on the site, answer as many of the questions above as you can. Include a copy of the URL with your report.

9. Survey. An automobile manufacturer wants to know what college students think about electric vehicles. They ask you to conduct a survey that asks students, "Do you think there will be more electric or gasoline powered vehicles on the road in 2025?" and "How likely are you to buy an electric vehicle in the next 10 years?" (scale of 1 = not at all likely to 5 = very likely).

10. Your survey. Think of a question that you'd like to know the answer to that might be answered with a survey. What are the questions? Identify the variables and answer the questions above.

11. World databank. The World Bank provides economic data on most of the world's countries at their website (databank.worldbank.org/data/home.aspx). Select 5 indicators that they provide and answer the questions above for these variables.

12. Arby's menu. A listing posted by the Arby's restaurant chain gives, for each of the sandwiches it sells, the type of meat in the sandwich, number of calories, and serving size in ounces. The data might be used to assess the nutritional value of the different sandwiches.

13. MBA admissions. A school in the northeastern United States is concerned with the recent drop in female students in its MBA program. It decides to collect data from the admissions office on each applicant, including: sex of each applicant, age of each applicant, whether or not the applicant was accepted, whether or not the applicant attended, and the reason for not attending (if the applicant did not attend). The school hopes to find commonalities among the female accepted students who have decided not to attend the business program.

14. MBA admissions II. An internationally recognized MBA program outside of Paris intends to also track the GPA of the MBA students and compares MBA performance to standardized test scores over a six-year period (2009–2014).

15. Pharmaceutical firm. Scientists at a major pharmaceutical firm conducted an experiment to study the effectiveness of an herbal compound to treat the common cold. They exposed volunteers to a cold virus, then gave them either the herbal compound or a sugar solution known to have no effect on colds. Several days later they assessed each patient's condition using a cold severity scale ranging from 0 to 5. They found no evidence of the benefits of the compound.

16. Startup company. A startup company is building a database of customers and sales information. For each customer, it records name, ID number, region of the country (1 = East, 2 = South, 3 = Midwest, 4 = West), date of last purchase, amount of purchase, and item purchased.

17. Vineyards. Business analysts hoping to provide information helpful to grape growers sent out a questionnaire to a sample of growers requesting these data about vineyards: size, number of years in existence, state, varieties of grapes grown, average case price, gross sales, and percent profit.

18. Spectrem Group polls. The Spectrem provides services for the affluent and retirement markets. In a recent survey, they found that millionaires tend to prefer dogs to cats from a question asking them to list the pets they own. They also found that senior executives are more likely to buy treats and toys for their pet than regular investors by asking, "What services and products do you buy for your pet?" (www.spectrem.com/news/life-ruff-ruff-529).

19. EPA. The Environmental Protection Agency (EPA) tracks fuel economy of automobiles. Among the data EPA analysts collect from the manufacturer are the manufacturer (Ford, Toyota, etc.), vehicle type (car, SUV, etc.), weight, horsepower, and gas mileage (mpg) for city and highway driving.

20. Consumer Reports. *Consumer Reports* published an article comparing smartphones. It listed 46 phones, giving brand, price, display size, operating system (Android, iOS, or Windows Phone), camera image size (megapixels), and whether it had a memory card slot.

21. Zagat. Zagat.com provides ratings from customer experiences on restaurants. For each restaurant, the percentage of customers that liked it, the average cost and ratings of the food, decor, and service (all on a 30-point scale) are reported.

22. L.L. Bean. L.L. Bean is a large U.S. retailer that depends heavily on its catalog sales. It collects data internally and tracks the number of catalogs mailed out, the number of square inches in each catalog, and the sales ($ thousands) in the four weeks following each mailing. The company is interested in learning more about the relationship (if any) among the timing and space of their catalogs and their sales.

23. Stock market. An online survey of students in a large MBA Statistics class at a business school in the northeastern United States asked them to report their total personal investment in the stock market ($), total number of different stocks currently held, total invested in mutual funds ($), and the name of each mutual fund in which they have invested. The data were used in the aggregate for classroom illustrations.

24. Theme park sites. A study on the potential for developing theme parks in various locations throughout Europe in 2013 collects the following information: the country where the proposed site is located, estimated cost to acquire site, size of population within a one-hour drive of the site, size of the site, and availability of mass transportation within five minutes of the site. The data will be used to present to prospective developers.

25. Taxi data. The market share analysis of rides in New York City was based in part on the data from the New York City Taxi and Limousine Commission. Data on each ride can be found on the website www.nyc.gov/html/tlc/html/about/trip_record_data.shtml. Because there are over 10,000,000 rides a month, the monthly files are large—up to 2 GB each. For each ride they contain information on the location, costs, and date, among other variables. Here are 13 columns and the first 11 rows (of 11,934,338!) for Yellow Taxis in the month of April 2016. (For a fascinating analysis of taxi data in New York and Chicago, visit the website toddwschneider.com/)

VendorID	TPEP_ pickup	TPEP_ dropof	Passenger_ count	Trip_ distance	Pickup_ longitude	Pickup_ latitude	Dropoff_ longitude	Dropoff_ latitude	Fare_ amount	Tip_ amount	Tolls_ amount	Total_ amount
1	4/1/16 0:00	4/1/16 0:01	1	0.5	−73.976883	40.7584953	−73.977669	40.7539024	3.5	0	0	4.8
1	4/1/16 0:00	4/1/16 0:12	2	2.2	−73.985207	40.7572937	−73.989288	40.7326584	10	2.25	0	13.55
2	4/1/16 0:00	4/1/16 0:10	2	0.96	−73.979202	40.7588692	−73.990677	40.7513199	8.5	0	0	9.8
2	4/1/16 0:00	4/1/16 0:10	5	1.54	−73.984856	40.7677231	−73.990829	40.7511864	8.5	1.96	0	11.76
2	4/1/16 0:00	4/1/16 0:00	2	10.45	−73.863739	40.7694702	−73.976814	40.7752838	34	8.07	5.54	48.41
1	4/1/16 0:00	4/1/16 0:15	1	3.5	−73.973373	40.7570763	−73.933472	40.766304	14	3	0	18.3
1	4/1/16 0:00	4/1/16 0:08	1	4.4	−73.790092	40.6470833	−73.793915	40.6673737	13.5	0	0	14.8
1	4/1/16 0:00	4/1/16 0:03	1	0.6	−73.988899	40.7454262	−73.991821	40.7384453	4.5	1.15	0	6.95
2	4/1/16 0:00	4/1/16 0:03	2	0.81	−73.985275	40.747364	−73.985657	40.7550812	4.5	1	0	6.8
1	4/1/16 0:00	4/1/16 0:04	1	0.8	0	0	−73.977692	40.7538757	5	0	0	6.3
1	4/1/16 0:00	4/1/16 0:06	2	1.8	−73.979752	40.7809486	−73.966621	40.8028374	7.5	0	0	8.8

ID	Age	Plan to Purchase Car?	City or Rural?	Mobile Device	Education	Gender	Latitude	Longitude	Country	Town Size	Household Size
00001700-9f84-0134-2d50-0aaafcbd6b1f	29	yes	city	mobile	high	female	1.2855	103.8565	Singapore	City with 5 million–10 million people	4
0001a0c0-a08e-0134-cf68-0a62e1402143	39	yes	city	mobile	high	female	−12.0678	−77.0886	Peru	Town with 1 000–50 000 people	5 or more
000497f0-9efa-0134-9d13-0aaafcbd6b1f	19	no	city	mobile	low	female	−33.0422	−71.3733	Chile	City with 250 000–1 million people	5 or more
000501c0-ba4c-0134-49bc-0aeaf0818377	27	no	city	desktop	medium	female	4.6492	−74.0628	Colombia	City with more than 10 million people	2
0007a460-9ef0-0134-0666-0a62e1402143	35	yes	city	desktop	high	female	41.0214	28.9684	Turkey	City with more than 10 million people	5 or more
000861c0-a289-0134-30ba-0a62e1402143	53	no	rural	mobile	high	male	33.7208	130.6997	Japan	Town with 1 000–50 000 people	2
0008dbc0-ac5e-0134-cb4a-0aaafcbd6b1f	21	yes	city	tablet	high	female	43.122	−79.805	Canada	City with 250 000–1 million people	4
000920d0-9f42-0134-54fc-0aaafcbd6b1f	19	no	city	mobile	high	female	3.0833	101.5333	Malaysia	City with 50 000–250 000 people	2
000ae030-b561-0134-aeb9-0aaafcbd6b1f	44	yes	city	mobile	high	female	1.2855	103.8565	Singapore	City with 50 000–250 000 people	2
000cb8d0-9df1-0134-4a2a-0aaafcbd6b1f	20	no	city	mobile	high	female	14.5955	120.9721	Philippines	City with 250 000–1 million people	3

26. Dalia Research. The data set from Dalia Research (you'll learn more about Dalia in Chapter 2) contains 763 variables, including demographic information on the 43,034 respondents and survey questions on a variety of topics from intention to purchase a car to quantity of bottled water consumption. Above is a small piece of that data set.

When you organize data in a spreadsheet, it is important to lay it out as a data table. For each of these examples in Exercises 27 to 30, show how you would lay out these data. Indicate the headings of columns and what would be found in each row.

27. Mortgages. For a study of mortgage loan performance: loan number, last 4 digits of borrower's social security number, amount of the loan, the name of the borrower.

28. Employee performance. Data collected to determine performance-based bonuses: employee ID, average contract closed (in $), supervisor's rating (1–10), years with the company.

29. Company performance. Data collected for financial planning: weekly sales, week (week number of the year), sales predicted by last year's plan, difference between predicted sales and realized sales.

30. Command performance. Data collected on investments in Broadway shows: number of investors, total invested, name of the show, profit/loss after one year.

For the following examples in Exercises 31 to 34, indicate whether the data are time series or cross-sectional.

31. Car sales. Number of cars sold by each salesperson in a dealership in September.

32. Motorcycle sales. Number of motorcycles sold by a dealership in each month of 2014.

33. Forestry. Average diameter of trees brought to a sawmill in each week of a year.

34. Baseball. Attendance at the third World Series game recording the age of each fan.

JUST CHECKING ANSWERS

1 The row refers to an order. You can tell because there is a unique purchase order number (first column), but not unique customers. Some customers made more than one purchase.

2 Who—policies on churches and schools

   What—policy number, years claim free, net property premium ($), net liability premium ($), total property value ($000), median age in ZIP code, school?, territory, coverage

   How—company records

   When—not given

3 Policy number: identifier (categorical)

   Years claim free: quantitative

   Net property premium: quantitative ($)

   Net liability premium: quantitative ($)

   Total property value: quantitative ($)

   Median age in ZIP code: quantitative

   School?: categorical (true/false)

   Territory: categorical

   Coverage: categorical

CHAPTER 2

Visualizing and Describing Categorical Data

Dalia Research

Market research uses consumer experience and opinion to inform smart business decisions. Traditional market research methods include face-to-face interviews, focus groups, surveys, and experiments, all of which can help us understand the opinions and behavior of consumers. But these methods tend to be labor-intensive and thus expensive and out of reach for many small firms, including startups.

Dalia Research, founded in Berlin in 2013, uses mobile technology to collect consumer data from around the world much faster and cheaper than previously possible. Rather than focusing on traditional in-person interviews, Dalia distributes surveys through a network of more than 40,000 apps and websites used by nearly 500 million people. To ensure that results are representative, Dalia targets a highly diverse set of demographic groups using a wide variety of apps and websites—from news to shopping to sports and games. In this way, Dalia can generate up to 21 million responses every month from people living in as many as 150 different countries. Dalia claims that, with this technology, they "can ask the world a question and get representative responses from countries all around the world in a matter of days."

In 2015, Dalia was voted the most innovative European startup in the Insight Innovation (IIeX) competition and, in 2017, they were ranked as Germany's 6th fastest growing startup.

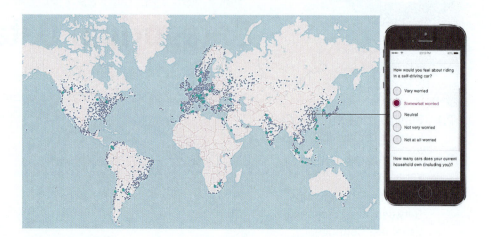

Peer-to-peer businesses are disrupting markets all over the world. AirBnB, eBay, Kiva, Lending Club and Bitcoin are just a few of the companies involved. In transportation, traditional cabs and limosines have seen their markets invaded worldwide. A Yellow Cab medallion, the license that a cab needs to operate in New York City, cost $1.05 million in 2014, but now sells for less than $250,000. That's a drop of over 75%. The market share of cabs dropped from about 84% in April 2015 to 64% a year later. What has caused this disruption to the cab industry? You probably know the answer already, since many millennials use ride-hailing apps from companies like Uber and Lyft, and smaller companies such as Via and Juno as well (see Figure 2.1).

FIGURE 2.1 A ring chart shows the decreased market share of taxis in New York City from April 2015 to April 2016. Ring charts are a variant of pie charts (see page 27). (Source: www.nyc.org)

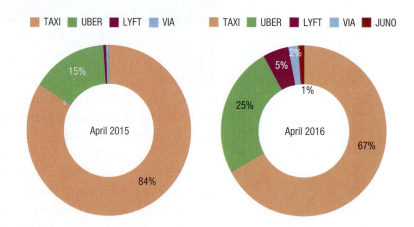

2.1   Summarizing a Categorical Variable

Kelly is an analyst for Analysis Group, an economic consulting firm based in North America. Having heard about the disruption of ride-hailing apps in New York, a European consortium is interested in assessing the impact globally. Kelly is assigned to look into the data from Europe and compare it to data from

WHO	Urban smartphone users
WHAT	Have you used a ride-hailing app to request transportation in the last year?
WHEN	Current
WHERE	Worldwide
HOW	Data compiled by Dalia Research
WHY	To understand customer use of ride-hailing apps in order to understand market disruption of the taxi industry

New York City. Kelly downloads data from the New York City Limousine and Taxi commission (www.nyc.gov), and contacts Dalia, which has recently surveyed urban smartphone users worldwide on a variety of issues including use of ride-hailing apps. Dalia sends her the first 1000 or so respondents collected from five countries Kelly wants to study. Each row corresponds to a respondent and contains information on the respondent's country, gps location (longitude and latitude) and whether he or she has ever used a ride-hailing app. Kelly uses the gps data to make a map, coloring those who have used a ride-hailing app in red and those who haven't in blue (see Figure 2.2).

From the ring chart (Figure 2.1) it seems clear that the Yellow Cab market share in New York has decreased. Looking at the map of the Dalia data (Figure 2.2) Kelly thinks there may be a higher percentage of ride sharing users in Eastern Europe than in the West, but she'd like to know for sure. Data visualizations like these are powerful, but usually it's better to start simply. Kelly would like to summarize the variables and display the information in a way that can easily communicate the results to others.

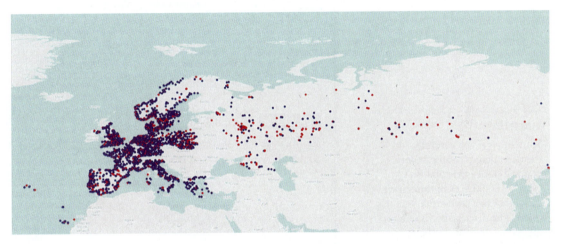

FIGURE 2.2   A map of Europe displaying the respondents from a recent Dalia survey. The red dots represent people who have used a ride-hailing app. Those who haven't are shown in blue. (Source: Dalia Research, personal communication.) (Data in **Dalia**)

Frequency Tables

A **frequency table** records the counts for each of the categories of a categorical variable. Some tables reports percentages instead of counts, and many report both. For example, the data on rides for hire from New York City for April 2016 are shown in Table 2.1 (along with the percent of trips).[1]

TABLE 2.1   A frequency table of the number of rides in April 2016 in New York City by company (green cabs included in Yellow Cab total).

Company	Trips	Percent of Trips
Yellow Cab	12,681,766	66.84
Uber	4,826,280	25.44
Lyft	871,980	4.60
Via	445,980	2.35
Juno	147,180	0.78

[1] Crain's New York Business (www.crainsnewyork.com/article/20170411/TRANSPORTATION/170419978/have-taxis-finally-hit-rock-bottom)

IN PRACTICE 2.1   Gaining insights from counts

The Super Bowl, the championship game of the National Football League of the United States, is an important annual social event for Americans, with tens of millions of viewers. The ads that air during the game are expensive: A 30-second ad during the 2017 Super Bowl cost about $5 to $5.5 million. The high price of these commercials makes them high-profile and much anticipated, and so the advertisers feel pressure to be innovative, entertaining, and often humorous. Some people, in fact, watch the Super Bowl mainly for the commercials. Polls often ask whether respondents are more interested in the game or the commercials. Here are 40 responses from one such poll (NA/Don't Know = No Answer or Don't Know):

Won't Watch	Game	Commercials	Won't Watch	Game
Game	Won't Watch	Commercials	Game	Game
Commercials	Commercials	Game	Won't Watch	Commercials
Game	NA/Don't Know	Commercials	Game	Game
Won't Watch	Game	Game	Won't Watch	Game
Game	Won't Watch	Won't Watch	Game	Won't Watch
Won't Watch	Commercials	Commercials	Game	Won't Watch
NA/Don't Know	Won't Watch	Game	Game	Game

MANAGER   What did our survey say about why people watch the Super Bowl?

ANALYST   The plurality of respondents said that they watched for the game. Here is a table showing counts and percentages:

Response	Counts	Percentage
Commercials	8	20.0
Game	18	45.0
Won't Watch	12	30.0
No Answer/Don't Know	2	5.0
Total	**40**	**100.0**

Source: d25d2506sfb94s.cloudfront.net/cumulus_
uploads/document/9mdlll9bu0/Results%20for%
20YouGov%20NY%20(Super%20Bowl)%20016%
2001.27.2017.pdf

100.01%?

Sometimes if you carefully add the percentages of all categories, you will notice the total isn't exactly 100.00% even though we know that that's what the total has to be. The discrepancy is due to individual percentages being rounded. You'll often see this in tables of percents, sometimes with explanatory footnotes.

2.2   Displaying a Categorical Variable

The Three Rules of Data Analysis

To solve a business problem, there are three things you should always do with data:

1. **Make a picture.** Exploring your data with a display will reveal things you are not likely to see in a table of numbers.
2. **Make a picture.** A well-designed display will do much of the work of analyzing your data. It can help you *model* your data by showing the important features and patterns.
3. **Make a picture.** The best way to *report* to others what you find in your data is with well-chosen data visualizations.

These are the three rules of data analysis. These days, you can create data visualizations easily, so there is no reason not to follow the three rules. Some displays communicate information better than others. We'll discuss some general principles for displaying information honestly in this chapter. Data visualization has become a special discipline in its own right. A well-designed display can show features of even a large, complex data set. Figure 2.2 showed the spatial pattern of ride-hailing apps by displaying each respondent with a dot, located at the site of their response: blue for "no—never used a ride-hailing app" or red for "yes."

The Area Principle

We can't make just any display; a bad picture can distort our understanding rather than help it. For example, Figure 2.3 is a graph of the frequencies of Table 2.1. What impression do you get of the relative frequencies of the market shares of the different companies? You can easily see from both the table and the figure that the largest market share was held by Yellow Cab. But the impression given by Figure 2.3 doesn't seem to correspond well to the percentages to the left of the cars.

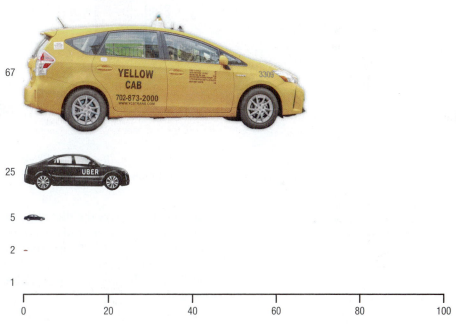

FIGURE 2.3   Although the length of each car corresponds to the correct percentage, the impression we get is all wrong because our brains compare the area (or volume) of the cars, not their length. The Uber market share in 2016 was 38% of the Yellow Cab share, but it looks much smaller.

Even though Yellow Cab still held the lion's share of the market in 2016, the cars in Figure 2.3 make the share look even larger. What's wrong? The lengths of the cars *do* match the percentages in the ring plot. But our eyes tend to be more impressed by the *area* (or perhaps even the *volume*) than by other aspects of each image, and it's that aspect of the image that we notice. Since Yellow Cab's market share was about 2.5 times as big as Uber's, the Yellow Cab is about 2.5 times as long as the Uber car, but it occupies more than 6 times the area. That just isn't a correct impression.

The best data displays observe a fundamental principle of graphing data called the **area principle**, which says that the area occupied by a part of the graph should correspond to the magnitude of the value it represents.

Bar Charts

Figure 2.4 gives us a chart that obeys the area principle. It's not as visually entertaining as the vehicles, but it does give a more *accurate* visual impression of the distribution. The height of each bar shows the count for its category. The bars are the same width, so their heights determine their areas, and the areas are proportional to the counts in each class. Now it's easy to see that Uber's rides are about 40% of Yellow Cab's. We can also see the relative sizes of the three smaller companies that were essentially invisible before. Bar charts make these kinds of comparisons easy and natural.

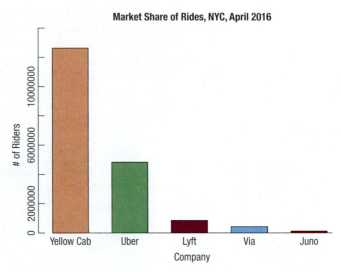

FIGURE 2.4 Rides in New York City in April 2016 by company. With the area principle satisfied, the true distribution is clear.

A **bar chart** displays the **distribution** of a categorical variable, showing the counts for each category next to each other for easy comparison. Bar charts should have small spaces between the bars to indicate that these are freestanding bars that could be rearranged into any order. The bars are lined up along a common base with labels for each category. The variable name is often used as a subtitle for the horizontal axis.

Bar charts are usually drawn vertically in columns, but sometimes, especially when the category names are long, they are drawn with

horizontal bars, like this.[2]

If we want to draw attention to the relative *proportion* of rides from each company, we could replace the counts with percentages and use a **relative frequency bar chart**, like the one shown in Figure 2.5.

---

[2]Excel refers to this display as a column chart when the bars are vertical and a bar chart when they are horizontal, but that's not standard statistics terminology.

FIGURE 2.5 The relative frequency bar chart looks the same as the bar chart (Figure 2.4) but shows the proportion of rides from each company rather than the counts.

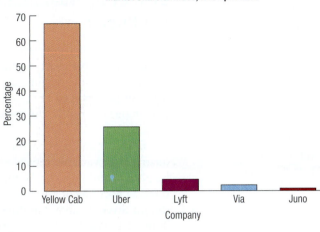

Market Share of Rides, NYC April 2016

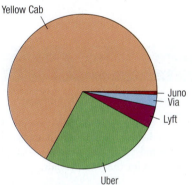

Market Share of Rides, NYC April 2016

FIGURE 2.6 A pie chart shows the proportion of rides from each company.

FIGURE 2.7 Pie charts and bar charts of three data sets. The pie charts look nearly the same, but the differences are clear in the bar charts.

Pie Charts

A **pie chart** shows how a whole group breaks into several categories. Pie charts show all the cases as a circle sliced into pieces whose areas are proportional to the fraction of cases in each category. A variant of the pie chart called a **ring chart** displays only the outer "crust" as we saw in Figure 2.1.

Because we're used to cutting up pies into 2, 4, or 8 pieces, pie charts are good for seeing relative frequencies near 1/2, 1/4, or 1/8. For example, in Figure 2.6, you can easily see that the slice representing Yellow Cab is well over half the total. Unfortunately, other comparisons are harder to make with pie charts.

For example, Figure 2.7 shows three pie charts that look pretty much alike along with bar charts of the same data. The bar charts show three distinctly different patterns, but it is almost impossible to see those in the pie charts.

If you want to make a pie chart or relative frequency bar chart, you'll need to also make sure that the categories don't overlap, so that no individual is counted in two categories. If the categories do overlap, it's misleading to make a pie chart, since the percentages won't add up to 100%.

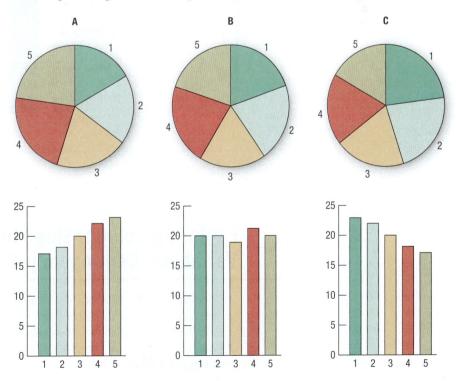

Company	Fare
Yellow Cab	$52.00
Uber	$68.37
Lyft	$56.25
Via	$42.71
Juno	$44.00

TABLE 2.2 A table (not a frequency table) of fares from South Street Seaport in New York City to JFK (11 AM Jan. 15, 2018).

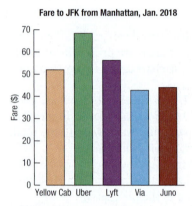

FIGURE 2.8 A bar chart of the fares listed in Table 2.2. We have kept the order of the categories the same as in Figure 2.4, but other orders are possible.

Displaying Quantitative Variables with Bar and Pie Charts

When we have a frequency table of counts, bar charts and pie charts are natural displays. For a bar chart, we put the categories on the *x*-axis and display the counts on the *y*-axis as the heights of the bars. Because there is a bar for each category, the bars can be arranged in various orders. (Although alphabetical order of the category names is rarely the most useful, it is the default used by most statistics software.)

Both bar and pie charts can be used for more than just counts. If we have any quantitative variable recorded for each category, we can display those values as heights of the bars (or, if appropriate, changing them into percentages of the total, as portions of a pie). Suppose we have fares to JFK airport from a location (South Street Seaport) in New York City for each of the five companies listed in Table 2.1. We could display these (or any other quantitative variable) in a bar chart as in Figure 2.8.

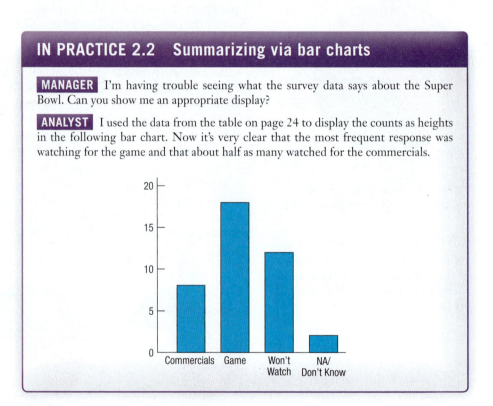

IN PRACTICE 2.2   Summarizing via bar charts

MANAGER I'm having trouble seeing what the survey data says about the Super Bowl. Can you show me an appropriate display?

ANALYST I used the data from the table on page 24 to display the counts as heights in the following bar chart. Now it's very clear that the most frequent response was watching for the game and that about half as many watched for the commercials.

2.3 Exploring Relationships Between Two Categorical Variables: Contingency Tables

Kelly downloads the data for the 13 countries shown in Figure 2.2 and arranges the two variables in a two-way table (Table 2.2).

Because they show how individuals are distributed along each variable depending on, or *contingent on*, the value of the other variable, tables like this are called **contingency tables**.

		Denmark	France	Germany	Greece	Italy	Netherlands	Norway	Poland	Portugal	Russia	Spain	Sweden	United Kingdom	Total
Used Ride-Hailing App?	No	845	898	871	916	874	866	806	734	828	494	807	854	810	**10603**
	Yes	206	166	137	120	136	135	250	273	192	511	209	203	215	**2753**
	Total	**1051**	**1064**	**1008**	**1036**	**1010**	**1001**	**1056**	**1007**	**1020**	**1005**	**1016**	**1057**	**1025**	**13356**

TABLE 2.3 Contingency table of *Ride-Hailing App?* and *Country*. The right margin Totals are the values of *No* and *Yes* from all 13 countries. The bottom margin Totals are the number of respondents from each *Country*. (Source: Dalia Research, personal communication.) (Data in **Dalia**)

Percent of What?

The English language can be tricky. If asked, "What percent of those answering 'Yes' were from Russia?" it's pretty clear that you should focus only on the *Yes* row. The question itself seems to restrict the *who* in the question to that row, so you should look at the number of those in each country among the 2753 people who replied "Yes." You'd find that in the row percentages.

But if you're asked, "What percent were Russians who replied 'yes'?" you'd have a different question. Be careful. That question really means "what percent of the entire sample were both from Russia and replying 'Yes'?", so the *who* is all respondents. The denominator should be 13,356, and the answer is the table percent.

Finally, if you're asked, "What percent of the Russians replied 'yes'?" you'd have a third question. Now the *who* is Russians. So the denominator is the 1005 Russians, and the answer is the column percent.

The margins of a contingency table give totals. The totals in the right-hand column of Table 2.3 show the frequency distribution of the variable *Ride-Hailing App?* We can see, for example, that most people surveyed still have not used such an app. The totals in the bottom row of the table show the frequency distribution of the variable *Country*—how many respondents Dalia obtained in each country. When presented like this, at the margins of a contingency table, the frequency distribution of either one of the variables is called its **marginal distribution**. The marginal distribution for a variable in a contingency table is the same as its frequency distribution.

Each **cell** of a contingency table (any intersection of a row and column of the table) gives the count for a combination of values of the two variables. For example, in Table 2.3 we can see that 810 respondents did not use an app in the United Kingdom (UK). Looking across the *Yes* row, you can see that the largest number of responses in that row (511) is from Russia. Are Brits less likely to use ride-hailing apps than Russians? Questions like this are more naturally addressed using percentages.

We can see that 137 Germans responded "yes." We could display this count as a percentage, but as a percentage of what? The total number of people in the survey? (137 is 1.03% of the total.) The number of Germans surveyed? (137 is 13.6% of the 1008 Germans surveyed.) The number of respondents who responded "yes"? (137 is 4.98% of all yes respondents.) Most statistics programs offer a choice of **total percent**, **row percent**, or **column percent** for contingency tables. Unfortunately, they often put them all together with several numbers in each cell of the table. The resulting table (Table 2.4) holds lots of information but is hard to understand.

	Denmark	France	Germany	Greece	Italy	Netherlands	Norway	Poland	Portugal	Russia	Spain	Sweden	United Kingdom	Total
No	845	898	871	916	874	866	806	734	828	494	807	854	810	**10603**
	6.33	6.72	6.52	6.86	6.54	6.48	6.03	5.50	6.20	3.70	6.04	6.39	6.06	100%
	80.40	84.40	86.41	88.42	86.53	86.51	76.33	72.89	81.18	49.15	79.43	80.79	79.02	79.39%
	7.97	8.47	8.21	8.64	8.24	8.17	7.60	6.92	7.81	4.66	7.61	8.05	7.64	79.39%
Yes	206	166	137	120	136	135	250	273	192	511	209	203	215	**2753**
	1.54	1.24	1.03	0.90	1.02	1.01	1.87	2.04	1.44	3.83	1.56	1.52	1.61	100%
	19.60	15.60	13.59	11.58	13.47	13.49	23.67	27.11	18.82	50.85	20.57	19.21	20.98	20.61%
	7.48	6.03	4.98	4.36	4.94	4.90	9.08	9.92	6.97	18.56	7.59	7.37	7.81	20.61%
Total	1051	1064	1008	1036	1010	1001	1056	1007	1020	1005	1016	1057	1025	13356

TABLE 2.4 Another contingency table of *Ride-Hailing App?* and *Country* showing the counts and the percentages these counts represent. For each count, there are three choices for the percentage: by row, by column, and by table total. There's probably too much information here for this table to be useful.

Yes	No	Total
511	494	**1005**
50.85	49.15	**100%**

TABLE 2.5 The conditional distribution of ride-hailing apps for *Russia*. These percentages are the column percentages for Russia from Table 2.4.

Conditional Distributions

The more interesting questions are contingent on something. We'd like to know, for example, whether these countries are similar in use of the ride-hailing apps. That's the kind of information that could inform a business decision. Table 2.5 shows the distribution of yes respondents conditional on country.

By comparing the frequencies conditional on *Country*, we can see interesting patterns. For example, by focusing on the tenth column of Table 2.3, we can see that Russia stands out as the country that has the highest percentage of people who have used the app. A distribution like this is called a **conditional distribution** because it shows the distribution of one variable for just those cases that satisfy a condition on another. In a contingency table, when the distribution of one variable is the same for all categories of another variable, we say that the two variables are **independent**. That tells us there's no association between these variables. We'll see a way to check for independence formally later in the book. For now, we'll just compare the distributions.

JUST CHECKING

So that they can balance their inventory, an optometry shop collects the following data for customers in the shop.

		Eye Condition			
		Nearsighted	Farsighted	Need Bifocals	Total
Sex	Males	6	20	6	32
	Females	4	16	12	32
	Total	10	36	18	64

1 What percent of females are farsighted?

2 What percent of nearsighted customers are female?

3 What percent of all customers are farsighted females?

4 What's the distribution of *Eye Condition*?

5 What's the conditional distribution of *Eye Condition* for males?

6 Compare the percent who are female among nearsighted customers to the percent of all customers who are female.

7 Does it seem that *Eye Condition* and *Sex* might be dependent? Explain.

2.4 Segmented Bar Charts and Mosaic Plots

Contingency tables like Tables 2.4 and 2.5 contain detailed information, but are not well-suited for communication. Visualizations of contingency tables like segmented or side-by-side bar charts and mosaic charts are an effective way of presenting the information and understanding the relationships between the variables. We'll return to the ride-sharing data for a moment, but let's start with a simpler example.

Everyone knows what happened in the North Atlantic on the night of April 14, 1912, as the *Titanic*, thought by many to be unsinkable, sank, leaving almost 1500 passengers and crew members on board to meet their icy fate. Women and children first was the rule for those commanding the lifeboats, but how did the class of ticket held enter into the order?

Table 2.6 shows some data about the passengers and crew aboard the *Titanic*.

TABLE 2.6 Part of a data table showing seven variables for 11 people aboard the *Titanic*. (Data in **Titanic**)

Name	Survived	Age	Adult/Child	Sex	Price(£)	Class
ABBING, Mr Anthony	Dead	42	Adult	Male	7.55	3
ABBOTT, Mr Ernest Owen	Dead	21	Adult	Male	0	Crew
ABBOTT, Mr Eugene Joseph	Dead	14	Child	Male	20.25	3
ABBOTT, Mr Rossmore Edward	Dead	16	Adult	Male	20.25	3
ABBOTT, Mrs Rhoda Mary "Rosa"	Alive	39	Adult	Female	20.25	3
ABELSETH, Miss Karen Marie	Alive	16	Adult	Female	7.65	3
ABELSETH, Mr Olaus Jörgensen	Alive	25	Adult	Male	7.65	3
ABELSON, Mr Samuel	Dead	30	Adult	Male	24	2
ABELSON, Mrs Hannah	Alive	28	Adult	Female	24	2
ABRAHAMSSON, Mr Abraham August Johannes	Alive	20	Adult	Male	7.93	3
ABRAHIM, Mrs Mary Sophie Halaut	Alive	18	Adult	Female	7.23	3

Only 31% of those aboard the *Titanic* survived. Was that survival rate the same for all ticket classes? Some accounts of the sinking of the *Titanic* suggest there might have been a relationship between the kind of ticket a passenger held and the passenger's chances of making it into a lifeboat. Table 2.7 shows a contingency table of the 2208 people on board the Titanic by *Survival* and ticket *Class*:

TABLE 2.7 A contingency table of *Class* by *Survival* with only counts and column percentages. Each column represents the conditional distribution of *Survival* for a given category of ticket *Class*.

			Class				
			First	Second	Third	Crew	Total
Survival	Alive	Count	201	119	180	212	712
		% of Column	62.0%	41.8%	25.4%	23.8%	32.3%
	Dead	Count	123	166	530	677	1496
		% of Column	38.0%	58.2%	74.6%	76.2%	67.7%
	Total	Count	324	285	710	889	2208
			100%	100%	100%	100%	100%

The changing percentages of survival across each row give the impression that ticket class mattered in whether a passenger survived. But, to make it more vivid, we can visualize the information in this table using side-by-side bar charts as in Figure 2.9 Now it's easy to compare the risks. Among first-class passengers, only 38% perished, compared to 58.2% for second-class ticket holders, 74.6% for those in third class, and 76.2% for crew members.

FIGURE 2.9 Side-by-side bar chart showing the conditional distribution of *Survival* for each category of ticket *Class*. The corresponding pie charts would have only two categories in each of four pies, so bar charts seem the better alternative.

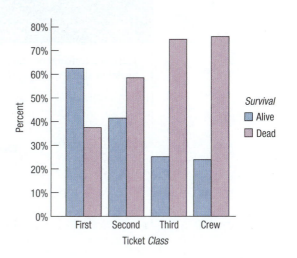

We could also display the *Titanic* information by dividing up bars in proportion to the relative frequencies. The resulting **segmented** (or **stacked**) **bar chart**, in Figure 2.10, treats each bar as the "whole" and divides it proportionally into segments corresponding to the percentage in each group. Now we see that the distributions of ticket *Class* are clearly different, indicating again that *Survival* was not independent of ticket *Class*. Notice that although the totals for survivors and nonsurvivors are quite different, the bars are the same height because we have converted the numbers to percentages. Compare this display with the side-by-side bar charts of the same data in Figure 2.9. Which graph do you find easier to understand?

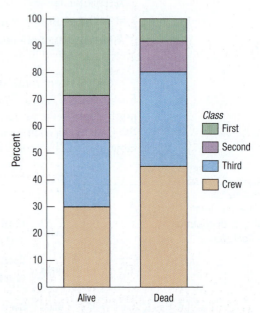

FIGURE 2.10 A segmented bar chart for *Class* by *Survival*. The segmented bar chart shows clearly that the marginal distributions of ticket *Class* differ between survivors and nonsurvivors.

IN PRACTICE 2.3   Insights about relationships of categorical variables from contingency tables and side-by-side bar charts

Here is a contingency table of the responses for 1008 adult U.S. respondents to the question about watching the Super Bowl discussed in the previous In Practice.

	Gender		
	Female	**Male**	**Total**
Game	198	277	475
Commercials	154	79	233
Won't Watch	160	132	292
NA/Don't Know	4	4	8
Total	516	492	1008

MANAGER The numbers are all here, but is there an association between what the viewers are interested in and their gender?

ANALYST Let's first look at the conditional distributions of the four responses for each Gender:

For Men:

Game = 277/492 = 56.3%

Commercials = 79/492 = 16.1%

Won't Watch = 132/492 = 26.8%

NA/Don't Know = 4/492 = 0.8%

For Women:

Game = 198/516 = 38.4%

Commercials = 154/516 = 29.8%

Won't Watch = 160/516 = 31.0%

NA/Don't Know = 4/516 = 0.8%

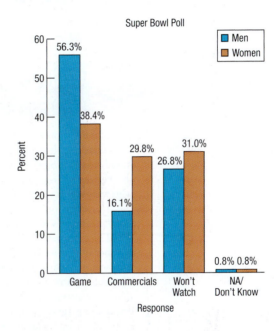

From the conditional distributions and the side-by-side bar charts, it seems that based on this poll, women were only slightly less interested than men in watching the Super Bowl telecast: 31% of the women said they didn't plan to watch, compared to just under 27% of men. Among those who planned to watch, however, there appears to be an association between the viewer's gender and what the viewer is most looking forward to. While more women are interested in the game (38%) than the commercials (30%), the margin among men is much wider: 56% of men said they were looking forward to seeing the game, compared to only 16% who cited the commercials.

Stacked Bar Charts with Quantitative Data

When we have a quantitative variable recorded for each level of a categorical variable, we can create a stacked bar chart of the values even though they are not counts. Be sure to label the axes appropriately and not as percentages.

A variant of the segmented bar chart, a **mosaic plot** looks like a segmented bar chart, but obeys the area principle better. Not only is each vertical bar proportional to the number of cases in its group, but each rectangle in the plot is proportional to the number of cases that fall into the corresponding cell of the contingency table. We can easily see now that only about a third of the people on the *Titanic* survived—something that we can't see in the segmented bar charts. Mosaic plots are increasingly popular for displaying contingency tables and are found in many software packages. They are especially useful when there are many categories, as the next two In Practice examples show, but unlike stacked bar charts, they are usually used only to display counts.

FIGURE 2.11 A mosaic plot for *Class* by *Survival*. The plot resembles the segmented bar chart in Figure 2.10, but now all areas are proportional to the number of cases corresponding to them. We can see the difference in the marginal distributions of ticket *Class* as before, but now we also see that only about a third of those on board survived.

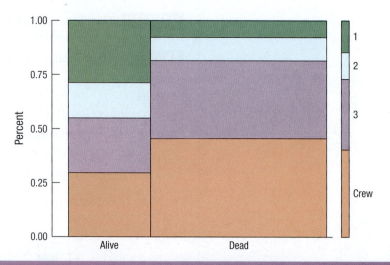

IN PRACTICE 2.4   Learning about associations in large data sets from mosaic plots

One of the authors has his four children on his family cell phone plan. He thought he had a good plan, one that covered everyone for 1500 text messages a month, until he received a monthly bill for $497.65, which somewhat exceeded the $149.95 he was expecting. From the Verizon website, he soon realized that the excess charges were due to his daughter who was away at college for the first time. The Verizon website allowed him to download the "metadata" on all calls and text messages. Here is a mosaic plot of the 3277 outgoing text messages by *Date* (on the *x*-axis) and proportion to each number (on the *y*-axis).

For each day (from 9/11 to 10/23), the width of each bar is proportional to the number of text messages sent. The height of each color within the bar represents the proportion of texts going to each of the most frequently texted numbers on that day. The colors show the most frequently texted phone numbers. The daughter explained that she was texting a lot when she first got to campus because she didn't know anyone and was texting her friends at other colleges. But she claimed that the number of texts had really "calmed down" recently.

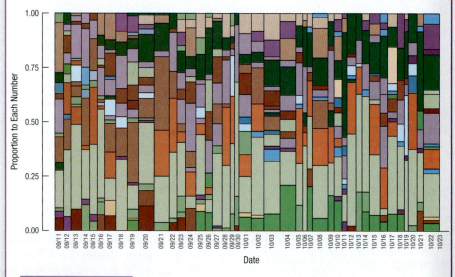

(FAMILY) MANAGER Do you see any evidence that the number of texts decreased over this period?

ANALYST No, if the number of texts were decreasing we should see wide bars on the left and narrower bars on the right. No such pattern is evident.

The father in this example realized that the number of texts was, in fact, not decreasing, and decided to see what other information about the patterns of text sending he could discover.

IN PRACTICE 2.5   Learning about associations in large data sets revisited

RECAP: The Verizon data from the previous example also includes the time of day. Here is a mosaic plot of the same 3277 outgoing texts by hour of the day (0 = midnight through 23 = 11 PM). The order of the hours in this plot goes from 3 AM (3) to 2 AM (2). Note: The first bar on the left contains the hours from 3 AM to 9 AM inclusive.

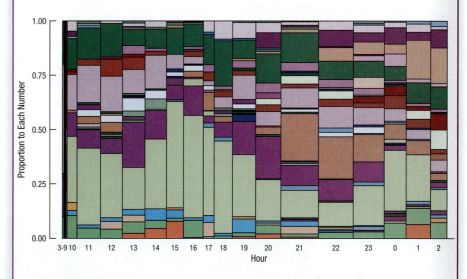

(FAMILY) MANAGER What can we learn about the daily habits of my daughter from the patterns in her texting?

ANALYST There is almost no activity between 3 and 9 AM. At 10 AM the texting starts (somewhat slowly as evidenced by the narrow bar at 10), then is fairly active and constant until 5 PM (17). The texting then increases, with a peak around 9 PM (21), tapering off at bit at midnight (0) to 2 AM. I asked a few questions about her daily activities. It turns out she has no early morning classes (as evidenced by the lack of activity until 10 AM), but she *does* have classes at 11, 12, and 1 PM (!). At 5 PM on most days she goes to the gym (notice the narrow bar at 17), and she claims to study from about 9 PM to midnight. As a teacher yourself, you shouldn't be surprised by this.

GUIDED EXAMPLE   Car Ownership and Countries

The use of apps to call for rides may be related to car ownership. Are markets where car ownership is less common more fertile ground for ride-hailing apps? Dalia also collected data on car ownership, asking "Do you own a car?" with possible responses "Yes," "No," and "No, but I have regular access to one." Kelly's client wants to know how car ownership varies across Europe. (Data in **Dalia**)

(continued)

| PLAN | • **Define** the problem—state the objectives of the study.
• **Identify** and define the variables.
• Provide the time frame of the data collection process. | The client wants to examine the distribution of responses to the question on car ownership and understand how they vary across countries. Dalia Research collected data on this question in the summer of 2017, obtaining approximately 1000 responses from urban smartphones users in each of the 13 countries in Europe used for the ride-hailing app analysis. We will use the data from that study.

The variable is *Car Ownership*. The responses are in nonoverlapping categories "Yes," "No," and "No, but I have regular access to one." |

| DO | • **Characterize** the variables and determine the appropriate analysis for data type.
• **Explore** the data via tables and graphics. For a large data set like this, we rely on technology to make tables and displays. | Both variables are categorical variables. *Car Ownership* can be treated as an ordered categorical variable, with "No, but I have regular access to one" falling between "Yes" and "No." To examine any differences in responses across countries, I will create a contingency table and a mosaic plot. Here are a contingency table of *Car Ownership* by *Country* and a corresponding mosaic plot: |

	Denmark	France	Germany	Greece	Italy	Netherlands	Norway	Poland	Portugal	Russia	Spain	Sweden	United Kingdom	Totals
Yes	533	741	576	539	752	571	650	625	668	393	633	539	412	**7632**
No, but I have regular access to one	194	90	134	204	142	161	175	147	125	159	157	211	193	**2092**
No	324	233	298	293	116	269	231	235	227	453	226	307	420	**3632**
Totals	**1051**	**1064**	**1008**	**1036**	**1010**	**1001**	**1056**	**1007**	**1020**	**1005**	**1016**	**1057**	**1025**	**13356**

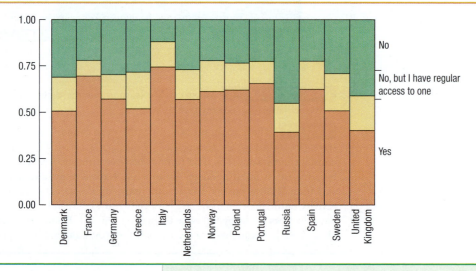

| REPORT | **Communicate and Present**
Summarize the charts and analysis in context. Make recommendations if possible and discuss further analysis that is needed. | **MEMO**

Re: Car ownership by country

Our analysis of the car ownership question shows three groups of countries in Europe with similar distributions. Russia and the UK have low ownership with about 40% of respondents responding yes. France, Italy, Spain, Poland and Portugal all have more than 60% ownership, with Italy the highest at nearly 75%. The other countries have between 50 and 60% ownership. France has a low percentage of non-owners with access to cars at 8.5%. All other countries have between 10 and 20% in that category. The enclosed tables and plots provide support for these conclusions. |

2.5 Three Categorical Variables

Studying the relationship between two variables can take us only so far. If a third variable is involved (as is often the case), the relationship between the first two variables may change depending on the level of the third. We saw that the *Survival* rate on the *Titanic* depended on the *Class* of steerage, but was the relationship between *Survival* and *Ticket Class* the same for men and women?

Mosaic plots and bar charts can often help to visualize these more complex relationships. Conditional distributions—separate contingency tables for each level of the third variable—can hold the details.

Bar charts, whether separate displays for each category of the third variable or side-by-side, can show the changing relationship of two variables across the levels of a third. Mosaic plots add additional information. Each rectangle in a mosaic plot is proportional to the number of cases corresponding to that combination of variable levels. We'll see examples of each in the next In Practice.

IN PRACTICE 2.6   Gaining insight by looking for associations among three variables at once

We've seen that survival on the *Titanic* depended on ticket class of individuals aboard. What visualization will help us to best investigate whether that relationship was the same for the two sexes? With three variables, bar charts and mosaic plots offer us many choices for best visualizing the complex relationships.

RESEARCHER I want to show the changing relationship between survival rate and ticket class for the two sexes. What would be some good ways to show this?

ANALYST With three variables we have lot of choices. Because we are most interested in survival rate, we'll keep that on the vertical axis. First, here are separate bar charts of *Survival* by *Ticket Class* for Males and Females.

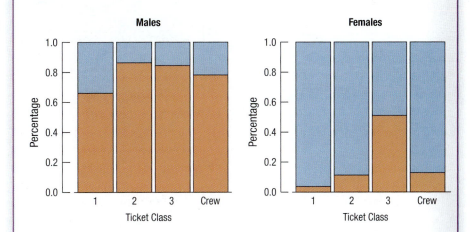

From the separate bar charts, we can see several things. First, it is clear how much higher, in general, the death rates (in orange) were for men, across all ticket classes. We can also see that the survival rates for men were fairly constant, with slightly higher survival rates for first class and crew. For women, not only were survival rates much higher, but the only group that suffered significant losses were women with third-class tickets, where the death rate approached 50%.

(continued)

By placing the bars for men and women side-by-side within each ticket class, we can highlight how different the survival rates were for the two sexes within each ticket class. For first and second class, and the crew, there were very few women lost, compared to substantial losses for men. For third class, the difference is smallest, with substantial losses for both sexes.

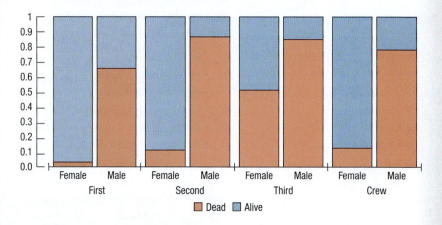

A mosaic plot adds an important piece of information. Even though most of the women lost held third-class tickets, we can now see that there were far fewer women on board. By comparing sizes of rectangles, we can see, for instance, that there were about as many women lost in third-class as there were men in first class.

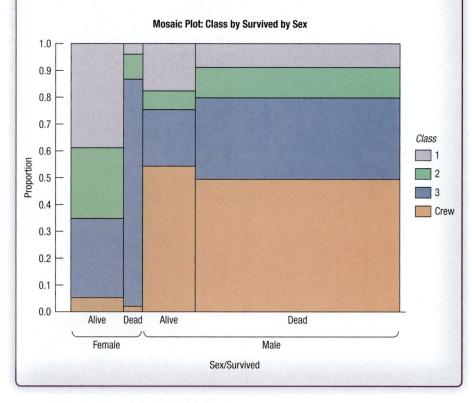

Mosaic Plot: Class by Survived by Sex

Whenever a third variable is involved, you should be cautious about looking at the overall percentages without considering the third variable. Summaries for a single variable that don't take account of others can be dangerous. Looking at only two variables can give paradoxical results and can lead to bad decisions. We'll see examples in the next section.

2.6   Simpson's Paradox

Here's an example showing that combining percentages across very different values or groups can give confusing results. Suppose there are two office supply sales representatives, Peter and Katrina. Peter argues that he's the better salesperson, since he managed to close 83% of his last 120 prospects compared with Katrina's 78%. But let's look at the data a little more closely. Here (Table 2.8) are the results for each of their last 120 sales calls, broken down by the product they were selling.

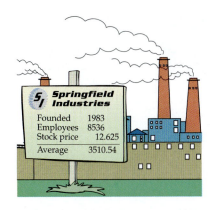

		Product		
		Keurig Coffee Pods	**Sonos Sound Systems**	**Overall**
Sales Rep	**Peter**	90 out of 100 90%	10 out of 20 50%	100 out of 120 83%
	Katrina	19 out of 20 95%	75 out of 100 75%	94 out of 120 78%

TABLE 2.8 Look at the percentages within each Product category. Who has a better success rate closing sales of coffee pods? Who has the better success rate closing sales of sound systems? Who has the better performance overall?

Look at the sales of the two products separately. For coffee pod sales, Katrina had a 95% success rate, and Peter only had a 90% rate. When selling sound systems, Katrina closed her sales 75% of the time, but Peter only 50%. So Peter has better "overall" performance, but Katrina is better selling each product. How can this be?

This problem is known as **Simpson's Paradox**, named for the statistician who described it in the 1960s. Since its discovery, there have been a few well-publicized cases of it (see Discrimination box below for an example). As we can see from Table 2.8, the problem results from inappropriately combining percentages of different groups. Katrina concentrates on selling sound systems, which are more expensive and so, more difficult. Her *overall* percentage is heavily influenced by her sound system average. Peter sells more coffee pods, which appear to be easier to sell. With their different patterns of selling, taking an overall percentage is misleading. Their manager should be careful not to conclude rashly that Peter is the better salesperson.

The lesson of Simpson's Paradox is to be sure to combine only comparable measurements for comparable individuals. Be especially careful when combining across different levels of a second variable. It's usually better to compare percentages *within* each level, rather than across levels.

> ### Discrimination?
> One famous example of Simpson's Paradox arose during an investigation of admission rates for men and women at the University of California at Berkeley's graduate schools. As reported in an article in *Science*, about 45% of male applicants were admitted, but only about 30% of female applicants got in. It looked like a clear case of discrimination. However, when the data were broken down by school (Engineering, Law, Medicine, etc.), it turned out that within each school, the women were admitted at nearly the same or, in some cases, much *higher* rates than the men. How could this be? Women applied in large numbers to schools with very low admission rates. (Law and Medicine, for example, admitted fewer than 10%.) Men tended to apply to Engineering and Science. Those schools have admission rates above 50%. When the total applicant pool was combined and the percentages were computed, the women had a much lower *overall* rate, but the combined percentage didn't really make sense.

⊘ WHAT CAN GO WRONG?

- **Don't violate the area principle.** This is probably the most common mistake in a graphical display. Violations of the area principle are often made for the sake of artistic presentation. Consider this pie chart of ways that respondents said they commute to work.

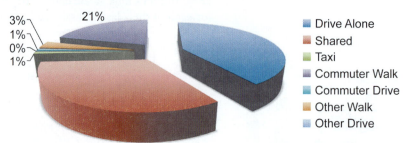

Would it surprise you to learn that the fraction who "Shared" rides to work is 33%, while the fraction who "Drive Alone" is 41%? This pie chart was made in Excel, but overuse of features that make it look interesting has hurt its ability to convey accurate information.

- **Keep it honest.** Here's a pie chart that displays data on the percentage of high school students who engage in specified dangerous behaviors as reported by the Centers for Disease Control. What's wrong with this plot?

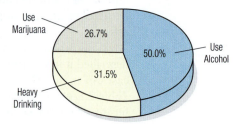

Try adding up the percentages. Or look at the 50% slice. Does it look right? Then think: What are these percentages of? Is there a "whole" that has been sliced up? In a pie chart, the proportions shown by each slice of the pie must add up to 100%, and each individual must fall into only one category. Of course, showing the pie on a slant makes it even harder to detect the error.

Here's another one. This chart shows the average number of texts in various time periods by American cell phone customers in the period 2001 to 2015.

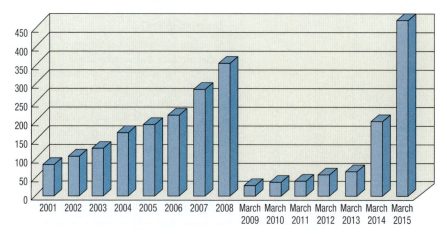

It may look as though text messaging decreased suddenly some time around 2009, which probably doesn't seem right to you. In fact, this chart has several problems. First, it's not a bar chart. Bar charts display counts, or values for categories. This bar chart is a plot of a quantitative variable (average number of texts) against time—which is not categorical. Of course, the real problem is that starting in 2009, they reported the data for only one month instead of for the entire year. Remarkably, the average number of texts per month in 2015 was already greater than the average number per year before 2008!

- **Don't confuse percentages.** Many percentages based on conditional and joint distributions sound similar, but are different (see Table 2.3):
  - The percentage of Russians who answered "Yes": This is 511/1005 or 50.9%—the column percent.
  - The percentage of those who answered "Yes" who were Russian: This is 511/2753 or 18.6%—the row percent.
  - The percentage of those who were Russian *and* answered "Yes": This is 511/13356 or 3.8%—the table percent.

  In each instance, pay attention to the wording that makes a restriction to a smaller group (those who are Russian, those who answered "Yes," and all respondents, respectively) before a percentage is found. This restricts the who of the problem and the associated denominator for the percentage. Your discussion of results must make these differences clear.

- **Don't forget to look at the variables separately, too.** When you make a contingency table or display a conditional distribution, be sure to also examine the marginal distributions. It's important to know how many cases are in each category.

- **Be sure to use enough individuals.** When you consider percentages, take care that they are based on a large enough number of individuals (or cases). Take care not to make a report such as this one:

  We found that 66.67% of the companies surveyed improved their performance by hiring outside consultants. The other company went bankrupt.

- **Don't overstate your case.** Independence is an important concept, but it is rare for two variables to be *entirely* independent. We can't conclude that one variable has no effect whatsoever on another. Usually, all we know is that little effect was observed in our study. Other studies of other groups under other circumstances could find different results.

ETHICS IN ACTION

Mount Ashland Promotions Inc. is organizing one of its most popular events, the ZenNaturals Annual Trade Fest. At this trade show, producers, manufacturers, and distributors in the natural foods market display the latest trends in organic foods, herbal supplements, and natural body care products. The Trade Fest attracts a wide variety of participants, from large distributors who display a wide range of products to small, independent companies.

As in previous years, Nina Li and her team at Mount Ashland are in charge of managing the event, which includes all advertising and publicity as well as arranging spots for exhibitors. The success of this event depends on Nina's ability to attract large numbers of small independent retailers in the natural foods market who are looking to expand their product lines. She knows that these small retailers tend to be zealously committed to the principles of healthful lifestyle.

(continued)

Moreover, many are members of the Organic Trade Federation (OTF), an organization that advocates ethical consumerism.

The OTF has been known to boycott trade shows that include too many products with controversial ingredients such as ginkgo biloba, hemp, or kava kava. Nina is aware that some herbal diet teas have been receiving lots of negative attention lately in trade publications and the popular press. These teas claim to be "thermogenic" or fat burning, and typically contain ma huang (or ephedra). Ephedra is particularly controversial, not only because it can be unsafe for people with certain existing health conditions, but because this fast-acting stimulant commonly found in diet and energy products is contrary to the OTF's principles and values.

Worried that too many products at the ZenNaturals Trade Fest may be thermogenic teas, Nina decides to take a closer look at vendors already committed to participate in the event. Based on the data that her team pulled together, she finds that more than 33% of them do indeed include teas in their product lines. She was quite surprised to find that this percentage is so high. She decides to categorize the vendors into four groups: (1) those selling herbal supplements only; (2) those selling organic foods and herbal supplements; (3) those selling organic foods, herbal supplements, and natural body care products; and (4) all others. She finds that only 2% of groups 1, 2, and 4 include tea in their product lines, while 34% of the third group do. Even though group 3 contains most of the vendors, Nina instructs her team to use the average percentage 10% in its communications, especially with the OTF, about the upcoming ZenNaturals Annual Trade Fest.

- **Identify the ethical dilemma in this scenario.**
- **What are the undesirable consequences?**
- **Propose an ethical solution that considers the welfare of all stakeholders.**

CHAPTER 2 FROM LEARNING TO EARNING

LEARNING OBJECTIVES

Make and interpret a frequency table for a categorical variable.
- We can summarize categorical data by counting the number of cases in each category, sometimes expressing the resulting distribution as percentages.

Make and interpret a bar chart or pie chart.
- We display categorical data using the area principle in either a **bar chart** or a **pie chart**.

Make and interpret a contingency table.
- When we want to see how two categorical variables are related, we put the counts (and/or percentages) in a two-way table called a **contingency table**.

Make and interpret bar charts and pie charts of marginal distributions.
- We look at the **marginal distribution** of each variable (found in the margins of the table). We also look at the **conditional distribution** of a variable within each category of the other variable.
- Comparing conditional distributions of one variable across categories of another tells us about the association between variables. If the conditional distributions of one variable are (roughly) the same for every category of the other, the variables are **independent**.

Make and interpret graphical displays for contingency tables.
- Bar charts (segmented or side-by-side) show the percentages or counts for the values of one variable conditional on the values of another.
- Mosaic plots represent the values in a contingency table because each rectangle is proportional to the number of cases in that cell of the table.

TERMS

Area principle In a statistical display, each data value is represented by the same amount of area.

Bar chart (relative frequency bar chart) A chart that represents the count (or percentage) of each category in a categorical variable as a bar, allowing easy visual comparisons across categories.

Cell	Each location in a contingency table, representing the values of two categorical variables, is called a cell.
Column percent	The proportion of each column contained in the cell of a frequency table.
Conditional distribution	The distribution of a variable restricting the *who* to consider only a smaller group of individuals.
Contingency table	A table displaying the frequencies (sometimes percentages) for each combination of two or more variables.
Distribution	The distribution of a variable is a list of:

- all the possible values of the variable
- the relative frequency of each value

Frequency table (relative frequency table)	A table that lists the categories in a categorical variable and gives the number (the percentage) of observations for each category.
Independent variables	Variables for which the conditional distribution of one variable is the same for each category of the other.
Marginal distribution	In a contingency table, the distribution of either variable alone. The counts or percentages are the totals found in the margins (usually the right-most column or bottom row) of the table.
Mosaic plot	A mosaic plot is a graphical representation of a (usually two-way) contingency table. The plot is divided into rectangles so that the area of each rectangle is proportional to the number of cases in the corresponding cell.
Pie chart	Pie charts show how a "whole" divides into categories by showing a wedge of a circle whose area corresponds to the proportion in each category.
Row percent	The proportion of each row contained in the cell of a frequency table.
Segmented (or stacked) bar chart	A segmented bar chart displays the conditional distribution of a categorical variable within each category of another variable.
Simpson's paradox	A phenomenon that arises when averages, or percentages, are taken across different groups, and these group averages appear to contradict the overall averages.
Total percent	The proportion of the total contained in the cell of a frequency table.

TECH SUPPORT   Displaying Categorical Data

Although every package makes a slightly different bar chart, they all have similar features:

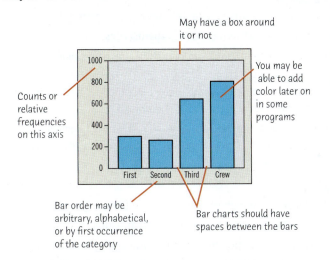

May have a box around it or not

You may be able to add color later on in some programs

Counts or relative frequencies on this axis

Bar order may be arbitrary, alphabetical, or by first occurrence of the category

Bar charts should have spaces between the bars

Sometimes the count or a percentage is printed above or on top of each bar to give some additional information. You may find that your statistics package sorts category names in annoying orders by default. For example, many packages sort categories alphabetically or by the order the categories are seen in the data set. Often, neither of these is the best choice.

EXCEL

Excel offers a versatile and powerful tool it calls a *PivotTable*. A pivot table can summarize, organize, and present data from an Excel spreadsheet. Pivot tables can be used to create frequency distributions and contingency tables. They provide a starting point for several kinds of displays. Pivot tables are linked to data in your Excel spreadsheet so they will update when you make changes to your data. They can also be linked directly to a *PivotChart* to display the data graphically. For a complete discussion of PivotTables and PivotCharts, see support.office.com/en-US/article/Overview-of-PivotTable-and-PivotChart-reports-527c8fa3-02c0-445a-a2db-7794676bce96

In a pivot table, all types of data are summarized into a row-by-column table format. Pivot table cells can hold counts, percentages, and descriptive statistics.

To create a pivot table:

- Open a data file in Excel. At least one of the variables in the dataset should be categorical.

- Choose **Insert > PivotChart > PivotChart & PivotTable** or **Insert > PivotChart** (Mac). Choose to put the pivot table in a new worksheet.

- The *PivotTable* builder will appear.

- The *PivotTable* builder has five boxes:

  - *Field List* (top): variables from the data set linked to the *PivotTable*. (The *Pivot-Table* tool calls the variables "fields.") Fields can be selected using the checkbox or dragged and dropped into one of the areas below in the *PivotTable* builder.

  - *Report Filters* (middle left): Variables placed here filter the data in the pivot table. When selected, the filter variable name appears above the pivot table. Use the drop-down list to the right of the variable name to choose values to display.

  - *Rows* (bottom left): Values of variables placed here become row labels in the pivot table.

  - *Columns* (middle right): Values of variables placed here become column labels in the pivot table.

  - *Values* (bottom right): Variables placed here are summarized in the cells of the table. Change settings to display count, sum, minimum, maximum, average, and more or to display percentages and ranks.

To create a frequency distribution pivot table:

- Drag a categorical variable from the Field List into **Rows**.

- Choose another variable from the data set and drag it into **Values**. Use a unique identifier variable (e.g., subject number) if possible.

- To change what fact or statistics about the **Values** variable is displayed, click the arrow next to the variable in the **Values** box and open the **Value Field Settings**. For a frequency distribution, select **count of [VARIABLE].** When changing **Value Field Settings**, note the tab **Show Values As**, which provides other display options (e.g., % of row, % of column).

The result will be a frequency table with a column for count.

To create a contingency table using *PivotTable*:

- Drag a categorical variable from the Field List into **Rows**.

- Drag a second categorical variable from the Field List into **Columns**.

3	Row Labels	Sum of Workers
4	16-24	16801
5	25-34	17375
6	35-44	15720
7	45-54	15827
8	55-64	9094
9	65 and older	2715
10	**Grand Total**	**77532**

- Choose another variable from the dataset and drag it into **Values**. The resulting pivot table is a row-by-column contingency table.

3	Sum of Workers	Column Labels				
4	Row Labels	Below Min-M	Below Min-W	HW-M	HW-W	Grand Total
5	16-24	384	738	7701	7978	16801
6	25-34	150	332	7864	9029	17375
7	35-44	71	170	7783	7696	15720
8	45-54	68	134	8260	7365	15827
9	55-64	35	72	4895	4092	9094
10	65 and older	22	50	1469	1174	2715
11	Grand Total	730	1496	37972	37334	77532

NOTE: As with the frequency distribution, you can use the **Value Field Settings** to change the type of summary.

To create a chart from a pivot table frequency distribution or contingency table on Windows:

- Place the cursor anywhere on the pivot table.

- On the Insert tab, pick **Recommended Charts**. PivotCharts are special charts that are linked to the PivotTable Data. For more information, see support.office.com/en-US/article/Create-a-PivotChart-c1b1e057-6990-4c38-b52b-8255538e7b1c

- Choose the type of chart: options include pie chart, bar chart, and segmented bar graph.

- Move the chart to a new worksheet by right-clicking the chart and selecting **Move chart**.

- In a bar chart created from a contingency table, by default, rows display on the *x*-axis and the columns are separate bars. To change this, right click on the chart, choose **Select data**, and then click **Switch Row/Column**.

- There is no PivotChart feature in Mac Excel 2016.

- On Macs, choose **Insert** and select your chart from the ribbon or choose a chart type from the **Chart** menu.

- You may wish to copy the data from the PivotTable to another area of your worksheet and use **Edit > Paste** Values to reformat the data so that it is in the proper format for the chart type you wish to create.

XLSTAT

To create a contingency table from unsummarized data:

- On the XLStat tab, choose **Preparing data**.

- From the menu, choose **Create a contingency table**.

- In the dialog box, enter your data range on the General tab. Your data should be in two columns, one of which is the row variable and the other is the column variable.

- On the Outputs tab, check the box next to **Contingency table** and optionally choose **Percentages/Row or Column** to see the conditional distributions.

JMP

JMP makes a bar chart and frequency table together.

- From the **Analyze** menu, choose **Distribution**.

- In the Distribution dialog, put (by dragging it or clicking on it) the name of the variable into the empty variable window beside the label **Y, Columns**; click **OK**.

To make a pie chart,

- Choose **Graph > Chart** menu.
- In the Chart dialog, select the variable name from the Columns list, click on the button labeled **Statistics**, and select **N** from the drop-down menu.
- Click the "**Categories, X, Levels**" button to assign the same variable name to the *x*-axis.

To make a contingency table and mosaic plot,

- From the **Analyze** menu, select **Fit Y by X**.
- Choose one variable as the Y, response variable, and the other as the X, factor variable. Both selected variables must be Nominal or Ordinal.
- JMP will make a mosaic plot and a contingency table.

JMP can make stacked and side-by-side bar charts:

- Select **Graph > Chart**.
- Select first grouping variable and click **Categories, X, Levels**.
- Select second grouping variable and click **Categories, X, Levels**.
- Select **Y variable** and click **Statistics**.
- Select **% of Total** (or **Mean** if 0/1 data) from the menu of statistics.
- Click **OK**.
- Select **Stack Bars** from the red triangle menu for stacked bar chart (default is side-by-side).

COMMENTS

JMP can also make bar charts and mosaic plots with more than two variables using the **Graph Builder**. See the **JMP** documentation for details: www.jmp.com/en_us/support/jmp-documentation.html

MINITAB

Minitab can make most of the plots discussed in this chapter. For details go to support.minitab.com/en-us/minitab/18/

- Choose the **Basic Statistics** or **Graphs** menu and select the display type of interest.
- To make a mosaic plot you must use a macro.
- Find instructions for downloading, installing, and using the macro at support.minitab.com/en-us/minitab/18/macro-library/macro-files/graphs-macros/mosaic/

In Minitab Express, find graphs in the **Graphs** menu. Both Bar Chart and Pie Chart offer options.

R

To make a bar chart or pie chart in **R**, you first need to create the frequency table for the desired variable(s).

If your data are in the data frame DATA and your variables are called X,Y, and Z, then

- tab=with(DATA, table(X)) will produce a frequency table for a single variable X.

- barplot(tab) will give a bar chart for X.
- Similarly, pie(tab) will give a pie chart.

To make a contingency table (with two or more variables),

- counts=with(DATA,table(X,Y))

A stacked bar chart of the contingency table can be made by:

- barplot(counts)

To make side-by-side bar charts, add beside=TRUE:

- barplot(counts,beside=TRUE)

Mosaicplots can be made via the mosaicplot function:

- with(DATA,mosaicplot(~X+Y))

or

- with(DATA,mosaicplot(~X+Y+Z))

COMMENTS

Plots can also be made via ggplot. See the documentation for ggplot2: ggplot2.org/.

SPSS

Most graphs in SPSS are made with the Chart Builder command:

Graphs > Chart Builder...

- Choose the **Gallery** tab in the lower panel of the dialog.
- From the menu on the left, choose **Bar** or **Pie/Polar**.
- In the resulting gallery, select the style of plot, drag it up and drop it into the Chart Preview Area.
- You will then be presented with an Element Properties dialog.
- Select variables from the Variables box in the Chart Builder dialog, the drag and drop them into the Chart Preview Area in the appropriate places.
- Indicate any special modifications in the Element Properties dialog. (None of those apply to methods of this chapter.)
- Click **Apply** and then **OK**.

An alternative is to use the SPSS Legacy Dialogs, where you will find a Pie command and a Bar command. Follow the instructions in the resulting dialogs.

STATCRUNCH

To make a bar chart or pie chart:

- Click on **Graph**.
- Choose the type of plot (**Bar Plot** or **Pie Chart**).
- Choose between raw data (**With Data**) or summaries of data (**With Summary**).
- Choose the variable name from the list of Columns; if using summaries, also choose the counts.

For bar graphs, select Type:

- **Frequency**, **Relative frequency**, **Percent**, **Relative frequency (within category)**, or **Percent (within category)**.
- Note that you may elect to group categories under a specified percentage as Other.
- Click on **Compute**!

To make a contingency table:

- Click on **Stat > Tables > Contingency > With Data** (or **With Summary**).
- Select Row variable and Column Variable (there are options for grouping and type of display).
- Click on **Compute!**

To make a stacked or side-by-side bar chart:

- Click on **Graph > Bar Plot > With Data** (or **With Summary**).

- Select **Column** variable.
- Select **Group by** for second variable.
- Select **Grouping option**. The default is **Split bars**—side-by-side—or select **Stack bars** or **Separate graph for each group**.
- Click on **Compute!**

COMMENTS
There are options for various percentages in the bar charts.

BRIEF CASE

Credit Card Bank

In Chapter 1, you identified the W's for the data in the file **Credit card bank**. For the categorical variables in the data set, create frequency tables, bar charts, and pie charts using your software. What might the bank want to know about these variables? Which of the tables and charts do you find most useful for communicating information about the bank's customers? Write a brief case report summarizing your analysis and results. (Data description in **Credit card bank info**)

CHAPTER 2 EXERCISES

SECTION 2.1

1. As part of the human resource group of your company you are asked to summarize the educational levels of the 512 employees in your division. From company records, you find that 164 have no college degree (None), 42 have an associate's degree (AA), 225 have a bachelor's degree (BA), 52 have a master's degree (MA), and 29 have PhDs. For the educational level of your division:

a) Make a frequency table.
b) Make a relative frequency table.

2. As part of the marketing group at Pixar, you are asked to find out the age distribution of the audience of Pixar's latest film. With the help of 10 of your colleagues, you conduct exit interviews by randomly selecting people to question at 20 different movie theaters. You ask them to tell you if they are younger than 6 years old, 6 to 9 years old, 10 to 14 years old, 15 to 21 years old, or older than 21. From 470 responses, you find out that 45 are younger than 6, 83 are 6 to 9 years old, 154 are 10 to 14, 18 are 15 to 21, and 170 are older than 21. For the age distribution:

a) Make a frequency table.
b) Make a relative frequency table.

SECTION 2.2

3. From the educational level data described in Exercise 1:

a) Make a bar chart using counts on the y-axis.
b) Make a relative frequency bar chart using percentages on the y-axis.
c) Make a pie chart.

4. From the age distribution data described in Exercise 2:

a) Make a bar chart using counts on the y-axis.
b) Make a relative frequency bar chart using percentages on the y-axis.
c) Make a pie chart.

5. For the educational levels described in Exercise 1:

a) Write two to four sentences summarizing the distribution.
b) What conclusions, if any, could you make about the educational level at other companies?

6. For the ages described in Exercise 2:

a) Write two to four sentences summarizing the distribution.
b) What possible problems do you see in concluding that the age distribution from these surveys accurately represents the ages of the national audience for this film?

SECTION 2.3

7. From Exercise 1, we also have data on how long each person has been with the company (tenure) categorized into three levels: less than 1 year, between 1 and 5 years, and more than 5 years. A table of the two variables together looks like:

	None	AA	BA	MA	PhD
<1 Year	10	3	50	20	12
1–5 Years	42	9	112	27	15
More Than 5 Years	112	30	63	5	2

a) Find the marginal distribution of the tenure. (*Hint*: Find the row totals.)
b) Verify that the marginal distribution of the education level is the same as that given in Exercise 1.

8. In addition to their age levels, the movie audiences in Exercise 2 were also asked if they had seen the movie before (Never, Once, More than Once). Here is a table showing the responses by age group:

	Under 6	6–9	10–14	15–21	Over 21
Never	39	60	84	16	151
Once	3	20	38	2	15
More Than Once	3	3	32	0	4

a) Find the marginal distribution of their previous viewing of the movie. (*Hint:* Find the row totals.)
b) Verify that the marginal distribution of the ages is the same as that given in Exercise 2.

SECTION 2.4

9. For the table in Exercise 7:

a) Find the column percentages.
b) Looking at the column percentages in part a, does the *tenure* distribution (how long the employee has been with the company) for each educational level look the same? Comment briefly.
c) Make a segmented or stacked bar chart showing the *tenure* distribution for each educational level.
d) Is it easier to see the differences in the distributions using the column percentages or the segmented bar chart?
e) How would a mosaic plot help to accurately display these data?

10. For the table in Exercise 8:

a) Find the column percentages.
b) Looking at the column percentages in part a, does the distribution of how many times someone has seen the movie look the same for each age group? Comment briefly.
c) Make a segmented bar chart, showing the distribution of viewings for each age level.
d) Is it easier to see the differences in the distributions using the column percentages or the segmented bar chart?
e) How would a mosaic plot represent these data more appropriately?

CHAPTER EXERCISES

11. Graphs in the news. Find a bar graph of categorical data from a business publication (e.g., *Bloomberg Businessweek*, *Fortune*, *The Wall Street Journal*, etc.).

a) Is the graph clearly labeled?
b) Does it violate the area principle?
c) Does the accompanying article tell the W's of the variable?
d) Do you think the article correctly interprets the data? Explain.

12. Graphs in the news, part 2. Find a pie chart of categorical data from a business publication (e.g., *Bloomberg Businessweek*, *Fortune*, *The Wall Street Journal*, etc.).

a) Is the graph clearly labeled?
b) Does it violate the area principle?
c) Does the accompanying article tell the W's of the variable?
d) Do you think the article correctly interprets the data? Explain.

13. Tables in the news. Find a frequency table of categorical data from a business publication (e.g., *Bloomberg Businessweek*, *Fortune*, *The Wall Street Journal*, etc.).

a) Is it clearly labeled?
b) Does it display percentages or counts?
c) Does the accompanying article tell the W's of the variable?
d) Do you think the article correctly interprets the data? Explain.

14. Tables in the news, part 2. Find a contingency table of categorical data from a business publication (e.g., *Bloomberg Businessweek*, *Fortune*, *The Wall Street Journal*, etc.).

a) Is it clearly labeled?
b) Does it display percentages or counts?
c) Does the accompanying article tell the W's of the variable?
d) Do you think the article correctly interprets the data? Explain.

15. U.S. market share. Multinational corporations face stiff competition in the carbonated drink category (also known as soda or pop, depending on where you live). Data were collected on the 2015 U.S. market share of leading sellers of carbonated soft drinks, summarized in the following pie chart:

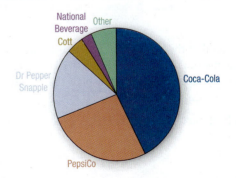

a) Is this an appropriate display for these data? Explain.
b) Which company had the largest share of the market?

16. Brand value. Corporations are also very interested in the value of their brand. The following chart displays the value of the top 6 carbonated soft drink brands in 2015 as collected by Millward Brown (www.millwardbrown .com/brandz/top-global-brands/2015/brand-categories/ soft-drinks)

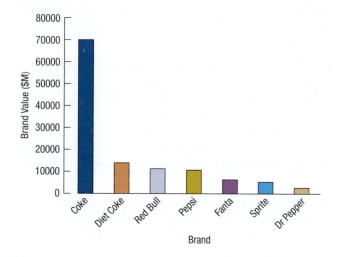

a) Is this an appropriate display for these data? Explain.
b) Which brand had the smallest brand value?
c) Which brand had the larger market value—Pepsi or Red Bull?

17. Market share again. Here's a bar chart of the data in Exercise 15.

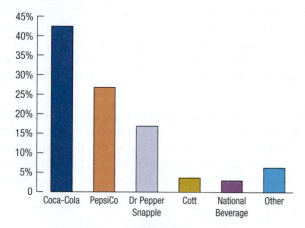

a) Compared to the pie chart in Exercise 15, which is better for displaying the relative portions of market share? Explain.
b) What is missing from this display that might make it somewhat misleading?

18. World market share again. Here's a pie chart of the data in Exercise 16.

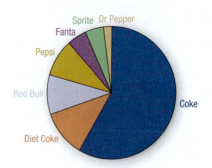

a) Which display of these data is best for comparing the market value of these brands? Explain.
b) Does Pepsi or Red Bull have a larger market value? Is that comparison easier to make with the pie chart or the bar chart of Exercise 16?

19. Insurance company. An insurance company is updating its payouts and cost structure for their insurance policies. Of particular interest to them is the risk analysis for customers currently on heart or blood pressure medication. The Centers for Disease Control and Prevention (www.cdc.gov) lists causes of death in the United States during one year as follows.

Cause of Death	Percent
Heart disease	30.3
Cancer	23.0
Circulatory diseases and stroke	8.4
Respiratory diseases	7.9
Accidents	4.1

a) Is it reasonable to conclude that heart or respiratory diseases were the cause of approximately 38% of U.S. deaths during this year?
b) What percent of deaths were from causes not listed here?
c) Create an appropriate display for these data.

20. Financial satisfaction In 2014, Pew Research Center released the results of a survey among U.S. adults that asked nearly 2000 people how satisfied they are with their current financial situation (www.pewsocialtrends .org/datasets/). Responses were collected by gender, using a five-point scale ranging from "Very Satisfied" to "Very Dissatisfied," with an option to refuse to answer. The tabulated results appear in the contingency table below:

Gender	Very satisfied	Somewhat satisfied	Somewhat dissatisfied	Very dissatisfied	No Answer	Total
Male	325	397	171	132	29	1054
Female	285	335	163	134	23	940
Total	610	732	334	266	52	1994

a) Compare the distribution of opinions between males and females in the survey. Is it reasonable for someone to conclude that females are less satisfied than males with their financial situation?

b) Would it be reasonable to conclude that there are more than 50% males in the United States from the data? Why or why not?

21. B2B. Business-to-business sales are a huge fraction of the economy of every country. As a result, there is a whole industry dedicated to tracking the market share of business products and services. Companies are interested in these market shares to track competitors and to decide which products are popular (and adopt them). Computer Profile surveyed 3500 Dutch companies to see what vendor they were using for video conferencing (www.computerprofile .com/analytics-papers/cisco-leader-voip-solutions-dutch-business-market/). Results showed market shares for Polycom = 31%, Cisco = 33%, Lifesize = 11%, and Siemens = 3%, with others making up the remainder. Create an appropriate graphical display of this information and write a sentence or two that might appear in a news-paper article about the market share.

T 22. Toy makers. The Toy Association tracks sales of toys using a tracking survey that represents approximately 80% of U.S. toy sales. Projected to the entire industry, the fol-lowing table breaks down U.S. toy sales by category.

a) Create an appropriate graphical display of this informa-tion and write a sentence or two that might appear in a newspaper article about the market for toys.

b) Does it appear that the relative sizes of the categories are the same in 2016 as they were in 2013?

Traditional Toy Categories	2013 ($B)	2016 ($B)
Action Figures & Accessories	$1.25	$1.44
Art & Crafts	$1.03	$0.98
Building Sets	$1.66	$1.97
Dolls	$2.31	$2.88
Games/Puzzles	$1.36	$1.95
Infant/Toddler/Preschool Toys	$3.06	$3.19
Youth Electronics	$0.55	$0.61
Outdoor & Sports Toys	$3.04	$3.73
Plush	$0.93	$1.08
Vehicles	$1.33	$1.45
All Other Toys	$1.06	$1.09

23. Job satisfaction. Pew Research published a study on Americans' satisfaction with their current job (www .pewsocialtrends.org/2016/10/06/3-how-americans-view-their-jobs/). They found that 49% of American workers say they are very satisfied with their current job, 30% are

somewhat satisfied, 9% are somewhat dissatisfied, and 6% are very dissatisfied.

a) What do you notice about the percentages listed? How could this be?

b) Make a bar chart to display the results and label it clearly.

c) Would a pie chart be an effective way of communicating this information? Why or why not?

24. Small business hiring. The Wells Fargo/Gallup Small Business Index survey from Exercise 23 also asked 604 small businesses about their cash flow over the next 12 months. 13% responded "Very Good," 37% "Somewhat good," 21% "Neither good nor poor," 20% "Somewhat poor," and 7% "Very poor."

a) What do you notice about the percentages listed?

b) Make a bar chart to display the results and label it clearly.

c) Would a pie chart be an effective way of communicating this information? Why or why not?

d) Write a couple of sentences on the responses of small business owners about their cash flow in the next 12 months.

25. Environmental hazard 2016. Data from the Interna-tional Tanker Owners Pollution Federation Limited (www .itopf.com) give the cause of spillage for 460 large oil tanker accidents from 1970 to 2016. Here are the displays. Write a brief report interpreting what the displays show. Is a pie chart an appropriate display for these data? Why or why not?

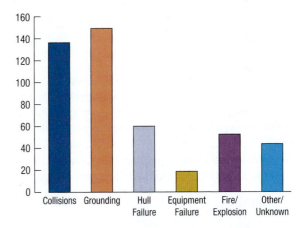

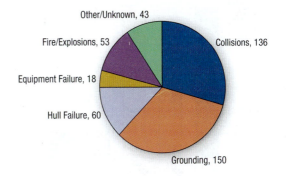

26. Olympic medals. In the history of the modern Olympics, the United States has won more medals than any other country. But the United States has a large population. Perhaps a better measure of success is the number of medals won *per capita*—that is the number of medals divided by the population. By that measure, the leading countries are Liechtenstein (255.42 medals/cap), Norway (95.271), Finland (86.514), and Sweden (66.455). The following table summarizes the medals/capita counts for the 100 countries with the most medals.

a) Try to make a display of these data. What problems do you encounter?

b) Can you find a way to organize the data so that the graph is more successful?

Medals/capita	# Countries	Medals/capita	# Countries
0	72	130	0
10	13	140	0
20	3	150	0
30	3	160	0
40	2	170	0
50	0	180	0
60	1	190	0
70	0	200	0
80	1	210	0
90	1	220	0
100	0	230	0
110	0	240	0
120	0	250	1

27. Importance of wealth. GfK Roper Reports Worldwide surveyed people, asking them "How important is acquiring wealth to you?" The percent who responded that it was of more than average importance were: 71.9% China, 59.6% France, 76.1% India, 45.5% U.K., and 45.3% U.S. There were about 1500 respondents per country. A report showed the following bar chart of these percentages.

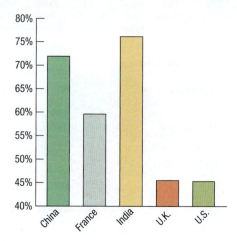

a) How much larger is the proportion of those who said acquiring wealth was important in India than in the United States?

b) Is that the impression given by the display? Explain.

c) How would you improve this display?

d) Make an appropriate display for the percentages.

e) Write a few sentences describing what you have learned about attitudes toward acquiring wealth.

28. Importance of power. In the same survey as that discussed in Exercise 27, GfK Roper Consulting also asked "How important is having control over people and resources to you?" The percent who responded that it was of more than average importance are given in the following table:

China	49.1%
France	44.1%
India	74.2%
U.K.	27.8%
U.S.	36.0%

Here's a pie chart of the data:

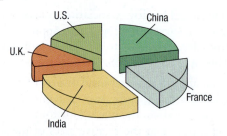

a) List the errors you see in this display.

b) Make an appropriate display for the percentages.

c) Write a few sentences describing what you have learned about attitudes toward acquiring power.

29. GE financials. GE derives revenue from eight operating segments, including three iconic divisions: Power, Aviation, and Healthcare. The following table shows the percentage of all revenue derived from these sources for the period from 2011 to 2015.

	2015	2014	2013	2012	2011
Power	18%	18%	17%	18%	18%
Aviation	21%	20%	19%	2%	17%
Healthcare	15%	16%	16%	16%	16%
Other	46%	46%	48%	64%	48%

a) Are these row or column percentages?

b) Make an appropriate display of these data.

c) Write a brief summary of this information.

30. Real estate pricing. A study of a sample of 1057 houses in upstate New York reports the following percentages of houses falling into different Price and Size categories.

	Price			
	Low	Med Low	Med High	High
Small	61.5%	35.2%	5.2%	2.4%
Med Small	30.4%	45.3%	26.4%	4.7%
Med Large	5.4%	17.6%	47.6%	21.7%
Large	2.7%	1.9%	20.8%	71.2%

(row label: **Size** on the left side)

a) Are these column, row, or total percentages? How do you know?

b) What percent of the highest priced houses were small?

c) From this table, can you determine what percent of all houses were in the low price category?

d) Among the lowest priced houses, what percent were small or medium small?

e) Write a few sentences describing the association between *Price* and *Size*.

31. Stock performance. The following table displays information for 470 of the S&P 500 stocks, on how their one-day change on a day on which the S&P 500 index gained 1.23% compared with their year-to-date change.

	Year to Date	
	Positive Change	Negative Change
Positive Change	164	233
Negative Change	48	25

(row label: **Single Day** on the left side)

a) What percent of the companies reported a positive change in their stock price over the year to date?

b) What percent of the companies reported a positive change in their stock price over both time periods?

c) What percent of the companies reported a negative change in their stock price over both time periods?

d) What percent of the companies reported a positive change in their stock price over one period and a negative change in the other period?

e) Among those companies reporting a positive change in their stock price over the prior day what percentage also reported a positive change over the year to date?

f) Among those companies reporting a negative change in their stock price over the prior day what percentage reported a positive change over the year to date?

g) What relationship, if any, do you see between the performance of a stock on a single day and its year-to-date performance?

32. New product. A company started and managed by business students is selling campus calendars. The students have conducted a market survey with the various campus constituents to determine sales potential and identify which market segments should be targeted. (Should they advertise in the Alumni Magazine and/or the local newspaper?) The following table shows the results of the market survey.

	Buying Likelihood			
	Unlikely	Moderately Likely	Very Likely	Total
Students	197	388	320	905
Faculty/Staff	103	137	98	338
Alumni	20	18	18	56
Town Residents	13	58	45	116
Total	333	601	481	1415

(row label: **Campus Group** on the left side)

a) What percent of all these respondents are alumni?

b) What percent of these respondents are very likely to buy the calendar?

c) What percent of the respondents who are very likely to buy the calendar are alumni?

d) Of the alumni, what percent are very likely to buy the calendar?

e) What is the marginal distribution of the campus constituents?

f) What is the conditional distribution of the campus constituents among those very likely to buy the calendar?

g) Does this study present any evidence that this company should focus on selling to certain campus constituents?

T 33. Foreclosures 2016. The government and many companies are interested in the number of people who lose their home because they are unable to pay. The process of losing a home has three stages, which begin with a "foreclosure filing." At some later point, the person may begin to pay again or the process will complete, becoming a "completed foreclosure." At that point, the person will be given a date by which they must move out of the house. When people move out and the house becomes the property of the bank, it is called a "home repossession." Below is a table showing the number of homes in each stage for the past several years (www.statisticbrain.com/home-foreclosure-statistics/).

Year	2012	2013	2014	2015	2016
Foreclosure Filings	2,300,000	1,369,405	1,117,426	1,147,365	956,864
Completed Foreclosures	2,100,000	921,064	575,378	575,378	427,997
Home Repossessions	700,000	463,108	327,069	327,069	203,108

a) What percent of Home Repossessions over these 5 years occurred in 2016?

b) What percent of all Foreclosure Filings occurred in 2012?

c) What percent of Completed Foreclosures occurred in 2015?

d) How did the percentage of Home Repossessions change between 2012 and 2016?

e) Is there anything about the data that makes you wonder about its accuracy?

34. Appl financials. Apple, Inc., divides their expenses into four categories: Cost of Revenue; Research & Development; Selling, General, & Administrative; and Income Taxes. The table below shows these categories for Apple from 2014 to 2016.

	2014	2015	2016
Cost of Revenue	112,258,000	140,089,000	131,376,000
Research & Development	6,041,000	8,067,000	10,045,000
Selling, General, & Administrative	11,993,000	14,329,000	14,194,000
Income Tax Expense	13,973,000	19,121,000	15,685,000

a) What percent of total costs and expenses was Research & Development in 2014? In 2016?
b) What percent of total costs and expenses were Taxes in 2015? In 2016?
c) Have Selling, General, & Administrative costs grown over this time period?
d) Compute the percentage of total costs associated with each of the four categories for each year in a contingency table.
e) Produce a visualization that compares the percentage cost breakdown across all of the years.

T 35. Movie ratings. The movie ratings system is a voluntary system operated jointly by the Motion Picture Association of America (MPAA) and the National Association of Theatre Owners (NATO). The ratings themselves are given by a board of parents who are members of the Classification and Ratings Administration (CARA). The board was created in response to outcries from parents in the 1960s for some kind of regulation of film content, and the first ratings were introduced in 1968. Here is information on the ratings of 340 movies that came out in 2016, also classified by their genre. (Data extracted from **Movies 06-15**)

	R or NC-17	PG-13	PG	G	Total
Action	15	18	1	0	34
Comedy	59	26	8	1	94
Drama	86	61	15	0	162
Thriller/Suspense	36	14	0	0	50
Total	196	119	24	1	340

a) Find the conditional distribution (in percentages) of movie ratings for action films.
b) Find the conditional distribution (in percentages) of movie ratings for PG-13 films.
c) Create a graph comparing the ratings for the four genres.
d) Are *Genre* and *Rating* independent? Write a brief summary of what these data show about movie ratings and the relationship to the genre of the film.

36. CyberShopping. It has become more common for shoppers to "comparison shop" using the Internet. Respondents to a Pew survey who owned cell phones were asked whether they had, in the past 30 days, looked up the price of a product while they were in a store to see if they could get a better price somewhere else. Here is a table of their responses by income level.

	<$30K	$30K–$49.9K	$50K–$74.9K	>$75K
Yes	207	115	134	204
No	625	406	260	417

(Source: www.pewinternet.org/Reports/2012/In-store-mobile-commerce.aspx)

a) Find the conditional distribution (in percentages) of income distribution for those who do not compare prices on the Internet.
b) Find the conditional distribution (in percentages) of income distribution for shoppers who do compare prices.
c) Create a graph comparing the income distributions of those who compare prices with those who don't.
d) Do you see any differences between the conditional distributions? Write a brief summary of what these data show about Internet use and its relationship to income.

37. MBAs. A survey of the entering MBA students at a university in the United States classified the country of origin of the students, as seen in the table.

	MBA Program		
	Two-Year MBA	Evening MBA	Total
Asia/Pacific Rim	31	33	64
Europe	5	0	5
Latin America	20	1	21
Middle East/Africa	5	5	10
North America	103	65	168
Total	164	104	268

(Origin, label on the left side)

a) What percent of all MBA students were from North America?
b) What percent of the Two-Year MBAs were from North America?
c) What percent of the Evening MBAs were from North America?
d) What is the marginal distribution of origin?
e) Obtain the column percentages and show the conditional distributions of origin by MBA Program.
f) Do you think that origin of the MBA student is independent of the MBA program? Explain.

38. MBAs, part 2. The same university as in Exercise 37 reported the following data on the gender of their students in their two MBA programs.

		Type		
		Two-Year	Evening	Total
Sex	Men	116	66	182
	Women	48	38	86
	Total	164	104	268

a) What percent of all MBA students are women?
b) What percent of Two-Year MBAs are women?
c) What percent of Evening MBAs are women?
d) Do you see evidence of an association between the *Type* of MBA program and the percentage of women students? If so, why do you believe this might be true?

T 39. Movies. The following table shows the number of films in each MPAA (www.mpaa.org) rating by year for each of the years between 2006 and 2015. (Data extracted from **Movies 06-15**)

Year	NC-17	R	PG-13	PG	G	Not Rated
2015	0	228	148	60	11	347
2014	1	224	143	64	12	291
2013	1	217	144	50	10	283
2012	2	218	140	62	14	273
2011	2	223	143	71	19	255
2010	2	194	82	48	5	207
2009	0	183	143	64	16	118
2008	2	233	165	58	18	240
2007	1	242	144	84	14	261
2006	0	221	140	66	16	274

a) What percent of all these films are G rated?
b) What percent of all films in 2008 were G rated?
c) What percent of all films were PG-13 and came out in 2012?
d) What percent of all films produced in 2009 or later were PG-13?
e) What percent of all films produced from 2006 to 2009 were rated PG-13, R or NC-17?
f) Compare the conditional distributions of the ratings for films produced in 2011 or later to those produced from 2006 to 2010. Write a couple of sentences summarizing what you see.

T 40. Movie admissions 2016. The following table shows attendance data collected by the Motion Picture Association of America during the period 2014 to 2016. Figures are the number (in millions) of frequent moviegoers in each age group.

	Age						
	2–11	12–17	18–24	25–39	40–49	50–59	60+
2016	3.1	5.4	7.2	8	3.3	4.2	5.1
2015	2.9	5.3	5.7	7.4	4.5	3.4	5.1
2014	2.7	5.5	7.0	7.1	5.7	4.2	5.3

a) What percent of all frequent moviegoers over the three year period were people between the ages of 12 and 24?
b) What percent of the frequent moviegoers in 2016 were people between the ages of 12 and 39?
c) What percent of *all* frequent moviegoers during this period were people between the ages of 18 and 24 who went to the movies in 2014?
d) What percent of frequent moviegoers in 2015 were people 60 years old and older?
e) What percent of *all* frequent moviegoers in the three year period were people 60 years old and older who went to the movies in 2015?
f) Compare the conditional distributions of the age groups across years. Write a couple of sentences summarizing what you see.

T 41. Tattoos. A study by the University of Texas Southwestern Medical Center examined 626 people to see if there was an increased risk of contracting hepatitis C associated with having a tattoo. If the subject had a tattoo, researchers asked whether it had been done in a commercial tattoo parlor or elsewhere. Write a brief description of the association between tattooing and hepatitis C, including an appropriate graphical display.

	Tattoo Done in Commercial Parlor	Tattoo Done Elsewhere	No Tattoo
Has Hepatitis C	17	8	18
No Hepatitis C	35	53	495

T 42. Poverty and region 2015. In 2015, the following data were reported by the U.S. Census Bureau. The data show the number of people (in thousands) living above and below the poverty line in each of the four regions of the United States (www.census.gov/content/dam/Census/library/publications/2016/demo/p60-256.pdf). Based on these data do you think there is an association between region and poverty? Explain.

Region	Below Poverty Level (000s)	Total (000s)
Northeast	6,891	55,779
Midwest	7,849	67,030
South	18,305	119,955
West	10,079	75,690

43. Being successful. Pew research surveyed 25- to 34-year-old adults in 2013 and asked them how important it is "to you personally" to have a high-paying job? Here is a table reporting the responses.

	Male	Female
Extremely important	163	139
Very important	346	273
Somewhat important	336	333
Not too important	87	53
Not at all important	5	4

a) What percent of women consider it very important or extremely important for them personally to have a high-paying job?
b) How does that compare to young men?
c) Do the distributions across all response categories look similar or different? Write a few sentences describing any associations you see.

T 44. Minimum wage workers. The U.S. Department of Labor (www.bls.gov) collects data on the number of U.S. workers who are employed at or below the minimum wage. Here is a table showing the number of hourly workers by *Age* and *Sex* and the number who were paid at or below the prevailing minimum wage:

Age	Hourly Workers (in thousands)		At or Below Minimum Wage (in thousands)	
	Men	Women	Men	Women
16–24	7978	7701	384	738
25–34	9029	7864	150	332
35–44	7696	7783	71	170
45–54	7365	8260	68	134
55–64	4092	4895	35	72
65+	1174	1469	22	50

a) What percent of the women were ages 16–24?
b) Using side-by-side bar graphs, compare the proportions of the men and women who worked at or below minimum wage at each *Age* group. Write a couple of sentences summarizing what you see.

45. Moviegoers and ethnicity. The Motion Picture Association of America studies the ethnicity of moviegoers to understand changes in the demographics of moviegoers over time. Here are the numbers of moviegoers (in millions) classified as to whether they were Hispanic, African-American, Caucasian, and Other for the year 2010. Also included are the numbers for the general U.S. population and the number of tickets sold.

	Caucasian	Hispanic	African-American	Other	Total
Population	204.6	49.6	37.2	18.6	310
Moviegoers	88.8	26.8	16.9	8.5	141
Tickets	728	338	143	91	1300
Total	1021.4	414.4	197.1	118.1	1751

a) Compare the conditional distribution of *Ethnicity* for all three groups: the entire population, moviegoers, and ticket holders.
b) Write a brief description of the association between population groups and *Ethnicity*.

46. Department store. A department store is planning its next advertising campaign. Since different publications are read by different market segments, they would like to know if they should be targeting specific age segments. The results of a marketing survey are summarized in the following table by *Age* and *Shopping Frequency* at their store.

		Age			
	Shopping	Under 30	30–49	50 and Over	Total
Frequency	Low	27	37	31	95
	Moderate	48	91	93	232
	High	23	51	73	147
	Total	98	179	197	474

a) Find the marginal distribution of *Shopping Frequency*.
b) Find the conditional distribution of *Shopping Frequency* within each age group.
c) Compare these distributions with a segmented bar graph.
d) Write a brief description of the association between *Age* and *Shopping Frequency* among these respondents.
e) Does this prove that customers ages 50 and over are more likely to shop at this department store? Explain.

47. Success II. Look back at the table in Exercise 43 concerning desires for success and a high-paying career. That table presented only the percentages, but Pew Research reported the numbers of respondents in the major categories:

	Women		Men	
Age	18–34	35–64	18–34	35–64
Count	610	571	703	605

With this additional information you should be able to answer these questions. (Note: Percentages were rounded to whole numbers, so estimated cell counts will have fractions. You need not round estimated cell counts to whole numbers for the purpose of answering these questions.)
a) What percentage of 18–34 year olds (both male and female) reported that being successful in a high-paying career or profession was "one of the most important things" to them personally?
b) What percentage of 18–34 year olds who said that such success was "one of the most important things" were women?

48. Income and pets. A company that distributes a variety of pet foods is planning their next advertising campaign. Since different publications are read by different market segments, they would like to know how pet ownership is distributed across different income segments. The U.S. Census Bureau (www.allcountries.org/uscensus/424_ household_pet_ownership_and_by_selected.html) reports the number of households owning various types of pets. Specifically, they keep track of dogs, cats, birds, and horses.

a) Do you think the income distributions of the households who own these different animals would be roughly the same? Why or why not?

Percent Distribution of Households Owning Pets

	Pets			
Income Range	Dog	Cat	Bird	Horse
Under $12,500	12.7	13.9	17.3	9.5
$12,500 to $24,999	19.1	19.7	20.9	20.3
$25,000 to $39,999	21.6	21.5	22.0	21.8
$40,000 to $59,999	21.5	21.2	17.5	23.1
$60,000 and over	25.2	23.7	22.3	25.4

b) The table shows the percentages of income levels for each type of animal owned. Are these row percentages, column percentages, or total percentages?
c) Do the data support that the pet food company should not target specific market segments based on household income? Explain.

49. Insurance company, part 2. An insurance company that provides medical insurance is concerned with recent data. They suspect that patients who undergo surgery at large hospitals have their discharges delayed for various reasons— which results in increased medical costs to the insurance company. The recent data for area hospitals and two types of surgery (major and minor) are shown in the following table.

	Discharge Delayed	
Procedure	Large Hospital	Small Hospital
Major Surgery	120 of 800	10 of 50
Minor Surgery	10 of 200	20 of 250

a) Overall, for what percent of patients was discharge delayed?
b) Were the percentages different for major and minor surgery?
c) Overall, what were the discharge delay rates at each hospital?
d) What were the delay rates at each hospital for each kind of surgery?
e) The insurance company is considering advising their clients to use large hospitals for surgery to avoid postsurgical complications. Do you think they should do this?
f) Explain, in your own words, why this confusion occurs.

50. Delivery service. A company must decide which of two delivery services they will contract with. During a recent trial period, they shipped numerous packages with each service and have kept track of how often deliveries did not arrive on time. Here are the data.

Delivery Service	Type of Service	Number of Deliveries	Number of Late Packages
Pack Rats	Regular	400	12
	Overnight	100	16
Boxes R Us	Regular	100	2
	Overnight	400	28

a) Compare the two services' overall percentage of late deliveries.
b) Based on the results in part a, the company has decided to hire Pack Rats. Do you agree they deliver on time more often? Why or why not? Be specific.
c) The results here are an instance of what phenomenon?

51. Graduate admissions. A 1975 article in the magazine *Science* examined the graduate admissions process at Berkeley for evidence of gender bias. The following table shows the number of applicants accepted to each of four graduate programs.

Program	Males Accepted (of Applicants)	Females Accepted (of Applicants)
1	511 of 825	89 of 108
2	352 of 560	17 of 25
3	137 of 407	132 of 375
4	22 of 373	24 of 341
Total	1022 of 2165	262 of 849

a) What percent of total applicants were admitted?
b) Overall, were a higher percentage of males or females admitted?
c) Compare the percentage of males and females admitted in each program.
d) Which of the comparisons you made do you consider to be the most valid? Why?

52. Simpson's Paradox. Develop your own table of data that is a business example of Simpson's Paradox. Explain the conflict between the conclusions made from the conditional and marginal distributions.

JUST CHECKING ANSWERS

1 50.0%   2 40.0%   3 25.0%

4 15.6% Nearsighted, 56.3% Farsighted, 18.8% Need Bifocals

5 18.8% Nearsighted, 62.5% Farsighted, 18.8% Need Bifocals

6 40% of the nearsighted customers are female, while 50% of customers are female.

7 Since nearsighted customers appear less likely to be female, it seems that they may not be independent. (But the numbers are small.)

CHAPTER 3

Describing, Displaying, and Visualizing Quantitative Data

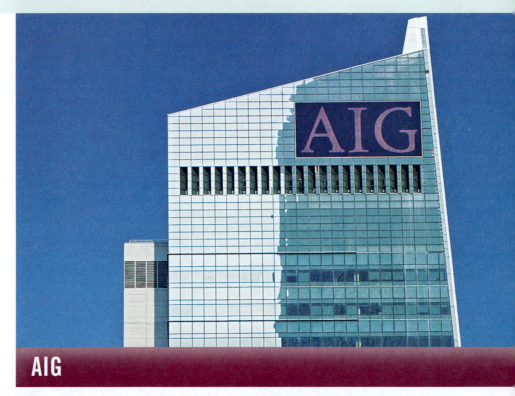

AIG

The American International Group (AIG) was once the 18th largest corporation in the world. AIG was founded nearly 100 years ago by Cornelius Vander Starr who opened an insurance agency in Shanghai, China. As the first Westerner to sell insurance to the Chinese, Starr grew his business rapidly until 1949 when Mao Zedong and the People's Liberation Army took over Shanghai. Starr moved the company to New York City, where it continued to grow, expanding its markets worldwide. In 2004, AIG stock hit an all-time high of $76.77, putting its market value at nearly $300 billion.

According to its own website, "By early 2007 AIG had assets of $1 trillion, $110 billion in revenues, 74 million customers and 116,000 employees in 130 countries and jurisdictions. Yet just 18 months later, AIG found itself on the brink of failure and in need of emergency government assistance." AIG was one of the largest beneficiaries of the U.S. government's Troubled Asset Relief Program (TARP), established in 2008 during the financial crisis to purchase assets and equity from financial institutions. TARP was an attempt to strengthen the financial sector and avoid a repeat of a depression as severe as the 1930s. Many banks quickly repaid the government part or all of the money given to them under the TARP program, but AIG, which received $170 billion, took until the end of 2012 to repay the government completely.

Even though AIG stock today is on solid financial footing, its stock price is only a fraction (adjusted for splits) of what it was before the 2008 crisis. Between 2007 and 2009 AIG stock lost more than 99% of its value, hitting $0.35 in early March. That same month AIG became embroiled in controversy when it disclosed that it had paid $218 million in bonuses to employees of its financial services division. AIG's drop in stock price represented a loss of nearly 300 billion dollars for investors.

Alex is working as an analyst at a small "hedge" fund. Their portfolio specializes in energy and banking. As part of his job, Alex provides background research on banks and insurance companies to find out information that will help the portfolio manager increase or decrease their holdings in particular companies. Alex wants to examine the history of the AIG collapse to learn how to predict such crises in the future. Were there warning signs in AIG's stock price data that investors should have heeded?

Whenever we have data, we begin in the same place; we display and summarize our data. Sometimes we can answer our questions about the data with simple visualizations. But often displays will surprise us. As the famous statistician John Tukey said:

> "The greatest value of a picture is when it forces us to notice what we never expected to see."

Alex will want to display data about AIG's stock price leading up to the crisis and possibly about other factors that may have been predictive.

How he chooses to display his data will depend on the nature of the data and his goals. In this example, he is looking for telltale signs of trouble that might have been missed by investors—and that he will want to be alert for in future investments. It is always a good idea to start by graphing and summarize data.[1] Later, we'll discuss ways to examine more complex questions and model relationships among variables and differences between groups of individuals. In all of these analyses, our underlying goal will be to understand the world so that we can make better business decisions.

One of the simplest ways to examine data is with a table of values—much the way data often appear in a spreadsheet. Table 3.1 gives the monthly average stock price (in dollars) for the six years leading up to the company's crisis. Were there clues to warn of problems?

	Jan.	Feb.	Mar.	Apr.	May	June	July	Aug.	Sept.	Oct.	Nov.	Dec.
2002	77.26	72.95	73.72	71.57	68.42	65.99	61.22	64.10	58.04	60.26	65.03	59.96
2003	59.74	49.57	49.41	54.38	56.52	57.88	59.80	61.51	59.39	60.93	58.73	62.37
2004	69.02	73.25	72.06	74.21	70.93	72.61	69.85	69.58	70.67	62.31	62.17	65.33
2005	66.74	68.96	61.55	51.77	53.81	55.66	60.27	60.86	60.54	62.64	67.06	66.72
2006	68.33	67.02	67.15	64.29	63.14	59.74	59.40	62.00	65.25	67.02	69.86	71.35
2007	70.45	68.99	68.14	68.25	71.78	71.75	68.64	65.21	66.02	66.12	56.86	58.13

TABLE 3.1 Monthly stock price in dollars of AIG stock for the period 2002 through 2007.

It's hard to tell very much from tables of values like this. You might get a rough idea of how much the stock cost—usually somewhere around $60 or so, but that's about it.

---

[1]Let's say this another way: It is always a *bad* idea not to start your investigation by visualizing and summarizing your data. However powerful your computer program may be, if you don't first look at your data, you risk missing the true story.

3.1   **Visualizing Quantitative Variables**

WHO	Months
WHAT	Monthly average price for AIG's stock (in dollars)
WHEN	2002 through 2007
WHERE	New York Stock Exchange
WHY	To examine AIG stock volatility

AIG's stock price is a *quantitative* variable, whose units are dollars. The values of a quantitative variable have no associated categories. Instead, we just slice up all the possible values into **bins** and then count the number of cases that fall into each bin. The bins, together with these counts, give the **distribution** of the quantitative variable and provide the building blocks for the display of the distribution, called a **histogram**.

Histograms

Here are the monthly prices of AIG stock displayed in a histogram.

FIGURE 3.1 Monthly average prices of AIG stock. The histogram displays the distribution of prices by showing for each "bin" of prices, the number of months having prices in that bin.

A histogram plots the bin counts as the heights of bars. It counts the number of cases that fall into each bin, and displays that count as the height of the corresponding bar. In Figure 3.1, each bin has a width of $5, so, for example, the height of the tallest bar says that there were 24 months whose average price of AIG stock was between $65 and $70. In this way, the histogram displays the entire distribution of prices. Unlike a bar chart, which puts gaps between bars to separate the categories, there are no gaps between the bars of a histogram unless there are actual gaps in the data. **Gaps** indicate a region where there are no values. Gaps can be important features of the distribution so watch out for them and point them out.

For categorical variables, each category got its own bar. The only choice was whether to combine categories for ease of display. For quantitative variables, we have to choose the width of the bins. It isn't hard to make a histogram by hand, but we almost always use software. Many statistics programs allow you to adjust the bin width yourself. How do you know what bin width is best? That requires judgment.

Does the distribution look as you expected? It's often a good idea to imagine what the distribution might look like before making a display. That way you're less likely to be fooled by errors either in your display or in the data themselves. From the histogram, we can see that in these months the AIG stock price was typically near $65 and usually between $55 and $75. That seems about right.

The vertical axis of a histogram shows the number of cases falling in each bin. An alternative is to report the percentage of cases in each bin, creating a **relative frequency histogram**. The shape of the two histograms is the same; only the vertical axis and labels are different. A relative frequency histogram is faithful to the area principle by displaying the *percentage* of cases in each bin instead of the count.

> When you look at a histogram, look for four characteristics:
>
> 1. Shape
>   a. Symmetry vs. skew
>   b. "Bumps" and valleys
>   c. Gaps
> 2. Center
> 3. Spread
>
> These characteristics will be much easier to discern when looking at a visualization of the data like a histogram than by looking at a table of the data.

FIGURE 3.2 A relative frequency histogram looks just like a frequency histogram except that the *y*-axis now shows the percentage of months in each bin.

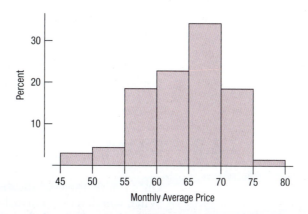

IN PRACTICE 3.1   Insights about distributions from histograms

The chief financial officer (CFO) of a music download site has just secured the rights to offer downloads of a new album. To see how well it's selling, she collects the number of downloads per hour for the past 24 hours: (Data in **Downloads**)

Hour	Downloads	Hour	Downloads
12:00 a.m.	36	12:00 p.m.	25
1:00 a.m.	28	1:00 p.m.	22
2:00 a.m.	19	2:00 p.m.	17
3:00 a.m.	10	3:00 p.m.	18
4:00 a.m.	5	4:00 p.m.	20
5:00 a.m.	3	5:00 p.m.	23
6:00 a.m.	2	6:00 p.m.	21
7:00 a.m.	6	7:00 p.m.	18
8:00 a.m.	12	8:00 p.m.	24
9:00 a.m.	14	9:00 p.m.	30
10:00 a.m.	20	10:00 p.m.	27
11:00 a.m.	18	11:00 p.m.	30

CFO I can't really tell how many downloads are happening each day. Can you find a way to help me better understand the number of downloads?

ANALYST I've collected the number of downloads into bins of five. The histogram shows that, for most hours of the day, we get between 10 and 30 downloads.

The histogram looks like this:

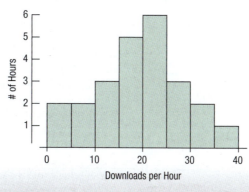

Before making a histogram, you should check the **Quantitative Data Condition**: The data must be values of a quantitative variable whose units are known.

Although a bar chart and a histogram may look similar, they're not the same display. You can't display categorical data in a histogram. Always check the condition that confirms what type of data you have before making your display.

3.2   Shape

Once you've displayed the distribution in a histogram, what can you say about it? When you describe a distribution, you should pay attention to three things: its **shape**, its **center**, and its **spread**.

We describe the shape of a distribution in terms of its modes, its symmetry, and whether it has any gaps or outlying values.

Mode

Does the histogram have a single, central hump (or peak) or several, separated humps? These humps are called **modes**. Formally, the mode is the single, most frequent value, but we rarely use the term that way.[2] The AIG stock prices have a single mode around $65. We often use modes to describe the shape of the distribution. A distribution whose histogram has one main hump, such as the one for the AIG stock prices, is called **unimodal**; distributions whose histograms have two humps are **bimodal**, and those with three or more are called **multimodal**. For example, here's a bimodal distribution.

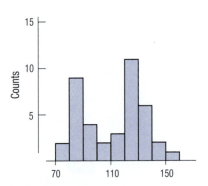

FIGURE 3.3   A bimodal distribution has two apparent modes.

A bimodal histogram is often an indication that there are two groups in the data. It's a good idea to investigate when you see bimodality. But don't get overly excited by minor fluctuations in the histogram, which may just be artifacts of where the bin boundaries fall. To be a true mode, the hump should still be there when you display the histogram with slightly different bin widths.

A distribution whose histogram doesn't appear to have any mode and in which all the bars are approximately the same height is called **uniform**. (Chapter 5 gives a more formal definition.)

---

[2]Technically, the mode is the value on the *x*-axis of the histogram below the highest peak, but when asked to identify the mode, most people would point to the peak itself.

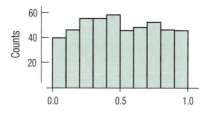

FIGURE 3.4 In a uniform distribution, bars are all about the same height. The histogram doesn't appear to have a mode.

Symmetry

Could you fold the histogram along a vertical line through the middle and have the edges match pretty closely, as in Figure 3.5, or are more of the values on one side, as in the histograms in Figure 3.6? A distribution is **symmetric** if the halves on either side of the center look, at least approximately, like mirror images.

FIGURE 3.5 A symmetric histogram can fold in the middle so that the two sides almost match.

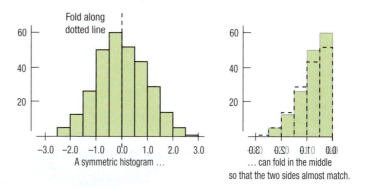
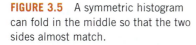

The (usually) thinner ends of a distribution are called the **tails**. If one tail stretches out farther than the other, the distribution is said to be **skewed** to the side of the longer tail.

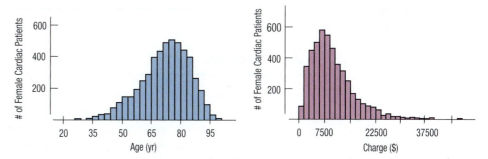

FIGURE 3.6 Two skewed histograms showing the age (left) and hospital charges (right) for all female heart attack patients in New York State in one year. The histogram of Age (in blue) is skewed to the left, while the histogram of Charges (in purple) is skewed to the right.

Outliers

Do any values appear to stick out? Often such values tell us something interesting or exciting about the data. You should always point out any stragglers or **outliers** that stand off away from the body of the distribution. For example, if you're studying the personal wealth of Americans and Bill Gates is in your sample, he would certainly be an outlier. Because his wealth would be so obviously atypical, you'd want to point it out as a special feature.

Outliers can affect almost every method we discuss in this book, so we'll always be on the lookout for them. An outlier can be the most informative part of your data,

Skewed Right or Left?
Amounts of things (dollars, employees, waiting times) can't be negative so they run up against zero. But they have no natural upper limit. So, they often have distributions that are skewed to the right. Grades on a test where most students do well are often skewed to the left with many scoring near the top, but a few straggling off to the low end.

or it might just be an error. Either way, you shouldn't throw it away without comment. Treat it specially and discuss it when you report your conclusions about your data. (Or find the error and fix it if you can.)

Using Your Judgment

How you characterize a distribution is often a judgment call. Do the two humps in the histogram really reveal two subgroups, or will the shape look different if you change the bin width slightly? Are those observations at the high end of the histogram truly unusual, or are they just the largest ones at the end of a long tail? These are matters of judgment on which different people can legitimately disagree. There's no automatic calculation or rule of thumb that can make the decision for you. Understanding your data and how they arose can help. What should guide your decisions is an honest desire to understand what is happening in the data. That's what you'll need to make sound business decisions.

Viewing a histogram at several different bin widths can help you to see how persistent some of the features are. Some technologies offer ways to change the bin width interactively to get multiple views of the histogram. If the number of observations in each bin is so small that moving a couple of values to the next bin changes your assessment of how many modes there are, be careful. Be sure to think about the data, where they came from, and what kinds of questions you hope to answer from them.

IN PRACTICE 3.2   Insights about distributions, II

CFO I'm starting to prepare my monthly report for investors. Tell me about the distribution of downloads from our site.

ANALYST It is unimodal and roughly symmetric with no outliers. I will report more later when I look at summary statistics.

3.3   Center

Look again at the AIG prices in Figure 3.1. If you had to pick one number to describe a *typical* price, what would you pick? When a histogram is unimodal and fairly symmetric, most people would point to the center of the distribution, where the histogram peaks. The typical price is around $65.00.

If we want to be more precise and *calculate* a number, we can *average* the data. In the AIG example, the average monthly price is $64.48, about what we might expect from the histogram. You probably know how to average values, but this is a good place to introduce notation that we'll use throughout the book. We'll call the generic variable x, and use the Greek capital letter sigma, Σ, to mean "sum" (sigma is "S" in Greek), and write:[3]

NOTATION ALERT

A bar over any symbol indicates the mean of that quantity.

$$\bar{x} = \frac{Total}{n} = \frac{\Sigma x}{n}.$$

---

[3]You may also see the variable called y and the equation written $\bar{y} = \dfrac{Total}{n} = \dfrac{\Sigma y}{n}$. We actually prefer to call a single variable y instead of x, because in the next chapter we'll need x to name a variable that predicts another (which we'll call y), but when you have only one variable either name is common. Most calculators call a single variable x.

According to this formula, we add up all the values of the variable, *x*, and divide that sum (*Total*, or Σx) by the number of data values, *n*. We call the resulting value the **mean** of *x*.[4]

Although the mean is a natural summary for unimodal, symmetric distributions, it can be misleading for skewed data or for distributions with gaps or outliers. The histogram of AIG monthly prices in Figure 3.1 is unimodal, and nearly symmetric, with a slight left skew. A look at the total volume of AIG stock sold each month for the same 6 years tells a very different story. Figure 3.7 shows a unimodal but strongly right-skewed distribution with two gaps. The mean monthly volume was 170.1 million shares. Locate that value on the histogram. Does it seem a little high as a summary of a typical month's volume? In fact, more than two out of three months have volumes that are less than that value. It might be better to use the **median**—the value that splits the histogram into two equal *areas*. The median is commonly used for variables such as cost or income, which are likely to be skewed. That's because the median is *resistant* to unusual observations and to the shape of the distribution. For the AIG monthly trading volumes, the median is 135.9 million shares, which seems like a more appropriate summary.

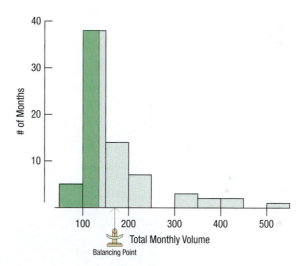

FIGURE 3.7   The median splits the area of the histogram in half at 135.9 million shares. The mean is the point on which the histogram would balance. Because the distribution is skewed to the right, the mean 170.1 million shares is *higher* than the median. The points at the right have pulled the mean toward them, away from the median.

Does it really make a difference whether we choose a mean or a median? The mean monthly price for the AIG stock is $64.48. Because the distribution of the prices is roughly symmetric, we'd expect the mean and median to be close. In fact, we compute the median to be $65.23. But for variables with skewed distributions, the story is quite different. For a right-skewed distribution like the monthly volumes in Figure 3.7, the mean is larger than the median: 170.1 compared to 135.9. The two give quite different summaries. The difference is due to the overall shape of the distributions.

---

[4]Once you've averaged the data, you might logically expect the result to be called the *average*. But average is used too colloquially, as in the "average" home buyer, where we don't sum up anything. Even though average *is* sometimes used in the way we intend, as in the Dow Jones Industrial Average (which is actually a weighted average) or a batting average, we'll usually use the term *mean* throughout the book.

> **BY HAND** **Finding the Median**
>
> Finding the median of a batch of n numbers is easy as long as you remember to order the values first. If n is odd, the median is the middle value. Counting in from the ends, we find this value in the $\frac{n+1}{2}$ position.
>
> When n is even, there are two middle values. So, in this case, the median is the average of the two values in positions $\frac{n}{2}$ and $\frac{n}{2} + 1$.
>
> Here are two examples:
>
> Suppose the batch has the values 14.1, 3.2, 25.3, 2.8, −17.5, 13.9, and 45.8. First we order the values: −17.5, 2.8, 3.2, 13.9, 14.1, 25.3, and 45.8. There are 7 values, so the median is the $(7 + 1)/2 = $ 4th value counting from the top or bottom: 13.9.
>
> Suppose we had the same batch with another value at 35.7. Then the ordered values are −17.5, 2.8, 3.2, 13.9, 14.1, 25.3, 35.7, and 45.8. The median is the average of the 8/2, or 4th, and the $(8/2) + 1$, or 5th, values. So the median is $(13.9 + 14.1)/2 = 14.0$.

The mean is the point at which the histogram would balance. A value far from the center has more leverage, pulling the mean in its direction. It's hard to argue that a summary that's been pulled aside by only a few outlying values or by a long tail is what we mean by the center of the distribution. That's why the median is usually a better choice for skewed data.

However, when the distribution is unimodal and symmetric, the mean offers better opportunities to calculate useful quantities and draw interesting conclusions. It will be the summary value we work with throughout the rest of the book, unless we specifically state otherwise.

> **IN PRACTICE 3.3** **Insights from measures of central tendency**
>
> **CFO** For my report, I'd like to summarize the downloads. What is a typical number of downloads per hour from our site?
>
> **ANALYST** The mean number is 18.7 downloads per hour. The median is 19.5 downloads per hour. Because the distribution is unimodal and roughly symmetric, we shouldn't be surprised that the two are close. There are a few more hours (in the middle of the night) with small numbers of downloads that pull the mean lower than the median, but either one seems like a reasonable summary to report.

3.4 Spread of the Distribution

We know that the typical price of the AIG stock is around $65, but knowing the mean or median alone doesn't tell us about the entire distribution. A stock whose price doesn't move away from its center isn't very interesting.[5] The more the data vary, the less a measure of center can tell us. We need to know how spread out the data are as well.

---

[5] And not much of an investment, either.

One simple measure of spread is the **range**, defined as the difference between the extremes:

$$\text{Range} = max - min.$$

For the AIG price data, the range is $77.26 − $49.41 = 27.85. Notice that the range is *a single number* that describes the spread of the data, not an interval of values—as you might think from its use in common speech. If there are any unusual observations in the data, the range is not resistant and will be influenced by them. Concentrating on the middle of the data avoids this problem.

The **lower quartile, Q1**, is defined as the value for which one quarter of the data lie below it and the **upper quartile, Q3**, is the value for which one quarter of the data lie above it. In this way, the quartiles frame the middle 50% of the data. The **interquartile range (IQR)** summarizes the spread by focusing on the middle half of the data. It's defined as the difference between the two quartiles:

$$\text{IQR} = Q3 - Q1.$$

BY HAND   Finding Quartiles

Quartiles are easy to find in theory, but more difficult in practice. The three quartiles, Q1 (lower quartile), Q2 (the median), and Q3 (the upper quartile), split the sorted data values into quarters. So, for example, 25% of the data values will lie at or below Q1. The problem lies in the fact that unless your sample size divides nicely by 4, there isn't just one way to split the data into quarters. The statistical software package SAS offers at least five different ways to compute quartiles. The differences are usually small, but can be annoying. Here are two of the most common methods for finding quartiles by hand or with a calculator:

1. The Tukey Method

    Split the sorted data at the median. (If *n* is odd, include the median with each half). Then find the median of each of these halves—use these as the quartiles.

    Example: The data set $\{14.1, 3.2, 25.3, 2.8, -17.5, 13.9, 45.8\}$

    First we order the values: $\{-17.5, 2.8, 3.2, 13.9, 14.1, 25.3, 45.8\}$.
    We found the median to be 13.9, so form two data sets:
    $\{-17.5, 2.8, 3.2, 13.9\}$ and $\{13.9, 14.1, 25.3, 45.8\}$. The medians of these are $3.0 = (2.8 + 3.2)/2$ and $19.7 = (14.1 + 25.3)/2$. So we let $Q1 = 3.0$ and $Q3 = 19.7$.

2. The TI calculator method

    The same as the Tukey method, except we *don't* include the median with each half. So for $\{14.1, 3.2, 25.3, 2.8, -17.5, 13.9, \text{ and } 45.8\}$ we find the two data sets:

    $\{-17.5, 2.8, 3.2\}$ and $\{14.1, 25.3, 45.8\}$ by not including the median in either.

    Now the medians of these are $Q1 = 2.8$ and $Q3 = 25.3$.

    Notice the effect on the IQR. For Tukey:

    $\text{IQR} = Q3 - Q1 = 19.7 - 3.0 = 16.7$, but for TI,
    $\text{IQR} = 25.3 - 2.8 = 22.5$.

For both of these methods, notice that the quartiles are either data values, or the average of two adjacent values. In Excel and other software, the quartiles are *interpolated*, so they may not be simple averages of two values. Be aware that there may be differences, but the idea is the same: the quartiles Q1, Q2, and Q3 split the data roughly into quarters.

> **Waiting in Line**
>
> Why do banks favor a single line that feeds several teller windows rather than separate lines for each teller? It does make the average waiting time slightly shorter, but that improvement is very small. The real difference people notice is that the time you can expect to wait is less variable when there is a single line, and people prefer consistency.

For the AIG data, Q1 = \$60.11, Q3 = \$69.01.[6] So the IQR = Q3 − Q1 = \$69.01 − \$60.11 = \$8.90.

The IQR is a reasonable summary of spread, but because it uses only the two quartiles of the data, it ignores much of the information about how individual values vary. By contrast, the standard deviation, takes into account how far each value is from the mean. Like the mean, the standard deviation is appropriate only for symmetric data and can be influenced by outlying observations.

As the name implies, the standard deviation uses the *deviations* of each data value from the mean. The average[7] of the *squared* deviations is called the **variance** and is denoted by s^2:

$$s^2 = \frac{\sum (x - \bar{x})^2}{n - 1}.$$

The variance plays an important role in statistics, but as a measure of spread, it has a problem. Whatever the units of the original data, the variance is in *squared* units. We want measures of spread to have the same units as the data, so we usually take the square root of the variance. That gives the **standard deviation**.

$$s = \sqrt{\frac{\sum (x - \bar{x})^2}{n - 1}}.$$

For the AIG stock prices, $s = \$6.12$.

IN PRACTICE 3.4   Describing variability of downloads

CFO Help me understand the variability of the downloads from our site and describe the spread of the number of downloads per hour.

ANALYST The range of downloads is 36 − 2 = 34 downloads per hour. The quartiles are 13 and 24.5, so the IQR is 24.5 − 13 = 11.5 downloads per hour. The standard deviation is 8.94 downloads per hour. Because the distribution is symmetric and unimodal, the standard deviation is a better measure of variability than the IQR.

JUST CHECKING

Thinking About Variation

1 The U.S. Census Bureau reports the median family income in its summary of census data. Why do you suppose they use the median instead of the mean? What might be the disadvantages of reporting the mean?

2 You've just bought a new car that claims to get a highway fuel efficiency of 31 miles per gallon (mpg). Of course, your mileage will "vary." If you had to guess, would you expect the IQR of gas mileage attained by all cars like yours to be 30 mpg, 3 mpg, or 0.3 mpg? Why?

3 A company selling a new Xbox controller advertises that the it has a mean lifetime of 5 years. If you were in charge of quality control at the factory, would you prefer that the standard deviation of life spans of the players you produce be 2 years or 2 months? Why?

---

[6]In general, we use the Tukey method in this book unless stated otherwise.
[7]For technical reasons, we divide by $n - 1$ instead of n to take this average. We'll discuss this more in Chapter 11.

3.5 Shape, Center, and Spread—A Summary

What should you report about a quantitative variable? Report the shape of its distribution, and include a center and a spread. But which measure of center and which measure of spread? The guidelines are pretty easy.

- If the shape is skewed, point that out and report the median and IQR. You may want to include the mean and standard deviation as well, explaining why the mean and median differ. The fact that the mean and median do not agree is a sign that the distribution may be skewed. A histogram will help you make the point.
- If the shape is unimodal and symmetric, report the mean and standard deviation and possibly the median and IQR as well. For unimodal symmetric data, the IQR is usually a bit larger than the standard deviation. If that's not true for your data set, look again to make sure the distribution isn't skewed or multimodal and that there are no outliers.
- If there are multiple modes, try to understand why. If you can identify a reason for separate modes, it may be a good idea to split the data into separate groups.
- If there are any clearly unusual observations, point them out. If you are reporting the mean and standard deviation, report them computed with and without the unusual observations. The differences may be revealing.
- Always pair the median with the IQR and the mean with the standard deviation. It's not useful to report a measure of center without a corresponding measure of spread. Reporting a center without a spread can lead you to think you know more about the distribution than you do. Reporting only the spread omits important information.

IN PRACTICE 3.5   Initial summary and description of a variable

CFO I'm preparing my final draft. Can you summarize the pattern of downloads from our site?

ANALYST The histogram that visualizes the distribution of downloads per hour appears on page 59 and shows the distribution to be unimodal and symmetric with no outliers. There are several hours in the middle of the night with very few downloads, but none seem to be so unusual as to be considered outliers. Because the distribution is unimodal and (roughly) symmetric, the mean and SD are appropriate as measures of central tendency and spread (variability). The mean number of downloads per hour is 18.7 and the standard deviation is 8.94.

3.6 Standardizing Variables

A real estate agent in California covers two markets. Palo Alto is next to Stanford University, filled with old homes and tree lined streets. The other is a newer neighborhood, in Foster City, created when part of the San Francisco Bay was filled in to create space for more housing.

Here are summaries of the listed prices of a sample of houses in these two neighborhoods as found on Zillow.com:

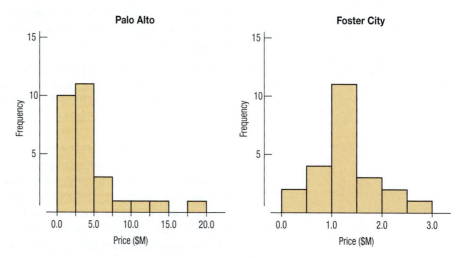

FIGURE 3.8 Prices of houses from samples from Palo Alto (left) and Foster City (right). Note that the horizontal scale is quite different for the two neighborhoods. Prices are in millions of dollars. (Data in **CA house prices**)

The average house in Palo Alto was listed at $4,541,390 with a standard deviation of $3,959,110, while the average Foster City house cost $1,256,910 with a standard deviation of $559,776. So, a $2,000,000 home in Foster City is on the expensive side, but for Palo Alto, that's rather inexpensive. (Believe it or not.)

Which would be more unusual, a $2M home in Foster City, or a $6M home in Palo Alto? Using the standard deviation as a way to measure distance helps us answer this question. In Foster City, a $2M home is $743,000 over the average. In Palo Alto, a $6M home is $1,486,100 over its average. That might seem more unusual. But look at the standard deviations. That excess of $743,000 is 1.3 standard deviations above the mean for Foster City. But in Palo Alto, the standard deviation is nearly $4M, so the $6M home is "only" 0.37 standard deviations above the mean.

Using the mean and standard deviation this way gives us a way to standardize values in different distributions to compare them.

How Does Standardizing Work?

We first need to find the mean and standard deviation of each variable for the prices in each town.

	Mean ($M)	SD ($M)
Palo Alto	4.541	3.959
Foster City	1.257	0.5598

> Standardizing lets us compare any quantities. We could ask, for example, whether a stock's low price was more extraordinary than the company's growth rate by finding z-scores for each.

Next we measure how *far* each of our values is from the mean of its variable. We subtract the mean and then divide by the standard deviation:

$$z = (x - \bar{x})/s.$$

We call the resulting value a **standardized value** and denote it with the letter z. Usually, we just call it a **z-score**. The z-score tells us how many standard deviations a value is from its mean.

Let's look at Palo Alto first.

To compute the z-score for the $6M house, take its value, subtract the mean (4.54139), and divide by the standard deviation, 3.95911:

$$z = (6 - 4.54139)/3.95911 = 0.368$$

So this house's price is 0.368 standard deviation *above* the mean price of all the houses we sampled in Palo Alto. How about that $2M home in Foster City? Standardizing it for the mean and standard deviation of Foster City prices, we find

$$z = (2 - 1.25691)/0.559776 = 1.33$$

So this house's price is more than a standard deviation above the mean for its location. Standardizing enables us to compare values from different distributions to see which is more unusual in context.

Standardizing into z-Scores:
- Shifts the mean to 0.
- Changes the standard deviation to 1.
- Does not change the shape.
- Removes the units.

IN PRACTICE 3.6   Compare disparate values

MANAGER We recently obtained data on a random sample of 350 houses that sold in our town. I know how to compute the mean and standard deviation of the houses, and I found that the average price was $175,000 with a standard deviation of $55,000. The size of the houses (in square feet) averaged 2100 sq. ft. with a standard deviation of 650 sq. ft. Which would be more unusual, a house that costs $340,000, or a 5000 sq. ft. house?

ANALYST The means and standard deviations have different units, so we need to standardize and compute z-scores to compare them. For the $340,000 house:

$$z = \frac{x - \bar{x}}{s} = \frac{(340,000 - 175,000)}{55,000} = 3.00$$

The house price is 3 standard deviations above the mean.
For the 5000 sq. ft. house:

$$z = \frac{x - \bar{x}}{s} = \frac{(5000 - 2100)}{650} = 4.46$$

This house is 4.46 standard deviations above the mean in size. That's more unusual than the house that costs $340,000.

3.7   Five-Number Summary and Boxplots

The **five-number summary** of a distribution reports its median, quartiles, and extremes (maximum and minimum). The five-number summary of the monthly trading volumes of AIG stock for the period 2002–2007 looks like this (in millions of shares).

Max	515.62
Q3	182.32
Median	135.87
Q1	121.04
Min	83.91

TABLE 3.2 The five-number summary of monthly trading volume of AIG shares (in millions of shares) for the period 2002–2007.

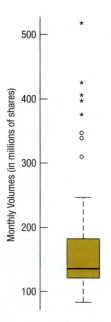

FIGURE 3.9 Boxplot of monthly volumes of AIG stock traded in the period 2002–2007 (in millions of shares).

The five-number summary provides a good overall look at the distribution. We can see that on half of the days the volume was between 121.04 and 182.32 million shares, and that it was never above 515.62 or below 83.91 million shares.

We can display the information from a five-number summary in a **boxplot** (see Figure 3.9), which is a powerful visualization of the data.

The central box shows the middle half of the data, between the quartiles. Because the top of the box is at the upper quartile (Q3) and the bottom is at Q1, the height of the box is equal to Q3 − Q1 which is the IQR. (For the AIG data, it's 61.28.) The median is displayed as a horizontal line. If the median is roughly centered between the quartiles, then the middle half of the data is roughly symmetric. If it is not centered, the distribution is skewed. In extreme cases, the median can coincide with one of the quartiles.

The whiskers reach out from the box to the most extreme values that are not considered outliers. The boxplot nominates points as outliers if they fall farther than 1.5 IQRs beyond either quartile (for the AIG data, 1.5 IQR = 1.5 × 61.28 = 91.92). The nominated cases are displayed individually, both to keep them out of the way for judging skewness and to encourage you to give them special attention. They may be mistakes or they may be the most interesting cases in your data. This rule is not a definition of what makes a point an outlier. It just nominates cases for special attention. And it is not a substitute for careful analysis and thought about whether an extreme value deserves to be treated specially.

Boxplots are especially useful for comparing several distributions side by side. From the shape of the box in Figure 3.9, we can see that the central part of the distribution of volume is skewed to the right (upward here) and the dissimilar length of the two whiskers shows that the skewness continues into the tails of the distribution. We also see several high-volume and some extremely high-volume months. Those months may warrant some inquiries into why trading volume was so high.

Why Use 1.5 IQRs for Nominating Outliers?

Nominate a point as a potential outlier if it lies farther than 1.5 IQRs beyond either the lower (Q1) or upper (Q3) quartile. Some boxplots also designate points as "far" outliers if they lie more than 3 IQRs from the quartiles (as in Figure 3.9). The prominent statistician John W. Tukey, the originator of the boxplot, was asked (by one of the authors) why the outlier nomination rule cut at 1.5 IQRs beyond each quartile. He answered that the reason was simple—1 IQR would be too small and 2 IQRs would be too large.

IN PRACTICE 3.7   Identifying potential outliers

MANAGER You created a histogram that helped me visualize the frequency of number of downloads per hour. Were there any strange or outlier points?

ANALYST The quartiles are 13 and 24.5 and the IQR is 11.5, and 1.5 × IQR = 17.25. A value would have to be larger than 24.5 + 17.25 = 41.75 downloads per hour or smaller than 13 − 17.25 = −4.25. The largest value was 36 downloads per hour and all values must be nonnegative, so there are no points nominated as outliers according to the 1.5 IQR rule.

GUIDED EXAMPLE Credit Card Bank Customers

To focus on the needs of particular customers, companies often segment their customers into groups with similar needs or spending patterns. A major credit card bank wanted to see how much a particular group of cardholders charged per month on their cards to understand the potential growth in their card use. The data for each customer was the amount he or she spent using the card during a recent three-month period. Boxplots are especially useful for one variable when combined with a histogram and numerical summaries. Let's summarize the spending of this market segment.

PLAN **Define** the problem—state the objectives of the study. **Identify** the *variable*. **Provide** the time frame of the data.	We want to summarize the average monthly charges (in dollars) made by 500 cardholders from a market segment of interest during a three-month period. The data are quantitative, so we'll use histograms and boxplots, as well as numerical summaries.

DO **Characterize** the variables and select an appropriate display based on the nature of the data and what you want to know about it.

Explore the data with tables and graphics.

REALITY CHECK It is always a good idea to anticipate the shape of the distribution so you can check whether the histogram is close to what you expected. Are these data reasonable amounts for customers to charge on their cards in a month? A typical value is a few hundred dollars. That seems like the right ballpark.

Note that outliers are often easier to see with boxplots than with histograms, but the histogram provides more details about the shape of the distribution. The computer program that made this boxplot "jitters" the outliers in the boxplot so they don't lie on top of each other, making them easier to see.

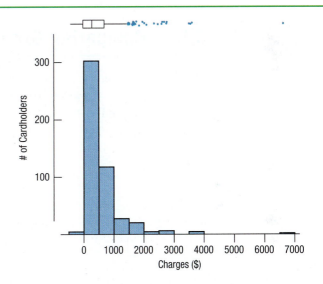

Both graphs show a distribution that is highly skewed to the right with several outliers and an extreme outlier near $7000.

Summary of Monthly Charges	
Count	500
Mean	544.749
Median	370.65
StdDev	661.244
IQR	624.125
Q1	114.54
Q3	738.665

The mean is much larger than the median. The data have a skewed distribution.

(continued)

REPORT

Communicate and Present Describe the shape, center, and spread of the distribution. Be sure to report on the symmetry, number of modes, and any gaps or outliers.

Recommend State a conclusion and any recommended actions or analysis.

MEMO

Re: Report on segment spending

The distribution of charges for this segment during this time period is unimodal and skewed to the right. For that reason, we have summarized the data with the median and interquartile range (IQR).

The median amount charged was $370.65. Half of the cardholders charged between $114.54 and $738.67.

In addition, there are several high outliers, with one extreme value at $6745.

There are also a few negative values. We suspect that these are people who returned more than they charged in a month, but because the values might be data errors, we suggest that they be checked.

Future analyses should look at whether charges during these three months were similar to charges in the rest of the year. We would also like to investigate if there is a seasonal pattern and, if so, whether it can be explained by our advertising campaigns or by other factors.

3.8 Comparing Groups

Stock prices can sometimes reflect turmoil within a company. Could an investor have seen signs of trouble in the AIG stock prices? Figure 3.10 shows the daily closing prices for the first two years of our data, 2002 and 2003:

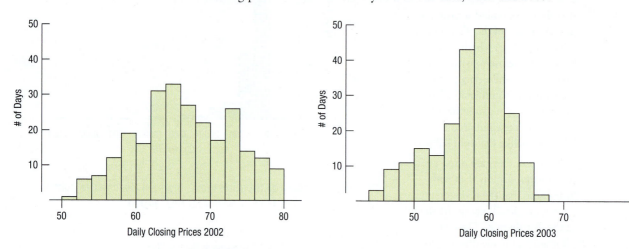

FIGURE 3.10 Daily closing prices of AIG on the NYSE for the two years 2002 and 2003. How do the two distributions differ?

Prices were generally lower in 2003 than 2002. The price distribution for 2002 appears to be symmetric with a center in the high $60s while the 2003 distribution is left skewed with a center below $60. For comparison, we displayed the two histograms on the same scale. Histograms with very different centers and spreads can appear similar unless you do that.[8]

Boxplots are a better choice when we compare several groups because they offer an ideal balance of information and simplicity, hiding the details while displaying the overall summary information.

---

[8]We didn't do that in Figure 3.8. If we only looked at the two histograms we might easily have missed how different Palo Alto and Foster City real estate prices are.

To compare several groups or categories, we place our boxplots side by side so we can compare their centers and spreads. We can see past any outliers in making these comparisons because the outliers are displayed individually. We can also begin to look for trends in both the centers and the spreads.

GUIDED EXAMPLE   AIG Stock Price

What really happened to the AIG stock price from the beginning of the period that our analyst, Alex, has been studying through the financial crisis of 2008/2009? Were there signs of trouble that a careful analyst might have noticed?

PLAN	
Define the problem and state the objectives. **Identify** the variables. **Provide** the time frame of the data.	We want to compare the daily prices of AIG shares traded on the NYSE from 2002 through 2009. The daily price is quantitative and measured in dollars. We can partition the values by year and use side-by-side boxplots to compare the daily prices across years.

DO	
Characterize the variables and determine the appropriate displays. **Explore** the data with tables and graphs	The prices of AIG stock are quantitative values recorded in dollars.

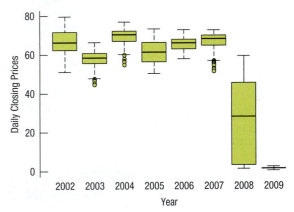

What happened in 2008? We'd better look there with a finer partition. Here are boxplots by month for 2008.

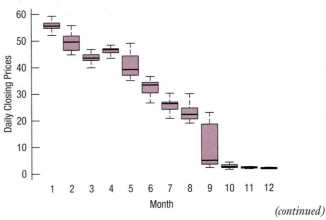

(continued)

Perhaps we need to consider another measure. Alex also has the daily stock opening prices for AIG during this period. They offer a way to consider the volatility of AIG prices as the difference between closing and opening prices on each day. We now know that 2007 and 2008 were the key years. So we'll make boxplots of the daily price spread, Close−Open, grouped by month for those years.

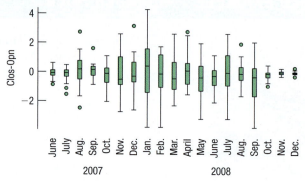

Almost a year before the September 2008 stock price crash, the daily volatility in the stock price grew substantially.

REPORT **Communicate and Present**
Report what you've learned about the data and any recommended action or analysis.

MEMO

Re: Research on price of AIG stock

We have examined the daily closing prices of AIG stock on the NYSE for the period 2002 through 2009. Prices were relatively stable for the period 2002 through 2007. Prices were a bit lower in 2003 but recovered and stayed generally above $60 for 2004 through 2007. However, in the fall of 2007, the daily fluctuations in stock price became much larger. Then throughout the first 9 months of 2008, prices dropped dramatically, and remained low throughout 2009. A boxplot by month during 2008 shows that the decline in price was sharpest in September. Most analysts point to that month as the beginning of the financial meltdown, but clearly there were signs in the price of AIG that trouble had been brewing for much longer. By October, and for the rest of the year, the price was very low with almost no variation.

IN PRACTICE 3.8 Comparing groups

CFO Is there a difference between the distribution of downloads during AM vs. PM hours? (See In Practice 3.1.)

ANALYST A powerful and easy way to compare two distributions is to use side-by-side boxplots. Examining the boxplots, we can see that there are generally more downloads in the afternoon than in the morning. The median number of afternoon downloads is around 22 as compared with 14 for the morning hours. The PM downloads are also much more consistent. The entire range of the PM hours, 15, is about the size of the IQR for AM hours. Both distributions appear to be fairly symmetric, although the AM hour distribution has some high points which seem to give some asymmetry.

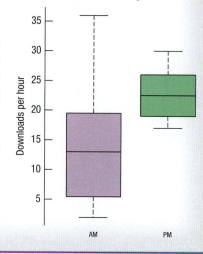

3.9   Identifying Outliers

We've just seen that the price of AIG shares dropped precipitously during the year 2008. Figure 3.11 shows the daily sales volume by month.

FIGURE 3.11 In January, there was a high-volume day of 38 million shares that is nominated as an outlier for that month. In February there were three outliers with a maximum of over 100 million shares. In most months one or more high-volume days are identified as outliers for their month. But none of these high-volume days would have been considered unusual during September, when the median daily volume of AIG stock was 170 million shares. Days that may have seemed ordinary for September if placed in another month would have seemed extraordinary and *vice versa*. That high-volume day in January certainly wouldn't stand out in September or even October or November, but for January it was remarkable.

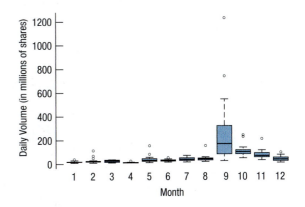

Cases that stand out from the rest of the data deserve our attention. Boxplots have a rule for nominating extreme cases to display as outliers, but that's just a rule of thumb—not a definition. The rule doesn't tell you what to do with them. It's never a substitute for careful thinking about the data and their context.

So, what *should* we do with outliers? The first thing to do is to try to understand them in the context of the data. Once you've identified likely outliers, you should always investigate them. Some outliers are not plausible and may simply be errors. A decimal point may have been misplaced, digits transposed, digits repeated or omitted, or the wrong value transcribed. Or, the units may be wrong. If you saw the number of AIG shares traded on the NYSE listed as 2 shares for a particular day, you'd know something was wrong. It could be that it was meant as 2 million shares, but you'd have to check to be sure. If you can identify the error, then you should certainly correct it.

Other outliers are not wrong; they're just different. These are the cases that often repay your efforts to understand them. You may learn more from the extraordinary cases than from summaries of the overall dataset.

What about those two days in September that stand out as extreme even during that volatile month? Those were September 15 and 16, 2008. On the 15th, 740 million shares of AIG stock were traded. That was followed by an incredible volume of over 1 billion shares of stock from a single company traded the following day. Here's how Barron's described the trading of September 16:

> ### Record Volume for NYSE Stocks, Nasdaq Trades Surge
> ### Beats Its July Record
>
> *Yesterday's record-setting volume of 8.14 billion shares traded of all stocks listed on the New York Stock Exchange was pushed aside today by 9.31 billion shares in NYSE Composite volume. The biggest among those trades was the buying and selling of American International Group, with 1.11 billion shares traded as of 4 p.m. today. The AIG trades were 12% of all NYSE Composite volume.*

IN PRACTICE 3.9   Initial description of a data set

MANAGER We just got a real estate report that lists the following prices for sales of single family homes in a small town in Virginia (rounded to the nearest thousand). Can you help me understand the prices in this town?

155,000	329,000	172,000	122,000	260,000
139,000	178,000	339,435,000	136,000	330,000
158,000	194,000	279,000	167,000	159,000
149,000	160,000	231,000	136,000	128,000

ANALYST A boxplot shows an extreme outlier:

That extreme point is a home whose sale price is listed at \$339.4M.

A check on the Internet shows that only one or two homes in the world sell for that amount and none are near here. This is clearly a mistake.

Setting aside this point, we find the following histogram and summary statistics:

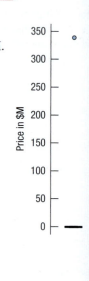

The distribution of prices is strongly skewed to the right. The median price is \$160,000. The minimum is \$122,000 and the maximum (without the outlier) is \$330,000. The middle 50% of house prices lie between \$144,000 and \$212,500 with an IQR of \$68,500. (Calculated using the Tukey method.)

3.10   Time Series Plots

A histogram can provide information about the distribution of a variable, but it can't show any pattern over time. A time series variable is a quantitative variable that has been measured or recorded at regular intervals over time. Usually, we require that the intervals are equally spaced, although values recorded for successive business days (skipping weekends and holidays) are usually treated as equally spaced. Whenever we have time series data, it is a good idea to look for patterns by plotting the data in time order.

When a time series has no strong trend or change in variability we say that it is **stationary**.[9] A histogram can provide a useful summary of a stationary series but generally misses what is really going on in a variable that changes over time.

---

[9]Sometimes we separate the properties and say the series is stationary with respect to the mean (if there is no trend) or stationary with respect to the variance (if the spread doesn't change). In the Guided Example, a time series of AIG stock differences in daily Opening and Closing prices would be stationary in its mean but not in its variance. But unless otherwise noted, we'll assume that all the statistical properties of a series that is called stationary are constant over time.

For example, when we examine the daily AIG prices for the year 2007 (Figure 3.12), we see that prices started to change during the last quarter, but a histogram wouldn't show that.

FIGURE 3.12 A time series plot of daily closing *Price* of AIG stock for the year 2007 shows the overall pattern and changes in variation.

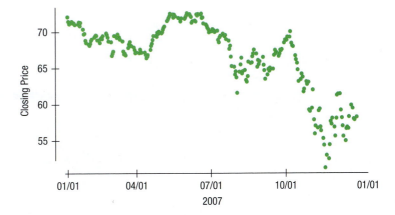

A display of values against time is called a **time series plot**. This plot reveals a pattern that we were unable to see in either a histogram or a boxplot. Now we can see that although the price rallied in the spring of 2007, after July there were already signs that the price might not stay above $60. By October, that pattern was clear.

Time series plots often show a great deal of point-to-point variation, as Figure 3.12 does, so you'll often see time series plots drawn with all the points connected (as in Figure 3.13), especially in financial publications.

FIGURE 3.13 The *Daily Prices* of Figure 3.12, drawn with lines connecting all the points. Sometimes this can help us see an underlying pattern.

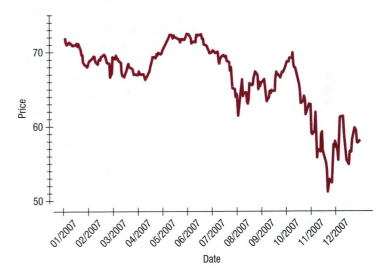

It may be better to smooth out the local point-to-point variability so we can see past this variation to understand any underlying trend. We will want to think about how the values vary around that trend—the time series version of center and spread. There are many ways for computers to find a smooth trace through a time series plot.

Figure 3.14 shows the daily prices of Figures 3.12 and 3.13 with a typical smoothing function, available in many statistics programs. With the smooth trace, it's a bit easier to see a pattern. The trace helps our eye follow the main trend and alerts us to points that don't fit the overall pattern.

It is always tempting to try to extend what we see in a timeplot into the future. Sometimes that makes sense. It's probably safe to predict more volume on the

FIGURE 3.14 The *2007 Daily Prices* of Figure 3.12, with a smooth trace added to help your eye see the long-term pattern.

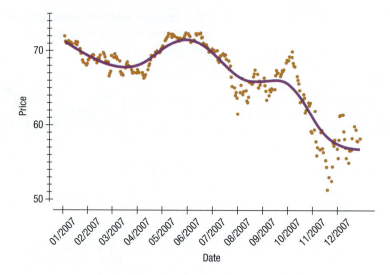

NYSE on triple witching days (when contracts expire) and less activity in the week between Christmas and New Year's Day.

Other patterns are riskier to extend into the future. If a stock's price has been rising, how long will it continue to go up? No stock has ever increased in value indefinitely, and no stock analyst has consistently been able to forecast when a stock's value will turn around. Stock prices, unemployment rates, and other economic, social, or psychological measures are much harder to predict than physical quantities. The path a ball will follow when thrown from a certain height at a given speed and direction is well understood. The path that interest rates will take is much less clear.

Unless you have strong (nonstatistical) reasons for doing otherwise, you should resist the temptation to think that any trend you see will continue indefinitely. Statistical models often tempt those who use them to think beyond the data. We'll pay close attention later in this book to understanding when, how, and how much we can justify doing that.

Look at the prices in Figures 3.12 through 3.14 and try to guess what happened in the subsequent months. Was that drop from October to December a sign of trouble ahead, or was the increase in December back to around $60 where the stock had comfortably traded for several years a sign that stability had returned to AIG's stock price? Perhaps those who picked up the stock for $51 in early November really got a bargain. Let's look ahead to 2008:

FIGURE 3.15 A time series plot of daily AIG *Price* in 2008 shows a general decline followed by a sharp collapse in September.

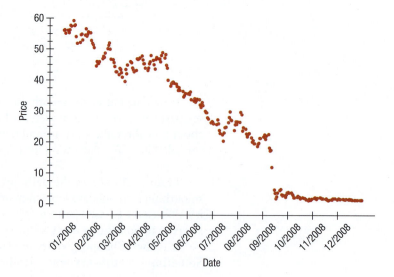

Even through the spring of 2008, although the price was gently falling, nothing prepared traders following only the time series plot for what was to follow. In September the stock lost nearly all of its value. But, by 2012, it was trading in the mid $30's.

IN PRACTICE 3.10   Insights from time series data

CFO Are there any interesting patterns in the hourly download data? (See In Practice 3.1.)

ANALYST Surprisingly, for this day, downloads were highest at midnight with about 36 downloads per hour, then dropped sharply until about 5–6 AM, when they reached their minimum at 2–3 per hour. They gradually increased to about 20 per hour by noon, and then stayed in the twenties until midnight, with a slight increase during the evening hours. When we ignored the time order, as we did earlier, we missed this pattern entirely.

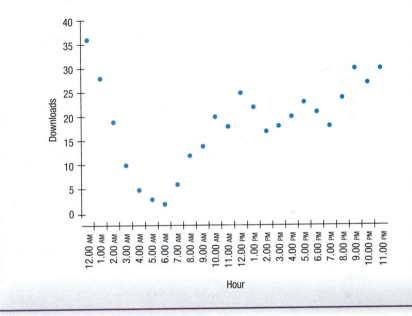

The histogram we saw in the beginning of the chapter (Figure 3.1) summarized the distribution of AIG stock prices fairly well because during that period the prices were fairly stable; the price series appears to be stationary. However, when the time series is not stationary as was the case for AIG prices after 2007, be careful. A histogram is unlikely to capture what is really of interest. Then, a time series plot is the best graphical display to use to display the behavior of the data.

*3.11 Transforming Skewed Data

When a distribution is skewed, it may not be appropriate to summarize the data simply with a center and spread, and it can be hard to decide whether the most extreme values are outliers or just part of the stretched-out tail. How can we say anything useful about such data? The secret is to apply a simple function to each data value. One function that can change the shape of a distribution is the logarithm function. Let's examine an example in which a set of data is severely skewed.

In 1980, the average CEO made about 42 times the average worker's salary. In the two decades that followed, CEO compensation soared when compared with the average worker's pay. What does the distribution of a sample of 434 companies' CEOs look like? Figure 3.16 shows a histogram of the CEO compensation from a recent year.

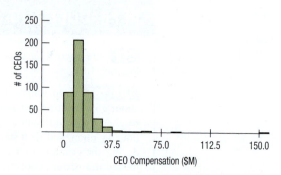

FIGURE 3.16   The total compensation for CEOs (in $M) of 434 of the largest companies is skewed and includes some extraordinarily large values.

These values are reported in *millions* of dollars. The boxplot indicates that some of the CEOs received extraordinarily high compensation. The reason that the histogram seems to leave so much of the area blank is that the largest observations are so far from the bulk of the data. This distribution is very skewed to the right.

Total compensation for CEOs consists of their base salaries, bonuses, and extra compensation, usually in the form of stock or stock options. Data that add together several variables, such as the compensation data, can easily have skewed distributions. It's often a good idea to separate the component variables and examine them individually, but we don't have that information for the CEOs.

Skewed distributions are difficult to summarize. It's hard to know what we mean by the "center" of a skewed distribution, so it's not obvious what value to use to summarize the distribution. What would you say was a typical CEO total compensation? The mean value in these data is $14.1M, but the median is "only" $11.9M.

One way to make a skewed distribution more symmetric is to **re-express**, or **transform**, the data by applying a simple function to all the data values. It is common to take the logarithm of variables like income, corporate earnings, and prices, which tend to be skewed to the right. Economists do this as a matter of course in many of their models.

Dealing with Logarithms

You may think of logarithms as something technical, but they are just a function that can make some values easier to work with. You know of scales that are re-expressed by logarithms (although you may not have realized it). Decibels for sound, Richter scale for earthquakes, and pH values for acidity are among the scales that come as logarithms of some measured quantity. Base 10 logs are the easiest to understand, but natural logs are often used as well. (Either one is fine.) You can think of the base 10 log of a number as roughly one less than the number of digits you need to write that number. So 100, which is the smallest number to require 3 digits, has a $\log_{10}$ of 2. And 1000 has a $\log_{10}$ of 3. The $\log_{10}$ of 500 is between 2 and 3, but you'd need a calculator to find that it's approximately 2.7. All salaries of "six figures" have $\log_{10}$ between 5 and 6. Fortunately, with technology, it is easy to re-express data by logs.

The histogram of the logs of the total CEO compensations in Figure 3.17 is nearly symmetric, so we can say that a typical log compensation is between 6.5 and 7.5. To be more precise, the mean log_{10} value is 7.07, while the median is 7.08. Note that nearly all the values are between 6.0 and 8.0—in other words, between $1,000,000 and $100,000,000 per year. Logarithmic transformations are common, but other transformations like square root and reciprocal are also used. Because computers and calculators are available to do the calculating, you should consider transformation as a helpful tool whenever you have skewed data.

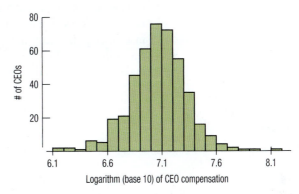

FIGURE 3.17 Taking logs makes the histogram of CEO total compensation nearly symmetric.

IN PRACTICE 3.11   Insights from skewed data

MANAGER *Fortune* magazine publishes a list of the 100 best companies to work for (money.cnn.com/magazines/fortune/bestcompanies/2010/). One statistic often looked at is the average annual pay for the most common job title at the company. Can we characterize those pay values?

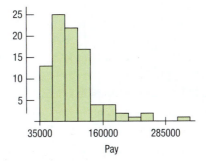   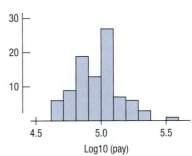

ANALYST I created a histogram of the average annual pay values. The pay values are skewed to the high end. Because of the high skew, I also created a histogram of the logarithm of the pay values. The logarithmic transformation makes the distribution more nearly symmetric, making it more appropriate to summarize with a mean and standard deviation.

⊘ WHAT CAN GO WRONG?

A data display should tell a story about the data. To do that it must speak in a clear language, making plain what variable is displayed, what any axis shows, and what the values of the data are. And it must be consistent in those decisions.

The task of summarizing a quantitative variable requires that we follow a set of rules. We need to watch out for certain features of the data that make summarizing them with a number dangerous. Here's some advice:

- **Don't make a histogram of a categorical variable.** Just because the variable contains numbers doesn't mean it's quantitative. Here's a histogram of the insurance policy numbers of some workers. It's not very informative because the policy numbers are categorical. A histogram of a categorical variable makes no sense. A bar chart or pie chart may do better.

FIGURE 3.18 It's not appropriate to display categorical data like policy numbers with a histogram.

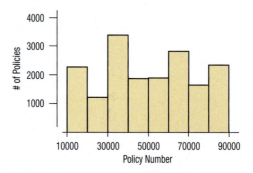

- **Choose a scale appropriate to the data.** Computer programs usually do a pretty good job of choosing histogram bin widths. Often, there's an easy way to adjust the width, sometimes interactively. Figure 3.19 shows the AIG price histogram with two other choices for the bin size. Neither seems to be the best choice.

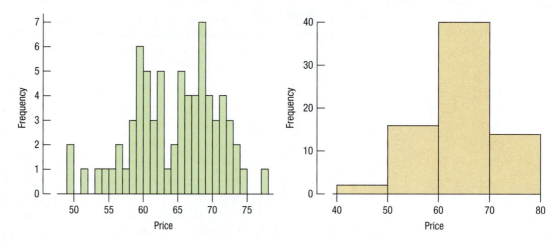

FIGURE 3.19 Changing the bin width changes how the histogram looks. The AIG stock prices look very different with these two choices.

- **Avoid inconsistent scales.** Parts of displays should be mutually consistent—it's not fair to change scales in the middle or to plot two variables on different scales on the same display. When comparing two groups, be sure to draw them on the same scale.

- **Label clearly.** Variables should be identified clearly and axes labeled so a reader knows what the plot displays.

Here's a remarkable example of a plot gone wrong. It illustrated a news story about rising college costs. It uses time series plots, but it gives a misleading impression. First, think about the story you're being told by this display. Then try to figure out what has gone wrong.

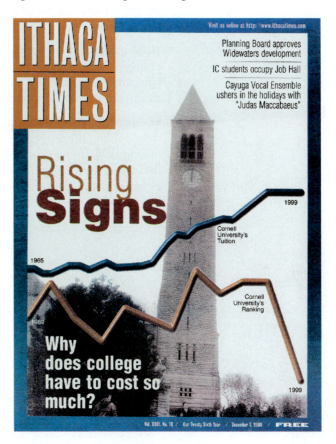

What's wrong? Just about everything.

- **The horizontal scales are inconsistent.** Both lines show trends over time, but for what years? The tuition sequence starts in 1965, but rankings are graphed from 1989. Plotting them on the same (invisible) scale makes it seem that they're for the same years.

- **The vertical axis isn't labeled.** That hides the fact that it's using two different scales. Does it graph dollars (of tuition) or ranking (of Cornell University)?

This display violates every rule we can think of. And it's even worse than that. It violates a rule that we didn't even consider. The two inconsistent scales for the vertical axis don't point in the same direction! The line for Cornell's rank shows that it has "plummeted" from 15th place to 6th place in academic rank. Most of us think that's an *improvement*, but that's not the message of this graph.

- **Do a reality check.** Don't let the computer (or calculator) do your thinking for you. Make sure the calculated summaries make sense. For example, does the mean look like it is in the center of the histogram? Think about the spread. An IQR of 50 mpg would clearly be wrong for a family car. And no measure of spread can be negative. The standard deviation can take the value 0, but only in the very unusual case that all the data values equal the same number. If you see the IQR or standard deviation equal to 0, it's probably a sign that something's wrong with the data.

- **Don't compute numerical summaries of a categorical variable.** The mean ZIP code or the standard deviation of Social Security numbers is not meaningful. If the variable is categorical, you should instead report summaries such as percentages. It is easy to make this mistake when you let technology do the summaries for you. After all, the computer doesn't care what the numbers mean.

- **Watch out for multiple modes.** If the distribution—as seen in a histogram, for example—has multiple modes, consider separating the data into groups. If you cannot separate the data in a meaningful way, you should not summarize the center and spread of the variable.

- **Beware of outliers.** If the data have outliers but are otherwise unimodal, consider holding the outliers out of the further calculations and reporting them individually. If you can find a simple reason for the outlier (for instance, a data transcription error), you should remove or correct it. If you cannot do either of these, then choose the median and IQR to summarize the center and spread.

ETHICS IN ACTION

Beth Tully owns Zenna's Café, an independent coffee shop located in a small Midwestern city. Since opening Zenna's in 2002, she has been steadily growing her business and now distributes her custom coffee blends to a number of regional restaurants and markets. She operates a microroaster that offers specialty grade Arabica coffees recognized by some as the best in the area.

In addition to providing the highest quality coffees, Beth also wants her business to be socially responsible. Toward that end, she pays fair prices to coffee farmers and donates funds to help charitable causes in Panama, Costa Rica, and Guatemala. In addition, she encourages her employees to get involved in the local community.

Recently, one of the well-known multinational coffeehouse chains announced plans to locate shops in her area. This chain is one of the few to offer Certified Free-Trade coffee products and work toward social justice in the global community. Consequently, Beth thought it might be a good idea for her to begin communicating Zenna's socially responsible efforts to the public, but with an emphasis on their commitment to the local community.

Three months ago she began collecting data on the number of volunteer hours donated by her employees per week. She has a total of 12 employees, of whom 10 are full time. Most employees volunteered less than 2 hours per week, but Beth noticed that one part-time employee volunteered more than 20 hours per week. She discovered that her employees collectively volunteered an average of 15 hours per month (with a median of 8 hours). She planned to report the average number and believed most people would be impressed with Zenna's level of commitment to the local community.

- **Identify the ethical dilemma in this scenario.**
- **What are the undesirable consequences?**
- **Propose an ethical solution that considers the welfare of all stakeholders.**

FROM LEARNING TO EARNING

LEARNING OBJECTIVES

Make and interpret histograms to display the distribution of a variable.

- We understand distributions in terms of their shape, center, and spread.

Describe the shape of a distribution.

- A **symmetric** distribution has roughly the same shape reflected around the center.
- A **skewed** distribution extends farther on one side than on the other.
- A **unimodal** distribution has a single major hump or mode; a bimodal distribution has two; multimodal distributions have more.
- **Outliers** are values that lie far from the rest of the data.

Compute the mean and median of a distribution, and know when it is best to use each to summarize the center.

- The **mean** is the sum of the values divided by the count. It is a suitable summary for unimodal, symmetric distributions.
- The **median** is the middle value; half the values are above and half are below the median. It is a better summary when the distribution is skewed or has outliers.

Compute the standard deviation and interquartile range (IQR), and know when it is best to use each to summarize the spread.

- The **standard deviation** is the square root of the average squared difference between each data value and the mean. It is the summary of choice for the spread of unimodal, symmetric variables.
- The **IQR** is the difference between the quartiles. It is often a better summary of spread for skewed distributions or data with outliers.

Standardize values and use them for comparisons of otherwise disparate variables.

- We standardize by finding **z-scores**. To convert a data value to its z-score, subtract the mean and divide by the standard deviation.
- z-scores have no units, so they can be compared to z-scores of other variables.
- The idea of measuring the distance of a value from the mean in terms of standard deviations is a basic concept in statistics and will return many times later in the course.

Find a five-number summary and, using it, make a boxplot. Use the boxplot's outlier nomination rule to identify cases that may deserve special attention.

- A **five-number summary** consists of the median, the quartiles, and the extremes of the data.
- A **boxplot** shows the quartiles as the upper and lower ends of a central box, the median as a line across the box, and "whiskers" that extend to the most extreme values that are not nominated as outliers.
- Boxplots display separately any case that is more than 1.5 IQRs beyond each quartile. These cases should be considered as possible outliers.

Use boxplots to compare distributions.

- Boxplots facilitate comparisons of several groups. It is easy to compare centers (medians) and spreads (IQRs).
- Because boxplots show possible outliers separately, any outliers don't affect comparisons.

Make and interpret time plots for time series data.

- Look for the trend and any changes in the spread of the data over time.

TERMS

Bin	In a histogram, the range of possible values are split into intervals called bins, over which the frequencies are displayed.
Bimodal	Distributions with two modes.
Boxplot	A boxplot displays the 5-number summary as a central box with whiskers that extend to the nonoutlying values. Boxplots are particularly effective for comparing groups.
Center	The middle of the distribution, usually summarized numerically by the mean or the median.
Distribution	The distribution of a variable gives:
	• possible values of the variable
	• frequency or relative frequency of each value or range of values
Five-number summary	A five-number summary for a variable consists of:
	• The minimum and maximum
	• The quartiles Q1 and Q3
	• The median
Gap	A region of a distribution where there are no values.
Histogram (relative frequency histogram)	A histogram uses adjacent bars to show the distribution of values in a quantitative variable. Each bar represents the frequency (relative frequency) of values falling in an interval of values.
Interquartile range (IQR)	The difference between the lower and upper quartiles. IQR = Q3 − Q1.
Mean	A measure of center found as $\bar{x} = \sum x / n$.
Median	The middle value with half of the data above it and half below it.
Mode	A peak or local high point in the shape of the distribution of a variable. The apparent location of modes can change as the scale of a histogram is changed.
Multimodal	Distributions with more than two modes.
Outliers	Extreme values that don't appear to belong with the rest of the data. They may be unusual values that deserve further investigation or just mistakes; there's no obvious way to tell.
Quartile	The lower quartile (Q1) is the value with a quarter of the data below it. The upper quartile (Q3) has a quarter of the data above it. The median and quartiles divide the data into four equal parts.
Range	The difference between the lowest and highest values in a data set: Range = *max* − *min*.
***Re-express or transform**	To re-express or transform data, take the logarithm, square root, reciprocal, or some other mathematical operation on all values of the data set. Re-expression can make the distribution of a variable more nearly symmetric and the spread of groups more nearly alike.
Shape	The visual appearance of the distribution. To describe the shape, look for:
	• single vs. multiple modes
	• symmetry vs. skewness
Skewed	A distribution is skewed if one tail stretches out farther than the other.
Spread	The description of how tightly clustered the distribution is around its center. Measures of spread include the IQR and the standard deviation.
Standard deviation	A measure of spread found as $s = \sqrt{\dfrac{\sum (x - \bar{x})^2}{n - 1}}$.
Standardized value	We standardize a value by subtracting the mean and dividing by the standard deviation for the variable. These values, called z-scores, have no units.
Stationary	A time series is said to be stationary if its statistical properties don't change over time.

Symmetric	A distribution is symmetric if the two halves on either side of the center look approximately like mirror images of each other.
Tail	The tails of a distribution are the parts that typically trail off on either side.
Time series plot	A time series plot displays the values of a time series plotted against time. Often, successive values are connected with lines to show trends more clearly.
Uniform	A distribution that's roughly flat is said to be uniform.
Unimodal	Having one mode. This is a useful term for describing the shape of a histogram when it's generally mound-shaped.
Variance	The standard deviation squared.
z-Score	A standardized value that tells how many standard deviations a value is from the mean; z-scores have a mean of 0 and a standard deviation of 1.

TECH SUPPORT   Displaying and Summarizing Quantitative Variables

Almost any program that displays data can make a histogram, but some will do a better job of determining where the bars should start and how they should partition the span of the data (see the figure below).

Many statistics packages offer a prepackaged collection of summary measures. The result might look like this:

```
Variable: Weight
N = 234
Mean = 143.3      Median = 139
St. Dev = 11.1    IQR = 14
```

Alternatively, a package might make a table for several variables and summary measures:

Variable	N	mean	median	stdev	IQR
Weight	234	143.3	139	11.1	14
Height	234	68.3	68.1	4.3	5
Score	234	86	88	9	5

It is usually easy to read the results and identify each computed summary statistic. You should be able to read the summary statistics produced by any computer package.

Packages often provide many more summary statistics than you need. Of course, some of these may not be appropriate when the data are skewed or have outliers. It is your responsibility to check a histogram and decide which summary statistics to use.

It is common for packages to report summary statistics to many decimal places of "accuracy." Of course, it is rare to find data that have such accuracy in the original measurements. The ability to calculate to six or seven digits beyond the decimal point doesn't mean that those digits have any meaning. Generally, it's a good idea to round these values, allowing perhaps one more digit of precision than was given in the original data.

Displays and summaries of quantitative variables are among the simplest things you can do in most statistics packages.

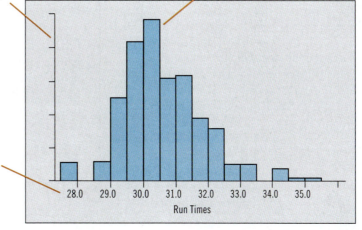

The vertical scale may be counts or proportions. Sometimes it isn't clear which. But the shape of the histogram is the same either way.

Most packages choose the number of bars for you automatically. Often you can adjust that choice.

The axis should be clearly labeled so you can tell what "pile" each bar represents. You should be able to tell the lower and upper bounds of each bar.

To make a histogram in Excel 2013 or 2016, use the Data Analysis add-in. If you have not installed and enabled that, you must do that first.

To install and enable the Data Analysis add-in,

- On the File tab, click **Options**, and then click **Add-Ins**.
- Near the bottom of the Excel Options dialog box, select **Add-ins** in the Manage box, and then click **OK**.
- In the Add-Ins dialog box, select the check box for Analysis ToolPak, and then click **OK**.
- If Excel displays a message that states it can't run this add-in and prompts you to install it, click **Yes** to install the add-in.

To make a histogram,

- From the Data option, select the **Data Analysis add-in**.
- From its menu, select **Histograms**.
- Indicate the range of the data whose histogram you wish to draw.
- Check **Labels** if your columns have names in the first cell.
- Check **Chart output** and click **OK**.
- Right-click on any bar of the resulting graph and, from the menu that drops down, select **Format Data Series …**
- Slide the Gap Width slider to **0%**, and click **Close**.
- In the pivot table on the left, use your pointing tool to slide the bottom of the table up to get rid of the "more" bin.
- Edit the bin names in Column A to properly identify the contents of each bin.

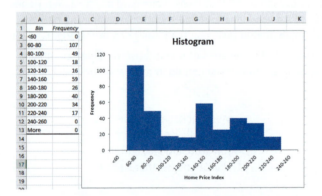

- You can right click on the legend or axis names to edit or remove them.

Alternatively, you can set up your own bin boundaries and count the observations falling within each bin using an Excel function such as FREQUENCY (Data array, Bins array). Consult your Excel manual or help files for details of how to do this.

To create a time series plot in Excel:

- Open a time-series data file sorted in ascending order by time.
- Highlight the column(s) holding the values of the quantitative variable(s) (the y-values) measured over a period of time.

- Choose **Insert** > **Charts** > **Line** > **2-D Line** or (2-D line with markers).
- Right click on the chart and choose **Select Data**.
- Right-click on the horizontal axis and select **Time** in the **Category** option of the **Number** menu option.

To make a boxplot:

- Choose **Visualizing data**, and then select **Univariate plots**.
- Enter the cell range of your data in the **Quantitative** or **Qualitative data** field.
- Select the type of chart on the **Charts** tab.

NOTE: XLStat scales side-by-side boxplots individually, so they are not suitable for comparing groups.

To make a histogram and find summary statistics:

- Choose **Distribution** from the **Analyze** menu.
- In the Distribution dialog, drag the name of the variable that you wish to analyze into the empty window beside the label "Y, Columns."
- Click **OK**. JMP computes standard summary statistics along with displays of the variables.

COMMENTS

Note that JMP displays histograms in a vertical orientation by default. To view the histogram in a horizontal orientation, choose **Red Triangle Menu** next to your variable name > **Display Options** > **Horizontal Layout**.

To make boxplots:

- Choose **Fit Y By X**. Assign a continuous response variable to Y, Response and a nominal group variable holding the group names to **X, Factor,** and click **OK**. JMP will offer (among other things) dotplots of the data. Click the red triangle and, under **Display Options**, select **Box Plots**. Note: If the variables are of the wrong type, the display options might not offer boxplots.

Alternatively

- Chose **Graph** > **Graph Builder**. Drag the quantitative variable to **Y** and the categorical variable to **X**. Right click on the points and change Points to **Box Plots**.

To make a time series plot in JMP:

- From the Analyze menu, choose **Fit Y by X**.
- Move the y variable (measured over time) into the Y, Response box.
- Move the x variable (time) into the X, Factor box.
- Press **OK**.
  - To connect the points select **Fit Each Value** from the red triangle next to Bivariate Fit.
- To put a smooth through the points, select either **Kernel Smoother** or **Fit Spline** under the red triangle.

COMMENTS

For either the **Kernel Smoother** or **Spline** a slider bar appears to adjust the amount of smoothing.

Alternatively,

- Select **Graph > Graph Builder**.
- Drag the y variable into the Y window and the x variable (time) into the X window.
- The default shows the points and a smoother.
  - Right click on the graph and select **Smoother > Change to > Line** to connect the points instead.

MINITAB

To make a histogram:

- Choose **Histogram** from the **Graph** menu.
- Select **Simple** for the type of graph and click **OK**.
- Enter the name of the quantitative variable you wish to display in the box labeled "Graph variables." Click **OK**.

If your data are frequency counts and values, then:

- Click **Data Options** and the **Frequency** tab.
- Enter the column that contains the frequency or counts data.

To make a boxplot:

- Choose **Boxplot** from the **Graph** menu and specify your data format.

To calculate summary statistics:

- Choose **Basic Statistics** from the **Stat** menu. From the **Basic Statistics** submenu, choose **Display Descriptive Statistics**.
- Assign variables from the variable list box to the Variables box. MINITAB makes a Descriptive Statistics table.

R

For a quantitative variable X:

- mean(X) gives the mean and sd(X) gives the standard deviation.
- hist(X) produces a histogram. The width and center options can be used to change the default breaks.

If the data for each group are in separate variables, Y1, Y2, Y3, . . .:

- **boxplot(Y1, Y2, Y3 . . .)** will produce side-by-side boxplots.

If the quantitative values are in variable Y and the grouping values are in categorical variable X:

- **boxplot(Y~X)** will produce side-by-side boxplots—one for each level of X.

COMMENTS

Your variables X and Y may be variables in a data frame. If so, and DATA is the name of the data frame, then you will need to use with (data,).

Many other summaries are available, including min(), max(), median(), and quantile(X, prob=p), where p is a probability between 0 and 1.

SPSS

To make a histogram or boxplot in SPSS open the Chart Builder from the Graphs menu.

- In the **Graphs** menu, choose **Legacy Dialogs**.
- Choose **Histogram** or **Boxplot** from the list of chart types.
- Drag the icon of the plot you want onto the canvas.
- Drag a scale variable to the y-axis drop zone.
- Click **OK**.

To make side-by-side boxplots, drag a categorical variable to the x-axis drop zone and click **OK**.

To calculate summary statistics:

- Choose **Explore** from the **Descriptive Statistics** submenu of the **Analyze** menu. In the **Explore** dialog, assign one or more variables from the source list to the Dependent List and click the **OK** button.

STATCRUNCH

For a quantitative variable, to calculate summaries:

- Click on **Stat**.
- Choose **Summary Stats > Columns**.
- Choose the variable name from the list of Columns.
- Click On **Compute!**

For a histogram, click on **Graph**.

- Choose **Histogram**.
- Choose the variable name from the list of Columns.
- Click on **Compute!**

For a boxplot, click on **Graph**.

- Choose **Boxplot**.
- Choose the variable name(s) from the list of Columns.
- Click on **Compute!**

COMMENTS

- You may need to hold down the Ctrl or Command key to choose more than one variable to summarize.
- You can use the Group by option to plot boxplots across levels of another variable.

BRIEF CASE

Detecting the Housing Bubble

The S&P/Case-Shiller Home Price Indices track changes in the value of residential real estate nationally and in 20 metropolitan regions. (Some of these indices are actually traded on the Chicago Mercantile Exchange.) The data set **Case-Shiller by City** gives the monthly index values for each of the 20 cities tracked by the Case-Shiller index and two national composite series. Examine these values and write a report on them.

Some suggestions: First consider the Composite.20 series, which combines (seasonally adjusted) data for the 20 cities. Describe the distribution of prices overall, then look at a time series plot and discuss the trend over time, especially the period from 2005 to 2008.

Then select several cities to compare. For example, you might compare Miami, Boston, and Detroit. Write a report discussing how trends in housing prices changed over time and how these changes differed from city to city.

CHAPTER 3 EXERCISES

SECTION 3.1

1. As part of the marketing team at an Internet music site, you want to understand who your customers are. You send out a survey to 25 customers (you use an incentive of $50 worth of downloads to guarantee a high response rate) asking for demographic information. One of the variables is the customer's age. For the 25 customers the ages are:

20	32	34	29	30
30	30	14	29	11
38	22	44	48	26
25	22	32	35	32
35	42	44	44	48

a) Make a histogram of the data using a bar width of 10 years.
b) Make a histogram of the data using a bar width of 5 years.
c) Make a relative frequency histogram of the data using a bar width of 5 years.

2. As the new manager of a small convenience store, you want to understand the shopping patterns of your customers. You randomly sample 20 purchases from yesterday's records (all purchases in U.S. dollars):

39.05	2.73	32.92	47.51
37.91	34.35	64.48	51.96
56.95	81.58	47.80	11.72
21.57	40.83	38.24	32.98
75.16	74.30	47.54	65.62

a) Make a histogram of the data using a bar width of $20.
b) Make a histogram of the data using a bar width of $10.
c) Make a relative frequency histogram of the data using a bar width of $10.

SECTION 3.2

3. For the histogram you made in Exercise 1a:

a) Is the distribution unimodal or multimodal?
b) Where is (are) the mode(s)?
c) Is the distribution symmetric?
d) Are there any outliers?

4. For the histogram you made in Exercise 2a:

a) Is the distribution unimodal or multimodal?
b) Where is (are) the mode(s)?
c) Is the distribution symmetric?
d) Are there any outliers?

SECTION 3.3

5. For the data in Exercise 1:

a) Would you expect the mean age to be smaller than, bigger than, or about the same size as the median? Explain.
b) Find the mean age.
c) Find the median age.

6. For the data in Exercise 2:

a) Would you expect the mean purchase to be smaller than, bigger than, or about the same size as the median? Explain.
b) Find the mean purchase.
c) Find the median purchase.

SECTION 3.4

7. For the data in Exercise 1:

a) Find the quartiles using your calculator.
b) Find the quartiles using the Tukey method (page 65).
c) Find the IQR using the quartiles from part b.
d) Find the standard deviation.

8. For the data in Exercise 2:

a) Find the quartiles using your calculator.
b) Find the quartiles using the Tukey method (page 65).
c) Find the IQR using the quartiles from part b.
d) Find the standard deviation.

SECTION 3.5

9. The histogram shows the December charges (in $) for 5000 customers from one marketing segment from a credit card company. (Negative values indicate customers who received more credits than charges during the month.)

a) Write a short description of this distribution (shape, center, spread, unusual features).
b) Would you expect the mean or the median to be larger? Explain.
c) Which would be a more appropriate summary of the center, the mean or the median? Explain.

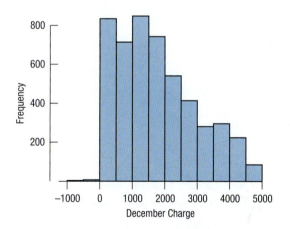

T 10. Adair Vineyard is a 10-acre vineyard in New Paltz, New York. The winery itself is housed in a 200-year-old historic Dutch barn, with the wine cellar on the first floor and the tasting room and gift shop on the second. Since they are relatively small and considering an expansion, they are curious about how their size compares to that of other vineyards. The histogram shows the sizes (in acres) of 36 wineries in upstate New York. (Data in **Vineyards**)

a) Write a short description of this distribution (shape, center, spread, unusual features).
b) Would you expect the mean or the median to be larger? Explain.
c) Which would be a more appropriate summary of the center, the mean or the median? Explain.

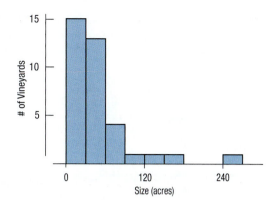

SECTION 3.6

11. Using the ages from Exercise 1:

a) Standardize the minimum and maximum ages using the mean from Exercise 5b and the standard deviation from Exercise 7d.
b) Which has the more extreme z-score, the min or the max?
c) How old would someone with a z-score of 3 be?

12. Using the purchases from Exercise 2:

a) Standardize the minimum and maximum purchase using the mean from Exercise 6b and the standard deviation from Exercise 8d.
b) Which has the more extreme z-score, the min or the max?
c) How large a purchase would a purchase with a z-score of 3.5 be?

SECTION 3.7

13. For the data in Exercise 1:

a) Draw a boxplot using the quartiles from Exercise 7b.
b) Does the boxplot nominate any outliers?
c) What age would be considered a high outlier?

14. For the data in Exercise 2:

a) Draw a boxplot using the quartiles from Exercise 8b.
b) Does the boxplot nominate any outliers?
c) What purchase amount would be considered a high outlier?

15. Here are summary statistics for the sizes (in acres) of upstate New York vineyards from Exercise 10.

Variable	N	Mean	StDev	Minimum	Q1	Median	Q3	Maximum
Acres	36	46.50	47.76	6	18.50	33.50	55	250

a) From the summary statistics, would you describe this distribution as symmetric or skewed? Explain.
b) From the summary statistics, are there any outliers? Explain.
c) Using these summary statistics, sketch a boxplot. What additional information would you need to complete the boxplot?

16. A survey of major universities asked what percentage of incoming freshmen usually graduate "on time" in 4 years. Use the summary statistics given to answer these questions.

	% on time
Count	48
Mean	68.35
Median	69.90
StdDev	10.20
Min	43.20
Max	87.40
Range	44.20
25th %tile	59.15
75th %tile	74.75

a) Would you describe this distribution as symmetric or skewed?
b) Are there any outliers? Explain.
c) Create a boxplot of these data.

SECTION 3.8

17. The survey from Exercise 1 had also asked the customers to say whether they were male or female. Here are the data:

Age	Sex	Age	Sex	Age	Sex	Age	Sex	Age	Sex
20	M	32	F	34	F	29	M	30	M
30	F	30	M	14	M	29	M	11	M
38	F	22	M	44	F	48	F	26	F
25	M	22	M	32	F	35	F	32	F
35	F	42	F	44	F	44	F	48	F

Construct boxplots to compare the ages of men and women and write a sentence summarizing what you find.

18. The store manager from Exercise 2 has collected data on purchases from weekdays and weekends. Here are some summary statistics (rounded to the nearest dollar):

Weekdays: $n = 230$
Min = 4, Q1 = 28, Median = 40, Q3 = 68, Max = 95
Weekends: $n = 150$
Min = 10, Q1 = 35, Median = 55, Q3 = 70, Max = 100

From these statistics, construct side-by-side boxplots and write a sentence comparing the two distributions.

19. Here are boxplots of the weekly sales (in $ U.S.) over a two-year period for a regional food store for two locations. Location #1 is a metropolitan area that is known to be residential where shoppers walk to the store. Location #2 is a suburban area where shoppers drive to the store. Assume that the two towns have similar populations and that the two stores are similar in square footage. Write a brief report discussing what these data show.

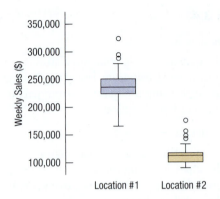

20. Recall the distributions of the weekly sales for the regional stores in Exercise 19. Following are boxplots of weekly sales for this same food store chain for three stores of similar size and location for two different states: Massachusetts (MA) and Connecticut (CT). Compare the distribution of sales for the two states and describe in a report.

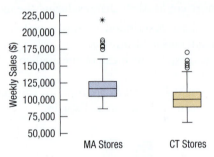

SECTION 3.9

T 21. The five-number summary for the total revenue (in $M) of the top 100 movies of 2015 looks like this: (Data selected from **Movies 06-15**)

Min	Q1	Med	Q3	Max
23.7	34.3	59.8	121.5	742.2

Are there any outliers in these data? How can you tell? What might your next steps in the analysis be?

22. The five-number summary for the ages of 100 respondents to a survey on cell phone use looks like this:

Min	Q1	Med	Q3	Max
13	24	38	49	256

Are there any outliers in these data? How can you tell? What might your next steps in the analysis be?

SECTION 3.10

23. Are the following data time series? If not, explain why.
a) Quarterly earnings of Microsoft Corp.
b) Unemployment in August 2010 by education level.
c) Time spent in training by workers in NewCo.
d) Numbers of e-mails sent by employees of SynCo each hour in a single day.

24. Are the following data time series? If not, explain why.

a) Reports from the Bureau of Labor Statistics on the number of U.S. adults who are employed full time in each major sector of the economy.

b) The quarterly Gross Domestic Product (GDP) of France from 1980 to the present.

c) The dates on which a particular employee was absent from work due to illness over the past two years.

d) The number of cases of flu reported by the CDC each week during a flu season.

SECTION 3.11

T 25. The histogram of the total revenues (in $M) of the movies in Exercise 21 looks like this:

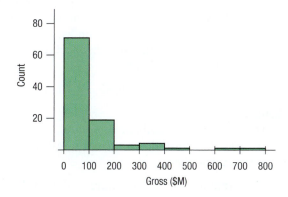

What might you suggest for the next step of the analysis?

26. The histogram of the ages of the respondents in Exercise 22 looks like this:

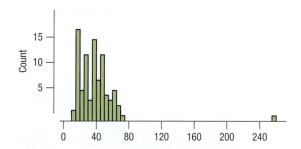

What might you suggest for the next step of the analysis?

CHAPTER EXERCISES

27. Statistics in business. Find a histogram that shows the distribution of a quantitative variable in a business publication (e.g., *The Wall Street Journal, Business Week*, etc.).

a) Does the article identify the W's?

b) Discuss whether the display is appropriate for the data.

c) Discuss what the display reveals about the variable and its distribution.

d) Does the article accurately describe and interpret the data? Explain.

28. Statistics in business, part 2. Find a graph other than a histogram that shows the distribution of a quantitative

variable in a business publication (e.g., *The Wall Street Journal, Business Week*, etc.).

a) Does the article identify the W's?

b) Discuss whether the display is appropriate for the data.

c) Discuss what the display reveals about the variable and its distribution.

d) Does the article accurately describe and interpret the data? Explain.

T 29. Shirt sizes. A clothing manufacturer wants to study men's neck sizes to plan how many shirts of different sizes to produce (shirt sizes are generally one-half inch larger than measured neck sizes and rounded to the nearest half inch). The following histogram shows the distribution of neck sizes of 248 random volunteers for a health study conducted in Utah.

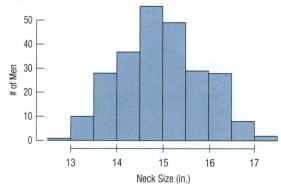

a) Write a short description of this distribution (shape, center, spread, unusual features).

b) What two bins hold the most values for neck size?

c) If we add half an inch to the neck size and round up to the nearest half inch to get the shirt size, what are the two most popular shirt sizes?

T 30. Gas prices 2017. The website LosAngelesGasPrices .com has current gasoline prices all over the United States. In the week of September 10, 2017, the following histogram shows the gas prices at 44 stations in the San Francisco Bay Area. Describe the shape of this distribution (shape, center, spread, unusual features).

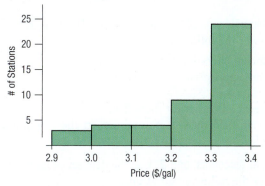

T 31. Mutual funds 2016. On December 30, 2016, the Standard and Poor's (S&P) 500 index hit an all-time high. During 2016, the S&P returned 12.25%. Here is a histogram of the 2016 net returns (total return – annual expenses) for

Money Magazine's 50 Best Mutual Funds and ETFs (time.com/money/4616747/best-mutual-funds-etfs-money-50/).

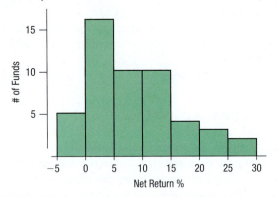

a) From the histogram, give a short summary of the distribution (shape, center, spread, unusual features).
b) In general, how did these funds perform compared to the S&P 500?

T **32. Car discounts.** A researcher, interested in studying gender differences in negotiations, collects data on the prices that men and women pay for new cars. Here is a histogram of the discounts (the amount in $ below the list price) that men and women received at one car dealership for the last 100 transactions (54 men and 46 women). Give a short summary of this distribution (shape, center, spread, unusual features). What do you think might account for this particular shape?

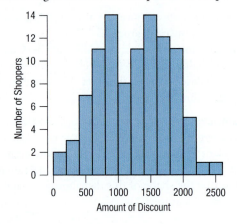

T **33. Mutual funds 2016, part 2.** Use the data set of Exercise 31 to answer the following questions.

a) Find the five-number summary for these data.
b) Find appropriate measures of center and spread for these data.
c) Create a boxplot for these data.
d) What can you see, if anything, in the histogram that isn't clear in the boxplot?

T **34. Car discounts, part 2.** Use the data set of Exercise 32 to answer the following questions.

a) Find the five-number summary for these data.
b) Create a boxplot for these data.
c) What can you see, if anything, in the histogram of Exercise 32 that isn't clear in the boxplot?

35. Gretzky. During his 20 seasons in the National Hockey League, Wayne Gretzky scored 50% more points than anyone else who ever played professional hockey. He accomplished this amazing feat while playing in 280 fewer games than Gordie Howe, the previous record holder. Here are the number of games Gretzky played during each season:

79, 80, 80, 80, 74, 80, 80, 79, 64, 78, 73, 78, 74, 45, 81, 48, 80, 82, 82, 70

a) Sketch a boxplot.
b) Briefly describe this distribution.
c) What unusual features do you see in this distribution? What might explain this?

36. McGwire. In his 16-year career as a player in major league baseball, Mark McGwire hit 583 home runs, placing him eighth on the all-time home run list (as of 2008). Here are the number of home runs that McGwire hit for each year from 1986 through 2001:

3, 49, 32, 33, 39, 22, 42, 9, 9, 39, 52, 58, 70, 65, 32, 29

a) Sketch a boxplot.
b) Briefly describe this distribution.
c) What unusual features do you see in this distribution? What might explain this?

37. Gretzky returns. Look once more at data of hockey games played each season by Wayne Gretzky, seen in Exercise 35.

a) Would you use the mean or the median to summarize the center of this distribution? Why?
b) Without actually finding the mean, would you expect it to be lower or higher than the median? Explain.
c) A student was asked to make a histogram of the data in Exercise 35 and produced the following. Comment.

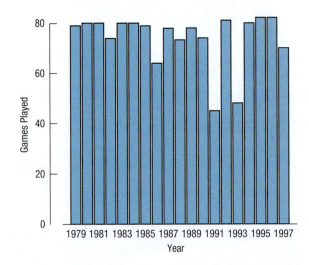

38. McGwire, again. Look once more at data of home runs hit by Mark McGwire during his 16-year career as seen in Exercise 36.

a) Would you use the mean or the median to summarize the center of this distribution? Why?
b) Find the median.
c) Without actually finding the mean, would you expect it to be lower or higher than the median? Explain.
d) A student was asked to make a histogram of the data in Exercise 36 and produced the following. Comment.

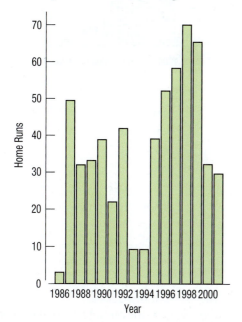

39. Pizza prices. The weekly prices of one brand of frozen pizza over a three-year period in Dallas are provided in the data file. Use the price data to answer the following questions.

a) Find the five-number summary for these data.
b) Find the range and IQR for these data.
c) Create a boxplot for these data.
d) Describe this distribution.
e) Describe any unusual observations.

40. Pizza prices, part 2. The weekly prices of one brand of frozen pizza over a three-year period in Chicago are provided in the data file. Use the price data to answer the following questions.

a) Find the five-number summary for these data.
b) Find the range and IQR for these data.
c) Create a boxplot for these data.
d) Describe the shape (center and spread) of this distribution.
e) Describe any unusual observations.

41. Transportation energy use. The U.S. Energy Information Administration (EIA) collects data on the total energy used per capita in transportation for each state and the District of Columbia. The data show the per capita consumption in the year 2015 in millions of BTU per person. Write a report on the transportation energy usage by states in the year 2015, being sure to include appropriate graphical displays and summary statistics.

State	Transportation	State	Transportation
Alabama	99.9	Montana	107.7
Alaska	232.5	Nebraska	106.1
Arizona	69.5	Nevada	73
Arkansas	92.4	New Hampshire	75.1
California	77.4	New Jersey	95.3
Colorado	74.8	New Mexico	101.7
Connecticut	63.5	New York	54.5
Delaware	69.7	North Carolina	69.6
District of Columbia	31	North Dakota	180.1
Florida	74.9	Ohio	80.7
Georgia	81.1	Oklahoma	122.8
Hawaii	101.9	Oregon	74.5
Idaho	90.3	Pennsylvania	69.6
Illinois	81.6	Rhode Island	58.2
Indiana	95.6	South Carolina	94.8
Iowa	96.4	South Dakota	116.7
Kansas	95.9	Tennessee	93.1
Kentucky	104.7	Texas	114.9
Louisiana	148.1	Utah	83.1
Maine	96.9	Vermont	78.4
Maryland	71.6	Virginia	83.2
Massachusetts	65.8	Washington	87
Michigan	74.5	West Virginia	98.1
Minnesota	80.4	Wisconsin	75.7
Mississippi	129	Wyoming	193.1
Missouri	90.6		

42. OECD GDP growth. Established in Paris in 1961, the Organization for Economic Cooperation and Development (OECD) (www.oecd.org) collects information on many economic and social aspects of countries around the world. Here are the 2016 GDP growth rates (in percentages) of 35 industrialized countries. Write a brief report on the 2016 GDP growth rates of these countries, being sure to include appropriate graphical displays and summary statistics.

Country	GDP Growth Rate	Country	GDP Growth Rate
Australia	2.44	Korea	2.83
Austria	1.61	Latvia	1.95
Belgium	1.19	Luxembourg	4.19
Canada	1.43	Mexico	2.04
Chile	1.59	Netherlands	2.13
Czech Republic	2.33	New Zealand	3.95
Denmark	1.29	Norway	1.08
Estonia	1.72	Poland	2.68
Finland	1.39	Portugal	1.4
France	1.1	Slovak Republic	3.29
Germany	1.78	Slovenia	2.49
Greece	−0.05	Spain	3.24
Hungary	1.86	Sweden	3.05
Iceland	7.2	Switzerland	1.31
Ireland	5.22	Turkey	3.07
Israel	4.04	United Kingdom	1.81
Italy	0.99	United States	1.62
Japan	1.04		

T **43. Golf courses.** A startup company is planning to build a new golf course. For marketing purposes, the company would like to be able to advertise the new course as one of the more difficult courses in the state of Vermont. One measure of the difficulty of a golf course is its length: the total distance (in yards) from tee to hole for all 18 holes. Here are the histogram and summary statistics for the lengths of all the golf courses in Vermont.

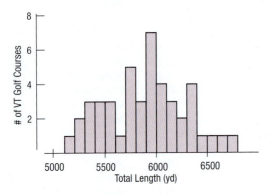

Count	45
Mean	5892.91 yd
StdDev	386.59
Min	5185
Q1	5585.75
Median	5928
Q3	6131
Max	6796

a) What is the range of these lengths?
b) Between what lengths do the central 50% of these courses lie?
c) What summary statistics would you use to describe these data?
d) Write a brief description of these data (shape, center, and spread).

44. Real estate. A real estate agent has surveyed houses in 20 nearby ZIP codes in an attempt to put together a comparison for a new property that she would like to put on the market. She knows that the size of the living area of a house is a strong factor in the price, and she'd like to market this house as being one of the biggest in the area. Here are a histogram and summary statistics for the sizes of all the houses in the area.

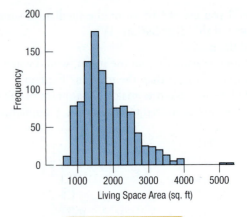

Count	1057
Mean	1819.498 sq. ft
StdDev	662.9414
Min	672
Q1	1342
Median	1675
Q3	2223
Max	5228
Missing	0

a) What is the range of these sizes?
b) Between what sizes do the central 50% of these houses lie?
c) What summary statistics would you use to describe these data?
d) Write a brief description of these data (shape, center, and spread).

T **45. Food sales.** Sales (in $) for one week were collected for 18 stores in a food store chain in the northeastern United States. The stores and the towns they are located in vary in size.

a) Make a suitable display of the sales from the data provided.
b) Summarize the central value for sales for this week with a median and mean. Why do they differ?
c) Given what you know about the distribution, which of these measures does the better job of summarizing the stores' sales? Why?
d) Summarize the spread of the sales distribution with a standard deviation and with an IQR.
e) Given what you know about the distribution, which of these measures does the better job of summarizing the spread of stores' sales? Why?
f) If we were to remove the outliers from the data, how would you expect the mean, median, standard deviation, and IQR to change?

T **46. Insurance profits.** Insurance companies don't know whether a policy they've written is profitable until the policy matures (expires). To see how they've performed recently, an analyst looked at mature policies and investigated the net profit to the company (in $).

a) Make a suitable display of the profits from the data provided.
b) Summarize the central value for the profits with a median and mean. Why do they differ?
c) Given what you know about the distribution, which of these measures might do a better job of summarizing the company's profits? Why?
d) Summarize the spread of the profit distribution with a standard deviation and with an IQR.
e) Given what you know about the distribution, which of these measures might do a better job of summarizing the spread in the company's profits? Why?
f) If we were to remove the outliers from the data, how would you expect the mean, median, standard deviation, and IQR to change?

T 47. iPod failures. In the early days of the iPod, MacInTouch (www.macintouch.com/reliability/ipodfailures.html) surveyed readers about reliability. Of the 8926 iPods owned at that time, 7510 were problem-free while the other 1416 failed. From the data, compute the failure rate for each of the 17 iPod models. Produce an appropriate graphical display of the failure rates and briefly describe the distribution. (To calculate the failure rate, divide the number failed by the sum of the number failed and the number OK for each model and then multiply by 100.)

T 48. OECD Unemployment 2016. The data set provided contains 2016 (4th quarter) unemployment rates for 38 developed countries (www.oecd.org). Produce an appropriate graphical display and briefly describe the distribution of unemployment rates. Report and comment on any outliers you may see.

49. Gas prices. A driver has recorded and posted on the Internet (www.randomuseless.info/gasprice/gasprice.html) the price he paid for gasoline at every purchase from 1979 to 2012. Since 1984 all purchases were self-serve and all were for premium (92–93 octane) gas. He has also standardized the prices to April 1979 dollars. Here are boxplots for 2003, 2006, 2009, and 2012:

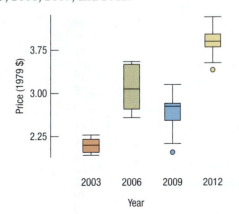

a) Compare the distribution of prices over the four years.
b) In which year were the prices least stable (most volatile)? Explain.

T 50. Fuel economy. American automobile companies are becoming more motivated to improve the fuel efficiency of the automobiles they produce. It is well known that fuel efficiency is impacted by many characteristics of the car. Describe what these boxplots tell you about the relationship between the number of cylinders a car's engine has and the car's fuel economy (mpg).

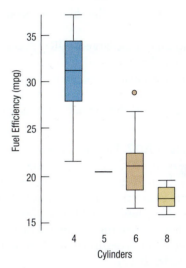

T 51. Wine prices 2013. The boxplots display bottle prices (in dollars) of dry Riesling wines produced by vineyards along three of the Finger Lakes in upstate New York.

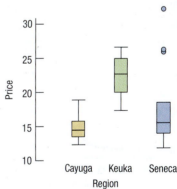

a) Which lake region produced the most expensive wine?
b) Which lake region produced the cheapest wine?
c) In which region were the wines generally more expensive?
d) Write a few sentences describing these prices.

T 52. Ozone. Historic ozone levels (in parts per billion, ppb) were recorded at sites in New Jersey monthly. Here are boxplots of the data for each month (over 46 years) lined up in order (January = 1).

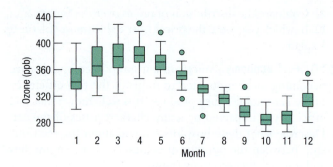

a) In what month was the highest ozone level ever recorded?
b) Which month has the largest IQR?
c) Which month has the smallest range?
d) Write a brief comparison of the ozone levels in January and June.
e) Write a report on the annual patterns you see in the ozone levels.

T 53. **Derby speeds 2017.** How fast do horses run? Kentucky Derby winners top 30 mph, as shown in the graph. This graph shows the percentage of Kentucky Derby winners that have run *slower* than a given speed. Note that few have won running less than 33 mph, but about 95% of the winning horses have run less than 37 mph. (A cumulative frequency graph like this is called an **ogive**.) (Data in **Kentucky Derby 2017**)

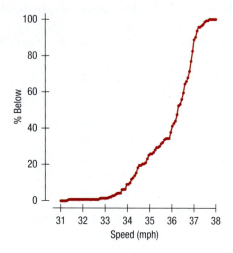

a) Estimate the median winning speed.
b) Estimate the quartiles.
c) Estimate the range and the IQR.
d) Create a boxplot of these speeds.
e) Write a few sentences about the speeds of the Kentucky Derby winners.

54. **Mutual funds, historical.** Here is an ogive of the distribution of monthly returns for a group of aggressive (or high growth) mutual funds over a period of 25 years. (Recall from Exercise 53 that an ogive, or cumulative relative frequency graph, shows the percent of cases at or

below a certain value. Thus this graph always begins at 0% and ends at 100%.)

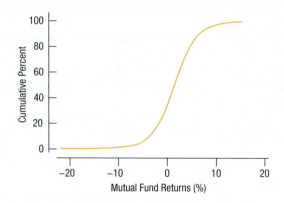

a) Estimate the median.
b) Estimate the quartiles.
c) Estimate the range and the IQR.

55. **Test scores.** Three statistics classes all took the same test. Here are histograms of the scores for each class.

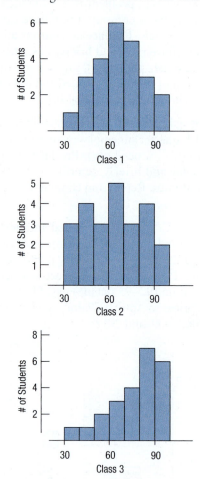

a) Which class had the highest mean score?
b) Which class had the highest median score?
c) For which class are the mean and median most different? Which is higher? Why?

d) Which class had the smallest standard deviation?
e) Which class had the smallest IQR?

56. Test scores, again. Look again at the histograms of test scores for the three statistics classes in Exercise 55.

a) Overall, which class do you think performed better on the test? Why?
b) How would you describe the shape of each distribution?
c) Match each class with the corresponding boxplot.

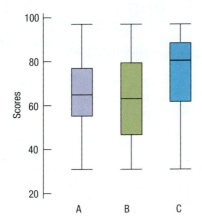

T 57. Quality control holes. Engineers at a computer production plant tested two methods for accuracy in drilling holes into a PC board. They tested how fast they could set the drilling machine by running 10 boards at each of two different speeds. To assess the results, they measured the distance (in inches) from the center of a target on the board to the center of the hole. The data and summary statistics are shown in the table.

	Fast	Slow
	0.000101	0.000098
	0.000102	0.000096
	0.000100	0.000097
	0.000102	0.000095
	0.000101	0.000094
	0.000103	0.000098
	0.000104	0.000096
	0.000102	0.975600
	0.000102	0.000097
	0.000100	0.000096
Mean	0.000102	0.097647
StdDev	0.000001	0.308481

Write a report summarizing the findings of the experiment. Include appropriate visual and verbal displays of the distributions, and make a recommendation to the engineers if they are most interested in the accuracy of the method.

T 58. Fire sale. A real estate agent notices that houses with fireplaces often fetch a premium in the market and wants to assess the difference in sales price of 60 homes that recently sold. The data and summary are shown in the table.

No Fireplace	Fireplace
142,212	134,865
206,512	118,007
50,709	138,297
108,794	129,470
68,353	309,808
123,266	157,946
80,248	173,723
135,708	140,510
122,221	151,917
128,440	235,105,000
221,925	259,999
65,325	211,517
87,588	102,068
88,207	115,659
148,246	145,583
205,073	116,289
185,323	238,792
71,904	310,696
199,684	139,079
81,762	109,578
45,004	89,893
62,105	132,311
79,893	131,411
88,770	158,863
115,312	130,490
118,952	178,767
	82,556
	122,221
	84,291
	206,512
	105,363
	103,508
	157,513
	103,861
Mean 116,597.54	7,061,657.74
Median 112,053	136,581

Write a report summarizing the findings of the investigation. Include appropriate visual and verbal displays of the distributions, and make a recommendation to the agent about the average premium that a fireplace is worth in this market.

59. Customer database. A philanthropic organization has a database of millions of donors that they contact by mail to raise money for charities. One of the variables in the database, *Title*, contains the title of the person or persons printed on the address label. The most common are Mr., Ms., Miss, and Mrs., but there are also Ambassador and Mrs., Your Imperial Majesty, and Cardinal, to name a few others. In all, there are over 100 different titles, each with a corresponding numeric code.

Code	Title	Code	Title
000	MR.	127	PRINCESS
001	MRS.	128	CHIEF
1002	MR. and MRS.	129	BARON
003	MISS	130	SHEIK
004	DR.	131	PRINCE AND PRINCESS
005	MADAME	132	YOUR IMPERIAL MAJESTY
006	SERGEANT	135	M. ET MME.
009	RABBI	210	PROF.
010	PROFESSOR	⋮	⋮
126	PRINCE		

An intern who was asked to analyze the organization's fundraising efforts presented these summary statistics for the variable *Title*.

Mean	54.41
StdDev	957.62
Median	1
IQR	2
n	94,649

a) What does the mean of 54.41 mean?
b) What are the typical reasons that cause measures of center and spread to be as different as those in this table?
c) Is that why these are so different?

60. CEOs. For each CEO, a code is listed that corresponds to the industry of the CEO's company. Here are a few of the codes and the industries to which they correspond:

Industry	Industry Code	Industry	Industry Code
Financial services	1	Energy	12
Food/drink/tobacco	2	Capital goods	14
Health	3	Computers/ communications	16
Insurance	4	Entertainment/ information	17
Retailing	6	Consumer non-durables	18
Forest products	9	Electric utilities	19
Aerospace/defense	11		

A recently hired investment analyst has been assigned to examine the industries and the compensations of the CEOs. To start the analysis, he produces the following histogram of industry codes.

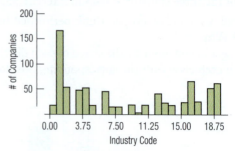

a) What might account for the gaps seen in the histogram?
b) What advice might you give the analyst about the appropriateness of this display?

T 61. Mutual fund types. The 70 mutual funds of Exercise 31 are classified into four types: U.S. Domestic Equity Funds, Bond Funds, International Funds, and Other Funds. Compare the 12 month returns of the four types of funds using an appropriate display and write a brief summary of the differences.

T 62. Car discounts, part 3. The discounts negotiated by the car buyers in Exercise 32 are classified by whether the buyer was Male (code = 0) or Female (code = 1). Compare the discounts of men vs. women using an appropriate display and write a brief summary of the differences.

63. Houses for sale. Each house listed on the multiple listing service (MLS) is assigned a sequential ID number. A recently hired real estate agent decided to examine the MLS numbers in a recent random sample of homes for sale by one real estate agency in nearby towns. To begin the analysis, the agent produces the following histogram of ID numbers.

a) What might account for the distribution seen in the histogram?
b) What advice might you give the analyst about the appropriateness of this display?

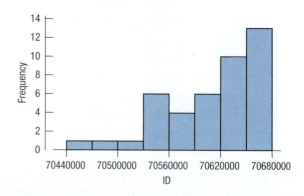

64. ZIP codes. Holes-R-Us, an Internet company that sells piercing jewelry, keeps transaction records on its sales. At a recent sales meeting, one of the staff presented the following histogram and summary statistics of the ZIP codes of the last 500 customers, so that the staff might understand where sales are coming from. Comment on the usefulness and appropriateness of this display.

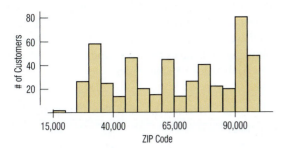

T **65. Hurricane history, tropical storms.** The North Atlantic hurricane database, or HURDAT, is a database of all tropical storms and hurricanes for the Atlantic Ocean, Gulf of Mexico, and Caribbean Sea, reporting numbers of storms each year since 1850. The older portion of the database reflects recent efforts to discover undocumented historical hurricanes in the late 19th and 20th centuries, which have greatly increased our knowledge of these past events. Recent catastrophic hurricanes such as Katrina, Harvey, and Irma have raised concerns that the number or intensity of Atlantic tropical storms and hurricanes has been increasing, possibly due to global climate change. Insurance companies are, of course, interested in this question. (Data in **Hurricane history**)

Here is a histogram of the data on tropical storms:

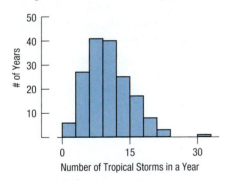

a) Describe the distribution.
Here is a time series plot of these data with a smooth trace added:

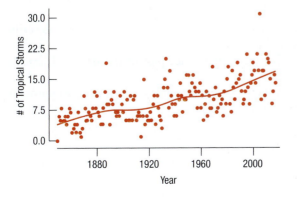

b) Discuss the time series plot. Does it support the claim of increasing numbers of tropical storms?
c) What can you see from the time series plot that you couldn't see in the histogram?

T **66. Hurricane history, major hurricanes.** The claims about climate change suggest two possible effects: more storms and bigger, stronger storms. Here are plots similar to those of Exercise 65, but for major hurricanes. (Data in **Hurricane history**)

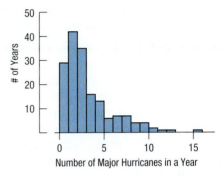

a) Describe the distribution.
Here is the time series plot of these data, along with a smooth trace.

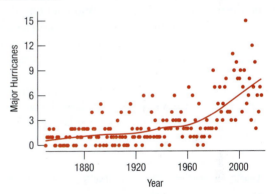

b) Discuss the time series plot. Does it support the claim of increasing numbers of major hurricanes?
c) What can you see from the time series plot that you couldn't see in the histogram? What can you see in the histogram that you can't see in the time series plot?

67. Productivity study. The National Center for Productivity releases information on the efficiency of workers. In a recent report, they included the following graph showing a rapid rise in productivity. What questions do you have about this?

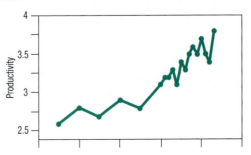

68. Productivity study revisited. A second report by the National Center for Productivity analyzed the relationship between productivity and wages. They used the graph from Exercise 67, with the x-axis labeled "wages." Comment on any problems you see with their analysis.

69. Real estate, part 2. The 1057 houses described in Exercise 44 have a mean price of $167,900, with a standard deviation of $77,158. The mean living area is 1819 sq. ft., with a standard deviation of 663 sq. ft. Which is more unusual, a house in that market that sells for $400,000 or a house that has 4000 sq. ft of living area? Explain.

T 70. Tuition 2016. In 2016, the mean tuition of private colleges and universities was $18,230, with a standard deviation of $7272. The mean tuition for public colleges and universities was $9624, with a standard deviation of $4669. The distribution of tuition in both groups is unimodal and symmetric. Which would be more unusual: to find a private institution with a tuition over $30,000 or to find a public institution with a tuition over $15,500? (Data in **Tuition 2016 all schools**)

T 71. Food consumption. FAOSTAT, the Food and Agriculture Organization of the United Nations, collects information on the production and consumption of more than 200 food and agricultural products for 200 countries around the world. Here are two tables, one for meat consumption (per capita in kg per year) and one for alcohol consumption (per capita in gallons per year). The United States leads in meat consumption with 267.30 pounds, while Ireland is the largest alcohol consumer at 55.80 gallons. Using z-scores, find which of these two countries is the larger consumer of both meat and alcohol together.

Country	Alcohol	Meat	Country	Alcohol	Meat
Australia	29.56	242.22	Luxembourg	34.32	197.34
Austria	40.46	242.22	Mexico	13.52	126.50
Belgium	34.32	197.34	Netherlands	23.87	201.08
Canada	26.62	219.56	New Zealand	25.22	228.58
Czech Republic	43.81	166.98	Norway	17.58	129.80
Denmark	40.59	256.96	Poland	20.70	155.10
Finland	25.01	146.08	Portugal	33.02	194.92
France	24.88	225.28	Slovakia	26.49	121.88
Germany	37.44	182.82	South Korea	17.60	93.06
Greece	17.68	201.30	Spain	28.05	259.82
Hungary	29.25	179.52	Sweden	20.07	155.32
Iceland	15.94	178.20	Switzerland	25.32	159.72
Ireland	55.80	194.26	Turkey	3.28	42.68
Italy	21.68	200.64	United Kingdom	30.32	171.16
Japan	14.59	93.28	United States	26.36	267.30

72. World Bank. The World Bank, through their Doing Business project (www.doingbusiness.org), ranks nearly 200 economies on the ease of doing business. One of their rankings measures the ease of starting a business and is made up (in part) of the following variables: number of required start up procedures, average start up time (in days), and average start up cost (in % of per capita income). The following table gives the mean and standard deviations of these variables for 95 economies.

	Procedures (#)	Time (Days)	Cost (%)
Mean	7.9	27.9	14.2
SD	2.9	19.6	12.9

Here are the data for three countries.

	Procedures	Time	Cost
Spain	10	47	15.1
Guatemala	11	26	47.3
Fiji	8	46	25.3

a) Use z-scores to combine the three measures.
b) Which country has the best environment after combining the three measures? Be careful—a lower rank indicates a better environment to start up a business.

T 73. Regular gas 2017. The data set provided contains U.S. regular retail gasoline prices (cents/gallon) from 2007 to August 2017, from a national sample of gasoline stations obtained from the U.S. Department of Energy.

a) Create a histogram of the data and describe the distribution.
b) Create a time series plot of the data and describe the trend.
c) Which graphical display seems the more appropriate for these data? Explain.

T 74. Home price index 2017. Standard and Poor's Case-Shiller Home Price Index measures the residential housing market in metropolitan regions across the United States. The national index, Composite.10, is a composite of 10 regions, and can be found in the data set provided for the years 1987 to 2017.

a) Create a histogram of the data and describe the distribution.
b) Create a time series plot of the data and describe the trend.
c) Which graphical display seems the more appropriate for these data? Explain.

T 75. Unemployment 2017. The histogram shows the monthly U.S. unemployment rate from January 2003 to August 2017.

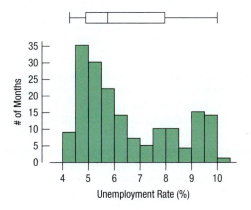

Here is the time series plot for the same data.

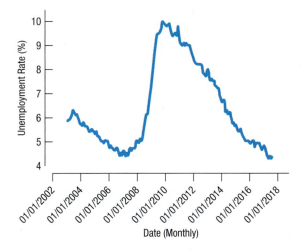

a) What features of the data can you see in the histogram that aren't clear in the time series plot?
b) What features of the data can you see in the time series plot that aren't clear in the histogram?
c) Which graphical display seems the more appropriate for these data? Explain.
d) Write a brief description of unemployment rates over this time period in the United States.

***76. Consumer Price Index (CPI) 2017.** Here is a histogram of the monthly CPI as reported by the Bureau of Labor Statistics (www.bls.gov/cpi) from January 2007 through August 2017.

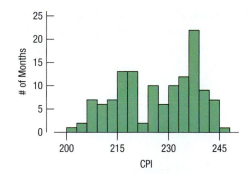

Here is the time series plot for the same data.

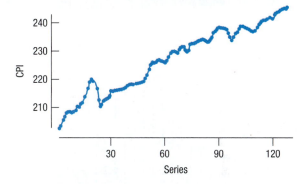

a) What features of the data can you see in the histogram that aren't clear from the time series plot?
b) What features of the data can you see in the time series plot that aren't clear in the histogram?
c) Which graphical display seems the more appropriate for these data? Explain.
d) Write a brief description of monthly CPI over this time period.

77. Assets. Here is a histogram of the assets (in millions of dollars) of 79 companies chosen from the *Forbes* list of the nation's top corporations.

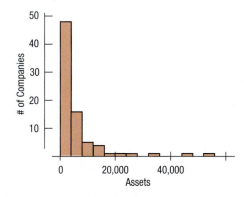

a) What aspect of this distribution makes it difficult to summarize, or to discuss, center and spread?
b) What would you suggest doing with these data if we want to understand them better?

78. Assets, again. Here are the same data you saw in Exercise 77 after re-expressions as the square root of assets and the logarithm of assets.

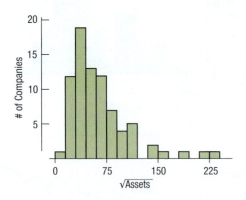

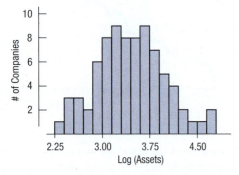

a) Which re-expression do you prefer? Why?
b) In the square root re-expression, what does the value 50 actually indicate about the company's assets?

JUST CHECKING ANSWERS

1 Incomes are probably skewed to the right and not symmetric, making the median the more appropriate measure of center. The mean will be influenced by the high end of family incomes and not reflect the "typical" family income as well as the median would. It will give the impression that the typical income is higher than it is.

2 An IQR of 30 mpg would mean that only 50% of the cars get gas mileages in an interval 30 mpg wide. Fuel economy doesn't vary that much. 3 mpg is reasonable. It seems plausible that 50% of the cars will be within about 3 mpg of each other. An IQR of 0.3 mpg would mean that the gas mileage of half the cars varies little from the estimate. It's unlikely that cars, drivers, and driving conditions are that consistent.

3 We'd prefer a standard deviation of 2 months. Making a consistent product is important for quality. Customers want to be able to count on the MP3 player lasting somewhere close to 5 years, and a standard deviation of 2 years would mean that life spans were highly variable.

CHAPTER 4

Correlation and Linear Regression

Zillow.com

Zillow.com is a real estate research site, founded in 2005 by Rich Barton and Lloyd Frink. Both are former Microsoft executives and founders of Expedia.com, the Internet-based travel agency. Zillow collects publicly available data and provides an estimate (called a Zestimate®) of a home's worth. The estimate is based on a model of the data that Zillow has been able to collect on a variety of predictor variables, including the past history of the home's sales, the location of the home, and characteristics of the house such as its size and number of bedrooms and bathrooms.

The site is enormously popular among both potential buyers and sellers of homes. According to DMR (Digital Marketing Ramblings, expandedramblings.com), Zillow is one of the most-visited U.S. real estate sites on the Web, with approximately 160 million visitors each month. As of early 2017, nearly 80% of all U.S. homes have been viewed on Zillow. In May 2017 Zillow announced the Zillow Prize, which will award $1,200,000 to the team that best improves Zillow's Zestimates. Chapter 5 will discuss more details.

ow exactly does Zillow figure the worth of a house? According to the Zillow.com site, "We compute this figure by taking zillions of data points—much of this data is public—and entering them into a formula. This formula is built using what our statisticians call 'a proprietary algorithm'—big words for 'secret formula.' When our statisticians developed the model to determine home values, they explored how homes in certain areas were similar (i.e., number of bedrooms and baths, and a myriad of other details) and then looked at the relationships between actual sale prices and those home details." These relationships form a pattern, and they use that pattern to develop a model to estimate a market value for a home.

As anyone who's ever looked at house prices knows, house prices depend on the local market. To control for that, we will restrict our attention to a single market, and use a random sample of 1728 home sales from the public records of sales in upstate New York, in the region around the city of Saratoga Springs. The first thing often mentioned in describing a house for sale is its size, or *Living Area*. Let's start with just one predictor variable. How well can *Living Area* predict home *Price*?

Figure 4.1 shows a plot of *Price* ($) against *Living Area* for the 1728 houses. Clearly price and house size are related. If you were asked to summarize the relationship, what would you say?

WHO	Houses
WHAT	Sale price (dollars) and other facts about the houses
WHERE	Upstate New York near Saratoga Springs
WHY	To understand what influences housing prices and how to predict them

FIGURE 4.1 *Price* ($) against *Living Area* for the 1728 houses. (Data in **Saratoga houses**)

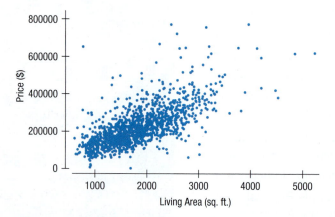

There is an overall trend; larger houses tend to cost more. But the relationship is far from perfect. This plot is an example of a **scatterplot**. It plots one quantitative variable against another. Just by looking at a scatterplot, you can see patterns, trends, relationships, and the occasional unusual cases standing apart from the general pattern.

Relationships between variables are often at the heart of what we'd like to learn from data. When we want to know if there is an **association** between two quantitative variables, scatterplots are the ideal way to visualize such associations.

4.1 Looking at Scatterplots

The Texas Transportation Institute (TTI), founded in 1950, studies and develops solutions to challenges faced by all forms of transportation. Although the goal is to solve the transportation problems of 2025, the TTI started collecting data on the relationship between freeway speed and the cost to society of freeway congestion as early as the year 2000. Figure 4.2 shows a scatterplot of the annual *Congestion Cost* Per Person of traffic delays (in dollars) in 65 cities in the United States against the Peak Period *Freeway Speed* (mph).

WHO	Cities in the United States
WHAT	*Congestion Cost Per Person* and *Peak Period Freeway Speed*
UNITS	*Congestion Cost Per Person* ($ per person per year); *Peak Period Freeway Speed* (mph)
WHEN	2000
WHERE	United States
WHY	To examine the relationship between congestion on the highways and its impact on society and business

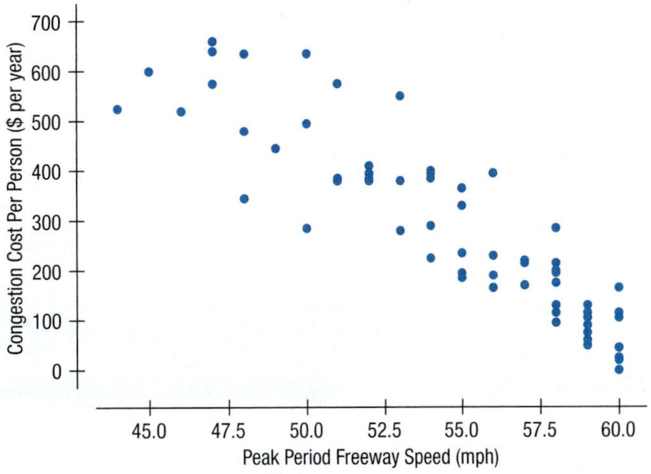

FIGURE 4.2 *Congestion Cost Per Person* ($ per year) of traffic delays against *Peak Period Freeway Speed* (mph) for 65 U.S. cities. (Data in **Congestion cost**)

If you want to describe the scatterplot of *Congestion Cost* against *Freeway Speed*, you might first mention the **direction** of the association. As the peak freeway speed goes up, the cost of congestion goes down. A pattern that runs from the upper left to the lower right  is said to be **negative**. A pattern running the other way, as we saw for the price and size of houses, is called **positive**.

> Look for **Direction**: What's the sign—positive, negative, or neither?

The second thing to look for in a scatterplot is its **form**. If there is a straight line relationship, it will appear as a cloud or swarm of points stretched out in a generally consistent, straight form. For example, the scatterplot of house prices (Figure 4.1) has an underlying **linear** form, although some points stray away from it.

Scatterplots can reveal many different kinds of patterns. Often they will not be straight, but straight line patterns are both the most common and the most useful for statistics.

If the relationship isn't straight, but curves gently, while still increasing or decreasing steadily,  we can often find ways to straighten it out by re-expressing one (or both) of the variables. But if it curves sharply—up and then

> Look for **Form**: Straight, curved, something exotic, or no pattern?

down, for example, —then you'll need more advanced methods.

The third feature to look for in a scatterplot is the **strength** of the relationship. At one extreme, do the points appear tightly clustered in a single stream  (whether straight, curved, or bending all over the place)? Or, at the other extreme, do the points seem to be so variable and spread out that we can barely discern any

> Look for **Strength**: How much scatter?

trend or pattern? 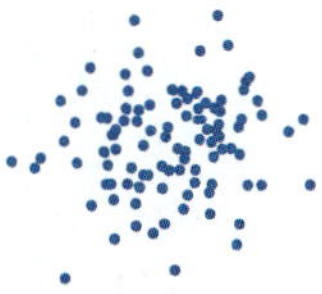 The traffic congestion plot shows moderate scatter around a generally straight form. That indicates that there's a moderately strong linear relationship between cost and speed.

Look for **Unusual Features**: Are there unusual observations or subgroups?

Finally, always look for the unexpected. Often the most interesting discovery in a scatterplot is something you never thought to look for. One example of such a surprise is an unusual observation, or **outlier**, standing away from the overall pattern of the scatterplot. Such a point is almost always interesting and deserves special attention. You may see entire clusters or subgroups that stand away or show a trend in a different direction than the rest of the plot. That should raise questions about why they are different. They may be a clue that you should split the data into subgroups instead of looking at them all together.

IN PRACTICE 4.1   Gaining insights about trends from scatterplots

The first automobile crash in New York City occurred in 1896, when a motor vehicle collided with a "pedalcycle" rider. Cycle/car accidents are a serious concern for insurance companies. Nearly 60,000 cyclists have died in traffic crashes in the United States since 1932. Demographic information such as the victim's age can be useful to insurers, who use it to set appropriate rates, and to retailers, who must plan what safety equipment to stock and how to present it to their customers. This becomes a more pressing concern when the demographic profiles change over time.

Here are data on the mean age of cyclists killed each year since 2000. (Source: National Highway Transportation Safety Agency, found at www-nrd.nhtsa.dot.gov) (Data in **Cyclists 2015**)

Year	Mean Age
2000	35
2001	36
2002	37
2003	36
2004	39
2005	39
2006	41
2007	40
2008	41
2009	41
2010	42
2011	43
2012	43
2013	44
2014	45
2015	45

MANAGER   I want to understand the trend in the average age of cyclists involved in fatal accidents. Can you produce an appropriate graphic?

ANALYST   The mean age of cyclist traffic deaths has been increasing almost linearly during this period. The trend is a strong one.

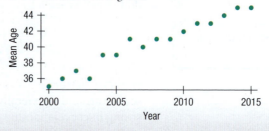

4.2 Assigning Roles to Variables in Scatterplots

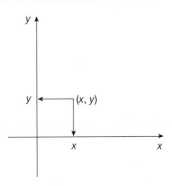

To make a scatterplot of two quantitative variables, assign one to the *y*-axis and the other to the *x*-axis.[1] As with any graph, be sure to label the axes clearly, and indicate the scales of the axes with numbers. Scatterplots display *quantitative* variables. Each variable has units, and these should appear with the display—usually near each axis. Each point is placed on a scatterplot at a position that corresponds to values of these two variables. Its horizontal location is specified by its *x*-value, and its vertical location is specified by its *y*-value variable. Together, these are known as *coordinates* and written (x, y).

Scatterplots made by computer programs (such as the two we've seen in this chapter) often do not—and usually should not—show the *origin*, the point at $x = 0$, $y = 0$ where the axes meet. If both variables have values near or on both sides of zero, then the origin will be part of the display. If the values are far from zero, though, there's no reason to include the origin. In fact, it's far better to focus on the part of the Cartesian plane that contains the data. In our example about house prices, none of the houses were free and all had some area so the computer drew the scatterplot in Figure 4.1 with axes that don't quite meet.

Which variable should go on the *x*-axis and which on the *y*-axis? What we want to know about the relationship can tell us how to make the plot. Zillow may have questions such as:

- How are prices related to the age of the house?
- Will increased accuracy in their price estimates be reflected in the number of visitors to the website?
- How does the number of photographs of a property affect the time viewers spend looking at it online?

In all of these examples, one variable plays the role of the **explanatory** or **predictor variable**, while the other takes on the role of the **response variable**. We place the explanatory variable on the *x*-axis and the response variable on the *y*-axis. When you make a scatterplot, you can assume that those who view it will think this way, so choose which variables to assign to which axes carefully.

The roles that we choose for variables have more to do with how we *think* about them than with the variables themselves. Just placing a variable on the *x*-axis doesn't necessarily mean that it explains or predicts *anything*, and the variable on the *y*-axis may not respond to it in any way. A real estate agent may want to predict prices using house size, which results in *Price* as the response variable as in Figure 4.1. But contractors and builders may be more interested in predicting the size of a house that can be built for a certain price, so for them, *Living Area* would be a natural response variable.

The *x*- and *y*-variables are sometimes referred to as the **independent** and **dependent** variables, respectively. The idea is that the *y*-variable *depends* on the *x*-variable and the *x*-variable acts *independently* to make *y* respond. These names, however, conflict with other uses of the same terms in statistics. Instead, we'll sometimes use the terms "explanatory" or "predictor variable" and "response variable" when we're discussing roles, but we'll often just say *x-variable* and *y-variable*.

René Descartes (1596–1650) was a philosopher, famous for the invention of the *Cartesian plane* and the statement *cogito, ergo sum*: I think, therefore I am.

NOTATION ALERT

So *x* and *y* are reserved letters as well, but not just for labeling the axes of a scatterplot. In statistics, the assignment of variables to the *x*- and *y*-axes (and choice of notation for them in formulas) often conveys information about their roles as predictor or response.

---

[1]René Descartes (1596–1650) was the first to use the coordinate system to associate points in the *x*–*y* plane with a pair of numbers. The playing field he defined in this way is formally called a Cartesian plane, in his honor. The *x*- and *y*-axes are also called the "ordinate" and the "abscissa"—but we can never remember which is which because statisticians don't generally use these terms. In statistics (and in all statistics computer programs) the axes are generally called "*x*" (abscissa) and "*y*" (ordinate) and are usually labeled with the names of the corresponding variables.

> ## IN PRACTICE 4.2   Understanding roles of variables
>
> **MANAGER** When examining the ages of victims in cycle/car accidents, why did you plot *year* on the *x*-axis and *mean age* on the *y*-axis? (See the example on page 108.)
>
> **ANALYST** To see how the age of accident victims might change over time, the year is the basis for prediction and the mean age of victims is the variable that is predicted.

4.3   Understanding Correlation

If you had to put a number (say, between 0 and 1) on the strength of the linear association between house prices and sizes in Figure 4.1, what would it be? Your measure shouldn't depend on the choice of units for the variables. Zillow could have reported the house sizes in square meters and the price in thousands of dollars, but regardless of the units, the scatterplot would look the same. When we change units, the direction, form, and strength won't change, so neither should our measure of the association's (linear) strength.

We saw a way to remove the units in the previous chapter. We can standardize each of the variables, finding $z_x = \left(\dfrac{x - \bar{x}}{s_x}\right)$ and $z_y = \left(\dfrac{y - \bar{y}}{s_y}\right)$. With these, we can compute a measure of strength that you've probably heard of—the **correlation coefficient**:

$$r = \frac{\sum z_x z_y}{n - 1}.$$

NOTATION ALERT

The letter *r* is always used for correlation, so you can't use it for anything else in statistics. Whenever you see an "*r*," it's safe to assume it's a correlation.

Keep in mind that the *x*'s and *y*'s are paired. For each house we have a price and a living area. To find the correlation we multiply each standardized value by the standardized value it is paired with and add up those *cross products*. We divide the total by the number of pairs minus one, $n - 1$.[2]

There are alternative formulas for the correlation in terms of the variables *x* and *y*. Here are two of the more common:

$$r = \frac{\sum (x - \bar{x})(y - \bar{y})}{\sqrt{\sum (x - \bar{x})^2 \sum (y - \bar{y})^2}} = \frac{\sum (x - \bar{x})(y - \bar{y})}{(n - 1)s_x s_y}.$$

These formulas can be more convenient for calculating correlation by hand, but the form using *z*-scores is best for understanding what correlation means. No matter which formula you use, the correlation between *Price* and *Living Area* for the Saratoga houses is 0.712.

> ## IN PRACTICE 4.3   Understanding the strength of a linear relationship through the correlation
>
> **MANAGER** As we think about life insurance for cyclists, I can't help but notice that the relationship between age and year for the cyclist accident data (p. 108) seems strong. Am I right?
>
> **ANALYST** Because the scatterplot shows that the relationship is linear, we can summarize the relationship with the correlation coefficient, which is 0.98. That indicates a strong linear association. Because this is a time series, we refer to it as a strong "trend."

---

[2]The same $n - 1$ we used for calculating the standard deviation.

Correlation Conditions

Correlation measures the strength of the *linear* association between two *quantitative* variables. Before you use correlation, you must check three *conditions:*

- **Quantitative Variables Condition:** Correlation applies only to quantitative variables. Don't apply correlation to categorical data masquerading as quantitative. Check that you know the variables' units and what they measure.
- **Linearity Condition:** Sure, you can *calculate* a correlation coefficient for any pair of variables. But correlation measures the strength only of the *linear* association and will be misleading if the relationship is not straight enough. What is "straight enough"? This question may sound too informal for a statistical condition, but that's really the point. We can't verify whether a relationship is linear or not. Very few relationships between variables are perfectly linear, even in theory, and scatterplots of real data are never perfectly straight. How nonlinear looking would the scatterplot have to be to fail the condition? This is a judgment call that you just have to think about. Do you think that the underlying relationship is curved? If so, then summarizing its strength with a correlation would be misleading.
- **Outlier Condition:** Unusual observations can distort the correlation and can make an otherwise small correlation look big or, on the other hand, hide a large correlation. It can even give an otherwise positive association a negative correlation coefficient (and vice versa). When you see an outlier, it's often a good idea to report the correlation both with and without the point.

Each of these conditions is easy to check with a scatterplot. Many correlations are reported without supporting data or plots. You should still think about the conditions. You should be cautious in interpreting (or accepting others' interpretations of) the correlation when you can't check the conditions for yourself.

Throughout this course, you'll see that doing statistics right means selecting the proper methods. That means you have to think about the situation at hand. An important first step is to check that the type of analysis you plan is appropriate. These conditions are just the first of many such checks.

JUST CHECKING

For the years 2004 to 2017, the daily stock prices of Google and Amazon have a correlation of 0.96.

1. Before drawing any conclusions from the correlation, what would you like to see? Why?
2. If your coworker tracks the same prices in euros, how will this change the correlation? Will you need to know the exchange rate between euros and U.S. dollars to draw conclusions?
3. If you standardize both prices, how will this affect the correlation?
4. In general, if on a given day the price of Google is relatively low, is the price of Amazon likely to be relatively low as well?
5. If on a given day the price of Google stock is high, is the price of Amazon stock definitely high as well?

GUIDED EXAMPLE   Holiday Spending

Do credit card customers who spend a lot on their cards during December holidays continue that spending after New Year's Day? To examine this question, an analyst took a random sample of 750 customers from her company's highest use segment and investigated the charges made on their cards in those two months. What is the relationship between January and December spending? (Data in **Holiday spending**)

(continued)

PLAN	**Define** the problem and state the objective.	Our objective is to investigate the association between the amount that a customer charges in January and the previous December. The customers have been randomly selected from among the highest use segment of customers. The variables measured are the total credit card charges (in $) in the two months of interest.
	Identify the quantitative variables to examine. Report the time frame over which the data have been collected and define each variable. (State the W's.)	Because we have two quantitative variables measured on the same cases, we can make a scatterplot. We'll use the charges in January as the response variable and the charges in December as the predictor.

DO	**Characterize** and **Explore** the variables.	✔ **Quantitative Variable Condition.** Both variables are quantitative. Both charges are measured in dollars.

December

min	Q1	median	Q3	max	mean	sd	n	missing
2.03	342.775	1043.255	2447.903	9889.98	1812.811	2036.493	750	0

January

min	Q1	median	Q3	max	mean	sd	n	missing
−125.5	222.2875	805.815	1879.448	9336.79	1309.675	1479.973	750	0

Summarize and visualize the variables.

The mean spending in December is $1812.81, which dropped to $1309.68 in January. Notice that there are some negative values in January, which means that some customers returned more than they spent in January.

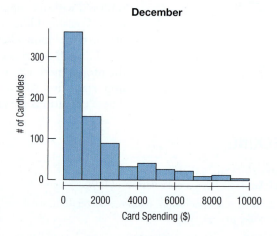

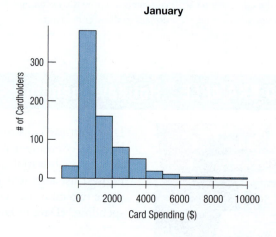

Both variables are skewed to the high end as we expect with a financial variable like spending.

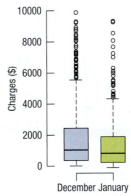

Boxplots of both variables show several outliers. However, there are no gaps in the histograms—which might indicate extraordinary values. Instead, these are simply the high-end spenders of right skewed distributions.

Make the scatterplot and clearly label the axes to identify the scale and units.

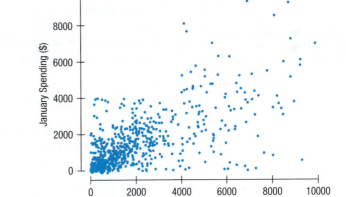

Model and check the conditions. Calculate the correlation.

✔ **Linearity Condition**. The scatterplot is straight enough.

✔ **Outlier Condition**. There are no obvious outliers, but there are several points that may be worth investigating.

The correlation is 0.688.

The positive correlation coefficient confirms the impression from the scatterplot.

REPORT

Present your conclusions. Describe the direction, form, and the strength of the plot, along with any unusual points or features. Be sure to state your interpretation in the proper context.

MEMO

Re: Credit card spending

We have examined the sample of customers from the credit card data. In particular, we looked at the charges made in December and January of last year. We noted that although January charges are lower, on average, there was a positive association between charges in the two months. The correlation was 0.688, which is moderately strong, and indicates some variation, as is also evident in the scatterplot.

We've concluded that although the observed pattern is positive, these data do not allow us to find the causes of this behavior.

Although January spending is generally somewhat lower, the data show that customers who spend more in December tend to spend more in January as well. There are some exceptions, which should be looked at in more detail.

Correlation Properties

Because correlation is so widely used as a measure of association it's a good idea to remember some of its basic properties. Here's a useful list of facts about the correlation coefficient:

- **The sign of a correlation coefficient gives the direction of the association.**
- **Correlation is always between −1 and +1.** Correlation *can* be exactly equal to −1.0 or +1.0, but watch out. These values are unusual in real data because they mean that all the data points fall *exactly* on a single straight line.
- **Correlation treats x and y symmetrically.** The correlation of x with y is the same as the correlation of y with x.
- **Correlation has no units.** This fact can be especially important when the data's units are somewhat vague to begin with (customer satisfaction, worker efficiency, productivity, and so on).
- **Correlation is not affected by changes in the center or scale of either variable.** Changing the units or baseline of either variable has no effect on the correlation coefficient because the correlation depends only on the z-scores.
- **Correlation measures the strength of the *linear* association between the two variables.** Variables can be strongly associated but still have a small correlation if the association is not linear.
- **Correlation is sensitive to unusual observations.** A single outlier can make a small correlation large or make a large one small.

Correlation Tables

Sometimes you'll see the correlations between each pair of variables in a dataset arranged in a table. The rows and columns of the table name the variables, and the cells hold the correlations.

	Price	Lot Size	Age	Land Value	Living Area
Price	1.000	0.158	−0.189	0.581	0.712
Lot Size	0.158	1.000	−0.016	0.059	0.163
Age	−0.189	−0.016	1.000	−0.022	−0.174
Land Value	0.581	0.059	−0.022	1.000	0.423
Living Area	0.712	0.163	−0.174	0.423	1.000

TABLE 4.1   A correlation table for some variables collected on the Saratoga houses.

Correlation tables are compact and give a lot of summary information at a glance. The diagonal cells of a correlation table always show correlations of exactly 1.000, and the upper half of the table is symmetrically the same as the lower half (can you see why?), so by convention, only the lower half is shown. A table like this can be an efficient way to start looking at a large dataset. But be sure to check for non-linearity and unusual observations, which could make the correlations in the table misleading or meaningless. Can you be sure, looking at Table 4.1, that all pairs of variables are linearly associated? Correlation tables are often produced by statistical software packages. Fortunately, these same packages often offer simple ways to make all the scatterplots you need to look at.[3]

---

[3] A table of scatterplots arranged just like a correlation table is sometimes called a *scatterplot matrix*, or SPLOM, and is easily created using a statistics package. It is a good idea to look at such a display if you plan to interpret the correlations in a correlation table.

4.4 Lurking Variables and Causation

An educational researcher finds a strong association between height and reading ability among elementary school students in a nationwide survey. Taller children tend to have higher reading scores. Does that mean that students' height *causes* their reading scores to go up? No matter how strong the correlation is between two variables, there's no simple way to show from observational data that one variable causes the other. A high correlation just increases the temptation to think and to say that the *x*-variable *causes* the *y*-variable. Just to make sure, let's repeat the point again.

No matter how strong the association, no matter how large the *r* value, no matter how straight the form, there is no way to conclude from a high correlation *alone* that one variable causes the other. There's always the possibility that some third variable—a **lurking variable**—is affecting both of the variables you have observed. In the reading score example, you may have already guessed that the lurking variable is the age of the child. Older children tend to be taller and have stronger reading skills. But even when the lurking variable isn't that obvious, resist the temptation to think that a high correlation implies causation. Here's another example.

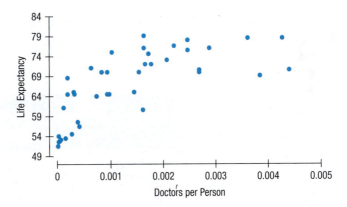

FIGURE 4.3 *Life Expectancy* and numbers of *Doctors per Person* in 40 countries shows a fairly strong, positive, somewhat linear relationship with a correlation of 0.705. (Data in **Doctors and life expectancy**)

Figure 4.3 shows the *Life Expectancy* (average of men and women, in years) for each of 40 countries of the world, plotted against the number of *Doctors per Person* in each country. The strong positive association ($r = 0.705$) seems to confirm our expectation that more *Doctors per Person* improves health care, leading to longer lifetimes and a higher *Life Expectancy*. Perhaps we should send more doctors to developing countries to increase life expectancy.

If we increase the number of doctors, will the life expectancy increase? That is, would adding more doctors *cause* greater life expectancy? Could there be another explanation of the association? Figure 4.4 shows another scatterplot. *Life Expectancy* is still the response, but this time the predictor variable is not the number of doctors, but the number of *Televisions per Person* in each country. The positive association in this scatterplot looks even *stronger* than the association in the previous plot. If we wanted to calculate a correlation, we should straighten the plot first, but even from this plot, it's clear that higher life expectancies are associated with more televisions per person. Should we conclude that increasing the number of televisions extends lifetimes? If so, we should send televisions instead of doctors to developing countries. Not only is the association with life expectancy stronger, but televisions are cheaper than doctors.

What's wrong with this reasoning? Maybe we were a bit hasty earlier when we concluded that doctors *cause* greater life expectancy. Maybe there's a lurking variable here. Countries with higher standards of living have longer life expectancies *and* more doctors (and more televisions per person). Could higher living standards cause changes in the other variables? If so, then improving living standards might be expected to prolong lives, increase the number of doctors, and increase the number of televisions. From this example, you can see how easy it is to fall into the

FIGURE 4.4 *Life Expectancy* and number of *Televisions per Person* shows a strong, positive (although clearly not linear) relationship. (Data in **Doctors and life expectancy**)

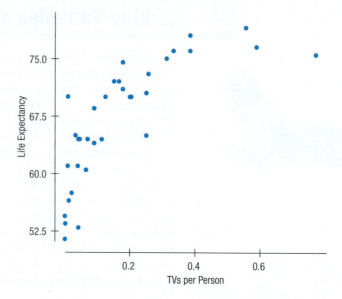

trap of mistakenly inferring causality from a correlation. For all we know, doctors (or televisions) *do* increase life expectancy. But we can't tell that by computing a correlation no matter how much we'd like to. Resist the temptation to conclude that *x* causes *y* from a correlation, no matter how obvious that conclusion seems to you.

> **IN PRACTICE 4.4   Gaining insight about causation from lurking variables**
>
> **MANAGER**   From the plot of **Mean Age** and **Year** (see page 108) it seems like older riders might be riding less safely than they used to. Can I conclude that from the strong correlation?
>
> **ANALYST**   No. You don't have data on the safety record of each age group. If the entire population of cyclists is aging then that would lead to the average age of cyclists in accidents increasing. In this case, the mean age of all cyclists is really a lurking variable.

4.5   The Linear Model

Let's return to the relationship between house price and size. In Figure 4.1 (repeated here) we saw a moderate, positive, linear relationship, so we can summarize its strength with a correlation. For this relationship, the correlation is 0.712.

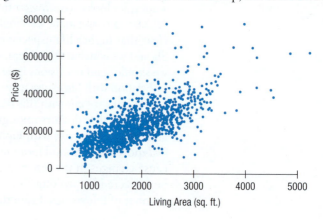

That's a strong correlation, but the strength of the relationship is only part of the picture. To be useful for decision making, we'll need to know more than the correlation. We'll need a model for the relationship between price and size. The correlation tells us the relationship is strong, but it doesn't tell us what it is.

To say more, we can model the relationship with a line and give the equation. Specifically, we can find a linear model to describe the relationship we saw in Figure 4.1 between *Price* and *Living Area*. A **linear model** is just an equation of a straight line through the data. The points in the scatterplot don't all line up, but a straight line can summarize the general pattern with only a few parameters. This model can help us understand how the variables are associated.

> " Statisticians, like artists, have the bad habit of falling in love with their models. "
>
> —George Box, famous statistician

Residuals

We know that a linear model won't be perfect. It will be a compromise. No matter what line we draw, it won't go through many of the points. The best line might not even hit *any* of the points. Then how can it be the "best" line? We want to find the line that somehow comes *closer* to all the points than any other line. Some of the points will be above the line and some below. Any linear model can be written as $\hat{y} = b_0 + b_1x$, where b_0 and b_1 are numbers estimated from the data and $\hat{y}$ (pronounced *y*-hat) is the **predicted value**. We use the *hat* to distinguish the predicted value from the observed value *y*. The difference between these two is called the **residual**:

$$e = y - \hat{y}.$$

The residual value tells us how far the model's prediction is from the observed value at that point. To find the residuals, we always subtract the predicted values from the observed ones.

Our question now is how to find the right line.

> **Positive or Negative?**
>
> A *negative* residual means the predicted value is too big—an overestimate. A *positive* residual shows the model makes an underestimate. These may actually seem backwards at first.

The Line of "Best Fit"

When we draw a line through a scatterplot, some residuals are positive, and some are negative. We can't assess how well the line fits by adding up all the residuals—the positive and negative ones would just cancel each other out. We need to find the line that's closest to all the points, and to do that, we need to make all the residuals positive. We faced the same issue when we calculated a standard deviation to measure spread. And we deal with it the same way here: by squaring the residuals to make them positive. The sum of all the squared residuals tells us how well the line we drew fits the data—the smaller the sum, the better the fit. A different line will produce a different sum, maybe bigger, maybe smaller. The **line of best fit** is the line for which the sum of the squared residuals is smallest—often called the **least squares line**.

This line has the special property that the variation of the data around the model, as seen in the residuals, is the smallest it can be for any straight line model for these data. No other line has this property. Speaking mathematically, we say that this line minimizes the sum of the squared residuals. You might think that finding this "least squares line" would be difficult. Surprisingly, it's not, although it was an exciting mathematical discovery when Legendre published it in 1805.

> **NOTATION ALERT**
>
> "Putting a hat on it" is standard statistics notation to indicate that something has been predicted by a model. Whenever you see a hat over a variable name or symbol, you can assume it is the predicted version of that variable or symbol.

4.6   Correlation and the Line

Any straight line can be written as:

$$y = b_0 + b_1x.$$

If we were to plot all the (x, y) pairs that satisfy this equation, they'd fall exactly on a straight line. Of course, with real data, the points won't all fall on the line.

Interpreting the Intercept

Suppose there's no house on a piece of property. Then the "size of the house" is 0 sq. ft. The model says that we should still expect to pay $13,439 for a house this size. Maybe the intercept can be interpreted this way, but we should always be cautious when extrapolating that far from the data we have. There are no empty lots in our data. The smallest house is 616 sq. ft. Intercepts often have no physical meaning and just serve as the starting point for the model.

So, we write our model as $\hat{y} = b_0 + b_1 x$, using $\hat{y}$ for the predicted values, because it's the predicted values (not the data values) that fall on the line. If the model is a good one, the data values will scatter closely around it.

For the Saratoga house data, the line is:

$$\widehat{Price} = 13{,}439 + 113.12 \ Living \ Area.$$

What does this mean? The **slope**, 113.12, says that we can expect a house that's one square foot bigger will be worth, on average, about $113.12 more. Slopes are always expressed in y-units per x-units. They tell you how the response variable changes for a one unit step in the predictor variable. So we'd say that the slope is $113.12 per square foot.

The **intercept**, $13,439, is the value of the line when the x-variable is zero. Of course we wouldn't use these data to predict such a price, because we don't have data for empty lots, so we should treat the intercept as just a "starting point" for our model.

JUST CHECKING

A scatterplot of sales per month (in thousands of dollars) vs. number of employees for all the outlets of a large computer chain shows a relationship that is straight, with only moderate scatter and no outliers. The correlation between *Sales* and *Employees* is 0.85, and the equation of the least squares model is:

$$\widehat{Sales} = 9.564 + 122.74 \ Employees.$$

6 What does the slope of 122.74 mean?

7 What are the units of the slope?

8 The outlet in Dallas, Texas, has 10 more employees than the outlet in Cincinnati. How much more *Sales* do you expect it to have?

9 Would you predict that an outlet with no employees would sell $9564 next month? Why or why not?

How do we find the slope and intercept of the least squares line? The model is built from the summary statistics we've used before. We use the correlation of y and x to tell us the strength and direction of the linear association. Correlation is found from the z-scores, so it has no units. We use the standard deviations of x and y, s_x and s_y, to provide the units of the variables, because standard deviations are measured in natural units. Finally, the means of x and y, $\bar{x}$ and $\bar{y}$, give the center of the point cloud, and we place the line to pass through the center. Putting that all together, the slope of the line is computed as:

$$b_1 = r\frac{s_y}{s_x}.$$

The correlation tells us the sign of the relationship, and the slope inherits this sign as well. If the correlation is positive, the scatterplot runs from lower left to upper right, and the slope of the line is positive. If the correlation is negative, then so is the slope of the line.

The best fit line goes through the middle of the data, so it predicts $\bar{y}$ for points whose x-value is $\bar{x}$. Putting that into our equation and using the slope we just found gives:

$$\bar{y} = b_0 + b_1\bar{x}$$

and we can rearrange the terms to find:

$$b_0 = \bar{y} - b_1\bar{x}.$$

It's easy to use the estimated linear model to predict the price of a house from its size. Consider, for example, a 3000 sq. ft. house at 100 Garnsey Lane in Schuylerville, NY, found on Zillow in July 2017. Our model predicts its price as:

$$\widehat{Price} = 13{,}439 + 113.12 \times 3000 = \$352{,}799.$$

In fact, the house's asking price is $364,500. The difference between the observed value and the value predicted by the regression equation, the residual, is $364,500 − $352,799 = $11,701.

Least squares lines are commonly called **regression lines**. "Regression" almost always means "the linear model fit by least squares." Clearly, regression and correlation are closely related. We'll need to check the same conditions before computing a regression as we did for correlation:

1. **Quantitative Variables Condition**
2. **Linearity Condition**
3. **Outlier Condition**

A little later in the chapter we'll add two more.

IN PRACTICE 4.5   Interpreting the equation of a linear model

MANAGER It looks to me like the data on cyclist accident deaths show a linear pattern. Can you fit a straight line and interpret the pattern for me?

ANALYST From the summary statistics,

$$b_1 = 0.979 \times \frac{3.22}{4.76} = 0.66$$

$$b_0 = 40.44 - 0.66 \times 2007.5 = -1284.51$$

$$\widehat{MeanAge} = -1284.51 + 0.66\,Year$$

The mean age of cyclists killed in vehicular accidents has increased by about 0.66 years of age (about 8 months) per year during the years observed by these data[4], but even though we fit a regression, we still don't know the reason for the increase.

Understanding Regression from Correlation

What happens to the regression equation if we standardize both the predictor and response variables and regress z_y on z_x? Standardized variables have standard deviation = 1 and mean = 0. So, the slope is $r\frac{1}{1} = r$, and the intercept is 0 (because both $\bar{y}$ and $\bar{x}$ are now 0). That leaves the simple equation

$$\hat{z}_y = r\,z_x.$$

Who Was First?

One of history's most famous disputes of authorship was between Gauss and Legendre over the method of "least squares." Legendre was the first to publish the solution to finding the best fit line through data in 1805, at which time Gauss claimed to have known it for years. There is some evidence that, in fact, Gauss may have been right, but he hadn't bothered to publish it, and had been unable to communicate its importance to other scientists.[5] Gauss later referred to the solution as "*our* method" (principium *nostrum*), which certainly didn't help his relationship with Legendre.

---

[4]As is often the case with calculations like these, statistical software will carry all intermediate steps to full precision. Our rounding each quantity to 2 decimal places makes it easier to follow, but changes the equation. From software, the equation is:

$$\widehat{MeanAge} = -1291.01 + 0.663\,Year$$

[5]Stigler, Steven M., "Gauss and the Invention of Least Squares," *Annals of Statistics*, 9, (3), 1981, pp. 465–474.

Although we don't usually standardize variables for regression, thinking in *z*-scores is a good way to understand correlation. The equation says that we'd expect a case that deviates by one standard deviation from the mean in *x* to have a value of *y* that is *r* standard deviations away from the mean in *y*.

Let's be more specific. For the Saratoga houses, the correlation is 0.712. So, we know immediately that:

$$\hat{z}_{Price} = 0.712\, z_{Living\ Area}.$$

That means that a house that is one standard deviation bigger than the mean house, about 620 sq feet, is predicted by our model to cost about 0.712 standard deviation or $70,000 more than the mean house.

4.7 Regression to the Mean

Sir Francis Galton was the first to speak of "regression," although others had fit lines to data by the same method.

Suppose you were told of a house for sale in Saratoga, and, without any additional information, you were asked to guess its price. What would be your guess? A good guess would be the mean price of those houses. Now suppose you are also told that this house's address is 1922 Sawyer Drive, and that 1922 is 2 standard deviations (SDs) above the mean house number. Would that change your guess? Probably not. The correlation between a house's address number and *Price* is near 0, so knowing its address number doesn't tell you anything about its *Price* and doesn't move your guess. (And the standardized regression equation, $\hat{z}_y = r\, z_x$, tells us that as well, since it says that we should move 0×2 SDs from the mean.)

On the other hand, if you were told that, measured in euros, the house's price was 2 SDs above the mean, you'd know the price in dollars. There's a perfect correlation between *Price* in dollars and *Price* in euros ($r = 1$), so you know it's 2 SDs above mean *Price* in dollars as well.

What if you were told that the house was 2 SDs above the mean in *Living Area*? Would you still guess that its price is average? You might guess that it costs more than average, but would you guess 2 SDs above the mean? When there was no correlation, we didn't move away from the mean at all. With a perfect correlation, we moved our guess the full 2 SDs. Any correlation between these extremes should lead us to move somewhere between 0 and 2 SDs above the mean. (To be exact, our best guess would be to move $r \times 2$ standard deviations away from the mean.)

Notice that if *x* is 2 SDs above its mean, we won't ever move more than 2 SDs away for *y*, since *r* can't be bigger than 1.0. So each predicted *y* tends to be closer to its mean (in standard deviations) than its corresponding *x* was. This property of the linear model is called **regression to the mean**. This is why the line is called the regression line.

Harold Hotelling was a prominent statistician and economic theorist. He taught statistics to (among others) Nobel prize winners Milton Friedman and Kenneth Arrow.

Business Tales About Regression to the Mean

During the Great Depression, Northwestern University professor Horace Secrist followed the fortunes of 49 department stores, measuring the ratio of net profit or loss to net sales. He divided the stores into four groups, took the average performance of each group, and followed those averages from 1920 to 1930. He found that stores that had been above average tended to perform worse, while those that were below average tended to improve.

A careful scientist, he then examined other types of business. All 73 of the different industries he examined showed the same pattern! He solicited comments and criticisms from economists and statisticians. He then published a book entitled *Triumph of Mediocrity in Business* (Secrist 1933) announcing his discovery. Initial reviews were favorable, but the prominent statistician Harold Hotelling pointed out in a scathing review that Secrist had simply rediscovered regression to the mean, which is a mathematical certainty and not a new principle of economics or business.

Although Secrist wrote 13 books on economics and statistics and was director of Northwestern University's bureau of business research, his name is still largely associated with the fallacious interpretation of regression to the mean.

More recently, the psychologist Daniel Kahneman, winner of the 2002 Nobel Prize in Economics, explained (see his book *Thinking, Fast and Slow*) that regression to the mean can make managers believe that praising employees who do well doesn't work, but punishing them when they do badly does. Employees who score a success are likely to do a bit less well the next time (just due to random fluctuation), whether they are praised or not. Those who make a big error are likely to do better next time, whether they were chastised or not. But managers like to believe that their management actions have consequences and will therefore conclude that praise causes workers to do worse, but criticism encourages workers to improve.

4.8 Checking the Model

The linear regression model may be the most widely used model in all of statistics and analytics. It has everything we could want in a model: two easily estimated parameters, a meaningful measure of how well the model fits the data, and the ability to predict new values. It even provides a self-check in plots of the residuals to help us avoid all kinds of mistakes. For the linear model, we start by checking the same conditions we checked earlier in this chapter for using correlation.

Linear models only make sense for quantitative data. The **Quantitative Data Condition** is pretty easy to check, but don't be fooled by categorical data recorded as numbers. You probably don't want to predict ZIP codes from credit card account numbers or house prices from address numbers.

The regression model *assumes* that the relationship between the variables is, in fact, linear—the **Linearity Assumption**. If you try to model a curved relationship with a straight line, you'll usually get what you deserve. We can't ever verify that the underlying relationship between two variables is truly linear, but an examination of the scatterplot will let you check the **Linearity Condition** as we did for correlation. If you don't judge the scatterplot to be straight enough, stop. You can't use a linear model for just *any* two variables, even if they are related. The two variables must have a *linear* association, or the model won't mean a thing and decisions you base on the model may be wrong. Some nonlinear relationships can be saved by re-expressing—or transforming—the data to make the scatterplot more linear. (See Section 4.11.)

Watch out for outliers. The Linearity Assumption also requires that no points lie far enough away to distort the line of best fit. Check the **Outlier Condition** to make sure no point needs special attention. Outlying values may have large residuals, and squaring makes their influence that much greater. Outlying points can dramatically change a regression model. Unusual observations can even change the sign of the slope, misleading us about the direction of the underlying relationship between the variables.

Assumptions and Conditions

Most models are useful only when specific assumptions are true. Of course, assumptions are hard—often impossible—to check. That's why we *assume* them. But we should check to see whether the assumptions are *reasonable*. Fortunately, there are often *conditions* that we can check. Checking the conditions provides information about whether the assumptions are reasonable, and whether it's safe to proceed with the model.

Check the Scatterplot!

Check the scatterplot. The shape must be linear, or you can't use regression for the variables in their current form. And watch out for outliers.

Another assumption that is usually made when fitting a linear regression is that the residuals are independent of each other. We don't strictly need this assumption to fit the line, but we will need it to draw conclusions beyond the data. We'll come back to it when we discuss inference. We can't be sure that the **Independence Assumption** is true, but we are more willing to believe that the cases are independent if the cases are a random sample from the population.

We can also check displays of the regression residuals for evidence of patterns, trends, or clumping, any of which would suggest a failure of independence. In the special case when we have a time series, a common violation of the Independence Assumption is for successive errors to be correlated with each other (autocorrelation). The error our model makes today may be similar to the one it made yesterday. We can check this violation by plotting the residuals against time and looking for patterns.

When our goal is just to explore and describe the relationship, independence isn't essential. However, when we want to go beyond the data at hand and make inferences for other situations (in Chapter 16) this will be a crucial assumption, so it's good practice to think about it even now, especially for time series. (See Chapter 20.)

We always check conditions with a scatterplot of the data, but we can learn even more after we've fit the regression model. There's extra information in the residuals that we can use to help us decide how reasonable our model is and how well the model fits. So, we plot the residuals and check the conditions again.

The residuals are the part of the data that *hasn't* been modeled. We can write

$$Data = Predicted + Residual$$

or, equivalently,

$$Residual = Data - Predicted.$$

Or, as we showed earlier, in symbols:

$$e = y - \hat{y}.$$

A scatterplot of the residuals versus the *x*-values should be a plot without patterns. It shouldn't have any interesting features—no direction, no shape. It should stretch horizontally, showing no bends, and it should have no outliers. If you see non-linearities, outliers, or clusters in the residuals, find out what the regression model missed.

Let's examine the residuals from our regression of house prices on living area.[6]

Why *e* for *Residual*?

The easy answer is that *r* is already taken for correlation, but the truth is that *e* stands for "error." It's not that the data point is a mistake but that statisticians often refer to variability not explained by a model as error.

FIGURE 4.5   Residuals of the regression model predicting house prices from size.

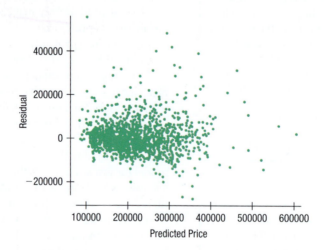

---

[6]Most computer statistics packages plot the residuals as we did in Figure 4.5, against the predicted values, rather than against *x*. When the slope is positive, the scatterplots are virtually identical except for the axes labels. When the slope is negative, the two versions are mirror images. Since all we care about is the patterns (or, better, lack of patterns) in the plot, either plot is useful.

Not only can the residuals help check the conditions, but they can also tell us how well the model performs. The better the model fits the data, the less the residuals will vary around the line. The standard deviation of the residuals, s_e, gives us a measure of how much the points spread around the regression line. Of course, for this summary to make sense, the residuals should all share the same underlying spread. So we must *assume* that the standard deviation around the line is the same wherever we want the model to apply.

This new assumption about the standard deviation around the line gives us a new condition, called the **Equal Spread Condition**. The associated question to ask is does the plot have a consistent spread or does it fan out? We check to make sure that the spread of the residuals is about the same everywhere. We can check that either in the original scatterplot of y against x or in the scatterplot of residuals (or, preferably, in both plots). We estimate the **standard deviation of the residuals** in almost the way you'd expect:

$$s_e = \sqrt{\frac{\sum e^2}{n - 2}}.$$

We don't need to subtract the mean of the residuals because $\bar{e} = 0$. Why divide by $n - 2$ rather than $n - 1$? We used $n - 1$ for s when we estimated the mean. Now we're estimating both a slope and an intercept. Looks like a pattern—and it is. We subtract one more for each parameter we estimate.

> **Equal Spread Condition**
>
> This condition requires that the scatter is about equal for all x-values. It's often checked using a plot of residuals against predicted values. The underlying assumption of equal variance is also called *homoscedasticity*.

For the Saratoga houses, the standard deviation of the errors is $69,100. When we predicted 110 Garnsey Lane, the residual was only $11.701, much less than the typical size of a residual.

IN PRACTICE 4.6 Gaining insights about the model by examining the residuals

MANAGER Did you assess your model of cyclists' ages on year to see if the assumptions were reasonable?

ANALYST The residuals show no pattern, as you can see from the plot of residuals vs. predicted values. There is one point that seems somewhat low, but it does not unduly affect the model and the model appears to be reasonable.

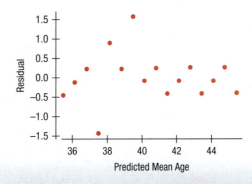

4.9   Variation in the Model and R^2

A publisher interested in assessing the cost of printing books wants to know how the thickness of a book is related to the number of pages. We certainly expect books with more pages to be thicker, but can we find a model to relate these two variables? Here's a scatterplot of the data:

FIGURE 4.6   Naturally enough, the thickness of a book grows with the number of pages. (Data in **Amazon books**)

WHO	Books sold by Amazon
WHAT	Thickness and Number of pages
UNITS	Inches and Counts
WHEN	2012
WHERE	Online
WHY	Originally collected as a class project

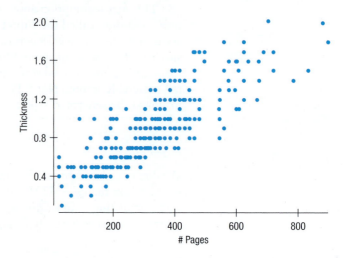

The regression model is

$$\widehat{Thickness} = 0.29 + 0.00183\ Pages$$

which says that books start out about 0.29 inch thick (due to covers and binding, perhaps) and then have about 0.00183 inch per page of thickness. We can see that the residuals vary less than the original thickness values did. That shows that we can get a better prediction of the thickness of a book by using a model rather than just using the mean to estimate the thickness of all the books.

FIGURE 4.7   Thickness and the regression residuals compared. The thickness values have their mean subtracted for the comparison. The smaller variation of the residuals shows the success of the regression model.

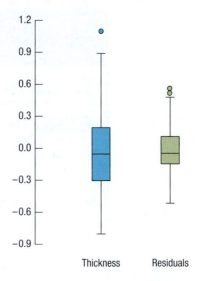

If the linear model were perfect, the residuals would all be zero and would have a standard deviation of 0. If knowing about the number of pages gave us no information about the thickness of a book, then we'd just use the mean thickness and not bother with the regression.

We can construct a measure that tells us where our model falls between being perfect and being useless. One measure we could use is the correlation between the data y and the predicted values $\hat{y}$. In a perfect regression model, the predictions would match the observed values and the correlation would be 1.0. In the worthless regression, we'd expect a correlation of 0.

All regression models fall somewhere between the two extremes of zero correlation and perfect correlation. We'd like to gauge where our model falls. But a regression model with correlation $+0.5$ is doing as well as one with correlation -0.5. They just have different directions. If we *square* the correlation coefficient, we'll get a value between 0 and 1, and the direction won't matter. But that's not the real reason for squaring the correlation. In fact, the squared correlation, r^2, gives the *fraction of the data's variation accounted for by the model*, and $1 - r^2$ is the fraction of the original variation left in the residuals. For the thickness and pages model, $r^2 = 0.809^2 = 0.654$, and $1 - r^2$ is 0.345, so 34.5% of the variability in *Thickness* has been left in the residuals.

All regression analyses include this statistic, although by tradition, it is written with a capital letter, R^2, and pronounced "**R-squared**." Because R^2 is a fraction of a whole, it is often given as a percentage.[7] An R^2 of 0% means that none of the variance in the data is in the model; all of it is still in the residuals. An R^2 of 100% sounds great, but means you've probably made a mistake.[8]

We can see how R^2 relates to the variance. The variance of *Thickness* is 0.136. The variance of the residuals is 0.0458.[9] That's $0.0458/0.136 = 0.3367$ or 33.67% of the variance of *Thickness* left behind in the residuals. So $100\% - 33.67\% = 66.32\%$ is the R^2 of the regression. The appropriate way to report this as part of a regression analysis is to say that 66.3% of the variance *is accounted for by the regression*.

r and R^2

Is a correlation of 0.80 twice as strong as a correlation of 0.40? Not if you think in terms of R^2. A correlation of 0.80 means an R^2 of $0.80^2 = 64\%$. A correlation of 0.40 means an R^2 of $0.40^2 = 16\%$—only a quarter as much of the variability accounted for. A correlation of 0.80 gives an R^2 *four* times as strong as a correlation of 0.40 and accounts for four times as much of the variability.

JUST CHECKING

Let's go back to our regression of Sales ($000) on number of employees.

$$\widehat{Sales} = 9.564 + 122.74 \, Employees$$

The R^2 value is reported as 72.25%.

10 What does the R^2 value mean about the relationship of *Sales* and *Employees*?

11 Is the correlation of *Sales* and *Employees* positive or negative? How do you know?

12 If we measured the *Sales* in thousands of euros instead of thousands of dollars, would the R^2 value change? How about the slope?

How Big Should R^2 Be?

The value of R^2 is always between 0% and 100%. But what is a "good" R^2 value? The answer depends on the kind of data you are analyzing and on what you want to do with it. Just as with correlation, there is no value for R^2 that automatically determines that the regression is "good." Data from scientific experiments often have R^2 in the 80% to 90% range and even higher. Data from observational studies and surveys, though, often show relatively weak associations because it's so difficult to measure reliable responses. An R^2 of 30% to 50% or even lower might be taken as evidence of a useful regression. The standard deviation of the residuals can give us more information about the usefulness of the regression by telling us how much scatter there is around the line.

Some Extreme Tales

One major company developed a method to differentiate between proteins. To do so, they had to distinguish between regressions with R^2 of 99.99% and 99.98%. For this application, 99.98% was not high enough.

The president of a financial services company reports that although his regressions give R^2 below 2%, they are highly successful because those used by his competition are even lower.

---

[7] By contrast, we usually give correlation coefficients as decimal values between -1.0 and 1.0.

[8] Well, actually, it means that you have a perfect fit. But perfect models don't happen with real data unless you accidentally try to predict a variable from itself.

[9] This isn't quite the same as squaring s_e which we discussed previously, but it's very close.

> ## IN PRACTICE 4.7   Understanding R^2
>
> **MANAGER** What's the R^2 for the regression of cyclist death ages vs. time that you found previously? And what exactly does it mean?
>
> **ANALYST** Because the correlation $r = 0.979$, R^2 is the square of this, or 0.958. It tells us that nearly 96% of the variation in the mean age of cyclist deaths can be accounted for by the trend over time.

As we've seen, an R^2 of 100% is a perfect fit, with no scatter around the line. The s_e would be zero. All of the variance would be accounted for by the model with none left in the residuals. This sounds great, but it's too good to be true for real data.[10]

4.10   Reality Check: Is the Regression Reasonable?

Statistics don't come out of nowhere. They are based on data. The results of a statistical analysis should reinforce common sense. If the results are surprising, then either you've learned something new about the world or your analysis is wrong.

Whenever you perform a regression, think about the coefficients and ask whether they make sense. Is the slope reasonable? Does the direction of the slope seem right? The small effort of asking whether the regression equation is plausible will be repaid whenever you catch errors or avoid saying something silly or absurd about the data. It's too easy to take something that comes out of a computer at face value and assume that it makes sense.

Always be skeptical and ask yourself if the answer is reasonable.

GUIDED EXAMPLE   Car Prices and Mileage

According to Trusted Choice, Independent Insurance Agents, the single most expensive cost of owning an automobile is depreciation. As soon as you drive it off the lot, the average new car loses 11% of its value and after just one year is worth only 75% of the original price. But how does the amount you drive affect the worth of the car over time? To answer that question, we collected recent sales offers on two different car models, the relatively expensive BMW M5 and the thrifty Honda Civic. For each model we found a random sample of cars with various miles driven that were for sale in 2017. (Data in **Used BMW M5 2017** and **Used Civics 2017**)

PLAN **Define** the problem and state the objective of the study. **Identify** the variables and their context.	We want to find out whether the mileage on the car's odometer is related to the asking price of a used car. We have two quantitative variables: the mileage (in miles) and the asking price ($). These data come from Kelley Blue Book and www.autotrader.com in mid 2017. There were 36 BMW M5s and 55 Honda Civics for sale in our region. We will build a regression for each car model separately.

---

[10]If you see an R^2 of 100%, it's a good idea to investigate what happened. You may have accidentally regressed two variables that measure the same thing.

DO **Characterize** the variables and determine the appropriate analysis.

Explore the dataset via graphics and summary statistics.

✔ **Quantitative Variables Condition**

Price

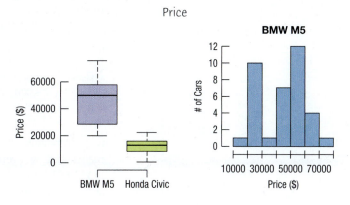

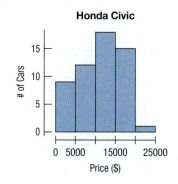

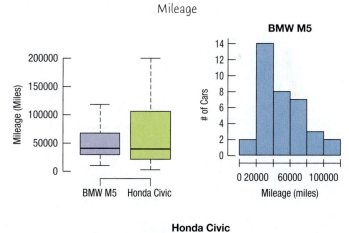

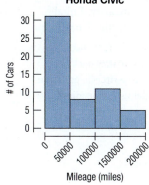

(continued)

| | BMW M5 | | Honda Civic | |
	Price	Mileage	Price	Mileage
Mean	$46,150.83	50874.89	$11,670.89	65276.20
SD	$16,073.40	2607.36	$5,145.78	54448.33
Min	$19,988.00	10919.00	$1,000.00	2500.00
Q1	$29,241.75	30189.75	$8,150.00	21700.00
Median	$49,743.00	40662.00	$12,500.00	39800.00
Q3	$57,811.75	67147.75	$15,350.00	106070.50
Max	$75,910.00	117329.00	$21,995.00	200000.00

Not surprisingly, the BMWs are, on average, much more expensive than the Hondas. An average used BMW M5 cost about $46,150 as compared to $11,671 for the Hondas. While both car models had a median mileage around 40,000 miles, the Honda's mileage had more variation and was more right skewed. The range of mileage for the BMWs was about 100,000 miles, while for the Hondas it was nearly 200,000 miles.

Make a scatterplot of the variables.

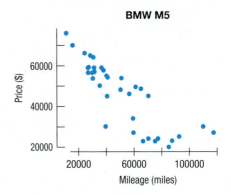

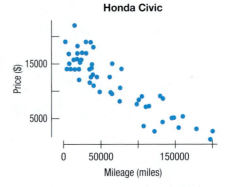

Check the **Linearity, Equal Spread,** and **Outlier Conditions.**

Model Find the regression line using a statistics package. Remember to write the equation of the model using meaningful variable names.

✔ **Linearity Condition** The scatterplots show a fairly strong negative association between *Price* and *Mileage* for both car models. The relationship for the Hondas is more linear.

✔ **Equal Spread Condition** The scatterplot for the Hondas shows equal spread across the x-values. The *Prices* of the BMWs seem to spread out a bit for the higher-mileage cars.

✔ **Outlier Condition** There appear to be a few possible mild outliers in the BMWs. One low-mileage BMW in particular seems to have an especially low price. Perhaps there is something else going on with that car. We will proceed with caution.

We have two quantitative variables that appear to satisfy the conditions, so we will model these relationship with a regression line.

Once you have the model, plot the residuals and check the Equal Spread Condition again.

Our software produces the following output.

BMW M5		Honda Civic	
Dependent variable is: Price		Dependent variable is: Price	
36 total cases		55 total cases	
R squared = 71.3%		R squared = 79.3	
s = 8737 with 36 − 2 = 34 df		s = 2363 with 55 − 2 = 53 df	
Variable	Coefficient	Variable	Coefficient
Intercept	72608.76	Intercept	17164.34
Mileage	−0.5200	Mileage	−0.0840

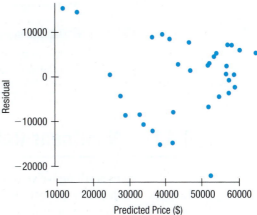

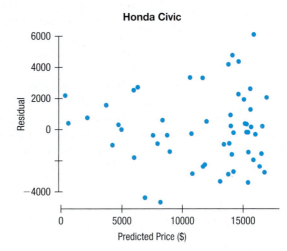

The residual plot for the Hondas appears generally patternless, with a slight increase in spread for the higher-priced cars. The BMWs show three possible outliers and inconsistent spread. We should be cautious in making predictions with these models.

REPORT   **Present** Interpret what you have found in the proper context.

MEMO

Re: Report on used car prices

We examined how well the mileage of a car can predict the asking price. The model for the BMW M5 is:

$$\widehat{Price} = \$72,609 - 0.520\ \$/mile \times Mileage.$$

The model for the Honda Civics is:

$$\widehat{Price} = \$17,164 - 0.084\ \$/mile \times Mileage.$$

(continued)

The model for the BMWs says that from a starting price of $72,609, the car loses about $0.52 for every mile driven, while for the Hondas, the starting price is only $17,164 and the decrease in price per mile is $0.084, about 1/6 of the loss per mile of the BMW. Of course, there are other factors involved and we cannot assign causality to the asking *Price* based on *Mileage*, and certainly not on *Mileage* alone.

The models assume that the decrease is linear and do not account for the known fact that the car loses approximately 11% of its value in the first mile. Thus, the intercepts would underestimate the price of a new car. It is also interesting to see that the average loss of $0.52 a mile for the BMW is close to the total reimbursement one would receive for business use of the car. The BMW owner would still be out of pocket for gas, insurance, registration and other expenses. The Honda Civic owner would be more than amply compensated.

4.11   Nonlinear Relationships

Everything we've discussed in this chapter requires that the underlying relationship between two variables be linear. But what should we do when the relationship is nonlinear and we can't use the correlation coefficient or a linear model? There are three basic approaches, each with its advantages and disadvantages.

Let's consider an example. The Human Development Index (HDI) was developed by the United Nations as a general measure of quality of life in countries around the world. It combines economic information (GDP), life expectancy, and education. The growth of cell phone usage has been phenomenal worldwide. Is cell phone usage related to the developmental state of a country? Figure 4.8 shows a scatterplot of number of *Cell Phones* vs. *HDI* for 152 countries of the world about 10 years ago.

We can look at the scatterplot and see that cell phone usage increases with increasing HDI. But the relationship is not straight. In Figure 4.8, we can easily see the bend in the form. But that doesn't help us summarize or model the relationship.

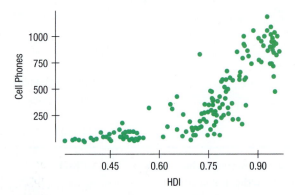

FIGURE 4.8   The scatterplot of number of *Cell Phones* (000s) vs. *HDI* for countries shows a bent relationship not suitable for correlation or regression.

You might think that we should just fit some curved function such as an exponential or quadratic to a shape like this. But using curved functions is complicated, and the resulting model can be difficult to interpret. And many of the convenient associated statistics (which we'll see in Chapters 16 and 17) are not appropriate for such models. So this approach isn't often used.

Another approach allows us to summarize the strength of the association between the variables even when we don't have a linear relationship. The **Spearman rank correlation**[11] works with the *ranks* of the data rather than their values. To find the ranks we simply count from the lowest value to the highest so that rank 1 is assigned to the lowest value, rank 2 to the next lowest, and so on. Using ranks for both variables generally straightens out the relationship, as Figure 4.9 shows.

FIGURE 4.9 Plotting the ranks results in a plot with a straight relationship.

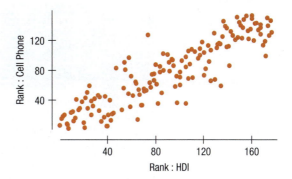

Now we can calculate a correlation on the ranks. The resulting correlation[12] summarizes the degree of relationship between two variables—but not, of course, of the degree of *linear* relationship. The Spearman correlation for these variables is 0.876. That says there's a reasonably strong relationship between *Cell Phones* and *HDI*. We don't usually fit a linear model to the ranks because that would be difficult to interpret and because the supporting statistics wouldn't be appropriate.

A third approach to a nonlinear relationship is to transform or re-express one or both of the variables by a function such as the square root, logarithm, or reciprocal. We saw in Chapter 3 that a transformation can improve the symmetry of the distribution of a single variable. In the same way—and often with the same transforming function—transformations can make a relationship more nearly linear. Figure 4.10, for example, shows the relationship between the log of the number of *Cell Phones* and the *HDI* for the same countries.

FIGURE 4.10 Taking the logarithm of *Cell Phones* results in a more nearly linear relationship.

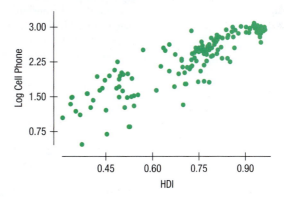

The advantage of re-expressing variables is that we *can* use regression models, along with all the supporting statistics still to come. The disadvantage is that we must interpret our results in terms of the re-expressed data, and it can be difficult to explain what we mean by the logarithm of the number of cell phones in a country. We can, of course, reverse the transformation to transform a predicted value or residual back to the original units. (In the case of a logarithmic transformation, calculate 10^y to get back to the original units.)

---

[11]Due to Charles Spearman, a psychologist who did pioneering work in intelligence testing.
[12]Spearman rank correlation is a *nonparametric* statistical method. You'll find other nonparametric methods in later chapters.

Which approach you choose is likely to depend on the situation and your needs. Statisticians, economists, and scientists generally prefer to transform their data, and many of their laws and theories include transforming functions.[13] But for just understanding the shape of a relationship, a scatterplot does a fine job, and as a summary of the strength of a relationship, a Spearman correlation is a good general-purpose tool.

IN PRACTICE 4.8   Improving understanding relationships between variables by re-expressing for linearity

MANAGER In preparation for our annual meeting, I want to look at the relationship between *Assets* and *Sales* as reported in other companies' annual financial statements to see where we stand. I made a scatterplot of those variables for 79 of the largest companies. (Data in **Companies**)

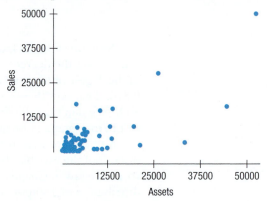

The Pearson correlation is 0.75, which seems to indicate a strong relationship, but I don't really understand it from this plot. Can you help me to see the relationship more clearly?

ANALYST The Pearson correlation is not appropriate for the original scatterplot because the relationship is not linear. The Spearman rank correlation of the original data is 0.50, which indicates a somewhat weaker relationship between the ranks. Alternatively we could take the logarithm of both variables to make the relationship easier to understand. The following scatterplot shows *Log(Sales)* against *Log(Assets)*.

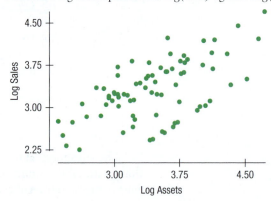

The Pearson correlation is now 0.58, about what the Spearman correlation indicated. There is a moderately strong, positive relationship between a company's *Assets* and *Sales*, but it's not linear.

---

[13]In fact, the HDI itself includes such transformed variables in its construction.

*4.12   Multiple Regression—A Glimpse Ahead

As we've seen, knowing the size of a house tells us something about what it should cost. A linear model for the relationship between two variables can provide insight and help predict the response variable under different scenarios for the predictor. But, the world of business and real decisions is usually more complex than a single y and x. If we really want to build a model for house prices, wouldn't we want to know its age, how many bathrooms it has, and whether it has air conditioning, in addition to its size? It turns out that it's not really very hard to add predictor variables to a linear model. Here is the model from Section 4.6 with only *Living Area* as the predictor: (Data in **Saratoga houses**)

$$\widehat{Price} = 13{,}439 + 113.12\,Living\,Area.$$

A 2000 sq. ft. house would be predicted to sell for $13,439 + 113.12 \$/sq. ft. \times 2000 sq. ft. = \$239,679.

What happens if we add the size of the lot? The model is probably much as you'd expect:

$$\widehat{Price} = 12{,}366 + 112.01\,Living\,Area + 6064.51\,Lot\,Size.$$

Lot sizes are measured in acres, so the same house with a half-acre lot would be worth, according to this new model, $12,366 + 112.01 \$/sq. ft. \times 2000 sq. ft. + 6064.51 \$/acre \times 0.50 acre = \$239,418, nearly the same as before.

This new model has taken some of the leftover variation from the first model, found in the residuals, and assigned some of it to the new variable. This new model adjusted the slope for *Living Area* once *Lot Size* is added because *Living Area* and *Lot Size* are related. This adjustment, or accounting for other variables in the model, is what makes multiple regression models versatile and useful.

When predictor variables are strongly related, the adjustment can seem surprising. Which of these houses do you think is worth more?

FIGURE 4.11   The house on the left has 8 bedrooms. The one on the right has 2. Which do you think is worth more?

It's not surprising that houses with more bedrooms tend to cost more. Figure 4.12 shows boxplots for houses with 2, 3, and 4 bedrooms (more than 95% of the houses).

It's not surprising that a linear model on bedrooms supports what we suspect:

$$\widehat{Price} = 59{,}862.96 + 48{,}217.81\,Bedrooms.$$

This model says that an additional bedroom, on average, is associated with an increase in price of about $48,000. Armed with this information the owner of a 1000 sq. ft. 2-bedroom house has a plan. He'll simply cut each bedroom into 4, advertise the house as an 8-bedroom house, and pocket an additional $289,306.86. Sound like a plan? Floor plans of before and after are shown in Figure 4.13.

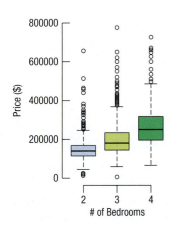

FIGURE 4.12   Side-by-side boxplots of *Price* against *Bedrooms* for houses with 2 to 4 bedrooms show that price increases, on average, with more bedrooms.

FIGURE 4.13 Floor plans of the 1000 sq. ft. home as a 2-bedroom house (original on the left) and as an 8-bedroom house on the right.

Of course, even if a bedroom measuring 3' by 4' were feasible, this doesn't make any sense. We know that linear models aren't causal and simply adding bedrooms won't increase the price, but how exactly does the multiple regression model take this into account? Let's fit a model with both *Bedrooms* and *Living Area* as predictors:

$$\widehat{Price} = 36{,}667.90 + 125.40 \, Living \, Area - 14196.77 \, Bedrooms.$$

With both predictors in the model, we now predict that a house of the *same size* with an additional bedroom will actually, on average, be associated with a *lower Price* of $14,196.77. The multiple regression model coefficients reflect the effect of each predictor *accounting for the presence of the other predictors*. Of course, more bedrooms typically mean a larger house, so this "decrease" in predicted price will, on average, be compensated for by a larger living area. The negative coefficient of bedrooms is for houses of a given size, not for houses in general. So, it's not a correct interpretation to say that houses with more bedrooms are associated with lower prices on average. That interpretation would be a mistake similar to the Simpson's Paradox problem we saw in Chapter 3.

With today's software, fitting a multiple regression model is no more difficult than fitting a simple linear model, but with more predictors multiple regression models are useful in far more real situations. Because they are so important, so powerful, and so common in business analysis, we'll devote Chapters 18 and 19 to multiple regression. However, like simple regression models, they can be misused and misinterpreted, issues that we'll discuss in great detail later.

⊘ WHAT CAN GO WRONG?

- **Don't say "correlation" when you mean "association."** How often have you heard the word "correlation"? Chances are pretty good that when you've heard the term, it's been misused. It's one of the most widely misused statistics terms, and given how often statistics are misused, that's saying a lot. One of the problems is that many people use the specific term *correlation* when they really mean the more general term *association*. Association is a deliberately vague term used to describe the relationship between two variables.

  Correlation is a precise term used to describe the strength and direction of a linear relationship between quantitative variables.

- **Don't correlate categorical variables.** Be sure to check the Quantitative Variables Condition. It makes no sense to compute a correlation of categorical variables.

- **Make sure the association is linear.** Not all associations between quantitative variables are linear. Correlation can miss even a strong nonlinear association. And linear regression models are never appropriate for relationships that are not linear. A company, concerned that customers might use ovens with imperfect temperature controls, performed a series of experiments[14] to assess the effect of baking temperature on the quality of brownies made from their freeze-dried reconstituted brownies. The company wants to understand the sensitivity of brownie quality to variation in oven temperatures around the recommended baking temperature of 325°F. The lab reported a correlation of −0.05 between the scores awarded by a panel of trained taste-testers and baking temperature and a regression slope of −0.02, so they told management that there is no relationship. Before printing directions on the box telling customers not to worry about the temperature, a savvy intern asks to see the scatterplot.

FIGURE 4.14 The relationship between brownie taste *Score* and *Baking Temperature* is strong, but not linear.

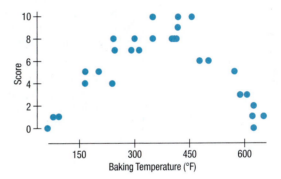

The plot actually shows a strong association—but not a linear one. Don't forget to check the Linearity Condition.

- **Beware of outliers.** You can't interpret a correlation coefficient or a regression model safely without a background check for unusual observations. Here's an example. The relationship between *IQ* and *Shoe Size* among comedians shows a surprisingly strong positive correlation of 0.50. To check assumptions, we look at the scatterplot.

FIGURE 4.15 *IQ* vs. *Shoe Size.*

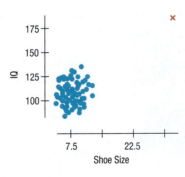

---

[14]Experiments designed to assess the impact of environmental variables outside the control of the company on the quality of the company's products were advocated by the Japanese quality expert Dr. Genichi Taguchi starting in the 1980s in the United States.

From this "study," what can we say about the relationship between the two? The correlation is 0.50. But who *does* that point in the upper right-hand corner belong to? The outlier is Bozo the Clown, known for his large shoes and widely acknowledged to be a comic "genius." Without Bozo the correlation is near zero.

Even a single unusual observation can dominate the correlation value. That's why you need to check the Unusual Observations Condition.

- **Don't confuse correlation with causation.** Once we have a strong correlation, it's tempting to try to explain it by imagining that the predictor variable has *caused* the response to change. Putting a regression line on a scatterplot tempts us even further. Humans are like that; we tend to see causes and effects in everything. Just because two variables are related does not mean that one *causes* the other.

Does Cancer Cause Smoking?

Even if the correlation of two variables is due to a causal relationship, the correlation itself cannot tell us what causes what.

Sir Ronald Aylmer Fisher (1890–1962) was one of the greatest statisticians of the 20th century. Fisher testified in court (paid by the tobacco companies) that a causal relationship might underlie the correlation of smoking and cancer:

> Is it possible, then, that lung cancer . . . is one of the causes of smoking cigarettes? I don't think it can be excluded . . . the pre-cancerous condition is one involving a certain amount of slight chronic inflammation . . .
>
> A slight cause of irritation . . . is commonly accompanied by pulling out a cigarette, and getting a little compensation for life's minor ills in that way. And . . . is not unlikely to be associated with smoking more frequently.

Ironically, the proof that smoking indeed is the cause of many cancers came from experiments conducted following the principles of experiment design and analysis that Fisher himself developed.

Scatterplots, correlation coefficients, and regression models never prove causation. This is, for example, partly why it took so long for the U.S. Surgeon General to get warning labels on cigarettes. Although there was plenty of evidence that increased smoking was *associated* with increased levels of lung cancer, it took years to provide evidence that smoking actually *causes* lung cancer. (The tobacco companies used this to great advantage.)

- **Watch out for lurking variables.** A scatterplot of the damage (in dollars) caused to a house by fire would show a strong correlation with the number of firefighters at the scene. Surely the damage doesn't cause firefighters. And firefighters actually do cause damage, spraying water all around and chopping holes, but does that mean we shouldn't call the fire department? Of course not. There is an underlying variable that leads to both more damage and more firefighters—the size of the blaze. You can often debunk claims made about data by finding a lurking variable behind the scenes.

- **Don't fit a straight line to a nonlinear relationship.** Linear regression is suited only to relationships that are, in fact, linear.

- **Beware of extraordinary points.** Data values can be extraordinary or unusual in a regression in two ways. They can have *y*-values that stand off from the linear pattern suggested by the bulk of the data. These are what we have been calling outliers; although with regression, a point can be an outlier by being far from the linear pattern even if it is not the largest or smallest y-value. Points can also be extraordinary in their x-values. Such points can exert a strong influence on the line. Both kinds of extraordinary points require attention.

- **Don't predict far beyond the data. A linear model will often do a reasonable job of summarizing a relationship in the range of observed *x*-values.** Once we have a working model for the relationship, it's tempting to use it. But beware of predicting y-values for x-values that lie too far outside the range of the original data. The model may no longer hold there, so such extrapolations too far from the data are dangerous.

- **Don't choose a model based on *R²* alone.** Although R^2 measures the *strength* of the linear association, a high R^2 does not demonstrate the *appropriateness* of the regression. A single unusual observation, or data that separate into two groups, can make the R^2 seem quite large when, in fact, the linear regression model is simply inappropriate. Conversely, a low R^2 value may be due to a single outlier. It may be that most of the data fall roughly along a straight line, with the exception of a single point. Always look at the scatterplot.

ETHICS IN ACTION

Rebekkah Greene, owner of Up with Life Café and Marketplace, is a true believer in the health and healing benefits of food. She offers her customers pure, wholesome, and locally sourced products. Recently, she decided to add a line of hearty "made to order" cereals that she prepares according to each customer's expressed preferences. To do this, she keeps a wide variety of ingredients on hand from which her customers can choose to "design" their own unique cereal mix. These not only include organic grains, nuts, and dried fruits typically found in cereals, like oat bran and wheat germ, but also a wide assortment of sprouted grains.

Rebekkah is following the lead of food innovators who understand that sprouting grains activates food enzymes, increases vitamin content, and decreases starch—all of which improve digestion and absorption. She finds that sprouted grains are particularly delicious choices for warm breakfast cereals. Being a purist, Rebekkah decided that she would take care of the sprouting process herself. She therefore invested in the equipment and designed a "sprouting" space with appropriate temperature and humidity controls.

At the onset, her "made to order" cereal mixes were a big hit. But after the novelty wore off, she noticed that sales began to decline. Since most of her regular customers are young to middle-aged women, Rebekkah now considered the possibility that most are weight conscious as well as health conscious. She suspects that many ultimately decided to give up eating cereal for breakfast, even if it can provide superior health benefits, to opt for lower-carb alternatives to maintain or lose weight.

Given her sizable investment in sprouting grains, Rebekkah realizes she needs to do something to get more of her cereals back on the breakfast table! She began to do some research on the topic to better educate her customers. While she found a number of studies suggesting that sprouted grains are particularly healthful, she focused her attention on findings that emphasize the relationship between eating breakfast (specifically cereal) and weight loss. In her weekly flyer on "Up with Life Food Facts" she cited one study she found in a dietetic association journal that showed regular cereal eaters had fewer weight problems than infrequent cereal eaters. She stressed this positive correlation in her advice to customers. *The more often you eat cereal for breakfast the more weight you can lose...more cereal = more weight lost!* She did fail to mention, however, that this particular study was funded by the big cereal companies.

- **Identify the ethical dilemma in this scenario.**
- **What are the undesirable consequences?**
- **Propose an ethical solution that considers the welfare of all stakeholders.**

4   FROM LEARNING TO EARNING

**LEARNING
OBJECTIVES**

Make a scatterplot to display the relationship between two quantitative variables.
- Look at the direction, form, and strength of the relationship, and any outliers that stand away from the overall pattern.

Provided the form of the relationship is linear, summarize its strength with a correlation, *r*.
- The sign of the correlation gives the direction of the relationship.
- $-1 \leq r \leq 1$; a correlation of 1 or -1 is a perfect linear relationship. A correlation of 0 is a lack of linear relationship.
- Correlation has no units, so shifting or scaling the data, standardizing, or even swapping the variables has no effect on the numerical value.
- A large correlation is not a sign of a causal relationship.

Model a linear relationship with a least squares regression model.
- The regression (best fit) line doesn't pass through all the points, but it is the best compromise in the sense that the sum of squares of the residuals is the smallest possible.
- The slope tells us the change in y per unit change in x.
- The R^2 gives the fraction of the variation in y accounted for by the linear regression model.

Recognize regression to the mean when it occurs in data.
- A deviation of one standard deviation from the mean in one variable is predicted to correspond to a deviation of r standard deviations from the mean in the other. Because r is never more than 1, we predict a change toward the mean.

Examine the residuals from a linear model to assess the quality of the model.
- When plotted against the predicted values, the residuals should show no pattern and no change in spread.

TERMS

Association
- **Direction:** A positive direction or association means that, in general, as one variable increases, so does the other. When increases in one variable generally correspond to decreases in the other, the association is negative.

- **Form:** The form we care about most is straight, but you should certainly describe other patterns you see in scatterplots.

- **Strength:** A scatterplot is said to show a strong association if there is little scatter around the underlying relationship.

Correlation coefficient   A numerical measure of the direction and strength of a linear association.
$$r = \frac{\sum z_x z_y}{n - 1}$$

**Explanatory or independent
variable (*x*-variable)**   The variable that accounts for, explains, predicts, or is otherwise responsible for the *y*-variable.

Intercept   The intercept, b_0, gives a starting value in *y*-units. It's the $\hat{y}$-value when x is 0.
$$b_0 = \bar{y} - b_1 \bar{x}$$

Least squares   A criterion that specifies the unique line that minimizes the variance of the residuals or, equivalently, the sum of the squared residuals.

**Linear model
(Line of best fit)**   The linear model of the form $\hat{y} = b_0 + b_1 x$ fit by least squares. Also called the regression line. To interpret a linear model, we need to know the variables and their units.

Lurking variable	A variable other than x and y that simultaneously affects both variables, accounting for the correlation between the two.
Outlier	A point that does not fit the overall pattern seen in the scatterplot.
Predicted value	The prediction for y found for each x-value in the data. A predicted value, $\hat{y}$, is found by substituting the x-value in the regression equation. The predicted values are the values on the fitted line; the points $(x, \hat{y})$ lie exactly on the fitted line.
Residual	The difference between the actual data value and the corresponding value predicted by the regression model—or, more generally, predicted by any model: $$e = y - \hat{y}.$$
Regression line	The particular linear equation that satisfies the least squares criterion, often called the line of best fit.
Regression to the mean	Because the correlation is always less than 1.0 in magnitude, each predicted y tends to be fewer standard deviations from its mean than its corresponding x is from its mean.
Response or dependent variable (y-variable)	The variable that the model is intended to explain or predict.
R^2	• The square of the correlation between y and x • The fraction of the variability of y accounted for by the least squares linear regression on x • An overall measure of how successful the regression is in linearly relating y to x
Scatterplot	A graph that shows the relationship between two quantitative variables measured on the same cases.
Slope	The slope, b_1, is given in y-units per x-unit. Differences of one unit in x are associated with differences of b_1 units in predicted values of y: $$b_1 = r\frac{s_y}{s_x}.$$
Spearman rank correlation	The correlation between the ranks of two variables may be an appropriate measure of the strength of a relationship when the form isn't straight.
Standard deviation of the residuals	s_e is found by: $$s_e = \sqrt{\frac{\sum e^2}{n-2}}.$$

TECH SUPPORT   Correlation and Regression

All statistics packages make a table of results for a regression. These tables may differ slightly from one package to another, but all are essentially the same—and all include much more than we need to know for now. Every computer regression table includes a section that looks something like this:

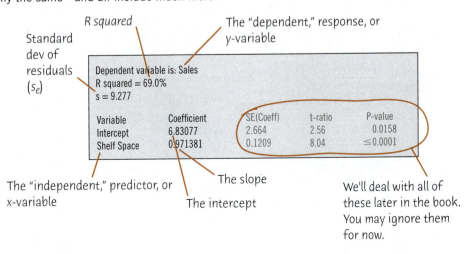

R squared

Standard dev of residuals (s_e)

The "dependent," response, or y-variable

Dependent variable is: Sales
R squared = 69.0%
s = 9.277

Variable	Coefficient	SE(Coeff)	t-ratio	P-value
Intercept	6.83077	2.664	2.56	0.0158
Shelf Space	0.971381	0.1209	8.04	≤ 0.0001

The "independent," predictor, or x-variable

The intercept

The slope

We'll deal with all of these later in the book. You may ignore them for now.

The slope and intercept coefficient are given in a table such as this one. Usually the slope is labeled with the name of the x-variable, and the intercept is labeled "Intercept" or "Constant." So the regression equation shown here is

$$\widehat{Sales} = 6.83077 + 0.971381 \; Shelf \; Space.$$

EXCEL

To make a scatterplot in Excel:

- Arrange data in worksheet so that x-variable and y-variable are in columns next to each other in that order.
- Highlight data in x-variable and y-variable column.
- Choose **Insert > Charts > Scatter > Scatter** (top left option). (Mac users choose **Scatter**.)
- The scatterplot appears. Shown here is a scatterplot of the Real Estate data.

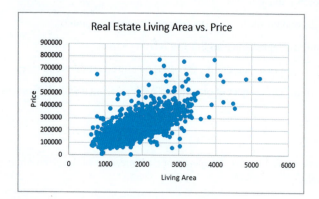

- To move the scatterplot to a new worksheet, right click on the chart and choose **Move Chart**.
- To add a linear regression line to a scatterplot, right click on a data point and choose **Add Trendline** or select the chart and click the plus sign that appears at the top right and toggle the **Trendline** option.)
- Design, Layout, and Format options are available by right clicking on that element in the chart or clicking on the plus sign that appears at the top right when the chart is selected. Use these to change chart layouts, labels, and colors.

- By default, Excel includes in the intercept in the plot. If your data values are all far from zero, you may need to re-format your scatterplot. (See the discussion of Format axis below.)

To carry out a Linear Regression in Excel:

- First, make sure that you've installed the Data Analysis add-in, as follows:
  - On the **File** tab, click **Options**, and then click **Add-Ins**.
  - Near the bottom of the **Excel Options** dialog box, select **Excel Add-ins** in the **Manage** box, and then click **Go**.
  - In the **Add-Ins** dialog box, select the check box for **Analysis ToolPak**, and then click **OK**.
  - If Excel displays a message that states it can't run this add-in and prompts you to install it, click **Yes** to install the add-in.
- Navigate to **Data > Data Analysis**.
- Select **Regression**.

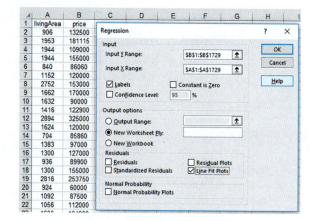

- Choose the cells of the spreadsheet holding the x- and y-variables.
- Check the **Labels** box if your data columns have variable names in the first row.
- Select where the output will appear.
- Check the **Line Fit Plots** box to display a scatterplot of the data with the Least Squares Regression Line.

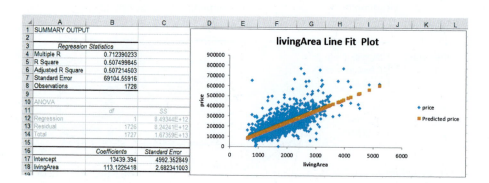

- The series displayed in red is the predicted values for price based on the Linear Regression Model. These points make up the Least Squares Regression Line.
- The R^2 value is in cell B5.
- The *y*-intercept and slope are in cells B17 and B18 respectively.
- The Design, Layout, and Format options are selected by right-clicking on that element within the chart. Use these to change chart layouts, labels, and colors.

But we aren't quite done yet. Excel always scales the axes of a scatterplot to show the origin (0, 0). But most data are not near the origin, so you may get a plot that, like this one, is bunched up in one corner.

- Right-click on the *x*-axis labels. From the menu that drops down, choose **Format axis**. . .
- Under **Axis Options**, set the *x*-axis minimum value. One useful trick is to use the dialog box itself as a straightedge to read over to the *x*-axis so you can estimate a good minimum value. Here 500 seems appropriate.
- Repeat the process with the *y*-axis if necessary.

XLStat

Choose the **XL Stat Tab** > **Modeling data** > **Linear regression**.

Input the ranges for the Y (dependent) and X (independent) variables.

Use the tabs in the dialog box to select options for output.

JMP

To make a scatterplot and compute correlation:

- Choose **Fit Y by X** from the **Analyze** menu.
- In the **Fit Y by X** dialog, drag the Y variable into the "**Y, Response**" box, and drag the X variable into the "**X, Factor**" box.
- Click the **OK** button.

Once JMP has made the scatterplot, click on the red triangle next to the plot title to reveal a menu of options.

- Select **Density Ellipse** and select **.95**. JMP draws an ellipse around the data and reveals the Correlation tab.
- Click the blue triangle next to Correlation to reveal a table containing the correlation coefficient.

To compute a regression,

- Choose **Fit Y by X** from the **Analyze** menu. Specify the Y variable in the—Select Columns box and click the **Y, Response** button.
- Specify the *x*-variable and click the **X, Factor** button.
- Click **OK** to make a scatterplot.
- In the scatterplot window, click on the red triangle beside the heading labeled "**Bivariate Fit...**" and choose **Fit Line**. JMP draws the least squares regression line on the scatterplot and displays the results of the regression in tables below the plot.

MINITAB

To make a scatterplot,

- Choose **Scatterplot** from the Graph menu.
- Choose **Simple** for the type of graph. Click **OK**.
- Enter variable names for the Y-variable and X-variable into the table. Click **OK**.

To compute a correlation coefficient,

- Choose **Basic Statistics** from the Stat menu.
- From the Basic Statistics submenu, choose **Correlation**. Specify the names of at least two quantitative variables in the "Variables" box.
- Click **OK** to compute the correlation table.

To compute a regression,

- Choose **Regression** from the Stat menu.
- From the Regression submenu, choose **Fitted Line Plot.**
- In the Fitted Line Plot dialog, click in the **Response Y** box, and assign the *y*-variable from the variable list.
- Click in the **Predictor X** box, and assign the *x*-variable from the Variable list. Make sure that the Type of Regression Model is set to Linear. Click the **OK** button.

R

To make a scatterplot of two variables, X and Y:

- **plot(X, Y)** or equivalently **plot(Y~X)** will produce the plot.
- **cor(X, Y)** finds the correlation.

  In the mosaic library, the syntax is cor (Y~X, data=DATA) even though correlation is symmetric with respect to Y and X.
- **lm(Y~X)** produces the linear model. (Also see below.)
- **summary(lm(Y~X))** produces more information about the model.

COMMENTS

Your variables X and Y may be variables in a data frame. If so, and DATA is the name of the data frame, then you will need to attach the data frame, or use

with(DATA,plot(Y~X)) or plot (Y~X,data=DATA).

For a linear model:

- **lm(Y~X,data=DATA)** is the preferred syntax. We strongly recommend against using the syntax lm (Y~X,) without including the data = statement.

Note: "lm" is short for "linear model".

SPSS

To make a scatterplot in SPSS, open the Chart Builder from the Graphs menu. Then

- Click the **Gallery** tab.
- Choose **Scatterplot** from the list of chart types.
- Drag the scatterplot onto the canvas.
- Drag a scale variable you want as the response variable to the *y*-axis drop zone.

- Drag a scale variable you want as the factor or predictor to the *x*-axis drop zone.
- Click **OK**.

To compute a correlation coefficient,

- Choose **Correlate** from the Analyze menu.
- From the Correlate submenu, choose **Bivariate**.
- In the Bivariate Correlations dialog, use the arrow button to move variables between the source and target lists. Make sure the Pearson option is selected in the Correlation Coefficients field.

To compute a regression, from the Analyze menu, choose

- **Regression > Linear** . . . In the Linear Regression dialog, specify the Dependent (*y*) and Independent (*x*) variables.
- Click the **Plots** button to specify plots and Normal Probability Plots of the residuals. Click **OK**.

STATCRUNCH

To make a scatterplot:

- Click on **Graph**.
- Choose **Scatter Plot**.
- Choose **X** and **Y** variable names from the list of **Columns**.
- Select other options as desired and then click on **Compute!**

To find a correlation:

- Click on **Stat**.
- Choose **Summary Stats > Correlation**.
- Choose two variable names from the list of **Columns**. (You may need to hold down the ctrl or command key to choose the second one.)
- Click on **Compute!**

To compute a regression,

- Click on **Stat**.
- Choose **Regression > Simple Linear**.
- Choose X and Y variable names from the list of columns.
- Click on **Compute!** to see the regression analysis.
- Click on **<** to see the scatterplot.

COMMENTS

Remember to check the scatterplot to be sure a linear model is appropriate.

Note that before choosing **Compute!**, you can select options from the **Transformation**, **Graphs**, and **Save** menus to transform *x* and *y* variables, ask for several plots, or save residuals or fitted values among other options.

BRIEF CASE

Fuel Efficiency

Both drivers and auto companies are motivated to raise the fuel efficiency of cars. Recent information posted by the U.S. government proposes some simple ways to increase fuel efficiency (see www.fueleconomy.gov): avoid rapid acceleration, avoid driving over 60 mph, reduce idling, and reduce the vehicle's weight. An extra 100 pounds can reduce fuel efficiency (mpg) by up to 2%. A marketing executive is studying the relationship between the fuel efficiency of cars (as measured in miles per gallon) and their weight to design a new compact car campaign. In the file **Fuel efficiency** you'll find data on the variables below.[15]

- Model of Car
- Engine Size
- Cylinders
- MSRP (Manufacturer's Suggested Retail Price in $)

- City (mpg)
- Highway (mpg)
- Country of origin
- Weight (lbs)
- Type (Car class)

Describe the relationship of *MSRP* and *Engine Size* with *Fuel Efficiency* (both City and Highway) in a written report. Only in the U.S. is fuel efficiency measured

---

[15]Data are from the 2004 model year and were compiled from www.Edmonds.com.

in miles per gallon. The rest of the world uses liters per 100 kilometers. To convert mpg to l/100 km, compute 235.215/mpg. Try that form of the variable and compare the resulting models. Be sure to plot the residuals.

Cost of Living

The Numbeo website (www.numbeo.com) provides access to a variety of data. One table lists prices of certain items in selected cities around the world. They also report an overall cost-of-living index for each city compared to the costs of hundreds of items in New York City. For example, London at 89.34 is nearly 11% cheaper than New York. You'll find the data for 511 cities as of mid 2017 in the file **Cost of living 2017**. Included are the *Cost of Living Index*, a *Rent Index*, a *Groceries Index*, a *Restaurant price Index*, and a *Local Purchasing Power Index* that measures the ability of the average wage earner in a city to buy goods and services. All indices are measured relative to New York City, which is scored 100.

Examine the relationship between the *Cost of Living Index* and the *Cost Index* for each of these individual items. Verify the necessary conditions and describe the relationship in as much detail as possible. (Remember to look at direction, form, and strength.) Identify any unusual observations.

Based on the correlations and linear regressions, which item would be the best predictor of overall cost in these cities? Which would be the worst? Are there any surprising relationships? Write a short report detailing your conclusions.

Mutual Funds

According to the U.S. Securities and Exchange Commission (SEC), a mutual fund is a professionally managed collection of investments for a group of investors in stocks, bonds, and other securities. The fund manager manages the investment portfolio and tracks the wins and losses. Eventually the dividends are passed along to the individual investors in the mutual fund. The first group fund was founded in 1924, but the spread of these types of funds was slowed by the stock market crash in 1929. Congress passed the Securities Act in 1933 and the Securities Exchange Act in 1934 to require that investors be provided disclosures about the fund, the securities, and the fund manager. The SEC drafted the Investment Company Act, which provided guidelines for registering all funds with the SEC. By the end of the 1960s, funds reported $48 billion in assets and, by October 2007 there were over 8000 mutual funds with combined assets under management of over $12 trillion.

Investors often choose mutual funds on the basis of past performance, and many brokers, mutual fund companies, and other websites offer such data. In the file **Mutual fund returns 2017**, you'll find the 1-month, 3-month, year-to-date (8-month), 1-year, 3-year, and 5-year returns of 98 Morningstar funds of various types. Which variable from the past (1-, 3-, or 5-year returns) provides the best predictions of the recent 3 months? Examine the scatterplots and regression models for predicting 3-month returns and write a short report containing your conclusions.

CHAPTER

4   EXERCISES

The calculations for correlation and regression models can be very sensitive to how intermediate results are rounded. If you find your answers using a calculator and writing down intermediate results, you may obtain slightly different answers than you would have had you used statistics software. Different programs can also yield different results. So your answers may differ in the trailing digits from those in the Appendix. That should not concern you. The meaningful digits are the first few; the trailing digits may be essentially random results of the rounding of intermediate results.

SECTION 4.1

1. Consider the following data from a small bookstore.

Number of Sales People Working	Sales (in $1000)
2	10
3	11
7	13
9	14
10	18
10	20
12	20
15	22
16	22
20	26
$\bar{x} = 10.4$	$\bar{y} = 17.6$
$SD(x) = 5.64$	$SD(y) = 5.34$

a) Prepare a scatterplot of *Sales* against *Number of Sales People Working*.
b) What can you say about the direction of the association?
c) What can you say about the form of the relationship?
d) What can you say about the strength of the relationship?
e) Does the scatterplot show any outliers?

T 2. Disk drives have been getting larger. Their capacity is now often given in *terabytes* (TB) where 1 TB = 1000 gigabytes, or about a trillion bytes. A search of prices for external disk drives on Amazon.com in mid-2016 found the following data: (Data in **Disk drives 2016**)

Capacity (TB)	Price ($)
0.5	59.99
1	79.99
2	111.97
3	109.99
4	149.99
6	423.34
8	596.11
12	1079.99
32	4461

a) Prepare a scatterplot of *Price* against *Capacity*.
b) What can you say about the direction of the association?
c) What can you say about the form of the relationship?
d) What can you say about the strength of the relationship?
e) Does the scatterplot show any outliers?

SECTION 4.2

3. The human resources department at a large multinational corporation wants to be able to predict average salary for a given number of years' experience. Data on salary (in $1000s) and years of experience were collected for a sample of employees.

a) Which variable is the explanatory or predictor variable?
b) Which variable is the response variable?
c) Which variable would you plot on the *y* axis?

4. A company that relies on Internet-based advertising linked to key search terms wants to understand the relationship between the amount it spends on this advertising and revenue (in $).

a) Which variable is the explanatory or predictor variable?
b) Which variable is the response variable?
c) Which variable would you plot on the *x* axis?

SECTION 4.3

5. If we assume that the conditions for correlation are met, which of the following are true? If false, explain briefly.

a) A correlation of -0.98 indicates a strong, negative association.
b) Multiplying every value of *x* by 2 will double the correlation.
c) The units of the correlation are the same as the units of *y*.

6. If we assume that the conditions for correlation are met, which of the following are true? If false, explain briefly.

a) A correlation of 0.02 indicates a strong positive association.
b) Standardizing the variables will make the correlation 0.
c) Adding an outlier can dramatically change the correlation.

SECTION 4.4

7. A larger firm is considering acquiring the bookstore of Exercise 1. An analyst for the firm, noting the relationship seen in Exercise 1, suggests that when they acquire the store they should hire more people because that will drive higher sales. Is his conclusion justified? What alternative explanations can you offer? Use appropriate statistics terminology.

8. A study finds that during blizzards, online sales are highly associated with the number of snow plows on the road; the more plows, the more online purchases. The director of an association of online merchants suggests that the organization should encourage municipalities to send out more plows whenever it snows because, he says, that will increase business. Comment.

SECTION 4.5

9. True or False. If False, explain briefly.

a) We choose the linear model that passes through the most data points on the scatterplot.
b) The residuals are the observed *y*-values minus the *y*-values predicted by the linear model.
c) Least squares means that the square of the largest residual is as small as it could possibly be.

10. True or False. If False, explain briefly.

a) Some of the residuals from a least squares linear model will be positive and some will be negative.
b) Least Squares means that some of the squares of the residuals are minimized.
c) We write $\hat{y}$ to denote the predicted values and y to denote the observed values.

SECTION 4.6

11. For the bookstore sales data in Exercise 1, the correlation of number of sales people and sales is 0.965.

a) If the number of people working is 2 standard deviations above the mean, how many standard deviations above or below the mean do you expect sales to be?
b) What value of sales does that correspond to?
c) If the number of people working is 1 standard deviation below the mean, how many standard deviations above or below the mean do you expect sales to be?
d) What value of sales does that correspond to?

12. For the hard drive data in Exercise 2, the correlation is 0.988 and other summary statistics are:

Capacity (in TB)	Price (in $)
$\bar{x} = 7.611$	$\bar{y} = 785.82$
$SD(x) = 9.854$	$SD(y) = 1418.67$

a) If a drive has a capacity of 17.46 TB (or 1 SD above the mean), how many standard deviations above or below the mean price of $785.82 do you expect the drive to cost?
b) What price does that correspond to?

13. For the bookstore of Exercise 1, the manager wants to predict *Sales* from *Number of Sales People Working*.

a) Find the slope estimate, b_1.
b) What does it mean, in this context?
c) Find the intercept, b_0.
d) What does it mean, in this context? Is it meaningful?
e) Write down the equation that predicts *Sales* from *Number of Sales People Working*.
f) If 18 people are working, what *Sales* do you predict?

g) If sales are actually $25,000 when 18 people are working, what is the value of the residual?
h) Have we overestimated or underestimated the sales?

14. For the disk drives in Exercise 2, we want to predict *Price* from *Capacity*.

a) Find the slope estimate, b_1 and interpret it in words.
b) Does the slope seem reasonable? Explain.
c) Find the intercept, b_0.
d) What does it mean, in this context? Is it meaningful?
e) Write down the equation that predicts *Price* from *Capacity*.
f) What would you predict for the price of a 3.0-TB disk?
g) What is the value of the residual you found in part f)?
h) Did the model overestimate or underestimate the pricing?

SECTION 4.7

15. A CEO complains that the winners of his "rookie junior executive of the year" award often turn out to have less impressive performance the following year. He wonders whether the award actually encourages them to slack off. Can you offer a better explanation?

16. An online investment blogger advises investing in mutual funds that have performed badly the past year because "regression to the mean tells us that they will do well next year." Is he correct?

SECTION 4.8

17. Here are the residuals for a regression of *Sales* on *Number of Sales People Working* for the bookstore of Exercise 1:

Sales People Working	Residual
2	0.07
3	0.16
7	−1.49
9	−2.32
10	0.77
10	2.77
12	0.94
15	0.20
16	−0.72
20	−0.37

a) What are the units of the residuals?
b) Which residual contributes the most to the sum that was minimized according to the Least Squares Criterion to find this regression?
c) Which residual contributes least to that sum?

18. Here are residual plots (residuals plotted against predicted values) for three linear regression models. Indicate which condition appears to be violated (linearity, outlier, or equal spread) in each case.

a)

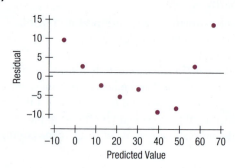

b)

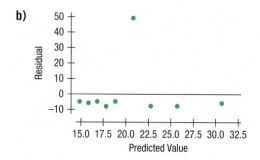

c)

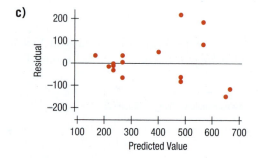

SECTION 4.9

19. For the regression model for the bookstore of Exercise 1, what is the value of R^2 and what does it mean?

20. For the disk drive data of Exercise 2 (as corrected in Exercise 12), find and interpret the value of R^2.

SECTION 4.11

21. When analyzing data on the number of employees in small companies in one town, a researcher took square roots of the counts. Some of the resulting values, which are reasonably symmetric were:

$$4, 4, 6, 7, 7, 8, 10$$

What were the original values, and how are they distributed?

22. You wish to explain to your boss what effect taking the base-10 logarithm of the salary values in the company's database will have on the data. As simple, example values you compare a salary of $10,000 earned by a part-time shipping clerk, a salary of $100,000 earned by a manager, and the CEO's $1,000,000 compensation package. Why might the average of these values be a misleading summary? What would the logarithms of these three values be?

CHAPTER EXERCISES

23. **Association.** Suppose you were to collect data for each pair of variables. You want to make a scatterplot. Which variable would you use as the explanatory variable and which as the response variable? Why? What would you expect to see in the scatterplot? Discuss the likely direction and form.

a) Cell phone bills: number of text messages, cost.
b) Automobiles: Fuel efficiency (mpg), sales volume (number of autos).
c) For each week: Ice cream cone sales, air conditioner sales.
d) Product: Price ($), demand (number sold per day).

24. **Association, part 2.** Suppose you were to collect data for each pair of variables. You want to make a scatterplot. Which variable would you use as the explanatory variable and which as the response variable? Why? What would you expect to see in the scatterplot? Discuss the likely direction and form.

a) T-shirts at a store: price each, number sold.
b) Real estate: house price, house size (square footage).
c) Economics: Interest rates, number of mortgage applications.
d) Employees: Salary, years of experience.

25. **Scatterplots.** Which of the scatterplots show:

a) Little or no association?
b) A negative association?
c) A linear association?
d) A moderately strong association?
e) A very strong association?

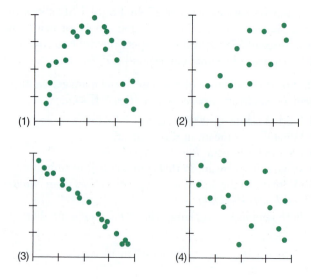

26. Scatterplots, part 2. Which of the scatterplots show:

a) Little or no association?
b) A negative association?
c) A linear association?
d) A moderately strong association?
e) A very strong association?

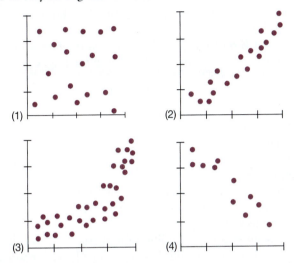

(1)   (2)

(3)   (4)

27. Manufacturing. A ceramics factory can fire eight large batches of pottery a day. Sometimes a few of the pieces break in the process. In order to understand the problem better, the factory records the number of broken pieces in each batch for three days and then creates the scatterplot shown.

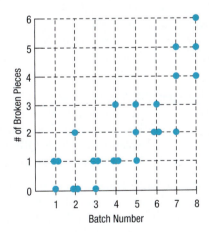

a) Make a histogram showing the distribution of the number of broken pieces in the 24 batches of pottery examined.
b) Describe the distribution as shown in the histogram. What feature of the problem is more apparent in the histogram than in the scatterplot?
c) What aspect of the company's problem is more apparent in the scatterplot?

28. Coffee sales. Owners of a new coffee shop tracked sales for the first 20 days and displayed the data in a scatterplot (by day).

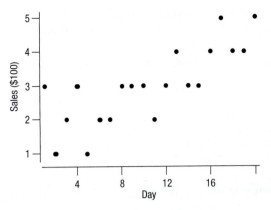

a) Make a histogram of the daily sales since the shop has been in business.
b) State one fact that is obvious from the scatterplot, but not from the histogram.
c) State one fact that is obvious from the histogram, but not from the scatterplot.

29. Matching. Here are several scatterplots. The calculated correlations are -0.923, -0.487, 0.006, and 0.777. Which is which?

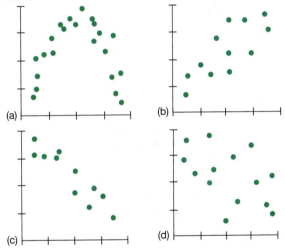

(a)   (b)

(c)   (d)

30. Matching, part 2. Here are several scatterplots. The calculated correlations are -0.977, -0.021, 0.736, and 0.951. Which is which?

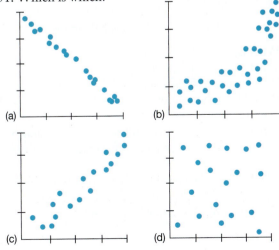

(a)   (b)

(c)   (d)

T 31. Pizza sales and price. A linear model fit to predict weekly *Sales* of frozen pizza (in pounds) from the average *Price* ($/unit) charged by a sample of stores in the city of Dallas in 39 recent weeks is: (Data in **Pizza prices**)

$$\widehat{Sales} = 141,865.53 - 24,369.49\ Price.$$

a) What is the explanatory variable?
b) What is the response variable?
c) What does the slope mean in this context?
d) What does the *y*-intercept mean in this context? Is it meaningful?
e) What do you predict the sales to be if the average price charged was $3.50 for a pizza?
f) If the sales for a price of $3.50 turned out to be 60,000 pounds, what would the residual be?

T 32. Quarterback performance 2017. The average salary for 30 top NFL quarterbacks in 2017 was just over $13,000,000. A linear model to predict *Salary* from *Total QBR* (an overall measure of performance based on game statistics) found the following:

$$\widehat{Salary} = 140,638.52 + 216,373.28\ *Total\ QBR.$$

a) What is the explanatory variable?
b) What is the response variable?
c) What does the slope mean in this context?
d) What does the *y*-intercept mean in this context? Is it meaningful?
e) What do you predict the *Salary* for a quarterback with a *Total QBR* of 60 points to be?
f) Tom Brady of the New England Patriots had a *Total QBR* of 83 and was paid $14,000,000 in 2016. What was his residual?
g) According to the model, was Brady over- or underpaid for the 2016 season? Explain.

T 33. Football salaries 2017. Is there a relationship between total team salary and the performance of teams in the National Football League (NFL)? For the 2016–2017 season, a linear model predicting *Wins* (out of 16 regular season games) from the total team *Salary* ($M) for the 32 teams in the league is:

$$\widehat{Wins} = -6.372 + 0.099\ Salary.$$

a) What is the explanatory variable?
b) What is the response variable?
c) What does the slope mean in this context?
d) What does the *y*-intercept mean in this context? Is it meaningful?
e) If one team spends $10 million more than another on salary, how many more games on average would you predict them to win?
f) The Dallas Cowboys spent $137 million on salaries and won 13 games. Did they do better or worse than predicted?
g) What was the Dallas Cowboys' residual?

h) The residual standard deviation is 2.92 games. What does that tell you about the likely practical use of this model for predicting wins?

T 34. Baseball salaries 2016. In 2016, the Los Angeles Dodgers spent nearly one quarter billion (!) dollars on salaries for their players (*Spotrac*). Is there a relationship between salary and team performance in Major League Baseball? For the 2016 season, a linear model fit to the number of *Wins* (out of 162 regular season games) from the team *Salary* ($M) for the 30 teams in the league is:

$$\widehat{Wins} = 63.81 + 0.136\ Salary.$$

a) What is the explanatory variable?
b) What is the response variable?
c) What does the slope mean in this context?
d) What does the *y*-intercept mean in this context? Is it meaningful?
e) If one team spends $10 million more than another on salaries, how many more games on average would you predict them to win?
f) If a team spent $100 million on salaries and won half (81) of their games, would they have done better or worse than predicted?
g) What would the residual of the team in part f be?
h) The R^2 for this model is 38.6% and the residual standard deviation is 8.5 games. How useful is this model likely to be for predicting the number of wins?

T 35. Pizza sales and price, part 2. For the data in Exercise 31, the average *Sales* was 52,697 pounds (SD = 10,261 pounds), and the correlation between *Price* and *Sales* was = −0.547. If the *Price* in a particular week was one SD higher than the mean *Price*, how much pizza would you predict was sold that week?

T 36. Quarterback performance 2017, part 2. The 30 quarterbacks in Exercise 32 had an average *Salary* of $13,788,022 (SD = $8,130,536). The correlation between *Salary* and *Total QBR* = 0.278. If a player had a Total QBR rating 1 SD below the average, what *Salary* would you predict for it?

37. Packaging. A CEO announces at the annual shareholders meeting that the new see-through packaging for the company's flagship product has been a success. In fact, he says, "There is a strong correlation between packaging and sales." Criticize this statement on statistical grounds.

38. Insurance. Insurance companies carefully track claims histories so that they can assess risk and set rates appropriately. The National Insurance Crime Bureau reports that Honda Accords, Honda Civics, and Toyota Camrys are the cars most frequently reported stolen, while Ford Tauruses, Pontiac Vibes, and Buick LeSabres are stolen least often. Is it correct to say that there's a correlation between the type of car you own and the risk that it will be stolen?

39. Sales by region. A sales manager for a major pharmaceutical company analyzes last year's sales data for her 96 sales representatives, grouping them by region (1 = East Coast United States; 2 = Mid West United States; 3 = West United States; 4 = South United States; 5 = Canada; 6 = Rest of World). She plots *Sales* (in $1000) against *Region* (1–6) and sees a strong negative correlation.

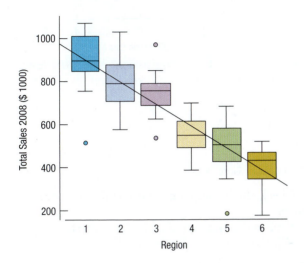

She fits a regression to the data and finds:

$$\widehat{Sales} = 1002.5 - 102.7\ Region.$$

The R^2 is 70.5%.

Write a few sentences interpreting this model and describing what she can conclude from this analysis.

40. Salary by job type. At a small company, the head of human resources wants to examine salary to prepare annual reviews. He selects 28 employees at random with job types ranging from 01 = Stocking clerk to 99 = President. He plots *Salary* ($) against *Job Type* and finds a strong linear relationship with a correlation of 0.96.

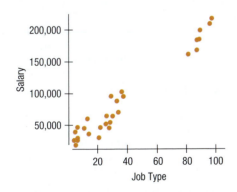

The regression output gives:

$$\widehat{Salary} = 15827.9 + 1939.1\ Job\ Type$$

Write a few sentences interpreting this model and describing what he can conclude from this analysis.

41. Carbon footprint 2015. The scatterplot shows, for 2015 cars, the carbon footprint (tons of CO_2 per mile) vs. the new Environmental Protection Agency (EPA) highway mileage for 69 family sedans as reported by the U.S. government (www.fueleconomy.gov/feg/byclass.htm); the cars in the lower right of the scatterplot plotted in red are all hybrids.

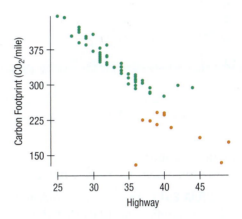

a) The correlation is −0.860. Describe the association.
b) Are the assumptions and conditions met for computing correlation?
c) Using technology, find the correlation of the data when the hybrid cards are not included with the others. Can you explain why it changes in that way?

42. EPA mpg 2013. In 2008, the EPA revised their methods for estimating the fuel efficiency (mpg) of cars—a factor that plays an increasingly important role in car sales. How do the new highway and city estimated mpg values relate to each other? Here's a scatterplot for 76 family sedans as reported by the U.S. government. These are the same cars as in Exercise 41.

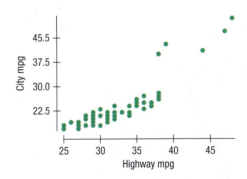

a) The correlation of these two variables is 0.896. Describe the association.
b) If the hybrids were removed from the data, what would you expect to happen to the slope (increase, decrease, or stay pretty much the same) and to the correlation (increase, decrease, the same)? Try it using technology. Report and discuss what you find.

43. Real estate. Is the number of total rooms in the house associated with the price of a house? Here is the scatterplot of a random sample of homes for sale:

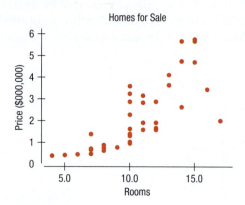

Homes for Sale

a) Is there an association?
b) Check the assumptions and conditions for correlation.

T 44. GDP and DJIA 2017. An economics student is studying the American economy and finds that the correlation between the inflation-adjusted Dow Jones Industrial Average and the Gross Domestic Product (GDP) (also inflation adjusted) is 0.85 for the years 1961 to 2016. (www.measuringworth.com). From that he concludes that there is a strong positive relationship between the two series and predicts that a drop in the GDP will make the stock market go down. Here is a scatterplot of the adjusted DJIA against the GDP (1961 to 2016) in constant (2010) $. Describe the relationship and comment on the student's conclusions.

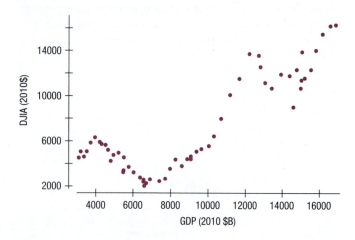

T 45. GDP growth 2017. Is economic growth in the developing world related to growth in the industrialized countries? Here's a scatterplot of the growth (in % of Gross Domestic Product) of the least developed countries (as classified by the UN) vs. the growth of the 19 European states. Each point represents one of the years from 1983 to 2016. The output of a regression analysis follows.

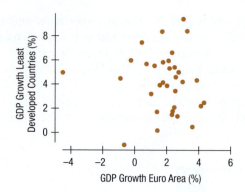

Dependent variable: GDP Growth Least Developed Countries
$R^2 = 0.002\%$
$s = 2.462$

Variable	Coefficient
Intercept	4.340
GDP Growth Euro Area	−0.066

a) Check the assumptions and conditions for the linear model.
b) Explain the meaning of R^2 in this context.
c) What are the cases in this model?

T 46. Euro-US GDP growth 2017. Is economic growth in Europe related to growth in the United States? Here's a scatterplot of the average growth in the 19 European countries (% of Gross Domestic Product) vs. the growth in the United States. Each point represents one of the years from 1961 to 2016.

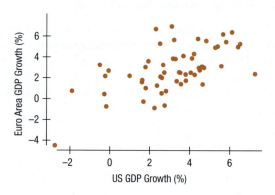

Dependent variable: European Countries GDP Growth
$R^2 = 35.09\%$
$s = 1.773$

Variable	Coefficient
Intercept	0.8703
U.S. GDP Growth	0.6230

a) Check the assumptions and conditions for the linear model.
b) Explain the meaning of R^2 in this context.

T 47. GDP growth 2017, part 2. From the linear model fit to the data on GDP growth in Exercise 45:

a) Write the equation of the regression line.
b) What is the meaning of the intercept? Does it make sense in this context?
c) Interpret the meaning of the slope.
d) In a year in which the European countries grow 4%, what do you predict for the least developed countries?
e) In 2007, the Euro Zone experienced a 3.02% growth, while the least developed countries grew at a rate of 9.41%. Is this more or less than you would have predicted?
f) What is the residual for this year?

T 48. Euro-US GDP growth 2017, part 2. From the linear model fit to the data on GDP growth of Exercise 46:

a) Write the equation of the regression line.
b) What is the meaning of the intercept? Does it make sense in this context?
c) Interpret the meaning of the slope.
d) In a year in which the United States grows at 0%, what do you predict for European growth?
e) In 2016, the United States experienced a 1.62% growth, while Europe grew at a rate of 1.75%. Is this more or less than you would have predicted?
f) What is the residual for this year?

T 49. Attendance 2016. American League baseball games are played under the designated hitter rule, meaning that pitchers, often weak hitters, do not come to bat. Baseball owners believe that the designated hitter rule means more runs scored, which in turn means higher attendance. Is there evidence that more fans attend games if the teams score more runs? Data collected from American League games during the 2016 season indicate a correlation of 0.432 between runs scored and the average number of people at the home games. (www.espn.com/mlb/attendance)

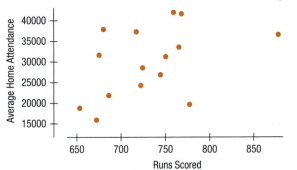

a) Does the scatterplot indicate that it's appropriate to calculate a correlation? Explain.
b) Describe the association between attendance and runs scored.
c) Does this association prove that the owners are right that more fans will come to games if the teams score more runs?

T 50. Second inning 2016. Perhaps fans are just more interested in teams that win. The displays below are based on American League teams for the 2016 season. (Data in **Attendance 2016**)

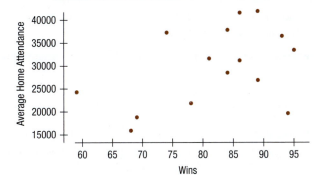

	Wins	Runs	Avg Home Att
Wins	1.000		
Runs	0.646	1.000	
Avg Home Att	0.457	0.431	1.000

a) Do winning teams generally enjoy greater attendance at their home games? Describe the association.
b) Is attendance more strongly associated with winning or scoring runs? Explain.
c) How strongly is scoring runs associated with winning games?

T 51. Mutual fund flows. As the nature of investing shifted in the 1990s (more day traders and faster flow of information using technology), the relationship between mutual fund monthly performance (*Return*) in percent and money flowing (*Flow*) into mutual funds ($ million) shifted. Using only the values for the 1990s (we'll examine later years in later chapters), answer the following questions. (You may assume that the assumptions and conditions for regression are met.)

The least squares linear regression is:

$$\widehat{Flow} = 9747 + 771\ Return.$$

a) Interpret the intercept in the linear model.
b) Interpret the slope in the linear model.
c) What is the predicted fund *Flow* for a month that had a market *Return* of 0%?
d) If during this month, the recorded fund *Flow* was $5 billion, what is the residual using this linear model? Did the model provide an underestimate or overestimate for this month?

52. Online clothing purchases. An online clothing retailer examined their transactional database to see if total yearly *Purchases* ($) were related to customers' *Incomes* ($). (You may assume that the assumptions and conditions for regression are met.)

The least squares linear regression is:

$$\widehat{Purchases} = -31.6 + 0.012\ Income.$$

a) Interpret the intercept in the linear model.

b) Interpret the slope in the linear model.

c) If a customer has an *Income* of $20,000, what is his predicted total yearly *Purchases*?

d) This customer's yearly *Purchases* were actually $100. What is the residual using this linear model? Did the model provide an underestimate or overestimate for this customer?

53. Residual plots. Tell what each of the following residual plots indicates about the appropriateness of the linear model that was fit to the data.

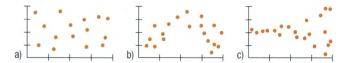

54. Residual plots, again. Tell what each of the following residual plots indicates about the appropriateness of the linear model that was fit to the data.

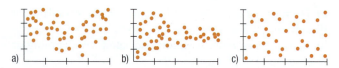

T 55. Consumer spending. An analyst at a large credit card bank is looking at the relationship between customers' charges to the bank's card in two successive months. He selects 150 customers at random, regresses charges in *March* ($) on charges in *February* ($), and finds an R^2 of 79%. The intercept is $730.20, and the slope is 0.79. After verifying all the data with the company's CPA, he concludes that the model is a useful one for predicting one month's charges from the other. Examine the data and comment on his conclusions.

56. Insurance policies. An actuary at a mid-sized insurance company is examining the sales performance of the company's sales force. She has data on the average size of the policy ($) written in two consecutive years by 200 salespeople. She fits a linear model and finds the slope to be 3.00 and the R^2 is 99.92%. She concludes that the predictions for next year's policy size will be very accurate. Examine the data and comment on her conclusions.

57. What slope? If you create a regression model for predicting the sales ($ million) from money spent on advertising the prior month ($ thousand), is the slope most likely to be closer to 0.03, 300, or 3000? Explain.

58. What slope, part 2? If you create a regression model for estimating a student's business school GPA (on a scale of 1–5) based on his math SAT (on a scale of 200–800), is the slope most likely to be closer to 0.01, 1, or 10? Explain.

59. Misinterpretations. An advertising agent who created a regression model using amount spent on *Advertising* to predict annual *Sales* for a company made these two statements. Assuming the calculations were done correctly, explain what is wrong with each interpretation.

a) My R^2 of 93% shows that this linear model is appropriate.

b) If this company spends $1.5 million on advertising, then annual sales will be $10 million.

60. More misinterpretations. An economist investigated the association between a country's *Literacy Rate* and *Gross Domestic Product (GDP)* and used the association to draw the following conclusions. Explain why each statement is incorrect. (Assume that all the calculations were done properly.)

a) The *Literacy Rate* determines 64% of the *GDP* for a country.

b) The slope of the line shows that an increase of 5% in *Literacy Rate* will produce a $1 billion improvement in *GDP*.

61. Business admissions. An analyst at a business school's admissions office claims to have developed a valid linear model predicting success (measured by starting salary ($) at time of graduation) from a student's undergraduate performance (measured by GPA). Describe how you would check each of the four regression conditions in this context.

62. School rankings. A popular magazine annually publishes rankings of both U.S. business programs and international business programs. The latest issue claims to have developed a linear model predicting the school's ranking (with "1" being the highest ranked school) from its financial resources (as measured by size of the school's endowment). Describe how you would apply each of the four regression conditions in this context.

T 63. Used BMW prices 2017. A business student needs cash, so he decides to sell his car. The car is a classic BMW "8 series" that was only made over the course of a few years in the 1990s. He would like to sell it on his own, rather than through a dealer so he'd like to predict the price he'll get for his car's model year.

a) Make a scatterplot for the data on used BMW 8's provided.

b) Describe the association between year and price.

c) Do you think a linear model is appropriate?

d) Computer software says that $R^2 = 17.2\%$. What is the correlation between year and price?

e) Explain the meaning of R^2 in this context.

f) Why doesn't this model explain 100% of the variability in the price of a used BMW 8 series?

T 64. Used BMW prices 2017, part 2. Use the advertised prices for BMW 8's given in Exercise 63 to create a linear model for the relationship between a car's *Model Year* and its *Price*.

a) Find the equation of the regression line.

b) Explain the meaning of the slope of the line.

c) Explain the meaning of the intercept of the line.

d) If you wanted to sell a 1997 BMW 8, what price seems appropriate?

e) You have a chance to buy one of two cars. They are about the same age and appear to be in equally good condition. Would you rather buy the one with a positive residual or the one with a negative residual? Explain.

T **65.** **Expensive cities.** Numbeo.com collects data from users in cities around the world on prices of a basket of goods and services and uses these data to determine a cost of living index. This index scales New York City as 100 and expresses the cost of living in other cities as a percentage of the New York cost. For example, in 2009, the cost of living index in Paris was 127.8, which means that it cost 27.8% more to live in Paris than New York that year. The scatterplot shows the index for 2017 plotted against the 2009 index for the 40 cities worldwide on which Numbeo collected data in both years.

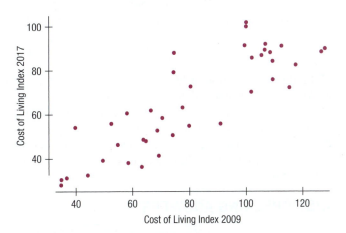

a) Describe the association between cost of living indices in 2009 and 2017.

b) The R^2 for the regression equation is 0.732. Interpret the value of R^2.

c) Find the correlation.

d) Using the data provided, find the least squares fit of the 2017 index to the 2009 index.

e) Predict the 2017 cost of living index of Paris and find its residual.

T **66.** **El Niño 2017.** Concern over the weather associated with El Niño has increased interest in the possibility that the climate on Earth is getting warmer. The most common theory relates an increase in atmospheric levels of carbon dioxide (CO_2), a greenhouse gas, to increases in temperature. Here is a scatterplot showing the mean annual CO_2 concentration in the atmosphere, measured in parts per million (ppm) at the top of Mauna Loa in Hawaii, each year from 1959 to 2016, and the global annual mean temperature (in degrees Celsius [C] from meteorological stations across the globe).

A regression predicting *Mean Temperature* from CO_2 produces the following output table (in part).

Dependent variable: Mean Temperature
R-squared = 89.5%

Variable	Coefficient
Intercept	9.786
CO_2	0.013

a) What is the correlation between CO_2 and *Mean Temperature*?

b) Explain the meaning of *R*-squared in this context.

c) Give the regression equation.

d) What is the meaning of the slope in this equation?

e) What is the meaning of the intercept of this equation?

f) Here is a scatterplot of the residuals vs. CO_2. Does this plot show evidence of the violations of any of the assumptions of the regression model? If so, which ones?

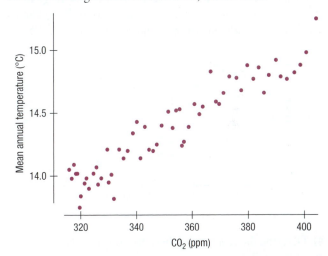

g) Suppose CO_2 levels reach 440 *ppm* in the future. What *Mean Temperature* does the model predict for that value?

T **67.** **Income and housing.** The Office of Federal Housing Enterprise Oversight (www.fhfa.gov) collects data on various aspects of housing costs around the United States. Here is a scatterplot of the *Housing Cost Index* versus the *Median Family Income* for each of the 50 states. The correlation is 0.624.

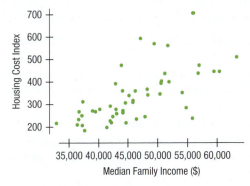

a) Describe the relationship between the *Housing Cost Index* and the *Median Family Income* by state.

b) If we standardized both variables, what would the correlation coefficient between the standardized variables be?

c) If we had measured *Median Family Income* in thousands of dollars instead of dollars, how would the correlation change?

d) Washington, DC, has a housing cost index of 548 and a median income of about $45,000. If we were to include DC in the dataset, how would that affect the correlation coefficient?

e) Do these data provide proof that by raising the median family income in a state, the housing cost index will rise as a result? Explain.

T 68. Interest rates and mortgages 2015. Since 1985, average mortgage interest rates have fluctuated from a low of nearly 3% to a high of over 14%. Is there a relationship between the amount of money people borrow and the interest rate that's offered? Here is a scatterplot of *Mortgage Loan Amount* in the United States (in trillions of dollars) versus yearly *Interest Rate* since 1985. The correlation is −0.85.

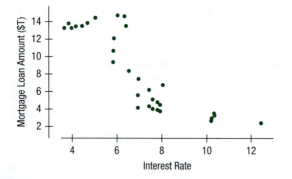

a) Describe the relationship between *Mortgage Loan Amount* and *Interest Rate*.

b) If we standardized both variables, what would the correlation coefficient between the standardized variables be?

c) If we were to measure *Mortgage Loan Amount* in billions of dollars instead of trillions of dollars, how would the correlation coefficient change?

d) Suppose that next year, interest rates were 11% and mortgages totaled $60 trillion. How would including that year with these data affect the correlation coefficient?

e) Do these data provide proof that if mortgage rates are lowered, people will take out larger mortgages? Explain.

T 69. Fuel economy 2016. Here are engine size (displacement, in liters) and gas mileage (estimated combined city and highway) for a random sample of 35 2016 model cars (taken from **Fuel Economy 2016** and identified in the data with *Sample* = "Yes").

a) Make a scatterplot for these data.

b) Describe the direction, form, and strength of the plot.

c) Find the correlation between engine size and miles per gallon.

d) Write a few sentences telling what the plot says about fuel economy.

T 70. Flights 2016. Here are the number of domestic flights flown in each year from 2000 to 2016 (www.transtats.bts.gov/homepage.asp):

Year	Flights
2000	7,905,617
2001	7,626,312
2002	8,085,083
2003	9,458,818
2004	9,968,047
2005	10,038,373
2006	9,712,750
2007	9,839,578
2008	9,378,227
2009	8,768,938
2010	8,702,365
2011	8,649,087
2012	8,446,201
2013	8,323,938
2014	8,107,802
2015	8,061,158
2016	4,036,068

a) Find the correlation of *Flights* with *Year*.

b) Make a scatterplot and describe the trend.

c) Why is the correlation you found in part a not a suitable summary of the strength of the association?

d) In turns out that the value reported for 2016 was only for the period January to June. What should we have done with that point?

JUST CHECKING ANSWERS

1. We know the scores are quantitative. We should check to see if the *Linearity Condition* and the *Outlier Condition* are satisfied by looking at a scatterplot of the two scores.

2. It won't change.

3. It won't change.

4. They are more likely to do poorly. The positive correlation means that low closing prices for Google are associated with low closing prices for Amazon.

5. No, the general association is positive, but daily closing prices may vary.

6. For each additional employee, monthly sales increase, on average, $122,740.

7. Thousands of $ per employee.

8. $1,227,400 per month.

9. No, the intercept doesn't really make sense here. A company with no employees is not likely to sell anything.

10. Differences in the number of employees account for about 71.4% of the variation in the monthly sales.

11. It's positive. The correlation and the slope have the same sign.

12. R^2, No. Slope, Yes.

CASE STUDY

Paralyzed Veterans of America

Philanthropic organizations often rely on contributions from individuals to finance the work that they do, and a national veterans' organization is no exception. The Paralyzed Veterans of America (PVA) was founded as a congressionally chartered veterans' service organization more than 60 years ago. It provides a range of services to veterans who have experienced spinal cord injury or dysfunction. Some of the services offered include medical care, research, education, and accessibility and legal consulting. In 2008, this organization had total revenue of more than $135 million, with more than 99% of this revenue coming from contributions.

An organization that depends so heavily on contributions needs a multifaceted fundraising program, and PVA solicits donations in a number of ways. From its website (www.pva.org), people can make a one-time donation, donate monthly, donate in honor or in memory of someone, and shop in the PVA online store. People can also support one of the charity events, such as its golf tournament, National Veterans Wheelchair Games, and Charity Ride.

Traditionally, one of PVA's main methods of soliciting funds was the use of return address labels and greeting cards (although still used, this method has declined in recent years). Typically, these gifts were sent to potential donors about every six weeks with a request for a contribution. From its established donors, PVA could expect a response rate of about 5%, which, given the relatively small cost to produce and send the gifts, kept the organization well funded.

But fundraising accounts for 28% of expenses, so PVA wanted to know who its donors are, what variables might be useful in predicting whether a donor is likely to give to an upcoming campaign, and what the size of that gift might be. Online is a dataset **Case study 1-PV**, which includes data designed to be very similar to part of the data that this organization works with. Here is a description of some of the variables. Keep in mind, however, that in the real dataset, there would be hundreds more variables given for each donor.

Variable Name	Units (if applicable)	Description	Remarks
Age	Years		
Own Home?	H = Yes; U = No or unknown		
Children	Counts		
Income		1 = Lowest ; 7 = Highest	Based on national medians and percentiles
Sex	M = Male; F = Female		
Total Wealth		1 = Lowest; 9 = Highest	Based on national medians and percentiles
Gifts to Other Orgs	Counts	Number of Gifts (if known) to other philanthropic organizations in the same time period	
Number of Gifts	Counts	Number of Gifts to this organization in this time period	
Time Between Gifts	Months	Time between first and second gifts	
Smallest Gift	$	Smallest Gift (in $) in the time period	See also Sqrt(Smallest Gift)
Largest Gift	$	Largest Gift (in $) in the time period	See also Sqrt(Largest Gift)
Previous Gift	$	Gift (in $) for previous campaign	See also Sqrt(Previous Gift)
Average Gift	$	Total amount donated divided by total number of gifts	See also Sqrt(Average Gift)

(continued)

Variable Name	Units (if applicable)	Description	Remarks
Current Gift	$	Gift (in $) to organization this campaign	See also Sqrt(Current Gift)
Sqrt(Smallest Gift)	Sqrt($)	Square Root of Smallest Gift in $	
Sqrt(Largest Gift)	Sqrt($)	Square Root of Largest Gift in $	
Sqrt(Previous Gift)	Sqrt($)	Square Root of Previous Gift in $	
Sqrt(Average Gift)	Sqrt($)	Square Root of Average Gift in $	
Sqrt(Current Gift)	Sqrt($)	Square Root of Current Gift in $	

Let's see what the data can tell us. Are there any interesting relationships between the current gift and other variables? Is it possible to use the data to predict who is going to respond to the next direct-mail campaign?

Recall that when variables are highly skewed or the relationship between variables is not linear, reporting a correlation coefficient is not appropriate. You may want to consider a transformed version of those variables (square roots are provided for all the variables concerning gifts) or a correlation based on the ranks of the values rather than the values themselves.

Suggested Study Plan and Questions

Write a report of what you discover about the donors to this organization. Be sure to follow the Plan, Do, Report outline for your report. Include a basic description of each variable (shape, center, and spread), point out any interesting features, and explore the relationships between the variables. In particular you should describe any interesting relationships between the current gift and other variables. Use these questions as a guide:

- Is the age distribution of the clients a typical one found in most businesses?
- Do people who give more often make smaller gifts on average?
- Do people who give to other organizations tend to give to this organization?

Describe the relationship between the Income and Wealth rankings. How do you explain this relationship (or lack of one)? (*Hint*: Look at the age distribution.)

What variables (if any) seem to have an association with the Current Gift? Do you think the organization can use any of these variables to predict the gift for the next campaign?

Optional: This file includes people who did not give to the current campaign. Do your answers to any of the questions above change if you consider only those who gave to this campaign?

CHAPTER 5

Randomness and Probability

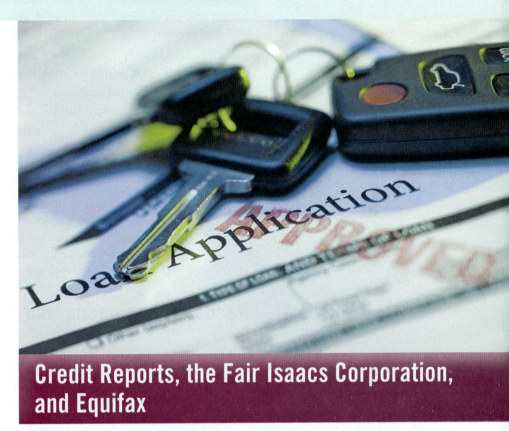

Credit Reports, the Fair Isaacs Corporation, and Equifax

You've probably never heard of the Fair Isaacs Corporation, but they probably know you. Whenever you apply for a loan, a credit card, or even a job, your credit "score" is used to determine whether you are a good risk. And because the most widely used credit scores are Fair Isaacs' FICO® scores, the company may well be involved in the decision. The Fair Isaacs Corporation (FICO) was founded in 1956, with the idea that data, used intelligently, could improve business decision making. Today, Fair Isaacs claims that their services provide companies around the world with information for more than 180 billion business decisions a year.

In 1989, Fair Isaacs invented the credit score, a number between 350 and 850 that summarizes your credit "worthiness." It's a snapshot of credit risk today based on your credit history and past behavior. Lenders of all kinds use credit scores to predict behavior, such as how likely you are to make your loan payments on time or to default on a loan. Lenders use the score to determine not only whether to give credit, but also the cost of the credit they'll offer. There are no established boundaries, but generally scores over 750 are considered excellent, and applicants with those scores get the best rates. An applicant with a score below 620 is generally considered to be a poor risk. Those with very low scores may be denied credit outright or only offered "subprime" loans at substantially higher rates.

Several companies now give consumers access to their credit scores and other credit history, but in 2017 Equifax became notorious for admitting to a security breach involving the credit information of approximately 143 million Americans. Though the attack was stated to have begun in mid-May, the breach was not observed until July 29, according to Equifax CEO Rick Smith and a subsequent report by Equifax. Information accessed by the hacker (or hackers) in the breach primarily includes first and last names, Social Security numbers, birth dates, addresses, and, in some instances, driver's license numbers and even credit card numbers.[1]

As a result of the breach, Equifax shares dropped 13 percent in early trading the day after the breach was made public and numerous lawsuits were filed against the company.

Companies have to manage risk to survive, but by its nature, risk carries uncertainty. A bank can't know for certain that you'll pay your mortgage on time—or at all. What can they do with events they can't predict? They start with the fact that, although individual outcomes cannot be anticipated with certainty, random phenomena do, in the long run, settle into patterns that are consistent and predictable. It's this property of random events that makes statistics practical.

5.1   Random Phenomena and Probability

When a customer calls the 800 number of a credit card company, he or she is asked for a card number before being connected with an operator. As the connection is made, the purchase records of that card and the demographic information of the customer are retrieved and displayed on the operator's screen. If the customer's FICO score is high enough, the operator may be prompted to "cross-sell" another service—perhaps a new "platinum" card for customers with a credit score of at least 750.

Of course, the company doesn't know which customers are going to call. Call arrivals are an example of a random phenomenon. With **random phenomena**, we can't predict the individual outcomes, but we can hope to understand characteristics of their long-run behavior. We don't know whether the *next* caller will qualify for the platinum card, but as calls come into the call center, the company will find that the percentage of platinum callers who qualify for cross-selling will settle into a pattern, like that shown in the graph in Figure 5.1.

Part of a call center operator's earnings might be based on the number of platinum cards she sells. To figure out what her potential bonus might be, an operator might first want to know what percentage of all callers qualifies. She decides to write down whether the caller from each call she gets today qualifies or not. The first caller today qualified. Then the next five callers' qualifications were no, yes, yes, no, and no. If we plot the percentage who qualify against the number of calls she's made so far the graph would start at 100% because the first caller qualified (1 out of 1, for 100%). The next caller didn't qualify, so the accumulated percentage dropped to 50% (1 out of 2). The third caller qualified (2 out of 3, or

---

FIGURE 5.1 The percentage of credit card customers who qualify for the premium card.

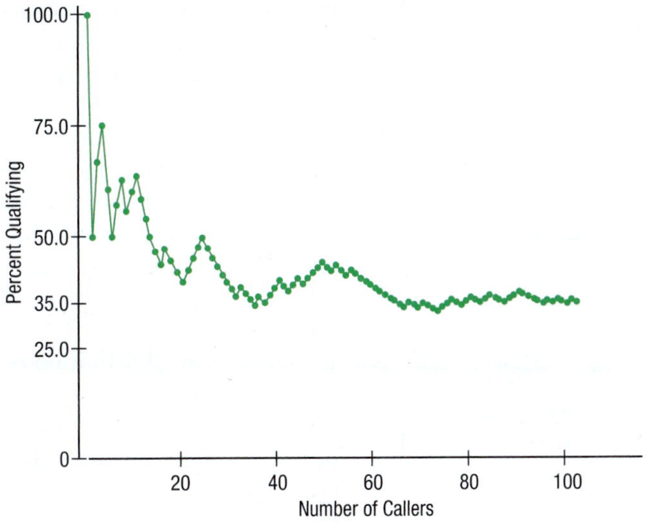

TABLE 5.1 Data on the first six callers showing their FICO score, whether they qualified for the platinum card offer, and a running percentage of number of callers who qualified.

Call	FICO Score	Qualify?	Running % Qualify
1	750	Yes	100
2	640	No	50
3	765	Yes	66.7
4	780	Yes	75
5	680	No	60
6	630	No	50
⋮	⋮	⋮	⋮

67%), then yes again (3 out of 4, or 75%), then no twice in a row (3 out of 5, for 60%, and then 3 out of 6, for 50%), and so on (Table 5.1). Each new call is a smaller fraction of the total number, so the percentages change less after each call. After a while, the graph starts to settle down and we can see that the fraction of customers who qualify is about 35% (Figure 5.1).

When talking about long-run behavior, it helps to define our terms. For any random phenomenon, each attempt, or **trial**, generates an **outcome**. For the call center, each call is a trial. Something happens on each trial, and we call whatever happens the outcome. Here the outcome is whether the caller qualifies or not. We use the more general term **event** to refer to outcomes or combinations of outcomes. For example, suppose we categorize callers into 6 risk categories and number these outcomes from 1 to 6 (of increasing credit worthiness). The three outcomes 4, 5, or 6 could make up the event "caller is at least a category 4."

We sometimes talk about the collection of *all possible outcomes*, a special event that we'll refer to as the **sample space**. We denote the sample space **S**; you may also see the Greek letter Ω used. But whatever symbol we use, the sample space is the set that contains all the possible outcomes. For the calls, if we let Q = qualified and N = not qualified, the sample space is simple: **S** = {Q, N}. If we look at two calls together, the sample space has four outcomes: **S** = {QQ, QN, NQ, NN}. If we were interested in at least one qualified caller from the two calls, we would be interested in the event (call it **A**) consisting of the three outcomes QQ, QN, and NQ, and we'd write **A** = {QQ, QN, NQ}.

Although we may not be able to predict a *particular* individual outcome, such as which incoming call represents a potential upgrade sale, we can say a lot about the long-run behavior. Look back at Figure 5.1. If you were asked for the

> A **random phenomenon** consists of **trials**. Each trial has an **outcome**. Outcomes combine to make **events**.

Probability as Long-Run Frequency

The **probability** of an event is its long-run relative frequency. A relative frequency is a fraction, so we can write it as $\frac{35}{100}$, as a decimal, 0.35, or as a percentage, 35%.

Law of Large Numbers (LLN)

The *long-run relative frequency* of repeated, independent events eventually produces the *true relative frequency* as the number of trials increases.

probability that a random caller will qualify, you might say that it was 35% because, in the *long run*, the percentage of the callers who qualify is about 35%. That's exactly what we mean by **probability**.

When we think about what happens with a series of trials, it really simplifies things if the individual trials are independent. Roughly speaking, **independence** means that the outcome of one trial doesn't influence or change the outcome of another. Recall, that in Chapter 2, we called two variables *independent* if the value of one categorical variable did not influence the value of another categorical variable. (We checked for independence by comparing relative frequency distributions across variables.) There's no reason to think that whether the one caller qualifies influences whether another caller qualifies, so these are independent trials. We'll see a more formal definition of independence later in the chapter.

You might think that we just got lucky when the percentage of the qualifying calls settled down to a number. But for independent events, we can depend on a principle called the **Law of Large Numbers (LLN)**, which states that if the events are independent, then as the number of trials increases, the long-run relative frequency of any outcome gets closer and closer to a single value. This gives us the guarantee we need and makes probability a useful concept.

Because the LLN guarantees that relative frequencies settle down in the long run, we can give a name to the value that they approach. We call it the probability of that event. For the call center, we can write $P(\text{qualified}) = 0.35$. Because it is based on repeatedly observing the event's outcome, this definition of probability is often called **empirical probability**.

5.2   The Nonexistent Law of Averages

> " Slump? I ain't in no slump. I just ain't hittin'. "
>
> —Yogi Berra

You may think it's obvious that the frequency of repeated events settles down in the long run to a single number. The discoverer of the Law of Large Numbers thought so, too. The way Jacob Bernoulli put it was: *"For even the most stupid of men is convinced that the more observations have been made, the less danger there is of wandering from one's goal."*

The Law of Large Numbers is often misunderstood to be a "law of averages." Many people believe, for example, that an outcome of a random event that hasn't occurred in many trials is "due" to occur. The original "dogs of the Dow" strategy for buying stocks recommended buying the 10 worst performing stocks of the 30 that make up the Dow Jones Industrial Average, figuring that these "dogs" were bound to do better next year. The thinking was that, since the relative frequency will settle down to the probability of that outcome in the long run, we'll have some "catching up" to do. That may seem logical, but random events don't work that way. In fact, Louis Rukeyser (the former host of *Wall Street Week*) said of the "dogs of the Dow" strategy, "that theory didn't work as promised."

Here's why. We actually know very little about the behavior of random events in the short run. The fact that we are seeing independent random events makes each individual result impossible to predict. Relative frequencies even out *only* in the long run. And the long run referred to in the LLN is really long. The "Large" in the law's name means *infinitely* large. Sequences of random events don't compensate in the short run and don't need to do so to get back to the right long-run probability. Any short-run deviations will be overwhelmed in the long run. If the probability of an outcome doesn't change and the events are independent, the probability of any outcome in another trial never changes, no matter what has happened in other trials.

Many people confuse the Law of Large numbers with the so-called Law of Averages, which says that things have to even out in the short run. But even though the Law of Averages doesn't exist at all, you'll hear people talk about it as if it does. Is a good hitter in baseball who has struck out the last six times *due* for a hit his next time up? If the stock market has been down for the last three sessions, is it *due* to increase today? No. This isn't the way random phenomena work. There is no Law of Averages for short runs—no "Law of Small Numbers." A belief in such a "law" can lead to poor business decisions.

Keno and the Law of Averages

Of course, sometimes an apparent drift from what we expect means that the probabilities are, in fact, not what we thought. If you get 10 heads in a row, maybe the coin has heads on both sides! Here's a true story that illustrates this.

Keno is a simple casino game in which numbers from 1 to 80 are chosen. The numbers, as in most lottery games, are supposed to be equally likely. Payoffs are made depending on how many of those numbers you match on your card. A group of graduate students from a statistics department decided to take a field trip to Reno. They (*very discreetly*) wrote down the outcomes of the games for a couple of days, then drove back to test whether the numbers were, in fact, equally likely. It turned out that some numbers were *more likely* to come up than others. Rather than bet on the Law of Averages and put their money on the numbers that were "due," the students put their faith in the LLN—and all their (and their friends') money on the numbers that had come up before. After they pocketed more than $50,000, they were escorted off the premises and invited never to show their faces in that casino again. Not coincidentally, the ringleader of that group currently makes his living on Wall Street.

> In addition, in time, if the roulette-betting fool keeps playing the game, the bad histories [outcomes] will tend to catch up with him.
>
> —Nassim Nicholas Taleb in *fooled by randomness*

The Law of Averages Debunked

You've just flipped a fair coin and seen six heads in a row. Does the coin "owe" you some tails? Suppose you spend that coin and your friend gets it in change. When she starts flipping the coin, should she expect a run of tails? Of course not. Each flip is a new event. The coin can't "remember" what it did in the past, so it can't "owe" any particular outcomes in the future. Just to see how this works in practice, we simulated 100,000 flips of a fair coin on a computer. In our 100,000 "flips," there were 2981 streaks of at least 5 heads. The "Law of Averages" suggests that the next flip after a run of 5 heads should be tails more often to even things out. Actually, in this particular simulation the next flip was heads more often than tails: 1550 times to 1431 times. That's 51.9% heads. You can perform a similar simulation easily.

JUST CHECKING

1 It has been shown that the stock market fluctuates randomly. Nevertheless, some investors believe that they should buy right after a day when the market goes down because it is bound to go up soon. Explain why this is faulty reasoning.

5.3   Different Types of Probability

Model-Based (Theoretical) Probability

> **Model-Based Probability**
> We can write:
> $$P(\mathbf{A}) = \frac{\text{\# of outcomes in } \mathbf{A}}{\text{total \# of outcomes}}$$
> and call this the **(theoretical) probability** of the event.

We've discussed *empirical probability*—the relative frequency of an event's occurrence as the probability of an event. There are other ways to define probability as well. Probability was first studied extensively by a group of French mathematicians who were interested in games of chance. Rather than experiment with the games and risk losing their money, they developed mathematical models of probability. To make things simple (as we usually do when we build models), they started by looking at games in which the different outcomes were equally likely.

Fortunately, many games of chance are like that. Any of 52 cards is equally likely to be the next one dealt from a well-shuffled deck. Each face of a die is equally likely to land up (or at least it should be).

When we have equally likely outcomes, we write the **(theoretical) probability** of an event **A**, as $P(A) =$ # of outcomes in **A**/total # of outcomes possible. When outcomes are equally likely, the probability that one of them occurs is easy to compute—it's just 1 divided by the number of possible outcomes. So the probability of rolling a 3 with a fair die is one in six, which we write as $1/6$. The probability of picking the ace of spades from a well-shuffled deck is $1/52$.

It's almost as simple to find probabilities for events that are made up of several equally likely outcomes. We just count all the outcomes that the event contains. The probability of the event is the number of outcomes in the event divided by the total number of possible outcomes.

For example, Pew Research reports that of 10,190 randomly generated working phone numbers called for a survey, the initial results of the calls were as follows:

Result	Number of Calls
No Answer	311
Busy	61
Answering Machine	1336
Callbacks	189
Other Non-Contacts	893
Contacted Numbers	7400

The phone numbers were generated randomly, so each was equally likely. To find the probability of a contact, we just divide the number of contacts by the number of calls: $7400/10,190 = 0.7262$.

But don't get trapped into thinking that random events are always equally likely. The chance of winning a lottery—especially lotteries with very large payoffs—is small. Regardless, people continue to buy tickets.

Personal Probability

What's the probability that gold will sell for more than $2000 an ounce at the end of next year? You may be able to come up with a number that seems reasonable. Of course, no matter what your guess is, your probability should be between 0 and 1. In our discussion of probability, we've defined probability in two ways: (1) in terms of the relative frequency—or the fraction of times—that an event occurs in the long run or (2) as the number of outcomes in the event divided by the total number of outcomes. Neither situation applies to your assessment of gold's chances of selling for more than $2000.

We use the *language* of probability in everyday speech to express a degree of uncertainty without necessarily basing it on long-run relative frequencies. Your personal assessment of an event expresses your uncertainty about the outcome. We call this kind of probability a subjective, or **personal probability**.

Although personal probabilities may be based on experience, they are typically not based on long-run relative frequencies or on equally likely events. But, like the two other probabilities we defined, they need to satisfy the same rules as both empirical and theoretical probabilities that we'll discuss in the next section.

5.4   Probability Rules

For some people, the phrase "50/50" means something vague like "I don't know" or "whatever." But when we discuss probabilities, 50/50 has the precise meaning that two outcomes are *equally likely*. Speaking vaguely about probabilities can get you into trouble, so it's wise to develop some formal rules about how probability works. These rules apply to probability whether we're dealing with empirical, theoretical, or personal probability.

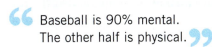

" Baseball is 90% mental. The other half is physical. "

—Yogi Berra

Rule 1. If the probability of an event occurring is 0, the event won't occur; likewise if the probability is 1, the event will *always* occur. Even if you think an event is very unlikely, its probability can't be negative, and even if you're sure it will happen, its probability can't be greater than 1. So we require that:

A probability is a number between 0 and 1.
For any event A, $0 \leq P(A) \leq 1$.

Rule 2. If a random phenomenon has only one possible outcome, it's not very interesting (or very random). So we need to distribute the probabilities among all the outcomes a trial can have. How can we do that so that it makes sense? For example, consider the behavior of a certain stock. The possible daily outcomes might be:

A: The stock price goes up.
B: The stock price goes down.
C: The stock price remains the same.

When we assign probabilities to these outcomes, we should be sure to distribute all of the available probability. Something always occurs, so the probability of *something* happening is 1. This is called the **Probability Assignment Rule**:

The probability of the set of all possible outcomes must be 1.
$$P(S) = 1$$

where **S** is the sample space.

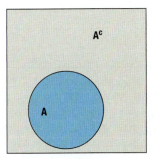

The set **A** and its complement **A**^{C}. Together, they make up the entire sample space **S**.

Rule 3. Suppose the probability that you get to class on time is 0.8. What's the probability that you don't get to class on time? Yes, it's 0.2. The set of outcomes that are *not* in the event **A** is called the "complement" of **A** and is denoted **A**^{C}. This leads to the **Complement Rule**:

The probability of an event occurring is 1 minus the probability
that it doesn't occur.
$$P(A) = 1 - P(A^C)$$

IN PRACTICE 5.1   Applying the complement rule

Lee's Lights sells lighting fixtures. Some customers are there only to browse, so Lee records the behavior of all customers for a week to assess how likely it is that a customer will make a purchase. Lee finds that of 1000 customers entering the store during the week, 300 make purchases. Lee concludes that the probability of a customer making a purchase is 0.30.

MANAGER (LEE) What is the probability that a walk-in customer *doesn't* make a purchase?

ANALYST We know the probability of a purchase is 30%. Because "no purchase" is the complement of "purchase,"

$$P(\text{no purchase}) = 1 - P(\text{purchase})$$
$$= 1 - 0.30 = 0.70$$

There is a 70% chance a walk-in customer won't make a purchase.

Rule 4. Whether or not a caller qualifies for a platinum card is a random outcome. Suppose the probability of qualifying is 0.35. What's the chance that the next two callers qualify? The **Multiplication Rule** says that to find the probability that two independent events occur, we multiply the probabilities. For two independent events **A** and **B**, the probability that both **A** *and* **B** occur is the product of the probabilities of the two events:

$$P(A \text{ and } B) = P(A) \times P(B), \text{ provided that A and B are independent.}$$

Thus if **A** = {customer 1 qualifies} and **B** = {customer 2 qualifies}, the chance that both qualify is:

$$0.35 \times 0.35 = 0.1225$$

Of course, to calculate this probability, we have used the assumption that the two events are independent. We'll expand the Multiplication Rule to be more general later in this chapter.

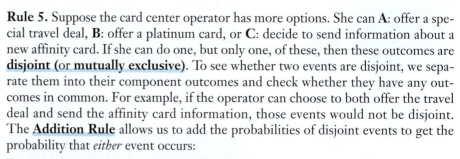

IN PRACTICE 5.2   Using the multiplication rule

Lee knows that the probability that a customer will make a purchase is 30%.

MANAGER (LEE)   What is the probability that the next two customers both make purchases?

ANALYST   If we can assume that customers behave independently, then we can use the Multiplication Rule.

$P(\text{first customer makes a purchase } and \text{ second customer makes a purchase})$
$= P(\text{purchase}) \times P(\text{purchase})$
$= 0.30 \times 0.30 = 0.09$

There's about a 9% chance that the next two customers will both make purchases.

Rule 5. Suppose the card center operator has more options. She can **A**: offer a special travel deal, **B**: offer a platinum card, or **C**: decide to send information about a new affinity card. If she can do one, but only one, of these, then these outcomes are **disjoint (or mutually exclusive)**. To see whether two events are disjoint, we separate them into their component outcomes and check whether they have any outcomes in common. For example, if the operator can choose to both offer the travel deal and send the affinity card information, those events would not be disjoint. The **Addition Rule** allows us to add the probabilities of disjoint events to get the probability that *either* event occurs:

$$P(A \text{ or } B) = P(A) + P(B), \text{ provided that A and B are disjoint.}$$

Thus the probability that the caller *either* is offered a platinum card *or* is sent the affinity card information is the sum of the two probabilities, since the events are disjoint.

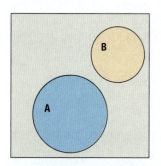

Two disjoint sets, **A** and **B**.

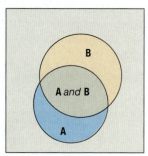

Two sets **A** and **B** that are not disjoint. The event (**A** *and* **B**) is their intersection.

IN PRACTICE 5.3   Using the addition rule

Some customers prefer to see the merchandise but then make their purchase later using Lee's Lights' website. Lee offers a promotion to attempt to track customer behavior. Customers leaving the store without making a purchase are offered a "bonus code" to use at the Internet site. Using these codes, Lee determines that there's a 9% chance of a customer making a purchase using the code later. We know that about 30% of customers make purchases when they enter the store.

> **MANAGER (LEE)**   What is the probability that a customer who enters the store will not make a purchase at all?
>
> **ANALYST**   We can use the Addition Rule because the alternatives "no purchase at all," "purchase in the store," and "purchase online" are disjoint events.
>
> $$P(\text{purchase in the store } or \text{ online}) = P(\text{purchase in store}) + P(\text{purchase online})$$
> $$= 0.30 + 0.09 = 0.39$$
>
> $$P(\text{no purchase at all}) = P(\text{not (purchase in the store } or \text{ purchase online)})$$
> $$= 1 - P(\text{in store } or \text{ online})$$
> $$= 1 - 0.39 = 0.61$$

NOTATION ALERT

You may see the event (**A** or **B**) written as (**A** $\cup$ **B**). The symbol $\cup$ means "union" and represents the outcomes in event **A** or event **B**. Similarly the symbol $\cap$ means intersection and represents outcomes that are in *both* event **A** and event **B**. You may see the event (**A** *and* **B**) written as (**A** $\cap$ **B**).

Rule 6. Suppose we would like to know the probability that either of the next two callers qualifies for a platinum card? We know $P(\mathbf{A}) = P(\mathbf{B}) = 0.35$, but $P(\mathbf{A} \text{ or } \mathbf{B})$ is not simply the sum $P(\mathbf{A}) + P(\mathbf{B})$ because the events $\mathbf{A}$ and $\mathbf{B}$ are not disjoint in this case. Both customers could qualify. So we need a new probability rule.

We can't simply add the probabilities of $\mathbf{A}$ and $\mathbf{B}$ because that would count the outcome of *both* customers qualifying twice. So, if we started by adding the two probabilities, we could compensate by subtracting out the probability that both qualify. In other words,

$$P(\text{customer A } or \text{ customer B qualifies}) =$$
$$P(\text{customer A qualifies}) + P(\text{customer B qualifies}) - P(\text{both customers qualify})$$
$$= (0.35) + (0.35) - (0.35 \times 0.35) \text{ (since events are independent)}$$
$$= (0.35) + (0.35) - (0.1225)$$
$$= 0.5775$$

It turns out that this method works in general. We add the probabilities of two events and then subtract out the probability of their intersection. This gives us the **General Addition Rule**, which does not require disjoint events:

$$P(\mathbf{A} \textit{ or } \mathbf{B}) = P(\mathbf{A}) + P(\mathbf{B}) - P(\mathbf{A} \textit{ and } \mathbf{B}) \text{ for any two events A and B.}$$

IN PRACTICE 5.4   Using the general addition rule

MANAGER (LEE)   Often there are two customers in the store at the same time. I'd expect that our chance of making at least one sale would be 60% = 30% + 30%. But I see in our data that this isn't the case. Are our salespeople doing something wrong? When two customers enter the store together, what is the probability that *at least one* of them makes a purchase?

ANALYST   I've looked at the data and the salespeople are not at fault.[2] The problem is that the probabilities of the two customers making purchases are not disjoint; either or both could choose to make a purchase. According to the data, there's a 20% chance that both will make a purchase, so when you added the probabilities together you were double-counting. (Even with four customers in the store we couldn't add 0.30 + 0.30 + 0.30 + 0.30 and be certain of a purchase.) We must use the General Addition Rule.

$$P(\text{at least one purchases}) = P(\text{A purchases } or \text{ B purchases})$$
$$= P(\text{A purchases}) + P(\text{B purchases})$$
$$- P(\text{A and B both purchase})$$
$$= 0.30 + 0.30 - 0.20 = 0.40$$

---

[2]The analyst also wonders how this manager got the job.

JUST CHECKING

2 Even successful companies sometimes make products with high failure rates. One (in) famous example is the Apple 40GB click wheel iPod, which used a tiny disk drive for storage. According to Macintouch.com, 30% of those devices eventually failed. It is reasonable to assume that the failures were independent. What would a store that sold these devices have seen?

   a) What is the probability that a particular 40GB click wheel iPod failed?

   b) What is the probability that two 40GB click wheel iPods sold together *both* failed?

   c) What is the probability that the store's first failure problem was the third one they sold?

   d) What is the probability the store had a failure problem with at least one of the five that they sold on a particular day?

GUIDED EXAMPLE   M&M's Modern Market Research

In 1941, when M&M's® milk chocolate candies were introduced to American GIs in World War II, there were six colors: brown, yellow, orange, red, green, and violet. Mars®, the company that manufactures M&M's, has used the introduction of a new color as a marketing and advertising event several times in the years since then. In 1980, the candy went international, adding 16 countries to their markets. In 1995, the company conducted a "worldwide survey" to vote on a new color. Over 10 million people voted to add blue. They even got the lights of the Empire State Building in New York City to glow blue to help announce the addition. In 2002, they used the Internet to help pick a new color. Children from over 200 countries were invited to respond via the Internet, telephone, or mail. Millions of voters chose among purple, pink, and teal. The global winner was purple, and for a brief time, purple M&M's could be found in packages worldwide (although in 2013, the colors were brown, yellow, red, blue, orange, and green). In the United States, 42% of those who voted said purple, 37% said teal, and only 19% said pink. But in Japan the percentages were 38% pink, 36% teal, and only 16% purple. Let's use Japan's percentages to ask some questions.

1. What's the probability that a Japanese M&M's survey respondent selected at random preferred either pink or teal?
2. If we pick two respondents at random, what's the probability that they *both* selected purple?
3. If we pick three respondents at random, what's the probability that *at least one* preferred purple?

| **PLAN** | **Setup** The probability of an event is its long-term relative frequency. This can be determined in several ways: by looking at many replications of an event, by deducing it from equally likely events, or by using some other information. Here, we are told the relative frequencies of the three responses. | The M&M's website reports the proportions of Japanese votes by color. These give the probability of selecting a voter who preferred each of the colors:

$$P(pink) = 0.38$$ $$P(teal) = 0.36$$ $$P(purple) = 0.16$$ |

Make sure the probabilities are legitimate. Here, they're not. Either there was a mistake or the other voters must have chosen a color other than the three given. A check of other countries shows a similar deficit, so probably we're seeing those who had no preference or who wrote in another color.

Each is between 0 and 1, but these don't add up to 1. The remaining 10% of the voters must have not expressed a preference or written in another color. We'll put them together into "other" and add $P(other) = 0.10$

With this addition, we have a legitimate assignment of probabilities.

Question 1: What's the probability that a Japanese M&M's survey respondent selected at random preferred either pink or teal?

PLAN	**Setup** Decide which rules to use and check the conditions they require.	The events "pink" and "teal" are individual outcomes (a respondent can't choose both colors), so they are disjoint. We can apply the General Addition Rule anyway.

DO	**Mechanics** Show your work.	$$P(pink\ or\ teal) = P(pink) + P(teal)$$ $$- P(pink\ and\ teal)$$ $$= 0.38 + 0.36 - 0 = 0.74$$ The probability that both pink and teal were chosen is zero, since respondents were limited to one choice.

REPORT	**Conclusion** Interpret your results in the proper context.	The probability that the respondent said pink or teal is 0.74.

Question 2: If we pick two respondents at random, what's the probability that they both said purple?

PLAN	**Setup** The word "both" suggests we want $P(\mathbf{A}\ and\ \mathbf{B})$, which calls for the Multiplication Rule. Check the required condition.	**Independence** It's unlikely that the choice made by one respondent affected the choice of the other, so the events seem to be independent. We can use the Multiplication Rule.

DO	**Mechanics** Show your work.
	
	For both respondents to pick purple, each one has to pick purple.
		$P(both\ purple)$
		$= P(first\ respondent\ picks\ purple\ and$
		    $second\ respondent\ picks\ purple)$
		$= P(first\ respondent\ picks\ purple)$
		    $\times\ P(second\ respondent\ picks\ purple)$
		$= 0.16 \times 0.16 = 0.0256$

REPORT	**Conclusion** Interpret your results in the proper context.	The probability that both respondents pick purple is 0.0256.

(continued)

Question 3: If we pick three respondents at random, what's the probability that at least one preferred purple?

PLAN	**Setup** The phrase "at least one" often flags a question best answered by looking at the complement, and that's the best approach here. The complement of "at least one preferred purple" is "none of them preferred purple."	$$P(\text{at least one picked purple})$$ $$= P(\{\text{none picked purple}\}^c)$$ $$= 1 - P(\text{none picked purple}).$$
	Check the conditions.	**Independence.** These are independent events because they are choices by three random respondents. We can use the Multiplication Rule.
DO	**Mechanics** We calculate P(none purple) by using the Multiplication Rule.	$$P(\text{none picked purple}) = P(\text{first not purple})$$ $$\times\, P(\text{second not purple})$$ $$\times\, P(\text{third not purple})$$ $$= [P(\text{not purple})]^3.$$ $$P(\text{not purple}) = 1 - P(\text{purple})$$ $$= 1 - 0.16 = 0.84.$$ So $P(\text{none picked purple}) = (0.84)^3 = 0.5927.$
	Then we can use the Complement Rule to get the probability we want.	$$P(\text{at least 1 picked purple})$$ $$= 1 - P(\text{none picked purple})$$ $$= 1 - 0.5927 = 0.4073.$$
REPORT	**Conclusion** Interpret your results in the proper context.	There's about a 40.7% chance that at least one of the respondents picked purple.

5.5   Joint Probability and Contingency Tables

As part of a Pick Your Prize Promotion, a chain store invited customers to choose which of three prizes they'd like to win (while providing name, address, phone number, and e-mail address). At one store, the responses could be placed in the contingency table in Table 5.2.

		Prize Preference			
		MP3	**Camera**	**Bike**	**Total**
Sex	**Man**	117	50	60	227
	Woman	130	91	30	251
	Total	247	141	90	478

TABLE 5.2 Prize preference for 478 customers.

If the winner is chosen at random from these customers, the probability we select a woman is just the corresponding relative frequency (since we're equally likely to select any of the 478 customers). There are 251 women in the data out of a total of 478, giving a probability of:

$$P(\text{woman}) = 251/478 = 0.525$$

A **marginal probability** uses a marginal frequency (from either the Total row or Total column) to compute the probability.

This is called a **marginal probability** because it depends only on totals found in the margins of the table. The same method works for more complicated events. For example, what's the probability of selecting a woman whose preferred prize is the camera? Well, 91 women named the camera as their preference, so the probability is:

$$P(\text{woman } and \text{ camera}) = 91/478 = 0.190$$

Probabilities such as these are called **joint probabilities** because they give the probability of two events occurring together.

The probability of selecting a customer whose preferred prize is a bike is:

$$P(\text{bike}) = 90/478 = 0.188$$

IN PRACTICE 5.5 Marginal probabilities

Lee suspects that men and women make different kinds of purchases at Lee's Lights (see In Practice 5.1 on page 163). The table shows the purchases made by the last 100 customers.

	Utility Lighting	Fashion Lighting	Total
Men	40	20	60
Women	10	30	40
Total	50	50	100

MANAGER (LEE) What's the probability that one of our customers is a woman? What is the probability that a random customer is a man who purchases fashion lighting?

ANALYST From the marginal totals we can see that 40% of our customers are women, so the probability that a customer is a woman is 0.40. The cell of the table for Men who purchase Fashion lighting has 20 of the 100 customers, so the probability of that event is 0.20.

5.6 Conditional Probability and the General Multiplication Rule

Since our sample space is these 478 customers, we can recognize the relative frequencies as probabilities. What if we are given the information that the selected customer is a woman? Would that change the probability that the selected customer's preferred prize is a bike? You bet it would! The pie charts in Figure 5.2 on the next page show that women are much less likely to say their preferred prize is a bike than are men. When we restrict our focus to women, we look only at the women's row of the table, which gives the conditional distribution of preferred prizes given "woman." Of the 251 women, only 30 of them said their preferred prize was a bike. We write the probability that a selected customer wants a bike *given* that we have selected a woman as:

$$P(\text{bike}|\text{woman}) = 30/251 = 0.120$$

For men, we look at the conditional distribution of preferred prizes given "man" shown in the top row of the table. There, of the 227 men, 60 said their

Women

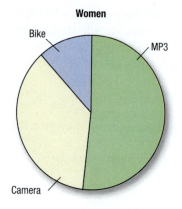

Men

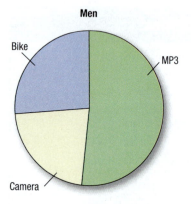

FIGURE 5.2 Conditional distributions of *Prize Preference* for *Women* and for *Men*.

Independence

If we had to pick one key idea in this chapter that you should understand and remember, it's the definition and meaning of independence.

preferred prize was a bike. So, $P(\text{bike}|\text{man}) = 60/227 = 0.264$, more than twice the women's probability (see Figure 5.2).

In general, when we want the probability of an event from a *conditional* distribution, we write $P(\mathbf{B}|\mathbf{A})$ and pronounce it "the probability of **B** *given* **A**." A probability that takes into account a given *condition* such as this is called a **conditional probability**.

Let's look at what we did. We worked with the counts, but we could work with the probabilities just as well. There were 30 women who selected a bike as a prize, and there were 251 women customers. So we found the probability to be 30/251. To find the probability of the event **B** *given* the event **A**, we restrict our attention to the outcomes in **A**. We then find in what fraction of *those* outcomes **B** also occurred. Formally, we write:

$$P(\mathbf{B}|\mathbf{A}) = \frac{P(\mathbf{A} \text{ and } \mathbf{B})}{P(\mathbf{A})}$$

We can use the formula directly with the probabilities derived from the contingency table (Table 5.2) to find:

$$P(\text{bike}|\text{woman}) = \frac{P(\text{bike and woman})}{P(\text{woman})} = \frac{30/478}{251/478} = \frac{30}{251} = 0.120 \text{ as before.}$$

The formula for conditional probability requires one restriction. The formula works only when the event that's given has probability greater than 0. The formula doesn't work if $P(\mathbf{A})$ is 0 because that would mean we had been "given" the fact that **A** was true even though the probability of **A** is 0, which would be a contradiction.

Rule 7. Remember the Multiplication Rule for the probability of **A** *and* **B**? It said

$$P(\mathbf{A} \text{ and } \mathbf{B}) = P(\mathbf{A}) \times P(\mathbf{B})$$

when **A** and **B** are independent. Now we can write a more general rule that doesn't require independence. In fact, we've already written it. We just need to rearrange the equation a bit.

The equation in the definition for conditional probability contains the probability of **A** *and* **B**. Rearranging the equation gives the **General Multiplication Rule** for compound events that does not require the events to be independent:

$$P(\mathbf{A} \text{ and } \mathbf{B}) = P(\mathbf{A}) \times P(\mathbf{B}|\mathbf{A}) \text{ for any two events A and B.}$$

The probability that two events, **A** and **B**, both occur is the probability that event **A** occurs multiplied by the probability that event **B** also occurs *given* that event **A** occurs.

Of course, there's nothing special about which event we call **A** and which one we call **B**. We should be able to state this the other way around. Indeed we can. It is equally true that:

$$P(\mathbf{A} \text{ and } \mathbf{B}) = P(\mathbf{B}) \times P(\mathbf{A}|\mathbf{B}).$$

Let's return to the question of just what it means for events to be independent. We said informally in Chapter 2 that what we mean by independence is that the outcome of one event does not influence the probability of the other. With our new notation for conditional probabilities, we can write a formal definition. Events **A** and **B** are **independent** whenever:

$$P(\mathbf{B}|\mathbf{A}) = P(\mathbf{B}).$$

Now we can see that the Multiplication Rule for independent events is just a special case of the General Multiplication Rule. The general rule says

$$P(\mathbf{A} \text{ and } \mathbf{B}) = P(\mathbf{A}) \times P(\mathbf{B}|\mathbf{A})$$

whether the events are independent or not. But when events **A** and **B** are independent, we can write $P(\mathbf{B})$ for $P(\mathbf{B}|\mathbf{A})$ and we get back our simple rule:

$$P(\mathbf{A} \textit{ and } \mathbf{B}) = P(\mathbf{A}) \times P(\mathbf{B}).$$

Sometimes people use this statement as the definition of independent events, but we find the other definition more intuitive. When events are independent, the fact that one has occurred does not affect the probability of the other.

Using our earlier example, is the probability of the event *choosing a bike* independent of the sex of the customer? We need to check whether

$$P(\text{bike}|\text{man}) = \frac{P(\text{bike } \textit{and } \text{man})}{P(\text{man})} = \frac{0.126}{0.475} = 0.264$$

is the same as $P(\text{bike}) = 0.188$.

Because these probabilities aren't equal, we can say that prize preference is *not* independent of the sex of the customer. Whenever at least one of the joint probabilities in the table is *not* equal to the product of the marginal probabilities, we say that the variables are not independent.

IN PRACTICE 5.6   Multiplying probabilities

MANAGER   I see from the margins of the table (see In Practice 5.5) that the chance that one of our customers is a woman is 40% and the chance of a fashion light sale is 50%. So I figure that the chance that a female customer would purchase fashion lighting would be 50% × 40% = 20%. Should I tell that to Marketing?

ANALYST   That would only be the right way to figure if the chance of a fashion lighting purchase was independent of the gender of the customer. But that doesn't appear to be true in our data. The correct way to make the calculation when we don't have independence is

$$P(\text{Woman } \textit{and } \text{Fashion}) = P(\text{Woman}) \times P(\text{Fashion}|\text{Woman})$$
$$= 0.40 \times 0.30/0.40 = 0.30$$

Looking at the contingency table, I see that this is the value in the cell for Woman and Fashion.

Independent vs. Disjoint

Are disjoint events independent? Both concepts seem to have similar ideas of separation and distinctness about them, but in fact disjoint events *cannot* be independent.[3] Let's see why. Consider the two disjoint events {you get an A in this course} and {you get a B in this course}. They're disjoint because they have no outcomes in common. Suppose you learn that you *did* get an A in the course. Now what is the probability that you got a B? You can't get both grades, so it must be 0.

Think about what that means. The fact that the first event (getting an A) occurred changed the probability for the second event (down to 0). So these events aren't independent.

Mutually exclusive events can never be independent. They have no outcomes in common, so knowing that one occurred means the other didn't. A common error

---

[3]Technically two disjoint events *can* be independent, but only if the probability of one of the events is 0. For practical purposes, we can ignore this case, since we don't anticipate collecting data about things that don't happen.

is to treat disjoint events as if they were independent and apply the Multiplication Rule for independent events. Don't make that mistake.

Are events A and B independent or disjoint?	
Independent	Check whether $P(\mathbf{B}\,|\,\mathbf{A}) = P(\mathbf{B})$ or Check whether $P(\mathbf{A}\,|\,\mathbf{B}) = P(\mathbf{A})$ or Check whether $P(\mathbf{A}\ and\ \mathbf{B}) = P(\mathbf{A}) \times P(\mathbf{B})$
Disjoint	Check whether $P(\mathbf{A}\ and\ \mathbf{B}) = 0$ or Check whether events A and B overlap in a sample space diagram or Check whether the two events can occur together

IN PRACTICE 5.7   Conditional probability

MANAGER (LEE) If a customer purchases a Fashion light, what is the probability that the customer is a woman?

ANALYST Using the table from In Practice 5.5 on page 169,

$$P(\text{Woman}\,|\,\text{Fashion}) = P(\text{Woman}\ and\ \text{Fashion})/P(\text{Fashion})$$
$$= 0.30/0.50 = 0.60$$

5.7   Constructing Contingency Tables

Sometimes we're given probabilities without a contingency table. You can often construct a simple table to correspond to the probabilities.

A survey of real estate in upstate New York classified homes into two price categories (Low—less than $175,000 and High—over $175,000). It also noted whether the houses had at least 2 bathrooms or not (True or False). We are told that 56% of the houses had at least 2 bathrooms, 62% of the houses were Low priced, and 22% of the houses were both. That's enough information to fill out the table. Translating the percentages to probabilities, we have:

		At Least 2 Bathrooms		
		True	**False**	**Total**
Price	**Low**	0.22		0.62
	High			
	Total	0.56		1.00

The 0.56 and 0.62 are marginal probabilities, so they go in the margins. What about the 22% of houses that were both low priced and had at least 2 bathrooms? That's a *joint* probability, so it belongs in the interior of the table.

Because the cells of the table show disjoint events, the probabilities always add to the marginal totals going across rows or down columns.

		At Least 2 Bathrooms		
		True	**False**	**Total**
Price	**Low**	0.22	0.40	0.62
	High	0.34	0.04	0.38
	Total	0.56	0.44	1.00

Now, finding any other probability is straightforward. For example, what's the probability that a high-priced house has at least 2 bathrooms?

$$P(\text{at least 2 bathrooms} \mid \text{high-priced})$$
$$= P(\text{at least 2 bathrooms } and \text{ high-priced}) / P(\text{high-priced})$$
$$= 0.34/0.38 = 0.895 \text{ or } 89.5\%.$$

JUST CHECKING

3 Suppose a supermarket is conducting a survey to find out the busiest time and day for shoppers. Survey respondents are asked (1) whether they shopped at the store on a weekday or on the weekend and (2) whether they shopped at the store before or after 5 PM. The survey revealed that:

- 48% of shoppers visited the store before 5 PM
  27% of shoppers visited the store on a weekday (Mon.–Fri.)
- 7% of shoppers visited the store before 5 PM on a weekday.

a) Make a contingency table for the variables *time of day* and *day of week*.

b) What is the probability that a randomly selected shopper who shops on a weekday also shops before 5 PM?

c) Are time and day of the week disjoint events?

d) Are time and day of the week independent events?

5.8 Probability Trees

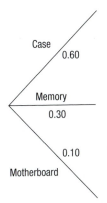

Some business decisions involve more subtle evaluation of probabilities. Given the probabilities of various outcomes, we can use a picture called a probability tree or **tree diagram** to help think through the decision-making process. A tree shows sequences of events as paths that look like branches of a tree. This can enable us to compare several possible scenarios. Here's a manufacturing example.

Personal electronic devices, such as smartphones and tablets, are getting more capable all the time. Manufacturing components for these devices is a challenge, and at the same time, consumers are demanding more and more functionality and increasing sturdiness. Microscopic and even submicroscopic flaws that can cause intermittent performance failures can develop during their fabrication. Defects will always occur, so the quality engineer in charge of the production process must monitor the number of defects and take action if the process seems out of control.

Let's suppose that the engineer is called down to the production line because the number of defects has crossed a threshold and the process has been declared to be out of control. She must decide between two possible actions. She knows that a small adjustment to the robots that assemble the components can fix a variety of problems, but for more complex problems, the entire production line needs to be shut down in order to pinpoint the problem. The adjustment requires that production be stopped for about an hour. But shutting down the line takes at least an entire shift (8 hours). Naturally, her boss would prefer that she make the simple adjustment. But without knowing the source or severity of the problem, she can't be sure whether that will be successful.

If the engineer wants to predict whether the smaller adjustment will work, she can use a probability tree to help make the decision. Based on her experience, the engineer thinks that there are three possible problems: (1) the motherboards could have faulty connections, (2) the memory could be the source of the faulty connections, or (3) some of the cases may simply be seating incorrectly in the assembly line. She knows from past experience how often these types of problem crop up and how likely it is that just making an adjustment will fix each type of problem. *Motherboard* problems are rare (10%), *memory* problems have been showing up about 30% of the time, and *case* alignment issues occur most often (60%). We can put those probabilities on the first set of branches in Figure 5.3.

FIGURE 5.3 Possible problems and their probabilities.

Notice that we've covered all the possibilities, and so the probabilities sum to one. To this diagram we can now add the *conditional* probabilities that a minor adjustment will fix each type of problem. Most likely the engineer will rely on her experience or assemble a team to help determine these probabilities. For example, the engineer knows that motherboard connection problems are not likely to be fixed with a simple adjustment: $P(\text{Fix}\,|\,\text{Motherboard}) = 0.10$. After some discussion, she and her team determine that $P(\text{Fix}\,|\,\text{Memory}) = 0.50$ and $P(\text{Fix}\,|\,\text{Case alignment}) = 0.80$. At the end of each branch representing the problem type, we draw two possible outcomes (*Fixed* or *Not Fixed*) and write the conditional probabilities on the branches.

FIGURE 5.4 Extending the tree diagram, we can show both the problem class and the outcome probabilities. The outcome (Fixed or Not fixed) probabilities are conditional on the problem type, and they change depending on which branch we follow.

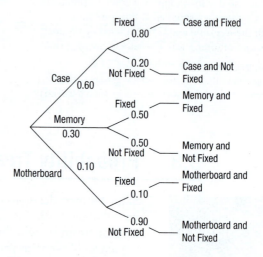

At the end of each second branch, we write the *joint event* corresponding to the combination of the two branches. For example, the top branch is the combination of the problem being Case alignment, and the outcome of the small adjustment is that the problem is now Fixed. For each of the joint events, we can use the General Multiplication Rule to calculate their joint probability. For example:

$$P(\textit{Case and Fixed}) = P(\textit{Case}) \times P(\textit{Fixed}\,|\,\textit{Case})$$
$$= 0.60 \times 0.80 = 0.48$$

We write this probability next to the corresponding event. Doing this for all branch combinations gives us Figure 5.5.

FIGURE 5.5 We can find the probabilities of compound events by multiplying the probabilities along the branch of the tree that leads to the event, just the way the General Multiplication Rule specifies.

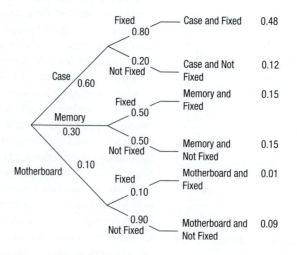

All the outcomes at the far right are disjoint because at every node, all the choices are disjoint alternatives. And those alternatives are *all* the possibilities, so the probabilities on the far right must add up to one.

Because the final outcomes are disjoint, we can add up any combination of probabilities to find probabilities for compound events. In particular, the engineer can answer her question: What's the probability that the problem will be fixed by a simple adjustment? She finds all the outcomes on the far right in which the problem was fixed. There are three (one corresponding to each type of problem), and she adds their probabilities: $0.48 + 0.15 + 0.01 = 0.64$. So 64% of all problems are fixed by the simple adjustment. The other 36% require a major investigation.

*5.9 Reversing the Conditioning: Bayes' Rule

The engineer in our story decided to try the simple adjustment and, fortunately, it worked. Now she needs to report to the quality engineer on the next shift what she thinks the problem was. Was it more likely to be a case alignment problem or a motherboard problem? We know the probabilities of those problems beforehand, but they change now that we have more information. What are the likelihoods that each of the possible problems was, in fact, the one that occurred?

Unfortunately, we can't read those probabilities from the tree in Figure 5.5. For example, the tree gives us $P(Fixed\ and\ Case) = 0.48$, but we want $P(Case\,|\,Fixed)$. We know $P(Fixed\,|\,Case) = 0.80$, but that's not the same thing. It isn't valid to reverse the order of conditioning in a conditional probability statement. To "turn the probability around," we need to go back to the definition of conditional probability.

$$P(Case\,|\,Fixed) = \frac{P(Case\ and\ Fixed)}{P(Fixed)}$$

We can read the probability in the numerator from the tree, and we've already calculated the probability in the denominator by adding all the probabilities on the final branches that correspond to the event *Fixed*. Putting those values in the formula, the engineer finds:

$$P(Case\,|\,Fixed) = \frac{0.48}{0.48 + 0.15 + 0.01} = 0.75$$

She knew that 60% of all problems were due to case alignment, but now that she knows the problem has been fixed, she knows more. Given the additional information that a simple adjustment was able to fix the problem, she now can increase the probability that the problem was case alignment to 0.75.

It's usually easiest to solve problems like this by reading the appropriate probabilities from the tree. However, we can write a general formula for finding the reverse conditional probability. To understand it, let's review our example again. Let $\mathbf{A}_1 = \{Case\}$, $\mathbf{A}_2 = \{Memory\}$, and $\mathbf{A}_3 = \{Motherboard\}$ represent the three types of problems. Let $\mathbf{B} = \{Fixed\}$, meaning that the simple adjustment fixed the problem. We know $P(\mathbf{B}\,|\,\mathbf{A}_1) = 0.80$, $P(\mathbf{B}\,|\,\mathbf{A}_2) = 0.50$, and $P(\mathbf{B}\,|\,\mathbf{A}_3) = 0.10$. We want to find the reverse probabilities, $P(\mathbf{A}_i\,|\,\mathbf{B})$, for the three possible problem types. From the definition of conditional probability, we know (for any of the three types of problems):

$$P(\mathbf{A}_i\,|\,\mathbf{B}) = \frac{P(\mathbf{A}_i\ and\ \mathbf{B})}{P(\mathbf{B})}$$

We still don't know either of these quantities, but we use the definition of conditional probability again to find $P(\mathbf{A}_i \ and \ \mathbf{B}) = P(\mathbf{B}|\mathbf{A}_i)P(\mathbf{A}_i)$, both of which we know. Finally, we find $P(\mathbf{B})$ by adding up the probabilities of the three events.

$$P(\mathbf{B}) = P(\mathbf{A}_1 \ and \ \mathbf{B}) + P(\mathbf{A}_2 \ and \ \mathbf{B}) + P(\mathbf{A}_3 \ and \ \mathbf{B}) =$$
$$P(\mathbf{B}|\mathbf{A}_1)P(\mathbf{A}_1) + P(\mathbf{B}|\mathbf{A}_2)P(\mathbf{A}_2) + P(\mathbf{B}|\mathbf{A}_3)P(\mathbf{A}_3)$$

In general, we can write this for n events $\mathbf{A}_i$ that are mutually exclusive (each pair is disjoint) and exhaustive (their union is the whole space). Then:

$$P(\mathbf{A}_i|\mathbf{B}) = \frac{P(\mathbf{B}|\mathbf{A}_i)P(\mathbf{A}_i)}{\sum_j P(\mathbf{B}|\mathbf{A}_j)P(\mathbf{A}_j)}$$

This formula is known as Bayes' rule, after the Reverend Thomas Bayes (1702–1761), even though historians don't really know if Bayes first came up with the reverse conditioning probability. When you need to find reverse conditional probabilities, we recommend drawing a tree and finding the appropriate probabilities as we did at the beginning of the section, but the formula gives the general rule.

⊘ WHAT CAN GO WRONG?

- **Beware of probabilities that don't add up to 1.** To be a legitimate assignment of probability, the sum of the probabilities for all possible outcomes must total 1. If the sum is less than 1, you may need to add another category ("other") and assign the remaining probability to that outcome. If the sum is more than 1, check that the outcomes are disjoint. If they're not, then you can't assign probabilities by counting relative frequencies. (And if they are, you must locate the error.)

- **Don't add probabilities of events if they're not disjoint.** Events must be disjoint to use the Addition Rule. The probability of being under 80 *or* a female is not the probability of being under 80 *plus* the probability of being female. That sum may be more than 1.

- **Don't multiply probabilities of events if they're not independent.** The probability of selecting a customer at random who is over 70 years old *and* retired is not the probability the customer is over 70 years old *times* the probability the customer is retired. Knowing that the customer is over 70 changes the probability of his or her being retired. You can't multiply these probabilities. The multiplication of probabilities of events that are not independent is one of the most common errors people make in dealing with probabilities.

- **Don't confuse disjoint and independent.** Disjoint events *can't* be independent. If $\mathbf{A}$ = {you get a promotion} and $\mathbf{B}$ = {you don't get a promotion}, $\mathbf{A}$ and $\mathbf{B}$ are disjoint. Are they independent? If you find out that $\mathbf{A}$ is true, does that change the probability of $\mathbf{B}$? Yes, if $\mathbf{A}$ is true, then $\mathbf{B}$ cannot be true, so they are not independent.

ETHICS IN ACTION

Fabrizio Rivetti is an entrepreneur who has recently started a wine importing business. While he currently has an exclusive relationship with only one premier winery in Tuscany, he is hoping to expand his importing business to include other wineries as well as artisan Italian food products, such as cheeses and specialty meats.

With plans to expand, Fabrizio is in need of extra funds. As a first step, he approaches a friend and fellow entrepreneur who has considerable experience dealing with angel investors, Chas Mulligan. Chas has successfully obtained funds from angel investors for his social networking startup company, so Fabrizio is hopeful that Chas can provide some sound advice. Chas explains to Fabrizio that most angel investors bear considerable risk and consequently favor ventures that are in high-growth areas, such as software, health care, and biotech. He also mentions that many angel investors, like venture capitalists, want to exercise some control over the startup companies in which they invest, either by securing a seat on the company's board of directors or having veto power.

Fabrizio is now a bit unsure about seeking angel investments, so Chas puts him in contact with a consultant, Paula Foxx, who can help him make the right decision. Paula is well connected with a network of angel investors, understands the types of startups they prefer to invest in, and, most importantly, knows how to prepare the perfect pitch. At their first meeting, Paula is quick to inform Fabrizio of her consultancy fee schedule. Next, she assures Fabrizio that she is acquainted with a number of angels whom she believes might be interested in his wine importing business. Fabrizio expresses to Paula his reservations about sharing too much control of his startup with investors, and is particularly wary of granting investors veto power.

He is reluctant to hire Paula on the spot, so Paula suggests they meet again after she has had the opportunity to pull together data on some of her most successful clients. Paula's objective is to direct clients to angels who tend to make large initial investments. In this way, her clients reach their goals more quickly and she can spend less time with each client. She decides to compile some data only for angel investors who have made significant initial investments in her clients' startups (in excess of $250,000). She came up with the following contingency table for this group of investors.

		Veto Power?		
		Yes	No	Total
Board Seat?	Yes	0.05	0.45	0.50
	No	0.45	0.05	0.50
	Total	0.50	0.50	1.00

She was happy to find that 50% did not get veto power and 50% did not sit on the board. By multiplying these two probabilities, she arrived at a figure she thought would help persuade Fabrizio to pursue angels and hire her to do so. She planned to tell him that 25% of angels who make large investments are not interested in either veto power or a seat on the board in the startups they fund. She called her administrative assistant to arrange another meeting with Fabrizio as soon as possible.

- **Identify the ethical dilemma in this scenario.**
- **What are the undesirable consequences?**
- **Propose an ethical solution that considers the welfare of all stakeholders.**

5 FROM LEARNING TO EARNING

LEARNING OBJECTIVES   **Apply the facts about probability to determine whether an assignment of probabilities is legitimate.**

- Probability is long-run relative frequency.
- Individual probabilities must be between 0 and 1.
- The sum of probabilities assigned to all outcomes must be 1.

Understand the Law of Large Numbers and that the common understanding of the "Law of Averages" is false.

Know the rules of probability and how to apply them.

- The **Complement Rule** says that $P(not\ \mathbf{A}) = P(\mathbf{A^C}) = 1 - P(\mathbf{A})$.
- The **Multiplication Rule** for independent events says that $P(\mathbf{A}\ and\ \mathbf{B}) = P(\mathbf{A}) \times P(\mathbf{B})$ provided events **A** and **B** are independent.
- The **General Multiplication Rule** says that $P(\mathbf{A}\ and\ \mathbf{B}) = P(\mathbf{A}) \times P(\mathbf{B}|\mathbf{A})$ for any events **A** and **B**.
- The **Addition Rule** for disjoint events says that $P(\mathbf{A}\ or\ \mathbf{B}) = P(\mathbf{A}) + P(\mathbf{B})$ provided events A and B are disjoint.
- The **General Addition Rule** says that $P(\mathbf{A}\ or\ \mathbf{B}) = P(\mathbf{A}) + P(\mathbf{B}) - P(\mathbf{A}\ and\ \mathbf{B})$ for any events **A** and **B**.

Know how to construct and read a contingency table.

Know how to define and use independence.

- Events A and B are independent if $P(\mathbf{A}|\mathbf{B}) = P(\mathbf{A})$.

Know how to construct tree diagrams and use them to calculate and understand conditional probabilities.

Know how to use Bayes' Rule to compute conditional probabilities.

TERMS

Addition Rule
If **A** and **B** are disjoint events, then the probability of **A** *or* **B** is
$$P(\mathbf{A}\ or\ \mathbf{B}) = P(\mathbf{A}) + P(\mathbf{B}).$$

Complement Rule
The probability of an event occurring is 1 minus the probability that it doesn't occur:
$$P(\mathbf{A}) = 1 - P(\mathbf{A^C}).$$

Conditional probability
$$P(\mathbf{B}|\mathbf{A}) = \frac{P(\mathbf{A}\ and\ \mathbf{B})}{P(\mathbf{A})}.$$
$P(\mathbf{B}|\mathbf{A})$ is read "the probability of **B** *given* **A**."

Disjoint (or mutually exclusive) events
Two events are disjoint if they have no outcomes in common. If **A** and **B** are disjoint, then the fact that **A** occurs tells us that **B** cannot occur. Disjoint events are also called "mutually exclusive."

Empirical probability
When the probability comes from the long-run relative frequency of the event's occurrence, it is an empirical probability.

Event
A collection of outcomes. Usually, we identify events so that we can attach probabilities to them. We denote events with bold capital letters such as **A**, **B**, or **C**.

General Addition Rule
For any two events, **A** and **B**, the probability of **A** *or* **B** is:
$$P(\mathbf{A}\ or\ \mathbf{B}) = P(\mathbf{A}) + P(\mathbf{B}) - P(\mathbf{A}\ and\ \mathbf{B}).$$

General Multiplication Rule
For any two events, **A** and **B**, the probability of **A** *and* **B** is:
$$P(\mathbf{A}\ and\ \mathbf{B}) = P(\mathbf{A}) \times P(\mathbf{B}|\mathbf{A}).$$

Independence (informally)
Two events are *independent* if the fact that one event occurs does not change the probability of the other.

Independence (used formally)
Events **A** and **B** are independent when $P(\mathbf{B}|\mathbf{A}) = P(\mathbf{B})$.

Joint probabilities
The probability that two events both occur.

Law of Large Numbers (LLN)
The Law of Large Numbers states that the *long-run relative frequency* of repeated, independent events settles down to the *true relative frequency* as the number of trials increases.

Marginal probability
In a joint probability table a marginal probability is the probability distribution of either variable separately, usually found in the rightmost column or bottom row of the table.

Multiplication Rule	If **A** and **B** are independent events, then the probability of **A** *and* **B** is:
	$$P(\mathbf{A}\text{ and }\mathbf{B}) = P(\mathbf{A}) \times P(\mathbf{B}).$$
Outcome	The outcome of a trial is the value measured, observed, or reported for an individual instance of that trial.
Personal probability	When the probability is subjective and represents one's personal degree of belief, it is called a personal probability.
Probability	The probability of an event is a number between 0 and 1 that reports the likelihood of the event's occurrence. A probability can be derived from a model (such as equally likely outcomes), from the long-run relative frequency of the event's occurrence, or from subjective degrees of belief. We write $P(\mathbf{A})$ for the probability of the event **A**.
Probability Assignment Rule	The probability of the entire sample space must be 1:
	$$P(S) = 1.$$
Random phenomenon	A phenomenon is random if we know what outcomes *could* happen, but not which particular values *will* happen in any given trial.
Sample space	The collection of all possible outcome values. The sample space has a probability of 1.
Theoretical probability	When the probability comes from a mathematical model (such as, but not limited to, equally likely outcomes), it is called a theoretical probability.
Trial	A single attempt or realization of a random phenomenon.
Tree diagram (or probability tree)	A display of conditional events or probabilities that is helpful in thinking through conditioning.

TECH SUPPORT   Generating Random Numbers

Most statistics packages generate single or lists of random numbers. You may find them useful for introducing randomness in a study or drawing a random sample. Excel can generate random numbers with the **RAND( )** function.

EXCEL

To generate a random number in Excel:

- In a cell, type **=RAND( )**. A random number between 0 and 1 (a real number to 9 decimal places) appears in the cell.
- To generate more random numbers, copy and paste this cell or select it and **Fill Down** to obtain more random values.
- To generate a random number within a range, type **=RAND( )*(b − a) + a** into the formula bar where **a** is the number at the low end of the range and **b** is the number at the high end of the range.
- You can also use the function **=RANDBETWEEN(a, b)** to generate an integer between a and b.

Random numbers are re-generated each time a change is made to the spreadsheet. To avoid this:

- Highlight the cell containing the random number.
- Copy the value and paste into same cell using the **Paste Values: Values** command.

All statistics programs generate "pseudo-random" numbers. That is, they use an algorithm that produces numbers that are almost indistinguishable from truly random values, but, because they are generated by an algorithm, are not truly random. You can obtain truly random numbers online at the site www.random.org.

BRIEF CASE

Global Markets

A global survey firm reports data from surveys taken in several countries. The data file **Global** holds data for 800 respondents in each of five countries. The variables provide demographic information (sex, age, education, marital status) and responses to questions of interest to marketers on personal finance and purchasing.

Write a report that discusses how decisions about personal finance and shopping vary by country and by sex. You'll want to make contingency tables of some variables and consider the contingent probabilities that they show. You may also want to restrict your attention to one country and then consider relationships between variables within that country.

CHAPTER 5 EXERCISES

SECTION 5.1

1. Indicate which of the following represent independent events. Explain briefly.

a) The gender of customers using an ATM machine.
b) The last digit of the social security numbers of students in a class.
c) The scores you receive on the first midterm, second midterm, and the final exam of a course.

2. Indicate which of the following represent independent events. Explain briefly.

a) Prices of houses on the same block.
b) Successive measurements of your heart rate as you exercise on a treadmill.
c) Measurements of the heart rates of all students in the gym.

SECTION 5.2

3. In many state lotteries, you can choose which numbers to play. Consider a common form in which you choose 5 numbers. Which of the following strategies can improve your chance of winning? If the method works, explain why. If not, explain why using appropriate statistics terms.

a) Always play 1, 2, 3, 4, 5.
b) Choose the numbers that did come up in the most recent lottery drawing because they are "hot."

4. For the same kind of lottery as in Exercise 3, which of the following strategies can improve your chance of winning? If the method works, explain why. If not, explain why using appropriate statistics terms.

a) Choose randomly from among the numbers that have *not* come up in the last 3 lottery drawings because they are "due."
b) Generate random numbers using a computer or calculator and play those.

SECTION 5.4

5. A recent survey found that, despite airline requests, about 40% of passengers don't fully turn off their cell phones during takeoff and landing (although they may put them in "airplane mode"). The two passengers across the aisle (in seats A and B) clearly do not know each other.

a) What is the probability that the passenger in seat A does not turn off his phone?
b) What is the probability that he does turn off his phone?
c) What is the probability that both of them turn off their phones?
d) What is the probability that at least one of them turns off his or her phone?

6. At your school, 10% of the class are marketing majors. If you are randomly assigned to two partners in your statistics class,

a) What is the probability that the first partner will be a marketing major?
b) What is the probability that the first partner won't be a marketing major?
c) What is the probability that both will be marketing majors?
d) What is the probability that at least one will be a marketing major?

SECTION 5.5

7. The following contingency table shows opinion about global warming among U.S. adults, broken down by political party affiliation (based on a poll in October 2012 by Pew Research found at www.people-press.org/2012/10/15/more-say-there-is-solid-evidence-of-global-warming/).

		Opinion on Global Warming		
		Nonissue	Serious Concern	Total
Political Party	Democratic	85	415	500
	Republican	290	210	500
	Independent	70	130	200
	Total	445	755	1200

a) What is the probability that a U.S. adult selected at random from these 1200 respondents believes that global warming is a serious issue?
b) What type of probability did you find in part a?
c) What is the probability that a U.S. adult selected at random is a Republican and believes that global warming is a serious issue?
d) What type of probability did you find in part c?

8. Multigenerational families can be categorized as having two adult generations, such as parents living with adult children, "skip" generation families, such as grandparents living with grandchildren, and three or more generations living in the household. Pew Research surveyed multigenerational households. This table is based on their reported results.

	2 Adult Gens	2 Skip Gens	3 or More Gens	
White	509	55	222	786
Hispanic	139	11	142	292
Black	119	32	99	250
Asian	61	1	48	110
	828	99	511	1438

a) What is the probability that a multigenerational family is Hispanic?
b) What is the probability that a multigenerational family selected at random is a Black, two-adult-generation family?
c) What type of probability did you find in parts a and b?

SECTION 5.6

9. Using the table from Exercise 7,

a) What is the probability that a randomly selected U.S. adult who is a Republican believes that global warming is a serious issue?

b) What is the probability that a randomly selected U.S. adult is a Republican given that he or she believes global warming is a serious issue?
c) What is $P(\text{Serious Concern} \mid \text{Democratic})$?

10. Using the table from Exercise 8,

a) What is the probability that a randomly selected Black multigenerational family is a two-adult-generation family?
b) What is the probability that a randomly selected multigenerational family is White, given that it is a "skip" generation family?
c) What is $P(3 \text{ or more Generations} \mid \text{Asian})$?

SECTION 5.7

11. A national survey indicated that 30% of adults conduct their banking online. It also found that 40% are under the age of 50, and that 25% are under the age of 50 and conduct their banking online.

a) What percentage of adults do not conduct their banking online?
b) What type of probability is the 25% mentioned above?
c) Construct a contingency table showing all joint and marginal probabilities.
d) What is the probability that an individual conducts banking online given that the individual is under the age of 50?
e) Are *Banking online* and *Age* independent? Explain.

12. Facebook reports that 70% of their users are from outside the United States and that 50% of their users log on to Facebook every day. Suppose that 20% of their users are United States users who log on every day.

a) What percentage of Facebook's users are from the United States?
b) What type of probability is the 20% mentioned above?
c) Construct a contingency table showing all the joint and marginal probabilities.
d) What is the probability that a user is from the United States given that he or she logs on every day?
e) Are *From United States* and *Log on Every Day* independent? Explain.

SECTION 5.8

13. Summit Projects provides marketing services and website management for many companies that specialize in outdoor products and services. To understand customer Web behavior, the company experiments with different offers and website design. The results of such experiments can help to maximize the probability that customers purchase products during a visit to a website. Possible actions by the website include offering the customer an instant discount, offering the customer free shipping, or doing nothing. A recent experiment found that customers make purchases 6% of the time when offered the instant discount, 5% when offered free shipping, and 2% when no special offer was given. Suppose 20% of the customers are offered the discount and an additional 30% are offered free shipping.

a) Construct a probability tree for this experiment.
b) What percent of customers who visit the site made a purchase?
c) Given that a customer made a purchase, what is the probability that they were offered free shipping?

14. The company in Exercise 13 performed another experiment in which they tested three website designs to see which one would lead to the highest probability of purchase. The first (design A) used enhanced product information, the second (design B) used extensive iconography, and the third (design C) allowed the customer to submit their own product ratings. After 6 weeks of testing, the designs delivered probabilities of purchase of 4.5%, 5.2%, and 3.8%, respectively. Equal numbers of customers were sent randomly to each website design.

a) Construct a probability tree for this experiment.
b) What percent of customers who visited the site made a purchase?
c) What is the probability that a randomly selected customer was sent to design C?
d) Given that a customer made a purchase, what is the probability that the customer had been sent to design C?

SECTION 5.9

15. According to U.S. Census data, 68% of the civilian U.S. labor force self-identifies as White, 11% as Black, and the remaining 21% as Hispanic/Latino or Other. Among Whites in the labor force, 54% are Male, and 46% Female. Among Blacks, 52% are Male and 48% Female, and among Hispanic/Latino/Other, 58% are Male and 42% are Female.

a) Polling companies need to sample an appropriate number of respondents of each gender from each ethnic group. For a randomly selected U.S. worker, fill in the probabilities in this tree:

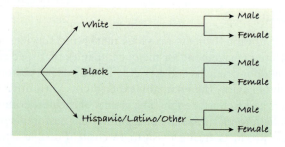

b) What is the probability that a randomly selected worker is a Black Female?
c) For a randomly selected worker, what is $P(Female \mid White)$?
d) For a randomly selected worker, what is $P(White \mid Female)$?

16. U.S. Customs and Border Protection has been testing automated kiosks that may be able to detect lies (www .wired.com/threatlevel/2013/01/ff-lie-detector/all/). One measurement used (among several) is involuntary eye movements. Using this method alone, tests show that it can detect 60% of lies, but incorrectly identifies 15% of true statements as lies. Suppose that 95% of those entering the country tell the truth. The immigration kiosk asks questions such as "Have you ever been arrested for a crime?" Naturally, all the applicants answer "No," but the kiosk identifies some of those answers as lies, and refers the entrant to a human interviewer.

a) Here is the outline of a probability tree for this situation. Fill in the probabilities:

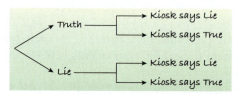

b) What is the probability that a random person will be telling the truth and will be cleared by the kiosk?
c) What is the probability that a person who is rejected by the kiosk was actually telling the truth?

CHAPTER EXERCISES

17. What does it mean? Part 1. Respond to the following questions:

a) A casino claims that its roulette wheel is truly random. What should that claim mean?
b) A reporter on *Market Place* says that there is a 50% chance that the NASDAQ will hit a new high in the next month. What is the meaning of such a phrase?

18. What does it mean? Part 2. Respond to the following questions:

a) After an unusually dry autumn, a radio announcer is heard to say, "Watch out! We'll pay for these sunny days later on this winter." Explain what he's trying to say, and comment on the validity of his reasoning.
b) A batter who had failed to get a hit in seven consecutive times at bat then hits a game-winning home run. When talking to reporters afterward, he says he was very confident that last time at bat because he knew he was "due for a hit." Comment on his reasoning.

19. Airline safety. Even though commercial airlines have excellent safety records, in the weeks following a crash, airlines often report a drop in the number of passengers, probably because people are afraid to risk flying.

a) A travel agent suggests that since the law of averages makes it highly unlikely to have two plane crashes within a few weeks of each other, flying soon after a crash is the safest time. What do you think?

b) If the airline industry proudly announces that it has set a new record for the longest period of safe flights, would you be reluctant to fly? Are the airlines due to have a crash?

20. Economic predictions. An investment newsletter makes general predictions about the economy to help their clients make sound investment decisions.

a) Recently they said that because the stock market had been up for the past three months in a row that it was "due for a correction" and advised their client to reduce their holdings. What "law" are they applying? Comment.
b) They advised buying a stock that had gone down in the past four sessions because they said that it was clearly "due to bounce back." What "law" are they applying? Comment.

21. Fire insurance. Insurance companies collect annual payments from homeowners in exchange for paying to rebuild houses that burn down.

a) Why should you be reluctant to accept a $3000 payment from your neighbor to replace his house should it burn down during the coming year?
b) Why can the insurance company make that offer?

22. Casino gambling. Recently, the International Gaming Technology company issued the following press release:

(LAS VEGAS, Nev.)—Cynthia Jay was smiling ear to ear as she walked into the news conference at the Desert Inn Resort in Las Vegas today, and well she should. Last night, the 37-year-old cocktail waitress won the world's largest slot jackpot—$34,959,458—on a Megabucks machine. She said she had played $27 in the machine when the jackpot hit. Nevada Megabucks has produced 49 major winners in its 14-year history. The top jackpot builds from a base amount of $7 million and can be won with a 3-coin ($3) bet.

a) How can the Desert Inn afford to give away millions of dollars on a $3 bet?
b) Why did the company issue a press release? Wouldn't most businesses want to keep such a huge loss quiet?

23. Toy company. A toy company is preparing to market an electronic game for young children that "randomly" generates a color. They suspect, however, that the way the random color is determined may not be reliable, so they ask the programmers to perform tests and report the frequencies of each outcome. Are each of the following probability assignments possible? Why or why not?

	Red	Yellow	Green	Blue
a)	0.25	0.25	0.25	0.25
b)	0.10	0.20	0.30	0.40
c)	0.20	0.30	0.40	0.50
d)	0	0	1.00	0
e)	0.10	0.20	1.20	−1.50

Probabilities of ...

24. Store discounts. Many stores run "secret sales": Shoppers receive cards that determine how large a discount they get, but the percentage is revealed by scratching off that black stuff (what *is* that?) only after the purchase has been totaled at the cash register. The store is required to reveal (in the fine print) the distribution of discounts available. Are each of these probability assignments plausible? Why or why not?

	10% Off	20% Off	30% Off	50% Off
a)	0.20	0.20	0.20	0.20
b)	0.50	0.30	0.20	0.10
c)	0.80	0.10	0.05	0.05
d)	0.75	0.25	0.25	−0.25
e)	1.00	0	0	0

Probabilities of ...

25. Quality control. A tire manufacturer recently announced a recall because 2% of its tires are defective. If you just bought a new set of four tires from this manufacturer, what is the probability that at least one of your new tires is defective?

26. Pepsi promotion. For a sales promotion, the manufacturer places winning symbols under the caps of 10% of all Pepsi bottles. If you buy a six-pack of Pepsi, what is the probability that you win something?

27. Auto warranty. In developing their warranty policy, an automobile company estimates that over a 1-year period 17% of their new cars will need to be repaired once, 7% will need repairs twice, and 4% will require three or more repairs. If you buy a new car from them, what is the probability that your car will need:

a) No repairs?
b) No more than one repair?
c) Some repairs?

28. Consulting team. You work for a large global management consulting company. Of the entire work force of analysts, 55% have had no experience in the telecommunications industry, 32% have had limited experience (less than 5 years), and the rest have had extensive experience (5 years or more). On a recent project, you and two other analysts were chosen at random to constitute a team. It turns out that part of the project involves telecommunications. What is the probability that the first teammate you meet has:

a) Extensive telecommunications experience?
b) Some telecommunications experience?
c) No more than limited telecommunications experience?

29. Auto warranty, part 2. Consider again the auto repair rates described in Exercise 27. If you bought two new cars, what is the probability that:

a) Neither will need repair?
b) Both will need repair?
c) At least one car will need repair?

30. Consulting team, part 2. You are assigned to be part of a team of three analysts of a global management consulting company as described in Exercise 28. What is the probability that of your other two teammates:

a) Neither has any telecommunications experience?
b) Both have some telecommunications experience?
c) At least one has had extensive telecommunications experience?

31. Auto warranty, again. You used the Multiplication Rule to calculate repair probabilities for your cars in Exercise 29.

a) What must be true about your cars in order to make that approach valid?
b) Do you think this assumption is reasonable? Explain.

32. Final consulting team project. You used the Multiplication Rule to calculate probabilities about the telecommunications experience of your consulting teammates in Exercise 30.

a) What must be true about the groups in order to make that approach valid?
b) Do you think this assumption is reasonable? Explain.

33. Real estate. In a sample of real estate ads, 64% of homes for sale had garages, 21% have swimming pools, and 17% have both features. What is the probability that a home for sale has:

a) A pool, a garage, or both?
b) Neither a pool nor a garage?
c) A pool but no garage?

34. Human resource data. Employment data at a large company reveal that 72% of the workers are married, 44% are college graduates, and half of the college grads are married. What's the probability that a randomly chosen worker is:

a) Neither married nor a college graduate?
b) Married but not a college graduate?
c) Married or a college graduate?

35. Mars product information. The Mars company says that before the introduction of purple, yellow made up 20% of their plain M&M candies, red made up another 20%, and orange, blue, and green each made up 10%. The rest were brown.

a) If you picked an M&M at random from a pre-purple bag of candies, what is the probability that it was:
  i) Brown?
  ii) Yellow or orange?
  iii) Not green?
  iv) Striped?

b) Assuming you had an infinite supply of M&M's with the older color distribution, if you picked three M&M's in a row, what is the probability that:
  i) They are all brown?
  ii) The third one is the first one that's red?
  iii) None are yellow?
  iv) At least one is green?

36. American Red Cross. The American Red Cross must track their supply and demand for various blood types. They estimate that about 45% of the U.S. population has Type O blood, 40% Type A, 11% Type B, and the rest Type AB.

a) If someone volunteers to give blood, what is the probability that this donor:
  i) Has Type AB blood?
  ii) Has Type A or Type B blood?
  iii) Is not Type O?
b) Among four potential donors, what is the probability that:
  i) All are Type O?
  ii) None have Type AB blood?
  iii) Not all are Type A?
  iv) At least one person is Type B?

37. More Mars product information. In Exercise 35, you calculated probabilities of getting various colors of M&M's.

a) If you draw one M&M, are the events of getting a red one and getting an orange one disjoint or independent or neither?
b) If you draw two M&M's one after the other, are the events of getting a red on the first and a red on the second disjoint or independent or neither?
c) Can disjoint events ever be independent? Explain.

38. American Red Cross, part 2. In Exercise 36, you calculated probabilities involving various blood types.

a) If you examine one donor, are the events of the donor being Type A and the donor being Type B disjoint or independent or neither? Explain your answer.
b) If you examine two donors, are the events that the first donor is Type A and the second donor is Type B disjoint or independent or neither?
c) Can disjoint events ever be independent? Explain.

39. Tax accountant. A recent study of IRS audits showed that, for estates worth less than $5 million, about 1 out of 7 of all estate tax returns are audited, but that probability increases to 50% for estates worth over $5 million. Suppose a tax accountant has three clients who have recently filed returns for estates worth more than $5 million. What are the probabilities that:

a) All three will be audited?
b) None will be audited?
c) At least one will be audited?
d) What did you assume in calculating these probabilities?

40. Casinos. Because gambling is big business, calculating the odds of a gambler winning or losing in every game is crucial to the financial forecasting for a casino. A standard slot machine has three wheels that spin independently. Each has 10 equally likely symbols: 4 bars, 3 lemons, 2 cherries, and a bell. If you play once, what is the probability that you will get:

a) 3 lemons?
b) No fruit symbols?
c) 3 bells (the jackpot)?
d) No bells?
e) At least one bar (an automatic loser)?

41. Spam filter. A company has recently replaced their e-mail spam filter because investigations had found that the volume of spam e-mail was interrupting productive work on about 15% of workdays. To see how bad the situation was, calculate the probability that during a 5-day work week, e-mail spam would interrupt work:

a) On Monday and again on Tuesday?
b) For the first time on Thursday?
c) Every day?
d) At least once during the week?

42. Tablet tech support. The technical support desk at a college has set up a special service for tablets. A survey shows that 54% of tablets on campus run Apple's iOS, 43% run Google's Android OS, and 3% run Microsoft's Windows. Assuming that users of each of the operating systems are equally likely to call in for technical support what is the probability that of the next three calls:

a) All are iOS?
b) None are Android?
c) At least one is a Windows machine?
d) All are Windows machines?

43. Casinos, part 2. In addition to slot machines, casinos must understand the probabilities involved in card games. Suppose you are playing at the blackjack table, and the dealer shuffles a deck of cards. The first card shown is red. So is the second and the third. In fact, you are surprised to see 5 red cards in a row. You start thinking, "The next one is due to be black!"

a) Are you correct in thinking that there's a higher probability that the next card will be black than red? Explain.
b) Is this an example of the Law of Large Numbers? Explain.

44. Inventory. A shipment of road bikes has just arrived at The Spoke, a small bicycle shop, and all the boxes have been placed in the back room. The owner asks her assistant to start bringing in the boxes. The assistant sees 20 identical-looking boxes and starts bringing them into the shop at random. The owner knows that she ordered 10 women's and 10 men's bicycles, and so she's surprised to find that the first six are all women's bikes. As the seventh box is brought in, she starts thinking, "This one is bound to be a men's bike."

a) Is she correct in thinking that there's a higher probability that the next box will contain a men's bike? Explain.
b) Is this an example of the Law of Large Numbers? Explain.

45. U.S. economic conditions 2017. A Gallup Poll in September 2017 asked U.S. adults to rate economic conditions in the country today as "excellent," "good," "only fair," or "poor." The results are below:

Current Economic Conditions	
Response	Number of Respondents
Excellent/Good	1190
Only Fair	1575
Poor	735
Total	**3500**

If we select a person at random from this sample of 1500 adults:

a) What is the probability that the person responded "Poor"?
b) What is the probability that the person responded "Fair" or "Poor"?

46. More economic conditions 2017. Exercise 45 shows the results of a Gallup Poll about U.S. economic conditions. Suppose we select three adults at random from this sample.

a) What is the probability that all three responded "Poor"?
b) What is the probability that none responded "Poor"?
c) What assumption did you make in computing these probabilities?
d) Explain why you think that assumption is reasonable.

47. Owning guns. The General Social Survey, run annually, asked respondents "Do you have in your home (or garage) any guns or revolvers?" The responses are given in the table (sda.berkeley.edu/cgi-bin/hsda?harcsda+gss10).

Gun Ownership	
Response	Number of Respondents
Yes	410
No	815
Don't Know/Refused	45
Total	**1270**

a) If we select a random person from this sample of 1270 adults, what is the probability that their response will be "No"?
b) What is the probability that their response will be "Don't know/refused"?
c) Show another way to calculate the probability in part b. (Hint: Use the complement.)

48. Gun ownership, part 2. Exercise 47 shows the results of a poll that asked about gun ownership. Suppose we select three adults at random from this sample.

a) What is the probability that all three respond "Yes"?
b) What is the probability that none responded "Yes"?
c) What assumption did you make in computing these probabilities?
d) Explain why you think that assumption is reasonable.

49. Contract bidding. As manager for a construction firm, you are in charge of bidding on two large contracts. You believe the probability you get contract #1 is 0.8. If you get contract #1, the probability you also get contract #2 will be 0.2, and if you do not get #1, the probability you get #2 will be 0.4.

a) Sketch the probability tree.
b) What is the probability you will get both contracts?
c) Your competitor hears that you got the second contract but hears nothing about the first contract. Given that you got the second contract, what is the probability that you also got the first contract?

50. Extended warranties. A company that manufactures and sells consumer video cameras sells two versions of their popular hard disk camera, a basic camera for $750, and a deluxe version for $1250. About 75% of customers select the basic camera. Of those, 60% purchase the extended warranty for an additional $200. Of the people who buy the deluxe version, 90% purchase the extended warranty.

a) Sketch the probability tree for total purchases.
b) What is the percentage of customers who buy an extended warranty?
c) What is the expected revenue of the company from a camera purchase (including warranty if applicable)?
d) Given that a customer purchases an extended warranty, what is the probability that he or she bought the deluxe version?

51. News Report 2017. A Pew Research report on September 13, 2017, reported that 61% of 18–29 year olds watch TV using online streaming services. (By contrast, only 5% of those 65 and older watch online.) The table below shows the proportions within each age group using various sources to watch TV, as well as the percentage of the U.S. population that each age group represents.

	Age Group			
	18–29	30–49	50–64	65+
Cable or satellite	0.31	0.52	0.70	0.84
Online streaming	0.61	0.37	0.10	0.05
Digital antenna	0.05	0.07	0.15	0.07
Percent of U.S. population	16.5	27.1	19.0	13.0

a) What is the probability that a randomly selected person in the United States is under 18 years old?
b) Given that a person is 55 years old, what is the probability that they watch TV via online streaming?
c) What is the probability that a randomly selected person in the United States is 18–29 years old and watches TV online?
d) What is the probability that a randomly selected person in the United States is 18 or older and watches TV via cable or satellite?

52. Titanic survival. Of the 2201 people on the RMS *Titanic*, only 711 survived. The practice of "women and children first" was first used to describe the chivalrous actions of the sailors during the sinking of the HMS *Birkenhead* in 1852, but became popular after the sinking of the *Titanic*, during which 53% of the children and 73% of the women survived, but only 21% of the men survived. Part of the protocol stated that passengers enter lifeboats by ticket class as well. Here is a table showing survival by ticket class.

	First	Second	Third	Crew	Total
Alive	203	118	178	212	711
	28.6%	16.6%	25.0%	29.8%	100%
Dead	122	167	528	673	1490
	8.2%	11.2%	35.4%	45.2%	100%

a) Find the conditional probability of survival for each type of ticket.
b) Draw a probability tree for this situation.
c) Given that a passenger survived, what is the probability they had a first-class ticket?

53. Coffeehouse survey. A Mintel report on coffeehouses asked consumers if they were spending more time in coffeehouses. The table below gives the responses classified by age:

a) What is the probability that a randomly selected respondent is spending more time at coffeehouses and donut shops this year than last year?
b) What is the probability that the person is younger than 25 years old?
c) What is the probability that the person is younger than 25 years old and is spending more time at coffeehouses and donut shops compared to last year?
d) What is the probability that the person is younger than 25 years old *or* is spending more time at coffeehouses and donut shops compared to last year?

	Age						
	18–24	**25–34**	**35–44**	**45–54**	**55–64**	**65+**	**Total**
I am spending less time at coffeehouses and donut shops this year than last year.	78	93	102	104	68	48	493
I am spending about the same time at coffeehouses and donut shops this year as last year.	82	109	106	89	75	67	528
I am spending more time at coffeehouses and donut shops this year than last year.	30	30	18	19	11	6	114
Total	190	232	226	212	154	121	1135

Source: 2011 Mintel Report. Reprinted by permission of Mintel, a leading market research company (www.mintel.com).

54. Electronic communications. A Mintel study asked consumers if electronic communications devices influenced whether or not they bought a certain car. The table below gives the results classified by household income:

If we select a person at random from this sample:

a) What is the probability that electronic communication devices somewhat influenced their decisions?
b) What is the probability that the person is earning at least $100K?
c) What is the probability that the person was somewhat influenced by electronic communications *and* earns at least $100K?
d) What is the probability that electronic communications somewhat influenced the purchase *or* that the person earns at least $100K?

Communications influence on car purchase, by household income, July 2011				
	Income			
Communication (e.g., hands-free calling):	**<$50K**	**$50K–99.9K**	**$100K+**	**Total**
Very Much	30	57	41	128
Somewhat	26	39	62	127
Not At All	23	39	35	97
Total	79	135	138	352

Source: Mintel.

55. Red Cross Rh. Exercises 36 and 38 discussed the challenges faced by the Red Cross in finding enough blood of various types. But blood typing also depends on the Rh factor, which can be negative or positive. Here is a table of the estimated proportions worldwide for blood types categorized on both type and Rh factor:

	Blood Type			
	O	**A**	**B**	**AB**
Rh +	36.44%	28.27%	20.59%	5.06%
Rh −	4.33%	3.52%	1.39%	0.45%

For a randomly selected human, what is the probability that he …

a) Is Rh negative given that he is type O?
b) Is type O given that he is Rh negative?
c) A person with Type A^- blood can accept donated blood only of types A^- and O^-. What is the probability that a randomly selected donor can donate to a recipient given that the recipient's blood type is A^-?

56. Automobile inspection. Twenty percent of cars that are inspected have faulty pollution control systems. The cost of repairing a pollution control system exceeds $100 about 40% of the time. When a driver takes her car in for inspection, what's the probability that she will end up paying more than $100 to repair the pollution control system?

57. Pharmaceutical company. A U.S. pharmaceutical company is considering manufacturing and marketing a pill that will help to lower both an individual's blood pressure and cholesterol. The company is interested in understanding the demand for such a product. The joint probabilities that an adult American man has high blood pressure, high cholesterol, or both are shown in the table.

		Blood Pressure	
		High	**OK**
Cholesterol	**High**	0.11	0.21
	OK	0.16	0.52

a) What's the probability that an adult American male has both conditions?
b) What's the probability that an adult American male has high blood pressure?
c) What's the probability that an adult American male with high blood pressure also has high cholesterol?
d) What's the probability that an adult American male has high blood pressure if it's known that he has high cholesterol?

58. International relocation. A European department store is developing a new advertising campaign for their new U.S. location, and their marketing managers need to understand their target market better. A survey of adult shoppers found the probabilities that an adult would shop at their new U.S. store classified by age is shown below.

		Shop		
		Yes	No	Total
Age	<20	0.26	0.04	0.30
	20–40	0.24	0.10	0.34
	>40	0.12	0.24	0.36
	Total	0.62	0.38	1.00

a) What's the probability that a survey respondent will shop at the U.S. store?
b) What is the probability that a survey respondent will shop at the store given that they are younger than 20 years old?
c) What is the probability that a survey respondent who is older than 40 shops at the store?
d) What is the probability that a survey respondent is younger than 20 or will shop at the store?

59. Pharmaceutical company, again. Given the table of probabilities compiled for marketing managers in Exercise 57, are high blood pressure and high cholesterol independent? Explain.

60. International relocation, again. Given the table of probabilities compiled for a department store chain in Exercise 58, are age and shopping at the department store independent? Explain.

61. Coffeehouse survey, part 2. Look again at the data from the coffeehouse survey in Exercise 53.

a) If we select a person at random, what's the probability we choose a person between 18 and 24 years old who is spending more time at coffeehouses?
b) Among the 18- to 24-year olds, what is the probability that the person responded that they are not spending more time at coffeehouses?
c) What's the probability that a person who spends the same amount of time at coffeehouses is between 35 and 44 years old?
d) If the person responded that they spend more time, what's the probability that they are at least 65 years old?
e) What's the probability that a person at least 65 years old spends the same amount of time?
f) Are the responses to the question and age independent?

62. Electronic communications, part 2. Look again at the data in the electronic communications in Exercise 54.

a) If we select a respondent at random, what's the probability that we choose a person earning less than $50 K and responded "somewhat"?

b) Among those earning $50–99.9K, what is the probability that the person responded "not at all"?
c) What's the probability that a person who responded "very much" was earning at least $100K?
d) If the person responded "very much," what is the probability that they earn between $50K and 99.9K?
e) Are the responses to the question and income level independent?

63. Real estate, part 2. In the real estate research described in Exercise 33, 64% of homes for sale have garages, 21% have swimming pools, and 17% have both features.

a) What is the probability that a home for sale has a garage, but not a pool?
b) If a home for sale has a garage, what's the probability that it has a pool, too?
c) Are having a garage and a pool independent events? Explain.
d) Are having a garage and a pool mutually exclusive? Explain.

64. Polling. Professional polling organizations face the challenge of selecting a representative sample of U.S. adults by telephone. This has been complicated by people who only use cell phones and by others whose landline phones are unlisted. A careful survey by Democracy Corps determined the following proportions:

Cell phone only	39%
Both cell and landline	29%
Landline only listed	22%
Landline only unlisted	7%

a) What's the probability that a randomly selected U.S. adult has a landline?
b) What's the probability that a U.S. adult has a landline given that he or she has a cell phone?
c) Are having a cell phone and a landline independent? Explain.
d) Are having a cell phone and a landline disjoint? Explain.

65. Property values. The following table shows a sample of property listings and values from one neighborhood (one ZIP code) in the Washington, DC, area in September 2017:

Property Values in This Neighborhood of Washington, DC

Price	Number of Bedrooms	Number of Stories	Garage	Number of Baths
$1.8MM	4	3	1	3
$1.1MM	3	2	1	3
$430K	1	1	0	1
$339K	1	1	0	1
$255K	0	1	0	1
$200K	0	1	0	1
$169K	0	1	0	1

a) In this sample, what proportion of homes is valued at $500K or less?

b) Are the number of bedrooms and property values independent? Explain.

66. Property values, part 2. A sample of 1800 homes in a different neighborhood of Washington, DC, in 2017 produced the data in the table for the number of bedrooms and house price. Is the price of the house independent of whether it has 3 or more bedrooms?

Property Values in the Washington, DC, Area

		3 or More Bedrooms	
		Yes	No
House Price	Less than $300K	238	528
	$300–450K	302	344
	$450–600K	289	99

67. Used cars. A business student is searching for a used car to purchase, so she posts an ad to a website saying she wants to buy a used Jeep between $18,000 and $20,000. From Kelley's BlueBook.com, she learns that there are 149 cars matching that description within a 30-mile radius of her home. If we assume that those are the people who will call her and that they are equally likely to call her:

		Price		
		$18,000–$18,999	$19,000–$19,999	Total
Car Make	Commander	3	6	9
	Compass	6	1	7
	Grand Cherokee	33	33	66
	Liberty	17	6	23
	Wrangler	33	11	44
	Total	92	57	149

a) What is the probability that the first caller will be a Jeep Liberty owner?

b) What is the probability that the first caller will own a Jeep Liberty that costs between $18,000 and $18,999?

c) If the first call offers her a Jeep Liberty, what is the probability that it costs less than $19,000?

d) Suppose she decides to ignore calls with cars whose cost is ≥$19,000. What is the probability that the first call she takes will offer to sell her a Jeep Liberty?

68. CEO relocation. The CEO of a mid-sized company has to relocate to another part of the country. To make it easier, the company has hired a relocation agency to help purchase a house. The CEO has 5 children and so has specified that the house have at least 5 bedrooms, but hasn't put any other constraints on the search. The relocation agency has narrowed the search down to the houses in the table and has selected one house to showcase to the CEO and family on their trip out to the new site. The agency doesn't know it, but the family has its heart set on a Cape Cod house with a fireplace. If the agency selected the house at random, without regard to this:

		Fireplace?		
		No	Yes	Total
House Type	Cape Cod	7	2	9
	Colonial	8	14	22
	Other	6	5	11
	Total	21	21	42

a) What is the probability that the selected house is a Cape Cod?

b) What is the probability that the house is a Colonial with a fireplace?

c) If the house is a Cape Cod, what is the probability that it has a fireplace?

d) What is the probability that the selected house is what the family wants?

*69. Computer reliability. Laptop computers have been growing in popularity according to a study by Current Analysis Inc. Laptops now represent more than half the computer sales in the United States. A campus bookstore sells both types of computers and in the last semester sold 56% laptops and 44% desktops. Reliability rates for the two types of machines are quite different, however. In the first year, 5% of desktops require service, while 15% of laptops have problems requiring service.

a) Sketch a probability tree for this situation.

b) What percentage of computers sold by the bookstore last semester required service?

c) Given that a computer required service, what is the probability that it was a laptop?

JUST CHECKING ANSWERS

1 The probability of going up on the next day is not affected by the previous day's outcome.

2 a) 0.30
   b) $0.30(0.30) = 0.09$
   c) $(1 - 0.30)^2(0.30) = 0.147$
   d) $1 - (1 - 0.30)^5 = 0.832$

3 a)

		Weekday		
		Yes	No	Total
Before Five	Yes	0.07	0.41	0.48
	No	0.20	0.32	0.52
	Total	0.27	0.73	1.00

   b) $P(\mathbf{BF}|\mathbf{WD}) = P(\mathbf{BF}\ and\ \mathbf{WD})/P(\mathbf{WD}) = 0.07/0.27 = 0.259$
   c) No, shoppers can do both (and 7% do).
   d) To be independent, we'd need $P(\mathbf{BF}|\mathbf{WD}) = P(\mathbf{BF})$. $P(\mathbf{BF}|\mathbf{WD}) = 0.259$, but $P(\mathbf{BF}) = 0.48$. They do not appear to be independent.

CHAPTER 6

Random Variables and Probability Models

Metropolitan Life Insurance Company

In 1863, at the height of the U.S. Civil War, a group of businessmen in New York City decided to form a new company to insure Civil War soldiers against disabilities and injuries suffered from the war. After the war ended, they changed direction and decided to focus on selling life insurance. The new company was named Metropolitan Life (MetLife) because the bulk of the company's clients were in the "metropolitan" area of New York City.

Although an economic depression in the 1870s put many life insurance companies out of business, MetLife survived, modeling their business on similar successful programs in England. Taking advantage of spreading industrialism and the selling methods of British insurance agents, the company soon was enrolling as many as 700 new policies per day. By 1909, MetLife was the nation's largest life insurer in the United States.

During the Great Depression of the 1930s, MetLife expanded their public service by promoting public health campaigns, focusing on educating the urban poor in major U.S. cities about the risk of tuberculosis. Because the company invested primarily in urban and farm mortgages, as opposed to the stock market, they survived the crash of 1929 and ended up investing heavily in the postwar U.S. housing boom. They were the principal investors in both the Empire State Building (1929) and Rockefeller Center (1931). During World War II, the company was the single largest contributor to the Allied cause, investing more than half of their total assets in war bonds.

Today, in addition to life insurance, MetLife manages pensions and investments. In 2000, the company held an initial public offering and entered the retail banking business in 2001 with the launch of MetLife Bank. The company's public face is well known because of their use of Snoopy, the dog from the cartoon strip *Peanuts*.

Importance of Insurance

Most people don't give insurance a second thought—they simply have health, life, auto, and possibly homeowner's or renter's insurance. However, the insurance industry is enormous: In 2015, the total value of life, health, and property insurance assets in the United States alone was over $7 trillion, and total insurance premiums in these sectors accounted for nearly 7% of GDP. (www.treasury.gov/initiatives/fio/reports-and-notices/Documents/FIO%20Annual%20Report%202013.pdf)

Insurance companies make bets all the time. For example, they bet that you're going to live a long life. Ironically, you bet that you're going to die sooner. Both you and the insurance company want the company to stay in business, so it's important to find a "fair price" for your bet. Of course, the right price for *you* depends on many factors, and nobody can predict exactly how long you'll live. But when the company averages its bets over enough customers, it can make reasonably accurate estimates of the amount it can expect to collect on a policy before it has to pay out the benefit. To do that effectively, it must model the situation with a probability model. Using the resulting probabilities, the company can find the fair price of almost any situation involving risk and uncertainty.

Here's a simple example. An insurance company offers a "death and disability" policy that pays $100,000 when a client dies or $50,000 if the client is permanently disabled. It charges a premium of $500 per year for this benefit. Is the company likely to make a profit selling such a plan? To answer this question, the company needs to know the *probability* that a client will die or become disabled in any year. From such actuarial information and the appropriate model, the company can calculate the expected value of this policy.

6.1 Expected Value of a Random Variable

To model the insurance company's risk, we need to define a few terms. The amount the company pays out on an individual policy is an example of a **random variable**, called that because its value is based on the outcome of a random event. We use a capital letter, in this case, X, to denote a random variable. We'll denote a particular *value* that it can have by the corresponding lowercase letter, in this case, x. For the insurance company, x can be $100,000 (if you die that year), $50,000 (if you are disabled), or $0 (if neither occurs). Because we can list all the outcomes, we call this random variable a **discrete random variable**. A random variable that can take on any value (possibly bounded on one or both sides) is called a **continuous random variable**. Continuous random variables are common in business applications for modeling physical quantities like heights and weights, and monetary quantities such as profits, revenues, and spending.

Sometimes it is obvious whether to treat a random variable as discrete or continuous, but at other times the choice is more subtle. Age, for example, might be viewed as discrete if it is measured only to the nearest decade with possible values 10, 20, 30, ... In a scientific context, however, it might be measured more precisely and treated as continuous.

For both discrete and continuous variables, the collection of all the possible values and the probabilities associated with them is called the **probability model** for the random variable. For a discrete random variable, we can list the probability of all possible values in a table, or describe it by a formula. For example, to model

NOTATION ALERT

The most common letters for random variables are *X*, *Y*, and *Z*, but any capital letter can be used.

the possible outcomes of a fair die, we can let X be the number showing on the face. The probability model for X is simply:

DIE ROLL	1	2	3	4	5	6
Probability	1/6	1/6	1/6	1/6	1/6	1/6

TABLE 6.1

or, simply as:

$$P(X = x) = \begin{cases} 1/6 & \textit{if } x = 1, 2, 3, 4, 5, \textit{ or } 6 \\ 0 & \textit{otherwise} \end{cases}$$

Both of these representations say the same thing. The formula is read: "The probability that the outcome (the die roll, represented by X) takes on the value x is equal to $1/6$ for each possible outcome (x can take on values from 1 to 6 pips showing on the die), and all other outcomes have 0 probability (showing that the die was a "standard" 6-sided die (not an 8- or 10-sided die, for example). You can see how much information is contained in the mathematical notation, which we use to succinctly express the relationship. Imagine how long the table would be for a typical Powerball Lottery!

Suppose in our insurance risk example that the death rate in any year is 1 out of every 1000 people and that another 2 out of 1000 suffer some kind of disability. The loss (the payout in $), which we'll denote as X, is a discrete random variable. It's random because it depends on the outcome of a random event (becoming disabled or dying), and it's discrete because it takes on only 3 possible values—$0, $50,000 or $100,000. We can display the probability model for X in a table, as in Table 6.2.

Policyholder Outcome	Payout x (cost)	Probability $P(X = x)$
Death	100,000	$\dfrac{1}{1000}$
Disability	50,000	$\dfrac{2}{1000}$
Neither	0	$\dfrac{997}{1000}$

TABLE 6.2 Probability model for an insurance policy.

Of course, we can't predict exactly what *will* happen during any given year, but we can say what we *expect* to happen—in this case, what we expect the profit of a policy will be. The expected value of a policy is a **parameter** (a numerically valued attribute) of the probability model. In fact, it's the mean. We'll signify this with the notation $E(X)$, for expected value (or sometimes μ to indicate that it is a mean). This isn't an average of data values, so we won't estimate it. Instead, we calculate it directly from the probability model for the random variable. Because it comes from a model and not data, we use the Greek letter μ to denote the parameter (and *not* $\bar{y}$ or $\bar{x}$).[1]

To see what the insurance company can expect, think about some convenient number of outcomes. For example, imagine that they have exactly 1000 clients and that the outcomes in one year followed the probability model exactly: 1 died, 2 were disabled, and 997 survived unscathed. Then our expected payout would be:

$$\mu = E(X) = \frac{100,000(1) + 50,000(2) + 0(997)}{1000} = 200$$

So our expected payout comes to $200 per policy.

NOTATION ALERT

The expected value (or mean) of a random variable is written $E(X)$ or μ. (Be sure not to confuse the mean of a random variable, calculated from probabilities, with the mean of a collection of data values which is denoted by $\bar{y}$ or $\bar{x}$.)

---

[1]The convention is to use Greek letters when a quantity is not estimated from data.

Instead of writing the expected value as one big fraction, we can rewrite it as separate terms, each divided by 1000.

$$\mu = E(X) = \$100{,}000\left(\frac{1}{1000}\right) + \$50{,}000\left(\frac{2}{1000}\right) + \$0\left(\frac{997}{1000}\right)$$

$$= \$200$$

Writing it this way, we can see that for each policy, there's a 1/1000 chance that we'll have to pay \$100,000 for a death and a 2/1000 chance that we'll have to pay \$50,000 for a disability. Of course, there's a 997/1000 chance that we won't have to pay anything.

So the **expected value** of a (discrete) random variable is found by multiplying each possible value of the random variable by the probability that it occurs and then summing all those products. This gives the general formula for the expected value of a discrete random variable:[2]

$$E(X) = \Sigma x P(x).$$

Translating the formula to English, it reads: The expected value of the random variable X (the disability policy) is obtained by taking each outcome (x is the cost of an outcome) and multiplying by the probability of that outcome occurring ($P(x)$), and adding these quantities for all possible outcomes (the summation sign).

Be sure that *every* possible outcome is included in the sum. Verify that you have a valid probability model to start with—the probabilities should each be between 0 and 1 and should sum to one. (Recall the rules of probability in Chapter 5.)

IN PRACTICE 6.1   Expected value of a lottery

MANAGER   Our charity is going to raise money by running a lottery. We plan to sell 500 tickets for \$3 each, and to offer a grand prize of \$250 and four second prizes of \$50 each. We need to raise \$1000. Can we expect to do so?

ANALYST   To figure out whether the lottery will make money, we need to compute the expected value of a ticket.

Each ticket has a 1/500 chance of winning the grand prize of \$250, a 4/500 chance of winning \$50, and a 495/500 chance of winning nothing. We represent the outcome of the lottery as a random variable, X, and we compute the expected value of a ticket by multiplying each outcome by its probability. So $E(X) = (1/500) \times \$250 + (4/500) \times \$50 + (495/500) \times \$0 = \$0.50 + \$0.40 + \$0.00 = \$0.90$. We need to include the cost, which is not a random variable because we pay it with certainty. Including the cost, the expected value of buying a ticket is $\$0.90 - \$3 = -\$2.10$. Although no single person will lose \$2.10 (they lose \$3, win \$50, or win \$250), \$2.10 is the amount, on average, that the lottery gains per ticket. Therefore, we can expect to make $500 \times \$2.10 = \$1050$. Regulators and savvy consumers also analyze games of chance from the perspective of the ticket buyer. This lottery has a payout of only 30% of the money collected, which is quite low. However, given that we are a charity, people are likely to view the ticket more like a donation than a casino game and not worry about the payout ratio.

---

[2]The concept of expected values for continuous random variables is similar, but the calculation requires calculus and is beyond the scope of this text.

6.2   Standard Deviation of a Random Variable

Of course, this expected value (or mean) is not what actually happens to any *particular* policyholder. No individual insurance policy actually costs the company $200. We are dealing with random events, so some policyholders receive big payouts and others nothing. Because the insurance company must anticipate this variability, it needs to know the standard deviation of the random variable.

For data, we calculate the standard deviation by first computing the deviation of each data value from the mean and squaring it. We perform a similar calculation when we compute the **standard deviation** of a (discrete) random variable as well. First, we find the deviation of each payout from the mean (expected value). (See Table 6.3.)

Policyholder Outcome	Payout x (cost)	Probability $P(X = x)$	Deviation $(x - EV)$
Death	100,000	$\dfrac{1}{1000}$	$(100{,}000 - 200) = 99{,}800$
Disability	50,000	$\dfrac{2}{1000}$	$(50{,}000 - 200) = 49{,}800$
Neither	0	$\dfrac{997}{1000}$	$(0 - 200) = -200$

TABLE 6.3   Deviations between the expected value and each payout (cost).

Next, we square each deviation. The **variance** is the expected value of those squared deviations. If you remember that the variance of a quantitative variable also involves summing (adding up) the squared deviation of each point from the mean of the distribution, this procedure should look familiar. In Table 6.3, we use the expected value as the mean to compute the deviation. To find the variance we multiply each squared deviation by the appropriate probability and sum those products:

$$Var(X) = 99{,}800^2\left(\frac{1}{1000}\right) + 49{,}800^2\left(\frac{2}{1000}\right) + (-200)^2\left(\frac{997}{1000}\right)$$

$$= 14{,}960{,}000.$$

Finally, we take the square root to get the standard deviation:

$$SD(X) = \sqrt{14{,}960{,}000} \approx \$3868$$

The insurance company can expect an average payout of $200 per policy, with a standard deviation of $3868.

We call this spread (the standard deviation) "risk," and you can see why. The company charges $500 for each policy and expects to pay out $200 per policy. Sounds like an easy way to make $300. (In fact, most of the time—probability 997/1000—the company pockets the entire $500.) But would you be willing to take on this risk yourself and sell all your friends policies like this? The problem is that occasionally the company loses big, which is why the standard deviation is so high. (If losses were limited to $10,000 at the maximum, the standard deviation would be much lower.) With a probability of 1/1000, it will pay out $100,000, and with a probability of 2/1000, it will pay out $50,000. That may be more risk than you're willing to take on. The standard deviation of $3868 gives an indication of the uncertainty of the profit, and that seems like a fairly large spread (risk) for an average profit of $300.

Here are the formulas for these arguments. Because these are parameters of our probability model, the variance and standard deviation can also be written as

σ^2 and σ, respectively (sometimes with the name of the random variable as a subscript). You should recognize both kinds of notation:

$$\sigma^2 = Var(X) = \sum (x - \mu)^2 P(x) = \sum (x - E(X))^2 P(x), \text{ and}$$

$$\sigma = SD(X) = \sqrt{Var(X)}.$$

IN PRACTICE 6.2   Quantifying risk

MANAGER Analyze the lottery from the perspective of a potential ticket buyer. How should the buyer look at the risk?

ANALYST We already computed the expected value of the lottery to be −$2.10 for the buyer. We now need to compute the standard deviation of buying a ticket.

$$\sigma^2 = Var(X) = \sum (x - E(X))^2 P(x) = \sum (x - 2.10)^2 P(x)$$

$$= (250 - 2.10)^2 \frac{1}{500} + (50 - 2.10)^2 \frac{4}{500} + (0 - 2.10)^2 \frac{495}{500}$$

$$= 61{,}454.41 \times \frac{1}{500} + 2{,}294.41 \times \frac{4}{500} + 4.41 \times \frac{495}{500}$$

$$= 145.63$$

so $\sigma = \sqrt{145.63} = \$12.07$

That's a lot of variation for a mean of −$2.10, which reflects the fact that there is a small chance that you'll win a lot but a large chance you'll win nothing. Note that almost all of the variation in this case is an improvement over losing $3, which is what happens in 495/500 cases. Some financial analysts treat this "upside" variation differently and do not call it "risk."

GUIDED EXAMPLE   Computer Inventory

As the head of inventory for a computer company, you've had a challenging couple of weeks. One of your warehouses recently had a fire, and you had to flag all the computers stored there to be recycled. On the positive side, you were thrilled that you had managed to ship two computers to your biggest client last week. But then you discovered that your assistant hadn't heard about the fire and had mistakenly transported a whole truckload of computers from the damaged warehouse into the shipping center. It turns out that 30% of all the computers shipped last week were damaged. You don't know whether your biggest client received two damaged computers, two undamaged ones, or one of each. Computers were selected at random from the shipping center for delivery.

If your client received two undamaged computers, everything is fine. If the client gets one damaged computer, it will be returned at your expense—$100— and you can replace it. However, if both computers are damaged, the client will cancel all other orders this month, and you'll lose $10,000.

(continued)

Question: What is the expected value and the standard deviation of your loss under this scenario?

PLAN	**Setup** State the problem.	We want to analyze the potential consequences of shipping damaged computers to a large client. We'll look at the expected value and standard deviation of the amount we'll lose.

Let X = amount of loss. We'll denote the receipt of an undamaged computer by **U** and the receipt of a damaged computer by **D**. The three possibilities are: two undamaged computers (**U** and **U**), two damaged computers (**D** and **D**), and one of each (**UD** or **DU**). Because the computers were selected randomly and the number in the warehouse is large, we can assume independence.

DO **Model** List the possible values of the random variable, and compute all the values you'll need to determine the probability model.

Because the events are independent, we can use the Multiplication Rule (Chapter 5) and find:

$$P(\mathbf{UU}) = P(\mathbf{U}) \times P(\mathbf{U})$$
$$= 0.7 \times 0.7 = 0.49$$
$$P(\mathbf{DD}) = P(\mathbf{D}) \times P(\mathbf{D})$$
$$= 0.3 \times 0.3 = 0.09$$

So, $P(\mathbf{UD}\ or\ \mathbf{DU}) = 1 - (0.49 + 0.09) = 0.42$

We have the following model for all possible values of X.

Outcome	x	$P(X = x)$
Two damaged	10,000	$P(\mathbf{DD}) = 0.09$
One damaged	100	$P(\mathbf{UD}\ or\ \mathbf{DU}) = 0.42$
Neither damaged	0	$P(\mathbf{UU}) = 0.49$

Mechanics Find the expected value.

$$E(X) = 0(0.49) + 100(0.42) + 10{,}000(0.09)$$
$$= \$942.00$$

Find the variance.

$$Var(X) = (0 - 942)^2 \times (0.49)$$
$$+ (100 - 942)^2 \times (0.42)$$
$$+ (10{,}000 - 942)^2 \times (0.09)$$
$$= 8{,}116{,}836$$

Find the standard deviation.

$$SD(X) = \sqrt{8{,}116{,}836} = \$2849.01$$

REPORT **Conclusion** Interpret your results in context.

MEMO

Re: Damaged computers

The recent shipment of two computers to our large client may have some serious problems. Even though there is about a 50% chance that they will receive two perfectly good computers, there is a 9% chance that they will receive two damaged computers and will cancel the rest of their monthly order. We have analyzed the expected loss to the firm as $942 with a standard deviation of $2849.01. The large standard deviation reflects the fact that there is a real possibility of losing $10,000 from the mistake.

Both numbers seem reasonable. The expected value of $942 is between the extremes of $0 and $10,000, and there's great variability in the outcome values.

REALITY
CHECK

6.3   Properties of Expected Values and Variances

Our example insurance company expected to pay out an average of $200 per policy, with a standard deviation of about $3868. The expected profit then was $500 − $200 = $300 per policy. Suppose that the company decides to lower the price of the premium by $50 to $450. It's pretty clear that the expected profit would drop an average of $50 per policy, to $450 − $200 = $250.

What about the standard deviation? We know that adding or subtracting a constant from data shifts the mean but doesn't change the variance or standard deviation. The same is true of random variables:[3]

$$E(X \pm c) = E(X) \pm c,$$
$$Var(X \pm c) = Var(X), \text{ and}$$
$$SD(X \pm c) = SD(X).$$

What if the company decides to *double* all the payouts—that is, pay $200,000 for death and $100,000 for disability? This would double the average payout per policy and also increase the variability in payouts. In general, multiplying each value of a random variable by a constant multiplies the mean by that constant and multiplies the variance by the *square* of the constant:

$$E(aX) = aE(X), \text{ and}$$
$$Var(aX) = a^2 Var(X).$$

Taking square roots of the last equation shows that the standard deviation is multiplied by the absolute value of the constant:

$$SD(aX) = |a|SD(X).$$

This insurance company sells policies to more than just one person. We've just seen how to compute means and variances for one person at a time. What happens to the mean and variance when we have a collection of customers? The profit on a group of customers is the *sum* of the individual profits, so we'll need to know how to find expected values and variances for sums. To start, consider a simple case with just two customers who we'll call Mr. Ecks and Ms. Wye. With an expected payout of $200 on each policy, we might expect a total of $200 + $200 = $400 to be paid out on the two policies—nothing surprising there. In other words, we have the **Addition Rule for Expected Values of Random Variables**: *The expected value of the sum (or difference) of random variables is the sum (or difference) of their expected values:*

$$E(X \pm Y) = E(X) \pm E(Y).$$

The variability is another matter. Is the risk of insuring two people the same as the risk of insuring one person for twice as much? We wouldn't expect both clients to die or become disabled in the same year. In fact, because we've spread the risk, the standard deviation should be smaller. Indeed, this is the fundamental principle behind insurance. By spreading the risk among many policies, a company can keep the standard deviation quite small and predict costs more accurately. It's much less risky to insure thousands of customers than one customer when the total expected payout is the same, assuming that the events are independent. Catastrophic events such as hurricanes or earthquakes that affect large numbers of customers at the same time destroy the independence assumption, and often the insurance company along with it.

But how much smaller is the standard deviation of the sum? It turns out that, if the random variables are independent, we have the **Addition Rule for Variances**

---

[3]The rules in this section are true for both discrete *and* continuous random variables.

of (Independent) Random Variables: *The variance of the sum or difference of two independent random variables is the sum of their individual variances:*

$$Var(X \pm Y) = Var(X) + Var(Y)$$

if X and Y are independent.

MATH BOX   Pythagorean theorem of statistics

We often use the standard deviation to measure variability, but when we add independent random variables, we use their variances. Think of the Pythagorean Theorem. In a right triangle (only), the *square* of the length of the hypotenuse is the sum of the *squares* of the lengths of the other two sides:

$$c^2 = a^2 + b^2.$$

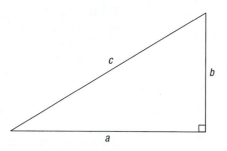

For independent random variables (only), the *square* of the standard deviation of their sum is the sum of the *squares* of their standard deviations:

$$SD^2(X + Y) = SD^2(X) + SD^2(Y).$$

It's simpler to write this with *variances*:

$$Var(X + Y) = Var(X) + Var(Y),$$

but we'll use the standard deviation formula often as well:

$$SD(X + Y) = \sqrt{Var(X) + Var(Y)}.$$

For Mr. Ecks and Ms. Wye, the insurance company can expect their outcomes to be independent, so (using X for Mr. Ecks's payout and Y for Ms. Wye's):

$$
\begin{aligned}
Var(X + Y) &= Var(X) + Var(Y) \\
&= 14,960,000 + 14,960,000 \\
&= 29,920,000.
\end{aligned}
$$

Remember, only variances add, not standard deviations.

Let's compare the variance of writing two independent policies to the variance of writing only one for twice the size. If the company had insured only Mr. Ecks for twice as much, the variance would have been

$$Var(2X) = 2^2 Var(X) = 4 \times 14,960,000 = 59,840,000, \text{ or}$$

twice as big as with two independent policies, even though the expected payout is the same.

Of course, variances are in squared units. The company would prefer to know standard deviations, which are in dollars. The standard deviation of the payout for two independent policies is $SD(X + Y) = \sqrt{Var(X + Y)} = \sqrt{29,920,000} \approx \$5470$. But the standard deviation of the payout for a single policy of twice the size is twice the standard deviation of a single policy: $SD(2X) = 2SD(X) = 2(\$3868) = \$7736$ or about 40% more than the standard deviation of the sum of the two independent policies.

If the company has two customers, then it will have an expected annual total payout (cost) of $400 with a standard deviation of about $5470. If they write one policy with an expected annual payout of $400, they increase the standard deviation by about 40%. Spreading risk by insuring many independent customers is one of the fundamental principles in insurance and finance.

Let's review the rules of expected values and variances for sums and differences.

- The expected value of the sum of two random variables is the sum of the expected values.
- The expected value of the difference of two random variables is the difference of the expected values:

$$E(X \pm Y) = E(X) \pm E(Y).$$

- If the random variables are independent, the variance of their sum or difference is always the sum of the variances:

$$Var(X \pm Y) = Var(X) + Var(Y).$$

Do we always *add* variances? Even when we take the *difference* of two random quantities? Yes! Think about the two insurance policies. Suppose we want to know the mean and standard deviation of the *difference* in payouts to the two clients. Since each policy has an expected payout of $200, the expected difference is $200 - \$200 = \$0$. If we computed the variance of the difference by subtracting variances, we would get $0 for the variance. But that doesn't make sense. Their difference won't always be exactly $0. In fact, the difference in payouts could range from $100,000 to $-100,000$, a spread of $200,000. The variability in differences *increases* as much as the variability in sums. If the company has two customers, the difference in payouts has a mean of $0 and a standard deviation of about $5470.

For Random Variables, Does $X + X + X = 3X$?

Maybe, but be careful. As we've just seen, insuring one person for $300,000 is not the same risk as insuring three people for $100,000 each. When each instance represents a different outcome for the same random variable, though, it's easy to fall into the trap of writing all of them with the same symbol. Don't make this common mistake. Make sure you write each instance as a *different* random variable. Just because each random variable describes a similar situation doesn't mean that each random outcome will be the same. What you really mean is $X_1 + X_2 + X_3$. Written this way, it's clear that the sum shouldn't necessarily equal 3 times *anything*.

IN PRACTICE 6.3 Diversification of investments

MANAGER We are considering investing $1000 into one or possibly two different investment funds. Historically, each has delivered 5% a year in profit with a standard deviation of 3%. So, a $1000 investment would produce $50 with a standard deviation of $30.

What are the relative advantages and disadvantages of putting $1000 into one, or splitting the $1000 and putting $500 into each?

ANALYST To analyze the different investment options, we need to compare the means and standard deviation of the returns. Let X = amount gained by putting $1000 into one

$$E(X) = 0.05 \times 1000 = \$50 \text{ and } SD(X) = 0.03 \times 1000 = \$30.$$

Let W = amount gained by putting $500 into each. W_1 and W_2 are the amounts invested in each fund. $E(W_1) = E(W_2) = 0.05 \times 500 = \$25$. So $E(W) = E(W_1) + E(W_2) = \$25 + \$25 = \$50$. The expected values of the two strategies are the same. You expect on average to earn $50 on $1000.

$$
\begin{aligned}
SD(W) &= \sqrt{SD^2(W_1) + SD^2(W_2)} = \sqrt{Var(W_1) + Var(W_2)} \\
&= \sqrt{(0.03 \times 500)^2 + (0.03 \times 500)^2} \\
&= \sqrt{15^2 + 15^2} \\
&= \$21.21
\end{aligned}
$$

(continued)

The standard deviation of the amount earned is $21.21 by splitting the investment amount compared to $30 for investing in one. The expected values are the same. Spreading the investment into more than one vehicle *reduces* the variation. On the other hand, keeping it all in one vehicle increases the chances of both extremely good and extremely bad returns. Which one is better depends on an individual's appetite for risk.[4]

Covariance

In Chapter 4 we saw that the association of two variables could be measured with their correlation. What about random variables? We can talk about the correlation between random variables, too. But it's easier to start with a related concept called covariance.

If X is a random variable with expected value $E(X) = \mu$ and Y is a random variable with expected value $E(X) = \nu$, then the **covariance** of X and Y is defined as

$$Cov(X, Y) = E((X - \mu)(Y - \nu)).$$

Reading the formula in English, it says that the covariance between X and Y is the expected value of the product of the two variables after centering them at their means.

The covariance gives us the extra information we need to find the variance of the sum or difference of two random variables when they are *not* independent:

$$Var(X \pm Y) = Var(X) + Var(Y) \pm 2Cov(X, Y).$$

When X and Y are independent, their covariance is zero, so we have the Pythagorean Theorem of statistics, as we saw earlier. When the variables are positively associated, the variance of their sum (or difference) is increased. This is why it's riskier to invest in two things that are related and less risky to diversify by finding two investments that are nearly independent (and thus have covariance near zero.)

The covariance, like the correlation, measures how X and Y vary together (*co = together*). Unlike the correlation, the covariance has units and doesn't have to be between -1 and 1, which makes it harder to interpret. To fix this "problem," we divide the covariance by each of the standard deviations to get the **correlation**:

$$Corr(X, Y) = \frac{Cov(X, Y)}{\sigma_X \sigma_Y}.$$

This is the random variable analogue of the correlation coefficient, r, which we saw in Chapter 4 for data. For random variables, correlation is usually denoted with the Greek letter ρ.

JUST CHECKING

1 Suppose that the time it takes a customer to get and pay for seats at the ticket window of a baseball park is a random variable with a mean of 100 seconds and a standard deviation of 50 seconds. When you get there, you find only two people in line in front of you.

a) How long do you expect to wait for your turn to get tickets?

b) What's the standard deviation of your wait time?

c) What assumption did you make about the two customers in finding the standard deviation?

---

[4]The assumption of independence is crucial, but not always (or ever) reasonable. As a March 3, 2010, article on *CNN Money* stated:

"It's only when economic conditions start to return to normal . . . that investors, and investments, move independently again. That's when diversification reasserts its case. . . ."

money.cnn.com/2010/03/03/pf/funds/diversification.moneymag/index.htm

6.4   Bernoulli Trials

When Google Inc. designed their web browser, *Chrome*, they worked hard to minimize the probability that their browser would have trouble displaying a website. Before releasing the product, they had to test many websites to discover those that might fail. Although web browsers are relatively new, *quality control inspection* such as this is common throughout manufacturing worldwide and has been in use in industry for nearly 100 years.

The developers of *Chrome* sampled websites, recording whether the browser displayed the website correctly or had a problem. We call the act of inspecting a website a trial. There are two possible outcomes—either the website is displayed correctly or it isn't. The developers thought that whether any particular website displayed correctly was independent from other sites. Situations like this occur often and are called **Bernoulli trials**. To summarize, trials are Bernoulli if:

- There are only two possible outcomes (called *success* and *failure*) for each trial.
- The probability of success, denoted p, is the same on every trial. (The probability of failure, $1 - p$ is often denoted q.)
- The trials are independent. Finding that one website does not display correctly does not change what might happen with the next website.

NOTATION ALERT
Now we have two more reserved letters. Whenever we deal with Bernoulli trials, p represents the probability of success, and q represents the probability of failure. (Of course, $q = 1 - p$.)

Common examples of Bernoulli trials include tossing a coin, collecting responses on Yes/No questions from surveys, or even shooting free throws in a basketball game. Bernoulli trials are remarkably versatile and can be used to model a wide variety of real-life situations. The specific question you might ask in different situations will give rise to different random variables that, in turn, have different probability models.

Of course, the *Chrome* developers wanted to find websites that wouldn't display so they could fix any problems in the browser. So for them a "success" was finding a failed website. The labels "success" and "failure" are often applied arbitrarily, so be sure you know what they mean in any particular situation.

One of the important requirements for Bernoulli trials is that the trials be independent. Sometimes that's a reasonable assumption. Is it true for our example? It's easy to imagine that related sites might have similar problems, but if the sites are selected at random, whether one has a problem should be independent of others.

The 10% Condition: Bernoulli trials must be independent. In theory, we need to sample from a population that's infinitely big. However, if the population is finite, it's still okay to proceed as long as the sample is smaller than 10% of the population. In Google's case, they just happened to have a directory of millions of websites, so most samples would easily satisfy the 10% condition.

6.5   Discrete Probability Models

Sam Savage, Professor at the University of Chicago, says in his book, *The Flaw of Averages,* that plans based only on averages are, on average, wrong. Unfortunately, many business owners make decisions based on averages—the average amount sold last year, the average number of customers seen last month, etc. But averages are just too simple to represent real-world business practice. Fortunately, we can do better by modeling business situations with a probability model. Probability models can play an important role in helping decision makers predict both the outcomes and the consequences of their decision alternatives. In this section we'll see that some fairly simple models let us model a wide variety of business phenomena.

Daniel Bernoulli (1700–1782) was the nephew of Jacob, whom you saw in Chapter 5. He was the first to work out the mathematics for what we now call Bernoulli trials.

The Uniform Model

We'll start with the simplest probability model of all, the Uniform model. When we first studied probability in Chapter 5, we saw that equally likely events were the simplest case. For example, a single die can turn up 1, 2, . . . , 6 on one toss. A probability model for the toss is Uniform because each of the outcomes has the same probability $(1/6)$ of occurring. Similarly if X is a random variable with possible outcomes 1, 2, . . . , n and $P(X = i) = 1/n$ for each value of i, then we say X has a **discrete Uniform distribution**, $U[1, \ldots, n]$.

Unfortunately, some business decision makers take only one step away from averages and assume that all their unknown outcomes are equally likely. That can put them with the lottery ticket purchaser who thought her chances were 50/50: "either I win or I don't." Let's look at some more realistic (and more useful) probability models.

The Geometric Model

What's the probability that when Google tests *Chrome* on new websites, the first website that fails to display is the second one that they test? They can use Bernoulli trials to build a probability model. Let X denote the number of trials (websites) until the first such "success." For X to be 2, the first website must have displayed correctly (which has probability $1 - p$), and then the second one must have not displayed correctly—a success, with probability p.[5] Since the trials are independent, these probabilities can be multiplied, and so $P(X = 2) = (1 - p)(p)$ or qp. Maybe Google won't find a success until the fifth trial. What are the chances of that? *Chrome* would have to display the first four websites correctly and then choke on the fifth one, so $P(X = 5) = (1 - p)^4(p) = q^4p$.

Whenever the question is how long (how many trials) it will take to achieve the first success, the model that gives this probability is the **Geometric probability model**. Geometric models are completely specified by one parameter, p, the probability of success. We denote them Geom(p).

Geometric Probability Model for Bernoulli Trials: Geom(p)

p = probability of success (and $q = 1 - p$ = probability of failure)
X = number of trials until the first success occurs

$$P(X = x) = q^{x-1}p$$

Expected value: $\mu = \dfrac{1}{p}$

Standard deviation: $\sigma = \sqrt{\dfrac{q}{p^2}}$

The Geometric distribution can tell Google something important about its software. No large complex program is entirely free of bugs. So before releasing a program or upgrade, developers typically ask not whether it is free of bugs, but how long it is likely to be until the next bug is discovered. If the expected number of trials until the next bug discovery is high enough, then it makes business sense to ship the product rather than wait for that next bug report.

---

[5]This is an example of applying the term "success" to something we care about—a *failure* of the browser. Don't be confused.

The Binomial Model

Suppose Google tests 5 websites. What's the probability that *exactly* 2 of them have problems (2 "successes")? The Geometric model tells how long it should take until the first success. Now we want to find the probability of getting exactly 2 successes among the 5 trials. We are still talking about Bernoulli trials, but we're asking a different question.

This time we're interested in the *number of successes* in the 5 trials, which we'll denote by X. We want to find $P(X = 2)$. Whenever the random variable of interest is the number of successes in a series of Bernoulli trials, it's called a Binomial random variable. It takes two parameters to define this **Binomial probability model**: the number of trials, n, and the probability of success, p. We denote this model Binom (n, p).

Suppose that in an early phase of development, 10% of the sites exhibited some sort of problem so that $p = 0.10$. Exactly 2 successes in 5 trials means 2 successes and 3 failures. It seems logical that the probability should be $(p)^2(1 - p)^3$. Unfortunately, it's not *quite* that easy. That calculation would give you the probability of finding two successes and then three failures—*in that order*. But you could find the two successes in a lot of other ways, for example in the 2nd and 4th website you test. The probability of that sequence is $(1 - p)p(1 - p)p(1 - p)$ which is also $p^2(1 - p)^3$. In fact, as long as there are two successes and three failures, the probability will always be the same, regardless of the order of the sequence of successes and failures. The probability will be $(p)^2(1 - p)^3$. To find the probability of getting 2 successes in 5 trials in any order, we just need to know how many ways that outcome can occur.

Fortunately, all the sequences that lead to the same number of successes are *disjoint*. (For example, if your successes came on the first two trials, they couldn't come on the last two.) So once we find all the different sequences, we can add up their probabilities. And since the probabilities are all the same, we just need to find how many sequences there are and multiply $(p)^2(1 - p)^3$ by that number.

Each different order in which we can have k successes in n trials is called a "combination." The total number of ways this can happen is written $\binom{n}{k}$ or $_nC_k$ and pronounced "n choose k:"

$$\binom{n}{k} = {_nC_k} = \frac{n!}{k!(n - k)!} \text{ where } n! = n \times (n - 1) \times \cdots \times 1.^6$$

For 2 successes in 5 trials,

$$\binom{5}{2} = \frac{5!}{2!(5 - 2)!} = \frac{(5 \times 4 \times 3 \times 2 \times 1)}{(2 \times 1 \times 3 \times 2 \times 1)} = \frac{(5 \times 4)}{(2 \times 1)} = 10.$$

So there are 10 ways to get 2 successes in 5 websites, and the probability of each is $(p)^2(1 - p)^3$. To find the probability of exactly 2 successes in 5 trials, we multiply the probability of any particular order by the number of possible different orders:

$P(\textit{exactly 2 successes in 5 trials}) = 10p^2(1 - p)^3 = 10(0.10)^2(0.90)^3 = 0.0729$

In general, we can write the probability of exactly k successes in n trials as

$P(X = k) = \binom{n}{k}p^k q^{n-k}$.

If the probability that any single website has a display problem is 0.10, what's the expected number of websites with problems if we test 100 sites? You probably

---

[6]You can demonstrate this formula for yourself by working out all possible sequences of 2, 3, and 4 successes and failures (e.g., SSS, SSF, SFS, . . . , etc., for $n = 3$) and seeing how many contain exactly k successes.

said 10. We suspect you didn't use the formula for expected value that involves multiplying each value times its probability and adding them up. In fact, there is an easier way to find the expected value for a Binomial random variable. You just multiply the probability of success by n. In other words, $E(X) = np$. We prove this in the next Math Box.

The standard deviation is less obvious and you can't just rely on your intuition. Fortunately, the formula for the standard deviation also boils down to something simple: $SD(X) = \sqrt{npq}$. If you're curious to know where that comes from, it's in the Math Box, too.

In our website example, with $n = 100$, $E(X) = np = 100(0.10) = 10$ so we expect to find 10 successes out of the 100 trials. The standard deviation is

$$\sqrt{100 \times 0.10 \times 0.90} = 3 \text{ websites.}$$

Binomial Model for Bernoulli Trials: Binom (n, p)

n = number of trials
p = probability of success (and $q = 1 - p$ = probability of failure)
X = number of successes in n trials

$$P(X = x) = \binom{n}{x} p^x q^{n-x}, \text{ where } \binom{n}{x} = \frac{n!}{x!(n-x)!}$$

Mean: $\mu = np$
Standard deviation: $\sigma = \sqrt{npq}$

MATH BOX   Mean and standard deviation of the Binomial model

To derive the formulas for the mean and standard deviation of the Binomial model we start with the most basic situation.

Consider a single Bernoulli trial with probability of success p. Let's find the mean and variance of the number of successes. We assign a value of 1 to a success and 0 to a failure.

Here's the probability model for the number of successes:

	Failure	Success
Outcome x	0	1
$P(X = x)$	q	p

Find the expected value:

$$E(X) = 0q + 1p$$
$$E(X) = p$$

Now the variance:

$$Var(X) = (0 - p)^2 q + (1 - p)^2 p$$
$$= p^2 q + q^2 p$$
$$= pq(p + q)$$
$$= pq(1)$$
$$Var(X) = pq$$

What happens when there is more than one trial? A Binomial model simply counts the number of successes in a series of n independent Bernoulli trials. That makes it easy to find the mean and standard deviation of a Binomial random variable, Y.

$$Let\ Y = X_1 + X_2 + X_3 + \cdots + X_n$$
$$E(Y) = E(X_1 + X_2 + X_3 + \cdots + X_n)$$
$$= E(X_1) + E(X_2) + E(X_3) + \cdots + E(X_n)$$
$$= p + p + p + \cdots + p \ (\text{There are } n \text{ terms.})$$

So, as we thought, the mean is $E(Y) = np$.

And since the trials are independent, the variances add:

$$Var(Y) = Var(X_1 + X_2 + X_3 + \cdots + X_n)$$
$$= Var(X_1) + Var(X_2) + Var(X_3) + \cdots + Var(X_n)$$
$$= pq + pq + pq + \cdots + pq \ (\text{Again, } n \text{ terms.})$$
$$Var(Y) = npq$$

Voila! The standard deviation is $SD(Y) = \sqrt{npq}$.

GUIDED EXAMPLE   The American Red Cross

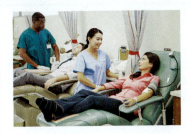

Every two seconds someone in America needs blood.

The American Red Cross is a nonprofit organization that runs like a large business. It serves over 3000 hospitals around the United States, providing a wide range of high-quality blood products and blood donor and patient testing services. It collects blood from over 4 million donors, provides blood to millions of patients, and is dedicated to meeting customer needs.

Balancing supply and demand is complicated not only by the logistics of finding donors that meet health criteria, but also by the fact that the blood type of donor and patient must be matched. People with O-negative blood are called "universal donors" because O-negative blood can be given to patients with any blood type. Only about 6% of people have O-negative blood, which presents a challenge in managing and planning. This is especially true, since, unlike a manufacturer who can balance supply by planning to produce or to purchase more or less of a key item, the Red Cross gets its supply from volunteer donors who show up more-or-less at random (at least in terms of blood type). Modeling the arrival of samples with various blood types helps the Red Cross managers to plan their blood allocations.

Here's a small example of the kind of planning required. Of the next 20 donors to arrive at a blood donation center, how many universal donors can be expected? Specifically, what are the mean and standard deviation of the number of universal donors? What is the probability that there are 2 or 3 universal donors?

Question 1: What are the mean and standard deviation of the number of universal donors?

Question 2: What is the probability that there are exactly 2 or 3 universal donors out of the 20 donors?

PLAN	**Define** the problem and state the objective	We want to know the mean and standard deviation of the number of universal donors among 20 people and the probability that there are 2 or 3 of them.
	Identify the success and failure outcomes, and check to see that these are Bernoulli trials.	✔ There are two outcomes:
		success = O-negative
	Define the random variable, and specify the model.	failure = other blood types

(continued)

✔ $p = 0.06$

✔ **10% Condition**: Fewer than 10% of all possible donors have shown up.

Let X = number of O-negative donors among $n = 20$ people.

We can model X with a Binom(20, 0.06).

DO **Characterize and Model** Find the expected value and standard deviation. Calculate the probability of 2 or 3 successes.	$E(X) = np = 20(0.06) = 1.2$ $SD(X) = \sqrt{npq} = \sqrt{20(0.06)(0.94)} \approx 1.06$ $P(X = 2 \text{ or } 3) = P(X = 2) + P(X = 3)$ $\qquad = \binom{20}{2}(0.06)^2(0.94)^{18}$ $\qquad\quad + \binom{20}{3}(0.06)^3(0.94)^{17}$ $\qquad \approx 0.2246 + 0.0860$ $\qquad = 0.3106$	
REPORT **Conclusion** Interpret your results in context.	**MEMO** **Re: Blood drive** In groups of 20 randomly selected blood donors, we'd expect to find an average of 1.2 universal donors, with a standard deviation of 1.06. About 31% of the time, we'd expect to find exactly 2 or 3 universal donors among the 20 people.	

The Poisson Model

Simeon Denis Poisson was a French mathematician interested in rare events. He originally derived his model to approximate the Binomial model when the probability of a success, p, is very small and the number of trials, n, is very large. Poisson's contribution was providing a simple approximation to find that probability. When you see the formula, however, you won't necessarily see the connection to the Binomial.

Not all discrete events can be modeled as Bernoulli trials. Sometimes we're interested simply in the number of events that occur over a given interval of time or space. For example, we might want to model the number of customers arriving in our store in the next ten minutes, the number of visitors to our website in the next minute, or the number of defects that occur in a computer monitor of a certain size. In cases like these, the number of occurrences can be modeled by a **Poisson model**. The Poisson's parameter, the mean of the distribution, is usually denoted by λ.

Poisson Probability Model for Occurrences: Poisson (λ)

λ = mean number of occurrences

X = number of occurrences

$$P(X = x) = \frac{e^{-\lambda}\lambda^x}{x!}$$

Expected value: $E(X) = \lambda$

Standard deviation: $SD(X) = \sqrt{\lambda}$

For example, data show an average of about 4 hits per minute to a small business website during the afternoon hours from 1:00 to 5:00 PM. We can use the Poisson model to find the probability of any number of hits arriving. For example, if we let X be the number of hits arriving in the next minute, then $P(X = x) = \dfrac{e^{-\lambda}\lambda^{x}}{x!} = \dfrac{e^{-4}4^{x}}{x!}$, using the given average rate of 4 per minute. So, the probability of no hits during the next minute would be $P(X = 0) = \dfrac{e^{-4}4^{0}}{0!} = e^{-4} = 0.018$ (the constant e is the base of the natural logarithms and is approximately 2.72).

One interesting and useful feature of the Poisson model is that it scales according to the interval size. For example, suppose we want to know the probability of no hits to our website in the next 30 seconds. Since the mean rate is 4 hits per minute, it's 2 hits per 30 seconds, so we can use the model with $\lambda = 2$ instead. If we let Y be the number of hits arriving in the next 30 seconds, then:

$$P(Y = 0) = \frac{e^{-2}2^{0}}{0!} = e^{-2} = 0.135.$$

(Recall that $0! = 1$.) The Poisson model has been used to model phenomena such as customer arrivals, hot streaks in sports, and disease clusters.

Whenever or wherever rare events happen closely together, people want to know whether the occurrence happened by chance or whether an underlying change caused the unusual occurrence. The Poisson model can be used to find the probability of the occurrence and can be the basis for making the judgment.

> **W. S. Gosset,** the quality control chemist at the Guinness brewery in the early 20th century who developed the methods of Chapters 11 and 12, was one of the first to use the Poisson in industry. He used it to model and predict the number of yeast cells so he'd know how much to add to the stock. The Poisson is a good model to consider whenever your data consist of counts of occurrences. It requires only that the events be independent and that the mean number of occurrences stays constant.

---

e and Compound Interest

The constant e equals $2.7182818\ldots$ (to 7 decimal places). One of the places e originally turned up was in calculating how much money you'd earn if you could get interest compounded more often. If you earn 100% per year simple interest, at the end of the year, you'd have twice as much money as when you started. But if the interest were compounded and paid at the end of every month, each month you'd earn 1/12 of 100% interest. At the year's end you'd have $(1 + 1/12)^{12} = 2.613$ times as much instead of 2. If the interest were paid every day, you'd get $(1 + 1/365)^{365} = 2.715$ times as much. If the interest were paid every second, you'd get $(1 + 1/3153600)^{3153600} = 2.7182812$ times as much. This is where e shows up. If you could get the interest compounded continually, you'd get e times as much. In other words, as n gets large, the limit of $(1 + 1/n)^{n} = e$. This unexpected result was discovered by Jacob Bernoulli in 1683.

JUST CHECKING

Roper Worldwide reports that they are able to contact 76% of the randomly selected households drawn for a telephone survey.

2 Explain why these phone calls can be considered Bernoulli trials.

3 Which of the models of this chapter (Geometric, Binomial, or Poisson) would you use to model the number of successful contracts from a list of 1000 sampled households?

4 Roper also reports that even after they contacted a household, only 38% of the contacts agreed to be interviewed. So the probability of getting a completed interview from a randomly selected household is only 0.29 (38% of 76%). Which of the models of this chapter would you use to model the number of households Roper has to call before they get the first completed interview?

IN PRACTICE 6.4 Probability in customer acquisition

A venture capital firm has a list of potential investors who have previously invested in new technologies. On average, these investors invest about 5% of the time. A new client of the firm is interested in finding investors for a mobile phone application that enables financial transactions, an application that is finding increasing acceptance in much of the developing world. An analyst at the firm is about to start calling potential investors.

MANAGER I have a number of questions about the likelihood of our company acquiring investors.

1. What is the probability that the first person she calls will want to invest?
2. What is the probability that none of the first five people she calls will be interested?
3. How many people will she have to call until the probability of finding someone interested is at least 0.50?
4. How many investors will she have to call, on average, to find someone interested?
5. If she calls 10 investors, what is the probability that exactly 2 of them will be interested?
6. What assumptions are you making to answer these questions?

ANALYST To answer your questions, I need to work with probability models.

1. Each investor has a 5% or 1/20 chance of wanting to invest, so the chance that the first person she calls is interested is 1/20.
2. P (first one not interested) $= 1 - 1/20 = 19/20$. Assuming the trials are independent, P(none are interested) $= P$ (1st not interested) $\times P$ (2nd not interested) $\times \cdots \times P$ (5th not interested) $= (19/20)^5 = 0.774$.
3. By trial and error, $(19/20)^{13} = 0.513$ and $(19/20)^{14} = 0.488$, so she would need to call 14 people to have the probability of *no one* interested drop below 0.50, therefore making the probability that someone is interested greater than 0.50.
4. This uses a Geometric model. Let $X =$ number of people she calls until the first interested person. $E(X) = 1/p = 1/(1/20) = 20$ people.
5. Using the Binomial model, let $Y =$ number of people interested in 10 calls, then

$$P(Y = 2) = \binom{10}{2}p^2(1 - p)^8 = \frac{10 \times 9}{2}(1/20)^2(19/20)^8 = 0.0746.$$

6. We are assuming that the trials are independent and that the probability of being interested in investing is the same for all potential investors.

⊘ WHAT CAN GO WRONG?

- **Probability models are still just models.** Models can be useful, but they are not reality. Think about the assumptions behind your models. Question probabilities as you would data.

- **If the model is wrong, so is everything else.** Before you try to find the mean or standard deviation of a random variable, check to make sure the probability model is reasonable. As a start, the probabilities should all be between 0 and 1 and they should add up to 1. If not, you may have calculated a probability incorrectly or left out a value of the random variable.

- **Watch out for variables that aren't independent.** You can add expected values of *any* two random variables, but you can only add variances of independent random variables. Suppose a survey includes questions about the number of hours of sleep people get each night and also the number of hours they are awake each day. From their answers, we find the mean and standard deviation of hours asleep and hours awake. The expected total must be 24 hours; after all, people are either asleep or awake. The means still add just fine. Since all the totals are exactly 24 hours, however, the standard deviation of the total will be 0. We can't add variances here because the number of hours you're awake depends on the number of hours you're asleep. Be sure to check for independence before adding variances.

- **Don't write independent instances of a random variable with notation that looks like they are the same variables.** Make sure you write each instance as a different random variable. Just because each random variable describes a similar situation doesn't mean that each random outcome will be the same. These are *random* variables, not the variables you saw in algebra. Write $X_1 + X_2 + X_3$ rather than $X + X + X$.

- **Don't forget:** Variances of independent random variables add. Standard deviations don't.

- **Don't forget:** Variances of independent random variables add, even when you're looking at the difference between them.

- **Be sure you have Bernoulli trials.** Be sure to check the requirements first: two possible outcomes per trial ("success" and "failure"), a constant probability of success, and independence. Remember that the 10% Condition provides a reasonable substitute for independence.

ETHICS IN ACTION

Kurt Williams was about to open a new SEP IRA account and was interested in exploring various investment options. Although he had some ideas about how to invest his money, Kurt thought it best to seek the advice of a professional, so he made an appointment with Keith Klingman, a financial advisor at James, Morgan, and Edwards, LLC.

Prior to their first meeting, Kurt told Keith that he preferred to keep his investments simple and wished to allocate his money to only two funds. Also, he mentioned that while he was willing to take on some risk to yield higher returns, he was concerned about taking on too much risk given the recent volatility in the markets. After their conversation, Keith began to prepare for their first meeting.

Because Kurt was interested in investing his SEP IRA money in only two funds, Keith decided to compile figures on the expected annual return and standard deviation (a measure of risk) for a potential SEP IRA account consisting of different combinations of two funds. If X and Y represent the annual returns for two different funds, Keith knew he could represent the expected annual return for any combination of funds as $aX + (1 - a)Y$, where a is the fraction of funds Kurt will allocate to X.

Keith calculated the expected annual return using the formula $E(aX + (1 - a)Y) = aE(X) + (1 - a)E(Y)$. Keith knew that this formula would be true for all funds X and Y even if their performances were correlated. To find the variance if the combined investment he calculated $Var(aX + (1 - a)Y) = a^2 Var(X) + (1 - a)^2 Var(Y)$.

Keith knew that the variance calculation assumed that the two funds were independent, but he figured that the formula was close enough even if the funds' performances were correlated, and he wanted to keep the presentation to Kurt simple.

Keith presented a variety of combinations of funds and allocations to Kurt. Because some equity funds delivered the best expected return, Keith advised Kurt to put all his money in two equity funds (funds that also generated higher brokerage fees) rather than allocating any money to a simple fixed income fund. Kurt was surprised to see that even under various market conditions, all the equity fund combinations seemed fairly safe in terms of volatility as evidenced by the fairly low standard deviations of the combined funds, and Keith assured him that these scenarios were realistic.

- **Identify the ethical dilemma in this scenario.**

- **What are the undesirable consequences?**

- **Propose an ethical solution that considers the welfare of all stakeholders.**

FROM LEARNING TO EARNING

LEARNING OBJECTIVES

Understand how probability models relate values to probabilities.

- For discrete random variables, probability models assign a probability to each possible outcome.

Know how to find the mean, or expected value, of a discrete probability model from $\mu = \sum x P(X = x)$ and the standard deviation from $\sigma = \sqrt{\sum (x - \mu)^2 P(x)}$.

Foresee the consequences of shifting and scaling random variables, specifically

$$E(X \pm c) = E(X) \pm c \qquad E(aX) = aE(X)$$

$$Var(X \pm c) = Var(X) \qquad Var(aX) = a^2 Var(X)$$

$$SD(X \pm c) = SD(X) \qquad SD(aX) = |a| SD(X)$$

Understand that when adding or subtracting random variables the expected values add or subtract as well: $E(X \pm Y) = E(X) \pm E(Y)$. However, when adding or subtracting independent random variables, the variances *add*:

$$Var(X \pm Y) = Var(X) + Var(Y)$$

Be able to explain the properties and parameters of the Uniform, the Binomial, the Geometric, and the Poisson distributions.

TERMS

Addition Rule for Expected Values of Random Variables

$$E(X \pm Y) = E(X) \pm E(Y)$$

Addition Rule for Variances of (Independent) Random Variables

(Pythagorean Theorem of Statistics)

If X and Y are *independent*: $Var(X \pm Y) = Var(X) + Var(Y)$,

and $SD(X \pm Y) = \sqrt{Var(X) + Var(Y)}$.

Bernoulli trials

A sequence of n trials are called Bernoulli trials if:

1. There are exactly two possible outcomes (usually denoted *success* and *failure*).
2. The probability of success is constant.
3. The trials are independent.

Binomial probability model

A Binomial model is appropriate for a random variable that counts the number of successes in a series of Bernoulli trials.

Changing a random variable by a constant

$$E(X \pm c) = E(X) \pm c \qquad Var(X \pm c) = Var(X) \qquad SD(X \pm c) = SD(X)$$

$$E(aX) = aE(X) \qquad Var(aX) = a^2 Var(X) \qquad SD(aX) = |a| SD(X)$$

Correlation

The correlation between two random variables X and Y is defined as $Corr(X, Y) = \dfrac{Cov(X, Y)}{\sigma_X \sigma_Y}$ and measures the strength of the linear association between them. It is a number between -1 and 1 where the extremes correspond to perfect negative and positive linear association respectively.

Continuous random variable

A random variable that can take on any value (possibly bounded on one or both sides).

Covariance

The covariance of random variables X and Y is $Cov(X, Y) = E((X - \mu)(Y - \nu))$ where $\mu = E(X)$ and $\nu = E(Y)$. In general (no need to assume independence) $Var(X \pm Y) = Var(X) + Var(Y) \pm 2Cov(X, Y)$

Discrete random variable

A random variable that can take one of a finite number[7] of distinct outcomes.

---

[7]Technically, there could be an infinite number of outcomes as long as they're *countable*. Essentially, that means we can imagine listing them all in order, like the counting numbers 1, 2, 3, 4, 5, . . .

Expected value	The expected value of a random variable is its theoretical long-run average value, the center of its model. Denoted μ or $E(X)$, it is found (if the random variable is discrete) by summing the products of variable values and probabilities:

$$\mu = E(X) = \Sigma x P(x)$$

Geometric probability model	A model appropriate for a random variable that counts the number of Bernoulli trials until the first success.
Parameter	A numerically valued attribute of a model, such as the values of μ and σ representing the mean and standard deviation.
Poisson model	A discrete model often used to model the number of arrivals of events such as customers arriving in a queue or calls arriving into a call center.
Probability model	A function that associates a probability P with each value of a discrete random variable X, denoted $P(X = x)$, or with any interval of values of a continuous random variable.
Random variable	Assumes any of several different values as a result of some random event. Random variables are denoted by a capital letter, such as X.
Standard deviation of a random variable	Describes the spread in the model and is the square root of the variance.
Uniform model, Uniform distribution	For a discrete uniform distribution over a set of n values, each value has probability $1/n$.
Variance of a random variable	The variance of a random variable is the expected value of the squared deviations from the mean. For discrete random variables, it can be calculated as:

$$\sigma^2 = Var(X) = \Sigma (x - \mu)^2 P(x).$$

TECH SUPPORT   Random Variables and Probability Models

Most statistics packages (and graphics calculators) offer functions that compute probabilities for various probability models. The important differences among these functions are in what they are named and the order of their arguments. In these functions, **"pdf"** stands for **"probability density function"**—what we've been calling a probability model. The letters **"cdf"** stand for **"cumulative distribution function,"** the technical term when we want to accumulate probabilities over a range of values. These technical terms show up in many of the function names. Many packages allow the computation of a probability given a value based on a given distribution and also the calculation of a value based on the probability.

For example, in Excel, Binomdist(x, n, prob, cumulative) computes Binomial probabilities. If cumulative is set to false, the calculation is only for one value of x.

EXCEL

The following commands can be used to calculate Binomial and Poisson distribution probabilities. In Excel, the value for "cumulative" will give either a cdf (cumulative = TRUE) or a pdf (cumulative = FALSE). The commands can either be typed directly into a cell or into the function bar at the top of the screen.

Excel Syntax	Example Syntax	Result	Probability Statement
BINOM.DIST(number of successes, trials, probability of success, cumulative)	=BINOM.DIST(5,20,0.06,TRUE)	0.9991	P(X≤5)
	=BINOM.DIST(5,20,0.06,FALSE)	0.0048	P(X<5)
BINOM.INV(trials, probability of success, probability)	=BINOM.INV(20,0.06,0.9991)	5.0000	P(X=?)=0.9991
	=POISSON.DIST(2,4,TRUE)	0.2381	P(X≤2)
POISSON.DIST(number of occurrences, mean number of occurrences, cumulative)	=POISSON.DIST(2,4,FALSE)	0.1465	P(X<2)

R

The library stats contains the pdfs and cdfs of several common distributions:

- **library(stats)**

- **dbinom(x, n, p)** # Gives $P(X = x)$ for Binomial with n and p

- **pbinom(x, n, p)** # Gives the cumulative distribution function $P(X \geq x)$ for the Binomial

- **dpois(x, mean)** # Gives $P(X = x)$ for the Poisson

- **ppois(x, mean)** # Gives the cumulative distribution function $P(X \geq x)$ for the Poisson

- Create a new data table: **File > New > New Data Table.**
- Right click on the header Column 1 and select **Formula.**
- Select **Discrete Probability.**
- Select any of:
  - Binomial Probability (prob, n, k) for the pdf
  - Binomial Distribution (prob, n, k) for the cdf
  - Poisson Probability (λ) for the pdf
  - Poisson Distribution (λ) for the cdf
- Click **OK** twice. The probability will be displayed in the first row of Column 1.

- Choose **Probability Distributions** from the Calc menu.
- Choose **Binomial** from the Probability Distributions submenu.
- To calculate the probability of getting *x* successes in *n* trials, choose **Probability.**
- To calculate the probability of getting *x* or fewer successes among *n* trials, choose **Cumulative Probability.**
- For Poisson, choose **Poisson** from the Probability Distribution submenu.

- In Data View, type values of the parameters for the desired distribution in the first row. For example, for a Binomial PDF, type the number of successes in the first column, first row; trials in second column, first row; and probability of success in the third column, first row.
- Choose **Transform: Compute Variable.**
- Type a name for the variable that will contain the result.

- In the box under Numeric Expression, type the desired probability to be calculated, using the labels for the variables where the parameter values are stored:
  - PDF.BINOM(x, n, prob)
  - CDF.BINOM(x, n, prob)
  - PDF.Poisson(x, mean)
  - CDF.Poisson(x, mean)
- Click **OK** and the probability will be calculated and stored in the next column. Adjust the column width to show more decimals—the value will be rounded to 2 decimal places by default.

To calculate Binomial probabilities:

- Click on **Stat.**
- Choose **Calculators > Binomial.**
- Enter the parameters, **n** and **p.**
- Choose a specific outcome ($=$) or a lower tail ($\le$ or $<$) or upper tail ($\ge$ or $>$) sum.
- Enter the number of successes **x.**
- Click on **Compute.**

To calculate Poisson probabilities:

- Click on **Stat.**
- Choose **Calculators > Poisson.**
- Enter the mean.
- Choose a specific outcome ($=$) or a lower tail ($\le$ or $<$) or upper tail ($\ge$ or $>$) sum.
- Enter the number of successes **x.**
- Click on **Compute.**

BRIEF CASE

Investment Options

A young entrepreneur has just raised $30,000 from investors, and she would like to invest it while she continues her fund-raising in hopes of starting her company one year from now. She wants to do due diligence and understand the risk of each of her investment options. After speaking with her colleagues in finance, she believes that she has three choices: (1) she can purchase a $30,000 certificate of deposit (CD); (2) she can invest in a mutual fund with a balanced portfolio; or (3) she can invest in a growth stock that has a greater potential payback but also has greater volatility. Each of her options will yield a different payback on her $30,000, depending on the state of the economy.

During the next year, she knows that the CD yields a constant annual percentage rate, regardless of the state of the economy. If she invests in a balanced mutual fund, she estimates that she will earn as much as 12% if the economy remains strong, but could possibly lose as much as 4% if the economy takes a downturn. Finally, if she invests all $30,000 in a growth stock, experienced investors tell her that she can earn as much as 40% in a strong economy, but may lose as much as 40% in a poor economy.

Estimating these returns, along with the likelihood of a strong economy, is challenging. Therefore, a "sensitivity analysis" is often conducted, where figures are computed using a range of values for each of the uncertain parameters in the problem. Following this advice, this investor decides to compute measures for a range of interest rates for CDs, a range of returns for the mutual fund, and a range of returns for the growth stock. In addition, the likelihood of a strong economy is unknown, so she will vary these probabilities as well.

Assume that the probability of a strong economy over the next year is 0.3, 0.5, or 0.7. To help this investor make an informed decision, evaluate the expected value and volatility of each of her investments using the following ranges of rates of growth:

CD: Look up the current annual rate for the return on a 3-year CD and use this value $\pm 0.5\%$.

Mutual Fund: Use values of 8%, 10%, and 12% for a strong economy and values of 0%, −2%, and −4% for a weak economy.

Growth Stock: Use values of 10%, 25%, and 40% in a strong economy and values of −10%, −25%, and −40% in a weak economy.

Discuss the expected returns and uncertainty of each of the alternative investment options for this investor in each of the scenarios you analyzed. Be sure to compare the volatility of each of her options.

CHAPTER 6 EXERCISES

SECTION 6.1

1. A company's employee database includes data on whether or not the employee includes a dependent child in his or her health insurance.

a) Is this variable discrete or continuous?
b) What are the possible values it can take on?

2. The database also, of course, includes each employee's compensation.

a) Is this variable discrete or continuous?
b) What are the possible values it can take on?

3. Suppose that the probabilities of a customer purchasing 0, 1, or 2 books at a book store are 0.5, 0.3, and 0.2, respectively. What is the expected number of books a customer will purchase?

4. A day trader buys an option on a stock that will return $100 profit if the stock goes up today and lose $400 if it

goes down. If the trader thinks there is a 75% chance that the stock will go up,

a) What is her expected value of the option's profit?
b) What do you think of this option?

SECTION 6.2

5. Find the standard deviation of the book purchases in Exercise 3.

6. Find the standard deviation of the day trader's option value in Exercise 4.

7. An orthodontist has three financing packages, and each has a different service charge. He estimates that 30% of patients use the first plan, which has a $10 finance charge; 50% use the second plan, which has a $20 finance charge; and 20% use the third plan, which has a $30 finance charge.

a) Find the expected value of the service charge.
b) Find the standard deviation of the service charge.

8. A marketing agency has developed three vacation packages to promote a timeshare plan at a new resort. They estimate that 20% of potential customers will choose the Day Plan, which does not include overnight accommodations; 40% will choose the Overnight Plan, which includes one night at the resort; and 40% will choose the Weekend Plan, which includes two nights.

a) Find the expected value of the number of nights potential customers will need.

b) Find the standard deviation of the number of nights potential customers will need.

SECTION 6.3

9. Given independent random variables, X and Y, with means and standard deviations as shown, find the mean and standard deviation of each of the variables in parts a to d.

a) $3X$
b) $Y + 6$
c) $X + Y$
d) $X - Y$

	Mean	SD
X	10	2
Y	20	5

10. Given independent random variables, X and Y, with means and standard deviations as shown, find the mean and standard deviation of each of the variables in parts a to d.

a) $X - 20$
b) $0.5Y$
c) $X + Y$
d) $X - Y$

	Mean	SD
X	80	12
Y	12	3

11. A broker has calculated the expected values of two different financial instruments X and Y. Suppose that $E(X) = \$100, E(Y) = \$90, SD(X) = \$12$, and $SD(Y) = \$8$. Find each of the following.

a) $E(X + 10)$ and $SD(X + 10)$
b) $E(5Y)$ and $SD(5Y)$
c) $E(X + Y)$ and $SD(X + Y)$
d) What assumption must you make in part c?

12. A company selling glass ornaments by mail-order expects, from previous history, that 6% of the ornaments it ships will break in shipping. You purchase two ornaments as gifts and have them shipped separately to two different addresses. What is the probability that both arrive safely? What did you assume?

SECTION 6.4

13. Which of these situations fit the conditions for using Bernoulli trials? Explain.

a) You are rolling 5 dice and need to get at least two 6s to win the game.
b) We record the distribution of home states of customers visiting our website.

c) A committee consisting of 11 men and 8 women selects a delegation of 4 to attend a professional meeting at random. What is the probability they choose all women?

d) A study (softwaresecure.typepad.com/multiple_choice/2007/05/cheat_cheat_nev.html) found that 56% of M.B.A. students admit to cheating. A business school dean surveys all the students in the graduating class and gets responses that admit to cheating from 250 of 481 students.

14. At the airport entry sites, a computer is used to randomly decide whether a traveler's baggage should be opened for inspection. If the chance of being selected is 12%, can you model your chance of having your baggage opened with a Bernoulli model? Check each of the conditions specifically.

SECTION 6.5

15. At many airports, a traveler entering the U.S. is sent randomly to one of several stations where his passport and visa are checked. If each of the 6 stations is equally likely, can the probabilities of which station a traveler will be sent be modeled with a Uniform model?

16. Through the career services office, you have arranged preliminary interviews at four companies for summer jobs. Each company will either ask you to come to their site for a follow-up interview or not. Let X be the random variable equal to the total number of follow-up interviews that you might have.

a) List all the possible values of X.
b) Is the random variable discrete or continuous?
c) Do you think a uniform distribution might be appropriate as a model for this random variable? Explain briefly.

17. The U.S. Census Bureau's 2012 Survey of Business Owners (www.census.gov/newsroom/press-releases/2015/cb15-209.html) showed that 35.8% of all non-farm businesses are owned by women. You are phoning local businesses and assume that the national percentage is true in your area. You wonder how many calls you will have to make before you find one owned by a woman. What probability model should you use? (Specify the parameters as well.)

18. As in Exercise 17, you are phoning local businesses. You call three firms. What is the probability that all three are owned by women?

19. A manufacturer of clothing knows that the probability of a button flaw (broken, sewed on incorrectly, or missing) is 0.002. An inspector examines 50 shirts in an hour, each with 6 buttons. Using a Poisson probability model:

a) What is the probability that she finds no button flaws?
b) What is the probability that she finds at least one?

20. Replacing the buttons with snaps increases the probability of a flaw to 0.003, but the inspector can check 70 shirts an hour (still with 6 snaps each). Now what is the probability she finds no snap flaws?

CHAPTER EXERCISES

21. New website. You have just launched the website for your company that sells nutritional products online. Suppose X = the number of different pages that a customer hits during a visit to the website.

a) Assuming that there are n different pages in total on your website, what are the possible values that this random variable may take on?
b) Is the random variable discrete or continuous?

22. New website, part 2. For the website described in Exercise 21, let Y = the total time (in minutes) that a customer spends during a visit to the website.

a) What are the possible values of this random variable?
b) Is the random variable discrete or continuous?

23. Repairs. The probability model below describes the number of repair calls that an appliance repair shop may receive during an hour.

Repair Calls	0	1	2	3
Probability	0.1	0.3	0.4	0.2

a) How many calls should the shop expect per hour?
b) What is the standard deviation?

24. Software company. A small software company will bid on a major contract. It anticipates a profit of $50,000 if it gets it, but thinks there is only a 30% chance of that happening.

a) What's the expected profit?
b) Find the standard deviation for the profit.

25. Commuting to work. A commuter must pass through five traffic lights on her way to work and will have to stop at each one that is red. After keeping a record for several months, she developed the following probability model for the number of red lights she hits:

X = # of Red	0	1	2	3	4	5
$p(X = x)$	0.05	0.25	0.35	0.15	0.15	0.05

a) How many red lights should she expect to hit each day?
b) What's the standard deviation?

26. Defects. A consumer organization inspecting new cars found that many had appearance defects (dents, scratches, paint chips, etc.). While none had more than three of these defects, 7% had three, 11% had two, and 21% had one defect.

a) Find the expected number of appearance defects in a new car.
b) What is the standard deviation?

27. Fishing tournament. A sporting goods manufacturer was asked to sponsor a local boy in two fishing tournaments. They claim the probability that he will win the first tournament is 0.4. If he wins the first tournament, they estimate the probability that he will also win the second is 0.2. They guess that if he loses the first tournament, the probability that he will win the second is 0.3.

a) According to their estimates, are the two tournaments independent? Explain your answer.
b) What's the probability that he loses both tournaments?
c) What's the probability he wins both tournaments?
d) Let random variable X be the number of tournaments he wins. Find the probability model for X.
e) What are the expected value and standard deviation of X?

28. Contracts. Your company bids for two contracts. You believe the probability that you get contract #1 is 0.8. If you get contract #1, the probability that you also get contract #2 will be 0.2, and if you do not get contract #1, the probability that you get contract #2 will be 0.3.

a) Are the outcomes of the two contract bids independent? Explain.
b) Find the probability you get both contracts.
c) Find the probability you get neither contract.
d) Let X be the number of contracts you get. Find the probability model for X.
e) Find the expected value and standard deviation of X.

29. Battery recall. A company has discovered that a recent batch of batteries had manufacturing flaws, and has issued a recall. You have 10 batteries covered by the recall, and 3 are dead. You choose 2 batteries at random from your package of 10.

a) Has the assumption of independence been met? Explain.
b) Create a probability model for the number of good batteries chosen.
c) What's the expected number of good batteries?
d) What's the standard deviation?

30. Grocery supplier. A grocery supplier believes that the mean number of broken eggs per dozen is 0.6, with a standard deviation of 0.5. You buy 3 dozen eggs without checking them.

a) How many broken eggs do you expect to get?
b) What's the standard deviation?
c) Is it necessary to assume the cartons of eggs are independent? Why?

31. Commuting, part 2. A commuter finds that she waits an average of 14.8 seconds at each of five stoplights, with a standard deviation of 9.2 seconds. Find the mean and the standard deviation of the total amount of time she waits at all five lights. What, if anything, did you assume?

32. Defective pixels. For warranty purposes, analysts want to model the number of defects on a screen of the new tablet they are manufacturing. Let X = the number of defective pixels per screen. If X can be modeled by:

X = # of Defective Pixels	0	1	2	3	4 or more
$P(X = x)$	0.95	0.04	0.008	0.002	0

a) What is the expected number of defective pixels per screen?
b) What is the standard deviation of the number of defective pixels per screen?
c) What is the expected number of defective pixels in the next 100 screens?
d) What is the standard deviation of the number of defective pixels in the next 100 screens?

33. Repair calls. Suppose that the appliance shop in Exercise 23 plans an 8-hour day.

a) Find the mean and standard deviation of the number of repair calls they should expect in a day.
b) What assumption did you make about the repair calls?
c) Use the mean and standard deviation to describe what a typical 8-hour day will be like.
d) At the end of a day, a worker comments, "Boy, I'm tired. Today was sure unusually busy!" How many repair calls would justify such an observation?

34. Casino. At a casino, people play the slot machines in hopes of hitting the jackpot, but most of the time, they lose their money. A certain machine pays out an average of $0.92 (for every dollar played), with a standard deviation of $120.

a) Why is the standard deviation so large?
b) If a gambler plays 5 times, what are the mean and standard deviation of the casino's profit?
c) If gamblers play this machine 1000 times in a day, what are the mean and standard deviation of the casino's profit?

35. Bike sale. A bicycle shop plans to offer 2 specially priced children's models at a sidewalk sale. The basic model will return a profit of $120 and the deluxe model $150. Past experience indicates that sales of the basic model will have a mean of 5.4 bikes with a standard deviation of 1.2, and sales of the deluxe model will have a mean of 3.2 bikes with a standard deviation of 0.8 bikes. The cost of setting up for the sidewalk sale is $200.

a) Define random variables and use them to express the bicycle shop's net profit.
b) What's the mean of the net profit?
c) What's the standard deviation of the net profit?
d) Do you need to make any assumptions in calculating the mean? How about the standard deviation?

36. Farmers' market. A farmer has 100 lb of apples and 50 lb of potatoes for sale. The market price for apples (per pound) each day is a random variable with a mean of 0.5 dollar and a standard deviation of 0.2 dollar. Similarly, for a pound of potatoes, the mean price is 0.3 dollar and the standard deviation is 0.1 dollar. It also costs him 2 dollars to bring all the apples and potatoes to the market. The market is busy with eager shoppers, so we can assume that he'll be able to sell all of each type of produce at that day's price.

a) Define your random variables, and use them to express the farmer's net income.
b) Find the mean of the net income.
c) Find the standard deviation of the net income.
d) Do you need to make any assumptions in calculating the mean? How about the standard deviation?

37. Cancelled flights. Mary is deciding whether to book the cheaper flight home college after her final exams, but she's unsure when her last exam will be. She thinks there is only a 20% chance that the exam will be scheduled after the last day she can get a seat on the cheaper flight. If it is and she has to cancel the flight, she will lose $150. If she can take the cheaper flight, she will save $100.

a) If she books the cheaper flight, what can she expect to gain, on average?
b) What is the standard deviation?

38. Day trading. An option to buy a stock is priced at $200. If the stock closes above 30 on May 15, the option will be worth $1000. If it closes below 20, the option will be worth nothing, and if it closes between 20 and 30 (inclusively), the option will be worth $200. A trader thinks there is a 50% chance that the stock will close in the 20–30 range, a 20% chance that it will close above 30, and a 30% chance that it will fall below 20 on May 15.

a) How much does she expect to gain?
b) What is the standard deviation of her gain?
c) Should she buy the stock option? Discuss the pros and cons in terms of your answers to (a) and (b).

39. eBay. A collector purchased a quantity of action figures and is going to sell them on eBay. He has 19 Hulk figures. In recent auctions, the mean selling price of similar figures has been $12.11, with a standard deviation of $1.38. He also has 13 Iron Man figures which have had a mean selling price of $10.19, with a standard deviation of $0.77. His insertion fee will be $0.55 on each item, and the closing fee will be 8.75% of the selling price. He assumes all will sell without having to be relisted.

a) Define your random variables, and use them to create a random variable for the collector's net revenue.
b) Find the mean (expected value) of the net revenue.
c) Find the standard deviation of the net revenue.
d) Do you have to assume independence for the sales on eBay? Explain.

40. Real estate. A real-estate broker in Washington, DC, purchased 3 two-bedroom houses in a depressed market for a combined cost of $1,000,000. He expects the cleaning and repair costs on each house to average $100,000 with a standard deviation of $15,000. When he sells them, after subtracting taxes and other closing costs, he expects to realize an average of $475,000 per house, with a standard deviation of $12,500.

a) Define your random variables, and use them to create a random variable for the broker's net profit.
b) Find the mean (expected value) of the net profit.
c) Find the standard deviation of the net profit.
d) Do you have to assume independence for the repairs and sale prices of the houses? Explain.

41. Bernoulli. Can we use probability models based on Bernoulli trials to investigate the following situations? Explain.

a) Each week a doctor rolls a single die to determine which of his six office staff members gets the preferred parking space.
b) A medical research lab has samples of blood collected from 120 different individuals. How likely is it that the majority of them are Type A blood, given that Type A is found in 43% of the population?
c) From a workforce of 13 men and 23 women, all five promotions go to men. How likely is that, if promotions are based on qualifications rather than gender?
d) We poll 500 of the 3000 stockholders to see how likely it is that the proposed budget will pass.
e) A company realizes that about 10% of its packages are not being sealed properly. In a case of 24 packages, how likely is it that more than 3 are unsealed?

42. Bernoulli, part 2. Can we use probability models based on Bernoulli trials to investigate the following situations? Explain.

a) You survey 500 potential customers to determine their color preference.
b) A manufacturer recalls a doll because about 3% have buttons that are not properly attached. Customers return 37 of these dolls to the local toy store. How likely are they to find any buttons not properly attached?
c) A city council of 11 Republicans and 8 Democrats picks a committee of 4 at random. How likely are they to choose all Democrats?
d) An executive reads that 74% of employees in his industry are dissatisfied with their jobs. How many dissatisfied employees can he expect to find among the 481 employees in his company?

43. Closing sales. A salesman normally makes a sale (closes) on 80% of his presentations. Assuming the presentations are independent, find the probability of each of the following.

a) He fails to close for the first time on his fifth attempt.

b) He closes his first presentation on his fourth attempt.
c) The first presentation he closes will be on his second attempt.
d) The first presentation he closes will be on one of his first three attempts.

44. Computer chip manufacturer. Suppose a computer chip manufacturer rejects 2% of the chips produced because they fail presale testing. Assuming the bad chips are independent, find the probability of each of the following.

a) The fifth chip they test is the first bad one they find.
b) They find a bad one within the first 10 they examine.
c) The first bad chip they find will be the fourth one they test.
d) The first bad chip they find will be one of the first three they test.

45. Side effects. Researchers testing a new medication find that 7% of users have side effects. To how many patients would a doctor expect to prescribe the medication before finding the first one who has side effects?

46. Credit cards. College students are a major target for advertisements for credit cards. At a university, 65% of students surveyed said they had opened a new credit card account within the past year. If that percentage is accurate, how many students would you expect to survey before finding one who had not opened a new account in the past year?

47. Missing pixels. A company that manufactures large LCD screens knows that not all pixels on their screen light, even if they spend great care when making them. In a sheet 6 ft by 10 ft (72 in. by 120 in.) that will be cut into smaller screens, they find an average of 4.7 blank pixels. They believe that the occurrences of blank pixels are independent. Their warranty policy states that they will replace any screen sold that shows more than 2 blank pixels.

a) What is the mean number of blank pixels per square foot?
b) What is the standard deviation of blank pixels per square foot?
c) What is the probability that a 2 ft by 3 ft screen will have at least one defect?
d) What is the probability that a 2 ft by 3 ft screen will be replaced because it has too many defects?

48. Bean bags. Cellophane that is going to be formed into bags for items such as dried beans or bird seed is passed over a light sensor to test if the alignment is correct before it passes through the heating units that seal the edges. Small adjustments can be made by the machine automatically. But if the alignment is too bad, the process is stopped and an operator has to manually adjust it. These misalignment stops occur randomly and independently. On one line, the average number of stops is 52 per 8-hour shift.

a) What is the mean number of stops per hour?
b) What is the standard deviation of stops per hour?

49. Hurricane insurance. An insurance company needs to assess the risks associated with providing hurricane insurance. During the 18 years from 2000 to 2017, Florida has been affected by 29 hurricanes. If hurricanes are independent and the mean has not changed, what is the probability of having a year in Florida with each of the following?

a) No hits?
b) Exactly 1 hit?
c) More than 1 hit?

50. Hurricane insurance, part 2. During the 18 years from 2000 through 2017, there were 128 major hurricanes in the Atlantic basin. Assume that hurricanes are independent and the mean has not changed.

a) What is the mean number of major hurricanes per year?
b) What is the standard deviation of the annual frequency of major hurricanes?
c) What is the probability of having a year with no major hurricanes?
d) What is the probability of going three years in a row without a major hurricane?

51. Lefties. A manufacturer of game controllers is concerned that their controller may be difficult for left-handed users. They set out to find lefties to test. About 13% of the population is left-handed. If they select a sample of five customers at random in their stores, what is the probability of each of these outcomes?

a) The first lefty is the fifth person chosen.
b) There are some lefties among the 5 people.
c) The first lefty is the second or third person.
d) There are exactly 3 lefties in the group.
e) There are at least 3 lefties in the group.
f) There are no more than 3 lefties in the group.

52. Arrows. An Olympic archer is able to hit the bull's-eye 80% of the time. Assume each shot is independent of the others. If she shoots 6 arrows, what's the probability of each of the following results?

a) Her first bull's-eye comes on the third arrow.
b) She misses the bull's-eye at least once.
c) Her first bull's-eye comes on the fourth or fifth arrow.
d) She gets exactly 4 bull's-eyes.
e) She gets at least 4 bull's-eyes.
f) She gets at most 4 bull's-eyes.

53. Satisfaction survey. A cable provider wants to contact customers in a particular telephone exchange to see how satisfied they are with the new digital TV service the company has provided. All numbers are in the 452 exchange, so there are 10,000 possible numbers from 452-0000 to 452-9999. If they select the numbers with equal probability:

a) What distribution would they use to model the selection?

b) What is the probability the number selected will be an even number?
c) What is the probability the number selected will end in 000?

54. Manufacturing quality. In an effort to check the quality of their cell phones, a manufacturing manager decides to take a random sample of 10 cell phones from yesterday's production run, which produced cell phones with serial numbers ranging (according to when they were produced) from 43005000 to 43005999. If each of the 1000 phones is equally likely to be selected:

a) What distribution would they use to model the selection?
b) What is the probability that a randomly selected cell phone will be one of the last 100 to be produced?
c) What is the probability that the first cell phone selected is either from the last 200 to be produced or from the first 50 to be produced?
d) What is the probability that the first two cell phones are both from the last 100 to be produced?

55. Web visitors. A website manager has noticed that during the evening hours, about 3 people per minute check out from their shopping cart and make an online purchase. She believes that each purchase is independent of the others and wants to model the number of purchases per minute.

a) What model might you suggest to model the number of purchases per minute?
b) What is the probability that in any 1 minute at least one purchase is made?
c) What is the probability that no one makes a purchase in the next 2 minutes?

56. Quality control. The manufacturer in Exercise 54 has noticed that the number of faulty cell phones in a production run of cell phones is usually small and that the quality of one day's run seems to have no bearing on the next day.

a) What model might you use to model the number of faulty cell phones produced in one day?
b) If the mean number of faulty cell phones is 2 per day, what is the probability that no faulty cell phones will be produced tomorrow?
c) If the mean number of faulty cell phones is 2 per day, what is the probability that 3 or more faulty cell phones were produced in today's run?

57. Lefties, redux. Consider our group of 5 people from Exercise 51.

a) How many lefties do you expect?
b) With what standard deviation?
c) If we keep picking people until we find a lefty, how long do you expect it will take?

58. More arrows. Consider our archer from Exercise 52.

a) How many bull's-eyes do you expect her to get?
b) With what standard deviation?
c) If she keeps shooting arrows until she hits the bull's-eye, how long do you expect it will take?

59. Still more lefties. Suppose we choose 12 people instead of the 5 chosen in Exercise 57.

a) Find the mean and standard deviation of the number of right-handers in the group.
b) What's the probability that they're not all right-handed?
c) What's the probability that there are no more than 10 righties?
d) What's the probability that there are exactly 6 of each?
e) What's the probability that the majority is right-handed?

60. Still more arrows. Suppose the archer from Exercise 58 shoots 10 arrows.

a) Find the mean and standard deviation of the number of bull's-eyes she may get.
b) What's the probability that she never misses?
c) What's the probability that there are no more than 8 bull's-eyes?
d) What's the probability that there are exactly 8 bull's-eyes?
e) What's the probability that she hits the bull's-eye more often than she misses?

61. Car dealership. Jeff, a sales manager of a car dealership, believes that his sales force sells a car to 35% of the customers who stop by the showroom. He needs the dealership to make 50 sales this month to get a special bonus of $100,000. Approximately 120 customers visit the showroom each month. You may assume that customers entering the dealership are independent of one another.

a) What is the probability that he will make his bonus?

b) What is the probability that he will sell between 40 and 50 cars?
c) Assume that Jeff can choose to either increase the motivation of his sales force so that they increase the probability of a sale to 40%, or to increase the number of people walking into the showroom to 140. Which makes it more likely that Jeff will sell 50 cars?
d) A marketing consultant suggests that she can produce an ad campaign that will increase the number of people walking into the showroom to 140 at a cost of $15,000. Assuming that Jeff is risk-neutral and has the budget, should Jeff accept this offer? (Hint: Jeff stands to make $100,000 if he hits his bonus. The increase in probability of making his bonus can be used to compute the expected value using a probability tree.)
e) What is the maximum amount that Jeff should be willing to pay to increase the number of people entering the showroom to 140 (assuming that he is risk-neutral and perfectly rational)?
f) If 20% of customers are "Big Spenders" who earn the firm a lot of money, what is the probability that Jeff will see at least 1 "Big Spender" in the next 10 customers (not see one that buys, but just see one)?

JUST CHECKING ANSWERS

1 a) $100 + 100 = 200$ seconds
  b) $\sqrt{50^2 + 50^2} = 70.7$ seconds
  c) The times for the two customers are independent.

2 There are two outcomes (contact, no contact), the probability of contact stays constant at 0.76, and random calls should be independent.

3 Binomial

4 Geometric

CHAPTER 7

The Normal and Other Continuous Distributions

The NYSE

The New York Stock Exchange (NYSE) was founded in 1792 by 24 stockbrokers who signed an agreement under a buttonwood tree on Wall Street in New York. The first offices were in a rented room at 40 Wall Street. In the 1830s traders who were not part of the Exchange did business in the street. They were called "curbstone brokers." It was the curbstone brokers who first made markets in gold and oil stocks and, after the Civil War, in small industrial companies such as the emerging steel, textile, and chemical industries.

By 1903 the New York Stock Exchange was established at its current home at 18 Broad Street. The curbstone brokers finally moved indoors in 1921 to a building on Greenwich street in lower Manhattan. In 1953 the curb market changed its name to the American Stock Exchange. In 1993 the American Stock Exchange pioneered the market for derivatives by introducing the first exchange-traded fund, Standard & Poor's Depositary Receipts (SPDRs).

The NYSE Euronext holding company was created in 2007 as a combination of the NYSE Group, Inc., and Euronext N.V. And in 2008, NYSE Euronext merged with the American Stock Exchange. The combined exchange is the world's largest and most liquid exchange group.

7.1   The Standard Deviation as a Ruler

Investors have always sought ways to help them decide when to buy and when to sell. Such measures have become increasingly sophisticated. But all rely on identifying when the stock market is in an unusual state—either unusually undervalued (buy!) or unusually overvalued (sell!). One such measure is the Cyclically Adjusted Price/Earnings Ratio (CAPE10) developed by Yale professor Robert Shiller. The CAPE10 is based on the standard Price/Earnings (P/E) ratio of stocks, but designed to smooth out short-term fluctuations by "cyclically adjusting" them. The CAPE10 has been as low as 4.78, in 1920, and as high as 44.20, in late 1999. The long-term average CAPE10 (since year 1881) is 16.78.

Investors who follow the CAPE10 use the metric to signal times to buy and sell. One mutual fund strategy buys only when the CAPE10 is 33% lower than the long-term average and sells (or "goes into cash") when the CAPE10 is 50% higher than the long-term average. Between January 1, 1971, and October 23, 2009, this strategy would have outperformed such standard measures as the Wiltshire 5000 in both average return and volatility, but it is important to note that the strategy would have been completely in cash from just before the stock market crash of 1987 all the way to March of 2009! Shiller popularized the strategy in his book *Irrational Exuberance*. Figure 7.1 shows a time series plot of the CAPE10 values for the New York Stock Exchange from 1880 until the beginning of 2013. Generally, the CAPE10 hovers around 15. But occasionally, it can take a large excursion. One such time was in 1999 and 2000, when the CAPE10 exceeded 40. But was this just a random peak or were these values really extraordinary?

WHO	Months
WHAT	CAPE10 values for the NYSE
WHEN	1880 through mid 2017
WHY	Investment guidance (Data in **CAPE10 2017**)

FIGURE 7.1   CAPE10 values for the NYSE from 1881 to 2017.

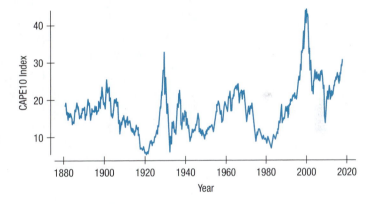

To answer this question, we can look at the overall distribution of CAPE10 values. Figure 7.2 shows a histogram of the same values. Now we don't see patterns over time, but we may be able to make a better judgment of whether values are extraordinary.

Overall, the main body of the distribution looks unimodal and reasonably symmetric. But then there's a tail of values that trails off to the high end. How can we assess how extraordinary they are?

Investors follow a wide variety of measures that record various aspects of stocks, bonds, and other investments. They are usually particularly interested in identifying times when these measures are extraordinary because those often represent times of increased risk or opportunity. But these are quantitative values, not categories.

How can we characterize the behavior of a random variable that can take on any value in a range of values? The distributions of Chapter 6 won't provide the tools we need, but many of the basic concepts still work. The random variables we need are *continuous*.

FIGURE 7.2 The distribution of the CAPE10 values shown in Figure 7.1.

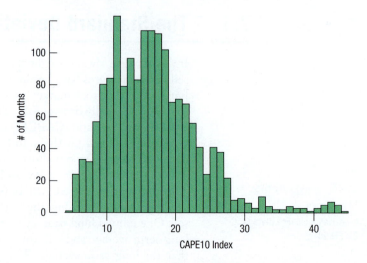

We saw in Chapter 3 that z-scores provide a standard way to compare values. In a sense, we use the standard deviation as a ruler, asking how many standard deviations a value is from the mean. That's what a z-score reports: the number of standard deviations away from the mean. We can convert the CAPE10 values to z-scores by subtracting their mean (16.78) and dividing by their standard deviation (6.68). Figure 7.3 shows the resulting distribution.

FIGURE 7.3 The CAPE10 values as z-scores.

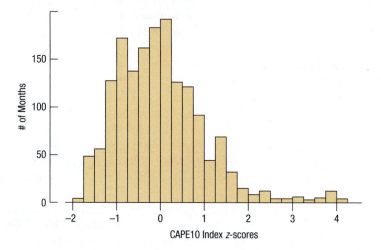

It's easy to see that the z-scores have the same distribution as the original values, but now we can also see that the largest of them is above 4. How extraordinary is it for a value to be four standard deviations away from the mean? Fortunately, there's a fact about unimodal, symmetric distributions that can guide us.[1]

The 68–95–99.7 Rule

In a unimodal, symmetric distribution, about 68% of the values fall within 1 standard deviation of the mean, about 95% fall within 2 standard deviations of the mean, and about 99.7%—almost all—fall within 3 standard deviations of the mean. Calling this rule the **68–95–99.7 Rule** provides a mnemonic for these three values.[2]

---

[1] All of the CAPE10 values in the right tail occurred after 1993. Until that time the distribution of CAPE10 values was quite symmetric and clearly unimodal.
[2] This rule is also called the "Empirical Rule" because it originally was observed without any proof. It was first published by Abraham de Moivre in 1733, 75 years before the underlying reason for it—which we're about to see—was known.

FIGURE 7.4 The 68–95–99.7 Rule tells us how much of most unimodal, symmetric models is found within one, two, or three standard deviations of the mean.

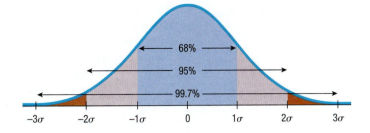

7.2 The Normal Distribution

NOTATION ALERT

$N(\mu, \sigma)$ always denotes a Normal. The μ, pronounced "mew," is the Greek letter for "m," and always represents the mean in a model. The σ, sigma, is the lowercase Greek letter for "s," and always represents the standard deviation in a model.

Is Normal Normal?

Don't be misled. The name "Normal" doesn't mean that these are the *usual* shapes for histograms. The name follows a tradition of positive thinking in mathematics and statistics in which functions, equations, and relationships that are easy to work with or have other nice properties are called "normal," "common," "regular," "natural," or similar terms. It's as if by calling them ordinary, we could make them actually occur more often and make our lives simpler.

Is the Standard Normal a Standard?

Yes. We call it the "Standard Normal" because it models standardized values. It is also a "standard" because this is the particular Normal model that we almost always use.

The 68–95–99.7 Rule is useful in describing how unusual a z-score is. But often in business we want a more precise answer than one of these three values. To say more about how big we expect a z-score to be, we need to *model* the data's distribution.

There is no universal standard for z-scores, but there is a model that shows up over and over in statistics. You've probably heard of "bell-shaped curves." Statisticians call them Normal (or Gaussian) distributions. **Normal distributions** are appropriate models for distributions whose shapes are unimodal and roughly symmetric. There is a Normal distribution for every possible combination of mean and standard deviation. We write $N(\mu, \sigma)$ to represent a Normal distribution with a mean of μ and a standard deviation of σ. We use Greek symbols here because this mean and standard deviation are parameters of the model, not summaries based on data. We can compute z-scores based on this model by using the parameters μ and σ. We still call these standardized values z-scores. We write

$$z = \frac{y - \mu}{\sigma}.$$

Standardized values have mean 0 and standard deviation 1, so by doing this to our values, we'll need only one model—the model $N(0, 1)$. The Normal distribution with mean 0 and standard deviation 1 is called the **standard Normal distribution** (or the **standard Normal model**). We've seen that in the Normal model, events farther than 3 standard deviations from the mean are rare. A z-score with magnitude more than 3 occurs only with probability about 0.003. Larger z-scores are even rarer. The probability of a z-score with magnitude 4 or more is about 0.00006 (or 6 in 100,000). A z-score with magnitude 5 or more occurs with probability less than 1 in a million (0.0000057) and 6 or more occurs only in about 2 in a billion cases. The Normal is often used as a model for events (especially in finance), but keep in mind that it may underestimate the probability of a rare event. (In finance such events are sometimes referred to as "black swans.")[3]

So be careful. You shouldn't use a Normal model for just any data set. Remember that standardizing won't change the shape of the distribution. If the distribution is not unimodal and symmetric to begin with, standardizing won't make it Normal.

JUST CHECKING

1 Your accounting teacher has announced that the lower of your two tests will be dropped. You got a 90 on test 1 and an 80 on test 2. You're all set to drop the 80 until she announces that she grades "on a curve." She standardized the scores in order to decide which is the lower one. If the mean on the first test was 88 with a standard deviation of 4 and the mean on the second was 75 with a standard deviation of 5,

a) Which one will be dropped?   b) Does this seem "fair"?

---

[3]Nicholas Taleb, in his book *The Black Swan: The Impact of the Highly Improbable*, uses the black swan as a metaphor for a disruptive event that comes as a surprise because its probability was underestimated.

The Normal distribution differs from the discrete probability distributions we saw in Chapter 6 because now, the random variable can take on any value. So, we need a **continuous random variable**. For any continuous random variable, the distribution of its probability can be shown with a curve called the **probability density function (pdf)**, usually denoted as $f(x)$. The curve we use to work with the Normal distribution is called the Normal probability density function.

The probability density function (pdf) doesn't give the probability directly as the probability models for discrete random variables did. Instead the pdf gives the probability from the area below its curve. For the standard Normal, shown in Figure 7.5, we can see that the area below the curve between −1 and 1 is about 68%, which is where the 68–95–99.7 Rule comes from.

FIGURE 7.5 The standard Normal density function (with mean 0 and standard deviation 1). The probability of finding a z-score in any interval is the area over that interval under the curve. For example, the probability that the z-score falls between −1 and 1 is about 68%, which can be seen approximately from the density function or found more precisely from a table or technology.

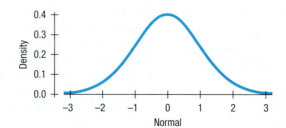

It's important to remember that the probability density function $f(x)$ isn't equal to $P(X = x)$. In fact, for a continuous random variable, X, $P(X = x)$ is 0 for every value of x! That may seem strange at first, but since the probability is the area under the curve over an interval, as the interval gets smaller and smaller, the probability does too. Finally, when the interval is just a point, there is no area—and no probability. (See the box below.)

How Can *Every* Value Have Probability 0?

We can find a probability for any interval of z-scores. But the probability for a single z-score is zero. How can that be? Let's look at the standard Normal random variable, Z. We could find (from a table, website, or computer program) that the probability that Z lies between 0 and 1 is 0.3413.

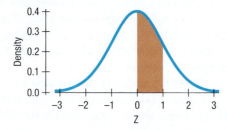

That's the area under the Normal pdf (in red) between the values 0 and 1.

So, what's the probability that Z is between 0 and 1/10?

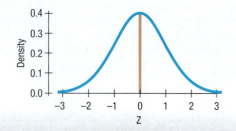

That area is only 0.0398. What is the chance then that Z will fall between 0 and 1/100? There's not much area—the probability is only 0.0040. If we kept going, the probability would keep getting smaller. The probability that Z is between 0 and 1/100,000 is less than 0.0001.

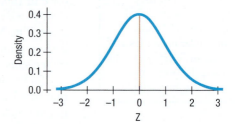

So, what's the probability that Z is *exactly* 0? Well, there's *no* area under the curve right at $x = 0$, so the probability is 0. It's only intervals that have positive probability, but that's OK. In real life we never mean exactly 0.0000000000 or any other value. If you say "exactly 164 pounds," you might really mean between 163.5 and 164.5 pounds or even between 163.99 and 164.01 pounds, but realistically not 164.000000000 . . . pounds.

IN PRACTICE 7.1   An extraordinary day for the Dow?

After the financial crisis of 2007/2008, the Dow Jones Industrial Average (DJIA) bottomed out at 7278 on March 20, 2009, but has steadily improved since, creating one of the longest bull markets in history. It closed above 20,000 for the first time in early 2017. During this bull market, from March 20, 2009, to September 2017, a histogram of day-to-day changes in the DJIA looked like this: (Data in **DJIA 2017**)

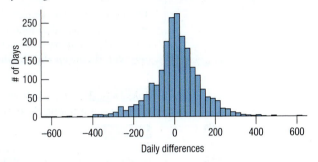

MANAGER   Some of our clients are nervous about a large drop in the Dow. I remember a drop last year of over 600 points in one day. How rare an event is that?

ANALYST   The distribution of daily differences over the past 8 years is roughly unimodal and symmetric with a mean of about 7 points and standard deviation of 123. A drop of 600 points would be nearly 5 standard deviations below the mean. If we use the Normal model, an event like that would occur very rarely, about one in a million days. But very rare events often occur more frequently than the Normal model predicts, so we should be cautious.

Finding Normal Percentiles

Finding the probability that a value is at least 1 SD above the mean is easy. We know that 68% of the values lie within 1 SD of the mean, so 32% lie farther away. Since the Normal distribution is symmetric, half of those 32% (or 16%) are more than 1 SD above the mean. But what if we want to know the percentage of observations that fall more than 1.8 SD above the mean? We already know that no more than 16% of observations have z-scores above 1. By similar reasoning, no more than 2.5% of the observations have a z-score above 2. Can we be more precise with our answer than "between 16% and 2.5%"?

FIGURE 7.6   A table of Normal percentiles (Table Z in Appendix B) lets us find the percentage of individuals in a standard Normal distribution falling below any specified z-score value.

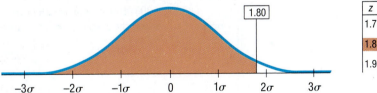

With a z-score we can use the standard Normal distribution to find the probabilities we're interested in. These days, we can find probabilities associated with z-scores using technology such as calculators, statistical software, and websites. We can also look up these values in a table of **Normal percentiles**.[4] Tables use the standard Normal distribution, so we'll have to convert our data to z-scores before using the table. Our value 1.8 SD above the mean is a z-score of 1.80. To use a table, as shown in Figure 7.6, find the z-score by looking down the left column for the first

---

[4]See Table Z in Appendix B. Many calculators and statistics computer packages do this as well.

two digits (1.8) and across the top row for the third digit, 0. The table gives the percentile as 0.9641. That means that 96.4% of the z-scores are less than 1.80. Since the total area is always 1, and $1 - 0.9641 = 0.0359$ we know that only 3.6% of all observations from a Normal distribution have z-scores higher than 1.80.

IN PRACTICE 7.2   GMAT scores and the Normal model

The Graduate Management Admission Test (GMAT) has scores from 200 to 800. Scores are supposed to follow a distribution that is roughly unimodal and symmetric and is designed to have an overall mean of 500 and a standard deviation of 100. In any one year, the mean and standard deviation may differ from these target values by a small amount, but we can use these values as good overall approximations.

MANAGER A new applicant to our company earned a 600 on the GMAT. Where does she stand among all those who took the GMAT?

ANALYST From what I can learn about the GMAT, the distribution is unimodal and symmetric, so I can approximate the distribution with a Normal model. The scores have a mean of 500 and an SD of 100.

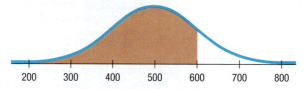

A score of 600 is 1 SD above the mean. That corresponds to one of the points in the 68–95–99.7% Rule. About 32% $(100\% - 68\%)$ of those who took the test were more than one standard deviation from the mean, but only half of those were on the high side. So about 16% (half of 32%) of the test scores were better than 600.

IN PRACTICE 7.3   More GMAT scores

MANAGER We have a whole new group of applicants with GMAT scores between 450 and 600. What percentage of all test takers does that correspond to?

ANALYST To find percentages from Normal models, I usually use technology or a website directly, but it might be useful to go through the details and use a table. The first step is to find the z-scores associated with each value. Standardizing the scores we are given, we find that for 600, $z = (600 - 500)/100 = 1.0$ and for 450, $z = (450 - 500)/100 = -0.50$. I labeled the axis below the picture both in the original values and the z-scores, as the following picture shows.

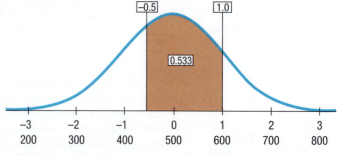

From Table Z, we find the area $z \le 1.0 = 0.8413$, which means that 84.13% of scores fall below 1.0, and the area $z \le -0.50 = 0.3085$, which means that 30.85% of the values fall below -0.5, so the proportion of z-scores *between* them is $84.13\% - 30.85\% = 53.28\%$. So, the Normal model estimates that these scores are very typical—over half, about 53.3%, of GMAT scores fall between 450 and 600.

Finding areas from z-scores is the simplest way to work with the Normal distribution. Sometimes we start with areas and need to work backward to find the corresponding z-score or even the original data value. For instance, what z-score represents the first quartile, Q1, in a Normal distribution? In our first set of examples, we knew the z-score and used the table or technology to find the percentile. Now we want to find the cut point for the 25th percentile. Make a picture, shading the leftmost 25% of the area. Look in Table Z for an area of 0.2500. The exact area is not there, but 0.2514 is the closest number. That shows up in the table with −0.6 in the left margin and 0.07 in the top margin. The z-score for Q1, then, is approximately $z = -0.67$. Computers and calculators can determine the cut point more precisely (and more easily).[5]

IN PRACTICE 7.4   An exclusive MBA program

MANAGER Another applicant says that her MBA program admits only people with GMAT scores among the top 10%. How high a GMAT score does it take to be eligible?

ANALYST The program takes the top 10%, so their cutoff score is the 90th percentile. Draw an approximate picture like this one.

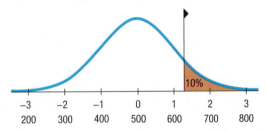

	0.07	0.08	0.09
1.0	0.8577	0.8599	0.8621
1.1	0.8790	0.8810	0.8830
1.2	0.8980	0.8997	0.9015
1.3	0.9147	0.9162	0.9177
1.4	0.9292	0.9306	0.9319

From our picture we can see that the z-value is between 1 and 1.5 (if we've judged 10% of the area correctly), and so the cutoff score is between 600 and 650 or so. Using Table Z, I located 0.90 in the *interior* of the table to find the corresponding z-score (see table above). Here the 1.2 is in the left margin, and the 0.08 is in the margin above the entry. Putting them together gives 1.28. Then I converted the z-score back to the original units. A z-score of 1.28 is 1.28 standard deviations above the mean. Since the standard deviation is 100, that's 128 GMAT points. The cutoff is 128 points above the mean of 500, or 628. Because the program wants GMAT scores in the top 10%, the cutoff is 628. (Actually GMAT scores are reported only in multiples of 10, so she'd have to score at least a 630.)

GUIDED EXAMPLE   Cereal Company

A cereal manufacturer has a machine that fills the boxes. Boxes are labeled "16 oz," so the company wants to have that much cereal in each box. But since no packaging process is perfect, there will be minor variations. If the machine is set at exactly 16 oz and the Normal distribution applies (or at least the distribution is roughly symmetric), then about half of the boxes will be underweight, making consumers unhappy and exposing the company to bad publicity and possible lawsuits. To prevent underweight boxes, the manufacturer has to set the mean a little higher than 16.0 oz. Based on their experience with the packaging machine, the company believes that the amount of cereal

(continued)

---

[5]We'll often use those more precise values in our examples. If you're finding the values from the table you may not get *exactly* the same number to all decimal places as your classmate who's using a computer package.

in the boxes fits a Normal distribution with a standard deviation of 0.2 oz. The manufacturer decides to set the machine to put an average of 16.3 oz in each box. Let's use that model to answer a series of questions about these cereal boxes.

Question 1: What fraction of the boxes will be underweight?

PLAN **Setup** State the variable and the objective. **Model** Check to see if a Normal distribution is appropriate. Specify which Normal distribution to use.	The variable is weight of cereal in a box. We want to determine what fraction of the boxes risk being underweight. We have no data, so we cannot make a histogram. But we are told that the company believes the distribution of weights from the machine is Normal. We use an $N(16.3, 0.2)$ model.
DO **Mechanics** Make a graph of this Normal distribution. Locate the value you're interested in on the picture, label it, and shade the appropriate region.	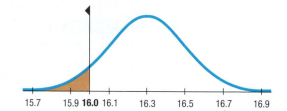
REALITY CHECK Estimate from the picture the percentage of boxes that are underweight. (This will be useful later to check that your answer makes sense.) Convert your cutoff value into a z-score. Look up the area in the Normal table, or use technology.	(It looks like a low percentage—maybe less than 10%.) We want to know what fraction of the boxes will weigh less than 16 oz. $$z = \frac{y - \mu}{\sigma} = \frac{16 - 16.3}{0.2} = -1.50$$ $$P(y < 16) = P(z < -1.50) = 0.0668$$
REPORT **Conclusion** Summarize and **present** your conclusion in the context of the problem.	**MEMO** **Re: Underweight boxes** We estimate that approximately 6.7% of the boxes will contain less than 16 oz of cereal.

Question 2: The company's lawyers say that 6.7% is too high. They insist that no more than 4% of the boxes can be underweight. So the company needs to set the machine to put a little more cereal in each box. What mean setting do they need?

PLAN **Setup** State the variable and the objective. **Model** Check to see if a Normal model is appropriate. Specify which Normal distribution to use. This time you are not given a value for the mean!	The variable is weight of cereal in a box. We want to determine a setting for the machine. We have no data, so we cannot make a histogram. But we are told that a Normal model applies. We don't know μ, the mean amount of cereal. The standard deviation for this machine is 0.2 oz. The model, then, is $N(\mu, 0.2)$.
REALITY CHECK We found out earlier that setting the machine to $\mu = 16.3$ oz made 6.7% of the boxes too light. We'll need to raise the mean a bit to reduce this fraction.	We are told that no more than 4% of the boxes can be below 16 oz.

DO	**Mechanics** Make a graph of this Normal distribution. Center it at μ (since you don't know the mean) and shade the region below 16 oz.	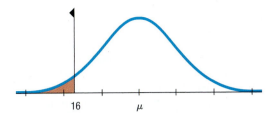

The z-score that has 0.04 area to the left of it is $z = -1.75$.

Using the Normal table, a calculator, or software, find the z-score that cuts off the lowest 4%.

Use this information to find μ. It's located 1.75 standard deviations to the right of 16.

Since 16 must be 1.75 standard deviations below the mean, we need to set the mean at $16 + 1.75 \cdot 0.2 = 16.35$.

REPORT	**Conclusion** **Summarize** and **present** your conclusion in the context of the problem.	**MEMO** **Re: Underweight boxes II** The company must set the machine to average 16.35 oz of cereal per box.

Question 3: The company president vetoes that plan, saying the company should give away less free cereal, not more. Her goal is to set the machine no higher than 16.2 oz and still have only 4% underweight boxes. The only way to accomplish this is to reduce the standard deviation. What standard deviation must the company achieve, and what does that mean about the machine?

PLAN	**Setup** State the variable and the objective.	The variable is weight of cereal in a box. We want to determine the necessary standard deviation to have only 4% of boxes underweight.

Model Check that a Normal model is appropriate.

Specify which Normal distribution to use. This time you don't know σ.

REALITY CHECK We know the new standard deviation must be less than 0.2 oz.

The company believes that the weights are described by a Normal distribution.

Now we know the mean, but we don't know the standard deviation. The model is therefore $N(16.2, \sigma)$.

DO	**Mechanics** Make a graph of this Normal distribution. Center it at 16.2, and shade the area you're interested in. We want 4% of the area to the left of 16 oz.	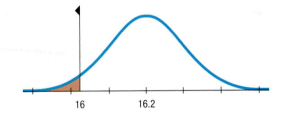

Find the z-score that cuts off the lowest 4%.

Solve for σ. (Note that we need 16 to be 1.75 σ's below 16.2, so 1.75 σ must be 0.2 oz. You could just start with that equation.)

We already know that the z-score with 4% below it is $z = -1.75$.

$$z = \frac{y - \mu}{\sigma}$$

$$-1.75 = \frac{16 - 16.2}{\sigma}$$

$$1.75\sigma = 0.2$$

$$\sigma = 0.114$$

REPORT	**Conclusion** **Summarize** and **present** your conclusion in the context of the problem. As we expected, the standard deviation is lower than before— actually, quite a bit lower.	**MEMO** **Re: Underweight boxes III** The company must get the machine to box cereal with a standard deviation of only 0.114 oz. This means the machine must be more consistent (by nearly a factor of 2) in filling the boxes.

JUST CHECKING

2 As a group, the Dutch are among the tallest people in the world. The average Dutch man is 184 cm tall—just over 6 feet (and the average Dutch woman is 170.8 cm tall—just over 5′7″). If a Normal model is appropriate and the standard deviation for men is about 8 cm, what percentage of all Dutch men will be over 2 meters (6′6″) tall?

3 Suppose it takes you 20 minutes, on average, to drive to work, with a standard deviation of 2 minutes. Suppose a Normal model is appropriate for the distributions of driving times.

a) How often will you arrive at work in less than 22 minutes?

b) How often will it take you more than 24 minutes?

c) Do you think the distribution of your driving times is unimodal and symmetric?

d) What does this say about the accuracy of your prediction? Explain.

7.3 Normal Probability Plots

Before using a Normal model you should check that the data follow a distribution that is at least close to Normal. You can check that the histogram is unimodal and symmetric, but there is also a specialized graphical display that can help you to decide whether the Normal model is appropriate: the **Normal probability plot**. If the distribution of the data is roughly Normal, the plot is roughly a diagonal straight line. Deviations from a straight line indicate that the distribution is not Normal. This plot is usually able to show deviations from Normality more clearly than the corresponding histogram, but it's usually easier to understand *how* a distribution fails to be Normal by looking at its histogram. Normal probability plots are difficult to make by hand, but are provided by most statistics software.

Some data on a car's fuel efficiency provide an example of data that are nearly Normal. The overall pattern of the Normal probability plot is straight. The two trailing low values correspond to the values in the histogram that trail off the low end. They're not quite in line with the rest of the data set. The Normal probability plot shows us that they're a bit lower than we'd expect of the lowest two values in a Normal distribution. (Data in **Nissan**)

FIGURE 7.7 Histogram and Normal probability plot for gas mileage (mpg) recorded for a Nissan Maxima. The vertical axes are the same, so each dot on the probability plot would fall into the bar on the histogram immediately to its left.

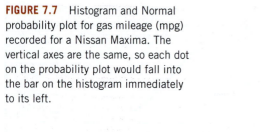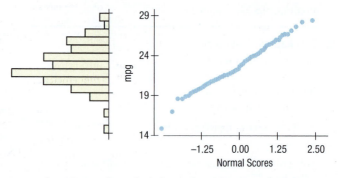

By contrast, the Normal probability plot of a sample of men's *Weights* in Figure 7.8 from a study of lifestyle and health is far from straight. The weights

FIGURE 7.8 Histogram and Normal probability plot for men's weights. Note how a skewed distribution corresponds to a bent probability plot.

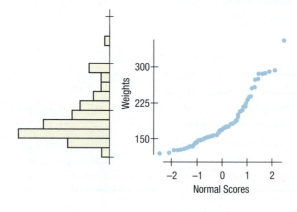

are skewed to the high end, and the plot is curved. We'd conclude from these pictures that approximations using the Normal model for these data would not be very accurate.

IN PRACTICE 7.5   Using a Normal probability plot

MANAGER The CAPE10 is a pretty good market indicator. Can I use the Normal model to tell our clients when an unusual value of the index occurs?

ANALYST A Normal probability plot of the historical CAPE10 prices looks like this:

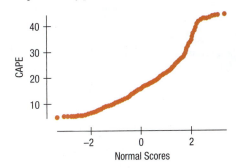

The bent shape of the probability plot indicates a deviation from Normality. The upward bend is because the distribution is skewed to the high end. The "kink" in that bend suggests a collection of values that don't continue that skewness consistently. We should probably not use a Normal model for these data.

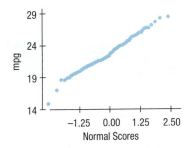

FIGURE 7.9 A Normal probability plot lines up the sorted data values against the Normal scores that we'd expect for a sample of that size. The straighter the line, the closer the data are to a Normal model. The mileage data look quite Normal.

How Does a Normal Probability Plot Work?

Figure 7.9 shows a Normal probability plot for 100 fuel efficiency measures for a car. The smallest of these has a z-score of -3.16. The Normal model can tell us what value to expect for the smallest z-score in a batch of 100 if a Normal model were appropriate. That turns out to be -2.58. So our first data value is smaller than we would expect from the Normal.

We can continue this and ask a similar question for each value. For example, the 14th-smallest fuel efficiency has a z-score of almost exactly -1, and that's just what we should expect (-1.1 to be exact). The easiest way to make the comparison, of course, is to graph it.[6] If our observed values look like a sample from a Normal model, then the probability plot stretches out in a straight line from lower left to upper right. But if our values deviate from what we'd expect, the plot will bend or have jumps in it. The values we'd expect from a Normal model are called Normal scores, or sometimes nscores. You can't easily look them up in the table, so probability plots are best made with technology and not by hand.

The best advice on using Normal probability plots is to see whether they are straight. If so, then your data look like data from a Normal model. If not, make a histogram to understand how they differ from the model.

7.4   The Distribution of Sums of Normals

Another reason Normal models show up so often is that they have some special properties. An important one is that the sum or difference of two independent Normal random variables is also Normal.

---

[6]Sometimes the Normal probability plot switches the two axes, putting the data on the x-axis and the z-scores on the y-axis.

A company manufactures small sound systems. At the end of the production line, the sound systems are packaged and prepared for shipping. Stage 1 of this process is called "packing." Workers must collect all the system components (a main unit, two speakers, a power cord, an antenna, and some wires), put each in plastic bags, and then place everything inside a protective form. The packed form then moves on to Stage 2, called "boxing," in which workers place the form and a packet of instructions in a cardboard box and then close, seal, and label the box for shipping.

The company says that times required for the packing stage are unimodal and symmetric and can be described by a Normal distribution with a mean of 9 minutes and standard deviation of 1.5 minutes. (See Figure 7.10.) The times for the boxing stage can also be modeled as Normal, with a mean of 6 minutes and standard deviation of 1 minute.

FIGURE 7.10 The Normal model for the packing stage with a mean of 9 minutes and standard deviation of 1.5 minutes.

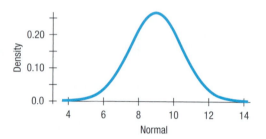

The company is interested in the total time that it takes to get a system through both packing and boxing, so they want to model the sum of the two random variables. Fortunately, the special property that adding independent Normals yields another Normal allows us to apply our knowledge of Normal probabilities to questions about the sum or difference of independent random variables. To use this property of Normals, we'll need to check two assumptions: that the variables are independent and that they can be modeled by the Normal distribution.

GUIDED EXAMPLE   Packaging Sound Systems

Consider the company that manufactures and ships small sound systems that we discussed previously.

If the time required to pack the sound systems can be described by a Normal distribution, with a mean of 9 minutes and standard deviation of 1.5 minutes, and the times for the boxing stage can also be modeled as Normal, with a mean of 6 minutes and standard deviation of 1 minute, what is the probability that packing an order of two systems takes over 20 minutes? What percentage of the sound systems takes longer to pack than to box?

Question 1: What is the probability that packing an order of two systems takes more than 18 minutes?

PLAN **Setup** State the problem.	We want to estimate the probability that packing an order of two systems takes more than 18 minutes.
Variables Define your random variables.	Let P_1 = time for packing the first system P_2 = time for packing the second system T = total time to pack two systems
Write an appropriate equation for the variables you need.	$T = P_1 + P_2$

Think about the model assumptions.	✔ **Normal Model Assumption.** We are told that packing times are well modeled by a Normal model, and we know that the sum of two Normal random variables is also Normal.	
	✔ **Independence Assumption.** There is no reason to think that the packing time for one system would affect the packing time for the next, so we can reasonably assume the two are independent.	

DO **Mechanics** Find the expected value. (Expected values always add.)

$$E(T) = E(P_1 + P_2)$$
$$= E(P_1) + E(P_2)$$
$$= 9 + 6 = 15 \text{ minutes}$$

Find the variance.

For sums of independent random variables, variances add. (In general, we don't need the variables to be Normal for this to be true—just independent.)

Since the times are independent,

$$Var(T) = Var(P_1 + P_2)$$
$$= Var(P_1) + Var(P_2)$$
$$= 1.5^2 + 1^2$$
$$Var(T) = 3.25$$
$$SD(T) = \sqrt{3.25} \approx 1.80 \text{ minutes}$$

Find the standard deviation.

Now we use the fact that both random variables follow Normal distributions to say that their sum is also Normal.

We can model the time, T, with a $N(15, 1.80)$ model.

Sketch a picture of the Normal distribution for the total time, shading the region representing over 20 minutes.

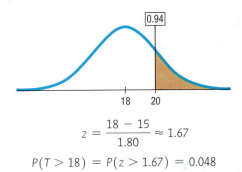

Find the z-score for 20 minutes.

$$z = \frac{18 - 15}{1.80} \approx 1.67$$

Use technology or a table to find the probability.

$$P(T > 18) = P(z > 1.67) = 0.048$$

REPORT **Conclusion** Interpret your result in context.

MEMO

Re: Computer systems packing

Using past history to build a model, we find slightly more than a 4.8% chance that it will take more than 18 minutes to pack an order of two systems.

Question 2: What percentage of systems take longer to pack than to box?

PLAN **Setup** State the question.

We want to estimate the percentage of the sound systems that takes longer to pack than to box.

Variables Define your random variables.

Let P = time for packing a system

B = time for boxing a system

D = difference in times to pack and box a system

Write an appropriate equation.

$D = P - B$

What are we trying to find? Notice that we can tell which of two quantities is greater by subtracting and asking whether the difference is positive or negative.

A system that takes longer to pack than to box will have $P > B$, and so D will be positive. We want to find $P(D > 0)$.

(continued)

Remember to think about the assumptions.

✔ **Normal Model Assumption.** We are told that both random variables are well modeled by Normal distributions, and we know that the difference of two Normal random variables is also Normal.

✔ **Independence Assumption.** There is no reason to think that the packing time for a system will affect its boxing time, so we can reasonably assume the two are independent.

DO   **Mechanics** Find the expected value.

$$E(D) = E(P - B)$$
$$= E(P) - E(B)$$
$$= 9 - 6 = 3 \text{ minutes}$$

For the difference of independent random variables, the variance is the sum of the individual variances.

Since the times are independent,

$$Var(D) = Var(P - B)$$
$$= Var(P) + Var(B)$$
$$= 1.5^2 + 1^2$$

$$Var(D) = 3.25$$

Find the standard deviation.

State what model you will use.

$$SD(D) = \sqrt{3.25} \approx 1.80 \text{ minutes}$$

We can model D with $N(3, 1.80)$.

Sketch a picture of the Normal distribution for the difference in times and shade the region representing a difference greater than zero.

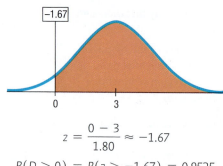

Find the z-score. Then use a table or technology to find the probability.

$$z = \frac{0 - 3}{1.80} \approx -1.67$$

$$P(D > 0) = P(z > -1.67) = 0.9525$$

REPORT   **Conclusion** Interpret your result in context.

MEMO

Re: Sound systems packing

In our second analysis, we found that just over 95% of all the sound systems will require more time for packing than for boxing.

7.5   The Normal Approximation for the Binomial

Recall That This Notation:

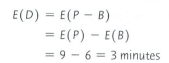

means "1000 choose 120".

We first saw this notation in Chapter 6 on page 203. Look back there if you need a reminder.

In the previous chapter we modeled the number of successes of a series of trials with a Binomial. Suppose we send out 1000 flyers advertising a free cup of coffee at our new cafe and we think that the probability that someone will come is about 0.10. We might want to know the chance that at least 120 people will come to claim their coffee. We could use the Binomial to calculate that with $n = 1000$ and $p = 0.10$. We know that the probability that exactly 120 people will come is $\binom{1000}{120} \times (0.10)^{120} \times (0.90)^{880}$ (about 0.005). But that's not the answer. We want to know the probability that *at least* 120 will show up, so we have to calculate a probability for 121, 122, 123, . . . and all the way up to 1000. There must be a better way. And there is. The Normal distribution can approximate the Binomial.

The Binomial model for our cafe has mean $np = 100$ and standard deviation $\sqrt{npq} \approx 9.5$. We might just try to approximate its distribution with a Normal distribution using the same mean and standard deviation. Remarkably enough, that turns out to be a very good approximation. Using that mean and standard deviation, we can find the *probability*:

$$P(X \geq 120) = P\left(z \geq \frac{120 - 100}{9.5}\right) \approx P(z \geq 2.11) \approx 0.0174$$

There seems to be only about a 1.7% chance that at least 120 people will show up. (Adding up all 881 probabilities using the Binomial agrees with this to 3 decimal places!)

We can't always use a Normal distribution to make estimates of Binomial probabilities. The success of the approximation depends on the sample size. Suppose we are searching for a prize in cereal boxes, where the probability of finding a prize is 20%. If we buy five boxes, the actual Binomial probabilities that we get 0, 1, 2, 3, 4, or 5 prizes are 33%, 41%, 20%, 5%, 1%, and 0.03%, respectively. The histogram just below shows that this probability model is skewed. We shouldn't try to estimate these probabilities by using a Normal model.

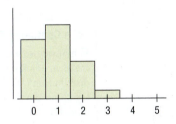

But if we open 50 boxes of this cereal and count the number of prizes we find, we'll get the histogram below. It is centered at $np = 50(0.2) = 10$ prizes, as expected, and it appears to be fairly symmetric around that center.

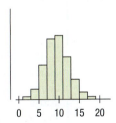

A Normal distribution is a close enough approximation to the Binomial only for a large enough number of trials. And what we mean by "large enough" depends on the probability of success. We'd need a larger sample if the probability of success were very low (or very high). It turns out that a Normal distribution works pretty well if we expect to see at least 10 successes and 10 failures. We can check the Success/Failure Condition.

Success/Failure Condition: A Binomial model is approximately Normal if we expect at least 10 successes and 10 failures:

$$np \geq 10 \text{ and } nq \geq 10.$$

Why 10? Well, actually it's 9, as revealed in the following Math Box.

MATH BOX   Why check $np \geq 10$?

It's easy to see where the magic number 10 comes from. You just need to remember how Normal models work. The problem is that a Normal model extends infinitely in both directions. But a Binomial model must have between 0 and n successes, so if we use a Normal to approximate a Binomial, we have to cut off its tails. That's not very important if the center of the Normal model is so far from 0 and n that the lost tails have only a negligible area. More than three standard deviations should do it because a Normal model has little probability past that.

So the mean needs to be at least 3 standard deviations from 0 and at least 3 standard deviations from n. Let's look at the 0 end.

We require:	$\mu - 3\sigma > 0$
Or, in other words:	$\mu > 3\sigma$
For a Binomial that's:	$np > 3\sqrt{npq}$
Squaring yields:	$n^2p^2 > 9npq$
Now simplify:	$np > 9q$
Since $q \leq 1$, we require:	$np > 9$

For simplicity we usually demand that np (and nq for the other tail) be at least 0 to use the Normal approximation which gives the Success/Failure Condition.[7]

*The Continuity Correction

When we use a continuous model to model a set of discrete events, we may need to make an adjustment called the **continuity correction**. We approximated the Binomial distribution (50, 0.2) with a Normal distribution. But what does the Normal distribution say about the probability that $X = 10$? Every specific value in the Normal probability model has probability 0. That's not the answer we want.

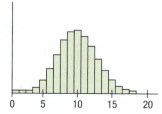

Because X is really discrete, it takes on the exact values 0, 1, 2, . . . , 50, each with positive probability. The histogram holds the secret to the correction. Look at the bin corresponding to $X = 10$ in the histogram. It goes from 9.5 to 10.5. What we really want is to find the area under the Normal curve *between* 9.5 and 10.5. So when we use the Normal distribution to approximate discrete events, we go halfway to the next value on the left and/or the right. We approximate $P(X = 10)$ by finding $P(9.5 \leq X \leq 10.5)$. For a Binomial $(50, 0.2)$, $\mu = 10$ and $\sigma = 2.83$.

$$\text{So } P(9.5 \leq X \leq 10.5) = P\left(\frac{9.5 - 10}{2.83} \leq z \leq \frac{10.5 - 10}{2.83}\right)$$

$$\approx P(-0.177 \leq z \leq 0.177)$$

$$\approx 0.1405$$

By comparison, the *exact* Binomial probability is 0.1398.

---

[7]Looking at the final step, we see that we need $np > 9$ in the worst case, when q (or p) is near 1, making the Binomial model quite skewed. When q and p are near 0.5—for example, between 0.4 and 0.6—the Binomial model is nearly symmetric, and $np > 5$ ought to be safe enough. Although we'll always check for 10 expected successes and failures, keep in mind that for values of p near 0.5, we can be somewhat more forgiving.

> ## IN PRACTICE 7.6   Gaining business insights from using the Normal distribution
>
> **MANAGER**   In our production of TV panels, for both our LCD and LED TV lines, some panels have stuck or "dead" pixels that have defective transistors and are permanently unlit. If a panel has too many dead pixels, we have to throw it out. Our production team tells us that when the production line is working correctly, the probability of rejecting a panel is 0.07. I have a few questions about the process.
>
> 1. How many screens do we expect to reject in a day's production run of 500 screens? What is the standard deviation?
> 2. If we reject 40 screens today, is that a large enough number to indicate that something may have gone wrong with the production line?
> 3. In the past week of 5 days of production, we've rejected 200 screens—an average of 40 per day. Should that raise concerns?
>
> **ANALYST**   Given the information from production, I've made some probability calculations to answer your questions:
>
> 1. $\mu = 0.07 \times 500 = 35$ is the expected number of rejects
>
> $\sigma = \sqrt{npq} = \sqrt{500 \times 0.07 \times 0.93} \approx 5.7$ is the standard deviation of the number of rejects/day
>
> 2. $P(X \geq 40) = P\left(z \geq \dfrac{40 - 35}{5.7}\right) \approx P(z \geq 0.877) \approx 0.19$, not an extraordinarily large number of rejects
>
> 3. Using the Normal approximation:
>
> $\mu = 0.07 \times 2500 = 175$
>
> $\sigma = \sqrt{2500 \times 0.07 \times 0.93} \approx 12.757$
>
> $P(X \geq 200) = P\left(z \geq \dfrac{200 - 175}{12.757}\right) \approx P(z \geq 1.96) \approx 0.025$
>
> Yes, this seems to be a number of rejects that would occur by chance rarely if nothing were wrong. I would tell production to look for a possible cause for the change.

7.6   Other Continuous Random Variables

Many phenomena in business can be modeled by continuous random variables. The Normal model is important, but it is only one of many different models. Entire courses are devoted to studying which models work well in different situations, but we'll introduce just two others that are commonly used: the uniform and the exponential.

The Uniform Distribution

We've already seen the discrete version of the uniform probability model. A continuous **uniform** shares the principle that all events should be equally likely, but with a continuous distribution we can't talk about the probability of a particular value because each value has probability zero. Instead, for a continuous random variable X, we say that the probability that X lies in any interval depends only on the length of that interval. Not surprisingly the density function of a continuous uniform random variable looks flat. It can be defined by the formula

$$f(x) = \begin{cases} \dfrac{1}{b-a} & if\ a \le x \le b \\ 0 & otherwise \end{cases}$$

FIGURE 7.11 The density function of a continuous uniform random variable on the interval from *a* to *b*.

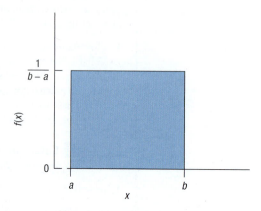

From Figure 7.11, it's easy to see that the probability that *X* lies in any interval between *a* and *b* is the same as any other interval of the same length. In fact, the probability is just the ratio of the length of the interval to the total length: $b - a$. In other words:

For values c and d ($c \le d$) both within the interval $[a, b]$:

$$P(c \le X \le d) = \frac{(d-c)}{(b-a)}$$

As an example, suppose you arrive at a bus stop and want to model how long you'll wait for the next bus. The sign says that busses arrive about every 20 minutes, but no other information is given. You might assume that the arrival is equally likely to be anywhere in the next 20 minutes, and so the density function would be

$$f(x) = \begin{cases} \dfrac{1}{20} & if\ \ 0 \le x \le 20 \\ 0 & otherwise \end{cases}$$

and would look as shown in Figure 7.12.

FIGURE 7.12 The density function of a continuous uniform random variable on the interval [0,20]. Notice that the mean (the balancing point) of the distribution is at 10 minutes and that the area of the box is 1.

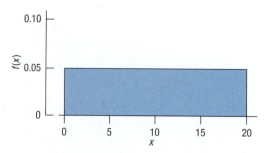

Just as the mean of a data distribution is the balancing point of a histogram, the mean of any continuous random variable is the balancing point of the density function. Looking at Figure 7.12, we can see that the balancing point is halfway between the end points at 10 minutes. In general, the expected value is:

$$E(X) = \frac{a + b}{2}$$

for a uniform distribution on the interval (a, b). With $a = 0$ and $b = 20$, the expected value would be 10 minutes.

The variance and standard deviation are less intuitive:

$$Var(X) = \frac{(b - a)^2}{12}; SD(X) = \sqrt{\frac{(b - a)^2}{12}}.$$

Using these formulas, our bus wait will have an expected value of 10 minutes with a standard deviation of $\sqrt{\frac{(20 - 0)^2}{12}} = 5.77$ minutes.

The Exponential Model

We saw in Chapter 6 that the Poisson distribution is a good model for the arrival, or occurrence, of events. We found, for example, the probability that x visits to our website will occur within the next minute. The **Exponential distribution** with parameter λ can be used to model the time *between* those events. Its density function has the form:

$$f(x) = \lambda e^{-\lambda x} \quad for \; x \geq 0 \; and \; \lambda > 0$$

The use of the parameter λ again is not coincidental. It highlights the relationship between the exponential and the Poisson.

FIGURE 7.13 The exponential density function with $\lambda = 1$.

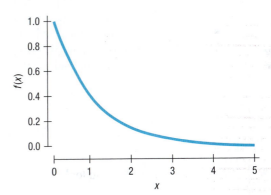

If a discrete random variable can be modeled by a Poisson model with rate λ, then the times between those events can be modeled by an exponential model with the same parameter λ. The mean of the exponential is $1/\lambda$. The inverse relationship between the two means makes intuitive sense. If λ increases and we expect *more* hits per minute, then the expected time between hits should go down. The standard deviation of an exponential random variable is $1/\lambda$.

Like any continuous random variable, probabilities of an exponential random variable can be found only through the density function. Fortunately, the area under the exponential density between any two values, s and t ($s \leq t$), has a particularly easy form:

$$P(s \leq X \leq t) = e^{-\lambda s} - e^{-\lambda t}.$$

In particular, by setting s to be 0, we can find the probability that the waiting time will be less than t from

$$P(X \leq t) = P(0 \leq X \leq t) = e^{-\lambda 0} - e^{-\lambda t} = 1 - e^{-\lambda t}.$$

The function $P(X \leq t) = F(t)$ is called the **cumulative distribution function (cdf)** of the random variable X. If arrivals of hits to our website can be well modeled by a Poisson with $\lambda = 4$/minute, then the probability that we'll have to wait less than 20 seconds (1/3 of a minute) for the next hit is $F(1/3) = P(0 \leq X \leq 1/3) = 1 - e^{-4/3} = 0.736$. That seems about right. Arrivals are coming about every 15 seconds on average, so we shouldn't be surprised that nearly 75% of the time we won't have to wait more than 20 seconds for the next hit.

⊘ WHAT CAN GO WRONG?

- **Probability models are still just models.** Models can be useful, but they are not reality. Think about the assumptions behind your models. Question probabilities as you would data.

- **Don't assume everything's Normal.** Just because a random variable is continuous or you happen to know a mean and standard deviation doesn't mean that a Normal model will be useful. You must think about whether the **Normality Assumption** is justified. Using a Normal model when it really does not apply will lead to wrong answers and misleading conclusions.

   A sample of CEOs has a mean total compensation of $10,307,311.87 with a standard deviation of $17,964,615.16. Using the Normal model rule, we should expect about 68% of the CEOs to have compensations between −$7,657,303.29 and $28,271,927.03. In fact, more than 90% of the CEOs have annual compensations in this range. What went wrong? The distribution is skewed, not symmetric. Using the 68–95–99.7 Rule for data like these will lead to silly results.

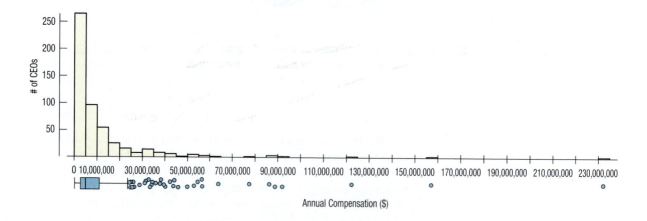

- **Don't use the Normal approximation with small n.** To use a Normal approximation in place of a Binomial model, there must be at least 10 expected successes and 10 expected failures.

ETHICS IN ACTION

Green River Army Depot's main business is the repair and refurbishment of electronics, mainly satellite and communication systems, in partnership with the Department of Defense (DOD). Recently, DOD has put a great deal of effort into continuous quality improvement, focusing on the length of time it takes to complete a project.

Dave Smith, head of the Productivity and Quality Improvement (PQI) directorate, is responsible for (among other things) facilitating lean improvement events throughout the Depot. These events bring together cross-functional teams with the goal of streamlining processes. PQI staff guide these teams in value stream mapping, identifying non–value added activities, and redesigning processes to eliminate waste. Dave is concerned that his group may not meet the new standards for quality which have specified that 97% of all projects must be completed within 60 days of their start dates.

In preparation for a meeting with the Depot commander, Dave decides to review data on lean improvement events. He finds that of the past 137 projects, 30% went beyond 60 days. The commander suggests that Dave be "creative" in his presentation of the statistics to make it look like the group is actually in compliance with the DOD.

The completion times are very skewed to the high end, which doesn't surprise Dave in the least. After all, no project can take less than 0 time, but a few always seem to go on for a much longer time than planned. He is pleased to find that the average completion time is only 40 days and that the standard deviation is 10 days. Dave knows that a Normal model is a poor representation of the completion times because of the skewness, but decides to use a $N(40,10)$ model. With this model, only about 2.5% of the projects would be expected to take more than 60 days!

He explains his model to this supervisor who is pleased with the results. Even though they know the data don't fit the model well, they also know that the DOD analysts are very familiar with Normal models and will be pleased to know that they are in compliance using it.

- **Identify the ethical dilemma in this scenario.**
- **What are the undesirable consequences?**
- **Propose an ethical solution that considers the welfare of all stakeholders.**

CHAPTER

7 FROM LEARNING TO EARNING

LEARNING OBJECTIVES

Recognize Normally distributed data by making a histogram and checking whether it is unimodal, symmetric, and bell-shaped, or by making a Normal probability plot using technology and checking whether the plot is roughly a straight line.

- The Normal model is a distribution that will be important for much of the rest of this course.
- Before using a Normal model, we should check that our data are plausibly from a Normally distributed population.
- A Normal probability plot provides evidence that the data are Normally distributed if it is linear.

Understand how to use the Normal model to judge whether a value is extreme.

- Standardize values to make z-scores and obtain a standard scale. Then refer to a standard Normal distribution.
- Use the 68–95–99.7 Rule as a rule-of-thumb to judge whether a value is extreme.

Know how to refer to tables or technology to find the probability of a value randomly selected from a Normal model falling in any interval.

- Know how to perform calculations about Normally distributed values and probabilities.

Recognize when independent random Normal quantities are being added or subtracted.

- The sum or difference will also follow a Normal model.
- The *variance* of the sum or difference will be the sum of the individual variances.
- The mean of the sum or difference will be the sum or difference, respectively, of the means.

Recognize when other continuous probability distributions are appropriate models.

TERMS

68–95–99.7 Rule (or Empirical Rule)
In a Normal model, 68% of values fall within one standard deviation of the mean, 95% fall within two standard deviations of the mean, and 99.7% fall within three standard deviations of the mean. This is also approximately true for most unimodal, symmetric distributions.

*Continuity correction
An adjustment made when a continuous model is used to model a set of discrete events.

Continuous random variable
A random variable that can take any numeric value within a range of values. The range may be infinite or bounded at either or both ends.

Cumulative distribution function (cdf)
A function for a continuous probability model that gives the probability of all values below a given value.

Exponential distribution
A continuous distribution appropriate for modeling the times between events whose occurrences follow a Poisson model.

Normal distribution
A unimodal, symmetric, "bell-shaped" distribution that appears throughout statistics.

Normal percentile
The Normal percentile corresponding to a z-score gives the percentage of values in a standard Normal distribution found at that z-score or below.

Normal probability plot
A display to help assess whether a distribution of data is approximately Normal. If the plot is nearly straight, the data satisfy the Nearly Normal Condition.

Probability density function (pdf)
A function for any continuous probability model that gives the probability of a random value falling between any two values as the area under the pdf between those two values.

Standard Normal model or Standard Normal distribution
A Normal model, $N(\mu, \sigma)$ with mean $\mu = 0$ and standard deviation $\sigma = 1$.

Uniform distribution
A continuous distribution that assigns a probability to any range of values (between 0 and 1) proportional to the difference between the values.

TECH SUPPORT   Probability Calculations and Plots

The best way to tell whether your data can be modeled well by a Normal model is to make a picture or two. We've already talked about making histograms. Normal probability plots are almost never made by hand because the values of the Normal scores are tricky to find. But most statistics software can make Normal plots, though various packages call the same plot by different names and array the information differently.

EXCEL

Excel offers a "Normal probability plot" as part of the Regression command in the Data Analysis extension, but (as of this writing) it is not a correct Normal probability plot and should not be used.

As discussed in Chapter 6, functions that calculate probabilities for continuous probability distributions will calculate either pdf ("probability density function"—what we've been calling a probability model) or cdf ("cumulative distribution function"—accumulate probabilities over a range of values). These technical terms show up in many of the function names. Excel uses the "cumulative" part of the command to determine whether you want a probability as your result (cumulative = true; this is the cdf) or a number as your result given a probability (cumulative = false; this is the pdf).

To calculate Continuous Distribution Probabilities in Excel:

Distribution	Excel Syntax	Example Syntax	Result	Probability Statement
Normal	NORM.DIST(x,mean,std. dev., cumulative)	=NORM.DIST(30,20,10,TRUE)	0.8413	$P(X<30)$, N(20,10)
$N(\mu, \sigma)$	NORM.INV(probability,mean,std. dev.)	=NORM.INV(0.1,20,10)	7.1845	$P(X<?)=0.10$, N(20,10)
Standard Normal	NORM.S.DIST(z,cumulative)	=NORM.S.DIST(-1.645,TRUE)	0.0500	$P(Z<-1.645)$
N(0, 1)	NORM.S.INV(probability)	=NORM.S.INV(0.05)	-1.6449	$P(Z<?)=0.05$
Exponential	EXPON.DIST(x, lambda, cumulative)	=EXPON.DIST(2,4/3,TRUE)	0.9305	$P(X<2)$, $\lambda=4/3$

Note that the commands here are for Excel 2016. These functions are available in earlier versions of Excel with similar commands. In general, the functions ending in DIST will calculate a probability given a value from the distribution and the INV functions will calculate a value given a probability. When using the function bar or typing into a cell, Excel will search the functions to find what matches the typed characters, and this can be used to find the proper function.

XLSTAT

XLStat can make Normal probability plots (XLStat calls these Q-Q plots):

- Select **Visualizing data**, and then **Univariate plots**.
- On the General tab, click the **Quantitative** data box and then select the data on your worksheet.
- Click **OK**.
- If prompted, click **Continue**.

JMP

To make a "Normal Quantile Plot" in JMP,

- Make a histogram using **Distributions** from the **Analyze** menu.
- Click on the drop-down menu next to the variable name.
- Choose **Normal Quantile Plot** from the drop-down menu.
- JMP opens the plot next to the histogram.

COMMENTS

JMP places the ordered data on the vertical axis and the Normal scores on the horizontal axis. The vertical axis aligns with the histogram's axis, a useful feature.

MINITAB

To make a "Normal Probability Plot" in MINITAB,

- Choose **Probability Plot** from the **Graph** menu.
- Select "Single" for the type of plot. Click **OK**.
- Enter the name of the variable in the "Graph variables" box. Click **OK**.

COMMENTS

MINITAB places the ordered data on the horizontal axis and the Normal scores on the vertical axis.

R

To make a Normal probability (Q-Q) plot for Y:

- **qqnorm(Y)** will produce the plot.

To standardize a variable Y:

- **Z = (Y − mean(Y))/sd(Y)** will create a standardized variable Z.

COMMENTS

By default, R places the ordered data on the vertical axis and the Normal scores on the horizontal axis, but that can be reversed by setting **datax = TRUE** inside qqnorm.

SPSS

To make a Normal "Q-Q plot" in SPSS,

- Choose **Descriptives > Q-Q Plots** from the **Analyze** menu.
- Select the variable to be displayed and add to "Variable".
- Make sure that "Normal" is selected under "Test Distribution". Leave all other defaults set.

COMMENTS

SPSS places the ordered data on the horizontal axis and the Normal scores on the vertical axis.

STATCRUNCH

To make a Normal probability plot:

- Click on **Graph**.
- Choose **QQ Plot**.
- Choose the variable name from the list of Columns.
- Click on **Compute!**

To work with Normal percentiles:

- Click on **Stat**.
- Choose **Calculators > Normal**.
- Choose a lower tail ($\leq$) or upper tail ($\geq$) region.
- Enter the z-score cutoff, and then click on **Compute** to find the probability.

OR

Enter the desired probability, and then click on **Compute** to find the z-score cutoff.

BRIEF CASE

Price/Earnings and Stock Value

The CAPE10 index is based on the Price/Earnings (P/E) ratios of stocks. We can examine the P/E ratios without applying the smoothing techniques used to find the CAPE10. The file **CAPE10 2017** holds the data, giving dates, various economic variables, CAPE10 values, and P/E values.

Examine the P/E values. Split the data into two periods: 1881–1989 and 1990 to the present. Would you judge that a Normal model would be appropriate for those values from the 1880s through the 1980s? Explain (and show the plots you made).

Now consider the more recent P/E values in this context. Do you think they have been extreme? What years, if any, appear to be particularly problematic? Explain.

CHAPTER 7 EXERCISES

Normal model calculations can be performed using a variety of technology or with the tables in Appendix B. Different methods may yield slightly different results.

SECTION 7.1

1. An incoming MBA student took placement exams in economics and mathematics. In economics, she scored 82 and in math 86. The overall results on the economics exam had a mean of 72 and a standard deviation of 8, while the mean math score was 68, with a standard deviation of 12. On which exam did she do better compared with the other students?

2. The first statistics exam had a mean of 65 and a standard deviation of 10 points; the second had a mean of 80 and a standard deviation of 5 points. Derrick scored an 80 on both tests. Julie scored a 70 on the first test and a 90 on the second. They both totaled 160 points on the two exams, but Julie claims that her total is better. Explain.

3. Your company's Human Resources department administers a test of "Executive Aptitude." They report test grades as z-scores, and you got a score of 2.20. What does this mean?

4. After examining a child at his 2-year checkup, the boy's pediatrician said that the z-score for his height relative to American 2-year-olds was -1.88. Write a sentence to explain to the parents what that means.

5. Your company will admit to the executive training program only people who score in the top 3% on the executive aptitude test discussed in Exercise 3.

a) With your z-score of 2.20, did you make the cut?
b) What do you need to assume about test scores to find your answer in part a?

6. The pediatrician in Exercise 4 explains to the parents that the most extreme 5% of cases often require special treatment or attention.

a) Does this child fall into that group?
b) What do you need to assume about the heights of 2-year-olds to find your answer to part a?

SECTION 7.2

7. The Environmental Protection Agency (EPA) fuel economy estimates for automobiles suggest a mean of 24.8 mpg and a standard deviation of 6.2 mpg for highway driving. Assume that a Normal model can be applied.

a) Draw the model for auto fuel economy. Clearly label it, showing what the 68–95–99.7 Rule predicts about miles per gallon.
b) In what interval would you expect the central 68% of autos to be found?
c) About what percent of autos should get more than 31 mpg?
d) About what percent of cars should get between 31 and 37.2 mpg?
e) Describe the gas mileage of the worst 2.5% of all cars.

8. Some IQ tests are standardized to a Normal model with a mean of 100 and a standard deviation of 16.

a) Draw the model for these IQ scores. Clearly label it, showing what the 68–95–99.7 Rule predicts about the scores.
b) In what interval would you expect the central 95% of IQ scores to be found?
c) About what percent of people should have IQ scores above 116?

d) About what percent of people should have IQ scores between 68 and 84?
e) About what percent of people should have IQ scores above 132?

9. What percent of a standard Normal model is found in each region? Be sure to draw a picture first.

a) $z > 1.5$
b) $z < 2.25$
c) $-1 < z < 1.15$
d) $|z| > 0.5$

10. What percent of a standard Normal model is found in each region? Draw a picture first.

a) $z > -2.05$
b) $z < -0.33$
c) $1.2 < z < 1.8$
d) $|z| < 1.28$

11. In a standard Normal model, what value(s) of z cut(s) off the region described? Don't forget to draw a picture.

a) the highest 20%
b) the highest 75%
c) the lowest 3%
d) the middle 90%

12. In a standard Normal model, what value(s) of z cut(s) off the region described? Remember to draw a picture first.

a) the lowest 12%
b) the highest 30%
c) the highest 7%
d) the middle 50%

SECTION 7.3

13. Speeds of cars were measured as they passed one point on a road to study whether traffic speed controls were needed. Here's a histogram and normal probability plot of the measured speeds. Is a Normal model appropriate for these data? Explain.

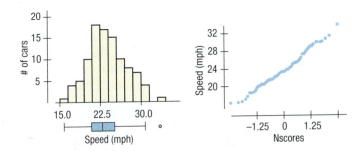

14. Has the Consumer Price Index (CPI) fluctuated around its mean according to a Normal model? Here are some displays. Is a Normal model appropriate for these data? Explain.

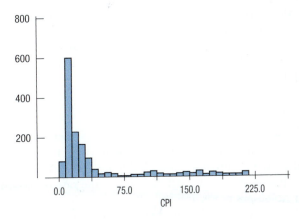

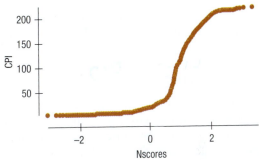

SECTION 7.4

15. For a new type of tire, a NASCAR team found the average distance a set of tires would run during a race is 168 miles, with a standard deviation of 14 miles. Assume that tire mileage is independent and follows a Normal model.

a) If the team plans to change tires twice during a 500-mile race, what is the expected value and standard deviation of miles remaining after two changes?
b) What is the probability they won't have to change tires a third time (and use a fourth set of tires) before the end of a 500-mile race?

16. In the 4×100 medley relay event, four swimmers swim 100 yards, each using a different stroke. A college team preparing for the conference championship looks at the times their swimmers have posted and creates a model based on the following assumptions:

- The swimmers' performances are independent.
- Each swimmer's times follow a Normal model.
- The means and standard deviations of the times (in seconds) are as shown here.

Swimmer	Mean	SD
1 (backstroke)	50.72	0.24
2 (breaststroke)	55.51	0.22
3 (butterfly)	49.43	0.25
4 (freestyle)	44.91	0.21

a) What are the mean and standard deviation for the relay team's total time in this event?

b) The team's best time so far this season was 3:19.48. (That's 199.48 seconds.) What is the probability that they will beat that time in the next event?

SECTION 7.5

17. Because many passengers who make reservations do not show up, airlines often overbook flights (sell more tickets than there are seats). A Boeing 767-400ER holds 245 passengers. If the airline believes the rate of passenger no-shows is 5% and sells 255 tickets, is it likely they will not have enough seats and someone will get bumped?

a) Use the Normal model to approximate the Binomial to determine the probability of at least 246 passengers showing up.

b) Should the airline change the number of tickets they sell for this flight? Explain.

18. Shortly after the introduction of the Belgian euro coin, newspapers around the world published articles claiming the coin is biased. The stories were based on reports that someone had spun the coin 250 times and gotten 140 heads—that's 56% heads.

a) Use the Normal model to approximate the Binomial to determine the probability of spinning a fair coin 250 times and getting at least 140 heads.

b) Do you think this is evidence that spinning a Belgian euro is unfair? Would you be willing to use it at the beginning of a sports event? Explain.

SECTION 7.6

19. A cable provider wants to contact customers in a particular telephone exchange to see how satisfied they are with the new digital TV service the company has provided. All numbers are in the 452 exchange, so there are 10,000 possible numbers from 452-0000 to 452-9999. If they select the numbers with equal probability:

a) What distribution would they use to model the selection?

b) The new business "incubator" was assigned the 200 numbers between 452-2500 and 452-2699, but these businesses don't subscribe to digital TV. What is the probability that the randomly selected number will be for an incubator business?

c) Numbers above 9000 were only released for domestic use last year, so they went to newly constructed residences. What is the probability that a randomly selected number will be one of these?

20. In an effort to check the quality of their cell phones, a manufacturing manager decides to take a random sample of 10 cell phones from yesterday's production run, which produced cell phones with serial numbers ranging (according to when they were produced) from 43005000 to 43005999. If each of the 1000 phones is equally likely to be selected:

a) What distribution would they use to model the selection?

b) What is the probability that a randomly selected cell phone will be one of the last 100 to be produced?

c) What is the probability that the first cell phone selected is either from the last 200 to be produced or from the first 50 to be produced?

21. Lifetimes of electronic components can often be modeled by an exponential model. Suppose quality control engineers want to model the lifetime of a hard drive to have a mean lifetime of 3 years.

a) What value of λ should they use?

b) With this model, what would the probability be that a hard drive lasts 5 years or less?

22. Suppose occurrences of sales on a small company's website are well modeled by a Poisson model with $\lambda = 5$/hour.

a) If a sale just occurred, what is the expected waiting time until the next sale?

b) What is the probability that the next sale will happen in the next 6 minutes?

CHAPTER EXERCISES

For Exercises 23–30, use the 68–95–99.7 Rule to approximate the probabilities rather than using technology to find the values more precisely. Answers given for probabilities or percentages from Exercise 31 on assume that a calculator or software has been used. Answers found from using Z-tables may vary slightly.

23. Mutual fund returns. In the first quarter of 2017, a group of domestic equity mutual funds had a mean return of 6.2% with a standard deviation of 1.8%. If a Normal model can be used to model them, what percent of the funds would you expect to be in each region?

Be sure to draw a picture first.

a) Returns of 8.0% or more

b) Returns of 6.2% or less

c) Returns between 2.6% and 9.8%

d) Returns of more than 11.6%

24. Human resource testing. Although controversial and the subject of some recent law suits (e.g., *Satchell et al. v. FedEx Express*), some human resource departments administer standard IQ tests to all employees. The Stanford-Binet test scores are well modeled by a Normal model with mean 100 and standard deviation 16. If the applicant pool is well modeled by this distribution, a randomly selected applicant would have what probability of scoring in the following regions?

a) 100 or below

b) Above 148

c) Between 84 and 116

d) Above 132

25. Mutual funds, again. From the mutual funds in Exercise 23 with quarterly returns that are well modeled by a Normal model with a mean of 6.2% and a standard deviation of 1.8%, find the cutoff return value(s) that would separate the

a) highest 50%.
b) highest 16%.
c) lowest 2.5%.
d) middle 68%.

26. Human resource testing, again. For the IQ test administered by human resources and discussed in Exercise 24, what cutoff value would separate the

a) lowest 0.15% of all applicants?
b) lowest 16%?
c) middle 95%?
d) highest 2.5%?

27. Currency exchange rates. The monthly exchange rates for the five-year period October 2012 to October 2017 between the euro (EUR) and the British pound (GBP) can be modeled by a Normal distribution with mean 1.24 euros (to pounds) and standard deviation 0.09 euro. Given this model, what is the probability that on a randomly selected day during this period, the pound was worth

a) less than 1.24 euros?
b) more than 1.33 euros?
c) less than 1.06 euros?
d) Which would be more unusual, a day on which the pound was worth less than 1.10 euros or more than 1.40 euros?

28. Stock prices. For the 71 trading days from January 3, 2017, to April 18, 2017, the daily closing price of IBM stock (in $) is well modeled by a Normal model with mean $174.85 and standard deviation $4.51. According to this model, what is the probability that on a randomly selected day in this period the stock price closed

a) above $179?
b) below $184?
c) between $161 and $188?
d) Which would be more unusual, a day on which the stock price closed above $180 or below $165?

29. Currency exchange rates, again. For the model of the EUR/GBP exchange rate discussed in Exercise 27, what would the cutoff rates be that would separate the

a) highest 16% of EUR/GBP rates?
b) lowest 50%?
c) middle 95%?
d) lowest 2.5%?

30. Stock prices, again. According to the model in Exercise 28, what cutoff value of price would separate the

a) lowest 16% of the days?
b) highest 0.15%?
c) middle 68%?
d) highest 50%?

31. Mutual fund probabilities. According to the Normal model $N(0.062, 0.018)$ describing mutual fund returns in the 1st quarter of 2013 in Exercise 23, what percent of this group of funds would you expect to have return

a) over 6.8%?
b) between 0% and 7.6%?
c) more than 1%?
d) less than 0%?

32. Normal IQs. Based on the Normal model $N(100, 16)$ describing IQ scores from Exercise 24, what percent of applicants would you expect to have scores

a) over 80?
b) under 90?
c) between 112 and 132?
d) over 125?

33. Mutual funds, once more. Based on the model $N(0.062, 0.018)$ for quarterly returns from Exercise 23, what are the cutoff values for the

a) highest 10% of these funds?
b) lowest 20%?
c) middle 40%?
d) highest 80%?

34. More IQs. In the Normal model $N(100, 16)$ for IQ scores from Exercise 24, what cutoff value bounds the

a) highest 5% of all IQs?
b) lowest 30% of the IQs?
c) middle 80% of the IQs?
d) lowest 90% of all IQs?

35. Mutual funds, finis. Consider the Normal model $N(0.062, 0.018)$ for returns of mutual funds in Exercise 23 one last time.

a) What value represents the 40th percentile of these returns?
b) What value represents the 99th percentile?
c) What's the IQR of the quarterly returns for this group of funds?

36. IQs, finis. Consider the IQ model $N(100, 16)$ one last time.

a) What IQ represents the 15th percentile?
b) What IQ represents the 98th percentile?
c) What's the IQR of the IQs?

37. Parameters. Every Normal model is defined by its parameters, the mean and the standard deviation. For each model described here, find the missing parameter. As always, start by drawing a picture.

a) $\mu = 20$, 45% above 30; $\sigma = ?$
b) $\mu = 88$, 2% below 50; $\sigma = ?$
c) $\sigma = 5$, 80% below 100; $\mu = ?$
d) $\sigma = 15.6$, 10% above 17.2; $\mu = ?$

38. Parameters, again. Every Normal model is defined by its parameters, the mean and the standard deviation. For each model described here, find the missing parameter. Don't forget to draw a picture.

a) $\mu = 1250$, 35% below 1200; $\sigma = ?$
b) $\mu = 0.64$, 12% above 0.70; $\sigma = ?$
c) $\sigma = 0.5$, 90% above 10.0; $\mu = ?$
d) $\sigma = 220$, 3% below 202; $\mu = ?$

39. SAT or ACT? Each year thousands of high school students take either the SAT or ACT, standardized tests used in the college admissions process. Combined SAT scores can go as high as 1600, while the maximum ACT composite score is 36. Since the two exams use very different scales, comparisons of performance are difficult. (A convenient rule of thumb is $SAT = 40 \times ACT + 150$; that is, multiply an ACT score by 40 and add 150 points to estimate the equivalent SAT score.) Assume that one year the combined SAT can be modeled by $N(1000, 200)$ and the ACT can be modeled by $N(27, 3)$. If an applicant to a university has taken the SAT and scored 1260 and another student has taken the ACT and scored 33, compare these students scores using z-values. Which one has a higher relative score? Explain.

40. Economics. Anna, a business major, took final exams in both Microeconomics and Macroeconomics and scored 83 on both. Her roommate Megan, also taking both courses, scored 77 on the Micro exam and 95 on the Macro exam. Overall, student scores on the Micro exam had a mean of 81 and a standard deviation of 5, and the Macro scores had a mean of 74 and a standard deviation of 15. Which student's overall performance was better? Explain.

41. Low job satisfaction. Suppose that job satisfaction scores can be modeled with $N(100, 12)$. Human resource departments of corporations are generally concerned if the job satisfaction drops below a certain score. What score would you consider to be unusually low? Explain.

42. Low return. Exercise 23 proposes modeling quarterly returns of a group of mutual funds with $N(0.062, 0.018)$. The manager of this group of funds would like to flag any fund whose return is unusually low for a quarter. What level of return would you consider to be unusually low? Explain.

43. Management survey. A survey of 200 middle managers showed a distribution of the number of hours of exercise they participated in per week with a mean of 3.66 hours and a standard deviation of 4.93 hours.

a) According to the Normal model, what percent of managers will exercise fewer than one standard deviation below the mean number of hours?
b) For these data, what does that mean? Explain.
c) Explain the problem in using the Normal model for these data.

44. Customer database. A large philanthropic organization keeps records on the people who have contributed to their cause. In addition to keeping records of past giving, the organization buys demographic data on neighborhoods from the U.S. Census Bureau. Eighteen of these variables concern the ethnicity of the neighborhood of the donor. Here is a histogram and summary statistics for the percentage of whites in the neighborhoods of 500 donors.

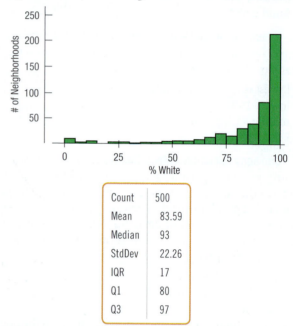

Count	500
Mean	83.59
Median	93
StdDev	22.26
IQR	17
Q1	80
Q3	97

a) Which is a better summary of the percentage of white residents in the neighborhoods, the mean or the median? Explain.
b) Which is a better summary of the spread, the IQR or the standard deviation? Explain.
c) From a Normal model, about what percentage of neighborhoods should have a percent white residents within one standard deviation of the mean?
d) What percentage of neighborhoods actually have a percent white within one standard deviation of the mean?
e) Explain the problem in using the Normal model for these data.

45. Drug company. Manufacturing and selling drugs that claim to reduce an individual's cholesterol level is big business. A company would like to market their drug to women if their cholesterol is in the top 15%. Assume the cholesterol levels of adult American women can be described by a Normal model with a mean of 188 mg/dL and a standard deviation of 24.

a) Draw and label the Normal model.
b) What percent of adult women do you expect to have cholesterol levels over 200 mg/dL?
c) What percent of adult women do you expect to have cholesterol levels between 150 and 170 mg/dL?
d) Estimate the interquartile range of the cholesterol levels.
e) Above what value are the highest 15% of women's cholesterol levels?

46. Tire company. A tire manufacturer believes that the tread life of its snow tires can be described by a Normal model with a mean of 32,000 miles and a standard deviation of 2500 miles.

a) If you buy a set of these tires, would it be reasonable for you to hope that they'll last 40,000 miles? Explain.
b) Approximately what fraction of these tires can be expected to last less than 30,000 miles?
c) Approximately what fraction of these tires can be expected to last between 30,000 and 35,000 miles?
d) Estimate the IQR for these data.
e) In planning a marketing strategy, a local tire dealer wants to offer a refund to any customer whose tires fail to last a certain number of miles. However, the dealer does not want to take too big a risk. If the dealer is willing to give refunds to no more than 1 of every 25 customers, for what mileage can he guarantee these tires to last?

47. Claims. Two companies make batteries for cell phone manufacturers. One company claims a mean life span of 2 years, while the other company claims a mean life span of 2.5 years (assuming average use of minutes/month for the cell phone).

a) Explain why you would also like to know the standard deviations of the battery life spans before deciding which brand to buy.
b) Suppose those standard deviations are 1.5 months for the first company and 9 months for the second company. Does this change your opinion of the batteries? Explain.

T 48. Car speeds. The police department of a major city needs to update its budget. For this purpose, they need to understand the variation in their fines collected from motorists for speeding. As a sample, they recorded the speeds of cars driving past a location with a 20 mph speed limit, a place that in the past has been known for producing fines. The mean of 100 readings was 23.84 mph, with a standard deviation of 3.56 mph. (The police actually recorded every car for a two-month period. These are 100 representative readings.)

a) How many standard deviations from the mean would a car going the speed limit be?
b) Which would be more unusual, a car traveling 34 mph or one going 10 mph?

49. CEOs. A business publication recently released a study on the total number of years of experience in industry among CEOs. The mean is provided in the article, but not the standard deviation. Is the standard deviation most likely to be 6 months, 6 years, or 16 years? Explain which standard deviation is correct and why.

50. Stocks. A newsletter for investors recently reported that the average stock price for a blue chip stock over the past 12 months was $72. No standard deviation was given. Is the standard deviation more likely to be $6, $16, or $60? Explain.

51. Cereal. The amount of cereal that can be poured into a small bowl varies with a mean of 1.5 ounces and a standard deviation of 0.3 ounce. A large bowl holds a mean of 2.5 ounces with a standard deviation of 0.4 ounce. You open a new box of cereal and pour one large and one small bowl.

a) How much more cereal do you expect to be in the large bowl?
b) What's the standard deviation of this difference?
c) If the difference follows a Normal model, what's the probability the small bowl contains more cereal than the large one?
d) What are the mean and standard deviation of the total amount of cereal in the two bowls?
e) If the total follows a Normal model, what's the probability you poured out more than 4.5 ounces of cereal in the two bowls together?
f) The amount of cereal the manufacturer puts in the boxes is a random variable with a mean of 16.3 ounces and a standard deviation of 0.2 ounce. Find the expected amount of cereal left in the box and the standard deviation.

52. Pets. The American Veterinary Association claims that the annual cost of medical care for dogs averages $100, with a standard deviation of $30, and for cats averages $120, with a standard deviation of $35.

a) What's the expected difference in the cost of medical care for dogs and cats?
b) What's the standard deviation of that difference?
c) If the costs can be described by Normal models, what's the probability that medical expenses are higher for someone's dog than for her cat?
d) What concerns do you have?

53. More cereal. In Exercise 51 we poured a large and a small bowl of cereal from a box. Suppose the amount of cereal that the manufacturer puts in the boxes is a random variable with mean 16.2 ounces and standard deviation 0.1 ounce.

a) Find the expected amount of cereal left in the box.
b) What's the standard deviation?
c) If the weight of the remaining cereal can be described by a Normal model, what's the probability that the box still contains more than 13 ounces?

54. More pets. You're thinking about getting two dogs and a cat. Assume that annual veterinary expenses are independent and have a Normal model with the means and standard deviations described in Exercise 52.

a) Define appropriate variables and express the total annual veterinary costs you may have.
b) Describe the model for this total cost. Be sure to specify its name, expected value, and standard deviation.
c) What's the probability that your total expenses will exceed $400?

55. Bikes. Bicycles arrive at a bike shop in boxes. Before they can be sold, they must be unpacked, assembled, and tuned (lubricated, adjusted, etc.). Based on past experience, the shop manager makes the following assumptions about how long this may take:

- The times for each setup phase are independent.
- The times for each phase follow a Normal model.
- The means and standard deviations of the times (in minutes) are as shown:

Phase	Mean	SD
Unpacking	3.5	0.7
Assembly	21.8	2.4
Tuning	12.3	2.7

a) What are the mean and standard deviation for the total bicycle setup time?
b) A customer decides to buy a bike like one of the display models but wants a different color. The shop has one, still in the box. The manager says they can have it ready in half an hour. Do you think the bike will be set up and ready to go as promised? Explain.

56. Bike sale. The bicycle shop in Exercise 55 estimates using current labor costs that unpacking a bike costs $0.82 on average with a standard deviation of $0.16. Assembly costs $8.00 on average with a standard deviation of $0.88 and tuning costs $4.10 with a standard deviation of $0.90. Because the costs are directly related to the times, you can use the same assumptions as in Exercise 55.

a) Define your random variables, and use them to express the total cost of the bike set up.
b) Find the mean set up cost.
c) Find the standard deviation of the set up cost.
d) If the next shipment is 40 bikes, what is the probability that the total set up cost will be less than $500?

57. Coffee and doughnuts. At a certain coffee shop, all the customers buy a cup of coffee; some also buy a doughnut. The shop owner believes that the number of cups he sells each day is normally distributed with a mean of 320 cups and a standard deviation of 20 cups. He also believes that the number of doughnuts he sells each day is independent of the coffee sales and is normally distributed with a mean of 150 doughnuts and a standard deviation of 12.

a) The shop is open every day but Sunday. Assuming day-to-day sales are independent, what's the probability he'll sell more than 2000 cups of coffee in a week?
b) If he makes a profit of 50 cents on each cup of coffee and 40 cents on each doughnut, can he reasonably expect to have a day's profit of over $300? Explain.
c) What's the probability that on any given day he'll sell a doughnut to more than half of his coffee customers?

58. Weightlifting. The Atlas BodyBuilding Company (ABC) sells "starter sets" of barbells that consist of one bar, two 20-pound weights, and four 5-pound weights. The bars weigh an average of 10 pounds with a standard deviation of 0.25 pound. The weights average the specified amounts, but the standard deviations are 0.2 pound for the 20-pounders and 0.1 pound for the 5-pounders. We can assume that all the weights are normally distributed.

a) ABC ships these starter sets to customers in two boxes: The bar goes in one box and the six weights go in another. What's the probability that the total weight in that second box exceeds 60.5 pounds? Define your variables clearly and state any assumptions you make.
b) It costs ABC $0.40 per pound to ship the box containing the weights. Because it's an odd-shaped package, though, shipping the bar costs $0.50 a pound plus a $6.00 surcharge. Find the mean and standard deviation of the company's total cost for shipping a starter set.
c) Suppose a customer puts a 20-pound weight at one end of the bar and the four 5-pound weights at the other end. Although he expects the two ends to weigh the same, they might differ slightly. What's the probability the difference is more than a quarter of a pound?

59. Lefties. A lecture hall has 200 seats with folding arm tablets, 30 of which are designed for left-handers. The typical size of classes that meet there is 188, and we can assume that about 13% of students are left-handed. Use a Normal approximation to find the probability that a right-handed student in one of these classes is forced to use a lefty arm tablet.

60. Seatbelts. Police estimate that 80% of drivers wear their seatbelts. They set up a safety roadblock, stopping cars to check for seatbelt use. If they stop 120 cars, what's the probability they find at least 20 drivers not wearing their seatbelt? Use a Normal approximation.

61. Rickets. Vitamin D is essential for strong, healthy bones. Although the bone disease rickets was largely eliminated in England during the 1950s, some people there are concerned that this generation of children is at increased risk because they are more likely to watch TV or play computer games than spend time outdoors. Recent research indicated that about 20% of British children are deficient in vitamin D. A company that sells vitamin D supplements tests 320 elementary school children in one area of the country. Use a Normal approximation to find the probability that no more than 50 of them have vitamin D deficiency.

62. Tennis. A tennis player has taken a special course to improve her serving. She thinks that individual serves are independent of each other. She has been able to make a successful first serve 70% of the time. Use a Normal approximation to find the probability she'll make at least 65 of her first serves out of the 80 she serves in her next match if her success percentage has not changed.

63. Wheel defects. Defects can occur anywhere on the wheel of a car during the manufacturing process. If X is the angle where the defect occurs, measured from a reference line, then X can be modeled as a uniform random variable on the interval from 0 to 360 degrees.

a) What is the probability that the defect is found between 0 and 180 degrees?

b) What is the probability that the defect is found between 0 and 45 degrees or between 315 and 360 degrees?

64. Quitting time. My employee seems to leave work anytime between 5 PM and 6 PM, uniformly.

a) What is the probability he will still be at work at 5:45 PM?

b) What is the probability he will still be at work at 5:45 PM every day this week (M–F)?

c) What did you assume to calculate b?

65. Web visitors. A website manager has noticed that during the evening hours, about 3 people per minute check out from their shopping cart and make an online purchase. She believes that each purchase is independent of the others.

a) What model might you suggest to model the number of purchases per minute?

b) What model would you use to model the time between events?

c) What is the mean time between purchases?

d) What is the probability that the time to the next purchase will be between 1 and 2 minutes?

66. Monitoring quality. A cell phone manufacturer samples cell phones from the assembly to test. She noticed that the number of faulty cell phones in a production run of cell phones is usually small and that the quality of one day's run seems to have no bearing on the next day.

a) What model might you use to model the number of faulty cell phones produced in one day?

She wants to model the time between the events of producing a faulty phone. The mean number of defective cell phones is 2 per day.

b) What model would you use to model the time between events?

c) What would the probability be that the time to the next failure is 1 day or less?

d) What is the mean time between failures?

JUST CHECKING ANSWERS

1 a) On the first test, the mean is 88 and the SD is 4, so $z = (90 - 88)/4 = 0.5$. On the second test, the mean is 75 and the SD is 5, so $z = (80 - 75)/5 = 1.0$. The first test has the lower z-score, so it is the one that will be dropped.

b) The second test is 1 standard deviation above the mean, farther away than the first test, so it's the better score relative to the class.

2 The mean is 184 centimeters, with a standard deviation of 8 centimeters. 2 meters is 200 centimeters, which is 2 standard deviations above the mean. We expect 2.28% of the men to be above 2 meters.

3 a) We know that 68% of the time we'll be within 1 standard deviation (2 min) of 20. So 32% of the time we'll arrive in less than 18 or more than 22 minutes. Half of those times (16%) will be greater than 22 minutes, so 84% will be less than 22 minutes.

b) 24 minutes is 2 standard deviations above the mean. From Table Z we find that 2.28% of the times will be more than 24 minutes.

c) Traffic incidents may occasionally increase the time it takes to get to school, so the driving times may be skewed to the right, and there may be outliers.

d) If so, the Normal model would not be appropriate and the percentages we predict would not be accurate.

CHAPTER 8

Data Sources: Observational Studies and Surveys

Roper Polls

Public opinion polls are a relatively new phenomenon. In 1948, as a result of telephone surveys of likely voters, all of the major organizations—Gallup, Roper, and Crossley—consistently predicted, throughout the summer and into the fall, that Thomas Dewey would defeat Harry Truman in the November presidential election. By October the results seemed so clear that *Fortune* magazine declared, "Due to the overwhelming evidence, *Fortune* and Mr. Roper plan no further detailed reports on change of opinion in the forthcoming presidential campaign. . . ."

Of course, Harry Truman went on to win the 1948 election, and the picture of Truman in the early morning after the election holding up the *Chicago Tribune* (printed the night before), with its headline declaring Dewey the winner, has become legend.

The public's faith in opinion polls plummeted after the election, but Elmo Roper vigorously defended the pollsters. Roper was a principal and founder of one of the first market research firms, Cherington, Wood, and Roper, and director of the *Fortune Survey*, which was the first national poll to use scientific sampling techniques. He argued that rather than abandoning polling, business leaders should learn what had gone wrong in the 1948 polls so that market research could be improved. His frank admission of the mistakes made in those polls helped to restore confidence in polling as a business tool.

For the rest of his career, Roper split his efforts between two projects, commercial polling and public opinion. He established the Roper Center for Public Opinion Research at Williams College as a place to house public opinion archives, convincing fellow polling leaders Gallup and Crossley to participate as well. Now located at Cornell University, the Roper Center is one of the world's leading archives of social science data. Roper's market research efforts started as Roper Research Associates and later became the Roper Organization, which was acquired in 2005 by GfK. Founded in Germany in 1934 as the Gesellschaft für Konsumforschung (literally, "Society for Consumption Research"), GfK now stands for "growth from knowledge." It is the fourth largest international market research organization, with over 130 companies in 70 countries and more than 7700 employees worldwide.

GfK Roper Consulting conducts a yearly, global study to examine cultural, economic, and social information that may be crucial to companies doing business worldwide. These companies use the information provided by GfK Roper to help make marketing and advertising decisions in different markets around the world.

How do the researchers at GfK Roper know that the responses they get reflect the real attitudes of consumers? After all, they don't ask everyone, but they don't want to limit their conclusions to just the people they surveyed. Generalizing from the data at hand to the world at large is something that market researchers, investors, and pollsters do every day.

8.1 Observational Studies and Found Data

Data are everywhere. IBM estimates that 90% of all data in the world were generated in the past two years. We currently generate about 2.5 billion terabytes (TB) a day (a TB is 1000 gigabytes). Most of these data are simply recording an event: a text message (about 15.2 million per minute), an Uber trip (about 46,000/min), a tweet (456,000/min), an Instagram post (47,000/min), or a Google search (3.6 million/min).[1]

We've discussed visualizing, analyzing, and modeling data, but we haven't talked about where data come from. And that matters. The conclusions you can draw from data and the soundness of your business decisions are limited by how your data were collected and their quality. You should ask about your data's "pedigree" as part of your analysis. Start with the five W's, especially how, where, and why the data were collected. And be skeptical of the suggestion that large amounts of data substitute for knowing their pedigree. A large amount of unreliable or biased data is just as unreliable as a smaller amount.

Can you trust your data? Companies and government agencies collect data in many different ways. Recording customer transactions or "loyalty cards" enables a company to record every purchase. A company might study such transactional data to identify associations between customer behavior and demographic information about the customer. For example, they might notice that customers with pets tend

---

[1] www.iflscience.com/technology/how-much-data-does-the-world-generate-every-minute/

to spend more on home cleaning supplies. But, because these data have no structure, it would be dangerous to conclude that owning a pet *causes* increased spending.

What's wrong with concluding that owning a pet causes purchases of cleaning supplies? That claim depends on there being no other differences between the groups that could account for the differences in purchasing behavior. But there are lots of variables that might cause differences. Perhaps more affluent families both have pets and spend more freely. Or maybe families with children both spend more on cleaning supplies and tend to have pets.

When it is practical, a somewhat better approach is to observe individuals, recording the variables of interest, and seeing how things turn out. This kind of study, in which individuals are observed and outcomes are measured, is called an **observational study**.

For example, if a home improvement store thought pet ownership might be a way to identify profitable customers, it might start by selecting a random sample of new customers and ask whether they have a pet. Analysts could then track their spending on home improvement and compare those who own pets to those who don't.

A study like this, in which individuals are followed to observe future outcomes is called a **prospective** study. One that identified pet owners and reviewed previous purchasing behavior would be called a **retrospective** study.

Observational studies are used widely in public health and marketing. Those that study rare outcomes, such as specific diseases, are often retrospective. They first identify people with the disease and then look into their history and heritage in search of things that may be related to their condition. But retrospective studies have a restricted view of the world because they are usually limited to a small part of the entire population. And because retrospective records are based on historical data and memories, they can have errors. (Do you recall *exactly* what you ate even yesterday? How about last Wednesday?)

Although an observational study may identify important variables related to an outcome of interest, there is no guarantee that we have found the right or the most important related variables. Perhaps people who own a home with a yard are more likely to have a pet and spend more on home improvement. It may be this fact—whether we know it or not—that drives spending on home improvement.

Observational studies, with appropriate caution and under certain circumstances, can be used to demonstrate causal relationships. However, getting to a causal explanation from observational data is extremely difficult under the best of conditions—and impossible in many cases. There is an entire field called causal inference that attempts to infer causes from observational studies, through careful reasoning and extensive case matching. These methods are extremely technical and they lie beyond the methods of this book. When it is important to identify factors that cause an outcome, the most effective approach is a designed experiment. A **designed experiment** differs from observational studies because the factors are actively manipulated with the intention of affecting the outcomes. Experimental designs are the subject of the next chapter.

> ### Retrospective Studies Can Give Valuable Clues
>
> For rare illnesses, it's not practical to draw a large enough sample to see many ill respondents, so the only option remaining is to develop retrospective data. For example, researchers can interview those who have become ill. The likely causes of both Legionnaires' disease and HIV were identified from such retrospective studies of the small populations who were first infected. But to confirm the causes, researchers needed laboratory-based experiments.

IN PRACTICE 8.1   Gaining insights from observational studies

Amtrak launched its high-speed train, the Acela, in December 2000. It is the only high-speed line in the United States and it is by far the most profitable of all Amtrak lines. The Acela line generates about one quarter of Amtrak's entire revenue.[2] It is

---

[2]reasonrail.blogspot.fr/2014/11/amtrak-routes-by-2014-cost-recovery.html

often used by business professionals because of its fast travel times, business class seats, and free Wi-Fi. The manager you work for at Amtrak wants to boost Acela's ridership among Millennials. You examine a sample of last year's customers for whom you have demographic information and find that only 5% of last year's riders were 21 years old or younger, but of those, 90% used the Internet while on board as opposed to 37% of riders older than 21 years.

MANAGER That's great. So, if we increase the quality and speed of the Wi-Fi service on board, will we attract more young riders?

ANALYST Not necessarily. This is only a retrospective observational study. Although I compared the rates of Internet use between those older and younger than 21 years, I can't come to any conclusions about why they chose to ride the Acela. We certainly can't conclude that changing our Wi-Fi quality will boost their ridership based on these data. On the other hand, we could possibly design an experiment to try to determine the effect of Wi-Fi quality on usership by millennials.

Big Data and Data on the Web

In recent years, it has become common to work with large amounts of routinely collected transactional data or data available on the Internet—commonly called "big data." And such data are increasingly being "mined" to make business and policy decisions. But even when the data are of high quality and record what they claim to record, it can be hazardous to use such data to infer conclusions. "Found" data have not been collected with the aim of learning anything specific. It can be dangerous to use them as if they were collected with such a purpose. One hazard is that variables that should have been measured to obtain an accurate view of patterns and relationships, and that would therefore have been included in a designed study, might not be available in found data. Another is that when there is a large amount of data, the sheer size of the dataset can make conclusions appear to be convincing. You should be very cautious with such data.

8.2 Sample Surveys

Data collected to understand a larger population or estimate some attributes of the population are often found by a **sample survey**. A **sample survey** asks questions of potential respondents and records their responses in an attempt to understand the larger population.

Three Ideas of Sampling

Idea 1: Sample—Examine a Part of the Whole

We'd like to know about an entire collection of individuals, called a **population**, but examining all of them is usually impractical, if not impossible. So we settle for examining a smaller group of individuals—a **sample**—selected from the population. For the Roper researchers the population of interest is the entire world, but it's not practical, cost-effective, or feasible to survey everyone. So they examine a sample selected from the population.

We take samples all the time. For example, if a restaurant chef wants to be sure that the vegetable soup she's cooking is up to her standards, she'll taste a spoonful. She doesn't need to consume the whole pot. She can trust that the taste will *represent* the flavor of the population—the entire pot. The idea of tasting is that a small sample, if selected properly, can represent the larger population.

> **The W's and Sampling**
>
> The population we are interested in is usually determined by the *why* of our study. The participants or cases in the sample we draw will be the *who*. *When* and *how* we draw the sample may depend on what is practical.

Sampling is common in many aspects of business practice. For example, auditors may sample some records rather than reading through all of them. Manufacturers monitor quality by testing a small sample off the line.

The GfK Roper Reports® Worldwide poll is an example of a **sample survey**, designed to ask questions of a small group of people in the hope of learning something about the entire population. Most likely, you've never been selected to be part of a national opinion poll. That's true of most people. So how can the pollsters claim that a sample represents the entire population? As we'll see, a representative sample can often provide a good idea of what the entire population is like. But the sample must be selected with care.

Selecting a sample to represent the population fairly is easy in theory, but in practice, it's more difficult than it sounds. For example, a sample may fail to represent part of the population. If a retail business samples customers as they come in the door, they may be missing an important part of their potential customer population—those who choose to shop elsewhere. Samples that over- or underemphasize some characteristics of the population are said to be biased. When a sample is **biased**, the summary characteristics of a sample differ from the corresponding characteristics of the population it is trying to represent, so they can produce misleading information. Conclusions based on biased samples are inherently flawed. There is usually no way to fix bias after the sample is drawn and no way to salvage useful information from it.

To make the sample as representative as possible, the best strategy is to select individuals for the sample *at random*. This may seem almost careless at first, but, as we will see, it is essential.

Idea 2: Randomize

Think back to our soup example. Suppose the chef adds some salt to the pot (the population). If she samples from the top before stirring, she'll get the misleading idea that the soup is salty. If she samples from the bottom, she'll get the equally misleading idea that it's bland. But by stirring the soup, she'll randomly distribute the salt throughout the soup making each spoonful a more representative sample of the soup, so each taste is more typical of the saltiness of the whole pot. Deliberate randomization is one of the great tools of statistics.

Randomization can also protect against factors that you aren't aware of. Suppose, while the chef isn't looking, an assistant adds a handful of peas to the soup. The peas sink to the bottom of the pot, mixing with the other vegetables. Stirring in the salt *also* randomizes the peas throughout the pot, making the sample taste more typical of the overall pot *even though the chef didn't know the peas were there*. So randomizing protects us by giving us a representative sample even for effects we were unaware of.

For a survey, we select participants at random, and this helps us represent *all* the features of our population, making sure that *on average* the sample looks like the rest of the population.

The essential feature of randomness is that the selection is "fair." We have discussed many facets of randomness in Chapter 5, and we can use some of those concepts here. What makes the sample fair is that each participant has an equal chance to be selected.

- **Why not match the sample to the population?** Rather than randomizing, we could try to design a sample to include every possible, relevant characteristic: income level, age, political affiliation, marital status, number of children, place of residence, etc. But we can't possibly think of all the things that might be important. Even if we could, we wouldn't be able to match our sample to the population for all these characteristics.

How well can a sample represent the population from which it was selected? Here's an example using the database of the Paralyzed Veterans of America, a philanthropic organization with a donor list of about 3.5 million people. We've taken two samples, each of 8000 individuals at random from the population. Table 8.1 shows how the means and proportions match up on seven variables.

	A	B	C	D	E	F	G	H
1		Age (yr)	White (%)	Female (%)	# of children	Income Bracket (1-7)	Wealth Bracket (1-9)	Homeowner? (% Yes)
2	Sample 1	61.4	85.12	56.2	1.54	3.91	5.29	71.36
3	Sample 2	61.2	84.44	56.4	1.51	3.88	5.33	72.30

TABLE 8.1 Means and proportions for seven variables from two samples of size 8000 from the Paralyzed Veterans of America data. We drew these samples using Microsoft Excel's RAND function (Excel 2016), but you can use almost any statistics software to draw similar random samples. The fact that the summaries of the variables from these two samples are so similar gives us confidence that either one would be representative of the entire population.

The two samples match closely in every category. You can see how well randomizing has stirred the population. We didn't preselect the samples for these variables, but randomizing has matched the results closely. The two samples don't vary much from each other, so we can assume that they don't differ much from the rest of the population either.

Idea 3: The Sample Size Is What Matters

You probably weren't surprised by the idea that a sample can represent the whole. And the idea of sampling randomly to make the sample fair makes sense too. But the third important idea of sampling often surprises people. The third idea is that the *size of the sample* determines what we can conclude from the data *regardless of the size of the population*. Many people think that to provide a good representation of the population, the sample must be a large percentage, or *fraction*, of the population, but in fact all that matters is the size of the sample. The size of the *population* doesn't matter at all.[3] A random sample of 100 students in a college represents the student body just about as well as a random sample of 100 voters represents the entire electorate of the United States. This is perhaps the most surprising idea in designing surveys.

Think about the pot of soup again. The chef is probably making a large pot of soup. But she doesn't need a really big spoon to decide how the soup tastes. She'll get the same information from an ordinary spoonful no matter how large the pot—as long as the pot is sufficiently stirred. That's what randomness does for us. What *fraction* of the population you sample doesn't matter. It's the **sample size** itself that's important. This idea is of key importance to the design of any sample survey, because it determines the balance between how well the survey can measure the population and how much the survey costs.

How big a sample do you need? That depends on what you're estimating, but too small a sample won't be representative of the population. To get an idea of what's really in the soup, you need a large enough taste to be a *representative* sample

[3]Well, that's not exactly true. If the population is smaller than about 10 times the size of the sample it *can* matter. It doesn't matter whenever, as usual, our sample is a very small fraction of the population.

from the pot, including, say, a selection of the vegetables. For a survey that tries to find the proportion of the population falling into a category, you'll usually need at least several hundred respondents.

- **What do the professionals do?** How do professional polling and market research companies do their work? The most common polling method today is to contact respondents by telephone. But technology is changing the way polling can be done. We learned about Dalia back in Chapter 2. Dalia samples from a sampling frame of up to 500 million people across 150 countries, accessing them by way of any of about 40,000 apps on their mobile devices. Dalia partners with the publishers of these apps to offer rewards for participation in the form of access to premium content, extra lives in games, gift cards, or charitable donations. Dalia uses stratification to invite a representative sample that matches known distributions in the population of interest. For example, they will sample the number of women in a narrow age range from a specified region based on census data that specify what fraction of the population fits those criteria. By contacting sampled individuals electronically, Dalia can complete a survey in less time, less expensively, and for a larger sample than with previous methodologies.

Do these methods work? The Pew Research Center for the People and the Press reports on survey completion rates about every three years. Pew reports that by 2012 a telephone survey could contact about 62% of households whose phone numbers had been randomly generated. However, only 14% of those contacts yielded an interview, amounting to only 9% of the households originally sampled. By contrast, Dalia reports Internet penetration of more than 85% in many countries (www.internetworldstats.com/top20.htm), and smartphone penetration is especially high in developing countries compared to computer or landline use. Nevertheless, Pew concludes that "telephone surveys that include landlines and cell phones and are weighted to match the demographic composition of the population continue to provide accurate data on most political, social and economic measures." (www.people-press.org/2012/05/15/assessing-the-representativeness-of-public-opinion-surveys/)

A Census—Does It Make Sense?

Why bother determining the right sample size? If you plan to open a store in a new community, why draw a sample of residents to understand their interests and needs? Wouldn't it be better to just include everyone and make the "sample" be the entire population? Such a special sample is called a **census**. Although a census would appear to provide the best possible information about the population, there are a number of reasons why it might not.

First, it can be difficult to complete a census. There always seem to be some individuals who are hard to locate or hard to measure. Do you really need to contact the folks away on vacation when you collect your data? How about those with no telephone or mailing address? The cost of locating the last few cases may far exceed the budget. It can also be just plain impractical to take a census. The quality control manager for Hostess® Twinkies® doesn't want to taste *all* the Twinkies on the production line to determine their quality. Aside from the fact that nobody could eat that many Twinkies, it would defeat their purpose: There would be none left to sell.

Second, the population you're studying may change. For example, in any human population, babies are born, people travel, and folks die during the time it takes to complete the census. News events and advertising campaigns can cause sudden shifts in opinions and preferences. A sample, surveyed in a shorter time frame, may actually generate more accurate information.

Finally, taking a census can be cumbersome. A census usually requires a team of pollsters and the cooperation of the population. Even with both, it's almost impossible to avoid errors. Because it tries to count everyone, the U.S. Census records too many college students. Many are included both by their families and in a report filed by their schools. Errors of this sort, of both under- and overcounting, can be found throughout the U.S. Census.

IN PRACTICE 8.2   Identifying the sample

A nonprofit organization has taken over the historic State Theater and hopes to preserve it with a combination of attractive shows and fundraising. The board of directors of the organization has asked a team of student consultants to help them design a survey to better understand the customer base likely to purchase tickets. Fortunately, the theater's computerized ticket system records contact and some demographic information for ticket purchasers, and that database of 7345 customers is available.

BOARD OF DIRECTORS Why can't we just perform a census?

CONSULTANTS The population of interest is all potential ticket purchasers. A census would have to reach all potential purchasers. We don't know who they are or have any way to contact them. We do have information about those who have purchased tickets and we can hope that potential purchasers would be like them.

8.3 Populations and Parameters

GfK Roper Reports Worldwide reports that 60.5% of people over 50 worry about food safety, but only 43.7% of teens do. What does this claim mean? We can be sure the Roper researchers didn't take a census. So they can't possibly know *exactly* what percentage of teenagers worry about food safety. So what does "43.7%" mean?

To generalize from a sample to the world at large, we need a model of reality. Such a model doesn't need to be complete or perfect. Just as a model of an airplane in a wind tunnel can tell engineers what they need to know about aerodynamics even though it doesn't include every rivet of the actual plane, models of data can give us summaries that we can learn from and use even though they don't fit each data value exactly. It's important to remember that they're only models of reality and not reality itself. But without models, what we can learn about the world at large is limited to only what we can say about the data we have at hand.

Models use mathematics to represent reality. We call the key numbers in those models **parameters**. Sometimes a parameter used in a model for a population is called (redundantly) a **population parameter**.

But let's not forget about the data. We use the data to try to estimate values for the population parameters. Any summary found from the data is a **statistic**. Those statistics that estimate population parameters are particularly interesting. Sometimes—and especially when we match statistics with the parameters they estimate—we use the term **sample statistic**.

We draw samples because we can't work with the entire population. We hope that the statistics we compute from the sample will estimate the corresponding parameters accurately. A sample that does this is said to be **representative**.

Statistic

Any quantity that we calculate from data could be called a "statistic." But in practice, we usually obtain a statistic from a sample and use it to estimate a population parameter.

Parameter

Population model parameters are not just unknown—usually they are unknowable. We take a sample and use the sample statistics to estimate them.

JUST CHECKING

1 Various claims are often made for surveys. Why is each of the following claims not correct?

a) It is always better to take a census than to draw a sample.

b) Stopping customers as they are leaving a restaurant is a good way to sample opinions about the quality of the food.

c) We drew a sample of 100 from the 3000 students in a school. To get the same level of precision for a town of 30,000 residents, we'll need a sample of 1000.

d) A poll taken at a popular website garnered 12,357 responses. The majority of respondents said they enjoy doing statistics. With a sample size that large, we can be sure that most Americans feel this way.

e) The true percentage of all Americans who enjoy statistics is called a "population statistic."

8.4   Common Sampling Designs

We've said that every individual in the population should have an equal chance of being selected in a sample. That makes the sample fair, but it's not quite enough to ensure that the sample is representative. Consider, for example, a market analyst who samples customers by drawing at random from product registration forms, half of which arrived by mail and half by online registration. She flips a coin. If it comes up heads, she'll draw 100 mail returns; tails, she'll draw 100 electronic returns. Each customer has an equal chance of being selected, but if tech-savvy customers are different, then the samples are hardly representative.

Simple Random Sample (SRS)

To make the sample representative, we must ensure that our sampling method gives each *combination* of individuals an equal chance as well. A sample drawn in this way is called a **simple random sample**, usually abbreviated **SRS**. An SRS is the sampling method on which the theory of working with sampled data is based and thus the standard against which we measure other sampling methods.

We'd like to select from the population, but often we don't have a list of all the individuals in the population. The list we actually draw from is called a **sampling frame**. A store may want to survey all its regular customers. But it can't draw a sample from the population of all regular customers, because it doesn't have such a list. The store may have a list of customers who have registered as "frequent shoppers." That list can be the sampling frame from which the store can draw its sample.

Of course, whenever the sampling frame and the population differ (as they almost always will), we must deal with the differences. Are the opinions of those who registered as frequent shoppers different from the opinions of the rest of the regular shoppers? What about customers who used to be regulars but haven't shopped there recently? The answers to questions like these about the sampling frame may depend on the purpose of the survey and may impact the conclusions that one can draw.

Once we have a sampling frame, we need to *randomize* it so we can choose an SRS. Fortunately, random numbers are readily available these days in spreadsheets, statistics programs, and even on the Internet. Before this technology existed, people used to literally draw numbers out of a hat to randomize. But now, the easiest way to randomize your sampling frame is to match it with a parallel list of random numbers and then sort the random numbers, carrying along the cases so that they get "shuffled" into random order. Then you can just pick cases off the top of the randomized list until you have enough for your sample.

Samples drawn at random generally differ one from another. If we were to repeat the sampling process, a new draw of random numbers would select different people for our sample. These differences would lead to different values for the variables we measure. We call these sample-to-sample differences **sampling variability**. Sometimes they are called **sampling error** even though no error has taken place. Surprisingly, sampling variability isn't a problem; it's an opportunity. If different samples from a population vary little from each other, then most likely the underlying population harbors little variation. If the samples show much sampling variability, the underlying population probably varies a lot. In the coming chapters, we'll spend much time and attention working with sampling variability to better understand what we are trying to measure.

Sampling Errors vs. Bias

Referring to sample-to-sample variability as sampling error, makes it sound like it's some kind of mistake. It's not. We understand that samples will vary, so "sampling errors" are to be expected. It's bias we must strive to avoid. Bias means our sampling method distorts our view of the population. Of course, bias leads to mistakes. Even more insidious, bias introduces errors that we cannot correct with subsequent analysis.

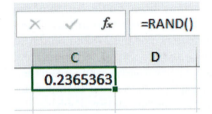

A Different Answer Every Time?

The RAND() function in Excel can take you by surprise. Every time the spreadsheet reopens, you get a new column of random numbers. But don't worry. Once you've shuffled the rows, you can ignore the new numbers. The order you got by shuffling won't keep changing. (Image created in Microsoft Excel)

IN PRACTICE 8.3   Choosing a random sample

Continuing In Practice from page 259, the student consultants select 200 ticket buyers at random from the database. First, the State Theater database is placed in a spreadsheet. Next, to draw random numbers, the students use the Excel command RAND( ). (They type =RAND() in the top cell of a column next to the data and then use *Fill Down* to populate the column down to the bottom.) They then sort the spreadsheet to put the random column in order and select ticket buyers from the top of the randomized spreadsheet until they complete 200 interviews. This makes it easy to select more respondents when (as always happens) some of the people they select can't be reached by telephone or decline to participate.

BOARD OF DIRECTORS   If we draw another sample will we get the same results? Also, next year, our database will have twice as many records. Will we need a sample that is twice as large?

CONSULTANTS   With random samples, we expect results to vary from one sample to another. We call that *sampling error* or *sampling variability*. We call the list from which we sample respondents our *sampling frame*. But a larger sampling frame does not require a larger sample. The size of the sample is all that matters.

The sampling frame is the customer database.

The size of the sample is all that matters, not the size of the population. We would need a sample of 200.

The differences in the responses from one sample to another are called sampling error, or sampling variability.

Simple random sampling is not the only fair way to sample. More complicated designs may save time or money or avert sampling problems. All statistical sampling designs have in common the idea that chance, rather than human choice, is used to select the sample.

Stratified Sampling

Designs that are used to sample from large populations—especially populations residing across large areas—are often more complicated than simple random samples. Sometimes we slice the population into homogeneous groups, called **strata**, and then use simple random sampling within each stratum, combining the results at the end. This is called **stratified random sampling**.

Why would we want to stratify? Suppose we want to survey how shoppers feel about a potential new anchor store at a large suburban mall. The shopper population is 60% women and 40% men, and we suspect that men and women have different views on their choice of anchor stores. If we use simple random sampling to select 100 people for the survey, we could end up with 70 men and 30 women or 35 men and 65 women. Our resulting estimates of the attractiveness of a new anchor store could vary widely. To help reduce this sampling variability, we can force a representative balance, selecting 40 men at random and 60 women at random. This would guarantee that the proportions of men and women within our sample match the proportions in the population, and that should make such samples more accurate in representing population opinion.

You can imagine that stratifying by race, income, age, and other characteristics can be helpful, depending on the purpose of the survey. When we use a sampling method that restricts by strata, additional samples are more like one another, so statistics calculated for the sampled values will vary less from one sample to another. This reduced sampling variability is the most important benefit of stratifying, but the analysis of data sampled with these designs is beyond the scope of our text.

Cluster and Multistage Sampling

Sometimes dividing the sample into homogeneous strata isn't practical, and even simple random sampling may be difficult. For example, suppose we wanted to assess the reading level of a product instruction manual based on the length of the sentences. Simple random sampling could be awkward; we'd have to number each sentence and then find, for example, the 576th sentence or the 2482nd sentence, and so on. Doesn't sound like much fun, does it?

We could make our task much easier by picking a few pages at random and then counting the lengths of the sentences on those pages. That's easier than picking individual sentences and works if we believe that the pages are all reasonably similar to one another in terms of reading level. Splitting the population in this way into parts or **clusters** that each represent the population can make sampling more practical. We select one or a few clusters at random and perform a census within each of them. This sampling design is called **cluster sampling**. If each cluster fairly represents the population, cluster sampling will generate an unbiased sample.

What's the difference between cluster sampling and stratified sampling? We stratify to ensure that our sample represents different groups in the population, and sample randomly within each stratum. This reduces the sample-to-sample variability. Strata are homogeneous, but differ from one another. By contrast, clusters are more or less alike, each heterogeneous and resembling the overall population. We cluster to save money or even to make the study practical.

Sometimes we use a variety of sampling methods together. In trying to assess the reading level of our instruction manual, we might worry that the "quick start" instructions are easy to read, but the "troubleshooting" chapter is more difficult. If so, we'd want to avoid samples that selected heavily from any one chapter. To guarantee a fair mix of sections, we could randomly choose one section from each chapter of the manual. Then we would randomly select a few pages from each of those sections. If altogether that made too many sentences, we might select a few sentences at random from each of the chosen pages. So, what is our sampling strategy? First we stratify by the chapter of the manual and randomly choose a section to represent each stratum. Within each selected section, we choose pages as clusters. Finally, we consider an SRS of sentences within each cluster. Sampling schemes that combine several methods are called **multistage samples**. Most surveys conducted by professional polling organizations and market research firms use some combination of stratified and cluster sampling as well as simple random samples.

Strata or Clusters?

We create strata by dividing the population into groups of similar individuals so that each stratum is different from the others. (For example, we often stratify by age, race, or sex.) By contrast, we create clusters that all look pretty much alike, each representing the wide variety of individuals seen in the population.

IN PRACTICE 8.4   More complex designs

The theater board wants to encourage people to come from out of town to attend theater events. They know that, in general, about 40% of ticket buyers are from out of town. These customers often purchase dinner at a local restaurant or stay overnight in a local inn, generating business for the town.

BOARD OF DIRECTORS We would like to encourage local businesses to advertise in the theater program. They will want to know about out-of-town customers. Will they be properly represented in the sample?

CONSULTANTS The data includes ZIP codes, so we can identify out-of-town customers. We propose a stratified sample, consisting of a sample of 80 out-of-town customers and a sample of 120 local customers.

By stratifying, we can guarantee that 40% of the sample is from out of town, reflecting the overall proportions among ticket buyers. If out-of-town customers differ in important ways from local ticket buyers, a stratified sample will reduce the variation in the estimates for each group so that the combined estimates can be more precise.

Systematic Samples

Sometimes we draw a sample by selecting individuals systematically. For example, a **systematic sample** might select every tenth person on an alphabetical list of employees. To make sure our sample is random, we still must start the systematic selection with a randomly selected individual—not necessarily the first person on the list. When there is no reason to believe that the order of the list could be associated in any way with the responses measured, systematic sampling can give a representative sample. Systematic sampling can be much less expensive than true random sampling. When you use a systematic sample, you should justify the assumption that the systematic method is not associated with any of the measured variables.

Think about the reading level sampling example again. Suppose we have chosen a section of the manual at random, then three pages at random from that section, and now we want to select a sample of 10 sentences from the 73 sentences found on those pages. Instead of numbering each sentence so we can pick a simple random sample, it would be easier to sample systematically. A quick calculation shows $73/10 = 7.3$, so we can get our sample by picking every seventh sentence on the page. But where should you start? At random, of course. We've accounted for $10 \times 7 = 70$ of the sentences, so we'll throw the extra three into the starting group and choose a sentence at random from the first 10. Then we pick every seventh sentence after that and record its length.

JUST CHECKING

2 We need to survey a random sample of the 300 passengers on a flight from San Francisco to Tokyo. Name each sampling method described.

   a) Pick every tenth passenger as people board the plane.
   b) From the boarding list, randomly choose five people flying first class and 25 of the other passengers.
   c) Randomly generate 30 seat numbers and survey the passengers who sit there.
   d) Randomly select a seat position (right window, right center, right aisle, etc.) and survey all the passengers sitting in those seats.

GUIDED EXAMPLE   Market Demand Survey

In a course at a business school in the United States, the students form business teams, propose a new product, and use seed money to launch a business to sell the product on campus.

Before committing funds for the business, each team must complete the following assignment: "Conduct a survey to determine the potential market demand on campus for the product you are proposing to sell." Suppose your team's product is a 500-piece jigsaw puzzle of the map of your college campus. Design a marketing survey and discuss the important issues to consider.

(continued)

PLAN

Define the problem—state the goals and objectives of the survey.

Characterize the Population and parameters. Identify the population to be studied and the associated sampling frame. What are the parameters of interest?

Sampling Plan Specify the sampling method and the planned sample size, *n*. Specify how the sample was actually drawn. What is the sampling frame?

The description should, if possible, be complete enough to allow someone to replicate the procedure, drawing another sample from the same population in the same manner. A good description of the procedure is essential, even if it could never practically be repeated. The question you ask is important, so state the wording of the question clearly. Be sure that the question is useful in helping you with the overall goal of the survey.

Our team designed a study to find out how likely students at our school are to buy our proposed product—a 500-piece jigsaw puzzle of the map of our college campus.

The population studied will be students at our school. We have obtained a list of all students currently enrolled to use as the sampling frame. The parameter of interest is the proportion of students likely to buy this product. We'll also collect some demographic information about the respondents.

We will select a simple random sample of 200 students. The sampling frame is the master list of students we obtained from the registrar. We decided against stratifying by sex or class because we thought that students were all more or less alike in their likely interest in our product.

We will ask the students we contact:

Do you solve jigsaw puzzles for fun?

Then we will show them a prototype puzzle and ask:

If this puzzle sold for $10, would you purchase one?

We will also record the respondent's sex and class.

DO

Sampling Practice Specify *when*, *where*, and *how* the sampling will be performed. Specify any other details of your survey, such as how respondents were contacted, any incentives that were offered to encourage them to respond, how nonrespondents were treated, and so on.

The survey will be administered in the middle of the fall semester during October. We have a master list of registered students, which we will randomize by matching it with random numbers from www.random.org and sorting on the random numbers, carrying the names. We will contact selected students by phone or e-mail and arrange to meet with them. If a student is unwilling to participate, the next name from the randomized list will be substituted until a sample of 200 participants is found.

We will meet with students in an office set aside for this purpose so that each will see the puzzle under similar conditions.

REPORT

Communicate and Present This report should include a discussion of all the elements needed to design the study. It's good practice to discuss any special circumstances or other issues that may need attention.

MEMO

Re: Survey plans

Our team's plans for the puzzle market survey call for a simple random sample of students. Because subjects need to be shown the prototype puzzle, we must arrange to meet with selected participants. We have arranged an office for that purpose.

We will also collect demographic information so we can determine whether there is in fact a difference in interest level among classes or between men and women.

The Real Sample

We have been discussing sampling in a somewhat idealized setting. In the real world, things can be a bit messier. Here are some things to consider.

The population may not be as well defined as it seems. For example, if a company wants the opinions of a typical mall "shopper," who should they sample? Should they only ask shoppers carrying a purchase? Should they include people eating at the food court? How about teenagers just hanging out in the mall? Even when the population is clear, it may not be possible to establish an appropriate sampling frame.

Usually, the practical sampling frame is not the group you *really* want to know about. For example, election polls want to sample from those who will actually vote in the next election—a group that is particularly tricky to identify before election day. The sampling frame limits what your survey can find out.

Then there's your target sample. These are the individuals selected according to your sample design for whom you *intend* to measure responses. You're not likely to get responses from all of them. ("I know it's dinner time, but I'm sure you wouldn't mind answering a few questions. It'll only take 20 minutes or so. Oh, you're busy?") Nonresponse is a problem in many surveys.

Sample designs are usually about the target sample. But in the real world, you won't get responses from everyone your design selects. So in reality, your sample consists of the actual respondents. These are the individuals about whom you *do* get data and can draw conclusions. Unfortunately, they might not be representative of either the sampling frame or the population.

At each step, the group we can study may be constrained further. The *who* of our study keeps changing, and each constraint can introduce biases. A careful study should address the question of how well each group matches the population of interest. The *who* in an SRS is the population of interest from which we've drawn a representative sample. That's not always true for other kinds of samples.

When people (or committees!) decide on a survey, they often fail to think through the important questions about who are the *who* of the study and whether they are the individuals from whom the answers would be interesting or have meaningful business consequences. This is a key step in performing a survey and should not be overlooked.

What's the Sample?

The population we want to study is determined by asking *why*. When we design a survey, we use the term "sample" to refer to the individuals selected, from whom we hope to obtain responses. Unfortunately, the real sample is just those we can reach to obtain responses—the *who* of the study. These are slightly different uses of the same term *sample*. The context usually makes clear which we mean, but it's important to realize that the difference between the two samples could undermine even a well-designed study.

8.5 The Valid Survey

It isn't sufficient to draw a sample and start asking questions. You want to feel confident your survey can yield the information you need about the population you are interested in. We want a *valid survey*.

To help ensure a valid survey, you need to ask four questions:

- What do I want to know?
- Who are the right respondents?
- What are the right questions?
- What will be done with the results?

These questions may seem obvious, but there are a number of specific pitfalls to avoid:

Know what you want to know. Far too often, decision makers decide to perform a survey without any clear idea of what they hope to learn. Before considering a survey, you must be clear about what you hope to learn and what population you want to learn about. If you don't know that, you can't even judge whether you have a valid survey. The survey *instrument*—the questionnaire itself—can be a source of errors. Perhaps the most common error is to ask unnecessary questions. The longer the survey, the fewer people will complete it, leading to greater nonresponse bias.

For each question on your survey, you should ask yourself whether you really want to know this and know what you would do with the responses if you had them. If you don't have a good use for the answer to a question, don't ask it.

Use the right sampling frame. A valid survey obtains responses from appropriate respondents. Be sure you have a suitable sampling frame. Have you identified the population of interest and sampled from it appropriately? A company looking to expand its base might survey customers who returned warrantee registration cards—after all, that's a readily available sampling frame—but if the company wants to know how to make its product more attractive, it needs to survey customers who rejected its product in favor of a competitor's product. This is the population that can tell the company what about its product needs to change to capture a larger market share. The errors in the presidential election polls of 1948 were likely due to the use of telephone samples in an era when telephones were not affordable by the less affluent—who were the folks most likely to vote for Truman.

It is equally important to be sure that your respondents actually know the information you hope to discover. Your customers may not know much about the competing products, so asking them to compare your product with others may not yield useful information.

Ask specific rather than general questions. It is better to be specific. "Do you usually recall TV commercials?" won't be as useful as "How many TV commercials can you recall from last night?" or better, yet, "Please describe for me all the TV commercials you can recall from your viewing last night."

Watch for biases. Even with the right sampling frame, you must beware of bias in your sample. If customers who purchase more expensive items are less likely to respond to your survey, this can lead to **nonresponse bias**. Although you can't expect all mailed surveys to be returned, if those individuals who don't respond have common characteristics, your sample will no longer represent the population you hope to learn about. Surveys in which respondents volunteer to participate, such as online surveys, suffer from **voluntary response bias**. Individuals with the strongest feelings on either side of an issue are more likely to respond; those who don't care may not bother.

Be careful with question phrasing. Questions must be carefully worded. A respondent may not understand the question—or may not understand the question the way the researcher intended it. For example, "Does anyone in your family own a Ford truck?" leaves the term "family" unclear. Does it include only spouses and children or parents and siblings, or do in-laws and second cousins count too? A question like "Was your Twinkie fresh?" might be interpreted quite differently by different people.

Be careful with answer phrasing. Respondents and survey-takers may also provide inaccurate responses, especially when questions are politically or sociologically sensitive. This also applies when the question does not take into account all possible answers, such as a true-false or multiple-choice question to which there may be other answers. Or the respondent may not know the correct answer to the question on the survey. In 1948, there were four major candidates for President,[4] but some survey respondents might not have been able to name them all. A survey question that just asked "Who do you plan to vote for?" might have underrepresented the less prominent candidates. And one that just asked "What do you think of Wallace?" might yield inaccurate results from voters who simply didn't know who he was. We refer to inaccurate responses (intentional or unintentional) as **measurement errors**. One way to cut down on measurement errors is to provide a range of possible responses. But be sure to phrase them in neutral terms.

---

[4]Harry Truman, Thomas Dewey, Strom Thurmond, and Henry Wallace.

The best way to protect a survey from measurement errors is to perform a pilot test. In a **pilot test**, a small sample is drawn from the sampling frame, and a draft form of the survey instrument is administered. A pilot test can point out flaws in the instrument. For example, during a staff cutback at one of our schools, a researcher surveyed faculty members to ask how they felt about the reduction in staff support. The scale ran from "It's a good idea" to "I'm very unhappy." Fortunately, a pilot study showed that everyone was very unhappy or worse. The scale was re-tuned to run from "unhappy" to "ready to quit."

IN PRACTICE 8.5   Survey design

BOARD OF DIRECTORS   We are confused by some of the technical terms. Can you explain the population, sampling frame, target sample, and sample to us? Are there concerns about which customers we can contact?

CONSULTANTS   The population is all potential ticket buyers.

The sampling frame consists of only those who have previously purchased tickets. Anyone who wasn't attracted to previous productions wouldn't be surveyed. That could keep the board from learning of ways to make the theater's offering more attractive to those who hadn't purchased tickets before.

The target sample is those selected from the database who can be contacted by telephone. Those with unlisted numbers or who had declined to give their phone number can't be contacted. It may be more difficult to contact those with caller ID.

The actual sample will be those previous customers selected at random from the database who can be reached by telephone and who agree to complete the survey.

8.6   How to Sample Badly

Bad sample designs yield worthless data. Many of the most convenient forms of sampling can be seriously biased. And there is no way to correct for the bias from a bad sample. So it's wise to pay attention to sample design—and to beware of reports based on poor samples.

Voluntary Response Sample

One of the most common dangerous sampling methods is the voluntary response sample. In a **voluntary response sample**, a large group of individuals is invited to respond, and all who do respond are counted. This method is used by call-in shows, 900 numbers, Internet polls, and letters written to members of Congress. Voluntary response samples are almost always biased, and so conclusions drawn from them are almost always wrong.

It's often hard to define the sampling frame of a voluntary response study. Practically, the frames are groups such as Internet users who frequent a particular website or viewers of a particular TV show. But those sampling frames don't correspond to the population you are likely to be interested in.

Even if the sampling frame is of interest, voluntary response samples are often biased toward those with strong opinions or those who are strongly motivated—and especially from those with strong negative opinions. A request that travelers who have used the local airport visit a survey site to report on their experiences is much more likely to hear from those who had long waits, cancelled flights, and lost luggage than from those whose flights were on time and carefree. The resulting voluntary response bias invalidates the survey.

Convenience Sampling

Another sampling method that doesn't work is convenience sampling. As the name suggests, in **convenience sampling** we simply include the individuals who are convenient. Unfortunately, this group may not be representative of the population. A survey of 437 potential home buyers in Orange County, California, found, among other things, that

> *all but 2 percent of the buyers have at least one computer at home, and 62 percent have two or more. Of those with a computer, 99 percent are connected to the Internet (Jennifer Hieger, "Portrait of Homebuyer Household: 2 Kids and a PC," Orange County Register, July 27, 2001).*

Later in the article, we learn that the survey was conducted via the Internet. That was a convenient way to collect data and surely easier than drawing a simple random sample, but perhaps home builders shouldn't conclude from this study that *every* family has a computer and an Internet connection.

Many surveys conducted at shopping malls suffer from the same problem. People in shopping malls are not necessarily representative of the population of interest. Mall shoppers tend to be more affluent and include a larger percentage of teenagers and retirees than the population at large. To make matters worse, survey interviewers tend to select individuals who look "safe," or easy to interview.

Convenience sampling is not just a problem for beginners. In fact, convenience sampling is a widespread problem in the business world. When a company wants to find out what people think about its products or services, it may turn to the easiest people to sample: its own customers. But the company will never learn how those who *don't* buy its product feel about it.

Do you use the Internet?

Click here ◯ for yes
Click here ◯ for no

Internet Surveys

Internet convenience surveys are often worthless. As voluntary response surveys, they have no well-defined sampling frame (all those who use the Internet and visit their site?) and thus report no useful information. Do not use them.

Bad Sampling Frame?

An SRS from an incomplete sampling frame introduces bias because the individuals included may differ from the ones not in the frame. It may be easier to sample workers from a single site, but if a company has many sites and they differ in worker satisfaction, training, or job descriptions, the resulting sample can be biased. There is serious concern among professional pollsters that the increasing numbers of people who can be reached only by cell phone may bias telephone-based market research and polling.

Undercoverage

Many survey designs suffer from **undercoverage**, in which some portion of the population is not sampled at all or has a smaller representation in the sample than it has in the population. Undercoverage can arise for a number of reasons, but it's always a potential source of bias. Are people who use answering machines to screen callers (and are thus less available to blind calls from market researchers) different from other customers in their purchasing preferences?

IN PRACTICE 8.6 Common mistakes in survey design

BOARD OF DIRECTORS Why not simply post someone at the door to ask theater goers their opinions? Another Board member asks, wouldn't it be even easier to post a questionnaire on the theater website and invite responses there? A third Board member suggests that rather than working with random numbers, we simply phone every 200th person on the list of past customers.

CONSULTANTS Questioning customers at the door would be a convenience sample. It would be cheap and fast but is likely to be biased by the nature and quality of the particular performance where the survey takes place.

Inviting responses on the website would be a voluntary response sample. Only customers who frequented the website and decided to respond would be surveyed. This might, for example, underrepresent older customers or those without home Internet access.

Sampling every 200th name from the customer list would be a systematic sample. It is slightly easier than randomizing. If the order of names on the list is unrelated to any questions asked, then this might be an acceptable method. But if, for example, the list is kept in the order of first purchases (when a customer's name and information were added to the database), then there might be a relationship between opinions and location on the list.

⊘ WHAT CAN GO WRONG?

- **Nonrespondents.** No survey succeeds in getting responses from everyone. The problem is that those who don't respond may differ from those who do. And if they differ on just the variables we care about, the lack of response will bias the results. Rather than sending out a large number of surveys for which the response rate will be low, it is often better to design a smaller, randomized survey for which you have the resources to ensure a high response rate.

- **Long, dull surveys.** Surveys that are too long are more likely to be refused, reducing the response rate and biasing all the results. Keep it short.

- **Response bias.** Response bias includes the tendency of respondents to tailor their responses to please the interviewer and the consequences of slanted question wording.

- **Push polls.** Push polls, which masquerade as surveys, present one side of an issue before asking a question. For example, a question like

  Would the fact that the new store that just opened by the mall sells mostly goods made overseas by workers in sweatshop conditions influence your decision to shop there rather than in the downtown store that features American-made products?

  is designed not to gather information, but to spread ill-will toward the new store.

THE WIZARD OF ID   parker and hart

The Wizard of Id © 2001 John L. Hart/Distributed by Creators Syndicate. Reprinted with permission. All rights reserved.

HOW TO THINK ABOUT BIASES

- **Look for biases in any survey.** If you design a survey of your own, ask someone else to help look for biases that may not be obvious to you. Do this *before* you collect your data. There's no way to recover from a biased sample or a survey that asks biased questions.

  A bigger sample size for a biased study just gives you a bigger useless study. A really big sample gives you a really big useless study.

- **Spend your time and resources reducing biases.** No other use of resources is as worthwhile as reducing the biases.

- **If you possibly can, pretest or pilot your survey.** Administer the survey in the exact form that you intend to use it to a small sample drawn from the population you intend to sample. Look for misunderstandings, misinterpretation, confusion, or other possible biases. Then redesign your survey instrument.

- **Always report your sampling methods in detail.** Others may be able to detect biases where you did not expect to find them.

ETHICS IN ACTION

The Lackawax River Group is interested in applying for state funds to continue their restoration and conservation of the Lackawax River, a river that has been polluted from years of industry and agricultural discharge. While they have managed to gain significant support for their cause through education and community involvement, the executive committee is now interested in presenting the state with more compelling evidence.

They decided to survey local residents regarding their attitudes toward the proposed expansion of the river restoration and conservation project. With limited time and money (the deadline for the grant application was fast approaching), the executive committee was delighted that one of its members, Harry Greentree, volunteered to undertake the project.

Harry owned a local organic food store and agreed to have a sample of his shoppers interviewed during the next one-week period. One committee member questioned whether a representative sample of residents could be found in this way, but the other members of the committee thought that the customers of Harry's store were likely to be just the kind of well-informed residents whose opinions they wanted to hear. The only instruction the committee decided to give was that the shoppers be selected in a systematic fashion, for instance, by interviewing every fifth person who entered the store. Harry had no problem with this request and was eager to help the Lackawax River Group.

- **Identify the ethical dilemma in this scenario.**
- **What are the undesirable consequences?**
- **Propose an ethical solution that considers the welfare of all stakeholders.**

CHAPTER

8 FROM LEARNING TO EARNING

LEARNING OBJECTIVES

Recognize observational studies.

- A retrospective study looks at an outcome in the present and looks for facts in the past that relate to it.
- A prospective study selects subjects and follows them as events unfold.

Know the three ideas of sampling.

- Examine a part of the whole: A sample can give information about the population.
- Randomize to make the sample representative.
- The sample size is what matters. It's the size of the sample—and not its fraction of the larger population—that determines the precision of the statistics it yields.

Be able to draw a simple random sample (SRS) using a table of random digits or a list of random numbers from technology or an Internet site.

- In a **simple random sample** (SRS), every possible group of *n* individuals has an equal chance of being our sample.

Know the definitions of other sampling methods:

- **Stratified samples** can reduce sampling variability by identifying homogeneous subgroups and then randomly sampling within each.
- **Cluster samples** randomly select among heterogeneous subgroups that each resemble the population at large, making our sampling tasks more manageable.
- **Systematic samples** can work in some situations and are often the least expensive method of sampling. But we still want to start them randomly.
- **Multistage samples** combine several random sampling methods.

Identify and avoid causes of bias.

- **Nonresponse bias** can arise when sampled individuals will not or cannot respond.
- **Response bias** arises when respondents' answers might be affected by external influences, such as question wording or interviewer behavior.
- **Voluntary response samples** are almost always biased and should be avoided and distrusted.
- **Convenience samples** are likely to be flawed for similar reasons.
- **Undercoverage** occurs when individuals from a subgroup of the population are selected less often than they should be.

TERMS

Bias	Any systematic failure of a sampling method to represent its population.
Census	An attempt to collect data on the entire population of interest.
Cluster	A subset of a population aggregated into larger sampling units. These units, chosen for reasons of cost or practicality, are often natural groups thought to be representative of the population.
Cluster sampling	A sampling design in which groups, or clusters, representative of the population are chosen at random and a census is then taken of each.
Convenience sampling	A sample that consists of individuals who are conveniently available.
Measurement error	Any inaccuracy in a response, from any source, whether intentional or unintentional.
Multistage sample	A sampling scheme that combines several sampling methods.
Nonresponse bias	Bias introduced to a sample when a large fraction of those sampled fails to respond.
Observational study	A study based on data in which no manipulation of factors has been employed.
Parameter	A numerically valued attribute of a model for a population. We rarely expect to know the value of a parameter, but we do hope to estimate it from sampled data.
Pilot test	A small trial run of a study to check that the methods of the study are sound.
Population	The entire group of individuals or instances about whom we hope to learn.
Population parameter	A numerically valued attribute of a model for a population.
Prospective study	An observational study in which subjects are followed to observe future outcomes. Because no treatments are deliberately applied, a prospective study is not an experiment. Nevertheless, prospective studies typically focus on estimating differences among groups that might appear as the groups are followed during the course of the study.

Randomization	A defense against bias in the sample selection process, in which each individual is given a fair, random chance of selection.
Representative sample	A sample from which the statistics computed accurately reflect the corresponding population parameters.
Response bias	Anything in a survey design that influences responses.
Retrospective study	An observational study in which subjects are selected and then their previous conditions or behaviors are determined. Because retrospective studies are not based on random samples, they usually focus on estimating differences between groups or associations between variables.
Sample	A subset of a population, examined in hope of learning about the population.
Sample size	The number of individuals in a sample.
Sample survey	A study that asks questions of a sample drawn from some population in the hope of learning something about the entire population.
Sampling frame	A list of individuals from which the sample is drawn. Individuals in the population of interest but who are not in the sampling frame cannot be included in any sample.
Sampling variability (or sampling error)	The natural tendency of randomly drawn samples to differ, one from another.
Simple random sample (SRS)	A sample in which each set of n elements in the population has an equal chance of selection.
Statistic, sample statistic	A value calculated for sampled data, particularly one that corresponds to, and thus estimates, a population parameter. The term "sample statistic" is sometimes used, usually to parallel the corresponding term "population parameter."
Strata	Subsets of a population that are internally homogeneous but may differ one from another.
Stratified random sample	A sampling design in which the population is divided into several homogeneous subpopulations, or strata, and random samples are then drawn from each stratum.
Systematic sample	A sample drawn by selecting individuals systematically from a sampling frame.
Undercoverage	A sampling scheme that biases the sample in a way that gives a part of the population less representation than it has in the population.
Voluntary response bias	Bias introduced to a sample when individuals can choose on their own whether to participate in the sample.
Voluntary response sample	A sample in which a large group of individuals are invited to respond and decide individually whether or not to participate. Voluntary response samples are generally worthless.

TECH SUPPORT

Computer-generated random numbers are usually quite good enough for drawing random samples. But there is little reason not to use the truly random values available on the Internet. Here's a convenient way to draw an SRS of a specified size using a computer-based sampling frame. The sampling frame can be a list of names or identification numbers arrayed, for example, as a column in a spreadsheet, statistics program, or database:

1. Generate random numbers of enough digits so that each exceeds the size of the sampling frame list by several digits. This makes duplication unlikely. (For example, in Excel, use the RAND function described in detail in Technology Help, Chapter 5, to fill a column with random numbers between 0 and 1. With many digits they will almost surely be unique.)

2. Assign the random numbers arbitrarily to individuals in the sampling frame list. For example, put them in an adjacent column.

3. Sort the list of random numbers, *carrying* along the sampling frame list.

4. Now the first n values in the sorted sampling frame column are an SRS of n values from the entire sampling frame.

Most statistics packages also offer commands to sample from your data, but you should be careful to see that they do what you intend.

BRIEF CASE

Market Survey Research

You are part of a marketing team that needs to research the potential of a new product. Your team decides to e-mail an interactive survey to a random sample of consumers. Write a short questionnaire that will generate the information you need about the new product. Select a sample of 200 using an SRS from your sampling frame. Discuss how you will collect the data and how the responses will help your market research.

The GfK Roper Reports Worldwide Survey

GfK Roper Consulting conducts market research for multinational companies who want to understand attitudes in different countries so they can market and advertise more effectively to different cultures. Every year they conduct a poll worldwide, which asks hundreds of questions of people in approximately 30 different countries. Respondents are asked a variety of questions about food. Some of the questions are simply yes/no (agree/disagree) questions: Please tell me whether you agree or disagree with each of these statements about your appearance: (Agree = 1; Disagree = 2; Don't know = 9).

> The way you look affects the way you feel.
>
> I am very interested in new skin care breakthroughs.
>
> People who don't care about their appearance don't care about themselves.

> Other questions are asked on a 5-point scale (Please tell me the extent to which you disagree or agree with it using the following scale: Disagree completely = 1; Disagree somewhat = 2; Neither disagree nor agree = 3; Agree somewhat = 4; Agree completely = 5; Don't know = 9).

> Examples of such questions include:
>
> I read labels carefully to find out about ingredients, fat content, and/or calories.
>
> I try to avoid eating fast food.
>
> When it comes to food I'm always on the lookout for something new.

Think about designing a survey on such a global scale:

- What is the population of interest?
- Why might it be difficult to select an SRS from this sampling frame?
- What are some potential sources of bias?
- Why might it be difficult to ensure a representative number of men and women and all age groups in some countries?
- What might be a reasonable sampling frame?

CHAPTER 8 EXERCISES

SECTION 8.1

1. For the following observational studies, indicate whether they are prospective or retrospective.

a) A company looked at a sample of returned registration cards to estimate the income level of households that purchased their product.

b) A retail outlet encouraged customers to join their "frequent buyers" program and studied whether those who joined were more likely to make use of discount coupons than those who were not members.

2. For the following observational studies, indicate whether they are prospective or retrospective studies.

a) An airline was concerned that new security measures might discourage air travelers. A year after the new security restrictions were put into place, the airlines compared the miles traveled by their frequent fliers before and after the change.

b) Does giving children a flu shot protect parents? Researchers questioned a random sample of families at the end of a flu season. They asked whether the children had been immunized, whether the parents had received flu shots, and who in the family had contracted the flu.

SECTION 8.2

3. Indicate whether each statement below is true or false. If false, explain why.

a) We can eliminate sampling error by selecting an unbiased sample.

b) Randomization helps to ensure that our sample is representative.

c) Sampling error refers to sample-to-sample differences and is also known as sampling variability.

d) It is better to try to match the characteristics of the sample to the population rather than relying on randomization.

4. Indicate whether each statement below is true or false. If false, explain why.

a) To get a representative sample, you must sample a large fraction of the population.

b) Using modern methods, it is best to select a representative subset of a population systematically.

c) A census is the only true representative sample.

d) A random sample of 100 students from a school with 2000 students has the same precision as a random sample of 100 from a school with 20,000 students.

SECTION 8.3

5. An environmental advocacy group is interested in the perceptions of farmers about global climate change. Specifically, they wish to determine the percentage of organic farmers who are concerned that climate change will affect their crop yields. They use an alphabetized list of members of the Northeast Organic Farming Association (www.nofa .org), a nonprofit organization of over 5000 members with chapters in Connecticut, Massachusetts, New Hampshire, New Jersey, New York, Rhode Island, and Vermont. They use Excel to generate a randomly shuffled list of the members. They then select members to contact from this list until they have succeeded in contacting 150 members.

a) What is the population?
b) What is the sampling frame?
c) What is the population parameter of interest?

6. An airline company is interested in the opinions of their frequent flyer customers about their proposed new routes. Specifically they want to know what proportion of them plan to use one of their new hubs in the next six months. They take a random sample of 10,000 from the database of all frequent flyers and send them an e-mail message with a request to fill out a survey in exchange for 1500 miles.

a) What is the population?
b) What is the sampling frame?
c) What is the population parameter of interest?

SECTION 8.4

7. As discussed in the chapter, GfK Roper Consulting conducts a global consumer survey to help multinational companies understand different consumer attitudes throughout the world. In India, the researchers interviewed 1000 people aged 13–65 (www.gfkamerica.com). Their sample is designed so that they get 500 males and 500 females.

a) Are they using a simple random sample? How do you know?
b) What kind of design do you think they are using?

8. For their class project, a group of Business students decides to survey the student body to assess opinions about a proposed new student coffee shop to judge how successful it might be. Their sample of 200 contained 50 first-year students, 50 sophomores, 50 juniors, and 50 seniors.

a) Do you think the group was using an SRS? Why?
b) What kind of sampling design do you think they used?

9. The environmental advocacy group from Exercise 5 that was interested in gauging perceptions about climate change among organic farmers has decided to use a different method to sample. Instead of randomly selecting members from a shuffled list, they listed the members in alphabetical order and took every tenth member until they succeeded in contacting 150 members. What kind of sampling method have they used?

10. The airline company from Exercise 6, interested in the opinions of their frequent flyer customers about their proposed new routes, has decided that different types of customers might have different opinions. Of their customers, 50% are silver-level, 30% are blue, and 20% are red. They first compile separate lists of silver, blue, and red members and then randomly select 5000 silver members, 3000 blue members, and 2000 red members to e-mail. What kind of sampling method have they used?

For Exercises 11 and 12, identify the following if possible. (If not, say why.)

a) The population
b) The population parameter of interest
c) The sampling frame
d) The sample
e) Any potential sources of bias you can detect and any problems you see in generalizing to the population of interest

11. A business magazine mailed a questionnaire to the human resources directors of all *Fortune* 500 companies, and received responses from 23% of them. Those responding reported that they did not find that such surveys intruded significantly on their workday.

12. A question posted on the Lycos website asked visitors to the site to say whether they thought that businesses should be required to pay for their employees' health insurance.

SECTION 8.5

13. An intern for the environmental group in Exercise 5 has decided to make the survey process simpler by calling 150 of the members who attended the recent symposium on coping with climate change that was recently held in Burlington, VT. He has all the phone numbers, so it will be easy to contact them. He will start calling members from the top of the list, which was generated as the members enrolled for the symposium. He has written a script to read to them that follows,

"As we learned in Burlington, climate change is a serious problem for farmers. Given the evidence of impact on crops, do you agree that the government should be doing more to fight global warming?"

a) What is the population of interest?
b) What is the sampling frame?
c) Point out any problems you see either with the sampling procedure and/or the survey itself. What are the potential impacts of these problems?

14. The airline company in Exercise 6 has realized that some of its customers don't have e-mail or don't read it regularly. They decide to restrict the mailing only to customers who have recently registered for a "Win a trip to Miami" contest, figuring that those with Internet access are more likely to read and to respond to their e-mail. They send an e-mail with the following message:

"Did you know that National Airlines has just spent over $3 million refurbishing our brand new hub in Miami? By answering the following question, you may be eligible to win $1000 worth of coupons that can be spent in any of the fabulous restaurants or shops in the Miami airport. Might you possibly think of traveling to Miami in the next six months on your way to one of your destinations?"

a) What is the population?
b) What is the sampling frame?
c) Point out any problems you see either with the sampling procedure and/or the survey itself. What are the potential impacts of these problems?

15. An intern is working for Pacific TV (PTV), a small cable and Internet provider, and has proposed some questions that might be used in the survey to assess whether customers are willing to pay $50 for a new service.

Question 1: If PTV offered state-of-the-art, high-speed Internet service for $50 per month, would you subscribe to that service?

Question 2: Would you find $50 per month—less than the cost of a daily cappuccino—an appropriate price for high-speed Internet service?

a) Do you think these are appropriately worded questions? Why or why not?
b) Which one has more neutral wording? Explain.

16. Here are more proposed survey questions for the survey in Exercise 15:

Question 3: Do you find that the slow speed of DSL Internet access reduces your enjoyment of web services?

Question 4: Given the growing importance of high-speed Internet access for your children's education, would you subscribe to such a service if it were offered?

a) Do you think these are appropriately worded questions? Why or why not?
b) Suggest a question with better wording.

SECTION 8.6

17. Indicate whether each statement below is true or false. If false, explain why.

a) A local television news program that asks viewers to call in and give their opinion on an issue typically results in a biased voluntary response sample.
b) Convenience samples are generally representative of the population.
c) Measurement error is the same as sampling error.
d) A pilot test can be useful for identifying poorly worded questions on a survey.

18. Indicate whether each statement below is true or false. If false, explain why.

a) Asking viewers to call into an 800 number is a good way to produce a representative sample.
b) When writing a survey, it's a good idea to include as many questions as possible to ensure efficiency and to lower costs.
c) A recent poll on a website was valid because the sample size was over 1,000,000 respondents.
d) Malls are not necessarily good places to conduct surveys because people who frequent malls may not be representative of the population at large.

19. For your marketing class, you'd like to take a survey from a sample of all the Catholic Church members in your city to assess the market for a DVD about Pope Francis's first year as pope. A list of churches shows 17 Catholic churches within the city limits. Rather than try to obtain a list of all members of all these churches, you decide to pick 3 churches at random. For those churches, you'll ask to get a list of all current members and contact 100 members at random.

a) What kind of design have you used?
b) What could go wrong with the design that you have proposed?

20. The U.S. Fish and Wildlife Service plans to study the fishing industry around Saginaw Bay. To do that, they decide to randomly select five fishing boats at the end of a randomly chosen fishing day and count the numbers and types of all the fish on those boats.

a) What kind of design have they used?
b) What could go wrong with the design that they have proposed?

CHAPTER EXERCISES

21. Software licenses. The website www.gamefaqs.com asked, as their question of the day to which visitors to the site were invited to respond, "*Do you ever read the end-user license agreements when installing software or games?*" Of the 98,574 respondents, 63.47% said they never read those agreements—a fact that software manufacturers might find important.

a) What kind of sample was this?
b) How much confidence would you place in using 63.47% as an estimate of the fraction of people who don't read software licenses?

22. Drugs in baseball. Major League Baseball, responding to concerns about their "brand," tests players to see whether they are using performance-enhancing drugs. Officials select a team at random, and a drug-testing crew shows up unannounced to test all 40 players on the team. Each testing day can be considered a study of drug use in Major League Baseball.

a) What kind of sample is this?
b) Is that choice appropriate?

23. Pew. Pew Research Center publishes polls on issues important in the news and about American life at its website, www.pewinternet.org. At the end of a report about a survey you can find a paragraph such as this one:

These readings come from a national survey conducted between November 14 and December 9, 2012 of U.S. adults on landline and cell phones and in English and in Spanish. The results reported here come from the 1,802 respondents who are internet users and the margin of error is +/−2.6 percentage points.

a) For this survey, identify the population of interest.
b) Pew performs its surveys by phoning numbers generated at random by a computer program. What is the sampling frame? Does this seem representative of the population?

24. Defining the survey. At its website (www.gallup.com) the Gallup World Poll reports results of surveys conducted in various places around the world. At the end of one of these reports about the reliability of electric power in Africa, they describe their methods, including explanations such as the following:

Results are based on face-to-face interviews with 1,000 adults, aged 15 and older, conducted in 2010 in Botswana, Burkina Faso, Cameroon, Central African Republic, Chad, Ghana, Kenya, Liberia, Mali, Niger, Nigeria, Senegal, Sierra Leone, South Africa, Tanzania, Uganda, and Zimbabwe. For results based on the total sample of national adults, one can say with 95% confidence that the maximum margin of sampling error ranges from ± 3.4 percentage points to ± 4.0 percentage points. The margin of error reflects the influence of data weighting. In addition to sampling error, question wording and practical difficulties in conducting surveys can introduce error or bias into the findings of public opinion polls.[5]

a) Gallup is interested in the opinions of Africans. What kind of survey design are they using?
b) Some of the countries surveyed have large populations. (South Africa is estimated to have over 50 million people.) Some are quite small. (Zimbabwe has fewer than 13,000,000 people.) Nonetheless, Gallup sampled 1000 adults in each

[5]Copyright © 2011 Gallup Inc. All rights reserved. The content is used with permission; however, Gallup retains all rights of republication.

country. How does this affect the precision of its estimates for these countries?

25–32. Survey details. *For the following reports about statistical studies, identify the following items (if possible). If you can't tell, then say so—this often happens when we read about a survey.*

a) The population
b) The population parameter of interest
c) The sampling frame
d) The sample
e) The sampling method, including whether or not randomization was employed
f) Any potential sources of bias you can detect and any problems you see in generalizing to the population of interest

25. Teens and technology. Pew Internet & American Life Project surveyed 802 pairs of parents and teens (aged 12–17). They report that 93% of teens have access to a computer. 25% of teens access the Internet primarily on their cell phone rather than on a computer.

26. Global warming. The Gallup Poll interviewed 1022 randomly selected U.S. adults aged 18 and older, March 7–10, 2013. Gallup reports that when asked whether respondents thought that global warming was due primarily to human activities, 57% of respondents said it was.

27. At the bar. Researchers waited outside a bar they had randomly selected from a list of such establishments. They stopped every tenth person who came out of the bar and asked whether he or she thought drinking and driving was a serious problem.

28. Election poll. Hoping to learn what issues may resonate with voters in the coming election, the campaign director for a mayoral candidate selects one block at random from each of the city's election districts. Staff members go there and interview all the residents they can find.

29. Toxic waste. The Environmental Protection Agency took soil samples at 16 locations near a former industrial waste dump and checked each for evidence of toxic chemicals. They found no elevated levels of any harmful substances.

30. Housing discrimination. Inspectors send trained "renters" of various races and ethnic backgrounds, and of both sexes to inquire about renting randomly assigned advertised apartments. They look for evidence that landlords deny access illegally based on race, sex, or ethnic background.

31. Quality control. A company packaging snack foods maintains quality control by randomly selecting 10 cases from each day's production and weighing the bags. Then they open one bag from each case and inspect the contents.

32. Contaminated milk. Dairy inspectors visit farms unannounced and take samples of the milk to test for contamination. If the milk is found to contain dirt, antibiotics, or other foreign matter, the milk will be destroyed and the farm is considered to be contaminated pending further testing.

33. Instant poll. A local TV station conducted an "Instant Poll" to predict the winner in the upcoming mayoral election. Evening news viewers were invited to phone in their votes, with the results to be announced on the late-night news. Based on the phone calls, the station predicted that Amabo would win the election with 52% of the vote. They were wrong: Amabo lost, getting only 46% of the vote. Do you think the station's faulty prediction is more likely to be a result of bias or sampling error? Explain.

34. Paper poll. Prior to the mayoral election discussed in Exercise 33, the newspaper also conducted a poll. The paper surveyed a random sample of registered voters stratified by political party, age, sex, and area of residence. This poll predicted that Amabo would win the election with 52% of the vote. The newspaper was wrong: Amabo lost, getting only 46% of the vote. Do you think the newspaper's faulty prediction is more likely to be a result of bias or sampling error? Explain.

35. Cable company market research. A local cable TV company, Pacific TV (PTV), with customers in 15 towns is considering offering high-speed Internet service on its cable lines. Before launching the new service they want to find out whether customers would pay the $75 per month that they plan to charge. An intern has prepared several alternative plans for assessing customer demand. For each, indicate what kind of sampling strategy is involved and what (if any) biases might result.

a) Put a big ad in the newspaper asking people to log their opinions on the PTV website.
b) Randomly select one of the towns and contact every cable subscriber by phone.
c) Send a survey to each customer and ask him or her to fill it out and return it.
d) Randomly select 20 customers from each town. Send them a survey, and follow up with a phone call if they do not return the survey within a week.

36. Cable company market research, part 2. Four new sampling strategies have been proposed to help PTV determine whether enough cable subscribers are likely to purchase high-speed Internet service. For each, indicate what kind of sampling strategy is involved and what (if any) biases might result.

a) Run a poll on the local TV news, asking people to dial one of two phone numbers to indicate whether they would be interested.
b) Hold a meeting in each of the 15 towns, and tally the opinions expressed by those who attend the meetings.
c) Randomly select one street in each town and contact each of the households on that street.
d) Go through the company's customer records, selecting every 40th subscriber. Send employees to those homes to interview the people chosen.

37. Amusement park riders. An amusement park has opened a new roller coaster. It is so popular that people are waiting for up to three hours for a two-minute ride. Concerned about how patrons (who paid a large amount to enter the park and ride on the rides) feel about this, they survey every tenth person in line for the roller coaster, starting from a randomly selected individual.

a) What kind of sample is this?
b) Is it likely to be representative?
c) What is the sampling frame?

38. Playground. Some people have been complaining that the children's playground at a municipal park is too small and is in need of repair. Managers of the park decide to survey city residents to see if they believe the playground should be rebuilt. They hand out questionnaires to parents who bring children to the park. Describe possible biases in this sample.

39. Another ride. The survey of patrons waiting in line for the roller coaster in Exercise 37 asks whether they think it is worthwhile to wait a long time for the ride and whether they'd like the amusement park to install still more roller coasters. What biases might cause a problem for this survey?

40. Playground bias. The survey described in Exercise 38 asked,

Many people believe this playground is too small and in need of repair. Do you think the playground should be repaired and expanded even if that means imposing an entrance fee to the park?

Describe two ways this question may lead to response bias.

41. (Possibly) Biased questions. Examine each of the following questions for possible bias. If you think the question is biased, indicate how and propose a better question.

a) Should companies that pollute the environment be compelled to pay the costs of cleanup?
b) Should a company enforce a strict dress code?

42. More possibly biased questions. Examine each of the following questions for possible bias. If you think the question is biased, indicate how and propose a better question.

a) Do you think that price or quality is more important in selecting a tablet computer?
b) Given humanity's great tradition of exploration, do you favor continued funding for space flights?

43. Phone surveys. Anytime we conduct a survey, we must take care to avoid undercoverage. Suppose we plan to select 500 names from the city phone book, call their homes between noon and 4 p.m., and interview whoever answers, anticipating contacts with at least 200 people.

a) Why is it difficult to use a simple random sample here?
b) Describe a more convenient, but still random, sampling strategy.

c) What kinds of households are likely to be included in the eventual sample of opinion? Who will be excluded?
d) Suppose, instead, that we continue calling each number, perhaps in the morning or evening, until an adult is contacted and interviewed. How does this improve the sampling design?
e) Random-digit dialing machines can generate the phone calls for us. How would this improve our design? Is anyone still excluded?

44. Cell phone survey. What about drawing a random sample only from cell phone exchanges? Discuss the advantages and disadvantages of such a sampling method compared with surveying randomly generated telephone numbers from non–cell phone exchanges. Do you think these advantages and disadvantages have changed over time? How do you expect they'll change in the future?

45. Change. How much change do you have on you right now? Go ahead, count it.

a) How much change do you have?
b) Suppose you check on your change every day for a week as you head for lunch and average the results. What parameter would this average estimate?
c) Suppose you ask 10 friends to average *their* change every day for a week, and you average those 10 measurements. What is the population now? What parameter would this average estimate?
d) Do you think these 10 average change amounts are likely to be representative of the population of change amounts in your class? In your college? In the country? Why or why not?

46. Fuel economy. Occasionally, when I fill my car with gas, I figure out how many miles per gallon my car got. I wrote down those results after six fill-ups in the past few months. Overall, it appears my car gets 28.8 miles per gallon.

a) What statistic have I calculated?
b) What is the parameter I'm trying to estimate?
c) How might my results be biased?
d) When the Environmental Protection Agency (EPA) checks a car like mine to predict its fuel economy, what parameter is it trying to estimate?

47. Accounting. Between quarterly audits, a company likes to check on its accounting procedures to address any problems before they become serious. The accounting staff processes payments on about 120 orders each day. The next day, the supervisor rechecks 10 of the transactions to be sure they were processed properly.

a) Propose a sampling strategy for the supervisor.
b) How would you modify that strategy if the company makes both wholesale and retail sales, requiring different bookkeeping procedures?

48. Happy workers? A manufacturing company employs 14 project managers, 48 foremen, and 377 laborers. In an effort to keep informed about any possible sources of employee discontent, management wants to conduct job satisfaction interviews with a simple random sample of employees every month.

a) Do you see any danger of bias in the company's plan? Explain.
b) How might you select a simple random sample?
c) Why do you think a simple random sample might not provide the best estimate of the parameters the company wants to estimate?
d) Propose a better sampling strategy.
e) Listed below are the last names of the project managers. Use random numbers to select two people to be interviewed. Be sure to explain your method carefully.

Barrett	Bowman	Chen
DeLara	DeRoos	Grigorov
Maceli	Mulvaney	Pagliarulo
Rosica	Smithson	Tadros
Williams	Yamamoto	

49. Quality control. Sammy's Salsa, a small local company, produces 20 cases of salsa a day. Each case contains 12 jars and is imprinted with a code indicating the date and batch number. To help maintain consistency, at the end of each day, Sammy selects three bottles of salsa, weighs the contents, and tastes the product. Help Sammy select the sample jars. Today's cases are coded 07N61 through 07N80.

a) Carefully explain your sampling strategy.
b) Show how to use random numbers to pick the three jars for testing.
c) Did you use a simple random sample? Explain.

50. Fish quality. Concerned about reports of discolored scales on fish caught downstream from a newly sited chemical plant, scientists set up a field station in a shoreline public park. For one week they asked fishermen there to bring any fish they caught to the field station for a brief inspection. At the end of the week, the scientists said that 18% of the 234 fish that were submitted for inspection displayed the discoloration. From this information, can the researchers estimate what proportion of fish in the river have discolored scales? Explain.

51. Sampling methods. Consider each of these situations. Do you think the proposed sampling method is appropriate? Explain.

a) We want to know what percentage of local doctors accept Medicaid patients. We call the offices of 50 doctors randomly selected from local Yellow Pages listings.
b) We want to know what percentage of local businesses anticipate hiring additional employees in the upcoming month. We randomly select a page in the Yellow Pages and call every business listed there.

52. More sampling methods. Consider each of these situations. Do you think the proposed sampling method is appropriate? Explain.

a) We want to know if business leaders in the community support the development of an "incubator" site at a vacant lot on the edge of town. We spend a day phoning local businesses in the phone book to ask whether they'd sign a petition.
b) We want to know if travelers at the local airport are satisfied with the food available there. We go to the airport on a busy day and interview every tenth person in line in the food court.

JUST CHECKING ANSWERS

1 a) It can be hard to reach all members of a population, and it can take so long that circumstances change, affecting the responses. A well-designed sample is often a better choice.

   b) This sample is probably biased—people who didn't like the food at the restaurant might not choose to eat there.

   c) No, only the sample size matters, not the fraction of the overall population.

   d) Students who frequent this website might be more enthusiastic about statistics than the overall population of statistics students. A large sample cannot compensate for bias.

   e) It's the population "parameter." "Statistics" describe samples.

2 a) systematic
   b) stratified
   c) simple
   d) cluster

CHAPTER 9

Data Sources: Experiments

Capital One

Not everyone graduates first in their class at a prestigious business school. But even doing that won't guarantee that the first company you start will become a Fortune 500 company within a decade. Richard Fairbank managed to do both. When he graduated from Stanford Business School in 1981, he wanted to start his own company, but, as he said in an interview with the *Stanford Business Magazine*, he had no experience, no money, and no business ideas. So he went to work for a consulting firm. Wanting to be on his own, he left in 1987 and landed a contract to study the operations of a large credit card bank in New York. It was then that he realized that the secret lay in data. He and his partner, Nigel Morris, asked themselves, "Why not use the mountains of data that credit cards produce to design cards with prices and terms to satisfy different customers?" But they had a hard time selling this idea to the large credit card issuers. At the time all cards carried the same interest rate—19.8% with a $20 annual fee, and almost half of the population didn't qualify for a card. And credit issuers were naturally resistant to new ideas.

Finally, Fairbank and Morris signed on with Signet, a regional bank that hoped to expand its modest credit card operation. Using demographic and financial data about Signet's customers, they designed and tested combinations of card features that allowed them to offer credit to customers who previously didn't qualify. Signet's credit card business grew and, by 1994, was spun off as Capital One with a market capitalization of $1.1B. Twenty years later, Capital One's revenues were $24.1B and its market capitalization was $33.7B.

Fairbank also introduced "scientific testing." Capital One designs experiments to gather data about customers. For example, customers who hear about a better deal than the one their current card offers may phone, threatening to switch to another bank unless they get a better deal. To help identify which potential card-hoppers were serious, Fairbank designed an experiment. When a card-hopper called, the customer service agent's computer randomly ordered one of three actions: match the claimed offer, split the difference in rates or fees, or just say no. In that way the company could gather data on who switched, who stayed, and how they behaved. When a potential card-hopper phones, the computer could give the operator a script specifying the terms to offer—or instruct the operator to bid the card-hopper a pleasant good-bye.

Fairbank attributes the phenomenal success of Capital One to their use of such experiments. According to Fairbank, "Anyone in the company can propose a test and, if the results are promising, Capital One will rush the new product or approach into use immediately." Why does this work for Capital One? Because, as Fairbank says, "We don't hesitate because our testing has already told us what will work."

Capital One weathered the financial crisis of 2008 better than most banks, selling their mortgage business and repaying the federal bailout by July 2009. In February 2012, it acquired ING Bank and in November announced that ING Direct would become Capital One 360. The firm was named by *Fortune* as one of the top 100 companies to work for in 2013. However, the previous July, Capital One was fined by the Consumer Financial Protection Bureau for "misleading millions of customers" about paying for extra services like payment protection and credit monitoring when receiving a new card. The company agreed to refund $140M to customers and pay $55M in fines.[1]

Fairbank started his analysis at Signet by looking for factors—variables in the data—that could help identify profitable customers. For this search he used the most convenient data he could find—the records of customers' transactions and interactions with customer service that had already been collected. As we have seen, found data such as these transactional data can be useful as an initial stage in understanding business circumstances. As we saw in the last chapter, this type of backward-looking search in data that have already been collected is an example of a retrospective observational study.

Retrospective observational studies are common in business because they are so practical. The data on which they are based are already available. But they make a weak basis for business decisions for a number of reasons. First, markets and customers are always changing, so the business environment may have changed since the data were first collected. Second, even if the world were completely stable, it would be impossible to be sure that the relationships seen between variables were a sound basis for action. Fairbank might have found, for example, that people who carry

---

[1]business.time.com/2012/07/19/cfpb-orders-capital-one-to-return-140-million-to-customers/

more than one credit card were more profitable than those who used a single card. But would this correlation imply that he should entice customers who carry only one card to get a second one? Couldn't it simply be true that people who spend more (and are thus more profitable to the bank) tend to have more than one card?

Although observational studies cannot give us the answer to questions like these, they can help to generate hypotheses. Fairbank did gain some insights from his observational study. But instead of *conclusions* on which he could make a sound decision, the study provided new hypotheses—theories that he could test as he took his next steps. To establish a causal relationship between factors that he could control (such as attributes of the cards or a willingness to extend credit to a new segment of the population) and identified responses (such as profitability, willingness to accept a card offer, or likelihood of failing to pay debts) he needed to collect new data. And the best way to generate data that can establish causal relationships is through designed, randomized experiments.

A retrospective observational study uses found data, but an experiment *randomly* assigns participants (in Fairbank's case, customers or potential customers) to particular treatments (such as card contract offers or even card colors or pictures). Random assignment is almost magic. It makes it possible to compare the responses among participants assigned to different treatments, and to conclude that those treatments *caused* the differences that were found.

Fairbank revolutionized the credit card industry through his use and advocacy of designed experiments at Capital One. In the 1980s, Capital One ran thousands of experiments on their customers, testing products and combinations of offers to determine which features caused the best results. This continues to this day. In 2011, the company opened Capital One Labs in San Francisco, and now has opened offices in New York and Washington, DC, as well. At these offices, the company can run experiments and test products using the latest technology.

You see the evidence of banking experiments in your mailbox every day. Nearly every credit card offer you receive is a "treatment" made up of different factors. The choices of percentage rate, benefits, and fees are often part of an experiment to determine their impact on card acquisition. On the Internet, vendors may randomly send you to a different site than other potential customers, to test which of two website designs encourages more "click-through" to the purchasing pages or which combination of price and special offer sells best.

You might think that the success of Capital One and a few other prominent firms, which have used experiments to beat the competition, would have made experiments the norm in business, but this is not the case. Despite their well-publicized success, experiments have been slow to penetrate many businesses.

In fact, recent developments are encouraging firms to go in the wrong direction! The lure of Big Data entices many firms to rely on observational data to hunt for correlations among variables. Some articles that you may have seen (and many software vendors) even suggest that analyses of massive datasets are all you need as a basis for business decisions. But, of course, this is nonsense. More data does not change the fact that correlation does not imply causation. And a designed experiment is the surest way to understand causal relationships between factors and responses. An understanding of the value and effectiveness of designed experiments is one of the most important lessons of this course.

JUST CHECKING

In early 2007, a larger-than-usual number of cats and dogs developed kidney failure; many died. Initially, researchers didn't know why, so they used an observational study to investigate.

1 Suppose that, as a researcher for a pet food manufacturer, you are called on to plan a study seeking the cause of this problem. Specify how you might proceed. Would your study be prospective or retrospective?

9.1 Randomized, Comparative Experiments

Experiments are a critical tool for understanding what products and ideas will work in the marketplace. An **experiment** is a study in which the experimenter *manipulates* attributes of what is being studied and observes the consequences. Usually, the attributes, called **factors**, are manipulated by being set to particular **levels** and then allocated or assigned to individuals. An experimenter identifies at least one factor to manipulate and at least one response variable to measure. Observed **responses** can be quantitative measurements such as the amount of a product sold or categorical responses like whether the customer purchased the product or not. (However, we will restrict attention to quantitative responses in this text.) The combination of factor levels assigned to a subject is called that subject's **treatment**.

The individuals on whom or which we experiment are known by a variety of terms. Humans who are experimented on are commonly called **subjects** or **participants**. Other individuals (rats, products, fiscal quarters, company divisions) are commonly referred to by the more generic term **experimental units**.

You have probably already been the subject of marketing experiments. Every credit card offer you receive is actually a combination of various factors that specify a "treatment" assigned to you. It defines the specific offer you get. For example, at Capital One, the factors might include *Annual Fee, Interest Rate,* and *Communication Channel* (how the offer is delivered to you: by e-mail, direct mail, phone, etc.). A customer's treatment might be the combination of *no Annual Fee* and a *moderate Interest Rate* with the offer being sent by *e-mail*. Other customers receive different treatments. The possible responses might be categorical (do you accept the offer of that card?) or quantitative (how much do you spend with that card during the first three months you have it?).

Two key features distinguish an experiment from observational studies and other types of investigations. First, the experimenter actively and deliberately manipulates the factors to specify the treatment. Second, the experiment assigns the subjects to those treatments at *random*. The importance of **random assignment** may not be immediately obvious. Experts, such as business executives and physicians, may think that they know how different subjects will respond to various treatments. In particular, marketing executives may want to send what they consider the best offer to their best customers, but this would make fair comparisons of treatments impossible. Without random assignment, we can't perform the analyses that allow us to conclude that differences among the treatments were responsible for any differences we observed in the responses. By using random assignment to ensure that the groups receiving different treatments are comparable, the experimenter can be sure that these differences are *due* to the differences in treatments. There are many stories of experts who were certain they knew the effect of a treatment and were proven wrong by a properly designed study. In business, it is important to get the facts rather than to just rely on what you may think you know from experience.

IN PRACTICE 9.1 Gaining insight from a marketing experiment

MANAGER You told me that most young riders of the Acela train use the Internet while on board (see In Practice 8.1). I am looking for ways to get more young people to ride the Acela. Can you analyze our customer database to figure out what to offer them?

ANALYST We cannot use our customer database to answer your question because everyone has been treated the same way. We need to conduct a prospective designed experiment to see if the young riders can be induced to ride more often if we provide incentives.

(continued)

I know that we recently purchased a mailing list of 16,000 college students. I've designed an experiment to manipulate the type of offer (the *factor*) at four different levels, each sent to 25% of the mailing list. The levels are (names in italics): (1) 10% off coupon for their next Acela ride (*Coupon*), (2) a 5000-mile Amtrak bonus card (*Card*), (3) a free Netflix download during their next Acela trip (*Movie*), and (4) no special offer (*No Offer*). We will monitor the four groups to see which group travels the most during the 12 months after sending the offer, and we will use *Miles Traveled* over the 12 months as the response variable. I'll use the results to assess whether the cost of the incentive is justified by their increased ridership.

9.2   The Four Principles of Experimental Design

When designing an experiment, there are four **principles of experimental design** to keep in mind:

1. **Control.** Controlling external sources of variation helps ensure that any differences seen are due to the experimental factors being tested and not extraneous changes in the environment. Environmental conditions can't be controlled in the usual sense, but, by making conditions as similar as possible for all treatment groups, the experimenter reduces the influence of other changes. In a test of a new credit card, the effect of a possible change to the economic environment can be controlled by sending all offers to customers at the same time and in the same manner. Otherwise, events like a sudden spike or drop in gas prices or a terrorist attack could influence customers in different ways, making it difficult to distinguish the effects of the treatments from the other effects. By controlling extraneous sources of variation the experimenter reduces the variability of the responses, making it easier to discern differences among the treatment groups.

   There is a second meaning of control in experiments. A bank testing the new creative idea of offering a card with special discounts on chocolate to attract more customers will want to compare its performance against one of their standard cards. Such a baseline measurement is called a control treatment, and the group that receives it is called the **control group**.

2. **Randomize.** In any true experiment, subjects are assigned treatments at random. Randomization allows us to equalize the effects of unknown or uncontrollable sources of variation even when they aren't controlled. Although randomization can't eliminate the effects of these sources, it spreads them out across the treatment levels so that we can see past them. Randomization also makes it possible to use the powerful methods of inference to draw conclusions from your study. Randomization protects us even from effects we didn't know about. Perhaps women are more likely to respond to the chocolate benefit card. We don't need to test equal numbers of men and women—our mailing list may not have that information—but if we randomize, that tendency won't contaminate our results. There's an adage that says "Control what you can, and randomize the rest."

3. **Replicate.** Replication shows up in different ways in experiments. Because we need to estimate the variability of our measurements, we must make more than one observation at each level of each factor. Sometimes that just means making repeated observations. But, as we'll see later, some experiments combine two or more factors in ways that may permit a single observation for each *treatment*— that is, each combination of factor levels. When such an experiment is repeated in its entirety, it is said to be *replicated*. Repeated observations at each treatment are called **replicates**. If the number of replicates is the same for each treatment combination, we say that the experiment is **balanced**. An important advantage

of balanced designs, especially those with more than one factor, is the ease of interpreting the effects. Unbalanced designs with more than one factor are more complicated, and their analysis is beyond the scope of this text.

A second kind of replication is to repeat the entire experiment for a different group of subjects, under different circumstances, or at a different time. Experiments do not require, and often can't obtain, representative random samples from an identified population. Experiments study the consequences of different levels of their factors. They rely on the random assignment of treatments to the subjects to generate the sampling distributions and to control for other possibly contaminating variables. When we detect a significant difference in response among treatment groups, we can conclude that it is due to the difference in treatments.

However, we should take care in generalizing that result too broadly if we've only studied a specialized population. A special offer of accelerated checkout lanes for regular customers may attract more business in December, but it may not be effective in July. Replication in a variety of circumstances increases our confidence that our results apply to other situations and populations.

4. **Block.** Sometimes we can identify a factor not under our control whose effect we don't care about, but which we suspect might have an effect either on our response variable or on the ways in which the factors we are studying affect that response. Perhaps men and women will respond differently to our chocolate offer. Or maybe customers with young children at home behave differently than those without. Platinum card members may be tempted by a premium offer much more than standard card members. Factors like these can account for some of the variation in our observed responses because subjects at different levels respond differently. But we can't *assign* them at random to subjects. So we deal with them by grouping, or **blocking**, our subjects together and, in effect, analyzing the experiment accounting for each block. Such factors are called **blocking factors**, and their levels are called **blocks**. Blocking in an experiment is like stratifying in a survey design. Blocking reduces variation by comparing subjects within these more homogeneous groups. That makes it easier to discern any differences in response due to the factors of interest. In addition, we may want to study the effect of the blocking factor itself. Blocking is an important compromise between randomization and control. However, unlike the first three principles, blocking is not required in all experiments.

JUST CHECKING

Following concerns over the contamination of its pet foods by melamine, which had been linked to kidney failure, a manufacturer now claims its products are safe. You are called on to design the study to demonstrate the safety of the new formulation.

2 Identify the treatment and response.

3 How would you implement control, randomization, and replication?

IN PRACTICE 9.2 Understanding experimental design principles

MANAGER Can you explain to me how we know that your experiment about young riders will get us the information we want?

ANALYST Of course. The experiment follows the three required principles of experimental design (blocking is optional). Specifically,

(continued)

Control: It is impossible to control other factors that may influence a person's decision to use the Acela. I decided to restrict attention to college and university students, and I sent all offers out at the same time to reduce variation. I also used a control group—one that receives no offer—which will be used to compare to the other three treatment levels.

Randomization: Although I can't control the other factors (besides *Offer*) that may influence a person's decision to use the Acela, by randomizing which students receive which offer, I hope that the influences of all those other factors will average out, enabling me to see the "pure" effect of the four treatments.

Replication: I've replicated by sending each type of offer to 4000 students. I hope that the response is high enough that will be able to see differences in *Miles Traveled* among the groups. This experiment is balanced, since the number of subjects is the same for all four treatments.

Blocking: I have not used blocking in the experiment. Possible blocking factors might include demographic variables such as the region of the student's home or college, their sex, or their parent's income, but I have not used those factors in the design.

9.3 Experimental Designs

One Factor Designs

The most common experimental design used in business is the single factor experiment with two levels. They are widely used and have many names including **A/B tests**, **bucket tests** or *split-run tests*. Sometimes they are called **champion/ challenger designs** when they're used to test a new idea (the challenger) against the current version (the champion). In this case, the customers offered the champion are the control group, and the customers offered the challenger (a special deal, a new offer, a new service, etc.) are the test group. A diagram of this design is shown in Figure 9.1. The single factor design is an example of a **completely randomized design**—a design where all the treatment combinations are assigned to the participants completely at random.

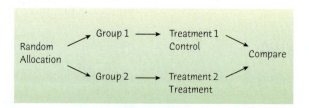

FIGURE 9.1 The simplest randomized design has two groups randomly assigned two different treatments.

Randomized Block Designs

It is not always possible to have completely random assignment of experimental units to treatments because some factors cannot be randomly assigned. For example, we can't randomly assign factors based on people's behavior, age, sex, and other attributes. Nonetheless, if we believe that these factors are important, we can break the population into groups based on the uncontrollable factor. The resulting groups are called blocks. Once we have a blocking factor, we then randomize subjects to the treatments *within each block*. This is called a **randomized block design**. In the experiment diagrammed in Figure 9.2, a marketer wanted to know the effect of two types of offers in each of two segments: a high spending group and a low spending group. The marketer selected 12,000 customers *from each group* at random and then randomly assigned the three treatments to the 12,000 customers *in each group* so that 4000 customers in each segment received each of the three treatments. A display makes the process clearer.

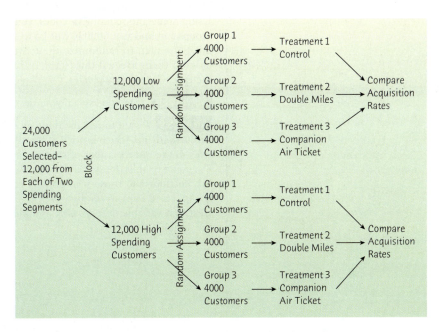

FIGURE 9.2   This example of a randomized block design shows that customers are randomized to treatments within each segment, or block.

Multi-Factor Designs

An experiment with more than one factor is called a **factorial design**. A full factorial design contains treatments that represent all possible combinations of all levels of all factors. Each specific combination of factors is called a treatment. The number of treatments can quickly become very large. With only three factors, one at 3 levels, one at 4, and one at 5, there would be $3 \times 4 \times 5 = 60$ different treatments.

Because of the possibility for huge numbers of treatments (and the requirement for very large numbers of experimental units, if we want appropriate replication), researchers typically limit the number of levels to just a few. Alternatively, advanced experimental designs allow researchers to use fewer treatments at the cost of some information loss.

It may seem that the added complexity of multiple factors is not worth the trouble. In fact, just the opposite is true. Testing multiple factors in a single experiment makes more efficient use of the available subjects. And testing factors together is the only way to see what happens at *combinations* of the levels.

An experiment to test the effectiveness of offering a $150 rebate on a new credit card may find that it increases customer spending by 1%. Another experiment finds that lowering the interest rate increases spending by 2%. But unless some customers were offered *both* the $150 rebate *and* the lower interest rate, the analyst can't learn whether offering both together would lead to still greater spending or less.

When the combination of two factors has a different effect than you would expect by adding the effects of the two factors together, that phenomenon is called an **interaction**. If the experiment does not contain both factors, it is impossible to see interactions. That can be a major omission because such effects can have the most important and surprising consequences in business.

IN PRACTICE 9.3 Designing an experiment

Continuing In Practice 9.2 (page 285), you are considering splitting up the students to be experimented on into two groups before mailing the offers: those who live or go to school in the Northeast corridor, where the Acela operates, and those who don't. Using home and school ZIP codes, you split the original 12,000 students into those groups and find that 6000 live or go to school in the Northeast corridor and 6000 do not.* You plan to randomize the treatments within those two groups and you'll monitor them to see if this factor, *NE corridor,* affects their *Miles Traveled* as well as the type of offer they receive.

MANAGER Can you explain your design to me in words and/or pictures?

ANALYST I want to test the three incentive: *Coupon,* *Card,* and *Movie,* against what we currently do, which is none of the above. So I'll randomly send those three incentives to the same number of students and use a fourth group as a control. But first I'm going to split the students into two blocks, those who live or go to school in the NE corridor and those who don't. I could just restrict the experiment to the first group, but I want to see how well the incentives work (if at all) on the others. I'll treat that variable, *NE corridor,* as a blocking variable. Here's a diagram explaining the design:

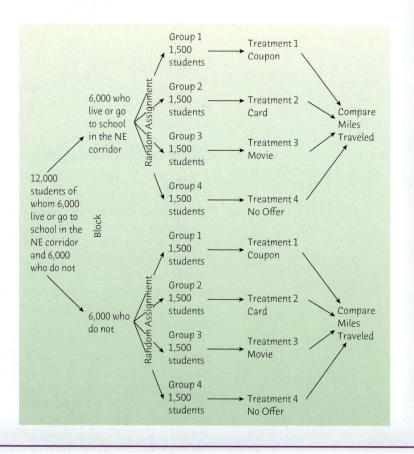

---

*There is no requirement that the block sizes must be equal. However, an analysis with unequal block sizes is more complicated.

GUIDED EXAMPLE   Designing a Direct Mail Experiment

At a major credit card bank, management has been pleased with the success of a recent campaign to cross-sell Silver card customers with the new SkyWest Gold card. But you, as a marketing analyst, think that the revenue of the card can be increased by adding three months of double miles on SkyWest to the offer, and you think the additional gain in charges will offset the cost of the double miles. You want to design a marketing experiment to find out what the difference will be in revenue if you offer the double miles. You've also been thinking about offering a new version of the miles called "use anywhere miles," which can be transferred to other airlines, so you want to test that version as well.

You also know that customers receive so many offers that they tend to disregard most of their direct mail. So, you'd like to see what happens if you send the offer in a shiny gold envelope with the SkyWest logo prominently displayed on the front. How can we design an experiment to see whether either of these factors has an effect on charges?

PLAN	**Define** and state the problem.	We want to study two factors to see their effect on the revenue generated for a new credit card offer.
	Response Specify the response variable.	Revenue is a percentage of the amount charged to the card by the cardholder. To measure the success, we will use the monthly charges of customers who receive the various offers. We will use the three months after the offer is sent out as the collection period and use the total amount charged per customer during this period as the response.
	Factors Identify the factors you plan to test. **Levels** Specify the levels of the factors you will use.	We will offer customers three levels of the factor *Miles* for the SkyWest Gold card: *Regular* (no additional) *Miles*, *Double Miles*, and *Double Use Anywhere Miles*. Customers will receive the offer in the *Standard Envelope* or the new SkyWest *Logo Envelope* (factor *Envelope*).
	Experimental Design Observe the principles of design: **Control** any sources of variability you know of and can control.	We will send out all the offers to customers at the same time (in mid September) and evaluate the response as total charges in the period October through December.
	Randomly assign experimental units to treatments to equalize the effects of unknown or uncontrollable sources of variation. **Replicate** results by placing more than one customer (usually many) in each treatment group.	A total of 30,000 current Silver card customers will be randomly selected from our customer records to receive one of the six offers. ✔ *Regular Miles* with *Standard Envelope* ✔ *Double Miles* with *Standard Envelope* ✔ *Double Use Anywhere Miles* with *Standard Envelope* ✔ *Regular Miles* with *Logo Envelope* ✔ *Double Miles* with *Logo Envelope* ✔ *Double Use Anywhere Miles* with *Logo Envelope*

(continued)

Make a Picture A diagram of your design can help you think about it.

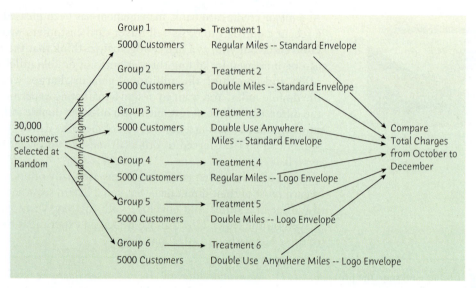

Specify any other details about the experiment. You must give enough details so that another experimenter could exactly replicate your experiment.

It's generally better to include details that might seem irrelevant because they may turn out to make a difference.

Specify how to measure the response.

On January 15, we will examine the total card charges for each customer for the period October 1 through December 31.

DO Write up the proposal to carry out the design and collect the data. At this stage of planning the do step is to get authorization to implement your proposal.

REPORT **Communicate** the basic outline of your proposal. Include a brief description of the experimental design and a plan for its implementation. Discuss how the experiment will address the original problem you set out to solve.

MEMO

Re: Test mailing for creative offer and envelope

We designed an experiment to test whether several creative ideas from marketing will generate enough revenue to justify their cost. We tested two factors: *Envelope* at two levels (*Logo* and *Standard*) and Miles at three levels (*Regular, Double, Use Anywhere*) to create a 2 × 3 factorial design. We will select 30,000 current Silver card members, who will be randomly assigned to one of the 6 cells of the design. We will evaluate the results using cumulative revenue for the 3 months post-mailing, which was sent out. When the results are in, we will reconvene to analyze the results. Of particular interest are:

✔ Whether offering *Double Miles* is worth the cost of the miles

✔ Whether the *Double Use Anywhere Miles* are worth the cost

✔ Whether the *Logo Envelope* increased spending enough to justify the added expense

9.4 Issues in Experimental Design

Blinding and Placebos

Humans are notoriously susceptible to errors in judgment—all of us. When we know what treatment is assigned, it's difficult not to let that knowledge influence our response or our assessment of the response, even when we try to be careful.

Suppose you were trying to sell your new brand of cola to be stocked in a school's vending machines. You might hope to convince the committee designated to make the choice that students prefer your less expensive cola, or at least that they can't taste the difference. You could set up an experiment to see which of the three competing brands students prefer (or whether they can tell the difference at all). But people have brand loyalties. If they know which brand they are tasting, it might influence their rating. To avoid this bias, it would be better to disguise the brands as much as possible. This strategy is called **blinding** the participants to the treatment. Even professional taste testers in food industry experiments are blinded to the treatment to reduce any prior feelings that might influence their judgment.

But it isn't just the subjects who should be blind. Experimenters themselves often subconsciously behave in ways that favor what they believe. It wouldn't be appropriate for you to run the study yourself if you have an interest in the outcome. People are so good at picking up subtle cues about treatments that the best (in fact, the only) defense against such biases in experiments on human subjects is to keep anyone who could affect the outcome or the measurement of the response from knowing which subjects have been assigned to which treatments. So, not only should your cola-tasting subjects be blinded, but also you, as the experimenter, shouldn't know which drink is which—at least until you're ready to analyze the results.

There are two main classes of individuals who can affect the outcome of the experiment:

- Those who could influence the results (the subjects, treatment administrators, or technicians)
- Those who evaluate the results (judges, experimenters, etc.)

When all the individuals in either one of these classes are blinded, an experiment is said to be **single-blind**. When everyone in both classes is blinded, we call the experiment **double-blind**. Double-blinding is the gold standard for any experiment involving both human subjects and human judgment about the response. Double-blind studies are the gold standard for a reason: You cannot overcome the subtle influence that results from experimenter knowledge of the treatments because it is subconscious, and the influence is quite significant. An experiment showed, for example, that the mere knowledge on the part of dentists that their (actually identically treated) patients might have received a placebo before tooth removal massively increased their patient's pain 1.5 hours post-procedure (Gracely et al., 1985, *Lancet*)!

Often simply applying *any* treatment can induce an improvement. Every parent knows the medicinal value of a kiss to make a toddler's scrape or bump stop hurting. Some of the improvement seen with a treatment—even an effective treatment—can be due simply to the act of treating. To separate these two effects, we can sometimes use a control treatment that mimics the treatment itself. A "fake" treatment that looks just like the treatments being tested is called a **placebo**. Placebos are the best way to blind subjects so they don't know whether they have received the treatment or not. One common version of a placebo in drug testing is a "sugar pill." Especially when psychological attitude can affect the results, control group subjects treated with a placebo may show an improvement.

The fact is that subjects treated with a placebo sometimes improve. It's not unusual for 20% or more of subjects given a placebo to report reduction in pain, improved movement, or greater alertness or even to demonstrate improved health

---

Blinding by Misleading

Social science experiments can sometimes blind subjects by disguising the purpose of a study. One of the authors participated as an undergraduate volunteer in one such (now infamous) psychology experiment. The subjects were told that the experiment was about 3-D spatial perception and were assigned to draw a model of a horse and were randomly assigned to a room alone or in a group. While they were busy drawing, a loud noise and then groaning were heard coming from the room next door. The *real* purpose of the experiment was to see whether being in a group affects how people reacted to the apparent disaster. The horse was only a pretext. The subjects were blind to the treatment because they were misled.

Placebos and Authority

The placebo effect is stronger when placebo treatments are administered with authority or by a figure who appears to be an authority. "Doctors" in white coats generate a stronger effect than salespeople in polyester suits. But the placebo effect is not reduced much, even when subjects know that the effect exists. People often suspect that they've gotten the placebo if nothing at all happens. So, recently, drug manufacturers have gone so far in making placebos realistic that they cause the same side effects as the drug being tested! Such "active placebos" usually induce a stronger placebo effect. When those side effects include loss of appetite or hair, the practice may raise ethical questions.

or performance. This **placebo effect** highlights both the importance of effective blinding and the importance of comparing treatments with a control. Placebo controls are so effective that you should use them as an essential tool for blinding whenever possible.

JUST CHECKING

The pet food manufacturer we've been following hires you to perform the experiment to test whether their new formulation is safe and nutritious for cats and dogs.

4 How would you establish a control group?

5 Would you use blinding? How? (Can or should you use double-blinding?)

6 Both cats and dogs are to be tested. Should you block? Explain.

The best experiments are usually:

- Randomized
- Double-blind
- Comparative
- Placebo-controlled

Confounding

A credit card bank wanted to test the sensitivity of the market to two factors: the annual fee charged for a card and the annual percentage rate charged. The bank selected 100,000 people at random from a mailing list and sent out 50,000 offers with a low rate and no fee and 50,000 offers with a higher rate and a $50 annual fee. They discovered that people preferred the low-rate, no-fee card. No surprise. In fact, customers signed up for that card at over twice the rate as the other offer. But the question the bank really wanted to answer was: "How much of the change was due to the rate, and how much was due to the fee?" Unfortunately, there's simply no way to separate out the two effects with that experimental design.

If the bank had followed a factorial design in the two factors and sent out all four possible different treatments—low rate with no fee; low rate with $50 fee; high rate with no fee, and high rate with $50 fee—each to 25,000 people, it could have learned about both factors and could have also learned about the interaction between rate and fee. But we can't tease apart these two effects because the people who were offered the low rate were also offered the no-fee card. Whenever the effects of two (or more) variables on a response cannot be distinguished from each other, we say that the two factors are **confounded**.

Confounding can arise either because of lurking variables in an observational study experiment, or because of poor design in an experiment. When variables are confounded it can be difficult to know which variable is really responsible for the effect. A shock to the economic or political situation that occurs during a marketing experiment can overwhelm the effects of the factors being manipulated. In designed experiments, randomization will usually take care of confounding by distributing uncontrolled factors over the treatments at random. But be sure to watch out for potential confounding effects even in a well-designed experiment.

JUST CHECKING

A researcher wanted to test how much familiarity helps memory. He designed an experiment and gave subjects (sophomores in a U.S. university) the following two groups of cities to memorize. He recorded the number of correct responses.

A: Paris, Rome, London, New York, Moscow

B: Bandar Seri Begawan, Nouakchott, Ulaanbaatar, Podgorica, Jayawardenepura Kotte

7 What other factor(s) did the researcher unwittingly confound with familiarity?

9.5   Displaying Data from Designed Experiments

Does the Difference Make a Difference?

A coworker has a new design for your startup's webpage that he claims will keep people more interested in your company than the old design. He decides to run an A/B test, sending half of people searching for your company to the old site (A) and half to his new design (B). After a week, you examine the results and find that the average amount of time for A is 80 seconds. The new design (B) resulted in an average of 90 seconds.

That sounds good. But was that increase really due to the new website, or just to random variation? If the website has only a small effect, it will be hard to tell the difference. If the amount of time people spend on your site is highly variable, that makes it hard to tell the difference as well. And if you try to make a decision based on only on a few subjects, that makes things ever worse. These three factors—size of the effect, variability, and the number of runs—all affect your ability to draw conclusions.

Observations vary. Suppose we display the results using boxplots. Figure 9.3 shows two possible pairs where the response variable is *Amount of Time* spent on the site. In the left pair, suppose the boxplot in green shows the results for the green A site and the orange boxplot shows results for site B. It looks pretty convincing. Now look at the pair on the right. The actual mean difference (10 seconds) is the same but there's so much variability in the times that the effect is hard to see.[2] Later, we'll see how to use the standard deviation of the difference as a measure to judge whether the difference is large enough to be fairly sure that it didn't occur just by natural variation. When an observed difference is large enough in standard deviations to be convincing, we say it's statistically significant. We'll put numbers on this concept later, but we'd say the difference is statistically significant in the left pair and not statistically significant in the right pair.

Later chapters show how statistical tests quantify this intuition. For now, the important point is that a difference is statistically significant if we don't believe that it's likely to have occurred only by chance.

Boxplots are great for visualizing changes in a response for different levels of a single quantitative factor, but when the experiment involves more than one factor, we have to be careful to think about all the factors together.

In our direct mail example from the Guided Example on page 289, we looked at two factors: *Miles* and *Envelope*. *Miles* had three levels: *Regular Miles*, *Double Miles*, and *Double Use Anywhere Miles*. The factor *Envelope* had two levels: *Standard* and new *Logo*. The three levels of *Miles* and the two levels of *Envelope* resulted in six treatment groups. Because this was a completely randomized design, 5000 customers were allocated at random to each treatment.

Three months after the offer was mailed out, the total charges on the card were recorded for each of the 30,000 cardholders in the experiment. The mean *Total Charges* for each treatment combination are shown in Table 9.1. Figure 9.4 shows boxplots of the six treatment groups' responses for each factor.

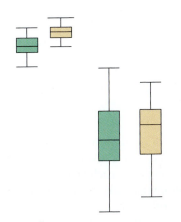

FIGURE 9.3 The boxplots in both pairs have centers the same distance apart, but when the spreads are large, the observed difference may be just from random fluctuation.

TABLE 9.1 Mean *Total Charges* by *Treatment* for the direct mail example on page 289. (Data in **Direct mail**)

		Envelope		
		Standard	**Logo**	**Means**
Miles	No Offer	1611	1762	**1687**
	Double Miles	1716	1874	**1795**
	Use Anywhere	1795	1979	**1887**
	Means	**1707**	**1872**	**1789**

---

[2]Of course the boxplots show medians at their centers, and we're trying to find differences among means. But for roughly symmetric distributions like these, the means and medians are very close.

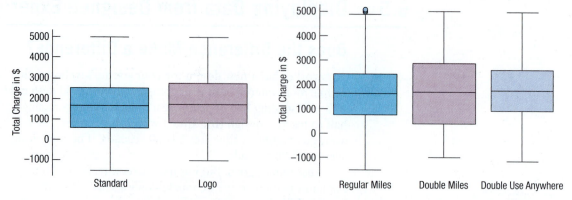

FIGURE 9.4 Boxplots of *Total Charge* by each factor. It is difficult to see the effects of the factors for several reasons. First, the other factor hasn't been accounted for; second, the effects are small compared to the overall variation in charges; third, an interaction between the predictor variables may mask the main effects; and finally, watch out for outliers in each treatment combination.

If you look closely at Figure 9.4, you may be able to discern a very slight increase in the *Total Charges* for some levels of the factors, but it's very difficult to see. There are several reasons for this. First, the variation due to each factor gets in the way of seeing the effect of the other factor. For example, each customer in the boxplot for the *Logo Envelope* got one of three different offers. If those offers had an effect on spending, then that increased the variation within the *Logo* treatment group. Second, as is typical in a marketing experiment of this kind, the effects are very small compared to the variability in people's spending. That's why companies use such a large sample size. And that's why we'll study efficient methods for determining important effects later in the text. Third, the main effects of the factors in a multi factor experiment may be masked by the interaction effect. We'll see how to display the interaction in the next section. Finally, watch out for outliers. It's a good idea to display the data in each cell using box plots or histograms to check for outliers.

Interaction Plots

Whenever we have more than one factor, we should investigate whether the effect of one factor is constant for all levels of the other. In other words, we should explore whether an interaction between the two factors affects the response. An **interaction plot**, as shown in Figure 9.5, is a plot of means for each treatment group. It is essential for visualizing interactions.

FIGURE 9.5 An interaction plot of the *Miles* and *Envelope* effects. The parallel lines show that the effects of the three *Miles* offers are roughly the same over the two different *Envelopes* and therefore that the interaction effect is small.

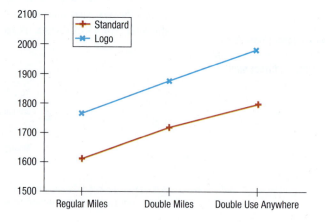

This plot displays means of the response at each treatment combination. The levels of one factor are shown on the *x*-axis. A separate line for each level of another factor connects the treatment means. When the effect of one factor on the response depends on the level of the other factor, the lines will not be parallel, giving evidence of an interaction between the factors.

This interaction plot shows the mean *Charges* at all six treatment groups. The levels of one of the factors, in this case *Miles*, are shown on the *x*-axis, and the mean *Charges* of the groups for each *Envelope* level are shown at each *Miles* level. The means of each level of *Envelope* are connected for ease of understanding. Notice that the effect of *Double Miles* over *Regular Miles* is about the same for both the *Standard* and *Logo Envelopes*. And the same is true for the *Double Use Anywhere* miles. This indicates that the effect of *Miles* is constant for the two different *Envelopes*. The lines are nearly parallel, which indicates that there is essentially no interaction effect.

To create the interaction plot in Figure 9.5, start with the table of means as in Table 9.1. Choose one factor to be on the *x*-axis. Here we have chosen *Miles*. Choose one level of the other factor to begin, say *Standard*, for *Envelope*. Plot the means for *Standard* for each level of *Miles*, connecting the points with a line. Here we've chosen red for *Standard*. Repeat with a different color for each level. Here there is only one other level, *Logo*, for which we've chosen blue. Many statistics packages offer interaction plots as part of advanced modeling methods such as multiple regression and ANOVA, but for now, it's important simply to understand what an interaction effect is and how to interpret interaction plots.

Later in the text we'll learn how to judge whether effects are statistically significant, meaning that they are enough so that we can be reasonably sure that the differences we see aren't just due to natural variation.

JUST CHECKING

Suppose that you had run the randomized block design from In Practice 9.3 (see page 288). You would have had two levels of the (blocking) factor *NE Corridor* (*NE* or *not*) and the same four levels of *Offer* (*Coupon, Card, Movie,* and *No Offer*).

8 What would a significant interaction effect between *NE Corridor* and *Offer*. mean? What would you tell the marketing group?

A marketing group at a small phone company designs an experiment to test two factors: 1. Data (100Mb or Unlimited). 2. Overseas calls (standard rates or free).

They offer the 4 treatment combinations at the same price randomly to 10,000 customers who go to their website. Historically about 4 to 5% of customers looking at their website sign up for one of the plans. During the experiment they find that 5% of the customers opt for the 100Mb standard rate combination, 6% for the Unlimited data, standard rate combination, 5% for the 100Mb free international plan, and 30% for the Unlimited data, free international calls plan.

9 Draw an interaction plot and explain the results of the experiment to the marketing group.

GUIDED EXAMPLE   A Follow-up Experiment

After analyzing the data, the bank decided to go with the *Logo* envelope, but a marketing specialist thought that more *Miles* might increase spending even more. A new test was designed to test both the type of *Miles* and the amount. Again, total *Charge* in three months is the response. (Data in **Direct mail follow up**)

(continued)

PLAN State the problem.

We want to study the two factors *Miles* and *Amount* to see their effect on the revenue generated for a new credit card offer.

Response Specify the response variable.

To measure the success, we will use the monthly charges of customers who receive the various offers. We will use the three months after the offer is sent out as the collection period and the total amount charged per customer during this period as the response.

Factors Identify the factors you plan to test.

We will offer each customer one of the two levels of the factor *Miles* for the SkyWest Gold card: *SkyWest Miles* or *Use Anywhere Miles*. Customers are offered three levels of *Miles*: *Regular Miles*, *Double Miles*, and *Triple Miles*.

Levels Specify the levels of the factors you will use.

We will send out all the offers to customers at the same time (in mid March) and evaluate the response as total charges in the period April through June.

Experimental Design Specify the design.

A total of 60,000 current Gold card customers will be selected from our customer records to be randomly assigned to receive one of the six offers.

✔ Regular SkyWest Miles

✔ Double SkyWest Miles

✔ Triple SkyWest Miles

✔ Regular Use Anywhere Miles

✔ Double Use Anywhere Miles

✔ Triple Use Anywhere Miles

Make a Picture A diagram of your design can help you think about it. We could also draw this diagram like the one on page 290 with 6 treatment groups, but now we are thinking of the design as having two distinct factors that we wish to evaluate individually, so this form gives the right impression.

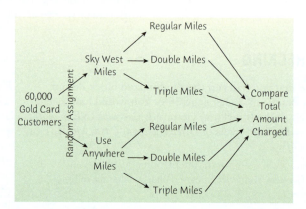

On June 15, we will examine the total card charges for each customer for the period April 1 through June 30.

We want to measure the effect of the two types of *Miles* and the three award amounts.

Specify any other experimental details. You must give enough details so that another experimenter could exactly replicate your experiment.

It's generally better to include details that might seem irrelevant than to leave out matters that could turn out to make a difference.

Specify how to measure the response and your hypotheses.

DO **Plot** Examine the boxplots and interaction plots, being careful to realize that an interaction effect may make the interpretation of the main effects problematic. Always be sure to examine the interaction plot before making conclusions about which factors influence the response.

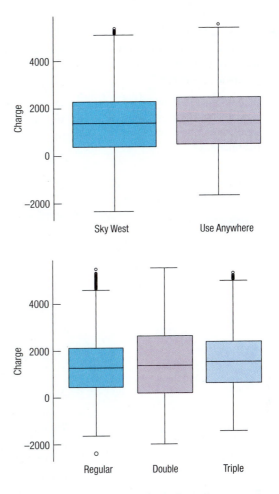

Boxplots by each factor show that there may be a slight increase in charges due to the *Use Anywhere Miles* and the *Amount of Miles* offered, but the differences are hard to see because of the intrinsic variation in *Charges*.

There are some outliers apparent in the boxplots, but none exerts a large influence on its group mean, so we will leave them in.

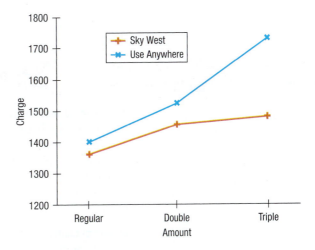

The interaction plot shows that offering *Triple Miles* may have a much larger effect for *Use Anywhere Miles* than for *Sky West Miles*.

(continued)

REPORT

To answer the initial question, we ask whether the differences we observe in the means of the groups are meaningful.

Because this is a randomized experiment, we can attribute significant differences to the treatments.

Be sure to make recommendations based on the context of your business decision.

MEMO

Re: Test mailing for creative offer and envelope

The mailing for testing the *Triple Miles* initiative went out in March, and results on charges from April through June were available in early July. We found that *Use Anywhere Miles* performed better than the standard *Sky West Miles*, but that the amount they increased charges depended on the amount offered.

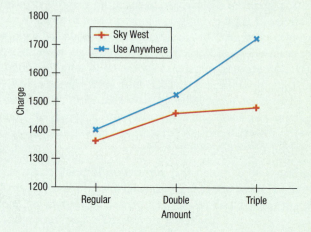

As we can see, Triple Miles for the Sky West Miles didn't increase Charge significantly and is probably not worth the added expense. However, Triple Miles for the Use Anywhere Miles generated an average $205 more in average Charge. Although we do not know whether the effects are statistically significant, we feel that the added revenue of the *Triple Miles* may justify their cost.

In summary, our preliminary recommendations are to offer *Triple Miles* for the *Use Anywhere Miles* offers for our Gold Card customers but keep the *Double Miles* offer for the *Sky West Miles*.

⊘ WHAT CAN GO WRONG?

- **Don't give up just because you can't run an experiment.** Sometimes we can't run an experiment because we can't identify or control the factors. Sometimes it would simply be unethical to run the experiment. (Consider randomly assigning employees to two environments—one where workers were exposed to massive amounts of cigarette smoke and one a smoke-free environment—to see differences in health and productivity.) If we can't perform an experiment, often an observational study is a good choice.

- **Beware of confounding.** Use randomization whenever possible to ensure that the factors not in your experiment are not confounded with your treatment levels. Be alert to confounding that cannot be avoided, and report it along with your results.

- **Bad things can happen even to good experiments.** Protect yourself by recording additional information. An experiment in which the air-conditioning failed for two weeks, affecting the results, was saved by recording the temperature (although that was not originally one of the factors) and estimating the effect the higher temperature had on the response.[3] It's generally good practice to collect as much information as possible about your experimental units and the circumstances of the experiment. For example, in the direct mail experiment, it would be wise to record details of the general economy and any global events (such as a sharp downturn in the stock market) that might affect customer behavior.

- **Don't spend your entire budget on the first run.** Just as it's a good idea to pretest a survey, it's always wise to try a small pilot experiment before running the full-scale experiment. You may learn, for example, how to choose factor levels more effectively, about effects you forgot to control, and about unanticipated confounding.

- **Be wary of generalizing to situations other than the one at hand.** Think hard about how the data were generated to understand the breadth of conclusions you are entitled to draw.

- **When there is an interaction between factors, be careful in interpreting the effect of the individual factors on the response variable.** Look at this interaction plot:

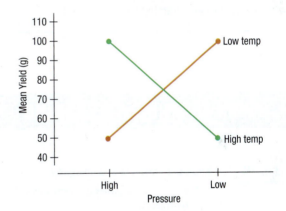

FIGURE 9.6 An interaction plot of *Yield by Temperature* and *Pressure*. There is no simple effect of *Pressure* because the average *Yield* at the two pressures is the same. That doesn't mean that *Pressure* has no effect on the *Yield*. In the presence of an interaction, be careful when interpreting the effect of individual factors.

The experiment was run at two temperatures and two pressure levels. High amounts of material were produced at high pressure with high temperature and at low pressure with low temperature. What's the effect of *Temperature*? Of *Pressure*? When looked at individually, each factor appears to have no effect on *Yield*, but it would be silly (and wrong) to say that neither *Temperature* nor *Pressure* was important. The real story is in the interaction. (See Figure 9.6.)

[3]R. D. DeVeaux and M. Szelewski, "Optimizing Automatic Splitless Injection Parameters for Gas Chromatographic Environmental Analysis," *Journal of Chromatographic Science* 27, no. 9 (1989): 513–518.

ETHICS IN ACTION

A large U.S. multinational that provides field services to energy companies worldwide operates in approximately 50 countries and employs nearly 85,000 people. While very profitable, this company has had its share of controversies. The most publicized involved allegations of misconduct with government contracts and inattention to safety resulting in incidents where employees were injured and the environment negatively impacted. Consequently, its top level executives became quite concerned after several of its employees in the United States filed complaints with the human resources department about the safety issues in the company.

To be proactive and potentially avoid more public scrutiny, management appointed Beth Morgan-Brown, head of corporate human resources, to coordinate an effort to investigate this issue more broadly. In the first phase of the investigation, she conducted interviews and reviewed files. As Beth had suspected, the Southeast region of the U.S. was particularly problematic. Beth had always believed that HR in that regional corporate office did not provide adequate safety training for management.

So, she developed a set of videos to see if they would better inform management of the serious safety issues in the field. She randomly selected 100 managers in each of the South East and West regions, assigning half of them in each region to receive the video training and the other half to receive no training. At the end of the training period she gave each manager a set of questions about safety to test their knowledge.

To her surprise, the managers in the South East who received the training actually did worse than those in the South East who received no training, but in the West, the trained managers did much better than those in the Western control group. On average overall, however, the trained managers did not do significantly better than the control group, and so Beth reported to corporate that the training was unsuccessful.

- **Identify the ethical dilemma in this scenario.**
- **What are the undesirable consequences?**
- **Propose an ethical solution that considers the welfare of all stakeholders.**

CHAPTER

9 FROM LEARNING TO EARNING

LEARNING OBJECTIVES

Know the elements of a designed randomized experiment.

- *Experimental units* (sometimes called *subjects* or *participants*) are assigned at random to *treatments*.
- The experimenter manipulates *factors*, setting them to specified *levels* to establish the treatments.
- A quantitative *response variable* is measured or observed for each experimental unit.
- We can attribute differences in the response to the differences among the treatments.

State and apply the Four Principles of Experimental Design.

- *Control* sources of variation other than the factors being tested. Make the conditions as similar as possible for all treatment groups except for differences among the treatments.
- *Randomize* the assignment of subjects to treatments. *Balance* the design by assigning the same number of subjects to each treatment.
- *Replicate* the experiment on more than one subject.
- *Block* the experiment by grouping together subjects who are similar in important ways that you cannot control.

Work with *Blinding* and *Control groups*.

- A *single-blind* study is one in which either all those who can affect the results or all those who evaluate the results are kept ignorant of which subjects receive which treatments.
- A *double-blind* study is one in which both those classes of actors are ignorant of the treatment assignment.

- A *control group* is assigned to a null treatment or to the best available alternative treatment.
- Control subjects are often administered a *placebo* or null treatment that mimics the treatment being studied but is known to be inactive.

TERMS

A/B test	An *A/B test* design offers two alternative treatments to judge which is better.
Balanced	An experiment design is said to be *balanced* if an equal number of experimental units receive each treatment. Balance is a desirable feature because balanced designs are easier to analyze.
Blind, Blinding	Any individual associated with an experiment who is not aware of how subjects have been allocated to treatment groups is said to be blinded.
Blocking, Blocking Factor	When groups of experimental units are similar, it is often a good idea to gather them together into the same level of a factor. The factor is called a blocking factor and its levels are called blocks. By blocking we isolate the variability attributable to the differences between the blocks so that we can see the differences in the means due to the treatments more clearly.
Bucket test	Compares two alternative treatments, another name for an A/B test.
Champion/challenge design	An A/B test that compares a new treatment (the challenger) with an established one (the champion).
Confounded	When a factor is associated with another factor in such a way that their effects cannot be separated, we say that these two factors are confounded.
Control	When we limit the levels of a factor not explicitly part of the experiment design, we have controlled that factor. (By contrast, the factors we are testing are said to be *manipulated*.)
Control group	The experimental units assigned to a baseline treatment level, typically either the default treatment, which is well understood, or a null, placebo treatment. Their responses provide a basis for comparison.
Designs	• **Randomized block design:** The randomization occurs only within blocks. • **Completely randomized design:** All experimental units have an equal chance of receiving any treatment. • **Factorial design:** Includes more than one factor in the same design and includes every combination of all the levels of each factor.
Double-blind, Single-blind	There are two classes of individuals who can affect the outcome of an experiment: those who could *influence the results* (subjects, treatment administrators, or technicians) those who *evaluate the results* (judges, treating physicians, etc.) When every individual in *either* of these classes is blinded, an experiment is said to be single-blind. When everyone in *both* classes is blinded, we call the experiment double-blind.
Experiment	An experiment *manipulates* factor levels to create treatments, *randomly assigns* subjects to these treatment levels, and then *compares* the responses of the subject groups across treatment levels.
Experimental units	Individuals on whom an experiment is performed. Usually called subjects or participants when they are human.
Factor	A variable whose levels are controlled by the experimenter. Experiments attempt to discover the effects that differences in factor levels may have on the responses of the experimental units.
Interaction	When the effects of the levels of one factor change depending on the level of the other factor, the two factors are said to interact. When interaction terms are present, it is misleading to talk about the main effect of one factor because how large it is *depends* on the level of the other factor.
Interaction plot	A plot that shows the means at each treatment combination, highlighting the factor effects and their behavior at all the combinations.
Level	The specific values that the experimenter chooses for a factor are called the levels of the factor.

Placebo	A treatment that mimics the treatment to be studied, designed so that all groups think they are receiving the same treatment. Many subjects respond to such a treatment (a response known as a *placebo effect*). Only by comparing with a placebo can we be sure that the observed effect of a treatment is not due simply to the placebo effect.
Placebo effect	The tendency of many human subjects (often 20% or more of experiment subjects) to show a response even when administered a placebo.
Principles of experimental design	• **Control** aspects of the experiment that we know may have an effect on the response, but that are not the factors being studied. • **Randomize** subjects to treatments to even out effects that we cannot control. • **Replicate** over as many subjects as possible. Results for a single subject are just anecdotes. • **Block** to reduce the effects of identifiable attributes of the subjects that cannot be controlled.
Random assignment	To be valid, an experiment must assign experimental units to treatment groups at random. This is called random assignment.
Replicates	One result is an anecdote; not data. Multiple cases should be treated in each treatment level of an experiment. These are referred to as *replicates*.
Response	A variable whose values are compared across different treatments. In a randomized experiment, large response differences can be attributed to the effect of differences in treatment level.
Subjects or Participants	When the experimental units are people, they are usually referred to as subjects or participants.
Treatment	The process, intervention, or other controlled circumstance applied to randomly assigned experimental units. Treatments are the different levels of a single factor or are made up of combinations of levels of two or more factors.

BRIEF CASE

Design a Multifactor Experiment

Design, carry out, and analyze your own multifactor experiment. The experiment doesn't have to involve human subjects. In fact, an experiment designed to find the best settings for microwave popcorn, the best paper airplane design, or the optimal weight and placement of coins on a toy car to make it travel farthest and fastest down an incline are all fine ideas. Be sure to define your response variable of interest before you start the experiment and detail how you'll perform the experiment, specifically including the elements you control, how you use randomization, and how many times you replicate the experiment. Make plots of your data and come to preliminary conclusions about which effects look important. Write up your conclusions and any recommendation for further testing.

CHAPTER 9 EXERCISES

SECTION 9.1

1. For the following experiment, identify the experimental units, the treatments, the response, and the random assignment.

A commercial food lab compared recipes for chocolate chip cookies. They baked cookies with different kinds of chips (milk chocolate, dark chocolate, and semi-sweet). All other ingredients and amounts were the same. Ten trained tasters rated the cookies on a scale of 1 to 10. The cookies were presented to the tasters in a random order.

2. For the following experiment, identify the experimental units, the treatments, the response, and the random assignment.

An investment club decided to compare investment strategies. Starting with nine equal investment amounts, three invested in the "dogs of the Dow"—stocks in the Dow Industrial average that had been underperforming relative to the rest of the Dow average. The relative amounts to invest in each of the stocks were chosen randomly and differently for each fund. Three funds invested following the advice of a TV investment show host, again choosing the specific stocks and allocations randomly for the three funds. And three funds invested by throwing darts at a page from the *Wall Street Journal* that listed stocks on the NYSE, and invested in each of the stocks hit by a dart, throwing a different set of darts for each of the three funds. At the end of six months the funds were compared.

SECTION 9.2

3. For the cookie recipe experiment of Exercise 1, identify how Control, Randomization, and Replication were used.

4. For the investment experiment of Exercise 2, identify how Control, Randomization, and Replication were used.

SECTION 9.3

5. An Internet sale site randomly sent customers to one of three versions of its welcome page. It recorded how long each visitor stayed in the site.

Here is a diagram of that experiment. Fill in the parts of the experiment.

6. Analysts from the Internet company of Exercise 5 are now concerned that customers who come directly to their site (by typing their URL into a browser) might respond differently than those referred to the site from other sites (such as search engines). They decide to block according to how the customer arrived at their site.

Here is a diagram of that experiment. Fill in the parts.

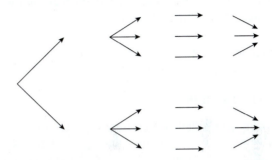

SECTION 9.4

7. For the following experiment, indicate whether it was single-blind, double-blind, or not blinded at all. Explain your reasoning.

Makers of a new frozen entrée arranged for it to be served to randomly selected customers at a restaurant in place of the equivalent entrée ordinarily prepared in the kitchen. After their meal, the customers were asked about the quality of the food.

8. For the following experiment, indicate whether it was single-blind, double-blind, or not blinded at all. Explain your reasoning.

Does a "stop smoking" program work better if it costs more? Smokers responding to an advertisement offering to help them stop smoking were randomly offered a program costing $100 or the same program costing $250. The offer was made individually to each client by presenting a sealed envelope so the clerk providing the offer did not know the details of the offer. At the end of the program (a course and films along with diet and smoking cessation aids), clients were followed for six months to see if they had indeed quit smoking.

9. Is the experiment of Exercise 1 blind? Could it be made double blind? Explain.

10. Is the experiment of Exercise 5 blind? Could it be made double blind? Explain.

SECTION 9.5

11. In the experiment described in Exercise 1, in fact the study also compared the use of butter or margarine in the recipes. The design was balanced, with each combination of chip type and oil type tested.

a) What were the factors and factor levels?
b) What were the treatments?
c) If an interaction was found to be significant, what would that mean?

12. The investment club described in Exercise 2 decided to repeat their experiment in a different way. Three members of the club took responsibility for one of each of the three investment "strategies," making the final choices and allocations of investment dollars. For this new experiment:

a) What were the subjects?
b) What were the factors and factor levels?
c) What were the treatments?

CHAPTER EXERCISES

13. Laundry detergents. A consumer group wants to test the efficacy of a new laundry detergent. They take 16 pieces of white cloth and stain each with the same amount of grease. They decide to try it using both hot and cold water settings and at both short and long washing times. Half of the 16 pieces will get the new detergent, and half will get a standard detergent. They'll compare the shirts by using an optical scanner to measure whiteness.

a) What are the factors they are testing?
b) Identify all the factor levels.
c) What is/are the response(s)?

14. Sales scripts. An outdoor products company wants to test a new website design where customers can get information about their favorite outdoor activity. They randomly send half of the customers coming to the website to the new design. They want to see whether the Web visitors spend more time at the site and whether they make a purchase.

a) What are the factors they are testing?
b) Identify all the factor levels.
c) What is/are the response(s)?

15. Laundry detergents, part 2. One member of the consumer group in Exercise 13 is concerned that the experiment will take too long and makes some suggestions to shorten it. Comment briefly on each idea.

a) Cut the runs to 8 by testing only the new detergent. Compare the results to results on the standard detergent published by the manufacturer.
b) Cut the runs to 8 by testing only in hot water.
c) Keep the number of runs at 16, but save time by running all the standard detergent runs first to avoid swapping detergents back and forth.

16. Swimsuits. A swimsuit manufacturer wants to test the speed of its newly designed $550 suit. They design an experiment by having 6 randomly selected Olympic swimmers swim as fast as they can with their old swimsuit first and then swim the same event again with the new, expensive swim suit. They'll use the difference in times as the response variable. Criticize the experiment and point out some of the problems with generalizing the results.

Ⓣ 17. Mozart. Will listening to a Mozart piano sonata make you smarter? In a published study, Rauscher, Shaw, and Ky reported that when students were given a spatial reasoning section of a standard IQ test, those who listened to Mozart for 10 minutes improved their scores more than those who simply sat quietly.

a) These researchers said the differences were statistically significant. Explain what that means in this context.
b) Steele, Bass, and Crook tried to replicate the original study. The subjects were 125 college students who participated in the experiment for course credit. Subjects first took the test. Then they were assigned to one of three groups: listening to a Mozart piano sonata, listening to music by Philip Glass, and sitting for 10 minutes in silence. Three days after the treatments, they were retested. Draw a diagram displaying the design of this experiment.
c) The boxplots show the differences in score before and after treatment for the three groups. Did the Mozart group show improvement?
d) Do you think the results prove that listening to Mozart is beneficial? Explain.

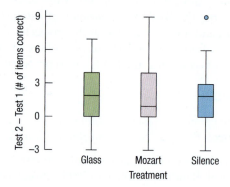

18. More Mozart. An advertisement selling specially designed CDs of Mozart's music specifically because they will "strengthen your mind, heal your body, and unlock your creative spirit" claims that "in Japan, a brewery actually reported that their best sake is made when Mozart is played near the yeast." Suppose you wished to design an experiment to test whether this is true. Assume you have the full cooperation of the sake brewery. Specify how you would design the experiment. Indicate factors and response and how they would be measured, controlled, or randomized.

19. Cereal marketing. The makers of Frumpies, "the breakfast of rug rats," want to improve their marketing, so they consult you.

a) They first want to know what fraction of children, ages 10 to 13, like their celery-flavored cereal. What kind of study should they perform?
b) They are thinking of introducing a new flavor, maple-marshmallow Frumpies and want to know whether children will prefer the new flavor to the old one. Design a completely randomized experiment to investigate this question.
c) They suspect that children who regularly watch the Saturday morning cartoon show starring Frump, the flying teenage warrior rabbit who eats Frumpies in every episode, may respond differently to the new flavor. How would you take that into account in your design?

20. Wine marketing. A Danish study published in the *Archives of Internal Medicine* casts significant doubt on suggestions that adults who drink wine have higher levels of "good" cholesterol and fewer heart attacks. These researchers followed a group of individuals born at a Copenhagen hospital between 1959 and 1961 for 40 years. Their study found that in this group the adults who drank wine were richer and better educated than those who did not.

a) What kind of study was this?
b) It is generally true that people with high levels of education and high socioeconomic status are healthier than others. How does this call into question the supposed health benefits of wine?
c) Can studies such as these prove causation (that wine helps prevent heart attacks, that drinking wine makes one richer, that being rich helps prevent heart attacks, etc.)? Explain.

21. SAT prep courses. Can special study courses actually help raise SAT scores? One organization says that the 30 students they tutored achieved an average gain of 60 points when they retook the test.

a) Explain why this does not necessarily prove that the special course caused the scores to go up.
b) Propose a design for an experiment that could test the effectiveness of the tutorial course.
c) Suppose you suspect that the tutorial course might be more helpful for students whose initial scores were particularly low. How would this affect your proposed design?

22. Safety switch. An industrial machine requires an emergency shutoff switch that must be designed so that it can be easily operated with either hand. Design an experiment to find out whether workers will be able to deactivate the machine as quickly with their left hands as with their right hands. Be sure to explain the role of randomization in your design.

T 23. Cars (fuel efficiency). These boxplots show the relationship between the number of cylinders in a car's engine and its fuel economy from a study conducted by a major car manufacturer.

a) Is this an experiment? Explain.
b) Do the boxplots indicate that cars with more cylinders tend to use more fuel?

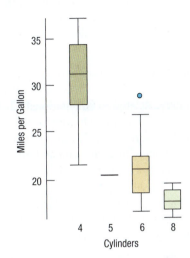

T 24. Wine production. The boxplots display case prices (in dollars) of wine produced by wineries along three of the Finger Lakes in upstate New York.

a) Is this an experiment? Explain.
b) Does there seem to be evidence that prices may differ by location? Explain.

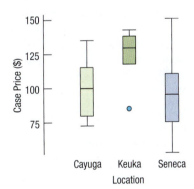

25. Shoes. A running-shoe manufacturer wants to test the effect of its new sprinting shoe on 100-meter dash times. The company sponsors 5 athletes who are running the 100-meter dash in the 2012 Summer Olympic games. To test the shoe, it has all 5 runners run the 100-meter dash with a competitor's shoe and then again with their new shoe. The company uses the difference in times as the response variable.

a) Suggest some improvements to the design.
b) Why might the shoe manufacturer not be able to generalize the results they find to all runners?

26. Swimsuits. A swimsuit manufacturer wants to test the speed of its newly designed suit. The company designs an experiment by having 6 randomly selected Olympic swimmers swim as fast as they can with their old swimsuit first and then swim the same event again with the new, expensive swimsuit. The company will use the difference in times as the response variable. Criticize the experiment and point out some of the problems with generalizing the results.

27. Skydiving, anyone? A humor piece published in the *British Medical Journal* ("Parachute Use to Prevent Death and Major Trauma Related to Gravitational Challenge: Systematic Review of Randomized Control Trials," Gordon, Smith, and Pell, *BMJ*, 2003:327) notes that we can't tell for sure whether parachutes are safe and effective because there has never been a properly randomized, double-blind, placebo-controlled study of parachute effectiveness in skydiving. (Yes, this is the sort of thing statisticians find funny. . . .) Suppose you were designing such a study.

a) What is the factor in this experiment?
b) What experimental units would you propose?[4]
c) What would serve as a placebo for this study?
d) What would the treatments be?
e) What would the response variable be?
f) What sources of variability would you control?
g) How would you randomize this "experiment"?
h) How would you make the experiment double-blind?

28. Coupons and gender. A supermarket wants to see the effects of coupons on spending. They believe that male and female heads of households will respond differently to the coupons. The supermarket chooses 200 males and 200 females, and sends half of each group the coupon, while half receive nothing. The outcome measure is expenditures in the following week.

a) What type of experimental design is this?
b) What are the factors?
c) What is the response variable?
d) Does this experiment satisfy the principles needed for a well-designed experiment?

29. Coupons and gender, part 2. The analyst who designed the experiment in Exercise 28 obtained the data, which is plotted are in the graph below.

a) Is there an interaction effect that is large enough to be worrisome?
b) The regional manager of the chain is having trouble interpreting the results. What conclusions would you draw from the experiment?
c) Is this experiment blinded?

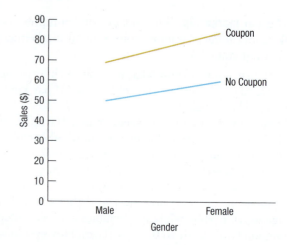

30. Diet and blood pressure. An experiment showed that subjects fed the DASH diet were able to lower their blood pressure by an average of 6.7 points compared to a group fed a "control diet." All meals were prepared by dietitians.

a) Why were the subjects randomly assigned to the diets instead of letting people pick what they wanted to eat?
b) Why were the meals prepared by dieticians?
c) Why did the researchers need the control group? If the DASH diet group's blood pressure was lower at the end of the experiment than at the beginning, wouldn't that prove the effectiveness of that diet?
d) What additional information would you want to know in order to decide whether an average reduction in blood pressure of 6.7 points was statistically significant?

T 31. Contrast baths. Contrast bath treatments use the immersion of an injured limb alternately in water of two contrasting temperatures. Those who use the method claim that it can reduce swelling. Researchers compared three treatments: (1) contrast baths and exercise, (2) contrast baths alone, and (3) exercise alone. (R. G. Janssen, D. A. Schwartz, and P. F. Velleman, "A Randomized Controlled Study of Contrast Baths on Patients with Carpal Tunnel Syndrome," *Journal of Hand Therapy*, 2009.) They report the following boxplots comparing the change in hand volume after treatment:

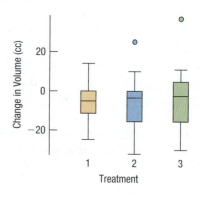

---
[4]Don't include your statistics instructor!

a) The researchers conclude that the differences were not statistically significant. Explain what that means in context.
b) The title says that the study was randomized and controlled. Explain what that probably means for this study.
c) The study did not use a placebo treatment. What was done instead? Do you think that was an appropriate choice? Explain.

32. Wine. A Danish study published in the *Archives of Internal Medicine* casts significant doubt on suggestions that adults who drink wine have higher levels of "good" cholesterol and fewer heart attacks. These researchers followed a group of individuals born at a Copenhagen hospital between 1959 and 1961 for 40 years. Their study found that in this group the adults who drank wine were richer and better educated than those who did not.

a) What kind of study was this?
b) It is generally true that people with high levels of education and high socioeconomic status are healthier than others. How does this call into question the supposed health benefits of wine?
c) Can studies such as these prove causation (that wine helps prevent heart attacks, that drinking wine makes one richer, that being rich helps prevent heart attacks, etc.)? Explain.

33. Swimming. Recently, a group of adults who swim regularly for exercise were evaluated for depression. It turned out that these swimmers were less likely to be depressed than the general population. The researchers said the difference was statistically significant.

a) What does "statistically significant" mean in this context?
b) Is this an experiment or an observational study? Explain.
c) News reports claimed this study proved that swimming can prevent depression. Explain why this conclusion is not justified by the study. Include an example of a possible lurking variable.
d) But perhaps it is true. We wonder if exercise can ward off depression, and whether anaerobic exercise (like weight training) is as effective as aerobic exercise (like swimming). We find 120 volunteers not currently engaged in a regular program of exercise. Design an appropriate experiment.

34. Gamers. A small maker of video games designs a pricing experiment. They know that some teens self-identify as "gamers," while others do not. They market a new video game to gamers and non-gamers, and they send half of each group a rebate worth $10. The results are plotted below.

a) At a company meeting, management says that the data show that rebates work. Is this interpretation correct? Why or why not?
b) Is there an interaction effect? How do you know?
c) Would the rebate strategy be better targeted at gamers or non-gamers?

d) Does this experiment satisfy the principles necessary for a properly designed experiment?
e) Is this experiment double-blind?

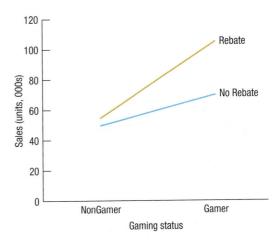

35. Mac and cheese. Kraft foods wants to see whether a coupon will affect sales for macaroni and cheese. Kraft picks a single grocery store in Philadelphia in which to test two coupon types: "buy one, get one free" and "$.50 off." They also want to test whether it matters on which day of the week the coupon gets delivered: Wednesday or Friday. They choose randomly assigned customers to one of the four conditions. They measure success by total sales of Kraft Macaroni and Cheese at the store.

a) What type of experimental design is this?
b) Do you have any concerns about the design?
c) Does this experiment satisfy the necessary conditions for a properly designed experiment?
d) The analyst computes the means for each cell, which appear in the table below. Based on the data, the analyst claims that it does not make a difference whether the coupon is delivered on Wednesday or Friday. Is the analyst correct? Why or why not? Does it help to create the interaction plot?

		Coupon Type		
		Buy-One-Get-One	$.50 off	Mean
Day of Week	Wednesday	500	450	475
	Friday	350	600	475
	Mean	425	525	

36. Data plans. Verizon Wireless wants to test new package deals. They are considering offering three levels of data per month (5 Gb, 10 Gb, Unlimited) and two different international calling options (no international calling, discounted international). They randomly assigned 10,000 customers to receive an offer for each of the six cells corresponding to all combinations of data and international calling. The outcome was the number of customers converting to the offer. Results appear in the table below.

a) Does this experiment satisfy the principles of good design?
b) Is there an interaction effect?
c) Interpret the results in managerial terms.

		Data Plan		
		5 Gb	**10 Gb**	**Unlimited**
International	**No International**	200	300	500
	Discounted International	300	500	1000

37. Gourmet foodies? Giant food stores serves two customer segments: "Budget Shoppers" and "Foodies." Giant sends 1000 of each type of customer one of two circulars: Deep Discounts or Gourmet Food. The response is the total amount spent at Giant stores over the next week.

a) What type of experimental design is this?
b) Draw the diagram associated with this design.
c) Does this design have any issues that should be worrisome?
d) The Giant analyst plots the means of each treatment condition in the interaction plot below. She concludes that "Foodies are wealthier, and spend more on food in general. Nonetheless, each segment is affected positively by the advertisement that most appeals to them, and negatively by less appealing ads. This accounts for the 'crossover' pattern: Foodies decrease spending but the Budget segment increases spending when sent the Deep Discount circular. The reverse is true for the Gourmet Food circular." Critique the analyst's conclusions.

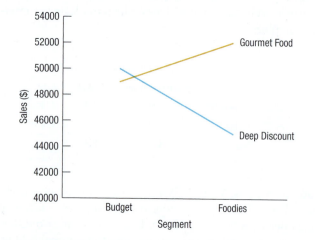

38. Dowsing. Before drilling for water, many rural homeowners hire a dowser (a person who claims to be able to sense the presence of underground water using a forked stick). Suppose we wish to set up an experiment to test one

dowser's ability. We get 20 identical containers, fill some with water, and ask him to tell which ones they are.

a) How will we randomize this procedure?
b) The dowser correctly identifies the contents of 12 out of 20 containers. Do you think this level of success is more likely due to chance or skill? Explain.
c) How many correct identifications (out of 20) would the dowser have to make to convince you that the forked-stick trick works? Explain.

39. Healing. A medical researcher suspects that giving post-surgical patients large doses of vitamin E will speed their recovery times by helping their incisions heal more quickly. Design an experiment to test this conjecture. Be sure to identify the factors, levels, treatments, response variable, and the role of randomization.

40. Reading. Some schools teach reading using phonics (the sounds made by letters) and others using whole language (word recognition). Suppose a school district wants to know which method works better. Suggest a design for an appropriate experiment.

41. Gas mileage. Do cars get better gas mileage with premium instead of regular unleaded gasoline? It might be possible to test some engines in a laboratory, but we'd rather use real cars and real drivers in real day-to-day driving, so we get 20 volunteers. Design the experiment.

42. Weekend deaths. A study published in the *New England Journal of Medicine* (Aug. 2001) suggests that it's dangerous to enter a hospital on a weekend. During a 10-year period, researchers tracked over 4 million emergency admissions to hospitals in Ontario, Canada. Their findings revealed that patients admitted on weekends had a much higher risk of death than those who went on weekdays.

a) What kind of study was this? Explain.
b) If you think you're quite ill on a Saturday, should you wait until Monday to seek medical help? Explain.
c) Suggest some possible explanations for this troubling finding.

43. Shingles. A research doctor has discovered a new ointment that she believes will be more effective than the current medication in the treatment of shingles (a painful skin rash). Eight patients have volunteered to participate in the initial trials of this ointment. You are the statistician hired as a consultant to help design an experiment.

a) Describe how you will conduct this experiment.
b) Suppose the eight patients' last names start with the letters A to H. Using the random numbers listed below, show which patients you will assign to each treatment. Explain your randomization procedure clearly.

41098 18329 78458 31685 55259

c) Can you make this experiment double-blind? How?

d) The initial experiment revealed that males and females may respond differently to the ointment. Further testing of the drug's effectiveness is now planned, and many patients have volunteered. What changes in your first design, if any, would you make for this second stage of testing?

44. Beetles. Hoping to learn how to control crop damage by a certain species of beetle, a researcher plans to test two different pesticides in small plots of corn. A few days after application of the chemicals, he'll check the number of beetle larvae found on each plant. The researcher wants to know whether either pesticide works and whether there is a significant difference in effectiveness between them. Design an appropriate experiment.

45. SAT prep. Can special study courses actually help raise SAT scores? One organization says that the 30 students they tutored achieved an average gain of 60 points when they retook the test.

a) Explain why this does not necessarily prove that the special course caused the scores to go up.

b) Propose a design for an experiment that could test the effectiveness of the tutorial course.

c) Suppose you suspect that the tutorial course might be more helpful for students whose initial scores were particularly low. How would this affect your proposed design?

46. Safety switch. An industrial machine requires an emergency shutoff switch that must be designed so that it can be easily operated with either hand. Design an experiment to find out whether workers will be able to deactivate the machine as quickly with their left hands as with their right hands. Be sure to explain the role of randomization in your design.

47. Washing clothes. A consumer group wants to test the effectiveness of a new "organic" laundry detergent and make recommendations to customers about how to best use the product. They intentionally stain 30 white T-shirts with grass in order to see how well the detergent will clean them. They want to try the detergent in cold water and in hot water on both the "regular" and "delicates" wash cycles. Design an appropriate experiment, indicating the number of factors, levels, and treatments. Explain the role of randomization in your experiment.

JUST CHECKING ANSWERS

1 Gather reports from veterinarians and pet hospitals. Look into the histories of sick animals. This would be a retrospective observational study.

2 Treatment: Feed the new food and a previously tested, known to be safe, food to pets.

Response: Judge the health of the animals, possibly by having a veterinarian examine them before and after the feeding trials.

3 Control by choosing similar animals. Perhaps choose just one breed and test animals of the same age and health. Treat them otherwise the same in terms of exercise, attention, and so on.

Randomize by assigning animals to treatments at random.

Replicate by having more than one animal fed each formulation.

4 A control group could be fed a standard laboratory food, if we have one known to be safe. Otherwise we could prepare a special food in our test kitchens to be certain of its safety.

5 The veterinarian evaluating the animals should be blind to the treatments. For double-blinding, all technicians handling the animals should also be blinded. That would require making the control food look as much like the test food as possible.

6 Yes. Test dogs and cats separately.

7 Word length and familiarity

8 A significant interaction effect implies that the effect of one factor is not the same for the levels of another. Thus, it is saying that the effect of the four offers is not the same for those living in the NE corridor as it is for those who do not. This could impact where Amtrak decides to advertise the offers, or to whom they decide to send them.

9 Only the combination of unlimited data and free international calls seems to have changed the response rate. There is a strong interaction between the data and international calls offers.

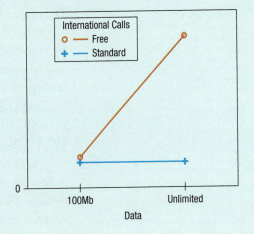

CHAPTER 10

Sampling Distributions and Confidence Intervals for Proportions

Marketing Credit Cards: The MBNA Story

When Delaware substantially raised its interest rate ceiling in 1981, banks and other lending institutions rushed to establish corporate headquarters there. One of these was the Maryland Bank National Association, which established a credit card branch in Delaware using the name MBNA. Starting in 1982 with 250 employees in a vacant supermarket in Ogletown, Delaware, MBNA grew explosively in the next two decades.

One of the reasons for this growth was MBNA's use of affinity groups—issuing cards endorsed by alumni associations, sports teams, interest groups, and labor unions, among others. MBNA sold the idea to these groups by letting them share a small percentage of the profit. By 2006, MBNA had become Delaware's largest private employer. At its peak, MBNA had more than 50 million cardholders and had outstanding credit card loans of $82.1 billion, making MBNA the third-largest U.S. credit card bank.

"In American corporate history, I doubt there are many companies that burned as brightly, for such a short period of time, as MBNA," said Rep. Mike Castle, R-Del.[1] MBNA was bought by Bank of America in 2005 for $35 billion. Bank of America kept the brand briefly before issuing all cards under its own name in 2007.

---

[1]Delaware *News Online*, January 1, 2006.

nlike the early days of the credit card industry when MBNA established itself, the environment today is intensely competitive, with companies constantly looking for ways to attract new customers and to maximize the profitability of the customers they already have. Many of the large companies have millions of customers, so instead of trying out a new idea with all their customers, they almost always conduct a pilot study or trial first, conducting a survey or an experiment on a sample of their customers.

Credit card companies make money on their cards in three ways: They earn a percentage of every transaction, they charge interest on balances that are not paid in full, and they collect fees (yearly fees, late fees, etc.). To generate all three types of revenue, the marketing departments of credit card banks constantly seek ways to encourage customers to increase the use of their cards.

A marketing specialist at one company has an idea of offering double air miles to their customers with an airline-affiliated card if they increase their spending by at least $800 in the month following the offer. Of course, offering double miles is not free. The company has to pay the airline for the added miles they give away. Her finance department tells her that if 20% of all customers increase spending by $800 then, based on past behavior, the double miles offer will be profitable. Unfortunately, she can't know what *all* customers will do until it's too late. So, she decides to send the offer to a random sample of 1000 customers. In that sample, she finds that 211 (21.1%) of the cardholders increase their spending by more than the required $800. Is that good enough? Could another sample of 1000 *different* people show 19.5%? If results vary from sample to sample how can we make good decisions? Variation like this is sometimes called **sampling error** even though no error has been committed. A better name for this variation that you'd expect to see from sample to sample might be **sampling variability**.

Even though we can't control this variability we can *predict* exactly how much different proportions will vary from sample to sample. This will enable us to make sound business decisions based on a single sample.

WHO	Cardholders of a bank's credit card
WHAT	Proportion of cardholders who increase their spending by at least $800 in the subsequent month
WHEN	Now
WHERE	United States
WHY	To predict costs and benefits of a program offer

10.1 The Distribution of Sample Proportions

Our marketing manager can't know p, the actual proportion of all cardholders who will increase their spending by more than $800. Her experiment with 1000 cardholders provides only one sample proportion, $\hat{p} = \dfrac{211}{1000} = 0.211$. So how can this single experiment provide useful information?

If we could see how proportions vary across all possible samples that she could have taken, that might help us make decisions about what a *single* experiment can tell us. One way to do that is to *simulate* lots of samples of the same size using the same population proportion. Here's a histogram of 10,000 sample proportions, each for a random sample of size 1000, using $p = 0.2$ as the true proportion:

FIGURE 10.1 A histogram of 10,000 samples of size 1000 with a true proportion of 0.20. Most of the samples have proportions between 0.175 and 0.225 and nearly all have proportions between 0.16 and 0.24.

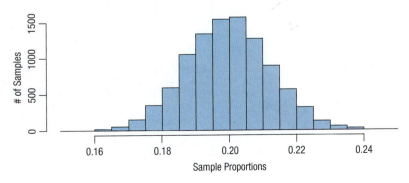

Imagine

We see only the sample we actually drew. If we *imagine* the results of all the other possible samples we could have drawn (by modeling or simulating them), we can learn more.

The Sampling Distribution for a Proportion

We have now answered the question raised at the start of the chapter. To discover how variable a sample proportion is, we need to know the proportion and the size of the sample. That's all.

Effect of Sample Size

Because n is in the denominator of $SD(\hat{p})$, the larger the sample, the smaller the standard deviation. We need a small standard deviation to make sound business decisions, but larger samples cost more. That tension is a fundamental issue in statistics.

What can we see about this distribution? First, not every sample has a sample proportion equal to 0.2. We know that sample proportions vary, and this distribution shows that variation. For example, we can see that sample proportions bigger than 0.24 and smaller than 0.16 are rare, and that most of the sample proportions are between 0.18 and 0.22. From the 10,000 samples, we can also compute the standard deviation of these sample proportions to see how much they vary. In this simulation the standard deviation is 0.0126, or 1.26%. The 68–95–99.7 Rule tells us to expect 95% of the sample proportions to be within 2×0.0126 of the mean (which is 0.20). That is, we expect 95% of the sample proportions to be in the interval (0.175, 0.225) and 99.7% within 3×0.0126 of 0.20 (0.162, 0.238). This matches the histogram pretty well.

The histogram in Figure 10.1 shows a simulation of the **sampling distribution** of $\hat{p}$. The theoretical sampling distribution is the distribution of all the sample proportions that would arise from all possible samples of the same size with a constant probability of a "success."

We actually didn't need to simulate this sampling distribution. We know, from Chapter 7, that the number of successes can be modeled by a Binomial, which, in turn, can be modeled by a Normal distribution as long as np and nq are large enough. The sample proportion is just the number of successes, X, divided by n, so if the distribution of X is Normal, the distribution of $\hat{p}$ should have the same shape. And we know that it should be centered at the true proportion p and have standard deviation $\sqrt{\dfrac{pq}{n}}$. Let's see how well that matches our simulation: $\sqrt{\dfrac{pq}{n}} = \sqrt{\dfrac{(0.2)(0.8)}{1000}} = 0.0126$. Pretty good! With a sample size this large, the Normal approximation really works well.

So, we can say that the sampling distribution of a sample proportion from a sample of size n with true proportion p is Normal with mean p and standard deviation $\sqrt{\dfrac{pq}{n}}$. Here's a picture of that sampling distribution model:

FIGURE 10.2   A Normal model centered at p with a standard deviation of $\sqrt{\dfrac{pq}{n}}$ is a good model for a collection of proportions found for many random samples of size n from a population with success probability p.

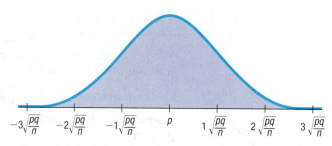

$$-3\sqrt{\dfrac{pq}{n}} \quad -2\sqrt{\dfrac{pq}{n}} \quad -1\sqrt{\dfrac{pq}{n}} \quad p \quad 1\sqrt{\dfrac{pq}{n}} \quad 2\sqrt{\dfrac{pq}{n}} \quad 3\sqrt{\dfrac{pq}{n}}$$

The Sampling Distribution Model for a Proportion

Provided that the sampled values are independent and the sample size is large enough, the sampling distribution of $\hat{p}$ is modeled by a Normal model with mean $\mu(\hat{p}) = p$ and standard deviation $SD(\hat{p}) = \sqrt{\dfrac{pq}{n}}$.

IN PRACTICE 10.1   The distribution of a sample proportion

A supermarket has installed "self-checkout" stations that allow customers to scan and bag their own groceries. These are popular, but because customers occasionally encounter a problem, a staff member must be available to help out. The manager wants to estimate what proportion of customers need help so that he can optimize the number of self-check stations per staff member. He collects data from the stations for 30 days, recording the proportion of customers on each day that need help and makes a histogram of the observed proportions.

MANAGER I see that the proportions are different from day to day. How can we make sense of them?

ANALYST We can assume that each day's proportion is independent of the other days—that is, knowing what happens on one day won't tell us what happens on another. There's a theorem that says the proportions will tend to follow a Normal, or bell-shaped, distribution. There is a possible problem with assuming independence from day to day. For example, shoppers on weekends might be less experienced than regular weekday shoppers and would then need more help.

JUST CHECKING

1 You want to poll a random sample of 100 shopping mall customers about whether they like the proposed location for the new coffee shop on the third floor, with a panoramic view of the food court. Of course, you'll get just one number, your sample proportion, $\hat{p}$. But if you imagined all the possible samples of 100 customers you could draw and imagined the histogram of all the sample proportions from these samples, what shape would it have?

2 Where would the center of that histogram be?

3 If you think that about half the customers are in favor of the plan, what would the standard deviation of the sample proportions be?

How Good Is the Normal Model?

We've seen that the sampling distribution of proportions follows the 68–95–99.7 Rule well. But do all sample proportions really work like this? Stop and think for a minute about what we're claiming. We've said that if we draw repeated random samples of the same size, n, from some population and measure the proportion, $\hat{p}$, we get for each sample, then the collection of these proportions will pile up around the underlying population proportion, p, in such a way that a histogram of the sample proportions can be modeled well by a Normal model.

There must be a catch. Suppose the samples were of size 2, for example. Then the only possible numbers of successes could be 0, 1, or 2, and the proportion values would be 0, 0.5, and 1. There's no way the histogram could ever look like a Normal model with only three possible values for the variable (Figure 10.3).

Well, there *is* a slight catch. The claim is only approximately true. But, the model becomes a better and better representation of the distribution of the sample proportions as the sample size gets bigger.[2] That's one reason we require np and nq to be at least 10. But the distributions of proportions from samples of the size you're likely to see in business do have histograms that are remarkably close to a Normal model.

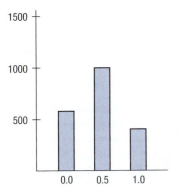

FIGURE 10.3 Proportions from samples of size 2 can take on only three possible values. A Normal model does not work well here.

IN PRACTICE 10.2 Sampling distribution for proportions

Spectrum provides cable, phone, and Internet services to customers, some of whom subscribe to "packages" including several services. Nationwide, suppose that 30% of their customers are "package subscribers" and subscribe to all three types of service. A local manager in Phoenix, Arizona, wonders if the proportion in his region is the same as the national proportion.

(continued)

---

[2]Formally, we say the claim is true in the limit as the sample size (n) grows.

> **MANAGER** I plan to survey 100 customers at random from our subscriber list. What should that sample tell us about our customer base?
>
> **ANALYST** We can tell quite a lot from the sample. If it is taken at random, then I expect the respondents will be mutually independent. Then because 30% of customers nationwide are package subscribers, we would expect the same for the sample proportion.
>
> The standard deviation is $SD(\hat{p}) = \sqrt{\dfrac{pq}{n}} = \sqrt{\dfrac{(0.3)(0.7)}{100}} = 0.046$.
>
> The shape of the sampling distribution of the proportion is Normal.
>
> **MANAGER** We've observed 49 customers who are package subscribers. Should we be surprised?
>
> **ANALYST** 49 customers results in a sample proportion of 0.49. The mean is 0.30 with a standard deviation of 0.046. This sample proportion is more than 4 standard deviations higher than the mean: $\dfrac{(0.49 - 0.30)}{0.046} = 4.13$. It would be very unusual to find such a large proportion in a random sample. Either it is a very unusual sample, or the proportion in your region is not the same as the national average.

Assumptions and Conditions

Most models are useful only when specific assumptions are true. In the case of the model for the distribution of sample proportions, there are two assumptions:

Independence Assumption: The sampled values must be *independent* of each other.

Sample Size Assumption: The sample size, n, must be *large* enough.

Of course, the best we can do with assumptions is to think about whether they are likely to be true, and we should do so. However, we often can check corresponding *conditions* that provide information about the assumptions as well. Think about the Independence Assumption and check the following corresponding conditions before using the Normal model to model the distribution of sample proportions:

Randomization Condition: If your data come from an experiment, subjects should have been randomly assigned to treatments. If you have a survey, your sample should be a simple random sample of the population. If some other sampling design was used, be sure the sampling method was not biased and that the data are representative of the population.

10% Condition: If sampling has not been made with replacement (that is, returning each sampled individual to the population before drawing the next individual), then the sample size, n, should be no larger than 10% of the population. If it is, you must adjust the size of the confidence interval with methods more advanced than those found in this book.

Success/Failure Condition: The Success/Failure Condition says that the sample size must be big enough so that both the number of "successes," np, and the number of "failures," nq, are expected to be at least 10. Expressed without the symbols, this condition just says that we need to expect at least 10 successes and at least 10 failures to have enough data for sound conclusions. For the bank's credit card promotion example, we labeled as a "success" a cardholder who increases monthly spending by at least $800 during the trial. The bank observed 211 successes and 789 failures. Both are at least 10, so there are certainly enough successes and enough failures for the condition to be satisfied.[3]

These two conditions seem to contradict each other. The Success/Failure Condition wants a big sample size. How big depends on *p*. If *p* is near 0.5, we need a sample of only 20 or so. If *p* is only 0.01, however, we'd need 1000. But the 10% Condition says that the sample size can't be too large a fraction of the population. Fortunately, the tension between them isn't usually a problem in practice. Often, as in polls that sample from all U.S. adults, or industrial samples from a day's production, the populations are much larger than 10 times the sample size.

IN PRACTICE 10.3   Assumptions and conditions for sample proportions

The analyst conducting the Spectrum survey says that, unfortunately, only 20 of the customers he tried to contact actually responded, but that of those 20, 8 are package subscribers.

MANAGER I have been expecting 30% of customers to be subscribers. Was it unusual to find 8 subscribers out of 20? Can we be sure?

ANALYST We would have expected $0.30 \times 20 = 6$ package subscribers but, because 6 is less than 10, we should be cautious in using the Normal as a model for the sampling distribution of proportions. (The number of *observed* successes, 8, is also less than 10.)

GUIDED EXAMPLE   Foreclosures

An analyst at a home loan lender was looking at a package of 90 mortgages that the company had recently purchased in central California. The analyst was aware that in that region about 13% of the homeowners with current mortgages will default on their loans in the next year and the houses will go into foreclosure. In deciding to buy the collection of mortgages, the finance department assumed that no more than 15 of the mortgages would go into default. Any amount above that will result in losses for the company. In the package of 90 mortgages, what's the probability that there will be more than 15 foreclosures?

| **PLAN** **Define** the problem. | We want to find the probability that in a group of 90 mortgages, more than 15 will default. Since 15 out of 90 is 16.7%, we need the probability of finding more than 16.7% defaults out of a sample of 90, if the proportion of defaults is 13%. |

(continued)

---

[3]The Success/Failure Condition is about the number of successes and failures we *expect*, but if the number of successes and failures that *occurred* is ≥10, then you can use that.

DO **Model** Check the conditions.

✔ **Independence Assumption** If the mortgages come from a wide geographical area, one homeowner defaulting should not affect the probability that another does. However, if the mortgages come from the same neighborhood(s), the Independence Assumption may fail and our estimates of the default probabilities may be wrong.

✔ **Randomization Condition.** For the question asked, these 90 mortgages in the package can be considered as a random sample of mortgages in the region. If there are too many failures, we may doubt that they are a representative sample.

✔ **10% Condition.** The 90 mortgages are less than 10% of the population.

✔ **Success/Failure Condition**

$$np = 90(0.13) = 11.7 \geq 10$$
$$nq = 90(0.87) = 78.3 \geq 10$$

Identify the parameters and the sampling distribution model.

The population proportion is $p = 0.13$. The conditions are satisfied, so we'll model the sampling distribution of $\hat{p}$ with a Normal model, with mean 0.13 and standard deviation

$$SD(\hat{p}) = \sqrt{\frac{pq}{n}} = \sqrt{\frac{(0.13)(0.87)}{90}} \approx 0.035.$$

Our model for $\hat{p}$ is $N(0.13, 0.035)$. We want to find $P(\hat{p} > 0.167)$.

Explore Make a picture. Sketch the model and shade the area we're interested in, in this case the area to the right of 16.7%.

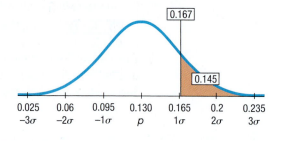

Mechanics Use the standard deviation as a ruler to find the z-score of the cutoff proportion. Find the resulting probability from a table, a computer program, or a calculator.

$$z = \frac{\hat{p} - p}{SD(\hat{p})} = \frac{0.167 - 0.13}{0.035} = 1.06$$

$$P(\hat{p} > 0.167) = P(z > 1.06) = 0.1446$$

REPORT **Communicate and Present** Interpret the probability in the context of the question.

MEMO

Re: Mortgage defaults

Assuming that the 90 mortgages we recently purchased are a random sample of mortgages in this region, there is about a 14.5% chance that we will exceed the 15 foreclosures that Finance has determined as the break-even point.

10.2 A Confidence Interval for a Proportion

To plan their inventory and production needs, businesses use a variety of forecasts about the economy. One important attribute is consumer confidence in the overall economy. Tracking changes in consumer confidence over time can help businesses gauge whether the demand for their products is on an upswing or about to experience a downturn. The Gallup Poll periodically asks a random sample of U.S. adults whether they think economic conditions are getting better, getting worse, or staying about the same. When Gallup polled 3559 respondents in April 2013 (during the week ending April 21), only 1495 thought economic conditions in the United States were getting better—a sample proportion of $\hat{p} = 1495/3559 = 42\%$. We (and Gallup) hope that this observed proportion is close to the population proportion, p, but we know that a second sample of 3559 adults wouldn't have a sample proportion of exactly 42.0%. In fact, Gallup did sample another group of adults just a few days later and found a slightly different sample proportion.

What can we say about consumer confidence in the entire population when the proportion that we measure keeps bouncing around from sample to sample? That's where the sampling distribution model can help. By knowing how much they vary and the shape of their distribution, we'll get a clearer idea of where the true proportion might be and how much we know about it. So, what do we know about our sampling distribution model? We know that it's centered at the true proportion, p, of all U.S. adults who think the economy is improving. But we don't know p. It probably isn't 42.0%. That's the $\hat{p}$ from our sample. What we do know is that the sampling distribution model of $\hat{p}$ is centered at p, and we know that the standard deviation of the sampling distribution is $\sqrt{\dfrac{pq}{n}}$. We also know that the shape of the sampling distribution is approximately Normal, when the sample is large enough.

This is all fine in the model world, but we need to solve problems in the real world. In the real world, we don't know p. (If we did, we wouldn't have bothered to take a sample.) And so, we don't know $\sqrt{pq/n}$ either. But, we'll do the best we can and *estimate* it by using $\sqrt{\hat{p}\hat{q}/n}$. That may not seem like a big deal, but it gets a special name. Whenever we estimate the standard deviation of a sampling distribution, we call it a **standard error (SE)**. Using $\hat{p}$, we find the standard error:

$$SE(\hat{p}) = \sqrt{\frac{\hat{p}\hat{q}}{n}} = \sqrt{\frac{(0.42)(1 - 0.42)}{3559}} = 0.008$$

Now, we use that to draw our best guess of the sampling distribution for the true proportion who think the economy is getting better as shown in Figure 10.4.

FIGURE 10.4 The sampling distribution of sample proportions from samples of size 3559 is centered at the true proportion, p, with a standard deviation of 0.008.

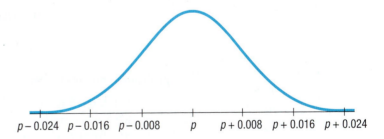

Because the sampling distribution is Normal, we expect that about 68% of all samples of 3559 U.S. adults taken in April 2013 would have sample proportions within 1 standard deviation of p. And about 95% of all these samples will have proportions within $p \pm 2$ SEs. But where is *our* sample proportion in this picture? And what value does p really have? We still don't know!

We do know that for 95% of random samples, $\hat{p}$ will be no more than 2 SEs away from p. So here's the key to using sampling distributions. Let's reverse it and look at it from $\hat{p}$'s point of view. If I'm $\hat{p}$, there's a 95% chance that p is no more than 2 SEs away from me. If I reach out 2 SEs, or 2×0.008, away from me on both sides, I'm 95% sure that p will be within my grasp.

FIGURE 10.5 Reaching out 2 *SEs* on either side of $\hat{p}$ makes us 95% confident we'll trap the true proportion, *p*.

ACME *p*-trap: Guaranteed*
to capture *p*.

*with 95% confidence

$\hat{p} - 2\ SE$ $\hat{p}$ $\hat{p} + 2\ SE$

What Can We Say About a Proportion?

So what can we really say about *p*? Of course, I'm not *sure* that my interval catches *p*. And I don't know its true value, but I can state a probability that I've covered the true value in an interval. Here's a list of things we'd like to be able to say and the reasons we can't say most of them:

1. **"42.0% of *all* U.S. adults thought the economy was improving."** It would be nice to be able to make absolute statements about population values with certainty, but we just don't have enough information to do that. There's no way to be sure that the population proportion is the same as the sample proportion; in fact, it almost certainly isn't. Observations vary. Another sample would yield a different sample proportion.

2. **"It is *probably* true that 42.0% of all U.S. adults thought the economy was improving."** No. In fact, we can be pretty sure that whatever the true proportion is, it's not exactly 42.0%, so the statement is not true.

3. **"We don't know exactly what proportion of U.S. adults thought the economy was improving, but we know that it's within the interval 42.0% ± 2 × 0.8%. That is, it's between 40.4% and 43.6%."** This is getting closer, but we still can't be certain. We can't know for sure that the true proportion is in this interval—or in any particular range.

4. **"We don't know exactly what proportion of U.S. adults thought the economy was improving, but the interval from 40.4% to 43.6% *probably* contains the true proportion."** Close! Now, we've fudged twice—first by giving an interval and second by admitting that we only think the interval "probably" contains the true value.

That last statement is true, but it's a bit wishy-washy. We can tighten it up by quantifying what we mean by "probably." We saw that 95% of the time when we reach out 2 SEs from $\hat{p}$, we capture *p*, *so we can be 95% confident that this is one of those times*. After putting a number on the probability that this interval covers the true proportion, we've given our best guess of where the parameter is and how certain we are that it's within some range.

5. **"We are 95% confident that between 40.4% and 43.6% of U.S. adults thought the economy was improving."** Statements like this are called **confidence intervals**. They don't tell us everything we might want to know, but they're the best we can do.

Each confidence interval discussed in this text has a name. You'll see many different kinds of confidence intervals in the following chapters. Some will be about more than *one* sample, some will be about statistics other than *proportions*, and some

> Far better an approximate answer to the right question, . . . than an exact answer to the wrong question.
>
> —John W. Tukey

will use models other than the Normal. The interval calculated and interpreted here is an example of a **one-proportion z-interval**.[4] We'll lay out the formal definition in the next few pages.

IN PRACTICE 10.4   Finding a 95% confidence interval for a proportion

The Chamber of Commerce of a mid-sized city has supported a proposal to change the zoning laws for a new part of town. The new regulations would allow for mixed commercial and residential development. The vote on the measure is scheduled for three weeks from today, and the president of the Chamber of Commerce is concerned that they may not have the majority of votes that they will need to pass the measure. She commissions a survey that asks likely voters if they plan to vote for the measure. Of the 516 people selected at random from likely voters, 289 said they would likely vote for the measure.

CHAMBER PRESIDENT I know that a survey will have a margin of error. What can you tell me about the true proportion of voters who will vote for the measure?

ANALYST We would estimate the proportion and margin of error like this:

$$\hat{p} = \frac{289}{516} = 0.56 \qquad \text{So, } SE(\hat{p}) = \sqrt{\frac{\hat{p}\hat{q}}{n}} = \sqrt{\frac{(0.56)(0.44)}{516}} = 0.022$$

A 95% confidence interval for p can be found from $\hat{p} \pm 2\,SE(\hat{p}) = 0.56 \pm 2(0.022) = (0.516, 0.604)$ or 51.6% to 60.4%.

We are 95% confident that the true proportion of voters who plan to vote for the measure is between 51.6% and 60.4%. This assumes that the sample we have is representative of all likely voters.

What Does "95% Confidence" Really Mean?

What do we mean when we say we have 95% confidence that our interval contains the true proportion? Formally, what we mean is that "95% of samples of this size will produce confidence intervals that capture the true proportion." This is correct but a little long-winded, so we sometimes say "we are 95% confident that the true proportion lies in our interval." Our uncertainty is about whether the particular sample we have at hand is one of the successful ones or one of the 5% that fail to produce an interval that captures the true value. In this chapter, we have seen how proportions vary from sample to sample. If other pollsters had selected their own samples of adults, they would have found some who thought the economy was getting better, but each sample proportion would almost certainly differ from ours. When they each tried to estimate the true proportion, they'd center their confidence intervals at the proportions they observed in their own samples. Each would have ended up with a different interval.

Figure 10.6 shows the confidence intervals produced by simulating 20 samples. The purple dots are the simulated proportions of adults in each sample who thought the economy was improving, and the orange segments show the confidence intervals found for each simulated sample. The green line represents the true percentage of adults who thought the economy was improving. You can see that most of the simulated confidence intervals include the true value—but one missed. (Note that it is the *intervals* that vary from sample to sample; the green line doesn't move.)

---

[4]In fact, this confidence interval is so standard for a single proportion that you may see it simply called a "confidence interval for the proportion."

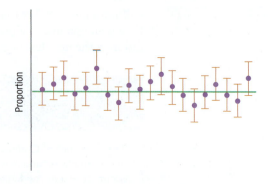

FIGURE 10.6 The horizontal green line shows the true proportion of people in April 2013 who thought the economy was improving. Most of the 20 simulated samples shown here produced 95% confidence intervals that captured the true value, but one missed.

Of course, a huge number of possible samples *could* be drawn, each with its own sample proportion. This simulation approximates just some of them. Each sample can be used to make a confidence interval. That's a large pile of possible confidence intervals, and ours is just one of those in the pile. Did *our* confidence interval "work"? We can never be sure because we'll never know the true proportion of all U.S. adults who thought in April 2013 that the economy was improving. However, the Normal model assures us that 95% of the intervals in the pile are winners, covering the true value, and only 5%, on average, miss the target. That's why we're 95% *confident* that our interval is a winner.

The statements we made about what all U.S. adults thought about the economy were possible because we used a Normal model for the sampling distribution. But is that model appropriate?

As we've seen, all statistical models make assumptions. If those assumptions are not true, the model might be inappropriate, and our conclusions based on it may be wrong. Because the confidence interval is built on the Normal model for the sampling distribution, the assumptions and conditions are the same as those we discussed in Section 10.1. But, because they are so important, we'll go over them again.

You can never be certain that an assumption is true, but you can decide intelligently whether it is reasonable. When you have data, you can often decide whether an assumption is plausible by checking a related condition in the data. However, you'll want to make a statement about the world at large, not just about the data. So the assumptions you make are not just about how the data look, but about how representative they are.

Here are the assumptions and the corresponding conditions to check before creating (or believing) a confidence interval about a proportion.

Independence Assumption

You first need to think about whether the Independence Assumption is plausible. You can look for reasons to suspect that it fails. You might wonder whether there is any reason to believe that the data values somehow affect each other. (For example, might any of the adults in the sample be related?) This condition depends on your knowledge of the situation. It's not one you can check by looking at the data. However, now that you have data, there are two conditions that you can check:

- **Randomization Condition:** Were the data sampled at random or generated from a properly randomized experiment? Proper randomization can help ensure independence.
- **10% Condition:** Samples are almost always drawn without replacement. Usually, you'd like to have as large a sample as you can. But if you sample from a small population, the probability of success may be different for the last few individuals you draw than it was for the first few. For example, if most of the women have already been sampled, the chance of drawing a woman from the remaining population is lower. If the sample exceeds 10% of the population,

you will have to adjust the margin of error with methods more advanced than those found in this text. But if less than 10% of the population is sampled, it is safe to proceed without adjustment.

Sample Size Assumption

The model we use for inference is based on the Normal model. So, the sample must be large enough for the Normal sampling model to be appropriate. It turns out that we need more data when the proportion is close to either extreme (0 or 1). This requirement is easy to check with the following condition:

- **Success/Failure Condition:** We must expect our sample to contain at least 10 "successes" and at least 10 "failures." Recall that by tradition we arbitrarily label one alternative (usually the outcome being counted) as a "success" even if it's something bad. The other alternative is then a "failure." So we check that both $n\hat{p} \geq 10$ and $n\hat{q} \geq 10$.

IN PRACTICE 10.5   Assumptions and conditions for a confidence interval for proportions

We previously reported a confidence interval to the president of the Chamber of Commerce.

CHAMBER PRESIDENT Can we really trust this estimate? Were the assumptions and conditions for making this interval satisfied?

ANALYST Because the sample was randomized, we assume that the responses of the people surveyed were independent so the Randomization Condition is met. We assume that 516 people represent fewer than 10% of the likely voters in the town so the 10% Condition is met. Because 289 people said they were likely to vote for the measure and thus 227 said they were not, both are much larger than 10 so the Success/Failure Condition is also met.

All the conditions to make a confidence interval for the proportion appear to have been satisfied.

10.3 Margin of Error: Certainty vs. Precision

We've just claimed that at a certain confidence level we've captured the true proportion of all U.S. adults who thought the economy was improving in April 2013. Our confidence interval stretched out the same distance on either side of the estimated proportion with the form:

$$\hat{p} \pm 2\,SE(\hat{p}).$$

The *extent* of that interval on either side of $\hat{p}$ is called the **margin of error (ME)**. In general, confidence intervals look like this:

$$estimate \pm ME.$$

The margin of error for our 95% confidence interval was 2 SEs. What if we wanted to be more confident? To be more confident, we'd need to capture p more often, and to do that, we'd need to make the interval wider. For example, if we want to be 99.7% confident, the margin of error will have to be 3 SEs.

The more confident we want to be, the larger the margin of error must be. We can be 100% confident that any proportion is between 0% and 100%, but that's

> **Confidence Intervals**
>
> We'll see many confidence intervals in this text. All have the form:
>
> $$estimate \pm ME.$$
>
> For proportions at 95% confidence:
>
> $$ME \approx 2\,SE(\hat{p}).$$

FIGURE 10.7 Reaching out 3 SEs on either side of $\hat{p}$ makes us 99.7% confident we'll trap the true proportion p. Compare the width of this interval with the interval in Figure 10.5.

$\hat{p} - 3\ SE$ $\hat{p}$ $\hat{p} + 3\ SE$

not very useful. Or we could give a narrow confidence interval, say, from 41.98% to 42.02%. But we couldn't be very confident about a statement this precise. Every confidence interval is a balance between certainty and precision.

The tension between certainty and precision is always there. There is no simple answer to the conflict. Fortunately, in most cases we can be both sufficiently certain and sufficiently precise to make useful statements. The choice of confidence level is somewhat arbitrary, but you must choose the level yourself. The data can't do it for you. The most commonly chosen confidence levels are 90%, 95%, and 99%, but any percentage can be used. (In practice, though, using something like 92.9% or 97.2% might be viewed with suspicion.)

Critical Values

In our opening example, our margin of error was 2 SEs, which produced a 95% confidence interval. To change the confidence level, we'll need to change the *number* of SEs to correspond to the new level. A wider confidence interval means more confidence. For any confidence level, the number of SEs we must stretch out on either side of $\hat{p}$ is called the **critical value**. Because it is based on the Normal model, we denote it z^*. For any confidence level, we can find the corresponding critical value from a computer, a calculator, or a Normal probability table, such as Table Z in the back of the book.

For a 95% confidence interval, the precise critical value is $z^* = 1.96$. That is, 95% of a Normal model is found within ± 1.96 standard deviations of the mean. We've been using $z^* = 2$ from the 68–95–99.7 Rule because 2 is very close to 1.96 and is easier to remember. Usually, the difference is negligible, but if you want to be precise, use 1.96.[5]

Suppose we could be satisfied with 90% confidence. What critical value would we need? We can use a smaller margin of error. Our greater precision is offset by

Some common confidence levels and their associated critical values:

CI	z^*
90%	1.645
95%	1.960
99%	2.576

---

[5] It's been suggested that since 1.96 is both an unusual value and so important in statistics, you can recognize someone who's had a statistics course by just saying "1.96" and seeing whether they react.

our acceptance of being wrong more often (that is, having a confidence interval that misses the true value). Specifically, for a 90% confidence interval, the critical value is only 1.645 because for a Normal model, 90% of the values are within 1.645 standard deviations from the mean (Figure 10.8). By contrast, suppose your boss demands more confidence. If she wants an interval in which she can have 99% confidence, she'll need to include values within 2.576 standard deviations, creating a wider confidence interval.

FIGURE 10.8 For a 90% confidence interval, the critical value is 1.645 because for a Normal model, 90% of the values fall within 1.645 standard deviations of the mean.

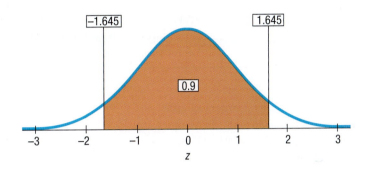

> **One-Proportion *z*-Interval**
>
> When the conditions are met, we are ready to find the confidence interval for the population proportion, p. The confidence interval is $\hat{p} \pm z^* \times SE(\hat{p})$, where the standard deviation of the proportion is estimated by $SE(\hat{p}) = \sqrt{\dfrac{\hat{p}\hat{q}}{n}}$.

IN PRACTICE 10.6 Finding confidence intervals for proportions with different levels of confidence

CHAMBER PRESIDENT How about an interval about which we can be 99% confident? Would that be better?

ANALYST In Practice 10.5 (on page 321) used 2 as the value of z^* for 95% confidence. A more precise value would be 1.96 for 95% confidence. For 99% confidence, the critical z-value is 2.576. So, a 99% confidence interval for the true proportion is

$$\hat{p} \pm 2.576 \, SE(\hat{p}) = 0.56 \pm 2.576(0.022) = (0.503, 0.617)$$

The confidence interval is now wider: 50.3% to 61.7%.

The Chamber of Commerce needs at least 50% for the vote to pass. At a 99% confidence level, it looks as if the measure will pass. However, we must assume that the sample is representative of the voters in the actual election and that people vote in the election as they said they will when they took the survey.

GUIDED EXAMPLE   Public Opinion

In March of 2013, workers in the greeting card company Edit66, based in the southern French town of Cabestany, took their bosses hostage. Company chiefs Paul Denis and Merthus Bezemer had informed employees who were to be laid off that they would not receive severance pay that they are legally entitled to. The workers refused to allow their bosses to leave the premises. The town's mayor Jean Vila supported the action. (www.english.rfi.fr/economy/20130329-greeetings-card-workers-kidnap-bosses-over-unpaid-layoff-pay) There had been a number of similar "bossnappings" in France in 2009. Incidents occurred

(continued)

WHO	Adults in France
WHAT	Proportion who sympathize with the practice of bossnapping
WHEN	April 2–3, 2009
WHERE	France
HOW	1010 adults were randomly sampled by the French Institute of Public Opinion (I'Ifop) for the magazine *Paris Match*
WHY	To investigate public opinion of bossnapping

at SONY, 3M, and Caterpillar plants in France. A poll taken by *Le Parisien* in April 2009 found 45% of the French "supportive" of such action. A similar poll taken by *Paris Match*, April 2–3, 2009, found 30% "approving" and 63% were "understanding" or "sympathetic" of the action. Only 7% condemned the practice of "bossnapping."

The *Paris Match* poll was based on a random representative sample of 1010 adults. What can we conclude about the proportion of all French adults who sympathize with (without supporting outright) the practice of bossnapping?

To answer this question, we'll build a confidence interval for the proportion of all French adults who sympathize with the practice of bossnapping. As with other procedures, there are three steps to building and summarizing a confidence interval for proportions: Plan, Do, and Report.

PLAN **Define** the question.

Identify the *parameter* you wish to estimate. Identify the *population* about which you wish to make statements.

Choose and state a confidence level.

We want to find an interval that is likely with 95% confidence to contain the true proportion, *p*, of French adults who sympathize with the practice of bossnapping. We have a random sample of 1010 French adults, with a sample proportion of 63%.

DO **Model** Think about the assumptions and check the conditions to decide whether we can use the Normal model.

✓ **Independence Assumption**: A French polling agency, l'Ifop, phoned a random sample of French adults. It is unlikely that any respondent influenced another.

✓ **Randomization Condition**: l'Ifop drew a random sample from all French adults. We don't have details of their randomization but assume that we can trust it.

✓ **10% Condition**: Although sampling was necessarily without replacement, there are many more French adults than were sampled. The sample is certainly less than 10% of the population.

✓ **Success/Failure Condition**:

$n\hat{p} = 1010 \times 0.63 = 636 \geq 10$ and
$n\hat{q} = 1010 \times 0.37 = 374 \geq 10$,

so the sample is large enough.

State the sampling distribution model for the statistic. Choose your method.

The conditions are satisfied, so I can use a Normal model to find a one-proportion z-interval.

Mechanics Construct the confidence interval. First, find the standard error. (Remember: It's called the "standard error" because we don't know *p* and have to use $\hat{p}$ instead.)

$n = 1010, \hat{p} = 0.63$, so

$$SE(\hat{p}) = \sqrt{\frac{0.63 \times 0.37}{1010}} = 0.015$$

Next, find the margin of error. We could informally use 2 for our critical value, but 1.96 is more accurate.[6]

Because the sampling model is Normal, for a 95% confidence interval, the critical value $z^* = 1.96$. The margin of error is:

$$ME = z^* \times SE(\hat{p}) = 1.96 \times 0.015 = 0.029$$

---

[6]If you are following along on your calculator and not rounding off (as we have done for this example), you'll get $SE = 0.0151944$ and a ME of 0.0297804.

Write the confidence interval.

REALITY CHECK Check that the interval is plausible. We may not have a strong expectation for the center, but the width of the interval depends primarily on the sample size—especially when the estimated proportion is near 0.5.

So the 95% confidence interval is:

$$0.63 \pm 0.029 \ or \ (0.601, 0.659).$$

The confidence interval covers a range of about plus or minus 3%. That's about the width we might expect for a sample size of about 1000 (when $\hat{p}$ is reasonably close to 0.5).

REPORT **Communicate and Present**
Interpret the confidence interval in the proper context. We're 95% confident that our interval captured the true proportion.

MEMO

Re: Bossnapping survey

The polling agency l'Ifop surveyed 1010 French adults and asked whether they approved, were sympathetic to, or disapproved of recent bossnapping actions. Although we can't know the true proportion of French adults who were sympathetic (without supporting outright), based on this survey we can be 95% confident that between 60.1% and 65.9% of all French adults were. Because this is an ongoing concern, we may want to repeat the survey to obtain more current data. We may also want to keep these results in mind for future corporate public relations.

JUST CHECKING

Think some more about the 95% confidence interval we just created in the guided example for the proportion of French adults who were sympathetic to bossnapping.

4 If we wanted to be 98% confident, would our confidence interval need to be wider or narrower?

5 Our margin of error was about $\pm 3\%$. If we wanted to reduce it to $\pm 2\%$ without increasing the sample size, would our level of confidence be higher or lower?

6 If the organization had polled more people, would the interval's margin of error have likely been larger or smaller?

10.4 Choosing the Sample Size

Every confidence interval must balance precision—the width of the interval—against confidence. Although it is good to be precise and comforting to be confident, there is a trade-off between the two. A confidence interval that says that the percentage is between 10% and 90% wouldn't be of much use, although you could be quite confident that it covered the true proportion. An interval from 43% to 44% is reassuringly precise, but not if it carries a confidence level of 35%. It's a rare study that reports confidence levels lower than 80%. Levels of 95% or 99% are more common.

The time to decide whether the margin of error is small enough to be useful is when you design your study. Don't wait until you compute your confidence interval. To get a narrower interval without giving up confidence, you need to have less variability in your sample proportion. How can you do that? Choose a larger sample.

Consider a company planning to offer a new service to their customers. Product managers want to estimate the proportion of customers who are likely to purchase this new service to within 3% with 95% confidence. How large a sample do they need? Let's look at the margin of error:

$$ME = z^* \sqrt{\frac{\hat{p}\hat{q}}{n}}$$

$$0.03 = 1.96 \sqrt{\frac{\hat{p}\hat{q}}{n}}.$$

What $\hat{p}$ Should We Use?

Often you'll have an estimate of the population proportion based on experience or perhaps on a previous study. If so, use that value as $\hat{p}$ in calculating what size sample you need. If not, the cautious approach is to use $\hat{p} = 0.5$. That will determine the largest sample necessary regardless of the true proportion. It's the *worst case* scenario.

They want to find n, the sample size. To find n, they need a value for $\hat{p}$. They don't know $\hat{p}$ because they don't have a sample yet, but they can probably guess a value. The worst case—the value that makes the SD (and therefore n) largest—is 0.50, so if they use that value for $\hat{p}$, they'll certainly be safe.

The company's equation, then, is:

$$0.03 = 1.96\sqrt{\frac{(0.5)(0.5)}{n}}.$$

To solve for n, just multiply both sides of the equation by $\sqrt{n}$ and divide by 0.03:

$$0.03\sqrt{n} = 1.96\sqrt{(0.5)(0.5)}$$

$$\sqrt{n} = \frac{1.96\sqrt{(0.5)(0.5)}}{0.03} \approx 32.67$$

Then square the result to find n:

$$n \approx (32.67)^2 \approx 1067.1$$

That method will probably give a value with a fraction. To be safe, always round up. The company will need at least 1068 respondents to keep the margin of error as small as 3% with a confidence level of 95%.

Unfortunately, bigger samples cost more money and require more effort. Because the standard error declines only with the *square root* of the sample size, to cut the standard error (and thus the ME) in half, you must *quadruple* the sample size.

Generally, a margin of error of 5% or less is acceptable, but different circumstances call for different standards. The size of the margin of error may be a marketing decision or one determined by the amount of financial risk you (or the company) are willing to accept. Drawing a large sample to get a smaller ME, however, can run into trouble. It takes time to survey 2400 people, and a survey that extends over a week or more may be trying to hit a target that moves during the time of the survey. A news event or new product announcement can change opinions in the middle of the survey process.

Keep in mind that the sample size for a survey is the number of respondents, not the number of people to whom questionnaires were sent or whose phone numbers were dialed. Also keep in mind that a low response rate turns any study essentially into a voluntary response study, which is of little value for inferring population values. It's almost always better to spend resources on increasing the response rate than on surveying a larger group. A complete or nearly complete response by a modest-size sample can yield useful results.

Why 1000?

Public opinion polls often use a sample size of 1000, which gives an ME of about 3% (at 95% confidence) when p is near 0.5. But businesses and nonprofit organizations often use much larger samples to estimate the response to a direct mail campaign. Why? Because the proportion of people who respond to these mailings is very low, often 5% or even less. An ME of 3% may not be precise enough if the response rate is that low. Instead, an ME like 0.1% would be more useful, and that requires a very large sample size.

Surveys are not the only place where proportions pop up. Credit card banks sample huge mailing lists to estimate what proportion of people will accept a credit card offer. Even pilot studies may be mailed to 50,000 customers or more. Most of these customers don't respond. But in this case, that doesn't make the sample smaller. In fact, they did respond in a way—they just said "No thanks." To the bank, the response rate[7] is $\hat{p}$. With a typical success rate below 1%, the bank needs a very small margin of error—often as low as 0.1%—to make a sound business decision. That calls for a large sample, and the bank should take care when estimating the size needed. For our election poll example, we used $p = 0.5$, both because it's safe and because we honestly believed p to be near 0.5. If the bank used 0.5, they'd get an absurd answer. Instead they base their calculation on a value of p that they expect to find from their experience.

---

[7]Be careful. In marketing studies like this *every* mailing yields a response—"yes" or "no"—and response rate means the success rate, the proportion of customers who accept the offer. That's a different use of the term response rate from the one used in survey response.

How Much Difference Can It Make?

A credit card company is about to send out a mailing to test the market for a new credit card. From that sample, they want to estimate the true proportion of people who will sign up for the card nationwide. To be within a tenth of a percentage point, or 0.001 of the true acquisition rate with 95% confidence, how big does the test mailing have to be? Similar mailings in the past lead them to expect that about 0.5% of the people receiving the offer will accept it. Using those values, they find:

$$ME = 0.001 = z^* \sqrt{\frac{pq}{n}} = 1.96 \sqrt{\frac{(0.005)(0.995)}{n}}$$

$$(0.001)^2 = 1.96^2 \frac{(0.005)(0.995)}{n} \Rightarrow n = \frac{1.96^2(0.005)(0.995)}{(0.001)^2}$$

$$= 19{,}111.96 \text{ or about } 19{,}112$$

That's a perfectly reasonable size for a trial mailing. But if they had used 0.50 for their estimate of p they would have found:

$$ME = 0.001 = z^* \sqrt{\frac{pq}{n}} = 1.96 \sqrt{\frac{(0.5)(0.5)}{n}}$$

$$(0.001)^2 = 1.96^2 \frac{(0.5)(0.5)}{n} \Rightarrow n = \frac{1.96^2(0.5)(0.5)}{(0.001)^2} = 960{,}400.$$

Quite a different result!

IN PRACTICE 10.7   Sample size calculations for a confidence interval for a proportion

CHAMBER PRESIDENT   I'm worried that the 99% confidence interval $(0.503, 0.617)$, which has a width of 0.114, is too wide.

How large a sample would we need to take to have a 99% interval half as wide? One quarter as wide? What if we wanted a 99% confidence interval that was plus or minus 3 percentage points? How large a sample would we need?

ANALYST   Because the formula for the confidence interval is dependent on the inverse of the square root of the sample size:

$$\hat{p} \pm z^* \sqrt{\frac{\hat{p}\hat{q}}{n}},$$

a sample size four times as large will produce a confidence interval *half* as wide. The original 99% confidence interval had a sample size of 516. If you want it half as wide, you will need about $4 \times 516 = 2064$ respondents. To get it a quarter as wide you'd need $4^2 \times 516 = 8256$ respondents!

If you want a 99% confidence interval that's plus or minus 3 percentage points, we must calculate

$$\hat{p} \pm z^* \sqrt{\frac{\hat{p}\hat{q}}{n}} = \hat{p} \pm 0.03$$

so

$$2.576 \sqrt{\frac{(0.5)(0.5)}{n}} = 0.03$$

(continued)

which means that

$$n \approx \left(\frac{2.576}{0.03}\right)^2 (0.5)(0.5) = 1843.27$$

Rounding up, we'd need 1844 respondents. We used 0.5 because we didn't have any information about the election before taking the survey. Using $p = 0.56$ instead would give $n = 1817$.

⊘ WHAT CAN GO WRONG?

- **Don't confuse the sampling distribution with the distribution of the sample.** When you take a sample, you always look at the distribution of the values, usually with a histogram, and you may calculate summary statistics. Examining the distribution of the sample like this is wise. But that's not the sampling distribution. The sampling distribution is an imaginary collection of the values that a statistic might have taken for all the random samples—the one you got and the ones that you didn't get. Use the sampling distribution model to make statements about how the statistic varies.

- **Beware of observations that are not independent.** The CLT depends crucially on the assumption of independence. Unfortunately, this isn't something you can check in your data. You have to think about how the data were gathered. Good sampling practice and well-designed randomized experiments ensure independence.

- **Watch out for small samples.** The CLT tells us that the sampling distribution model is Normal if n is large enough. The Success/Failure Condition assures us that if we have at least 10 successes and failures, the Normal model will work well for modeling the sampling distribution of the sample proportion. If the population proportion is near 0.50, we could get by with even fewer successes and failures, but the Success/Failure Condition is conservative and will protect us no matter how large or small the true underlying proportion happens to be.

Confidence intervals are powerful tools. Not only do they tell us what is known about the parameter value, but—more important—they also tell us what we *don't* know. In order to use confidence intervals effectively, you must be clear about what you say about them.

- **Be sure to use the right language to describe your confidence intervals.** Technically, you should say "I am 95% confident that the interval from 40.4% to 43.6% captures the true proportion of U.S. adults who thought the economy was improving in April 2013." That formal phrasing emphasizes that *your confidence (and your uncertainty) is about the interval, not the true proportion.* But you may choose a more casual phrasing like "I am 95% confident that between 40.4% and 43.6% of U.S. adults thought the economy was improving in April 2013." Because you've made it clear that the uncertainty is yours and you didn't suggest that the randomness is in the true proportion, this is OK. Keep in mind that it's the interval that's random. It's the focus of both our confidence and our doubt.

- **Don't suggest that the parameter varies.** A statement like "there is a 95% chance that the true proportion is between 40.4% and 43.6%" sounds as though you think the population proportion wanders around and sometimes happens to fall between 40.4% and 43.6%. When you interpret a confidence interval, make it clear that *you* know that the population parameter is fixed and that it is the interval that varies from sample to sample.

- **Don't claim that other samples will agree with yours.** Keep in mind that the confidence interval makes a statement about the true population proportion. An interpretation such as "in 95% of samples of U.S. adults the proportion who thought the economy was improving in April 2013 will be between 40.4% and 43.6%" is just wrong. The interval isn't about sample proportions but about the population proportion. There is nothing special about the sample we happen to have; it doesn't establish a standard for other samples.

- **Don't be certain about the parameter.** Saying "between 40.4% and 43.6% of U.S. adults thought the economy was improving in April 2013" asserts that the population proportion cannot be outside that interval. Of course, you can't be absolutely certain of that (just pretty sure).

- **Don't forget: It's about the parameter.** Don't say "I'm 95% confident that $\hat{p}$ is between 40.4% and 43.6%." Of course, you are—in fact, we calculated that our sample proportion was 42.0%. So we already *know* the sample proportion. The confidence interval is about the (unknown) population parameter, p.

- **Don't claim to know too much.** Don't say "I'm 95% confident that between 40.4% and 43.6% of all U.S. adults think the economy is improving." Gallup sampled adults during April 2013, and public opinion shifts over time.

- **Do take responsibility.** Confidence intervals are about *un*certainty. *You* are the one who is uncertain, not the parameter. You have to accept the responsibility and consequences of the fact that not all the intervals you compute will capture the true value. In fact, about 5% of the 95% confidence intervals you find will fail to capture the true value of the parameter. You *can* say "I am 95% confident that between 40.4% and 43.6% of U.S. adults thought the economy was improving in April 2013."

Confidence intervals and margins of error depend crucially on the assumptions and conditions. When they're not true the results may be invalid. For your own surveys, follow the survey designs from Chapter 8. For surveys you read about, be sure to:

- **Watch out for biased sampling.** Just because we have more statistical machinery now doesn't mean we can forget what we've already learned. A questionnaire that finds that 85% of people enjoy filling out surveys still suffers from nonresponse bias even though now we're able to put confidence intervals around this (biased) estimate.

- **Think about independence.** The assumption that the values in a sample are mutually independent is one that you usually cannot check. It always pays to think about it, though.

- **Be careful of sample size.** The validity of the confidence interval for proportions may be affected by sample size. Avoid using the confidence interval on "small" samples.

ETHICS IN ACTION

Gold Key Agency is a regional real estate brokerage firm that features properties in northern Pennsylvania and southern New York. Ann Sheridan has been with the agency for about five years, working out of its Bradford County, PA, office. One of her current clients, Ben Rhodes, has been looking at a fairly large parcel of land with an old farmhouse to renovate. He seems very interested and she has met with him several times, but he has expressed some concern about gas drilling in the region.

Ann is well aware of how natural gas drilling in the area has affected the real estate business. Large reserves located in the Marcellus shale formation, now accessible as a result of advances in horizontal drilling and hydraulic fracturing, or "fracking," has created an economic boom: new jobs, an influx of workers, and prosperity to landowners who have leased to gas drilling companies. At the same time, it has had undesirable consequences.

Because drilling companies are not required by law to disclose the chemicals used in fracking, many fear its potential negative effects on the surrounding environment. Indeed, there is evidence that some property values have actually decreased, particularly those depending on well water. Demonstrations in the media of how well water contaminated by fracking chemicals "ignites" has further heightened anxiety. Moreover, some banks and credit unions are reluctant to grant mortgages on properties leased for gas drilling.

Ann is getting ready to meet yet again with Ben. She really wants to close this deal, so she decides to gather some information to help persuade Ben to make the purchase. Ann collects both the selling price and appraised value for each of 20 properties recently sold by agents in her office. She finds that only one of them sold for below its appraised value. Based on these data, Ann constructs a 95% confidence interval and finds the upper limit to be 15%. That value is small enough to please her, so she doesn't bother to look more closely at whether her method is appropriate for her data. Assuming that one of Ben's concerns may be that property values in the region may decline in the future, she plans to use this figure to reassure him. She will tell him that she is 95% sure that no more than 15% of properties in the area run the risk of selling for less than its appraised value. She hopes this will convince Ben to finally make an offer on the property.

- **Identify the ethical dilemma in this scenario.**
- **What are the undesirable consequences?**
- **Propose an ethical solution that considers the welfare of all stakeholders.**

CHAPTER

10   FROM LEARNING TO EARNING

LEARNING OBJECTIVES

Model the variation in statistics from sample to sample with a sampling distribution.
- The sampling distribution of the sample proportion is Normal as long as the sample size is large enough.

Understand that, usually, the mean of a sampling distribution is the value of the parameter estimated.
- For the sampling distribution of $\hat{p}$, the mean is p.

Interpret the standard deviation of a sampling distribution.
- The standard deviation of a sampling model is the most important information about it.
- The standard deviation of the sampling distribution of a proportion is $\sqrt{\dfrac{pq}{n}}$ where $q = 1 - p$.

Construct a confidence interval for a proportion, p, as the statistic, $\hat{p}$, plus and minus a margin of error.
- The margin of error consists of a **critical value** based on the sampling model times a **standard error** based on the sample.
- The critical value is found from the Normal model.
- The standard error of a sample proportion is calculated as $\sqrt{\dfrac{\hat{p}\hat{q}}{n}}$.

Interpret a confidence interval correctly.

- You can claim to have the specified level of confidence that the interval you have computed actually covers the true value.

Understand the importance of the sample size, *n*, in improving both the certainty (confidence level) and precision (margin of error).

- For the same sample size and proportion, more certainty requires less precision and more precision requires less certainty.

Know and check the assumptions and conditions for finding and interpreting confidence intervals.

- Independence Assumption or Randomization Condition
- 10% Condition
- Success/Failure Condition

Be able to invert the calculation of the margin of error to find the sample size required, given a proportion, a confidence level, and a desired margin of error.

TERMS

Confidence interval
An interval of values usually of the form

$$estimate \pm margin\ of\ error$$

found from data in such a way that a particular percentage of all random samples can be expected to yield intervals that capture the true parameter value.

Critical value
The number of standard errors to move away from the estimate (mean of the sampling distribution) to correspond to the specified level of confidence. The critical value, denoted z^*, is usually found from a table or with technology.

Margin of error (ME)
In a confidence interval, the extent of the interval on either side of the estimate (the observed statistic value). A margin of error is typically the product of a critical value from the sampling distribution and a standard error from the data. A small margin of error corresponds to a confidence interval that pins down the parameter precisely. A large margin of error corresponds to a confidence interval that gives relatively little information about the estimated parameter.

One-proportion *z*-interval
A confidence interval for the true value of a proportion. The confidence interval is

$$\hat{p} \pm z^*SE(\hat{p})$$

where z^* is a critical value from the Standard Normal model corresponding to the specified confidence level and $SE(\hat{p}) = \sqrt{\dfrac{\hat{p}\hat{q}}{n}}$.

Sampling distribution
The distribution of a statistic over many independent samples of the same size from the same population.

Sampling distribution model for a proportion
If the Independence Assumption and Randomization Condition are met and we expect at least 10 successes and 10 failures, then the sampling distribution of a proportion is well modeled by a Normal model with a mean equal to the true proportion value, p, and a standard deviation equal to $\sqrt{\dfrac{pq}{n}}$.

Sampling error
Sampling variability
The variability we expect to see from sample to sample is often called the sampling error, although sampling variability is a better term.

Standard error (SE)
When the standard deviation of the sampling distribution of a statistic is estimated from the data, the resulting statistic is called a standard error (SE).

TECH SUPPORT   Confidence Intervals for Proportions

Confidence intervals for proportions are so easy and natural that many statistics packages don't offer special commands for them. Most statistics programs want the "raw data" for computations. For proportions, the raw data are the "success" and "failure" status for each case. Usually, these are given as 1 or 0, but they might be category names like "yes" and "no." Often we just know the proportion of successes, $\hat{p}$, and the total count, n. Computer packages don't usually deal with summary data like this easily, but the statistics routines found on many graphing calculators allow you to create confidence intervals from summaries of the data—usually all you need to enter are the number of successes and the sample size.

In some programs you can reconstruct variables of 0's and 1's with the given proportions. But even when you have (or can reconstruct) the raw data values, you may not get *exactly* the same margin of error from a computer package as you would find working by hand. The reason is that some packages make approximations or use other methods. The result is very close but not exactly the same. Fortunately, statistics means never having to say you're certain, so the approximate result is good enough.

EXCEL

Inference methods for proportions are not part of the standard Excel tool set, but you use Excel's equations to calculate a confidence interval for a proportion in Excel:

◢	A	B	C	D	E
1	z-Estimate of a Proportion				
2					
3	Sample Proportion	0.63	Confidence Interval Estimate		
4	Sample Size	1010	0.63	±	0.0298
5	Confidence Level	0.95	Lower Confidence Limit		0.6002
6			Upper Confidence Limit		0.6598

- Enter the sample proportion in cell B3.
- Enter the sample size in cell B4.
- Enter the confidence level in cell B5.
- In cell C4, type: "=b3".
- In cell E4, type "=NORM.S.INV(0.5+B5/2)*(SQRT(B3*(1−B3)/B4))".
- Type "=C4−E4" in cell E5.
- Type "=C4+E4" in cell E6.

COMMENTS

The method shown here will work for summarized data. When working with raw data, use the COUNTIF function in Excel to quickly count values to compute the sample proportion. You can also use the Pivot Table to quickly summarize the data.

JMP

For a categorical variable that holds category labels, the **Distribution** platform includes tests and intervals for proportions.

For raw data:

- Right-click on the column containing data.
- Identify "Modeling Type" as Nominal.
- Choose **Analyze > Distribution**.
- Select data column as **Y, Columns** and click **OK**.
- Expand menu next to variable name in output.
- Select **Confidence Interval** and choose confidence level.

COMMENTS

JMP uses slightly different methods for proportion inferences than those discussed in this text. Your answers are likely to be slightly different, especially for small samples.

MINITAB

Choose **Basic Statistics** from the **Stat** menu.

- Choose **1Proportion** from the Basic Statistics submenu.
- If you have a large sample, change method to Normal distribution.
- If the data are category names in a variable, assign the variable from the variable list box to the **Samples in columns** box.
- If you have summarized data, click the **Summarized Data** button and fill in the number of trials and the number of successes.
- Click the **Options** button and specify the remaining details. Leave the Alternative as $\neq$.

COMMENTS

When working from a variable that names categories, MINITAB treats the last category as the "success" category. You can specify how the categories should be ordered.

R

The standard libraries in R do not contain a function for the confidence of a proportion, but a simple function can be written to do so. For example:

```
pconfint=function(phat,n,conf=.95)
    {
        se = sqrt(phat*(1−phat)/n)
        al2 = 1−(1−conf)/2
        zstar = qnorm(al2)
        ul = phat+zstar*se
        ll = phat·zstar*se
        return(c(ll,ul))
    }
```

For example, pconfint(0.3,500) will give a 95% confidence interval for p based on 150 successes out of 500.

SPSS

SPSS does not find confidence intervals for proportions.

To create a confidence interval for a proportion using summaries:

- Click on **Stat**.
- Choose **Proportion Stats > One sample > With summary**.
- Enter the **Number of successes** (x) and **Number of observations** (n).
- Indicate **Confidence Interval** (Standard-Wald), and then enter the **Level** of confidence.
- Click on **Compute!**

To create a confidence interval for a proportion using data:

- Click on **Stat**.
- Choose **Proportion Stats > One sample > With data**.
- Choose the variable **Column** listing the Outcomes.
- Enter the outcome to be considered a Success.
- Indicate **Confidence Interval**, and then enter the **Level** of confidence.
- Click on **Compute!**

BRIEF CASE

Has Gold Lost its Luster?

In 2011, when the Gallup organization polled investors, 34% rated gold the best long-term investment. But in April of 2017 Gallup surveyed a random sample of U.S. adults (news.gallup.com/poll/208820/americans-favor-real-estate-long-term-investment.aspx). Respondents were asked to select the best long-term investment from a list of possibilities. Only 183 of the 1019 respondents chose gold as the best long-term investment. By contrast, only 51 chose bonds.

Compute the standard error for each sample proportion. Compute and describe a 95% confidence interval in the context of the question.

Do you think opinions about the value of gold as a long-term investment have really changed from the old 34% favorability rate, or do you think this is just sample variability? Explain.

Forecasting Demand

Utilities must forecast the demand for energy use far into the future because it takes decades to plan and build new power plants. Ron Baker, who worked for New York State Electric and Gas (NYSEG), had the job of predicting the proportion of homes that would choose to use electricity to heat their homes. He was prepared to report a confidence interval for the true proportion, but after seeing his preliminary report, his management demanded a single number as his prediction. Help Ron explain to his management why a confidence interval for the desired proportion would be more useful for planning purposes. Explain how the precision of the interval and the confidence we can have in it are related to each other. Discuss the business consequences of an interval that is too narrow and the consequences of an interval with too low a confidence level.

CHAPTER 10 EXERCISES

SECTION 10.1

1. An investment website can tell what devices are used to access the site. The site managers wonder whether they should enhance the facilities for trading via "smartphones" so they want to estimate the proportion of users who access the site that way (even if they also use their computers sometimes). They draw a random sample of 200 investors from their customers. Suppose that the true proportion of smartphone users is 36%.

a) What would you expect the shape of the sampling distribution for the sample proportion to be?

b) What would be the mean of this sampling distribution?

c) If the sample size were increased to 500, would your answers change? Explain.

2. The proportion of adult women in the United States is approximately 51%. A marketing survey telephones 400 people at random.

a) What proportion of women in the sample of 400 would you expect to see?

b) How many women, on average, would you expect to find in a sample of that size? (*Hint:* Multiply the expected proportion by the sample size.)

3. The investment website of Exercise 1 draws a random sample of 200 investors from their customers. Suppose that the true proportion of smartphone users is 36%.

a) What would the standard deviation of the sampling distribution of the proportion of smartphone users be?

b) What is the probability that the sample proportion of smartphone users is greater than 0.36?

c) What is the probability that the sample proportion is between 0.30 and 0.40?

d) What is the probability that the sample proportion is less than 0.28?

e) What is the probability that the sample proportion is greater than 0.42?

4. The proportion of adult women in the United States is approximately 51%. A marketing survey telephones 400 people at random.

a) What is the sampling distribution of the observed proportion that are women?

b) What is the standard deviation of that proportion?

c) Would you be surprised to find 53% women in a sample of size 400? Explain.

d) Would you be surprised to find 48% women in a sample of size 400? Explain.

e) Would you be surprised to find that there were fewer than 160 women in the sample? Explain.

5. A real estate agent wants to know how many owners of homes worth over $1,000,000 might be considering putting their home on the market in the next 12 months. He surveys 40 of them and finds that 10 of them are considering such a move. Are all the assumptions and conditions for finding the sampling distribution of the proportion satisfied? Explain briefly.

6. A tourist agency wants to know what proportion of visitors to the Eiffel Tower are from the Far East. To find out they survey 100 people in the line to purchase tickets to the top of the tower one Sunday afternoon in May. Are all the assumptions and conditions for finding the sampling distribution of the proportion satisfied? Explain briefly.

7. A marketing researcher for a phone company surveys 100 people and finds that that proportion of clients who are likely to switch providers when their contract expires is 0.15.

a) What is the standard deviation of the sampling distribution of the proportion?

b) If she wants to reduce the standard deviation by half, how large a sample would she need?

8. A market researcher for a provider of iPhone accessories wants to know the proportion of customers who own cars to assess the market for a new iPhone dashboard mount. A survey of 500 customers indicates that 76% own cars.

a) What is the standard deviation of the sampling distribution of the proportion?

b) How large would the standard deviation have been if he had surveyed only 125 customers (assuming the proportion is about the same)?

SECTION 10.2

9. For each situation below identify the population and the sample and identify p and $\hat{p}$ if appropriate and what the value of $\hat{p}$ is. Would you trust a confidence interval for the true proportion based on these data? Explain briefly why or why not.

a) As concertgoers enter a stadium, a security guard randomly inspects their backpacks for alcoholic beverages. Of the 130 backpacks checked so far, 17 contained alcoholic beverages of some kind. The guards want to estimate the percentage of all backpacks of concertgoers at this concert that contain alcoholic beverages.

b) The website of the English newspaper *The Guardian* asked visitors to the site to say whether they approved of recent "bossnapping" actions by British workers who were outraged over being fired. Of those who responded, 49.2% said "Yes. Desperate times, desperate measures."

c) An airline wants to know the weight of carry-on baggage that customers take on their international routes, so they take a random sample of 50 bags and find that the average weight is 17.3 pounds.

10. For each situation below identify the population and the sample and explain what p and $\hat{p}$ represent and what the value of $\hat{p}$ is. Would you trust a confidence interval for the true proportion based on these data? Explain briefly why or why not.

a) A marketing analyst conducts a large survey of her customers to find out how much money they plan to spend at the company website in the next 6 months. The average amount reported from the 534 respondents is $145.34.

b) A campus survey on a large campus (40,000 students) is trying to find out whether students approve of a new parking policy allowing students to park in previously inaccessible parking lots, but for a small fee. Surveys are sent out by mail and e-mail to all students. Of the 243 surveys returned, 134 are in favor of the change.

c) The human resources department of a large Fortune 100 company wants to find out how many employees would take advantage of an on-site day care facility. They send out an e-mail to 500 employees and receive responses from 450 of them. Of those responding, 75 say that they would take advantage of such a facility.

11. A survey of 200 students is selected randomly on a large university campus. They are asked if they use a laptop in class to take notes. The result of the survey is that 70 of the 200 students responded "yes."

a) What is the value of the sample proportion $\hat{p}$?
b) What is the standard error of the sample proportion?
c) Construct an approximate 95% confidence interval for the true proportion p by taking ± 2 SEs from the sample proportion.

12. From a survey of 250 coworkers you find that 155 would like the company to provide on-site day care.

a) What is the value of the sample proportion $\hat{p}$?
b) What is the standard error of the sample proportion?
c) Construct an approximate 95% confidence interval for the true proportion p by taking ± 2 SEs from the sample proportion.

13. From a survey of coworkers you find that 48% of 200 have already received this year's flu vaccine. An approximate 95% confidence interval is (0.409, 0.551). Which of the following are true? If not, explain briefly.

a) 95% of the coworkers fall in the interval (0.409, 0.551).
b) We are 95% confident that the proportion of coworkers who have received this year's flu vaccine is between 40.9% and 55.1%.
c) There is a 95% chance that a random selected coworker has received the vaccine.
d) There is a 48% chance that a random selected coworker has received the vaccine.
e) We are 95% confident that between 40.9% and 55.1% of the samples will have a proportion near 48%.

14. From the survey in Exercise 11, which of the following are true? If they are not true, explain briefly why not.

a) 95% of the 200 students are in the interval (0.283, 0.417).
b) The true proportion of students who use laptops to take notes is captured in the interval (0.283, 0.417) with probability 0.95.
c) There is a 35% chance that a student uses a laptop to take notes.
d) There is a 95% chance that the student uses a laptop to take notes 35% of the time.
e) We are 95% confident that the true proportion of students who use laptops to take notes is captured in the interval (0.283, 0.417).

SECTION 10.3

15. From the survey in Exercise 11,

a) How would the confidence interval change if the confidence level had been 90% instead of 95%?
b) How would the confidence interval change if the sample size had been 300 instead of 200? (Assume the same sample proportion.)

c) How would the confidence interval change if the confidence level had been 99% instead of 95%?
d) How large would the sample size have to be to make the margin of error half as big in the 95% confidence interval?

16. As in Exercise 13, from a survey of coworkers you find that 48% of 200 have already received this year's flu vaccine. An approximate 95% confidence interval is (0.409, 0.551).

a) How would the confidence interval change if the sample size had been 800 instead of 200?
b) How would the confidence interval change if the confidence level had been 90% instead of 95%?
c) How would the confidence interval change if the confidence level had been 99% instead of 95%?

SECTION 10.4

17. Suppose you want to estimate the proportion of traditional college students on your campus who own their own car. You have no preconceived idea of what that proportion might be.

a) What sample size is needed if you wish to be 95% confident that your estimate is within 0.02 of the true proportion?
b) What sample size is needed if you wish to be 99% confident that your estimate is within 0.02 of the true proportion?
c) What sample size is needed if you wish to be 95% confident that your estimate is within 0.05 of the true proportion?

18. As in Exercise 17, you want to estimate the proportion of traditional college students on your campus who own their own car. However, from some research on other college campuses, you believe the proportion will be near 20%.

a) What sample size is needed if you wish to be 95% confident that your estimate is within 0.02 of the true proportion?
b) What sample size is needed if you wish to be 99% confident that your estimate is within 0.02 of the true proportion?
c) What sample size is needed if you wish to be 95% confident that your estimate is within 0.05 of the true proportion?

19. It's believed that as many as 25% of adults over age 50 never graduated from high school. We wish to see if this percentage is the same among the 25 to 30 age group.

a) How many of this younger age group must we survey in order to estimate the proportion of nongrads to within 6% with 90% confidence?
b) Suppose we want to cut the margin of error to 4%. What's the necessary sample size?
c) What sample size would produce a margin of error of 3%?

20. In preparing a report on the economy, we need to estimate the percentage of businesses that plan to hire additional employees in the next 60 days.

a) How many randomly selected employers must we contact in order to create an estimate in which we are 98% confident with a margin of error of 5%?

b) Suppose we want to reduce the margin of error to 3%. What sample size will suffice?

c) Why might it not be worth the effort to try to get an interval with a margin of error of 1%?

CHAPTER EXERCISES

21. Send money. When they send out their fundraising letter, a philanthropic organization typically gets a return from about 5% of the people on their mailing list. To see what the response rate might be for future appeals, they did a simulation using samples of size 20, 50, 100, and 200. For each sample size, they simulated 1000 mailings with success rate $p = 0.05$ and constructed the histogram of the 1000 sample proportions, shown below. Explain what these histograms say about the sampling distribution model for sample proportions. Be sure to talk about shape, center, and spread.

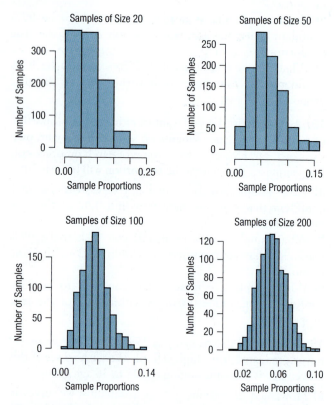

22. Character recognition. An automatic character recognition device can successfully read about 85% of handwritten loan applications. To estimate what might happen when this device reads a stack of applications, the company did a simulation using samples of size 20, 50, 75, and 100. For each sample size, they simulated 1000 samples with success rate $p = 0.85$ and constructed the histogram of the 1000 sample proportions, shown here. Explain what these histograms say about the sampling distribution model for sample proportions. Be sure to talk about shape, center, and spread.

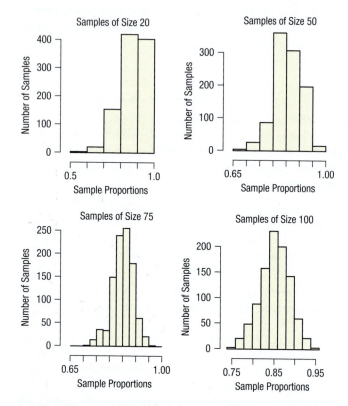

23. Send money, again. The philanthropic organization in Exercise 21 expects about a 5% success rate when they send fundraising letters to the people on their mailing list. In Exercise 21 you looked at the histograms showing distributions of sample proportions from 1000 simulated mailings for samples of size 20, 50, 100, and 200. The sample statistics from each simulation were as follows:

n	mean	st. dev.
20	0.0497	0.0479
50	0.0516	0.0309
100	0.0497	0.0215
200	0.0501	0.0152

a) According to the Normal model, what should the theoretical mean and standard deviations be for these sample sizes?

b) How close are those theoretical values to what was observed in these simulations?

c) Looking at the histograms in Exercise 21, at what sample size would you be comfortable using the Normal model as an approximation for the sampling distribution?

d) What does the Success/Failure Condition say about the choice you made in part c?

24. Character recognition, again. The automatic character recognition device discussed in Exercise 22 successfully reads about 85% of handwritten loan applications. In Exercise 22 you looked at the histograms showing distributions of sample proportions from 1000 simulated samples of size 20, 50, 75, and 100. The sample statistics from each simulation were as follows:

n	mean	st. dev.
20	0.8481	0.0803
50	0.8507	0.0509
75	0.8481	0.0406
100	0.8488	0.0354

a) According to the Normal model, what should the theoretical mean and standard deviations be for these sample sizes?
b) How close are those theoretical values to what was observed in these simulations?
c) Looking at the histograms in Exercise 22, at what sample size would you be comfortable using the Normal model as an approximation for the sampling distribution?
d) What does the Success/Failure Condition say about the choice you made in part c?

25. Stock picking. In a large Business Statistics class, the professor has each person select stocks by throwing 16 darts at pages of the *Wall Street Journal*. They then check to see whether their stock picks rose or fell the next day and report their proportion of "successes." As a lesson, the professor has selected pages of the *Journal* for which exactly half the publicly traded stocks went up and half went down. The professor then makes a histogram of the reported proportions.

a) What shape would you expect this histogram to be? Why?
b) Where do you expect the histogram to be centered?
c) How much variability would you expect among these proportions?
d) Explain why a Normal model should not be used here.

26. Quality management. Manufacturing companies strive to maintain production consistency, but it is often difficult for outsiders to tell whether they have succeeded. Sometimes, however, we can find a simple example. The candy company that makes M&M's candies claims that 10% of the candies it produces are green and that bags are packed randomly. We can check on their production controls by sampling bags of candies. Suppose we open bags containing about 50 M&M's and record the proportion of green candies.

a) If we plot a histogram showing the proportions of green candies in the various bags, what shape would you expect it to have?
b) Can that histogram be approximated by a Normal model? Explain.
c) Where should the center of the histogram be?
d) What should the standard deviation of the proportion be?

27. Bigger portfolio. The class in Exercise 25 expands its stock-picking experiment.

a) The students use computer-generated random numbers to choose 25 stocks each. Use the 68–95–99.7 Rule to describe the sampling distribution model.
b) Confirm that you can use a Normal model here.
c) They increase the number of stocks picked to 64 each. Draw and label the appropriate sampling distribution model. Check the appropriate conditions to justify your model.
d) Explain how the sampling distribution model changes as the number of stocks picked increases.

28. More quality. Would a bigger sample help us to assess manufacturing consistency? Suppose instead of the 50-candy bags of Exercise 26, we work with bags that contain 200 M&M's each. Again we calculate the proportion of green candies found.

a) Explain why it's appropriate to use a Normal model to describe the distribution of the proportion of green M&M's they might expect.
b) Use the 68–95–99.7 Rule to describe how this proportion might vary from bag to bag.
c) How would this model change if the bags contained even more candies?

29. A winning investment strategy? One student in the class of Exercise 25 claims to have found a winning strategy. He watches a cable news show about investing and *during the show* throws his darts at the pages of the *Journal*. He claims that of 200 stocks picked in this manner, 58% were winners.

a) What do you think of his claim? Explain.
b) If there are 100 students in the class, are you surprised that one was this successful? Explain.

30. Even more quality. In a really large bag of M&M's, we found 12% of 500 candies were green. Is this evidence that the manufacturing process is out of control and has made too many greens? Explain.

31. Speeding. State police believe that 70% of the drivers traveling on a major interstate highway exceed the speed limit. They plan to set up a radar trap and check the speeds of 80 cars.

a) Using the 68–95–99.7 Rule, draw and label the distribution of the proportion of these cars the police will observe speeding.
b) Do you think the appropriate conditions necessary for your analysis are met? Explain.

32. Smoking, 2016. The Centers for Disease Control and Prevention (www.cdc.gov/tobacco/data_statistics/fact_sheets/adult_data/cig_smoking/index.htm) reported that in 2016, 15.5% of American adults smoked cigarettes. Describe the sampling distribution model for the proportion of smokers among a randomly selected group of 100 adults. Be sure to discuss your assumptions and conditions.

33. Vision. It is generally believed that nearsightedness affects about 12% of all children. A school district has registered 170 incoming kindergarten children.

a) Can you use the Normal Model to describe the sampling distribution model for the sample proportion of children who are nearsighted? Check the conditions and discuss any assumptions you need to make.

b) Sketch and clearly label the sampling model, based on the 68–95–99.7 Rule.

c) How many of the incoming students might the school expect to be nearsighted? Explain.

34. Mortgages 2013. In early 2013 Realty Trac reported that foreclosures had settled down to 1 in 859 homes per month for a rate of 0.116%, far below the 1.6% seen during the financial crisis of 2007–2008. Suppose a large bank holds 9455 of these mortgages.

a) Can you use the Normal model to describe the sampling distribution model for the sample proportion of foreclosures? Check the conditions and discuss any assumptions you need to make.

b) Sketch and clearly label the sampling model, based on the 68–95–99.7 Rule.

c) How many of these homeowners might the bank expect will default on their mortgages? Explain.

35. Loans. Based on past experience, a bank believes that 7% of the people who receive loans will not make payments on time. The bank has recently approved 200 loans.

a) What are the mean and standard deviation of the proportion of clients in this group who may not make timely payments?

b) What assumptions underlie your model? Are the conditions met? Explain.

c) What's the probability that over 10% of these clients will not make timely payments?

36. Contacts. The campus representative for Lens.com wants to know what percentage of students at a university currently wear contact lens. Suppose the true proportion is 30%.

a) We randomly pick 100 students. Let $\hat{p}$ represent the proportion of students in this sample who wear contacts. What's the appropriate model for the distribution of $\hat{p}$? Specify the name of the distribution, the mean, and the standard deviation. Be sure to verify that the conditions are met.

b) What's the approximate probability that more than one third of this sample wear contacts?

37. Back to school? Best known for its testing program, ACT, Inc., also compiles data on a variety of issues in education. In 2012 the company reported that the national college freshman-to-sophomore retention rate at four-year colleges was about 80.0%. Consider colleges with freshman classes of 400 students. Use the 68–95–99.7 Rule to describe the sampling distribution model for the percentage of those students we expect to return to that school for their sophomore years. Do you think the appropriate conditions are met?

38. Binge drinking. A national study found that 44% of college students engage in binge drinking (5 drinks at a sitting for men, 4 for women). Use the 68–95–99.7 Rule to describe the sampling distribution model for the proportion of students in a randomly selected group of 200 college students who engage in binge drinking. Do you think the appropriate conditions are met?

39. Back to school, again. Based on the 80% national retention rate described in Exercise 37, does a college where 551 of the 603 freshmen returned the next year as sophomores have a right to brag that it has an unusually high retention rate? Explain.

40. Binge sample. After hearing of the national result that 44% of students engage in binge drinking (5 drinks at a sitting for men, 4 for women), a professor surveyed a random sample of 244 students at his college and found that 96 of them admitted to binge drinking in the past week. Should he be surprised at this result? Explain.

41. Polling. Just before a referendum on a school budget, a local newspaper polls 400 voters in an attempt to predict whether the budget will pass. Suppose that the budget actually has the support of 52% of the voters. What's the probability the newspaper's sample will lead them to predict defeat? Be sure to verify that the assumptions and conditions necessary for your analysis are met.

42. Seeds. Information on a packet of seeds claims that the germination rate is 92%. What's the probability that more than 95% of the 160 seeds in the packet will germinate? Be sure to discuss your assumptions and check the conditions that support your model.

43. Apples. When a truckload of apples arrives at a packing plant, a random sample of 150 is selected and examined for bruises, discoloration, and other defects. The whole truckload will be rejected if more than 5% of the sample is unsatisfactory. Suppose that in fact 8% of the apples on the truck do not meet the desired standard. What's the probability that the shipment will be accepted anyway?

44. Genetic defect. It's believed that 4% of children have a gene that may be linked to type 1 diabetes. Researchers hoping to track 20 of these children for several years test 732 newborns for the presence of this gene. What's the probability that they find enough subjects for their study?

45. Catalog sales. A catalog sales company promises to deliver orders placed on the Internet within 3 days. Follow-up calls to a few randomly selected customers show that a 95% confidence interval for the proportion of all orders that arrive on time is 88% ± 6%. What does this mean? Are the conclusions in parts a–e correct? Explain.

a) Between 82% and 94% of all orders arrive on time.

b) 95% of all random samples of customers will show that 88% of orders arrive on time.

c) 95% of all random samples of customers will show that 82% to 94% of orders arrive on time.

d) The company is 95% sure that between 82% and 94% of the orders placed by the customers in this sample arrived on time.

e) On 95% of the days, between 82% and 94% of the orders will arrive on time.

46. Belgian euro. Two students made worldwide head-lines by spinning a Belgian euro 250 times and getting 140 heads—that's 56%. That makes the 90% confidence interval (51%, 61%). What does this mean? Are the con-clusions in parts a–e correct? Explain your answers.

a) Between 51% and 61% of all euros are unfair.

b) We are 90% sure that in this experiment this euro landed heads between 51% and 61% of the spins.

c) We are 90% sure that spun euros will land heads between 51% and 61% of the time.

d) If you spin a euro many times, you can be 90% sure of getting between 51% and 61% heads.

e) 90% of all spun euros will land heads between 51% and 61% of the time.

47. Confidence intervals. Several factors are involved in the creation of a confidence interval. Among them are the sample size, the level of confidence, and the margin of error. Which statements are true?

a) For a given sample size, higher confidence means a smaller margin of error.

b) For a specified confidence level, larger samples provide smaller margins of error.

c) For a fixed margin of error, larger samples provide greater confidence.

d) For a given confidence level, halving the margin of error requires a sample twice as large.

48. Confidence intervals, again. Several factors are involved in the creation of a confidence interval. Among them are the sample size, the level of confidence, and the margin of error. Which statements are true?

a) For a given sample size, reducing the margin of error will mean lower confidence.

b) For a certain confidence level, you can get a smaller margin of error by selecting a bigger sample.

c) For a fixed margin of error, smaller samples will mean lower confidence.

d) For a given confidence level, a sample 9 times as large will make a margin of error one third as big.

49. Cars. A student is considering publishing a new maga-zine aimed directly at owners of Japanese automobiles. He wanted to estimate the fraction of cars in the United States that are made in Japan. The computer output summarizes the results of a random sample of 50 autos. Explain care-fully what it tells you.

```
z-interval for proportion
With 90.00% confidence
0.29938661 < p(japan) < 0.46984416
```

50. Quality control. For quality control purposes, 900 ceramic tiles were inspected to determine the proportion of defective (e.g., cracked, uneven finish, etc.) tiles. Assum-ing that these tiles are representative of all tiles manufac-tured by an Italian tile company, what can you conclude based on the computer output?

```
z-interval for proportion
With 95.00% confidence
0.025 < p(defective) < 0.035
```

51. E-mail. A small company involved in e-commerce is interested in statistics concerning the use of e-mail. A poll found that 38% of a random sample of 1012 adults, who use a computer at their home, work, or school, said that they do not send or receive e-mail.

a) Find the margin of error for this poll if we want 90% confidence in our estimate of the percent of American adults who do not use e-mail.

b) Explain what that margin of error means.

c) If we want to be 99% confident, will the margin of error be larger or smaller? Explain.

d) Find that margin of error.

e) In general, if all other aspects of the situation remain the same, will smaller margins of error involve greater or less confidence in the interval?

52. Biotechnology. A biotechnology firm in Boston is plan-ning its investment strategy for future products and research labs. A poll found that only 8% of a random sample of 1012 U.S. adults approved of attempts to clone a human.

a) Find the margin of error for this poll if we want 95% confidence in our estimate of the percent of American adults who approve of cloning humans.

b) Explain what that margin of error means.

c) If we only need to be 90% confident, will the margin of error be larger or smaller? Explain.

d) Find that margin of error.

e) In general, if all other aspects of the situation remain the same, would smaller samples produce smaller or larger margins of error?

53. Teenage drivers. An insurance company checks police records on 582 accidents selected at random and notes that teenagers were at the wheel in 91 of them.

a) Create a 95% confidence interval for the percentage of all auto accidents that involve teenage drivers.

b) Explain what your interval means.

c) Explain what "95% confidence" means.

d) A politician urging tighter restrictions on drivers' licenses issued to teens says, "In one of every five auto accidents, a teenager is behind the wheel." Does your confidence interval support or contradict this statement? Explain.

54. Advertisers. Direct mail advertisers send solicitations ("junk mail") to thousands of potential customers in the hope that some will buy the company's product. The response rate is usually quite low. Suppose a company wants to test the response to a new flyer and sends it to 1000 people randomly selected from their mailing list of over 200,000 people. They get orders from 123 of the recipients.

a) Create a 90% confidence interval for the percentage of people the company contacts who may buy something.
b) Explain what this interval means.
c) Explain what "90% confidence" means.
d) The company must decide whether to now do a mass mailing. The mailing won't be cost-effective unless it produces at least a 5% return. What does your confidence interval suggest? Explain.

55. Retailers. Some food retailers propose subjecting food to a low level of radiation in order to improve safety, but sale of such "irradiated" food is opposed by many people. Suppose a grocer wants to find out what his customers think. He has cashiers distribute surveys at checkout and ask customers to fill them out and drop them in a box near the front door. He gets responses from 122 customers, of whom 78 oppose the radiation treatments. What can the grocer conclude about the opinions of all his customers?

56. Local news. The mayor of a small city has suggested that the state locate a new prison there, arguing that the construction project and resulting jobs will be good for the local economy. A total of 183 residents show up for a public hearing on the proposal, and a show of hands finds 31 in favor of the prison project. What can the city council conclude about public support for the mayor's initiative?

57. Internet music. In a survey on downloading music, the Gallup Poll asked 703 Internet users if they "ever downloaded music from an Internet site that was not authorized by a record company, or not," and 18% responded "yes." Construct a 95% confidence interval for the true proportion of Internet users who have downloaded music from an Internet site that was not authorized.

58. Economy worries. During the week of April 15, 2013, a Gallup Poll asked 1500 U.S. adults, aged 18 or over, how they rated economic conditions. Only 17% rated the economy as Excellent/Good. Construct a 95% confidence interval for the true proportion of Americans who rated the U.S. economy as Excellent/Good.

59. International business. In Canada, the vast majority (90%) of companies in the chemical industry are ISO 14001 certified. The ISO 14001 is an international standard for environmental management systems. An environmental group wished to estimate the percentage of U.S. chemical companies that are ISO 14001 certified. Of the 550 chemical companies sampled, 385 are certified.

a) What proportion of the sample reported being certified?
b) Create a 95% confidence interval for the proportion of U.S. chemical companies with ISO 14001 certification. (Be sure to check conditions.) Compare to the Canadian proportion.

60. Worldwide survey. GfK Roper surveyed people worldwide, asking them, "How important is acquiring wealth to you?" Of 1535 respondents in India, 1168 said that it was of more than average importance. In the United States, of 1317 respondents, 596 said it was of more than average importance.

a) What proportion thought acquiring wealth was of more than average importance in each country's sample?
b) Create a 95% confidence interval for the proportion who thought it was of more than average importance in India. (Be sure to test conditions.) Compare that to a confidence interval for the U.S. population.

61. Business ethics. In a survey on corporate ethics, a poll split a sample at random, asking 538 faculty and corporate recruiters the question: "Generally speaking, do you believe that MBAs are more or less aware of ethical issues in business today than five years ago?" The other half were asked: "Generally speaking, do you believe that MBAs are less or more aware of ethical issues in business today than five years ago?" These may seem like the same questions, but sometimes the order of the choices matters. In response to the first question, 53% thought MBA graduates were more aware of ethical issues, but when the question was phrased differently, this proportion dropped to 44%.

a) What kind of bias may be present here?
b) Each group consisted of 538 respondents. If we combine them, considering the overall group to be one larger random sample, what is a 95% confidence interval for the proportion of the faculty and corporate recruiters that believe MBAs are more aware of ethical issues today?
c) How does the margin of error based on this pooled sample compare with the margins of error from the separate groups? Why?

62. Middle Eastern entrepreneurs. In 2012, Gallup published a report entitled "Qatar's Rising Entrepreneurial Spirit" in which they concluded that the 33% of 1057 Qatari youth they surveyed who responded that they plan to start their own business was the highest in the region. They conducted a variety of face to face and phone interviews with Qatari youth during their survey. They noted that the margin of error was between 6.6 and 7.8 percentage points, and that "in addition to sampling error, question wording and practical difficulties in conducting surveys can introduce error or bias into the findings of public opinion polls."

a) What kinds of bias might they be referring to?
b) Does their margin of error suggest that this was a simple random sample? Explain.

63. Pharmaceutical company. A pharmaceutical company is considering investing in a "new and improved" vitamin D supplement for children. Vitamin D, whether ingested as a dietary supplement or produced naturally when sunlight falls upon the skin, is essential for strong, healthy bones. The bone disease rickets was largely eliminated in England during the 1950s, but now there is concern that a generation of children more likely to watch TV or play computer games than spend time outdoors is at increased risk. A recent study of 2700 children randomly selected from all parts of England found 20% of them deficient in vitamin D.

a) Find a 98% confidence interval for the proportion of children in England who are deficient in vitamin D.
b) Explain carefully what your interval means.
c) Explain what "98% confidence" means.
d) Does the study show that computer games are a likely cause of rickets? Explain.

64. Real estate survey. A real estate agent looks over the 15 listings she has in a particular ZIP code in California and finds that 80% of them have swimming pools.

a) Check the assumptions and conditions for inference on proportions.
b) If it's appropriate, find a 90% confidence interval for the proportion of houses in this ZIP code that have swimming pools. If it's not appropriate, explain why.

65. Benefits survey. A paralegal at the Vermont State Attorney General's office wants to know how many companies in Vermont provide health insurance benefits to all employees. She chooses 12 companies at random and finds that all 12 offer benefits.

a) Check the assumptions and conditions for inference on proportions.
b) If conditions are met, find a 95% confidence interval for the true proportion of companies that provide health insurance benefits to all their employees. If conditions are not met, explain why.

66. Awareness survey. A telemarketer at a credit card company is instructed to ask the next 18 customers that call into the 800 number whether they are aware of the new Platinum card that the company is offering. Of the 18, 17 said they were aware of the program.

a) Check the assumptions and conditions for inference on proportions.
b) If conditions are met, find a 95% confidence interval for the true proportion of customers who are aware of the new card. If conditions are not met, explain why.

67. IRS. In a random survey of 226 self-employed individuals, 20 reported having had their tax returns audited by the IRS in the past year. Estimate the proportion of self-employed individuals nationwide who've been audited by the IRS in the past year.

a) Check the assumptions and conditions (to the extent you can) for constructing a confidence interval.

b) Construct a 95% confidence interval.
c) Interpret your interval.
d) Explain what "95% confidence" means in this context.

68. Internet music, again. A Gallup Poll (Exercise 57) asked Americans if the fact that they can make copies of songs on the Internet for free made them more likely—or less likely—to buy a performer's CD. Only 13% responded that it made them "less likely." The poll was based on a random sample of 703 Internet users.

a) Check that the assumptions and conditions are met for inference on proportions.
b) Find the 95% confidence interval for the true proportion of all U.S. Internet users who are "less likely" to buy CDs.

69. Politics. A recent poll of 1005 U.S. adults split the sample into four age groups: ages 18–29, 30–49, 50–64, and 65+. In the youngest age group, 62% said that they thought the United States was ready for a woman president, as opposed to 35% who said, "no, the country was not ready" (3% were undecided). The sample included 250 18- to 29-year-olds.

a) Do you expect the 95% confidence interval for the true proportion of all 18- to 29-year-olds who think the United States is ready for a woman president to be wider or narrower than the 95% confidence interval for the true proportion of all U.S. adults? Explain.
b) Find the 95% confidence interval for the true proportion of all 18- to 29-year-olds who believe the United States is ready for a woman president.

70. More Internet music. A random sample of 168 students was asked how many songs were in their digital music library and what fraction of them was legally purchased. Overall, they reported having a total of 117,079 songs, of which 23.1% were legal. The music industry would like a good estimate of the proportion of songs in students' digital music libraries that are legal.

a) Think carefully. What is the parameter being estimated? What is the population? What is the sample size?
b) Check the conditions for making a confidence interval.
c) Construct a 95% confidence interval for the fraction of legal digital music.
d) Explain what this interval means. Do you believe that you can be this confident about your result? Why or why not?

71. CDs. A company manufacturing CDs is working on a new technology. A random sample of 703 Internet users were asked: "As you may know, some CDs are being manufactured so that you can only make one copy of the CD after you purchase it. Would you buy a CD with this technology, or would you refuse to buy it even if it was one you would normally buy?" Of these users, 64% responded that they would buy the CD.

a) Create a 90% confidence interval for this percentage.
b) If the company wants to cut the margin of error in half, how many users must they survey?

72. Internet music, last time. The research group that conducted the survey in Exercise 70 wants to provide the music industry with definitive information, but they believe that they could use a smaller sample next time. If the group is willing to have twice as big a margin of error, how many songs must be included?

73. Graduation. As in Exercise 19, we hope to estimate the percentage of adults aged 25 to 30 who never graduated from high school. What sample size would allow us to increase our confidence level to 95% while reducing the margin of error to only 2%?

74. Better hiring info. Editors of the business report in Exercise 20 are willing to accept a margin of error of 4% but want 99% confidence. How many randomly selected employers will they need to contact?

75. Pilot study. A state's environmental agency worries that a large percentage of cars may be violating clean air emissions standards. The agency hopes to check a sample of vehicles in order to estimate that percentage with a margin of error of 3% and 90% confidence. To gauge the size of the problem, the agency first picks 60 cars and finds 9 with faulty emissions systems. How many should be sampled for a full investigation?

76. Another pilot study. During routine conversations, the CEO of a new start-up reports that 22% of adults between the ages of 21 and 39 will purchase her new product. Hearing this, some investors decide to conduct a large-scale study, hoping to estimate the proportion to within 4% with 98% confidence. How many randomly selected adults between the ages of 21 and 39 must they survey?

77. Approval rating. A newspaper reports that the governor's approval rating stands at 65%. The article adds that the poll is based on a random sample of 972 adults and has a margin of error of 2.5%. What level of confidence did the pollsters use?

78. Amendment. The Board of Directors of a publicly traded company says that a proposed amendment to their bylaws is likely to win approval in the upcoming election because a poll of 1505 stock owners indicated that 52% would vote in favor. The Board goes on to say that the margin of error for this poll was 3%.

a) Explain why the poll is actually inconclusive.
b) What confidence level did the pollsters use?

T 79. Holiday shopping. The data set provided contains credit card purchases of 500 customers in the month before Christmas, randomly chosen from a segment of a major credit card issuer. The marketing department is considering a special offer for customers who spend more than $1000 per month on their card. From these data construct a 95% confidence interval for the proportion of customers in this segment who will qualify.

T 80. Advertising. A philanthropic organization knows that its donors have an average age near 60 and is considering taking out an ad in the *American Association of Retired People (AARP)* magazine. An analyst wonders what proportion of their donors are actually 50 years old or older. He takes a random sample of the records of 500 donors. From the data provided, construct a 95% confidence interval for the proportion of donors who are 50 years old or older.

JUST CHECKING ANSWERS

1 A Normal model (approximately).
2 At the actual proportion of all customers who like the new location.
3 $SD(\hat{p}) = \sqrt{\dfrac{(0.5)(0.5)}{100}} = 0.05$
4 Wider
5 Lower
6 Smaller

Real Estate Simulation

Many variables important to the real estate market are skewed, limited to only a few values or considered as categorical variables. Yet, marketing and business decisions are often made based on means and proportions calculated over many homes.

Data on 1063 houses sold recently in the Saratoga, New York, area are in the file **Saratoga house prices**. Let's investigate how the sampling distribution of proportions approaches the Normal.

Part 1: Proportions

The variable *Fireplace* is a dichotomous variable where 1 = *has a fireplace* and 0 = *does not have a fireplace*.

- Calculate the proportion of homes that have fireplaces for all 1063 homes. Using this value, calculate what the standard error of the sample proportion would be for a sample of size 50.

- Using the software of your choice, draw 100 samples of size 50 from this population of homes, find the proportion of homes with fireplaces in each of these samples, and make a histogram of these proportions.

- Compare the mean and standard deviation of this (sampling) distribution to what you previously calculated.

- Examine the distribution of the sampled proportions. What do you expect it to look like? How closely does it match the theoretical distribution?

Part 2: Confidence Intervals for Proportion

Of the 1063 homes in the data set, 635, or 59.7% have fireplaces.

- Using appropriate software, draw 100 samples of size 25 from the data and compute 90% confidence intervals for the true proportion.

- How many of these contain 59.7%?

- Repeat this for 100 samples of size 100.

- Write up a short report explaining the main differences between the two sets of intervals.

CHAPTER 11

Confidence Intervals for Means

Guinness & Co.

In 1759, when Arthur Guinness was 34 years old, he signed a 9000-year lease on a run-down, abandoned brewery in Dublin. The brewery covered four acres and consisted of a mill, two malt houses, stabling for 12 horses, and a loft that could hold 200 tons of hay. This was a huge business risk. Brewing was a difficult and competitive market. Gin, whiskey, and the traditional London porter were the drinks of choice.

In addition to the lighter ales that Dublin was known for, Guinness began to brew dark porters to compete directly with those of the English brewers. Forty years later, Guinness stopped brewing light Dublin ales altogether to concentrate on his stouts and porters. Upon his death in 1803, his son Arthur Guinness II took over the business, and a few years later the company began to export Guinness stout to other parts of Europe. By the 1830s, the Guinness St. James's Gate Brewery had become the largest in Ireland. In 1886, the Guinness Brewery, with an annual production of 1.2 million barrels, was the first major brewery to be incorporated as a public company on the London Stock Exchange. During the 1890s, the company began to employ scientists. One of those, William S. Gosset, was hired as a chemist to test the quality of the brewing process. Gosset was both an early pioneer of quality improvement methods in industry and a statistician whose work made modern statistical inference possible.[1]

As a chemist at Guinness, Gosset was in charge of quality control. His job was to make sure that the quality of the stout would meet the standards of the brewery's discerning customers. It's easy to understand why testing a large amount of stout might be difficult, not to mention dangerous to one's health. So to test for quality, Gosset was limited to samples of only 3 or 4 observations. Working with such small samples, he began to notice that his tests for quality weren't quite right. When the batches that he rejected were sent back to the laboratory for more extensive testing, too often his conclusions turned out to be wrong. As a practicing statistician, Gosset knew he had to be wrong *some* of the time, but it concerned him that he was wrong more often than theory predicted. Gosset took a leave from Guinness to earn one of the first advanced degrees in statistics, and in the process developed methods that are fundamental to statistics practice. We'll see Gosset's insights later in this chapter.

11.1   The Central Limit Theorem

We've learned a lot about proportions. We know that when we sample at random, the proportions we get will vary from sample to sample. We also know that the Normal model does a remarkably good job at summarizing all that variation. Could something that simple work for means? We won't keep you in suspense. It turns out that means also have a sampling distribution that we can model with a Normal model. There's a theoretical result that proves it, but we can understand it from a simulation, too.

Simulating the Sampling Distribution of a Mean

Employees at a large office in an urban area were asked how long they spent commuting to work that day. Here is a histogram of the distribution of times in minutes.

FIGURE 11.1 Commuting times of 5000 representative workers in a Manhattan office. (Data in **Population commute times**)

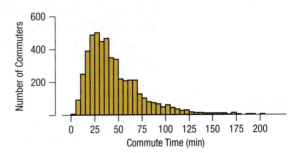

The distribution is skewed to the right, as you would probably expect. Nobody can commute instantly, and some folks have quite a long trip.

The distribution above is a census of all 5000 employees, but typically, only a random sample of employees is interviewed to save time and money. Human Resources (HR) wants to report the mean commuting time to the Vice President,

---
[1]Source: Guinness & Co., www.guinness.com/global/story/history.

using only the smaller sample. How much does the mean of a sample differ from the "true" mean of the entire population? Let's use simulation to understand how the means of samples behave.

If HR were to select a single employee at random, their commute time would be that sample's mean (since there is only one value). Here's a simulation of 10,000 such samples of size 1:

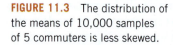

FIGURE 11.2 The distribution of the means of 10,000 "samples" of one commuter looks like the population distribution.

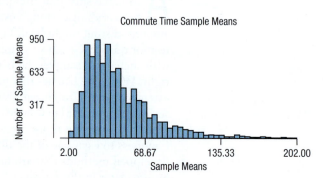

It looks a lot like the population of 5000, but here there are 10,000 "means," so it isn't quite the same.

Few people would be comfortable with a sample of size 1. What about samples of 5 workers? Here is how means of random samples of 5 are distributed when we simulate 10,000 samples:

FIGURE 11.3 The distribution of the means of 10,000 samples of 5 commuters is less skewed.

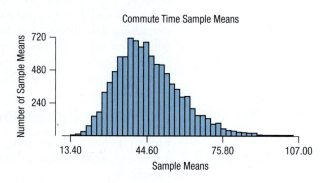

The distribution of the sample means is less skewed and smoother than the population distribution. But samples of 5 are still small. What if we sampled 20 workers, (and again simulated to repeat the random sample 10,000 times)? What would the means look like then?

FIGURE 11.4 The distribution of the means of 10,000 samples of 20 commuters.

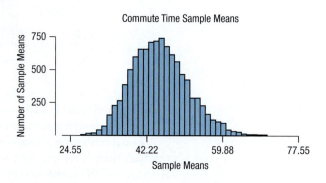

This distribution is unimodal and nearly symmetric. Notice also how much less the means vary. Where for small samples they went from near 0 to more than 200 minutes, now they are roughly between 24 and 77.

Let's try samples of 50:

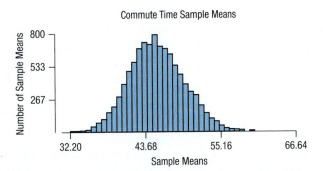

Commute Time Sample Means

FIGURE 11.5   The distribution of the means of 10,000 samples of 50 commuters is nearly Normal and much less variable than the data (in Figure 11.1).

Now the Normal shape of the distribution of the means is quite clear. It is also clear that the means vary much less than the original data.

Do sample means always behave like this? Does the Normal model emerge magically to describe how sample means vary from sample to sample?

The Central Limit Theorem

The simulation may look like a special situation. But it turns out that what we see when we sampled the commute times is true for means of repeated samples for almost every situation. The result is even more remarkable than it may at first appear. It is true for sufficiently large samples from almost any population. That is, there are almost no special conditions at all.

Let's say that again: The sampling distribution of *any* mean becomes Normal as the sample size grows. All we need is for the observations to be mutually independent. We don't even care about the shape of the population distribution![2] This surprising fact was proved in a fairly general form in 1810 by Pierre-Simon Laplace, and caused quite a stir (at least in mathematics circles) because it is so unintuitive. Laplace's result is called the **Central Limit Theorem**[3] (CLT).

Not only does the distribution of means of many random samples get closer and closer to a Normal model as the sample size grows, but *this is true regardless of the shape of the population distribution!* Even if we sample from a skewed or bimodal population, the Central Limit Theorem tells us that means of repeated random samples will tend to follow a Normal model as the sample size grows. Of course, it works better and faster the closer the population distribution is to a Normal model. If the data come from a population that's exactly Normal to start with, then the observations themselves are Normal. If we take samples of size 1, their "means" are just drawn from the observations themselves—so, of course, they have a Normal sampling distribution. We've seen that it works for a moderately skewed population distribution, but the theorem works even for a population that is very skewed (like the CEO data from Chapter 3, for example), although then it may take a sample size of hundreds of observations for the Normal model to work well.

For example, think about a real bimodal population, one that consists of only 0s and 1s. The CLT says that even means of samples from this population will follow a Normal sampling distribution model. But wait. Suppose we have a

Pierre-Simon Laplace, 1749–1827.

❝ The theory of probabilities is at bottom nothing but common sense reduced to calculus. ❞

—Laplace, in Théorie Analytique des Probabilitiés, 1812

---

[2] Technically, the data must come from a population with a finite variance.

[3] The word "central" in the name of the theorem means "fundamental." It doesn't refer to the center of a distribution.

categorical variable and we assign a 1 to each individual in the category and a 0 to each individual not in the category. Then we find the mean of these 0s and 1s. That's the same as counting the number of individuals who are in the category and dividing by n. That mean will be the *sample proportion*, $\hat{p}$, of individuals who are in the category (a "success"). So maybe it wasn't so surprising after all that proportions, like means, have Normal sampling distribution models; proportions are actually just a special case of Laplace's remarkable theorem. Of course, for such an extremely bimodal population, we need a reasonably large sample size—and that's where the Success/Failure Condition for proportions comes in.

> **The Central Limit Theorem (CLT)**
> The mean of a random sample has a sampling distribution whose shape can be approximated by a Normal model. The larger the sample, the better the approximation will be.

Be careful. We have been slipping smoothly between the real world, in which we draw random samples of data, and a magical mathematical-model world, in which we describe how the sample means and proportions we observe in the real world might behave if we could see the results from every random sample that we might have drawn. Now we have *two* distributions to deal with. The first is the real-world distribution of the sample, which we might display with a histogram (for quantitative data) or with a bar chart or table (for categorical data). The second is the math-world *sampling distribution* of the statistic, which we can approximate with a simulation, as we did earlier, or model with a Normal model based on the Central Limit Theorem. Don't confuse the two.

For example, don't mistakenly think the CLT says that the *data* are Normally distributed as long as the sample is large enough. In fact, we expect that the larger the sample, the more the distribution of the data will look like the distribution of the population from which it is drawn—skewed, bimodal, whatever—but not necessarily Normal. You can collect a sample of CEO salaries for all the companies in the world, but the histogram will never look Normal. It will be skewed to the right. The Central Limit Theorem doesn't talk about the distribution of the data from the sample. It talks about the sample *means* and sample *proportions* of many different random samples drawn from the same population. Of course, we never actually draw all those samples, so the CLT is talking about an imaginary distribution—the sampling distribution model.

When the population shape is not unimodal and symmetric, we need larger samples for the sampling distribution to resemble the Normal. But when the sample is large enough, the CLT applies to means and proportions from almost any dataset.

JUST CHECKING

> **The Central Limit Theorem**
>
> A supermarket manager examines the amount spent by customers using a self-checkout station. He finds that the distribution of these amounts is unimodal but skewed to the high end because some customers make unusually expensive purchases. He finds the mean spent on each of the 30 days studied and makes a histogram of those values.
>
> 1 What shape would you expect for this histogram?
>
> 2 If, instead of averaging all customers on each day, he selects the first 10 for each day and just averages those, how would you expect his histogram of the means to differ from the one in (1)?

11.2   The Sampling Distribution of the Mean

The CLT says that the sampling distribution of any mean or proportion is approximately Normal. But which Normal? We know that any Normal model is specified by its mean and standard deviation. For proportions, the sampling distribution is centered at the population proportion. For means, it's centered at the population mean. What else would we expect?

What about the standard deviations? We noticed in our simulation that the histograms got narrower as the number of commuters we averaged increased. This shouldn't be surprising. Means vary less than the individual observations. Think about it for a minute. Which would be more surprising, having *one* person in your statistics class who is over 6′9″ tall or having the *mean* of 100 students taking the course be over 6′9″? The first event is fairly rare.[4] You may have seen somebody this tall in one of your classes sometime. But finding a class of 100 whose mean height is over 6′9″ tall just won't happen. Why? *Means have smaller standard deviations than individuals.*

> The n's justify the means.
>
> Statistics pun
> (Fortunately, there aren't many.)

Specifically, the Normal model for the sampling distribution of the mean has a standard deviation $SD(\bar{y}) = \dfrac{\sigma}{\sqrt{n}}$ where we write σ for the standard deviation of the population, as we did in Chapter 7. To emphasize that this standard deviation is a *parameter* of the sampling distribution model for the sample mean, $\bar{y}$, we write $SD(\bar{y})$ or $\sigma(\bar{y})$.

The Sampling Distribution Model for a Mean

When a random sample is drawn from any population with mean μ and standard deviation σ, its sample mean, $\bar{y}$, has a sampling distribution with the same mean μ but whose standard deviation is $\dfrac{\sigma}{\sqrt{n}}$, and we write $\sigma(\bar{y}) = SD(\bar{y}) = \dfrac{\sigma}{\sqrt{n}}$. No matter what population the random sample comes from, the shape of the sampling distribution is approximately Normal as long as the sample size is large enough. The larger the sample used, the more closely the Normal approximates the sampling distribution model for the mean.

We now have two closely related sampling distribution models. Which one we use depends on which kind of data we have.

- When we have categorical data, we calculate a sample proportion, $\hat{p}$. Its sampling distribution follows a Normal model with a mean at the population proportion, p, and a standard deviation $SD(\hat{p}) = \sqrt{\dfrac{pq}{n}} = \dfrac{\sqrt{pq}}{\sqrt{n}}$.

- When we have quantitative data, we calculate a sample mean, $\bar{y}$. Its sampling distribution has a Normal model with a mean at the population mean, μ, and a standard deviation $SD(\bar{y}) = \dfrac{\sigma}{\sqrt{n}}$.

The means of these models are easy to remember, so all you need to be careful about is the standard deviations. Remember that these are standard deviations of the *statistics* $\hat{p}$ and $\bar{y}$. They both have a square root of n in the denominator.

---

[4]If students are a random sample of adults, fewer than 1 out of 10,000 should be taller than 6′9″. Why might college students not really be a random sample with respect to height? Even if they're not a perfectly random sample, a college student over 6′9″ tall is still rare.

That tells us that the larger the sample, the less either statistic will vary. The only difference is in the numerator. If you just start by writing $SD(\bar{y})$ for quantitative data and $SD(\hat{p})$ for categorical data, you'll be able to remember which formula to use.

IN PRACTICE 11.1 Working with the sampling distribution of the mean

The weights of boxes shipped by a company follow a unimodal, symmetric distribution with a mean of 12 lbs and a standard deviation of 4 lbs. Boxes are shipped in palettes of 10 boxes.

MANAGER It is a problem for the company if palettes exceed the shipper's limit of 150 lbs. What is the probability that a palette will exceed that limit?

ANALYST Asking the probability that the total weight of a sample of 10 boxes exceeds 150 lbs is the same as asking the probability that the *mean* weight exceeds 15 lbs. First I'll check the conditions. I will assume that the 10 boxes on the palette are a random sample from the population of boxes and that their weights are mutually independent. We know that the underlying distribution of weights is unimodal and symmetric, so a sample of 10 boxes should be large enough.

Under these conditions, the CLT says that the sampling distribution of $\bar{y}$ has a Normal model with mean 12 and standard deviation

$$SD(\bar{y}) = \frac{\sigma}{\sqrt{n}} = \frac{4}{\sqrt{10}} = 1.26 \text{ and } z = \frac{\bar{y} - \mu}{SD(\bar{y})} = \frac{15 - 12}{1.26} = 2.38$$

$$P(\bar{y} > 15) = P(z > 2.38) = 0.0087$$

So the chance that the shipper will reject a palette is only 0.0087—less than 1%.

11.3 How Sampling Distribution Models Work

Both of the sampling distributions we've looked at are Normal. We know for proportions, $SD(\hat{p}) = \sqrt{\dfrac{pq}{n}}$, and for means, $SD(\bar{y}) = \dfrac{\sigma}{\sqrt{n}}$. These are great if we know, or can pretend that we know, p or σ, and sometimes we'll do that.

Often we know only the observed proportion, $\hat{p}$, or the sample standard deviation, s. So of course we just use what we know, and we estimate. That may not seem like a big deal, but it gets a special name. Whenever we estimate the standard deviation of a sampling distribution, we call that estimated standard deviation a **standard error (SE)**.

For a sample proportion, $\hat{p}$, the standard error is:

$$SE(\hat{p}) = \sqrt{\frac{\hat{p}\hat{q}}{n}}.$$

For the sample mean, $\bar{y}$, the standard error is:

$$SE(\bar{y}) = \frac{s}{\sqrt{n}}.$$

You may see a "standard error" reported by a computer program in a summary or offered by a calculator. It's safe to assume that if no statistic is specified, what was meant is $SE(\bar{y})$, the standard error of the mean.

JUST CHECKING

3 The entrance exam for business schools, the GMAT, given to 100 students had a mean of 520 and a standard deviation of 120. What was the standard error for the mean of this sample of students?

4 As the sample size increases, what happens to the standard error, assuming the standard deviation remains constant?

5 If the sample size is doubled, what is the impact on the standard error?

To keep track of how the concepts we've seen combine, we can draw a diagram relating them. At the heart is the idea that *the statistic itself (the sample proportion or the sample mean) is a random quantity*. We can't know what our statistic will be because it comes from a random sample. A different random sample would have given a different result. This sample-to-sample variability is what generates the sampling distribution, the distribution of all the possible values that the statistic could have had.

We could simulate that distribution by pretending to take lots of samples. Fortunately, for the mean and the proportion, the CLT tells us that we can model their sampling distribution directly with a Normal model.

The two basic truths about sampling distributions are:

1. Sampling distributions arise because samples vary. Each random sample will contain different cases and, so, a different value of the statistic.
2. Although we can always simulate a sampling distribution, the Central Limit Theorem saves us the trouble for means and proportions.

When we don't know σ, we estimate it with the standard deviation of the one real sample. That gives us the standard error, $SE(\bar{y}) = \dfrac{s}{\sqrt{n}}$.

Figure 11.6 diagrams the process.

FIGURE 11.6 We start with a population model, which can have any shape. It can even be bimodal or skewed (as this one is). We label the mean of this model μ and its standard deviation, σ.

We draw one real sample (solid line) of size n and show its histogram and summary statistics. We *imagine* (or simulate) drawing many other samples (dotted lines), which have their own histograms and summary statistics.

We (imagine) gathering all the means into a histogram.

The CLT tells us we can model the shape of this histogram with a Normal model. The mean of this Normal is μ, and the standard deviation is

$$SD(\bar{y}) = \frac{\sigma}{\sqrt{n}}.$$

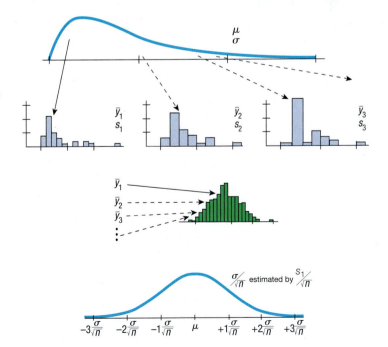

11.4   Gosset and the *t*-Distribution

You've learned how to create confidence intervals for proportions. Now we want to do the same thing for means. For proportions we found the confidence interval as

$$\hat{p} \pm ME.$$

The margin of error (*ME*) was equal to a critical value, z^*, times $SE(\hat{p})$. Our confidence interval for means will look very similar:

$$\bar{y} \pm ME.$$

And our *ME* will be a critical value times $SE(\bar{y})$. So let's put the pieces together.

The Central Limit Theorem gives us a sampling distribution and a standard deviation for the mean. All we need is a random sample of quantitative data and the true value of the population standard deviation σ.

But wait. That could be a problem. To compute $\sigma/\sqrt{n}$ we need to know σ. How are we supposed to know σ? Suppose we told you that for 25 young executives the mean value of their stock portfolios is \$125,672. Would that tell you the value of σ? No, the standard deviation depends on how similarly the executives invest, not on how well they invested (the mean tells us that). But we need σ because it's the numerator of the standard deviation of the sample mean: $SD(\bar{y}) = \dfrac{\sigma}{\sqrt{n}}$. So what can we do? The obvious answer is to use the sample standard deviation, s, from the data instead of σ. The result is the standard error: $SE(\bar{y}) = \dfrac{s}{\sqrt{n}}$.

A century ago, people just plugged the standard error into the Normal model, assuming it would work. And for large sample sizes it *did* work pretty well. But they began to notice problems with smaller samples. The extra variation in the standard error was wreaking havoc with the margins of error.

Gosset was the first to investigate this phenomenon. He realized that not only do we need to allow for the extra variation with larger margins of error, but we also need a new sampling distribution model. In fact, we need a whole *family* of models, depending on the sample size, n. These models are unimodal, symmetric, and bell-shaped, but the smaller our sample, the more we must stretch out the tails. Gosset's work transformed statistics, but most people who use his work don't even know his name.

To find the sampling distribution of $\dfrac{\bar{y}}{s/\sqrt{n}}$, Gosset simulated it *by hand*. He drew paper slips of small samples from a hat *hundreds of times* and computed the means and standard deviations with a mechanically cranked calculator. Today, you could repeat in seconds on a computer the experiment that took him over a year. Gosset's work was so meticulous that not only did he get the shape of the new histogram approximately right, but he even figured out the exact formula for it from his sample. The formula was not confirmed mathematically until years later by Sir Ronald Aylmer Fisher.

Gosset's *t*

Gosset made decisions about the stout's quality by using statistical inference. He knew that if he used a 95% confidence interval, he would fail to capture the true quality of the batch about 5% of the time. However, the lab told him that he was in fact rejecting about 15% of the good batches. Gosset knew something was wrong, and it bugged him.

Gosset took time off from his job to study the problem and earn a graduate degree in the emerging field of statistics. He figured out that when he used the standard error $\dfrac{s}{\sqrt{n}}$, the shape of the sampling model was no longer Normal. He even figured out what the new model was. We now call that model the *t*-distribution.

The Guinness Company didn't give Gosset a lot of support for his work. In fact, it had a policy against publishing results. Gosset had to convince the company that he was not publishing an industrial secret and (as part of getting permission to publish) had to use a pseudonym. The pseudonym he chose was "Student," and ever since, the model he found has been known as **Student's *t***.

NOTATION ALERT

Ever since Gosset, the letter *t* has been reserved in statistics for his distribution.

Using a Known Standard Deviation

Variation is inherent in manufacturing, even under the most tightly controlled processes. To ensure that parts do not vary too much, however, quality professionals monitor the processes by selecting samples at regular intervals. The mean performance of these samples is measured, and if it lies too far from the desired target mean, the process may be stopped until the underlying cause of the problem can be determined. In silicon wafer manufacturing, the thickness of the film is a crucial measurement. To assess a sample of wafers, quality engineers compare the mean thickness of the sample to the target mean. But, they don't estimate the standard deviation of the mean by using the standard error derived from the same sample. Instead they base the standard deviation of the mean on the historical process standard deviation, estimated from a vast collection of similar parts. In this case, the standard deviation can be treated as "known" and the Normal model can be used for the sampling distribution instead of the *t*-distribution.

Gosset's model is bell-shaped, but the details change with the sample sizes (Figure 11.7). In fact, the Student's *t*-models form a family of related distributions that depend on a parameter known as **degrees of freedom**. We often denote degrees of freedom as df and the models as t_{df}, with the numerical value of the degrees of freedom as a subscript. Compared with the Normal model, *t*-models with only a few degrees of freedom have a narrower peak and have fatter tails. (See Figure 11.7.) (That's what makes the margin of error bigger.) As the degrees of freedom increase, the *t*-models look more and more like the Normal model. In fact, the *t*-model with infinite degrees of freedom is exactly Normal.[5] This is great news if you happen to have an infinite number of data values. That's not likely, but fortunately, above a few hundred degrees of freedom it's very hard to tell the difference. Of course, in the rare situation that you *know* σ, it would be foolish not to use that information. If you don't have to estimate σ, you can use the Normal model. Typically that value of σ would be based on (lots of) experience, or on a theoretical model. Usually, however, you'll estimate σ by *s* from the data and use the *t*-model.

z or t?

If you know σ, use *z*. (But that almost never happens.) Whenever you use *s* to estimate σ, use *t*.

Practical Sampling Distribution Model for Means

When certain conditions are met, the standardized sample mean,

$$t = \frac{\bar{y} - \mu}{SE(\bar{y})}$$

follows a Student's *t*-model with $n - 1$ degrees of freedom. We find the standard error from:

$$SE(\bar{y}) = \frac{s}{\sqrt{n}}.$$

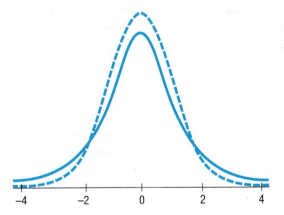

FIGURE 11.7 The *t*-model (solid curve) with 2 degrees of freedom has fatter tails than the Normal model (dashed curve). So the 68–95–99.7 Rule doesn't work for *t*-models with only a few degrees of freedom.

---

[5]Formally, in the limit as the number of degrees of freedom goes to infinity.

11.5   A Confidence Interval for Means

To make confidence intervals, we need to use Gosset's model. Which one? Well, for means, it turns out the right value for degrees of freedom is df $= n - 1$.

One-Sample *t*-Interval

When the assumptions and conditions are met, we are ready to find the **one-sample *t*-interval for the population mean**, μ. The confidence interval is:

$$\bar{y} \pm t^*_{n-1} \times SE(\bar{y})$$

where the standard error of the mean is:

$$SE(\bar{y}) = \frac{s}{\sqrt{n}}.$$

The critical value t^*_{n-1} depends on the particular confidence level, C, that you specify and on the number of degrees of freedom, $n - 1$, which we get from the sample size.

---

*Degrees of Freedom—Why *n* − 1?

The reason we use $n - 1$ degrees of freedom for the t is closely related to why we used $n - 1$ when we calculated the standard deviation. We promised back then to say more about that choice later, and this seems like a good time to bring it up.

If only we knew the true population mean, μ, we would find the sample standard deviation using n instead of $n - 1$ as:

$$s = \sqrt{\frac{\sum (y - \mu)^2}{n}} \text{ and we'd call it } s.$$

We have to use $\bar{y}$ instead of μ, though, and that causes a problem. For any sample, $\bar{y}$ is as close to the data values as possible in the sense that the sum of squared deviations from the sample mean is as small as possible. We say that the mean is a "least squares" statistic. Any other value—and in particular, the population mean, μ—will give a larger sum of squared deviations. So if we use $\sum (y - \bar{y})^2$ instead of $\sum (y - \mu)^2$ in the equation to calculate s, our standard deviation estimate will actually be too small. The amazing mathematical fact is that we can compensate for the fact that $\sum (y - \bar{y})^2$ is too small just by dividing by $n - 1$ instead of by n. So that's what the $n - 1$ is doing in the denominator of s. We call $n - 1$ the degrees of freedom.

When Gosset corrected the Normal model for the extra uncertainty, the margin of error got bigger because more uncertainty calls for a wider margin of error. When you use Gosset's model instead of the Normal model, your confidence intervals will be just a bit wider. That's just the correction you need. By using the t-model, you've compensated for the extra variability in precisely the right way.

Finding *t**-Values

The Student's t-models are different for each value of degrees of freedom. We might print a table like Table Z (in Appendix B) for each degrees of freedom value, but that's a lot of pages and not likely to be a bestseller. One way to shorten the text is to limit ourselves to the most commonly used confidence levels, typically, 80%, 90%, 95%, and 99%. So statistics texts usually have one table of t-model critical values for a selected set of confidence levels. This one does too; see Table T in Appendix B.

The *t*-tables run down the page for as many degrees of freedom as can fit, and, as you can see from Figure 11.8, they are much easier to use than the Normal tables. But there is only room on the page for a limited number of degrees of freedom. Of course, for *enough* degrees of freedom, the *t*-model gets closer and closer to the Normal, so the tables give a final row with the critical values from the Normal model and label it "∞ df." You can also find tables on the Internet,[6] and these often allow other confidence levels and extend for any number of degrees of freedom.

FIGURE 11.8 Part of Table T in Appendix B.

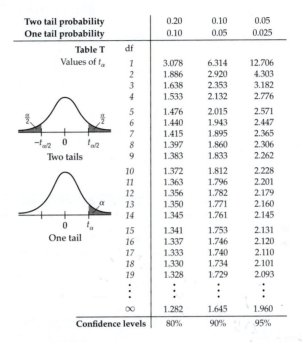

| Two tail probability | | 0.20 | 0.10 | 0.05 |
One tail probability		0.10	0.05	0.025
Table T	df			
Values of t_α	1	3.078	6.314	12.706
	2	1.886	2.920	4.303
	3	1.638	2.353	3.182
	4	1.533	2.132	2.776
	5	1.476	2.015	2.571
	6	1.440	1.943	2.447
	7	1.415	1.895	2.365
	8	1.397	1.860	2.306
	9	1.383	1.833	2.262
	10	1.372	1.812	2.228
	11	1.363	1.796	2.201
	12	1.356	1.782	2.179
	13	1.350	1.771	2.160
	14	1.345	1.761	2.145
	15	1.341	1.753	2.131
	16	1.337	1.746	2.120
	17	1.333	1.740	2.110
	18	1.330	1.734	2.101
	19	1.328	1.729	2.093
	⋮	⋮	⋮	⋮
	∞	1.282	1.645	1.960
Confidence levels		80%	90%	95%

IN PRACTICE 11.2   Finding a confidence interval for the mean

According to the Environmental Defense Fund, "Americans are eating more and more salmon, drawn to its rich taste and health benefits. Increasingly they are choosing *farmed* salmon because of its wide availability and low price. But in the last few years, farmed salmon has been surrounded by controversy over its health risks and the ecological impacts of salmon aquaculture operations. Studies have shown that some farmed salmon is relatively higher in contaminants like PCBs than wild salmon, and there is mounting concern over the industry's impact on wild salmon populations." (Data in **Salmon**)

PURCHASE MANAGER   I have read this study of contaminants in farmed salmon in which fish from many sources were analyzed for 14 organic contaminants.[7] One of those was the insecticide mirex, which has been shown to be carcinogenic and is suspected of being toxic to the liver, kidneys, and endocrine system. I know that the Environmental Protection Agency recommends to recreational fishers a "screening value" that mirex concentration be no larger than 0.08 ppm. Can we be confident that the fish we purchase are safe for our customers?

(continued)

[6]For example, at astools.datadesk.com

[7]Ronald A. Hites, Jeffery A. Foran, David O. Carpenter, M. Coreen Hamilton, Barbara A. Knuth, and Steven J. Schwager, "Global Assessment of Organic Contaminants in Farmed Salmon," *Science* 9, January 2004: Vol. 303, no. 5655, pp. 226–229.

ANALYST Summaries for 150 mirex concentrations (in parts per million) from a variety of farmed salmon sources were reported as:

$$n = 150; \quad \bar{y} = 0.0913 \text{ ppm}; \quad s = 0.0495 \text{ ppm}$$

Because $n = 150$, there are 149 df. (There isn't an entry in Table T for 149 df, but I can use the next *smaller* value to be conservative.) I find $t^*_{140, 0.025} = 1.977$ (from technology, $t^*_{149, 0.025} = 1.976$), so a 95% confidence interval is

$$\bar{y} \pm t^* \times SE(\bar{y}) = \bar{y} \pm 1.977 \times \frac{s}{\sqrt{n}} = 0.0913 \pm 1.977\frac{0.0495}{\sqrt{150}} = (0.0833, 0.0993)$$

If this sample is representative (as the authors claim it is), we can be 95% confident that it contains the true value of the mean mirex concentration. Because the interval from 0.0833 to 0.0993 ppm is entirely above the recommended value set by the EPA, we have reason to believe that the true mirex concentration exceeds the EPA guidelines. We may want to purchase wild salmon or find a fish farm that tests for safe levels of contaminants.

11.6 Assumptions and Conditions

Gosset found the *t*-model by simulation. Years later, when Sir Ronald Fisher showed mathematically that Gosset was right (and, incidentally, named the distribution "*t*"), he needed to make some assumptions to make the proof work. These are the assumptions we need in order to use the Student's *t*-models.

Independence Assumption

The data values should be independent. There's really no way to check independence of the data by looking at the sample, but we should think about whether the assumption is reasonable.

Randomization Condition: The data arise from a random sample or suitably randomized experiment. Randomly sampled data—and especially data from a Simple Random Sample (SRS)—are ideal.

When a sample is drawn without replacement, technically we ought to confirm that we haven't sampled a large fraction of the population, which would threaten the independence of our selections. In that case, we can check the following condition.

10% Condition: The sample size should be no more than 10% of the population. In practice, though, we often don't mention the 10% Condition when estimating means. Why not? When we made inferences about proportions, this condition was crucial because we usually had large samples. But for means our samples are generally smaller, so this problem arises only if we're sampling from a small population (and then there's a correction formula we could use).

Normal Population Assumption

Student's *t*-models won't work for data that are badly skewed. How skewed is too skewed? Well, formally, we assume that the data are from a population that follows a Normal model. Practically speaking, there's no way to be certain this is true.

And it's almost certainly *not* true. Models are idealized; real data are, well, real. The good news, however, is that even for small samples, it's sufficient to check a condition.

We Don't *Want* to Stop

We check conditions hoping that we can make a meaningful analysis of our data. The conditions serve as *disqualifiers*—we keep going unless there's a serious problem. If we find minor issues, we note them and express caution about our results. If the sample is not an SRS, but we believe it's representative of some populations, we limit our conclusions accordingly. If there are outliers, rather than stop, we perform the analysis both with and without them. If the sample looks bimodal, we try to analyze subgroups separately. Only when there's major trouble—like a strongly skewed small sample or an obviously nonrepresentative sample—are we unable to proceed at all.

Nearly Normal Condition. The data come from a distribution that is unimodal and symmetric. This is a much more practical condition and one we can check by making a histogram.[8] For small samples, it can be hard to see any distribution shape in the histogram. Unfortunately, the condition matters most when it's hardest to check.

For very small samples ($n < 15$ or so), the data should follow a Normal model pretty closely. Of course, with so little data, it's rather hard to tell. But if you do find outliers or strong skewness, don't use these methods.

For moderate sample sizes (n between 15 and 40 or so), the t methods will work well as long as the data are unimodal and reasonably symmetric. Make a histogram to check.

When the sample size is larger than 40 or 50, the t methods are safe to use unless the data are extremely skewed.[9] Make a histogram anyway. If you find outliers in the data and they aren't errors that are easy to fix, it's always a good idea to perform the analysis twice, once with and once without the outliers, even for large samples. The outliers may well hold additional information about the data, so they deserve special attention. If you find multiple modes, you may well have different groups that should be analyzed and understood separately.

If the data are extremely skewed, the mean may not be the most appropriate summary. But when our data consist of a collection of instances whose *total* is the business consequence—as when we add up the profits (or losses) from many transactions or the costs of many supplies—then the mean is just that total divided by n. And that's the value with a business consequence. Fortunately, in this instance, the Central Limit Theorem comes to our rescue. Even when we must sample from a very skewed distribution, the sampling distribution of our sample mean will be close to Normal, so we can use Student's t methods without much worry as long as the sample size is *large enough*.

How large is large enough? Figure 11.9 shows a histogram of CEO compensations ($000) for *Fortune* 500 companies.

FIGURE 11.9 It's hard to imagine a distribution more skewed than these annual compensations from the *Fortune* 500 CEOs.

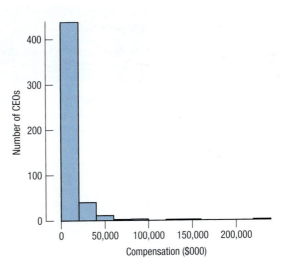

[8]Or we could check a Normal probability plot.

[9]You may see the "rule" that for samples bigger than 30 you should use the Normal model. This rule appears to have arisen because printed t-tables generally ran out of room on the page at about 30 df, rather than for good statistical reasons. With the availability of t-tables on the Internet and the fact that statistics programs can deal with any number of degrees of freedom, this rule is out of date. You may notice that even table T in the back of this text provides values up to 1000 df.

Although this distribution is very skewed, the Central Limit Theorem will make the sampling distribution of the means of samples from this distribution more and more Normal as the sample size grows. Figure 11.10 is a histogram of the means of many samples of 100 CEOs:

FIGURE 11.10 Even samples as small as 100 from the CEO dataset produce means whose sampling distribution is nearly Normal. Larger samples will have sampling distributions even more Normal.

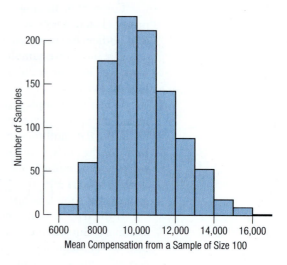

Often, in modern business applications, even if we have a sample of many hundreds, or thousands, we should still be on guard for outliers and multiple modes and we should think about whether the observations are independent. But if the mean is of interest, the Central Limit Theorem works quite well in ensuring that the sampling distribution of the mean will be close to the Normal for samples of this size.

IN PRACTICE 11.3 Checking the assumptions and conditions for a confidence interval for means

Researchers purchased whole farmed salmon from 51 farms in eight regions in six countries. The histogram shows the concentrations of the insecticide mirex in the 150 samples of farmed salmon we examined in the previous example. (Data in **Salmon**)

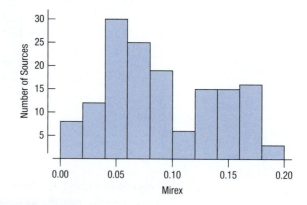

PURCHASING MANAGER Before I decide to change our purchasing I'd like to be sure that your confidence interval is valid. Are the assumptions and conditions for making a confidence interval for the mean mirex concentration satisfied?

> **ANALYST** Here are the assumptions and conditions that I checked:
> - ✓ **Independence Assumption:** The fish were raised in many different places, and samples were purchased independently from several sources.
> - ✓ **Randomization Condition:** The fish were selected randomly from those available for sale.
> - ✓ **Nearly Normal Condition:** The histogram of the data looks bimodal. While it might be interesting to learn the reason for that and possibly identify the subsets, we can proceed because the sample size is large.
>
> It's okay to use these data about farm-raised salmon to make a confidence interval for the mean. I think we can trust the results.

JUST CHECKING

> **The alumni organization of your university is trying to get information on the success of their recent graduates, so they have surveyed a sample of graduates. We know that incomes are likely to be skewed to the right (although perhaps not as much as the salaries of CEOs!).**
>
> **6** If they are successful at obtaining the salaries of only 20 recent graduates, what should they be concerned about when reporting a confidence interval for mean salaries of all recent grads?
>
> **7** Why do they need to base these confidence intervals on *t*-models?
>
> **8** If they manage to get 60 salaries instead of 20, how will this affect their confidence interval?

GUIDED EXAMPLE   Insurance Profits

Insurance companies take risks. When they insure a property or a life, they must price the policy in such a way that their expected profit enables them to survive. They can base their projections on actuarial tables, but the reality of the insurance business often demands that they discount policies to a variety of customers and situations. Managing this risk is made even more difficult by the fact that until the policy expires, the company won't know if they've made a profit, no matter what premium they charge.

A manager wanted to see how well one of her sales representatives was doing, so she selected 30 matured policies that had been sold by the sales rep and computed the (net) profit (premium charged minus paid claims), for each of the 30 policies.

The manager would like you, as a consultant, to construct a 95% confidence interval for the mean profit of the policies sold by this sales rep. (Data in **Insurance profits sales rep**)

Profit (in $) from 30 Policies		
222.80	463.35	2089.40
1756.23	−66.20	2692.75
1100.85	57.90	2495.70
3340.66	833.95	2172.70
1006.50	1390.70	3249.65
445.50	2447.50	−397.10
3255.60	1847.50	−397.31
3701.85	865.40	186.25
−803.35	1415.65	590.85
3865.90	2756.94	578.95

(continued)

PLAN	**Define** and state the problem. **Characterize** the variables and their context. **Explore** the data. Check the distribution shape and look for skewness, multiple modes, and outliers.	We wish to find a 95% confidence interval for the mean profit of policies sold by this sales rep. We have data for 30 matured policies. Here's a boxplot and histogram of these values. 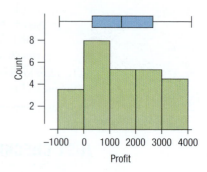 The sample appears to be unimodal and fairly symmetric with profit values between −$1000 and $4000 and no outliers.

DO	Compute basic statistics and construct the confidence interval.	Using software, we obtain the following basic statistics: $$n = 30$$ $$\bar{y} = \$1438.90$$ $$s = \$1329.60$$
	Model Think about the assumptions and check the conditions.	✔ **Independence Assumption** This is a random sample so observations should be independent. ✔ **Randomization Condition** This sample was selected randomly from the matured policies sold by the sales representative of the company. ✔ **Nearly Normal Condition** The distribution of profits is unimodal and fairly symmetric without strong skewness.
	State the sampling distribution model for the statistic. Remember that the standard error of the mean is equal to the standard deviation divided by the square root of n. The critical value we need to make a 95% confidence interval comes from a Student's t-table, a computer program, or a calculator. We have $30 - 1 = 29$ degrees of freedom. So we look up the corresponding t^*-value in Table Z.	We will use a Student's t-model with $n - 1 = 30 - 1 = 29$ degrees of freedom and find a one-sample t-interval for the mean. The standard error of the mean is: $$SE(\bar{y}) = \frac{s}{\sqrt{n}} = \frac{1329.60}{\sqrt{30}} = \$242.75$$ There are $30 - 1 = 29$ degrees of freedom. The manager has specified a 95% level of confidence, so the critical value (from Table T) is 2.045. The margin of error is: $$ME = 2.045 \times SE(\bar{y})$$ $$= 2.045 \times 242.75$$ $$= \$496.42$$ The 95% confidence interval for the mean profit is: $$\$1438.90 \pm \$496.42$$ $$= (\$942.48, \$1935.32)$$

REPORT **Communicate and Present**

Interpret the confidence interval in the proper context.

When we construct confidence intervals in this way, we expect 95% of them to cover the true mean and 5% to miss the true value. That's what "95% confident" means.

MEMO

Re: Profit from policies

From our analysis of the selected policies, we are 95% confident that the true mean profit of policies sold by this sales rep is contained in the interval from $942.48 to $1935.32.

Caveat: Insurance losses are notoriously subject to outliers. One very large loss could influence the average profit substantially. However, there were no such cases in this dataset.

Cautions About Interpreting Confidence Intervals

Confidence intervals for means offer new, tempting, wrong interpretations. Here are some ways to keep from going astray:

- *Don't say,* "*95% of all the policies* sold by this sales rep have profits between $942.48 and $1935.32." The confidence interval is about the *mean*, not about the measurements of individual policies.
- *Don't say,* "We are 95% confident that *a randomly selected policy* will have a net profit between $942.48 and $1935.32." This false interpretation is also about individual policies rather than about the *mean* of the policies. We are 95% confident that the *mean* profit of all (similar) policies sold by this sales rep is between $942.48 and $1935.32.
- *Don't say,* "The mean profit is $1438.90 *95% of the time.*" That's about means, but still wrong. It implies that the true mean varies, when in fact it is the confidence interval that would have been different had we gotten a different sample.
- *Finally, don't say,* "*95% of all samples* will have mean profits between $942.48 and $1935.32." That statement suggests that *this* interval somehow sets a standard for every other interval. In fact, this interval is no more (or less) likely to be correct than any other. You could say that 95% of all possible samples would produce intervals that contain the true mean profit. (The problem is that because we'll never know what the true mean profit is, we can't know if our sample was one of those 95%.)

So, what *should* you say? Since 95% of random samples yield an interval that captures the true mean, you should say:

- "I am 95% confident that the interval from $942.48 to $1935.32 contains the mean profit of all policies sold by this sales representative." It's also okay to make this a little less formal by saying something like:
- "I am 95% confident that the mean profit for all policies sold by this sales rep is between $942.48 and $1935.32."

Remember: Your uncertainty is about the interval, not the true mean. The interval varies randomly. The true mean profit is neither variable nor random—just unknown.

JUST CHECKING

9 The alumni organization finds a confidence interval for the mean starting salary of their recent graduates to be ($55,000, $62,000). They release a statement to prospective students saying that 95% of them will earn between $55,000 and $62,000 their first year on the job. Why is this wrong?

Sample Size

How large a sample do we need? More information is always better, but acquiring more observations costs money, effort, and time. So how much data is enough?

As we make plans to collect data, we should have some idea of how small a margin of error is required to be able to draw a conclusion or detect a difference we want to see. If the size of the effect we're studying is large, then we may be able to tolerate a larger ME. If we need greater precision, however, we'll want a smaller ME, and, of course, that means a larger sample size. Armed with the ME and confidence level, we can find the sample size we'll need. Almost.

We know that for a mean, $ME = t^*_{n-1} \times SE(\bar{y})$ and that $SE(\bar{y}) = \dfrac{s}{\sqrt{n}}$, so we can determine the sample size by solving this equation for n:

$$ME = t^*_{n-1} \times \frac{s}{\sqrt{n}}.$$

The good news is that we have an equation; the bad news is that we won't know most of the values we need to compute it. When we thought about sample size for proportions, we ran into a similar problem. There we had to guess a working value for p to compute a sample size. Here, we need to know s, and if we're thinking about a very small sample, we need to know how many degrees of freedom to use. As an approximation for the critical value of t for 95% confidence (for the number of df we are likely to see), we can use 2.0 instead of t^*. That's much simpler to calculate, and it's a pretty good approximation for the number of degrees of freedom we're likely to see. We don't know s until we get some data, but we want to calculate the sample size *before* collecting the data. We might be able to make a good guess, and that is often good enough for this purpose. If we have no idea what the standard deviation might be or if the sample size really matters (for example, because each additional individual is very expensive to sample or experiment on), it might be a good idea to run a small *pilot study* to get some feeling for the size of the standard deviation.

There are software packages available that can compute sample sizes for confidence intervals. You'll need to specify the margin of error you want to see, the confidence level you want, and a value for the standard deviation. It's important to keep in mind that all sample size calculations are approximate. You'll either need to assume a value for the standard deviation, or run a pilot study to estimate it. And you won't know the *actual* margin of error until after you've collected the data.

JUST CHECKING

> **You've seen an ad for some software that claims to lower the time it takes to download movies. It costs $49.95, so you're thinking about testing it on a few movies to see if it really works before you buy. Right now it takes you about 20 minutes on average to download a 2-hour movie. The standard deviation is about 5 minutes.**
>
> **10** Suppose the standard deviation of the time it takes this software is only 2 minutes instead of 5. Will this widen or narrow your confidence interval for the mean time it takes to download a movie? Why?

IN PRACTICE 11.4   Finding the sample size for a confidence interval for means

In the 150 samples of farmed salmon (see pages 355–356), the mean concentration of mirex was 0.0913 ppm with a standard deviation of 0.0495 ppm. A 95% confidence interval for the mean mirex concentration was found to be (0.0833, 0.0993).

PURCHASING MANAGER   I would feel more comfortable with an interval that had a margin of error of 0.004. How much larger must the sample be for that?

ANALYST   We will assume that the standard deviation is 0.0495 ppm. The margin of error is equal to the critical value times the standard error. Using 2 for t^*, we find:

$$0.004 = 2 \times \frac{0.0495}{\sqrt{n}}$$

Solving for n, we find:

$$\sqrt{n} = 2 \times \frac{0.0495}{0.004}$$

or

$$n = \left(2 \times \frac{0.0495}{0.004} \right)^2 = 612.56$$

We would need a sample of at least 613 to have a good chance of getting a margin of error of 0.004.

11.7   Visualizing Confidence Intervals for the Mean

When we simulated the sampling distribution of means of samples drawn from the population of commuters, we saw that the most common values for the means were in the middle of the distributions, with less common ones showing up in the tails.

Of course, each simulation is different, but Figure 11.11 shows another simulation of the means of 10,000 samples of size 50. Once again we see that the sampling distribution of the means looks quite close to a Normal.

FIGURE 11.11   Means of 10,000 random samples of size 50 from the population of 5000 commuters show a unimodal and almost symmetric distribution. Here the middle 95% of the values are highlighted.

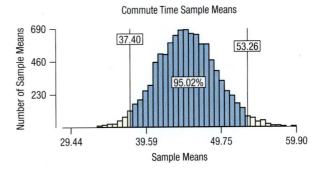

Figure 11.11 colors the part of the histogram containing the middle 95% of the simulated means. The interval shown—in this example from 37.40 to 53.26—is an interval of length 15.86 minutes that holds the 95% *most likely values* for the mean. But, this isn't a confidence interval. A confidence interval tries to capture the population mean by using a sample. Here we "cheated." We used the population itself, so this interval is centered right at the population mean. That's not how a confidence

interval works, but it gives us a visual way to think about how a confidence interval works. Look at all the samples in the colored area. If we took an interval of the same length (15.86) minutes and centered it at each of those means, those confidence intervals would all capture the population mean. Only the 5% noncolored samples have means too far away for this to work. That's what we mean by a 95% confidence interval. It works for 95% of all random samples. (Too bad we'll never know if our sample is one of them!).

Now there's a catch. How do we know the length of the interval to place on top of our sample mean? That's where Gosset comes in. He figured out the theoretical distribution (the t) used to find the right margin of error. It's a theoretical result, but it works remarkably well in practice.

*Bootstrapping

Recently a trick using computer simulation was found that lets us generate a picture like the one in Figure 11.11 with only one sample, without using Gosset's distribution. Let's suppose we started with just one sample of 50 commuters. Here are their commuting times: (Data in **Commute times sample50**)

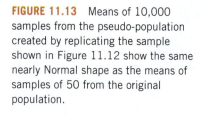

FIGURE 11.12 A sample of 50 commute times shows the same skewness to the right.

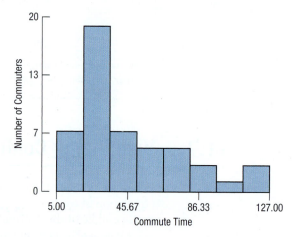

Now we'd like to take a different sample from the population, but usually we can't. Instead, we make a pseudo-population by creating many, many copies of this sample. This invented population isn't the same as the original one, but it does resemble it. Next we'll repeat what we did for Figure 11.11, but instead of using the real population we'll take 10,000 samples from this pseudo-population.[10] Here's the histogram of those means:

FIGURE 11.13 Means of 10,000 samples from the pseudo-population created by replicating the sample shown in Figure 11.12 show the same nearly Normal shape as the means of samples of 50 from the original population.

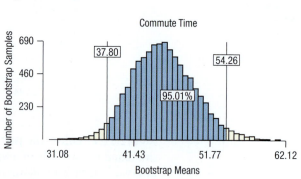

---

[10]It isn't necessary to actually construct the pseudo-population. The same result comes from sampling from the data *with replacement*—that is, each time a value is sampled, it is thrown back in so it can possibly be sampled again.

Wow. We get a sampling distribution that looks remarkably like the one we got by honestly sampling from the population—with one big difference. This one isn't centered at the population mean, but at the mean of our sample. And when we identify the middle 95% of these means as the most plausible values for the mean, we get a confidence interval centered at the sample mean. Now here's the amazing part: Notice that the interval is the right length (or very close). We've managed to find the right margin of error without Gosset's distribution and without having to know the population. It's as if we pulled ourselves up by our bootstraps—and that's what the statistician Brad Effron thought when he discovered it. So he called it the **bootstrap**. The samples are called **bootstrap samples** and the repeated sampling from the pseudo-population is called **resampling**. Because this interval has the right margin of error and is centered at our sample's mean, it's a confidence interval for the population mean—called, remarkably enough—a **bootstrap confidence interval**. And, of course, by choosing a different percentage of means in the middle, we can make a confidence interval for any level of confidence that we like. We just must be sure to take enough samples. Typically, 1000 or more is good enough.

Notice that because our simulated intervals are based on random simulations, they aren't exactly the same. That should remind us that confidence intervals are themselves random objects. And they must be random because they are based on means and standard deviations, which vary from sample to sample.

Bootstrap confidence intervals are available in many statistics programs. Of course, you can't compute them by hand. They have the advantage that, unlike confidence intervals based on Student's *t*, there is no need to assume that the underlying population is Normal. They have the disadvantage that they need a computer and are random—and thus not entirely reproducible.

Note also that, although you needn't check for near-Normality, you do need to check for outliers and multiple modes, either of which will mess up a bootstrap confidence interval (as it would a Student's *t*-interval). Behavior like that in your data always needs to be dealt with before you proceed in any analysis.

Comparing the Methods

We now have two ways to identify an interval that contains plausible values for the population mean. For a particular sample, these methods won't give exactly the same answer. In fact, the bootstrap method will give a slightly different interval each time we run the resampling program. This time it gave a 95% interval from 37.80 to 54.26 minutes and the *t*-interval, based on the CLT, would be from 36.93 to 53.51 minutes. The difference in the intervals is a helpful reminder that confidence intervals are *random*. That is, we expect confidence intervals to vary from sample to sample. And for bootstraps, from run to run. But that's OK. All we are claiming is that, in the long run, about 95% of these intervals will include the true mean, and certainly two different, but similar, intervals can each do that.

Thoughts About Confidence Intervals

The 5000 employees whose commute times we've examined are a diverse group. Some live virtually next to the office in Lower Manhattan, commuting only a minute or two to work, and others live far out on Long Island or in New Jersey and Pennsylvania, commuting several hours a day. On average, they commute about 45.4 minutes a day.

We have two very different methods for finding a confidence interval for the mean given a random sample. One is based on the Central Limit Theorem, using Gosset's *t* correction when estimating the standard deviation of the mean. The other, based on the bootstrap, resamples the data to estimate how much the sample mean varies and looks at the histogram of the bootstrap means. It constructs the confidence interval by identifying the central values of this histogram as the plausible values for the true mean.

Does it make any difference which method you use? Well, yes and no. Yes, in the sense that you'll get slightly different answers. In fact, if you repeat the bootstrap, you (or your classmates) will get slightly different answers each time you resample, even with the same data. And of course, if you draw a new sample from the population, you'll get a new confidence interval no matter which method you use. But really the answer is no, it doesn't make much difference to decisions about the real world. A confidence interval for the mean is simply a carefully stated guess about where we think the mean might be, along with an indication of how successful we think that guess might be.

There are always constraints on what we can know about a population from a sample. Some arise from the size of the sample, others from the quality of the data and how the data were gathered. A confidence interval communicates some of those constraints, but you should keep in mind the limits of your data.

For example, the t-interval for the mean commute times for our sample gives (36.93, 53.51) minutes as the 95% confidence interval. Since we know $\mu = 45.43$, we can see that it "worked." One bootstrap interval that we ran gave (37.80, 54.26) minutes. Most software reports intervals like this to ridiculous fake precision. For example:

```
95 percent confidence interval:
36.926695 53.513305

sample estimates:
mean of x = 45.22
```

The commuters reported their commute time in minutes. (And some may have rounded to the nearest quarter hour.) So five decimal places (about 600 microseconds) is a "precision" that just isn't available from the data, nor one that makes any sense.

Similarly, it makes very little difference whether you choose a 95% confidence level or use 98% or 93%. Most people have little intuition for the differences among those.

The *important point* about confidence intervals is not their precision. A confidence interval is, by nature, random. It changes with the sample and, for the bootstrap, with each simulation as well. But every confidence interval contains both our best guess of the mean and how precise we think that guess is.

In the example, we can see that the mean commute time may be about 5 minutes shorter or longer than the sample mean of about 45.0 minutes. That's probably all the HR Department wanted to know.

People often misinterpret confidence intervals. When we asked employees of the company what the 95% interval 37.80 and 54.26 minutes meant, most answered "95% of us commute between about 38 and 54 minutes to work." That would imply that most of the employees live in this ring around Lower Manhattan. See picture to the left.

That's clearly not right. It's the *mean* commute time that we've captured, not the commuters' times themselves. We've seen that people's commute times vary widely, from a few minutes to several hours. A larger sample would make the confidence interval even smaller, but wouldn't make people live nearer to each other.

It's important to know how confidence intervals are constructed and to check the assumptions and conditions to be sure that they are valid. Remember that they represent our best *guess* of where we think the mean is—and how confident we are in that guess.

⊘ WHAT CAN GO WRONG?

First, you must decide when to use Student's *t* methods.

- **Don't confuse proportions and means.** When you treat your data as categorical, counting successes and summarizing with a sample proportion, make inferences using the Normal model methods. When you treat your data as quantitative, summarizing with a sample mean, make your inferences using Student's *t* methods.

Student's *t* methods work only when the Normal Population Assumption is true. Naturally, many of the ways things can go wrong turn out to be ways that the Normal Population Assumption can fail. It's always a good idea to look for the most common kinds of failure. It turns out that you can even fix some of them.

- **Beware of multimodality.** The Nearly Normal Condition clearly fails if a histogram of the data has two or more modes. When you see this, look for the possibility that your data come from two groups. If so, your best bet is to try to separate the data into groups. (Use the variables to help distinguish the modes, if possible. For example, if the modes seem to be composed mostly of men in one and women in the other, split the data according to the person's sex.) Then you can analyze each group separately.

- **Beware of skewed data.** Make a histogram of the data. If the data are severely skewed, you might try re-expressing the variable. Re-expressing may yield a distribution that is unimodal and symmetric, making it more appropriate for the inference methods for means. Re-expression cannot help if the sample distribution is not unimodal.

> **What to Do with Outliers**
>
> As tempting as it is to get rid of annoying values, you can't just throw away outliers and not discuss them. It is not appropriate to lop off the highest or lowest values just to improve your results. The best strategy is to report the analysis with *and* without the outliers and comment on any differences.

- **Investigate outliers.** The Nearly Normal Condition also fails if the data have outliers. If you find outliers in the data, you need to investigate them. Sometimes, it's obvious that a data value is wrong and the justification for removing or correcting it is clear. When there's no clear justification for removing an outlier, you might want to run the analysis both with and without the outlier and note any differences in your conclusions. Any time data values are set aside, you *must* report on them individually. Often they will turn out to be the most informative part of your report on the data.[11]

Of course, Normality issues aren't the only risks you face when doing inferences about means.

- **Watch out for bias.** Measurements of all kinds can be biased. If your observations differ from the true mean in a systematic way, your confidence interval may not capture the true mean. And there is no sample size that will save you. A bathroom scale that's 5 pounds off will be 5 pounds off even if you weigh yourself 100 times and take the average. We've seen several sources of bias in surveys, but measurements can be biased, too. Be sure to think about possible sources of bias in your measurements.

---

[11] This suggestion may be controversial in some disciplines. Setting aside outliers is seen by some as unethical because the result is likely to be a narrower confidence interval or a smaller P-value. But an analysis of data with outliers left in place is *always* wrong. The outliers violate the Nearly Normal Condition and also the implicit assumption of a homogeneous population, so they invalidate inference procedures. An analysis of the nonoutlying points, along with a separate discussion of the outliers, is often much more informative, and can reveal important aspects of the data.

- **Make sure data are independent.** Student's *t* methods also require the sampled values to be mutually independent. We check for random sampling. You should also think hard about whether there are likely violations of independence in the data collection method. If there are, be very cautious about using these methods.

ETHICS IN ACTION

It has been three years since Mohammed Al-Tamimi opened his computer repair business, Mo's Mending Station. Unlike the well-known Nerd Squad of the big electronics retailer, Mo's Mending Station fixes only computers and does not deal with any other electronics such as TVs, phones, cameras, or appliances. Nor does Mo's provide any in-home services, such as networking or computer setup. Mo's main objective is clear: to provide standard repair services for computers and laptops, virus and spyware removal, and data recovery, each at a fixed low price. He charges the competitive rate of $45 per hour for more complicated computer issues.

Mo's slogan is "*Get twice the nerd at half the cost!*" This strategy has worked well, allowing Mohammed to grow his business to include six repair technicians and one office manager. However, recent monthly receipts indicate that the demand for Mo's services may be slowing down. Worried that the Mending Station might be losing its competitive price advantage, Mohammed gathers his staff together for a brainstorming session. Ed Ramsey, who has been with Mo's since it opened, mentions the possibility that the Mending Station's low prices may give some potential customers the impression that it offers poor quality service. He suggests hiring a local advertising firm to help brand Mo's Mending Station as affordable AND high quality by emphasizing its team of professional,

experienced, and friendly repair technicians. In other words, put the focus on "*twice the nerd*" rather than "*half the cost.*"

Mohammed thinks that this is a great idea and wonders if they can also prepare some statistics to strengthen the message. Because customer receipts include both when a computer is brought to Mo's (date and time) as well as when the repair is finished, he asks his office manager to select a sample so they can estimate the average service time. Based on 36 receipts, she finds a mean service time of 2 hours and 10 minutes with a standard deviation of 30 minutes. Further statistical analysis yielded a 95% confidence interval for the mean service time of 1.99 to 2.33 hours. Mohammed plans to advertise that 95% of his customers can expect to get their computers back from repair in between 1.99 and 2.33 hours! He is anxious to include this claim in all of the Mending Station's future marketing communication materials.

- **Identify the ethical dilemma in this scenario.**
- **Has Mohammed interpreted the confidence interval correctly?**
- **What are the undesirable consequences?**
- **Propose an ethical solution that considers the welfare of all stakeholders.**

LEARNING OBJECTIVES

Know the sampling distribution of the mean.

- To apply the Central Limit Theorem for the mean in practical applications, we must estimate the standard deviation. This *standard error* is

$$SE(\bar{y}) = \frac{s}{\sqrt{n}}$$

- When we use the SE, the sampling distribution that allows for the additional uncertainty is Student's *t*.

Construct confidence intervals for the true mean, μ.
- A confidence interval for the mean has the form $\bar{y} \pm ME$.
- The margin of error is $ME = t^*_{df} SE(\bar{y})$.

Find t^*-values by technology or from tables.
- When constructing confidence intervals for means, the correct degrees of freedom is $n - 1$.

Check the Assumptions and Conditions before using any sampling distribution for inference.

Write clear summaries to interpret a confidence interval.

Be able to perform a hypothesis test for a mean.
- The null hypothesis has the form $H_0: \mu = \mu_0$.
- We refer the test statistic $t = \dfrac{\bar{y} - \mu_0}{SE(\bar{y})}$ to the Student's t-distribution with $n - 1$ degrees of freedom.

TERMS

Bootstrap
A general method of statistical inference that uses computer simulation to resample from the available data to approximate the sampling distribution of a statistic.

Bootstrap confidence interval
A bootstrap confidence interval is found by identifying the central C% of a bootstrap distribution based on the available data.

Bootstrap sample
One of the (typically at least 1000) samples drawn from a pseudo-population (or, equivalently, sampled with replacement) from a sample of data. A bootstrap sample is typically of the same size as the sample itself.

Central Limit Theorem
The Central Limit Theorem (CLT) states that the sampling distribution model of the sample mean (and proportion) from a random sample is approximately Normal for large n, regardless of the distribution of the population, as long as the observations are independent.

Degrees of freedom (df)
A parameter of the Student's t-distribution that depends upon the sample size. Typically, more degrees of freedom reflects increasing information from the sample.

One-sample t-interval for the mean
A one-sample t-interval for the population mean is:
$$\bar{y} \pm t^*_{n-1} \times SE(\bar{y}) \text{ where } SE(\bar{y}) = \frac{s}{\sqrt{n}}.$$
The critical value t^*_{n-1} depends on the particular confidence level, C, that you specify and on the number of degrees of freedom, $n - 1$.

Pseudo-population
A conceptual construction consisting of repeating a sample many times. The pseudo-population has the same mean and standard deviation as the original sample, and is a population for which the original sample is the most likely sample to be drawn at random. Sampling from the pseudo-population generates a bootstrap sample. An equivalent way to draw bootstrap samples that is more practical is to use resampling.

Resampling
A common way to perform bootstrap calculations is to repeatedly sample from your data *with replacement*, thus re-sampling the data.

Sampling distribution model for a mean
If the independence assumption and randomization condition are met and the sample size is large enough, the sampling distribution of the sample mean is well modeled by a Normal model with a mean equal to the population mean, and a standard deviation equal to $\dfrac{\sigma}{\sqrt{n}}$.

Standard error
An estimate of the standard deviation of a statistic's sampling distribution based on the data.

Student's t
A family of distributions indexed by its degrees of freedom. The t-models are unimodal, symmetric, and bell-shaped, but generally have fatter tails and a narrower center than the Normal model. As the degrees of freedom increase, t-distributions approach the Normal model.

TECH SUPPORT   Confidence Intervals for Means

Statistics packages offer convenient ways to make histograms of the data. Even better for assessing near-Normality is a Normal probability plot. When you work on a computer, there is simply no excuse for skipping the step of plotting the data to check that it is nearly Normal. *Beware:* statistics packages don't agree on whether to place the Normal scores on the *x*-axis (as we have done) or the *y*-axis. Read the axis labels.

Any standard statistics package can compute a confidence interval.

The commands to do inference for means on common statistics programs and calculators are not always obvious. (By contrast, the resulting output is usually clearly labeled and easy to read.) The guides for each program can help you start navigating.

EXCEL

Specify formulas. Find $t*$ with the T.INV(alpha, df) function.

COMMENTS

Not really automatic. For the examples in this chapter, substitute 0.05 for "alpha" in the T.INV command.

JMP

- From the Analyze menu, select **Distribution**.
- For a confidence interval, scroll down to the Moments section to find the interval limits.
- Then fill in the resulting dialog.

COMMENTS

"Moment" is a fancy statistical term for means, standard deviations, and other related statistics.

MINITAB

- From the Stat menu, choose the **Basic Statistics** submenu.
- From that menu, choose **1-sample t. . . .**
- Then fill in the dialog.

COMMENTS

The dialog offers a clear choice between confidence interval and test (which we'll discuss in the next chapter).

	A	B	C	D	E	F
1	t-Estimate of a Mean					
2						
3	Sample Mean	15.02	Confidence Interval Estimate			Syntax for Column E
4	Sample St. Dev.	8.31	15.02	±	1.81	=ABS(T.INV((1-B6)/2,(B5-1))*(B4/B5^0.5))
5	Sample Size	83	Lower Confidence Limit		13.21	=B3-E4
6	Confidence Level	0.95	Upper Confidence Limit		16.83	=B3+E4

XLSTAT

To find a one sample *z*-interval or a one sample *t*-interval:

- Choose **Parametric Tests**, and then **One-sample t-test and z-test**.
- Under the **General** tab, enter your data cell range and choose either **z-test** or **Student's t-test**.
- On the **Options** tab, choose the **Alternative hypothesis** of Mean 1 ≠ **Theoretical mean**.
- For calculating just a confidence interval, you can leave the **Theoretical mean** field blank.
- Under **Significance Level**, enter in the desired level of significance. The output will yield the $(1 - \alpha)100\%$ confidence level.

R

To produce a confidence interval (default is 95%), create a vector of data in x and then:

- **t.test**(x, alternative = c("two.sided", "less", "greater"), mu = 0, conf.level = 0.95)

Provides the confidence interval for a specified alternative along with additional statistics for performing a hypothesis test (as we'll see in the next chapter).

SPSS

From the Analyze menu, choose the **Compare Means** submenu.
Alternatively:

- From the Analyze Menu, choose **Descriptive Statistics**.
- Choose **Explore**.
- Click the **Statistics** button to change confidence level and choose **Statistics** only if no plots are desired.

To do inference for a mean using summaries:

- Click on **Stat**.
- Choose **T Stats > One Sample > with Summary**.
- Enter the Sample mean, Sample std dev, and Sample size.
- Under **Perform**: indicate **Confidence interval** for μ, and then enter the **Level** of confidence.
- Click on **Compute**!

To do inference for a mean using data:

- Click on **Stat**.
- Choose **T Statistics > One Sample > with Data**.
- Choose the variable by selecting a **Column**.
- Under **Perform**: indicate **Confidence interval**, and then enter the **Level** of confidence.
- Click on **Compute**!

BRIEF CASE

Real Estate

A real estate agent is trying to understand the pricing of homes in her area, a region comprised of small to midsize towns and a small city. For each of 1200 homes recently sold in the region, the file **Real estate sample 1200** holds the following variables:

- *Sale Price* (in \$)
- *Lot size* (size of the lot in acres)
- *Waterfront* (Yes, No)
- *Age* (in years)
- *Central Air* (Yes, No)
- *Fuel Type* (Wood, Oil, Gas, Electric, Propane, Solar, Other)
- *Condition* (1 to 5, 1 = Poor, 5 = Excellent)
- *Living Area* (living area in square feet)
- *Pct College* (% in ZIP code who attend a four-year college)
- *Full Baths* (number of full bathrooms)
- *Half Baths* (number of half bathrooms)
- *Bedrooms* (number of bedrooms)
- *Fireplace* (1 = Yes, 0 = No)

The agent has a family interested in a four-bedroom house. Using confidence intervals, how should she advise the family on what the average price of a four-bedroom house might be in this area? Compare that to a confidence interval for two-bedroom homes. How much more, on average, does a house that has central air conditioning sell for? Restrict your attention to two-bedroom houses and answer the question again. What about four-bedroom houses? Repeat this investigation for houses with and without fireplaces. What cautions might you give the agent before coming to any overall conclusions?

Explore other questions that might be useful for the real estate agent in knowing how different categorical factors affect the sale price and write up a short report on your findings.

Donor Profiles

A philanthropic organization collects and buys data on their donor base. The full database contains about 4.5 million donors and over 400 variables collected

(continued)

BRIEF CASE *(continued)*

on each, but the dataset **Donor profiles** is a sample of 916 donors and includes the variables:

- *Age* (in years)
- *Homeowner* (H = Yes, U = Unknown)
- *Gender* (F = Female, M = Male, U = Unknown)
- *Wealth* (Ordered categories of total household wealth from 1 = Lowest to 9 = Highest)
- *Children* (Number of children)
- *Donated Last* (0 = Did not donate to last campaign, 1 = Did donate to last campaign)
- *Amt Donated Last* ($ amount of contribution to last campaign)

The analysts at the organization want to know how much people donate on average to campaigns, and what factors might influence that amount. Compare the confidence intervals for the mean *Amt Donated Last* by those known to own their homes with those whose homeowner status is unknown. Perform similar comparisons for *Gender* and two of the *Wealth* categories. Write up a short report using graphics and confidence intervals for what you have found. (Be careful not to make inferences directly about the differences between groups. We'll discuss that in Chapter 13. Your inference should be about single groups.)

(The distribution of *Amt Donated Last* is highly skewed to the right, and so the median might be thought to be the appropriate summary. But the median is $0.00 so the analysts must use the mean. From simulations, they have ascertained that the sampling distribution for the mean is unimodal and symmetric for samples larger than 250 or so. Note that small differences in the mean could result in millions of dollars of added revenue nationwide. The average cost of their solicitation is $0.67 per person to produce and mail.)

CHAPTER 11 EXERCISES

SECTION 11.1

1. Games for the iPad have a distribution of prices that is skewed to the high end.

a) Explain why this is what you would expect.
b) Members of the iPad gamers club each own about 50 games. Pat is one such member. What would you expect the shape of the distribution of game prices on her iPad to be?
c) Each club member computes the average price of his or her games. What shape would you expect the distribution of these averages to have?

2. For a sample of 36 houses, what would you expect the distribution of the sale prices to be? A real-estate agent has been assigned 10 houses at random to sell this month. She wants to know whether the mean price of those houses is typical. What, if anything, does she need to assume about the distribution of prices to be able to use the Central Limit Theorem? Are those assumptions reasonable?

3. According to the Gallup Poll, 27% of U.S. adults have high levels of cholesterol. Gallup reports that such elevated levels "could be financially devastating to the U.S. healthcare system" and are a major concern to health insurance providers. According to recent studies, cholesterol levels in healthy U.S. adults average about 215 mg/dL with a standard deviation of about 30 mg/dL and are roughly Normally distributed. If the cholesterol levels of a sample of 42 healthy U.S. adults is taken,

a) What shape should the sampling distribution of the mean have?
b) What would the mean of the sampling distribution be?
c) What would its standard deviation be?
d) If the sample size were increased to 100, how would your answers to parts a–c change?

4. As in Exercise 3, cholesterol levels in healthy U.S. adults average about 215 mg/dL with a standard deviation of about 30 mg/dL and are roughly Normally distributed.

If the cholesterol levels of a sample of 42 healthy US adults is taken, what is the probability that the mean cholesterol level of the sample

a) Will be no more than 215?
b) Will be between 205 and 225?
c) Will be less than 200?
d) Will be greater than 220?

SECTION 11.3

5. Organizers of a fishing tournament believe that the lake holds a sizable population of largemouth bass. They assume that the weights of these fish have a model that is skewed to the right with a mean of 3.5 pounds and a standard deviation of 2.32 pounds.

a) Explain why a skewed model makes sense here.
b) Explain why you cannot use a Normal model to determine the probability that a largemouth bass randomly selected ("caught") from the lake weighs over 3 pounds.
c) Each contestant catches 5 fish each day. Can you determine the probability that someone's catch averages over 3 pounds? Explain.
d) The 12 contestants competing each caught the limit of 5 fish. What's the standard deviation of the mean weight of the 60 fish caught?
e) Would you be surprised if the mean weight of the 60 fish caught in the competition was more than 4.5 pounds? Use the 68–95–99.7 Rule.

6. In 2008 and 2009, Systemax bought two failing electronics stores, Circuit City and CompUSA. They kept both the names active for several years during which time customers could purchase products from either website. If we take a random sample of a mixture of those purchases from the two websites, the distribution of the amounts purchased will be bimodal.

a) As their sample size increases, what's the expected shape of the distribution of amounts purchased in the sample?
b) As the sample size increases, what's the expected shape of the sampling model for the mean amount purchased of the sample?

SECTION 11.4

7. A survey of 25 randomly selected customers found the following ages (in years):

20	32	34	29	30
30	30	14	29	11
38	22	44	48	26
25	22	32	35	32
35	42	44	44	48

The mean was 31.84 years and the standard deviation was 9.84 years.

a) What is the standard error of the mean?
b) How would the standard error change if the sample size had been 100 instead of 25? (Assume that the sample standard deviation didn't change.)

8. A random sample of 20 purchases showed the following amounts (in $):

39.05	2.73	32.92	47.51
37.91	34.35	64.48	51.96
56.95	81.58	47.80	11.72
21.57	40.83	38.24	32.98
75.16	74.30	47.54	65.62

The mean was $45.26 and the standard deviation was $20.67.

a) What is the standard error of the mean?
b) How would the standard error change if the sample size had been 5 instead of 20? (Assume that the sample standard deviation didn't change.)

9. For the data in Exercise 7:

a) How many degrees of freedom does the t-statistic have?
b) How many degrees of freedom would the t-statistic have if the sample size had been 100?

10. For the data in Exercise 8:

a) How many degrees of freedom does the t-statistic have?
b) How many degrees of freedom would the t-statistic have if the sample size had been 5?

SECTION 11.5

11. Find the critical value t^* for:

a) a 95% confidence interval based on 24 df.
b) a 95% confidence interval based on 99 df.

12. Find the critical value t^* for:

a) a 90% confidence interval based on 19 df.
b) a 90% confidence interval based on 4 df.

13. For the ages in Exercise 7:

a) Construct a 95% confidence interval for the mean age of all customers, assuming that the assumptions and conditions for the confidence interval have been met.
b) How large is the margin of error?
c) How would the confidence interval change if you had assumed that the standard deviation was known to be 10.0 years?

14. For the purchase amounts in Exercise 8:

a) Construct a 90% confidence interval for the mean purchases of all customers, assuming that the assumptions and conditions for the confidence interval have been met.
b) How large is the margin of error?
c) How would the confidence interval change if you had assumed that the standard deviation was known to be $20?

SECTION 11.6

15. For the confidence intervals of Exercise 13, a histogram of the data looks like this:

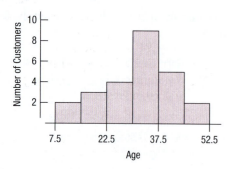

Check the assumptions and conditions for your inference.

16. For the confidence intervals of Exercise 14, a histogram of the data looks like this:

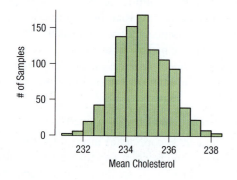

Check the assumptions and conditions for your inference.

*SECTION 11.7

T ***17.** **Framingham cholesterol.** The Framingham Heart Study recorded the cholesterol levels of more than 1400 participants in Framingham, MA (Data in **Framingham**). To find a bootstrap confidence interval for the mean cholesterol, a student took 1000 bootstrap samples, calculated the mean of each, and found the following histogram of the bootstrap means:

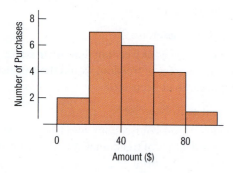

Summary statistics of the means show:

0.5%	1%	2%	2.5%	5%	95%	97.5%	98%	99%	99.5%
231.890	232.130	232.370	232.434	232.769	236.763	237.130	237.281	237.526	237.873

a) Use the data above to construct a 95% confidence interval for the mean cholesterol.
b) Interpret the interval you constructed in part a.
c) What assumptions did you make, if any, in interpreting the interval?

T ***18.** **Student survey.** A business statistics class conducted a student survey in which 299 students were randomly selected and asked a variety of questions. One of the questions asked "How many friends do you have on Facebook?" To find a confidence interval for the mean number, a student drew 1000 bootstrap samples of the data and obtained the following histogram and summary statistics:

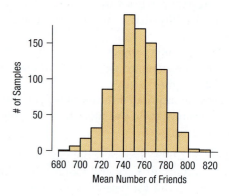

Summary statistics of the means show:

0.5%	1%	2%	2.5%	5%	95%	97.5%	98%	99%	99.5%
698.301	702.498	707.779	709.967	718.279	785.623	792.099	793.411	797.358	800.702

a) Use the data above to construct a 98% confidence interval for the mean number of Facebook friends a student has.
b) Interpret the interval you constructed in part a.
c) What assumptions did you make, if any, in interpreting the interval?

CHAPTER EXERCISES

19. *t-models.* Using the *t*-tables, software, or a calculator, estimate:

a) the critical value of *t* for a 90% confidence interval with df = 17.
b) the critical value of *t* for a 98% confidence interval with df = 88.

20. *t*-models, part 2. Using the *t* tables, software, or a calculator, estimate:

a) the critical value of *t* for a 95% confidence interval with df = 7.

b) the critical value of *t* for a 99% confidence interval with df = 102.

21. Confidence intervals. Describe how the width of a 95% confidence interval for a mean changes as the standard deviation (*s*) of a sample increases, assuming sample size remains the same.

22. Confidence intervals, part 2. Describe how the width of a 95% confidence interval for a mean changes as the sample size (*n*) increases, assuming the standard deviation remains the same.

23. Confidence intervals and sample size. A confidence interval for the price of gasoline from a random sample of 30 gas stations in a region gives the following statistics:

$$\bar{y} = \$4.49 \quad s = \$0.29$$

a) Find a 95% confidence interval for the mean price of regular gasoline in that region.

b) Find the 90% confidence interval for the mean.

c) If we had the same statistics from a sample of 60 stations, what would the 95% confidence interval be now?

24. Confidence intervals and sample size, part 2. A confidence interval for the price of gasoline from a random sample of 30 gas stations in a region gives the following statistics:

$$\bar{y} = \$4.49 \quad SE(\bar{y}) = \$0.06$$

a) Find a 95% confidence interval for the mean price of regular gasoline in that region.

b) Find the 90% confidence interval for the mean.

c) If we had the same statistics from a sample of 60 stations, what would the 95% confidence interval be now?

25. Marketing livestock feed. A feed supply company has developed a special feed supplement to see if it will promote weight gain in livestock. Their researchers report that the 77 cows studied gained an average of 56 pounds and that a 95% confidence interval for the mean weight gain this supplement produces has a margin of error of ±11 pounds. Staff in their marketing department wrote the following conclusions. Did anyone interpret the interval correctly? Explain any misinterpretations.

a) 95% of the cows studied gained between 45 and 67 pounds.

b) We're 95% sure that a cow fed this supplement will gain between 45 and 67 pounds.

c) We're 95% sure that the average weight gain among the cows in this study was between 45 and 67 pounds.

d) The average weight gain of cows fed this supplement is between 45 and 67 pounds 95% of the time.

e) If this supplement is tested on another sample of cows, there is a 95% chance that their average weight gain will be between 45 and 67 pounds.

26. Meal costs. A company is interested in estimating the costs of lunch in their cafeteria. After surveying employees, the staff calculated that a 95% confidence interval for the mean amount of money spent for lunch over a period of six months is ($780, $920). Now the organization is trying to write its report and considering the following interpretations. Comment on each.

a) 95% of all employees pay between $780 and $920 for lunch.

b) 95% of the sampled employees paid between $780 and $920 for lunch.

c) We're 95% sure that employees in this sample averaged between $780 and $920 for lunch.

d) 95% of all samples of employees will have average lunch costs between $780 and $920.

e) We're 95% sure that the average amount all employees pay for lunch is between $780 and $920.

27. CEO compensation. A sample of 20 CEOs from the Forbes 500 shows total annual compensations ranging from a minimum of $0.1 to $62.24 million. The average for these 20 CEOs is $7.946 million. The histogram and boxplot are as follows:

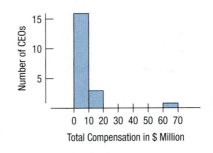

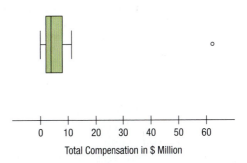

Based on these data, a computer program found that a confidence interval for the mean annual compensation of all Forbes 500 CEOs is (1.69, 14.20) $M. Why should you be hesitant to trust this confidence interval?

28. Credit card charges. A credit card company takes a random sample of 100 cardholders to see how much they charged on their card last month. A histogram and boxplot are as follows:

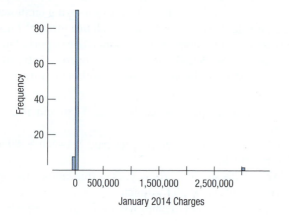

January 2014 Charges

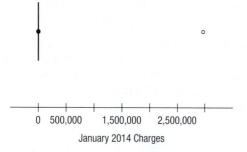

January 2014 Charges

A computer program found that the 95% confidence interval for the mean amount spent in January 2014 is (−$28,366.84, $90,691.49). Explain why the analysts didn't find the confidence interval useful, and explain what went wrong.

29. Parking. Hoping to lure more shoppers downtown, a city builds a new public parking garage in the central business district. The city plans to pay for the structure through parking fees. For a random sample of 44 weekdays, daily fees collected averaged $126, with a standard deviation of $15.

a) What assumptions must you make in order to use these statistics for inference?
b) Find a 90% confidence interval for the mean daily income this parking garage will generate.
c) Explain in context what this confidence interval means.
d) Explain what 90% confidence means in this context.
e) The consultant who advised the city on this project predicted that parking revenues would average $128 per day. Based on your confidence interval, what do you think of the consultant's prediction? Why?

30. Housing. In 2012, a large number of foreclosed homes in the Washington, DC, metro area were sold. In one community, a sample of 30 foreclosed homes sold for an average of $443,705 with a standard deviation of $196,196.

a) What assumptions and conditions must be checked before finding a confidence interval for the mean? How would you check them?
b) Find a 95% confidence interval for the mean value per home.
c) Interpret this interval and explain what 95% confidence means.
d) Suppose nationally, the average foreclosed home sold for $350,000. Do you think the average sale price in the sampled community differs significantly from the national average? Explain.

31. Parking, part 2. Suppose that for budget planning purposes the city in Exercise 29 needs a better estimate of the mean daily income from parking fees.

a) Someone suggests that the city use its data to create a 95% confidence interval instead of the 90% interval first created. How would this interval be better for the city? (You need not actually create the new interval.)
b) How would the 95% confidence interval be worse for the planners?
c) How could they achieve a confidence interval estimate that would better serve their planning needs?

32. Housing, part 2. In Exercise 30, we found a 95% confidence interval to estimate the average value of foreclosed homes.

a) Suppose the standard deviation of the values was $300,000 instead of the $196,196 used for that interval. What would the larger standard deviation do to the width of the confidence interval (assuming the same level of confidence)?
b) Your classmate suggests that the margin of error in the interval could be reduced if the confidence level were changed to 90% instead of 95%. Do you agree with this statement? Why or why not?
c) Instead of changing the level of confidence, would it be more statistically appropriate to draw a bigger sample?

33. State budgets. States that rely on sales tax for revenue to fund education, public safety, and other programs often end up with budget surpluses during economic growth periods (when people spend more on consumer goods) and budget deficits during recessions (when people spend less on consumer goods). Fifty-one small retailers in a state with a growing economy were recently sampled. The sample showed a mean increase of $2350 in additional sales tax revenue collected per retailer compared to the previous quarter. The sample standard deviation = $425.

a) Find a 95% confidence interval for the mean increase in sales tax revenue.
b) What assumptions have you made in this inference? Do you think the appropriate conditions have been satisfied?
c) Explain what your interval means and provide an example of what it does not mean.

34. State budgets, part 2. Suppose the state in Exercise 33 sampled 16 small retailers instead of 51, and for the sample of 16, the sample mean increase again equaled $2350 in additional sales tax revenue collected per retailer compared to the previous quarter. Also assume the sample standard deviation = $425.

a) What is the standard error of the mean increase in sales tax revenue collected?
b) What happens to the accuracy of the estimate when the interval is constructed using the smaller sample size?
c) Find and interpret a 95% confidence interval.
d) How does the margin of error for the interval constructed in Exercise 33 compare with the margin of error constructed in this exercise? Explain statistically how sample size changes the accuracy of the constructed interval. Which sample would you prefer if you were a state budget planner? Why?

T 35. Departures 2016. What are the chances your flight will leave on time? The U.S. Bureau of Transportation Statistics of the Department of Transportation publishes information about airline performance. Here are a histogram and summary statistics for the percentage of flights departing on time each month from 1995 through November 2016. (Data in **Late arrivals 2016**)

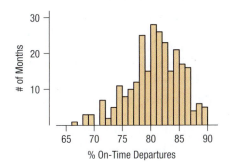

n	263
$\bar{y}$	80.72
s	4.57

There is no evidence of a trend over time. (The correlation of % On-Time Departure with time is $r = -0.073$.)

a) Check the assumptions and conditions for inference.
b) Find a 90% confidence interval for the mean percentage of flights that depart on time.
c) Interpret this interval for a traveler planning to fly.

T 36. Late arrivals 2016. Will your flight get you to your destination on time? The U.S. Bureau of Transportation Statistics reported the percentage of flights that were late each month from 1995 through early 2016. Here's a histogram, along with some summary statistics:

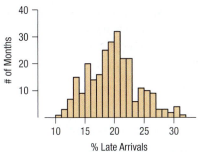

n	263
$\bar{y}$	19.76
s	4.22

We can consider these data to be a representative sample of all months. There is no evidence of a time trend.

a) Check the assumptions and conditions for inference about the mean.
b) Find a 99% confidence interval for the true percentage of flights that arrive late.
c) Interpret this interval for a traveler planning to fly.

T 37. Computer lab fees. The technology committee has stated that the average time spent by students per lab visit has increased, and the increase supports the need for increased lab fees. To substantiate this claim, the committee randomly samples 12 student lab visits and notes the amount of time spent using the computer. The times in minutes are as follows:

Time	
52	74
57	53
54	136
76	73
62	8
52	62

a) Plot the data. Are any of the observations outliers? Explain.
b) The previous mean amount of time spent using the lab computer was 55 minutes. Find a 95% confidence interval for the true mean. What do you conclude about the claim? If there are outliers, find intervals with and without the outliers present.

38. Cell phone batteries. A company that produces cell phones claims its standard phone battery lasts longer on average than other batteries in the market. To support this claim, the company publishes an ad reporting the results of a recent experiment showing that under normal usage, their batteries last at least 35 hours. To investigate this claim, a consumer advocacy group asked the company for the raw data. The company sends the group the following results:

35, 34, 32, 31, 34, 34, 32, 33, 35, 55, 32, 31

Find a 95% confidence interval and state your conclusion. Explain how you dealt with the outlier, and why.

39. Growth and air pollution. Government officials have difficulty attracting new business to communities with troubled reputations. Nevada has been one of the fastest growing states in the country for a number of years. Accompanying the rapid growth are massive new construction projects. Since Nevada has a dry climate, the construction creates visible dust pollution. High pollution levels may paint a less than attractive picture of the area, and can also result in fines levied by the federal government. As required by government regulation, researchers continually monitor pollution levels. In the most recent test of pollution levels, 121 air samples were collected. The dust particulate levels must be reported to the federal regulatory agencies. In the report sent to the federal agency, it was noted that the mean particulate level = 57.6 micrograms/cubic liter of air, and the 95% confidence interval estimate is 52.06 mg to 63.07 mg. A graph of the distribution of the particulate amounts was also included and is shown below.

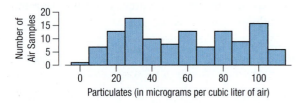

a) Discuss the assumptions and conditions for using Student's *t* inference methods with these data.

b) Do you think the confidence interval noted in the report is valid? Briefly explain why or why not.

40. Convention revenues. At one time, Nevada was the only U.S. state that allowed gambling. Although gambling continues to be one of the major industries in Nevada, the proliferation of legalized gambling in other areas of the country has required state and local governments to look at other growth possibilities. The convention and visitor's authorities in many Nevada cities actively recruit national conventions that bring thousands of visitors to the state. Various demographic and economic data are collected from surveys given to convention attendees. One statistic of interest is the amount visitors spend on slot machine gambling. Nevada often reports the slot machine expenditure

as amount spent per hotel guest room. A recent survey of 500 visitors asked how much they spent on gambling. The average expenditure per room was $180.

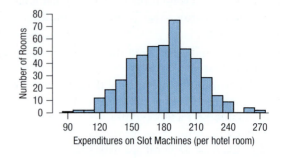

Casinos will use the information reported in the survey to estimate slot machine expenditure per hotel room. Do you think the estimates produced by the survey will accurately represent expenditures? Explain using the statistics reported and graph shown.

41. Traffic speed. Police departments often try to control traffic speed by placing speed-measuring machines on roads that tell motorists how fast they are driving. Traffic safety experts must determine where machines should be placed. In one recent test, police recorded the average speed clocked by cars driving on one busy street close to an elementary school. For a sample of 25 speeds, it was determined that the average amount over the speed limit for the 25 clocked speeds was 11.6 mph with a standard deviation of 8 mph. The 95% confidence interval estimate for this sample is 8.30 mph to 14.90 mph.

a) What is the margin of error for this problem?

b) The researchers commented that the interval was too wide. Explain specifically what should be done to reduce the margin of error to no more than ±2 mph.

42. Traffic speed, part 2. The speed-measuring machines must measure accurately to maximize effectiveness in slowing traffic. The accuracy of the machines will be tested before placement on city streets. To ensure that error rates are estimated accurately, the researchers want to take a large enough sample to ensure usable and accurate interval estimates of how much the machines may be off in measuring actual speeds. Specifically, the researchers want the margin of error for a single speed measurement to be no more than ±1.5 mph.

a) Discuss how the researchers may obtain a reasonable estimate of the standard deviation of error in the measured speeds.

b) Suppose the standard deviation for the error in the measured speeds equals 4 mph. At 95% confidence, what sample size should be taken to ensure that the margin of error is no larger than ±1.0 mph?

43. Tax audits. Certified public accountants are often required to appear with clients if the IRS audits the client's tax return. Some accounting firms give the client an option to pay a fee when the tax return is completed that guarantees tax advice and support from the accountant if the client were audited. The fee is charged up front like an insurance premium and is less than the amount that would be charged if the client were later audited and then decided to ask the firm for assistance during the audit. A large accounting firm is trying to determine what fee to charge for next year's returns. In previous years, the actual mean cost to the firm for attending a client audit session was $650. To determine if this cost has changed, the firm randomly samples 32 client audit fees. The sample mean audit cost was $680 with a standard deviation of $75.

a) Develop a 95% confidence interval estimate for the mean audit cost.

b) Based on your confidence interval, what do you think of the claim that the mean cost has changed?

44. Tax audits, part 2. While reviewing the sample of audit fees, a senior accountant for the firm notes that the fee charged by the firm's accountants depends on the complexity of the return. A comparison of actual charges therefore might not provide the information needed to set next year's fees. To better understand the fee structure, the senior accountant requests a new sample that measures the time the accountants spent on the audit. Last year, the average hours charged per client audit was 3.25 hours. A new sample of 10 audit times shows the following times in hours:

4.2, 3.7, 4.8, 2.9, 3.1, 4.5, 4.2, 4.1, 5.0, 3.4

a) Assume the conditions necessary for inference are met. Find a 90% confidence interval estimate for the mean audit time.

b) Based on your answer to part a, do you think that the audit times have, in fact, increased?

Ⓣ 45. Wind power. Should you generate electricity with your own personal wind turbine? That depends on whether you have enough wind on your site. To produce enough energy, your site should have an annual average wind speed of at least 8 miles per hour, according to the Wind Energy Association. One candidate site was monitored for a year, with wind speeds recorded every 6 hours. A total of 1114 readings of wind speed averaged 8.019 mph with a standard deviation of 3.813 mph. You've been asked to make a statistical report to help the landowner decide whether to place a wind turbine at this site. (Data in **Wind speed**)

a) Discuss the assumptions and conditions for using Student's *t* inference methods with these data. Here are some plots that may help you decide whether the methods can be used:

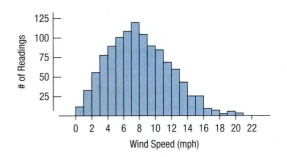

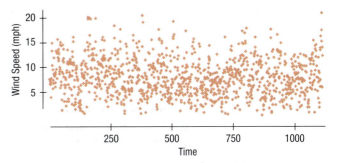

b) What would you tell the landowner about whether this site is suitable for a small wind turbine? Explain

46. Real estate crash? After the sub-prime crisis of late 2007, real estate prices fell almost everywhere in the United States. In 2006–2007 before the crisis, the average selling price of homes in a region in upstate New York was $191,300. A real estate agency wants to know how much the prices have fallen since then. They collect a sample of 1231 homes in the region in mid-2013 and find the average asking price to be $178,613.50 with a standard deviation of $92,701.56. You have been retained by the real estate agency to report on the current situation.

a) Discuss the assumptions and conditions for using *t*-methods for inference with these data. Here are some plots that may help you decide what to do.

b) What would you report to the real estate agency about the current situation?

Ⓣ 47. Yogurt. *Consumer Reports* tested 11 brands of vanilla yogurt and found these numbers of calories per serving:

130 160 150 120 120 110 170 160 110 130 90

a) Check the assumptions and conditions for inference.

b) Create a 95% confidence interval for the average calorie content of vanilla yogurt.

c) A diet guide claims that you will get an average of 120 calories from a serving of vanilla yogurt. What does this evidence indicate? Use your confidence interval to test an appropriate hypothesis and state your conclusion.

T **48. Golf drives 2015.** How far do professional golfers drive a ball? (For non-golfers, the drive is the shot hit from a tee at the start of a hole and is typically the longest shot.) Here's a histogram of the average driving distances of the 199 leading professional golfers in 2016 along with summary statistics (www.pgatour.com).

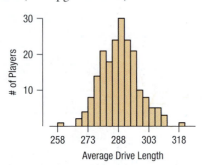

n	199
$\bar{y}$	288.685
s	9.281

a) Find a 95% confidence interval for the mean drive distance.
b) Interpreting this interval raises some problems. Discuss.
c) The data are the mean driving distance for each golfer. Is that another concern in interpreting the interval?

JUST CHECKING ANSWERS

1 Normal. It doesn't matter that the sample is drawn from a skewed distribution; the CLT tells us that the means can be modeled with a Normal model as long as the sample size is large enough.

2 I would expect the histogram to be skewed. A sample of 10 is fairly small. With a skewed population the CLT requires a larger sample size before the sampling distribution of the mean will appear to be Normal.

3 $SE(\bar{y}) = 120/\sqrt{100} = 12$

4 Decreases.

5 The standard error decreases by $1/\sqrt{2}$.

6 Because the distribution is right skewed, the confidence interval based on only 20 observations is not likely to be accurate.

7 They don't know the population standard deviation, so they must use the sample SD as an estimate. The additional uncertainty is taken into account by *t*-models.

8 With a sample size of 60, the conditions are more nearly satisfied because the sampling distribution of the mean is closer to the Normal model, so the confidence interval should be accurate. It will also be narrower than the one based on 20.

9 The confidence interval is about the *mean* starting salary, not about individuals.

10 It will narrow it because the standard error will go down proportionally.

CHAPTER

12

Testing Hypotheses

Casting Ingots

Ingots are huge pieces of metal, sometimes weighing more than 20,000 pounds, made in a giant mold. They must be cast in one large piece for use in fabricating large structural parts for cars and planes. As the liquid metal cools, cracks can develop on the surface of the ingot, which can propagate into the zone required for the part, compromising its integrity. Airplane manufacturers insist that metal for their planes be defect-free, so the ingot must be made over if any cracking is detected.

Even though the metal from the cracked ingot is recycled, the cost runs into the tens of thousands of dollars to recast an ingot, not to mention the energy waste. About 2/3 of all aluminum ingots produced in the United States use a process called the "direct chill" method designed to reduce recasting. Metal manufacturers would like to avoid cracking if at all possible. But the casting process is complicated and not everything is completely under control. It's estimated that about 5% of aluminum ingots need to be recast because of cracking. That rate depends on the size of the ingot cast. In one plant that specializes in very large (over 30,000 lb) ingots designed for the airplane industry, about 20% of the ingots have had some kind of surface crack. In an attempt to reduce the cracking proportion, the plant engineers and chemists recently tried out some changes in the casting process. Since then, 400 ingots have been cast and only 68 (17%) of them have cracked. Has the new method worked? Has the cracking rate really decreased, or was 17% just due to luck? Is the 17% cracking rate merely a result of natural sampling variability, or is this enough evidence to justify a change to the new method?

People want to make informed decisions like this all the time. Does the new website design increase our click-through rate? Has the "click-it or ticket" campaign increased compliance with seat belt laws? Did the Super Bowl ad we bought actually increase sales? To answer such questions so that we can make intelligent decisions, we test *hypotheses*.

> " Half the money I spend on advertising is wasted; the trouble is I don't know which half. "
>
> —John Wanamaker
> (attributed)

12.1 Hypotheses

Hypothesis

n.; pl. {Hypotheses}. A supposition; a proposition or principle which is supposed or taken for granted, in order to draw a conclusion or inference for proof of the point in question; something not proved, but assumed for the purpose of argument.

—*Webster's Unabridged Dictionary, 1913*

NOTATION ALERT

Capital H is the standard letter for hypotheses. H_0 always labels the null hypothesis, and H_A labels the alternative hypothesis.

If the changes they made lowered the cracking rate from 20%, management will need to decide whether the costs of the new method warrant the changes. Managers are naturally cautious, and because humans are natural skeptics, they assume the new method makes no difference—but they hope the data can convince them otherwise. The starting hypothesis to be tested is called the **null hypothesis**—null because it assumes that nothing has changed. We denote it H_0. It specifies a parameter—here the proportion of cracked ingots—and a value—that the cracking rate is 20%. We usually write this in the form H_0: *parameter = hypothesized value*. So, for the ingots we would write H_0: $p = 0.20$.

The **alternative hypothesis**, which we denote H_A, is not a single value, but contains all the other values of the parameter. We can write H_A: $p \neq 0.20$.

What would convince you that the cracking rate had actually changed? If the rate dropped from 20% to 19.8%, would that convince you? After all, observed proportions do vary, so even if the changes had no effect, you'd expect some difference. What if it dropped to 1%? Would random fluctuation account for a change that big? That's the crucial question in a hypothesis test. As usual in statistics, when thinking about the size of a change, we *naturally* think of using its standard deviation to measure that change.[1] We ask how many standard deviations the observed value is from the hypothesized value, and we know how to find the standard deviation of a proportion:

$$SD(\hat{p}) = \sqrt{\frac{pq}{n}} = \sqrt{\frac{(0.20)(0.80)}{400}} = 0.02.$$

> **Why Is This a Standard Deviation and Not a Standard Error?**
>
> Remember that we reserve the term "standard error" for the *estimate* of the standard deviation of the sampling distribution. But we're not estimating here—we have a value of p from our null hypothesis model. To remind us that the parameter value comes from the null hypothesis, it is sometimes written as p_0 and the standard deviation as $SD(\hat{p}) = \sqrt{p_0 q_0 / n}$. That's different than when we found a confidence interval for p. In that case we couldn't assume that we knew its value, so we estimated the standard deviation from the sample value $\hat{p}$.

If the changes have no effect, then the true cracking rate is still 0.20, and for samples of 400, the standard deviation of $\hat{p}$ is 0.02. We know from the sampling distribution of $\hat{p}$ that in 95% of samples of this size, the engineers will see a

---

[1] It's Chapter 12. Did you?

cracking rate within 0.04 of 0.20 just by chance. In other words, they expect to see between 64 and 96 cracked ingots (see Figure 12.1). The engineers saw 68 cracked ingots out of 400 (a rate of 0.17). Given an assumed rate of 0.20, is that a surprising number? Would you say that the cracking rate has changed?

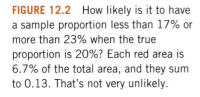

FIGURE 12.1 A simulation of 10,000 samples of 400 ingots with a cracking rate of 20% shows how we should expect the number of cracked ingots to vary.

Now that we have the Central Limit Theorem we don't need to rely on simulation. The CLT tells us that we can use the Normal model to find the probability instead. The engineers observed a cracking rate of 0.17—a difference of 0.03 from the standard (null hypothesis) value of 0.20. Using the fact that the standard deviation is 0.02, we can find the area in the two tails of the Normal model that lie more than 0.03 away from 0.20 (see Figure 12.2). That tells us how rare our observed rate is.

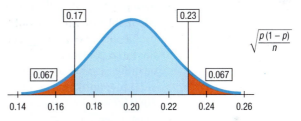

FIGURE 12.2 How likely is it to have a sample proportion less than 17% or more than 23% when the true proportion is 20%? Each red area is 6.7% of the total area, and they sum to 0.13. That's not very unlikely.

You know how to find that probability using either technology, such as the app at www.astools.datadesk.com, Microsoft Excel (=norm.dist command), or Table Z at the back of the text. As you can see in Figure 12.2, the probability comes to about 0.13. In other words, a sample of 400 ingots with a cracking rate this far from 0.20 would happen about 13% of the time just by chance. That doesn't seem very unusual, so the observed proportion of 0.17, even though it's lower, doesn't provide evidence that the new method changed the cracking rate.

IN PRACTICE 12.1   Was there a change? Framing a hypothesis

Summit Projects was a full-service interactive agency, based in Hood River, OR, that offered companies a variety of website services. One of Summit's clients, Smart-Wool®, produces and sells wool apparel, including the famous SmartWool socks. After Summit redesigned SmartWool's apparel website, analysts at SmartWool wondered whether traffic has changed since the new website went live.

MANAGER From the old site, we turned about 15% of the visits into sales. I'm hoping the new design gives us a better rate, but I'm interested in knowing if there's any real change.

ANALYST You need to conduct a hypothesis test. Let p = proportion of visits that result in a sale. Then

$$H_0: p = 0.15 \text{ vs. } H_A: p \neq 0.15.$$

A Trial as a Hypothesis Test

Management would be really interested to learn that the engineers' changes changed the cracking rate. But to test it, they assumed that the rate had *not* changed. Does this reasoning seem backward? That could be because we usually prefer to think about getting things right rather than getting them wrong. But, you've seen this reasoning before in a different context. This is the logic of jury trials.

Let's suppose a defendant has been accused of robbery. In British common law and those systems derived from it (including U.S. law), the null hypothesis is that the defendant is innocent. Instructions to juries are quite explicit about this.

How is the null hypothesis tested? The prosecution first collects evidence. ("If the defendant were innocent, wouldn't it be remarkable that the police found him at the scene of the crime with a bag full of money in his hand, a mask on his face, and a getaway car parked outside?") For us, the data are the evidence.

The next step is to judge the evidence. Evaluating the evidence is the responsibility of the jury in a trial, but it falls on your shoulders in hypothesis testing. The jury considers the evidence in light of the *presumption* of innocence and judges whether the evidence against the defendant would be plausible *if the defendant were in fact innocent*.

Like the jury, you ask, "Could these data plausibly have happened by chance if the null hypothesis were true?" If they are very unlikely to have occurred, then the evidence raises a reasonable doubt about the null hypothesis.

Sometimes, you must make a decision. The standard of "beyond a reasonable doubt" is wonderfully ambiguous because it leaves the jury to decide the degree to which the evidence contradicts the hypothesis of innocence. Juries don't explicitly use probability to help them decide whether to reject that hypothesis. But when you ask the same question of your null hypothesis, you have the advantage of being able to quantify exactly how surprising the evidence would be if the null hypothesis were true.

How unlikely is unlikely? Some people set rigid standards, like 1 time out of $20(0.05)$ or 1 time out of $100(0.01)$.[2] But if *you* have to make the decision, you must judge for yourself in each situation whether the probability of observing your data is small enough to constitute "reasonable doubt."

12.2   P-Values

To test a hypothesis we must answer the question "Are the data surprising, given the null hypothesis?" So we need *probability*–specifically, the probability of seeing data like these (or something even less likely) *given* the null hypothesis. In the ingots example, this came to 0.13. This probability is the value on which we base our decision, so statisticians give it a special name: the **P-value**.[3] Usually, you'll use a sampling distribution model or a simulation to find P-values. Either way, the computer will do the heavy lifting.

When a P-value is very low, there are only two possibilities. Either the null hypothesis is correct and we've just seen something remarkable, or the null hypothesis is wrong (and the reason for a low P-value is that the model was wrong). Now we have a choice. Should we decide that a rare event has happened to us, or should we trust that the data were not unusual and that our null model was wrong? We don't believe in rare events,[4] so a low enough P-value leads us to reject the null

---

[2]See Section 12.6 for warnings about bright line decisions like this.

[3]You'd think if it were that special it would have a better name, but "P-value" is about as creative as statisticians get.

[4]Or at least we don't think that they don't happen to us.

> If the People fail to satisfy their burden of proof, you must find the defendant not guilty.
>
> —NY state jury instructions

Beyond a Reasonable Doubt

We ask whether the data were unlikely beyond a reasonable doubt. We've just calculated that probability. The probability that the observed statistic value (or an even more extreme value) could occur if the null model were true—in the ingots example, 0.13—is the P-value.

> The null hypothesis is never proved or established, but is possibly disproved, in the course of experimentation. Every experiment may be said to exist only in order to give the facts a chance of disproving the null hypothesis.
>
> —Sir Ronald Fisher, The Design of Experiments

Don't "Accept" the Null Hypothesis

Think about the null hypothesis H_0: All swans are white. Does collecting a sample of 100 white swans prove the null hypothesis? The data are *consistent* with this hypothesis and seem to lend support to it, but they don't *prove* it. In fact, all we can do is disprove the null hypothesis—for example, by finding just one non-white swan.

hypothesis. There is no hard and fast rule about how low the P-value has to be. In fact, it depends on the consequences of our decision and the size of the change we've observed.

When the P-value is high, we haven't seen anything unlikely or surprising at all. The data are consistent with the model from the null hypothesis, and we have no reason to reject it. Does that mean we've proved it? No. Many other models could be consistent with the data we've seen, so *we haven't proven anything*. The most we can say is that the null model doesn't appear to be false. Formally, we "fail to reject" the null hypothesis. That's a pretty weak conclusion, but it's all we can do with a high P-value.

IN PRACTICE 12.2   Using P-values to make decisions

The SmartWool analyst in In Practice 12.1 collects a representative sample of visits since the new website has gone online.

MANAGER   Since we made the switch, 270 people (out of 1500) have made a purchase. That's 18%. Is that a big enough change from the original 15% rate for us to conclude that this wasn't just due to chance?

ANALYST   The difference (0.03) is 3.18 standard deviations larger than 0, with a P-value of about 0.0011. That's strong evidence that the difference is not due to chance. So we conclude that the proportion of sales has changed.

What to Do with an "Innocent" Defendant

Back to the jury trial. The jury assumes the defendant is innocent, but when the evidence is not strong enough to reject that hypothesis, they say "not guilty." They do not claim that the null hypothesis is true and say that the defendant is innocent. All they say is that they have not seen sufficient evidence to convict. The defendant may, in fact, be innocent, but the jury has no way to be sure.

In the same way, when the P-value is large, the most we can do is to "fail to reject" our null hypothesis. We never declare the null hypothesis to be true (or "accept" the null), because we simply do not know whether it's true or not. (But, unlike a jury trial, there is no "double indemnity" in science. More data may become available in the future.)

JUST CHECKING

1 A research team wants to know if aspirin helps to thin blood. The null hypothesis says that it doesn't. They test 12 patients, observe the proportion with thinner blood, and get a P-value of 0.32. They proclaim that aspirin doesn't work. What would you say?

2 An allergy drug has been tested and found to give relief to 75% of the patients in a large clinical trial. Now the scientists want to see if the new, improved version works even better. What would the null hypothesis be?

3 The new drug is tested and the P-value is 0.0001. What would you conclude about the new drug?

Alternative Alternatives

Tests on the ingot data can be viewed in two different ways. We know the old cracking rate is 20%, so the null hypothesis is

$$H_0: p = 0.20.$$

But we have a choice of alternative hypotheses. A metallurgist working for the company might be interested in *any* change in the cracking rate due to the new process. Even if the rate got worse, she might learn something useful from it. In that case, she's interested in possible changes on both sides of the null hypothesis. So she would write her alternative hypothesis as

$$H_A: p \neq 0.20.$$

An alternative hypothesis such as this is known as a **two-sided alternative** because we are equally interested in deviations on either side of the null hypothesis value. For two-sided alternatives, the P-value is the probability of deviating in *either* direction from the null hypothesis value.

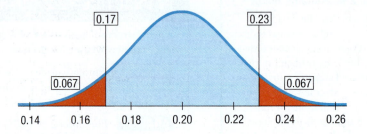

But management wants to know only if the cracking rate has *decreased* to below 20%. Knowing how to *increase* the cracking rate probably doesn't interest them. To make that explicit, they could write their alternative hypothesis as

$$H_A: p < 0.20.$$

An alternative hypothesis that focuses on deviations from the null hypothesis value in only one direction is called a **one-sided alternative**.[5]

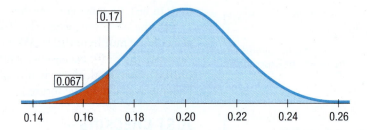

For a hypothesis test with a one-sided alternative, the P-value is the probability of deviating *only in the direction of the alternative* away from the null hypothesis value. For the same data, the one-sided P-value is half the two-sided P-value. So, a one-sided test will reject the null hypothesis more often. This is good and bad. It's great that it rejects the null hypothesis more often when it's false, but it also rejects it more often when it's true. We discuss this issue in detail in the next chapter. A two-sided test is always more conservative. Because its P-value is twice as big as either one-sided alternative, it will reject the null hypothesis less often. Unless you can justify the choice of a one-sided test, it's usually better to assume the alternative is two-sided. One advantage of a two-sided test is that the results are easily matched to the confidence interval. See Section 12.5.

---

[5]These are also called a **two- and one-tailed alternatives**, because the probabilities we care about are found in the tails of the sampling distribution.

12.3 The Reasoning of Hypothesis Testing

As the subsequent chapters will show, the reasoning of hypothesis testing is essentially the same no matter what we test. For example, we'll test proportions, means, differences between groups, and even regression coefficients, but the logic stays the same. Here's a path to follow.

1. Setup

First, we state the null hypothesis. That's usually the skeptical claim that nothing's different. Are we considering a (New! Improved!) possibly better method? The null hypothesis says, "Oh yeah? Convince me!" To convert a skeptic, we must pile up enough evidence against the null hypothesis that we can reasonably reject it.

In statistical hypothesis testing, hypotheses are almost always about model parameters. To assess how unlikely our data may be, we need a null model. The null hypothesis specifies a particular parameter value to use in our model. In the usual shorthand, we write H_0: *parameter* = *hypothesized value*. The alternative hypothesis, H_A, contains the values of the parameter we consider plausible when we reject the null.

> **Confusing?**
>
> Hypothesis testing can be confusing because it seems *backward*.
> 1. Assume that the null hypothesis is true (even though you may think this to be unlikely).
> 2. Decide what would be "surprising," *if* the null hypothesis were actually true.
> 3. Collect data.
> 4. Compute a statistic. Compare the statistic to the criterion from #2. If you are "surprised," reject the null (something is likely going on that is not the null, because observing the data you got if the null were true is unlikely).

> **How to Say It**
>
> You might think that the 0 in H_0 should be pronounced as "zero" or "0," but it's actually pronounced "naught" as in "all is for naught."

> ### IN PRACTICE 12.3 More practice in writing hypotheses
>
> A large city's Department of Motor Vehicles claimed that 80% of candidates pass driving tests, but a newspaper reporter's survey of 90 randomly selected local teens who had taken the test found that only 61 had passed.
>
> **DMV MANAGER** Does this finding suggest that the passing rate for teenagers is lower than the official rate that we report? How would I write the hypotheses to test this?
>
> **ANALYST** Because you want to know if the rate is lower, we'll write a one-sided hypothesis. Let p = the proportion of teens that pass. Then:
>
> $$H_0: p = 0.80$$
> $$H_A: p < 0.80$$

2. Model

To plan a statistical hypothesis test, specify the *model* you will use to test the null hypothesis and the parameter of interest. Of course, all models require assumptions, so you will need to state them and check any corresponding conditions.

Your Model step should end with a statement such as

Because the conditions are satisfied, I can model the sampling distribution of the proportion with a Normal model.

Watch out, though. Your Model step could end with

Because the conditions are not satisfied, I can't proceed with the test.

If that's the case, stop and reconsider.

Because the test about a single proportion is based on the Normal model, it is called a **one-proportion z-test**.[6] Each test in the text has a name that you should include in your report. Some tests will be about more than one sample, some will involve statistics other than proportions or means, and some will use models other than the Normal. For each test, be sure to check the appropriate assumptions and conditions. This will usually require a plot of your data.

When the Conditions Fail . . .

You might proceed with caution, explicitly stating your concerns. Or you may need to do the analysis with and without an outlier, or on different subgroups, or after re-expressing the response variable. Or you may not be able to proceed at all.

One-Proportion z-Test

The conditions for the one-proportion z-test are the same as for the one-proportion z-interval. We test the hypothesis $H_0: p = p_0$ using the statistic $z = \dfrac{(\hat{p} - p_0)}{SD(\hat{p})}$. We use the hypothesized proportion to find the standard deviation, $SD(\hat{p}) = \sqrt{\dfrac{p_0 q_0}{n}}$.

When the conditions are met and the null hypothesis is true, this statistic follows the standard Normal model, so we can use that model to obtain a P-value.

IN PRACTICE 12.4 Checking the conditions

RECAP A large city's DMV claimed that 80% of candidates pass driving tests. A reporter has results from a survey of 90 randomly selected local teens who had taken the test.

MANAGER I know it's not always appropriate to do a statistical test of hypothesis. Are we ok here?

ANALYST Yes. Here are the conditions I checked:

✔ **Randomization Condition:** The 90 teens surveyed were a random sample of local teenage driving candidates.

✔ **10% Condition:** 90 is fewer than 10% of the teenagers who take driving tests in a large city.

✔ **Success/Failure Condition:** We expect $np_0 = 90(0.80) = 72$ successes and $nq_0 = 90(0.20) = 18$ failures. Both are at least 10.

Because the conditions are satisfied, it's okay to use a Normal model and perform a one-proportion z-test.

3. Mechanics

The "mechanics" are the calculation of our test statistic and P-value. Different tests will have different formulas, different test statistics, and different sampling distributions. Usually, the mechanics are handled by a statistics program.

---

[6]It's also called the "one-sample test for a proportion."

Conditional Probability

Did you notice that a P-value is a conditional probability? It's the probability that the observed results could have happened *if* (or given that) the null hypothesis were true.

IN PRACTICE 12.5   Finding a P-value

RECAP A large city's DMV claimed that 80% of candidates pass driving tests, but a survey of 90 randomly selected local teens who had taken the test found only 61 who passed.

MANAGER How do our results compare with the official claim? If we perform a test, is the difference between our results and the city's claim statistically significant?

ANALYST Well, we have $n = 90$, $x = 61$, and a hypothesized $p = 0.80$.

The proportion of teens that passed in the sample is:

$$\hat{p} = \frac{61}{90} \approx 0.678$$

$$SD(\hat{p}) = \sqrt{\frac{p_0 q_0}{n}} = \sqrt{\frac{(0.8)(0.2)}{90}} \approx 0.042$$

$$z = \frac{\hat{p} - p_0}{SD(\hat{p})} = \frac{0.678 - 0.800}{0.042} \approx -2.90$$

P-value $= P(z < -2.90) = 0.002$

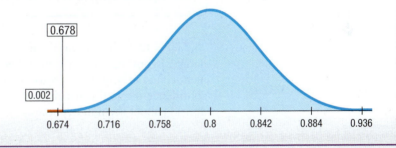

The picture shows that a proportion that low is unlikely to have occurred by chance if the teens' passing proportion was the same 80%. The P-value of 0.002 provides strong evidence that the teens' true passing proportion is lower. We say that this result is "statistically significant."

4. Conclusion

The conclusion in a hypothesis test is always a statement about the null hypothesis. The conclusion must state either that we reject or that we fail to reject the null hypothesis. And, as always, the conclusion should be stated in context.

How Much Does It Cost?

Formal tests of a null hypothesis base the decision of whether to reject the null hypothesis solely on the size of the P-value. But in real life, we want to evaluate the costs of our decisions as well. How much would you be willing to pay for a faster computer? Shouldn't your decision depend on how much faster? And on how much more it costs? Costs are not just monetary either. Would you use the same standard of proof for testing the safety of an airplane as for the speed of your new computer?

Your conclusion about the null hypothesis should never be the end of a testing procedure. Usually there are actions to take or policies to change. In our ingot example, management must decide whether to continue the changes proposed by the engineers. The decision always includes the practical consideration of whether the new method is worth the cost. Suppose management decides to reject the null hypothesis of 20% cracking in favor of the alternative that the percentage has changed. They must still evaluate how much the new method changes the cracking rate and how much it would cost to accomplish that change. The *size of the effect* is always a concern when we test hypotheses. A good way to look at the **effect size** is to examine a confidence interval.

IN PRACTICE 12.6   Stating the conclusion

RECAP   A large city's DMV claimed that 80% of candidates pass driving tests. Data from a reporter's survey of randomly selected local teens who had taken the test produced a P-value of 0.002.

MANAGER   OK, great. I think I've got it. But can you say it again in plain English so I can tell the reporter what we found?

ANALYST   Because the P-value of 0.002 is very small, these survey data provide strong evidence that the passing rate for teenagers taking the driving test is lower than 80%.

   If the passing rate for teenage driving candidates were actually 80%, we'd expect to see passing rates this low in only about 1 in 500 (0.2%) samples of this size. This seems quite unlikely, casting doubt that our stated success rate applies to teens.

Table 12.1 summarizes the hypothesis testing process. Remember that by their nature, hypothesis tests result in black-and-white decisions. This is where judgment comes in. Looking at associated costs and the range of possible values from a confidence interval is usually better than relying simply on a reject/don't reject decision about the null hypothesis.

		The Hypothesis Testing Process
PLAN	Setup	State your problem and identify the variables. Be sure that the identity of the cases and what the variables measure are both clear.
	Hypotheses	State your hypotheses: • The null hypothesis, H_0, identifies a parameter and proposes a value for it. • The alternative hypothesis, H_A, specifies what kind of deviations from the null model would be of interest.
	Model	Specify the statistic and its sampling distribution model. The sampling distribution model comes from theory and will usually be something you look up. It will likely require you to make assumptions about your data. You can often determine if an assumption is plausible by checking related conditions—usually with graphical displays. If the required assumptions are not plausible, STOP. You can't test your hypothesis with this method or with these data. Otherwise, state clearly what method you will use.
DO	Mechanics	Calculate the test statistic. Usually, you'll use technology to do the work.
	Find the P-value	Find the probability of observing the statistic value you found (or values even less likely). The sampling distribution model provides this probability. The hypothesized parameter value will be needed for the sampling distribution model, and the alternative hypothesis will indicate what part of the distribution is of interest. Usually, we can use technology to find this probability. The probability is called the P-value. You should report it along with your decision.

	Reasoning	Is the P-value small? Then **reject** the null hypothesis.
		   If the null hypothesis were true then we have observed a rare event, and we don't want to base decisions on rare events.
		Is the P-value large? Then **fail to reject** the null hypothesis.
		   We don't know whether the null hypothesis is true, so we can't "accept" it. But we lack strong enough evidence to declare it false.

REPORT	Conclusion	You must decide for yourself what probability would be so small that you would find the data too unlikely to have occurred by chance. Although there are some common values (10%, 5%, and 1% are all used), your business decision should be based on the circumstances of the test, including considerations of the costs involved, whether your test conclusion proves to be correct or not. Report your conclusions in plain English, using language based on the context of the problem, not statistical jargon.

TABLE 12.1   The hypothesis testing process. These are the basic steps involved from the initial planning phase to explaining your results to others.

GUIDED EXAMPLE   Credit Card Promotion

A credit card company plans to offer a special incentive program to customers who charge at least $500 next month. The marketing department has pulled a sample of 500 customers from the same month last year and noted that the mean amount charged was $478.19 and the median amount was $216.48. The finance department says that the only relevant quantity is the proportion of customers who spend more than $500. If that proportion is not more than 25%, the program will lose money.

Among the 500 customers, 148 or 29.6% of them charged $500 or more. Has the goal that 25% of all customers charging at least $500 been met?

PLAN	**Setup** State the problem and discuss the variables and the context.	We want to know whether 25% or more of the customers will spend $500 or more in the next month and qualify for the special program. We will use the data from the same month a year ago to estimate the proportion and see whether the proportion was at least 25%.

The statistic is $\hat{p} = 0.296$, the proportion of customers who charged $500 or more.

$$H_0: p = 0.25$$
$$H_A: p > 0.25$$

Hypotheses The null hypothesis is that the proportion qualifying is 25%. The alternative is that it is higher. It's clearly a one-sided test.

Model Check the conditions.

✔ **Independence Assumption.** Customers are not likely to influence one another when it comes to spending on their credit cards.

✔ **Randomization Condition.** This is a random sample from the company's database.

✔ **Success/Failure Condition.** We expect 125 successes and 375 failures, both at least 10. The sample is large enough.

✔ **10% Condition.** The sample of 500 customers is less than 10% of all our customers.

State your method.

Under these conditions, the sampling model is Normal. We'll compute a one-proportion z-test.

DO	**Mechanics** Write down the given information and determine the sample proportion. Find the test statistic and its P-value.	$n = 500$, so

$$\hat{p} = \frac{148}{500} = 0.296 \text{ and}$$

$$SD(\hat{p}) = \sqrt{\frac{(0.25)(0.75)}{500}} = 0.01936$$

so the test statistic is $z = \dfrac{0.296 - 0.250}{0.01936} = 2.38$

From technology or from Table Z at the back of the text, we find that the probability of a z-score ≥ 2.38 is 0.0087, so that is our P-value.

REPORT	**Communicate and Present Your Conclusion** Link the test to your decision about the null hypothesis, then state your conclusion in context.	**MEMO** **Re: Credit card promotion** If the true proportion of customers charging $500 or more were actually 25%, the probability of seeing a success rate at least as large as the 29.6% that we did observe is about 0.0087. This is strong evidence that the true proportion is greater than our target of 25%. However, business judgment is called for to determine whether to go ahead with the new promotion.

Here's a portion of table Z that gives the probability we needed for the hypothesis test. At $z = 2.38$, the table gives the percentile as 0.9913. The upper-tail probability (shaded red) is, therefore, $1 - 0.9913 = 0.0087$; so, for our test, that's the P-value we need.

FIGURE 12.3 A portion of a Normal table with the look-up for $z = 2.38$ indicated. It's usually easier to use technology to find P-values.

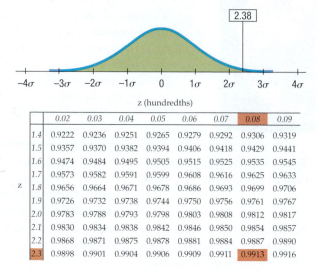

z	0.02	0.03	0.04	0.05	0.06	0.07	0.08	0.09
1.4	0.9222	0.9236	0.9251	0.9265	0.9279	0.9292	0.9306	0.9319
1.5	0.9357	0.9370	0.9382	0.9394	0.9406	0.9418	0.9429	0.9441
1.6	0.9474	0.9484	0.9495	0.9505	0.9515	0.9525	0.9535	0.9545
1.7	0.9573	0.9582	0.9591	0.9599	0.9608	0.9616	0.9625	0.9633
1.8	0.9656	0.9664	0.9671	0.9678	0.9686	0.9693	0.9699	0.9706
1.9	0.9726	0.9732	0.9738	0.9744	0.9750	0.9756	0.9761	0.9767
2.0	0.9783	0.9788	0.9793	0.9798	0.9803	0.9808	0.9812	0.9817
2.1	0.9830	0.9834	0.9838	0.9842	0.9846	0.9850	0.9854	0.9857
2.2	0.9868	0.9871	0.9875	0.9878	0.9881	0.9884	0.9887	0.9890
2.3	0.9898	0.9901	0.9904	0.9906	0.9909	0.9911	0.9913	0.9916

12.4   A Hypothesis Test for the Mean

A hospital in Nashville is considering changes to the prenatal care they offer. They collected the gestation times of 70 pregnancies that ended in live births. The established human gestation time is 266 days. Were their mean gestation times different? (Data in **Nashville**)

The test called for here is based on Student's t because it is a test about the mean and we don't know the standard deviation. It is called a **one-sample t-test for the mean**. The rubric for testing says to first state the hypotheses.

1. **Hypotheses.** The parameter of interest is the mean gestation time, and the null value is given by general medical knowledge. We can write

$$H_0: \mu = 266 \text{ vs. } H_A: \mu \neq 266.$$

2. **Model.** In Chapter 11, we used Student's t to build confidence intervals for the mean. That's what we'll do for hypothesis tests as well—and for the same reason we had then: We don't know the standard deviation, σ. We don't have a random sample, but we think it is representative. The values are almost surely independent. A histogram of the data is unimodal and nearly symmetric with no outliers. The sample mean, $\bar{y}$, is 260.31 and the standard deviation, s, is 15.26 days.

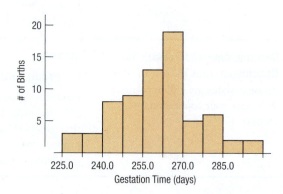

3. **Mechanics.** The calculations are similar to those for a confidence interval:

$$t = \frac{(\bar{y} - \mu_0)}{s/\sqrt{n}} = \frac{260.31 - 266}{15.2577/\sqrt{70}} = -3.118.$$

The t distribution on $n - 1 = 69$ df looks like this:

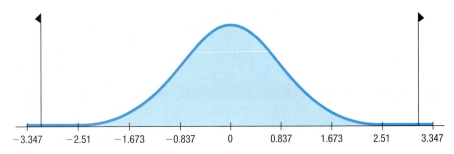

$$-3.347 \quad -2.51 \quad -1.673 \quad -0.837 \quad 0 \quad 0.837 \quad 1.673 \quad 2.51 \quad 3.347$$

which shows the P-value to be 0.0027.

4. **Conclusion.** With a P-value this small, we reject the null hypothesis. In fact, a 95% confidence interval is $(256.7, 264.0)$ days, so plausible values for the mean gestation time are below the standard mean of 266. However, all of the plausible values are within about a week of normal gestation, so the hospital administrators may not see this as a reason for alarm.

One-Sample t-Test for the Mean

The assumptions and conditions for the one-sample t-test for the mean are the same as for the one-sample t-interval (see Chapter 11). We test the hypothesis $H_0: \mu = \mu_0$ using the statistic

$$t_{n-1} = \frac{\bar{y} - \mu_0}{SE(\bar{y})}.$$

The standard error of $\bar{y}$ is $SE(\bar{y}) = \dfrac{s}{\sqrt{n}}.$

When the conditions are met and the null hypothesis is true, this statistic follows a Student's t-model with $n - 1$ degrees of freedom. We use that model to obtain a P-value.

IN PRACTICE 12.7   Making decisions using a one-sample t-test for the mean

RECAP   In Practice 11.2 considered a study in which researchers tested 150 farm-raised salmon for organic contaminants. They found the mean concentration of the carcinogenic insecticide mirex to be 0.0913 parts per million, with standard deviation 0.0495 ppm. As a safety recommendation to recreational fishers, the Environmental Protection Agency's (EPA) recommended "screening value" for mirex is 0.08 ppm. (Data in **Salmon**)

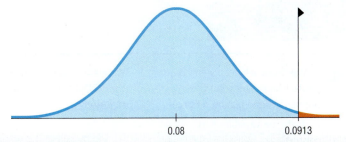

$$0.08 \qquad\qquad 0.0913$$

(continued)

MANAGER Are the farmed salmon we buy contaminated beyond the level permitted by the EPA?

ANALYST (We've already checked the conditions; see page 398.)

$$H_0: \mu = 0.08$$
$$H_A: \mu > 0.08$$

These data satisfy the conditions for inference; I'll do a one-sample *t*-test for the mean:

$$n = 150, df = 149$$
$$\bar{y} = 0.0913, s = 0.0495$$
$$SE(\bar{y}) = \frac{0.0495}{\sqrt{150}} = 0.0040$$
$$t_{149} = \frac{0.0913 - 0.08}{0.0040} = 2.825$$

P-value = 0.0027 (from technology)

With a P-value that low, I reject the null hypothesis and conclude that, in farm-raised salmon, the mirex contamination level does not conform to the EPA screening value. In fact, we already knew this. The confidence interval we found in Chapter 11 showed that the plausible values for the mean mirex contamination are in the interval (0.0834, 0.0992) ppm—showing all values above the EPA screening value.

When σ is Known

If the hospital administrators use the established value of 14 days for the standard deviation of healthy gestation times, as they did for the confidence interval, they can use a *z*-test instead of a *t*-test. Practically, this will make little difference, but, when the science is solid, it removes the variability that results from estimating the standard deviation from samples. In this case, instead of a $t_{69} = -3.118$ they would find

$$z = \frac{260.31 - 266}{14/\sqrt{70}} = -3.40$$

which would lead to the same conclusion (that the mean gestation time of the hospital is not 266 days) with a slightly smaller P-value.

JUST CHECKING

4 The research team that wants to know if aspirin helps to thin blood also measures the plasma viscosity (PV) of the 12 patients before and after taking aspirin. The mean of the 12 differences (after − before) is 0.8 standard errors below 0 for a one-sided P-value of 0.22. They claim that on the basis of this trial, aspirin does not reduce PV. What would you say?

5 A marketing team wants to test whether their Facebook page increases revenue. They find that people who "like" their page spend more, on average, than their other customers by about $5.06 a month. The P-value is 0.049. They tell management that they have strong evidence that the Facebook page is working and is worth the time and effort to maintain it. What would you say?

GUIDED EXAMPLE Insurance Profits Revisited

Let's apply the one-sample *t*-test to the 30 mature policies sampled by the manager in Chapter 11 (data in **Insurance profits sales rep**). From these 30 policies, the management would like to know if there's evidence that the mean profit of policies sold by this sales rep is less than $1500.

| **PLAN** | **Setup** State what we want to know. Make clear what the population and parameter are.

Identify the variables and context. | We want to test whether the mean profit of the sales rep's policies is less than $1500. We have a random sample of 30 mature policies from which to judge.

$H_O: \mu = \$1500$
$H_A: \mu < \$1500$ |

Hypotheses We give benefit of the doubt to the sales rep. The null hypothesis is that the true mean profit is equal to $1500. Because we're interested in whether the profit is less, the alternative is one-sided.

We checked the histogram of these data in the Guided Example in Chapter 11 and saw that it had a unimodal, symmetric distribution.

Make a graph. Check the distribution for skewness, multiple modes, and outliers.

Model Check the conditions.

We checked the Randomization and Nearly Normal Conditions in the Chapter 11 Guided Example.

State the sampling distribution model.

The conditions are satisfied, so we'll use a Student's t-model with $n - 1 = 29$ degrees of freedom and a one-sample t-test for the mean.

Choose your method.

DO **Mechanics** Compute the sample statistics. Be sure to include the units when you write down what you know from the data.

Using software, we obtain the following basic statistics:

$$n = 30$$
$$\text{Mean} = \$1438.90$$
$$s = \$1329.60$$
$$t = \frac{1438.90 - 1500}{1329.60/\sqrt{30}} = -0.2517$$

The t-statistic calculation is just a standardized value. We subtract the hypothesized mean and divide by the standard error.

(The observed mean is less than one standard error below the hypothesized value.)

We assume the null model is true to find the P-value. Make a picture of the t-model, centered at μ_0. Since this is a lower-tail test, shade the region to the left of the observed average profit.

The P-value is the probability of observing a sample mean as small as $1438.90 (or smaller) *if* the true mean were $1500, as the null hypothesis states. We can find this P-value from a table, calculator, or computer program.

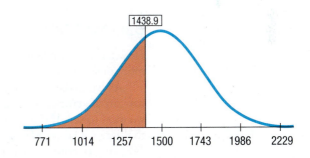

P-value = $P(t_{29} < -0.2517) = 0.4015$ (or from a table $0.1 < P$)

REPORT **Conclusion** Link the P-value to your decision about H_0, and state your conclusion in context.

MEMO

Re: Sales performance

The mean profit on 30 sampled contracts closed by the sales rep in question has fallen below our standard of $1500, but there is not enough evidence in this sample of policies to indicate that the true mean is below $1500. If the mean were $1500, we would expect a sample of size 30 to have a mean this low about 40.15% of the time.

Notice that the way this hypothesis was set up, the sales rep's mean profit would have to be well below $1500 to reject the null hypothesis. Because the null hypothesis was that the mean was $1500 and the alternative was that it was less, this setup gave some benefit of the doubt to the sales rep. There's nothing intrinsically wrong with that, but keep in mind that it's always a good idea to make sure that the hypotheses are stated in ways that will guide you to make the right business decision.

IN PRACTICE 12.8 Making a decision by testing a mean

RECAP Summit Projects recently redesigned a client company's website and wants to show that sales have increased.

CLIENT Can you demonstrate that your expensive redesign has had the result you promised?

ANALYST I have selected 58 sales records at random from 2000 of your company's access logs. I find a mean amount spent of $26.05 with a standard deviation of $10.20.

Your question amounts to asking that we test the hypothesis that the mean is $24.85 (as it was before the redesign) against the alternative that it has increased.

We can write: $H_0: \mu = \$24.85$ *vs.* $H_A: \mu > \$24.85$. Then

$$t = \frac{(26.05 - 24.85)}{10.2/\sqrt{58}} = 0.896.$$

Because you are concerned only with an improvement in sales, I will use an alternative hypothesis that is *one-sided*. I find $P(t > 0.896)$ with 57 degrees of freedom. From technology, $P(t > 0.896) = 0.1870$, a large P-value. This would not be a surprising value if the hypothesized mean of $24.85 were the true value. Therefore I *fail to reject* the null hypothesis and conclude that there is not sufficient evidence to suggest that the mean has increased from 24.85. It appears that our redesign may not have had the promised effect, so we will be refunding your money.

Sample Size

How large a sample do we need? More information is always better, but acquiring more observations costs money, effort, and time. So how much data is enough?

As we make plans to collect data, we should have some idea of how small a margin of error is required to be able to draw a conclusion or detect a difference we want to see. If the size of the effect we're studying is large, then we may be able to tolerate a larger ME. If we need greater precision, however, we'll want a smaller ME, and, of course, that means a larger sample size. Armed with the ME and confidence level, we can find the sample size we'll need. Almost.

We know that for a mean, $ME = t_{n-1}^* \times SE(\bar{y})$ and that $SE(\bar{y}) = \dfrac{s}{\sqrt{n}}$, so we can determine the sample size by solving this equation for n:

$$ME = t_{n-1}^* \times \frac{s}{\sqrt{n}}.$$

The good news is that we have an equation; the bad news is that we won't know most of the values we need to compute it. When we thought about sample size for proportions, we ran into a similar problem. There we had to guess a working value for p to compute a sample size. Here, we need to know s, and if we're thinking about a very small sample, we need to know how many degrees of freedom to use. As an approximation for the critical value of t for 95% confidence (for the number of df we are likely to see), we can use 2.0 instead of t^*. That's much simpler to calculate, and it's a pretty good approximation for the number of degrees of freedom we're likely to see. We don't know *s* until we get some data, but we want to calculate the sample size *before* collecting the data. We might be able to make a good guess, and that is often good enough for this purpose. If we have no idea what the standard deviation might be or if the sample size really matters (for example, because each additional individual is very expensive to sample or experiment on), it might be a good idea to run a small *pilot study* to get some feeling for the size of the standard deviation.

There are software packages available that can compute sample sizes for both confidence intervals and tests. For a confidence interval, you'll need to specify the margin of error you want to see, the confidence level you want, and a value for the standard deviation. For a hypothesis test, you'll need to specify your value for alpha, the standard deviation, and the power you want the test to have for the effect size that you want to be able to detect. (Chapter 13 discusses the power of a test.) It's important to keep in mind that all sample size calculations are approximate. You'll either need to assume a value for the standard deviation, or run a pilot study to estimate it. And you won't know the *actual* margin of error or the power of the test until after you've collected the data.

JUST CHECKING

You've seen an ad for some software that claims to lower the time it takes to download movies. It costs $49.95, so you're thinking about testing it on a few movies to see if it really works before you buy. Right now it takes you about 20 minutes on average to download a 2-hour movie. The standard deviation is about 5 minutes.

6 For which situation would you need a larger sample size to see if the software works: the software really reduces the time by 2 minutes or by 10 minutes on average? Why?

7 Suppose the standard deviation of the time it takes this software is only 2 minutes instead of 5. Will this widen or narrow your confidence interval for the mean time it takes to download a movie? Why?

IN PRACTICE 12.9   Finding the sample size for a confidence interval for means

In the 150 samples of farmed salmon (see page 397), the mean concentration of mirex was 0.0913 ppm with a standard deviation of 0.0495 ppm. A 95% confidence interval for the mean mirex concentration was found to be (0.0833, 0.0993).

MANAGER   If I wanted more precision about the amount of mirex in the salmon, how large a sample would we need to produce a 95% confidence interval with a margin of error of 0.004?

ANALYST   I will assume that the standard deviation is 0.0495 ppm. The margin of error is equal to the critical value times the standard error. Using 2 for t^*, we find:

$$0.004 = 2 \times \frac{0.0495}{\sqrt{n}}$$

Solving for *n*, we find:

$$\sqrt{n} = 2 \times \frac{0.0495}{0.004}$$

or

$$n = \left(2 \times \frac{0.0495}{0.004} \right)^2 = 612.56$$

We would need a sample of at least 613 to have a good chance of getting a margin of error of 0.004.

12.5 Intervals and Tests

Carl Wunderlich (1815–1877), the father of clinical thermometry.

As we saw from several examples in Chapter 11, a decision about the null hypothesis can often be made by simply looking at the confidence interval. The confidence interval contains all the plausible values of the parameter. If it doesn't contain the hypothesized value, then that value isn't plausible, and we should reject the null hypothesis. Confidence intervals and significance tests are built from the same calculations. In fact, they are really just two ways of looking at the same question.

Confidence intervals and hypothesis tests look at the same problem from two different perspectives. The confidence interval is *data-centric*. Its center is the statistic computed from the data. It then finds an interval of plausible values for the parameter by extending around that statistic. When testing a hypothesis using a confidence interval, we ask if the proposed parameter value is consistent with our interval and we reject the null hypothesis if that proposed value is not in the interval. By contrast, a hypothesis test is *model-centric*. It starts with a model centered at the *proposed null parameter value*, and asks if the *data* are consistent with that model. If the data are too unusual (as measured by the model), then we reject the hypothesis. So, they are both doing the same thing, but from different points of view.

How is the confidence level related to the P-value? To be precise, a level C confidence interval contains *all* of the plausible null hypothesis values that would *not* be rejected if you use a P-value of $(1 - C)$ as the cutoff for deciding to reject H_0.

When you've performed a hypothesis test, the corresponding confidence interval can provide additional information. By providing the plausible values for the parameter, it can help you judge the importance of your result. If your hypothesized value was far from the observed statistic (and you therefore rejected your null hypothesis), the null value has no information about your data, so a confidence interval provides the *only* information about plausible values.

Here's an example. Fifty-two healthy adults had their temperatures taken orally (data in **Normal temperature**). We all "know" that "normal" body temperature is 98.6°F (or 37°C), but the mean of these 52 temperatures is only 98.285°F. The 98.6 number comes from the work of Carl Wunderlich, a German medical professor of the mid-19th century who measured the temperatures of tens of thousands of patients over an 18-year period using a foot-long thermometer than took 20 minutes to get a stable reading. Could 98.6 and Wunderlich be wrong? In fact, some research published nearly 30 years ago in the *Journal of the American Medical Association*[7] asked the same question.

Summary	Temperature
Count	52
Mean	98.285
Median	98.200
MidRange	98.600
StdDev	0.6824
Range	2.800
IntQRange	1.050

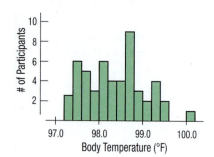

We'll examine Wunderlich's hypothesis in two ways: by constructing a confidence interval for the true mean and by performing a hypothesis test of $\mu = 98.6$. We'll use 99% as our confidence level, which equates to a level of significance of 0.01. The confidence interval is

$$\bar{y} \pm t_{51,0.005} \frac{s}{\sqrt{n}} = 98.285 \pm 2.676 \frac{0.6824}{\sqrt{52}} = (98.032, 98.538).$$

As we can see, the upper end misses 98.6 by nearly a half a degree.

What does a hypothesis test say about it?

$$t = \frac{98.285 - 98.6}{0.6824/\sqrt{52}} = -3.3387$$

$$df = 51, \text{P-value} = 0.0016$$

The hypothesis test rejects the null hypothesis of 98.6 with a P-value just over 0.001, strong evidence that the mean is not 98.6. We'll return to this example on the next page.

---

[7]Philip A. Mackowiak, MD; Steven S. Wasserman, PhD; and Myron M. Levine, MD; *Journal of the American Medical Association* 268: 1578–1580 (1992).

The Special Case of Proportions

The relationship between confidence intervals and hypothesis tests works for almost every inference procedure we'll see in this text. We use the standard error of the statistic as a ruler for both. For the confidence interval, we reach out a number (often near 2) of standard errors on each side of the statistic. For a hypothesis test, we measure how many standard errors away our data lie from the hypothesized value and compute a P-value. But proportions are a little special. When we test a hypothesis about a proportion, not only do we use the hypothesized null value as the center of our null distribution, but we use it to compute the spread of that distribution as well. In this case, we're not estimating anything, so we call it a standard deviation, not a standard error, and write it as

$$SD(\hat{p}) = \sqrt{\frac{pq}{n}}.$$

But when we construct a confidence interval, there's no null hypothesis value. So we use the observed proportion, $\hat{p}$, and calculate its standard error: $SE(\hat{p}) = \sqrt{\frac{\hat{p}\hat{q}}{n}}$.

Does this make a difference? Usually no. When the observed proportion is near the hypothesized value, the SE and SD are very similar, so the usual relationship between the test and the interval works reasonably well. But if the hypothesized value is quite far from the observed value, the relationship between test and interval breaks down.

Here's an example: Suppose you want to test whether the coin that is flipped to determine who kicks off in your school's football games is fair. The natural null hypothesis is $H_0: p = 0.50$. Suppose you flip the coin 100 times, and get only 3 Heads. There's no way that could happen with a fair coin. That's 9.4 standard deviations below 50%, with a P-value of about 10^{-25}. You would obviously claim that the coin is rigged. With only 3 "successes" you can't make a confidence interval using the methods of this chapter. But that's no reason not to test the hypothesis—and that's why the Success/Failure Condition for a hypothesis test of a proportion uses np_0 and not $n\hat{p}$. When testing a hypothesis, you should always use the null value of p when calculating $SD(\hat{p})$.

*Bootstrap Hypothesis Tests and Intervals

In Chapter 11, we saw that a "bootstrap" confidence interval can be found by repeated sampling from a pseud-population based on a single sample as if we had many samples from the underlying population. For each sample, we compute the mean and make a histogram of those means. For a 99% confidence interval, we'd find the central 99% of the values. Here's a histogram of the means of 10,000 resamples of the temperatures.

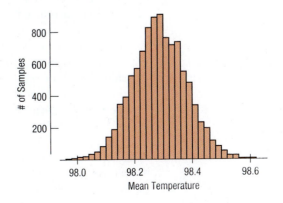

From the 0.5th and 99.5th percentiles, a 99% confidence interval finds

0.5%	99.5%
98.04231	98.53078

very close to our t-based interval.

Because 98.6 is not in the confidence interval, we can reject the null hypothesis that the true mean is 98.6. And because the confidence level is 0.99, we know that the P-value is less than 0.01, but we can't pin it down more precisely than that.

If we want more information about the P-value, we'll need to shift our distribution to center it at the null hypothesis. The distribution we used to create the confidence interval was centered at the mean of our sample, 98.285°F. To adjust the distribution to our null hypothesis mean of 98.6°F, we can add 0.315 to each of the bootstrap means. That will shift the distribution without changing its standard deviation. The shifted bootstrap distribution looks like this:

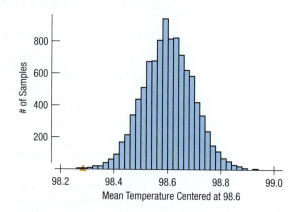

The P-value for this hypothesis test is then chance of seeing a sample mean that is sufficiently extreme for this shifted distribution. So we ask, "How many times was there a value as far from 98.6 as the sample mean we did observe?" That value is shown in red on the histogram. In this example, the answer is 9 times out of 10,000, which gives a bootstrap P-value of 0.0009. The t-based P-value was 0.0016, so the two methods draw essentially the same conclusion:[8] We reject the hypothesis that the true mean temperature of healthy adults is 98.6°F. In fact, modern research has concluded that the mean human body temperature is about 98.2°F for temperatures taken orally (as Wunderlich did).

Here are the steps to follow to use the bootstrap to test a hypothesis $H_0: \mu = \mu_0$.

1. Find the sample mean, $\bar{y}$, from your data. Add $(\mu_0 - \bar{y})$ to each observation in your sample to shift the center of this sample to μ_0. Bootstrap this shifted sample k times, recording the mean each time. (Equivalently, bootstrap the original sample k times, record the means, and then add $(\mu_0 - \bar{y})$ to each mean.) *Note:* You get to choose k. Typical values for k are at least 1000 or even 10,000.
2. You have produced a simulated sampling distribution centered at the null hypothesis value of μ_0. Find the proportion of times the bootstrapped sample means fall as far or farther from the mean of this sampling distribution as the original observed sample mean, $\bar{y}$. That proportion is a P-value. *Note:* It is considered bad form to report a P-value of zero even if no resampled means are that extreme. After all, there is always the possibility that with more trials you'd see a sample mean that extraordinary.

---

[8]With only 52 observations, we couldn't draw meaningful differences between these P-values even if we wanted to.

GUIDED EXAMPLE   Tests and Intervals

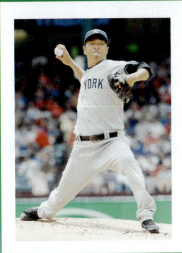

Anyone who plays or watches sports has heard of the "home field advantage." Tournaments in many sports are designed to try to neutralize the advantage of the home team or player. Most people believe that teams tend to win more often when they play at home. But do they?

If there were no home field advantage, the home teams would win about half of all games played. To test this, we'll use the games in the Major League Baseball 2017 season. That year, there were 2430 regular-season games. It turns out that the home team won 1311 of the 2430 games, or 53.95% of the time.

(Baseball) Manager Could this deviation from 50% be explained just from natural sampling variability, or is it evidence to suggest that there really is a home field advantage, at least in professional baseball?

PLAN	
Setup State what we want to know.	I want to know whether in professional baseball, playing at home makes a difference in the likelihood of winning. The data are all 2430 games from the 2017 Major League Baseball season. The variable is whether or not the home team won. The parameter of interest is the proportion of home team wins. If there's no advantage, I'd expect that proportion to be 0.50.
Define the variables and discuss the W's.	
Hypotheses The null hypothesis makes the claim of no difference from the baseline. Here, that means no home field advantage.	$$H_0: p = 0.50$$ $$H_A: p \neq 0.50$$
Model Think about the assumptions and check the appropriate conditions. This is not a random sample. If we wanted to talk only about this season there would be no inference. So, we view the 2430 games here not as a random sample, but as a representative collection of games. Our inference is about all years of Major League Baseball.	✔ **Independence Assumption**: Generally, the outcome of one game has no effect on the outcome of another game. But this may not be strictly true. For example, if a key player is injured, the probability that the team will win in the next couple of games may decrease slightly, but independence is still roughly true. The data come from one entire season, but I expect other seasons to be similar. I'm not just interested in 2017, and those games, while not randomly selected, should be a reasonable representative sample of all Major League Baseball games in the recent past and near future. ✔ **10% Condition**: We are interested in home field advantage for Major League Baseball for all seasons. While not a random sample, these 2430 games are fewer than 10% of all games played over the years. ✔ **Success/Failure Condition**: Both $np_0 = 2430(0.50) = 1215$ and $nq_0 = 2430(0.50) = 1215$ are at least 10.
Specify the sampling distribution model. State what test you plan to use.	Because the conditions are satisfied, I'll use a Normal model for the sampling distribution of the proportion and do a **one-proportion z-test**.

(continued)

DO	**Mechanics** The null model gives us the mean; because we are working with proportions, the mean gives us the standard deviation.	The null model is a Normal distribution with a mean of 0.50 and a standard deviation of

$$SD(\hat{p}) = \sqrt{\frac{p_0 q_0}{n}} = \sqrt{\frac{(0.5)(1 - 0.5)}{2430}}$$

$$= 0.010143.$$

Next, we find the z-score for the observed proportion, to find out how many standard deviations it is from the hypothesized proportion.

The observed proportion, $\hat{p}$, is 0.5395.

So the z-value is

$$z = \frac{0.5395 - 0.5}{0.010143} = 3.89.$$

From the z-score, we can find the P-value, which tells us the probability of observing a value that extreme (or more).

The sample proportion lies 3.89 standard deviations above the mean.

The corresponding P-value is less than 0.0001.

The probability of observing a value 3.89 or more standard deviations away from the mean of a Normal model can be found to be less than 0.0001.

REPORT	**Communicate and Present Your Conclusions** State your conclusion about the parameter—in context, of course!

MEMO

Re: Home field advantage

The P-value of 0.0001 says that if the true proportion of home team wins were 0.50, then an observed value of 0.5395 (or **more extreme**) would occur less than one time in 1000. With a P-value so small, I reject H_0. I have reasonable evidence that the true proportion of home team wins is **not** 50%.

Question: OK, but how big a difference are we talking about? Just knowing that there is an effect is only part of the answer. Let's find a confidence interval for the home field advantage.

PLAN	**Model** Think about the assumptions and check the conditions.

✔ **Success/Failure Condition:** There were 1311 home team wins and 1119 losses, both at least 10.

The conditions are identical to those for the hypothesis test, with one difference: Now we are not given a hypothesized proportion, p_0, so we must instead work with the observed results.

Specify the sampling distribution model.

Tell what method you plan to use.

The conditions are satisfied, so I can model the sampling distribution of the proportion with a Normal model and find a **one-proportion z-interval**.

DO	**Mechanics** We can't find the sampling model standard deviation from the null model proportion. (In fact, we've just rejected it.) Instead, we find the standard error of $\hat{p}$ from the *observed* proportions. Other than that substitution, the calculation looks the same as for the hypothesis test.

$$SE(\hat{p}) = \sqrt{\frac{\hat{p}\hat{q}}{n}} = \sqrt{\frac{(0.5395)(1 - 0.5395)}{2430}}$$

$$= 0.01011$$

The sampling model is Normal, so for a 95% confidence interval, the critical value $z^* = 1.96$.

With this large a sample size, the difference is negligible, but in smaller samples, it could make a bigger difference.

The margin of error is

$$ME = z^* \times SE(\hat{p}) = 1.96 \times 0.01011 = 0.0198.$$

So the 95% confidence interval is

$$0.5395 \pm 0.0198 \text{ or } (0.5197, 0.5593).$$

REPORT   **Conclusion** Confidence intervals help us think about the size of the effect. Here we can see that the home field advantage may affect enough games to make a real difference.

> **MEMO**
> **Re: Home field advantage**
> I am 95% confident that, in professional baseball, home teams win between 51.97% and 55.93% of the games.
>
> In a season of 162 games, the low end of this interval, 51.97% of the 81 home games, would mean about one and a half extra home victories, on average. The upper end, 55.93%, would mean more than 4 extra wins.

12.6 P-Values and Decisions: What to Tell About a Hypothesis Test

REPORT MORE

Hypothesis tests are particularly useful when we must make a decision. Is the defendant guilty or not? Should we choose print advertising or television? The absolute nature of the hypothesis test decision, however, makes some people (including the authors) uneasy. Whenever possible, it's a good idea to report a confidence interval for the parameter of interest as well.

How small should the P-value be to reject the null hypothesis? A jury needs enough evidence to show the defendant guilty "beyond a reasonable doubt." How does that translate to P-values? The answer is that there is no good, universal answer. How small the P-value has to be to reject the null hypothesis is highly context-dependent. When we're screening for a disease and want to be sure we treat all those who are sick, we may be willing to reject the null hypothesis of no disease with a P-value as large as 0.10. That would mean that 10% of the healthy people would be treated as sick and subjected to further testing. We might rather treat (or recommend further testing for) the occasional healthy person than fail to treat someone who was really sick. But a long-standing hypothesis, believed by many to be true, needs stronger evidence (and a correspondingly small P-value) to reject it.

See if you require the same P-value to reject each of the following null hypotheses:

Don't We Want to Reject the Null?

Often the folks who collect the data or perform the experiment hope to reject the null. (They hope the new drug is better than the placebo, or the new ad campaign is better than the old one.) But when we practice statistics, we can't allow that hope to affect our decision. The essential attitude for a hypothesis tester is skepticism. Until we become convinced otherwise, we cling to the null's assertion that there's nothing unusual, no effect, no difference, etc. As in a jury trial, the burden of proof rests with the alternative hypothesis—innocent until proven guilty. When you test a hypothesis, you must act as judge and jury, but you are not the prosecutor.

- A renowned musicologist claims that she can distinguish between the works of Mozart and Haydn simply by hearing a randomly selected 20 seconds of music from any work by either composer. What's the null hypothesis? If she's just guessing, she'll get 50% of the pieces correct, on average. So our null hypothesis is that p equals 50%. If she's for real, she'll get more than 50% correct. Now, we present her with 10 pieces of Mozart or Haydn chosen at random. She gets 9 out of 10 correct. It turns out that the P-value associated with that result is 0.011. (In other words, if you tried to just guess, you'd get at least 9 out of 10 correct only about 1% of the time.) What would *you* conclude? Most people would probably reject the null hypothesis and be convinced that she has some ability to do as she claims. Why? Because the P-value is small and we don't have any particular reason to doubt the alternative.

- On the other hand, imagine a student who bets that he can make a flipped coin land the way he wants just by thinking hard. To test him, we flip a fair coin 10 times. Suppose he gets 9 out of 10 right. This also has a P-value of 0.011. Are you willing now to reject this null hypothesis? Are you convinced that he's not just lucky? What amount of evidence *would* convince you? We require more evidence if rejecting the null hypothesis would contradict long-standing beliefs or other scientific results. Of course, with sufficient evidence we would revise our opinions (and scientific theories). That's how science makes progress.

❝ An extraordinary claim requires extraordinary proof. ❞

—Marcello Truzzi

The above saying—"An extraordinary claim requires extraordinary proof"— is often quoted by scientists without attributing it to Truzzi. But he appears to have published it first (in "On the Extraordinary: An Attempt at Clarification," *Zetetic Scholar*, Vol. 1, No. 1, p. 11, 1978).

Another factor in choosing a P-value is the importance of the issue being tested. Consider the following two tests:

- A researcher claims that the proportion of college students who hold part-time jobs now is higher than the proportion known to hold such jobs a decade ago. You might be willing to believe the claim (and reject the null hypothesis of no change) with a P-value of 0.05.
- An engineer claims that even though there were several problems with the rivets holding the wing on an airplane in their fleet, they've retested the proportion of faulty rivets and now the P-value is small enough to reject the null hypothesis that the proportion is the same. What P-value would be small enough to get you to fly on that plane?

Your conclusion about any null hypothesis should always be accompanied by the P-value of the test and, ideally, a confidence interval. Don't just declare the null hypothesis rejected or not rejected. Report the P-value to show the strength of the evidence against the hypothesis and a confidence interval to show the effect size. This will let each reader decide whether or not to reject the null hypothesis and whether or not to consider the result important.

When you reject a null hypothesis you conclude that the parameter value lies in the alternative. But the alternative is absurdly large—usually every possible value except the null. A confidence interval is based on the observed data and provides a much more useful set of plausible values. In fact, it's likely that you didn't believe the null value anyway. (Is the coin *exactly* fair? Is $P(\text{head}) = 0.5000000\ldots$ and not 0.50000001?) So what are hypothesis tests good for? Well, sometimes we need to make a decision. Setting an arbitrary threshold for the P-value provides a "bright line" decision rule. And the P-value provides useful information about how far the data are from the null value.

P-values have become controversial because some people base decisions solely on their P-values without regard to assumptions, conditions, effect size, or cost. The American Statistical Association recently published a statement about P-values.[9] They recommend six principles underlying the proper interpretation of P-values:

1. P-values can indicate how incompatible the data are with a specified statistical model.
2. P-values do not measure the probability that the studied hypothesis is true, or the probability that the data were produced by random chance alone.
3. Scientific conclusions and business or policy decisions should not be based only on whether a P-value passes a specific threshold.
4. Proper inference requires full reporting and transparency.
5. A P-value, or statistical significance, does not measure the size of an effect or the importance of a result.
6. By itself, a P-value does not provide a good measure of evidence regarding a model or hypothesis.

JUST CHECKING

8 A bank is testing a new method for getting delinquent customers to pay their past-due credit card bills. The standard way was to send a letter (costing about $0.40) asking the customer to pay. That worked 30% of the time. They want to test a new method that involves sending a DVD to customers encouraging them to contact the bank and set up a payment plan. Developing and sending the video costs about $10.00 per customer. What is the parameter of interest? What are the null and alternative hypotheses?

9 The bank sets up an experiment to test the effectiveness of the DVD. They mail it out to several randomly selected delinquent customers and keep track of how many actually do contact the bank to arrange payments. The bank's statistician calculates a P-value of 0.003. What does this P-value suggest about the DVD?

10 The statistician tells the bank's management that the results are clear and that they should switch to the DVD method. Do you agree? What else might you want to know?

---

[9] You have seen these issues discussed already in the chapter. For more details, see the paper at www.amstat.org/asa/files/pdfs/P-ValueStatement.pdf.

⊘ WHAT CAN GO WRONG?

Hypothesis tests are so widely used—and so widely misused—that we've devoted all of Chapter 13 to discussing the pitfalls involved, but there are a few issues that we can talk about already.

- **Don't base your null hypothesis on what you see in the data.** You are not allowed to look at the data first and then adjust your null hypothesis so that it will be rejected. When your sample value turns out to be $\hat{p} = 51.8\%$, with a standard deviation of 1%, don't form a null hypothesis like $H_0: p = 49.8\%$, knowing that you can reject it. You should always *Think* about the situation you are investigating and make your null hypothesis describe the "nothing interesting" or "nothing has changed" scenario. No peeking at the data!

- **Don't make your null hypothesis what you want to show to be true.** Remember, the null hypothesis is the status quo, the nothing-is-strange-here position a skeptic would take. You wonder whether the data cast doubt on that. You can reject the null hypothesis, but you can never "accept" or "prove" the null.

- **Don't forget to check the conditions.** The reasoning of inference depends on randomization. No amount of care in calculating a test result can recover from biased sampling. The probabilities we compute depend on the Independence Assumption. And the sample must be large enough to justify the use of the null model.

- **Don't accept the null hypothesis.** You may not have found enough evidence to reject it, but you surely have *not* proven it's true!

- **If you fail to reject the null hypothesis, don't think that a bigger sample would be more likely to lead to rejection.** If the results you looked at were "almost" significant, it's enticing to think that because you would have rejected the null had these same observations come from a larger sample, then a larger sample would surely lead to rejection. Don't be misled. Remember, each sample is different, and a larger sample won't necessarily duplicate your current observations. Indeed, the Central Limit Theorem tells us that statistics will vary *less* in larger samples. We should therefore expect such results to be less extreme. Maybe they'd be statistically significant but maybe (perhaps even probably) not. Even if you fail to reject the null hypothesis, it's a good idea to examine a confidence interval. If none of the plausible parameter values in the interval would matter to you (for example, because none would be *practically* significant), then even a larger study with a correspondingly smaller standard error is unlikely to be worthwhile.

ETHICS IN ACTION

I t has been three years since Mohammed Al-Tamimi opened his computer repair business, Mo's Mending Station. Unlike the well-known Nerd Squad of the big electronics retailer, Mo's Mending Station fixes only computers and does not deal with any other electronics such as TVs, phones, cameras, or appliances. Nor does Mo's provide any in-home services, such as networking or computer setup. Mo's main objective is clear: to provide standard repair services for computers and laptops, virus and spyware removal, and data recovery, each at a fixed low price. He charges the competitive rate of $45 per hour for more complicated computer issues.

Mo's slogan is "*Get twice the nerd at half the cost!*" This strategy has worked well, allowing Mohammed to grow his business to include six repair technicians and one office manager. However, recent monthly receipts indicate that the demand for Mo's services may be slowing down. Worried that the Mending Station might be losing its competitive price advantage, Mohammed gathers his staff together for a brainstorming session. Ed Ramsey, who has been with Mo's since it opened, mentions the possibility that the Mending Station's low prices may give some potential customers the impression that it offers poor quality service. He suggests hiring a local advertising firm to help brand Mo's Mending Station as affordable AND high quality by emphasizing its team of professional, experienced, and friendly repair technicians. In other words, put the focus on "*twice the nerd*" rather than "*half the cost.*"

Mohammed thinks that this is a great idea and wonders if they can also prepare some statistics to strengthen the message. Because customer receipts include both when a computer is brought to Mo's (date and time) as well as when the repair is finished, he asks his office manager to select a sample so they can estimate the average service time. Based on 36 receipts, she finds a mean service time of 2 hours and 10 minutes with a standard deviation of 30 minutes. Further statistical analysis yielded a 95% confidence interval for the mean service time of 1.99 to 2.33 hours. Mohammed plans to advertise that 95% of his customers can expect to wait between 1.99 and 2.33 hours to get their computers back from repair! He is anxious to include this claim in all of the Mending Station's future marketing communication materials.

- **Identify the ethical dilemma in this scenario.**
- **Has Mohammed interpreted the confidence interval correctly?**
- **What are the undesirable consequences?**
- **Propose an ethical solution that considers the welfare of all stakeholders.**

CHAPTER

12   FROM LEARNING TO EARNING

LEARNING OBJECTIVES

Know how to formulate a null and an alternative hypothesis for a question of interest.
- The null hypothesis specifies a parameter and a (null) value for that parameter.
- The alternative hypothesis specifies a range of plausible values should we reject the null.

Be able to perform a hypothesis test for a proportion.
- The null hypothesis has the form $H_0: p = p_0$.
- We find the standard deviation of the sampling distribution of the sample proportion by assuming that the null hypothesis is true:

$$SD(\hat{p}) = \sqrt{\frac{p_0 q_0}{n}}.$$

- We refer the statistic $z = \dfrac{\hat{p} - p_0}{SD(\hat{p})}$ to the standard Normal model.

Be able to perform a hypothesis test for a mean.

- To apply the Central Limit Theorem for the mean in practical applications, we must estimate the standard deviation. This *standard error* is

$$SE(\bar{y}) = \frac{s}{\sqrt{n}}$$

- When we use the SE, the sampling distribution that allows for the additional uncertainty is Student's t-model on $n - 1$ degrees of freedom.

- We refer the test statistic $t = \dfrac{\bar{y} - \mu_0}{SE(y)}$ to the Student's t distribution with $n - 1$ degrees of freedom.

- Find critical values by technology or from tables.

- Check the assumptions and conditions before using any sampling distribution for inference.

Write clear summaries to interpret a confidence interval or state a hypothesis test's conclusion.

Understand P-values.

- A P-value is the estimated probability of observing a statistic value at least as far from the (null) hypothesized value as the one we have actually observed.

- A small P-value indicates that the statistic we have observed would be unlikely were the null hypothesis true. That leads us to doubt the null.

- A large P-value just tells us that we have insufficient evidence to doubt the null hypothesis. In particular, it does not prove the null to be true.

Know the reasoning of hypothesis testing.

- State the **hypotheses**.
- Determine (and check assumptions for) the sampling distribution **model**.
- Calculate the test statistic—the **mechanics**.
- State your **conclusions and decisions**.

Be able to decide on a two-sided or one-sided alternative hypothesis, and justify your decision.

Know that confidence intervals and hypothesis tests go hand in hand in helping us think about models.

- A hypothesis test makes a yes/no decision about the plausibility of the value of a parameter value.
- A confidence interval shows us the range of plausible values for the parameter.

TERMS

Alternative hypothesis The alternative hypothesis proposes what we should conclude if we reject the null hypothesis.

Effect size The difference between the null hypothesis value and the true value of a model parameter.

Hypothesis A model or proposition that we adopt in order to test.

Null hypothesis The claim being assessed in a hypothesis test that states "no change from the traditional value," "no effect," "no difference," or "no relationship." For a claim to be a testable null hypothesis, it must specify a value for some population parameter that can form the basis for assuming a sampling distribution for a test statistic.

One-proportion z-test A test of the null hypothesis that the proportion of a single sample equals a specified value ($H_0: p = p_0$) by referring the statistic $z = \dfrac{\hat{p} - p_0}{SD(\hat{p})}$ to a Standard Normal model.

One-sample t-test for the mean The one-sample t-test for the mean tests the hypothesis $H_0: \mu = \mu_0$ using the statistic

$$t_{n-1} = \frac{\bar{y} - \mu_0}{SE(\bar{y})}.$$

The standard error of $\bar{y}$ is

$$SE(\bar{y}) = \frac{s}{\sqrt{n}}.$$

One-sided alternative (One-tailed alternative)	An alternative hypothesis is one-sided (e.g., $H_A: p > p_0$ or $H_A: p < p_0$) when we are interested in deviations in *only one* direction away from the hypothesized parameter value.
P-value	The probability of observing a value for a test statistic at least as far from the hypothesized value as the statistic value actually observed if the null hypothesis is true. A small P-value indicates either that the observation is improbable or that the probability calculation was based on incorrect assumptions. The assumed truth of the null hypothesis is the assumption under suspicion.
Two-sided alternative (Two-tailed alternative)	An alternative hypothesis is two-sided ($H_A: p \neq p_0$) when we are interested in deviations in *either* direction away from the hypothesized parameter value.

TECH SUPPORT   Hypothesis Tests

Hypothesis tests for proportions are so easy and natural that many statistics packages don't offer special commands for them. Most statistics programs want to know the "success" and "failure" status for each case. Usually these are given as 1 or 0, but they might be category names like "yes" and "no." Often you just know the proportion of successes, $\hat{p}$, and the total count, n. Computer packages don't usually deal naturally with summary data like these, but the statistics routines found on many graphing calculators do. These calculators allow you to test hypotheses from summaries of the data—usually, all you need to enter are the number of successes and the sample size.

In some programs you can reconstruct the original values. But even when you have reconstructed (or can reconstruct) the raw data values, often you won't get exactly the same test statistic from a computer package as you would find working by hand. The reason is that when the packages treat the proportion as a mean, they make some approximations. The result is very close, but not exactly the same.

For quantitative data, statistics packages offer convenient ways to make histograms of the data. Even better for assessing near-Normality is a Normal probability plot. When you work on a computer, there is simply no excuse for skipping the step of plotting the data to check that it is nearly Normal. *Beware:* Statistics packages don't agree on whether to place the Normal scores on the x-axis (as we have done) or the y-axis. Read the axis labels.

Any standard statistics package can compute a hypothesis test for a mean. Here's what the package output might look like in general (although no package we know gives the results in exactly this form):[11]

Null hypothesis   Alternative hypothesis

```
Test Ho: μ(sleep) = 7 vs Ha:  μ(sleep) < 7
Sample Mean = 6.6400
t = -1.6737 w/24 df
P-value = 0.05359
```

The t-statistic (and its degrees of freedom)

The P-value is usually given last

The package computes the sample mean and sample standard deviation of the variable and finds the P-value from the *t*-distribution based on the appropriate number of degrees of freedom. All modern statistics packages report P-values. The package may also provide additional information such as the sample mean, sample standard deviation, *t*-statistic value, and degrees of freedom. These are useful for interpreting the resulting P-value and telling the difference between a meaningful result and one that is merely statistically significant. Statistics packages that report the estimated standard deviation of the sampling distribution usually label it "standard error" or "*SE*."

Inference results are also sometimes reported in a table. You may have to read carefully to find the values you need. Often, test results and the corresponding confidence interval bounds are given together. And often you must read carefully to find the alternative hypotheses. Here's an example of that kind of output:

---

[11]Many statistics packages keep as many as 16 digits for all intermediate calculations. However, for reporting, the rule-of-thumb that says to report one more decimal place for a statistic than are in the original data is a good one.

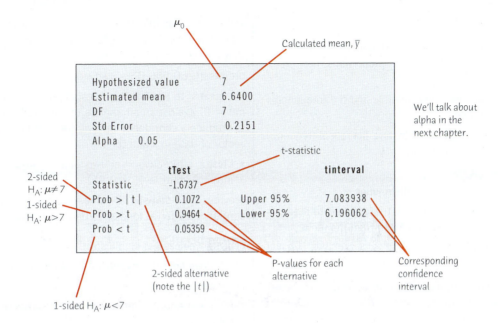

μ_0

Calculated mean, $\bar{y}$

Hypothesized value	7
Estimated mean	6.6400
DF	7
Std Error	0.2151
Alpha	0.05

We'll talk about alpha in the next chapter.

t-statistic

	tTest		**tinterval**
2-sided $H_A: \mu \neq 7$	Statistic	-1.6737	
1-sided $H_A: \mu > 7$	Prob > |t|	0.1072	Upper 95% 7.083938
	Prob > t	0.9464	Lower 95% 6.196062
	Prob < t	0.05359	

2-sided alternative (note the \|t\|)

P-values for each alternative

Corresponding confidence interval

1-sided $H_A: \mu < 7$

EXCEL

Inference methods for proportions are not part of the standard Excel tool set.

To find a one-sample *t*-interval and one-sample *t*-test for the mean using Excel, follow these examples:

	A	B	C	D	E	F
1	t-Estimate of a Mean					
2						
3	Sample Mean	15.02	Confidence Interval Estimate			Syntax for Column E
4	Sample St. Dev.	8.31	15.02	±	1.81	=ABS(T.INV((1-B6)/2,(B5-1))*(B4/B5^0.5))
5	Sample Size	83	Lower Confidence Limit		13.21	=B3-E4
6	Confidence Level	0.95	Upper Confidence Limit		16.83	=B3+E4

	A	B	C	D	E
1	t-Test of a Mean				
2					Syntax for Column D
3	Sample Mean	460.38	t-Stat	1.89	=(B3-B6)/(B4/B5^0.5)
4	Sample St. Dev.	38.83	P(T<=t) One-tailed	0.0323	=1-(T.DIST(ABS(D3),B5-1,1))
5	Sample Size	50	t Critical Lower One-tail	-1.6766	=T.INV(B7,B5-1)
6	Hypothesized Mean	450	t Critical Upper One-tail	1.6766	=ABS(T.INV(B7,B5-1))
7	Alpha	0.05	P(T<=t) Two-tailed	0.0646	=2*D4
8			t Critical Two-tail ±	2.0096	=ABS(T.INV(B7/2,B5-1))

XLSTAT

To find a one sample *z* interval or a one sample *t* interval:

- Choose **Parametric Tests**, and then **One-sample t-test and z-test**.
- Under the **General** tab, enter your data cell range and choose either **z-test** or **Student's t test**.
- On the **Options** tab, choose the **Alternative hypothesis** of **Mean 1 ≠ Theoretical mean**.
- For calculating just a confidence interval, you can leave the **Theoretical mean** field blank. If you are also conducting a hypothesis test, enter in the theoretical mean here.

- Under **Significance Level**, enter in the desired level of significance. The output will yield the $(1 - \alpha)100\%$ confidence level.

To conduct a one-mean *z* test or a one-mean *t* test:

- Choose **Parametric Tests**, and then **One-sample t-test and z-test**.
- Complete the dialog box as you did for a confidence interval.
- Fill in the field for **Theoretical mean** with the population mean from your null hypothesis.

JMP

For a categorical variable that holds category labels, the Distribution platform includes tests of proportions. For summarized data:

- Put the category names in one variable and the frequencies in an adjacent variable.
- Designate the frequency column to have the role of frequency. Then use the Distribution platform.

For quantitative variables:

- From the Analyze menu, select **Distribution**.
- For a hypothesis test, click the red triangle next to the variable's name and choose **Test Mean** from the menu.
- Then fill in the resulting dialog.

COMMENTS

JMP uses slightly different methods for proportion inferences than those discussed in this text. Your answers are likely to be slightly different.

MINITAB

For proportions:

- Choose **Basic Statistics** from the Stat menu.
- Choose **1Proportion** from the Basic Statistics submenu.
- If you have a large sample, change method to Normal distribution.
- If the data are category names in a variable, assign the variable from the variable list box to the Samples in columns box.
- If you have summarized data, click the **Summarized Data** button and fill in the number of trials and the number of successes.

For means:

- From the Stat menu, choose the **Basic Statistics** submenu.
- From that menu, choose **1-sample t. . . .**
- Then fill in the dialog.
- Click the **Options** button and specify the remaining details.
- Click the **OK** button.

COMMENTS

When working from a variable that names categories, Minitab treats the last category as the "success" category. You can specify how the categories should be ordered.

COMMENTS

The dialog offers a clear choice between confidence interval and test.

R

For proportions, Iin library(stats):

- prop.test(X, n, p = NULL, alternative = c("two.sided," "less," "greater"), conf.level = 0.95, correct=FALSE)

will test the hypothesis that $p = p_0$ against various alternatives. For example with 260 successes out of 500, to test that $p = 0.5$ vs. $p \neq 0.5$, use:

prop.test(260,500,0.5, "two.sided," correct=FALSE)

For means, to test the hypothesis that $\mu =$ mu (default is mu = 0) against an alternative (default is two-sided) and to produce a confidence interval (default is 95%), create a vector of data in x and then:

- **t.test**(x, alternative = c("two.sided", "less", "greater"), mu = 0, conf.level = 0.95)

provides the t-statistic, P-value, degrees of freedom, and the confidence interval for a specified alternative.

SPSS

SPSS does not offer hypothesis tests for proportions.

For means:

- From the Analyze menu, choose the **Compare Means** submenu.
- From that, choose the **One-Sample t-test** command.

COMMENTS

The commands suggest neither a single mean nor an interval. But the results provide both a test and an interval.

STATCRUNCH

To test a hypothesis for a proportion using summaries:

- Click on **Stat**.
- Choose **Proportion Stats > One Sample > With Summary**.
- Enter the **# of successes** (x) and **# of observations** (n).
- Under **Perform**: indicate **Hypothesis Test** for p, then enter the hypothesized Null proportion, and choose the alternative hypothesis.
- Click on **Compute!**

To test a hypothesis for a proportion using data:

- Click on **Stat**.
- Choose **Proportion Stats > One Sample > With Data**.
- Choose the variable from **Values in**:
- Enter the outcome to be considered a Success.
- Under **Perform**: indicate **Hypothesis Test** for p, then enter the hypothesized Null proportion, and choose the alternative hypothesis.
- Click on **Compute!**

To do inference for a mean using summaries:

- Click on **Stat**.
- Choose **T Stats > One Sample > With Summary**.
- Enter the Sample mean, Sample std dev, and Sample size.

- Under **Perform**: indicate **Hypothesis Test** for μ, then enter the hypothesized Null mean, and choose the alternative hypothesis.

OR

Indicate **Confidence Interval**, and then enter the Level of confidence.

- Click on **Compute**!

To do inference for a mean using data:

- Click on **Stat**.

- Choose **T Stats** > **One Sample** > **With Data**.
- Choose the variable of interest under **Select Column(s)**.
- Under **Perform**: indicate **Hypothesis Test**, then enter the hypothesized Null mean, and choose the alternative hypothesis.

OR

Indicate **Confidence Interval**, and then enter the Level of confidence.

- Click on **Compute**!

BRIEF CASE

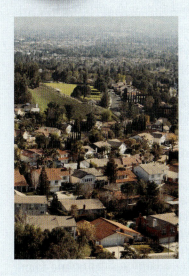

Real Estate

In the last chapter, you looked at the data file **Real estate sample 1200**, which holds the following variables:

- *Sale Price* (in $)
- *Lot size* (size of the lot in acres)
- *Waterfront* (Yes, No)
- *Age* (in years)
- *Central Air* (Yes, No)
- *Fuel Type* (Wood, Oil, Gas, Electric, Propane, Solar, Other)
- *Condition* (1 to 5, 1 = Poor, 5 = Excellent)
- *Living Area* (living area in square feet)
- *Pct College* (% in ZIP code who attend a four-year college)
- *Full Baths* (number of full bathrooms)
- *Half Baths* (number of half bathrooms)
- *Bedrooms* (number of bedrooms)
- *Fireplace* (Yes, No)

Re-examine your findings from the last chapter, but this time, phrase your questions in terms of hypotheses to test and write your conclusions accordingly. Write up a short report to a real estate agent of your major findings.

Donor Profiles

In Chapter 11, you examined a philanthropic organization that collects and buys data on their donor base. The data set **Donor profiles** contained a sample of 916 donors and includes the variables:

- *Age* (in years)
- *Homeowner* (H = Yes, U = Unknown)
- *Gender* (F = Female, M = Male, U = Unknown)
- *Wealth* (Ordered categories of total household wealth from 1 = Lowest to 9 = Highest)
- *Children* (Number of children)
- *Donated Last* (0 = Did not donate to last campaign, 1 = Did donate to last campaign)
- *Amt Donated Last* ($ amount of contribution to last campaign)

Re-examine your findings from the last chapter, but this time, phrase your questions in terms of hypotheses to test and write your conclusions accordingly. Write up a short report to the company on your major findings about potential donors.

SECTION 12.1

1. Better than aspirin? A very large study showed that aspirin reduced the rate of first heart attacks by 44%. A pharmaceutical company thinks they have a drug that will be more effective than aspirin, and plans to do a randomized clinical trial to test the new drug. What is the null hypothesis the company will use?

2. Psychic. A friend of yours claims to be psychic. You are skeptical. To test this you take a stack of 100 playing cards and have your friend try to identify the suit (hearts, diamonds, clubs, or spades), without looking, of course! State the null hypothesis for your experiment.

3. Parameters and hypotheses. For each of the following situations, define the parameter (proportion or mean) and write the null and alternative hypotheses in terms of parameter values. Example: We want to know if the proportion of up days in the stock market is 50%. Answer: Let $p =$ the proportion of up days. $H_0: p = 0.5$ vs. $H_A: p \neq 0.5$.

a) A casino wants to know if their slot machine really delivers the 1 in 100 win rate that it claims.

b) Last year, customers spent an average of $35.32 per visit to the company's website. Based on a random sample of purchases this year, the company wants to know if the mean this year has changed.

c) A pharmaceutical company wonders if their new drug has a cure rate different from the 30% reported by the placebo.

d) A bank wants to know if the percentage of customers using their website has changed from the 40% that used it before their system crashed last week.

4. Hypotheses and parameters. As in Exercise 3, for each of the following situations, define the parameter and write the null and alternative hypotheses in terms of parameter values.

a) Seat-belt compliance in Massachusetts was 65% in 2008. The state wants to know if it has changed.

b) Last year, a survey found that 45% of the employees were willing to pay for on-site day care. The company wants to know if that has changed.

c) Regular card customers have a default rate of 6.7%. A credit card bank wants to know if that rate is different for their Gold card customers.

d) Regular card customers have been with the company for an average of 17.3 months. The credit card bank wants to know if their Gold card customers have been with the company on average the same amount of time.

SECTION 12.2

5. Better than aspirin again? Referring to the study of Exercise 1:

a) Is the alternative to the null hypothesis more naturally one-sided or two-sided? Explain.

b) The P-value from a clinical trial testing the hypothesis is 0.0028. What do you conclude?

c) What would you have concluded if the P-value had been 0.28?

6. GRE performance. A test preparation company claims that more than 50% of the students who take their GRE prep course improve their scores by at least 10 points.

a) Is the alternative to the null hypothesis more naturally one-sided or two-sided? Explain.

b) A test run with randomly selected participants gives a P-value of 0.981. What do you conclude?

c) What would you have concluded if the P-value had been 0.019?

SECTION 12.3

7. Hispanic origin. According to the 2010 Census, 16% of the people in the United States are of Hispanic or Latino origin. One county supervisor believes her county has a different proportion of Hispanic people than the nation as a whole. She looks at their most recent survey data, which was a random sample of 437 county residents, and found that 44 of those surveyed are of Hispanic origin.

a) State the hypotheses.

b) Name the model and check appropriate conditions for a hypothesis test.

c) Draw and label a sketch, and then calculate the test statistic and P-value.

d) State your conclusion.

8. Empty houses. According to the 2010 Census, 11.4% of all housing units in the United States were vacant. A county supervisor wonders if her county is different from this. She randomly selects 850 housing units in her county and finds that 129 of the housing units are vacant.

a) State the hypotheses.

b) Name the model and check appropriate conditions for a hypothesis test.

c) Draw and label a sketch, and then calculate the test statistic and P-value.

d) State your conclusion.

SECTION 12.4

9. GRE performance again. Instead of advertising the percentage of customers who improve by at least 10 points, a manager suggests testing whether the mean score improves at all. For each customer they record the difference in score before and after taking the course (After − Before).

a) State the null and alternative hypotheses.
b) The P-value from the test is 0.65. Does this provide any evidence that their course works?
c) From part b, what can you tell, if anything, about the mean difference in the sample scores?

10. Marriage. In 1960, census results indicated that the age at which American men first married had a mean of 23.3 years. It is widely suspected that young people today are waiting longer to get married. We want to find out if the mean age of first marriage has increased since then.

a) Write appropriate hypotheses.
b) We plan to test our hypothesis by selecting a random sample of 40 men who married for the first time last year. Do you think the necessary assumptions for inference are satisfied? Explain.
c) Describe the approximate sampling distribution model for the mean age in such samples.
d) The men in our sample married at an average age of 24.2 years, with a standard deviation of 5.3 years. That results in a t-statistic of 1.074. What is the P-value for this?
e) Explain (in context) what this P-value means.
f) What's your conclusion?

11. Pizza. A researcher tests whether the mean cholesterol level among those who eat frozen pizza exceeds the value considered to indicate a health risk. She gets a P-value of 0.07. Explain in this context what the "7%" represents.

12. Golf balls. The United States Golf Association (USGA) sets performance standards for golf balls. For example, the initial velocity of the ball may not exceed 250 feet per second when measured by an apparatus approved by the USGA. Suppose a manufacturer introduces a new kind of ball and provides a sample for testing. Based on the mean speed in the test, the USGA comes up with a P-value of 0.34. Explain in this context what the "34%" represents.

SECTION 12.5

13. Bad medicine. Occasionally, a report comes out that a drug that cures some disease turns out to have a nasty side effect. For example, some antidepressant drugs may cause suicidal thoughts in younger patients. A researcher wants to study such a drug and look for evidence of a side effect.

a) If the test yields a low P-value and the researcher rejects the null hypothesis, but there is actually no ill side effect of the drug, what are the consequences of such an error?

b) If the test yields a high P-value and the researcher fails to reject the null hypothesis, but there *is* a bad side effect of the drug, what are the consequences of such an error?

14. Expensive medicine. Developing a new drug can be an expensive process, resulting in high costs to patients. A pharmaceutical company has developed a new drug to reduce cholesterol, and it will conduct a clinical trial to compare the effectiveness to the most widely used current treatment. The results will be analyzed using a hypothesis test.

a) If the test yields a low P-value and the researcher rejects the null hypothesis that the new drug is not more effective, but it actually is not better, what are the consequences of such an error?
b) If the test yields a high P-value and the researcher fails to reject the null hypothesis, but the new drug *is* more effective, what are the consequences of such an error?

CHAPTER EXERCISES

15. Hypotheses. Write the null and alternative hypotheses you would use to test each of the following situations:

a) A governor is concerned about his "negatives"—the percentage of state residents who express disapproval of his job performance. His political committee pays for a series of TV ads, hoping that they can keep the negatives below 30%. They will use follow-up polling to assess the ads' effectiveness.
b) Is a coin fair?
c) Only about 20% of people who try to quit smoking succeed. Sellers of a motivational tape claim that listening to the recorded messages can help people quit.

16. More hypotheses. Write the null and alternative hypotheses you would use to test each situation.

a) In the 1950s, only about 40% of high school graduates went on to college. Has the percentage changed?
b) Twenty percent of cars of a certain model have needed costly transmission work after being driven between 50,000 and 100,000 miles. The manufacturer hopes that a redesign of a transmission component has solved this problem.
c) We field-test a new-flavor soft drink, planning to market it only if we are sure that over 60% of the people like the flavor.

17. Negatives. After the political ad campaign described in Exercise 15, part a, pollsters check the governor's negatives. They test the hypothesis that the ads produced no change against the alternative that the negatives are now below 30% and find a P-value of 0.22. Which conclusion is appropriate? Explain.

a) There's a 22% chance that the ads worked.
b) There's a 78% chance that the ads worked.
c) There's a 22% chance that their poll is correct.
d) There's a 22% chance that natural sampling variation could produce poll results like these if there's really no change in public opinion.

18. Dice. The seller of a loaded die claims that it will favor the outcome 6. We don't believe that claim, and roll the die 200 times to test an appropriate hypothesis. Our P-value turns out to be 0.03. Which conclusion is appropriate? Explain.

a) There's a 3% chance that the die is fair.
b) There's a 97% chance that the die is fair.
c) There's a 3% chance that a loaded die could randomly produce the results we observed, so it's reasonable to conclude that the die is fair.
d) There's a 3% chance that a fair die could randomly produce the results we observed, so it's reasonable to conclude that the die is loaded.

19. Relief. A company's old antacid formula provided relief for 70% of the people who used it. The company tests a new formula to see if it is better and gets a P-value of 0.27. Is it reasonable to conclude that the new formula and the old one are equally effective? Explain.

20. Cars. A survey investigating whether the proportion of today's high school seniors who own their own cars is higher than it was a decade ago finds a P-value of 0.017. Is it reasonable to conclude that more high schoolers have cars? Explain.

21. He cheats? A friend of yours claims that when he tosses a coin he can control the outcome. You are skeptical and want him to prove it. He tosses the coin, and you call heads; it's tails. You try again and lose again.

a) Do two losses in a row convince you that he really can control the toss? Explain.
b) You try a third time, and again you lose. What's the probability of losing three tosses in a row if the process is fair?
c) Would three losses in a row convince you that your friend controls the outcome? Explain.
d) How many times in a row would you have to lose to be pretty sure that this friend really can control the toss? Justify your answer by calculating a probability and explaining what it means.

22. Candy. Someone hands you a box of a dozen chocolate-covered candies, telling you that half are vanilla creams and the other half peanut butter. You pick candies at random and discover the first three you eat are all vanilla.

a) If there really were 6 vanilla and 6 peanut butter candies in the box, what is the probability that you would have picked three vanillas in a row?
b) Do you think there really might have been 6 of each? Explain.
c) Would you continue to believe that half are vanilla if the fourth one you try is also vanilla? Explain.

23. Smartphones. Many people have trouble setting up all the features of their smartphones, so a company has developed what it hopes will be easier instructions. The goal is

to have at least 96% of customers succeed. The company tests the new system on 200 people, of whom 188 were successful. Is this strong evidence that the new system fails to meet the company's goal? A Student's test of this hypothesis is shown. How many mistakes can you find?

$H_0: \hat{p} = 0.96$

$H_A: \hat{p} \neq 0.96$

SRS, $0.96(200) > 10$

$\frac{188}{200} = 0.94; \quad SD(\hat{p}) = \sqrt{\frac{(0.94)(0.06)}{200}} = 0.017$

$z = \frac{0.96 - 0.94}{0.017} = 1.18$

$P = P(z > 1.18) = 0.12$

There is strong evidence the new instructions don't work.

24. Obesity 2016. In 2016, the Centers for Disease Control and Prevention reported that 36.5% of adults in the United States are obese. A county health service planning a new awareness campaign polls a random sample of 750 adults living there. In this sample, 228 people were found to be obese based on their answers to a health questionnaire.

Do these responses provide strong evidence that the 36.5% figure is not accurate for this region? Correct the mistakes you find in a student's attempt to test an appropriate hypothesis.

$H_0: \hat{p} = 0.365$

$H_A: \hat{p} < 0.365$

SRS, $750 \geq 10$

$\frac{228}{750} = 0.304; \quad SD(\hat{p}) = \sqrt{\frac{(0.304)(0.696)}{750}} = 0.017$

$z = \frac{0.304 - 0.365}{0.017} = -3.588$

$P = P(z > -3.588) = 0.9998$

There is more than a 99.98% chance that the stated percentage is correct for this region.

25. Dowsing. In a rural area, only about 30% of the wells that are drilled find adequate water at a depth of 100 feet or less. A local man claims to be able to find water by "dowsing"—using a forked stick to indicate where the well should be drilled. You check with 80 of his customers and find that 27 have wells less than 100 feet deep. What do you conclude about his claim?

a) Write appropriate hypotheses.
b) Check the necessary assumptions and conditions.
c) Perform the mechanics of the test. What is the P-value?
d) Explain carefully what the P-value means in context.
e) What's your conclusion?

26. Abnormalities. In the 1980s, it was generally believed that congenital abnormalities affected about 5% of the nation's children. Some people believe that the increase in the number of chemicals in the environment has led to an increase in the incidence of abnormalities. A recent study examined 384 children and found that 46 of them showed signs of an abnormality. Is this strong evidence that the risk has increased?

a) Write appropriate hypotheses.
b) Check the necessary assumptions and conditions.
c) Perform the mechanics of the test. What is the P-value?
d) Explain carefully what the P-value means in context.
e) What's your conclusion?
f) Do environmental chemicals cause congenital abnormalities?

27. Absentees. The National Center for Education Statistics monitors many aspects of elementary and secondary education nationwide. Their 1996 numbers are often used as a baseline to assess changes. In 1996, 34% of students had not been absent from school even once during the previous month. In a 2000 survey, responses from 8302 students showed that this figure had slipped to 33%. Officials would, of course, be concerned if student attendance were declining. Do these figures give evidence of a change in student attendance?

a) Write appropriate hypotheses.
b) Check the assumptions and conditions.
c) Perform the test and find the P-value.
d) State your conclusion.
e) Do you think this difference is meaningful? Explain.

28. Educated mothers. The National Center for Education Statistics monitors many aspects of elementary and secondary education nationwide. Their 1996 numbers are often used as a baseline to assess changes. In 1996, 31% of students reported that their mothers had graduated from college. In 2000, responses from 8368 students found that this figure had grown to 32%. Is this evidence of a change in education level among mothers?

a) Write appropriate hypotheses.
b) Check the assumptions and conditions.
c) Perform the test and find the P-value.
d) State your conclusion.
e) Do you think this difference is meaningful? Explain.

29. Contributions, please. The Paralyzed Veterans of America recently sent letters to a random sample of 100,000 potential donors and received 4781 donations. They've had a contribution rate of 5% in past campaigns, but a staff member worries that the rate is lower now that they've redesigned their letter. Is there evidence that the 4.78% they received is evidence of a real drop in the contribution rate?

a) What are the hypotheses?
b) Are the assumptions and conditions for inference met?
c) Do you think the rate would drop? Explain.

30. Take the offer. First USA tested the effectiveness of a double miles campaign by recently sending out offers to a random sample of 50,000 cardholders. Of those, 1184 registered for the promotion. Even though this is nearly a 2.4% rate, a staff member suspects that the success rate for the full campaign will be no different than the standard 2% rate that they are used to seeing in similar campaigns. What do you predict?

a) What are the hypotheses?
b) Are the assumptions and conditions for inference met?
c) Do you think the rate would change if they use this fund-raising campaign? Explain.

31. Pollution. A company with a fleet of 150 cars found that the emissions systems of 7 out of the 22 they tested failed to meet pollution control guidelines. Is this strong evidence that more than 20% of the fleet might be out of compliance? Test an appropriate hypothesis and state your conclusion. Be sure the appropriate assumptions and conditions are satisfied before you proceed.

32. Scratch and dent. An appliance manufacturer stockpiles washers and dryers in a large warehouse for shipment to retail stores. Sometimes in handling them the appliances get damaged. Even though the damage may be minor, the company must sell those machines at drastically reduced prices. The company goal is to keep the level of damaged machines below 2%. One day an inspector randomly checks 60 washers and finds that 5 of them have scratches or dents. Is this strong evidence that the warehouse is failing to meet the company goal? Test an appropriate hypothesis and state your conclusion. Be sure the appropriate assumptions and conditions are satisfied before you proceed.

33. Twins. A national vital statistics report indicated that about 3% of all births produced twins. Is the rate of twin births the same among very young mothers? Data from a large city hospital found that only 7 sets of twins were born to 469 teenage girls. Test an appropriate hypothesis and state your conclusion. Be sure the appropriate assumptions and conditions are satisfied before you proceed.

34. Football 2016. During the first 15 weeks of the 2016 season, the home team won 137 of the 238 regular-season National Football League games. Is this strong evidence of a home field advantage in professional football? Test an appropriate hypothesis and state your conclusion. Be sure the appropriate assumptions and conditions are satisfied before you proceed.

35. WebZine. A magazine is considering the launch of an online edition. The magazine plans to go ahead only if it's convinced that more than 25% of current readers would subscribe. The magazine contacted a simple random sample of 500 current subscribers, and 137 of those surveyed expressed interest. What should the company do? Test an appropriate hypothesis and state your conclusion. Be sure the appropriate assumptions and conditions are satisfied before you proceed.

36. Seeds. A garden center wants to store leftover packets of vegetable seeds for sale the following spring, but the center is concerned that the seeds may not germinate at the same rate a year later. The manager finds a packet of last year's green bean seeds and plants them as a test. Although the packet claims a germination rate of 92%, only 171 of 200 test seeds sprout. Is this evidence that the seeds have lost viability during a year in storage? Test an appropriate hypothesis and state your conclusion. Be sure the appropriate assumptions and conditions are satisfied before you proceed.

37. Women executives. A company is criticized because only 13 of 43 people in executive-level positions are women. The company explains that although this proportion is lower than it might wish, it's not a surprising value given that only 40% of all its employees are women. What do you think? Test an appropriate hypothesis and state your conclusion. Be sure the appropriate assumptions and conditions are satisfied before you proceed.

38. Jury. Census data for a certain county show that 19% of the adult residents are Hispanic. Suppose 72 people are called for jury duty and only 9 of them are Hispanic. Does this apparent underrepresentation of Hispanics call into question the fairness of the jury selection system? Explain.

39. Dropouts 2015. Some people are concerned that new tougher standards and high-stakes tests adopted in many states have driven up the high school dropout rate. The National Center for Education Statistics (nces.ed.gov/fastfacts/) reported that the high school dropout rate for the year 2015 was 5.9%. One school district whose dropout rate has always been very close to the national average reports that 107 of their 1782 high school students dropped out last year. Is this evidence that their dropout rate may be increasing? Explain.

40. Acid rain. A study of the effects of acid rain on trees in the Hopkins Forest shows that 25 of 100 trees sampled exhibited some sort of damage from acid rain. This rate seemed to be higher than the 15% quoted in a recent *Environmetrics* article on the average proportion of damaged trees in the Northeast. Does the sample suggest that trees in the Hopkins Forest are more susceptible than trees from the rest of the region? Comment, and write up your own conclusions based on an appropriate confidence interval as well as a hypothesis test. Include any assumptions you made about the data.

41. Lost luggage. An airline's public relations department says that the airline rarely loses passengers' luggage. It further claims that on those occasions when luggage is lost, 90% is recovered and delivered to its owner within 24 hours. A consumer group that surveyed a large number of air travelers found that only 103 of 122 people who

lost luggage on that airline were reunited with the missing items by the next day. Does this cast doubt on the airline's claim? Explain.

42. TV ads. A startup company is about to market a new computer printer. It decides to gamble by running commercials during the Super Bowl. The company hopes that name recognition will be worth the high cost of the ads. The goal of the company is that over 40% of the public recognize its brand name and associate it with computer equipment. The day after the game, a pollster contacts 420 randomly chosen adults and finds that 181 of them know that this company manufactures printers. Would you recommend that the company continue to advertise during Super Bowls? Explain.

43. John Wayne. Like a lot of other Americans, John Wayne died of cancer. But is there more to this story? In 1955, Wayne was in Utah shooting the film *The Conqueror*. Across the state line, in Nevada, the United States military was testing atomic bombs. Radioactive fallout from those tests drifted across the filming location. A total of 46 of the 220 people working on the film eventually died of cancer. Cancer experts estimate that one would expect only about 30 cancer deaths in a group this size.

a) Is the death rate among the movie crew unusually high?
b) Does this prove that exposure to radiation increases the risk of cancer?

44. AP Stats 2017. The College Board reported that 53.8% of all students who took the 2017 AP Statistics exam earned scores of 3 or higher. One teacher wondered if the performance of her school was better. She believed that year's students to be typical of those who will take AP Stats at that school and was pleased when 30 of her 54 students achieved scores of 3 or better.

a) How many standard errors above the national rate did her students score? Does that seem like a lot? Explain.
b) Can she claim that her school is better? Explain.

45. Tax audits. Certified public accountants are often required to appear with clients if the IRS audits the client's tax return. Some accounting firms give the client an option to pay a fee when the tax return is completed that guarantees tax advice and support from the accountant if the client were audited. The fee is charged up front like an insurance premium and is less than the amount that would be charged if the client were later audited and then decided to ask the firm for assistance during the audit. A large accounting firm is trying to determine what fee to charge for next year's returns. In previous years, the actual mean cost to the firm for attending a client audit session was $650. To determine if this cost has changed, the firm randomly samples 32 client audit fees. The sample mean audit cost was $680 with a standard deviation of $85.

a) Develop a 95% confidence interval estimate for the mean audit cost.

b) Based on your confidence interval, what do you think of the claim that the mean cost has changed?

46. Hot dogs. A nutrition lab tested 40 hot dogs to see if their mean sodium content was less than the 325-mg upper limit set by regulations for "reduced sodium" franks. The mean sodium content for the sample was 322.0 mg with a standard deviation of 18 mg. Assume that the assumptions and conditions for the test are met.

a) Test the hypothesis that the mean sodium content meets the regulation.

b) Will a larger sample size ensure that the regulations are met?

47. Safe pizza? A researcher tests whether the mean cholesterol level among those who eat frozen pizza exceeds the value considered to indicate a health risk. She gets a P-value of 0.04. Explain in this context what the "4%" represents.

T 48. Computer lab fees. A college's technology committee wants to perform a test to see if the mean amount of time students are spending in the computer lab has increased from 55 minutes. Here are the data from a random sample of 12 students.

Time	
52	74
57	53
54	136
76	73
62	8
52	62

a) Plot the data. Are any of the observations outliers? Explain.

b) What do you conclude about the claim? If there are outliers, perform the test with and without the outliers present.

T 49. Package weights. Students investigated the packaging of potato chips. They purchased 6 bags of Lay's Ruffles marked with a net weight of 28.3 grams. They carefully weighed the contents of each bag, recording the following weights (in grams): 29.3, 28.2, 29.1, 28.7, 28.9, 28.5. (Data in **Ruffles**)

a) Do these data satisfy the assumptions for inference? Explain.

b) Find the mean and standard deviation of the weights.

c) Test the hypothesis that the net weight is as claimed.

T 50. Package weights again. Some students checked 6 bags of Doritos marked with a net weight of 28.3 grams. They carefully weighed the contents of each bag, recording the

following weights (in grams): 29.2, 28.5, 28.7, 28.9, 29.1, 29.5. (Data in **Doritos**)

a) Do these data satisfy the assumptions for inference? Explain.

b) Find the mean and standard deviation of the weights.

c) Test the hypothesis that the net weight is as claimed.

T 51. Popcorn. Yvon Hopps ran an experiment to determine optimum power and time settings for microwave popcorn. His goal was to find a combination of power and time that would deliver high-quality popcorn with less than 10% of the kernels left unpopped, on average. Experiments of this kind are commonly conducted by companies to refine their package instructions. After experimenting with several bags, he determined that power 9 at 4 minutes was the best combination. To be sure that the method was successful, he popped 8 more bags of popcorn (selected at random) at this setting. All were of high quality, with the following percentages of uncooked popcorn: 7, 13.2, 10, 6, 7.8, 2.8, 2.2, 5.2. Use a test of hypothesis to decide if Yvon has met his goal.

T 52. Ski wax. Bjork Larsen was trying to decide whether to use a new racing wax for cross-country skis. He decided that the wax would be worth the price if he could average less than 55 seconds on a course he knew well, so he planned to study the wax by racing on the course 8 times. His 8 race times were 56.3, 65.9, 50.5, 52.4, 46.5, 57.8, 52.2, and 43.2 seconds. Should he buy the wax? Explain by performing an appropriate hypothesis test.

T 53. Advertising. In 1998, in a famous advertising campaign, the Nabisco Company announced a "1000 Chips Challenge," claiming that every 18-ounce bag of their Chips Ahoy! cookies contained at least 1000 chocolate chips. Dedicated statistics students at the Air Force Academy purchased some randomly selected bags of cookies and counted the chocolate chips. Some of their data are given below. (Data in **Chips Ahoy!**)

| 1219 | 1214 | 1087 | 1200 | 1419 | 1121 | 1325 | 1345 |
| 1244 | 1258 | 1356 | 1132 | 1191 | 1270 | 1295 | 1135 |

a) Check the assumptions and conditions for inference. Comment on any concerns you have.

b) Test their claim by performing an appropriate hypothesis test.

T 54. Yogurt. As we saw in Chapter 11, Exercise 51, *Consumer Reports* tested 11 brands of vanilla yogurt and found these numbers of calories per serving:

| 130 | 160 | 150 | 120 | 120 | 110 | 170 | 160 | 110 | 130 | 90 |

a) Check the assumptions and conditions.

b) A diet guide claims that you will get an average of 120 calories from a serving of vanilla yogurt. Use an appropriate hypothesis test to comment on their claim.

T 55. Maze. Here are the data from the researcher studying the reaction times of rats. He has a requirement that the maze take about a minute to complete on average.

Time (sec)	
38.4	57.6
46.2	55.5
62.5	49.5
38.0	40.9
62.8	44.3
33.9	93.8
50.4	47.9
35.0	69.2
52.8	46.2
60.1	56.3
55.1	

a) Plot the data. Do you think the conditions are satisfied? Explain.

b) Do you think this maze meets the requirement that the maze takes at most a minute to complete, on average? Perform the test with and without the outlier and write a couple of sentences to the experimenter about whether the maze meets the requirement.

T 56. Facebook friends. According to www.marketingcharts.com/, the average 18–24-year old has 649 Facebook friends. The student who collected the survey data in **Student survey** wanted to test if the mean number is higher at his school. Using his data, test an appropriate hypothesis and write a couple of sentences summarizing what you discover.

T *57. Maze revisited. A student resampled the **Maze** times from Exercise 55 1000 times. The histogram shows the distributions of the means, and a summary of the quantiles is shown below it.

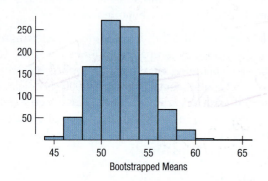

0.05%	0.1%	0.5%	1%	5%	50%	95%	99%	99.5%	99.9%	99.95%
44.657	44.985	45.271	46.119	47.642	52.021	57.220	59.363	59.939	62.088	63.132

a) Find a 99% bootstrap confidence interval for the true mean time it takes to complete the maze.

b) Why is the sampling distribution slightly skewed to the right?

c) How does the skewness affect the confidence interval?

d) What does the confidence interval say about the hypothesis that it takes a minute on average?

T *58. Facebook friends again. A bootstrap test of the hypothesis in Exercise 56 produced the following distribution (shifted to center the histogram at the hypothesized mean of 649): (Data in **Student survey**)

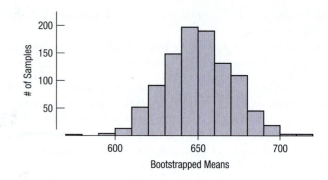

a) What is the P-value of this test?

b) Write a sentence or two with your conclusion.

JUST CHECKING ANSWERS

1 You can't conclude that the null hypothesis is true. You can conclude only that the experiment was unable to reject the null hypothesis. They were unable, on the basis of 12 patients, to show that aspirin was effective.

2 The null hypothesis is $H_0: p = 0.75$.

3 With a P-value of 0.0001, this is very strong evidence against the null hypothesis. We can reject H_0 and conclude that the improved version of the drug gives relief to a higher proportion of patients.

4 You can't conclude that the null hypothesis is true. You can conclude only that the experiment was unable to reject the null hypothesis. They were unable, on the basis of 12 patients, to show that aspirin was effective in lowering the mean PV level.

5 The P-value shows some (weak) evidence that the mean might be higher. However, this is not a random sample of customers. People who spend more at their website might be more inclined to "like" their page. There is no evidence that the presence of the Facebook page is causing the spending to increase, or that even if it is increasing that it's worth the investment.

6 2 minutes. You'll need a larger sample size to see a smaller effect size because the sample mean is likely to be closer to the hypothesized mean if the effect size is smaller.

7 It will narrow it because the standard error will go down proportionately.

8 The parameter of interest is the proportion, p, of all delinquent customers who will pay their bills. $H_0: p = 0.30$ and $H_A: p > 0.30$.

9 The very low P-value leads us to reject the null hypothesis. There is strong evidence that the DVD is more effective in getting people to start paying their debts than just sending a letter had been.

10 All we know is that there is strong evidence to suggest that $p > 0.30$. We don't know how much higher than 30% the new proportion is. We'd like to see a confidence interval to see if the new method is worth the cost.

CHAPTER 13

More About Tests and Intervals

Traveler's Insurance

Fire devastated many U.S. cities in the 18th, 19th, and early 20th centuries. The Great Chicago Fire of 1871 is perhaps the most famous, destroying over 3 square miles of downtown Chicago. But fire also burned major portions of New York (three times), New Orleans (twice), Detroit, Savannah, Pittsburgh, Troy, and, of course, San Francisco in 1906. Business owners needed protection from these disasters.

Benjamin Franklin was an early advocate of providing insurance to protect against the losses from fire, and in 1752 helped form an insurance company. In 1853, the St. Paul Fire and Marine Insurance Company was founded. Two years later it paid its first claim after a fire that started in a bakery destroyed a row of offices. Unlike several competitors, it paid all its Chicago Fire claims in full, establishing its reputation. After the San Francisco earthquake and fire it issued the following statement: "We will not only pay in full, but will continue business with a substantial surplus, and be prepared in the future, as in the past, to meet every claim presented properly."

Fire was not the only hazard that people needed insurance for. Ten Hartford, Connecticut, businessmen founded the Travelers Insurance Company in 1864, "for the purpose of insuring travelers against loss of life or personal injury while journeying by railway or steamboat." It expanded coverage two years later to provide protection against all kinds of accidents. In 1912 they paid more than $1 million to beneficiaries due to the sinking of the *Titanic*.

In 2004, these two giant insurance providers merged to form the St. Paul Travelers Companies, Inc. Three years later the company simplified its name to the Travelers Companies and re-acquired its famous red umbrella symbol.

In 2009 Travelers became one of the 30 Dow Jones Industrials. Today it has assets of over $105 billion and employs 30,000 people in the U.S., Canada, Ireland, and the U.K.[1]

How do insurance companies decide how much to charge for protection and what the chances are that they will be able to cover the costs associated with disasters? Actuaries are the people who measure and manage risk. They put a price on risk by estimating the likelihood of rare events and the costs of insuring against them. That takes financial, statistical, and business skills. It also makes them invaluable to many businesses.

Natural disasters can change the assessment of risk, and hence the price, of an insurance policy. After hurricanes like Harvey in Texas, Hurricane Irma in the Caribbean, and Hurricane Maria in the U.S. Virgin islands and Puerto Rico, flood insurance costs often increase dramatically, sometimes forcing residents to leave their coastal homes. Events of human origin, such as changes in laws affecting safety, can also affect insurance prices, and actuaries must analyze the changes and predict the possible increases in liability to the insurance companies.

In 2000, Florida changed its motorcycle helmet law. No longer were riders 21 and older required to wear helmets. Under the new law, those under 21 still had to wear helmets, but a report by the Preusser Group (www.preussergroup.com) suggested that helmet use may have declined in this group, too. To assess the impact to motorcycle insurers, actuaries must be able to estimate, among other things, the number of riders who will actually take advantage of the new law by not wearing helmets, thereby increasing their risk of both death and injury.

It isn't practical to survey young motorcycle riders. (For example, how can you construct a sampling frame? If you contacted licensed riders, would they admit to riding illegally without a helmet?) So, the researchers adopted a different strategy. Police reports of motorcycle accidents record whether the rider wore a helmet and give the rider's age. Before the change in the helmet law, 60% of youths involved in a motorcycle accident had been wearing their helmets. The Preusser study looked at accident reports during 2001–2003, the three years following the law change, considering these riders to be a representative sample of the larger population. They observed 781 young riders who were involved in accidents. Of these, 396 (or 50.7%) were wearing helmets. Is this evidence of a decline in helmet-wearing, or just the natural fluctuation of such statistics?

WHO	Florida motorcycle riders aged 20 and younger involved in motorcycle accidents
WHAT	% wearing helmets
WHEN	2001–2003
WHERE	Florida
WHY	Assessment of injury rates commissioned by the National Highway Traffic Safety Administration (NHTSA)

The Society of Actuaries and the Casualty Actuarial Society

Actuaries are rather rare themselves; only about 21,000 work in the United States. Perhaps because of this, they are very well paid. In fact according to Beanactuary.org, experienced actuarial "fellows have the potential to earn from $150,000 to $250,000 annually, and many actuaries earn more than that." Yahoo! Finance listed actuary as "the best job of 2013" ahead of biomedical engineer and financial planner. (Lumberjack, oil rig worker, and mail carrier were among the worst 10.)

If you're enjoying this course, you may want to look into a career as an actuary. Contact the Society of Actuaries or the Casualty Actuarial Society, the two societies that represent actuaries and administer the sequence of exams that qualify you to be considered as an actuary. The full process typically takes from 6 to 10 years, but you can begin a career as an actuary by passing the first two exams and preparing for the other exams while you work as an actuarial assistant.

[1] www.travelers.com

13.1 How to Think About P-Values

A P-value is a conditional probability. It tells us the probability of getting results at least as unusual as the observed statistic, *given* that the null hypothesis is true. We can write P-value = $P($observed statistic value [or even more extreme]$|H_0)$.

Writing the P-value this way helps to make clear that the P-value is *not* the probability that the null hypothesis is true. It is a probability about the data. Let's say that again:

The P-value is not the probability that the null hypothesis is true.

The P-value is not even the conditional probability that the null hypothesis is true given the data. We would write that probability as $P(H_0|$ observed statistic value$)$. This is a conditional probability but in reverse. Perhaps equally annoying, the P-value also is not the probability that the alternative hypothesis is true. You can see this by noting that the alternative hypothesis does not appear in the statement of the conditional probability. It would be nice to know both of these probabilities, but it's impossible to calculate either without making additional assumptions. As we saw in Chapter 5, reversing the order in a conditional probability is difficult, and the results can be counterintuitive.

We can find the P-value, $P($observed statistic value$|H_0)$, because H_0 gives the parameter values that we need to calculate the required probability. But there's no direct way to find $P(H_0|$observed statistic value$)$ or $P(H_A|$observed statistic$)$.[2] As tempting as it may be to say that a P-value of 0.03 means there's a 3% chance that the null hypothesis is true, that just isn't right. What we can say is, given that the null hypothesis is true, there's a 3% chance of observing the statistic value that we have actually observed (or one more unlike the null value).

Which Conditional?

Suppose that a political science major is offered the chance to be a White House intern. There would be a very high probability that next summer she'd be in Washington, D.C. That is, $P($Washington$|$Intern$)$ would be high. But if we find a student in Washington, D.C., is it likely that she's a White House intern? Almost surely not; $P($Intern$|$Washington$)$ is low. You can't switch around conditional probabilities. The P-value is $P($data$|H_0)$. We might wish we could report $P(H_0|$data$)$, but these two quantities are NOT the same.

What to Do with a Small P-Value

We know that a small P-value means that the result we just observed is unlikely to occur if the null hypothesis is true. So we have evidence against the null hypothesis. An even smaller P-value implies stronger evidence against the null hypothesis, but it doesn't mean that the null hypothesis is "less true."

> The wise man proportions his belief to the evidence.
>
> —David Hume,
> "Enquiry Concerning Human Understanding," 1748

How Guilty Is the Suspect?

We might like to know $P(H_0|$data$)$, but when you think about it, we can't talk about the probability that the null hypothesis is true. The null is not a random event, so either it is true or it isn't. The data, however, are random in the sense that if we were to repeat a randomized experiment or draw another random sample, we'd get different data and expect to find a different statistic value. So we can talk about the probability of the data given the null hypothesis, and that's the P-value.

But it does make sense that the smaller the P-value, the more confident we can be in declaring that we doubt the null hypothesis. Think again about the jury trial from Chapter 12. Our null hypothesis is that the defendant is innocent. Then the evidence starts rolling in. A car the same color as his was parked in front of the bank. Well, there are lots of cars that color. The probability of that happening (given his innocence) is pretty high, so we're not persuaded that he's guilty. The bank's security camera showed the robber was male and about the defendant's height and weight. Hmmm. Could that be a coincidence? If he's innocent, then it's a little less likely that the car and description would

(continued)

---

[2]The approach to statistical inference known as Bayesian Statistics addresses the question in just this way, but it requires more advanced mathematics and more assumptions.

both match, so our P-value goes down. We're starting to question his innocence a little. Witnesses said the robber wore a blue jacket just like the one the police found in a garbage can behind the defendant's house. Well, if he's innocent, then that doesn't seem very likely, does it? If he's really innocent, the probability that all of these could have happened is getting pretty low. Now our P-value may be small enough to be called "beyond a reasonable doubt" and lead to a conviction. Each new piece of evidence strains our skepticism a bit more. The more compelling the evidence—the more *unlikely* it would be were he innocent—the more convinced we become that he's guilty.

But even though it may make us more confident in declaring him guilty, additional evidence does not make *him* any guiltier. Either he robbed the bank or he didn't. Additional evidence (like the teller picking him out of a police lineup) just makes us more confident that we did the right thing when we convicted him. The lower the P-value, the more comfortable we feel about our decision to reject the null hypothesis, but the null hypothesis doesn't get any more false.

> " You're so guilty now. "
> —Rearview Mirror

How small the P-value has to be for you to reject the null hypothesis depends on a lot of things, not all of which can be precisely quantified. Your belief in the null hypothesis will influence your decision. Your trust in the data, in the experimental method if the data come from a planned experiment, in the survey protocol if the data come from a designed survey, all influence your decision. The P-value should serve as a measure of the strength of the evidence against the null hypothesis, but should never serve as a hard and fast rule for decisions. You have to take that responsibility on yourself.

As a review, let's look at the helmet law example discussed earlier. Did helmet wearing among young riders decrease after the law allowed older riders to ride without helmets? What is the evidence?

GUIDED EXAMPLE   Did a Proportion Change?

Question: Did helmet use in Florida decline among riders under the age of 21 subsequent to the change in the helmet laws?

PLAN	**Define** and state the problem and discuss the variables and the W's.	I want to know whether the rate of helmet wearing among Florida's motorcycle riders under the age of 21 decreased after the law changed to allow older riders to go without helmets. The proportion before the law was passed was 60% so I'll use that as my null hypothesis value. The alternative is one-sided because I'm interested only in seeing if the rate decreased. I have data from accident records showing 396 of 781 young riders were wearing helmets.

Hypotheses The null hypothesis is established by the rate set before the change in the law. The study was concerned with safety, so they'll want to know of any decline in helmet use, making this a lower-tail test.

$$H_0\text{: } p = 0.60$$
$$H_A\text{: } p < 0.60$$

Model Check the conditions.

✔ **Independence Assumption**: The data are for riders involved in accidents during a three-year period. Individuals are assumed to be independent of one another.

✔ **Randomization Condition**: No randomization was applied, but we are considering these riders involved in accidents to be a representative sample of all riders. We should take care in generalizing our conclusions.

✔ **10% Condition**: These 781 riders are a small sample of a larger population of all young motorcycle riders.

✔ **Success/Failure Condition**: We'd expect $np = 781(0.6) = 468.6$ helmeted riders and $nq = 781(0.4) = 312.4$ non-helmeted. Both are at least 10.

Specify the sampling distribution model and name the test.	The conditions are satisfied, so I can use a Normal model and perform a **one-proportion z-test**.

DO

Mechanics Find the standard deviation of the sampling model using the hypothesized proportion.

There were 396 helmet wearers among the 781 accident victims.

$$\hat{p} = \frac{396}{781} = 0.507$$

$$SD(\hat{p}) = \sqrt{\frac{p_0 q_0}{n}} = \sqrt{\frac{(0.60)(0.40)}{781}} = 0.0175$$

Find the z-score for the observed proportion.

$$z = \frac{\hat{p} - p_0}{SD(\hat{p})} = \frac{0.507 - 0.60}{0.0175} = -5.31$$

Make a picture. Sketch a Normal model centered at the hypothesized helmet rate of 60%. This is a lower-tail test, so shade the region to the left of the observed rate.

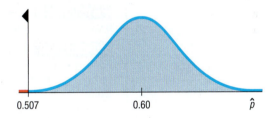

Given this z-score, the P-value is obviously very low.

The observed helmet rate is 5.31 standard deviations below the former rate. The corresponding P-value is less than 0.001.

Find a confidence interval for the proportion.

A 95% confidence interval for the true rate is:

$$\hat{p} \pm z^* \sqrt{\frac{\hat{p}\hat{q}}{n}} = 0.507 \pm 1.96(0.0179) = (0.472, 0.542)$$

REPORT

Communicate and Present your results. Link the P-value to your decision about the null hypothesis, and then state your conclusion in context.

MEMO

Re: Helmet compliance rate

We examined data from motorcycle accidents to assess whether compliance with the helmet law had declined among riders under 21 after the change in the law.

The very small P-value says that if the true rate of helmet-wearing among riders under 21 were still 60%, the probability of observing a rate no higher than 50.7% in a sample like this is less than 1 chance in 1000, so I reject the null hypothesis. There is strong evidence that there has been a decline in helmet use among riders under 21. For prediction purposes, a 95% confidence interval for the true compliance rate of under 21 riders is from 47.2% to 54.2%.

There is strong evidence that the rate is no longer 60%, but the small P-value by itself says nothing about how much lower the rate might be. The confidence interval provides that information; the rate seems to be closer to 50% now. Whether a change from 60% to 50% makes an important difference in safety is a judgment that depends on the situation, but not on the P-value. Not coincidentally, on July 1, 2008, Florida required a motorcycle "endorsement" for all motorcycle riders. For riders under 21, that requires a motorcycle safety course. Although only about 70% of motorcycle riders are endorsed, the percentage of unendorsed riders involved in crashes dropped considerably after 2008.[3]

IN PRACTICE 13.1   Thinking about the P-value

Many medications have side effects, some of them serious. During a clinical trial, pharmaceutical companies watch for serious side effects and are obligated to report such findings to the U.S. Food and Drug Administration (FDA). The diabetes drug Avandia was approved to treat Type 2 diabetes in 1999. But a 2007 article in the *New England Journal of Medicine* (*NEJM*) raised concerns that the drug might carry an increased risk of heart attack. The article's author, Dr. Steven E. Nissen, reported that the seven-year risk of heart attack in diabetes patients taking the drug Avandia was increased from the baseline of 20.2% to an estimated risk of 28.9% and said the P-value was 0.03.

PHYSICIAN   I accept 0.202 as a baseline. How should I understand the P-value of 0.03 when I read the *NEJM* study? Should I change my practice?

CONSULTANT   The P-value = $P(\hat{p} \geq 28.9\% \,|\, p = 20.2\%)$. That is, it's the probability of seeing such a high heart attack rate among the people studied if, in fact, taking Avandia really didn't increase the risk at all. The P-value of 0.03 means that there would be a very small chance of observing a rate of heart attacks that high, by chance alone, if the true rate of heart attacks were 20.2%, and so we conclude that the heart attack rate with Avandia is higher.

What to Do with a High P-Value

Insurance companies constantly evaluate medical procedures to make sure their cost is justified. One controversial therapy is therapeutic (or healing) touch (TT), which is taught in many schools of nursing. In therapy, the practitioner moves her hands near, but does not touch, a patient in an attempt to manipulate a "human energy field." Therapeutic touch practitioners believe that by adjusting this field they can promote healing. However, no instrument has ever detected a human energy field, and no experiment has ever shown that TT practitioners can detect such a field.

In 1998, the *Journal of the American Medical Association* published a paper reporting work by a then nine-year-old girl.[4] She had performed a simple experiment in which she challenged 15 TT practitioners to detect whether her unseen hand was hovering over their left or right hand (selected by the flip of a coin).

The practitioners "warmed up" with a period during which they could see the experimenter's hand, and each said that they could detect the girl's human energy field. Then a screen was placed so that the practitioners could not see the girl's

---

[3]www.ridesmartflorida.com

[4]L. Rosa, E. Rosa, L. Sarner, and S. Barrett, "A Close Look at Therapeutic Touch," *JAMA* 279(13) [1 April 1998]: 1005–1010.

hand, and they attempted 10 trials each. Overall, of 150 trials, the TT practitioners were successful only 70 times—a success proportion of 46.7%.

The null hypothesis here is that the TT practitioners were just guessing. If that were the case, since the hand was chosen using a coin flip, the practitioners would guess correctly 50% of the time. So the null hypothesis is that $p = 0.5$ and the alternative that they could actually detect a human energy field is (one-sided) $p > 0.5$.

What would constitute evidence that they weren't guessing? Certainly, a very high proportion of correct guesses out of 150 would convince most people. Exactly how high the proportion of correct guesses has to be for you to reject the null hypothesis depends on how small a P-value you need to be convinced (which, in turn, depends on how often you're willing to make mistakes—a topic we'll discuss later in the chapter).

But let's look again at the TT practitioners' proportion. Does it provide any evidence that they weren't guessing? The proportion of correct guesses is 46.7%—that's *less* than the hypothesized value, not greater! When we find $SD(\hat{p}) = 0.041$ (or 4.1%) we can see that 46.7% is almost 1 SD *below* the hypothesized proportion:

$$SD(\hat{p}) = \sqrt{\frac{p_0 q_0}{n}} = \sqrt{\frac{(0.5)(0.5)}{150}} \approx 0.041$$

The observed proportion, $\hat{p}$, is 0.467.

$$z = \frac{\hat{p} - p_0}{SD(\hat{p})} = \frac{0.467 - 0.5}{0.041} = -0.805$$

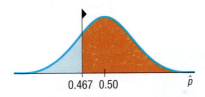

The observed success rate is 0.805 standard deviations below the hypothesized mean.

$$P = P(z > -0.805) = 0.790$$

If the practitioners had been highly successful, the researchers would have seen a low P-value and would have concluded that they could actually detect a human energy field.

But that's not what happened. What they observed was a $\hat{p} = 0.467$ success rate. The P-value for this proportion is greater than 0.5 because the observed value is on the "wrong" side of the null hypothesis value. Wrong, that is, if you wanted to find evidence against the null hypothesis. To convince anyone that they can detect a human energy field, the practitioners should be doing better than guessing, not worse!

Obviously, the null hypothesis won't be rejected with a large P-value; to reject it, the P-value would have to be quite small. But a P-value of 0.790 seems so big it is almost strange. In fact, for a one-sided test, any time the test statistic is on the "wrong" side of the hypothesis, we know immediately that the P-value is at least 0.50 and we know that we have no evidence to reject the null hypothesis.

Big P-values just mean that what we've observed isn't surprising. That is, the results are in line with our assumption that the null hypothesis models the world, so we have no reason to reject it. A big P-value doesn't prove that the null hypothesis is true, but it certainly offers no evidence that it's *not* true. When we see a large P-value, all we can say is that we "don't reject the null hypothesis."

IN PRACTICE 13.2 More about p-values

RECAP The question of whether the diabetes drug Avandia increased the risk of heart attack was raised by a study in the *New England Journal of Medicine*. This study estimated the seven-year risk of heart attack to be 28.9% and reported a P-value of 0.03 for a test of whether this risk was higher than the baseline seven-year risk of 20.2%. An earlier study (the ADOPT study) had estimated the seven-year risk to be 26.9% and reported a P-value of 0.27.

PHYSICIAN I recall seeing an earlier study in which the baseline risk was reported as 26.9%. Does that matter?

CONSULTANT The earlier study was called the ADOPT study. That study used a baseline risk of 26.9%, which results in a P-value of 0.27. This means that a heart attack rate at least as high as the one they observed could be expected in 27% of similar experiments even if, in fact, there were no increased risk from taking Avandia. That's not remarkable enough to reject the null hypothesis. In other words, the ADOPT study wasn't convincing.

13.2 Alpha Levels and Significance

Sometimes we need to make a firm decision about whether or not to reject the null hypothesis. A jury must *decide* whether the evidence reaches the level of "beyond a reasonable doubt." A business must *select* a Web design. You need to decide which section of a statistics course to enroll in.

When the P-value is small, it tells us that our data are rare *given the null hypothesis*. As humans, we are suspicious of rare events. If the data are "rare enough" under the null hypothesis (i.e., assuming that the null is true), we just don't think that could have happened due to chance. Since the data *did* happen, something must be wrong. All we can do now is to reject the null hypothesis.

But how rare is "rare"? How low does the P-value have to be?

We can define "rare event" arbitrarily by setting a threshold for our P-value as we saw in Chapter 12. If our P-value falls below that point, we'll reject the null hypothesis. We call such results *statistically significant*. The threshold is called an **alpha level**. Not surprisingly, it's labeled with the Greek letter α. Common α-levels are 0.10, 0.05, 0.01, and 0.001. You have the option—almost the *obligation*—to consider your alpha level carefully and choose an appropriate one for the situation. If you're assessing the safety of air bags, you'll want a low alpha level; even 0.01 might not be low enough. If you're just wondering whether folks prefer their pizza with or without pepperoni, you might be happy with $\alpha = 0.10$. It can be hard to justify your choice of α, though, so often we arbitrarily choose 0.05.

Sir Ronald Fisher (1890–1962) was one of the founders of modern statistics.

> **Where Did the Value 0.05 Come From?**
>
> In 1931, in a famous book called *The Design of Experiments*, Sir Ronald Fisher discussed the amount of evidence needed to reject a null hypothesis. He said that it was *situation dependent*, but remarked, somewhat casually, that for many scientific applications, 1 out of 20 *might be* a reasonable value, especially in a *first* experiment—one that will be followed by confirmation. Since then, some people—indeed some entire disciplines—have acted as if the number 0.05 were sacrosanct.

NOTATION ALERT

The first Greek letter, α, is used in statistics for the threshold value of a hypothesis test. You'll hear it referred to as the alpha level. Common values are 0.10, 0.05, 0.01, and 0.001.

The alpha level is also called the **significance level**. When we reject the null hypothesis, we say that the test is "significant at that level." For example, we might say that we reject the null hypothesis "at the 5% level of significance." You must select the alpha level *before* you look at the data. Otherwise you can be accused of finagling the conclusions by tuning the alpha level to the results after you've seen the data.

What can you say if the P-value does not fall below α? When you have not found sufficient evidence to reject the null according to the standard you have established, you should say: "The data have failed to provide sufficient evidence to reject the null hypothesis." Don't say: "We accept the null hypothesis." You certainly haven't proven or established the null hypothesis; it was assumed to begin with. You *could* say that you have *retained* the null hypothesis, but it's better to say that you've failed to reject it.

> ### It Could Happen to You!
> Of course, if the null hypothesis is true, no matter what alpha level you choose, you still have a probability α of rejecting the null hypothesis by mistake. When we do reject the null hypothesis, no one ever thinks that *this* is one of those rare times. As statistician Stu Hunter notes, "The statistician says 'rare events do happen—but not to me!'"

> ### Conclusion
> If the P-value $< \alpha$, then reject H_0.
> If the P-value $\geq \alpha$, then fail to reject H_0.

Look again at the home field advantage example in Chapter 12. The P-value was <0.001. This is so much smaller than any reasonable alpha level that we can reject H_0. We concluded: "We reject the null hypothesis. There is sufficient evidence to conclude that there is a home field advantage over and above what we expect with random variation." On the other hand, when testing the success rate in the therapeutic touch example, the P-value was 0.790, a very high P-value. In this case we can say only that we have failed to reject the null hypothesis that $p = 0.50$. We certainly can't say that we've proved it, or even that we've accepted it.

The automatic nature of the reject/fail-to-reject decision when we use an alpha level may make you uncomfortable. If your P-value falls just slightly above your alpha level, you're not allowed to reject the null. Yet a P-value just barely below the alpha level leads to rejection. If this bothers you, you're in good company. Many statisticians think it better to report the P-value than to choose an alpha level and carry the decision through to a final reject/fail-to-reject verdict. So when you declare your decision, it's always a good idea to report the P-value as an indication of the strength of the evidence against the null hypothesis.

> ### Practical vs. Statistical Significance
> A large insurance company mined its data and found a statistically significant ($P = 0.04$) difference between the mean value of policies sold in 2001 and those sold in 2002. The difference in the mean values was $0.98. Even though it was statistically significant, management did not see this as an important difference when a typical policy sold for more than $1000. On the other hand, a marketable improvement of 10% in relief rate for a new pain medicine may not be statistically significant unless a large number of people are tested. The effect, which is economically significant, might not be statistically significant. So, always think carefully about the practical consequences of a hypothesis test conclusion.

> ### It's in the Stars
> Some disciplines carry the idea further and code P-values by their size. In this scheme, a P-value between 0.05 and 0.01 gets highlighted by a single asterisk (*). A P-value between 0.01 and 0.001 gets two asterisks (**), and a P-value less than 0.001 gets three (***). This can be a convenient summary of the weight of evidence against the null hypothesis, but it isn't wise to take the distinctions too seriously and make black-and-white decisions near the boundaries. The boundaries are a matter of tradition, not science; there is nothing special about 0.05. A P-value of 0.051 should be looked at seriously and not casually thrown away just because it's larger than 0.05, and one that's 0.009 is not very different from one that's 0.011.

Sometimes it's best to report that the conclusion is not yet clear and to suggest that more data be gathered. (In a trial, a jury may "hang" and be unable to return a verdict.) In such cases, it's an especially good idea to report the P-value, since it's the best summary we have of what the data say or fail to say about the null hypothesis.

What do we mean when we say that a test is statistically significant? All we mean is that the test statistic had a P-value lower than our alpha level. Don't be lulled into thinking that "statistical significance" necessarily carries with it any practical importance or impact.

For large samples, even small, unimportant ("insignificant") deviations from the null hypothesis can be statistically significant. On the other hand, if the sample is not large enough, even large, financially or scientifically important differences may not be statistically significant.

When you report your decision about the null hypothesis, it's good practice to report the effect size (the magnitude of the difference between the observed statistic value and the null hypothesis value in the data units) along with the P-value.

IN PRACTICE 13.3   Changing the evidence needed after the fact

RECAP The manager at Summit Projects (see In Practice 12.8) is convinced that the mean sales have increased and wants to adjust the α-level. Recall that the mean before the new web design was $24.85 and the sample mean from 58 pulled records after the new design was $26.05. The P-value was 0.1870.

MANAGER We increased the mean sales by $1.20 a person. That's nearly a 5% increase just from the new design. You told me that the result wasn't statistically significant. What if I change the α-level to 0.20. Wouldn't that give me significance?

ANALYST Technically it would, but it's a really bad idea. First, 0.20 is a very high α-level. Using that, you will decide that mean sales have increased when they actually haven't 20% of the time. It's probably a good idea to construct a confidence interval to see how large or small the mean might plausibly be (see In Practice 13.4).

13.3   Critical Values

When building a confidence interval, we calculated the margin of error as the product of an estimated standard error for the statistic and a critical value. For proportions, we found a **critical value**, z^*, to correspond to our selected confidence level. For means, we found the critical value t^* based on both the confidence level and the degrees of freedom. Critical values can also be used as a shortcut for hypothesis tests. Before computers and calculators were common, P-values were hard to find. It was easier to select a few common alpha levels (0.05, 0.01, 0.001, for example) and learn the corresponding critical values for the Normal model (that is, the critical values corresponding to confidence levels 0.95, 0.99, and 0.999, respectively). Rather than find the probability that corresponded to your observed statistic, you'd just calculate how many standard deviations it was away from the hypothesized value and compare that value directly against these z^* values. (Remember that whenever we measure the distance of a value from the mean in standard deviations, we are finding a z-score.) Any z-score larger in magnitude (that is, more extreme) than a particular critical value has to be less likely, so it will have a P-value smaller than the corresponding alpha.

If we were willing to settle for a flat reject/fail-to-reject decision, comparing an observed z-score with the critical value for a specified alpha level would give a shortcut path to that decision. For the home field advantage example, if we choose $\alpha = 0.05$, then in order to reject H_0, our z-score has to be larger than the one-sided critical value of 1.645. The observed proportion was 4.74 standard deviations above 0.5, so we clearly reject the null hypothesis. This is perfectly correct and does give us a yes/no decision, but it gives us less information about the hypothesis because we don't have the P-value to think about. With technology, P-values are easy to find. And since they give more information about the strength of the evidence, you should report them.

Quick Decisions

If you need to make a decision on the fly with no technology, remember "2." That's our old friend from the 68–95–99.7 Rule. It's roughly the critical value for testing a hypothesis against a two-sided alternative at $\alpha = 0.05$ using z. In fact, it's just about the t^* critical value with 60 degrees of freedom. The exact critical value for z^* is 1.96, but 2 is close enough for most decisions.

Here are the traditional z^* critical values from the Normal model:[5]

Using Critical Values

We can repeat the tests in In Practice 12.2 and 12.8 using critical values. Remember that the z-value for testing the null hypothesis was 3.182. For the test of proportions, the critical z^*-values at $\alpha = 0.05$ are ± 1.96. Because 3.182 is much larger than 1.96, we reject the null hypothesis. For the one-sided test of means, with $n = 58$, the critical t^*-value at $\alpha = 0.05$ is 1.676 (using df = 50 from a table) or 1.672 (using df = 57 from technology). In either case, the t-value of 0.896 is smaller than the critical value, so we fail to reject the null hypothesis, as before.

α	1-sided	2-sided
0.05	1.645	1.96
0.01	2.33	2.576
0.001	3.09	3.29

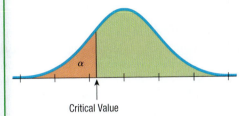

FIGURE 13.1 When the alternative is one-sided, the critical value puts all of α on one side.

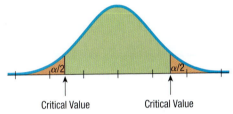

FIGURE 13.2 When the alternative is two-sided, the critical value splits α equally into two tails.

When testing means, you'll need to know both the α-level and the degrees of freedom to find the t^* critical value. With large n, the t^* critical values will be close to the z^* critical values (above) that you use for testing proportions.

13.4 Confidence Intervals and Hypothesis Tests

We've attached symbols to many of the p's. Let's keep them straight.

- p is a population parameter—the true proportion in the population.
- p_0 is a hypothesized value of p.
- $\hat{p}$ is an observed proportion.
- p^* is a critical value of a proportion corresponding to a specified α.

Confidence intervals and hypothesis tests are built from the same calculations. They have the same assumptions and conditions. You can approximate a hypothesis test by examining the confidence interval. Just ask whether the null hypothesis value is consistent with a confidence interval for the parameter at the corresponding confidence level. Because confidence intervals are naturally two-sided, they correspond to two-sided tests. For example, a 95% confidence interval corresponds to a two-sided hypothesis test at $\alpha = 5\%$. In general, a confidence interval with a confidence level of $C\%$ corresponds to a two-sided hypothesis test with an α-level of $100 - C\%$.

A Technical Note

For means, you can test a hypothesis by seeing if the null value falls in the appropriate confidence interval. However, for proportions, this isn't *exactly* true. For a confidence interval, we estimate the standard deviation of $\hat{p}$ from $\hat{p}$ itself, making it a *standard error*. For the corresponding hypothesis test, we use the model's *standard deviation* for $\hat{p}$ based on the null hypothesis value p_0. When $\hat{p}$ and p_0 are close, these calculations give similar results. When they differ, you're likely to reject H_0 (because the observed proportion is far from your hypothesized value). In that case, you're better off building your confidence interval with a standard error estimated from the data rather than rely on the model you just rejected.

---

[5]In a sense, these are the flip side of the 68–95–99.7 Rule. There we chose simple statistical distances from the mean and recalled the areas of the tails. Here we select convenient tail areas (0.05, 0.01, and 0.001, either on one side or adding both together), and record the corresponding statistical distances.

FIGURE 13.3 The 90% confidence interval is symmetric and leaves 5% on each side. Because the hypothesized value of 0.50 is not a plausible value, we can reject the null hypothesis at $\alpha = 0.05$.

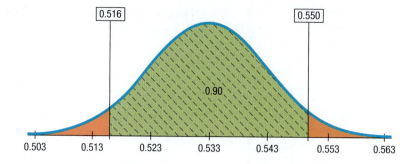

If you are performing a one-sided test at level 0.05, you leave 5% on one side of the null hypothesis. The critical value will then match up with a 90% confidence interval, since that interval leaves 5% on *each* side. Figure 13.3 shows an example. A 90% confidence for the home field advantage is (0.516, 0.550). This contains the plausible values of the true proportion of wins by a home team. Since 0.50 is *not* in the interval, and all values are above 0.05, we can reject the null hypothesis at $\alpha = 0.05$. We use a 90% confidence interval because we wanted a one-sided conclusion.

JUST CHECKING

1 Recall Just Checking 12.9 in which a bank is testing a new method for getting delinquent customers to pay their past-due credit card bills. The bank sets up an experiment to test the effectiveness of the DVD. The DVD is mailed to several randomly selected delinquent customers, and employees keep track of how many customers then contact the bank to arrange payments. The bank just got back the results on their test of the DVD strategy. A 90% confidence interval for the success rate is (0.35, 0.45). Their old send-a-letter method had worked 30% of the time. Can you reject the null hypothesis and conclude that the method increases the proportion at $\alpha = 0.05$? Explain.

2 Given the confidence interval the bank found in the trial of the DVD mailing, what would you recommend be done? Should the bank scrap the DVD strategy?

3 The mileage rewards program at a major airline company has just completed a test market of a new arrangement with a hotel partner to try to increase engagement of valued customers with the program. The cost to the rewards program of the hotel offer is $35.00 per customer. From the test market, a 95% confidence interval for the revenue generated is ($37.95, $55.05). What does that say about the viability of the new arrangement?

GUIDED EXAMPLE   Credit Card Promotion

The credit card company we met on page 391 wanted to test whether at least 25% of their customers charged $500 or more.

Among the 500 customers, 148 or 29.6% of them charged $500 or more. Instead of a hypothesis test, let's use a confidence interval to test whether the goal of 25% for all customers was met.

PLAN	**Define** and state the problem, and discuss the variables and the context.	We want to know whether 25% or more of the customers will spend $500 or more in the next month and qualify for the special program. We will use the data from the same month a year ago to estimate the proportion and see whether the proportion was at least 25%.

Hypotheses The null hypothesis is that the proportion qualifying is 25%. The alternative is that it is higher. It's a one-sided test, so if we use a confidence interval, we'll have to be careful about what level we use.

The statistic is $\hat{p} = 0.296$, the proportion of customers who charged $500 or more.

$$H_0: p = 0.25$$
$$H_A: p > 0.25$$

Model Check the conditions. (Because this is a confidence interval, we use the observed successes and failures to check the Success/Failure Condition.)

✔ **Independence Assumption.** Customers are not likely to influence one another when it comes to spending on their credit cards.

✔ **Randomization Condition.** This is a random sample from the company's database.

✔ **10% Condition.** The sample is less than 10% of all customers.

✔ **Success/Failure Condition.** There were 148 successes and 352 failures, both at least 10. The sample is large enough.

State your method. Here we are using a confidence interval to test a hypothesis.

Under these conditions, the sampling model is Normal. We'll create a one-proportion z-interval.

DO	Write down the given information and determine the sample proportion.

$n = 500$, so

$$\hat{p} = \frac{148}{500} = 0.296 \text{ and}$$

$$SE(\hat{p}) = \sqrt{\frac{\hat{p}\hat{q}}{n}} = \sqrt{\frac{(0.296)(0.704)}{500}} = 0.020$$

$$ME = z^* \times SE(\hat{p})$$
$$= 1.645(0.020) = 0.033$$

To use a confidence interval, we need a confidence level that corresponds to the alpha level of the test. The level wasn't specifically given, but 0.05 is a typical alpha level to use. If we use $\alpha = 0.05$, we should construct a 90% confidence interval because this is a one-sided test. That will leave 5% on *each* side of the observed proportion. Determine the standard error of the sample proportion and the margin of error. The critical value is $z^* = 1.645$.

The confidence interval is estimate ± margin of error.

The 90% confidence interval is 0.296 ± 0.033 or $(0.263, 0.329)$.

REPORT	**Communicate** your conclusions clearly. Link the confidence interval to your decision about the null hypothesis, then state your conclusion in context.

MEMO

Re: Credit card promotion

Our study of a sample of customer records indicates that between 26.3% and 32.9% of customers charge $500 or more. We are 90% confident that this interval includes the true value. Because the minimum suitable value of 25% is below this interval, we conclude that it is not a plausible value, and so we reject the null hypothesis that only 25% of the customers charge more than $500 a month. The goal appears to have been met assuming that the month we studied is typical.

> **IN PRACTICE 13.4**   **Decision making with confidence intervals**
>
> **MANAGER** I'm not sure I understood when you said that a confidence interval might shed more light on our mean sales after the web design. Can you be more specific?
>
> **ANALYST** Yes, I recommended against using an α-level of 0.20 because of the high probability of making an error. Let's construct a 90% confidence interval for the mean sales based on our 58 recent purchases.
>
> $$(\bar{y} - t^*SE(\bar{y}), \bar{y} + t^*SE(\bar{y})) = \left(26.05 - 1.672 \times \frac{10.2}{\sqrt{58}}, 26.05 + 1.672 \times \frac{10.2}{\sqrt{(58)}}\right)$$
>
> $$= (23.81, 28.29)$$
>
> The hypothesized value of $24.85 is in this interval, so we fail to reject the null hypothesis. But, more important, notice that it's plausible that the mean sales actually went down. Even a drop of $1.00 in the mean is plausible. On the other hand, an increase of over $3 is plausible, too. We should take a larger sample if we want more precise information.

13.5   Two Types of Errors

Nobody's perfect. Even with lots of evidence, we can still make the wrong decision. In fact, when we perform a hypothesis test, we can make mistakes in *two* ways:

I. The null hypothesis is true, but we mistakenly reject it.
II. The null hypothesis is false, but we fail to reject it.

These two types of errors are known as **Type I** and **Type II errors**, respectively. One way to keep the names straight is to remember that we start by assuming the null hypothesis is true, so a Type I error is the first kind of error we could make. For the Summit manager in In Practice 13.3, a Type I error would be deciding that the mean had increased when it actually hadn't.

In medical disease testing, the null hypothesis is usually the assumption that a person is healthy. The alternative is that he or she has the disease we're testing for. So a Type I error is a *false positive*—a healthy person is diagnosed with the disease. A Type II error, in which an infected person is diagnosed as disease free, is a *false negative*. These errors have other names, depending on the particular discipline and context.

Which type of error is more serious depends on the situation. In a jury trial, a Type I error occurs if the jury convicts an innocent person. A Type II error occurs if the jury fails to convict a guilty person. Which seems more serious? In medical diagnosis, a false negative could mean that a sick patient goes untreated. A false positive might mean that the person receives unnecessary treatments or even surgery.

In business planning, a false-positive result could mean that money will be invested in a project that turns out not to be profitable. A false-negative result might mean that money won't be invested in a project that would have been profitable. Which error is worse, the lost investment or the lost opportunity? The answer always depends on the situation, the cost, and your point of view.

Here's an illustration of the situations:

How often will a Type I error occur? It happens when the null hypothesis is true but we've had the bad luck to draw an unusual sample. To reject H_0, the P-value must fall below α. When H_0 is true, that happens *exactly* with probability α. So when you choose level α, you're setting the probability of a Type I error to α.

What if H_0 is not true? Then we can't possibly make a Type I error. You can't get a false positive from a sick person. A Type I error can happen only when H_0 is true.

When H_0 is false and we reject it, we have done the right thing. A test's ability to detect a false hypothesis is called the **power** of the test. In a jury trial, power is a measure of the ability of the criminal justice system to convict people who are guilty. We'll have a lot more to say about power soon.

When H_0 is false but we fail to reject it, we have made a Type II error. We assign the letter β to the probability of this mistake. What's the value of β? That's harder to assess than α because we don't know what the value of the parameter really is. When H_0 is true, it specifies a single parameter value. But when H_0 is false, we don't have a specific one; we have many possible values. We can compute the probability β for any parameter value in H_A, but the choice of which one to pick is not always clear.

One way to focus our attention is by thinking about the *effect size*. That is, ask: "How big a difference would matter?" Suppose a charity wants to test whether placing personalized address labels in the envelope along with a request for a donation increases the response rate above the baseline of 5%. If the minimum response that would pay for the address labels is 6%, they would calculate β for the alternative $p = 0.06$.

Of course, we could reduce β for *all* alternative parameter values by increasing α. By making it easier to reject the null, we'd be more likely to reject it whether it's true or not. The only way to reduce *both* types of error is to collect more evidence or, in statistical terms, to collect more data. Otherwise, we just wind up trading off one kind of error against the other. Whenever you design a survey or experiment, it's a good idea to calculate β (for a reasonable α-level). Use a parameter value in the alternative that corresponds to an effect size that you want to be able to detect. Too often, studies fail because their sample sizes are too small to detect the change they are looking for.

JUST CHECKING

4 Remember our bank that's sending out DVDs to try to get customers to make payments on delinquent loans? It is looking for evidence that the costlier DVD strategy produces a higher success rate than the letters it has been sending. Explain what a Type I error is in this context and what the consequences would be to the bank.

5 What's a Type II error in the bank experiment context and what would the consequences be?

6 If the DVD strategy *really* works well—actually getting 60% of the people to pay off their balances—would the power of the test be higher or lower compared to a 32% payoff rate? Explain briefly.

7 Recall the mileage program test market of Question 3. Suppose after completing the hotel partnership, the mean revenue per customer is $40.26. Has a Type I or Type II error been made? Explain.

IN PRACTICE 13.5   Assessing decision-making errors

Suppose that a year later, a full accounting of all the transactions at Summit Projects (see pages 385 and 396) finds that 26.5% of visits resulted in sales and they had an average purchase amount of $26.25.

MANAGER   I see that our results are not exactly what you predicted. I understand that we can't expect a perfect prediction, but would you say that any errors have been made?

ANALYST   We rejected the null hypothesis that $p = 0.15$ and in fact $p = 0.265$, so we did not make a Type I error (the only error we could have made when rejecting the null hypothesis). For the mean amount, we failed to reject that the mean had increased from $24.85 but actually the mean had increased to $26.25 so we made a Type II error—we failed to reject the null hypothesis when it was false. Our confidence interval indicated that this was a possibility.

13.6   Power

Power and Effect Size

When planning a study, it's wise to think about the size of the effect we're looking for. We've called the effect size the difference between the null hypothesis and the observed statistic. In planning, it's the difference between the null hypothesis and a particular alternative we're interested in. It's easier to see a larger effect size, so the power of the study will increase with the effect size.

Once the study has been completed we'll base our business decision on the observed effect size, the difference between the null hypothesis and the observed value.

Remember, we can never prove a null hypothesis true. We can only fail to reject it. But when we fail to reject a null hypothesis, it's natural to wonder whether we looked hard enough. Might the null hypothesis actually be false and our test too weak to tell?

When the null hypothesis actually *is* false, we hope our test is strong enough to reject it. Suppose your restaurant gets an average rating of 7.3 on Trip Advisor. You want to see if a new seasonal menu can boost that. After you introduce the new menu, the average of the ratings by the first five customers is 7.8. That's slightly higher than the old average, but a confidence interval for the mean rating contains 7.3 and the P-value is 0.4. You can't reject the null hypothesis of no change, but you still wonder if the increase was due to chance or to the new menu. Is a sample of five customers really large enough to tell? We know that a sample that small is likely to give a wide confidence interval. Even so, if those five customers had averaged a 9.8 rating, you'd probably be convinced it was the due to the new menu. That's because when the change is big enough, a wide confidence interval is OK. Our ability to decide whether we've just seen a random fluctuation or a true difference depends on the sample size, the amount of variation among customers, and the actual size of the difference. So, before starting your trials, you'd like to know whether you'll have enough observations to have a good chance of discerning a real difference.

The power of the test gives us a way to think about that. The power of a test is the probability that it correctly rejects a false null hypothesis. When the power is high, we can be confident that we've looked hard enough. We know that β is the probability that a test *fails* to reject a false null hypothesis, so the power of the test is the complement, $1 - \beta$. We might have just written $1 - \beta$, but power is such an important concept that it gets its own name.

Whenever a study fails to reject its null hypothesis, the test's power comes into question. Was the sample size big enough to detect an effect had there been one? Might we have missed an effect large enough to be interesting just because we failed to gather sufficient data or because there was too much variability in the data we could gather? Might the problem be that the experiment simply lacked adequate power to detect their ability?

When we calculate power, we base our calculation on the smallest effect that might influence our business decision. The value of the power depends on how large this effect is. For proportions, that effect size is $p - p_0$; for means it's $\mu - \mu_0$. The power depends directly on the effect size. It's easier to see larger effects, so the further p_0 is from p (or μ is from μ_0), the greater the power.

How can we decide what power we need? Choice of power is more a financial or scientific decision than a statistical one because to calculate the power, we need to specify the alternative parameter value we're interested in. In other words, power is calculated for a particular effect size, and it changes depending on the size of the effect we want to detect.

Graph It!

It makes intuitive sense that the larger the effect size, the easier it should be to see it. Obtaining a larger sample size decreases the probability of a Type II error, and so it increases the power. Finally, it should also makes sense that the more we're willing to accept a Type I error, the less likely we will be to make a Type II error.

Figure 13.5 may help you visualize the relationships among these concepts. Although we'll use proportions to show the ideas, a similar picture and similar statements also hold true for means. Suppose we are testing $H_0: p = p_0$ against the alternative $H_A: p > p_0$. We'll reject the null if the observed proportion, $\hat{p}$, is big enough. By *big enough*, we mean $\hat{p} > p^*$ for some critical value p^* (shown as the red region in the right tail of the upper curve). The upper model shows a picture of the sampling distribution model for the proportion when the null hypothesis is true. If the null were true, then this would be a picture of that truth. We'd make a Type I error whenever the sample gave us $\hat{p} > p^*$ because we would reject the (true) null hypothesis. Unusual samples like that would happen only with probability α.

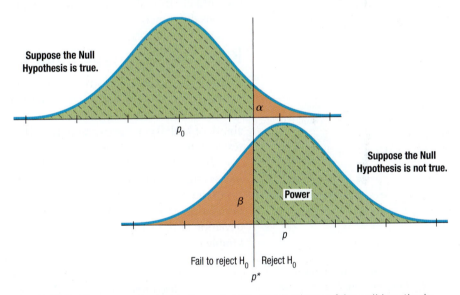

FIGURE 13.5 The power of a test is the probability that it rejects a false null hypothesis. The upper figure shows the null hypothesis model. We'd reject the null in a one-sided test if we observed a value in the red region to the right of the critical value, p^*. The lower figure shows the model if we assume that the true value is p. If the true value of p is greater than p_0, then we're more likely to observe a value that exceeds the critical value and make the correct decision to reject the null hypothesis. The power of the test is the green region on the right of the lower figure. Of course, even drawing samples whose observed proportions are distributed around p, we'll sometimes get a value in the red region on the left and make a Type II error of failing to reject the null.

In reality, though, the null hypothesis is rarely *exactly* true. The lower probability model supposes that H_0 is not true. In particular, it supposes that the true value is p, not p_0. It shows a distribution of possible observed $\hat{p}$ values around this true value. Because of sampling variability, sometimes $\hat{p} < p^*$ and we fail to reject the (false) null hypothesis. Then we'd make a Type II error. The area under the curve to the left of p^* in the bottom model represents how often this happens. The probability is β. In this picture, β is less than half, so most of the time we *do* make the right decision. The *power* of the test—the probability that we make the right decision—is shown as the region to the right of p^*. It's $1 - \beta$.

We calculate p^* based on the upper model because p^* depends only on the null model and the alpha level. No matter what the true proportion, p^* doesn't change. After all, we don't *know* the truth, so we can't use it to determine the critical value. But we always reject H_0 when $\hat{p} > p^*$.

How often we reject H_0 when it's *false* depends on the effect size. We can see from the picture that if the true proportion were further from the hypothesized value, the bottom curve would shift to the right, making the power greater.

We can see several important relationships from this figure:

- Power = $1 - \beta$.
- Moving the critical value (p^* in the case of proportions) to the right reduces α, the probability of a Type I error, but increases β, the probability of a Type II error. It correspondingly reduces the power.
- The larger the true effect size, the real difference between the hypothesized value and the true population value, the smaller the chance of making a Type II error and the greater the power of the test.

If the two proportions (or means) are very far apart, the two models will barely overlap, and we would not be likely to make any Type II errors at all—but then, we are unlikely to really need a formal hypothesis testing procedure to see such an obvious difference.

Reducing Both Type I and Type II Errors

Figure 13.5 seems to show that if we reduce Type I errors, we automatically must increase Type II errors. But there is a way to reduce both. Can you think of it?

If we can make both curves narrower, as shown in Figure 13.6, then the probability of both Type I errors and Type II errors will decrease, and the power of the test will increase.

How can we do that? The only way is to reduce the standard deviations by increasing the sample size. (Remember, these are pictures of sampling distribution models, not of data.) Increasing the sample size works regardless of the true population parameters. But recall the curse of diminishing returns. The standard deviation of the sampling distribution model decreases only as the *square root* of the sample size, so to halve the standard deviations, we must *quadruple* the sample size.

FIGURE 13.6 Making the standard deviations smaller increases the power without changing the alpha level or the corresponding *z* critical value. The proportions are just as far apart as in Figure 13.5, but the error rates are reduced. A similar picture could be drawn for testing means.

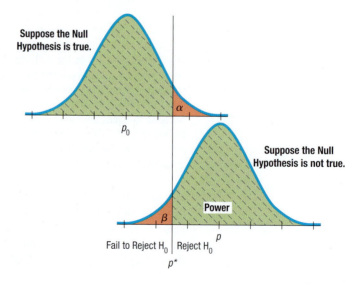

⊘ WHAT CAN GO WRONG? (RECAP)

- **Don't confuse proportions and means.** When you treat your data as categorical, counting successes and summarizing with a sample proportion, make inferences using the Normal model methods. When you treat your data as quantitative, summarizing with a sample mean, make your inferences using Student's t methods.

- **Don't base your null hypotheses on what you see in the data.** You are not allowed to look at the data first and then adjust your null hypothesis so that it will be rejected. If the mean spending of 10 customers turns out to be $\bar{y} = \$24.94$ with a standard error of \$5, don't form a null hypothesis just big enough so you'll be able to reject it like $H_0: \mu = \$26.97$. The null hypothesis should not be based on the data you collect. It should describe the "nothing interesting" or "nothing has changed" situation.

- **Don't base your alternative hypothesis on the data either.** You should always think about the situation you are investigating and base your alternative hypothesis on that. Are you interested only in knowing whether something has *increased*? Then write a one-tail (upper tail) alternative. Or would you be equally interested in a change in either direction? Then you want a two-tailed alternative. You should decide whether to do a one- or two-tailed test based on what results would be of interest to you, not on what you might see in the data.

- **Don't make your null hypothesis what you want to show to be true.** Remember, the null hypothesis is the status quo, the nothing-is-strange-here position a skeptic would take. You wonder whether the data cast doubt on that. You can reject the null hypothesis, but you can never "accept" or "prove" the null.

- **Don't forget to check the conditions.** The reasoning of inference depends on randomization. No amount of care in calculating a test result can save you from a biased sample. The probabilities you compute depend on the Independence Assumption. And your sample must be large enough to justify your use of a Normal model.

- **Don't believe too strongly in arbitrary alpha levels.** There's not really much difference between a P-value of 0.051 and a P-value of 0.049, but sometimes it's regarded as the difference between night (having to retain H_0) and day (being able to shout to the world that your results are "statistically significant"). It may just be better to report the P-value and a confidence interval and let the world (perhaps your manager or client) decide along with you.

- **Don't confuse practical and statistical significance.** A large sample size can make it easy to discern even a trivial change from the null hypothesis value. On the other hand, you could miss an important difference if your test lacks sufficient power.

- **Don't forget that in spite of all your care, you might make a wrong decision.** No one can ever reduce the probability of a Type I error (α) or of a Type II error (β) to zero (but increasing the sample size helps).

ETHICS IN ACTION

Many retailers have recognized the importance of staying connected to their in-store customers via the Internet. Retailers not only use the Internet to inform their customers about specials and promotions, but also to send them e-coupons redeemable for discounts.

Shellie Cooper, longtime owner of a small organic food store, specializes in locally produced organic foods and products. Over the years Shellie's customer base has been quite stable, consisting mainly of health-conscious individuals who tend not to be very price sensitive, opting to pay higher prices for better-quality local, organic products.

Faced with increasing competition from grocery chains offering more organic choices, however, Shellie is now thinking of offering coupons. She needs to decide between the newspaper and the Internet. She recently read that the percentage of consumers who use printable Internet coupons is on the rise but, at 15%, is much less than the 40% who clip and redeem newspaper coupons. Nonetheless, she's interested in learning more about the Internet and sets up a meeting with Jack Kasor, a Web consultant. She discovers

that for an initial investment and continuing monthly fee, Jack would design Shellie's website, host it on his server, and broadcast e-coupons to her customers at regular intervals. While she was concerned about the difference in redemption rates for e-coupons vs. newspaper coupons, Jack assured her that e-coupon redemptions are continuing to rise and that she should expect between 15% and 40% of her customers to redeem them. Shellie agreed to give it a try.

After the first six months, Jack informed Shellie that the proportion of her customers who redeemed e-coupons was significantly greater than 15%. He determined this by selecting several broadcasts at random and found the number redeemed (483) out of the total number sent (3000). Shellie thought that this was positive and made up her mind to continue the use of e-coupons.

- **Identify the ethical dilemma in this scenario.**
- **What are the undesirable consequences?**
- **Propose an ethical solution that considers the welfare of all stakeholders.**

CHAPTER 13 FROM LEARNING TO EARNING

LEARNING OBJECTIVES

Understand P-values in greater depth.
- A P-value is the conditional probability of observing a statistic value at least as far from the (null) hypothesized value as the one we have actually observed given that the null hypothesis is true.
- A small P-value indicates that the statistic we have observed would be unlikely were the null hypothesis true. That leads us to doubt the null.
- A large P-value just tells us that we have insufficient evidence to doubt the null hypothesis. In particular, it does not prove the null to be true.

Compare P-values to a predetermined α-level to decide whether to reject the null hypothesis.

Be aware of the risks of making errors when testing hypotheses.
- A Type I error can occur when rejecting a null hypothesis if that hypothesis is, in fact, true.
- A Type II error can occur when failing to reject a null hypothesis if that hypothesis is, in fact, false.

Understand the concept of the power of a test.
- We are particularly concerned with power when we fail to reject a null hypothesis.
- The power of a test reports, for a specified effect size, the probability that the test would reject a false null hypothesis.
- Remember that increasing the sample size will generally improve the power of any test.

TERMS

Alpha level
The threshold P-value that determines when we reject a null hypothesis. Using an alpha level of α, if we observe a statistic whose P-value based on the null hypothesis is less than α, we reject that null hypothesis.

Critical value
The value in the sampling distribution model of the statistic whose P-value is equal to the alpha level. Any statistic value further from the null hypothesis value than the critical value will have a smaller P-value than α and will lead to rejecting the null hypothesis. The critical value is often denoted with an asterisk, as z^* or t^*, for example.

Power
The probability that a hypothesis test will correctly reject a false null hypothesis. To find the power of a test, we must specify a particular alternative parameter value as the "true" value. For any specific value in the alternative, the power is $1 - \beta$.

Significance level
Another term for the alpha level, used most often in a phrase such as "at the 5% significance level."

Type I error
The error of rejecting a null hypothesis when in fact it is true (also called a "false positive"). The probability of a Type I error is α.

Type II error
The error of failing to reject a null hypothesis when in fact it is false (also called a "false negative"). The probability of a Type II error is commonly denoted β and depends on the effect size.

BRIEF CASE

Confidence Intervals and Hypothesis Tests

Using the **Paralyzed Veterans** dataset, construct a 95% confidence interval for the mean age of a potential donor to the Paralyzed Veterans. Test the hypothesis that the mean age is 62 years old. Discuss what the confidence interval says about the hypothesis test. Is the difference meaningful as well? Now take a sample of size 20 from the dataset and repeat both the confidence interval and the hypothesis test. Discuss how sample size affects the probability of making errors and the power of a test.

CHAPTER 13 EXERCISES

SECTION 13.1

1. Which of the following are true? If false, explain briefly.
a) A P-value of 0.01 means that the null hypothesis is false.
b) A P-value of 0.01 means that the null hypothesis has a 0.01 chance of being true.
c) A P-value of 0.01 is evidence against the null hypothesis.
d) A P-value of 0.01 means we should definitely reject the null hypothesis.

2. Which of the following are true? If false, explain briefly.
a) If the null hypothesis is true, you'll get a high P-value.
b) If the null hypothesis is true, a P-value of 0.01 will occur about 1% of the time.
c) A P-value of 0.90 means that the null hypothesis has a good chance of being true.
d) A P-value of 0.90 is strong evidence that the null hypothesis is true.

SECTION 13.2

3. Which of the following statements are true? If false, explain briefly.

a) Using an alpha level of 0.05, a P-value of 0.04 results in rejecting the null hypothesis.
b) The alpha level depends on the sample size.
c) With an alpha level of 0.01, a P-value of 0.10 results in rejecting the null hypothesis.
d) Using an alpha level of 0.05, a P-value of 0.06 means the null hypothesis is true.

4. Which of the following statements are true? If false, explain briefly.

a) It is better to use an alpha level of 0.05 than an alpha level of 0.01.
b) If we use an alpha level of 0.01, then a P-value of 0.001 is statistically significant.
c) If we use an alpha level of 0.01, then we reject the null hypothesis if the P-value is 0.001.
d) If the P-value is 0.01, we reject the null hypothesis for any alpha level greater than 0.01.

SECTION 13.3

5. For each of the following situations, find the critical value(s) for z or t.

a) $H_0: p = 0.5$ vs. $H_A: p \neq 0.5$ at $\alpha = 0.05$.
b) $H_0: p = 0.4$ vs. $H_A: p > 0.4$ at $\alpha = 0.05$.
c) $H_0: \mu = 10$ vs. $H_A: \mu \neq 10$ at $\alpha = 0.05$; $n = 36$.
d) $H_0: p = 0.5$ vs. $H_A: p > 0.5$ at $\alpha = 0.01$; $n = 345$.
e) $H_0: \mu = 20$ vs. $H_A: \mu < 20$ at $\alpha = 0.01$; $n = 1000$.

6. For each of the following situations, find the critical value for z or t.

a) $H_0: \mu = 105$ vs. $H_A: \mu \neq 105$ at $\alpha = 0.05$; $n = 61$.
b) $H_0: p = 0.05$ vs. $H_A: p > 0.05$ at $\alpha = 0.05$.
c) $H_0: p = 0.6$ vs. $H_A: p \neq 0.6$ at $\alpha = 0.01$.
d) $H_0: p = 0.5$ vs. $H_A: p < 0.5$ at $\alpha = 0.01$; $n = 500$.
e) $H_0: p = 0.2$ vs. $H_A: p < 0.2$ at $\alpha = 0.01$.

SECTION 13.4

7. Suppose that you are testing the hypotheses $H_0: p = 0.20$ vs. $H_A: p \neq 0.20$. A sample of size 250 results in a sample proportion of 0.25.

a) Construct a 95% confidence interval for p.
b) Based on the confidence interval, at $\alpha = 0.05$ can you reject H_0? Explain.
c) What is the difference between the standard error and standard deviation of the sample proportion?
d) Which is used in computing the confidence interval?

8. Suppose that you are testing the hypotheses $H_0: p = 0.40$ vs. $H_A: p > 0.40$. A sample of size 200 results in a sample proportion of 0.55.

a) Construct a 90% confidence interval for p.
b) Based on the confidence interval, at $\alpha = 0.05$ can you reject H_0? Explain.
c) What is the difference between the standard error and standard deviation of the sample proportion?
d) Which is used in computing the confidence interval?

9. Suppose that you are testing the hypotheses $H_0: \mu = 16$ vs. $H_A: \mu < 16$. A sample of size 25 results in a sample mean of 16.5 and a standard deviation of 2.0.

a) What is the standard error of the mean?
b) What is the critical value of t^* for a 90% confidence interval?
c) Construct a 90% confidence interval for μ.
d) Based on the confidence interval, at $\alpha = 0.05$ can you reject H_0? Explain.

10. Suppose that you are testing the hypotheses $H_0: \mu = 80$ vs. $H_A: \mu \neq 80$. A sample of size 61 results in a sample mean of 75 and a standard deviation of 1.5.

a) What is the standard error of the mean?
b) What is the critical value of t^* for a 95% confidence interval?
c) Construct a 95% confidence interval for μ.
d) Based on the confidence interval, at $\alpha = 0.05$ can you reject H_0? Explain.

SECTION 13.5

11. For each of the following situations, state whether a Type I, a Type II, or neither error has been made. Explain briefly.

a) A bank wants to know if the enrollment on their website is above 30% based on a small sample of customers. They test $H_0: p = 0.3$ vs. $H_A: p > 0.3$ and reject the null hypothesis. Later they find out that actually 28% of all customers enrolled.

b) A student tests 100 students to determine whether other students on her campus prefer Coke or Pepsi and finds no evidence that preference for Coke is not 0.5. Later, a marketing company tests all students on campus and finds no difference.

c) A human resource analyst wants to know if the applicants this year score, on average, higher on their placement exam than the 52.5 points the candidates averaged last year. She samples 50 recent tests and finds the average to be 54.1 points. She fails to reject the null hypothesis that the mean is 52.5 points. At the end of the year, they find that the candidates this year had a mean of 55.3 points.

d) A pharmaceutical company tests whether a drug lifts the headache relief rate from the 25% achieved by the placebo. They fail to reject the null hypothesis because the P-value is 0.465. Further testing shows that the drug actually relieves headaches in 38% of people.

12. For each of the following situations, state whether a Type I, a Type II, or neither error has been made.

a) A test of $H_0: \mu = 25$ vs. $H_A: \mu > 25$ rejects the null hypothesis. Later it is discovered that $\mu = 24.9$.

b) A test of $H_0: p = 0.8$ vs. $H_A: p < 0.8$ fails to reject the null hypothesis. Later it is discovered that $p = 0.9$.

c) A test of $H_0: p = 0.5$ vs. $H_A: p \neq 0.5$ rejects the null hypothesis. Later it is discovered that $p = 0.65$.

d) A test of $H_0: p = 0.7$ vs. $H_A: p < 0.7$ fails to reject the null hypothesis. Later is it discovered that $p = 0.6$.

SECTION 13.6

13. Most car engines need at least 87 octane to avoid "knocking" or "pinging," terms used to describe the pre-ignition that can happen when a fuel's octane is too low. An engineer is designing an experiment to raise the octane of an ethanol-based fuel. From previous studies, she thinks that with 8 experimental runs, she will have a power of 0.90 to detect a real increase of 3 points in the mean octane.

a) If the actual increase is only 1 point, will the power be increased or decreased?

b) If she wants the power to be the same, but she is interested in detecting an increase of only 1 point, what will she need to do?

14. A marketing analyst at an Internet book store is testing a new web design which she hopes will increase sales. She wants to randomly send n customers to the new site. She's hoping for an increase of 10% in sales from the new site. She calculates a power of 0.43 for that increase from a sample of 150 customers. Explain to her why she should consider a larger sample size.

CHAPTER EXERCISES

15. Alpha. A researcher developing scanners to search for hidden weapons at airports has concluded that a new device is significantly better than the current scanner. He made this decision based on a test using $\alpha = 0.05$. Would he have made the same decision at $\alpha = 0.10$? How about $\alpha = 0.01$? Explain.

16. Alpha, again. Analysts evaluating a new program to encourage customer retention in a test market find no evidence of an increased rate of retention in a test of 2000 customers. They based this conclusion on a test using $\alpha = 0.01$. Would they have made the same decision at $\alpha = 0.05$? How about $\alpha = 0.001$? Explain.

17. Measles. Health researchers at a large HMO base their cost predictions for measles on the belief that 98% of children have been vaccinated against measles. A random survey of medical records at many schools across the country found that, among more than 13,000 children, only

97.4% had been vaccinated. A statistician would reject the 98% hypothesis with a P-value of $P < 0.0001$.

a) Explain what the P-value means in this context.

b) The result is statistically significant, but is it important? Comment.

18. Computer skills. A new program may reduce the proportion of employees who fail a computer skills course. The company that developed this program supplied materials and teacher training for a large-scale test involving nearly 8500 employees in several different sites. Statistical analysis of the results showed that the percentage of employees who did not pass the course was reduced from 15.9% to 15.1%. The hypothesis that the program produced no improvement was rejected with a P-value of 0.023.

a) Explain what the P-value means in this context.

b) Even though this program has been shown to be significantly better statistically, why might you not recommend that your company adopt it?

19. Groceries. Yahoo surveyed 2400 U.S. men. Of the men, 1224 identified themselves as the primary grocery shopper in their household.

a) Estimate the percentage of all American males who identify themselves as the primary grocery shopper. Use a 98% confidence interval being sure to check the conditions.

b) A grocery store owner believed that only 45% of men are the primary grocery shopper for their family, and targets his advertising accordingly. He wishes to conduct a hypothesis test to see if the fraction is in fact higher than 45%. What does your confidence interval indicate? Explain.

c) What is the level of significance of this test? Explain.

20. Hard times. A random poll of 800 working men found that 9% had taken on a second job to help pay the bills. (www.careerbuilder.com)

a) Estimate the true percentage of men that are taking on second jobs by constructing a 95% confidence interval.

b) A pundit on a TV news show claimed that only 6% of working men had a second job. Use your confidence interval to test whether his claim is plausible given the poll data.

21. Convenient alpha. An enthusiastic junior executive has run a test of his new marketing program. He reports that it resulted in a "significant" increase in sales. A footnote on his report explains that he used an alpha level of 7.2% for his test. Presumably, he performed a hypothesis test against the null hypothesis of no change in sales.

a) If instead he had used an alpha level of 5%, is it more or less likely that he would have rejected his null hypothesis? Explain.

b) If he chose the alpha level 7.2% so that he could claim statistical significance, explain why this is not an ethical use of statistics.

22. Safety. The manufacturer of a new sleeping pill suspects that it may increase the risk of sleepwalking, which could be dangerous. A test of the drug fails to reject the null hypothesis of no increase in sleepwalking when tested at $\alpha = 0.01$.

a) If the test had been performed at $\alpha = 0.05$, would the test have been more or less likely to reject the null hypothesis of no increase in sleepwalking?

b) Which alpha level do you think the company should use? Why?

23. Sales increase. A software engineer at Neverware, a company that replaces computers in schools with terminals connected to a server, is testing a new server to see if mean download times are decreased with the new server. When he compares a random sample of 20 times to the previous standard he gets a t-statistic of -15.

a) Explain what the t-statistic means in this context.

b) Look up the 0.001 lower critical value for a t-statistic with 19 df and state your conclusion about the test.

c) Why did you probably not need to look up the critical value in part b to reach your conclusion?

24. Web finder. Zocdoc.com provides a service to find and make appointments with medical professionals across the United States. Suppose an analyst looking to see if a new web design had improved the percentage of people successfully making appointments found a z-score of 10.23.

a) Explain what the z-statistic means in this context.

b) Look up the 0.001 upper critical value for a z-statistic and state your conclusion about the test.

c) Why did you probably not need to look up the critical value in part b to reach your conclusion?

25. Measles revisited. The analyst in Exercise 17 finds a 98% confidence interval for the true proportion of vaccinated children to be (0.9707, 0.9773).

a) Explain why she can reject the null hypothesis that $p = 0.98$ vs. $p < 0.98$ at $\alpha = 0.01$.

b) Explain why the difference may or may not be important.

26. Computer skills again. The health care analyst in Exercise 18 finds a 90% confidence interval for the true proportion of employees who fail the course to be (14.46%, 15.74%).

a) Explain why she can reject the null hypothesis that $p = 0.159$ vs. $p < 0.159$ at $\alpha = 0.05$.

b) Explain why the difference may or may not be important.

c) Could you reject the hypothesis that $p = 0.157$? Explain.

27. Loans. Before lending someone money, banks must decide whether they believe the applicant will repay the loan. One strategy used is a point system. Loan officers assess information about the applicant, totaling points they award for the person's income level, credit history, current debt burden, and so on. The higher the point total, the more convinced the bank is that it's safe to make the loan. Any applicant with a lower point total than a certain cutoff score is denied a loan.

We can think of this decision as a hypothesis test. Since the bank makes its profit from the interest collected on repaid loans, their null hypothesis is that the applicant will repay the loan and therefore should get the money. Only if the person's score falls below the minimum cutoff will the bank reject the null and deny the loan. This system is reasonably reliable, but, of course, sometimes there are mistakes.

a) When a person defaults on a loan, which type of error did the bank make?

b) Which kind of error is it when the bank misses an opportunity to make a loan to someone who would have repaid it?

c) Suppose the bank decides to lower the cutoff score from 250 points to 200. Is that analogous to choosing a higher or lower value of α for a hypothesis test? Explain.

d) What impact does this change in the cutoff value have on the chance of each type of error?

28. Spam. Spam filters try to sort your e-mails, deciding which are real messages and which are unwanted. One method used is a point system. The filter reads each incoming e-mail and assigns points to the sender, the subject, key words in the message, and so on. The higher the point total, the more likely it is that the message is unwanted. The filter has a cutoff value for the point total; any message rated lower than that cutoff passes through to your inbox, and the rest, suspected to be spam, are diverted to the junk mailbox.

We can think of the filter's decision as a hypothesis test. The null hypothesis is that the e-mail is a real message and should go to your inbox. A higher point total provides evidence that the message may be spam; when there's sufficient evidence, the filter rejects the null, classifying the message as junk. This usually works pretty well, but, of course, sometimes the filter makes a mistake.

a) When the filter allows spam to slip through into your inbox, which kind of error is that?

b) Which kind of error is it when a real message gets classified as junk?

c) Some filters allow the user (that's you) to adjust the cutoff. Suppose your filter has a default cutoff of 50 points, but you reset it to 60. Is that analogous to choosing a higher or lower value of α for a hypothesis test? Explain.

d) What impact does this change in the cutoff value have on the chance of each type of error?

29. Second loan. Exercise 27 describes the loan score method a bank uses to decide which applicants it will lend money. Only if the total points awarded for various aspects of an applicant's financial condition fail to add up to a minimum cutoff score set by the bank will the loan be denied.

a) In this context, what is meant by the power of the test?
b) What could the bank do to increase the power?
c) What's the disadvantage of doing that?

30. More spam. Consider again the points-based spam filter described in Exercise 28. When the points assigned to various components of an e-mail exceed the cutoff value you've set, the filter rejects its null hypothesis (that the message is real) and diverts that e-mail to a junk mailbox.

a) In this context, what is meant by the power of the test?
b) What could you do to increase the filter's power?
c) What's the disadvantage of doing that?

31. Homeowners. According to the U.S. Census Bureau (www.census.gov/housing/hvs/files/currenthvspress.pdf), in 2017, 63.9% of American families owned their homes. Census data reveal that the ownership rate in one small city is even lower. The city council is debating a plan to offer tax breaks to first-time home buyers in order to encourage people to become homeowners. They decide to adopt the plan on a 2-year trial basis and use the data they collect to make a decision about continuing the tax breaks. Since this plan costs the city tax revenues, they will continue to use it only if there is strong evidence that the rate of home ownership is increasing.

a) In words, what will their hypotheses be?
b) What would a Type I error be?
c) What would a Type II error be?
d) For each type of error, tell who would be harmed.
e) What would the power of the test represent in this context?

32. Alzheimer's. Testing for Alzheimer's disease can be a long and expensive process, consisting of lengthy tests and medical diagnosis. A group of researchers (Solomon et al., 1998) devised a 7-minute test to serve as a quick screen for the disease for use in the general population of senior citizens. A patient who tested positive would then go through the more expensive battery of tests and medical diagnosis. The authors reported a false-positive rate of 4% and a false-negative rate of 8%.

a) Put this in the context of a hypothesis test. What are the null and alternative hypotheses?
b) What would a Type I error mean?
c) What would a Type II error mean?
d) Which is worse here, a Type I or Type II error? Explain.
e) What is the power of this test?

33. Testing cars. A clean air standard requires that vehicle exhaust emissions not exceed specified limits for various pollutants. Many states require that cars be tested annually to be sure they meet these standards. Suppose state regulators double-check a random sample of cars that a suspect repair shop has certified as okay. They will revoke the shop's license if they find significant evidence that the shop is certifying vehicles that do not meet standards.

a) In this context, what is a Type I error?
b) In this context, what is a Type II error?
c) Which type of error would the shop's owner consider more serious?
d) Which type of error might environmentalists consider more serious?

34. Quality control. Production managers on an assembly line must monitor the output to be sure that the level of defective products remains small. They periodically inspect a random sample of the items produced. If they find a significant increase in the proportion of items that must be rejected, they will halt the assembly process until the problem can be identified and repaired.

a) In this context, what is a Type I error?
b) In this context, what is a Type II error?
c) Which type of error would the factory owner consider more serious?
d) Which type of error might customers consider more serious?

35. Cars, again. As in Exercise 33, state regulators are checking up on repair shops to see if they are certifying vehicles that do not meet pollution standards.

a) In this context, what is meant by the power of the test the regulators are conducting?
b) Will the power be greater if they test 20 or 40 cars? Why?
c) Will the power be greater if they use a 5% or a 10% level of significance? Why?
d) Will the power be greater if the repair shop's inspectors are only a little out of compliance or a lot? Why?

36. Production. Consider again the task of the quality control inspectors in Exercise 34.

a) In this context, what is meant by the power of the test the inspectors conduct?
b) They are currently testing 5 items each hour. Someone has proposed that they test 10 instead. What are the advantages and disadvantages of such a change?
c) Their test currently uses a 5% level of significance. What are the advantages and disadvantages of changing to an alpha level of 1%?
d) Suppose that, as a day passes, one of the machines on the assembly line produces more and more items that are defective. How will this affect the power of the test?

37. Equal opportunity? A company is sued for job discrimination because only 19% of the newly hired candidates were minorities when 27% of all applicants were minorities. Is this strong evidence that the company's hiring practices are discriminatory?

a) Is this a one-tailed or a two-tailed test? Why?
b) In this context, what would a Type I error be?
c) In this context, what would a Type II error be?
d) In this context, what is meant by the power of the test?
e) If the hypothesis is tested at the 5% level of significance instead of 1%, how will this affect the power of the test?
f) The lawsuit is based on the hiring of 37 employees. Is the power of the test higher than, lower than, or the same as it would be if it were based on 87 hires?

38. Stop signs. Highway safety engineers test new road signs, hoping that increased reflectivity will make them more visible to drivers. Volunteers drive through a test course with several of the new- and old-style signs and rate which kind shows up the best.

a) Is this a one-tailed or a two-tailed test? Why?
b) In this context, what would a Type I error be?
c) In this context, what would a Type II error be?
d) In this context, what is meant by the power of the test?
e) If the hypothesis is tested at the 1% level of significance instead of 5%, how will this affect the power of the test?
f) The engineers hoped to base their decision on the reactions of 50 drivers, but time and budget constraints may force them to cut back to 20. How would this affect the power of the test? Explain.

39. Software for learning. A statistics professor has observed that for several years students score an average of 105 points out of 150 on the semester exam. A salesman suggests that he try a statistics software package that gets students more involved with computers, predicting that it will increase students' scores. The software is expensive, and the salesman offers to let the professor use it for a semester to see if the scores on the final exam increase significantly. The professor will have to pay for the software only if he chooses to continue using it.

a) Is this a one-tailed or two-tailed test? Explain.
b) Write the null and alternative hypotheses.
c) In this context, explain what would happen if the professor makes a Type I error.
d) In this context, explain what would happen if the professor makes a Type II error.
e) What is meant by the power of this test?

40. Software, part II. 203 students signed up for the Stats course in Exercise 39. They used the software suggested by the salesman, and scored an average of 108 points on the final with a standard deviation of 8.7 points.

a) Should the professor spend the money for this software? Support your recommendation with an appropriate test.
b) Does this improvement seem to be practically significant?

41. Collections. Credit card companies lose money on cardholders who fail to pay their minimum payments. They use a variety of methods to encourage their delinquent cardholders to pay their credit card balances, such as letters, phone calls, and eventually the hiring of a collection agency. To justify the cost of using the collection agency, the agency must collect an average of at least $200 per customer. After a trial period during which the agency attempted to collect from a random sample of 100 delinquent cardholders, the 90% confidence interval on the mean collected amount was reported as ($190.25, $250.75). Given this, what recommendation(s) would you make to the credit card company about using the collection agency?

42. Free gift. A philanthropic organization sends out "free gifts" to people on their mailing list in the hope that the receiver will respond by sending back a donation. Typical gifts are mailing labels, greeting cards, or post cards. They want to test out a new gift that costs $0.50 per item to produce and mail. They mail it to a "small" sample of 2000 customers and find a 90% confidence interval of the mean donation to be ($0.489, $0.879). As a consultant, what recommendation(s) would you make to the organization about using this gift?

43. TV safety. The manufacturer of a metal stand for home TV sets must be sure that its product will not fail under the weight of the TV. Since some larger sets weigh nearly 300 pounds, the company's safety inspectors have set a standard of ensuring that the stands can support an average of over 500 pounds. Their inspectors regularly subject a random sample of the stands to increasing weight until they fail. They test the hypothesis $H_0: \mu = 500$ against $H_A: \mu > 500$, using the level of significance $\alpha = 0.01$. If the sample of stands fails to pass this safety test, the inspectors will not certify the product for sale to the general public.

a) Is this an upper-tail or lower-tail test? In the context of the problem, why do you think this is important?
b) Explain what will happen if the inspectors commit a Type I error.
c) Explain what will happen if the inspectors commit a Type II error.

44. Catheters. During an angiogram, heart problems can be examined via a small tube (a catheter) threaded into the heart from a vein in the patient's leg. It's important that the company that manufactures the catheter maintain a diameter of 2.00 mm. (The standard deviation is quite small.)

Each day, quality control personnel make several measurements to test $H_0: \mu = 2.00$ against $H_A: \mu \neq 2.00$ at a significance level of $\alpha = 0.05$. If they discover a problem, they will stop the manufacturing process until it is corrected.

a) Is this a one-sided or two-sided test? In the context of the problem, why do you think this is important?
b) Explain in this context what happens if the quality control people commit a Type I error.
c) Explain in this context what happens if the quality control people commit a Type II error.

45. TV safety, revisited. The manufacturer of the metal TV stands in Exercise 43 is thinking of revising its safety test.

a) If the company's lawyers are worried about being sued for selling an unsafe product, should they increase or decrease the value of α? Explain.
b) In this context, what is meant by the power of the test?
c) If the company wants to increase the power of the test, what options does it have? Explain the advantages and disadvantages of each option.

46. Catheters, again. The catheter company in Exercise 44 is reviewing its testing procedure.

a) Suppose the significance level is changed to $\alpha = 0.01$. Will the probability of a Type II error increase, decrease, or remain the same?
b) What is meant by the power of the test the company conducts?
c) Suppose the manufacturing process is slipping out of proper adjustment. As the actual mean diameter of the catheters produced gets farther and farther above the desired 2.00 mm, will the power of the quality control test increase, decrease, or remain the same?
d) What could they do to improve the power of the test?

47. Two coins. In a drawer are two coins. They look the same, but one coin produces heads 90% of the time when spun while the other one produces heads only 30% of the time. You select one of the coins. You are allowed to spin it *once* and then must decide whether the coin is the 90%- or the 30%-head coin. Your null hypothesis is that your coin produces 90% heads.

a) What is the alternative hypothesis?
b) Given that the outcome of your spin is tails, what would you decide? What if it were heads?
c) How large is α in this case?
d) How large is the power of this test? (*Hint:* How many possibilities are in the alternative hypothesis?)
e) How could you lower the probability of a Type I error and increase the power of the test at the same time?

48. Faulty or not? You are in charge of shipping computers to customers. You learn that a faulty RAM chip was

put into some of the machines. There's a simple test you can perform, but it's not perfect. All but 4% of the time, a good chip passes the test, but unfortunately, 35% of the bad chips pass the test, too. You have to decide on the basis of one test whether the chip is good or bad. Make this a hypothesis test.

a) What are the null and alternative hypotheses?
b) Given that a computer fails the test, what would you decide? What if it passes the test?
c) How large is α for this test?
d) What is the power of this test? (*Hint:* How many possibilities are in the alternative hypothesis?)

49. Collections, part 2. The owner of the collection agency in Exercise 41 is quite certain that they can collect more than $200 per customer on average. He urges that the credit card company run a larger trial. Do you think a larger trial might help the company make a better decision? Explain.

50. Free gift, part 2. The philanthropic organization of Exercise 42 decided to go ahead with the new gift. In mailings to 98,000 prospects, the new mailing yielded an average of $0.78. If they had decided based on their initial trial *not* to use this gift, what kind of error would they have made? What aspects of their initial trial might have suggested to you (as their consultant) that a larger trial would be worthwhile?

51. Pricing for competitiveness. SLIX wax is developing a new high performance fluorocarbon wax for cross country ski racing designed to be used under a wide variety of conditions. In order to justify the price marketing wants, the wax needs to be very fast. Specifically, the mean time to finish their standard test course should be less than 55 seconds for the former Olympic champion who is now their consultant. To test it, the consultant will ski the course 8 times.

a) The champion's times are 56.3, 65.9, 50.5, 52.4, 46.5, 57.8, 52.2, and 43.2 seconds to complete the test course. Should they market the wax? Explain.
b) Suppose they decide not to market the wax after the test, but it turns out that the wax really does lower the champion's average time to less than 55 seconds. What kind of error have they made? Explain the impact to the company of such an error.

52. Popcorn. Pop's Popcorn, Inc., needs to determine the optimum power and time settings for their new licorice-flavored microwave popcorn. They want to find a combination of power and time that delivers high-quality popcorn with less than 10% of the kernels left unpopped, on average—a value that their market research says is demanded by their customers. Their research department experiments with several settings and determines that power 9 at 4 minutes is optimum. Their tests confirm that this setting meets the less than 10% requirement. They change the instructions on the box and promote a new money back guarantee of less than 10% unpopped kernels.

a) If, in fact, the setting results in more than 10% kernels unpopped, what kind of error have they made? What will the consequence be for the company?

b) To reduce the risk of making an error, the president (Pop himself) tells them to test 8 more bags of popcorn (selected at random) at the specified setting. They find the following percentage of unpopped kernels: 7, 13.2, 10, 6, 7.8, 2.8, 2.2, 5.2. Does this provide evidence that the setting meets their goal of less than than 10% unpopped? Explain.

JUST CHECKING ANSWERS

1 Yes. At $\alpha = 0.05$, you can reject the null hypothesis because 0.30 is not contained in the 90% confidence interval—it's evidence that sending the DVDs is more effective than sending letters.

2 The confidence interval is from 35% to 45%. So there is strong evidence that the new success rate is higher than 30% but probably not higher than 45%. However, the DVD strategy is more expensive and may not be worth it. The bank should consider whether the DVD strategy is justified even if the success rate is only 35%.

3 The confidence interval suggests that at 95% confidence, even in the worst case, the arrangement will generate a mean profit of at least $37.95 − $35.00 = $2.95 per customer. On the other hand, it may generate a profit as high as $55.05 − $35.00 = $20.05 per customer.

4 A Type I error would mean deciding that the DVD success rate is higher than 30%, when it isn't. The bank would adopt a more expensive method for collecting payments that's no better than its original, less expensive strategy.

5 A Type II error would mean deciding that there's not enough evidence to say the DVD strategy works when in fact it does. The bank would fail to discover an effective method for increasing revenue from delinquent accounts.

6 Higher; the larger the effect size, the greater the power. It's easier to detect an improvement to a 60% success rate than to a 32% rate.

7 No error has been made. The confidence interval from the test market suggested that the mean revenue was above the $35 cost per customer, and in fact that's what happened.

Comparing Two Means

Visa Global Organization

Today, more than one billion people and 24 million merchants use the Visa card in 170 countries worldwide. But back in the early 1950s when the idea of cashless transactions first took hold, only Diners Club and some retailers, notably oil companies, issued charge cards. The vast majority of purchases were made by cash or personal check. Bank of America pioneered its BankAmericard program in Fresno, California, in 1958, and American Express issued the first plastic card in 1959. The idea of a credit "card" really gained momentum a decade later when a group of banks formed a joint venture to create a centralized system of payment. National BankAmericard, Inc. (NBI) took ownership of the credit card system in 1970 and for simplicity and marketability changed its name to Visa in 1976. (The name Visa is pronounced nearly the same way in every language.) That year, Visa processed 679,000 transactions—a volume that is processed on average every four minutes today. As technology changed, so did the credit card industry. By 1986, cardholders were able to use their Visa cards to get cash from ATMs. But card fraud continues to be a concern. Fraud losses totaled $16.31B for all card issuers in the United States alone in 2014. With the transition to EMV (chip) technology, companies may be able to control fraud more effectively.

Now a global organization, Visa is divided into several regional entities including: Visa Asia Pacific, Visa Canada, Visa Europe, and Visa USA. In the fiscal year ending September 2017, Visa's global network processed more than 160 billion transactions for a total volume of 10.2 trillion.[1]

The credit card business can be very profitable. According to the Federal Reserve Bank,[2] credit card debt hit $1 trillion for the first time in September 2017, for an average household debt of $7454. But, since many households have no debt, that average is misleading. Among households that carry credit card debt, the average debt was more than $16,000 in 2017. Not surprisingly, the credit card business is also intensely competitive. Rival banks and lending agencies are constantly trying to create new products and offers to win new customers, keep current customers, and provide incentives for current customers to charge more on their cards.

Are some credit card promotions more effective than others? For example, do customers spend more using their credit card if they know they will be given "double miles" or "double coupons" toward flights, hotel stays, or store purchases? To answer questions such as this, credit card issuers often perform experiments on a sample of customers, making some of them an *offer* of an incentive, while other customers receive no offer. Promotions cost the company money, so the company needs to estimate the size of any increased revenue to judge whether it is sufficient to cover their expenses. By comparing the performance of the two offers on the sample, they can decide whether the new offer would provide enough potential profit if they were to "roll it out" and offer it to their entire customer base.

Experiments that compare two groups are common throughout both science and industry. Other applications include comparing the effects of a new drug with the traditional therapy, the fuel efficiency of two car engine designs, or the sales of new products on two different customer segments. Usually the experiment is carried out on a subset of the population, often a much smaller subset. Using statistics, we can make statements about whether the means of the two groups differ in the population at large, and how large that difference might be.

14.1 Comparing Two Means

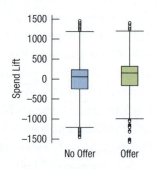

FIGURE 14.1 Side-by-side boxplots show a small increase in spending for the group that received the promotion.

The natural display for comparing the distributions of two groups is side-by-side boxplots (see Figure 14.1). For the credit card promotion, the company judges results of an A/B test by comparing the *mean* spend lift (the change in spending from before receiving the promotion to after receiving it) for the two samples. If the difference in spend lift between the group that received the promotion and the group that didn't is high enough, this will be viewed as evidence that the promotion worked. Looking at the two boxplots, it's not obvious that there's much of a difference. Can we conclude that the slight increase seen for those who received the promotion is more than just random fluctuation? We'll need statistical inference.

For two groups, the statistic of interest is the difference in the observed means of the offer and no offer groups: $\bar{y}_{Offer} - \bar{y}_{No\ Offer}$. We've offered the promotion to a random sample of cardholders and used another sample of cardholders, who got no special offer, as a control group. We know what happened in our samples, but what we'd really like to know is the difference of the means in the population at large: $\mu_{Offer} - \mu_{No\ Offer}$.

[1]Sources: Visa International Service Association, www.corporate.visa.com; s1.q4cdn.com/050606653/files/doc_financials/2017/New/Visa-Inc.-2017-Operational-Performance-Data.pdf.

[2]www.federalreserve.gov/releases/g19/current/.

We compare two means in much the same way as we compared a single mean to a hypothesized value. But now both means are statistics, each with its own standard deviation, and the population model parameter of interest is the *difference* between the means. In our example, it's the true difference between the mean spend lift for customers offered the promotion and for customers for whom no offer was made. We estimate the difference with $\bar{y}_{Offer} - \bar{y}_{No\ Offer}$. How can we tell if a difference we observe in the sample means indicates a real difference in the underlying population means? We'll need to know the sampling distribution model and standard deviation of the difference. Once we know those, we can build a confidence interval and test a hypothesis just as we did for a single mean.

We have data on 500 randomly selected customers who were offered the promotion and another randomly selected 500 who were not. It's easy to find the mean and standard deviation of the spend lift for each of these groups. From these, we can find the standard deviation of each mean, but that's not what we want. We need the standard deviation of the *difference* in the means. For that, we can use a simple rule: *If the sample means come from independent samples, the variance of their sum or difference is the sum of their variances.*

> ### Variances Add for Sums *and* Differences
> At first, it may seem that this can't be true for differences as well as for sums. Here's some intuition about why variation increases even when we subtract two random quantities. Grab a full box of cereal. The label claims that it contains 16 ounces of cereal. We know that's not exact. There's a random quantity of cereal in the box with a mean (presumably) of 16 ounces and some variation from box to box. Now pour a 2-ounce serving of cereal into a bowl. Of course, your serving isn't exactly 2 ounces. There's some variation there, too. How much cereal would you guess was left in the box? Can you guess as accurately as you could for the full box? *After* you pour your bowl, the amount of cereal in the box is still a random quantity (with a smaller mean than before), but you've made it *more variable* because of the uncertainty in the amount you poured. Notice that we don't add the *standard deviations* of these two random quantities. It's the *variance* of the amount of cereal left in the box that's the sum of the two variances.

As long as the two groups are independent, we find the standard deviation of the *difference* between the two sample means by adding their variances and then taking the square root:

$$SD(\bar{y}_1 - \bar{y}_2) = \sqrt{Var(\bar{y}_1) + Var(\bar{y}_2)}$$

$$= \sqrt{\left(\frac{\sigma_1}{\sqrt{n_1}}\right)^2 + \left(\frac{\sigma_2}{\sqrt{n_2}}\right)^2}$$

$$= \sqrt{\frac{\sigma_1^2}{n_1} + \frac{\sigma_2^2}{n_2}}$$

Of course, usually we don't know the true standard deviations of the two groups, σ_1 and σ_2, so we substitute the estimates, s_1 and s_2, and find a *standard error*:

$$SE(\bar{y}_1 - \bar{y}_2) = \sqrt{\frac{s_1^2}{n_1} + \frac{s_2^2}{n_2}}.$$

Just as we did for one mean, we'll use the standard error to judge how big the difference really is. You shouldn't be surprised that, just as for a single mean, the difference in the means divided by the standard error of that difference has a sampling model that follows a Student's *t*-distribution.

To do inference, we'll need the degrees of freedom for the Student's *t*-model. The formula is straightforward but doesn't help our understanding much, so we

An Easier Rule?

The formula for the degrees of freedom of the sampling distribution of the difference between two means is hard to remember. So some books teach an easier rule: The number of degrees of freedom is always at *least* the smaller of $n_1 - 1$ and $n_2 - 1$ and at most $n_1 + n_2 - 2$. The problem is that if you need to use this rule, you'll have to be conservative and use the lower value. And *that* approximation can be a poor choice because it can give less than *half* the degrees of freedom you're entitled to from the correct formula. So, we don't recommend using it unless you have lots of data.

leave it to the computer or calculator. (If you are curious and really want to see the formula, look in the footnote.[3])

A Sampling Distribution for the Difference Between Two Means

We denote the difference in the means of two groups by the Greek letter delta:

$$\mu_1 - \mu_2 = \Delta$$

When the conditions are met (see Section 14.3), the standardized sample difference between the means of two independent groups,

$$t = \frac{(\bar{y}_1 - \bar{y}_2) - \Delta}{SE(\bar{y}_1 - \bar{y}_2)},$$

can be modeled by a Student's t-model with a number of degrees of freedom found with a special formula. We estimate the standard error with

$$SE(\bar{y}_1 - \bar{y}_2) = \sqrt{\frac{s_1^2}{n_1} + \frac{s_2^2}{n_2}}.$$

IN PRACTICE 14.1 Sampling distribution of the difference of two means

The owner of a large car dealership wants to understand the negotiation process for buying a new car. Cars are given a "sticker price," but a potential buyer may negotiate a better price. He wonders if there is a difference in how men and women negotiate and who, if either, obtains the larger discount.

OWNER I want to know the mean difference of the discounts received by men and women. What is its standard error? If there is no difference between them, does this seem like an unusually large value?

CONSULTANT I have drawn a random sample of 100 customers from the last six months' sales and find that 54 were men and 46 were women. On average the 54 men received an average discount of $962.96 with a standard deviation of $458.95; the 46 women received an average discount of $1262.61 with a standard deviation of $399.70. The mean difference is $1262.61 - $962.96 = $299.65. The women received, on average, a discount that was larger by $299.65. The standard error is

$$SE(\bar{y}_{Women} - \bar{y}_{Men}) = \sqrt{\frac{s_{Women}^2}{n_{Women}} + \frac{s_{Men}^2}{n_{Men}}} = \sqrt{\frac{(399.70)^2}{46} + \frac{(458.95)^2}{54}} = \$85.87$$

So, the difference is $299.65/85.87 = 3.49 standard errors away from 0. That sounds like a reasonably large number of standard errors for a Student's t-statistic with 97.94 degrees of freedom (using the df formula).

---

[3]The result is due to Satterthwaite and Welch.

Satterthwaite, F. E. (1946). "An Approximate Distribution of Estimates of Variance Components," *Biometrics Bulletin* 2: 110–114.

Welch, B. L. (1947). "The Generalization of Student's Problem When Several Different Population Variances Are Involved," *Biometrika* 34: 28–35.

$$df = \frac{\left(\frac{s_1^2}{n_1} + \frac{s_2^2}{n_2}\right)^2}{\frac{1}{n_1 - 1}\left(\frac{s_1^2}{n_1}\right)^2 + \frac{1}{n_2 - 1}\left(\frac{s_2^2}{n_2}\right)^2}$$

This approximation formula usually doesn't even give a whole number. If you are using a table, you'll need a whole number, so round down to be safe. If you are using technology, the approximation formulas that computers and calculators use for the Student's t-distribution can deal with fractional degrees of freedom.

14.2   The Two-Sample *t*-Test

Now we've got everything we need to construct the hypothesis test, and you already know how to do it. It's the same idea we used when testing one mean against a hypothesized value. Here, we start by hypothesizing a value for the true difference of the means. We'll call that hypothesized difference Δ_0. (It's so common for that hypothesized difference to be zero that we often just assume $\Delta_0 = 0$.) We then divide the difference in the means from our samples by its standard error and use that ratio to find a P-value from a Student's *t*-model. The test is called the **two-sample *t*-test**.

> **Two-Sample *t*-Test**
>
> When the appropriate assumptions and conditions are met, we test the hypothesis:
>
> $$H_0: \mu_1 - \mu_2 = \Delta_0$$
>
> where the hypothesized difference Δ_0 is almost always 0. We use the statistic:
>
> $$t = \frac{(\bar{y}_1 - \bar{y}_2) - \Delta_0}{SE(\bar{y}_1 - \bar{y}_2)}.$$
>
> The standard error of $\bar{y}_1 - \bar{y}_2$ is:
>
> $$SE(\bar{y}_1 - \bar{y}_2) = \sqrt{\frac{s_1^2}{n_1} + \frac{s_2^2}{n_2}}.$$
>
> When the null hypothesis is true, the statistic can be closely modeled by a Student's *t*-distribution with a number of degrees of freedom given by a special formula. We use that model to compare our *t*-ratio with a critical value for *t* or to obtain a P-value.

The Two-Sample *t*-Methods

Two-sample *t*-methods assume that the two groups are independent. This is a crucial assumption. If it's not met, it is not safe to use these methods. One common way for groups to fail independence is when each observation in one group is related to one (and only one) observation in the other group—for example, if we test the *same* subjects before and after an event, or if we measure a variable on both husbands and wives. In that case, the observations are said to be matched or **paired** and you'll need to use the paired *t*-methods discussed in Section 14.7.

Sometimes you may see the two-sample *t*-methods referred to as the two **independent** samples *t*-methods for emphasis. In this text, however, when we say two-sample, we'll always assume that the groups are independent.

> ### IN PRACTICE 14.2   Gaining insight from the *t*-test for the difference of two means
>
> **OWNER**   OK, I can see (on page 450) that there is a difference between the average discount obtained by men and by women, but might that just be due to the random sample of car buyers you chose? How can I be confident that the difference is real so I can base sound business decisions on it?
>
> **CONSULTANT**   What you are asking for is a hypothesis test. We set that up by assuming (or pretending) that the difference is zero and then testing whether the data contradict that assumption. The calculations look like this:
>
> The null hypothesis is: $H_0: \mu_{Women} - \mu_{Men} = 0$ vs.
>
> $$H_A: \mu_{Women} - \mu_{Men} \neq 0.$$
>
> The difference in the sample means, $\bar{y}_{Women} - \bar{y}_{Men}$, is $299.65 with a standard error of 85.87. The *t*-statistic is that difference divided by the standard error:
>
> $t = \dfrac{\bar{y}_{Women} - \bar{y}_{Men}}{SE(\bar{y}_{Women} - \bar{y}_{Men})} = \dfrac{299.65}{85.87} = 3.49$. The approximation formula gives 97.94
>
> degrees of freedom. The P-value (from technology) for $t = 3.49$ with 97.94 df is 0.00073. That P-value is so small that we can reject the null hypothesis. There is strong evidence to suggest that the difference in mean discount received by men and women is not 0.

14.3   Assumptions and Conditions

Before we can perform a two-sample *t*-test, we have to check the assumptions and conditions.

Independence Assumption

We can't *assume* that the data, taken as one big group, come from a homogeneous population because that would mean assuming the means were equal—and we're trying to test that. But we can assume that the data in *each group* must be drawn independently and at random from each group's own homogeneous population separately, or generated by a randomized comparative experiment. We should think about whether the Independence Assumption is reasonable. We can also check two conditions:

> **Randomization Condition:** Data collected with suitable randomization are likely to be independent. For surveys, are the data a representative random sample? For experiments, was the experiment randomized?

> **10% Condition:** We usually check this condition for differences of means only if we have a very small population or an extremely large sample. We needn't worry about it at all for randomized experiments.

Normal Population Assumption

With Student's *t*-models, we need the assumption that the underlying populations are *each* Normally distributed. So we check one condition.

> **Nearly Normal Condition:** We must check Normality for *both* groups; a violation by either one violates the condition. As we saw for single sample means, the Normality Assumption matters most when sample sizes are small. When either group is small ($n < 15$), you should not use these methods if the histogram or Normal probability plot shows skewness or outliers. For *n*'s closer to 40, a mildly skewed histogram is OK, but you should remark on any outliers you find and not work with severely skewed data. When both groups are bigger than that, the Central Limit Theorem starts to work, so the Nearly Normal Condition for the data matters less. Even in large samples, however, you should still be on the lookout for outliers, extreme skewness, and multiple modes.

Independent Groups Assumption

To use the two-sample *t*-methods, the two groups we are comparing must be independent of each other. In fact, the test is sometimes called the two *independent samples t*-test. No statistical test can verify that the groups are independent. You have to think about how the data were collected. The assumption would be violated, for example, if one group were comprised of husbands and the other group, their wives. Similarly, if we compared subjects' performances before some treatment with their performances afterward, we'd expect a relationship of each "before" measurement with its corresponding "after" measurement. When the observational units in the two groups are related or matched, *the two-sample methods of this section can't be applied.* Instead, we need the methods of Section 14.7.

JUST CHECKING

Many office "coffee stations" collect voluntary payments for the food consumed. Researchers at the University of Newcastle upon Tyne performed an experiment to see whether the image of eyes watching would change employee behavior.[4] Each week on the cupboard behind the "honesty box," they alternated pictures of eyes looking at the viewer with pictures of flowers. They measured the consumption of milk to approximate the amount of food consumed and recorded the contributions (in £) each week per liter of milk. The table summarizes their results.

	Eyes	Flowers
n (# weeks)	5	5
$\bar{y}$	0.417 £/liter	0.151 £/liter
s	0.1811	0.067

1 What null hypothesis were the researchers testing?

2 Check the assumptions and conditions needed to test whether there really is a difference in behavior due to the difference in pictures.

3 What alternative hypothesis would you test?

4 The P-value of the test was less than 0.05. State a brief conclusion.

IN PRACTICE 14.3 Checking assumptions and conditions for a two-sample *t*-test

OWNER Do you really expect me to believe your conclusion that the mean discounts negotiated by men and by women are not the same (on p. 451)? I think it might be due to anomalies in your sample data.

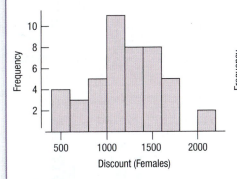

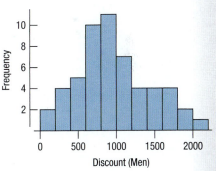

CONSULTANT I drew the samples at random, so the Randomization Condition is satisfied. There is no reason to think that the men's and women's responses are related (as they might be if they were husband and wife pairs) so the Independent Group Assumption is plausible. Because both groups have more than 40 observations, it is OK that the distributions of the discounts are mildly skewed. There are no obvious outliers (there is a small gap in the women's distribution, but the observations are not far from the center), so all the assumptions and conditions seem to be satisfied. I have no real concerns about the conclusion that the mean difference is not 0. I recommend that you can safely base business decisions on this conclusion.

---

[4]Melissa Bateson, Daniel Nettle, and Gilbert Roberts, "Cues of Being Watched Enhance Cooperation in a Real-World Setting," *Biol. Lett.* Doi:10.1098/rsbl.2006.0509.

GUIDED EXAMPLE Credit Card Promotions and Spending

Our preliminary market research has suggested that a new incentive may increase customer spending. However, before we invest in this promotion on the entire population of cardholders, let's test a hypothesis on a sample. To judge whether the incentive works, we will examine the change in spending (called the *spend lift*) over a six-month period. We will see whether the *spend lift* for the group that received the offer was greater than the *spend lift* for the group that received no offer. If we observe differences, how can we decide whether these differences are important (or real) enough to justify our costs?

PLAN **Define** and state what we want to know. Identify the *parameter* we wish to estimate. Here our parameter is the difference in the means, not the individual group means. Identify the *population(s)* about which we wish to make statements. Identify the variables and context.	We want to know if cardholders who are offered a promotion spend more on their credit card. We have the spend lift (in $) for a random sample of 500 cardholders who were offered the promotion and for a random sample of 500 customers who were not. H_0: The mean spend lift for the group who received the offer is the same as for the group who did not: H_0: $\mu_{Offer} - \mu_{No\ Offer} = 0$ H_A: The mean spend lift for the group who received the offer is higher: H_A: $\mu_{Offer} - \mu_{No\ Offer} > 0$

DO **Display** the data and check the assumptions and conditions. Make a graph to compare the two groups and check the distribution of each group. For completeness, we should report any outliers. If any outliers are extreme enough, we should consider performing the test both with and without the outliers and reporting the difference.	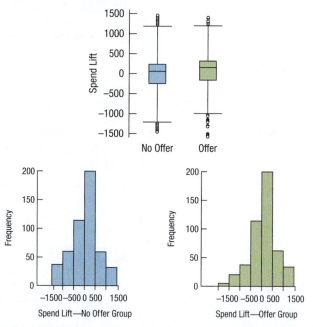 The boxplots and histograms show the distribution of both groups. It looks like the distribution for each group is unimodal and fairly symmetric. The boxplots indicate several outliers in each group, but we have no reason to delete them, and their impact is minimal.

Model Check the assumptions and conditions.

✔ **Independence Assumption.** We have no reason to believe that the spending behavior of one customer would influence the spending behavior of another customer in the same group. The data report the "spend lift" for each customer for the same time period.

✔ **Randomization Condition.** The customers who were offered the promotion were selected at random.

✔ **Nearly Normal Condition.** The samples are large, so we are not overly concerned with this condition, and the boxplots and histograms show unimodal, symmetric distributions for both groups.

✔ **Independent Groups Assumption.** Customers were assigned to groups at random. There's no reason to think that those in one group can affect the spending behavior of those in the other group.

Under these conditions, it's appropriate to use a Student's t-model.

State the sampling distribution model for the statistic. Here the degrees of freedom will come from the approximation formula in footnote 3.

Specify your method.

Mechanics List the summary statistics. Be sure to include the units along with the statistics. Use meaningful subscripts to identify the groups.

We will use a two-sample t-test.

We know $n_{No\ Offer} = 500$ and $n_{Offer} = 500$.
From technology, we find:

$$\bar{y}_{No\ Offer} = \$7.69 \qquad \bar{y}_{Offer} = \$127.61$$
$$s_{No\ Offer} = \$611.62 \quad s_{Offer} = \$566.05$$

The observed difference in the two means is:

$$\bar{y}_{Offer} - \bar{y}_{No\ Offer} = \$127.61 - \$7.69 = \$119.92$$

The groups are independent, so:

Use the sample standard deviations to find the standard error of the sampling distribution.

$$SE(\bar{y}_{Offer} - \bar{y}_{No\ Offer}) = \sqrt{\frac{(566.05)^2}{500} + \frac{(611.62)^2}{500}}$$
$$= \$37.27$$

The observed t-value is:

$$t = 119.92/37.27 = 3.218$$

with 992.0 df (from technology).

The best alternative is to let the computer use the approximation formula for the degrees of freedom and find the P-value.

(To use critical values, we could find that the one-sided 0.01 critical value for a t with 992.0 df is $t^* = 2.33$.)

Our observed t-value is larger than this, so we could reject the null hypothesis at the 0.01 level.)

Using software to obtain the P-value, we get:

```
Promotional Group    N      Mean      StDev
        No          500      7.69     611.62
        Yes         500    127.61     566.05

Difference = mu(1) − mu(0)
Estimate for difference: 119.9231
t = 3.2178, df = 992.007
One-sided P-value = 0.0006669
```

(continued)

MEMO

Re: Credit card promotion

Our analysis of the credit card promotion experiment found that customers offered the promotion spent more than those not offered the promotion. The difference was statistically significant, with a P-value < 0.001. So we conclude that this promotion will increase spending. The difference in spend lift averaged $119.92, but our analyses so far have not determined how much income this will generate for the company and thus whether the estimated increase in spending is worth the cost of the offer.

14.4   A Confidence Interval for the Difference Between Two Means

We rejected the null hypothesis that customers who were offered a promotion would spend the same amount, on average, as customers who had not been offered the promotion. Because the company took a random sample of customers for each group, and our P-value was convincingly small, we concluded that the difference in mean spending between the two groups is not zero for the population. So, should the company offer the promotion to all customers?

A hypothesis test really says nothing about the size of the difference. All it says is that the observed difference is large enough that we can be confident that the real (population) difference isn't zero. That's what the term "statistically significant" means. It doesn't say that the difference is important, financially significant, or interesting. Rejecting a null hypothesis simply says that a value as extreme as the observed statistic is unlikely to have been observed if the null hypothesis were true. That leaves only two alternative conclusions. Either the sample we used was extraordinarily unusual (and we've already checked that there were no outliers and the distribution was reasonable) or the null hypothesis was false. Statisticians acknowledge that rare events do happen (rarely), but we choose to reject the null hypothesis instead of believing that a rare event happened to us this time.

So, what recommendations can we make to the company? Almost every business decision depends on looking at a range of likely scenarios—precisely the kind of information a confidence interval gives. We construct a confidence interval for the difference in means in the usual way, starting with our observed statistic, in this case $(\bar{y}_1 - \bar{y}_2)$. We then add and subtract a multiple of the standard error, $SE(\bar{y}_1 - \bar{y}_2)$, where the multiple is based on the Student's t-distribution with the same df formula we saw before.

The critical value t^*_{df} depends on the particular confidence level, and on the number of degrees of freedom.

> **Confidence Interval for the Difference Between the Means of Two Independent Groups**
>
> When the conditions are met, we are ready to find a **two-sample t-interval** for the difference between the means of two independent groups, $\mu_1 - \mu_2$. The confidence interval is:
>
> $$(\bar{y}_1 - \bar{y}_2) \pm t^*_{df} \times SE(\bar{y}_1 - \bar{y}_2),$$
>
> where the standard error of the difference of the means is:
>
> $$SE(\bar{y}_1 - \bar{y}_2) = \sqrt{\frac{s_1^2}{n_1} + \frac{s_2^2}{n_2}},$$
>
> and the degrees of freedom is found by the special formula (see p. 450).

> **IN PRACTICE 14.4   A confidence interval for the difference between the means of two independent groups**
>
> **OWNER**   OK, I'm convinced that there is a difference between the discounts women get and those that men get. But is that difference costing me money? Is it large enough that I should change how I train my sales force?
>
> **CONSULTANT**   I can't tell you exactly how big the difference is, but I can give you an interval that is likely to include the correct value. I hope that's good enough for your decision.

We've seen that the difference from our sample is $299.65 with a standard error of $85.87 and that the *t*-test we performed had 97.94 degrees of freedom. The 95% critical value for a *t* with 97.94 degrees of freedom is 1.984. Using these values, I can construct a 95% confidence interval for the true difference in the means of the groups:

$$\bar{y}_{Women} - \bar{y}_{Men} \pm t^*_{97.94} SE(\bar{y}_{Women} - \bar{y}_{Men}) = 299.65 \pm 1.984 \times 85.87$$
$$= (\$129.28, \$470.02)$$

We can be 95% confident that, on average, women received a discount that is between $129.28 and $470.02 larger than the men at this dealership.

GUIDED EXAMPLE   Confidence Interval for Credit Card Spending

We rejected the null hypothesis that the mean spending in the two groups was equal. But, to find out whether we should consider offering the promotion nationwide, we need to estimate the magnitude of the spend lift.

PLAN **Define** and state what we want to know.	We want to find a 95% confidence interval for the mean difference in spending between those who are offered a promotion and those who aren't.
Identify the *parameter* we wish to estimate. Here our parameter is the difference in the means, not the individual group means.	
Identify the *population(s)* about which we wish to make statements.	We looked at the boxplots and histograms of the groups and checked the conditions before. The same assumptions and conditions are appropriate here, so we can proceed directly to the confidence interval.
Identify the variables and context.	
Specify the method.	We will use a two-sample *t*-interval.

DO **Mechanics** Construct the confidence interval. Be sure to include the units along with the statistics. Use meaningful subscripts to identify the groups.	In our previous analysis, we found:

$$\bar{y}_{No\ Offer} = \$7.69 \qquad \bar{y}_{Offer} = \$127.61$$
$$s_{No\ Offer} = \$611.62 \qquad s_{Offer} = \$566.05$$

The observed difference in the two means is:

$$\bar{y}_{Offer} - \bar{y}_{No\ Offer} = \$127.61 - \$7.69 = \$119.92,$$

and the standard error is:

$$SE(\bar{y}_{Offer} - \bar{y}_{No\ Offer}) = \$37.27$$

Use the sample standard deviations to find the standard error of the sampling distribution.

The best alternative is to let the computer use the approximation formula for the degrees of freedom and find the confidence interval.

From technology, the df is 992.007, and the one-sided 0.025 critical value for *t* with 992.007 df is 1.96. So the 95% confidence interval is:

$$\$119.92 \pm 1.96(\$37.27) = (\$46.87, \$192.97)$$

Ordinarily, we rely on technology for the calculations. In our hand calculations, we rounded values at intermediate steps to show the steps more clearly. The computer keeps full precision and is the one you should report. The difference between the hand and computer calculations is about $0.08.

Using software to obtain these computations, we get:

```
95 percent confidence interval:
 (46.78784, 193.05837)
sample means:
No Offer    Offer
7.690882    127.613987
```

(continued)

REPORT **Communicate and present** your conclusions. Interpret the confidence interval in the proper context.

> **MEMO**
>
> **Re: Credit card promotion experiment**
>
> In our experiment, the promotion resulted in an increased spend lift of $119.92 on average. Further analysis gives a 95% confidence interval of ($46.79, $193.06). In other words, we expect with 95% confidence that under similar conditions, the mean spend lift that we achieve when we roll out the offer to all similar customers will be in this interval. We recommend that the company consider whether the values in this interval will justify the cost of the promotion program.

14.5   The Pooled *t*-Test

If you bought a used camera in good condition from a friend, would you pay the same as you would if you bought the same item from a stranger? A researcher at Cornell University[5] wanted to know how friendship might affect simple sales such as this. She randomly divided subjects into two groups and gave each group descriptions of items they might want to buy. One group was told to imagine buying from a friend whom they expected to see again. The other group was told to imagine buying from a stranger.

Here are the prices they offered to pay for a used camera in good condition.

Price Offered for a Used Camera ($)	
Buying from a Friend	**Buying from a Stranger**
275	260
300	250
260	175
300	130
255	200
275	225
290	240
300	

WHO	University students
WHAT	Prices offered to pay for a used camera ($)
WHEN	1990s
WHERE	Cornell University
WHY	To study the effects of friendship on transactions

The researcher who designed the friendship study was interested in testing the impact of friendship on negotiations. Previous theories had doubted that friendship had a measurable effect on pricing, but she hoped to find such an effect. The usual null hypothesis is that there's no difference in means and that's what we'll use for the camera purchase prices.

When we performed *t*-tests earlier in the chapter, we used an approximation formula that adjusts the degrees of freedom downward. Because this is an experiment rather than observational data from a sample survey, we might be willing to make another assumption. The null hypothesis says that whether you buy from a

---

[5]J. J. Halpern (1997). "The Transaction Index: A Method for Standardizing Comparisons of Transaction Characteristics Across Different Contexts," *Group Decision and Negotiation*, 6, no. 6: 557–572.

friend or a stranger should have no effect on the mean amount you're willing to pay for a camera. If it has no effect on the means, it would be reasonable to also assume that it doesn't affect the variance of the transactions.

If we're willing to *assume* that the variances of the groups are equal (at least when the null hypothesis is true), then we can use a slightly more powerful method. We **pool** the data to estimate a common variance:

$$s_{pooled}^2 = \frac{(n_1 - 1)\, s_1^2 + (n_2 - 1)\, s_2^2}{(n_1 - 1) + (n_2 - 1)}.$$

Then we substitute this pooled variance in place of each of the variances in the standard error formula, simplifying it:

$$SE_{pooled}(\bar{y}_1 - \bar{y}_2) = \sqrt{\frac{s_{pooled}^2}{n_1} + \frac{s_{pooled}^2}{n_2}} = s_{pooled}\sqrt{\frac{1}{n_1} + \frac{1}{n_2}}.$$

The formula for degrees of freedom for the Student's *t*-model is simpler, too:

$$df = (n_1 - 1) + (n_2 - 1).$$

Because pooled *t* assumes that the groups have the same variance, it is wise to check this **Equal Variance Assumption**. An easy way to do that is to compare their boxplots to check whether the boxes are of roughly equal size and that there are no extreme outliers in need of special attention.

Pooled *t*-Test and Confidence Interval for the Difference Between Means

The conditions for the **pooled *t*-test** for the difference between the means of two independent groups are the same as for the two-sample *t*-test with the additional assumption that the variances of the two groups are the same. We test the hypothesis:

$$H_0\colon \mu_1 - \mu_2 = \Delta_0,$$

where the hypothesized difference Δ_0 is almost always 0, using the statistic

$$t = \frac{(\bar{y}_1 - \bar{y}_2) - \Delta_0}{SE_{pooled}(\bar{y}_1 - \bar{y}_2)}.$$

The standard error of $\bar{y}_1 - \bar{y}_2$ is:

$$SE_{pooled}(\bar{y}_1 - \bar{y}_2) = s_{pooled}\sqrt{\frac{1}{n_1} + \frac{1}{n_2}},$$

where the pooled variance is:

$$s_{pooled}^2 = \frac{(n_1 - 1)\, s_1^2 + (n_2 - 1)\, s_2^2}{(n_1 - 1) + (n_2 - 1)}.$$

When the conditions are met and the null hypothesis is true, we can model this statistic's sampling distribution with a Student's *t*-model with $(n_1 - 1) + (n_2 - 1)$ degrees of freedom. We use that model to obtain a P-value for a test or a margin of error for a confidence interval.

The corresponding **pooled-*t* confidence interval** is:

$$(\bar{y}_1 - \bar{y}_2) \pm t_{df}^* \times SE_{pooled}(\bar{y}_1 - \bar{y}_2),$$

where the critical value t^* depends on the confidence level and is found with $(n_1 - 1) + (n_2 - 1)$ degrees of freedom.

GUIDED EXAMPLE   Role of Friendship in Negotiations

The usual null hypothesis in a pooled *t*-test is that there's no difference in means and that's what we'll use for the camera purchase prices.

PLAN	**Define** and state what we want to know.	We want to know whether people are likely to offer a different amount for a used camera when buying from a friend than when buying from a stranger. We wonder whether the difference between mean amounts is zero. We have bid prices from 8 subjects buying from a friend and 7 subjects buying from a stranger, found in a randomized experiment.
	Identify the *parameter* we wish to estimate. Here our parameter is the difference in the means, not the individual group means. Identify the variables and context.	

Hypotheses State the null and alternative hypotheses.

The research claim is that friendship changes what people are willing to pay. The natural null hypothesis is that friendship makes no difference.

We didn't start with any knowledge of whether friendship might increase or decrease the price, so we choose a two-sided alternative.

H_0: The difference in mean price offered to friends and the mean price offered to strangers is zero:

$$\mu_F - \mu_S = 0,$$

H_A: The difference in mean prices is not zero:

$$\mu_F - \mu_S \neq 0.$$

DO Make a graph. Boxplots are the display of choice for comparing groups. We'll also want to check the distribution of each group. Histograms may do a better job.

REALITY CHECK Looks like the prices are higher if you buy from a friend. The two ranges barely overlap, so we'll be pretty surprised if we don't reject the null hypothesis.

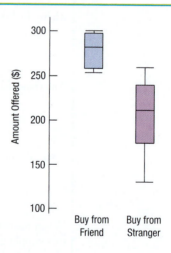

Model Think about the assumptions and check the conditions. (Because this is a randomized experiment, we haven't sampled at all, so the 10% Condition doesn't apply.)

✔ **Independence Assumption**. There is no reason to think that the behavior of one subject influenced the behavior of another.

✔ **Randomization Condition**. The experiment was randomized. Subjects were assigned to treatment groups at random.

✔ **Independent Groups Assumption**. Randomizing the experiment gives independent groups.

✔ **Nearly Normal Condition.** Histograms of the two sets of prices show no evidence of skewness or extreme outliers.

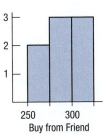
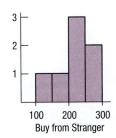

Buy from Friend   Buy from Stranger

State the sampling distribution model.

Specify the method.

Because this is a randomized experiment with a null hypothesis of no difference in means, we can make the Equal Variance Assumption. If, as we are assuming from the null hypothesis, the treatment doesn't change the means, then it is reasonable to assume that it also doesn't change the variances. Under these assumptions and conditions, we can use a Student's *t*-model to perform a pooled *t*-test.

Mechanics List the summary statistics. Be sure to use proper notation.

Use the null model to find the P-value. First determine the standard error of the difference between sample means.

From the data:

$$n_F = 8 \qquad n_S = 7$$
$$\bar{y}_F = \$281.88 \quad \bar{y}_S = \$211.43$$
$$s_F = \$18.31 \quad s_S = \$46.43$$

The pooled variance estimate is:

$$s_p^2 = \frac{(n_F - 1)s_F^2 + (n_S - 1)s_S^2}{n_F + n_S - 2}$$
$$= \frac{(8 - 1)(18.31)^2 + (7 - 1)(46.43)^2}{8 + 7 - 2}$$
$$= 1175.48$$

The standard error of the difference becomes:

$$SE_{pooled}(\bar{y}_F - \bar{y}_S) = \sqrt{\frac{s_p^2}{n_F} + \frac{s_p^2}{n_S}}$$
$$= 17.744$$

The observed difference in means is:

$$(\bar{y}_F - \bar{y}_S) = 281.88 - 211.43 = \$70.45$$

which results in a *t*-ratio

Find the *t*-value.

$$t = \frac{(\bar{y}_F - \bar{y}_S) - (0)}{SE_{pooled}(\bar{y}_F - \bar{y}_S)} = \frac{70.45}{17.744} = 3.97$$

Make a graph. Sketch the *t*-model centered at the hypothesized difference of zero. Because this is a two-tailed test, shade the region to the right of the observed difference and the corresponding region in the other tail.

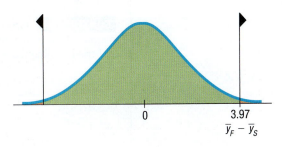

0   3.97
$\bar{y}_F - \bar{y}_S$

(continued)

A statistics program can find the P-value.

The computer output for a pooled *t*-test appears here.

```
Pooled T Test for friend vs. stranger

            N     Mean    StDev   SE Mean
Friend      8     281.9   18.3      6.5
Stranger    7     211.4   46.4      18

t = 3.9699, df = 13, P-value = 0.001600
Alternative hypothesis: true difference in means is not
equal to 0

95 percent confidence interval:
(32.11047, 108.78238)
```

REPORT **Communicate and present** your conclusions. Link the P-value to your decision about the null hypothesis and state the conclusion in context.

Be cautious about generalizing to items whose prices are outside the range of those in this study. The confidence interval can reveal more detailed information about the size of the difference. In the original article (referenced in footnote 5 in this chapter), the researcher tested several items and proposed a model relating the size of the difference to the price of the items.

MEMO

Re: Role of friendship in negotiations

Results of a small experiment show that people are likely to offer a different amount for a used camera when bargaining with a friend than when bargaining with a stranger. The difference in mean offers was statistically significant ($P = 0.0016$).

The confidence interval suggests that people tend to offer more to a friend than they would to a stranger. For the camera, the 95% confidence interval for the mean difference in price was $32.11 to $108.78, but we suspect that the actual difference may vary with the price of the item purchased.

When Should You Use the Pooled *t*-Test?

> Because the advantages of pooling are small, and you are allowed to pool only rarely (when the equal variances assumption is met), our advice is: ***don't***.
>
> **It's never wrong *not* to pool.**

When the variances of the two groups are in fact equal, the two methods give pretty much the same result. On average, pooled methods have a small advantage (slightly narrower confidence intervals, slightly more powerful tests), but the advantage is slight. When the variances are *not* equal, the pooled methods are just not valid and can give poor results. You have to use the two-sample methods instead. Pooled *t*-methods are most appropriate for experimental data, where the equal variance assumption is most plausible. But for most other data, we recommend using two-sample *t*.

IN PRACTICE 14.5 The pooled *t*-test

RECAP The consultant in In Practice 14.3 used a two-sample *t-test* to find a significant difference between the mean discounts offered men and women.

CONSULTANT Just to be sure, I've also performed a pooled *t*-test. I don't see any reason to believe that the variance of discounts should be different for men and women, so I tried pooling them. The pooled estimate of the common standard deviation is:

$$s_{pooled} = \sqrt{\frac{(n_{Women} - 1)s_{Women}^2 + (n_{Men} - 1)s_{Men}^2}{n_{Women} + n_{Men} - 2}}$$

$$= \sqrt{\frac{(46 - 1)(399.70)^2 + (54 - 1)(458.95)^2}{46 + 54 - 2}}$$

$$= 432.75$$

We use that to find the *SE* of the difference:

$$SE_{pooled}(\bar{y}_{Women} - \bar{y}_{Men}) = s_{pooled}\sqrt{\frac{1}{n_{Women}} + \frac{1}{n_{Men}}} = 432.75\sqrt{\frac{1}{46} + \frac{1}{54}} = \$86.83$$

(Without pooling, our estimate was $85.87.) This pooled t has $46 + 54 - 2 = 98$ degrees of freedom.

$$t_{98} = \frac{\bar{y}_{Women} - \bar{y}_{Men}}{SE_{pooled}(\bar{y}_{Women} - \bar{y}_{Men})} = \frac{299.65}{86.83} = 3.45$$

The P-value for a t of 3.45 with 98 degrees of freedom is (from technology) 0.0008. The two-sample t-test value was 0.0007. There is no practical difference between these, and we reach the same conclusion that the difference is not 0. The assumption of equal variances did not affect the conclusion.

14.6 Paired Data

The two-sample t-test depends crucially on the assumption that the two groups are independent of each other. One common violation of this assumption is when we have data on the *same* cases in two different circumstances. For example, we might want to compare the same customers' spending at our website last January to this January, or we might have each participant in a focus group rate two different product designs. Data such as these are said to be **paired**. When pairs arise from an experiment, the pairing is a type of *blocking*. A common form of blocking is to test subjects *before* and *after* a treatment. When pairing arises from an observational study, it is called *matching*.

In either case, when the data are paired, the groups are not independent, so you *should not* use the two-sample (or pooled two-sample) method. You must decide, from the way the data were collected whether the data are paired. Be careful. There is no statistical test to determine whether your data are paired. You must decide whether the data are paired from understanding how they were collected and what they mean (check the W's).

Once we recognize that our data are matched pairs, it makes sense to concentrate on the *differences* between the two measurements in each pair. That is, we look at the collection of pairwise differences in the measured variable. For example, when studying customer spending, we would analyze the *difference* between this January's and last January's spending for each customer. Because it is the *differences* we care about, we can analyze the data as a single variable holding those differences. With only one variable to consider, we can use a simple one-sample t-test. A **paired t-test** is just a one-sample t-test for the mean of the pairwise differences. The sample size is the number of pairs.

The assumptions and conditions for the test are exactly the same as the ones we used for the one-sample t-test. But now we have the additional assumption that the data are in fact paired.

> **Are the Data Paired?**
>
> To decide whether your data are paired you'll need to understand the business context of the data and how the data were collected. Pairing is not a choice, but a fact about the data. If the data are paired, you can't treat the groups as independent. But to be paired, the data must be related between the two groups in a way that you can justify. That justification may involve knowledge about the data not present in the variables themselves.

Paired Data Assumption

The data must be paired. When you have two groups with the same number of observations, it may be tempting to match them up, but that's not valid. Nor can you pair data just because they "seem to go together." To use paired methods you must determine from knowing how the data were collected that the individuals are paired. Usually the context will make it clear, but this can be a subtle decision that calls on your knowledge of the data.

Be sure to recognize paired data when you have it. Remember, two-sample t-methods aren't valid unless the groups are independent, and paired groups aren't independent.

Independence Assumption

For these methods, it's the *differences* that must be independent of each other. This is just the one-sample *t*-test assumption of independence, now applied to the differences. As always, randomization helps to ensure independence.

Randomization Condition. Randomness can arise in many ways. The *pairs* may be a random sample. For example, we may be comparing opinions of husbands and wives from a random selection of couples. In an experiment, the order of the two treatments may be randomly assigned, or the treatments may be randomly assigned to one member of each pair. In a before-and-after study, we may believe that the observed differences are a representative sample from a population of interest. What we want to know usually focuses our attention on where the randomness should be.

10% Condition. When we sample from a finite population, we should be careful not to sample more than 10% of that population. Sampling too large a fraction of the population calls the Independence Assumption into question. We don't usually check the 10% Condition, but it is a good idea to think about it.

Normal Population Assumption

The population of *differences* follow a Normal model. There is no need to check the distribution of the two individual groups. In fact, each group can be quite skewed and yet the differences can still be unimodal and symmetric.

Nearly Normal Condition. Make a histogram of the differences. The Normal population assumption matters less as we have more pairs to consider. You may be pleasantly surprised when you check this condition. Even if your original measurements are skewed or bimodal, the *differences* may be nearly Normal. After all, the individual who was way out in the tail on an initial measurement is likely to still be out there on the second one, giving a perfectly ordinary difference.

IN PRACTICE 14.6   Paired data

The owner of the car dealership (of the previous In Practice examples) is curious about the maximum discount his salesmen are willing to give to customers. In particular, two of his salespeople, Frank and Ray, seem to have very different ideas about how much discount to allow. To test his suspicion, he selects 30 cars from the lot and asks each to say how much discount he would allow a customer.

OWNER I have the data from my question to Frank and Ray. What test would you use to see whether their mean discounts are equal?.

CONSULTANT I'd use a paired *t*-test. The responses (maximum discount in $) are from the same 30 cars for each salesman, so the data are paired, not independent samples.

14.7   Paired *t*-Methods

The paired *t*-test is mechanically a one-sample *t*-test applied to the paired differences. Compare the mean difference to its standard error. If the ratio is large enough, reject the null hypothesis.

Paired *t*-Test

When the conditions are met, we are ready to test whether the mean paired difference is significantly different from a hypothesized value (called Δ_0). We test the hypothesis:

$$H_0: \mu_d = \Delta_0,$$

where the *d*'s are the pairwise differences and Δ_0 is almost always 0.

We use the statistic:

$$t = \frac{\bar{d} - \Delta_0}{SE(\bar{d})},$$

where $\bar{d}$ is the mean of the pairwise differences, *n* is the number of *pairs*, and

$$SE(\bar{d}) = \frac{s_d}{\sqrt{n}},$$

where s_d is the standard deviation of the pairwise differences.

When the conditions are met and the null hypothesis is true, the sampling distribution of this statistic is a Student's *t*-model with $n - 1$ degrees of freedom and we use that model to obtain the P-value.

Similarly, we can construct a confidence interval for the true mean difference. As in a one-sample *t*-interval, we center our estimate at the mean difference in our data. The margin of error on either side is the standard error multiplied by a critical *t*-value (based on our confidence level and the number of pairs we have).

Paired *t*-Interval

When the conditions are met, we are ready to find the confidence interval for the mean of the paired differences. The confidence interval is:

$$\bar{d} \pm t^*_{n-1} \times SE(\bar{d}),$$

where the standard error of the mean difference is $SE(\bar{d}) = \frac{s_d}{\sqrt{n}}$.

The critical value t^* from the Student's *t*-model depends on the particular confidence level that you specify and on the degrees of freedom, $n - 1$, based on the number of pairs, *n*.

JUST CHECKING

Think about each of the following situations. Would you use a two-sample *t* or paired *t*-method (or neither)? Why?

5 Random samples of 50 men and 50 women are surveyed on the amount they invest on average in the stock market on an annual basis. We want to estimate any gender difference in how much they invest.

6 Random samples of students were surveyed on their perception of ethical and community service issues both in their first year and fourth year at a university. The university wants to know whether their required programs in ethical decision-making and service learning change student perceptions.

7 A random sample of work groups within a company was identified. Within each work group, one male and one female worker were selected at random. Each was asked to rate the secretarial support that their work group received. When rating the same support staff, do men and women rate them equally on average?

8 A total of 50 companies are surveyed about business practices. Some are privately held and others are publicly traded. We wish to investigate differences between these two kinds of companies.

9 These same 50 companies are surveyed again one year later to see if their perceptions, business practices, and R&D investment have changed.

GUIDED EXAMPLE   Seasonal Spending

Economists and credit card banks know that people tend to spend more near the holidays in December. In fact, sales in the few days after Thanksgiving (the fourth Thursday of November in the United States) provide an indication of the strength of the holiday season sales and an early look at the strength of the economy in general. After the holidays, spending decreases substantially. Because credit card banks receive a percentage of each transaction, they need to forecast how much the average spending will increase or decrease from month to month. How much less do people tend to spend in January than December? For any particular segment of cardholders, a credit card bank could select two random samples—one for each month—and simply compare

(continued)

WHO	Cardholders in a particular market segment of a major credit card issuer
WHAT	Amount charged on their credit card in December and January
WHERE	United States
WHY	To estimate the amount of decrease in spending one could expect after the holiday shopping season

the average amount spent in January with that in December. A more sensible approach might be to select a single random sample and compare the spending between the two months for *each cardholder*. Designing the study in this way and examining the paired differences gives a more precise estimate of the actual change in spending.

Here we have a sample of 911 cardholders from a particular market segment and the amount they charged on their credit card in both December and the following January. We can test whether the mean difference in spending is 0 by using a paired *t*-test and create a **paired *t*-confidence interval** to estimate the true mean difference in spending between the two months.

PLAN	**Define** and state what we want to know. Identify the *parameter* we wish to estimate and the sample size.	We want to know how much we can expect credit card charges to change, on average, from December to January for this market segment. We have the total amount charged in December and January for n = 911 cardholders in this segment. We want to test whether the mean spending is the same for customers in the two months and find a confidence interval for the true mean difference in charges between these two months for all cardholders in this segment. Because we know that people tend to spend more in December, we will look at the difference: December spend − January spend and use a one-sided test. A positive difference will mean a decrease in spending.
	Hypotheses State the null and alternative hypotheses.	H_0: Mean spending was the same in December and January; the mean difference is zero: $\mu_d = 0$. H_A: Mean spending was greater in December than January; the mean difference was greater than zero: $\mu_d > 0$.

DO	Make a picture of the differences. Don't plot separate distributions of the two groups—that would entirely miss the pairing. For paired data, it's the Normality of the differences that we care about. Treat those paired differences as you would a single variable, and check the Nearly Normal Condition.	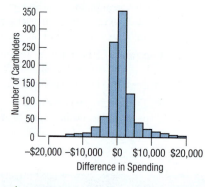 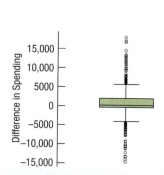
	Model Check the conditions. State why the data are paired. Simply having the same number of individuals in each group or displaying them in side-by-side columns doesn't make them paired. Think about what we hope to learn and where the randomization comes from.	✓ **Paired Data Assumption**: The data are paired because they are measurements on the same cardholders in two different months. ✓ **Independence Assumption**: The behavior of any individual is independent of the behavior of the others, so the differences are mutually independent. ✓ **Randomization Condition**: This was a random sample from a large market segment. ✓ **Nearly Normal Condition**: The distribution of the differences is unimodal and symmetric. Although the tails of the distribution are long, the distributions are symmetric. (This is typical of the behavior of credit card spending.) There are no isolated cases that would unduly dominate the mean difference, and our sample size is large so the Central Limit Theorem will protect us.

Specify the sampling distribution model.

The conditions are met, so we'll use a Student's *t*-model with $(n - 1) = 910$ degrees of freedom, perform a paired *t*-test, and find a paired *t*-confidence interval.

Choose the method.

The computer output tells us:

Mechanics *n* is the number of *pairs*, in this case, the number of cardholders.

$$n = 911 \ pairs$$

$$\bar{d} = \$788.18$$

$\bar{d}$ is the mean difference.

$$s_d = \$3740.22$$

s_d is the standard deviation of the differences.

Make a picture. Sketch a *t*-model centered at the observed mean of 788.18.

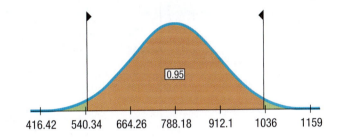

| 416.42 | 540.34 | 664.26 | 788.18 | 912.1 | 1036 | 1159 |

Find the standard error and the *t*-score of the observed mean difference. There is nothing new in the mechanics of the paired *t*-methods. These are the mechanics of the *t*-test and *t*-interval for a mean applied to the differences.

We estimate the standard error of $\bar{d}$ using:

$$SE(\bar{d}) = \frac{s_d}{\sqrt{n}} = \frac{3740.22}{\sqrt{911}} = \$123.919$$

We find $t = \dfrac{\bar{d} - 0}{SE(\bar{d})} = \dfrac{788.180}{123.919} = 6.36$

A *t*-statistic with 910 degrees of freedom and a value of 6.36 has a one-sided P-value <0.001.

The critical value for a 95% confidence interval is:

$$t^*_{910} = 1.96$$

The margin of error, $ME = t^*_{910} \times SE(\bar{d})$

$$= 1.96 \times 123.919 = 242.88$$

So a 95% CI is $\bar{d} \pm ME = (\$545.30, \$1031.06)$.

REPORT **Communicate and present** your conclusions. Link the results of the confidence interval to the context of the problem.

MEMO

Re: Credit card expenditure changes

In the sample of cardholders studied, the change in expenditures between December and January averaged $788.18, which means that, on average, cardholders spend $788.18 less in January than the month before. There is strong evidence to suggest that the mean difference is not zero and that customers really do spend more in December than January. Although we didn't measure the change for all cardholders in the segment, we can be 95% confident that the true mean decrease in spending from December to January was between $545.30 and $1031.06.

IN PRACTICE 14.7 The paired *t*-test

Here are some summary statistics:

OWNER OK, you said you'd use a paired *t*-test to compare Frank and Ray's mean discounts. What did you find?

CONSULTANT Let's look at the data from your experiment.

$$\bar{y}_{Frank} = \$414.48 \quad \bar{y}_{Ray} = \$478.88$$

$$SD_{Frank} = \$87.33 \quad SD_{Ray} = \$175.12$$

$$\bar{y}_{Diff} = \$64.40 \quad SD_{Diff} = \$146.74$$

The null hypothesis is that the mean maximum discount that Frank and Ray would give is the same.

I'll use a paired *t*-test because Frank and Ray were asked to give opinions about the same 30 cars.

$$t_{n-1} = \frac{\bar{d}}{SE(\bar{d})}$$

$$SE(\bar{d}) = \frac{s_d}{\sqrt{n}} = \frac{146.74}{\sqrt{30}} = \$26.79$$

$$t_{29} = \frac{64.40}{26.79} = 2.404$$

According to my Student's *t* app, this statistic has a (two-sided) P-value of 0.0228. With a P-value that small, I'll reject the null hypothesis that the mean difference is 0 and conclude that there is sufficient evidence to conclude that they are not the same.

To get more information, a 95% confidence interval:

$$t_{29}^* = 2.045 \text{ at } 95\% \text{ confidence}$$

$$\bar{d} \pm t_{29}^* \times SE(\bar{d}) = 64.40 \pm 2.045 \times 26.79$$

$$= (\$9.61, \$119.19)$$

shows that Ray gives, on average, somewhere between $9.61 and $119.19 more for his maximum discount than Frank does. So it seems that Ray's mean discount is greater, but I can't tell you where in that range the difference falls.

⊘ WHAT CAN GO WRONG?

- **Watch out for paired data when using the two-sample *t*-test.** The Independent Groups Assumption deserves special attention. Some research designs *deliberately* violate the Independent Groups Assumption by using pairing (or blocking) to reduce the variance of the tested statistic. If the samples are *not* independent, you can't use two-sample methods. This is probably the main thing that can go wrong when using two-sample methods.

- **Don't use individual confidence intervals for each group to test the difference between their means.** If you make 95% confidence intervals for the means of each group separately and you find that the intervals don't overlap, you can reject the hypothesis that the means are equal (at the corresponding α level).

But, if the intervals do overlap, that doesn't mean that you *can't* reject the null hypothesis. The margin of error for the difference between the means is smaller than the sum of the individual confidence interval margins of error. Comparing the individual confidence intervals is like adding the standard deviations. But we know that it's the variances that we add, and when we do it right, we actually get a more powerful test. So, don't test the difference between group means by looking at separate confidence intervals. Always make a two-sample *t*-interval or perform a two-sample *t*-test.

- **Look at the plots.** The usual (by now) cautions about checking for outliers and non-Normal distributions apply. The simple defense is to make and examine plots (side-by-side boxplots and histograms for two independent samples, histograms of the differences for paired data). You may be surprised how often this simple step saves you from the wrong or even absurd conclusions that can be generated by a single undetected outlier. You don't want to conclude that two methods have very different means just because one observation is atypical.

- **Don't use a paired *t*-method when the samples aren't paired.** When two groups don't have the same number of values, it's easy to see that they can't be paired. But just because two groups have the same number of observations doesn't mean they can be paired, even if they are shown side by side in a table. We might have 25 men and 25 women in our study, but they might be completely independent of one another. If they were siblings or spouses, we might consider them paired. Remember that you cannot *choose* which method to use based on your preferences. The realization that data are paired can be subtle and can depend on facts about how the data were collected that are not part of the data themselves. You must think carefully about your data, and you should explain your decision as part of your report.

- **Don't forget to look for outliers when using paired methods.** For two-sample *t*-methods watch out for outliers in *either* group. For paired *t*-methods, the outliers we care about now are in the differences. A subject who is extraordinary both before and after a treatment may still have a perfectly typical difference (one of the advantages of paired data designs). But one outlying difference can completely distort your conclusions. Be sure to plot the differences (even if you also plot the data) when using paired methods.

Do What We Say, Not What We Do

Precision machines used in industry often have a bewildering number of parameters that have to be set, so experiments are performed in an attempt to try to find the best settings. Such was the case for a hole-punching machine used by a well-known computer manufacturer to make printed circuit boards. The data were analyzed by one of the authors, but because he was in a hurry, he didn't look at the boxplots first and just performed *t*-tests on the experimental factors. When he found extremely small P-values even for factors that made no sense, he plotted the data. Sure enough, there was one observation 1,000,000 times bigger than the others. It turns out that it had been recorded in microns (millionths of an inch), while all the rest were in inches.

ETHICS IN ACTION

Joan Martinez is just beginning her third year as dean of the business school at a small regional university in the mid-west. When she joined, the university's president and academic provost expressed concern over dwindling enrollments in the MBA program, and made it clear to her that increasing MBA enrollment was to be her highest priority. She spent her first year evaluating the situation. She discovered that the main reason for the business school's declining enrollments in the MBA program is its location. The region had experienced an economic downturn that forced companies and businesses, many of which had tuition reimbursement programs for their employees, to close or relocate. Given the lack of prospects for increasing MBA enrollments in the traditional regional market, Joan made plans to start an online MBA program.

The university's administration was very enthusiastic about the initiative and approved funding for a new position, Online MBA Director. Joan hired Raj Patel to fill it. Raj not only had considerable experience with online MBA programs, but a proven track record for getting faculty support, something that Joan really needed. Faculty who teach the more quantitative, technical courses had already begun criticizing the initiative. They argued that it would be difficult to achieve desired student learning outcomes in these types of courses using the online mode of delivery. Therefore, Raj's first task as the new Online MBA Director was to change their beliefs.

He remembered that a faculty colleague from his former institution, Rob Lowry, taught finance in a hybrid format: the first half in a traditional classroom and the other half online. Raj contacted him to ask if he would share his test scores (without identifying students) for the mid-term (based on traditional in-class instruction) and the final (based upon online teaching). Rob agreed. Based on test scores for 40 students, Raj calculated the mid-term average as 78.65 and the final exam average as 72.55. Although students' test scores after online instruction were lower, the two-sample t-test revealed that the averages on the two exams were not significantly different ($t = 1.82$, $P\text{-value} = 0.073$). Raj felt that these results help make the case that online and in-class instruction are equivalent when it comes to student learning in quantitative business courses, and Joan agreed. She was happy to have these results in time for the next faculty meeting.

- **Identify the ethical dilemma in this scenario.**
- **What are the undesirable consequences?**
- **Propose an ethical solution that considers the welfare of all stakeholders.**

CHAPTER

14 FROM LEARNING TO EARNING

LEARNING OBJECTIVES

Know how to test whether the difference in the means of two independent groups is equal to some hypothesized value.

- The two-sample t-test is appropriate for independent groups. It uses a special formula for degrees of freedom.
- The assumptions and conditions are the same as for one-sample inferences for means with the addition of assuming that the groups are independent of each other.
- The most common null hypothesis is that the means are equal.

Be able to construct and interpret a confidence interval for the difference between the means of two independent groups.

- The confidence interval inverts the t-test in the natural way.

Know how and when to use pooled t inference methods.

- There is an additional assumption that the variances of the two groups are equal.
- This may be a plausible assumption in a randomized experiment.

Recognize when you have paired or matched samples and use an appropriate inference method.

- Paired t-methods are the same as one-sample t-methods applied to the pairwise differences.
- If data are paired they cannot be independent, so two-sample t and pooled-t methods would not be applicable.

TERMS

Paired data Data are paired when the observations are collected in pairs or the observations in one group are naturally related to observations in the other. The simplest form of pairing is to measure each subject twice—often before and after a treatment is applied. Pairing in experiments is a form of blocking and arises in other contexts. Pairing in observational and survey data is a form of matching.

Paired t-confidence interval A confidence interval for the mean of the pairwise differences between paired groups found as $\bar{d} \pm t^*_{n-1} \times SE(\bar{d})$, where $SE(\bar{d}) = \dfrac{s_d}{\sqrt{n}}$ and n is the number of pairs.

Paired t-test A hypothesis test for the mean of the pairwise differences of two groups. It tests the null hypothesis $H_0\colon \mu_d = \Delta_0$, where the hypothesized difference is almost always 0, using the statistic $t = \dfrac{\bar{d} - \Delta_0}{SE(\bar{d})}$ with $n - 1$ degrees of freedom, where $SE(\bar{d}) = \dfrac{s_d}{\sqrt{n}}$ and n is the number of pairs.

Pooled t-interval A confidence interval for the difference in the means of two independent groups used when we are willing and able to make the additional assumption that the variances of the groups are equal. It is found as:

$$(\bar{y}_1 - \bar{y}_2) \pm t^*_{df} \times SE_{pooled}(\bar{y}_1 - \bar{y}_2),$$

$$\text{where } SE_{pooled}(\bar{y}_1 - \bar{y}_2) = s_{pooled} \sqrt{\frac{1}{n_1} + \frac{1}{n_2}},$$

and the pooled variance is

$$s^2_{pooled} = \frac{(n_1 - 1)\, s_1^2 + (n_2 - 1)\, s_2^2}{(n_1 - 1) + (n_2 - 1)}.$$

The number of degrees of freedom is $(n_1 - 1) + (n_2 - 1)$.

Pooled t-test A hypothesis test for the difference in the means of two independent groups when we are willing and able to assume that the variances of the groups are equal. It tests the null hypothesis

$$H_0\colon \mu_1 - \mu_2 = \Delta_0,$$

where the hypothesized difference Δ_0 is almost always 0, using the statistic

$$t_{df} = \frac{(\bar{y}_1 - \bar{y}_2) - \Delta_0}{SE_{pooled}(\bar{y}_1 - \bar{y}_2)},$$

where the pooled standard error is defined as for the pooled interval and the degrees of freedom is $(n_1 - 1) + (n_2 - 1)$.

Pooling Data from two or more populations may sometimes be combined, or *pooled*, to estimate a statistic (typically a pooled variance) when we are willing to assume that the estimated value is the same in both populations. The resulting larger sample size may lead to an estimate with lower sample variance. However, pooled estimates are appropriate only when the required assumptions are true.

Two-sample t-interval A confidence interval for the difference in the means of two independent groups found as

$$(\bar{y}_1 - \bar{y}_2) \pm t^*_{df} \times SE(\bar{y}_1 - \bar{y}_2), \text{ where}$$

$$SE(\bar{y}_1 - \bar{y}_2) = \sqrt{\frac{s_1^2}{n_1} + \frac{s_2^2}{n_2}}$$

and the number of degrees of freedom is given by the approximation formula in footnote 3 of this chapter, or with technology.

Two-sample t-test A hypothesis test for the difference in the means of two independent groups. It tests the null hypothesis

$$H_0\colon \mu_1 - \mu_2 = \Delta_0,$$

where the hypothesized difference Δ_0 is almost always 0, using the statistic

$$t_{df} = \frac{(\bar{y}_1 - \bar{y}_2) - \Delta_0}{SE(\bar{y}_1 - \bar{y}_2)},$$

with the number of degrees of freedom given by the approximation formula in footnote 3 of this chapter, or with technology.

TECH SUPPORT   Comparing Two Groups

Two-Sample Methods

Here's some typical computer package output with comments:

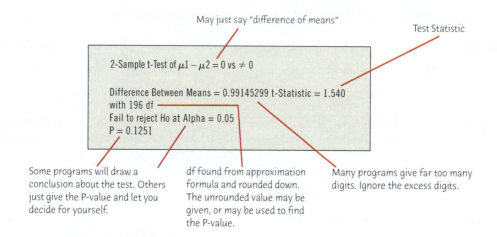

May just say "difference of means"

Test Statistic

2-Sample t-Test of $\mu1 - \mu2 = 0$ vs $\neq 0$

Difference Between Means = 0.99145299   t-Statistic = 1.540
with 196 df
Fail to reject Ho at Alpha = 0.05
P = 0.1251

Some programs will draw a conclusion about the test. Others just give the P-value and let you decide for yourself.

df found from approximation formula and rounded down. The unrounded value may be given, or may be used to find the P-value.

Many programs give far too many digits. Ignore the excess digits.

Some statistics software automatically tries to test whether the variances of the two groups are equal. Some automatically offer both the two-sample-*t* and pooled-*t* results. Ignore the test for the variances; it has little power in any situation in which its results could matter. If the pooled and two-sample methods differ in any important way, you should stick with the two-sample method. Most likely, the Equal Variance Assumption needed for the pooled method has failed.

The degrees of freedom approximation usually gives a fractional value. Most packages seem to round the approximate value down to the next smallest integer (although they may actually compute the P-value with the fractional value, gaining a tiny amount of power).

There are two ways to organize data when we want to compare two independent groups. The first, called **unstacked data**, lists the data in two columns, one for each group. Each list can be thought of as a variable. In this method, the variables in the credit card example would be "Offer" and "No Offer." Graphing calculators usually prefer this form, and some computer programs can use it as well.

The alternative way to organize the data is as **stacked data**. What is the response variable for the credit card experiment? It's the "Spend Lift"—the amount by which customers increased their spending. But the values of this variable in the unstacked lists are in both columns, and actually there's an experiment factor here, too—namely, whether the customer was offered the promotion or not. So we could put the data into two different columns, one with the "Spend Lift"s in it and one with a "Yes" for those who were offered the promotion and a "No" for those who weren't. The stacked data would look like this:

Spend Lift	Offer
969.74	Yes
915.04	Yes
197.57	No
77.31	No
196.27	Yes
…	…

This way of organizing the data makes sense as well. Now the factor and the response variables are clearly visible. You'll have to see which method your program requires. Some packages even allow you to structure the data either way.

The commands to do inference for two independent groups on common statistics technology are not always found in obvious places. The step-by-step instructions contain some starting guidelines.

Paired Methods

Most statistics programs can compute paired-*t* analyses. Some may want you to find the differences yourself and use the one-sample *t*-methods. Those that perform the entire procedure will need to know the two variables to compare. The computer, of course, cannot verify that the variables are naturally paired. Most programs will check whether the two variables have the same number of observations, but some stop there, and that can cause trouble. Most programs will automatically omit any pair that is missing a value for either variable. You must look carefully to see whether that has happened.

As we've seen with other inference results, some packages pack a lot of information into a simple table, but you must locate what you want for yourself. Here's a generic example with comments.

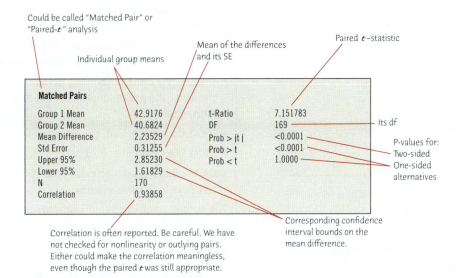

Could be called "Matched Pair" or "Paired-*t*" analysis

Individual group means

Mean of the differences and its SE

Paired *t*–statistic

Matched Pairs

Group 1 Mean	42.9176	t-Ratio	7.151783	
Group 2 Mean	40.6824	DF	169	Its df
Mean Difference	2.23529	Prob > |t|	<0.0001	
Std Error	0.31255	Prob > t	<0.0001	
Upper 95%	2.85230	Prob < t	1.0000	
Lower 95%	1.61829			
N	170			
Correlation	0.93858			

P-values for:
Two-sided
One-sided
alternatives

Correlation is often reported. Be careful. We have not checked for nonlinearity or outlying pairs. Either could make the correlation meaningless, even though the paired *t* was still appropriate.

Corresponding confidence interval bounds on the mean difference.

Other packages try to be more descriptive. It may be easier to find the results, but you may get less information from the output table.

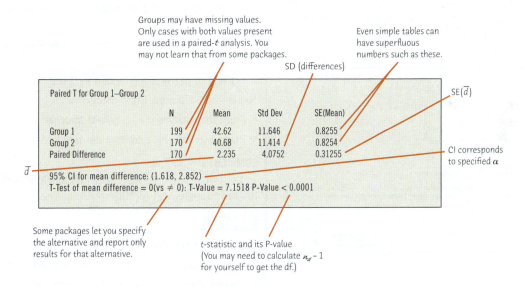

Groups may have missing values. Only cases with both values present are used in a paired-*t* analysis. You may not learn that from some packages.

SD (differences)

Even simple tables can have superfluous numbers such as these.

$SE(\bar{d})$

Paired T for Group 1–Group 2

	N	Mean	Std Dev	SE(Mean)
Group 1	199	42.62	11.646	0.8255
Group 2	170	40.68	11.414	0.8254
Paired Difference	170	2.235	4.0752	0.31255

$\bar{d}$

CI corresponds to specified α

95% CI for mean difference: (1.618, 2.852)
T-Test of mean difference = 0(vs ≠ 0): T-Value = 7.1518 P-Value < 0.0001

Some packages let you specify the alternative and report only results for that alternative.

t-statistic and its P-value
(You may need to calculate $n_d - 1$ for yourself to get the df.)

Computers make it easy to examine the boxplots of the two groups and the histogram of the differences—both important steps. Some programs offer a scatterplot of the two variables. That can be helpful. In terms of the scatterplot, a paired *t*-test is about whether the points tend to be above or below the 45° line $y = x$. (Note that pairing says nothing about whether the scatterplot should be straight. That doesn't matter for our *t*-methods.)

EXCEL

To perform a two-sample *t*-test in Excel using Data Analysis Tool Pack:

- In the **Data** menu, Choose **Data Analysis** (found under Analysis).
- Choose the appropriate *t*-test from the menu.
- Identify the following:
  - The cell range for the data in the two samples (for testing independent groups) or the difference data (for a paired *t*-test).
  - The hypothesized difference.

- Check the box next to Labels if the first row of the data contains labels, and identify where you would like the results to be placed.

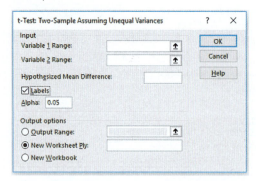

To perform a two-sample *t*-test using built-in formulas:

- From Formulas, choose **More Functions > Statistical > T.TEST**, and specify:
  - Array 1 and Array 2 = Location in the spreadsheet of the two groups to compare.
  - Tails of the distribution = 1 for one-tailed test and 2 for two-tailed test.
  - Type = 1 for a paired test, 2 for equal variance *t*-test, and 3 for unequal variance *t*-test.

Note that when Excel performs a two-sample *t*-test, it rounds the df from the special formula. We recommend the slightly more conservative approach of truncating and using the smaller number of df.

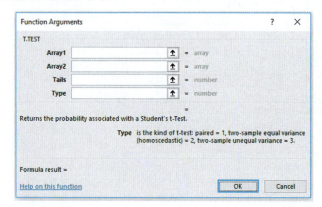

To perform a paired *t*-test in Excel:

- Enter paired data into two columns with one pair in each row.
- In another column, calculate the difference of the values in the two columns.
- Analyze the difference column using a one-sample *t*-test. An example is shown below:

	A	B	C	D	E
1	t-Test of a Mean				
2					Syntax for Column D
3	Sample Mean	460.38	t-Stat	1.89	=(B3-B6)/(B4/B5^0.5)
4	Sample St. Dev.	38.83	P(T<=t) One-tailed	0.0323	=1-(T.DIST(ABS(D3),B5-1,1))
5	Sample Size	50	t Critical Lower One-tail	-1.6766	=T.INV(B7,B5-1)
6	Hypothesized Mean	450	t Critical Upper One-tail	1.6766	=ABS(T.INV(B7,B5-1))
7	Alpha	0.05	P(T<=t) Two-tailed	0.0646	=2*D4
8			t Critical Two-tail ±	2.0096	=ABS(T.INV(B7/2,B5-1))

XLSTAT

To conduct a *t* test for the difference between two means:

- Choose **Parametric tests,** and then **Two-sample t-test and z-test.**
- If the two samples are in two separate columns in your workbook, choose the option **One column per sample.**
- If your data are *stacked* (one column lists the data, and the other the group identifier) choose the option **One column per variable.**
- If the data are paired, choose the option **Paired samples.**
- Enter the range of cell data.
- On the **Options** tab, for a test that is not pooled uncheck the box next to **Assume equality.**

The output yields the results of a hypothesis test and a confidence interval for the difference between means.

JMP

To conduct a two-sample *t*-test in JMP:

- From the **Analyze** menu, select **Fit X by Y.**
- Select variables: a **Y, Response** variable that holds the data and an **X, Factor** variable that holds the group names. Click OK, and JMP will make a dotplot. Be sure that the variable type for the **X, Factor** variable is set to nominal or ordinal.
- Click the Red triangle next to "Oneway Analysis..." and select:
  - *t* **Test** to perform a two-sample *t*-test.

To compute a paired *t*-test using JMP:

- From the **Analyze** menu, select **Matched Pairs.**
- Place two variables containing matched data into **Y, Column.**

COMMENTS

To perform a pooled *t*-test, select **Means/ANOVA/Pooled *t*** under the red triangle next to "Oneway Analysis..."

MINITAB

To perform a two-sample *t*-test in Minitab:

- From the **Stat** menu, choose the **Basic Statistics** submenu.
- Choose **2-sample t...** and fill in the dialog for:
  - Data in "one column" (unstacked data)
  - Data "two columns" (stacked data) or
  - Summarized data

To conduct a paired *t*-test using Minitab:

- From the **Stat** menu, choose the **Basic Statistics** submenu.
- Choose **Paired t** and fill in the dialog for:
  - Data in "two columns" or
  - Summarized data

Note: For two-sample *t*-tests, the **Graphs** button creates boxplots of your two samples and the **Options** button allows you to conduct either a one-sided or two-sided test or change the confidence level.

R

To test the hypothesis that $\mu_1 = \mu_2$ against an alternative (default is two-sided):

- Create a vector for the data of each group, say *X* and *Y*, and produce the confidence interval (default is 95%):
- t.test(X,Y, alternative = c("two.sided", "less", "greater"), conf.level = 0.95)

will produce the *t*-statistic, degrees of freedom, P-value, and confidence interval for a specified alternative.

COMMENTS

This is the same function as for the one-sample *t*-test, but with two vectors. In R, the default *t*-test does not assume equal variances in the two groups (default is **var.equal = FALSE**). To get the "pooled" *t*-test, add **var.equal = TRUE** to the function call.

To test the hypothesis that $\mu_1 = \mu_2$ for paired data against an alternative (default is two-sided), create a vector for the data of each group, such as x and y and produce the confidence interval (default is 95%):

- **t.test**(x,y, alternative = c("two.sided", "less", "greater"), paired = TRUE, conf.level = **0.95**)

will produce the *t*-statistic, degrees of freedom, P-value, and confidence interval for a specified alternative.

COMMENTS

This is the same function as for both the one- and two-sample *t*-test, but with paired=True.

STATCRUNCH

To do inference for the difference between two means using summaries:

- Click on **Stat**.
- Choose **T Stats > Two Sample > With Summary**.
- Enter the **Sample mean, Standard deviation**, and sample **Size** for each group.
- Indicate **Hypothesis Test**, then enter the hypothesized Null mean difference (usually 0), and choose the **Alternative** hypothesis.

OR

Indicate **Confidence Interval**, and then enter the **Level** of confidence.

- Click on **Compute!**

To do inference for the difference between two means using data:

- Click on **Stat**.
- Choose **T Stats > Two Sample > With Data**.
- Choose the variable Column for each group.
- Indicate **Hypothesis Test**, then enter the hypothesized **Null mean** difference (usually 0), and choose the **Alternative** hypothesis.

OR

Indicate **Confidence Interval**, and then enter the **Level** of confidence.

- Click on **Compute!**

To do inference for the mean of paired differences:

- Click on **Stat**.
- Choose **T Stats > Paired**.
- Choose the **Column** for each variable.
- Check **Save differences** so you can look at a histogram to be sure the Nearly Normal Condition is satisfied.
- Indicate **Hypothesis Test**, then enter the hypothesized **Null mean** difference (usually 0), and choose the **Alternative** hypothesis.

OR

Indicate **Confidence Interval**, and then enter the **Level** of confidence.

- Click on **Compute!**

SPSS

To conduct a two-sample *t*-test in SPSS:

- From the **Analyze** menu, choose the **Compare Means** submenu.
- Choose **Independent-Samples T Test.**
- Specify the data variable and grouping variable, click the button under the grouping variable, and identify numerical codes for groups.

Note: SPSS offers both the two-sample and pooled-*t* results in the same table. SPSS expects the data in one variable and group names in the other. If there are more than two group names in the group variable, only the two that are named in the dialog box will be compared.

To perform a paired *t*-test in SPSS:

- From the **Analyze** menu, choose the **Compare Means** submenu.
- Choose **Paired Samples T Test.**
- Highlight the two variables containing the paired data and add to the list.

BRIEF CASE

Real Estate

In Chapter 4, we examined the regression of the sales price of a home on its size and saw that larger homes generally fetch a higher price. How much can we learn about a house from the fact that it has a fireplace or more than the average number of bedrooms? Data for a random sample of 1063 homes from the upstate New York area can be found in the file **Saratoga house prices**. There are 6 quantitative variables: *Price($)*, *Living Area(sq.ft)*, *Bathrooms(#)*, *Bedrooms(#)*, *Lot Size(Acres)*, and *Age(years)*, and one categorical variable, *Fireplace*? ($1 = Yes; 0 = No$) denoting whether the house has at least one fireplace. We can use *t*-methods to see, for example, whether homes with fireplaces sell for more, on average, and by how much. For the quantitative variables, create new categorical variables by splitting them at the median or some other splitting point of your choice, and compare home prices above and below this value. For example, the median number of *Bedrooms* of these homes is 2. You might compare the prices of homes with 1 or 2 bedrooms to those with more than 2. Write up a short report summarizing the differences in mean price based on the categorical variables that you created.

Consumer Spending Patterns (Data Analysis)

You are on the financial planning team for monitoring a high spending segment of a credit card. You know that customers tend to spend more during December before the holidays, but you're not sure about the pattern of spending in the months after the holidays. Look at the dataset **Consumer spending post holiday**. It contains the monthly credit card spending of 1200 customers during the months December, January, February, March, and April. Report on the spending differences between the months. If you had failed to realize that these are paired data, what difference would that have made in your reported confidence intervals and tests?

CHAPTER 14 EXERCISES

SECTION 14.1

1. A developer wants to know if the houses in two different neighborhoods were built at roughly the same time. She takes a random sample of six houses from each neighborhood and finds their ages from local records. The table shows the data for each sample (in years).

Neighborhood 1	Neighborhood 2
57	50
60	43
46	35
62	53
67	46
56	55

a) Find the sample means for each neighborhood.
b) Find the estimated difference of the mean ages of the two neighborhoods.
c) Find the sample variances for each neighborhood.
d) Find the sample standard deviations for each neighborhood.
e) Find the standard error of the difference of the two sample means.

2. A market analyst wants to know if the new website he designed is showing increased page views per visit. A customer is randomly sent to one of two different websites, offering the same products, but with different designs. Here are the page views from five randomly chosen customers from each website:

Website A	Website B
9	10
4	13
14	2
7	3
2	7

a) Find the sample mean page views for each website.
b) Find the estimated difference of the sample mean page views of the two websites.
c) Find the sample variances for each website.
d) Find the sample standard deviations for each website.
e) Find the standard error of the difference of the sample means.

3. The developer in Exercise 1 hires an assistant to collect a random sample of houses from each neighborhood and finds that the summary statistics for the two neighborhoods look as follows:

Neighborhood 1	Neighborhood 2
$n_1 = 30$	$n_2 = 35$
$\bar{y}_1 = 57.2$ yrs	$\bar{y}_2 = 47.6$ yrs
$s_1 = 7.51$ yrs	$s_2 = 7.85$ yrs

a) Find the estimated mean age difference between the two neighborhoods.
b) Find the standard error of the estimated mean difference.
c) Calculate the t-statistic for the observed difference in mean ages, assuming that the true mean difference is 0.

4. Not happy with the previous results, the analyst in Exercise 2 takes a much larger random sample of customers from each website and records their page views. Here are the data:

Website A	Website B
$n_1 = 80$	$n_2 = 95$
$\bar{y}_1 = 7.7$ pages	$\bar{y}_2 = 7.3$ pages
$s_1 = 4.6$ pages	$s_2 = 4.3$ pages

a) Find the estimated mean difference in page visits between the two websites.
b) Find the standard error of the estimated mean difference.
c) Calculate the t-statistic for the observed difference in mean page visits assuming that the true mean difference is 0.

SECTION 14.2

5. For the data in Exercise 1, we want to test the null hypothesis that the mean age of houses in the two neighborhoods is the same. Assume that the data come from a population that is Normally distributed.

a) Using the values you found in Exercise 1, find the value of the t-statistic for the difference in mean ages for the null hypothesis.
b) Calculate the degrees of freedom from the formula in the footnote of page 450.
c) Calculate the degrees of freedom using the rule that $df = \min(n_1 - 1, n_2 - 1)$.
d) Find the P-value using the degrees of freedom from part b. (You can either round the number of df and use a table or use technology or a website).
e) Find the P-value using the degrees of freedom from part d.
f) What do you conclude at $\alpha = 0.05$?

6. For the data in Exercise 2, we want to test the null hypothesis that the mean number of page visits is the same for the two websites. Assume that the data come from a population that is Normally distributed.

a) Using the values you found in Exercise 2, find the value of the t-statistic for the difference in mean ages for the null hypothesis.
b) Calculate the degrees of freedom from the formula in the footnote of page 450.
c) Calculate the degrees of freedom using the rule that $df = \min(n_1 - 1, n_2 - 1)$.
d) Find the P-value using the degrees of freedom from part b. (You can either round the number of df and use a table or use technology or a website).
e) Find the P-value using the degrees of freedom from part c.
f) What do you conclude at $\alpha = 0.05$?

7. Using the data in Exercise 3, test the hypothesis that the mean age of houses in the two neighborhoods is the same. You may assume that the ages of houses in each neighborhood follow a Normal distribution.

a) Calculate the P-value of the statistic knowing that the approximation formula gives 62.2 df (you will need to round or use technology).
b) Calculate the P-value of the statistic using the rule that df is at least $min(n_1 - 1, n_2 - 1)$.
c) What do you conclude at $\alpha = 0.05$?

8. Using the data in Exercise 4, test the hypothesis that the mean number of page views from the two websites is the same. You may assume that the number of page views from each website follows a Normal distribution.

a) Calculate the P-value of the statistic knowing that the approximation formula gives 163.6 df.
b) Calculate the P-value of the statistic using the rule that df is at least $\min(n_1 - 1, n_2 - 1)$.
c) What do you conclude at $\alpha = 0.05$?

SECTION 14.4

9. Using the data in Exercise 1, and assuming that the data come from a distribution that is Normally distributed,

a) Find a 95% confidence interval for the mean difference in ages of houses in the two neighborhoods.
b) Is 0 within the confidence interval?
c) What does it say about the null hypothesis that the mean difference is 0?

10. Using the data in Exercise 2, and assuming that the data come from a distribution that is Normally distributed,

a) Find a 95% confidence interval for the mean difference in page views from the two websites.
b) Is 0 within the confidence interval?
c) What does it say about the null hypothesis that the mean difference is 0?

11. Using the summary statistics in Exercise 3, and assuming that the data come from a distribution that is Normally distributed,

a) Find a 95% confidence interval for the mean difference in ages of houses in the two neighborhoods using the df given in Exercise 7.
b) Why is the confidence interval narrower than the one you found in Exercise 9?
c) Is 0 within the confidence interval?
d) What does it say about the null hypothesis that the mean difference is 0?

12. Using the summary statistics in Exercise 4, and assuming that the data come from a distribution that is Normally distributed,

a) Find a 95% confidence interval for the mean difference in page views from the two websites.
b) Why is the confidence interval narrower than the one you found in Exercise 10?
c) Is 0 within the confidence interval?
d) What does it say about the null hypothesis that the mean difference is 0?

SECTION 14.5

13. For the data in Exercise 1,

a) Test the null hypothesis at $\alpha = 0.05$ using the pooled *t*-test. (Show the *t*-statistic, P-value, and conclusion.)
b) Find a 95% confidence interval using the pooled degrees of freedom.
c) Are your answers different from what you previously found in Exercise 9? Explain briefly why or why not.

14. For the data in Exercise 2,

a) Test the null hypothesis at $\alpha = 0.05$ using the pooled *t*-test. (Show the *t*-statistic, P-value, and conclusion.)
b) Find a 95% confidence interval using the pooled degrees of freedom.

c) Are your answers different from what you previously found in Exercise 10? Explain briefly why or why not.

15. For the data in Exercise 3,

a) Test the null hypothesis at $\alpha = 0.05$ using the pooled *t*-test. (Show the *t*-statistic, P-value, and conclusion.)
b) Find a 95% confidence interval using the pooled degrees of freedom.
c) Are your answers different from what you previously found in Exercise 11? Explain briefly why or why not.

16. For the data in Exercise 4,

a) Test the null hypothesis at $\alpha = 0.05$ using the pooled *t*-test. (Show the *t*-statistic, P-value, and conclusion.)
b) Find a 95% confidence interval using the pooled degrees of freedom.
c) Are your answers different from what you previously found in Exercise 12? Explain briefly why or why not.

SECTION 14.6

17. For each of the following scenarios, say whether the data should be treated as independent or paired samples. Explain briefly. If paired, explain what the pairing involves.

a) An efficiency expert claims that a new ergonomic desk chair makes typing at a computer terminal easier and faster. To test it, 15 volunteers are selected. Using both the new chair and their old chair, each volunteer types a randomly selected passage for 2 minutes and the number of correct words typed is recorded.
b) A developer wants to know if the houses in two different neighborhoods have the same mean price. She selects 10 houses from each neighborhood at random and tests the null hypothesis that the means are equal.
c) A manager wants to know if the mean productivity of two workers is the same. For a random selection of 30 hours in the past month, he compares the number of items produced by each worker in that hour.

18. For each of the following scenarios, say whether the data should be treated as independent or paired samples. Explain briefly. If paired, explain what the pairing involves.

a) An efficiency expert claims that a new ergonomic desk chair makes typing at a computer terminal easier and faster. To test it, 30 volunteers are selected. Half of the volunteers will use the new chair and half will use their old chairs. Each volunteer types a randomly selected passage for 2 minutes and the number of correct words typed is recorded.
b) A real estate agent wants to know how much extra a fireplace adds to the price of a house. She selects 25 city blocks. In each block, she randomly chooses a house with a fireplace and one without and records the assessment value.
c) A manager wants to know if the mean productivity of two workers is the same. For each worker, he randomly selects 30 hours in the past month and compares the number of items produced.

SECTION 14.7

19. A supermarket chain wants to know if their "buy one, get one free" campaign increases customer traffic enough to justify the cost of the program. For each of 10 stores they select two days at random to run the test. For one of those days (selected by a coin flip), the program will be in effect. They want to test the hypothesis that there is no mean difference in traffic against the alternative that the program increases the mean traffic. Here are the results in number of customer visits to the 10 stores:

Store #	With Program	Without Program
1	140	136
2	233	235
3	110	108
4	42	35
5	332	328
6	135	135
7	151	144
8	33	39
9	178	170
10	147	141

a) Are the data paired? Explain.
b) Compute the mean difference.
c) Compute the standard deviation of the differences.
d) Compute the standard error of the mean difference.
e) Find the value of the *t*-statistic.
f) How many degrees of freedom does the *t*-statistic have?
g) Is the alternative one- or two-sided? Explain.
h) What is the P-value associated with this *t*-statistic? (Assume that the other assumptions and conditions for inference are met.)
i) At $\alpha = 0.05$, what do you conclude?

20. A city wants to know if a new advertising campaign to make citizens aware of the dangers of driving after drinking has been effective. They count the number of drivers who have been stopped with more alcohol in their systems than the law allows for each day of the week in the week before and the week a month after the campaign starts. Here are the results:

Day of Week	Before	After
M	5	2
T	4	0
W	2	2
Th	4	1
F	6	8
S	14	7
Su	6	7

a) Are the data paired? Explain.
b) Compute the mean difference.
c) Compute the standard deviation of the differences.
d) Compute the standard error of the mean difference.
e) Find the value of the *t*-statistic.
f) How many degrees of freedom does the *t*-statistic have?
g) Is the alternative one- or two-sided? Explain.
h) What is the P-value associated with this *t*-statistic? (Assume that the other assumptions and conditions for inference are met.)
i) At $\alpha = 0.05$, what do you conclude?

21. In order to judge whether the program is successful, the manager of the supermarket chain in Exercise 19 wants to know the plausible range of values for the mean increase in customers using the program. Construct a 90% confidence interval.

22. A new operating system is installed in every workstation at a large company. The claim of the operating system manufacturer is that the time to shut down and turn on the machine will be much faster. To test it an employee selects 36 machines and tests the combined shut down and restart time of each machine before and after the new operating system has been installed. The mean and standard deviation of the differences (before – after) is 23.5 seconds with a standard deviation of 40 seconds.

a) What is the standard error of the mean difference?
b) How many degrees of freedom does the *t*-statistic have?
c) What is the 90% confidence interval for the mean difference?
d) What do you conclude at $\alpha = 0.05$?

CHAPTER EXERCISES

23. Hot dogs and calories. Consumers increasingly make food purchases based on nutrition values. *Consumer Reports* examined the calorie content of two kinds of hot dogs: meat (usually a mixture of pork, turkey, and chicken) and all beef. The researchers purchased samples of several different brands. The meat hot dogs averaged 111.7 calories, compared to 135.4 for the beef hot dogs. A test of the null hypothesis that there's no difference in mean calorie content yields a P-value of 0.124. What would you conclude?

24. Hot dogs and sodium. The *Consumer Reports* article described in Exercise 23 also listed the sodium content (in mg) for the various hot dogs tested. A test of the null hypothesis that beef hot dogs and meat hot dogs don't differ in the mean amounts of sodium yields a P-value of 0.110. What would you conclude?

25. Learning math. The Core Plus Mathematics Project (CPMP) is an innovative approach to teaching mathematics that engages students in group investigations and mathematical modeling. After field tests in 36 high schools over a three-year period, researchers compared the performances of CPMP students with those taught using a traditional curriculum. In one test, students had to solve applied algebra problems using calculators. Scores for 320 CPMP students were compared with those of a control group of 273 students in a traditional math program. Computer software was used to create a confidence interval for the difference in mean scores (*Journal for Research in Mathematics Education*, 31, no. 3, 2000).

```
Conf. level: 95%
Variable: μ(CPMP) − μ(Ctrl)
Interval: (5.573, 11.427)
```

a) What is the margin of error for this confidence interval?
b) If we had created a 98% confidence interval, would the margin of error be larger or smaller?
c) Explain what the calculated interval means in this context.
d) Does this result suggest that students who learn mathematics with CPMP will have (statistically) significantly higher mean scores in applied algebra than those in traditional programs? Explain.

26. Sales performance. A chain that specializes in healthy and organic food would like to compare the sales performance of two of its primary stores in the state of Massachusetts. These stores are both in urban, residential areas with similar demographics. A comparison of the weekly sales randomly sampled over a period of nearly two years for these two stores yields the following information:

Store	N	Mean	StDev	Minimum	Median	Maximum
Store #1	9	242170	23937	211225	232901	292381
Store #2	9	235338	29690	187475	232070	287838

a) Create a 95% confidence interval for the difference in the mean store weekly sales. (df from technology is 15.31)
b) Interpret your interval in context.
c) Does it appear that one store sells more on average than the other store?
d) What is the margin of error for this interval?
e) Would you expect a 99% confidence interval to be wider or narrower? Explain.
f) If you computed a 99% confidence interval, would your conclusion in part c change? Explain.

27. CPMP, again. During the study described in Exercise 25, students in both CPMP and traditional classes took another algebra test that did not allow them to use calculators. The table shows the results. Are the mean scores of the two groups significantly different? Assume that the assumptions for inference are satisfied.

Math Program	n	Mean	SD
CPMP	312	29.0	18.8
Traditional	265	38.4	16.2

a) Write an appropriate hypothesis.
b) Here is computer output for this hypothesis test. Explain what the P-value means in this context.

```
2-Sample t-Test of μ1 − μ2 ≠ 0
t-Statistic = −6.451 w/574.8761 df
P < 0.0001
```

c) State a conclusion about the CPMP program.

28. IT training costs. An accounting firm is trying to decide between IT training conducted in-house and the use of third party consultants. To get some preliminary cost data, each type of training was implemented at two of the firm's offices located in different cities. The table below shows the average annual training cost per employee at each location. Are the mean costs significantly different? Assume that the assumptions for inference are satisfied.

IT Training	n	Mean	SD
In-House	210	$490.00	$32.00
Consultants	180	$500.00	$48.00

a) Write the appropriate hypotheses.
b) Below is computer output for this hypothesis test. Explain what the P-value means in this context.

```
2-Sample t-Test of μ₁ − μ₂ ≠ 0
t-Statistic = −2.38 w/303 df
P = .018
```

c) State a conclusion about IT training costs.

29. CPMP and word problems. The study of the new CPMP mathematics methodology described in Exercise 25 also tested students' abilities to solve word problems. This table shows how the CPMP and traditional groups performed. What do you conclude? (Assume that the assumptions for inference are met.)

Math Program	n	Mean	SD
CPMP	320	57.4	32.1
Traditional	273	53.9	28.5

30. Statistical training. The accounting firm described in Exercise 28 is interested in providing opportunities for its auditors to gain more expertise in statistical sampling methods. They wish to compare traditional classroom instruction with online self-paced tutorials. Auditors were assigned at random to one type of instruction, and the auditors were then given an exam. The table shows how the two groups performed. What do you conclude? (Assume the assumptions for inference are met.)

Program	n	Mean	SD
Traditional	296	74.5	11.2
Online	275	72.9	12.3

31. Trucking company. A trucking company would like to compare two different routes for efficiency. Truckers are randomly assigned to two different routes. Twenty truckers following Route A report an average of 40 minutes, with a standard deviation of 3 minutes. Twenty truckers following Route B report an average of 43 minutes, with a standard deviation of 2 minutes. Histograms of travel times for the routes are roughly symmetric and show no outliers.

a) Find a 95% confidence interval for the difference in average time for the two routes.

b) Will the company save time by always driving one of the routes? Explain.

32. Change in sales. Suppose the specialty food chain from Exercise 26 wants to now compare the change in sales across different regions. An examination of the difference in sales over a 37-week period in a recent year for 8 stores in the state of Massachusetts compared to 12 stores in nearby states reveals the following descriptive statistics for relative increase in sales. (If these means are multiplied by 100, they show % increase in sales.)

State	N	Mean	StDev
MA	8	0.0738	0.0666
Other	12	0.0559	0.0503

a) Find the 90% confidence interval for the difference in relative increase in sales over this time period.

b) Is there a significant difference in increase in sales between these two groups of stores? Explain.

c) What would you like to see to check the conditions?

T 33. Cereal company. A food company is concerned about recent criticism of the sugar content of their children's cereals. The data show the sugar content (as a percentage of weight) of several national brands of children's and adults' cereals.

Children's cereals: 40.3, 55, 45.7, 43.3, 50.3, 45.9, 53.5, 43, 44.2, 44, 47.4, 44, 33.6, 55.1, 48.8, 50.4, 37.8, 60.3, 46.6

Adults' cereals: 20, 30.2, 2.2, 7.5, 4.4, 22.2, 16.6, 14.5, 21.4, 3.3, 6.6, 7.8, 10.6, 16.2, 14.5, 4.1, 15.8, 4.1, 2.4, 3.5, 8.5, 10, 1, 4.4, 1.3, 8.1, 4.7, 18.4

a) Write the null and alternative hypotheses.

b) Check the conditions.

c) Find the 95% confidence interval for the difference in means.

d) Is there a significant difference in mean sugar content between these two types of cereals? Explain.

34. Italian wines. Chemical analyses of 1599 red and 4898 white Italian wines revealed the following summary statistics for pH (a measure of acidity):

Type	Count	Mean	St Dev
Red	1599	3.311	0.154
White	4898	3.188	0.151

Is there a difference in pH between red and white wines?

a) Write the null and alternative hypotheses.

b) What conditions would you check?

c) Test the hypothesis and find the P-value.

d) Is there a significant difference in pH?

T 35. Bond funds. Morningstar (www.morningstar.com) selects mutual funds as "Medalist" funds expected to perform well over the long term. You have decided to invest in a bond fund and plan to limit your choice of funds to Morningstar "medalist" funds. But now you must choose between a taxable fund and a municipal bond fund that is at least partially tax-free. Which is better? Here are the % returns for the three-year period leading up to spring of 2013:

Taxable bond funds
    10.83, 6.45, 8.52, 10.9, 4.16, 10.48, 6.07, 2.69, 1.24, 1.58, 4.02, 5.64, 6.29, 12.36

Municipal bond funds
    8.34, 7.3, 6.07, 6.46, 5.77, 5.89, 5.76, 5.81, 5.12, 5.63 4.71, 5.22, 5.21, 3.12, 4.77, 2.2

a) Write the null and alternative hypotheses.

b) Check the conditions.

c) Test the hypothesis and find the P-value.

d) Is there a significant difference in 3-year returns between these two kinds of funds?

36. Technology adoption. The Pew Internet & American Life Project (www.pewinternet.org/) conducts surveys to gauge how the Internet and technology impact daily life of individuals, families, and communities. In a recent survey Pew asked respondents if they thought that computers and technology give people more or less control over their lives. Companies that are involved in innovative technologies use the survey results to better understand their target market. One might suspect that younger and older respondents might differ in their opinions of whether computers and technology give them more control over their lives. A subset of the data from this survey shows the mean ages of two groups of respondents, those who reported that they believed that computers and technology give them "more" control and those that reported "less" control.

Group	N	Mean	StDev	Min	Q1	Med	Q3	Max
More	74	54.42	19.65	18	41.5	53.5	68.5	99.0
Less	29	54.34	18.57	20	41.0	58.0	70.0	84.0

a) Write the null and alternative hypotheses.

b) Find the 95% confidence interval for the difference in mean age between the two groups of respondents.

c) Is there a significant difference in the mean ages between these two groups? Explain.

37. Product testing. A company is producing and marketing new reading activities for elementary school children that it believes will improve reading comprehension scores. A researcher randomly assigns third graders to an eight-week program in which some will use these activities and others will experience traditional teaching methods. At the end of the experiment, both groups take a reading comprehension exam. Do these results suggest that the new activities are better? Test an appropriate hypothesis and state your conclusion.

New Activities		Control	
24	54	10	42
33	56	17	42
43	57	20	42
43	58	26	43
43	59	28	48
46	61	33	53
49	62	37	55
52	67	37	55
53	71	41	60
			62
			85
			42
			42

38. Product placement. The owner of a small organic food store was concerned about her sales of a specialty yogurt manufactured in Greece. As a result of increasing fuel costs, she recently had to increase its price. To help boost sales, she decided to place the product on a different shelf (near eye level for most consumers) and in a location near other popular international products. She kept track of sales (number of containers sold per week) for six months after she made the change. These values are shown below, along with the sales numbers for the six months prior to making the change.

Before Change		After Change	
20	40	32	55
28	40	39	55
29	40	42	55
29	42	43	58
32	42	45	60
32	43	48	60
34	45	49	61
37	45	50	62
37	46	50	63
38	47	51	66
39	50	52	67
40	56	55	70

Do these results suggest that sales are better after the change in product placement? Test an appropriate hypothesis and state your conclusion. Be sure to check assumptions and conditions.

39. Named tropical cyclones 2017. It has been suggested that global climate change may be affecting the frequency of tropical storms. The data here show the number of tropical cyclones (including hurricanes) assigned official names by the National Hurricane Center. Is there evidence of a change? (Data extracted from **Hurricane history**)

1997–2006	2007–2017
9, 14, 16, 19, 17, 14, 21, 17, 31, 10	17, 17, 11, 21, 20, 19, 15, 9, 12, 16, 14

a) Write the null and alternative hypotheses.
b) Are the conditions for hypothesis testing satisfied?
c) If so, test the hypothesis.

40. Hurricanes 2017. Exercise 39 considered possible changes in the numbers of tropical cyclones that have grown large enough to be officially named. Regardless of the *number* of storms, has the *fraction* of named storms that grew to hurricane strength changed? Here are those fractions for the same periods as those considered in the previous exercise. (Data extracted from **Hurricane history**)

1997–2006	2007–2017
0.889, 1.000, 0.750, 0.789, 0.882, 0.857, 0.762, 0.882, 0.903, 1.000	0.882, 0.941, 0.818, 0.905, 0.950, 1.000, 0.933, 0.889, 0.917, 0.938, 0.929

a) Write the null and alternative hypotheses.
b) Are the conditions for hypothesis testing satisfied?
c) If so, test the hypothesis.

41. Ginkgo test. A pharmaceutical company is producing and marketing a ginkgo biloba supplement to enhance memory. In an experiment to test the product, subjects were assigned randomly to take ginkgo biloba supplements or a placebo. Their memory was tested to see whether it improved. Here are boxplots comparing the two groups and some computer output from a two-sample *t*-test computed for the data. (Data in **Memory**)

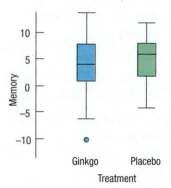

```
2-Sample t-Test of μ_G − μ_p > 0
Difference Between Means = −0.9914
t-Statistic = −1.540 w/196.61 df
P = 0.9374
```

a) Explain in this context what the P-value means.

b) State your conclusion about the effectiveness of ginkgo biloba.

c) Proponents of ginkgo biloba continue to insist that it works. What type of error do they claim your conclusion makes?

T **42. Designated hitter 2016.** American League baseball teams play their games with the designated hitter rule, meaning that pitchers do not bat. The league believes that replacing the pitcher, traditionally a weak hitter, with another player in the batting order produces more runs and generates more interest among fans. The data provided in the file **Attendance 2016** include the average numbers of runs scored per game (*Runs per game*) by American League and National League teams for the 2016 season (www.baseball-reference.com).

American League		National League	
Team	Runs/game	Team	Runs/game
Baltimore Orioles	4.59	Arizona Diamondbacks	4.64
Boston Red Sox	5.42	Atlanta Braves	4.03
Chicago White Sox	4.23	Chicago Cubs	4.99
Cleveland Indians	4.83	Cincinnati Reds	4.42
Detroit Tigers	4.66	Colorado Rockies	5.22
Houston Astros	4.47	Los Angeles Dodgers	4.48
Kansas City Royals	4.17	Miami Marlins	4.07
Los Angeles Angels	4.43	Milwaukee Brewers	4.14
Minnesota Twins	4.46	NY Mets	4.14
NY Yankees	4.20	Philadelphia Phillies	3.77
Oakland Athletics	4.03	Pittsburgh Pirates	4.50
Seattle Mariners	4.74	San Diego Padres	4.23
Tampa Bay Rays	4.15	San Francisco Giants	4.41
Texas Rangers	4.72	St Louis Cardinals	4.81
Toronto Blue Jays	4.69	Washington Nationals	4.71

a) Create an appropriate display of these data. What do you see?

b) With a 95% confidence interval, estimate the mean number of runs scored by American League teams.

c) With a 95% confidence interval, estimate the mean number of runs scored by National League teams.

d) Explain why you should not use two separate confidence intervals to decide whether the two leagues differ in average number of runs scored.

43. Productivity. A factory hiring people to work on an assembly line gives job applicants a test of manual agility.

This test counts how many strangely shaped pegs the applicant can fit into matching holes in a one-minute period. The table summarizes the data by gender of the job applicant. Assume that all conditions necessary for inference are met.

	Male	Female
Number of Subjects	50	50
Pegs Placed:		
Mean	19.39	17.91
SD	2.52	3.39

a) Find 95% confidence intervals for the average number of pegs that males and females can each place.

b) Those intervals overlap. What does this suggest about any gender-based difference in manual agility?

c) Find a 95% confidence interval for the difference in the mean number of pegs that could be placed by men and women.

d) What does this interval suggest about any gender-based difference in manual agility?

e) The two results seem contradictory. Which method is correct: doing two-sample inference, or doing one-sample inference twice?

f) Why don't the results agree?

T **44. Designated hitter 2016, part 2.** Do the data in Exercise 42 suggest that the American League's designated hitter rule may lead to more runs per game scored?

a) Write the null and alternative hypotheses.

b) Find a 95% confidence interval for the difference in mean runs per game, and interpret your interval.

c) Test the hypothesis stated above in part a and find the P-value.

d) Interpret the P-value and state your conclusion. Does the test suggest that the American League scores more runs on average?

T **45. Water hardness.** In an investigation of environmental causes of disease, data were collected on the annual mortality rate (deaths per 100,000) for males in 61 large towns in England and Wales. In addition, the water hardness was recorded as the calcium concentration (parts per million, ppm) in the drinking water. The dataset also notes for each town whether it was south or north of Derby. Is there a significant difference in mortality rates in the two regions? Here are the summary statistics.

```
Summary of:          mortality
For categories in:   Derby

Group     Count     Mean      Median    StdDev
North     34        1631.59   1631      138.470
South     27        1388.85   1369      151.114
```

a) Test appropriate hypotheses and state your conclusion.
b) The boxplots of the two distributions show a possible outlier among the data north of Derby. What effect might that have had on your test?

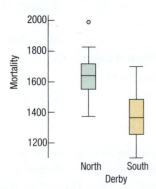

North   South
Derby

46. Technology investment. The Price-to-Book-value ratio is often used by investors to indicate whether a stock's price is particularly high or low relative to the value of the company. But different market sectors expect different Price/Book values. Here are data on technology companies (biz.yahoo.com/p/8conameu.html accessed in May 2013). We'll compare applications software companies with manufacturers of peripheral equipment. For both, we have taken the logarithm of the Price/Book ratio to make the distributions more nearly symmetric.

Group	Count	Mean	Median	StdDev
Peripherals	19	0.339035	0.264818	0.342258
Software	102	0.566206	0.516535	0.527435

a) State and test appropriate hypotheses and state your conclusion. (So you don't need to compute that strange degrees of freedom formula, the correct df is 36.)
b) Here are boxplots. What more do they tell you about the distributions? Do you think this changes your conclusions in part a?

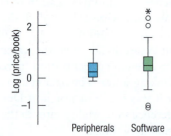

Peripherals   Software

47. Job satisfaction. A company institutes an exercise break for its workers to see if this will improve job satisfaction, as measured by a questionnaire that was given to a random sample of workers to assess their satisfaction.

Worker Number	Job Satisfaction Index	
	Before	After
1	34	33
2	28	36
3	29	50
4	45	41
5	26	37
6	27	41
7	24	39
8	15	21
9	15	20
10	27	37

a) Identify the procedure you would use to assess the effectiveness of the exercise program and check to see if the conditions allow for the use of that procedure.
b) Test an appropriate hypothesis and state your conclusion.

48. ERP effectiveness. When implementing a packaged Enterprise Resource Planning (ERP) system, many companies report that the module they first install is Financial Accounting. Among the measures used to gauge the effectiveness of their ERP system implementation is acceleration of the financial close process. Below is a sample of 8 companies that report their average time (in weeks) to financial close before and after the implementation of their ERP system.

Company	Before	After
1	6.5	4.2
2	7.0	5.9
3	8.0	8.0
4	4.5	4.0
5	5.2	3.8
6	4.9	4.1
7	5.2	6.0
8	6.5	4.2

a) Identify the procedure you would use to assess the effectiveness of the ERP system and check to see if the conditions allow for the use of that procedure.
b) Test an appropriate hypothesis and state your conclusion.

49. Delivery time. A small appliance company is interested in comparing delivery times of their product during two months. They are concerned that the summer slow-downs in August cause delivery times to lag during this month. Given the following delivery times (in days) of their appliances to the customer for a random sample of 6 orders each month, test if delivery times differ across these two months.

June	54	49	68	66	62	62
August	50	65	74	64	68	72

50. Branding. The *Journal of Applied Psychology* reported on a study that examined whether the content of TV shows influenced the ability of viewers to recall brand names of items featured in the commercials. The researchers randomly assigned volunteers to watch one of three programs, each containing the same nine commercials. One of the programs had violent content, another sexual content, and the third neutral content. After the shows ended, the subjects were asked to recall the brands of products that were advertised. The table shows summaries for how many brands were recalled.

	Program Type		
	Violent	**Sexual**	**Neutral**
n	108	108	108
Mean	2.08	1.71	3.17
SD	1.87	1.76	1.77

a) Do these results indicate that viewer memory for ads may differ depending on program content? Test the hypothesis that there is no difference in ad memory between programs with sexual content and those with violent content. State your conclusion.
b) Is there evidence that viewer memory for ads may differ between programs with sexual content and those with neutral content? Test an appropriate hypothesis and state your conclusion.

51. Ad campaign. You are a consultant to the marketing department of a business preparing to launch an ad campaign for a new product. The company can afford to run ads during one TV show, and has decided not to sponsor a show with sexual content (see Exercise 50). You create a confidence interval for the difference in mean number of brand names remembered between the groups watching violent shows and those watching neutral shows.

```
Two-Sample t
95% CI for μ_viol − μ_neut: (−1.578, −0.602)
```

a) At the meeting of the marketing staff, you have to explain what this output means. What will you say?
b) What advice would you give the company about the upcoming ad campaign?

52. Branding, part 2. In the study described in Exercise 50, the researchers also contacted the subjects again, 24 hours later, and asked them to recall the brands advertised.

Results for the number of brands recalled are summarized in the table.

	Program Type		
	Violent	**Sexual**	**Neutral**
No. of Subjects	101	106	103
Mean	3.02	2.72	4.65
SD	1.61	1.85	1.62

a) Is there a significant difference in viewers' abilities to remember brands advertised in shows with violent vs. neutral content?
b) Find a 95% confidence interval for the difference in mean number of brand names remembered between the groups watching shows with sexual content and those watching neutral shows. Interpret your interval in this context.

53. Ad recall. In Exercises 50 and 52, we see the number of advertised brand names people recalled immediately after watching TV shows and 24 hours later. Strangely enough, it appears that they remembered more about the ads the next day. Should we conclude this is true in general about people's memory of TV ads?

a) Suppose one analyst conducts a two-sample hypothesis test to see if memory of brands advertised during violent TV shows is higher 24 hours later. The P-value is 0.00013. What might she conclude?
b) Explain why her procedure was inappropriate. Which of the assumptions for inference was violated?
c) How might the design of this experiment have tainted these results?
d) Suggest a design that could compare immediate brand name recall with recall one day later.

54. Hybrid SUVs. The Chevy Tahoe Hybrid got a lot of attention when it first appeared. It is a relatively high-priced hybrid SUV that makes use of the latest technologies for fuel efficiency. One of the more popular hybrid SUVs on the market is the modestly priced Ford Escape Hybrid. A consumer group was interested in comparing the gas mileage of these two models. In order to do so, each vehicle was driven on the same 10 routes that combined both highway and city streets. The results showed that the mean mileage for the Chevy Tahoe was 29 mpg and for the Ford Escape it was 31 mpg. The standard deviations were 3.2 mpg and 2.5 mpg, respectively.

a) An analyst for the consumer group computed the two-sample *t* 95% confidence interval for the difference between the two means as (−0.71, 4.71). What conclusion would he reach based on this analysis?
b) Why is this procedure inappropriate? What assumption is violated?
c) In what way do you think this may have impacted the results?

55. The Internet. The National Assessment in Education Program compared science scores for students who had home Internet access with the scores of those who did not, as shown in the graph. They report that the differences are statistically significant.

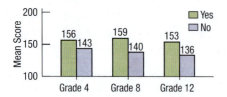

a) Explain what "statistically significant" means in this context.
b) If their conclusion is incorrect, which type of error did the researchers commit?
c) Does this prove that using the Internet at home can improve a student's performance in science?
d) What companies might be interested in this information?

56. Credit card debt public or private. The average credit card debt carried by college students was compared at public versus private universities. It was reported that a significant difference existed between the two types of institutions and that students at private universities carried higher credit card debt.

a) Explain what "statistically significant" means in this context.
b) If this conclusion is incorrect, which type of error was committed?
c) Does this prove that students who choose to attend public institutions will carry lower credit card debt?

57. Pizza sales. A national food product company believes that it sells more frozen pizza during the winter months than during the summer months. Average weekly sales for a sample of stores in the Baltimore area over a three-year period provided the following data for sales volume (in pounds) during the two seasons.

Season	N	Mean	StDev	Minimum	Maximum
Winter	38	31234	13500	15312	73841
Summer	40	22475	8442	12743	54706

a) How much difference is there between the mean amount of this brand of frozen pizza sold (in pounds) between the two seasons? (Assume that this time frame represents typical sales in the Baltimore area.)
b) Construct and interpret a 95% confidence interval for the difference between weekly sales during the winter and summer months.
c) Suggest factors that might have influenced the sales of the frozen pizza during the winter months.

58. More pizza sales. Here's some additional information about the pizza sales data presented in Exercise 57. It is generally thought that sales spike during the weeks leading up to AFC and NFC football championship games, as well as leading up to the Super Bowl at the beginning of February each year. If we omit those 6 weeks of sales from this three-year period of weekly sales, the summary statistics look like this.

Season	N	Mean	StDev	Minimum	Maximum
Winter	32	28995	9913	15312	48354
Summer	40	22475	8442	12743	54706

Do sales appear to be higher during the winter months after omitting those weeks most influenced by football championship games?

a) Write the null and alternative hypotheses.
b) Test the null hypotheses and state your conclusion.
c) Suggest additional factors that may influence pizza sales not accounted for in this exercise.

⊤ 59. Olympic heats 2012. In Olympic running events, preliminary heats are determined by random draw, so we should expect the ability level of runners in the various heats to be about the same, on average. The table gives the times (in seconds) for the 800-m men's run in the 2012 Olympics in London for preliminary heats 1 and 3. Is there any evidence that the mean time to finish is different for randomized heats? Explain. Be sure to include a discussion of assumptions and conditions for your analysis.

Country	Name	Time	Heat
BOT	Nigel Amos	105.9	1
BRA	Fabiano Pecanha	106.3	1
ESP	Luis Alberto Marco	106.9	1
USA	Khadevis Robinson	107.2	1
POL	Marcin Lewandowski	107.6	1
RUS	Ivan Tukhtachev	109.8	1
GUM	Derek Mandell	118.9	1
SUD	Abubaker Kaki	105.5	3
KEN	Timothy Kitum	105.7	3
KSA	Abdulaziz Ladan Mohammed	106.1	3
CUB	Andy González	106.2	3
GBR	Gareth Warburton	107.0	3
HUN	Tamás Kazi	107.1	3
GER	Sören Ludolph	108.6	3
VAN	Arnold Sorina	114.3	3

⊤ 60. Swimming heats 2016. In Exercise 59, we looked at the times in two different heats for the 800-m men's run from the 2012 Olympics. Unlike track events, swimming heats are *not* determined at random. Instead, swimmers are seeded so that better swimmers are placed in later heats. Here are the times (in seconds) for two heats of the women's 400-m freestyle at the 2016 Olympics.

Heat 2		
Country	Name	Time
SRB	Katarina Simonovic	120.1
CZE	Barbora Seemanova	120.3
MKD	Anastasia Bogdanovski	120.5
CUB	Elisbet Games	121.1
BAH	Joanna Evans	121.3
HON	Sara Pastrana	123.2
PER	Andrea Cedron Rodriguez	125.3

Heat 5		
Country	Name	Time
USA	Katie Ledecky	115
AUS	Emma McKeon	115.8
SWE	Michelle Coleman	116.5
AUS	Bronte Barratt	116.9
ESP	Melania Costa Schmid	118.2
JPN	Rikako Ikee	118.5
FRA	Coralie Balmy	118.8
GBR	Eleanor Faulkner	120.5

Do these results suggest that the mean times of heat 5 are faster than heat 2? Explain. Include a discussion of assumptions and conditions for your analysis.

61. Tee tests. Does it matter what kind of tee a golfer places the ball on? The company that manufactures "Stinger" tees claims that the thinner shaft and smaller head will lessen resistance and drag, reducing spin and allowing the ball to travel farther. Golf Laboratories, Inc., compared the distance traveled by golf balls hit off regular wooden tees to those hit off Stinger tees. All the balls were struck by the same golf club using a robotic device set to swing the club head at approximately 95 miles per hour. Summary statistics from the test are shown in the table. Assume that 6 balls were hit off each tee and that the data were suitable for inference. Is there evidence that balls hit off the Stinger tees would have a higher initial velocity?

		Total Distance (yards)	Ball Velocity (mph)	Club Velocity (mph)
Regular Tee	Mean	227.17	127.00	96.17
	SD	2.14	0.89	0.41
Stinger Tee	Mean	241.00	128.83	96.17
	SD	2.76	0.41	0.52

62. Tee tests, part 2. Given the test results on golf tees described in Exercise 61, is there evidence that balls hit off Stinger tees travel farther? Assume that 6 balls were hit off each tee and that the data are suitable for inference.

63. Marketing slogan. A company is considering marketing their classical music as "music to study by." Is this a valid slogan? In a study conducted by some statistics students, 62 people were randomly assigned to listen to rap music, music by Mozart, or no music while attempting to memorize objects pictured on a page. They were then asked to list all the objects they could remember. Here are summary statistics for each group.

	Rap	Mozart	No Music
Count	29	20	13
Mean	10.72	10.00	12.77
SD	3.99	3.19	4.73

a) Does it appear that it is better to study while listening to Mozart than to rap music? Test an appropriate hypothesis and state your conclusion.
b) Create a 90% confidence interval for the mean difference in memory score between students who study to Mozart and those who listen to no music at all. Interpret your interval.

64. Marketing slogan, part 2. Using the results of the experiment described in Exercise 63, does it matter whether one listens to rap music while studying, or is it better to study without music at all?

a) Test an appropriate hypothesis and state your conclusion.
b) If you concluded there is a difference, estimate the size of that difference with a 90% confidence interval and explain what your interval means.

T 65. Mutual fund returns 2017. You have heard that if you leave your money in mutual funds for a longer period of time, you will see a greater return. So you would like to compare the 1-year and 5-year returns of a random sample of mutual funds to see if indeed, your return is expected to be greater if you leave your money in the funds for 5 years.

a) Using the data provided, check the conditions for this test.
b) Write the null and alternative hypotheses for this test.
c) Test the hypothesis and find the P-value if appropriate.
d) Find a 95% confidence interval for the mean difference.

T 66. Mutual fund returns 2017, part 2. An investment blog suggests that you've been doing this all wrong and should invest in mutual funds only for the short term. So you decide to compare returns at 1 month and 3 months.

a) Using the data provided, check the conditions for this test.
b) Write the null and alternative hypotheses for this test.
c) Test the hypothesis and find the P-value if appropriate.
d) Find a 95% confidence interval for the mean difference.

T 67. **Attendance 2016.** For the same reasons identified in Exercise 42, a friend of yours claims that the attendance at Road (away) games is lower in the American League than in the National League. Using the **Attendance** 2016 data (same data as in Exercises 42 and 44), you decide to test your friend's theory.

a) Using the data provided in the file, check the conditions for this test.
b) Write the null and alternative hypotheses for this test.
c) Test the hypothesis and find the P-value.
d) What is your conclusion?
e) Use the pooled *t*-test to test the hypothesis and compare your answer to parts c and d.

T 68. **Cloud seeding.** It has long been a dream of farmers to summon rain when it is needed for their crops. Crop losses to drought have significant economic impact. One possibility is cloud seeding, in which chemicals are dropped into clouds in an attempt to induce rain. Simpson, Alsen, and Eden (*Technometrics*, 1975) report the results of trials in which clouds were seeded and the amount of rainfall recorded. The authors report on 26 seeded (Group 2) and 26 unseeded (Group 1) clouds. Each group has been sorted in order of the amount of rainfall, largest amount first. Here are two possible tests to study the question of whether cloud seeding works.

```
Paired t-Test of μ(1 − 2)
Mean of Paired Differences = −277.4
t-Statistic = −3.641 w/25 dfp = 0.0012
2-Sample t-test of μ1 − μ2
Difference Between Means = −277.4
t-Statistic = −1.998w/33 dfp = 0.0538
```

a) Which of these tests is appropriate for these data? Explain.
b) Using the test you selected, state your conclusion.

T 69. **Online insurance.** After seeing countless commercials claiming one can get cheaper car insurance from an online company, a local insurance agent was concerned that he might lose some customers. To investigate, he randomly selected profiles (type of car, coverage, driving record, etc.) for 10 of his clients and checked online price quotes for their policies. The comparisons are shown in the table.

Local	Online	PriceDiff
568	391	177
872	602	270
451	488	−37
1229	903	326
605	677	−72
1021	1270	−249
783	703	80
844	789	55
907	1008	−101
712	702	10

His statistical software produced the following summaries (where *PriceDiff* = *Local* − *Online*):

Variable	Count	Mean	StdDev
Local	10	799.200	229.281
Online	10	753.300	256.267
PriceDiff	10	45.900	175.663

At first, the insurance agent wondered whether there was some kind of mistake in this output. He thought the Pythagorean Theorem of Statistics should work for finding the standard deviation of the price differences—in other words, that

$$SD(Local − Online) = \sqrt{SD^2(Local) + SD^2(Online)}.$$

But when he checked, he found that

$$\sqrt{(229.281)^2 + (256.267)^2} = 343.864,$$

not 175.663 as given by the software. Tell him where his mistake is.

T 70. **Wind speed.** Alternative sources of energy are of increasing interest throughout the energy industry. Wind energy has great potential. But appropriate sites must be found for the turbines. To select the site for an electricity-generating wind turbine, wind speeds were recorded at several potential sites every 6 hours for a year. Two sites not far from each other looked good. Each had a mean wind speed high enough to qualify, but we should choose the site with a higher average daily wind speed. Because the sites are near each other and the wind speeds were recorded at the same times, we should view the speeds as paired. Here are the summaries of the speeds (in miles per hour):

Variable	Count	Mean	StdDev
site2	1114	7.452	3.586
site4	1114	7.248	3.421
site2 − site4	1114	0.204	2.551

Is there a mistake in this output? Why doesn't the Pythagorean Theorem of Statistics work here? In other words, shouldn't

$$SD(site2 − site4) = \sqrt{SD^2(site2) + SD^2(site4)}?$$

But $\sqrt{(3.586)^2 + (3.421)^2} = 4.956$, not 2.551 as given by the software. Explain why this happened.

T 71. **Online insurance, part 2.** In Exercise 69, we saw summary statistics for 10 drivers' car insurance premiums quoted by a local agent and an online company. Here are displays for each company's quotes and for the difference (*Local − Online*):

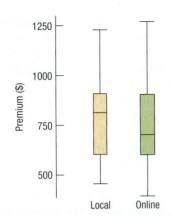

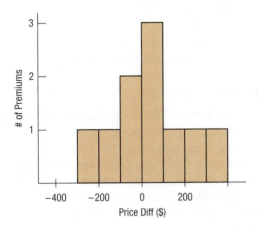

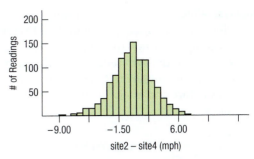

a) The boxplots show outliers for each site, yet the histogram shows none. Discuss why.

b) Which of the summaries would you use to select between these sites? Why?

c) Using the information you have, discuss the assumptions and conditions for paired t inference for these data. (*Hint:* Think hard about the Independence Assumption in particular.)

T 73. Online insurance, part 3. Exercises 69 and 71 give summaries and displays for car insurance premiums quoted by a local agent and an online company. Test an appropriate hypothesis to see if there is evidence that drivers might save money by switching to the online company.

T 74. Wind speed, part 3. Exercises 70 and 72 give summaries and displays for two potential sites for a wind turbine. Test an appropriate hypothesis to see if there is evidence that either of these sites has a higher average wind speed.

75. Employee athletes. An ergonomics consultant is engaged by a large consumer products company to see what they can do to increase productivity. The consultant recommends an "employee athlete" program, encouraging every employee to devote 5 minutes an hour to physical activity. The company worries that the gains in productivity will be offset by the loss in time on the job. They'd like to know if the program increases or decreases productivity. To measure it, they monitor a random sample of 145 employees who word process, measuring their hourly key strokes both before and after the program is instituted. Here are the data:

a) Which of the summaries would help you decide whether the online company offers cheaper insurance? Why?

b) The standard deviation of *PriceDiff* is quite a bit smaller than the standard deviation of prices quoted by either the local or online companies. Discuss why.

c) Using the information you have, discuss the assumptions and conditions for inference with these data.

T 72. Wind speed, part 2. In Exercise 70, we saw summary statistics for wind speeds at two sites near each other, both being considered as locations for an electricity-generating wind turbine. The data, recorded every 6 hours for a year, showed each of the sites had a mean wind speed high enough to qualify, but how can we tell which site is best? Here are some displays:

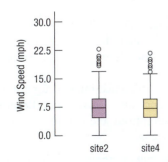

	Keystrokes per Hour		
	Before	**After**	**Difference (After − Before)**
Mean	1534.2	1556.9	22.7
SD	168.5	149.5	113.6
N	145	145	145

a) What are the null and alternative hypotheses?

b) What can you conclude? Explain.

c) Give a 95% confidence interval for the mean change in productivity (as measured by keystrokes per hour).

76. Employee athletes, part 2. A small company, on hearing about the employee athlete program (see Exercise 75) at the large company down the street, decides to try it as well. To measure the difference in productivity, they measure the average number of keystrokes per hour of 23 employees before and after the program is instituted. The data follow:

	Keystrokes per Hour		
	Before	**After**	**Difference (After − Before)**
Mean	1497.3	1544.8	47.5
SD	155.4	136.7	122.8
N	23	23	23

a) Is there evidence to suggest that the program increases productivity?
b) Give a 95% confidence interval for the mean change in productivity (as measured by keystrokes per hour).
c) Given this information and the results of Exercise 75, what recommendations would you make to the company about the effectiveness of the program?

T 77. Exercise equipment. A leading manufacturer of exercise equipment wanted to collect data on the effectiveness of their equipment. An August 2001 article in the journal *Medicine and Science in Sports and Exercise* compared how long it would take men and women to burn 200 calories during light or heavy workouts on various kinds of exercise equipment. The results summarized in the table are the average times for a group of physically active young men and women whose performances were measured on a representative sample of exercise equipment.

		Average Minutes to Burn 200 Calories			
		Hard Exertion		**Light Exertion**	
		Men	**Women**	**Men**	**Women**
Machine Type	Treadmill	12	17	14	22
	X-C Skier	12	16	16	23
	Stair Climber	13	18	20	37
	Rowing Machine	14	16	21	25
	Exercise Rider	22	24	27	36
	Exercise Bike	16	20	29	44

a) On average, how many minutes longer than a man must a woman exercise at a light exertion rate in order to burn 200 calories? Find a 95% confidence interval.
b) Estimate the average number of minutes longer a woman must work out at light exertion than at heavy exertion to get the same benefit. Find a 95% confidence interval.
c) These data are actually averages rather than individual times. How might this affect the margins of error in these confidence intervals?

T 78. Market value. Real estate agents want to set correctly the price of a house that's about to go on the real estate market. They must choose a price that strikes a balance between one that is so high that the house takes too long to sell and one that's so low that not enough value will go to the homeowner. One appraisal method is the "Comparative Market Analysis" approach by which the market value of a house is based on recent sales of similar homes in the neighborhood. Because no two houses are exactly the same, appraisers have to adjust comparable homes for such features as extra square footage, bedrooms, fireplaces, upgrading, parking facilities, swimming pool, lot size, location, and so on. The appraised market values and the selling prices of 45 homes from the same region are in the data file.

a) Test the hypothesis that on average, the market value and the sale price of homes from this region are the same.
b) Find a 95% confidence interval for the mean difference.
c) Explain your findings in a sentence or two in context.

T 79. Stopping distance. In an experiment on braking performance, a tire manufacturer measured the stopping distance for one of its tire models. On a test track, a car made repeated stops from 60 miles per hour. Twenty tests were run, 10 each on both dry and wet pavement, with results shown in the table. (Note that actual *braking distance*, which takes into account the driver's reaction time, is much longer, typically nearly 300 feet at 60 mph!)

Stopping Distance (ft)	
Dry Pavement	**Wet Pavement**
145	211
152	191
141	220
143	207
131	198
148	208
126	206
140	177
135	183
133	223

a) Find a 95% confidence interval for the mean dry pavement stopping distance. Be sure to check the appropriate assumptions and conditions, and explain what your interval means.
b) Find a 95% confidence interval for the mean increase in stopping distance on wet pavement. Be sure to check the appropriate assumptions and conditions, and explain what your interval means.

T 80. Stopping distances, again. For another test of the tires in Exercise 79, the company tried them on 10 different cars, recording the stopping distance for each car on both wet and dry pavement. Results are shown in the following table.

Stopping Distance (ft)		
Car #	Dry Pavement	Wet Pavement
1	150	201
2	147	220
3	136	192
4	134	146
5	130	182
6	134	173
7	134	202
8	128	180
9	136	192
10	158	206

a) Find a 95% confidence interval for the mean dry pavement stopping distance. Be sure to check the appropriate assumptions and conditions, and explain what your interval means.

b) Find a 95% confidence interval for the mean increase in stopping distance on wet pavement. Be sure to check the appropriate assumptions and conditions, and explain what your interval means.

T 81. Airline "bumping" 2017. Commercial airlines overbook flights, selling more tickets than they have seats, because a sizable number of reservation holders don't show up in time for their flights. But sometimes, there are more passengers wishing to board than there are seats. Most airlines try to entice travelers to voluntarily give up their seats in return for free travel or other awards, but they do have to "bump" some travelers involuntarily. Of course, they don't like to offend passengers by bumping, so they are constantly trying to improve their systems for predicting how many passengers will show up. Have the rates of "bumping" changed? Here are data on the number of passengers involuntarily denied boarding ("bumping" is not the approved term) per 10,000 passengers during the periods of January to June in 2016 and 2017 by airline.

Involuntary Denied Boarding/10K Enplanements		
Airline	2017	2016
1 Delta Airlines	0.07	0.09
2 Virgin America	0.27	0.13
3 JetBlue Airways	0.54	0.82
4 United Airlines	0.30	0.45
5 Hawaiian Airlines	0.11	0.04
6 Express Jet Airlines	0.67	1.58
7 Skywest Airlines	0.37	0.96
8 American Airlines	0.46	0.66
9 Alaska Airlines	0.35	0.41
10 Southwest Airlines	0.58	1.06
11 Frontier Airlines	0.45	0.63
12 Spirit Airlines	0.88	0.93

a) Are these paired data? Why or why not?

b) Was there a statistically significant change in the number of passengers involuntarily denied boarding per 10,000 passengers?

T 82. Grocery prices. WinCo Foods, a large discount grocery retailer in the western United States, promotes itself as the lowest priced grocery retailer. In newspaper ads WinCo Foods published a price comparison for products between WinCo and several competing grocery retailers. One of the retailers compared against WinCo was Walmart, also known as a low price competitor. WinCo selected a variety of products, listed the price of the product charges at each retailer, and showed the sales receipt to prove the prices at WinCo were the lowest in the area. A sample of the products and their price comparison at both WinCo and Walmart are shown in the following table:

Item	WinCo Price	Walmart Price
Bananas (lb)	0.42	0.56
Red Onions (lb)	0.58	0.98
Mini Peeled Carrots (1 lb bag)	0.98	1.48
Roma Tomatoes (lb)	0.98	2.67
Deli Tater Wedges (lb)	1.18	1.78
Beef Cube Steak (lb)	3.83	4.11
Beef Top Round London Broil (lb)	3.48	4.12
Pillsbury Devils Food Cake Mix (18.25 oz)	0.88	0.88
Lipton Rice and Sauce Mix (5.6 oz)	0.88	1.06
Sierra Nevada Pale Ale (12 – 12 oz bottles)	12.68	12.84
GM Cheerios Oat Clusters (11.3 oz)	1.98	2.74
Charmin Bathroom Tissue (12 roll)	5.98	7.48
Bumble Bee Pink Salmon (14.75 oz)	1.58	1.98
Pace Thick & Chunky Salsa, Mild (24 oz)	2.28	2.78
Nalley Chili, Regular w/Beans (15 oz)	0.78	0.78
Challenge Butter (lb quarters)	2.18	2.58
Kraft American Singles (12 oz)	2.27	2.27
Yuban Coffee FAC (36 oz)	5.98	7.56
Totino's Pizza Rolls, Pepperoni (19.8 oz)	2.38	2.42
Rosarita Refried Beans, Original (16 oz)	0.68	0.73
Barilla Spaghetti (16 oz)	0.78	1.23
Sun-Maid Mini Raisins (14 – .5 oz)	1.18	1.36
Jif Peanut Butter, Creamy (28 oz)	2.54	2.72
Dole Fruit Bowl, Mixed Fruit (4 – 4 oz)	1.68	1.98
Progresso Chicken Noodle Soup (19 oz)	1.28	1.38
Precious Mozzarella Ball, Part Skim (16 oz)	3.28	4.23
Mrs. Cubbison Seasoned Croutons (6 oz)	0.88	1.12
Kellogg's Raisin Bran (20 oz)	1.98	2.50
Campbell's Soup at Hand, Cream of Tomato (10.75 oz)	1.18	1.26

a) Do the prices listed indicate that, on average, prices at WinCo are lower than prices at Walmart?

b) At the bottom of the price list, the following statement appears: "Though this list is not intended to represent a typical weekly grocery order or a random list of grocery items, WinCo continues to be the area's low price leader." Why do you think WinCo added this statement?

c) What other comments could be made about the statistical validity of the test on price comparisons given in the ad?

JUST CHECKING ANSWERS

1 $H_0: \mu_{eyes} - \mu_{flowers} = 0$

2 ✓ **Independence Assumption:** The amount paid by one person should be independent of the amount paid by others.

  ✓ **Randomization Condition:** This study was observational. Treatments alternated a week at a time and were applied to the same group of office workers.

  ✓ **Nearly Normal Condition:** We don't have the data to check, but it seems unlikely there would be outliers in either group.

  ✓ **Independent Groups Assumptions:** The same workers were recorded each week, but week-to-week independence is plausible.

3 $H_A: \mu_{eyes} - \mu_{flowers} \neq 0$. An argument could be made for a one-sided test because the research hypothesis was that eyes would improve honest compliance.

4 Office workers' compliance in leaving money to pay for food at an office coffee station was different when a picture of eyes was placed behind the "honesty box" than when the picture was one of flowers.

5 These are independent groups sampled at random, so use a two-sample t confidence interval to estimate the size of the difference.

6 If the same random sample of students was sampled both in the first year and again in the fourth year of their university experience, then this would be a paired t-test.

7 A male and female are selected from each work group. The question calls for a paired t-test.

8 Since we have no reason to believe that public and private companies have equal variances, we should use a two-sample test.

9 Since the same 50 companies are surveyed twice to examine a change in variables over time, this would be a paired t-test.

CHAPTER 15

Inference for Counts: Chi-Square Tests

SAC Capital

Hedge funds, like mutual funds and pension funds, pool investors' money in an attempt to make profits. Unlike these other funds, however, hedge funds are not required to register with the U.S. Securities and Exchange Commission (SEC) because they issue securities in "private offerings" only to "qualified investors" (typically, investors with either $1 million in assets or annual income of at least $200,000).

Hedge funds don't necessarily "hedge" their investments against market moves. But typically these funds use multiple, often complex, strategies to exploit inefficiencies in the market. For these reasons, hedge fund managers have the reputation for being obsessive traders, and the SEC has recently begun to investigate their practices.

One of the most successful hedge funds is SAC Capital, which was founded by Steven (Stevie) A. Cohen in 1992 with nine employees and $25 million in assets under management (AUM). SAC Capital returned annual gains of 40% or more through much of the 1990s and is now reported to have more than 1000 employees and nearly $14 billion in assets under management. According to *Forbes*, Cohen's $9.3 billion fortune ranks him as the 41st wealthiest American and 117th richest person in the world.

Cohen, a legendary figure on Wall Street, is known for taking advantage of any information he can find and for turning that information into profit. Unlike most hedge funds, which trade by computer and pay fractions of a cent per trade, SAC still trades the "old fashioned way," paying 3 to 5¢. It is generally agreed to be the largest payer of fees on Wall Street, a largesse that may earn it tips from traders.

In March of 2013, SAC agreed to pay (without admitting guilt) a fine of $616 million—the largest fine in the history of the Securities and Exchange Commission—to settle charges of insider trading in just two trades. In October of 2013, SAC pleaded guilty and agreed to pay fines of $1.2B. The government also forced SAC to stop managing money for outside investors. But don't feel too sorry for Mr. Cohen. The firm will continue to manage his fortune of over $9B. He is still the 35th richest man in the United States.

In a business as competitive as hedge fund management, information is gold. Being the first to have information and knowing how to act on it can mean the difference between success and failure. Hedge fund managers look for small advantages everywhere, hoping to exploit inefficiencies in the market and to turn those inefficiencies into profit.

Wall Street has plenty of "wisdom" about market patterns. For example, investors are advised to watch for "calendar effects," certain times of year or days of the week that are particularly good or bad: "As goes January, so goes the year" and "Sell in May and go away." Some analysts claim that the "bad period" for holding stocks is from the sixth trading day of June to the fifth-to-last trading day of October. Of course, there is also Mark Twain's advice:

> October. This is one of the peculiarly dangerous months to speculate in stocks. The others are July, January, September, April, November, May, March, June, December, August, and February.
> —Mark Twain, *Pudd'nhead Wilson*, 1894

One common claim is that stocks show a weekly pattern. For example, some argue that there is a *weekend effect* in which stock returns on Mondays are often lower than those of the immediately preceding Friday. Are patterns such as this real? We have the data, so we can check. Between October 1, 1928, and January 12, 2018, there were 22,418 trading sessions. Let's first see how many trading days fell on each day of the week. It's not exactly 20% for each day because of holidays. The distribution of days is shown in Table 15.1.

Of these 22,418 trading sessions, 11,701, or about 52% of the days, saw a gain in the Dow Jones Industrial Average (DJIA). To test for a pattern, we need a model. The model comes from the supposition that any day is as likely to show a gain as any other. In any sample of positive or "up" days, we should expect to see the same distribution of days as in Table 15.1—in other words, about 19.28% of "up" days would be Mondays, 20.28% would be Tuesdays, and so on. Here is the distribution of days in one such random sample of 1000 "up" days.

Of course, we expect some variation. We wouldn't expect the proportions of days in the two tables to match exactly. In our sample, the percentage of Mondays in Table 15.2 is slightly lower than in Table 15.1, and the proportion of Fridays is a little higher. Are these deviations enough for us to declare that there is a recognizable pattern?

Day of the Week	Count	% of Days
Monday	4322	0.1928
Tuesday	4547	0.2028
Wednesday	4570	0.2039
Thursday	4500	0.2007
Friday	4479	0.1998

TABLE 15.1 The distribution of days of the week among the 22,418 trading days from October 1, 1928, to January 12, 2018. We expect about 20% to fall in each day, with minor variations due to holidays and other events.

TABLE 15.2 The distribution of days of the week for a sample of 1000 "up" trading days selected at random from October 1, 1928, to January 12, 2018. If there is no pattern, we would expect the proportions here to match fairly closely the proportions observed among all trading days in Table 15.1.

Day of the Week	Count	% of Days in the Sample of "Up" days
Monday	166	0.166
Tuesday	202	0.202
Wednesday	218	0.218
Thursday	192	0.192
Friday	222	0.222

15.1 Goodness-of-Fit Tests

To address this question, we test the table's **goodness-of-fit**, where *fit* refers to the null model proposed. Here, the null model is that there is no pattern, that the distribution of *up* days should be the same as the distribution of trading days overall. (If there were no holidays or other closings, that would just be 20% for each day of the week.)

Assumptions and Conditions

Data for a goodness-of-fit test are organized in tables, and the assumptions and conditions reflect that. Rather than having an observation for each individual, we typically work with summary counts in categories. Here, the individuals are trading days, but rather than list all 1000 trading days in the sample, we have totals for each weekday.

Counted Data Condition.   The data must be counts for the categories of a categorical variable. This might seem a silly condition to check. But many kinds of values can be assigned to categories, and it is unfortunately common to find the methods of this chapter applied incorrectly (even by business professionals) to proportions or quantities just because they happen to be organized in a two-way table. So check to be sure that you really have counts.

Independence Assumption

Independence Assumption.   The counts in the cells should be independent of each other. You should think about whether that's reasonable. If the data are a random sample you can simply check the Randomization Condition.

Randomization Condition.   The individuals counted in the table should be a random sample from some population. We need this condition if we want to generalize our conclusions to that population. We took a random sample of 1000 trading days on which the DJIA rose. That lets us assume that the market's performance on any one day is independent of performance on another. If we had selected 1000 consecutive trading days, there would be a risk that market performance on one day could affect performance on the next, or that an external event could affect performance for several consecutive days.

Sample Size Assumption

Sample Size Assumption.   We must have enough data for the methods to work. We usually just check the following condition:

Expected Cell Frequency Condition.   We should expect to see at least 5 individuals in each cell. The expected cell frequency condition should remind you of—and is, in fact, quite similar to—the condition that np and nq be at least 10 when we test proportions.

Expected Cell Frequencies

Companies often want to assess the relative successes of their products in different regions. However, a company whose sales regions had 100, 200, 300, and 400 representatives might not expect equal sales in all regions. They might expect observed sales to be proportional to the size of the sales force. The null hypothesis in that case would be that the proportions of sales were 1/10, 2/10, 3/10, and 4/10, respectively. With 500 total sales, their expected counts would be 50, 100, 150, and 200.

Chi-Square Model

We have observed a count in each category (weekday). We can compute the number of up days we'd *expect* to see for each weekday if the null model were true. For the trading days example, the expected counts come from the null hypothesis that the up days are distributed among weekdays just as trading days are. Of course, we could imagine almost any kind of model and base a null hypothesis on that model.

To decide whether the null model is plausible, we look at the differences between the expected values from the model and the counts we observe. We wonder: Are these differences so large that they call the model into question, or could they have arisen from natural sampling variability? We denote the *differences* between these observed and expected counts, $(Obs - Exp)$. As we did with variance, we square them. That gives us positive values and focuses attention on any cells with large differences. Because the differences between observed and expected counts generally get larger the more data we have, we also need to get an idea of the *relative* sizes of the differences. To do that, we divide each squared difference by the expected count for that cell.

The test statistic, called the **chi-square (or chi-squared) statistic**, is found by adding up the sum of the squares of the deviations between the observed and expected counts divided by the expected counts:

$$\chi^2 = \sum_{all\ cells} \frac{(Obs - Exp)^2}{Exp}.$$

The chi-square statistic is denoted χ^2, where χ is the Greek letter chi (pronounced kī). The resulting family of sampling distribution models is called the **chi-square models**.

The members of this family of models differ in the number of degrees of freedom. The number of degrees of freedom for a goodness-of-fit test is $k - 1$, where k is the number of cells—in this example, 5 weekdays.

We will use the chi-square statistic only for testing hypotheses, not for constructing confidence intervals. A small chi-square statistic means that our model fits the data well, so a small value gives us no reason to doubt the null hypothesis. If the observed counts don't match the expected counts, the statistic will be large. If the calculated statistic value is large enough, we'll reject the null hypothesis. So the chi-square test is always one-sided. What could be simpler? Let's see how it works.

> **NOTATION ALERT**
>
> We compare the counts *observed* in each cell with the counts we *expect* to find. The usual notation uses *Obs* and *Exp* as we've used here. The expected counts are found from the null model.

> **NOTATION ALERT**
>
> The only use of the Greek letter χ in statistics is to represent the chi-square statistic and the associated sampling distribution. This violates the general rule that Greek letters represent population parameters. Here we are using a Greek letter simply to name a family of distribution models and a statistic.

IN PRACTICE 15.1 Goodness-of-fit test

MANAGER I manage 8 call center operators at a telecommunications company. To develop new business, I have given each operator a list of randomly selected phone numbers of rival phone company customers. I have also provided the operators with a script that tries to convince the customers to switch providers. I'd like to know whether some of the operators are performing better than others.

The 120 new customer acquisitions are distributed as follows:

Operator	1	2	3	4	5	6	7	8
New Customers	11	17	9	12	19	18	13	21

ANALYST You have randomized the potential new customers to the operators so the Randomization Condition is satisfied. The data are counts and there are at least 5 expected counts in each cell, so we can apply a chi-square goodness-of-fit test to the null hypothesis that the operator performance is uniform and that each of the operators will convince the same number of customers. Specifically we expect each operator to have converted 1/8 of the 120 customers that switched providers.

Operator	1	2	3	4	5	6	7	8
Observed	11	17	9	12	19	18	13	21
Expected	15	15	15	15	15	15	15	15
Observed − Expected	−4	2	−6	−3	4	3	−2	6
$(Obs - Exp)^2$	16	4	36	9	16	9	4	36
$(Obs - Exp)^2/Exp$	$16/15 = 1.07$	$4/15 = 0.27$	$36/15 = 2.40$	$9/15 = 0.60$	$16/15 = 1.07$	$9/15 = 0.60$	$4/15 = 0.27$	$36/15 = 2.40$

$$\sum \frac{(Obs - Exp)^2}{Exp} = 1.07 + 0.27 + 2.40 + \cdots + 2.40 = 8.68$$

The number of degrees of freedom is $k - 1 = 7$.

$$P(\chi_7^2 > 8.68) = 0.2765$$

8.68 is not a surprising value for a chi-square statistic with 7 degrees of freedom. So, we fail to reject the null hypothesis that the operators actually find new customers at different rates. I conclude that the operators are performing at roughly the same level. Any differences are probably random fluctuations.

BY HAND The chi-square calculation

Here are the steps to calculate the chi-square statistic:

1. **Find the expected values.** These come from the null hypothesis model. Every null model gives a hypothesized proportion for each cell. The expected value is the product of the total number of observations times this proportion. (The result need not be an integer.)

2. **Compute the residuals.** Once you have expected values for each cell, find the residuals, $Obs - Exp$.

3. **Square the residuals.** $(Obs - Exp)^2$

4. **Compute the components.** Find $\dfrac{(Obs - Exp)^2}{Exp}$ for each cell.

5. **Find the sum of the components.** That's the chi-square statistic,
$$\chi^2 = \sum_{all\ cells} \frac{(Obs - Exp)^2}{Exp}.$$

6. **Find the degrees of freedom.** It's equal to the number of cells minus one.

7. **Test the hypothesis.** Large chi-square values mean lots of deviation from the hypothesized model, so they give small P-values. Look up the critical value from a table of chi-square values such as Table X in Appendix B, or use technology to find the P-value directly.

(continued)

The steps of the chi-square calculations are often laid out in tables and they are particularly easy to perform on a spreadsheet. Use one row for each category, and columns for observed counts, expected counts, residuals, squared residuals, and the contributions to the chi-square total:

	A	B	C	D	E	F	G
1	Day	Pop%	Obs	Exp	Resid	Resid^2	Component
2	Monday	0.19279	166	192.79	-26.8	717.70	3.722724726
3	Tuesday	0.20283	202	202.83	-0.8	0.69	0.00339644
4	Wednesday	0.20385	218	203.85	14.2	200.22	0.982205053
5	Thursday	0.20073	192	200.73	-8.7	76.21	0.379678673
6	Friday	0.19979	222	199.79	22.2	493.28	2.469012964

TABLE 15.3 Calculations for the chi-square statistic in the trading days example can be performed conveniently in Microsoft Excel 2016. Set up the calculation in the first row and Fill Down, and then find the sum of the rightmost column. The CHIDIST function looks up the chi-square total to find the P-value.

GUIDED EXAMPLE   Stock Market Patterns

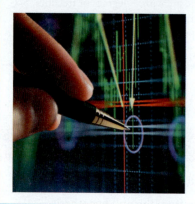

We have counts of the "up" days for each day of the week. The economic theory we want to investigate is whether there is a pattern in "up" days. So, our null hypothesis is that across all days in which the DJIA rose, the days of the week are distributed as they are across all trading days. (As we saw, the trading days are not quite *evenly* distributed because of holidays, so we use the *trading days* percentages as the null model.) The alternative hypothesis is that the observed percentages are *not* uniform. The test statistic looks at how closely the observed data match this idealized situation.

PLAN **Define** the problem and state what you want to know. Identify the variables and context. **Hypotheses** State the null and alternative hypotheses. For χ^2 tests, it's usually easier to state the hypotheses in words than in symbols.	We want to know whether the distribution for "up" days differs from the null model (the trading days distribution). We have the number of times each weekday appeared among a random sample of 1000 "up" days. H_0: The days of the work week are distributed among the up days as they are among all trading days. H_A: The trading days model does not fit the up days distribution.
DO **Model** Think about the assumptions and check the conditions.	✓ **Counted Data Condition** We have counts of the days of the week for all trading days and for the "up" days. ✓ **Independence Assumption** We have no reason to expect that one day's performance will affect another's, but to be safe we've taken a random sample of days. The randomization should make them far enough apart to alleviate any concerns about dependence. ✓ **Randomization Condition** We have a random sample of 1000 days from the time period. ✓ **Expected Cell Frequency Condition** All the expected cell frequencies are much larger than 5.

Specify the sampling distribution model.

Name the test you will use.

To find the expected number of days, we take the fraction of each weekday from all days and multiply by the number of "up" days.

For example, there were 4322 Mondays out of 22,418 trading days.

So, we'd expect there would be $1000 \times 4322/22418$ or 192.79 Mondays among the 1000 "up" days.

Each cell contributes a value equal to $\dfrac{(Obs - Exp)^2}{Exp}$ to the chi-square sum.

Add up these components. If you do it by hand, it can be helpful to arrange the calculation in a table or spreadsheet.

The P-value is the probability in the upper tail of the χ^2 model. It can be found using software or a table (see Table X in Appendix B).

Large χ^2 statistic values correspond to small P-values, which would lead us to reject the null hypothesis, but the value here is not particularly large.

The conditions are satisfied, so we'll use a χ^2 model with $5 - 1 = 4$ degrees of freedom and do a **chi-square goodness-of-fit test**.

The expected values are:

Monday	192.79
Tuesday	202.83
Wednesday	203.85
Thursday	200.73
Friday	199.79

And we observe:

Monday	166
Tuesday	202
Wednesday	218
Thursday	192
Friday	222

$$\chi^2 = \frac{(166 - 192.79)^2}{192.79} + \cdots + \frac{(222 - 199.79)^2}{199.79}$$
$$= 7.556$$

Using Table X in Appendix B, we find that for a significance level of 5% and 4 degrees of freedom, we'd need a value of 9.488 or more to have a P-value less than 0.05. Our value of 7.556 is less than that.

Using a computer to generate the P-value, we find:

$$\text{P-value} = P(\chi_4^2 > 7.556) = 0.1093$$

REPORT

Communicate and present Link the P-value to your decision. Be sure to say more than a fact about the distribution of counts. State your conclusion in terms of what the data mean.

MEMO

Re: Stock market patterns

Our investigation of whether there are day-of-the-week patterns in the behavior of the DJIA in which one day or another is more likely to be an "up" day found no evidence of such a pattern. Our statistical test indicated that a pattern such as the one found in our sample of trading days would happen by chance about 10% of the time.

We conclude that there is, unfortunately, no evidence of a pattern that could be used to guide investment in the market. We were unable to detect a "weekend" or other day-of-the-week effect in the market.

15.2   Interpreting Chi-Square Values

When we calculated χ^2 for the trading days example, we got 7.556. Even though the number of Mondays seemed low, the χ^2 value was not large for 4 degrees of freedom, so we were unable to reject the null hypothesis. In general, what *is* big for a χ^2 statistic?

Think about how χ^2 is calculated. In every cell, any deviation from the expected count contributes to the sum. Large deviations generally contribute more, but if there are a lot of cells, even small deviations can add up, making the χ^2 value larger. So the more cells there are, the higher the value of χ^2 has to be before it becomes significant. For χ^2, the decision about how big is big depends on the number of degrees of freedom.

Unlike the Normal and t families, χ^2 models are skewed. Curves in the χ^2 family change both shape and center as the number of degrees of freedom grows. For example, Figure 15.1 shows the χ^2 curves for 5 and for 9 degrees of freedom.

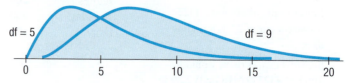

FIGURE 15.1   The χ^2 curves for 5 and 9 degrees of freedom.

Notice that the value $\chi^2 = 10$ might seem somewhat extreme when there are 5 degrees of freedom, but appears to be rather ordinary for 9 degrees of freedom. Here are two simple facts to help you think about χ^2 models:

- The mode is at $\chi^2 = \text{df} - 2$. (Look at the curves; their peaks are at 3 and 7.)
- The expected value (mean) of a χ^2 model is its number of degrees of freedom. That's a bit to the right of the mode—as we would expect for a distribution that is skewed to the right.

Goodness-of-fit tests are often performed by people who have a theory of what the proportions *should* be in each category and who believe their theory to be true. In some cases, unlike our market example, there isn't an obvious null hypothesis against which to test the proposed model. So, unfortunately, in those cases, the only null hypothesis available is that the proposed theory is true. And as we know, the hypothesis testing procedure allows us only to reject the null or fail to reject it. We can never confirm that a theory is in fact true; we can never confirm the null hypothesis.

At best, we can point out that the data are consistent with the proposed theory. But this doesn't prove the theory. The data *could* be consistent with the model even if the theory were wrong. In that case, we fail to reject the null hypothesis but can't conclude anything for sure about whether the theory is true.

15.3   Examining the Residuals

Chi-square tests are always one-sided. The chi-square statistic is always positive, and a large value provides evidence against the null hypothesis (because it shows that the fit to the model is *not* good), while small values provide little evidence that the model doesn't fit. In another sense, however, chi-square tests are really many-sided; a large statistic doesn't tell us *how* the null model doesn't fit. In our market theory example, if we had rejected the uniform model, we wouldn't have known *how* it failed. Was it because there were not enough Mondays represented, or was it that all five days showed some deviation from the uniform?

When we reject a null hypothesis in a goodness-of-fit test, we can examine the residuals in each cell to learn more. In fact, whenever we reject a null hypothesis, it's a good idea to examine the residuals. (We don't need to do that when we fail to reject because when the χ^2 value is small, all of its components must have been small.) Because we want to compare residuals for cells that may have very different counts, we standardize the residuals. We know the mean residual is zero,[1] but we

---

---

[1]Residual = Observed − Expected. Because the total of the expected values is the same as the observed total, the residuals must sum to zero.

need to know each residual's standard deviation. When we tested proportions, we saw a link between the expected proportion and its standard deviation. For counts, there's a similar link. To standardize a cell's residual, we divide by the square root of its expected value:[2]

$$\frac{(Obs - Exp)}{\sqrt{Exp}}.$$

Notice that these **standardized residuals** are the square roots of the components we calculated for each cell, with the plus $(+)$ or the minus $(-)$ sign indicating whether we observed more or fewer cases than we expected.

The standardized residuals give us a chance to think about the underlying patterns and to consider how the distribution differs from the model. Now that we've divided each residual by its standard deviation, they are z-scores. If the null hypothesis were true, we could even use the 68–95–99.7 Rule to judge how extraordinary the large ones are.

Ordinarily, you should only look at the residuals if the chi-square value is significantly large. But for illustration, we'll take a peek at the standardized residuals for the trading days data:

	Standardized Residual $= \dfrac{(Obs - Exp)}{\sqrt{Exp}}$
Monday	-1.9295
Tuesday	-0.0581
Wednesday	0.9908
Thursday	-0.6163
Friday	1.5710

TABLE 15.4 Standardized residuals.

As we would expect from the small chi-square value, none of these values is remarkable.

IN PRACTICE 15.2   Explaining a significant chi-square test using residuals

MANAGER Do any operators in our experiment stand out as having especially strong or weak performance?

ANALYST Because we failed to reject the null hypothesis, we don't expect any of the standardized residuals to be large, but we will examine them nonetheless.

The standardized residuals are the square roots of the components (from the bottom row of the table in In Practice 15.1 on page 497).

Standardized Residuals	-1.03	0.52	-1.55	-0.77	1.03	0.77	-0.52	1.55

As we expected, none of the residuals are large. Even though some of the operators enrolled more than twice the number of new customers as others, the variation is typical (within two standard deviations) of what we would expect if all their performances were, in fact, equal.

---

[2]It can be shown mathematically that the square root of the expected value estimates the appropriate standard deviation.

15.4   The Chi-Square Test of Homogeneity

Pew Research conducted a survey about social networking in several countries. The question of interest to businesses asked whether respondents had access to and used social networking. Responses were "yes" (use social networking), "no," and "not available." We organized the responses into a contingency table that looked like this: (Data in **Social networking**)

Country	No	Yes	N/A	Total
Britain	336	529	153	1018
Egypt	70	300	630	1000
Germany	460	340	200	1000
Russia	90	500	420	1010
U.S.	293	506	212	1011
Total	1249	2175	1615	5039

TABLE 15.5   Responses to a question about use and availability of social networking. ("N/A" = not available)

The natural question to ask is whether there are any differences among the countries (and, if so, what those are). We can start with a stacked bar chart.

FIGURE 15.2   The data of Table 15.5 in a stacked bar chart. The bars are easy to compare because they have roughly the same total counts.

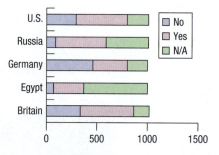

In Figure 15.2, Egypt stands out for having less availability of social networking. Germany may have an unusually large number of people saying they don't use social networking despite its availability.

But are the observed differences in the percentages real or just natural sampling variation? Our null hypothesis is that the proportions choosing each alternative are the same for each country. To test that hypothesis, we use a **chi-square test of homogeneity**. This is just another chi-square test. It turns out that the mechanics of the test of this hypothesis are nearly identical to the chi-square goodness-of-fit test we just saw in Section 15.1. The difference is that the goodness-of-fit test compared our observed counts to the expected counts from a *given* model. The test of homogeneity, by contrast, has a null hypothesis that the distributions are the same for all the groups. The test examines the differences between the observed counts and what we'd expect under that assumption of homogeneity.

For example, 529/1018, or 52%, of British respondents said that they use social networking. If the distributions were homogeneous across the five countries (as the null hypothesis asserts), then that proportion should be the same for all five countries. So 52% of the 1010 Russian respondents, or 525, would have said that they use social networking. That's the number we'd *expect* under the rule hypothesis.

Working in this way, we (or, more likely, the computer) can fill in expected values for each cell. The following table shows these expected values for each response and each country.

	No	Yes	N/A	Total
Britain	252.328	439.403	326.269	1018
Egypt	247.867	431.633	320.500	1000
Germany	247.867	431.633	320.500	1000
Russia	250.345	435.950	323.705	1010
U.S.	250.593	436.381	324.026	1011
Total	1249	2175	1615	5039

TABLE 15.6 Expected values for the responses. Because these are theoretical values, they don't have to be integers.

The term *homogeneity* refers to the hypothesis that things are the same. Here, we ask whether the distribution of responses is the same across the five countries. The chi-square test looks for differences large enough to step beyond what we might expect from random sample-to-sample variation. It can reveal a large deviation in a single category or small but persistent differences over all the categories—or anything in between.

Assumptions and Conditions

The assumptions and conditions are the same as for the chi-square test for goodness-of-fit. The **Counted Data Condition** says that these data must be counts. You can never perform a chi-square test on a quantitative variable. For example, if Pew had asked how many hours in a typical day respondents spent on social networking, we wouldn't be able to use a chi-square test to determine whether the mean time expenditures in the five countries were the same.[3]

Independence Assumption. The counts must be independent of each other. We can check the **Randomization Condition**. Here, we have random samples, so we *can* assume that the observations are independent.

The **Sample Size Assumption** can be checked with the **Expected Cell Frequency Condition**, which says that the expected count in each cell must be at least 5. Here, our samples are certainly large enough.

Following the pattern of the goodness-of-fit test, we compute the component for each cell of the table:

$$\text{Component} = \frac{(Obs - Exp)^2}{Exp}.$$

Summing these components across all cells gives the chi-square value:

$$\chi^2 = \sum_{all\ cells} \frac{(Obs - Exp)^2}{Exp}.$$

> **Large Samples and Chi-Square Tests**
>
> Whenever we test any hypothesis, a very large sample size means that small effects have a greater chance of being statistically significant. This is especially true for chi-square tests. So it's important to look at the effect sizes when the null hypothesis is rejected to see if the differences are practically significant. Don't rely only on the P-value when making a business decision. This applies to many of the examples in this chapter which have large sample sizes typical of those seen in today's business environment.

---

[3]To do that, you'd use a method called Analysis of Variance.

The degrees of freedom are different than they were for the goodness-of-fit test. For a test of homogeneity, there are $(R - 1) \times (C - 1)$ degrees of freedom, where R is the number of rows and C is the number of columns.

In our example, we have $4 \times 2 = 8$ degrees of freedom. We'll need the degrees of freedom to find a P-value for the chi-square statistic.

BY HAND   How to find expected values

In a contingency table, to test for homogeneity, we need to find the expected values when the null hypothesis is true. To find the expected value for row i and column j, we take:

$$Exp_{ij} = \frac{Total_{Row\ i} \times Total_{Col\ j}}{Table\ Total}$$

Here's an example:

Suppose we ask 100 people, 40 men and 60 women, to name their magazine preference: *Sports Illustrated*, *Cosmopolitan*, or *The Economist*, with the following result, shown in Microsoft Excel 2016 below.

	A	B	C	D	E
1	Actual	SI	Cosmo	Economist	Total
2	Men	25	5	10	40
3	Women	10	45	5	60
4	Total	35	50	15	100

Then, for example, the expected value under homogeneity for *Men* (row 1) who prefer *The Economist* (column 3) would be:

$$Exp_{13} = \frac{40 \times 15}{100} = 6$$

Performing similar calculations for all cells gives the expected values:

		SI	Cosmo	Economist	Total
6	Expected	SI	Cosmo	Economist	Total
7	Men	14	20	6	40
8	Women	21	30	9	60
9	Total	35	50	15	100

It is a simple matter to do these calculations in a spreadsheet (as we have done here).

For the social networking data, the chi-square value is 1049, with 8 degrees of freedom. We don't need a table to know that this is large enough to be statistically significant. So we can conclude that these five countries are not homogeneous in the use of social networking.

If you find that simply rejecting the hypothesis of homogeneity is a bit unsatisfying, you're in good company. It's hardly a shock that responses to this question differ from country to country especially with sample sizes this large. What we'd really like to know is where the differences were and how big they were. The test for homogeneity doesn't answer these interesting questions, but it does provide some evidence that can help us. A look at the standardized residuals can help identify cells that don't match the homogeneity pattern.

IN PRACTICE 15.3 . Testing homogeneity

MANAGER People constantly worry about the economy, and it matters a lot to our firm whether people have a positive or a negative view of their economic future. I just saw an article that compared Americans' attitudes toward the economy in spring 2017 to with those in spring 2009. Is the distribution of people's views of the economy different between the two time periods? I am attaching the data from the article. The question was, "Now thinking about our economic situation, how would you describe the current economic situation in (survey country)—is it very good, somewhat good, somewhat bad, or very bad?"

	Very Good	Somewhat Good	Somewhat Bad	Very Bad	Total
Spring 2017	27	147	81	39	294
Spring 2009	6	45	126	123	300
Totals	33(5.6%)	192(32.3%)	207(34.8%)	162(27.3%)	594

ANALYST What you want is called a test of homogeneity, testing whether the distribution of responses is the same for the two time periods. The data are counts, the Pew poll selected adults randomly (in each time period), and all expected cell frequencies are much greater than 5 (see table below), so we can proceed.

There are $(4 - 1) \times (2 - 1)$ or 3 degrees of freedom.

If the distributions were the same, we would expect each cell to have expected values that are 5.6%, 32.3%, 34.8%, and 27.3% of the row totals for Very Good, Somewhat Good, Somewhat Bad, and Very Bad, respectively. These values can be computed explicitly from:

$$Exp_{ij} = \frac{TotalRow_i \times TotalCol_j}{Table\ Total}$$

So, in the first cell (Spring 2017, Very Good):

$$Exp_{11} = \frac{TotalRow_1 \times TotalCol_1}{Table\ Total} = \frac{33 \times 294}{594} = 16.3$$

Expected counts for all cells are:

	Very Good	Somewhat Good	Somewhat Bad	Very Bad
Spring 2017	16.33	95.03	102.45	80.18
Spring 2009	16.33	95.03	102.45	80.18

The components $\frac{(Obs - Exp)^2}{Exp}$ are:

Components	Very Good	Somewhat Good	Somewhat Bad	Very Bad
Spring 2017	7.0	28.4	4.5	21.2
Spring 2009	7.0	28.4	4.5	21.2

Summing these gives $\chi^2 = 7.0 + 28.4 + \cdots + 21.2 = 120.8$, which, with 3 df, has a P-value of < 0.0001.

We, therefore, reject the hypothesis that the distribution of responses is the same for 2009 and 2017.

15.5 Comparing Two Proportions

	Female	Male	Total
Game	198	277	475
Commercials	154	79	233
Total	352	356	708

TABLE 15.7 Counts of respondents categorized by sex and whether they watch the Super Bowl primarily for the game or for the commercials.

In Chapter 2 we saw data from a survey comparing the reasons that men and women watch the Super Bowl. Advertisers spend huge amounts on Super Bowl ads and, consequently, care deeply about who watches them. If we extract the data on the 708 survey respondents who answered and said they would be watching the Super Bowl, we get the data in Table 15.7.

A chi-square test of homogeneity gives 37.26 with 1 degree of freedom. That has a P-value ≤ 0.0001, so we can reject the null hypothesis of no difference.

When we have a 2×2 table like this, we are really just comparing two proportions. In this example, $154/352 = 43.75\%$ of the women and $79/356 = 22.19\%$ of the men say they watch the Super Bowl primarily for the commercials. In this special case of testing the equality of two proportions, there is a z-test, which is equivalent and gives the same P-value.

Confidence Interval for the Difference of Two Proportions

The approach of working directly with proportions offers an advantage. As we saw, 43.75% of the women and 22.19% of the men watch the Super Bowl primarily for the commercials. That's a difference of 21.56%.

If we knew the standard error of that quantity, we could use a z-statistic to construct a confidence interval for the true difference in the population. It's not hard to find the standard error. All we need is the formula:[4]

$$SE(\hat{p}_1 - \hat{p}_2) = \sqrt{\frac{\hat{p}_1\hat{q}_1}{n_1} + \frac{\hat{p}_2\hat{q}_2}{n_2}}$$

The confidence interval has the same form as the confidence interval for a single proportion, with this new standard error:

$$(\hat{p}_1 - \hat{p}_2) \pm z^*SE(\hat{p}_1 - \hat{p}_2).$$

> **Confidence Interval for the Difference of Two Proportions**
>
> When the conditions are met, we can find the confidence interval for the difference of two proportions, $p_1 - p_2$. The confidence interval is
>
> $$(\hat{p}_1 - \hat{p}_2) \pm z^*SE(\hat{p}_1 - \hat{p}_2),$$
>
> where we find the standard error of the difference as
>
> $$SE(\hat{p}_1 - \hat{p}_2) = \sqrt{\frac{\hat{p}_1\hat{q}_1}{n_1} + \frac{\hat{p}_2\hat{q}_2}{n_2}}$$
>
> from the observed proportions.
>
> The critical value z^* depends on the particular confidence level that you specify.

For the Super Bowl survey, a 95% confidence interval for the true difference between the proportion of women and the proportion of men preferring the commercials is:

$$(0.4375 - 0.2219) \pm 1.96 \times \sqrt{\frac{0.4375 \times 0.5625}{352} + \frac{0.2219 \times 0.7781}{356}}$$

$$= 0.2156 \pm 0.0674$$

or from 14.82% to 28.30%.

---

[4]The standard error of the difference is found from the general fact that the variance of a difference of two independent quantities is the *sum* of their variances. See Chapter 6 for details.

We can be 95% confident that between 14.82% and 28.30% more women than men watch the Super Bowl for the commercials more than for the game.

This confidence interval helps us to address the question of whether the difference matters. That depends on the reason we are asking the question. The confidence interval shows the *effect size*—or at least the interval of plausible values for the effect size. A company planning to advertise on the Super Bowl might consider this difference large enough to consider in designing their ads. Be sure to consider the effect size whenever you make a business decision based on rejecting a null hypothesis.

IN PRACTICE 15.4   A confidence interval for the difference of proportions

MANAGER In the poll on the state of the economy, 59.2% of people responded that the economy was Very or Somewhat Good in Spring 2017, whereas only 17% responded that way in Spring 2009. The difference is 42%, but is there a way to get a range of plausible values for this difference?

ANALYST Yes, we can calculate a confidence interval for the difference in two proportions. I will use subscript "N" to mean "new" data and subscript "O" to mean "older" data.

The confidence interval can be found from:

$$(\hat{p}_N - \hat{p}_O) \pm z^* SE(\hat{p}_N - \hat{p}_O) \text{ where } SE(\hat{p}_N - \hat{p}_O) = \sqrt{\frac{\hat{p}_N \hat{q}_N}{n_N} + \frac{\hat{p}_O \hat{q}_O}{n_O}}$$

$$= \sqrt{\frac{(0.59)(0.41)}{294} + \frac{(0.17)(0.83)}{300}} = 0.0361.$$

Since we know the 95% confidence critical value for z is 1.96, we have:

$$0.422 \pm 1.96(0.0361) = (0.35, 0.49).$$

In other words, we are 95% confident that the proportion of people who think that the economy is either Very or Somewhat Good is between 35% and 49% higher in 2017 than in 2009.

15.6   Chi-Square Test of Independence

If the importance people place on their personal appearance varies a great deal by age, that might be crucial for the marketing department of a global cosmetics company. Fortunately, we have data. The GfK Roper Reports® Worldwide Survey asked 30,000 consumers in 23 countries about their attitudes on health, beauty, and other personal values. One question participants were asked was how important their personal appearance is to them.

We might think of the different age groups as categories to be compared with a test of homogeneity. But it makes more sense to think of *Age* as a second variable whose value has been measured for each respondent along with his or her response to the appearance question. Asking whether the distribution of responses changes with *Age* now raises the question of whether the variables personal *Appearance* and *Age* are independent. (Data in **Personal appearance**)

TABLE 15.8 Responses to the question about personal appearance by age group.

		Age						
		13–19	20–29	30–39	40–49	50–59	60+	Total
Appearance	7—Extremely Important	396	337	300	252	142	93	1520
	6	325	326	307	254	123	86	1421
	5	318	312	317	270	150	106	1473
	4—Average Importance	397	376	403	423	224	210	2033
	3	83	83	88	93	54	45	446
	2	37	43	53	58	37	45	273
	1—Not At All Important	40	37	53	56	36	52	274
	Total	1596	1514	1521	1406	766	637	7440

Whenever we have two variables in a contingency table like this, the natural test is a **chi-square test of independence**. Mechanically, this chi-square test is identical to a test of homogeneity. The difference between the two tests is in how we think of the data and, thus, what conclusion we draw.

Here we ask whether the response to the personal appearance question is independent of age. Remember, that for any two events, **A** and **B**, to be independent, the probability of event **A** given that event **B** occurred must be the same as the probability of event **A**. Here, this means the probability that a randomly selected respondent thinks personal appearance is extremely important doesn't depend on his or her age group. Of course, from a table based on data, the probabilities will never be exactly the same. But to tell whether they are different enough, we use a chi-square test of independence.

Here we have two categorical variables measured on a single population. For the homogeneity test, we had a single categorical variable measured independently on two or more populations. Now we ask a different question: "Are the variables independent?" rather than "Are the groups homogeneous?" These are subtle differences, but they are important when we draw conclusions.

> **Homogeneity or Independence?**
> The only difference between the test for homogeneity and the test for independence is in the decision you need to make.

Assumptions and Conditions

Of course, we still need counts and enough data so that the expected counts are at least five in each cell.

If we're interested in the independence of variables, we usually want to generalize from the data to some population. In that case, we'll need to check that the data are a representative random sample from that population.

GUIDED EXAMPLE   Personal Appearance and Age

We want to help marketers discover whether a person's age influences how they respond to the question: "How important is seeking the utmost attractive appearance to you?" We have the values of *Age* in six age categories. We will view *Age* as a variable, and ask whether the variables *Age* and *Appearance* are independent.

PLAN	**Setup** State what you want to know.	We want to know whether the categorical variables personal *Appearance* and *Age* are statistically independent. We have a contingency table of 7440 respondents from a sample of five countries.
	Identify the variables and context.	

Hypotheses State the null and alternative hypotheses.

We perform a test of independence when we suspect the variables may not be independent. We are making the claim that knowing the respondents' age will change the distribution of their response to the question about personal *Appearance*, and testing the null hypothesis that it is *not* true.

H$_O$: Personal *Appearance* and *Age* are independent.[5]

H$_A$: Personal *Appearance* and *Age* are not independent.

Model Check the conditions.

✔ **Counted Data Condition** We have counts of individuals categorized on two categorical variables.

✔ **Randomization Condition** These data are from a randomized survey conducted in 30 countries. We have data from five of them. Although they are not an SRS, the samples within each country were selected to avoid biases.

✔ **Expected Cell Frequency Condition** The expected values are all much larger than 5.

The table below shows the expected counts for each cell. The expected counts are calculated exactly as they were for a test of homogeneity; in the first cell, for example, we expect $\frac{1520}{7440} = 20.43\%$ of 1596, which is 326.065.

		Expected Values					
		Age					
		13–19	20–29	30–39	40–49	50–59	60 +
Appearance	7—Extremely Important	326.065	309.312	310.742	287.247	156.495	130.140
	6	304.827	289.166	290.503	268.538	146.302	121.664
	5	315.982	299.748	301.133	278.365	151.656	126.116
	4—Average Importance	436.111	413.705	415.617	384.193	209.312	174.062
	3	95.674	90.759	91.178	84.284	45.919	38.186
	2	58.563	55.554	55.811	51.591	28.107	23.374
	1—Not At All Important	58.777	55.758	56.015	51.780	28.210	23.459

The stacked bar graph shows that the response seems to be dependent on *Age*. Older people tend to think personal appearance is less important than younger people.

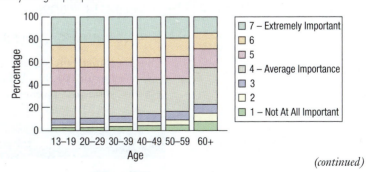

(continued)

---

[5]As in other chi-square tests, the hypotheses are usually expressed in words, without parameters. The hypothesis of independence itself tells us how to find expected values for each cell of the contingency table. That's all we need.

	Specify the model. Name the test you will use.	(The counts are shown in Table 15.8.) We'll use a χ^2 model with $(7-1) \times (6-1) = 30$ df and do a **chi-square test of independence**.
DO	**Mechanics** Calculate χ^2 and find the P-value using software. The shape of a chi-square model depends on its degrees of freedom. Even with 30 df, this chi-square statistic is extremely large, so the resulting P-value is small.	$$\chi^2 = \sum_{all\ cells} \frac{(Obs - Exp)^2}{Exp} = 170.7762$$ P-value $= P(\chi^2_{30} > 170.7762) < 0.001$
REPORT	**Conclusion** Link the P-value to your decision. State your conclusion.	**MEMO** **Re: Investigation of the relationship between age of consumer and attitudes about personal appearance** It appears from our analysis of the Roper survey that attitudes on personal *Appearance* are not independent of *Age*. It seems that older people find personal appearance less important than younger people do (on average in the five countries selected).

We rejected the null hypothesis of independence between *Age* and attitudes about personal *Appearance*. With a sample size this large, we can detect very small deviations from independence, so it's almost guaranteed that the chi-square test will reject the null hypothesis. Examining the residuals can help you see the cells that deviate farthest from independence. To make a meaningful business decision, you'll have to look at effect sizes as well as the P-value. We should also look at each country's data individually, since country to country differences could affect marketing decisions.

Suppose the company was specifically interested in deciding how to split advertising resources between the teen market and the 30- to 39-year-old market. How much of a difference is there between the proportions of those in each age group that rated personal *Appearance* as very important (responding either 6 or 7)?

For that we'll need to construct a confidence interval on the difference. From Table 15.8, we find that the percentages of those answering 6 and 7 are 45.18% and 39.91% for the teen and 30- to 39-year-old groups, respectively. The 95% confidence interval is:

$$(\hat{p}_1 - \hat{p}_2) \pm z^*SE(\hat{p}_1 - \hat{p}_2)$$

$$= (0.4518 - 0.3991) \pm 1.96 \times \sqrt{\frac{(0.4518)(0.5482)}{1596} + \frac{(0.3991)(0.6009)}{1521}}$$

$$= (0.018, 0.087), \text{ or } (1.8\% \text{ to } 8.7\%)$$

This is a statistically significant difference, but now we can see that the difference may be as small as 1.8%. When deciding how to allocate advertising expenditures, it is important to keep these estimates of the effect size in mind.

IN PRACTICE 15.5   A chi-square test of independence

MANAGER I saw a poll from the General Social Survey (University of Michigan) that discussed attitudes toward marijuana across different age groups in the United States. I am forwarding the table of results, below. Does attitude toward marijuana legalization depend on age, or are they independent? We have products for which it might matter what the consumer's view of marijuana legalization was. The question asked whether marijuana should be legal or not legal, with no intermediate categories.

	Age				
	<35	35–50	50–65	>65	Total
Legal	343	292	322	166	1123
Not legal	148	178	193	194	713
Total	491	470	515	360	1836

ANALYST Based on what you said, the null hypothesis is that *Opinion* and *Age* are independent. We can view this as a test of independence as opposed to a test of homogeneity if we view *Age* and *Opinion* as variables whose relationship we want to understand. This was a random sample and there are at least 5 expected responses in every cell. The expected values are calculated using the formula:

$$Exp_{ij} = \frac{TotalRow_i \times TotalCol_j}{Table\ Total} \Rightarrow$$

$$Exp_{11} = \frac{TotalRow_1 \times TotalCol_1}{Table\ Total} = \frac{491 \times 1123}{1836} = 300.3$$

The full table of expected values is:

	Age				
Expected Values	<35	35–50	50–65	>65	Total
Legal	300.3	287.5	315.0	220.2	1123
Not legal	190.7	182.5	200.0	139.8	713
Total	491.0	470.0	515.0	360.0	1836

The chi-square components are:

	Age			
Components	<35	35–50	50–65	>65
Legal	6.1	0.1	0.2	13.3
Not legal	9.6	0.1	0.2	21.0

There are $(r - 1) \times (c - 1) = 1 \times 3 = 3$ degrees of freedom. Summing all the components gives:

$$\chi_3^2 = 6.1 + 0.1 + \cdots + 21.0 = 50.5,$$

which has a P-value < 0.0001.

Thus, we reject the null hypothesis and conclude that *Age* and *Opinion* about *Marijuana* are not independent. Looking at the residuals,

	Age			
Residuals	<35	35–50	50–65	>65
Legal	2.5	0.3	0.4	−3.7
Not legal	−3.1	−0.3	−0.5	4.6

we see a pattern. These two variables fail to be independent because increasing age is associated with less favorable attitudes toward marijuana.

(continued)

Bar charts arranged in *Age* order make the pattern clear:

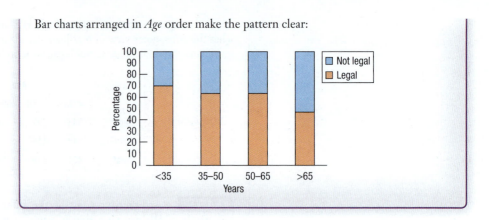

JUST CHECKING

Which of the three chi-square tests would you use in each of the following situations—goodness-of-fit, homogeneity, or independence?

1 A restaurant manager wonders whether customers who dine on Friday nights have the same preferences among the chef's four special entrées as those who dine on Saturday nights. One weekend he has the wait staff record which entrées were ordered each night. Assuming these customers to be typical of all weekend diners, he'll compare the distributions of meals chosen Friday and Saturday.

2 Company policy calls for parking spaces to be assigned to everyone at random, but you suspect that may not be so. There are three lots of equal size: lot A, next to the building; lot B, a bit farther away; and lot C on the other side of the highway. You gather data about employees at middle management level and above to see how many were assigned parking in each lot.

3 Is a student's social life affected by where the student lives? A campus survey asked a random sample of students whether they lived in a dormitory, in off-campus housing, or at home and whether they had been out on a date 0, 1–2, 3–4, or 5 or more times in the past two weeks.

Chi-Square Tests and Causation

Chi-square tests are common. Tests for independence are especially widespread. Unfortunately, many people interpret a small P-value as proof of causation. We know better. Just as correlation between quantitative variables does not demonstrate causation, a failure of independence between two categorical variables does not show a cause-and-effect relationship between them, nor should we say that one variable *depends* on the other.

The chi-square test for independence treats the two variables symmetrically. There is no way to differentiate the direction of any possible causation from one variable to the other. While we can see that attitudes on personal *Appearance* and *Age* are related, we can't say that getting older *causes* you to change attitudes. And certainly it's not correct to say that changing attitudes on personal appearance makes you older.

Of course, there's never any way to eliminate the possibility that a lurking variable is responsible for the observed lack of independence. In some sense, a failure of independence between two categorical variables is less impressive than a strong, consistent association between quantitative variables. Two categorical variables can fail the test of independence in many ways, including ways that show no consistent pattern of failure. Examination of the chi-square standardized residuals can help you think about the underlying patterns.

⊘ WHAT CAN GO WRONG?

- **Don't use chi-square methods unless you have counts.** All three of the chi-square tests apply only to counts. Other kinds of data can be arrayed in two-way tables. Just because numbers are in a two-way table doesn't make them suitable for chi-square analysis. Data reported as proportions or percentages can be suitable for chi-square procedures, *but only after they are converted to counts*. If you try to do the calculations without first finding the counts, your results will be wrong.

- **Beware large samples.** Beware *large* samples? That's not the advice you're used to hearing. The chi-square tests, however, are unusual. You should be wary of chi-square tests performed on very large samples. No hypothesized distribution fits perfectly, no two groups are exactly homogeneous, and two variables are rarely perfectly independent. The degrees of freedom for chi-square tests don't grow with the sample size. With a sufficiently large sample size, a chi-square test can always reject the null hypothesis. But we have no measure of how far the data are from the null model. There are no confidence intervals to help us judge the effect size except in the case of two proportions.

- **Don't say that one variable "depends" on the other just because they're not independent.** "Depend" can suggest a model or a pattern, but variables can fail to be independent in many different ways. When variables fail the test for independence, it may be better to say they are "associated."

ETHICS IN ACTION

Forever Youthful, Inc., specializes in products that contain biologically active ingredients with anti-aging properties often referred to as "cosmeceuticals." Forever Youthful, Inc., has been exclusively focused on skin care. Its line of luxurious creams, masks, and eye treatments, based on various combinations of antioxidants, peptides, and even growth factors, claim to reverse the signs of aging. Michele Kaplan, Vice President for Sales and Marketing, and her team have been very successful in partnering with high-end spas, resorts, and boutiques to deliver Forever Youthful skin care products to its target customer: older wealthy women. Consequently, Michele was the only top level executive to survive the recent restructuring at Forever Youthful after a new president and CEO, J. C. Burnett, was hired.

Under Burnett's leadership the company has begun to move in several different directions. An emerging trend in the anti-aging market is hair care, and Forever Youthful is about to launch a line of expensive shampoos, conditioners, and scalp treatments designed to make hair shiny, full, and younger looking. Michele is excited about the prospects for sales in this new market segment, and she believes the current strategy of targeting high-end distributors, in this case fashionable salons, would work best. However, the new leadership team is proposing that the hair care line of products be sold online direct to customers, arguing that this is more cost-effective because it doesn't require establishing relationships with hair

salons. Michele disagrees. She is concerned about the possible negative consequences of such a move, particularly on the brand's "elite" image, not to mention on her division.

To prove her point, Michele directed her research team to design some questions for gathering data from current and potential customers. Working with some of the businesses that sell Forever Youthful skin care products, clients were interviewed about their online purchasing behaviors and perceptions of brand image as they checked in for appointments. Demographic data were also collected. Based on a sample of 3500 clients, chi-square tests for independence were performed to determine if responses about online shopping and brand image were independent of age category. The results revealed what Michele had expected. Online purchasing behavior is dependent on age. Moreover, level of agreement with the statement "hair products sold online are of inferior quality to those sold in salons" also showed dependence on age. Because Forever Youthful targets older customers, Michele is hopeful that these findings will help convince the team that her strategy is best. She is now looking forward to the next leadership team meeting.

- **Identify the ethical dilemma in this scenario.**

- **What are the undesirable consequences?**

- **Propose an ethical solution that considers the welfare of all stakeholders.**

15   FROM LEARNING TO EARNING

LEARNING OBJECTIVES

Recognize when a chi-square test of goodness-of-fit, homogeneity, or independence is appropriate.

For each test, find the expected cell frequencies.

For each test, check the assumptions and corresponding conditions and know how to complete the test.

- Counted Data Condition.
- Independence Assumption; randomization makes independence more plausible.
- Sample Size Assumption with the Expected Cell Frequency Condition; expect at least 5 observations in each cell.

Interpret a chi-square test.

- Even though we might believe the model, we cannot prove that the data fit the model with a chi-square test because that would mean confirming the null hypothesis.

Examine the standardized residuals to understand what cells were responsible for rejecting a null hypothesis.

Compare two proportions.

State the null hypothesis for a test of independence and understand how that is different from the null hypothesis for a test of homogeneity.

- Both are computed the same way. You may not find both offered by your technology. You can use either one as long as you interpret your result correctly.

TERMS

Chi-square models

Chi-square models are skewed to the right. They are parameterized by their degrees of freedom and become less skewed with increasing degrees of freedom.

Chi-square (or chi-squared) statistic

The chi-square statistic is found by summing the chi-square components. Chi-square tests can be used to test goodness-of-fit, homogeneity, or independence.

Chi-square goodness-of-fit test

A test of whether the distribution of counts in one categorical variable matches the distribution predicted by a model. A chi-square test of goodness-of-fit finds

$$\chi^2 = \sum_{all\ cells} \frac{(Obs - Exp)^2}{Exp},$$

where the expected counts come from the predicting model. It finds a P-value from a chi-square model with $n - 1$ degrees of freedom, where n is the number of categories in the categorical variable.

Chi-square test of homogeneity

A test comparing the distribution of counts for two or more groups on the same categorical variable. A chi-square test of homogeneity finds

$$\chi^2 = \sum_{all\ cells} \frac{(Obs - Exp)^2}{Exp},$$

where the expected counts are based on the overall frequencies, adjusted for the totals in each group. We find a P-value from a chi-square distribution with $(R - 1) \times (C - 1)$ degrees of freedom, where R gives the number of categories (rows) and C gives the number of independent groups (columns).

Chi-square test of independence

A test of whether two categorical variables are independent. It examines the distribution of counts for one group of individuals classified according to both variables. A chi-square test of *independence* uses the same calculation as a test of homogeneity. We find a P-value from a chi-square distribution with $(R - 1) \times (C - 1)$ degrees of freedom, where R gives the number of categories in one variable and C gives the number of categories in the other.

Standardized residual   In each cell of a two-way table, a standardized residual is the square root of the chi-square component for that cell with the sign of the *Observed – Expected* difference:

$$\frac{(Obs - Exp)}{\sqrt{Exp}}$$

When we reject a chi-square test, an examination of the standardized residuals can sometimes reveal more about how the data deviate from the null model.

TECH SUPPORT Chi-Square

Most statistics packages associate chi-square tests with contingency tables. Often chi-square is available as an option only when you make a contingency table. This organization can make it hard to locate the chi-square test and may confuse the three different roles that the chi-square test can take. In particular, chi-square tests for goodness-of-fit may be hard to find or missing entirely. Chi-square tests for homogeneity are computationally the same as chi-square tests for independence, so you may have to perform the mechanics as if they were tests of independence and interpret them afterward as tests of homogeneity.

Most statistics packages work with data on individuals rather than with the summary counts. If the only information you have is the table of counts, you may find it more difficult to get a statistics package to compute chi-square. Some packages offer a way to reconstruct the data from the summary counts so that they can then be passed back through the chi-square calculation, finding the cell counts again. Many packages offer chi-square standardized residuals (although they may be called something else).

EXCEL

To perform a chi-square goodness-of-fit test using Excel:

If you have two parallel columns, one holding observed counts and the other expected counts, follow these steps:

- In columns D through F, you can use spreadsheet calculations and built-in functions to calculate (Obs-Exp), (Obs-Exp)^2, and (Obs-Exp)^2/Exp. Type the following into cells D2, E2, and F2, respectively:
  - =(B2-C2)
  - =D2^2
  - =E2/C2
- Copy the formulas from D2, E2, and F2 and paste into the remainder of the rows in columns D, E, and F.
- Using the =SUM function, add the values contained in the cells in column F to get the χ^2 value.
- The CHISQ.INV.RT and CHISQ.DIST.RT functions can then be used to calculate the critical value and P-value of the chi-square statistic that is calculated. See the image below for commands. Note that the function used to calculate degrees of freedom (=COUNT) should reflect rows containing data.

	A	B	C	D	E	F	G
1	Operator	Observed	Expected	(Obs-Exp)	(Obs-Exp)^2	(Obs-Exp)^2/Exp	Excel Syntax
2	1	11	15	-4	16	1.0667	
3	2	17	15	2	4	0.2667	
4	3	9	15	-6	36	2.4000	
5	4	12	15	-3	9	0.6000	
6	5	19	15	4	16	1.0667	
7	6	18	15	3	9	0.6000	
8	7	13	15	-2	4	0.2667	
9	8	21	15	6	36	2.4000	
10					*Chi-Square=*	8.6667	=SUM(F2:F9)
11					*Alpha=*	0.0500	[Enter Value]
12					*df=*	7	=COUNT(A2:A9)-1
13					χ^2 *critical=*	14.0671	=CHISQ.INV.RT(F11,F12)
14					*p-value=*	0.2775	=CHISQ.DIST.RT(F10,F12)

To perform a chi-square test of independence using Excel:

- Summarize raw data into a row by column pivot table—this will be the observed table. It should have row and column totals and a grand total.

- In the same spreadsheet, create a row by column table that mirrors the observed table without the rows and columns—this will be the expected table.

- In each corresponding cell in the expected table, calculate the expected value. In the example shown below, the formula in cell B11 is =(D5*B7)/D7; repeat this for all cells in the expected table.

- Create a third row by column table that mirrors the observed table without the rows and columns—this will be the table that holds the chi-square calculation for each cell.

- In each corresponding cell in the chi-square table, calculate the chi-square value. In the example shown here, the code for cell B15 =((POWER((B5-B11),2)/B11)); repeat this for all cells in the expected table.

- Below the table, designate cells to hold the values for alpha and degrees of freedom (recall that degrees of freedom for this statistic are [number of rows] $-1*$ [number of columns] -1), and then type in the code to calculate the chi-square value, critical chi-square value, and P-value.

	A	B	C	D
1				
2				
3	Pivot Table			
4		AC	No AC	Grand Total
5	New	43	38	81
6	Old	592	1055	1647
7	Grand Total	635	1093	1728
8				
9				
10	Expected Values	AC	No AC	
11	New	29.765625	51.234375	
12	Old	605.234375	1041.765625	
13				
14	(O-E)^2/E Values	AC	No AC	
15	New	5.884260171	3.418577501	
16	Old	0.289389844	0.168126762	
17				
18				
19	Chi-Square=	9.7604	=SUM(B15:C16)	
20	Alpha=	0.0500	[Enter Value]	
21	df=	1	[Enter Value]	
22	χ^2 critical=	3.8415	=CHISQ.INV.RT(B20,B21)	
23	p-value=	0.0018	=CHISQ.DIST.RT(B19,B21)	

COMMENTS

Excel offers the function CHISQ.TEST (actual_range, expected_range), which computes a chi-square P-value for independence. However, this command will only provide the P-value and no other values. Both ranges are of the form UpperLeftCell: LowerRightCell, specifying two rectangular tables. The two tables must be of the same size and shape. The function is called CHITEST in Excel versions earlier than 2010.

XLSTAT

To perform a chi-square goodness-of-fit test:

- Choose **Parametric Tests**, and then select **Multinomial goodness of fit test**.

- In one column you should have the observed frequencies of the categories of the variable. Enter this under **Frequencies**.

- In another column you should have either the expected frequencies or the proportions. Enter this under either **Expected frequencies** (or expected proportions) and choose the appropriate **data format**.

- Be sure to check the box that says **Chi-square test**.

- Enter in the desired **Significance level**.

- Select **OK**.

- Select **Continue** (if prompted).

To perform a chi-square test for homogeneity:

- Choose **Correlation/Association tests**, and then select **Tests on contingency tables**.

- If your data already are in a contingency table, choose the **Data format** option **Contingency table**.

- If your data are not in a contingency table, choose **Qualitative variables**.

- Enter the cell range of your data.

- On the **Options** tab, check **Chi-square test**.

- On the **Outputs** tab, choose **Proportions/Row** or **Proportions/ Column** if you wish to see the conditional distributions.

JMP

To perform a chi-square goodness-of-fit test:

- Select **Analyze > Distribution**.

- Choose a categorical variable for the **Y, Columns** dialog box.

- From the red triangle next to the variable, name, select **Test Probabilities** and enter the probabilities you want to test.

To perform other chi-square tests:

- Select **Analyze > Fit Y by X**.

- Choose one variable as the Y, response variable, and the other as the X, factor variable. Both selected variables must be Nominal or Ordinal.

- JMP will make a plot and a contingency table. Below the contingency table, **JMP** offers a **Tests** panel. In that panel, the Chi Square for independence is called **Pearson**. The table also offers the P-value.

- Click on the contingency Table title bar to drop down a menu that offers to include a **Deviation** and Cell **Chi square** in each cell of the table.

COMMENTS

JMP will perform a chi-square analysis for a **Fit Y by X** if both variables are nominal or ordinal (marked with an N or O), but not otherwise. Be sure the variables have the right type.

Deviations are the observed—expected differences in counts. Cell chi-squares are the squares of the standardized residuals. Refer to the deviations for the sign of the difference.

MINITAB

From the **Start** menu,

- Choose the **Tables** submenu.
- From that menu, choose **Chi Square Test**....
- In the dialog, identify the columns that make up the table. Minitab will display the table and print the chi-square value and its P-value.

COMMENTS

Alternatively, select the **Cross Tabulation** ... command to see more options for the table, including expected counts and standardized residuals.

R

Goodness-of-fit test:

To test the probabilities in a vector prob with observed values in a vector x:

- **chisq.test**(x,p=prob)

Test of independence or homogeneity:

With counts in a contingency table (a matrix called, say, con.table), the test of independence (or homogeneity) is found by

- **chisq.test**(con.table)

COMMENTS

Using the function xtabs you can create a contingency table from two variables x and y in a data frame called mydata by

- con.table = xtabs(~x+y,data=mydata) then
- **chisq.test**(con.table)

SPSS

- From the Analyze menu, choose the **Descriptive Statistics** submenu.
- From that submenu, choose **Crosstabs** . . . .

- In the Crosstabs dialog, assign the row and column variables from the variable list. Both variables must be categorical.
- Click the **Cells** button to specify that standardized residuals should be displayed.
- Click the **Statistics** button to specify a chi-square test.

COMMENTS

SPSS offers only variables that it knows to be categorical in the variable list for the Crosstabs dialog. If the variables you want are missing, check that they have the right type.

STATCRUNCH

To perform a goodness-of-fit test:

- Enter the observed counts in one column of a data table and the expected counts in another.
- Click on **Stat**.
- Choose **Goodness-of-fit** > **Chi-Square Test**.
- Choose the **Observed Column** and the **Expected Column**.
- Click on **Compute!**

COMMENTS

These chi-square tests may also be performed using the actual data table instead of summary counts. See the StatCrunch Help page for details.

To perform a test of homogeneity or independence:

- Create a table (without totals):
- Name the first column as one variable, and then enter the categories underneath.
- Name the adjacent columns as the categories of the other variable, entering the observed counts underneath.
- Click on **Stat**.
- Choose **Tables** > **Contingency** > **With Summary**.
- Choose the **Columns** holding counts.
- Choose the **Row labels column**.
- Enter the **Column variable** name.
- Click on **Compute!**

BRIEF CASE

Health Insurance

In 2010, the U.S. Congress passed the historic health care reform bill that will provide some type of coverage for the millions of Americans without health care insurance. Just how widespread is the lack of medical coverage in 2016, years after health care reform was passed? The media claim that the segments of the population most at risk are women, children, the elderly, and the poor. The tables give the number of uninsured (in thousands) by sex, by age, and by household income in 2016.[6] Using the appropriate summary statistics, graphical displays, statistical tests, and confidence intervals, investigate the accuracy of the media's statement using these data. Be sure to discuss your assumptions, methods, results, and conclusions. (Note: Some totals between tables may not match exactly due to rounding.)

	Gender		
	Male	Female	Total
Uninsured	15,143	12,909	28,052
Insured	141,796	150,524	292,320
Total	156,939	163,433	320,372

	Age			
	<18	18–64	65 +	Total
Uninsured	3,924	23,530	598	28,052
Insured	70,123	173,521	48,676	292,320
Total	74,047	197,051	49,274	320,372

	Income				
	Less than $25,000	$25,000 to $49,999	$50,000 to $74,999	$75,000 or more	Total
Uninsured	8,865	7,791	4,594	6,803	28,053
Insured	50,599	59,112	48,434	134,174	292,319
Total	59,464	66,903	53,028	140,977	320,372

Loyalty Program

A marketing executive tested two incentives to see what percentage of customers would enroll in a new Web-based loyalty program. The customers were asked to log on to their accounts on the Web and provide some demographic and spending information. As an incentive, they were offered either nothing (*No Offer*), free flight insurance on their next flight (*Free Insurance*), or a free companion airline ticket (*Free Flight*). The customers were segmented according to their past year's spending patterns as spending primarily in one of five areas: *Travel, Entertainment, Dining, Household*, or *Balanced*. The executive wanted to know whether the incentives resulted in different enrollment rates (*Response*). Specifically, she wanted to know how much higher the enrollment rate for the free flight was compared to the free insurance. She also wanted to see whether *Spending Pattern* was associated with *Response*. Using the data **Loyalty Program**, write up a report for the marketing executive using appropriate graphics, summary statistics, statistical tests, and confidence intervals.

---

[6]Source: U.S. Census Bureau, Current Population Survey, Annual Social and Economic Supplement, 2016 (www.census.gov/data/tables/time-series/demo/income-poverty/cps-hi/hi-01.html).

SECTION 15.1

1. If there is no seasonal effect on human births, we would expect equal numbers of children to be born in each season (winter, spring, summer, and fall). A student takes a census of her statistics class and finds that of the 120 students in the class, 25 were born in winter, 35 in spring, 32 in summer, and 28 in fall. She wonders if the excess in the spring is an indication that births are not uniform throughout the year.

a) What is the expected number of births in each season if there is no "seasonal effect" on births?
b) Compute the χ^2 statistic.
c) How many degrees of freedom does the χ^2 statistic have?

2. At a major credit card bank, the percentages of people who historically apply for the Silver, Gold, and Platinum cards are 60%, 30%, and 10%, respectively. In a recent sample of customers responding to a promotion, of 200 customers, 110 applied for Silver, 55 for Gold, and 35 for Platinum. Is there evidence to suggest that the percentages for this promotion may be different from the historical proportions?

a) What is the expected number of customers applying for each type of card in this sample if the historical proportions are still true?
b) Compute the χ^2 statistic.
c) How many degrees of freedom does the χ^2 statistic have?

SECTION 15.2

3. For the births in Exercise 1,

a) If there is no seasonal effect, about how big, on average, would you expect the χ^2 statistic to be (what is the mean of the χ^2 distribution)?
b) Does the statistic you computed in Exercise 1 seem large in comparison to this mean? Explain briefly.
c) What does that say about the null hypothesis?
d) Find the $\alpha = 0.05$ critical value for the χ^2 distribution with the appropriate number of df.
e) Using the critical value, what do you conclude about the null hypothesis at $\alpha = 0.05$?

4. For the customers in Exercise 2,

a) If the customers apply for the three cards according to the historical proportions, about how big, on average, would you expect the χ^2 statistic to be (what is the mean of the χ^2 distribution)?
b) Does the statistic you computed in Exercise 2 seem large in comparison to this mean? Explain briefly.

c) What does that say about the null hypothesis?
d) Find the $\alpha = 0.05$ critical value for the χ^2 distribution with the appropriate number of df.
e) Using the critical value, what do you conclude about the null hypothesis at $\alpha = 0.05$?

SECTION 15.3

5. For the data in Exercise 1,

a) Compute the standardized residual for each season.
b) Are any of these particularly large? (Compared to what?)
c) Why should you have anticipated the answer to part b?

6. For the data in Exercise 2,

a) Compute the standardized residual for each type of card.
b) Are any of these particularly large? (Compared to what?)
c) What does the answer to part b say about this new group of customers?

SECTION 15.4

7. An analyst at a local bank wonders if the age distribution of customers coming for service at his branch in town is the same as at the branch located near the mall. He selects 100 transactions at random from each branch and researches the age information for the associated customer. Here are the data:

	Age			
	Less Than 30	30–55	56 or Older	Total
In-Town Branch	20	40	40	100
Mall Branch	30	50	20	100
Total	50	90	60	200

a) What is the null hypothesis?
b) What type of test is this?
c) What are the expected numbers for each cell if the null hypothesis is true?
d) Find the χ^2 statistic.
e) How many degrees of freedom does it have?
f) Find the critical value at $\alpha = 0.05$.
g) What do you conclude?

8. A market researcher working for the bank in Exercise 2 wants to know if the distribution of applications by card is the same for the past three mailings. She takes a random sample of 200 from each mailing and counts the number applying for Silver, Gold, and Platinum. The data follow:

	Type of Card			
	Silver	Gold	Platinum	Total
Mailing 1	120	50	30	200
Mailing 2	115	50	35	200
Mailing 3	105	55	40	200
Total	340	155	105	600

a) What is the null hypothesis?
b) What type of test is this?
c) What are the expected numbers for each cell if the null hypothesis is true?
d) Find the χ^2 statistic.
e) How many degrees of freedom does it have?
f) Find the critical value at $\alpha = 0.05$.
g) What do you conclude?

SECTION 15.5

9. Markets have become interested in the potential of social networking sites. But they need to understand the demographics of social networking users. Pew Research has conducted surveys since 2012 that address these questions. (www.pewinternet.org/Reports/2013/Social-media-users/Social-Networking-Site-Users). In late 2012, the Pew Research survey found that 525 of 846 surveyed male Internet users use social networking. By contrast 679 of 956 female Internet users use social networking.

a) Find the proportions of male and female Internet users who said they use social networking.
b) What is the difference in proportions?
c) What is the standard error of the difference?
d) Find a 95% confidence interval for the difference between the proportions.

10. From the same survey as in Exercise 9, 294 of the 409 respondents who reported earning less than $30,000 per year said they were social networking users. At the other end of the income scale, 333 of the 504 respondents reporting earnings of $75,000 or more were social networking users.

a) Find the proportions of each income group who are social networking users.
b) What is the difference in proportions?
c) What is the standard error of the difference?
d) Find a 95% confidence interval for the difference between these proportions.

SECTION 15.6

11. A similar Pew poll in 2016 asked people how often they used the Internet. (Data in **Income and internet**)

	How often do you use the Internet?		
Household Income	Every day	At least once a week but not every day	Once a week or less
Less than $25,000	104	48	23
$25,000 to $49,999	154	35	15
$50,000 to $84,999	217	25	12
$85,000 to $124,999	214	23	7
$125,000 or more	160	17	1

a) Under the usual null hypothesis, what are the expected values?
b) Compute the χ^2 statistic.
c) How many degrees of freedom does it have?
d) What do you conclude?

12. As part of the poll in Exercise 11, Pew asked whether the respondent owned a smartphone. Are Internet use and smartphone ownership independent?

	How often do you use the Internet?		
Do you own a smartphone?	Every day	At least once a week but not every day	Once a week or less
Yes	694	71	18
No	150	74	38

a) Under the usual null hypothesis, what are the expected values?
b) Compute the χ^2 statistic.
c) How many degrees of freedom does it have?
d) What do you conclude?

CHAPTER EXERCISES

13. Concepts. For each of the following situations, state whether you'd use a chi-square goodness-of-fit test, chi-square test of homogeneity, chi-square test of independence, or some other statistical test.

a) A brokerage firm wants to see whether the type of account a customer has (Silver, Gold, or Platinum) affects the type of trades that customer makes (in person, by phone, or on the Internet). It collects a random sample of trades made for its customers over the past year and performs a test.
b) That brokerage firm also wants to know if the type of account affects the size of the account (in dollars). It performs a test to see if the mean size of the account is the same for the three account types.
c) The academic research office at a large community college wants to see whether the distribution of courses chosen (Humanities, Social Science, or Science) is different for its residential and nonresidential students. It assembles last semester's data and performs a test.

14. Concepts, part 2. For each of the following situations, state whether you'd use a chi-square goodness-of-fit test, a chi-square test of homogeneity, a chi-square test of independence, or some other statistical test.

a) Is the quality of a car affected by what day it was built? A car manufacturer examines a random sample of the warranty claims filed over the past two years to test whether defects are randomly distributed across days of the work week.

b) A researcher for the American Booksellers Association wants to know if retail sales/sq. ft. is related to serving coffee or snacks on the premises. She examines a database of 10,000 independently owned bookstores testing whether retail sales (dollars/sq. ft.) is related to whether or not the store has a coffee bar.

c) A researcher wants to find out whether education level (some high school, high school graduate, college graduate, advanced degree) is related to the type of transaction most likely to be conducted using the Internet (shopping, banking, travel reservations, auctions). He surveys 500 randomly chosen adults and performs a test.

15. Dice. After getting trounced by your little brother in a children's game, you suspect that the die he gave you is unfair. To check, you roll it 60 times, recording the number of times each face appears. Do these results cast doubt on the die's fairness?

Face	Count
1	11
2	7
3	9
4	15
5	12
6	6

a) If the die is fair, how many times would you expect each face to show?

b) To see if these results are unusual, will you test goodness-of-fit, homogeneity, or independence?

c) State your hypotheses.

d) Check the conditions.

e) How many degrees of freedom are there?

f) Find χ^2 and the P-value.

g) State your conclusion.

16. Online Mating. According to recent research (www .nas.org) married couples who met their spouse through an online dating service may have a different divorce rate than those who met "offline." ("Online Mating" from *Proceedings of the National Academy of Sciences of the United States of America*. Copyright © 2008 National Academy of Sciences. Reproduced by permission of the National Academy of Sciences.) The survey polled couples who married between 2005 and 2012. The baseline divorce rate

(by 2013) for offline marriages in this cohort is 7.73%. The report gives the following divorce statistics according to the online dating service where the couple met:

Service	Couples (n)	Divorces/Separations
eHarmony	791	29
Match	775	58
Plenty of Fish	201	20
Yahoo	227	12
Small Sites	777	37

a) If the divorce rate were the same for these couples as for those who met offline, how many divorces would you expect for each group of couples?

b) To test whether these couples are different from offline couples, will you perform a goodness-of-fit test, a test of homogeneity, or a test of independence?

c) State the hypotheses.

d) Check the conditions.

e) Find the standardized residuals and the chi-square components. (Hint: Use a spreadsheet to perform the calculations.)

f) State the number of degrees of freedom and find χ^2 and the P-value.

g) State your conclusion.

h) Online dating services are a billion-dollar business in the United States. Does it change your conclusion to know that the study was funded by eHarmony?

17. Quality control. A company advertises that its premium mixture of nuts contains 10% Brazil nuts, 20% cashews, 20% almonds, 10% hazelnuts, and that the rest are peanuts. You buy a large can and separate the various kinds of nuts. Upon weighing them, you find there are 112 grams of Brazil nuts, 183 grams of cashews, 207 grams of almonds, 71 grams of hazelnuts, and 446 grams of peanuts. You wonder whether your mix is significantly different from what the company advertises.

a) Explain why the chi-square goodness-of-fit test is not an appropriate way to find out.

b) What might you do instead of weighing the nuts to use a χ^2 test?

18. Sales rep travel. A sales representative who is on the road visiting clients thinks that, on average, he drives the same distance each day of the week. He keeps track of his mileage for several weeks and discovers that he averages 122 miles on Mondays, 203 miles on Tuesdays, 176 miles on Wednesdays, 181 miles on Thursdays, and 108 miles on Fridays. He wonders if this evidence contradicts his belief in a uniform distribution of miles across the days of the week. Is it appropriate to test his hypothesis using the chi-square goodness-of-fit test? Explain.

19. Maryland lottery. For a lottery to be successful, the public must have confidence in its fairness. One of the lotteries in Maryland is Pick-3 Lottery, where 3 random digits are drawn each day.[7] A fair game depends on every value (0 to 9) being equally likely at each of the three positions. If not, then someone detecting a pattern could take advantage of that and beat the lottery. To investigate the randomness, we'll look at data collected over a recent 32-week period. Although the winning numbers look like three-digit numbers, in fact, each digit is a randomly drawn numeral. We have 654 random digits in all. Are each of the digits from 0 to 9 equally likely? Here is a table of the frequencies. (Maryland State Lottery Agency, www.mdlottery.com)

Group	Count	%
0	62	9.480
1	55	8.410
2	66	10.092
3	64	9.786
4	75	11.468
5	57	8.716
6	71	10.856
7	74	11.315
8	69	10.550
9	61	9.327

a) Select the appropriate procedure.
b) Check the assumptions.
c) State the hypotheses.
d) Test an appropriate hypothesis and state your results.
e) Interpret the meaning of the results and state a conclusion.

20. Employment discrimination? Census data for New York City indicate that 29.2% of the under-18 population is white, 28.2% black, 31.5% Latino, 9.1% Asian, and 2% are of other ethnicities. The New York Civil Liberties Union points out that of 26,181 police officers, 64.8% are white, 14.5% black, 19.1% Hispanic, and 1.4% Asian. Do the police officers reflect the ethnic composition of the city's youth? (Equate Latino with Hispanic.)

a) Select the appropriate procedure.
b) Check the assumptions.
c) State the hypotheses.
d) Test an appropriate hypothesis and state your results.
e) Interpret the meaning of the results and state a conclusion.

T 21. Titanic. Here is a table showing who survived the sinking of the *Titanic* based on whether they were crew members or passengers booked in first-, second-, or third-class staterooms.

	Crew	First	Second	Third	Total
Alive	212	202	118	178	710
Dead	673	123	167	528	1491
Total	885	325	285	706	2201

a) If we draw an individual at random from this table, what's the probability that we will draw a member of the crew?
b) What's the probability of randomly selecting a third-class passenger who survived?
c) What's the probability of a randomly selected passenger surviving, given that the passenger was in a first-class stateroom?
d) If someone's chances of surviving were the same regardless of their status on the ship, how many members of the crew would you expect to have lived?
e) State the null and alternative hypotheses we would test here (and the name of the test).
f) Give the degrees of freedom for the test.
g) The chi-square value for the table is 187.8, and the corresponding P-value is barely greater than 0. State your conclusions about the hypotheses.

T 22. Promotion discrimination? The table shows the rank attained by male and female officers in the New York City Police Department (NYPD). Do these data indicate that men and women are equitably represented at all levels of the department? (All possible ranks in the NYPD are shown.) (Data in **NYPD**)

		Male	Female
Rank	Officer	21,900	4281
	Detective	4058	806
	Sergeant	3898	415
	Lieutenant	1333	89
	Captain	359	12
	Higher Ranks	218	10

a) What's the probability that a person selected at random from the NYPD is a female?
b) What's the probability that a person selected at random from the NYPD is a detective?
c) Assuming no bias in promotions, how many female detectives would you expect the NYPD to have?
d) To see if there is evidence of differences in ranks attained by males and females, will you test goodness-of-fit, homogeneity, or independence?

---

[7]Source: Maryland State Lottery Agency, www.mdlottery.com.

e) State the hypotheses.
f) Test the conditions.
g) How many degrees of freedom are there?
h) Find the chi-square value and the associated P-value.
i) State your conclusion.
j) If you concluded that the distributions are not the same, analyze the differences using the standardized residuals of your calculations.

23. Birth order and college choice. Students in an Introductory statistics class at a large university were classified by birth order and by the college they attend.

	Birth Order (1 = oldest or only child)				
	1	**2**	**3**	**4 or More**	**Total**
Arts and Sciences	34	14	6	3	57
Agriculture	52	27	5	9	93
Social Science	15	17	8	3	43
Professional	13	11	1	6	31
Total	114	69	20	21	224

Expected Values	Birth Order (1 = oldest or only child)			
	1	**2**	**3**	**4 or More**
Arts and Sciences	29.0089	17.5580	5.0893	5.3438
Agriculture	47.3304	28.6473	8.3036	8.7188
Social Science	21.8839	13.2455	3.8393	4.0313
Professional	15.7768	9.5491	2.7679	2.9063

a) What kind of chi-square test is appropriate—goodness-of-fit, homogeneity, or independence?
b) State your hypotheses.
c) State and check the conditions.
d) How many degrees of freedom are there?
e) The calculation yields $\chi^2 = 17.78$, with $P = 0.0378$. State your conclusion.
f) Examine and comment on the standardized residuals. Do they challenge your conclusion? Explain.

Standardized Residuals	Birth Order (1 = oldest or only child)			
	1	**2**	**3**	**4 or More**
Arts and Sciences	0.92667	−0.84913	0.40370	−1.01388
Agriculture	0.67876	−0.30778	−1.14640	0.09525
Social Science	−1.47155	1.03160	2.12350	−0.51362
Professional	−0.69909	0.46952	−1.06261	1.81476

24. Automobile manufacturers. *Consumer Reports* uses surveys given to subscribers of its magazine and website (www.ConsumerReports.org) to measure reliability in automobiles. This annual survey asks about problems that consumers have had with their cars, vans, SUVs, or trucks during the previous 12 months. Each analysis is based on the number of problems per 100 vehicles.

	Origin of Manufacturer			
	Asia	**Europe**	**U.S.**	**Total**
No Problems	88	79	83	250
Problems	12	21	17	50
Total	100	100	100	300

Expected Values			
	Asia	**Europe**	**U.S.**
No Problems	83.33	83.33	83.33
Problems	16.67	16.67	16.67

a) State your hypotheses.
b) State and check the conditions.
c) How many degrees of freedom are there?
d) The calculation yields $\chi^2 = 2.928$, with $P = 0.231$. State your conclusion.
e) Would you expect that a larger sample might find statistical significance? Explain.

T 25. Cranberry juice. It's common folk wisdom that cranberries can help prevent urinary tract infections in women. A leading producer of cranberry juice would like to use this information in their next ad campaign, so they need evidence of this claim. In 2001, the *British Medical Journal* reported the results of a Finnish study in which three groups of 50 women were monitored for these infections over 6 months. One group drank cranberry juice daily, another group drank a lactobacillus drink, and the third group drank neither of those beverages, serving as a control group. In the control group, 18 women developed at least one infection compared with 20 of those who consumed the lactobacillus drink and only 8 of those who drank cranberry juice. Does this study provide supporting evidence for the value of cranberry juice in warding off urinary tract infections in women?

a) Select the appropriate procedure.
b) Check the assumptions.
c) State the hypotheses.
d) Test an appropriate hypothesis and state your results.
e) Interpret the meaning of the results and state a conclusion.
f) If you concluded that the groups are not the same, analyze the differences using the standardized residuals of your calculations.

26. College value? In March and April of 2011, the Pew Research Center asked 2142 U.S. adults and 1055 college presidents whether they would "rate the job the higher education system is doing in providing value for the money spent by students and their families as" Excellent, Good, Only Fair, or Poor.

	Poor	Only Fair	Good	Excellent	No Answer/ Don't Know
U.S. Adults	321	900	750	107	64
College Presidents	32	222	622	179	0

Is there a difference in the distribution of responses between U.S. adults and college presidents?

a) Is this a test of independence or homogeneity?
b) Write appropriate hypotheses.
c) Check the necessary assumptions and conditions.
d) Find the P-value of your test.
e) State your conclusion and analysis.

27. Shopping. A survey of 430 randomly chosen adults finds that 47 of 222 men and 37 of 208 women had purchased books online.

a) Is there evidence that the sex of the person and whether they buy books online are associated?
b) If your conclusion in fact proves to be wrong, did you make a Type I or Type II error?
c) Give a 95% confidence interval for the difference in proportions of buying online for men and women.

28. Information technology. A recent report suggests that Chief Information Officers (CIOs) who report directly to Chief Financial Officers (CFOs) rather than Chief Executive Officers (CEOs) are more likely to have IT agendas that deal with cost cutting and compliance (SearchCIO.com, March 14, 2006). In a random sample of 535 companies, it was found that CIOs reported directly to CFOs in 173 out of 335 service firms and in 95 out of 200 manufacturing companies.

a) Is there evidence that type of business (service versus manufacturing) and whether or not the CIO reports directly to the CFO are associated?
b) If your conclusion proves to be wrong, did you make a Type I or Type II error?
c) Give a 95% confidence interval for the difference in proportions of companies in which the CIO reports directly to the CFO between service and manufacturing firms.

29. Fast food. GfK Roper Consulting gathers information on consumer preferences around the world to help companies monitor attitudes about health, food, and health care products. They asked people in many different cultures how they felt about the following statement: *I try to avoid eating fast foods.*

In a random sample of 800 respondents, 411 people were 35 years old or younger, and, of those, 197 agreed (completely or somewhat) with the statement. Of the 389 people over 35 years old, 246 people agreed with the statement.

a) Is there evidence that the percentage of people avoiding fast food is different in the two age groups?
b) Give a 90% confidence interval for the difference in proportions.

30. Libraries. Public libraries are not run for profit, but they must know their customers. A Pew Research survey in November 2012 found that 426 of 584 surveyed parents of young children had current library cards. 967 of 1668 adults without young children had library cards.

a) Is there evidence that the percentage of adults with library cards is different between these two groups?
b) Give a 95% confidence interval for the difference.
c) Do you think the difference should affect how a library markets its services?

31. Under water. In early 2012, the proportion of mortgages that were "under water"—a negative equity position in which the homeowner owes more than the value of the home—was highest in Nevada and Arizona (s.wsj .net/public/resources/documents/info-NEGATIVE_ EQUITY_0911.html). Lenders are also interested in homes at risk—those within 5% of being in a negative equity position. A sample of mortgages from these two states suggest that the problem may be less severe in Nevada. The sample found that 62 of 1369 Arizona mortgages were in a "near negative equity" state. A sample of 604 Nevada mortgages found 22 in a near negative equity state.

a) Is there evidence that the percentage of near negative equity mortgages is different in the two states?
b) Give a 90% confidence interval for the difference in proportions.

32. Labor force. Immigration reform has focused on dividing illegal immigrants into two groups: long-term and short-term. In a random sample of 958 construction workers from the Northeast, 66 are illegal short-term immigrants. In the Midwest, 42 out of a sample of 1070 are illegal short-term immigrants.

a) Is there evidence that the percentage of construction workers who are illegal short-term immigrants differs in the two regions?
b) Give a 90% confidence interval for the difference in proportions.

33. Seafood company. A large company in the northeastern United States that buys fish from local fishermen and distributes them to major companies and restaurants is considering launching a new ad campaign on the health benefits of fish. As evidence, they would like to cite the following study. Medical researchers followed 6272 Swedish men for 30 years to see if there was any association between the amount of fish in their diet and prostate cancer ("Fatty

Fish Consumption and Risk of Prostate Cancer," *Lancet*, June 2001).

	Prostate Cancer	
Fish Consumption	**No**	**Yes**
Never/Seldom	110	14
Small Part of Diet	2420	201
Moderate Part	2769	209
Large Part	507	42

a) Is this a survey, a retrospective study, a prospective study, or an experiment? Explain.
b) Is this a test of homogeneity or independence?
c) Do you see evidence of an association between the amount of fish in a man's diet and his risk of developing prostate cancer?
d) Does this study prove that eating fish does not prevent prostate cancer? Explain.

34. Investment options. A full service brokerage firm surveyed a random sample of 1200 clients asking them to indicate the likelihood that they would add inflation-linked annuities and bonds to their portfolios within the next year. The table below shows the distribution of responses by the investors' tolerance for risk. Test an appropriate hypothesis for the relationship between risk tolerance and the likelihood of investing in inflation-linked options.

	Risk Tolerance			
Likelihood of Investing in Inflation-Linked Options	**Averse**	**Neutral**	**Seeking**	**Total**
Certain Will Invest	191	93	40	324
Likely to Invest	82	106	123	311
Not Likely to Invest	64	110	101	275
Certain Will Not Invest	63	91	136	290
Total	**400**	**400**	**400**	**1200**

35. Being successful. Pew Research surveyed U.S. adults in December 2011. They asked how important it is "to you personally" to be successful in a high-paying career or profession. Among 18- to 34-year-old respondents, do men and women have the same ideas about the importance of this kind of success? Here's a table of the responses:

	F	M	Total
Most important	110	77	187
Very important	293	331	624
Somewhat important	158	218	376
Not important	49	77	126
Total	**610**	**703**	**1313**

a) Select the appropriate procedure.
b) Check the assumptions.
c) State the hypotheses.
d) Test an appropriate hypothesis and state your results.
e) Interpret the meaning of the results and state a conclusion.

36. Entrepreneurial executives. A leading CEO mentoring organization offers a program for chief executives, presidents, and business owners with a focus on developing entrepreneurial skills. Women and men executives that recently completed the program rated its value. Are perceptions of the program's value the same for men and women?

	Men	Women
Perceived Value		
Excellent	3	9
Good	11	12
Average	14	8
Marginal	9	2
Poor	3	1

a) Will you test goodness-of-fit, homogeneity, or independence?
b) Write appropriate hypotheses.
c) Find the expected counts for each cell, and explain why the chi-square procedures are not appropriate for this table.

37. Owning stocks. The Cornell National Social Survey[8] asked 1000 U.S. adults about their employment status and whether they owned stocks. This table gives the counts of the 938 respondents:

	Stocks		
Employed	**No**	**Yes**	**Total**
Yes	330	248	578
No	123	45	168
Retired	120	72	192
Total	**573**	**365**	**938**

Is there a relationship between employment status and stock ownership?

a) Select an appropriate procedure.
b) Check the assumptions.
c) Test the hypothesis.
d) Examine the residuals.
e) Discuss what you find.

---

[8]Cornell Survey Research Institute, 2009 and 2011.

38. Online shopping. A recent report concludes that while Internet users like the convenience of online shopping, they do have concerns about privacy and security (*Online Shopping*, Washington, DC, Pew Internet & American Life Project, February 2008). A random sample of adults were asked to indicate their level of agreement with the statement "I don't like giving my credit card number or personal information online." The table gives a subset of responses. Test an appropriate hypothesis for the relationship between age and level of concern about privacy and security online.

	Strongly Agree	Agree	Disagree	Strongly Disagree	Total
Ages 18–29	127	147	138	10	422
Ages 30–49	141	129	78	55	403
Ages 50–64	178	102	64	51	395
Ages 65 +	180	132	54	14	380
Total	626	510	334	130	1600

(rows grouped under "Age Category")

a) Select the appropriate procedure.
b) Check the assumptions.
c) State the hypotheses.
d) Test an appropriate hypothesis and state your results.
e) Interpret the meaning of the results and state a conclusion.

39. Entrepreneurial executives again. In some situations where the expected counts are too small, as in Exercise 36, we can complete an analysis anyway. We can often proceed after combining cells in some way that makes sense and also produces a table in which the conditions are satisfied. Here is a new table displaying the same data, but combining "Marginal" and "Poor" into a new category called "Below Average."

	Men	Women
Excellent	3	9
Good	11	12
Average	14	8
Below Average	12	3

(rows grouped under "Perceived Value")

a) Find the expected counts for each cell in this new table, and explain why a chi-square procedure is now appropriate.
b) With this change in the table, what has happened to the number of degrees of freedom?
c) Test your hypothesis about the two groups and state an appropriate conclusion.

40. Small business. The director of a small business development center located in a mid-sized city is reviewing data about its clients. In particular, she is interested in examining if the distribution of business owners across the various stages of the business life cycle is the same for white-owned and Hispanic-owned businesses. The data are shown below.

	White-Owned	Hispanic-Owned
Planning	11	9
Starting	14	11
Managing	20	2
Getting Out	15	1

(rows grouped under "Stage in Business")

a) Will you test goodness-of-fit, homogeneity, or independence?
b) Write the appropriate hypotheses.
c) Find the expected counts for each cell and explain why chi-square procedures are not appropriate for this table.
d) Create a new table by combining categories so that a chi-square procedure can be used.
e) With this change in the table, what has happened to the number of degrees of freedom?
f) Test your hypothesis about the two groups and state an appropriate conclusion.

T 41. Racial steering. A subtle form of racial discrimination in housing is "racial steering." Racial steering occurs when real estate agents show prospective buyers only homes in neighborhoods already dominated by that family's race. This violates the Fair Housing Act of 1968. Tenants at a large apartment complex filed a lawsuit alleging racial steering. The complex is divided into two parts: Section A and Section B. The plaintiffs claimed that white potential renters were steered to Section A, while African-Americans were steered to Section B. The following table displays the data that were presented in court to show the locations of recently rented apartments. Do you think there is evidence of racial steering?

	New Renters		
	White	Black	Total
Section A	87	8	95
Section B	83	34	117
Total	170	42	212

T 42. Titanic, again. Newspaper headlines at the time and traditional wisdom in the succeeding decades have held that women and children escaped the *Titanic* in greater proportion than men. Here's a table with the relevant data. Do you think that survival was independent of whether the person was male or female? Defend your conclusion.

	Female	Male	Total
Alive	343	367	710
Dead	127	1364	1491
Total	470	1731	2201

T **43. Racial steering, revisited.** Find a 95% confidence interval for the difference in the proportions of Black renters in the two sections for the data in Exercise 43.

T **44. *Titanic*, one more time.** Find a 95% confidence interval for the difference in the proportion of women who survived and the proportion of men who survived for the data in Exercise 44. (Assume the passengers on the *Titanic* were representative of others who might have taken the trip.)

45. Industry sector and outsourcing. Many companies have chosen to outsource segments of their business to external providers in order to cut costs and improve quality and/or efficiencies. Common business segments that are outsourced include Information Technology (IT) and Human Resources (HR). The data below show the types of outsourcing decisions made (no outsourcing, IT only, HR only, both IT and HR) by a sample of companies from various industry sectors.

<table>
<thead>
<tr><th></th><th></th><th>No Outsourcing</th><th>IT Only</th><th>HR Only</th><th>Both IT and HR</th></tr>
</thead>
<tbody>
<tr><td rowspan="4">Industry Sector</td><td>Health Care</td><td>810</td><td>6429</td><td>4725</td><td>1127</td></tr>
<tr><td>Financial</td><td>263</td><td>1598</td><td>549</td><td>117</td></tr>
<tr><td>Industrial Goods</td><td>1031</td><td>1269</td><td>412</td><td>99</td></tr>
<tr><td>Consumer Goods</td><td>66</td><td>341</td><td>305</td><td>197</td></tr>
</tbody>
</table>

Do these data highlight significant differences in outsourcing by industry sector?

a) Select the appropriate procedure.
b) Check the assumptions.
c) State the hypotheses.
d) Test an appropriate hypothesis and state your results.
e) Interpret the meaning of the results and state a conclusion.

46. Industry sector and outsourcing, part 2. Consider only the companies that have outsourced their IT and HR business segments. Do these data suggest significant differences between companies in the financial and industrial goods sectors with regard to their outsourcing decisions?

<table>
<thead>
<tr><th></th><th></th><th>IT Only</th><th>HR Only</th><th>Both IT and HR</th></tr>
</thead>
<tbody>
<tr><td rowspan="2">Industry Sector</td><td>Financial</td><td>1598</td><td>549</td><td>117</td></tr>
<tr><td>Industrial Goods</td><td>1269</td><td>412</td><td>99</td></tr>
</tbody>
</table>

a) Select the appropriate procedure.
b) Check the assumptions.

c) State the hypotheses.
d) Test an appropriate hypothesis and state your results.
e) Interpret the meaning of the results and state the conclusion.

47. Management styles. Use the survey results in the table below to investigate differences in employee job satisfaction among organizations in the United States with different management styles.

<table>
<thead>
<tr><th></th><th></th><th colspan="4">Employee Job Satisfaction</th></tr>
<tr><th></th><th></th><th>Very Satisfied</th><th>Satisfied</th><th>Somewhat Satisfied</th><th>Not Satisfied</th></tr>
</thead>
<tbody>
<tr><td rowspan="5">Management Styles</td><td>Exploitative Authoritarian</td><td>27</td><td>82</td><td>43</td><td>48</td></tr>
<tr><td>Benevolent Authoritarian</td><td>50</td><td>19</td><td>56</td><td>75</td></tr>
<tr><td>Laissez Faire</td><td>52</td><td>88</td><td>26</td><td>34</td></tr>
<tr><td>Consultative</td><td>71</td><td>83</td><td>20</td><td>26</td></tr>
<tr><td>Participative</td><td>101</td><td>59</td><td>20</td><td>20</td></tr>
</tbody>
</table>

a) Select the appropriate procedure.
b) Check the assumptions.
c) State the hypotheses.
d) Test an appropriate hypothesis and state your results.
e) Interpret the meaning of the results and state a conclusion.

48. Ranking companies. Every year, *Fortune* magazine lists the 100 best companies to work for, based on criteria such as pay, benefits, days off, and diversity. In 2018, the top three were Sales Force, Wegmans Food Markets, and Ultimate Software. In 2017, of the top 30, 10 were in the top third for most days off, 9 were in the middle third, and 11 were in the bottom third. Of the bottom 30 in rank, 7 were in the top third, 13 were in the middle third, and 10 were in the bottom third. Is there evidence that number of days off is related to overall ranking as best place to work?

a) Select the appropriate procedure.
b) Check the assumptions.
c) State the hypotheses.
d) Test an appropriate hypothesis and state your results.
e) Interpret the meaning of the results and state a conclusion.

49. Businesses and blogs. The Pew Internet & American Life Project routinely conducts surveys to gauge the impact of the Internet and technology on daily life. A recent survey asked respondents if they read online journals or blogs, an Internet activity of potential interest to many businesses. A subset of the data from this survey (*February–March 2007 Tracking Data Set*) shows responses to this question. Test whether reading online journals or blogs is independent of generation.

	Read Online Journal or Blog			
Generation	Yes, Yesterday	Yes, but Not Yesterday	No	Total
Gen-Y (18–30)	29	35	62	126
Gen X (31–42)	12	34	137	183
Trailing Boomers (43–52)	15	34	132	181
Leading Boomers (53–61)	7	22	83	112
Matures (62 +)	6	21	111	138
Total	69	146	525	740

50. CyberShopping. It has become more common for shoppers to "comparison shop" using the Internet. Respondents to a Pew survey in 2013 who owned cell phones were asked whether they had, in the past 30 days, looked up the price of a product while they were in a store to see if they could get a better price somewhere else. Here is a table of their responses by income level.

	<$30K	$30K–$49.9K	$50K–$74.9K	>$75K
Yes	207	115	134	204
No	625	406	260	417

a) Is the frequency of comparison shopping on the Internet independent of the income level of the respondent? Perform an appropriate chi-square test and state your conclusion.
b) Calculate and examine the standardized residuals. What pattern (if any, do they show that would be of interest to retailers concerned about cybershopping comparisons?

51. Information systems. In a recent study of enterprise resource planning (ERP) system effectiveness, researchers asked companies about how they assessed the success of their ERP systems. Out of 335 manufacturing companies surveyed, they found that 201 used return on investment (ROI), 100 used reductions in inventory levels, 28 used improved data quality, and 6 used on-time delivery. In a survey of 200 service firms, 40 used ROI, 40 used inventory levels, 100 used improved data quality, and 20 used on-time delivery. Is there evidence that the measures used to assess ERP system effectiveness differ between service and manufacturing firms? Perform the appropriate test and state your conclusion.

52. U.S. Gross Domestic Product. The U.S. Bureau of Economic Analysis provides information on the Gross Domestic Product Per Capita (GDP PC) in the United States by state (www.bea.gov). The Bureau recently released figures that showed the real (GDP PC) by state for 2016. Using the data in the table below examine if (GDP PC) and *Region* of the country are independent. (Alaska and Hawaii are part of the West Region. DC is included in the Mideast Region.)

	Above Median GDP PC?		
	No	Yes	Total
West (Far West, Southwest, and Rocky Mtn.)	7	8	15
Midwest (Great Lakes and Plains States)	5	7	12
Southeast	11	1	12
Northeast (Mideast and New England States)	3	9	12
Total	26	25	51

53. Economic growth. The U.S. Bureau of Economic Analysis also provides information on the growth of the U.S. economy (www.bea.gov). The Bureau recently released figures that they claimed showed a growth spurt in the western region of the United States. Using the table and map below, determine if the percent change in real GDP by state for 2005–2006 was independent of region of the country. (Alaska and Hawaii are part of the West Region. DC is included in the Mideast Region.)

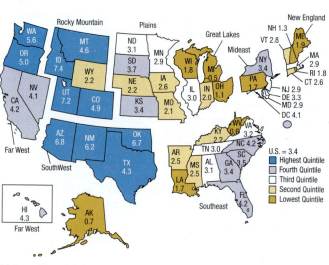

Percent Change in Real GDP by State, 2005–2006

U.S. Bureau of Economic Analysis

	GDP % Change		
	Top 40%	Bottom 60%	Total
West (Far West, Southwest, and Rocky Mtn.)	13	2	15
Midwest (Great Lakes and Plains States)	2	10	12
Southeast	4	8	12
Northeast (Mideast and New England States)	2	10	12
Total	21	30	51

54. Economic growth, revisited. The U.S. Bureau of Economic Analysis provides information on the GDP in the United States by metropolitan area (www.bea.gov). The Bureau recently released figures that showed the percent change in real GDP by metropolitan area for 2004–2005. Using the data in the following table, examine if there is independence of the growth in metropolitan GDP and region of the country. (Alaska and Hawaii are part of the West Region. Some of the metropolitan areas may have been combined for this analysis.)

	GDP Growth		
	Top Two Quintiles (top 40%)	Bottom Three Quintiles (bottom 60%)	Total
West (Far West, Southwest, and Rocky Mtn.)	62	46	108
Midwest (Great Lakes and Plains States)	9	87	96
Southeast	38	58	96
Northeast (Mideast and New England States)	12	36	48
Total	121	227	348

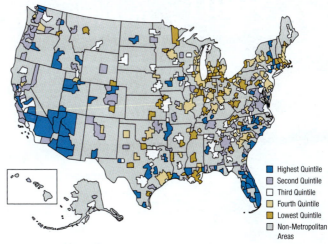

Legend:
- Highest Quintile
- Second Quintile
- Third Quintile
- Fourth Quintile
- Lowest Quintile
- Non-Metropolitan Areas

U.S. Bureau of Economic Analysis

JUST CHECKING ANSWERS

1 This is a test of homogeneity. The clue is that the question asks whether the distributions are alike.

2 This is a test of goodness-of-fit. We want to test the model of equal assignment to all lots against what actually happened.

3 This is a test of independence. We have responses on two variables for the same individuals.

Investment Strategy Segmentation

In the aftermath of the financial crisis of 2008, brokerage firms struggled to get individual investors back into the stock market. To gain competitive advantage, market analysts in nearly every industry group their customers into different segments by placing advertisements where they can have the greatest impact. The brokerage business is no different. Because different groups of people invest differently, customizing advertising to the needs of these groups leads to more efficient advertising placement and response. Brokerage firms get their information about the investment practices of individuals from a variety of sources, among which the U.S. Census Bureau figures prominently.

The U.S. Census Bureau, with the help of the Bureau of Labor Statistics (BLS) and the Internal Revenue Service (IRS), monitors the incomes and expenditures of Americans. A random sample of Americans are surveyed periodically about their investment practices. In the file **Case Study III** you'll find a random sample of 1000 people from the 48,842 records found in the file Census Income Data set on the University of California at Irvine machine learning repository. This subset was sampled from those that showed some level of investment in the stock market as evidenced by claiming *Capital Gains ($)*, *Capital Losses ($)*, or *Dividends ($)*. Included as well are the demographic variables for these people: *Age (years)*, *Sex (male/female)*, *Union Member (Yes/No)*, *Citizenship (several categories)*, *College (No College/Some)*, *Married (Married/Single)*, *Filer Status (Joint/Single)*.

To support her segmentation efforts, a market analyst at an online brokerage firm wants to study differences in investment behaviors. If she can find meaningful differences in the types and amounts of investing that various groups engage in, she can use that information to inform the advertising and marketing departments in their strategies to attract new investors. Using the techniques of Part III, including confidence intervals and hypothesis tests, what differences in investment behaviors can you find among the various demographic groups?

Some specific questions to consider:

1. Do men and women invest similarly? Construct confidence intervals for the differences in mean *Capital Gains*, *Capital Losses*, and *Dividends*.

   Be sure to make a suitable display to check assumptions and conditions. If you find outlier(s), consider the analysis with and without the outlier(s).

2. Make a suitable display to compare investment results for the various levels of *Citizenship*.

3. Do those who file singly have the same investment results as those who file jointly? Select, perform, and interpret an appropriate test.

4. Compare differences in investment results for the other demographic variables, being careful to check assumptions and conditions.

   Once again, make suitable displays. Are there outliers to be concerned with? Discuss.

Summarize your findings and conclusions about the investment practices of various groups. Write a short report in order to help the market analyst.

CHAPTER 16

Inference for Regression

Nambé Mills

Nambé (nam-BAY) Mills, Inc., was founded in 1951 near the tiny village of Nambé Pueblo, about 10 miles north of Santa Fe, New Mexico. Known for its elegant, functional cooking and tableware, Nambé Mills now sells its products in luxury stores throughout the world. Many of its products are made from an eight-metal alloy created at the Los Alamos National Laboratory (where the atomic bomb was developed during World War II) and now used exclusively by Nambé Mills. The alloy has the luster of silver and the solidity of iron, but its main component is aluminum. In fact, it does not contain silver, lead, or pewter (a tin and copper alloy), and it does not tarnish, unlike some of the bowls pictured above. Because it's a trade secret, Nambé Mills does not divulge the rest of the formula. Up to 15 craftsmen may be involved in the production process of an item, which includes molding, pouring, grinding, polishing, and buffing.

B ecause Nambé Mills's metal products are sand-cast, they must go through a lengthy production process. To rationalize its production schedule, management examined the total polishing times of 59 tableware items. Here's a scatterplot showing the retail price of the items and the amount of time (in minutes) spent in the polishing phase (Figure 16.1).

FIGURE 16.1 A scatterplot of *Price* ($) against polishing *Time* (minutes) for Nambé tableware products shows that the items that take longer to polish cost more, on average. (Data in **Nambe_2018**)

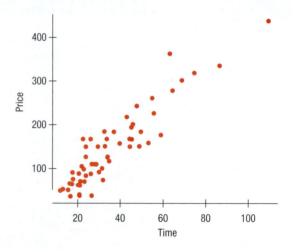

The equation of the least squares line for these data is:

$$\widehat{Price} = -4.871 + 4.200 \times Time$$

The slope says that, on average, the price increases by $4.20 for every extra minute of polishing time.

In Chapter 4, we used the regression line just as a description of the data at hand. Now we'd like to know what the regression model can tell us beyond the sample. To do that, we'll make confidence intervals and test hypotheses about the slope and intercept of the regression line as we've done for the mean and proportion of a sample.

> **The Regression Model**
>
> Remember that we find the least squares line as $\hat{y} = b_0 + b_1x$ where $b_1 = r\, s_y/s_x$ and $b_0 = \bar{y} - b_1\bar{x}$.

16.1 A Hypothesis Test and Confidence Interval for the Slope

Our data are a sample of 59 items. If we take another sample, we hope the regression line will be similar to the one we found here, but we know it won't be exactly the same. Observations vary from sample to sample. But we can imagine a true idealized line that models the relationship between *Price* and *Time*. Following our usual conventions, we write the model using Greek letters and consider the coefficients (slope and intercept) to be parameters: β_0 is the intercept, and β_1 is the slope. Corresponding to our fitted line of $\hat{y} = b_0 + b_1x$, we write $\mu_y = \beta_0 + \beta_1x$. We write μ_y instead of y because the regression model assumes that the *means* of the y-values for each value of x fall exactly on the line. We can picture the model as in Figure 16.2. The means are on the line, and the y-values at each x are distributed around them.

Now, if only we had all the values in the population, we could find the slope and intercept of this *idealized regression line* explicitly by using least squares.

Of course, the individual y's are not at these means. In fact, the line will miss most—and usually all—of the plotted points. Some y's lie above the line and some below the line, so like all models, this one makes errors. To account for each individual value of y in our model, we can include these errors, which we denote by ε:

$$y = \beta_0 + \beta_1x + \varepsilon.$$

> **NOTATION ALERT**
>
> We use lowercase Greek betas (β) to denote the coefficients in the regression model. We estimate them with the b's in the fitted regression equation. We used β earlier for the probability of a Type II error, but β here is not related to its earlier use. We use ε for the errors because these are the errors of the model—values we are not likely to know exactly.

This equation has an ε to soak up the deviation at each point, so the model gives a value of y for each value of x. To do hypothesis tests and make confidence intervals, we assume that the errors have a Normal distribution around the line at each x-value, as shown in Figure 16.2.

FIGURE 16.2 There's a distribution of *Prices* for each value of polishing *Time*. The regression model assumes that the means line up perfectly like this, and that the y-values are distributed with a Normal model around the line at each x-value.

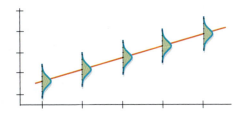

We estimate the β's by finding a regression line, $\hat{y} = b_0 + b_1 x$, as we did in Chapter 4. The residuals, $e = y - \hat{y}$ are the sample-based versions of the errors, ε. We'll use them to help us assess the regression model.

We know that least squares regression will give us reasonable estimates of the parameters of this model from a random sample of data. We also know that our estimates won't be exactly equal to the parameters in the idealized or "true" model. Our challenge is to account for the uncertainty in our estimates by making confidence intervals as we've done for means and proportions. For that, we need to find the standard errors of the slope and intercept.

We expect the estimated slope for any sample, b_1, to be close to—but not actually equal to—the model slope, β_1. Across many repeated samples, however, the mean of all the slopes would be very close to the true parameter value. If we could see the collection of slopes from many samples (imagined or real) we would see a distribution of values around the true slope. That's the sampling distribution of the slope.

What is the standard deviation of this distribution? That depends on several aspects of our situation: how much the data vary, how solid a basis we have for our estimate, and how much data we have.

- **Spread around the line.** Figure 16.3 shows samples from two populations. Which underlying population would give rise to the more consistent slopes?

FIGURE 16.3 Which of these scatterplots would give the more consistent regression slope estimate if we were to sample repeatedly from its underlying population?

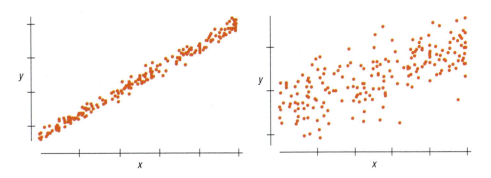

Less scatter around the line means the slope will be more consistent from sample to sample. In Chapter 4, we measured the spread around the line with the **residual standard deviation**:

$$s_e = \sqrt{\frac{\Sigma (y - \hat{y})^2}{n - 2}}.$$

The less scatter around the line, the smaller the residual standard deviation and the stronger the relationship between x and y.

- **Spread of the *x*'s:** Here are samples from two more populations (Figure 16.4). Which of these would yield more consistent slopes?

FIGURE 16.4 Which of these scatterplots would give the more consistent regression slope estimate if we were to sample repeatedly from the underlying population?

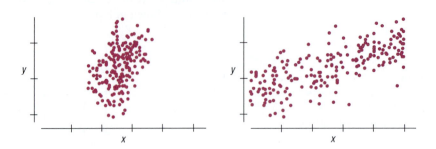

A plot like the one on the right has a broader range of *x*-values, so it gives a more stable base for the slope. We might expect the slopes of samples from situations like that to vary less from sample to sample. A large standard deviation of *x*, s_x, as in the figure on the right, provides a more stable regression.

- **Sample size.** What about the two scatterplots in Figure 16.5?

FIGURE 16.5 Which of these scatterplots would give the more consistent regression slope estimate if we were to sample repeatedly from the underlying population?

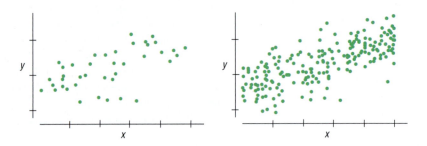

It shouldn't shock you that a larger sample size (scatterplot on the right) gives more consistent estimates from sample to sample.

Let's summarize what we've seen in these three figures:

The Standard Error of the Regression Slope

Three aspects of the scatterplot that affect the standard error of the regression slope are:

- Spread around the line: s_e
- Spread of *x*-values: s_x
- Sample size: n

These are in fact the *only* things that affect the standard error of the slope. The formula for the standard error of the slope is:

$$SE(b_1) = \frac{s_e}{s_x \sqrt{n-1}}.$$

The error standard deviation, s_e, is in the *numerator*, since a larger spread around the line *increases* the slope's standard error. On the other hand, the *denominator* has both a sample size term ($\sqrt{n-1}$) and s_x because increasing either of these *decreases* the slope's standard error.

Our goal is a hypothesis test or confidence interval for the slope. The standard deviation of the sampling distribution of the slope is one part, but we need to know the shape of the sampling distribution as well. Here the Central Limit Theorem and Gosset come to the rescue again. We do just what we've done with the mean and proportion. We standardize the estimated slope by subtracting the model value and dividing by the estimated standard error. And just as we did with the mean, we get a Student's t-model, this time with $n - 2$ degrees of freedom:

$$\frac{b_1 - \beta_1}{SE(b_1)} \sim t_{n-2}.$$

> ### The Sampling Distribution for the Regression Slope
>
> When the conditions are met, the standardized estimated regression slope,
>
> $$t = \frac{b_1 - \beta_1}{SE(b_1)},$$
>
> follows a Student's t-model with $n - 2$ degrees of freedom. We estimate the standard error with $SE(b_1) = \dfrac{s_e}{s_x \sqrt{n - 1}}$, where $s_e = \sqrt{\dfrac{\sum (y - \hat{y})^2}{n - 2}}$, n is the number of data values, and s_x is the standard deviation of the x-values.

What If the Slope Is 0?

If $b_1 = 0$, our prediction is $\hat{y} = b_0 + 0x$, and the equation collapses to just $\hat{y} = b_0$. Now x is nowhere in sight, so y doesn't depend on x at all.

In this case, b_0 would turn out to be $\bar{y}$. Why? Because we know that $b_0 = \bar{y} - b_1 \bar{x}$, and when $b_1 = 0$, that becomes simply $b_0 = \bar{y}$. It turns out, that when the slope is 0, the entire regression equation is just $\hat{y} = \bar{y}$, so for every value of x, we predict the mean value ($\bar{y}$) for y. This should match your intuition. If x doesn't give you any information about y, your best guess for y should be the mean.

Now that we have the standard error of the slope and its sampling distribution, we can test a hypothesis about it and make confidence intervals. The usual null hypothesis about the slope is that it's equal to 0. Why? Well, a slope of zero would say that y doesn't tend to change linearly when x changes—in other words, that there is no linear association between the two variables. If the slope were zero, there wouldn't be much left of our regression equation.

A null hypothesis of a zero slope questions the entire claim of a linear relationship between the two variables, and often that's just what we want to know. In fact, every software package or calculator that does regression simply assumes that you want to test the null hypothesis that the slope is really zero.

This is just like every other t-test we've seen: a difference between the statistic and its hypothesized value divided by its standard error. This test is the t-test that the regression slope is 0, usually referred to as the **t-test for the regression slope**.

Another use of these values might be to make a confidence interval for the slope. We can build a confidence interval in the usual way, as an estimate plus or minus a margin of error. As always, the margin of error is just the product of the standard error and a critical value.

The t-Test for the Regression Slope

When the assumptions and conditions are met, we can test the hypothesis H_0: $\beta_1 = 0$ vs. H_A: $\beta_1 \neq 0$ (or a one-sided alternative hypothesis) using the standardized estimated regression slope,

$$t = \frac{b_1 - \beta_1}{SE(b_1)},$$

which follows a Student's t-model with $n - 2$ degrees of freedom. We can use the t-model to find the P-value of the test.

> ### The Confidence Interval for the Regression Slope
>
> When the assumptions and conditions are met, we can find a confidence interval for β_1 from
>
> $$b_1 \pm t^*_{n-2} \times SE(b_1),$$
>
> where the critical value t^* depends on the confidence level and has $n - 2$ degrees of freedom.

The same reasoning applies for the intercept. We write:

$$\frac{b_0 - \beta_0}{SE(b_0)} \sim t_{n-2}.$$

We could use this statistic to construct confidence intervals and test hypotheses about the intercept, but often the value of the intercept isn't interesting. Most hypothesis tests and confidence intervals for regression are about the slope. But in case you really want to see the formula for the standard error of the intercept, we've parked it in a footnote.[1]

---

[1] $SE(b_0) = s_e \sqrt{\dfrac{1}{n} + \dfrac{\bar{x}^2}{\sum (x - \bar{x})^2}}$

Regression models are almost always estimated with a computer. The calculations are too long to do conveniently by hand for datasets of any reasonable size. No matter how the regression is computed, the results are usually presented in a table that has a standard form. Figure 16.6 shows a portion of a typical regression results table, along with annotations showing where the numbers come from.

FIGURE 16.6 A typical computer regression table presents regression results in a standard format.

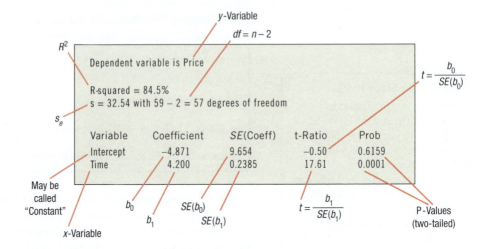

16.2 Assumptions and Conditions

Back in Chapter 4 when we fit lines to data, we needed both the **Linearity** and the **Equal Variance Assumptions**. Now, to make inferences about the coefficients of the line, we'll have to assume that the errors are independent and Normally distributed as well.

It is important to check the assumptions and their associated conditions in the right order, so we number the assumptions, and check conditions for each in that order: (1) Linearity Assumption, (2) Independence Assumption, (3) Equal Variance Assumption, and (4) Normal Population Assumption.

1. Linearity Assumption

If the true relationship of two quantitative variables is far from linear and we use a straight line to fit the data, our entire analysis will be useless, so we always check linearity first (and we check the **Quantitative Variable Condition** for both variables as well).

The **Linearity Condition** is satisfied if a scatterplot looks straight. It's generally not a good idea to draw a line through the scatterplot when checking. That can fool your eye into seeing the plot as straighter than it really is. Sometimes it's easier to see violations of this condition by looking at a scatterplot of the residuals against x or against the predicted values, $\hat{y}$. That plot should have no pattern if the condition is satisfied.

If the scatterplot shows a reasonably straight relationship, we can go on to some assumptions about the errors. If not, we stop here, or consider transforming the variables to make the scatterplot more linear.

2. Independence Assumption

The errors in the true underlying regression model (the ε's) must be independent of each other. As usual, there's no way to be sure that the Independence Assumption is true.

When we care about inference for the regression parameters, it's often because we think our regression model might apply to a larger population. In such cases, we can check the **Randomization Condition** that the individuals are a random sample from that population.

We can also check displays of the regression residuals for evidence of patterns, trends, or clumping, any of which would suggest a failure of independence. In the special case when we have a time series, a common violation of the Independence Assumption is for successive errors to be correlated (autocorrelated). (The error our model makes today may be similar to the one it made yesterday.) We can check this violation by plotting the residuals against time (usually the x-variable for a time series) and looking for patterns.

3. Equal Variance Assumption

The variability of y should be about the same for all values of x. In Chapter 4, we found the standard deviation of the residuals (s_e). Now we need this standard deviation to estimate the standard errors of the coefficients but the residual standard deviation only makes sense if the scatter of the residuals is the same everywhere (otherwise, what are we estimating?)

We check the **Equal Spread Condition** by looking at a scatterplot of residuals against either x or $\hat{y}$. Make sure the spread around the line is nearly constant. Be alert for a "fan" shape or other tendency for the variation to grow or shrink in one part of the scatterplot.

If the plot is reasonably straight, the data are independent, and the spread doesn't change, we can move on to the final assumption and its associated condition.

4. Normal Population Assumption

To use a Student's t-model for inference, we must assume the errors around the idealized regression line at each value of x follow a Normal model. As we did before when we used Student's t, we'll settle for the residuals satisfying the **Nearly Normal Condition**.[2] As we have noted before, the Normality Assumption becomes less important as the sample size grows because the model is about means, and the Central Limit Theorem takes over. You can check a histogram of the residuals or look at a **Normal probability plot** (see Section 7.3), which finds deviations from the Normal model more efficiently. Another common failure of Normality is the presence of an outlier. So, we still check the **Outlier Condition**.

Summary of Assumptions and Conditions

We don't expect the assumptions to be exactly true. As George Box said, "all models are wrong." But the linear model is often close enough to be useful as long as the assumptions of the model are reasonably met.

Before we compute the regression, we should check the Linearity Condition. (You can also look for outliers here.) Then, after we fit the model we should check the rest.

So we work in this order:

1. **Make a scatterplot of the data** to check the Linearity Condition and to look for outliers (and always check that the variables are quantitative as well). (This checks the **Linearity Assumption**.)
2. If the data show a reasonably straight relationship, **fit a regression and find the residuals, e, and predicted values, $\hat{y}$.**

> " Truth will emerge more readily from error than from confusion. "
>
> —Francis Bacon (1561–1626), English philosopher

---

[2]*This* is why we check the conditions in order. We check that the residuals are independent and that the variation is the same for all x's before we can lump all the residuals together to check the Normal Condition.

3. If you know when the measurements were made, **plot the residuals against time** to check for evidence of patterns that suggest they may not be independent (**Independence Assumption**).
4. **Make a scatterplot of the residuals against x or the predicted values.** This plot should have no pattern. Check in particular for any bend (which would suggest that the data weren't that straight after all), for any thickening (or thinning), and, of course, for any unusual observations. (If you discover any errors, correct them or omit those points, and go back to step 1. Otherwise, consider performing two regressions—one with and one without the unusual observations.) (**Equal Variance Assumption**)
5. If the scatterplots look OK, then **make a histogram and Normal probability plot of the residuals** to check the **Nearly Normal** and **Outlier Conditions** (**Normal Population Assumption**).

The entire next chapter is devoted to examining the conditions for regression.

GUIDED EXAMPLE   Nambé Mills

Now that we have a method to draw inferences from our regression equation, let's try it out on the Nambé Mills data. The slope of the regression gives the impact of *Time* on *Price*. Let's test the hypothesis that the slope is different from zero.

PLAN	**Setup** State the objectives.	We want to test the null hypothesis that the price of Nambé Mills items is not related to the time it takes to polish them. We have data for 59 items sold by Nambé Mills. The slope of this relationship will model the relationship between *Time* and *Price*. Our null hypothesis is that the slope of the regression is 0.

PLAN

Setup State the objectives.

Identify the parameter you wish to estimate. Here our parameter is the slope.

Identify the variables and their context.

Hypotheses Write the null and alternative hypotheses.

Model Check the assumptions and conditions.

Make graphs. Because our scatterplot of y versus x looks reasonably straight, we can find the least squares regression and plot the residuals.

We want to test the null hypothesis that the price of Nambé Mills items is not related to the time it takes to polish them. We have data for 59 items sold by Nambé Mills. The slope of this relationship will model the relationship between *Time* and *Price*. Our null hypothesis is that the slope of the regression is 0.

H_0: The *Price* of an item is not linearly related to the polishing *Time*: $\beta_1 = 0$.
H_A: The *Price* is related to the *Time*: $\beta_1 \neq 0$.

✓ **Linearity Condition**: There is no obvious curve in the scatterplot of y versus x.

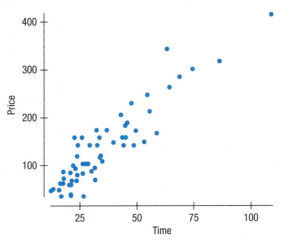

If it is appropriate, we check for suggestions that the Independence Assumption fails by plotting the residuals against time. Patterns or trends in that plot raise our suspicions.

✔ **Independence Assumption**: These data are on 59 different items manufactured by the company. There is no reason to suggest that the error in modeling the price of one item should be influenced by another.

✔ **Randomization Condition**: The data are *not* a random sample, but we assume they are representative of the prices and polishing times of Nambé Mills items.

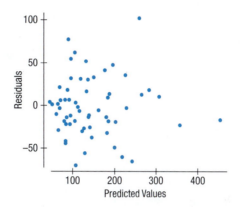

✔ **Equal Spread Condition**: The plot of residuals against the predicted values shows no obvious patterns. The spread is about the same for all predicted values, and the scatter appears random.

✔ **Nearly Normal Condition**: A histogram of the residuals is unimodal and symmetric, and the Normal probability plot is reasonably straight.

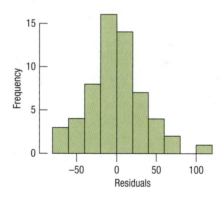

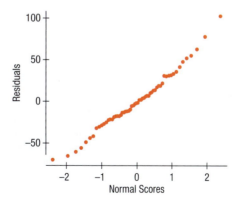

(continued)

State the sampling distribution model.

Choose the method.

Under these conditions, the sampling distribution of the regression slope can be modeled by a Student's t-model with $(n - 2) = 59 - 2 = 57$ degrees of freedom, so we'll proceed with a regression slope t-test.

DO

Mechanics The regression equation can be found from the formulas in Chapter 4, but regressions are almost always found from a computer program or calculator.

The P-values given in the regression output table are from the Student's t-distribution on $(n - 2) = 57$ degrees of freedom. They are appropriate for two-sided alternatives.

Create a confidence interval for the true slope. To obtain the t-value for 57 degrees of freedom, use the t-table at the back of your text. The estimated slope and SE for the slope are obtained from the regression output.

Interpret the interval.

Simply rejecting the standard null hypothesis doesn't guarantee that the size of the effect is large enough to be important.

Here's the computer output for this regression.

Variable	Coefficient	SE(coeff)	t-Ratio	P-Value
Intercept	−4.871	9.655	−0.50	0.6158
Time	4.200	0.2385	17.61	<0.0001

s = 34.54   R-Sq = 84.5%

The P-value < 0.0001 means that the association we see in the data is unlikely to have occurred by chance. Therefore, we reject the null hypothesis and conclude that there is strong evidence that the *Price* is linearly related to the polishing *Time*.

A 95% confidence interval for β_1 is:

$$b_1 \pm t^*_{n-2} \times SE(b_1) = (3.72, 4.68)\$/minute$$

We can be 95% confident that the price is higher on average, between $3.72 and $4.68 for each additional minute of polishing time. (Technically: we are 95% confident that the interval from $3.72 to $4.68 per minute captures the true rate at which the *Price* increases with polishing *Time*.)

REPORT

Communicate and present your results State the conclusion in the proper context.

MEMO

Re: Nambé Mills pricing

We investigated the relationship between polishing time and pricing of 59 Nambé Mills items. The regression analysis showed that, on average, the price is higher by $4.20 for every additional minute of polishing time. Assuming that these items are representative, we are 95% confident that the actual price of a metal item manufactured by Nambé Mills is higher by between $3.72 and $4.68 on average for each additional minute of polishing work required.

JUST CHECKING

Companies that market food items conduct research into how and how much people eat. They might, for example, study how big people's mouths tend to be. Researchers measured mouth volume by pouring water into the mouths of subjects who lay on their backs. Unless this is your idea of a good time, it would be helpful to have a model to estimate mouth volume more simply. Fortunately, mouth volume is related to height. (Mouth volume is measured in cubic centimeters and height in meters.)

> The data were checked and deemed suitable for regression. Take a look at the computer output below.
>
> ```
> Summary of Mouth Volume
> Mean          60.2704
> StdDev        16.8777
> ```
> ```
> Dependent variable is Mouth Volume
> R-squared = 15.3%
> s = 15.66 with 61 − 2 = 59 degrees of freedom
> ```
>
> | Variable | Coefficient | SE(coeff) | t-Ratio | P-Value |
> |----------|-------------|-----------|---------|---------|
> | Intercept | −44.7113 | 32.16 | −1.39 | 0.1697 |
> | Height | 61.3787 | 18.77 | 3.27 | 0.0018 |
>
> **1** What does the *t*-ratio of 3.27 for the slope tell about this relationship? How does the P-value help your understanding?
>
> **2** Would you say that measuring a person's height could reliably be used as a substitute for the wetter method of determining how big a person's mouth is? What numbers in the output helped you reach that conclusion?
>
> **3** What does the value of s_e add to this discussion?

*A Hypothesis Test for Correlation

We just tested whether the slope, β_1, was 0. To test it, we estimated the slope from the data and then, using its standard error and the *t*-distribution, measured how far the slope was from 0: $t = \dfrac{b_1 - 0}{SE(b_1)}$. What if we wanted to test whether the *correlation* between x and y is 0? We write ρ for the parameter (true population value) of the correlation, so we're testing $H_0: \rho = 0$. Remember that the regression slope estimate is $b_1 = r\dfrac{s_y}{s_x}$. The same is true for the parameter versions of these statistics: $\beta_1 = \rho\dfrac{\sigma_y}{\sigma_x}$. That means that if the slope is really 0, then the correlation has to be 0, too. So if we test $H_0: \beta_1 = 0$, that's really the same as testing $H_0: \rho = 0$. Sometimes a researcher, however, might want to test correlation without fitting a regression, so you'll see the test of correlation as a separate test (it's also slightly more general), but the results are mathematically the same even though the form looks a little different.

The *t*-Test for the Correlation Coefficient

When the conditions are met, we can test the hypothesis $H_0: \rho = 0$ vs. $H_A: \rho \neq 0$ using the test statistic:

$$t = r\sqrt{\frac{n-2}{1-r^2}},$$

which follows a Student's *t*-model with $n - 2$ degrees of freedom. We can use the *t*-model to find the P-value of the test.

IN PRACTICE 16.1 Testing correlation in survey results

BACKGROUND The Cornell National Social Survey (CNSS) is a national annual survey of a random sample of 1000 adults in the continental United States. Researchers in various disciplines can submit questions for the survey. According to the Cornell Survey Research Institute's site, sri.cornell.edu/sri/cnss.cfm, the survey is administered by telephone, using a random digit dial (RDD) method. The survey contains a small core of demographic questions, with all remaining questions being generated by Cornell researchers. The interviews average no more than 20 minutes in length and are conducted by the Survey Research Institute. The data are made available to the public and can be used by researchers and business professionals.

(continued)

MANAGER We need a marketing campaign for our electronics store. I found some data online from CNSS, and I computed the correlation between *Age* of respondents and their *Expenditures on Electronics* to be −0.142. Can I conclude that older people spend less on electronics?

ANALYST The sign seems to indicate that you are correct, but before concluding that the association is real, we want to test for statistical significance, to see how likely it would be to find a correlation of that size through chance alone (if the true correlation were zero). To test, we compute

$$t = -0.142\sqrt{\frac{1000 - 2}{1 - (-0.142)^2}} = -4.53,$$

which is a large enough value to be statistically significant. We can reject the null hypothesis that the true correlation, ρ, is zero.

A test that rejects the null hypothesis for the correlation tells us that there is a real linear relationship between the variables, but it doesn't tell enough. In the In Practice we conclude that the correlation isn't 0, but where do we go from here? For business decisions, we need to know more. We need the information provided by the full regression model. The test that the correlation is zero is equivalent to the test that the slope is zero, but the regression model helps us to understand what's going on and to make real decisions.

16.3 Standard Errors for Predicted Values

Often a business decision will depend not on the value of a slope coefficient, but on a predicted value of the response variable, y, for some given value of x. We saw how to find a predicted value for any value of x back in Chapter 4. This predicted value would be our best estimate, but we still want to know how likely it is that our estimate is correct. Now that we have standard errors, we can use them to construct confidence intervals for the predictions. That makes it possible to report our uncertainty about those predictions honestly—something we'd want to know before relying on them for a decision.

From our model of Nambé Mills items, we can use polishing *Time* to get a reasonable estimate of *Price*. Suppose a manager wanted to estimate the selling *Price* of an item that takes 40 minutes of *Time* to polish. A confidence interval can indicate how precise that prediction is. The precision depends on the question asked, however, and there are two different questions we could ask:

Do we want to know the mean *Price* for *all items* that have a polishing *Time* of 40 minutes?

or,

Do we want to estimate the *Price* for a *particular* item whose polishing *Time* is 40 minutes?

What's the difference between the two questions? The manufacturer might be more interested in the first question, which asks about the *mean Price* of all items that take a certain *Time* to polish. But a customer or sales manager might be more interested in the second question—estimating an *individual* item's *Price*. The predicted *Price* value is the same for both, but one question leads to a much more precise interval than the other. If your intuition says that it's easier to be more precise about the mean than about an individual, you're on the right track. Because, as we have seen, means vary much less than individuals, we can predict the *mean Price* for all items with the same polishing *Time* more precisely than we can predict the *Price* of a particular item with that polishing *Time*.

Let's start by predicting the mean *Price* for a new *Time*, one that was not necessarily part of the original dataset. To emphasize this, we'll call this x-value "x sub new" and write it x_ν.[3] As an example, we'll take x_ν to be 40 minutes. The regression equation predicts *Price* by $\hat{y}_\nu = b_0 + b_1 x_\nu$. Now that we have the predicted value, we can construct a confidence interval around this number. It has the usual form:

$$\hat{y}_\nu \pm t^*_{n-2} \times SE.$$

The t^*-value is the critical value (from Table T or technology) for $n - 2$ degrees of freedom and the specified confidence level.

The Confidence Interval for the Predicted Mean Value

When the conditions are met, we find the confidence interval for the predicted mean value μ_ν at a value x_ν as

$$\hat{y}_\nu \pm t^*_{n-2} \times SE,$$

where the standard error is

$$SE(\hat{\mu}_\nu) = \sqrt{SE^2(b_1) \times (x_\nu - \bar{x}^2) + \frac{s_e^2}{n}}.$$

This last equation says that the SE of the prediction (and thus the CI) will get wider when the SE of the slope increases (more uncertainty about the slope means more uncertainty about the prediction), when the x-value we are using to predict is farther from the mean of x (we are most certain predicting at the mean of x), and when the variance of the residuals increases (more scatter around the line).

Figure 16.7 shows the confidence intervals for the mean predictions. In this plot, the intervals for all the mean *Prices* at all values of *Time* are shown together as confidence bands. Notice that the bands get wider as we attempt to predict values that lie farther away from the mean *Time*. (That's due to the $(x_\nu - \bar{x})^2$ term in the SE formula.) As we move away from the mean x-value, there is more uncertainty associated with our prediction.

FIGURE 16.7 The confidence intervals for the mean *Price* at a given polishing *Time* are shown as the green dotted lines. Near the mean *Time* (35.8 minutes) our confidence interval for the mean *Price* is narrower than for values far from the mean, like 100 minutes.

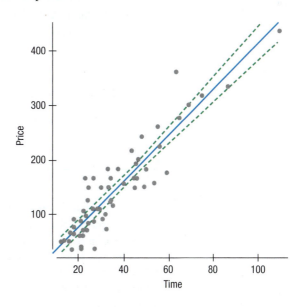

---

[3]Yes, this is a bilingual pun. The Greek letter ν is called "nu." Don't blame me; my co-author suggested this.

Like all confidence intervals, the width of these confidence intervals varies with the sample size. A larger sample would result in narrower intervals.

The last factor affecting our confidence intervals is the spread of the data around the line. If there were more spread around the line, predictions would be less certain, and the confidence interval bands would be wider.

From Figure 16.7, it's easy to see that most *points* don't fall within the confidence interval bands—and we shouldn't expect them to. These bands show confidence intervals for the *mean*. An even larger sample would have given even narrower bands. Then we'd expect an even smaller percentage of the points to fall within them.

If we want to capture an *individual* price, we need to use a wider interval, called a **prediction interval**. Figure 16.8 shows the prediction intervals for the Nambé Mills data. Prediction intervals are based on the same quantities as the confidence intervals, but the standard error includes an extra term for the spread around the line. As Figure 16.8 shows, these bands also widen as we move from the mean of *x*.

FIGURE 16.8 Prediction intervals (in red) estimate the interval that contains, say, 95% of the distribution of the *y*-values that might be observed at a given value of *x*. If the assumptions and conditions hold, then there's about a 95% chance that a particular *y*-value at x_ν will be covered by the interval.

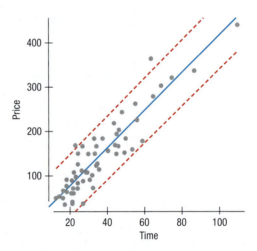

The Prediction Interval for an Individual Value

When the conditions are met, we can find the prediction interval for all values of *y* at a value x_ν as

$$\hat{y}_\nu \pm t^*_{n-2} \times SE,$$

where the standard error is

$$SE(\hat{y}_\nu) = \sqrt{SE^2(b_1) \times (x_\nu - \bar{x})^2 + \frac{s_e^2}{n} + s_e^2}.$$

The critical value t^* depends on the confidence level that you specify.

You can see that this interval is wider than the confidence interval for the predicted mean by exactly the final term: an addition of s_e^2. So, the larger standard deviation of the residuals, the less well we can predict a single point.

The good news about confidence intervals for prediction is that they are not hard to find and are provided by most statistics software. The bad news is that intervals for an individual predicted value can be quite wide—often so wide that they are not very useful for a business decision. By contrast, confidence intervals for the mean prediction are often narrow enough to be useful. But you must remember the difference between the two kinds of prediction intervals.

16.4 Using Confidence and Prediction Intervals

How well can our regression model predict the mean price for objects that take 25 minutes to polish? The regression output table provides most of the numbers we need.

Variable	Coefficient	SE(coeff)	t-Ratio	P-Value
Intercept	−4.871	9.654	−0.50	0.6159
Time	4.200	0.2385	17.61	<0.0001

s = 32.54 R-Sq = 84.5%

The regression model gives a predicted value at $x_\nu = 25$ minutes of:

$$-4.871 + 4.200(25) = \$100.13$$

Many statistics programs can also provide prediction confidence intervals. The 95% confidence interval for the mean price of items with a 25-minute polishing time is ($90.20, $110.06). That may be precise enough to support decisions about where to advertise these products, for example.

But the 95% confidence interval for a particular item with a 25-minute polishing time is ($34.22, $166.04). That's so wide that it serves more as a warning not to believe that the predicted value of $100.13 provides that much information about a single item. Figure 16.9 shows both intervals.

For the details of how the formulas lead to these intervals, see the Math Box.

FIGURE 16.9 A scatterplot of *Price* versus *Time* with a least squares regression line. The inner lines (green) near the regression line show the extent of the 95% confidence intervals, and the outer lines (red) show the prediction intervals. Most of the points are contained within the prediction intervals (as they should be), but not within the confidence interval for the means.

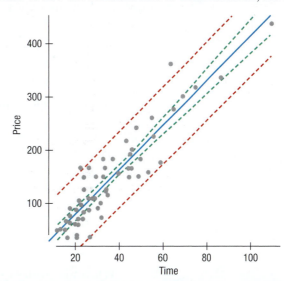

MATH BOX Finding confidence and prediction intervals

We find the standard errors from the formula using the values in the regression output and associated values. (The mean *Polishing Time* in these data is 35.82 minutes.)

$$SE(\hat{\mu}_\nu) = \sqrt{(SE^2(b_1))(x_\nu - \bar{x})^2 + \left(\frac{s_e}{\sqrt{n}}\right)^2}$$

$$= \sqrt{(0.2385)^2(25 - 35.82)^2 + \left(\frac{32.54}{\sqrt{59}}\right)^2} = \$4.96$$

The t^*-value that excludes 2.5% in either tail with $59 - 2 = 57$ df is (according to the tables) 2.002.

(continued)

Putting it all together, the margin of error is:

$$ME = 2.002(4.96) = \$9.93$$

So, the 95% confidence interval is

$$\$100.13 \pm 9.93 = (\$90.20, \$110.06)$$

To make a prediction interval for an *individual* item's price with a polishing time of 25 minutes, we use the formula

$$SE(\hat{y}_\nu) = \sqrt{\left(SE^2(b_1)\right)(x_\nu - \bar{x})^2 + \frac{s_e^2}{n} + s_e^2} = \$32.92,$$

and find the ME to be

$$ME = t^* \, SE(\hat{y}_\nu) = 2.002 \times 32.92 = \$65.91,$$

and so the prediction interval is

$$\hat{y} \pm ME = 100.13 \pm 65.91 = (\$34.22, \$166.04).$$

⊘ WHAT CAN GO WRONG?

With inference, we've put numbers on our estimates and predictions, but these numbers are only as good as the model. Here are the main things to watch out for:

- **Don't fit a linear regression to data that aren't straight.** This is the most fundamental assumption. If the relationship between x and y isn't approximately linear, there's no sense in fitting a straight line to it.

- **Watch out for changing spread.** The common part of confidence and prediction intervals is the estimate of the error standard deviation, the spread around the line. If it changes with x, the estimate won't make sense. Imagine making a prediction interval for these data:

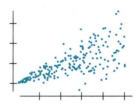

When x is small, we can predict y precisely, but as x gets larger, it's much harder to pin y down. Unfortunately, if the spread changes, the single value of s_e won't pick that up. The prediction interval will use the average spread around the line, with the result that we'll be too pessimistic about our precision for low x-values and too optimistic for high x-values. A re-expression of y is often a good fix for changing spread.

- **Watch out for non-Normal errors.** When we make a prediction interval for an individual y-value, the Central Limit Theorem can't come to our rescue. For us to believe the prediction interval, the errors must follow the Normal model. Check the histogram and Normal probability plot of the residuals to see if this assumption looks reasonable.

- **Watch out for one-tailed tests.** Because tests of hypotheses about regression coefficients are usually two-tailed, software packages report two-tailed P-values. If you are using that type of software to conduct a one-tailed test about the slope, you'll need to divide the reported P-value by two.

ETHICS IN ACTION

The need for senior care businesses that offer companionship and nonmedical home services is increasing as the U.S. population continues to age. One such franchise, Independent Senior Care, tries to set itself apart from its competitors by offering an additional service to prospective franchisees. In addition to standard information packets that provide tools, training, and mentorship opportunities, Independent Senior Care has an analyst on staff, Allen Ackman, to help prospective franchisees evaluate the feasibility of opening an elder care business in their area.

Allen was contacted recently by Kyle Sennefeld, a recent business school graduate with a minor in gerontology, who is interested in starting a senior care franchise in northeastern Pennsylvania. Allen decides to use a regression model that relates annual profit to the number of residents over the age of 65 that live within a 100-mile radius of a franchise location. Even though the R^2 for this model is small, the slope is statistically significant, and the model is easy to explain to prospective franchisees. Allen sends Kyle a report that estimates the annual profit at Kyle's proposed location. Kyle was excited to see that opening an Independent Senior Care franchise in northeastern Pennsylvania would be a good business decision.

- **Identify the ethical dilemma in this scenario.**
- **What are the undesirable consequences?**
- **Propose an ethical solution that considers the welfare of all stakeholders.**

CHAPTER

16 FROM LEARNING TO EARNING

LEARNING OBJECTIVES

Apply your understanding of inference for means using Student's t to make inference about regression coefficients.

Know the Assumptions and Conditions for inference about regression coefficients and how to check them, in this order:

- **Linearity Assumption,** checked with the Linearity Condition by examining a scatterplot of y vs. x or a scatterplot of the residuals plotted against the predicted values.
- **Independence Assumption,** which can't be checked, but is more plausible if the data were collected with appropriate randomization—the Randomization Condition.
- **Equal Variance Assumption,** which requires that the spread around the regression model be the same everywhere. We check it with the Equal Spread Condition, assessed with a scatterplot of the residuals versus the predicted values.
- **Normal Population Assumption,** which is required to use Student's t-models unless the sample size is large. Check it with the Nearly Normal Condition by making a histogram or normal probability plot of the residuals.

Know the components of the standard error of the slope coefficient:

- The standard deviation of the residuals, $s_e = \sqrt{\dfrac{\sum (y - \hat{y})^2}{n - 2}}$
- The standard deviation of x, $s_x = \sqrt{\dfrac{\sum (x - \bar{x})^2}{n - 1}}$
- The sample size, n

Be able to find and interpret the standard error of the slope.

- $SE(b_1) = \dfrac{s_e}{s_x \sqrt{n-1}}$

- The standard error of the slope is the estimated standard deviation of the sampling distribution of the slope.

State and test the standard null hypothesis on the slope.

- $H_0: \beta_1 = 0$. This would mean that x and y are not linearly related.

- We test this null hypothesis using the t-statistic $t = \dfrac{b_1 - 0}{SE(b_1)}$.

Construct and interpret a confidence interval for the predicted mean value corresponding to a specified value, x_ν.

- $\hat{y}_\nu \pm t^*_{n-2} \times SE(\hat{\mu}_\nu)$, where $SE(\hat{\mu}_\nu) = \sqrt{SE^2(b_1) \times (x_\nu - \bar{x})^2 + \dfrac{s_e^2}{n}}$.

Construct and interpret a confidence interval for an individual predicted value corresponding to a specified value, x_ν.

- $\hat{y}_\nu \pm t^*_{n-2} \times SE(\hat{y}_\nu)$, where $SE(\hat{y}_\nu) = \sqrt{SE^2(b_1) \times (x_\nu - \bar{x})^2 + \dfrac{s_e^2}{n} + s_e^2}$.

TERMS

Confidence interval for the predicted mean value

Different samples will give different estimates of the regression model and, so, different predicted values for the same value of x. We find a confidence interval for the mean of these predicted values at a specified x-value, x_ν, as

$$\hat{y}_\nu \pm t^*_{n-2} \times SE(\hat{\mu}_\nu),$$

where

$$SE(\hat{\mu}_\nu) = \sqrt{SE^2(b_1) \times (x_\nu - \bar{x})^2 + \dfrac{s_e^2}{n}}.$$

The critical value, t^*_{n-2}, depends on the specified confidence level and the Student's t-model with $n - 2$ degrees of freedom.

Confidence interval for the regression slope

When the assumptions are satisfied, we can find a confidence interval for the slope parameter from $b_1 \pm t^*_{n-2} \times SE(b_1)$. The critical value, t^*_{n-2}, depends on the confidence interval specified and on the Student's t-model with $n - 2$ degrees of freedom.

Prediction interval for a future observation

A confidence interval for individual values. Prediction intervals are to observations as confidence intervals are to parameters. They predict the distribution of individual values, while confidence intervals specify likely values for a true parameter. When the assumptions are satisfied, the prediction interval takes the form

$$\hat{y}_\nu \pm t^*_{n-2} \times SE(\hat{y}_\nu),$$

where

$$SE(\hat{y}_\nu) = \sqrt{SE^2(b_1) \times (x_\nu - \bar{x})^2 + \dfrac{s_e^2}{n} + s_e^2}.$$

The critical value, t^*_{n-2}, depends on the specified confidence level and the Student's t-model with $n - 2$ degrees of freedom. The extra s_e^2 in $SE(\hat{y}_\nu)$ makes the interval wider than the corresponding confidence interval for the mean.

Residual standard deviation

The measure, denoted s_e, of the spread of the data around the regression line:

$$s_e = \sqrt{\dfrac{\sum (y - \hat{y})^2}{n-2}} = \sqrt{\dfrac{\sum e^2}{n-2}}.$$

***t*-test for the regression slope**

The usual null hypothesis is that the true value of the slope is zero. The alternative is that it is not. A slope of zero indicates a complete lack of linear relationship between y and x.

To test $H_0: \beta_1 = 0$ we find

$$t = \frac{b_1 - 0}{SE(b_1)},$$

where $SE(b_1) = \dfrac{s_e}{s_x \sqrt{n - 1}}$, $s_e = \sqrt{\dfrac{\sum (y - \hat{y})^2}{n - 2}}$, n is the number of cases, and s_x is the standard deviation of the x-values. We find the P-value from the Student's t-model with $n - 2$ degrees of freedom.

TECH SUPPORT   Regression Analysis

All statistics packages make a table of results for a regression. These tables differ slightly from one package to another, but all are essentially the same.

All packages offer analyses of the residuals. With some, you must request plots of the residuals as you request the regression. Others let you find the regression first and then analyze the residuals afterward. Either way, your analysis is not complete if you don't check the residuals with a histogram or Normal probability plot and a scatterplot of the residuals against x or the predicted values.

You should, of course, always look at the scatterplot of your two variables before computing a regression.

Regressions are almost always found with a computer or calculator. The calculations are too long to do conveniently by hand for datasets of any reasonable size. No matter how the regression is computed, the results are usually presented in a table that has a standard form. Here's a portion of a typical regression results table, along with annotations showing where the numbers come from.

The regression table gives the coefficients (once you find them in the middle of all this other information). This regression (for different items than in the example in the text) predicts Price from Time. The regression equation is

$$\widehat{Price} = -2.891 + 2.492\ Time$$

and the R^2 for the regression is 84.5%.

The column of t-ratios gives the test statistics for the respective null hypotheses that the true values of the coefficients are zero. The corresponding P-values are also usually reported.

EXCEL

To perform a regression analysis in Excel:

- From **Data**, select **Data Analysis** and select **Regression**.
- Enter the data range holding the y-variable in the box labeled "Input Y range".
- Enter the range of cells holding the x-variable in the box labeled "Input X range".

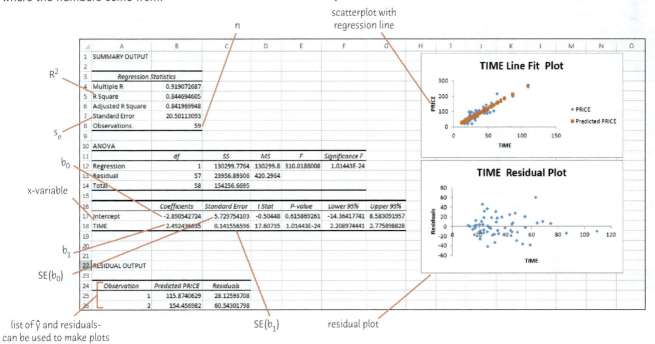

list of $\hat{y}$ and residuals-
can be used to make plots
of the residuals

- Select the **New Worksheet Ply** option to report results in a new worksheet (or identify output range in current worksheet or new workbook) and **Labels** if the first row of the data holds the variable labels.

- Select **Residuals**, **Residual Plots**, and **Line Fit Plots** options.

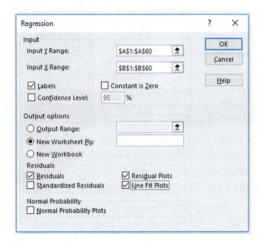

- After the plots are generated, you can delete the predicted values and/or add the least squares line, called a Trendline in Excel, on the Line Fit Plot.

- To obtain a histogram of the residuals, use residuals listed in Excel output to create a histogram using **Data > Data Analysis > Histogram**.

COMMENTS

The Y and X ranges do not need to be in the same rows of the spreadsheet, although they must cover the same number of cells. But it is a good idea to arrange your data in parallel columns as in a data table to reduce the chance of error. Although the dialog offers a Normal probability plot of the residuals, the data analysis add-in does not make a correct probability plot, so don't use this option.

JMP

To perform a regression analysis in JMP,

- From the **Analyze** menu, select **Fit Y by X**.

- Select variables: a **Y, Response** variable, and an **X, Factor** variable. Both must be continuous (quantitative).

- JMP makes a scatterplot.

- Click on the red triangle beside the heading labeled **Bivariate Fit...** and choose **Fit Line**. JMP draws the least squares regression line on the scatterplot and displays the results of the regression in tables below the plot.

- The portion of the table labeled "Parameter Estimates" gives the coefficients and their standard errors, *t*-ratios, and P-values.

COMMENTS

JMP chooses a regression analysis when both variables are "Continuous." If you get a different analysis, check the variable types.

The Parameter table does not include the residual standard deviation s_e. You can find that as Root Mean Square Error in the Summary of Fit panel of the output.

MINITAB

To compute a regression analysis in Minitab,

- Choose **Regression** from the **Stat** menu.

- Choose **Regression...** from the **Regression** submenu.

- In the Regression dialog, assign the Y-variable to the Response box and assign the X-variable to the Predictors box.

- Click the **Graphs** button.

- In the Regression-Graphs dialog, select **Standardized residuals**, and check **Normal plot of residuals**, **Residuals versus fits**, and **Residuals versus order**.

- Click the **OK** button to return to the Regression dialog.

- Click the **OK** button to compute the regression.

COMMENTS

You can also start by choosing a Fitted Line plot from the **Regression** submenu to see the scatterplot first—usually good practice.

R

Suppose the response variable *y* and predictor variables $x_1, \ldots, x_k$ are in a data frame called mydata. To fit a regression of *y* on x_1 and x_2:

- mylm = lm(y ~ x$_1$ + x$_2$, data = mydata).

- summary(mylm) # gives the details of the fit, including estimates, SEs, and the ANOVA table.

- plot(mylm) # gives a variety of plots.

- To fit the model with *all* the predictors in the data frame,

  mylm = lm(y ~., data = mydata) # The period means use all other variables.

COMMENTS

To get confidence or prediction intervals use:

- predict(mylm,interval = "confidence")

or

- predict(mylm, interval = "prediction").

Predictions on points not found in the original data frame can be found from predict as well. In the new data frame (called, say, mynewdata), there must be a predictor variable with the same name as the original "x" variable. Then predict(mylm, newdata=mynewdata) will produce predictions at all the "x" values of mynewdata.

To find a regression in SPSS,

- Choose **Regression** from the **Analyze** menu.
- Choose **Linear** from the **Regression** submenu.
- In the Linear Regression dialog that appears, select the Y-variable and move it to the dependent target. Then move the X-variable to the independent target.
- Click the **Plots** button.
- In the Linear Regression Plots dialog, choose to plot the *SRESIDs against the *ZPRED values.
- Click the **Continue** button to return to the Linear Regression dialog.
- Click the **OK** button to compute the regression.

- Click on **Stat**.
- Choose **Regression** > **Simple** Linear.
- Choose X and Y variable names from the list of columns.
- Indicate that you want to see a residuals plot and a histogram of the residuals.
- Click on **Compute**!
- Click on > to see any plots you chose.

COMMENTS

Be sure to check the conditions for regression inference by looking at both the residuals plot and a histogram of the residuals.

BRIEF CASE

Frozen Pizza

The product manager at a subsidiary of Kraft Foods, Inc., is interested in learning how sensitive sales are to changes in the unit price of a frozen pizza in Dallas, Denver, Baltimore, and Chicago. The product manager has been provided data on both *Price* and *Sales* volume every fourth week over a period of nearly four years for the four cities (**Pizza prices**).

Examine the relationship between *Price* and *Sales* for each city. Be sure to discuss the nature and validity of this relationship. Is it linear? Is it negative? Is it significant? Are the conditions of regression met? Some individuals in the product manager's division suspect that frozen pizza sales are more sensitive to price in some cities than in others. Is there any evidence to suggest that? Write up a short report on what you find. Include 95% confidence intervals for the mean *Sales* if the *Price* is $2.50 and discuss how that interval changes if the *Price* is $3.50.

Global Warming?

Every spring, Nenana, Alaska, hosts a contest in which participants try to guess the exact minute that a wooden tripod placed on the frozen Tanana River will fall through the breaking ice. The contest started in 1917 as a diversion for railroad engineers, with a jackpot of $800 for the closest guess. It has grown into an event in which hundreds of thousands of entrants enter their guesses on the Internet and vie for more than $300,000.

Because so much money and interest depends on the time of the ice breakup, it has been recorded to the nearest minute with great accuracy ever since 1917. (Data in **Nenana 2017**) And because a standard measure of breakup has been used throughout this time, the data are consistent. An article in *Science* ("Climate Change in Nontraditional Data Sets," *Science* 294, October 2001) used the data to investigate global warming. Researchers are interested in the following questions. What is the rate of change in the date of breakup over time (if any)? If the ice is breaking up earlier, what is your conclusion? Does this necessarily suggest global warming? What could be other reasons for this trend? What is the predicted breakup date for the year 2020? (Be sure to include an appropriate prediction or confidence interval.) Write up a short report with your answers.

CHAPTER

16   EXERCISES

SECTION 16.1

1. A website that rents movies online recorded the age and the number of movies rented during the past month for some of their customers. Here are their data:

Age	Rentals
35	9
40	8
50	4
65	3
40	10
30	12

Make a scatterplot for these data. What does it tell you about the relationship between these two variables? From computer output, the regression line has $b_0 = 18.9$ and $b_1 = -0.260$.

a) Use the estimated regression equation to predict *Rentals* for all six values of *Age*.
b) Find the residuals e_i.
c) Calculate the residual standard deviation, s_e.

2. A training center, wishing to demonstrate the effectiveness of their methods, tests some of their clients after different numbers of days of training, recording their scores on a sample test. Their data are:

Training Days	Correct Responses
1	4
4	6
8	7
10	9 .
12	10

The regression model they calculate is

$$\widehat{Correct\ responses} = 3.525 + 0.525\ Training\ days.$$

a) Use the model to predict the correct responses for each number of training days.
b) Find the residuals, e_i.
c) Calculate the residual standard deviation, s_e.

3. For the regression of Exercise 1, find the standard error of the regression slope. Show all three values that go into the calculation.

4. For the regression of Exercise 2, find the standard error of the regression slope. Show all three values that go into the calculation.

5. A dataset of 5 observations for *Concession Sales per person* ($) at a theater and *Minutes before the movie begins* results in the following estimated regression model:

$$\widehat{Sales} = 4.3 + 0.265\ Minutes.$$

The standard error of the regression slope is 0.0454.

a) Compute the value of the *t*-statistic to test if there is a significant relationship between *Sales* and *Minutes*.
b) What are the degrees of freedom associated with the *t*-statistic?
c) What is the P-value associated with the *t*-statistic?
d) At $\alpha = 0.05$, can you reject the standard null hypothesis for the slope? Explain.

6. A soap manufacturer tested a standard bar of soap to see how long it would last. A test subject showered with the soap each day for 15 days and recorded the *Weight* (in grams) of the soap after the shower. The resulting regression computer output looks, in part, like this:

```
Dependent variable is: Weight
R-squared = 99.5%
s = 2.949
```

Variable	Coefficient	SE(Coeff)	t-Ratio	P-Value
Intercept	123.141	1.382	89.1	<0.0001
Day	−5.57476	0.1068	−52.2	<0.0001

Find the following facts in this output, or determine them from what you know.

a) The standard deviation of the residuals
b) The slope of the regression line
c) The standard error of b_1
d) The P-value appropriate for testing $H_0: \beta_1 = 0$ versus $H_A: \beta_1 \neq 0$
e) Is the null hypothesis rejected at $\alpha = 0.05$?

SECTION 16.2

7. For the data from Exercise 1, which of the following conditions can you check from the scatterplot? Are satisfied?

a) Linearity
b) Independence
c) Equal Spread
d) Normal Population

8. Here's a scatterplot of the % of income spent on food versus household income for respondents to the Cornell National Social Survey:

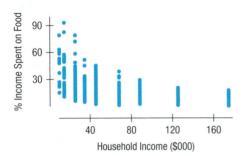

For each of the regression assumptions, state whether it is satisfied, not satisfied, or can't be determined from this plot.

a) Linearity
b) Independence
c) Equal Spread
d) Normal Population

SECTION 16.3

9. Here are data from a small bookstore.

Number of Salespeople Working	Sales (in $1000's)
2	10
3	11
7	13
9	14
10	18
10	20
12	20
15	22
16	22
20	26
$\bar{x} = 10.4$	$\bar{y} = 17.6$
$SD(x) = 5.64$	$SD(y) = 5.34$

The regression line is:

$$\widehat{Sales} = 8.10 + 0.9134\ Number\ of\ Salespeople\ Working.$$

The assumptions and conditions for regression are met, and from technology we learn that

$$SE(b_1) = 0.0873 \qquad s_e = 1.477$$

a) Find the predicted *Sales* on a day with 12 employees working.
b) Find a 95% confidence interval for the mean *Sales* on days that have 12 employees working.
c) Find the 95% prediction interval for *Sales* on a day with 12 employees working.

10. The study of external disk drives from Chapter 4, Exercise 2 (with the outlier removed) finds the following:

	Capacity (TB)	Price ($)
	0.15	35
	0.25	39.95
	0.32	49.95
	1	75
	2	110
	3	140
	4	325
Mean	1.53	110.7
SD	1.51	102.05

The least squares line was found to be: $\widehat{Price} = 15.112 + 62.417\ Capacity$ with $s_e = 42.037$ and $SE(b_1) = 11.328$.

a) Find the predicted *Price* of a 2 TB hard drive.
b) Find a 95% confidence interval for the mean *Price* of 2 TB disk drives.
c) Find the 95% prediction interval for the *Price* of a 2 TB hard drive.

SECTION 16.4

11. A survey designed to study how much households spend on eating out finds the following regression model,

$$\widehat{EatOut\ \$/wk} = 17.28 + 0.354\ HHIncome$$

relating the amount respondents said they spent individually to eat out each week to their household income in $1000's.

a) A 95% prediction interval for a customer with a household income of $80,000 is ($35.60, $55.60). Explain to the restaurant owner how she should interpret this interval.
b) A 95% confidence interval for the mean amount spent weekly to eat out by people with a household income of $80,000 is ($40.60, $50.60). Explain to a restaurant owner how to interpret this interval.
c) Now explain to her why these intervals are different.

12. In Exercise 5, we saw a regression to predict the sales per person at a movie theater in terms of the time (in minutes) before the show. The model was:

$$\widehat{Sales} = 4.3 + 0.265\ Minutes.$$

a) A 90% prediction interval for sales to a concessions customer 10 minutes before the movie starts is ($4.60, $9.30). Explain how to interpret this interval.
b) A 90% confidence interval for the mean of sales per person 10 minutes before the movie starts is ($6.65, $7.25). Explain how to interpret this interval.
c) Which interval is of particular interest to the concessions manager? Which one is of particular interest to you, the moviegoer?

SECTION 16.5

13. Recall the small bookstore we saw in Exercise 9. The regression line is:

$$\widehat{Sales} = 8.10 + 0.9134 \, Number\ of\ Sales\ People\ Working$$

and the assumptions and conditions for regression are met. Calculations with technology find that

$$s_e = 1.477.$$

a) Find the predicted sales on a day with 500 employees working.
b) Find a 95% prediction interval for the sales on a day with 500 employees working.
c) Are these predictions likely to be useful? Explain.

14. Look back at the prices for the external disk drives we saw in Exercise 10.

The least squares line is $\widehat{Price} = 15.112 + 62.417 \, Capacity$.

The assumptions and conditions for regression are met.

$$SE(b_1) = 11.328$$

a) Disk drives keep growing in capacity. Some tech experts now talk about *Petabyte* ($PB = 1000\ TB = 1,000,000\ GB$) drives. What does this model predict that a Petabyte-capacity drive will cost?
b) Find a 95% prediction interval for the price of a 1 PB drive.
c) Are these predictions likely to be useful? Explain.

CHAPTER EXERCISES

T 15. Online shopping. Several studies have found that the frequency with which shoppers browse Internet retailers is related to the frequency with which they actually purchase products and/or services online. Here are data showing the age of respondents and their answer to the question "How many minutes do you browse online retailers per week?"

Age	Browsing Time (min/wk)
22	492
50	186
44	180
32	384
55	120
60	120
38	276
22	480
21	510
45	252
52	126
33	360
19	570
17	588
21	498

a) Make a scatterplot for these data.
b) Do you think a linear model is appropriate? Explain.
c) Find the equation of the regression line.
d) Check the residuals to see if the conditions for inference are met.

T 16. Climate change 2016. The earth has been getting warmer. Most climate scientists agree that one important cause of the warming is the increase in atmospheric levels of carbon dioxide (CO_2), a greenhouse gas. Here is part of a regression analysis of the mean annual air temperature over both land and sea across the globe, in degrees Celsius on the mean annual CO_2 concentration in the atmosphere, measured in parts per thousand (ppt), at the top of Mauna Loa in Hawaii. The scatterplots and residuals plots indicated that the data were appropriate for inference and the response variable is *Temp* (temperature anomaly: deviation from long-term average).

```
Variable      Coeff      SE(Coeff)
Intercept    -3.179      0.1584
CO2           0.0099     0.0004

R-squared = 89.7%
s = 0.088 with 58 - 2 = 56 degrees of freedom
```

a) Write the equation of the regression line.
b) Find the value of the correlation. Is there evidence of an association between CO_2 level and global temperature?
c) Find the *t*-value and P-value for the slope. Is there evidence of an association between CO_2 level and global temperature? What do you know from the slope and *t*-test that you might not have known from the correlation?
d) Do you think predictions made by this regression will be very accurate? Explain.

T 17. Movie budgets. How does the cost of a movie depend on its length? Data on the cost (millions of dollars) and the running time (minutes) for major release films in one recent year are summarized in these plots and computer output:

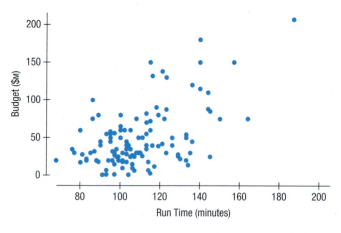

```
Dependent variable is: Budget($M)
R-squared = 15.4%
s = 32.95 with 120 − 2 = 118 degrees of freedom
```

Variable	Coefficient	SE(Coeff)	t-Ratio	P-Value
Intercept	−31.39	17.12	−1.83	0.0693
Run time	0.71	0.15	4.64	<0.0001

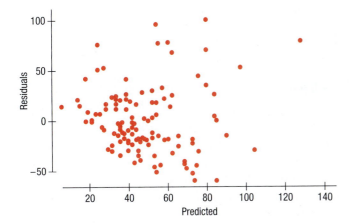

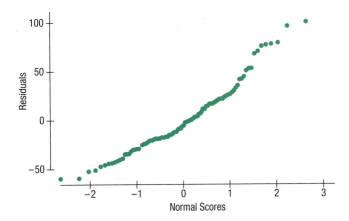

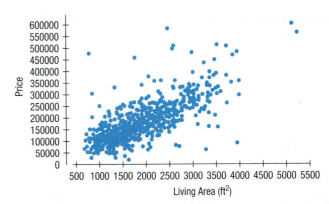

```
Dependent variable is: Price
R-squared = 57.6%
s = 50290 with 1057 − 2 = 1055 degrees of freedom
```

Variable	Coefficient	SE(Coeff)	t-Ratio	P-Value
Intercept	7239.28	4520.34	1.60	0.11
Living Area	88.30	2.33	37.8	<.0001

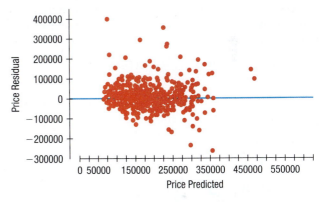

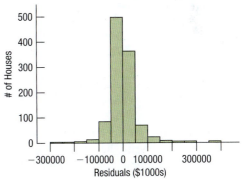

a) Explain in words and numbers what the regression says.
b) The intercept is negative. Discuss its value, taking note of the P-value.
c) The output reports $s = 32.95$. Explain what that means in this context.
d) What's the value of the standard error of the slope of the regression line?
e) Explain what that means in this context.

T 18. Housing prices. How does the price of a house depend on its size? Data from Saratoga, New York, on 1057 randomly selected houses that had been sold include data on price ($) and *Living Area* (ft^2), producing the following graphs and computer output:

a) Explain in words and numbers what the regression says.
b) Discuss the intercept, taking note of its P-value.
c) The output reports $s = 50,290$. Explain what that means in this context.
d) What's the value of the standard error of the slope of the regression line?
e) Explain what that means in this context.

T **19.** **Movie budgets, part 2.** Exercise 17 shows computer output examining the association between the length of a movie and its cost.

a) Check the assumptions and conditions for inference.
b) Find a 95% confidence interval for the slope and interpret it.

T **20.** **Housing prices, part 2.** Exercise 18 shows computer output examining the association between the sizes of houses and their sale prices.

a) Check the assumptions and conditions for inference.
b) Find a 95% confidence interval for the slope and interpret it.

T **21.** **Water hardness.** In an investigation of environmental causes of disease, data were collected on the annual mortality rate (deaths per 100,000) for males in 61 large towns in England and Wales. In addition, the water hardness was recorded as the calcium concentration (parts per million, or ppm) in the drinking water. Here are the scatterplot and regression analysis of the relationship between mortality and calcium concentration, where the dependent variable is *Mortality*.

```
Variable        Coeff       SE(Coeff)
Intercept      1676.36        29.30
Calcium          -3.226        0.485

R-squared = 42.9%
s = 143.0 with 61 - 2 = 59 degrees of freedom
```

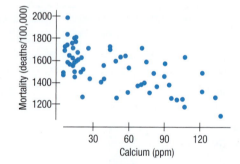

a) Is there an association between the hardness of the water and the mortality rate? Write the appropriate hypothesis.
b) Assuming the assumptions for regression inference are met, what do you conclude?
c) Create a 95% confidence interval for the slope of the true line relating calcium concentration and mortality.
d) Interpret your interval in context.

T **22.** **Mutual fund returns 2017.** The Brief Case for Chapter 4 listed the rate of return for 98 mutual funds over the previous 3-year and 5-year periods. It's common for advertisements to carry the disclaimer that "past returns may not be indicative of future performance." Do these data indicate that there was an association between 3-year and 5-year rates of return?

T **23.** **Retail trade index.** The index of deflated turnover for retail trade shows the activity in volume of the retail trade sector. The United Nations Statistics Division reports Retail trade deflated sales/turnover (seasonally adjusted) with 2005 = 100. The data file holds this index for 43 countries for the years 2007–2010.

a) Find a regression model predicting the *2010* index from the index in *2007* for the sample of 43 countries provided by UNSD.
b) Examine the residuals to determine if a linear regression is appropriate.
c) Test an appropriate hypothesis to determine if the association is significant.
d) What percentage of the variability in the *2010 Index* is accounted for by the regression model?

T **24.** **Male unemployment 2017.** Using unemployment data provided by the World Bank, investigate the association between the male unemployment rate in 2014 and 2017.

a) Find a regression model predicting the *2017* rate from the *2014* rate.
b) Examine the residuals to determine if a linear regression is appropriate.
c) Test an appropriate hypothesis to determine if the association is significant.
d) What percentage of the variability in the *2017* rate is accounted for by the *regression model*?

T **25.** **Used cars 2014.** Classified ads in a newspaper offered several used Toyota Corollas for sale. Listed below are the ages of the cars and the advertised prices.

Age (yr)	Prices Advertised ($)
9	11599
4	14998
4	12998
7	10998
3	15998
5	14559
5	11599
8	9998
9	9998
1	15998
5	12599
3	16998
5	13998

a) Make a scatterplot for these data.
b) Do you think a linear model is appropriate? Explain.
c) Find the equation of the regression line.
d) Check the residuals to see if the conditions for inference are met.

T 26. Property assessment. The following software results provide information about the size (in square feet) of 18 homes in Ithaca, New York, and the city's assessed value of those homes, where the response variable is *Assessment*.

Predictor	Coeff	SE(Coeff)	t-Ratio	P-Value
Intercept	37108.85	8664.33	4.28	0.0006
Size	11.90	4.29	2.77	0.0136

s = 4682.10   R-Sq = 32.5%

Variable	Mean	StdDev
Assessment	60946.7	5527.62
Size	2003.39	264.727

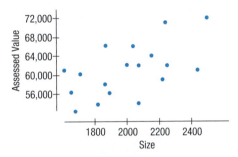

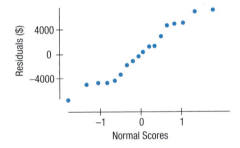

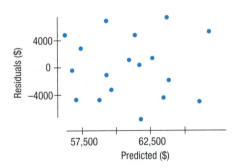

a) Explain why inference for linear regression is appropriate with these data.

b) Is there a significant linear association between the *Size* of a home and its *Assessment*? Test an appropriate hypothesis and state your conclusion.

c) What percentage of the variability in assessed value is accounted for by this regression?

d) Give a 90% confidence interval for the slope of the true regression line, and explain its meaning in the proper context.

e) From this analysis, can we conclude that adding a room to your house will increase its assessed value? Why or why not?

f) The owner of a home measuring 2100 square feet files an appeal, claiming that the $70,200 assessed value is too high. Do you agree? Explain your reasoning.

T 27. Used cars, part 2. Based on the analysis of used car prices you did for Exercise 25, if appropriate, create a 95% confidence interval for the slope of the regression line and explain what your interval means in context.

T 28. Assets and sales. A business analyst is looking at a company's assets and sales to determine the relationship (if any) between the two measures. She has data (in $million) from a random sample of 79 Fortune 500 companies, and obtained the linear regression below: (Data in **Companies**)

Predictor	Coeff	SE(Coeff)	t-Ratio	P-Value
Intercept	1867.4	804.5	2.32	0.0230
Sales	0.975	0.099	9.84	<0.0001

s = 6132.59   R-Sq = 55.7%

Use the data provided to find a 95% confidence interval for the slope of the regression line and interpret your interval in context.

T 29. Fuel economy and weight. A consumer organization has reported test data for 50 car models. We will examine the association between the weight of the car (in thousands of pounds) and the fuel efficiency (in miles per gallon). Use the data provided on the disk to answer the following questions, where the response variable is *Fuel Efficiency* (mpg). (Data in **Fuel economy**)

a) Create the scatterplot and obtain the regression equation.

b) Are the assumptions for regression satisfied?

c) Write the appropriate hypotheses for the slope.

d) Test the hypotheses and state your conclusion.

T 30. Auto batteries. *Consumer Reports* listed the price (in dollars) and power (in cold cranking amps) of auto batteries. We want to know if more expensive batteries are generally better in terms of starting power. Here are the regression and residual output, where the response variable is *Power*.

```
Dependent variable is: Power
R-squared = 25.2%
s = 116.0 with 33 − 2 = 31 degrees of freedom
```

Variable	Coefficient	SE(Coeff)	t-Ratio	P-Value
Intercept	384.594	93.55	4.11	0.0003
Price	4.146	1.282	3.23	0.0029

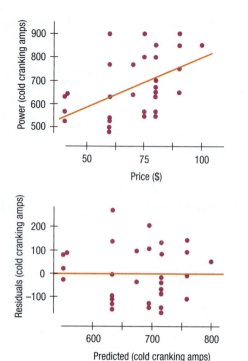

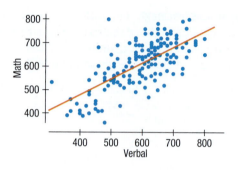

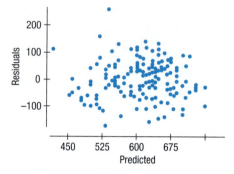

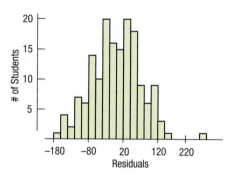

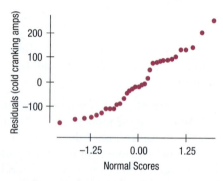

a) How many batteries were tested?

b) Are the conditions for inference satisfied? Explain.

c) Is there evidence of a linear association between the price and cranking power of auto batteries? Test an appropriate hypothesis and state your conclusion.

d) Is the association strong? Explain.

e) What is the equation of the regression line?

f) Create a 90% confidence interval for the slope of the true line.

g) Interpret your interval in this context.

T 31. SAT scores. How strong was the association between student scores on the Math and Verbal sections of the old SAT? Scores on this exam ranged from 200 to 800 and were widely used by college admissions offices. Here are summary statistics, regression analysis, and plots of the scores for a graduating class of 162 students at Ithaca High School, where the response variable is *Math Score*.

Predictor	Coeff	SE(Coeff)	t-Ratio	P-Value
Intercept	209.55	34.35	6.10	<0.0001
Verbal	0.675	0.057	11.88	<0.0001

s = 71.75   R-Sq = 46.9%

a) Is there evidence of a linear association between *Math* and *Verbal* scores? Write an appropriate hypothesis.

b) Discuss the assumptions for inference.

c) Test your hypothesis and state an appropriate conclusion.

T 32. Productivity 2016. How strong is the association between labor productivity and labor costs? Data from the Bureau of Labor Statistics for labor productivity, as measured by *Output per Employee*, and *Unit Labor Costs* across industries, are used to examine this relationship (ftp://ftp .bls.gov).

a) From a scatterplot, is there evidence of a linear association between *Labor Productivity* and *Unit Labor Costs*? Write an appropriate hypothesis.

b) Discuss the assumptions for inference.

c) Test your hypothesis and state an appropriate conclusion.

T 33. Football salaries 2017. Football owners are constantly in competition for good players. The more wins, the more likely that the team will provide good business returns for the owners. The resources that each of the 32 teams has in the National Football League (NFL) vary, but the draft system is designed to counteract the advantages that wealthy teams may have. Is it working or does the size of the payroll matter? Here is the regression output for the season between the team payroll and the number of wins. (See also Chapter 4, Exercise 33.)

Predictor	Coeff	SE(Coeff)	t-Ratio	P-Value
Intercept	−6.37	6.06	−1.05	0.30
Payroll($M)	0.10	0.04	2.34	0.03

s = 2.92 R-Sq = 15.4%

a) State the hypotheses about the slope.
b) Perform the hypothesis test and state your conclusion in context.
c) Using a statistics program and the data, check the assumptions and conditions.

T 34. Female president. The Gallup organization has, over six decades, periodically asked the following question:

If your party nominated a generally well-qualified person for president who happened to be a woman, would you vote for that person?

We wonder if the proportion of the public who have "no opinion" on this issue has changed over the years. Here is a regression for the proportion of those respondents whose response to this question about voting for a woman president was "no opinion." Assume that the conditions for inference are satisfied and that the response variable is proportion responding *No Opinion*.

Predictor	Coeff	SE(Coeff)	t-Ratio	P-Value
Intercept	7.693	2.445	3.15	0.0071
Year	−0.043	0.035	−1.21	0.2460

s = 2.28 R-Sq = 9.5%

a) State the hypotheses about the slope (both numerically and in words) that describes how voters' thoughts have changed about voting for a woman.
b) Assuming that the conditions for inference are satisfied, perform the hypothesis test and state your conclusion.
c) Examine the scatterplot corresponding to the regression for No Opinion. How does it change your opinion of the trend in "no opinion" responses? Do you think the true slope is negative as shown in the regression output?

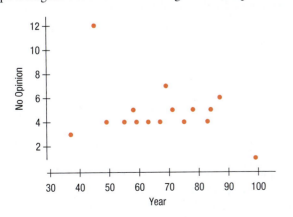

T 35. Fuel economy and weight, part 2. Consider again the data in Exercise 29 about the gas mileage and weights of cars.

a) Create a 95% confidence interval for the slope of the regression line.
b) Explain in this context what your confidence interval means.

T 36. SAT scores, part 2. Consider the high school SAT scores data from Exercise 31.

a) Find a 90% confidence interval for the slope of the true line describing the association between Math and Verbal scores.
b) Explain in this context what your confidence interval means.

T 37. Ozone. The Environmental Protection Agency is examining the relationship between the ozone level (in parts per million) and the population (in millions) of U.S. cities. Part of the regression analysis is shown.

Dependent variable is Ozone
R-squared = 84.4%
s = 5.454 with 16 − 2 = 14 df

Variable	Coeff	SE(Coeff)
Intercept	18.892	2.395
Pop	6.650	1.910

a) We suspect that the greater the population of a city, the higher its ozone level. Is the relationship statistically significant? Assuming the conditions for inference are satisfied, test an appropriate hypothesis and state your conclusion in context.
b) Do you think that the population of a city is a useful predictor of ozone level? Use the values of both R^2 and s in your explanation.

T 38. Sales and profits. A business analyst was interested in the relationship between a company's sales and its profits. She collected data (in millions of dollars) from a random sample of Fortune 500 companies and created the regression analysis and summary statistics shown. The assumptions for regression inference appeared to be satisfied.

	Profits	Sales
Count	79	79
Mean	209.839	4178.29
Variance	635,172	49,163,000
Std Dev	796.977	7011.63

Dependent variable is Profits
R-squared = 66.2% s = 466.2

Variable	Coefficient	SE(Coeff)
Intercept	−176.644	61.16
Sales	0.092498	0.0075

a) Is there a statistically significant association between sales and profits? Test an appropriate hypothesis and state your conclusion in context.
b) Do you think that a company's sales serve as a useful predictor of its profits? Use the values of both R^2 and s in your explanation.

T **39. Ozone, again.** Using a statistics program, consider again the relationship between the population and ozone level of U.S. cities that you analyzed in Exercise 37.

a) Give a 90% confidence interval for the approximate increase in ozone level associated with each additional million city inhabitants.

b) For the cities studied, the mean population was 1.7 million people. The population of Boston is approximately 0.6 million people. Predict the mean ozone level for cities of that size with an interval in which you have 90% confidence.

T **40. More sales and profits.** Using a statistics program, consider again the relationship between the sales and profits of Fortune 500 companies that you analyzed in Exercise 38.

a) Find a 95% confidence interval for the slope of the regression line. Interpret your interval in context.

b) Last year, the drug manufacturer Eli Lilly, Inc., reported gross sales of $23 billion (that's $23,000 million). Create a 95% prediction interval for the company's profits, and interpret your interval in context.

T **41. Tablet computers 2014.** In 2014, cnet.com listed the battery life (in hours) and maximum luminous intensity (i.e., screen brightness, in cd/m²) for a sample of tablet computers. We want to know if we can predict battery life from the maximum brightness. (reviews.cnet.com/8301-19736_7-20080768-251/cnet-updates-tablet-test-results/?tag=contentBody; contentHighlights)

```
Dependent variable is Video battery life (in hours)
R-squared = 11.3%
s = 2.13 with 34 − 2 = 32 degrees of freedom

Variable    Estimate   Std Error   t-Ratio   p-value
Intercept   5.387      1.727       3.12      0.0038
Brightness  0.009      0.004       2.02      0.0522
```

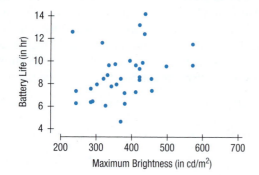

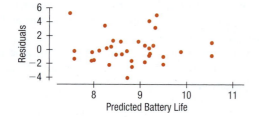

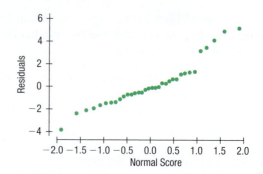

a) How many tablet computers were tested?

b) Are the conditions for inference satisfied? Explain.

c) Is there evidence of an association between maximum brightness of the screen and battery life? Test an appropriate hypothesis and state your conclusion.

d) Is the association strong? Explain.

e) What is the equation of the regression line?

f) Create a 95% confidence interval for the slope of the true line.

g) Interpret your interval in this context.

T **42. Income vs. hours 2013.** There are 168 hours in a week. If you spend all of it sleeping and having fun, you will earn very little money. On the other hand, if you spend much of it working, do you earn more? In other words, do people earn more money each year when they work a greater number of hours each week? The Current Population Survey contains the relevant data, which are in the included dataset.

a) Compute a regression of HH income on Hours Worked. State the null and alternative hypotheses associated with this regression.

b) Are the assumptions for regression satisfied?

c) What would you write to a manager regarding this analysis?

T **43. Cost of living 2017.** The *Worldwide Cost of Living Survey* published by Numbeo.com provides an index that expresses the cost of living in other cities as a percentage of the New York cost. For example, in 2017, the cost of living index in Geneva was 142, which means that it was 42% higher than New York. The data also contain separate indices for Groceries, Rent, and Restaurants. The output shows the regression of Total Cost of Living Index on Grocery Index.

```
Predictor       Estimate  Std Error  t-Ratio  P-Value
Intercept       9.79      0.85       11.6     <.0001
Groceries Index 0.87      0.01       70.1     <.0001

s = 6.86   R-Sq = 91%
```

a) State the hypotheses about the slope (both numerically and in words).

b) Perform the hypothesis test and state your conclusion in context.

c) Explain what the *R*-squared in this regression means.

d) Do these results indicate that the cost of groceries is the main determinant of the cost of living in a city? Explain.

44. Job growth. *Fortune Magazine* publishes the top 100 companies to work for every year. Among the information listed is the percentage growth in jobs at each company. The output below shows the regression of job growth (%) in the current year on job growth from two years prior. (One outlier has been omitted.) *Job Growth* in the more recent year is the response variable.

```
Dependent variable is: Job Growth
R-squared = 5.7%
s = 0.0738 with 68 - 2 = 6 degrees of freedom

Variable     Coeff    SE(Coeff)   t-Ratio   P-Value
Intercept    0.0628   0.009       7.00      <0.0001
Job Growth   0.2      0.100       2.00      0.0498
```

a) State the hypotheses about the slope (both numerically and in words).
b) Assuming that the assumptions for inference are satisfied, perform the hypothesis test and state your conclusion in context.
c) Explain what the *R*-squared in this regression means.
d) Do these results indicate that, in general, companies with a higher job growth in the earlier year had higher job growth in the later year? Explain.

T 45. Cost of living again. In Exercise 43, we examined the *Worldwide Cost of Living Survey* cost of living index. Now we use the Restaurant Price Index to predict total cost of living. Here are the results:

```
R-squared = 90%
s = 6.95 with 511 - 2 = 509 degrees of freedom

Predictor         Estimate  Std Error  t-Ratio  P-Value
Intercept         18.14     0.75       24.3     <.0001
Restaurant Price  0.80      0.01       69.1     <.0001
```

a) How do you interpret the coefficient of Restaurant price?
b) The R^2 of this regression is 90%, and the R^2 of the regression from Exercise 43 was 91%. How is it possible that both variables explain almost 90% of the variation in total cost of living?

T 46. Job growth, again. In Exercise 44, the company Zappos was omitted. Here is a scatterplot of the data with Zappos plotted as an *x*:

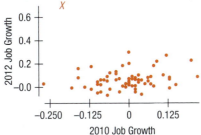

a) In words, what does the outlying point say about Zappos?
b) What effect would this point have on the regression, had it been left with the rest of the data?
c) Using the included data, find the regression with and without the outlier.

T 47. Old pitchers. Many factors may affect fans' decision to go to a ball game. Is it possible that fans prefer teams with an older pitching staff?

a) Examine a scatterplot of Attend/Game and PitchAge. Check the conditions for regression.
b) Do you think there is a linear association between Attendance and Pitcher Age?
c) Compute and discuss the regression model.

T 48. Little League product testing. Ads for a Little League instructional video claimed that the techniques would improve the performances of Little League pitchers. To test this claim, 20 Little Leaguers threw 50 pitches each, and we recorded the number of strikes. After the players participated in the training program, we repeated the test. The following table shows the number of strikes each player threw before and after the training. A test of paired differences failed to show that this training was effective in improving a player's ability to throw strikes. Is there any evidence that the *Effectiveness* (*After − Before*) of the video depends on the player's *Initial Ability* (*Before*) to throw strikes? Test an appropriate hypothesis and state your conclusion. Propose an explanation for what you find.

Number of Strikes (out of 50)			
Before	After	Before	After
28	35	33	33
29	36	33	35
30	32	34	32
32	28	34	30
32	30	34	33
32	31	35	34
32	32	36	37
32	34	36	33
32	35	37	35
33	36	37	32

T 49. Fuel economy and weight, part 3. Consider again the data in Exercise 29 about the fuel economy and weights of cars.

a) Create a 95% confidence interval for the average fuel efficiency among cars weighing 2500 pounds, and explain what your interval means.
b) Create a 95% prediction interval for the gas mileage you might get driving your new 3450-pound SUV, and explain what that interval means.

T 50. SAT scores, part 3. Consider the high school SAT scores data from Exercise 31 once more. The mean Verbal score was 596.30 and the standard deviation was 99.52.

a) Find a 90% confidence interval for the mean SAT Math score for all students with an SAT Verbal score of 500.
b) Find a 90% prediction interval for the Math score of the senior class president, if you know she scored 710 on the Verbal section.

T 51. Little League product testing, part 2. Using the same data provided in Exercise 48, answer the following questions.

a) Find the 95% prediction interval for the effectiveness of the video on a pitcher with an initial ability of 33 strikes.
b) Do you think predictions made by this regression will be very accurate? Explain.

T 52. Assets and sales, part 2. The analyst in Exercise 28 realized the data were in need of transformation because of the non-linearity between the variables. Economists commonly take the logarithm of these variables to make the relationship more nearly linear, and she did too. (These are base 10 logs.) The dependent variable is *LogSales*. The conditions for regression inference now appear to be satisfied. (Data in **Companies**)

```
Dependent variable is: LogSales
R-squared = 33.9%
s = 0.4278 with 79 − 2 = 77 degrees of freedom

Variable    Coefficient  SE(Coeff)  t-Ratio  P-Value
Intercept    1.303        0.3211     4.06     0.0001
LogAssets    0.578        0.0919     6.28     <0.0001
```

a) Is there a significant linear association between *LogAssets* and *LogSales*? Find the *t*-value and P-value to test an appropriate hypothesis and state your conclusion in context.
b) Do you think that a company's assets serve as a useful predictor of their sales?

T 53. All the efficiency money can buy 2013. A sample of 61 model-2013 cars from an online information service was examined to see how fuel efficiency (as highway mpg) relates to the cost (Manufacturer's Suggested Retail Price in dollars) of cars. (Data in **All the efficiency**) Here are displays and computer output:

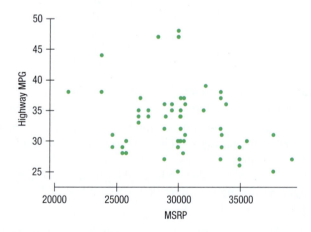

```
Dependent variable is: Highway MPG
R-squared = 10.36%
s = 4,870 with 61 − 2 = 59 degrees of freedom

Variable    Coefficient  SE(Coeff)  t-Ratio  P-Value
Intercept    45.6898      4.849       9.42    <0.0001
MSRP        −0.000416     0.000159   −2.61     0.0114
```

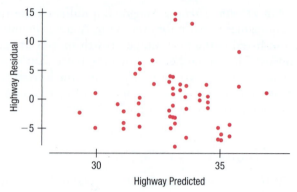

a) State what you want to know, identify the variables, and give the appropriate hypotheses.
b) Check the assumptions and conditions.
c) If the conditions are met, complete the analysis.

T 54. Energy use and recession. The Great Recession of 2008 changed spending and energy use habits worldwide. Based on data collected from the United Nations Millennium Indicators Database related to measuring the goal of *ensuring environmental sustainability*, investigate the association between energy use (kg oil equivalent per $1000 GDP) before (2006) and after (2010) the crisis, for a sample of 33 countries (unstats.un.org/unsd/mi/mi_goals.asp; accessed June 2013).

a) Find a regression model showing the relationship between *2010 Energy Use* (response variable) and *2006 Energy Use* (predictor variable).
b) Examine the residuals to determine if a linear regression is appropriate.
c) Test an appropriate hypothesis to determine if the association is significant.
d) What percentage of the variability in *2010 Energy Use* is explained by *2006 Energy Use*?

T 55. Youth unemployment 2016. Here is a scatterplot showing the regression line, 95% confidence intervals, and 95% prediction intervals, using youth unemployment data for a sample of 33 nations. The response variable is the *Male Rate*, and the predictor variable is the *Female Rate*.

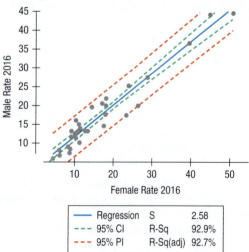

a) Explain the meaning of the 95% prediction intervals in this context.

b) Explain the meaning of the 95% confidence intervals in this context.

c) Using a statistics program, identify any unusual observations, and discuss their potential impact on the regression.

56. Youth unemployment, again. Here is a scatterplot showing the regression line, 95% confidence intervals, and 95% prediction intervals, using 2015 and 2016 male unemployment data for a sample of 33 nations. The response variable is the *2016-Male Rate*, and the predictor variable is the *2015-Male Rate*.

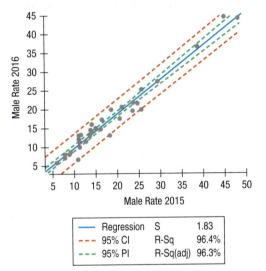

a) Explain the meaning of the 95% prediction intervals in this context.

b) Explain the meaning of the 95% confidence intervals in this context.

c) Using a statistics program, identify any unusual observations, and discuss their potential impact on the regression.

57. Energy use and recession, part 2. Examine the regression and scatterplot showing the regression line, 95% confidence intervals, and 95% prediction intervals using *2006* and *2010 energy use* (kg oil equivalent per $1000 GDP) for a sample of 31 countries first examined in Exercise 54. The response variable is *2010 Energy Use*.

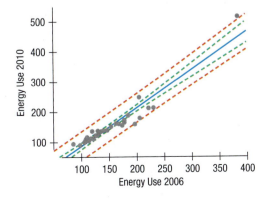

a) Explain the meaning of the 95% prediction intervals in this context.

b) Explain the meaning of the 95% confidence intervals in this context.

You can see the regression model in Exercise 54. The extraordinary point is Iceland. If we set it aside, the model looks like this

```
Response variable is: Energy Use 2010
R squared = 88.6%
s = 13.10 with 32 − 2 = 30 degrees of freedom
```

Variable	Coefficient	SE(Coeff)	t-Ratio	P-Value
Intercept	5.74436	9.061	0.634	0.5309
Energy 2006	0.921540	0.0605	15.2	<0.0001

c) How has setting aside Iceland changed the regression model? How is it likely to affect the intervals discussed in a) and b)?

58. Internet users 2014. The Internet has revolutionized business and offers unprecedented opportunities for globalization. However, the ability to access the Internet varies greatly among different regions of the world. One of the variables the United Nations collects data on each year is Internet Users per 100 Population (mdgs.un.org/unsd/mdg/Data.aspx) for various countries. Below is a scatterplot showing the regression line, 95% confidence intervals, and 95% prediction intervals using 2000 and 2014 Internet use (Internet users per 100 population) for a sample of 70 countries. The response variable is Internet Users per 100—2014.

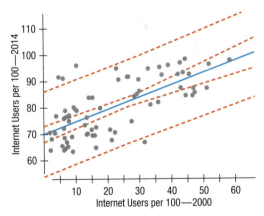

a) Working with the dataset with the same name as this exercise, find a regression model showing the relationship between personal computer adoption in Internet Users per 100—2014 (the response variable) and personal computer adoption in Internet Users per 100—2000 (the predictor variable).

b) Explain the meaning of the 95% prediction intervals in this context.

c) Explain the meaning of the 95% confidence intervals in this context.

T **59.** **Seasonal spending.** Spending on credit cards decreases after the Christmas spending season (as measured by amount charged on a credit card in December). The dataset with the same name as this exercise contains the monthly credit card charges of a random sample of 99 cardholders.

a) Build a regression model to predict January spending from December's spending.
b) How much, on average, will cardholders who charged $2000 in December charge in January?
c) Give a 95% confidence interval for the average January charges of cardholders who charged $2000 in December.
d) From part c, give a 95% confidence interval for the average decrease in the charges of cardholders who charged $2000 in December.
e) What reservations, if any, do you have about the confidence intervals you made in parts c and d?

T **60.** **Seasonal spending, part 2.** Financial analysts know that January credit card charges will generally be much lower than those of the month before. What about the difference between January and the next month? Does the trend continue? The dataset contains the monthly credit card charges of a random sample of 99 cardholders.

a) Build a regression model to predict February charges from January charges.
b) How much, on average, will cardholders who charged $2000 in January charge in February?
c) Give a 95% confidence interval for the average February charges of cardholders who charged $2000 in January.
d) From part c, give a 95% confidence interval for the average decrease in the charges of cardholders who charged $2000 in January.
e) What reservations, if any, do you have about the confidence intervals you made in parts c and d?

JUST CHECKING ANSWERS

1 A high t-ratio of 3.27 indicates that the slope is different from zero—that is, that there is a linear relationship between height and mouth size. The small P-value says that a slope this large would be very unlikely to occur by chance if, in fact, there was no linear relationship between the variables.

2 Not really. The R^2 for this regression is only 15.3%, so height doesn't account for very much of the variability in mouth size.

3 The value of s_e tells the standard deviation of the residuals. Mouth sizes have a mean of 60.3 cubic centimeters. A standard deviation of 15.7 in the residuals indicates that the errors made by this regression model can be quite large relative to what we are estimating. Errors of 15 to 30 cubic centimeters would be common.

Understanding Residuals

Kellogg's

John Harvey Kellogg was a physician who ran the Battle Creek Sanitarium. He was an advocate of vegetarian diets and of living without caffeine, alcohol, or sex. He was an early advocate of peanut butter, patenting one of the first devices for making it. But he is best remembered for his work with his brother Will Keith Kellogg. Together, in 1897, they founded the Sanitas Food Company to manufacture whole grain cereals.

At the start of the 20th century, breakfast was typically a large, high-fat meal of eggs and meat for the wealthy and a less nutritious meal of porridge or gruel for the poor. The Kellogg brothers introduced toasted corn flakes as a healthy and affordable alternative. But in 1906, they argued when Will wanted to add sugar to the recipe—an idea that horrified John Harvey. Will founded the Battle Creek Toasted Corn Flake Company, which eventually became the Kellogg Company, using its founder's "W. K. Kellogg" signature as a logo—a marketing concept that survives in the script "Kellogg's" on their boxes to this day.

True to its roots in healthy nutrition, Kellogg's brands include Kashi® health foods, Morningstar Farms® vegetarian foods, and Nutri-Grain® cereal bars. (However, they also make Cocoa Krispies®, Froot Loops®, Cheez-Its®, and Keebler® Cookies.) In 1923, Kellogg hired the first dietitian to work in the food industry, and in the 1930s, Kellogg was the first company to print nutrition information on their boxes. The W. K. Kellogg Institute for Food and Nutrition Research, a world-class research facility, opened in 1997. The company continues to advocate for healthy nutrition, offering advice and education on their website and partnering with organizations such as the American Heart Association.

Regression may be the most widely used statistics method. It is used every day throughout the world to help make good business decisions. The applications are limitless. It can be used to predict customer loyalty, staffing needs at hospitals, sales of automobiles, and almost anything that can be quantified. Because regression is so widely used, it's also widely abused and misinterpreted. This chapter presents examples of regressions in which things are not quite as simple as they may seem at first and shows how you can still use regression to discover what the data have to say.

The residuals from the fitting of a linear regression hold a remarkable amount of information about the model. Remember that a residual is the difference between the actual data and the value we predict for it: $e = y - \hat{y}$. Residuals can help tell you how well the model is performing and provide clues for fixing it if it's not working as well as it could. In this chapter, we'll show a variety of ways in which detecting patterns in the residuals can help you improve the model. Examining residuals can reveal more about the data than was apparent at first, or even second, glance. That's why no regression analysis is ever complete without a display of the residuals and a thorough examination of what they have to say.

17.1 Examining Residuals for Groups

WHO	Breakfast cereals
WHAT	Nutrition information
WHEN	Not stated
WHERE	U.S.

It seems that ever since the Kellogg brothers fought over sugar in breakfast cereals, it has been a concern. Using data from those nutrition labels introduced by Kellogg, we can examine the relationship between the calories in a serving and the amount of sugar (in grams). Figure 17.1 appears to satisfy the conditions for regression; the relationship is linear with no outliers. (Data in **Cereals**)

The least squares regression model,

$$\widehat{calories} = 89.5 + 2.50\,sugar$$

has an R^2 of 32%. Figure 17.2 shows the residuals.

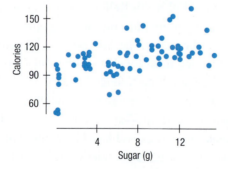

FIGURE 17.1 *Calories* versus *Sugar* content (grams) per serving of breakfast cereal.

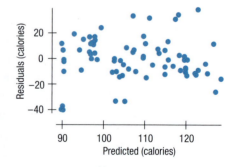

FIGURE 17.2 Residuals for the regression plotted against predicted *Calories*.

At first glance, Figure 17.2 seems to have no particular structure, and as you may remember from Chapter 4, that's exactly what we hope to see. But let's check a histogram of the residuals.

FIGURE 17.3 The distribution of the regression residuals shows modes above and below the central large mode. These may be worth a second look.

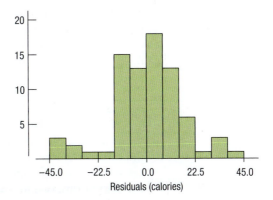

How would you describe the shape of the histogram in Figure 17.3? It looks like there might be small modes on either side of the central body of the data. A few cereals stand out with larger negative residuals—that is, fewer calories than we might have predicted. And a few stand out with larger positive residuals. Of course, the sample size here is not very large. We can't say for sure that there are three modes, but it's worth a closer look.

FIGURE 17.4 A scatterplot of the residuals vs. predicted values for the cereal regression. The green x's are cereals whose calorie content is higher than the linear model predicts. The red −'s show cereals with fewer calories than the model predicts. Is there something special about these cereals?

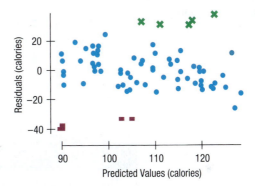

Let's look more carefully at the residuals. Figure 17.4 repeats the scatterplot of Figure 17.2, but with the points in those modes marked. Now we can see that those two groups stand away from the central pattern in the scatterplot. Doing a little more work and examining the dataset, we find that the high-residual cereals (green x's) are *Just Right Fruit & Nut*; *Muesli Raisins, Dates & Almonds*; *Peaches & Pecans*; *Mueslix Crispy Blend*; and *Nutri-Grain Almond Raisin*. Do these cereals have something in common? These high-calorie cereals all market themselves as "healthy." This might be surprising, but in fact, "healthy" cereals often contain more fat. They often contain nuts and oil which are "natural" and don't necessarily contain sugar, but are higher in fat than grain and sugar. So, they may have more calories than we might expect from looking at their sugar content alone.

The low-residual (red −'s) cereals are *Puffed Rice*, *Puffed Wheat*, three bran cereals, and *Golden Crisps*. These cereals have fewer calories than we would expect based on their sugar content. We might not have grouped these cereals together before. What they have in common is a low calorie count *relative to their sugar content*—even though their sugar contents are quite different. (They are low calorie because of their shape and structure.)

These observations may not lead us to question the overall linear model, but they do help us understand that other factors may be part of the story. An exploration of residuals often leads us to discover more about individual cases. When we discover groups in our data, we may decide to analyze them separately, using a different model for each group.

Often, more research can help us discover why certain cases tend to behave similarly. Here, certain cereals group together in the residual plot because cereal manufacturers aim cereals at different segments of the market. A common technique used to attract different customers is to place different types of cereals on certain shelves. Cereals for kids tend to be on the "kid's shelf," at their eye level. Toddlers aren't likely to grab a box from this shelf and beg, "Mom, can we please get this *All-Bran with Extra Fiber?*"

How can we take this extra information into account in our analysis? Figure 17.5 shows a scatterplot of *Calories* and *Sugar*, colored according to the shelf on which the cereals were found, with a separate regression line fit for each shelf. Now we can see that the top shelf is unlike the bottom two shelves. We might want to report two regressions, one for the top shelf and one for the bottom two shelves.[1]

FIGURE 17.5 *Calories* and *Sugars* colored according to the shelf on which the cereal was found in a supermarket, with regression lines fit for each shelf individually. Do these data appear homogeneous? That is, do the cereals seem to all be from the same population of cereals? Or are there kinds of cereals that we might want to consider separately?

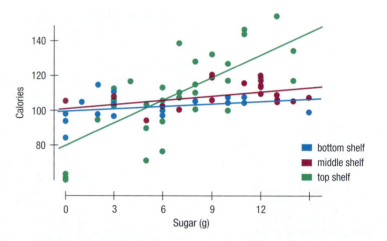

IN PRACTICE 17.1   Diamond prices

The price of a jewelry diamond depends on the 4 C's: Carat weight, Cut, Clarity, and Color. Diamond colors are assigned letters from D, for colorless stones, through K, for increasingly more yellow stones. A K-color stone is only faintly yellow and still considered jewelry quality.

CUSTOMER   I'm in the market for a diamond, but I want to know that I'm paying a fair price.

SALESPERSON   I have here a sample of diamond prices from a website. (Data in **Diamonds**) Here is a scatterplot of *Price* vs. *Carat Weight* with points colored according to *Color*:

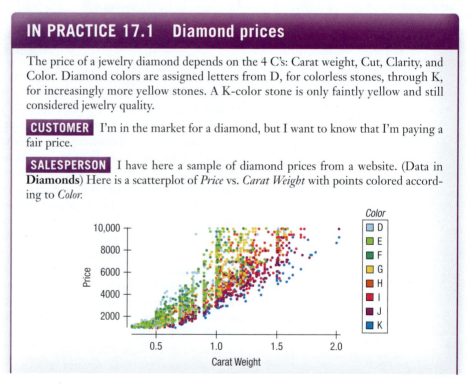

---

[1]Another alternative is to fit a multiple regression model by adding variables (called dummy or indicator variables) that distinguish the groups. This method will be discussed in Chapter 18.

The first decision to make is on the amount of color (or lack of) in the diamond that you want and are willing to pay for. As you can see from the graph, for a given *Carat Weight*, diamonds with better (earlier letter) colors are generally worth more. This is not true for every diamond, but it is generally true. There may be greater variability in the middle of the color range with H-color diamonds showing more variability than either D- or K-color stones. There is greater variability for larger (heavier) diamonds.

17.2   Extrapolation and Prediction

Linear models give a predicted value for each case in the data. Put a new *x*-value into the equation, and it gives a predicted value, $\hat{y}$, to go with it. But when the new *x*-value lies far from the data we used to build the regression, how trustworthy is the prediction?

The simple answer is that the farther the new *x*-value is from $\bar{x}$, the center of the *x*-values, the less trust we should place in the predicted value. Once we venture into new *x* territory, such a prediction is called an **extrapolation**. Extrapolations are dangerous because they require the additional—and questionable—assumption that nothing about the relationship between *x* and *y* changes, even at extreme values of *x* and beyond. Extrapolations can get us into deep trouble, especially if we try to predict far into the future.

As a cautionary example, let's examine oil prices from 1972 to 1981.[2] In the mid 1970s, in the midst of an energy crisis, oil prices surged, and long lines at gas stations were common. In 1970, the price of oil was about $3 a barrel. A few years later, it had surged to $15. In 1975, a survey of 15 top econometric forecasting models (built by groups that included Nobel prize–winning economists) found predictions for 1985 oil prices that ranged from $50 to $200 a barrel—which would be $181 to $726(!) dollars a barrel in 2005 dollars. (We shall use constant 2005 dollars from now on, to factor out inflation.) How close were these forecasts? Let's look at Figure 17.6. (Data extracted from **Oil prices 2016**)

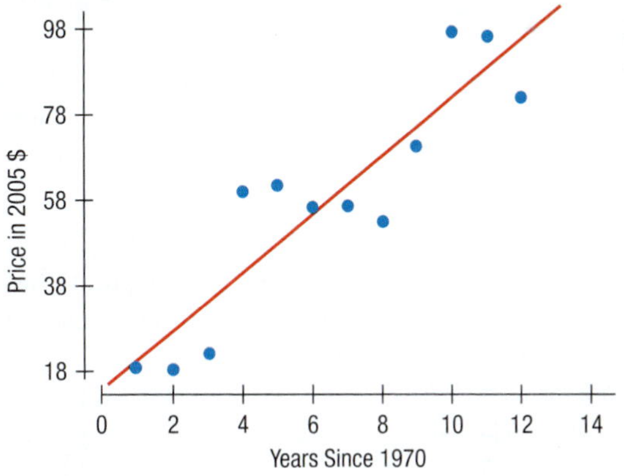

> ### When the Data Are Years
> We usually don't enter them as four-digit numbers. Here, we used 0 for 1970, 10 for 1980, and so on. It's common to assign 0 to the date of the first observation in our dataset if we are working with a time series. Another option is to enter two digits for the year, using 88 for 1988, for instance. Rescaling years like this often makes calculations easier and equations simpler. But be careful; if 1988 is 88, then 2004 is 104 (not 4).

FIGURE 17.6 The price of oil per barrel in constant (2005) dollars from 1971 to 1982 shows a linear trend increasing at about $7 a year.

The regression model for the *Price* of oil against *Time* (Years since 1970) for these data is

$$\widehat{Price} = 13.14 + 6.89\ Time,$$

which says that prices increased, on average, $6.89 per year, or nearly $69 in 10 years. If they continued to increase linearly, it would have been easy to predict oil prices. And indeed, many forecasters made that assumption. How well did they do?

---

[2]We will discuss special models for fitting data when *x* is time in Chapter 20, but simple regression models are often used. Even when using more sophisticated methods, the dangers of extrapolation don't disappear.

Well, in the period from 1982 to 1998, oil prices didn't exactly continue that steady increase. In fact, they went down so much that by 1998, prices (adjusted for inflation) were the lowest they'd been since before World War II (Figure 17.7).

FIGURE 17.7 Time series plot of price of oil in constant (2005) dollars shows a fairly constant decrease over time.

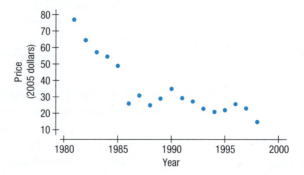

FIGURE 17.7 Time series plot of price of oil in constant (2005) dollars shows a fairly constant decrease over time.

For example, the average price of oil in 1985 turned out to be less than $30 per barrel—not quite the $100 predicted by the model. Extrapolating out beyond the original data by just four years produced some vastly inaccurate forecasts. While the time series plot in Figure 17.7 shows a fairly steady decline, this pattern clearly didn't continue (or oil would be free by now).

In the 1990s, the U.S. government decided to include scenarios in their forecasts. The result was that the Energy Information Administration (EIA) offered *two* 20-year forecasts for oil prices after 1998 in their Annual Energy Outlook (AEO). Both of these scenarios, however, called for relatively modest increases in oil prices (Figure 17.8).

FIGURE 17.8 This graph, adapted from one by the Energy Information Administration, shows oil prices from 1970 to 1998 with two sets of forecasts for the period 1999 to 2020.

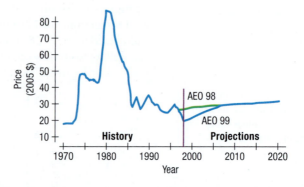

So, how accurate have these forecasts been? Let's compare these predictions to the actual prices. (Data in **Oil prices 2016**; see Figure 17.9.)

FIGURE 17.9 Here are the same EIA forecasts as in Figure 17.8, together with the actual prices from 1981 to 2016. Neither forecast predicted the sharp run-up in the first decade of the 21st century.

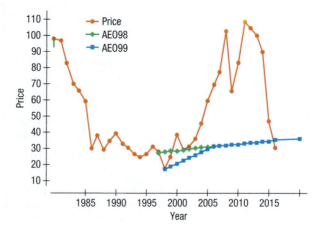

The experts seem to have missed the sharp run-up in oil prices in the first decade of the 21st century and the subsequent precipitous drop. It looks like the predictions were pretty good for 2016, but that's clearly a fortunate accident. Where do you think oil prices will go in the *next* decade? Your guess may be as good as anyone's. Clearly, these forecasts did not take into account many of the unforeseen global and economic events that occurred since 2000. Providing accurate long-term forecasts is extremely difficult.

Extrapolation far from the data is dangerous. Linear models are based on the x-values of the data at hand and cannot be trusted beyond that span. Some phenomena do exhibit a kind of structural regularity or inertia that allows us to guess that the currently observed systematic behavior will continue outside this range. When x is time, you should be especially wary. Such regularity can't be counted on in phenomena such as stock prices, sales figures, hurricane tracks, or public opinion.

Extrapolating from current trends is a mistake made not only by regression beginners or the naïve. Professional forecasters are prone to the same mistakes, and sometimes the errors are striking. However, because the temptation to predict the future is so strong, our more realistic advice is this:

If you extrapolate far into the future, be prepared for the actual values to be (possibly quite) different from your predictions.

> 66 Prediction is difficult, especially about the future. 99
>
> —Niels Bohr,
> Danish Physicist
> (who was probably quoting
> an old Danish saying)

IN PRACTICE 17.2 A big diamond

The Cullinan I diamond (the "Star of Africa") owned by the Queen of England is, at 530.20 carats, the largest D-color cut diamond in the world. It is mounted at the head of the scepter with the cross in the British crown jewels.

MANAGER We've received a request to estimate the value of the "Star of Africa" diamond. What does our model say?

ANALYST When we restrict our analysis of the diamonds we saw on page 568 to D-color diamonds, the regression model of *Price* on *Carat Weight* is

$$\widehat{Price} = -2129.14 + 8081.12 CaratWt$$

The predicted price from the model is $4,282,482. That's only about 1/100th of the $400 million price placed on the diamond. The rarity of such large diamonds makes them far more valuable than a model based on much smaller stones could predict. Extrapolation that far from the data on which a model is based is not likely to work well.

17.3 Unusual and Extraordinary Observations

Your credit card company makes money each time you use your card. To encourage you to use your card, the card issuer may offer you an incentive such as airline miles, rebates, or gifts.[3] Of course, this is profitable to the company only if the increased use brings in enough revenue to offset the cost of the incentives. New ideas for offers (referred to as "creatives") are typically tested on a sample of cardholders before they are rolled out to the entire segment or population, a process referred to as a "campaign." Typically, the new offer (the "challenger") is tested against a control group who may be offered nothing or the current best offer ("the champion").

---

[3]There are websites dedicated to finding credit card "deals." Search "credit card rewards."

One campaign offered one of the highest-performing market segments an incentive for three months: one redeemable anytime air mile for each dollar spent. After this challenger showed a significant increase in spending compared to the control group during the test period, it was adopted. Analysts hoped that the increase in spending they saw during the test period would continue, but they feared that some cardholders would only change their spending temporarily, with a resulting drop in spending afterward.

However, they were surprised to see that the increase in spending continued well beyond the test period. To investigate, they made a scatterplot like the one shown in Figure 17.10.

FIGURE 17.10   Spending after the test plotted against spending during the test period reveals a surprising value and a positive regression slope.

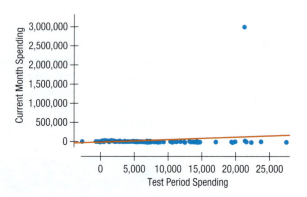

The outlying point, at the top of the graph, represents a cardholder who charged nearly $3 million in the month after the test period ended. Remarkably, the point was verified to be a real purchase! Nevertheless, this cardholder is clearly not typical of the rest of credit card users. To determine whether the spending increase persisted, we need to examine the plot without the outlying point (Figure 17.11).

FIGURE 17.11   A plot of current spending against the spending during the campaign period, with the outlier set aside. Now the slope is negative, and significantly so.

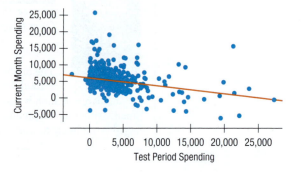

The plot does show that those with the largest charges during the test period actually spent less in the following month. Just one outlier was capable of changing the slope's direction from strongly negative to strongly positive.

Outliers, Leverage, and Influence

By providing a simple description of how data behave, models help us see when and how data values are unusual. In regression, a point can stand out in two ways. A case can have a large residual, as our $3 million spender certainly did. Points with y-values that are far from the regression model are called **outliers**. Because they are not like the other cases, they deserve special attention.

A data point can also be unusual if its x-value is far from the mean of the x-values. Such a point is said to have high **leverage**. The physical image of a lever

" For whoever knows the ways of Nature will more easily notice her deviations; and, on the other hand, whoever knows her deviations will more accurately describe her ways. "

—Francis Bacon (1561–1626)

is exactly right. The least squares line must pass through $(\bar{x}, \bar{y})$, so you can picture that point as the fulcrum of the lever. Just as sitting farther from the center of a seesaw gives you more leverage, points with values far from $\bar{x}$ pull more strongly on the regression line.

A point with high leverage has the potential to change the regression line but it doesn't always use that potential. If the point is consistent with the trend of the other points, it doesn't change our estimate of the line. By sitting so far from $\bar{x}$ though, it may appear to strengthen the relationship, inflating the correlation and R^2.

How can you tell if a high-leverage point changes the model? Just fit the linear model twice, both with and without the point in question. We say that a point is **influential** if omitting it from the analysis gives a very different model (as the high spender did for the credit card spending in Figure 17.10).[4]

Unusual points in a regression often tell us more about the data and the model than any other cases. Whenever you have—or suspect that you have—influential points, you should fit the linear model to the other cases alone and then compare the two regression models to understand how they differ. A model dominated by a single point is unlikely to be useful for understanding the rest of the cases or for predicting a value for a specified *x*. The best way to understand unusual points is against the background of the model established by the other data values. Although it is wise to compare a model fit with and without a possibly influential point, that doesn't mean you can just choose the model with the higher R^2. Don't give in to the temptation to delete points simply because they don't fit the line. That can give a false picture of how well the model fits the data. But often the best way to treat interesting cases and subgroups is to note that they are influential and to find out what makes them special.

Not all points with large influence have large residuals. Sometimes, their influence pulls the regression line so close that it makes the residual deceptively small. Influential points like that can have a shocking effect on the regression. Figure 17.12 shows IQ plotted against shoe size from a fanciful study of intelligence and foot size. The outlier is Bozo the clown, known for his large feet and hailed as a comic genius.

FIGURE 17.12 Bozo the clown's extraordinarily large shoes give his data point high-leverage in the regression of: $\hat{IQ} = 93.3 + 2.08$ *Shoe Size*, even though the R^2 is 25%. Wherever Bozo's IQ happens to be, the regression line will follow.

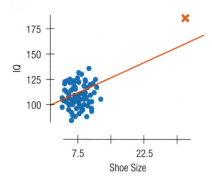

Although this is a silly example, it illustrates an important and common potential problem. Almost all of the variance accounted for ($R^2 = 25\%$) is due to *one* point, namely, Bozo. Without Bozo, there is little correlation between shoe size and IQ. If we run the regression after omitting Bozo, we get an R^2 of only 0.7%—a weak linear relationship (as one might expect). One single point exhibits a great influence on the regression analysis.

[4]Some texts use the term *influential point* for any observation that influences the slope, intercept, or R^2. We'll reserve the term for points that influence the slope.

JUST CHECKING

Each of these scatterplots shows an unusual point. For each, tell whether the point is a high-leverage point, would have a large residual, and/or is influential.

1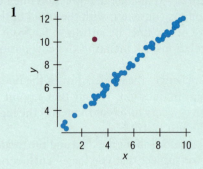

2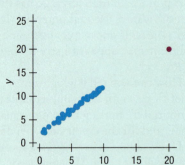

3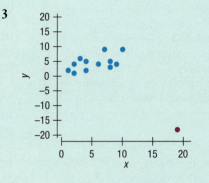

What should you do with a high-leverage point? Sometimes these values are important (they may be customers with extremely high incomes or employees with unusually long service to the company), and they may say more about the relationship between y and x than any of the other data values. However, at other times, high-leverage points are values that really don't belong with the rest of the data. Such points should probably be omitted, and a linear model found without them for comparison. When in doubt, it's usually best to fit regressions both with and without the points and compare the two models.

- **Warning:** Influential points can hide in plots of residuals. Points with high-leverage pull the line close to them, so they often have small residuals. You'll see influential points more easily in scatterplots of the original data, and you'll see their effects by finding a regression model with and without the points.

IN PRACTICE 17.3   Colored diamonds

JEWELRY STORE MANAGER   Some true diamonds are colored from inclusions or structural differences. Can the prices of these diamonds be predicted with the models we make for traditional clear diamonds? For example, does the model work for black diamonds and blue diamonds?

ANALYST   Let's look at the data. One online site lists a black diamond that weighs 2.94 carats for $3050. Black diamonds are true diamonds but may have formed from impacts of comets, asteroids, or meteors rather than from geological pressures deep underground. They are probably best compared to the most-colored K-quality diamonds. Here is a scatterplot of *Price* vs. *Carat Weight* for K-color diamonds. The black diamond (shown with a red x) has both high leverage and a large residual.

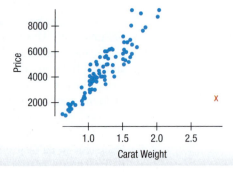

The same site lists a blue diamond that weighs 0.82 carat for $16,500. Blue diamonds are a luxury item, best compared to the best D-color clear diamonds. Here is a scatterplot of *Price* vs. *Carat Weight* for D-color diamonds with the blue diamond shown as a red **x**.

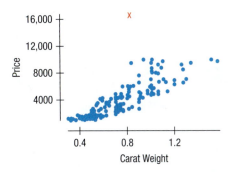

MANAGER Well, shouldn't we include those diamonds in the regression model?

ANALYST That would be a bad idea. The black diamond has high leverage because it is heavier than any of the other diamonds considered. It also has a large negative residual because it is much less expensive than a regression for K-color diamonds would predict. As a result, it would pull the regression line down, making the slope smaller.

The blue diamond has a large positive residual because it is much more expensive even than the regression on perfect D-color diamonds would predict. However, because its carat weight is in the middle of the range of weights considered for the regression, it has little leverage. Including this case will increase the intercept slightly, but won't change the slope very much. However, it would reduce the *R*-squared value.

17.4 Working with Summary Values

Scatterplots of statistics summarized over groups tend to show less variability than we would see if we measured the same variables on individuals. This is because the summary statistics themselves vary less than the data on the individuals.

Wind power is getting increasing attention as an alternative, carbon-free method of generating electricity. Of course, there must be enough wind to make it cost-effective. In a study to find a site for a wind generator, wind speeds were collected four times a day (at 6:00 A.M., noon, 6:00 P.M., and midnight) for a year at several possible sites. Figure 17.13 plots the wind speeds for two of these sites. The correlation is 0.736.

What would happen to the correlation if we used only one measurement per day? If, instead of plotting four data points for each day, we record an average speed for each day, the resulting scatterplot shows less variation, as Figure 17.14 shows. The correlation for these values increases to 0.844.

Let's average over an even longer time period. Figure 17.15 shows *monthly* averages for the year (plotted on the same scale). Now the correlation is 0.942.

What these scatterplots show is that summary statistics exhibit less scatter than the data on individuals on which they're based and can give us a false impression of how well a line summarizes the data. There's no simple correction for this phenomenon. If we're given summary data, we usually can't get the original values back. You should be a bit suspicious of conclusions based on regressions of summary data. They may look better than they really are.

Another way to reduce the number of points in a dataset is to select or sample points rather than average them. This can be especially important with data, such as the wind speeds, that are measured over time. For example, if instead of finding the *mean* for each day, we select just one of the four daily measurements—say the one

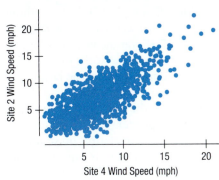

FIGURE 17.13 The wind speed at sites 2 and 4 are correlated. (Data in **Wind speed**)

made at noon on each day. We would have just as many points as in Figure 17.14, but the correlation is 0.730—essentially the same as for the full data. Figure 17.16 shows the relationship.

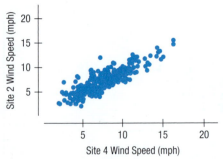

FIGURE 17.14 Daily average wind speeds show less variation.

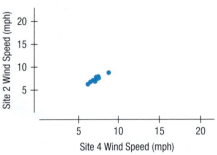

FIGURE 17.15 Monthly averages are even less variable.

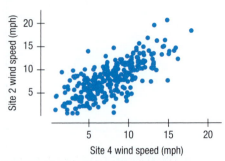

FIGURE 17.16 Selecting only the noon measurements doesn't reduce the variation. Compare this scatterplot to Figures 17.13 and 17.14.

17.5 Autocorrelation

> **Why Is Autocorrelation a Problem?**
>
> When data are highly correlated over time, each data point is similar to those around it. So each data point provides less additional information than if the points had been independent. All regression inference is based on independent errors so we need to check for autocorrelation.

Time series data that are collected at regular time points often have the property that points near each other in time will be related. When values at time t are correlated with values at time $t - 1$ we say the values are **autocorrelated** in the first order. If values are correlated with values two time periods back, we say second-order autocorrelation is present, and so on.

A regression model applied to autocorrelated data will have errors that are not independent, and that violates an assumption for regression. The statistical tests and confidence intervals for the slope depend on independence, and its violation can render these tests and intervals invalid. Fortunately, there is a statistic, called the Durbin-Watson statistic, that can detect first-order autocorrelation from the residuals of a regression analysis.

The Brief Case of Chapter 16 provided data on *Price* and *Sales* volume of frozen pizza for several cities for one week each month. We actually have the data for *every* week in the same three-year period. Here is the regression of *Sales* volume on *Price* for Dallas. (Data in **Pizza prices**)

	Coeff	SE(Coeff)	t-value	P-value
Intercept	139547	11302	12.347	<0.0001
Price	−33527	4308	−7.783	<0.0001

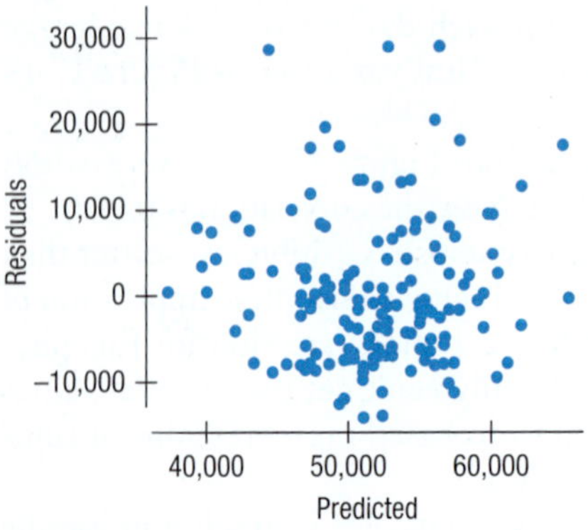

A plot of the residuals against predicted values (Figure 17.17) shows nothing particularly unusual. But because these data points are consecutive weekly data, we should investigate the residuals vs. time. In Figure 17.18 (on the next page) we've plotted the *Residuals* against *Week*, consecutively from week 1 to week 156.

It may not be obvious that there's a pattern here. Autocorrelation can be difficult to see in residuals. It does seem, however, that there is a tendency in Figure 17.18 for the residuals to be related to nearby points. Notice the overall positive trend. We shouldn't see such a trend in residuals that are independent of each other.

The **Durbin-Watson statistic** estimates the autocorrelation by summing squares of consecutive differences and comparing the sum with its expected value under the null hypothesis of no autocorrelation. The Durbin-Watson statistic is computed as follows:

FIGURE 17.17 A scatterplot of the residuals vs. predicted values for the 156 weeks of pizza sales data reveals no obvious patterns.

$$D = \frac{\sum_{t=2}^{n} (e_t - e_{t-1})^2}{\sum_{t=1}^{n} e_t^2}$$

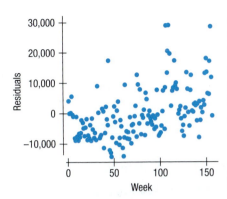

FIGURE 17.18 A scatterplot of the residuals against weeks for the 156 weeks of pizza sales data seems to show some trend.

Why 0 and 4?

Notice that if the adjacent residuals are equal (perfectly correlated), then the numerator and the value of D equals 0. If, on the other hand, the residuals are equal but have opposite signs (perfectly negatively correlated), then each difference is twice the residual. Then after squaring, the numerator will be 2^2, or four times the denominator.

where e_t is the residual at time t. The statistic always falls in the interval from 0 to 4. When the null hypothesis of no autocorrelation is true, the value of D should be 2. Values of D below 2 are evidence of positive autocorrelation, while values of D above 2 indicate possible negative autocorrelation. Positive autocorrelation is more common than negative autocorrelation. How far below or above 2 does D need to be to show "strong" or significant autocorrelation? It may be surprising, but the answer to this question depends only on the sample size, n, and the number of predictors in the regression model, k, which for simple regression is equal to 1.

A standard Durbin-Watson table (see Table D in Appendix B) shows the sample size down the left-hand column, so that each row corresponds to a different sample size n, with the number of predictors k across the top. For each k there are two columns: d_L and d_U. (The significance level of the table is also shown at the top of the page.) The test has several possible outcomes:

If $D < d_L$ (lower critical value), then there is evidence of positive autocorrelation.

If $d_L < D < d_U$, then the test is inconclusive.

If $D > d_U$ (upper critical value), then there is no evidence of positive autocorrelation.

To test negative autocorrelation, we use the same values of d_L and d_U, but we subtract them from 4:

If $D > 4 - d_L$ (lower critical value), then there is evidence of negative autocorrelation.

If $4 - d_L < D < 4 - d_U$, then the test is inconclusive.

If $D < 4 - d_U$ (upper critical value), then there is no evidence of negative autocorrelation.

We usually rely on technology to compute the statistic. For the pizza example, we have $n = 156$ weeks and one predictor (*Price*), so $k = 1$. The value of D is $D = 0.8812$. Using the table in Appendix B, we find the largest value of n listed is $n = 100$, and at $\alpha = 0.05$, $d_L = 1.65$. Because our value is less than that, we conclude that there is evidence of positive autocorrelation. (A software package would find the P-value to be <0.0001.) We conclude that the residuals are *not* independent but that residuals from one week have a positive correlation with the residuals from the preceding week. The standard errors and test for the slope are not valid since we don't have independence.

IN PRACTICE 17.4   Gemstone imports

The U.S. Geological Survey reports facts about a range of mineral and material commodities (minerals.usgs.gov/ds/2005/140/) including gemstones. From their report, we find that imports of gemstones increased between 1990 and 2015: (Data in **Gemstones**)

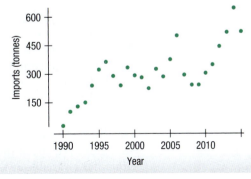

(continued)

A regression gives the following:

```
Response variable is:  Imports(tonnes)
R squared = 58.3%
s = 91.03 with 26 - 2 = 24 degrees of freedom

Variable     Coefficient    SE(Coeff)    t-ratio    P-value
Intercept    -27322.8         4767        -5.73     <0.0001
Year            13.798        2.380        5.80     <0.0001
```

The Durbin-Watson statistic is $D = 0.8604$.

MANAGER These data are measured over time. Is it still safe to interpret a regression for them?

ANALYST The data are a time series. For time series there is always a possibility of autocorrelation, which we test for with the Durbin-Watson statistic. A value of 0.8604 for a regression with $n = 26$ and one predictor is below the lower limit (d_L) for significance, which we can find from Table D in Appendix B to be 1.30. So we conclude that there is evidence of a positive autocorrelation in these data. We should not rely on the standard errors calculated for this regression.

Time series methods (see Chapter 20) attempt to deal with the problem of autocorrelation by modeling the errors. Another solution is to find a predictor variable that accounts for some of the autocorrelation and removes the dependence in the residuals (see Chapter 19). A simple solution that often works is to sample from the time series so that the values are more distant in time and thus less likely to be correlated. If we take every fourth week of data (as we did in Chapter 16), starting at week 4, from the Dallas pizza data, our regression becomes:

```
             Coeff     SE(Coeff)    t-ratio     P-value
Intercept    148350     22266        6.663      <0.0001
Price        -36762      8583       -4.283      0.000126
```

Now, $D = 1.617$. With $n = 39$, the upper critical value d_U is 1.54. Since our new value of D is larger than that, we see no evidence of autocorrelation. Output from technology shows the P-value:

```
Durbin-Watson test
D = 1.6165, P = 0.098740
```

We should feel more comfortable basing our confidence and prediction intervals on this model.

17.6 Transforming (Re-expressing) Data

Linearity

Increasing gas prices and concern for the environment have led to increased attention to automobile fuel efficiency. The most important factor in fuel efficiency is the weight of the car. (Consider the data in **Cars**.)

The relationship is strong ($R^2 = 81.6\%$), clearly negative, and apparently linear. The regression equation

$$\widehat{Fuel\ Efficiency} = 48.7 - 8.4\,Weight$$

says that fuel efficiency drops by 8.4 mpg per 1000 pounds, starting from a value of 48.7 mpg. We check the **Linearity Condition** by plotting the residuals versus either the x-variable or the predicted values.

The scatterplot of the residuals against *Weight* (Figure 17.20) holds a surprise. Residual plots should have no pattern, but this one has a bend. Look at Figure 17.19. The scatter of points isn't really straight. There's a slight bend to the plot, but the bend is much easier to see in the residuals.

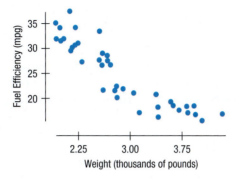

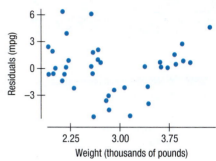

FIGURE 17.19 *Fuel Efficiency* (mpg) vs. *Weight* (thousands of pounds) shows a strong, apparently linear, negative trend.

FIGURE 17.20 Plotting residuals against weight reveals a bend. The bend can be seen if you look carefully at the original scatterplot, but here it's easier to see.

When the relationship isn't straight, we shouldn't fit a regression or summarize the strength of the association with correlation. But often we can make the relationship straighter. All we have to do is **re-express** (or **transform**) one or both of the variables with a simple function. In this case, there's a natural function. In the U.S., automobile fuel efficiency is measured in miles per gallon. But throughout the rest of the world, things are different. Not only do other countries use metric measures, and thus kilometers and liters, but they measure fuel efficiency in liters per 100 kilometers. That's the *reciprocal* of miles per gallon (times a scale constant). That is, the gas amount (gallons or liters) is in the numerator, and the distance (miles or kilometers) is now in the denominator.

There's no reason to prefer one form or the other, so let's try the (negative) reciprocal form. The residuals look better as well. (See Figures 17.21 and 17.22.)

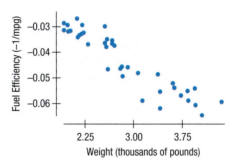

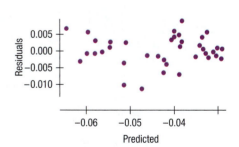

FIGURE 17.21 The reciprocal of *Fuel Efficiency* vs. *Weight* is straighter.

FIGURE 17.22 Residuals from the regression of *Fuel Efficiency* (− 1/mpg) on *Weight* show less bend.

There's a clear improvement using the reciprocal, so we should use the reciprocal as the response in our regression model.

Are we allowed to re-express fuel efficiency as its reciprocal? For these data, it seems like a good idea. After all, we chose a form of the variable used by most people in the world. The general idea of transforming data to improve and simplify its

WHO	77 large companies
WHAT	*Assets, Sales,* and *Market Sector*
UNITS	$1,000,000
WHEN	1986
WHY	To examine distribution of *Assets* for the top *Forbes* 500 companies

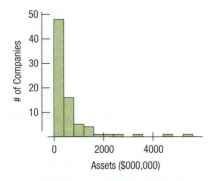

FIGURE 17.23 The distribution of the *Assets* of large companies is skewed to the right. Data on wealth often look like this.

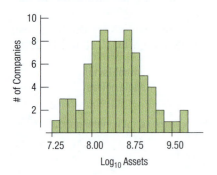

FIGURE 17.24 Taking logs makes the distribution more symmetric.

FIGURE 17.25 Assets of large companies by *Market Sector*. It's hard to compare centers or spreads, and there seem to be a number of high outliers.

structure extends beyond straightening scatterplots. In fact, you use re-expressions in everyday life. How fast can you go on a bicycle? If you measure your speed, you probably do it in distance per time (miles per hour or kilometers per hour). In 2005, during a 12-mile-long time trial in the Tour de France, Dave Zabriskie averaged nearly 35 mph (54.7 kph). You probably realize that's a tough act to follow. It's fast. You can tell that at a glance because you have no trouble thinking in terms of distance covered per time.

If you averaged 12.5 mph (20.1 kph) for a mile run, would that be fast? Would it be fast for a 100-meter dash? Even if you run the mile often, you probably have to stop and calculate. Although we measure speed of bicycles in distance per time, we don't usually measure running speed that way. Instead, we re-express it as the *reciprocal*—time per distance (minutes per mile, seconds per 100 meters, etc.). Running a mile in under 5 minutes (12 mph) is fast. A mile at 16 mph would be close to the world record (that's a 3-minute 45-second mile).

The point is that there is no single natural way to measure speed. In some cases, we use distance traveled per time, and in other cases, we use the reciprocal. It's just because we're used to thinking that way in each case, not because one way is correct. It's important to realize that the way these quantities are measured is not sacred. It's usually just convenience or custom. When we re-express a quantity to make it satisfy certain conditions, we may either leave it in those new units when we explain the analysis to others or convert it back to the original units.

Goals of Re-expression

We re-express data for several reasons. Each of these goals helps make the data more suitable for analysis by our methods. We'll illustrate each goal by looking at data about large companies. (Data in **Companies**)

Goal 1 *Make the distribution of a variable (as seen in its histogram, for example) more symmetric.* It's easier to summarize the center of a symmetric distribution, and for nearly symmetric distributions, we can use the mean and standard deviation. If the distribution is unimodal, then the resulting distribution may be closer to the Normal model, allowing us to use the 68–95–99.7 Rule.

Figure 17.23 shows the *Assets* of 77 large companies as reported by *Forbes*.

The skewed distribution is made much more symmetric by taking logs (see Figure 17.24).

Goal 2 *Make the spread of several groups (as seen in side-by-side boxplots) more alike,* even if their centers differ. Groups that share a common spread are easier to compare. We'll see methods later in the text that can be applied only to groups with a common standard deviation. We saw an example of re-expression for comparing groups with boxplots in Chapter 3.

Figure 17.25 shows the *Assets* of these companies by *Market Sector.*

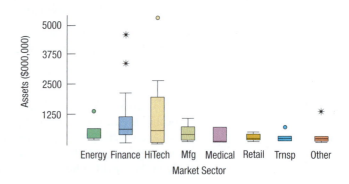

Taking logs makes the individual boxplots more symmetric and gives them spreads that are more nearly equal as Figure 17.26 shows.

FIGURE 17.26 After re-expressing using logs, it's much easier to compare across *Market Sectors*. The boxplots are more symmetric, most have similar spreads, and the companies that seemed to be outliers before are no longer extraordinary. Two new outliers have appeared in the finance sector. They are the only companies in that sector that are not banks.

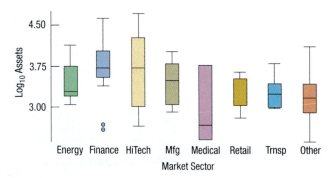

This makes it easier to compare *Assets* across *Market Sector*s. It can also reveal problems in the data. Some companies that looked like outliers on the high end turned out to be more typical. But two companies in the Finance sector now stick out. They are not banks. Unlike the rest of the companies in that sector, they may have been placed in the wrong sector, but we couldn't see that in the original data.

Goal 3 *Make the form of a scatterplot more nearly linear:* Linear scatterplots are easier to describe. The value of re-expressing data to straighten a relationship is that we can fit a linear model once the relationship is straight.

Figure 17.27 shows *Assets* plotted against the logarithm of *Sales*.

FIGURE 17.27 *Assets* vs. log *Sales* shows a positive association (bigger *Sales* goes with bigger *Assets*) with a bent shape.

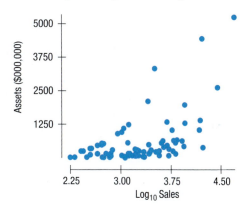

Note that the plot of *Assets* versus log *Sales* shows that the points go from tightly bunched at the left to widely scattered at the right—a "fan" shape. The plot's shape is bent. Taking logs makes the relationship much more linear (see Figure 17.28). If we re-express the company *Assets* using logarithms, we get a graph that shows a more linear association. Also note that the "fan" shape has disappeared and the variability at each value of x is about the same.

FIGURE 17.28 Log *Assets* vs. log *Sales* shows a positive linear association.

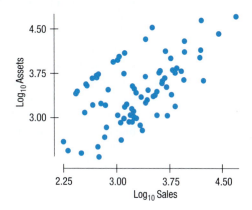

Goal 4 *Make the scatter in a scatterplot or residual plot spread out evenly rather than following a fan shape.* Having an even scatter is a condition of many methods of statistics, as we'll see in later chapters. This goal is closely related to Goal 2, but it often comes along with Goal 3. Indeed, a glance back at the scatterplot (Figure 17.27) shows that the plot for *Assets* is much more spread out on the right than on the left, while the plot for log *Assets* (Figure 17.28) has roughly the same variation in log *Assets* for any *x*-value.

IN PRACTICE 17.5   Re-expressing diamond prices

When we first looked at diamond prices (on page 568), we noted that we needed to model prices for different color diamonds separately. In other examples, we restricted attention to either the D- or K-color diamonds at either end of the color spectrum. Here is a scatterplot of *Price* vs. *Carat Weight* for the E- and F-color stones:

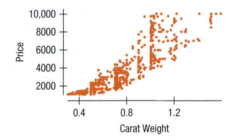

MANAGER I'd like to use the regression model for these stones as well. Is that OK?

ANALYST No, the plot of the data violates several conditions required for regression. The relationship is not straight. It also spreads out more on the right than on the left.

17.7   The Ladder of Powers

We've seen that taking logs or reciprocals can improve an analysis of relationships. Other transformations can be helpful too, but how do we know which re-expression to use? We could use trial and error to choose a re-expression, but there's an easier way. We can choose our re-expressions from a family of simple mathematical expressions that move data toward our goals in a consistent way. This family includes the most common ways to re-express data. More important, the members of the family line up in order, so that the farther you move away from the original data (the "1" position), the greater the effect on the data. This fact lets you search systematically for a transformation that works—stepping a bit farther from "1" or taking a step back toward "1" as you see the results.

Where to start? It turns out that certain kinds of data are more likely to be helped by particular re-expressions. Knowing that gives you a good place to start your search for a mathematical expression. We call this collection of re-expressions the **Ladder of Powers**. The following table shows some of the most useful powers with each one specified as a single value.

Power	Name	Comment
2	*The square of the data values, y^2*	Try this for unimodal distributions that are skewed to the left.
1	The raw data—no change at all. This is "home base." The farther you step from here up or down the ladder, the greater the effect.	Data that can take on both positive and negative values with no bounds are less likely to benefit from re-expression.
1/2	The square root of the data values $\sqrt{y}$	Counts often benefit from a square root re-expression. For counted data, start here.
"0"	Although mathematicians define the "0-th" power differently, for us the place is held by the logarithm.	Measurements that cannot be negative, and especially values that grow by percentage increases such as salaries or populations, often benefit from a log re-expression. When in doubt, start here. If your data have zeros, try adding a small constant to all values before finding the logs.
−1/2	The (negative) reciprocal square root $-1/\sqrt{y}$	An uncommon re-expression, but sometimes useful. Changing the sign to take the *negative* of the reciprocal square root preserves the direction of relationships, which can be a bit simpler.
−1	The (negative) reciprocal, $-1/y$	Ratios of two quantities (miles per hour, for example) often benefit from a reciprocal. (You have about a 50-50 chance that the original ratio was taken in the "wrong" order for simple statistical analysis and would benefit from re-expression.) Often, the reciprocal will have simple units (hours per mile). Change the sign if you want to preserve the direction of relationships. If your data have zeros, try adding a small constant to all values before finding the reciprocal.

The Ladder of Powers orders the *effects* that the re-expressions have on data. If you try, say, taking the square roots of all the values in a variable and it helps, but not enough, then moving farther down the ladder to the logarithm or reciprocal root will have a similar effect on your data, but even stronger. If you go too far, you can always back up. But don't forget—when you take a negative power, the *direction* of the relationship will change. You can always change the sign of the response if you want to keep the same direction.

IN PRACTICE 17.6 Finding a re-expression for diamond prices

MANAGER OK, you showed me (on page 582) that the relationship between *Price* and *Carat Weight* is not linear and spreads out toward the right side of the plot. What can we do to deal with these problems?

ANALYST There is a way to deal with these problems. We can re-express *Price*, hoping to improve these problems. Here are three possible re-expressions of *Price:* square root, $\log_{10}$, and (negative) reciprocal.

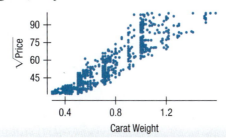

(continued)

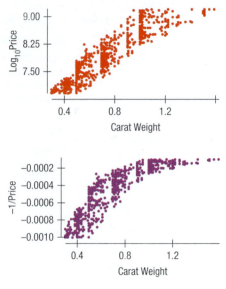

MANAGER I see that re-expression can help, but which of these does the best job of making the relationship linear? Does the plot indicate that we have satisfied the regression assumptions?

ANALYST My choice would be the logarithm. The relationship of $\log_{10}$ *Price* to *Carat Weight* is much more linear and the spread has evened out across the plot. A regression of $\log_{10}$ *Price* on *Carat Weight* would be appropriate.

GUIDED EXAMPLE   Commercial Real Estate

What determines the value of commercial real estate? In Chapter 4 we used a simple linear relationship with an R^2 of 62.4% to see that living area was a good predictor of the value of a family home. Does the same relationship hold for commercial property? Are other factors important?

We have available data on 286 commercial properties in and around a major U.S. city. (Data in **Commercial properties**)

PLAN **Define** the problem and state your objective. Identify the quantitative variables you wish to examine. Define each variable. (State the W's.)	Our objective is to investigate the association between the *Price* of a commercial property ($M) and its *Size* (square ft).
	We have data for 286 commercial properties in and around a major U.S. city. We will build and diagnose a regression model.
Plot the data.	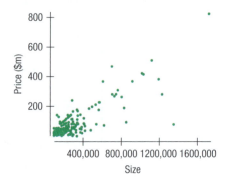

DO   Check the conditions for regression.

✔ **Quantitative Variable Condition**: Both variables are quantitative.

✔ **Linearity Condition**: The scatterplot is straight enough.

✔ **Outlier Condition**: There are no obvious outliers.

✔ **Equal Spread Condition**: The plot fans out to the right. That makes us suspect skewness, so we'll look at a histogram:

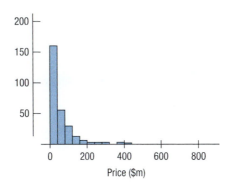

REALITY CHECK ✔   It isn't surprising to find that *Price* is skewed to the high end. Variables like this that cannot get too small but have no real limit on the upper end are often skewed like this.

The skewness of *Price* suggests a re-expression to make the distribution more nearly symmetric and to even out the spread in the scatterplot.

We will investigate re-expressions of the variables.

A histogram of $\text{Log}_{10}(\text{Price})$ is much more symmetric:

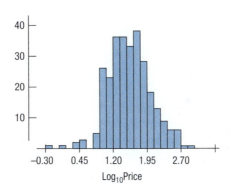

Log_{10} is easier to interpret than the natural log. The $\log_{10}$ of 1,000,000 is 6; the $\log_{10}$ of 10,000,000 is 7. So these prices are mostly between \$1M and \$100M, with some near \$1B ($\log_{10} = 9$).

The scatterplot of $\text{Log}_{10}(\text{Price})$ vs. *Size* is not straight:

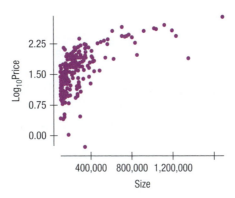

(continued)

It seems natural to try a square root re-expression for a variable like *Size* that is measured in squared units (ft^2):

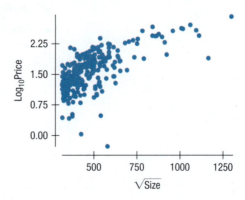

This is an improvement, but still not straight. We'll try the next two steps on the Ladder of Powers: log and $-1/\sqrt{y}$:

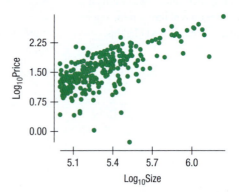

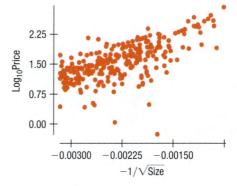

We change the sign when we take the reciprocal to preserve the direction—here a positive relationship.

The log and (negative) reciprocal root look good. We'll pick the reciprocal root but could just as well have used the log.

A regression fit to this relationship looks like this:

```
Dependent variable is: Log₁₀(Price)
R² = 45.7%    R²(adjusted) = 45.5%
s = 0.3484 with 286 − 2 = 284 df
```

Variable	Coeff	SE(Coeff)	t-ratio	P-value
Intercept	2.842	0.0857	33.2	<0.0001
$-1/\sqrt{Size}$	561.375	36.34	15.4	<0.0001

As often happens when we re-express data for one reason (in this example, to improve linearity and make the variables more nearly symmetric), we also improve other aspects of the data. Except for these outliers, the residuals have a more symmetric distribution and are more nearly Normal than they would have been for the original variables. When we test coefficients, one condition is that the residuals be nearly Normal, so this can be important.

A plot of the residuals shows some outliers:

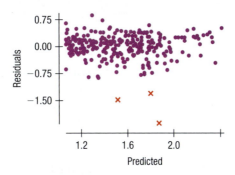

Without knowing more, we can't be sure why these properties appear to be so inexpensive. Perhaps they are an opportunity for a developer.

One suggestive observation is that two of them are among the oldest of the properties in our data, having been built before 1890. But two other properties are still older, and one of our outliers isn't old at all, so that's not a full explanation:

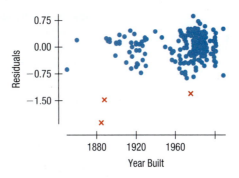

If we set aside the three outliers, the R^2 increases to 59.2%.

REPORT | **Communicate and present** the steps taken and what you learned about the data.

MEMO

Re: Commercial properties

Our regression analysis of commercial properties showed that the relationship between price and size was not linear—unlike what we found previously for residential properties. Re-expressing the variables, we found that the $\log_{10}$ of *Price* can be predicted from $1/\sqrt{Size}$ with an R^2 of 59.2%. That's not as strong a relationship as we found for residential properties.

We also found three outliers, which we set aside for further investigation. They may present investment opportunities because they appear to be unexpectedly inexpensive.

JUST CHECKING

4 You want to model the relationship between prices for various items in Paris and Hong Kong. The scatterplot of Hong Kong prices vs. Paris prices shows a generally straight pattern with a small amount of scatter. What re-expression (if any) of the Hong Kong prices might you start with?

5 You want to model the population growth of the United States over the past 200 years with a percentage growth that's nearly constant. The scatterplot shows a strongly upwardly curved pattern. What re-expression (if any) of the population might you start with?

⊘ WHAT CAN GO WRONG?

This entire chapter has warned about things that can go wrong in a regression analysis. So let's just recap. When you make a linear model:

- **Make sure the relationship is straight enough to fit a regression model.** Check the Linearity Condition on the scatterplot of y against x and always examine the residuals for evidence that the Linearity Assumption has failed. It's often easier to see deviations from a straight line in the residuals plot than in the scatterplot of the original data. Pay special attention to the most extreme residuals because they may have something to add to the story told by the linear model.

- **Be on guard for different groups.** Check for evidence that the data consist of separate subsets. If you find subsets that behave differently, consider fitting a different linear model to each subset.

- **Beware of extrapolating.** Beware of extrapolation beyond the x-values that were used to fit the model. Although it's common to use linear models to extrapolate, be cautious.

- **Beware of extrapolating far into the future.** Be especially cautious about extrapolating far into the future with linear models. A linear model assumes that changes over time will continue forever at the same rate you've observed in the past. Predicting the future is particularly tempting and particularly dangerous.

- **Look for unusual points.** Unusual points always deserve attention and may well reveal more about your data than the rest of the points combined. Always look for them and try to understand why they stand apart. Making a scatterplot of the data is a good way to reveal high-leverage and influential points. A scatterplot of the residuals against the predicted values is a good tool for finding points with large residuals.

- **Beware of high-leverage points, especially of those that are influential.** Influential points can alter the regression model a great deal. The resulting model may say more about one or two points than about the overall relationship.

- **Consider setting aside outliers and re-running the regression.** To see the impact of outliers on a regression, try running two regressions, one with and one without the extraordinary points, and then discuss the differences.

- **Treat unusual points honestly.** If you remove enough carefully selected points, you will eventually get a regression with a high R^2. But it won't get you very far. Some data are not simple enough for a linear model to fit very well. When that happens, report the failure and stop.

- **Be alert for autocorrelation.** Data measured over time may fail the Independence Assumption. A Durbin-Watson test can check for that.

- **Watch out when dealing with data that are summaries.** Be cautious in working with data values that are themselves summaries, such as means or medians. Such statistics are less variable than the data on which they are based, so they tend to inflate the impression of the strength of a relationship.

- **Re-express your data when necessary.** When the data don't have the right form for the model you are fitting, your analysis can't be valid. Be alert for opportunities to re-express data to achieve simpler forms

ETHICS IN ACTION

Most people older than 40 remember chia seeds as the source of "green hair" for a variety of animal-shaped terra-cotta figurines. While chia pets are still available (there is even one resembling President Trump), chia seeds are now more often recognized for being a super nutritious addition to smoothies, cereals, and energy bars. Chia seeds are rich in omega-3 fatty acids and antioxidants, as well as high in fiber and protein, and many large food companies have introduced them into their products. According to an article published in the *New York Times* business section (November 23, 2012), the demand for chia has grown dramatically because of its popularity among athletes and health-conscious individuals.

Max Rendall is excited about the new "super seed." As a chemist at a mid-sized university, he recently obtained funding from a major food manufacturer to research the purported health benefits of chia. In particular, his study examines the effectiveness of chia on lowering triglycerides. Triglycerides are fat in the blood, and higher levels increase the risk for heart disease. This type of research is not new for Max. He has regularly secured grants from private companies to investigate the health benefits of foods, among them cranberries, dark chocolate, and popcorn. And many of his findings have been reported in the popular press.

For this particular study, Max and his assistant Margaret recruited individuals with very high levels of blood triglycerides—above 500 mg/dL—and instructed them to consume chia seeds daily (in varying amounts) over a six-week period. Triglyceride levels of the study participants were measured at the beginning and end of the six weeks to determine the percentage change. The percentage change was then regressed against the average daily amount of chia consumed (in grams). The relationship was linear and significant. The more chia consumed, the greater the percentage drop in triglyceride levels.

However, while examining the residuals from the regression Margaret did notice an influential outlier; one individual in the study experienced an extreme drop in triglycerides. She brought this to Max's attention, and they decided to perform the regression analysis again, this time excluding the outlier. They were surprised at how much weaker the relationship was when this individual's data was removed. After some discussion, they thought it best not to exclude data points. After all, it had been difficult recruiting eligible participants for the study. Max and Margaret were quite happy with their findings, and knew that the sponsor of their research would be pleased as well.

- **Identify the ethical dilemma in this scenario.**
- **What are the undesirable consequences?**
- **Propose an ethical solution that considers the welfare of all stakeholders.**

CHAPTER

17 FROM LEARNING TO EARNING

LEARNING OBJECTIVES

Be skeptical of regression models. Always plot and examine the residuals for unexpected behavior.
Be alert to a variety of possible violations of the standard regression assumptions and know what to do when you find them.

Be alert for subgroups in the data.

- Often these will turn out to be separate groups that should not be analyzed together in a single analysis.
- Often identifying subgroups can help us understand what is going on in the data.

Be especially cautious about extrapolating beyond the data.

Look out for unusual and extraordinary observations.

- Cases that are extreme in x have high leverage and can affect a regression model strongly.
- Cases that are extreme in y have large residuals.
- Cases that have both high leverage and large residuals are influential. Setting them aside will change the regression model, so you should consider whether their influence on the model is appropriate or desirable.

Notice when you are working with summary values.

- Summaries vary less than the data they summarize, so they may give the impression of greater certainty than your model deserves.

Diagnose and treat nonlinearity.

- If a scatterplot of y vs. x isn't straight, a linear regression model isn't appropriate.
- Re-expressing one or both variables can often improve the straightness of the relationship.
- The powers, roots, and the logarithm provide an ordered collection of re-expressions so you can search up and down the "ladder of powers" to find an appropriate one.

TERMS

Autocorrelation	The correlation of a variable with itself, offset by one or more positions. Autocorrelation is especially important for variables measured over time.
Durbin-Watson Statistic	A statistic that tests the strength of autocorrelation in a variable. It is commonly applied to check whether regression residuals are not mutually independent for data measured over time.
Extrapolation	Although linear models provide an easy way to predict values of y for a given value of x, it is unsafe to predict for values of x far from the ones used to find the linear model equation. Be cautious when extrapolating.
Influential	If omitting a point from the data changes the regression model substantially, that point is considered influential.
Ladder of Powers	The powers to which we typically re-express values of a variable can by ordered according to the value of the exponent and with the logarithm at the "0" point. This ordering is called the ladder of powers.
Leverage	Data points whose x-values are far from the mean of x are said to exert leverage on a linear model. High-leverage points pull the line close to them, so they can have a large effect on the line, sometimes completely determining the slope and intercept. Points with high enough leverage can have deceptively small residuals.
Outlier	Any data point that stands away from the regression line by having a large residual is called an outlier.
Transformation (or Re-expression)	A function—typically a simple power or root—applied to the values of a quantitative variable to make its distribution more symmetric and/or to simplify its relationship with other variables.

TECH SUPPORT Examining Residuals

Most statistics technology offers simple ways to check whether your data satisfy the conditions for regression and to re-express the data when that is called for. We have already seen that these programs can make a simple scatterplot. They can also help us check the conditions by plotting residuals. Most statistics packages offer a way to re-express and compute with variables.

EXCEL

To save regression residuals in Excel:

- From **Data**, select **Data Analysis** and select **Regression**. Enter the data ranges and specify location for the output.
- Select **Residuals**, **Residual Plots**, and **Line Fit Plots**.

Residuals
☑ Residuals   ☑ Residual Plots
☐ Standardized Residuals ☑ Line Fit Plots

- Click **OK**.

At the end of the output, find the list of observations, predicted values, and residuals. They can be copied to a new worksheet to analyze residuals.

To create transformed variables in Excel:

- In a new column, use Excel's built-in functions to transform existing data.

	A	B	C	D
1	Weight	MPG	MPG²	
2	3252	22	=POWER(B2,2)	
3	3219	20	POWER(number, power)	

- Fill down to re-express the entire variable.

XLSTAT

To save residuals using XLSTAT:

- Choose the **Modeling data** menu, and then select **Linear regression**.
- On the **Charts** tab select **residuals**.

To create transformed variables using XLSTAT:

- Choose the **Preparing data** menu, and then select **Variables transformation**.
- Select variable name and location.
- Select **other** under transformation, and select desired transformation from **transformations tab**.
- Transformed variables can also be created using Excel's built-in functions.

JMP

- From the **Analyze** menu, choose **Fit Y by X**.
- Select **Fit Line**.
- Under Linear Fit, select **Plot Residuals**. You can also choose to **Save Residuals**.
- Subsequently, from the **Distribution** menu, choose **Normal quantile plot** or **histogram** for the residuals.

To re-express a variable in JMP,

- Double-click to the right of the last column of data to create a new column.
- Name the new column and select it.
- Choose **Formula** from the **Cols** menu.
- In the Formula dialog, choose the transformation and variable that you wish to assign to the new column.
- In JMP 11 and later you can also click on a variable in the dialog box to obtain a list of transformations.
- Click the **OK** button.

JMP places the re-expressed data in the new column.

COMMENTS

The log and square root re-expressions are found in the **Transcendental** menu of functions in the formula dialog.

MINITAB

To save residuals in MINITAB:

- From the **Stat** menu, choose **Regression**.
- From the Regression submenu, select **Fit Regression Model**.
- In the Regression dialog, enter the response variable name in the "Response" box and the predictor variable name in the "Predictor" box.
- To specify saved results, in the Regression dialog, click **Storage**.
- Check "Residuals". Click **OK**.
- To specify displays, in the Regression dialog, click **Graphs**.

- Under "Residual Plots", select "Individual plots" and check "Residuals versus fits". Click **OK**.
- Now back in the Regression dialog, click **OK**. Minitab computes the regression and the requested saved values and graphs.

To re-express a variable in MINITAB,

- Choose **Calculator** from the **Calc** menu.
- In the Calculator dialog, specify a name for the new re-expressed variable.
- Use the **Functions List**, the calculator buttons, and the **Variables list** box to build the expression. Click **OK**.

R

Suppose the response variable y and predictor variable x are in a data frame called mydata. After fitting a regression of y on x via:

- mylm=lm(y~x, data=mydata).
- summary(mylm) # gives the details of the fit, including the ANOVA table.
- plot(mylm) #gives a variety of plots.
- lm.influence(mylm) #gives a variety of regression diagnostic values.

To re-express a variable, you can make a new variable in the data frame as in mydata$logx=log(mydata$x) or, re-express the variable in the formula: mylm2=lm((y~I(log(x)),data=mydata).

COMMENTS

The I() function—(capital I)—"as.is" protects the variable from being misinterpreted. It's a good idea to use it whenever adding an expression inside a formula.

SPSS

To save residuals in SPSS:

- From the **Analyze** menu, choose **Regression**.
- From the Regression submenu, choose **Linear**. After assigning variables to their roles in the regression, click the **Plots ...** button.
- In the Plots dialog, you can specify a Normal probability plot of residuals and scatterplots of various versions of standardized residuals and predicted values.

To re-express a variable in SPSS, choose **Compute Variable** from the **Transform** menu.

- Enter a name in the Target Variable field.
- Use the calculator and Function List to build the expression.
- Move a variable to be re-expressed from the source list to the Numeric Expression field. Click the **OK** button.

COMMENTS

A plot of ***ZRESID** against ***PRED** will look most like the residual plots we've discussed. SPSS standardizes the residuals by dividing by their standard deviation. (There's no need to subtract their mean; it must be zero.) The standardization doesn't affect the scatterplot.

To perform a regression:

- Click on **Stat**.
- Choose **Regression > Simple Linear**.
- Choose the **Y variable** and the **X variable**.
- Choose **Graphs** and select desired graphs.
- Click on **Compute!**

COMMENTS

Residuals, Studentized residuals, predicted values, confidence intervals, prediction intervals, and a variety of diagnostics can be saved by

- Choose **Save**:
- Select the options you want.

BRIEF CASE

Gross Domestic Product

The gross domestic product (GDP) per capita is a widely used measure of a country's (or state's) economy. It is defined as the total market value of all goods and services produced within a country (or state) in a specified period of time. The most common computation of GDP includes five items: consumption, gross investment, government spending, exports, and imports (which negatively impact the total). The Census Bureau reports the GDP for each state in the United States quarterly. The government also reports annual personal income totals (seasonally adjusted in $millions) by state and each state's population. Let's examine how personal income is related to GDP at the state level. Use the data in the file **GDP by state** to investigate the relationship between GDP and personal income.

Find a model to predict *Personal Income* from *GDP*. Write a short report detailing what you find. Be sure to include appropriate plots, look for influential points, and consider transforming either or both variables.

Repeat the analysis after dividing both variables by state population in 2005 to create per capita versions of the variables. Discuss which regression you think best helps to describe how personal income and GDP are related. Be sure to examine the residuals and discuss the regression assumptions.

Energy Sources

Renewable sources of energy are of growing importance in the economy. The Energy Information Administration reports the amount of renewable energy generated (in thousands of kilowatt-hours) in each of the states both including and excluding hydroelectric generation. The data are in **Alternative Energy 2016**.

Consider the relationship of hydroelectric power with alternative energy from non-hydro sources. Find a model for this relationship. Be sure to deal with any extraordinary or influential points. You may want to transform one or both variables. Discuss your residual analysis and the regression assumptions.

Now graph the relationship between (re-expressed) hydroelectric power and wind-generated power. Locate subgroups of states within this plot and discuss how they differ. Do you think a single model for the relationship of these renewable sources is appropriate? Summarize your conclusions in a report.

SECTION 17.1

1. An analysis of spending by a sample of credit card bank cardholders shows that spending by cardholders in January (*Jan*) is related to their spending in December (*Dec*):

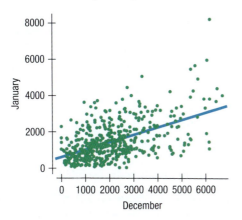

The assumptions and conditions of the linear regression seemed to be satisfied and an analyst was about to predict January spending using the model shown below:

$$\widehat{Jan} = \$612.07 + 0.403\ Dec$$

Another analyst worried that different types of cardholders might behave differently. She examined the spending patterns of the cardholders and placed them into five market *Segments*. When she plotted the data using different colors and symbols for the five different segments, she found the following:

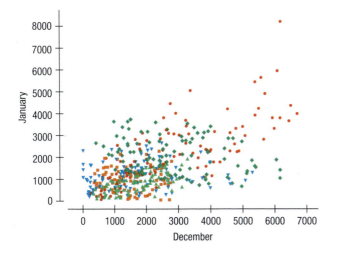

Look at this plot carefully and discuss why she might be worried about the predictions from the model $\widehat{Jan} = \$612.07 + 0.403\ Dec$.

2. A concert production company examined its records. The manager made the following scatterplot. The company places concerts in two venues, a smaller, more intimate theater (plotted with blue circles) and a larger auditorium-style venue.

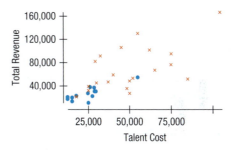

a) Describe the relationship between *Talent Cost* and *Total Revenue*. (Remember: direction, form, strength, outliers.)
b) How are the results for the two venues similar?
c) How are they different?

3. The analyst in Exercise 1 tried fitting the regression line to each market segment separately and found the following:

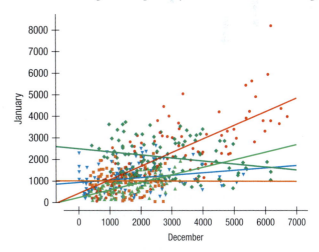

What does this say about her concern in Exercise 1? Was she justified in worrying that the overall model $\widehat{Jan} = \$612.07 + 0.403\ Dec$ might not accurately summarize the relationship? Explain briefly.

4. The concert production company of Exercise 2 made a second scatterplot, this time relating *Total Revenue* to *Ticket Sales*.

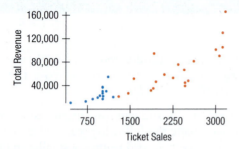

a) Describe the relationship between *Ticket Sales* and *Total Revenue*.
b) How are the results for the two venues similar?
c) How are they different?

SECTION 17.2

5. Here are the data from the small bookstore we saw in Chapter 15, Exercise 9.

Number of Sales People Working	Sales (in $1000)
2	10
3	11
7	13
9	14
10	18
10	20
12	20
15	22
16	22
20	26
$\bar{x} = 10.4$	$\bar{y} = 17.6$
$SD(x) = 5.64$	$SD(y) = 5.34$

The regression line is:

$$\widehat{Sales} = 8.10 + 0.913 \; Number \; of \; Sales \; People \; Working$$

and we can assume that the assumptions and conditions for regression are met. Calculations with technology find that

$$s_e = 1.477.$$

a) Find the predicted sales on a day with 500 employees working.
b) Is this prediction likely to be useful? Explain.

6. Here are prices for the external disk drives we saw in Chapter 15, Exercise 10:

Capacity (in TB)	Price (in $)
0.15	35.00
0.25	39.95
0.32	49.95
1.0	75.00
2.0	110.00
3.0	140.00
4.0	325.00
$\bar{x} = 1.53$	$\bar{y} = 110.7$
$SD(x) = 1.515$	$SD(y) = 102.049$

The least squares line is $\widehat{Price} = 15.11 + 62.417 \; Capacity$.

The assumptions and conditions for regression are met.

$$SE(b_1) = 11.33 \text{ and } s_e = 42.04$$

a) Disk drives keep growing in capacity. Some tech experts now talk about *Petabyte* (PB = 1000 TB = 1,000,000 GB) drives. What does this model predict that a Petabyte-capacity drive will cost?
b) Is this prediction likely to be useful? Explain.

7. A regression of *Total Revenue* on *Ticket Sales* by the concert production company of Exercises 2 and 4 finds the model

$$\widehat{Revenue} = -14,228 + 36.87 \; TicketSales$$

a) Management is considering adding a stadium-style venue that would seat 10,000. What does this model predict that revenue would be if the new venue were to sell out?
b) Why would it be a poor business decision to assume that this model accurately predicts revenue for this situation?

8. The production company of Exercise 7 offers advanced sales to "Frequent Buyers" through its website. Here's a relevant scatterplot:

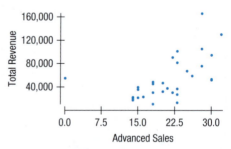

One performer refused to permit advanced sales. What effect has that point had on the regression to model *Total Revenue* from *Advanced Sales*?

SECTION 17.3

9. The bookstore in Exercise 5 decides to have a gala event in an attempt to drum up business. They hire 100 employees for the day and bring in a total of $42,000.

a) Find the regression line predicting *Sales* from *Number of people working* with the new point added.

b) What has changed from the original regression equation?
c) Is the new point a high leverage point or an influential point?
d) Does the new point have a large residual? Explain.

10. The data for hard drives in Exercise 6 originally included a 200 GB (0.2 TB) drive that sold for $299.00 (see Chapter 4, Exercise 2).

a) Find the regression line predicting *Price* from *Capacity* with this hard drive added.
b) What has changed from the original regression equation?
c) Is the new point a high leverage point or an influential point?
d) Does the new point have a large residual? Explain.

SECTION 17.5

11. A beverage company specializing in sales of champagne reports four years of quarterly sales as follows (in millions of $):

Quarter	Sales ($M)
1	12
2	41
3	15
4	48
5	25
6	55
7	23
8	69
9	51
10	80
11	54
12	87
13	64
14	94
15	62
16	108

The regression equation is *Predicted Sales* $= 14.15 + 4.87$ *Quarter*.

a) Find the residuals.
b) Plot the residuals against *Quarter*. Comment.
c) Compute the Durbin-Watson statistic.
d) At $\alpha = 0.05$, what are the values of d_L and d_U?
e) Is there evidence of positive autocorrelation? Explain.
f) Is there evidence of negative autocorrelation? Explain.

12. A company fits a regression to predict monthly *Orders* over a period of 48 months. The Durbin-Watson statistic on the residuals is 0.875.

a) At $\alpha = 0.01$, using $k = 1$ and $n = 50$, what are the values of d_L and d_U?
b) Is there evidence of positive autocorrelation? Explain.
c) Is there evidence of negative autocorrelation? Explain.

13. The manager of the concert production company considered in earlier exercises considers the regression of *Total Revenue* on *Ticket Sales* (see Exercise 4) and computes the Durbin-Watson statistic, obtaining a value of 0.51.

a) Consult Table D in Appendix B using $k = 1$ and $n = 45$ and complete the test at $\alpha = 0.05$.
b) Specify what this statistic tests and what the test says about these data.

14. The regression of *Total Revenue* on *Total Expenses* for the concerts of Exercise 13 gives the following model:

```
Dependent variable is: Total Revenue
R squared = 56.4%  R squared (adjusted) = 55.0%
s = 24269 with 34 - 2 = 32 degrees of freedom
```

Variable	Coefficient	SE(Coeff)	t-ratio	P-value
Intercept	-3688.54	9453	-0.390	0.6990
Total Expenses	0.731250	0.1137	6.43	<0.0001

a) The Durbin-Watson statistic for this analysis is 0.73. Consult Table D in Appendix B and complete the test at $\alpha = 0.05$.
b) What do you conclude from this test?

SECTION 17.6

15. A scatterplot of *Salary* against *Years Experience* for some employees, and the scatterplot of residuals against predicted *Salary* from the regression line are shown in the figures. On the basis of these plots, would you recommend a re-expression of either *Salary* or *Years Experience*? Explain.

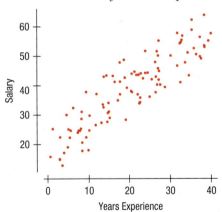

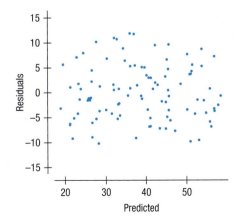

16. A study of homes looking at the relationship between *Age* of a home and *Price* produced the following scatterplot. A regression was fit to the data as shown below.

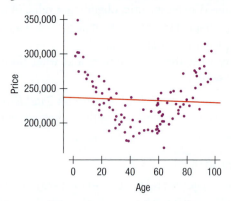

On the basis of this plot, would you advise using this regression? Explain.

17. A small company has developed an improved process for making solar panels. The company needs to set its prices and wants those prices to reflect the efficiencies of producing larger batches. The data show the following:

#Units	Cost per Unit
10	7.389
20	6.049
30	4.953
40	4.055
50	3.320
60	2.718
70	2.459
80	2.225
90	2.013
100	1.822
120	1.648
140	1.491
160	1.349
180	1.221
200	1.105

A scatterplot of *Cost per Unit* vs. *#Units* looks like this:

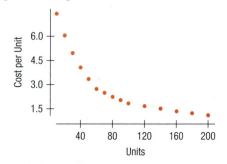

What should be done to make the relationship more nearly linear?

18. One possible model for the manufacturing process of Exercise 17 is the following:

```
Dependent variable is: Log(Cost per unit)
R squared = 90.1%  R squared (adjusted) = 89.3%
s = 0.0841 with 15 − 2 = 13 degrees of freedom
```

Variable	Coefficient	SE(Coeff)	t-ratio	P-value
Intercept	0.7618	0.0405	18.8	<0.0001
#Units	−0.0041	0.0004	−10.9	<0.0001

Using this model, predict the cost per unit in a batch of 300.

SECTION 17.7

19. A quickly growing company shows the following scatterplot of customers vs. time (in months).

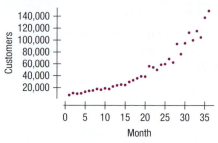

a) What re-expression might you suggest for the number of customers?
b) What power in the ladder of powers does that correspond to?

20. For the regression in Exercise 19:

A student tries taking the reciprocal of customers and produces the plot shown below:

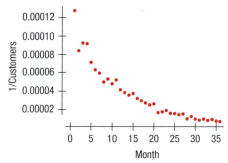

a) Would you recommend this transformation? Why or why not?
b) What would you suggest?

CHAPTER EXERCISES

T **21. Marriage age 2017.** Weddings are one of the fastest growing businesses; about $40 billion is spent on weddings in the United States each year. But demographics may be changing, and this could affect wedding retailers' marketing plans. Is there evidence that the age at which women get married has changed over the past 100 years? The scatterplot shows the trend in age at first marriage for American women. (U.S. Census Bureau; www.census.gov)

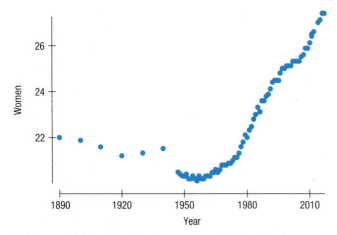

a) Do you think there is a clear pattern? Describe the trend.
b) Is the association strong?
c) Is the correlation high? Explain.
d) Do you think a linear model is appropriate for these data? Explain.

T 22. Smoking 2014. Even with campaigns to reduce smoking, Americans still consume more than four packs of cigarettes per month per adult (libraries.ucsd.edu/ssds/pub/CTS/tobacco/sales). The Centers for Disease Control and Prevention track cigarette smoking in the United States. How has the percentage of people who smoke changed since the danger became clear during the last half of the 20th century? The scatterplot shows percentages of smokers among men 18–24 years of age, as estimated by surveys. (Centers for Disease Control and Prevention; www.cdc.gov/nchs/)

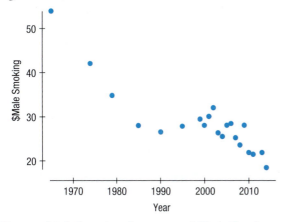

a) Do you think there is a clear pattern? Describe the trend.
b) Is the association strong?
c) Is a linear model appropriate for these data? Explain.

T 23. Human Development Index (HDI) 2016. The United Nations Development Programme (UNDP) collects data in the developing world to help countries solve global and national development challenges. In the UNDP annual Human Development Report, you can find data on over 100 variables for each of 197 countries worldwide. One summary measure used by the agency is the Human Development Index (HDI), which attempts to summarize

in a single number the progress in health, education, and economics of a country. In 2012, the HDI was as high as 0.955 for Norway and as low as 0.304 for the Congo and Niger. The gross national income per capita (GNI/cap), by contrast, is often used to summarize the *overall* economic strength of a country. Is the HDI related to the GNI/cap? (Data in **HDI 2016**)

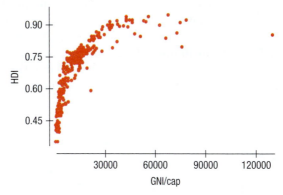

a) Explain why fitting a linear model to these data would be misleading.
b) If you fit a linear model to the data, what do you think a scatterplot of residuals versus predicted *HDI* will look like?
c) Qatar has an extraordinarily high GNI/cap and Equitorial Guinea has a very low *HDI* for its GNI/cap. Will setting these points aside improve the model substantially? Explain.

T 24. Human Development Index 2016, part 2. The United Nations Development Programme (UNDP) uses the Human Development Index (HDI) in an attempt to summarize in one number the progress in health, education, and economics of a country. The mean years of schooling is positively associated with HDI. Can that be used to predict the HDI? Here is a scatterplot:

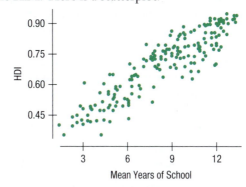

a) Would it be appropriate to fit a linear model to these data?
b) If you fit a linear model to the data, what do you think a scatterplot of residuals versus predicted *HDI* will look like?

25. Good model? In justifying his choice of a model, a consultant says "I know this is the correct model because $R^2 = 99.4\%$."

a) Is this reasoning correct? Explain.
b) Does this model allow the consultant to make accurate predictions? Explain.

26. Bad model? An intern who has created a linear model is disappointed to find that her R^2 value is a very low 13%.

a) Does this mean that a linear model is not appropriate? Explain.
b) Does this model allow the intern to make accurate predictions? Explain.

T 27. Movie budgets. Here's a scatterplot of the production budgets (in millions of dollars) vs. the running time (in minutes) for a collection of major movies. Dramas are plotted in red and all other genres are plotted in blue. A separate least squares regression line has been fitted to each group. For the following questions, just examine the plot:

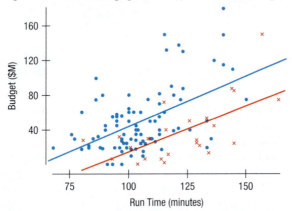

a) What are the units for the slopes of these lines?
b) In what way are dramas and other movies similar with respect to this relationship?
c) In what way are dramas different from other genres of movies with respect to this relationship?

T 28. Movie revenues. How does what a movie earns relate to its run time? Will audiences pay more for a longer film? Does the relationship depend on the type of film?

The scatterplot shows the relationship for the films in Exercise 27 between *U.S. Gross* earnings and *Run Time*. Dramas are plotted with purple dots, comedies with green squares, horror/thriller/action films with blue diamonds, and adventure movies with orange crosses. Regression lines have been drawn for each type of movie. (Data in **Movie budgets**)

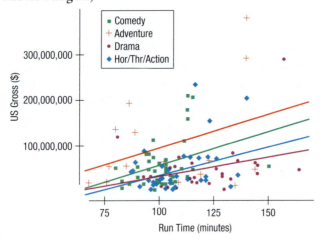

a) In what ways is the relationship between run times and U.S. Gross similar for the four kinds of films?
b) How do the gross receipts of adventure films (the red line on top) differ from those of comedies (the green line below the red)? Discuss both the slopes and the intercepts.
c) The film *Harry Potter and the Goblet of Fire* is the purple point in the upper right. If it were omitted from this analysis, how might that change your conclusions about dramas?

T 29. Oakland passengers. Much attention has been paid to the challenges faced by the airline industry. Patterns in customer demand are an important variable to watch. The scatterplot below shows the number of passengers departing from Oakland (CA) airport month by month from 1990 to 2007. Time is shown as years since 1990, with fractional years used to represent each month. (Data selected from **Oakland passengers 2016**)

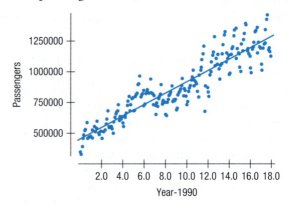

Here's a regression with the residuals plotted against the predicted values

```
R squared = 85.2%   s = 100359

Variable         Coefficient
Intercept          455650
year-1990           46131.3
```

a) Interpret the slope and intercept of the regression model.
b) What does the value of R^2 say about how successful the model is?
c) Interpret s_e in this context.
d) Would you use this model to predict the numbers of passengers in 2010 (*Years* − *1990* = 20)? Explain.

T **30. Tracking hurricanes 2016.** Like many businesses, The National Hurricane Center also participates in a program to improve the quality of data and predictions by government agencies. They report their errors in predicting the path of hurricanes. The following scatterplot shows the trend in 48-hour tracking errors since 1970. (www.nhc .noaa.gov/verification/pdfs/1970-present_OFCL_ATL_ annual_trk_errors_noTDs.pdf)

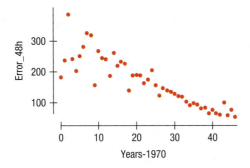

```
Response variable is: Error_48h
R squared = 78.1%   s = 38.00

Variable        Coefficient
Intercept       290.5
Year-1970        -5.16941
```

a) Interpret the slope and intercept of the regression model.
b) Interpret s_e in this context.
c) If the Center had a goal of achieving an average tracking error of 30 nautical miles by 2020, will they make it? Explain.
d) What cautions would you state about your conclusion?

31. Unusual points. Each of the four scatterplots a–d that follow shows a cluster of points and one "stray" point. For each, answer questions 1–4:

1) In what way is the point unusual? Does it have high leverage, a large residual, or both?
2) Do you think that point is an influential point?
3) If that point were removed from the data, would the correlation become stronger or weaker? Explain.
4) If that point were removed from the data, would the slope of the regression line increase, decrease, or remain the same? Explain.

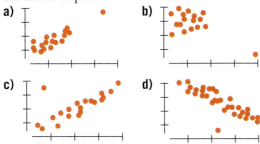

32. More unusual points. Each of the following scatterplots a–d shows a cluster of points and one "stray" point. For each, answer questions 1–4:

1) In what way is the point unusual? Does it have high leverage, a large residual, or both?
2) Do you think that point is an influential point?
3) If that point were removed from the data, would the correlation become stronger or weaker? Explain.
4) If that point were removed from the data, would the slope of the regression line increase, decrease, or remain the same? Explain.

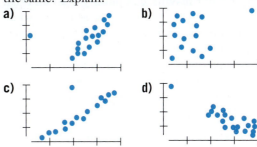

33. The extra point. The scatterplot shows five blue data points at the left. Not surprisingly, the correlation for these points is $r = 0$. Suppose *one* additional data point is added at one of the five positions suggested below in green. Match each point (a–e) with the correct new correlation from the list given.

1) -0.90
2) -0.40
3) 0.00
4) 0.05
5) 0.75

34. The extra point, part 2. The original five points in Exercise 33 produce a regression line with slope 0. Match each of the green points (a–e) with the slope of the line after that one point is added:

1) -0.45
2) -0.30
3) 0.00
4) 0.05
5) 0.85

35. What's the cause? A researcher gathering data for a pharmaceutical firm measures blood pressure and the percentage of body fat for several adult males and finds a strong positive association. Describe three different possible cause-and-effect relationships that might be present.

36. What's the effect? Published reports about violence in computer games have become a concern to developers and distributors of these games. One firm commissioned a study of violent behavior in elementary-school children. The researcher asked the children's parents how much time each child spent playing computer games and had their teachers rate each child's level of aggressiveness when playing with other children. The researcher found a moderately strong positive correlation between computer game time and aggressiveness score. But does this mean that playing computer games increases aggression in children? Describe three different possible cause-and-effect explanations for this relationship.

37. Heating cost. Small businesses must track every expense. A flower shop owner tracked her costs for heating and related it to the average daily Fahrenheit temperature, finding the model $\widehat{Cost} = 133 - 2.13\ Temp$. The residuals plot for her data is shown.

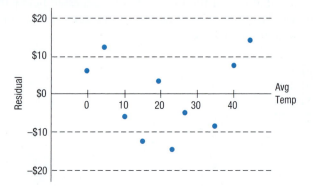

a) Interpret the slope of the line in this context.
b) Interpret the y-intercept of the line in this context.
c) During months when the temperature stays around freezing, would you expect cost predictions based on this model to be accurate, too low, or too high? Explain.
d) What heating cost does the model predict for a month that averages 10°?
e) During one of the months on which the model was based, the temperature did average 10°. What were the actual heating costs for that month?
f) Do you think the home owner should use this model? Explain.
g) Would this model be more successful if the temperature were expressed in degrees Celsius? Explain.

38. Fuel economy. How does the speed at which a car drives affect fuel economy? Owners of a taxi fleet, watching their bottom line sink beneath fuel costs, hired a research firm to tell them the optimal speed for their taxis to drive. Researchers drove a compact car for 200 miles at speeds ranging from 35 to 75 miles per hour. From their data, they created the model $\widehat{Fuel\ Efficiency} = 32 - 0.1\ Speed$ and created this residual plot:

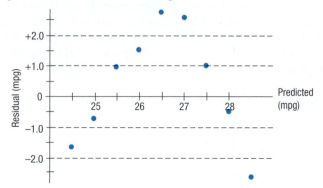

a) Interpret the slope of this line in context.
b) Explain why it's silly to attach any meaning to the y-intercept.
c) When this model predicts high *Fuel Efficiency*, what can you say about those predictions?
d) What *Fuel Efficiency* does the model predict when the car is driven at 50 mph?
e) What was the actual *Fuel Efficiency* when the car was driven at 45 mph?
f) Do you think there appears to be a strong association between *Speed* and *Fuel Efficiency*? Explain.
g) Do you think this is the appropriate model for that association? Explain.

39. Historical interest rates. Here's a plot showing the federal rate on 3-month Treasury bills from 1950 to 1980, and a regression model fit to the relationship between the *Rate* (in %) and *Years since 1950*. (www.gpoaccess.gov/eop/)

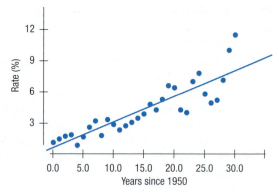

```
Dependent variable is: Rate
R-squared = 77.4%   s = 1.239

Variable      Coeff
Intercept     0.640282
Year-1950     0.247637
```

a) What is the correlation between *Rate* and *Year*?
b) Interpret the slope and intercept.
c) What does this model predict for the interest rate in the year 2000?
d) Would you expect this prediction to have been accurate? Explain.

T **40. Marriage age 2017, part 2.** In Exercise 21 we looked at the age at which women married as one of the variables considered by those selling wedding services. Another variable of concern is the *difference* in age of the two partners. The graph shows the ages of both men and women at first marriage. (www.census.gov)

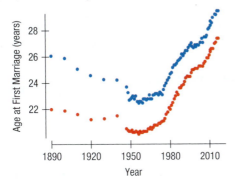

Clearly, the pattern for men is similar to the pattern for women. But are the two lines getting closer together?

Here is a timeplot showing the *difference* in average age (men's age – women's age) at first marriage, the regression analysis, and the associated residuals plot.

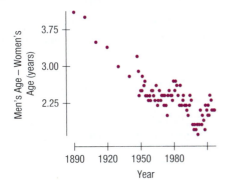

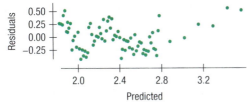

```
R squared = 69.9%   s = 0.2487

Variable      Coefficient
Intercept     29.6175
Year          −0.013782
```

a) What is the correlation between *Age Difference* and *Year*?
b) Interpret the slope of this line.
c) Predict the average age difference in 2025.
d) Describe reasons why you might not place much faith in that prediction.

41. Modern interest rates. In Exercise 39 you investigated the federal rate on 3-month Treasury bills between 1950 and 1980. The scatterplot below shows that the trend

changed dramatically after 1980, so we've built a new regression model that includes only the data since 1980 (from $x = 30$ and on in the plot below).

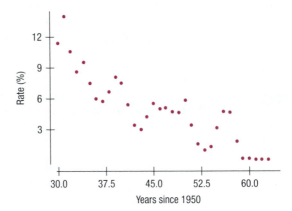

```
Dependent variable is: Rate
R-squared = 78.3%   s = 1.644

Variable      Coeff
Intercept     19.2024
Year-50       −0.30871
```

a) How does this model compare to the one in Exercise 39?
b) What does this model estimate the interest rate to have been in 2000? How does this compare to the rate you predicted in Exercise 39?
c) Do you trust this newer predicted value? Explain.
d) Given these two models, what would you predict the interest rate on 3-month Treasury bills will be in 2025?

T **42. Marriage age 2017, part 3.** Here is a regression of Women's age vs. Men's age, and a plot of the residuals.

```
Response variable is: Women
R squared = 96.7%   s = 0.4256

Variable      Coefficient
Intercept     −4.19569
Men            1.07254
```

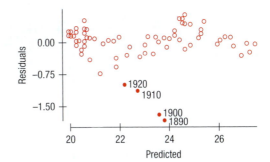

a) The residual plot shows 4 outliers, labeled according to the years they correspond to. Explain what they say about the data for those years.
b) Even though *Year* is not plotted here, you have enough information from the previously shown displays of these data to tell where the most recent points are on this plot of residuals. Explain.

43. Colorblind. Although some women are colorblind, this condition is found primarily in men. An advertisement for socks marked so they were easy for someone who was colorblind to match started out "There's a strong correlation between sex and colorblindness." Explain in statistics terms why this isn't a correct statement (whether or not it might be a good ad).

44. New homes. A real estate agent collects data to develop a model that will use the *Size* of a new home (in square feet) to predict its *Sale Price* (in thousands of dollars). Which of these is most likely to be the slope of the regression line: 0.008, 0.08, 0.8, or 8? Explain.

45. Residuals. Suppose you have fit a linear model to some data and now take a look at the residuals. For each of the following possible residuals plots, tell whether you would try a re-expression and, if so, why.

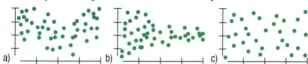

46. Residuals, part 2. Suppose you have fit a linear model to some data and now take a look at the residuals. For each of the following possible residuals plots, tell whether you would try a re-expression and, if so, why.

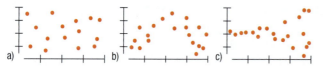

T 47. Oakland passengers, part 2. In Exercise 29, we created a linear model describing the trend in the number of passengers departing from Oakland (CA) airport each month from 1997 to 2007. Here's the residual plot, but with lines added to show the order of the values in time:

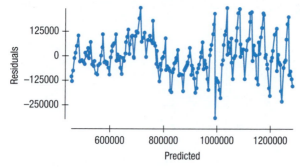

a) Can you account for the pattern shown here?
b) Would a re-expression help us deal with this pattern? Explain.

T 48. Home Depot sales. The home retail industry experienced relatively consistent annual growth until the economic crisis of 2006. Here is a scatterplot of the *Net Sales* ($B) of *The Home Depot* from 1995 through 2004, along with a regression and a time series plot of the residuals.

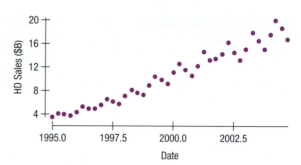

Dependent variable is: HDSales
R-squared = 95.5%
s = 1.044 with 40 − 2 = 38 degrees of freedom

Variable	Coeff	SE(Coeff)	t-ratio	P-value
Constant	−3234.87	114.4	−28.3	<0.0001
Date	1.62283	0.0572	28.4	<0.0001

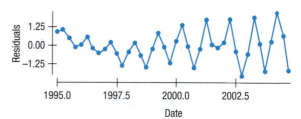

a) What does the R^2 value in the regression mean?
b) What features of the residuals should be noted with regards to this regression?
c) What features of the residuals might be dealt with by a re-expression? Which ones would not be helped by a re-expression?
d) Can you use the regression model to help in your understanding of the growth of this market?

49. Models. For each of the models listed below, predict y when $x = 2$.

a) $\hat{y} = 1.2 + 0.8x$
b) $\widehat{\ln y} = 1.2 + 0.8x$
c) $\widehat{\sqrt{y}} = 1.2 + 0.8x$
d) $\widehat{1/y} = 1.2 + 0.8x$
e) $\hat{y} = 1.2x^{0.8}$

50. More models. For each of the models listed below, predict y when $x = 2$.

a) $\hat{y} = 1.2 + 0.8 \log x$
b) $\log \hat{y} = 1.2 + 0.8x$
c) $\hat{y} = 1.2 + 0.8\sqrt{x}$
d) $\hat{y} = 1.2(0.8^x)$
e) $\hat{y} = 0.8x^2 + 1.2x + 1$

51. Models, again. Find the predicted value of y, using each model for $x = 10$.

a) $\hat{y} = 2 + 0.8 \ln x$
b) $\widehat{\log y} = 5 - 0.23x$
c) $\dfrac{1}{\sqrt{\hat{y}}} = 17.1 - 1.66x$

52. Models, last time. Find the predicted value of *y*, using each model when $x = 4$.

a) $\hat{y} = 10 + \sqrt{x}$

b) $\dfrac{1}{\hat{y}} = 14.5 - 3.45x$

c) $\sqrt{\hat{y}} = 3.0 + 0.5x$

T 53. Lobsters 2016. According to the Maine Department of Marine Resources, in 2016 more than 130,800,000 pounds of lobster were landed in Maine—a catch worth more than $533.09M. The lobster fishing industry is carefully controlled and licensed, and facts about it have been recorded for more than a century, so it is an important industry that we can examine in detail. We'll look at annual data (available at www.maine.gov/dmr) from 1950 through 2016.

The value of the annual lobster catch has grown. Here's a scatterplot of the value in millions of dollars over time:

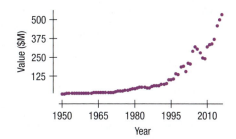

a) Which regression assumptions and conditions appear to be violated according to this plot?

Here's a scatterplot of the *log* of the value:

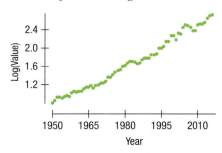

b) Discuss the same assumptions as in part a. Does taking logs make these data suitable for regression?

After performing a regression on the log values, we obtain the following plot of residuals:

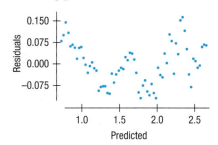

c) Discuss what this plot shows. Would a different transformation be likely to do better than the *log*? Explain.

T 54. Lobsters 2016, part 2. Lobster are caught in traps, which are baited and left in the open ocean. Licenses to fish for lobster are limited, there is a small additional fee for each trap in use, and there are limits on the numbers of traps that can be placed in each of seven fishing zones. But those limits have changed over time. Here's a scatterplot of the number of traps per licensed lobster fisher over time:

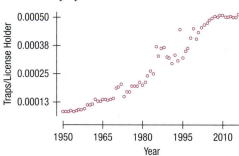

a) Does this plot satisfy the regression assumptions and conditions? Explain.

A regression of *Traps/Fisher* vs. *Year* yields the following plot of residuals:

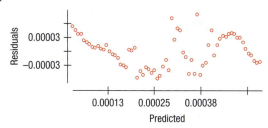

b) What can you see in the plots of residuals that may not have been clear in the original scatterplot of the data?

T 55. GDP and DJIA 2017. Does the Dow Jones Industrial Average (DJIA) reflect the economy as measured by the Gross Domestic Product (GDP)? Here's a plot and a regression. (Both are converted to 2010 dollars to remove the effects of inflation. GDP is in $B to make the numbers manageable.)

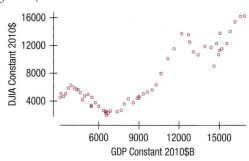

```
Response variable is: DJIA (2010$)
R squared = 72.5%   s = 2242

Variable          Coefficient
Intercept         -492.074
GDP(2010$B)          0.839340
```

a) Interpret the slope coefficient of this regression.

b) What does the R^2 report?

T **56. Lobsters 2016, part 3.** Of course, what matters most to the individual entrepreneur—the licensed commercial lobster fisher—is the price of lobster. Here's an analysis relating that price ($/lb) to the number of traps (millions) since 1950:

```
Dependent variable is: Price/lb
R squared = 92.8%
s = 0.3399

Variable      Coefficient
Intercept      -0.2750
Traps(M)        1.2522
```

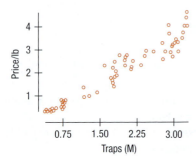

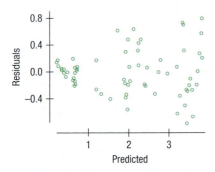

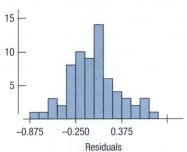

a) Are the assumptions and conditions for regression inference satisfied?

b) What does the coefficient of *Traps* mean in this model? Does it predict that licensing more traps would cause an increase in the price of lobster? Suggest some alternative explanations.

T **57. GDP 2017.** The scatterplot shows the gross domestic product (GDP) of the United States in trillions of (2010) dollars plotted against years since 1960. (Data in **GDP and DJIA 2017**)

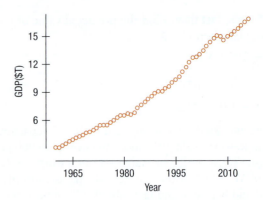

A linear model fit to the relationship looks like this: (We've included much of the regression table as you'd see it from a statistics program.)

```
Response variable is: GDP($T)
R squared = 98.0%  R squared (adjusted) = 98.0%
s = 0.6088 with 57 - 2 = 55 degrees of freedom

Variable     Coefficient   SE(Coeff)   t-ratio   P-value
Intercept     -500.348       9.744      -51.4    <0.0001
Year            0.256307     0.0049      52.3    <0.0001
```

a) Does the value 98.0% suggest that this is a good model? Explain.

b) Here's a scatterplot of the residuals. Now do you think this is a good model for these data? Explain?

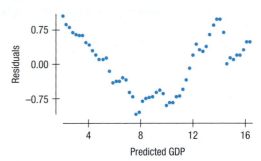

T **58. GDP 2017, part 2.** Consider again the post-1960 trend in U.S. GDP we examined in Exercise 57. Here are a regression and residual plot when we use the square root of GDP in the model. Is this a better model for GDP? Explain. (Data in **GDP and DJIA 2017**)

```
Response variable is: √GDP
R squared = 99.4%  R squared (adjusted) = 99.4%
s = 0.0554 with 57 - 2 = 55 degrees of freedom

Variable     Coefficient   SE(Coeff)   t-ratio   P-value
Intercept    -83.2810       0.8867      -93.9    <0.0001
Year           0.043374     0.0004       97.2    <0.0001
```

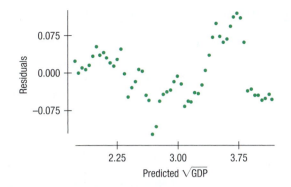

59. Logs (not logarithms). Many professions use tables to determine key quantities. The value of a log is based on the number of board feet of lumber the log may contain. (A board foot is the equivalent of a piece of wood 1 inch thick, 12 inches wide, and 1 foot long. For example, a $2'' \times 4''$ piece that is 12 feet long contains 8 board feet.) To estimate the amount of lumber in a log, buyers measure the diameter inside the bark at the smaller end. Then they look in a table based on the Doyle Log Scale. The table below shows the estimates for logs 16 feet long.

Diameter of Log	8″	12″	16″	20″	24″	28″
Board Feet	16	64	144	256	400	576

a) What transformation of *Board Feet* makes this relationship linear?
b) Based on a linear regression using this transformation, How much lumber would you estimate that a log 10 inches in diameter contains?
c) What does this model suggest about logs 36 inches in diameter?

60. Life expectancy U.S. Life insurance rates are based on life expectancy values compiled for large demographic groups. But with improvements in medical care and nutrition, life expectancies have been changing. Here is a table from the National Vital Statistics Report that gives the Life Expectancy for white males in the United States every decade during the last century (1 = 1900 to 1910, 2 = 1911 to 1920, etc.). Consider a linear model to predict future increases in life expectancy. Would re-expressing either variable make a better model?

Decade	1	2	3	4	5	6	7	8	9	10
Life exp.	48.6	54.4	59.7	62.1	66.5	67.4	68.0	70.7	72.7	74.9

61. OECD GDP. The Organization for Economic Cooperation and Development (OECD) is an organization comprised of thirty countries. To belong, a country must support the principles of representative democracy and a free market economy. How have these countries grown in the decade from 1988 to 1998–2000? Here are the GDP per capita for 24 of the OECD members (in year 2000 dollars). (www.sba.gov/advo/research/rs264tot.pdf)

Country	1988 GDP/Capita	1998–2000 GDP/Capita
Australia	18,558	23,713
Austria	25,626	31,192
Belgium	24,204	30,506
Canada	19,349	22,605
Denmark	31,517	38,136
Finland	25,682	31,246
France	24,663	29,744
Germany	27,196	32,256
Greece	10,606	13,181
Ireland	13,050	27,282
Italy	17,339	20,710
Japan	36,301	44,154
Korea	7038	12,844
Mexico	3024	3685
Netherlands	23,159	30,720
New Zealand	15,480	17,979
Norway	28,241	37,934
Portugal	8935	12,756
Spain	12,879	17,197
Sweden	26,634	30,873
Switzerland	43,375	46,330
Turkey	2457	2947
United Kingdom	17,676	22,153
United States	25,324	31,296

Make a model of 1998–2000 GDP/Capita in terms of 1988 GDP/Capita. Plot the residuals and discuss any concerns you may have.

T 62. Orange production. Orange growers know that the larger an orange the higher the price it will bring. But as the number of oranges on a tree increases, the fruit tends to be smaller. Here's a table of that relationship. Create a model for this relationship, and express any concerns you may have. (Data in **Oranges**)

Number of Oranges/Tree	Average Weight/ Fruit (lb)
50	0.60
100	0.58
150	0.56
200	0.55
250	0.53
300	0.52
350	0.50
400	0.49
450	0.48
500	0.46
600	0.44
700	0.42
800	0.40
900	0.38

JUST CHECKING ANSWERS

1 Not high-leverage, not influential, large residual
2 High-leverage, not influential, small residual
3 High-leverage, influential, not large residual
4 None
5 Logarithm

Multiple Regression

Zillow.com

Zillow.com is a real estate research site, founded in 2005 by Rich Barton and Lloyd Frink. Both are former Microsoft executives and founders of Expedia.com, the Internet-based travel agency. Zillow collects publicly available data and provides an estimate (called a Zestimate®) of a home's worth. The estimate is based on a model of the data that Zillow has been able to collect on a variety of predictor variables, including the past history of the home's sales, the location of the home, and characteristics of the house such as its size and number of bedrooms and bathrooms.

The site is enormously popular among both potential buyers and sellers of homes. According to Rismedia.com, Zillow is one of the most-visited U.S. real estate sites on the Web, with approximately 5 million unique users each month. These users include more than one-third of all mortgage professionals in the U.S.—or approximately 125,000—in any given month. Additionally, 90% of Zillow users are homeowners, and two-thirds are either buying and selling now, or plan to in the near future.

ow exactly does Zillow figure the worth of a house? According to the Zillow.com site, "We compute this figure by taking zillions of data points—much of this data is public—and entering them into a formula. This formula is built using what our statisticians call 'a proprietary algorithm'—big words for 'secret formula.' When our statisticians developed the model to determine home values, they explored how homes in certain areas were similar (i.e., number of bedrooms and baths, and a myriad of other details) and then looked at the relationships between actual sale prices and those home details." These relationships form a pattern, and they use that pattern to develop a model to estimate a market value for a home. In other words, the Zillow statisticians use a model, most likely a regression model, to predict home value from the characteristics of the house. We've seen how to predict a response variable based on a single predictor. That's been useful, but the types of business decisions we'll want to make are often too complex for simple regression.[1] In this chapter, we'll expand the power of the regression model to take into account many predictor variables into what's called a multiple regression model. With our understanding of simple regression as a base, getting to multiple regression isn't a big step, but it's an important and worthwhile one. Multiple regression is probably the most powerful and widely used statistical tool today.

As anyone who's ever looked at house prices knows, house prices depend on the local market. To control for that, we will restrict our attention to a single market. We have a random sample of 1057 home sales from the public records of sales in upstate New York, in the region around the city of Saratoga Springs. (Data in **Housing prices**) The first thing often mentioned in describing a house for sale is the number of bedrooms. Let's start with just one predictor variable. Can we use *Bedrooms* to predict home *Price*?

WHO	Houses
WHAT	Sale price (dollars) and other facts about the houses
WHERE	Upstate New York near Saratoga Springs
WHY	To understand what influences housing prices and how to predict them

FIGURE 18.1 Side-by-side boxplots of *Price* against *Bedrooms* show that price increases, on average, with more bedrooms.

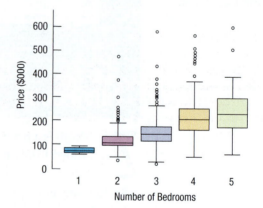

The number of *Bedrooms* is a quantitative variable, but it holds only a few values (from 1 to 5 in this dataset). So a scatterplot may not be the best way to examine the relationship between *Bedrooms* and *Price*. In fact, at each value for *Bedrooms* there is a whole distribution of prices. Side-by-side boxplots of *Price* against *Bedrooms* (Figure 18.1) show a general increase in price with more bedrooms, and an approximately linear growth.

Figure 18.1 also shows a clearly increasing spread from left to right, violating the Equal Spread Condition, and that's a possible sign of trouble. For now, we'll proceed cautiously. We'll fit the regression model, but we will be cautious about using inference methods for the model. Later we'll add more variables to increase the power and usefulness of the model.

---

[1]When we need to note the difference, a regression with a single predictor is called a **simple regression**.

SUMMARY OUTPUT				
Response Variable is Price				
Regression Statistics				
R Square	0.214			
Standard Error	68432.21			
Observations	1057			
	Coefficients	Standard Error	t Stat	P-value
Intercept	14349.48	9297.69	1.54	0.1230
Bedrooms	48218.91	2843.88	16.96	0.0000

A linear regression model of *Price* on *Bedrooms* gives the model

$$\widehat{Price} = 14349.48 + 48218.91 \times Bedrooms.$$

The model tells us that, on average, we'd expect the price to be higher by almost $50,000 for each bedroom in the house, as we can see from the slope value of $48,218.91. But the R^2 for this regression is only 21.4%. So the regression model accounts for about 21.4% of the variation in house prices. Perhaps some of the other facts about these houses can account for portions of the remaining variation.

The standard deviation of the residuals is $s = 68,432$, which tells us that the model only does a modestly good job of accounting for the price of a home. Approximating with the 68–95–99.7 Rule, we'd guess that only about 68% of home prices predicted by this model would be within $68,432 of the actual price. That's not likely to be close enough to be useful for a home buyer.

18.1 The Multiple Regression Model

For simple regression, we wrote the predicted values in terms of one predictor variable:

$$\hat{y} = b_0 + b_1 x.$$

To include more predictors in the model, we simply write the same regression model with more predictor variables. The resulting **multiple regression** looks like this:

$$\hat{y} = b_0 + b_1 x_1 + b_2 x_2 + \cdots + b_k x_k$$

where b_0 is still the intercept and each b_k is the estimated coefficient of its corresponding predictor x_k. Although the model doesn't look much more complicated than a simple regression, it isn't practical to determine a multiple regression by hand. This is a job for a statistics program on a computer. Remember that for simple regression, we found the coefficients for the model using the least squares solution, the one whose coefficients made the sum of the squared residuals as small as possible. For multiple regression, a statistics package does the same thing and can find the coefficients of the least squares model easily.

If you know how to find the regression of *Price* on *Bedrooms* using a statistics package, you can probably just add another variable to the list of predictors in your program to compute a multiple regression. A multiple regression of *Price* on the two variables *Bedrooms* and *Living Area* generates a multiple regression table like the one in Table 18.1.

```
Response variable: Price
R² = 57.8%
s = 50142.4 with 1057 − 3 = 1054 degrees of freedom
```

Variable	Coeff	SE(Coeff)	t-ratio	P-value
Intercept	20986.09	6816.3	3.08	0.0021
Bedrooms	−7483.10	2783.5	−2.69	0.0073
Living Area	93.84	3.11	30.18	<0.0001

TABLE 18.1 Multiple regression output for the linear model predicting *Price* from *Bedrooms* and *Living Area*.

You should recognize most of the numbers in this table, and most of them mean what you expect them to. The value of R^2 for a regression on two variables gives the fraction of the variability of *Price* accounted for by both predictor variables together. With *Bedrooms* alone predicting *Price*, the R^2 value was 21.4%, but this model accounts for 57.8% of the variability in *Price* and the standard deviation of the residuals is now $50,142.40. We shouldn't be surprised that the variability explained by the model has gone up. It was for this reason—the hope of accounting for some of that leftover variability—that we introduced a second predictor. We also shouldn't be surprised that the size of the house, as measured by *Living Area*, also contributes to a good prediction of house prices. Collecting the coefficients of the multiple regression of *Price* on *Bedrooms* and *Living Area* from Table 18.1, we can write the estimated regression as:

$$\widehat{Price} = 20{,}986.09 - 7{,}483.10 Bedrooms + 93.84 Living\ Area.$$

As before, we define the residuals as:

$$e = y - \hat{y}.$$

The standard deviation of the residuals is still denoted s (or also sometimes s_e to distinguish it from the standard deviation of y). The degrees of freedom is the number of observations ($n = 1057$) minus one for each coefficient estimated:

$$df = n - k - 1,$$

where k is the number of predictor variables and n is the number of cases. For this model, subtract 3 (the two coefficients and the intercept). To find the standard deviation of the residuals, use that number of degrees of freedom in the denominator:

$$s_e = \sqrt{\frac{\sum (y - \hat{y})^2}{n - k - 1}}.$$

For each predictor, the regression output shows a coefficient, its standard error, a *t*-ratio, and the corresponding P-value. As with simple regression, the **t-ratio** measures how many standard errors the coefficient is away from 0. Using a Student's t-model, we can find its P-value and use that to test the null hypothesis that the true value of the coefficient is 0.

What's different? With so much of the multiple regression looking just like simple regression, why devote an entire chapter to the subject?

There are several answers to this question. First, and most important, is that the meaning of the coefficients in the regression model has changed in a subtle, but important, way. Because that change is not obvious, multiple regression coefficients are often misinterpreted. And that can lead to dangerously wrong decisions.

Second, multiple regression is an extraordinarily versatile model, underlying many widely used statistics methods. A sound understanding of the multiple regression model will help you to understand these other applications as well.

Third, multiple regression offers you a first glimpse into statistical models that use more than two quantitative variables. The real world is complex. Simple models are a great start, but they're not detailed enough to be useful for understanding, predicting, and making business decisions in many real-world situations. Models that use several variables can be a big step toward realistic and useful modeling of complex phenomena and relationships.

IN PRACTICE 18.1 The multiple regression model

A large clothing store has recently sent out a special catalog of Fall clothes, and Leiram, its marketing analyst, wants to find out which customers responded to it and which ones bought the most. She plans to conduct an RFM (Recency, Frequency, Monetary) analysis. The RFM method is based on the principle that 80% of your business comes from the best 20% of your customers, and states that the following attributes will be useful predictors of who the best customers will be:

- How *recently* the customer has purchased (Recency)
- How *frequently* the customer shops (Frequency)
- How *much* the customer spends (Monetary)

For each customer, Leiram has information for the past 5 years on: *Date of Last Purchase*, *Number of Purchases*, and *Total Amount Spent*. In addition, she has demographic information including *Age, Marital Status, Sex, Income*, and *Number of Children*. She chooses a random sample of 149 customers who bought something from the catalog and who have purchased at least 3 times in the past 5 years (*Number of Purchases*). She wants to model how much they bought from the new catalog (*Respond Amount*).

Leiram fits the following multiple regression model to the response variable *Respond Amount*:

```
Response Variable: Respond Amount
R² = 91.48% Adjusted R² = 91.31%
s = 18.183 with 149 − 4 = 145 degrees of freedom

Variable              Coeff      SE(Coeff)   t-ratio    P-value
Intercept             111.01     6.459       17.187     <0.0001
Income                0.00091    0.00012     7.643      <0.0001
Total Amount Spent    0.154      0.00852     18.042     <0.0001
Number of Purchases   −14.81     0.716       −20.695    <0.0001
```

MANAGER This looks interesting. How much of the variation in *Respond Amount* is explained by this model? What does the term $s = 18.183$ mean? Which variables seem important in the model?

ANALYST (LEIRAM) This model has an R^2 of 91.48%, which means that the model has explained 91.48% of the variation in *Respond Amount* using the three predictors: *Income, Total Amount Spent*, and *Number of Purchases*. The term $s = 18.183$ means that the standard deviation of the residuals is about $18.18. Using the 68–95–99.7 Rule we know that most prediction errors will be no larger than about $36.36. All terms seem important in this model, since all three have very large *t*-ratios and correspondingly small P-values.

18.2 Interpreting Multiple Regression Coefficients

It makes sense that both the number of bedrooms and the size of the living area would influence the price of a house. We'd expect both variables to have a positive effect on price—houses with more bedrooms typically sell for more money, as do larger houses. But look at the coefficient for *Bedrooms* in the multiple regression equation. It's negative: −7483.10. How can it be that the coefficient of *Bedrooms* in the multiple regression is negative? And not just slightly negative, its *t*-ratio is large enough for us to be quite confident that the true value is really negative. Yet we saw the coefficient was clearly positive when *Bedrooms* was the sole predictor in the model (Figure 18.2).

The explanation of this apparent paradox is that in a multiple regression, coefficients have a more subtle meaning. Each coefficient takes into account the other predictor(s) in the model.

To see how variables can interact, let's look at a group of similarly sized homes and examine the relationship between *Bedrooms* and *Price* just for houses with 2500 to 3000 square feet of living area (Figure 18.3). For houses of this size, those with *fewer* bedrooms have a higher price, on average, than those with more bedrooms. This makes sense when we think about houses in terms of *both*. A 2500-square-foot

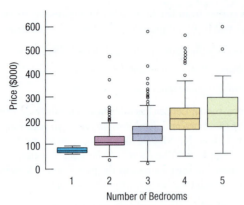

FIGURE 18.2 The slope of *Bedrooms* is positive. Each is worth about $48,000 in the price of a house as the simple regression model estimated.

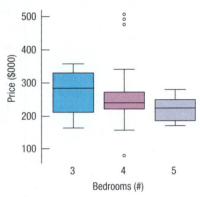

FIGURE 18.3 For the 96 houses with *Living Area* between 2500 and 3000 square feet, the slope of *Price* on *Bedrooms* is negative. If we restricted our data to homes of this size, we would predict that the houses with one more bedroom would have a *Price* about $17,800 lower.

house with five bedrooms would have either relatively small, cramped bedrooms or not much common living space. The same size house with only three bedrooms could have larger, more attractive bedrooms and still have adequate common living space. What the coefficient of *Bedrooms* says in the multiple regression is that, after accounting for living area, houses with more bedrooms tend to sell for a *lower* price—that the pattern for moderate-size homes is generally true across all sizes.

JUST CHECKING

Body fat percentage is an important health indicator, but it is difficult to measure accurately. One way to do so is via dual energy X-ray absorptiometry (DEXA) at a cost of several hundred dollars per image. Insurance companies want to know if body fat percentage can be estimated from easier-to-measure characteristics such as *Height* and *Weight*. A scatterplot of *Percent Body Fat* against *Height* for 250 adult men shows no pattern, and the correlation is -0.03, which is not statistically significant. A multiple regression using *Height (inches)*, *Age (years)*, and *Weight (pounds)* finds the following model: (Data in Bodyfat)

	Coeff	SE(Coeff)	t-ratio	P-value
Intercept	57.27217	10.39897	5.507	<0.0001
Height	−1.27416	0.15801	−8.064	<0.0001
Weight	0.25366	0.01483	17.110	<0.0001
Age	0.13732	0.02806	4.895	<0.0001

s = 5.382 on 246 degrees of freedom
Multiple R-squared: 0.584,
F-statistic: 115.1 on 3 and 246 DF, P-value: <0.0001

1 Interpret the R^2 of this regression model.

2 Interpret the coefficient of *Age*.

3 How can the coefficient of *Height* have such a small P-value in the multiple regression when the correlation between *Height* and *Percent Body Fat* was not statistically distinguishable from zero?

Of course, without taking *Living Area* into account, *Price* tends to go *up* with more bedrooms. But that's because *Living Area* and *Bedrooms* are related. Multiple regression coefficients must always be interpreted in terms of the other predictors in the model. That can make their interpretation more subtle, more complex, and more challenging, but it is also what makes multiple regression so versatile and effective. The more sophisticated interpretations are more appropriate.

People often make another error when interpreting coefficients. Regression coefficients should not be interpreted causally. A regression model describes the world as measured by the data, but it can't say very much about what would happen if things were changed. For example, this analysis cannot tell a homeowner how much the price of his home will change if he combines two of his four bedrooms into a new master bedroom. And it can't be used to predict whether adding a 100-square-foot child's bedroom onto the house would increase or decrease its value. The model simply reports the relationship between the number of *Bedrooms* and *Living Area* and *Price* for existing houses. As always with regression, you should be careful not to assume causation between the predictor variables and the response.

IN PRACTICE 18.2 Interpreting multiple regression coefficients

MANAGER In your regression model of *Respond Amount*, interpret the intercept and the regression coefficients of the three predictors.

ANALYST (LEIRAM) The model says that from a base of $111.01 of spending, customers (who have purchased at least 3 times in the last 12 months), on average, spent $0.91 for every $1000 of *Income* (after accounting for *Number of Purchases* and *Total Amount Spent*), $0.154 for every dollar they have spent in the past 5 years (after accounting for *Income* and *Number of Purchases*), but $14.81 less for every additional purchase that they've made in the last 5 years (after accounting for *Income* and *Total Amount Spent*). It is important to note especially that the coefficient in *Number of Purchases* is negative, but only after accounting for both *Income* and *Total Amount Spent*.

18.3 Assumptions and Conditions for the Multiple Regression Model

We can write the multiple regression model, numbering the predictors arbitrarily (the order doesn't matter), writing betas for the model coefficients (which we will estimate from the data), and including the errors in the model:

$$y = \beta_0 + \beta_1 x_1 + \beta_2 x_2 + \cdots + \beta_k x_k + \varepsilon.$$

The assumptions and conditions for the multiple regression model are nearly the same as for simple regression, but with more variables in the model, we'll have to make a few changes, as described in the following sections.

Linearity Assumption

We are fitting a linear model.[2] For that to be the right kind of model for this analysis, we need to verify an underlying linear relationship. But now we're thinking about several predictors. To confirm that the assumption is reasonable, we'll check the Linearity Condition for *each* of the predictors.

---

[2]By *linear* we mean that each *x* appears simply multiplied by its coefficient and added to the model, and that no *x* appears in an exponent or some other more complicated function. That ensures that as we move along any *x*-variable, our prediction for *y* will change at a constant rate (given by the coefficient) if nothing else changes.

Linearity Condition.   Scatterplots of *y* against each of the predictors are reasonably straight. The scatterplots need not show a strong (or any) slope; just check to make sure that there isn't a bend or other non-linearity. For the real estate data, the scatterplot is linear in both *Bedrooms* and *Living Area*.

As in simple regression, it's a good idea to check the residual plot for any violations of the Linearity Condition. Fit the regression and plot the residuals against the predicted values (Figure 18.4), checking to make sure there are no patterns—especially bends or other non-linearities.

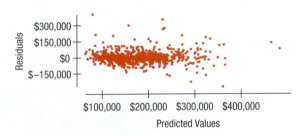

FIGURE 18.4   A scatterplot of residuals against the predicted values shows no obvious pattern.

Independence Assumption

As with simple regression, the errors in the true underlying regression model must be independent of each other. As usual, there's no way to be sure that the Independence Assumption is true, but you should think about how the data were collected to see if that assumption is reasonable. You should check the Randomization Condition as well.

Randomization Condition.   Ideally, the data should arise from a random sample or randomized experiment. Randomization assures us that the data are representative of some identifiable population. If you can't identify the population, you can interpret the regression model as a description of the data you have, but you can't interpret the hypothesis tests at all because such tests are about a regression model for a specific population. Regression methods are often applied to data that were not collected with randomization. Regression models fit to such data may still do a good job of modeling the data at hand, but without some reason to believe that the data are representative of a particular population, you should be reluctant to believe that the model generalizes to other situations.

We also check the regression residuals for evidence of patterns, trends, or clumping, any of which would suggest a failure of independence. In the special case when one of the *x*-variables is related to time (or is itself *Time*), be sure that the residuals do not have a pattern when plotted against that variable. In addition to checking the plot of residuals against the predicted values, we recommend that you check the individual plots of the residuals against each of the explanatory, or *x*, variables in the model. These individual plots can yield important information on necessary transformations, or re-expressions, for the predictor variables.

The real estate data were sampled from a larger set of public records for sales during a limited period of time. The error the model makes in predicting one is not likely to be related to the error it makes in predicting another.

Equal Variance Assumption

The variability of the errors should be about the same for all values of *each* predictor. To see whether this assumption is valid, look at scatterplots and check the Equal Spread Condition.

Equal Spread Condition.   The same scatterplot of residuals against the predicted values (Figure 18.4) is a good check of the consistency of the spread. We saw what appeared to be a violation of the Equal Spread Condition when *Price* was plotted against *Bedrooms* (Figure 18.2). But here in the multiple regression, the problem has dissipated when we look at the residuals. Apparently, much of the tendency of houses with more bedrooms to have greater variability in prices was accounted for in the model when we included *Living Area* as a predictor.

If residual plots show no pattern, if the errors are plausibly independent, and if the plots of residuals against each *x*-variable don't show changes in variation, you can feel good about interpreting the regression model. Before testing hypotheses, however, you must check one final assumption: the Normality Assumption.

Normality Assumption

We assume that the errors around the idealized regression model at any specified values of the *x*-variables follow a Normal model. We need this assumption so that we can use a Student's *t*-model for inference. As with other times when we've used Student's *t*, we'll settle for the residuals satisfying the Nearly Normal Condition. As with means, the assumption is less important as the sample size grows. For large datasets, you have to be careful only of extreme skewness or large outliers. These inference methods will work well even when the residuals are moderately skewed, if the sample size is large. If the distribution of residuals is unimodal and symmetric, there is little to worry about.[3]

Nearly Normal Condition.   Because there is only one set of residuals, this is the same set of conditions we had for simple regression. Look at a histogram or Normal probability plot of the residuals.

FIGURE 18.5   A histogram of the residuals shows a unimodal, symmetric distribution, but the tails seem a bit longer than one would expect from a Normal model. The Normal probability plot confirms that.

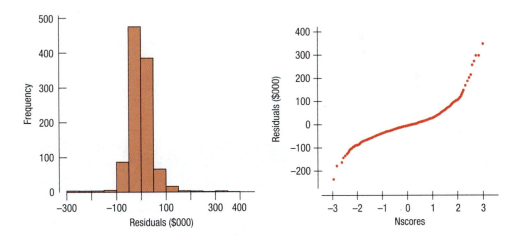

The histogram of residuals in the real estate example certainly looks unimodal and symmetric. The Normal probability plot has some bend on both sides, which indicates that the residuals in the tails straggle away from the center more than Normally distributed data would. However, as we have said before, the Normality Assumption becomes less important as the sample size grows, and here we have no skewness and more than 1000 cases. (The Central Limit Theorem helps our confidence intervals and tests based on the *t*-statistic to be valid when we have large samples.)

---

[3]The only time we need strict adherence to the Normality Assumption of the errors is when finding prediction intervals for individuals in multiple regression. Because they are based on individual Normal probabilities and not the Central Limit Theorem, the errors must closely follow a Normal model.

Let's summarize all the checks of conditions that we've made and the order in which we've made them.

1. Check the Linearity Condition with scatterplots of the *y*-variable against each *x*-variable.
2. If the scatterplots are straight enough, fit a multiple regression model to the data. (Otherwise, either stop or consider re-expressing an *x*-variable or the *y*-variable.)
3. Find the residuals and predicted values.
4. Make a scatterplot of the residuals against the predicted values (and ideally against each predictor variable separately). These plots should look patternless. Check, in particular, for any bend (which would suggest that the data weren't all that straight after all) and for any changes in variation. If there's a bend, consider re-expressing the *y*- and/or the *x*-variables. If the variation in the plot grows from one side to the other, consider re-expressing the *y*-variable. If you re-express a variable, start the model fitting over.
5. Think about how the data were collected. Was suitable randomization used? Are the data representative of some identifiable population? If the data are measured over time, check for evidence of patterns that might suggest they're not independent by plotting the residuals against time to look for patterns.
6. If the conditions check out this far, feel free to interpret the regression model and use it for prediction.
7. Make a histogram and Normal probability plot of the residuals to check the Nearly Normal Condition. If the sample size is large, the Normality is less important for inference, but always be on the lookout for skewness or outliers.

JUST CHECKING

4 Give two ways that we use histograms to support the construction, inference, and understanding of multiple regression models.

5 Give two ways that we use scatterplots to support the construction, inference, and understanding of multiple regression models.

6 What role does the Normal model play in the construction, inference, and understanding of multiple regression models?

IN PRACTICE 18.3   Assumptions and conditions for multiple regression

Here are plots of *Respond Amount* against the three predictors, a plot of the residuals against the predicted values from the multiple regression, a histogram of the residuals, and a Normal probability plot of the residuals. Recall that the data come from a random sample of customers who both responded to the catalog and who had purchased at least 3 times in the past 5 years.

MANAGER Do the assumptions and conditions for multiple regression appear to have been met?

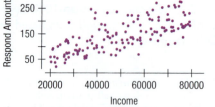

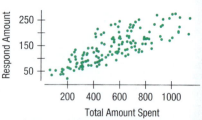

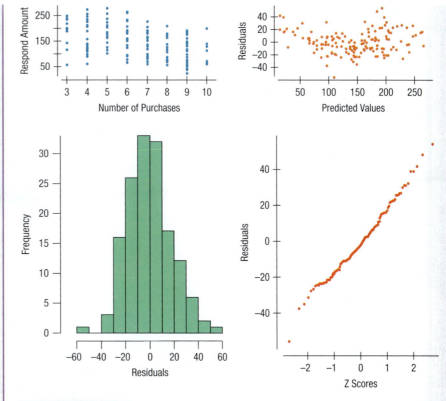

ANALYST (LEIRAM) Because the sample is random, the Randomization Condition is satisfied and we assume the responses are independent. The plots of *Respond Amount* against each predictor are reasonably linear with the possible exception of *Number of Purchases*. There may also be some curvature and increasing spread in the residual plot. The histogram of residuals is unimodal and symmetric with no extreme outliers. The Normal probability plot shows that the distribution is fairly Normally distributed. The conditions are not completely satisfied and we should proceed somewhat cautiously especially with regard to *Number of Purchases*.

GUIDED EXAMPLE   Housing Prices

Zillow.com attracts millions of users each month who are interested in finding out how much their house is worth. Let's see how well a multiple regression model can do. (We're still using the Saratoga Springs housing data in the file **Housing prices**.) The variables available include:

Price　　　The price of the house as sold in 2002
Living Area　The size of the living area of the house in square feet
Bedrooms　　The number of bedrooms
Bathrooms　The number of bathrooms (a half bath is a toilet and sink only)
Age　　　Age of the house in years
Fireplaces　Number of fireplaces in the house

PLAN	**Define** the problem—state the objective of the study. Identify the variables. **Identify** the variables.	We want to build a model to predict house prices for a region in upstate New York. We have data on *Price* ($), *Living Area* (sq ft), *Bedrooms* (#), *Bathrooms* (#), *Fireplaces* (#), and *Age* (in years).

(continued)

DO

Characterize and explore the variables.

Specify the Model. Think about the assumptions and check the conditions.

Linearity Condition

To fit a regression model, we first require linearity. Scatterplots (or side-by-side boxplots) of *Price* against all potential predictor variables are shown.

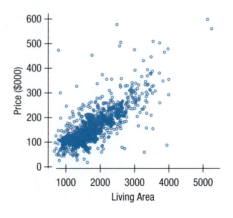

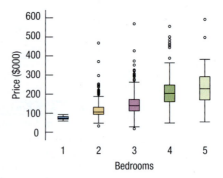

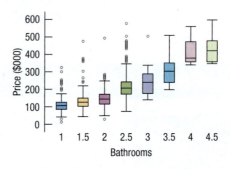

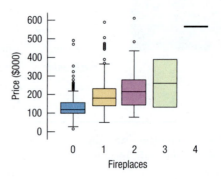

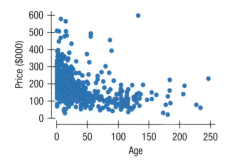

Remarks

There are a few anomalies in the plots that deserve discussion. The plot of *Price* against *Bathrooms* shows a positive relationship, but it is not quite linear. For now, we'll proceed cautiously. The plot of *Price* against *Fireplaces* shows an outlier—an expensive home with four fireplaces. We tried setting this home aside and running the regression without it, but its influence on the coefficients was not large, so we decided to include it in the model. The plot of *Price* against *Age* is not linear and varies more for new houses than for older ones. We may want to consider re-expressing *Age* to improve the linearity of the relationship. For now, we'll try a multiple regression to model *Price* based on all of the predictors. To interpret the P-values, we need to check:

✔ **Independence Assumption.** We can regard the house prices as being independent of one another. The error the regression model makes in predicting one isn't likely to be related to the error it will make in predicting another.

✔ **Randomization Condition.** These 1057 houses are a random sample of a much larger set.

✔ **Equal Spread Condition.** A scatterplot of residuals vs. predicted values shows no evidence of changing spread. There is a group of homes whose residuals are larger (both negative and positive) than the vast majority. This is also seen in the long tails of the histogram of residuals.

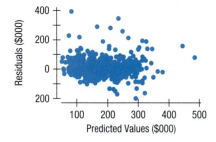

We need the Nearly Normal Condition only if we want to do inference and the sample size is not large. If the sample size is large, as it is here, we need the distribution to be Normal only if we plan to produce prediction intervals.

✔ **Nearly Normal Condition, Outlier Condition.** The histogram of residuals is unimodal and symmetric, but long tailed. The Normal probability plot supports that.

(continued)

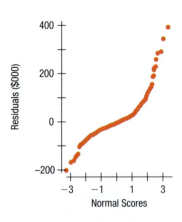
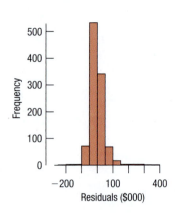

Under these conditions, we can proceed with caution to a multiple regression analysis. We will return to some of our concerns about curvature in some plots in the discussion.

Here is some computer output for the multiple regression, using all five predictors.

	Coeff	SE(Coeff)	t-ratio	P-value
Intercept	15712.702	7311.427	2.149	0.03186
Living Area	73.446	4.009	18.321	<0.0001
Bedrooms	−6361.311	2749.503	−2.314	0.02088
Bathrooms	19236.678	3669.080	5.243	<0.0001
Fireplaces	9162.791	3194.233	2.869	0.00421
Age	−142.740	48.276	−2.957	0.00318

Residual standard error: 48615.95 on 1051 degrees of freedom
Multiple R-squared: 0.6049

F = 321.8 on 5 and 1051 df P < 0.0001

The estimated equation is:

$$\widehat{Price} = 15{,}712.70 + 73.45\,Living\ Area - 6361.31\,Bedrooms + 19{,}236.68\,Bathrooms + 9162.79\,Fireplaces - 142.74\,Age$$

All of the P-values are small, which indicates that even with five predictors in the model, all are contributing. The R^2 value of 60.49% indicates that more than 60% of the overall variation in house prices has been accounted for by this model. The residual standard error of $48,620 gives us a rough indication that we can predict the price of a typical home to within about 2 × $48,620 = $97,240. That seems too large to be useful, but the model does give some idea of the price of a home.

Mechanics We always fit multiple regression models with computer software. An output table like this one isn't exactly what any of the major packages produce, but it is enough like all of them to look familiar.

REPORT

Present your Conclusions
Summarize your results and state any limitations of your model in the context of your original objectives.

MEMO

Re: Regression analysis of home price predictions

A regression model of *Price* on *Living Area, Bedrooms, Bathrooms, Fireplaces,* and *Age* accounts for 60.5% of the variation in the price of homes in upstate New York. The residual standard deviation is $48,620. A statistical test of each coefficient shows that each one is almost certainly not zero, so each of these variables appears to be a contributor to the price of a house.

This model reflects the common wisdom in real estate about the importance of various aspects of a home. An important variable not included is the location, which every real estate agent knows is crucial to pricing a house. This is ameliorated by the fact that all these houses are in the same general area. However, knowing more specific information about where they are located would almost certainly help the model. The price found from this model is to be used as a starting point for comparing a home with comparable homes in the area.

The model may be improved by re-expressing one or more of the predictors, especially *Age* and *Bathrooms*. We recommend caution in interpreting the coefficients across the entire range of these predictors.

18.4   Testing the Multiple Regression Model

There are several hypothesis tests in the multiple regression output, but all of them talk about the same thing. Each is concerned with whether the underlying model parameters (the slopes and intercept) are actually zero. The first of these hypotheses is one we skipped over for simple regression (for reasons that will be clear in a minute).

Now that we have more than one predictor, there's an overall test we should perform before we consider inference for the coefficients. We ask the global question: Is this multiple regression model any good at all? If home prices were set randomly or based on other factors than those we have as predictors, then the best estimate would just be the mean price.

To address the overall question, we'll test the null hypothesis that all the slope coefficients are zero:

$$H_0: \beta_1 = \cdots = \beta_k = 0 \text{ vs. } H_A: \text{ at least one } \beta \neq 0.$$

F-test for Simple Regression?

Why didn't we check the F-test for simple regression? In fact, we did. When you do a simple regression with statistics software, you'll see the F-statistic in the output. But for simple regression, it gives the same information as the *t*-test for the slope. It tests the null hypothesis that the slope coefficient is zero, and we already test that with the *t*-statistic for the slope. In fact, the square of that *t*-statistic is equal to the F-statistic for the simple regression, so it really is the identical test.

We can test this hypothesis with an **F-test**. (It's the generalization of the *t*-test to more than one predictor.) The sampling distribution of the statistic is labeled with the letter F (in honor of Sir Ronald Fisher). The F-distribution has two degrees of freedom, k, the number of predictors, and $n - k - 1$. In the Guided Example, there were $k = 5$ predictors and $n = 1057$ homes, which means that the F-value of 321.8 has 5 and $1057 - 5 - 1 = 1051$ degrees of freedom. The regression output (page 620) shows that it has a P-value < 0.0001. The null hypothesis is that all the coefficients are 0, in which case the regression model predicts no better than the mean. The alternative is that at least one coefficient is non-zero. The test is one-sided—bigger F-values mean smaller P-values. If the null hypothesis were true, the F-statistic would have a value near 1. The F-statistic here is quite large, so we can easily reject the null hypothesis and conclude that the multiple regression model for predicting house prices with these five variables is better than just using the mean.[4]

Once we check the F-test and reject its null hypothesis—and, if we are being careful, *only* if we reject that hypothesis—we can move on to checking the test statistics for the individual coefficients. Those tests look like what we did for the slope of a simple regression in Chapter 15. For each coefficient, we test the null hypothesis that the slope is zero against the (two-sided) alternative that it isn't zero. The regression table gives a standard error for each coefficient and the ratio of

---

[4]To know how big the F-value has to be, we need a table of F-values. There are F tables in the back of the text, and most regression tables include a P-value for the F-statistic.

the estimated coefficient to its standard error. If the assumptions and conditions are met (and now we need the Nearly Normal Condition or a large sample), these ratios follow a Student's t-distribution:

$$t_{n-k-1} = \frac{b_j - 0}{SE(b_j)}.$$

Where did the degrees of freedom $n - k - 1$ come from? We have a rule of thumb that works here. The degrees of freedom value is the number of data values minus the number of estimated coefficients, minus 1 for the intercept. For the house price regression on five predictors, that's $n - 5 - 1$. Almost every regression report includes both the t-statistics and their corresponding P-values.

We can build a confidence interval in the usual way, with an estimate plus or minus a margin of error. As always, the margin of error is the product of the standard error and a critical value. Here the critical value comes from the t-distribution on $n - k - 1$ degrees of freedom, and the standard errors are in the regression table. So a confidence interval for each slope β_j is:

$$b_j \pm t^*_{n-k-1} \times SE(b_j).$$

The tricky parts of these tests are that the standard errors of the coefficients now require harder calculations (so we leave it to technology), and the meaning of a coefficient, as we have seen, depends on all the other predictors in the multiple regression model.

That last point is important. If we fail to reject the null hypothesis for a multiple regression coefficient, it does *not* mean that the corresponding predictor variable has no linear relationship to y. It means that the corresponding predictor contributes nothing to modeling y *after allowing for all the other predictors*.

The multiple regression model looks so simple and straightforward. It *looks* like each β_j tells us the effect of its associated predictor, x_j, on the response variable, y. But that is not true. This is, without a doubt, the most common error that people make with multiple regression. In fact:

- The coefficient β_j in a multiple regression can be quite different from zero even when it is possible there is no simple linear relationship between y and x_j.
- It is even possible that the multiple regression slope changes sign when a new variable enters the regression. We saw this for the *Price* on *Bedrooms* real estate example when *Living Area* was added to the regression.

So we'll say it once more: The coefficient of x_j in a multiple regression depends as much on the *other* predictors as it does on x_j. Failing to interpret coefficients properly is the most common error in working with regression models.

IN PRACTICE 18.4 Testing a multiple regression model

Leiram tries another model, adding the variable *Age* to see if that improves the model:

```
Response Variable: Respond Amount
R² = 91.50%; Adjusted R² = 91.23%
s = 18.179 with 149 − 5 = 144 degrees of freedom
```

Variable	Coeff	SE(Coeff)	t-ratio	P-value
Intercept	114.91	9.244	12.439	<0.0001
Income	0.00091	0.00012	7.619	<0.0001
Total Amount Spent	0.154	0.00855	18.007	<0.0001
Number of Purchases	−14.79	0.719	−20.570	<0.0001
Age	−0.1264	0.2144	−0.5898	0.5563

MANAGER Has the variable *Age* improved the model? Should we leave the term in?

ANALYST (LEIRAM) Of course, we would like to see the residual plots, but given this output it appears that although the R^2 value has increased from 0.9148 to 0.9150, the *t*-ratio for *Age* is only -0.5898 with a P-value of 0.5563. This indicates that there is no evidence to suggest that the slope for *Age* is different from 0. We cannot reject that null hypothesis. There is no reason to leave *Age* in this model.

18.5 Adjusted R^2 and the F-statistic

In Chapter 16, for simple linear regression, we interpreted R^2 as the variation in *y* accounted for by the model. The same interpretation holds for multiple regression, where now the model contains more than one predictor variable. The R^2 value tells us how much (as a fraction or percentage) of the variation in *y* is accounted for by the model with all the predictor variables included.

There are some relationships among the standard error of the residuals, s_e, the F-ratio, and R^2 that are useful for understanding how to assess the value of the multiple regression model. To start, we can write the standard error of the residuals as:

$$s_e = \sqrt{\frac{SSE}{n - k - 1}},$$

where $SSE = \sum e^2$ is called the **Sum of Squared Residuals** (or errors—the E is for error). A larger SSE (and thus s_e) means that the residuals are more variable and that our predictions will be correspondingly less precise.

We can look at the total variation of the response variable, *y*, which is called the **Total Sum of Squares** and is denoted SST: $SST = \sum (y - \bar{y})^2$. For any regression model, we have no control over SST, but we'd like SSE to be as small as we can make it by finding predictor variables that account for as much of that variation as possible. In fact, we can write an equation that relates the total variation SST to SSE:

$$SST = SSR + SSE,$$

where $SSR = \sum (\hat{y} - \bar{y})^2$ is called the **Regression Sum of Squares** because it comes from the predictor variables and tells how much of the total variation in the response is due to the regression model. For a model to account for a large portion of the variability in *y*, SSR should be large and SSE should be small. In fact, R^2 is just the ratio of SSR to SST:

$$R^2 = \frac{SSR}{SST} = 1 - \frac{SSE}{SST}.$$

When the SSE is nearly 0, the R^2 value will be close to 1.

In Chapter 16, we saw that for the relationship between two quantitative variables, testing the standard null hypothesis about the correlation coefficient, $H_0: \rho = 0$, was equivalent to testing the standard null hypothesis about the slope, $H_0: \beta_1 = 0$. A similar result holds here for multiple regression. Testing the overall hypothesis tested by the F-statistic, $H_0: \beta_1 = \beta_2 = \cdots = \beta_k = 0$, is equivalent to testing whether the true multiple regression R^2 is zero. In fact, the F-statistic for testing that all the slopes are zero can be found as:

$$F = \frac{R^2/k}{(1 - R^2)/(n - k - 1)} = \frac{\dfrac{SSR}{SST}\dfrac{1}{k}}{\dfrac{SSE}{SST}\dfrac{1}{n - k - 1}} = \frac{SSR/k}{SSE/(n - k - 1)} = \frac{MSR}{MSE}.$$

Mean Squares

Whenever a sum of squares is divided by its degrees of freedom, the result is called a mean square. For example, the Mean Square for Error, which you may see written as MSE, is found as $SSE/(n - k - 1)$. It estimates the variance of the errors.

Similarly $SST/(n - 1)$ divides the total sum of square by *its* degrees of freedom. That is sometimes called the Mean Square for Total and denoted MST. We've seen this one before; the MST is just the variance of *y*.

And SSR/k is the Mean Square for Regression.

In other words, using an F-test to see whether any of the true coefficients is different from 0 is equivalent to testing whether the R^2 value is different from zero. A rejection of either hypothesis says that at least one of the predictors accounts for enough variation in y to distinguish it from noise. Unfortunately, the test doesn't say which slope is responsible. You must look at individual t-tests on the slopes to determine that. Because removing one predictor variable from the regression equation can change any number of slope coefficients, it is not straightforward to determine the right subset of predictors to use. We'll return to that problem when we discuss model selection in Chapter 19.

R^2 and Adjusted R^2

Adding a predictor variable to a multiple regression equation does not always increase the amount of variation accounted for by the model, but it can never reduce it. Adding new predictor variables will always keep the R^2 value the same or increase it. It can never decrease it. But, even if the R^2 value grows, that doesn't mean that the resulting model is a better model or that it has greater predictive ability. If you have a model with k predictors (all of which have statistically significant coefficients at some α level) and want to see if including a new variable, x_{k+1}, is warranted, you could fit the model with all $k + 1$ variables and simply test the slope of the added variable with a t-test of the slope.

This method can test whether the most recently added variable adds significantly to the model, but choosing the "best" subset of predictors is not necessarily straightforward. We'll discuss strategies for model selection in Chapter 19. The trade-off between a small (parsimonious) model and one that fits the data well is one of the great challenges of any serious model-building effort. Various statistics have been proposed to provide guidance for this search, and one of the most common is called adjusted R^2. **Adjusted R^2** imposes a "penalty" for each new term that's added to the model in an attempt to make models of different sizes (numbers of predictors) comparable. It differs from R^2 because it can shrink when a predictor is added to the regression model or grow when a predictor is removed if the predictor in question doesn't contribute usefully to the model. It can even be negative.

For a multiple regression with k predictor variables and n cases, it is defined as

$$R^2_{adj} = 1 - (1 - R^2)\frac{n - 1}{n - k - 1} = 1 - \frac{SSE/(n - k - 1)}{SST/(n - 1)}.$$

In the Guided Example, the regression of *Price* on *Bedrooms, Bathrooms, Living Area, Fireplaces*, and *Age* resulted in an R^2 of 0.6049. All the coefficients had P-values well below 0.05. The adjusted R^2 value for this model is 0.6030. Adding the variable *Lot Size* to the model gives the following regression model:

	Coeff	SE(Coeff)	t-ratio	P-value
Intercept	15360.011	7334.804	2.094	0.03649
Living Area	73.388	4.043	18.154	<0.00001
Bedrooms	−6096.387	2757.736	−2.211	0.02728
Bathrooms	18824.069	3676.582	5.120	<0.00001
Fireplaces	9226.356	3191.788	2.891	0.00392
Age	−152.615	48.224	−3.165	0.00160
Lot Size	847.764	1989.112	0.426	0.67005

Residual standard error: 48440 on 1041 degrees of freedom
Multiple R-squared: 0.6081, Adjusted R-squared: 0.6059
F-statistic: 269.3 on 6 and 1041 DF, P-value: <0.0001

The most striking feature of this regression table as compared to the one in the Guided Example on page 620, is that although most of the coefficients have changed very little, the coefficient of *Lot Size* is far from significant, with a P-value of 0.670. Yet, the adjusted R^2 value is actually higher than for the previous model. This is why we warn against putting too much faith in this statistic. Especially for large samples, the adjusted R^2 does not always adjust downward enough to make sensible model choices. The other problem with comparing these two models is that 9 homes had missing values for *Lot Size*, which means that we're not comparing the models on exactly the same dataset. When we matched the two models on the smaller dataset, the adjusted R^2 value actually did "make the right decision" but just barely—0.6059 versus 0.6060 for the model without *Lot Size*. One might expect a larger difference considering we added a variable whose *t*-ratio is much less than 1.

The lesson to be learned here is that there is no "correct" set of predictors to use for any real business decision problem, and finding a reasonable model is a process that takes a combination of science, art, business knowledge, and common sense. Look at the adjusted R^2 value for any multiple regression model you fit, but be sure to think about all the other reasons for including or not including any given predictor variable. We will have much more to say about this important subject in Chapter 19.

IN PRACTICE 18.5 R^2 and adjusted R^2

MANAGER The model for *Respond Amount* that included *Age* as a predictor (see In Practice 18.4 on page 622) had an adjusted R^2 value of 0.9123 (or 91.23%). The original model (see In Practice 18.1 on page 610) had an adjusted R^2 value of 0.9131. How is that consistent with the decision we made to drop *Age* from the model?

ANALYST (LEIRAM) The *t*-ratio indicated that the slope for *Age* was not significantly different from 0, so I recommend that we drop *Age* from the model. Although the R^2 value for the model that included *Age* was slightly higher, the adjusted R^2 value was slightly lower. Adjusted R^2 adds a penalty for each added term that allows us to compare models of different sizes. Because the adjusted R^2 value for the smaller model (without *Age*) is higher than the larger model (with *Age*), it indicates that the inclusion of *Age* is not justified, which is consistent with the recommendation from the *t*-ratio.

---

*18.6   The Logistic Regression Model

Business decisions often depend on whether something will happen or not. Will my customers leave my wireless service at the end of their subscription? How likely is it that my customers will respond to the offer I just mailed? The response variable is either Yes or No—a dichotomous response. By definition, that's a categorical response, so we can't use linear regression methods to predict it.

If we coded this categorical response variable by giving the Yes values the value 1 and the No values the value 0, we could "pretend" that it's quantitative and try to fit a linear model. Let's imagine that we're trying to model whether someone will respond to an offer based on how much they spent in the last year at our company. The regression of *Purchase (1 = Yes: 0 = No)* on *Spending* might look like Figure 18.6.

The model shows that as past spending increases, something having to do with responding to the offer increases. Look at *Spending* near $500. Nearly all the customers who spend that much responded to the offer, while for those customers who spent less than $100 last year, almost none responded. The line seems to show the proportion of those responding for different values of *Spending*. Looking at the plot, what would you predict the proportion of responders to be for those that spent about $225? You might say that the proportion was about 0.50.

FIGURE 18.6   A linear model of *Respond to Offer* shows that as *Spending* increases, the proportion of customers responding to the offer increases as well. Unfortunately, the line predicts values outside the interval (0,1), but those are the only sensible values for proportions or probabilities.

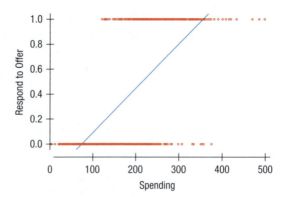

FIGURE 18.6   A linear model of *Respond to Offer* shows that as *Spending* increases, the proportion of customers responding to the offer increases as well. Unfortunately, the line predicts values outside the interval (0,1), but those are the only sensible values for proportions or probabilities.

What's wrong with this interpretation? We know proportions (or probabilities) must lie between 0 and 1. But the linear model has no such restrictions. The line crosses 1.0 at about $350 in *Spending* and goes below 0 at about $75 in *Spending*. However, by transforming the probability, we can make the model behave better and get more sensible predictions for all values of *Spending*. We could just cut off all values greater than 1 at 1 and all values less than 0 at 0. That would work fine in the middle, but we know that things like customer behavior don't change that abruptly. So we'd prefer a model that curves at the ends to approach 0 and 1 gently. That's likely to be a better model for what really happens. A simple function is all we need. There are several that can do the job, but one common model is the logistic regression model. Figure 18.7 shows a plot of the logistic regression model predictions for the same data.

FIGURE 18.7   A logistic regression model of *Respond to Offer* on *Spending* predicts values between 0 and 1 for the proportion of customers who *Respond* for all values of *Spending*.

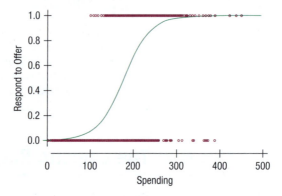

For many values of *Spending*, especially those near the mean value of *Spending*, the predictions of the probability of responding are similar for the linear and logistic models, but the logistic transformation approaches the limits at 0 and 1 smoothly. A logistic regression is an example of a non-linear regression model. The computer finds the coefficients by solving a system of equations that in some ways mimic the least squares calculations we did for linear regression. The **logistic regression** model looks like this:

$$\ln\left(\frac{p}{1-p}\right) = \beta_0 + \beta_1 x_1 + \cdots + \beta_k x_k$$

where $\ln(\ )$ denotes the natural logarithm and p is the probability of a "success."

In other words, it's not the probabilities themselves that are modeled by a (multiple) regression model, but a transformation (the logistic function) of the probabilities. When the probabilities are transformed back and plotted, we get an S-shaped curve (when plotted against each predictor), as seen in Figure 18.7.

As with multiple regression, computer output for a logistic regression model provides estimates for each coefficient, standard errors, and a test for whether the coefficient is zero. Unlike multiple regression, the coefficients for each variable are

tested with a chi-square statistic[5] rather than a t-statistic, and the overall R^2 is no longer available. (Some computer programs use a z-statistic to test individual coefficients. The tests are equivalent.) Because the probabilities are not a linear function of the predictors, it is more difficult to interpret the coefficients. The fitted logistic regression equation can be written:

$$\ln\left(\frac{\hat{p}}{1-\hat{p}}\right) = b_0 + b_1 x_1 + \cdots + b_k x_k.$$

Some researchers try to interpret the logistic regression equation directly by realizing that the expression on the left of the logistic regression equation, $\ln\left(\frac{\hat{p}}{1-\hat{p}}\right)$, can be thought of as the predicted log (base e) odds of the outcome. This is sometimes denoted $\text{logit}(\hat{p})$. The higher the log odds, the higher the probability. Negative log odds indicate that the probability is less than 0.5 because then $\frac{p}{1-p}$ will be less than 1 and thus have a negative logarithm. Positive log odds indicate a probability greater than 0.5. If the coefficient of a particular predictor is positive, it means that higher values of it are associated with higher log odds and thus a higher probability of the response. So, the *direction* is interpretable in the same way as a multiple regression coefficient. But an increase of one unit of the predictor *increases* the predicted *log odds* by an amount equal to the coefficient of that predictor, after allowing for the effects of all the other predictors. It does not increase the predicted *probability* by that amount.

The transformation back to probabilities is straightforward, but non-linear. Once you have fit the logistic regression equation

$$\ln\left(\frac{\hat{p}}{1-\hat{p}}\right) = \text{logit}(\hat{p}) = b_0 + b_1 x_1 + \cdots + b_k x_k,$$

you can find the individual probability estimates from the equation:

$$\hat{p} = \frac{1}{1 + e^{-(b_0 + b_1 x_1 + \cdots + b_k x_k)}} = \frac{e^{(b_0 + b_1 x_1 + \cdots + b_k x_k)}}{1 + e^{(b_0 + b_1 x_1 + \cdots + b_k x_k)}}.$$

Log Odds

Racetrack enthusiasts know that when p is a probability, $\frac{p}{1-p}$ is the *odds* in favor of a success. For example, when the probability of success, $p = 1/3$, we'd get the ratio $\frac{1/3}{2/3} = \frac{1}{2}$. We'd say that the odds in favor of success are 1:2 (or we'd probably say the odds *against* it are 2:1). Logistic regression models the *logarithm* of the odds as a linear function of x. In fact, nobody really thinks in terms of the log of the odds ratio. But it's the combination of that ratio and the logarithm that gets us the nice S-curved shape. What is important is that we can work backward from a log odds ratio to get the probability—which is often easier to think about.

The assumptions and conditions for fitting a logistic regression are similar to multiple regression. We still need the Independence Assumption and Randomization Condition. We no longer need the Linearity or Equal Spread Condition. However, it's a good idea to plot the response variable against each predictor variable to make sure that there are no outliers that could unduly influence the model. A customer who both spent $10,000 and responded to the offer could possibly change the shape of the curve shown in Figure 18.7. However, residual analysis for logistic regression models is beyond the scope of this text.

---

[5]Yes, the same sampling distribution model as we used in Chapter 15.

IN PRACTICE 18.6   Logistic regression

Leiram wants to build a model to predict *whether* a customer will respond to the new catalog offer. The variable *Respond* indicates 1 for responders and 0 for nonresponders. After trying several models, she settles on the following logistic regression model:

Response Variable: Respond

Variable	Coeff	SE(Coeff)	z-value	P-value
Intercept	−3.298	0.4054	−8.136	<0.0001
Age	0.08365	0.012226	6.836	<0.0001
Days Since Last Purchase	0.00364	0.000831	4.378	<0.0001

MANAGER   Explain to me how to use this model. Do we need both predictor variables? How can I use the model? For example, according to the model, who would be more likely to respond, a 20-year-old customer who has recently purchased another item, or a 50-year-old customer who has not purchased in a year?

ANALYST (LEIRAM)   The model says:

$$\text{logit}(\hat{p}) = -3.298 + 0.08365 \ \textit{Age} + 0.00364 \ \textit{Days Since Last Purchase},$$

which means that the probability of responding goes up with both *Age* and *Days Since Last Purchase*. Both terms have large z-values and correspondingly low P-values, which indicate that they contribute substantially to the model. We should keep both terms. Because both terms are positively associated with increasing (log) odds of purchasing, both an older person and one who has *not* purchased recently are more likely to respond. A 50-year-old who has not purchased recently would be more likely to respond than the 20-year-old who has.

GUIDED EXAMPLE   Time on Market

A real estate agent used information on 1115 houses, such as we used in our multiple regression Guided Example. She wants to predict whether a house sold in the first 3 months it was on the market based on other variables. The variables available include:

Sold	1 = Yes—the house sold within the first 3 months it was listed; 0 = No, it did not sell within 3 months.
Price	The price of the house as sold in 2002
Living Area	The size of the living area of the house in square feet
Bedrooms	The number of bedrooms
Bathrooms	The number of bathrooms (a half bath is a toilet and sink only)
Age	Age of the house in years
Fireplaces	Number of fireplaces in the house

PLAN   **Define** the problem. State the objective of the study. Identify the variables.

Model   Think about the assumptions and check the conditions.

We want to build a model to predict whether a house will sell within the first 3 months it's on the market based on *Price* ($), *Living Area* (sq ft), *Bedrooms* (#), *Bathrooms* (#), *Fireplaces* (#), and *Age* (years). Notice that now *Price* is a predictor variable in the regression.

Outlier Condition

To fit a logistic regression model, we check that there are no outliers in the predictors that may unduly influence the model.

Here are scatterplots of *Sold* (1 = Yes; 0 = No) against each predictor. (Plots of *Sold* against the variables *Bathrooms*, *Bedrooms*, and *Fireplaces* are uninformative because these predictors are discrete.)

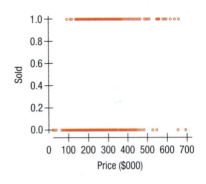

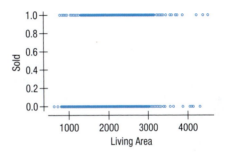

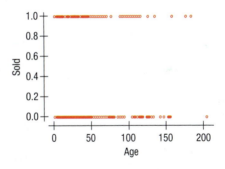

✔ **Outlier Condition.** There do not seem to be any outliers in the predictors. Of course, there can't be any in the response variable; it is only 0 or 1.

✔ **Independence Assumption.** We can regard the house prices as being independent of one another, since they come from a fairly large geographic area.

✔ **Randomization Condition.** These 1115 houses are a random sample from a larger collection of houses.

We can fit a logistic regression predicting *Sold* from the six predictor variables.

(continued)

DO

Mechanics We always fit logistic regression models with computer software. An output table like this one isn't exactly what any of the major packages produce, but it is enough like all of them to look familiar.

Here is the computer output for the logistic regression using all six predictors.

	Coeff	SE(Coeff)	z-value	P-value
Intercept	−3.222e+00	3.826e−01	−8.422	<0.0001
Living Area	−1.444e−03	2.518e−04	−5.734	<0.0001
Age	4.900e−03	2.823e−03	1.736	0.082609
Price	1.693e−05	1.444e−06	11.719	<0.0001
Bedrooms	4.805e−01	1.366e−01	3.517	0.000436
Bathrooms	−1.813e−01	1.829e−01	−0.991	0.321493
Fireplaces	−1.253e−01	1.633e−01	−0.767	0.442885

The estimated equation is:

$$\text{logit}(\hat{p}) = -3.22 - 0.00144 Living\ Area$$
$$+ 0.0049 Age + 0.0000169 Price$$
$$+ 0.481 Bedrooms - 0.181 Bathrooms$$
$$- 0.125 Fireplaces$$

Strategies for model selection will be discussed in Chapter 19.

Three of the P-values are quite small, two are large (*Bathrooms* and *Fireplaces*), and one is marginal (*Age*). After examining several alternatives, we chose the following model.

	Coeff	SE(Coeff)	z-value	P-value
Intercept	−3.351e+00	3.601e−01	−9.305	<0.0001
Living Area	−1.574e−03	2.342e−04	−6.719	<0.0001
Age	6.106e−03	2.668e−03	2.289	0.022102
Price	1.672e−05	1.428e−06	11.704	<0.0001
Bedrooms	4.631e−01	1.354e−01	3.421	0.000623

The estimated logit equation is:

$$\text{logit}(\hat{p}) = -3.351 - 0.00157 Living\ Area$$
$$+ 0.00611 Age + 0.0000167 Price$$
$$+ 0.463 Bedrooms$$

While interpretation is difficult, it appears that for a house of a given size (and age and bedrooms), higher-priced homes may have a higher chance of selling within 3 months. For a house of given size and price and age, having more bedrooms may be associated with a greater chance of selling within 3 months.

REPORT

Present your Conclusions
Summarize your results and state any limitations of your model in the context of your original objectives.

MEMO

Re: Logistic regression analysis of selling

A logistic regression model of *Sold* on various predictors was fit, and a model based on *Living Area, Bedrooms, Price,* and *Age* found that these four predictors were statistically significant in predicting the probability that a house will sell within 3 months. More thorough analysis to understand the meaning of the coefficients is needed, but each of these variables appears to be an important predictor of whether the house will sell quickly.

However, knowing more specific information about other characteristics of a house and where it is located would almost certainly help the model.

⊘ WHAT CAN GO WRONG?

Interpreting Coefficients

- **Don't claim to "hold everything else constant" for a single individual.** It's often meaningless to say that a regression coefficient says what we expect to happen if all variables but one were held constant for an individual and the predictor in question changed. While it's mathematically correct, it often just doesn't make any sense. For example, in a regression of salary on years of experience, years of education, and age, subjects can't gain a year of experience or get another year of education without getting a year older. Instead, we *can* think about all those who satisfy given criteria on some predictors and ask about the conditional relationship between *y* and one *x* for those individuals.

- **Don't interpret regression causally.** Regressions are usually applied to observational data. Without deliberately assigned treatments, randomization, and control, we can't draw conclusions about causes and effects. We can never be certain that there are no variables lurking in the background, causing everything we've seen. Don't interpret b_1, the coefficient of x_1 in the multiple regression, by saying: "If we were to change an individual's x_1 by 1 unit (holding the other *x*'s constant), it would change his *y* by b_1 units." We have no way of knowing what applying a change to an individual would do.

- **Be cautious about interpreting a regression model as predictive.** Yes, we do call the *x*'s predictors, and you can certainly plug in values for each of the *x*'s and find a corresponding *predicted value*, $\hat{y}$. But the term "prediction" suggests extrapolation into the future or beyond the data, and we know that we can get into trouble when we use models to estimate $\hat{y}$-values for *x*'s not in the range of the data. Be careful not to extrapolate very far from the span of your data. In simple regression, it was easy to tell when you extrapolated. With many predictor variables, it's often harder to know when you are outside the bounds of your original data.[6] We usually think of fitting models to the data more as modeling than as prediction, so that's often a more appropriate term.

- **Be careful when interpreting the signs of coefficients in a multiple regression.** Sometimes our primary interest in a predictor is whether it has a positive or negative association with *y*. As we have seen, though, the sign of the coefficient also depends on the other predictors in the model. Don't look at the sign in isolation and conclude that "the direction of the relationship is positive (or negative)." Just like the value of the coefficient, the sign is about the relationship after allowing for the linear effects of the other predictors. The sign of a variable can change depending on which other predictors are in or out of the model. For example, in the regression model for house prices, we saw the coefficient of *Bedrooms* change sign when *Living Area* was added to the model as a predictor. It isn't correct to say either that houses with more bedrooms sell for more on average or that they sell for less. The truth is more subtle and requires that we understand the multiple regression model.

- **If a coefficient's *t*-statistic is not significant, don't interpret it at all.** You can't be sure that the value of the corresponding parameter in the underlying regression model isn't really zero.

---

[6]With several predictors we can wander beyond the data because of the *combination* of values even when individual values are not extraordinary. For example, houses with 1 bathroom and houses with 5 bedrooms can both be found in the real estate records, but a single house with 5 bedrooms and only 1 bathroom would be quite unusual. The model we found is not appropriate for predicting the price of such an extraordinary house.

⊘ WHAT ELSE CAN GO WRONG?

- **Don't fit a linear regression to data that aren't straight.** This is the most fundamental regression assumption. If the relationship between the x's and y isn't approximately linear, there's no sense in fitting a linear model to it. What we mean by "linear" is a model of the form we have been writing for the regression. When we have two predictors, this is the equation of a plane, which is linear in the sense of being flat in all directions. With more predictors, the geometry is harder to visualize, but the simple structure of the model is consistent; the predicted values change consistently with equal size changes in any predictor.

    Usually we're satisfied when plots of y against each of the x's are straight enough. We'll also check a scatterplot of the residuals against the predicted values for signs of non-linearity.

- **Watch out for changing variance in the residuals.** The estimate of the error standard deviation shows up in all the inference formulas. But that estimate assumes that the error standard deviation is the same throughout the extent of the x's so that we can combine all the residuals when we estimate it. If s_e changes with any x, these estimates won't make sense. The most common check is a plot of the residuals against the predicted values. You can also check plots of residuals against several of the predictors. If they show a thickening and especially if they also show a bend, then consider re-expressing y.

- **Make sure the errors are nearly Normal.** All of our inferences require that, unless the sample size is large, the true errors be modeled well by a Normal model. Check the histogram and Normal probability plot of the residuals to see whether this assumption looks reasonable.

- **Watch out for high-influence points and outliers.** We always have to be on the lookout for a few points that have undue influence on our model, and regression is certainly no exception. Chapter 19 discusses this issue in greater depth.

ETHICS IN ACTION

Alpine Medical Systems, Inc., is a large provider of medical equipment and supplies to hospitals, doctors, clinics, and other health care professionals. Alpine's VP of Marketing and Sales, Kenneth Jadik, asked one of the company's analysts, Nicole Haly, to develop a model that could be used to predict the performance of the company's sales force.

Based on data collected over the past year, as well as records kept by Human Resources, she considered five potential independent variables: (1) gender, (2) starting base salary, (3) years of sales experience, (4) personality test score, and (5) high school grade point average. The dependent variable (sales performance) is measured as the sales dollars generated per quarter.

In discussing the results with Nicole, Kenneth asks to see the full regression model with all five independent variables

included. Kenneth notes that a t-test for the coefficient of gender shows no significant effect on sales performance and recommends that it be eliminated from the model. Nicole reminds him of the company's history of offering lower starting base salaries to women, recently corrected under court order. If instead, starting base salary is removed from the model, gender is statistically significant, and its coefficient indicates that women on the sales force outperform men (taking into account the other variables). Kenneth argues that because gender is not significant when all predictors are included, it is the variable that should be omitted.

- **Identify the ethical dilemma in this scenario.**
- **What are the undesirable consequences?**
- **Propose an ethical solution that considers the welfare of all stakeholders**

CHAPTER

18 FROM LEARNING TO EARNING

LEARNING OBJECTIVES

Know how to perform a multiple regression, using the technology of your choice.

- Technologies differ, but most produce similar-looking tables to hold the regression results. Know how to find the values you need in the output generated by the technology you are using.

Understand how to interpret a multiple regression model.

- The meaning of a multiple regression coefficient depends on the other variables in the model. In particular, it is the relationship of y to the associated x after removing the linear effects of the other x's.

Be sure to check the Assumptions and Conditions before interpreting a multiple regression model.

- The **Linearity Assumption** asserts that the form of the multiple regression model is appropriate. We check it by examining scatterplots. If the plots appear to be linear, we can fit a multiple regression model.
- The **Independence Assumption** requires that the errors made by the model in fitting the data be mutually independent. Data that arise from random samples or randomized experiments usually satisfy this assumption.
- The **Equal Variance Assumption** states that the variability around the multiple regression model should be the same everywhere. We usually check the **Equal Spread Condition** by plotting the residuals against the predicted values. This assumption is needed so that we can pool the residuals to estimate their standard deviation, which we will need for inferences about the regression coefficients.
- The **Normality Assumption** says that the model's errors should follow a Normal model. We check the **Nearly Normal Condition** with a histogram or normal probability plot of the residuals. We need this assumption to use Student's t models for inference, but for larger sample sizes, it is less important.

Know how to state and test hypotheses about the multiple regression coefficients.

- The standard hypothesis test for each coefficient is

$$H_0: \beta_j = 0 \text{ vs.}$$
$$H_A: \beta_j \neq 0$$

- We test these hypotheses by referring the test statistic

$$\frac{b_j - 0}{SE(b_j)}$$

to the Student's t-distribution on $n - k - 1$ degrees of freedom, where k is the number of coefficients estimated in the multiple regression.

Interpret other associated statistics generated by a multiple regression.

- R^2 is the fraction of the variation in y accounted for by the multiple regression model.
- Adjusted R^2 attempts to adjust for the number of coefficients estimated.
- The F-statistic tests the overall hypothesis that the regression model is of no more value than simply modeling y with its mean.
- The standard deviation of the residuals,

$$s_e = \sqrt{\frac{\sum e^2}{n - k - 1}}$$

provides an idea of how precisely the regression model fits the data.

TERMS

Adjusted R^2 An adjustment to the R^2 statistic that attempts to allow for the number of predictors in the model. It is sometimes used when comparing regression models with different numbers of predictors:

$$R^2_{adj} = 1 - (1 - R^2)\frac{n-1}{n-k-1} = 1 - \frac{SSE/(n-k-1)}{SST/(n-1)}.$$

F-test The F-test is used to test the null hypothesis that the overall regression is no improvement over just modeling y with its mean:

$$H_0: \beta_1 = \cdots = \beta_k = 0. \text{ vs } H_A: \text{ at least one } \beta \neq 0$$

If this null hypothesis is not rejected, then you should not proceed to test the individual coefficients.

*Logistic regression A regression model that models a binary (0/1) response variable based on quantitative predictor variables.

Multiple regression A linear regression with two or more predictors whose coefficients are found by least squares. When the distinction is needed, a least squares linear regression with a single predictor is called a *simple regression*. The multiple regression model is: $y = \beta_0 + \beta_1 x_1 + \cdots + \beta_k x_k + \varepsilon$.

Regression Sum of Squares, SSR A measure of the total variation in the response variable due to the model. $SSR = \sum(\hat{y} - \bar{y})^2$.

Sum of Squared Errors or Residuals, SSE A measure of the variation in the residuals. $SSE = \sum(y - \hat{y})^2$.

Total Sum of Squares, SST A measure of the variation in the response variable. $SST = \sum(y - \bar{y})^2$. Note that $\frac{SST}{n-1} = Var(y)$.

t-ratios for the coefficients The t-ratios for the coefficients can be used to test the null hypotheses that the true value of each coefficient is zero against the alternative that it is not. The t-distribution is also used in the construction of confidence intervals for each slope coefficient.

TECH SUPPORT   Regression Analysis

All statistics packages make a table of results for a regression. The table for multiple regression looks very similar to the table for simple regression.

Most packages offer to plot residuals against predicted values. Some will also plot residuals against the x's. With some packages, you must request plots of the residuals when you request the regression. Others let you find the regression first and then analyze the residuals afterward. Either way, your analysis is not complete if you don't check the residuals with a histogram or Normal probability plot and a scatterplot of the residuals against the x's or the predicted values. In most packages, the commands to obtain residuals and residual plots are the same for single and multiple regression.

Multiple regressions are always found with a computer or programmable calculator. Before computers were available, a full multiple regression analysis could take months or even years of work.

EXCEL

- Select **Data Analysis** from the **Analysis Group** on the Data Tab.
- Select **Regression** from the **Analysis Tools** list.
- Click the **OK** button.
- Enter the data range holding the y-variable in the box labeled **Y-range**.
- Enter the range of cells holding the x-variables in the box labeled **X-range**.
- Select the **New Worksheet Ply** option.
- Select **Residuals** options. Click the **OK** button.

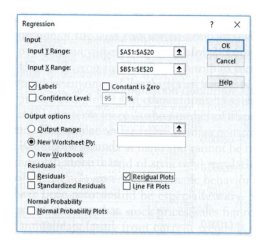

COMMENTS

Although the Excel Data Analysis dialog offers a Normal probability plot of the residuals, the data analysis add-in does not make a correct probability plot, so don't use this option.

XLSTAT

- In **Modeling Data** menu, choose **Linear Regression**.
- Enter y-variable and x-variable cell ranges.
- Specify desired statistics in Outputs and Charts tabs, respectively.

COMMENTS

For both Excel and XLStat, the Y and X cell ranges do not need to be in the same rows of the spreadsheet, although they must cover the same number of cells. It is a good idea to arrange your data in parallel columns as in a data table. The X-variables must be in adjacent columns. No cells in the data range may hold nonnumeric values or be left blank.

JMP

- From the **Analyze** menu, select **Fit Model**.
- Put the response variable in the **Y** dialog box and the predictor variables in the **Add** dialog box under **Construct Model Effects**.
- Click on **Run Model**.

COMMENTS

JMP chooses a regression analysis when the response variable is "Continuous." The predictors can be any combination of quantitative or categorical. If you get a different analysis, check the variable types.

MINITAB

- Choose **Regression** from the **Stat** menu.
- Choose **Fit Model ...** from the **Regression** submenu.

- In the Regression dialog, assign the Y-variable to the Response box and assign the X-variables to the Predictors box.
- Click the **Graphs** button.
- In the Regression-Graphs dialog, select **Standardized residuals**, and check **Normal plot of residuals** and **Residuals versus fits**.
- Click the **OK** button to return to the Regression dialog.
- Click the **OK** button to compute the regression.

R

Suppose the response variable y and predictor variables $x_1, \ldots, x_k$ are in a data frame called mydata. To fit a multiple regression of y on x_1 and x_2:

- mylm = lm(y ~ x_1 + x_2, data = mydata).
- summary(mylm) # gives the details of the fit, including the ANOVA table.
- plot(mylm) # gives a variety of plots.

To fit the model with *all* the predictors in the data frame,

- mylm = lm(y~., data = mydata) # The period means use all other variables.

COMMENTS

To get confidence or prediction intervals use:

- predict(mylm, interval = "confidence")

or

- predict(mylm, interval = "prediction".)

SPSS

- Choose **Regression** from the **Analyze** menu.
- Choose **Linear** from the **Regression** submenu.

- When the Linear Regression dialog appears, select the Y-variable and move it to the dependent target. Then move the X-variables to the independent target.
- Click the **Plots** button.
- In the Linear Regression Plots dialog, choose to plot the *SRESIDs against the *ZPRED values.
- Click the **Continue** button to return to the Linear Regression dialog.
- Click the **OK** button to compute the regression.

- To find a multiple regression of a response variable y on two factors, x_1 and x_2, from the Stat menu, choose **Regression > Multiple Linear**.
- In the dialog, specify the response (Y) variable. Specify the predictors (X variables) and Interactions (optional).
- Click **Compute!** to perform the regression.

COMMENTS

You can save residuals and predicted values among other quantities with the save options.

BRIEF CASE

Golf Success

Professional sports, like many other professions, require a variety of skills for success. That makes it difficult to evaluate and predict success. Fortunately, sports provide examples we can use to learn about modeling success because of the vast amount of data which are available. Here's an example.

What makes a golfer successful? The game of golf requires many skills. Putting well or hitting long drives will not, by themselves, lead to success. Success in golf requires a combination of skills. That makes multiple regression a good candidate for modeling golf achievement.

A number of Internet sites post statistics for the current PGA players. We have data for 190 top players of 2017 in the file **Golfers 2017**.

All of these players earned money on the tour, but the distribution of earnings is quite skewed. So it's a good idea to take log of Earnings as the response variable.

The variables in the data file include:

LogEarn	The logarithm of earnings
Greens in Regulation	Greens in Regulation. Percentage of holes played in which the ball is on the green with two or more strokes left for par.
Putt Average	Average number of putts per hole in which the green was reached in regulation.
Save %	Each time a golfer hits a bunker by the side of a green but needs only one or two additional shots to reach the hole, he is credited with a save. This is the percentage of opportunities for saves that are realized.
Yds/Drive	Average Drive Distance (yards). Measured as averages over pairs of drives in opposite directions (to account for wind).
Driving Acc	Drive Accuracy. Percent of drives landing on the fairway.

Investigate these data. Find a regression model to predict golfers' success (measured in log earnings). Write a report presenting your model including an assessment of its limitations. Note: Although you may consider several intermediate models, a good report is about the model you think best, not necessarily about all the models you tried along the way while searching for it.

SECTION 18.1

1. A house in the upstate New York area from which the chapter data was drawn has 2 bedrooms and 1000 square feet of living area. Using the multiple regression model found in the chapter,

$$\widehat{Price} = 20{,}986.09 - 7483.10 Bedrooms + 93.84 Living\ Area.$$

a) Find the price that this model estimates.
b) The house just sold for $135,000. Find the residual corresponding to this house.
c) What does that residual say about this transaction?

2. A candy maker surveyed chocolate bars available in a local supermarket and found the following least squares regression model:

$$\widehat{Calories} = 28.4 + 11.37 Fat(g) + 2.91 Sugar(g).$$

a) The hand-crafted chocolate she makes has 15 g of fat and 20 g of sugar. How many calories does the model predict for a serving?
b) In fact, a laboratory test shows that her candy has 227 calories per serving. Find the residual corresponding to this candy. (Be sure to include the units.)
c) What does that residual say about her candy?

SECTION 18.2

3. What can predict how much a motion picture will make? We have data on a number of recent releases that includes the *USGross* (in $M), the *Budget* ($M), the *Run Time* (minutes), and the average number of *Stars* awarded by reviewers. The first several entries in the data table look like this:

Movie	USGross ($M)	Budget ($M)	Run Time (minutes)	Stars
White Noise	56.094360	30	101	2
Coach Carter	67.264877	45	136	3
Elektra	24.409722	65	100	2
Racing Stripes	49.772522	30	110	3
Assault on Precinct 13	20.040895	30	109	3
Are We There Yet?	82.674398	20	94	2
Alone in the Dark	5.178569	20	96	1.5
Indigo	51.100486	25	105	3.5

We want a regression model to predict *USGross*. Parts of the regression output computed in Excel look like this:

```
Dependent variable is: USGross($)
R squared = 47.4% R squared (adjusted) = 46.0%
s = 46.41 with 120 - 4 = 116 degrees of freedom
```

Variable	Coefficient	SE(Coeff)	t-ratio	P-value
Intercept	-22.9898	25.70	-0.895	0.3729
Budget($)	1.13442	0.1297	8.75	<0.0001
Stars	24.9724	5.884	4.24	<0.0001
Run Time	-0.403296	0.2513	-1.60	0.1113

a) Write the multiple regression equation.
b) What is the interpretation of the coefficient of *Budget* in this regression model?

4. A middle manager at an entertainment company, upon seeing the analysis of Exercise 3, concludes that the longer you make a movie, the less money it will make. He argues that his company's films should all be cut by 30 minutes to improve their gross. Explain the flaw in his interpretation of this model.

SECTION 18.3

5. For the movies examined in Exercise 4, here is a scatterplot of *USGross* vs. *Budget*:

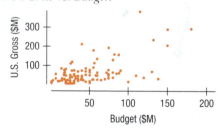

What (if anything) does this scatterplot tell us about the following assumptions and conditions for the regression?

a) Linearity Condition   **b)** Equal Spread Condition
c) Normality Assumption

6. For the movies regression, here is a histogram of the residuals. What does it tell us about these assumptions and conditions?

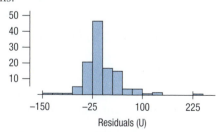

a) Linearity Condition   **b)** Nearly Normal Condition
c) Equal Spread Condition

SECTION 18.4

7. In the regression output for the movies of Exercise 3,

a) What is the null hypothesis tested for the coefficient of *Stars* in this table?
b) What is the *t*-statistic corresponding to this test?
c) What is the P-value corresponding to this *t*-statistic?
d) Complete the hypothesis test. Do you reject the null hypothesis?

8. a) What is the null hypothesis tested for the coefficient of *Run Time* in the regression of Exercise 3?
b) What is the *t*-statistic corresponding to this test?
c) Why is this *t*-statistic negative?
d) What is the P-value corresponding to this *t*-statistic?
e) Complete the hypothesis test. Do you reject the null hypothesis?

SECTION 18.5

9. In the regression model of Exercise 3,

a) What is the R^2 for this regression? What does it mean?
b) Why is the "Adjusted R Square" in the table different from the "R Square"?

10. Here is another part of the regression output for the movies in Exercise 3:

Source	Sum of Squares	df	Mean Square	F-ratio
Regression	224995	3	74998.4	34.8
Residual	249799	116	2153.44	

a) Using the values from the table, show how the value of R^2 could be computed. Don't try to do the calculation, just show what is computed.
b) What is the F-statistic value for this regression?
c) What null hypothesis can you test with it?
d) Would you reject that null hypothesis?

CHAPTER EXERCISES

The next 12 exercises consist of two sets of 6 (one even-numbered, one odd-numbered). Each set guides you through a multiple regression analysis. We suggest that you do all 6 exercises in a set. Remember that the answers to the odd-numbered exercises can be found in the back of the text.

T 11. Police Pay 2016. Is the amount of violent crime related to what police officers are paid? The data file holds data for each state of the United States. The variables are:

> *Violent Crime* (crimes per 100,000 population)
> *Police Officer Pay* (mean $)
> *High School Graduation Rate* (%)

One natural question to ask of these data is how police officer wages are related to violent crime across these states.

First, here are plots and background information.

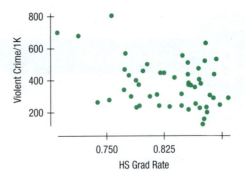

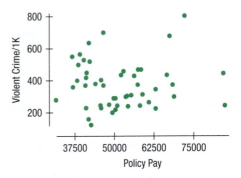

a) Name and check (to the extent possible) the regression assumptions and their corresponding conditions.
b) If we found a regression to predict *Violent Crime* just from *High School Graduation Rate*, what would the R^2 of that regression be?

	Violent Crime	Police Pay	HS Grad
Violent Crime	1.000		
Police Pay	0.036	1.000	
HS Grad Rate	−0.374	−0.163	1.0

T 12. Broadway shows. In 2016, 13.27 million people attended a Broadway show, paying an average of more than $100 per ticket. We'd like to understand this $1.4 billion business better. The Broadway League, Inc. (www.broadwayleague.com/research/statistics-broadway-nyc/), provides some historical and current data. The following variables are available for each year since the 1984–1985 season:

> *Season* (The initial year of the season, so the 1984–1985 season is 1984.)
> *Gross* ($M)
> *Attendance* (M) Note: Before 2009 this is Paid Attendance. Beginning 2009 it is Attendance.)
> *Playing weeks* (Total weeks during each show performed, summed over all shows; the best measure of Broadway's overall activity.)

Here are some plots and background information.

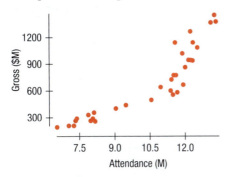

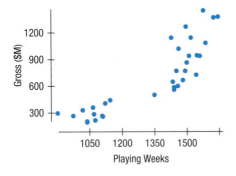

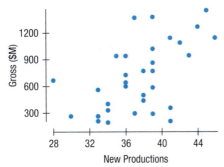

Correlations				
	Gross ($M)	Attendance	Playing Weeks	New Productions
Gross	1.000			
Attendance	0.905	1.000		
Playing Weeks	0.873	0.977	1.000	
New Productions	0.575	0.411	0.375	1.000

a) Name and check (to the extent possible) the regression assumptions.
b) If we found a regression of *Gross* receipts on *New Productions*, what would the R^2 of that regression be?

T 13. Police pay 2016, part 2. Here's a multiple regression model for the variables considered in Exercise 11.

```
Response variable is: Violent Crime/1K
R squared = 15.1%  R squared (adjusted) = 11.4%
s = 137.3 with  49 − 3 = 46 degrees of freedom
```

Variable	Coefficient	SE(Coeff)	t-ratio	P-value
Intercept	1305.51	346.5	3.77	0.0005
Police pay	−0.347222	1.690	−0.205	0.8381
HS Grad rate	−1097.36	385.8	−2.84	0.0066

a) Write the regression model.
b) What does the coefficient of *Police Pay* mean in the context of this regression model?
c) In a state in which the average police officer wage is $50,000 and the high school graduation rate is 80%, what does this model estimate the violent crime rate would be?
d) Is this likely to be a good prediction? Why do you think that?

T 14. Broadway shows, part 2. Here's a multiple regression model for the variables considered in Exercise 12:

```
Response variable is: Gross($M)
R squared = 86.9%  R squared (adjusted) = 85.6%
s = 146.9 with 33 − 4 = 29 degrees of freedom
```

Variable	Coefficient	SE(Coeff)	t-ratio	P-value
Intercept	−1596.40	280.8	−5.68	<0.0001
Attendance	163.515	57.88	2.83	0.0085
Playing weeks	−0.177197	0.5337	−0.332	0.7423
New Productions	21.7613	6.709	3.24	0.0030

a) Write the regression model.
b) What does the coefficient of *Attendance* mean in this regression?
c) In a season in which attendance was 13 million over 1500 playing weeks for 45 new productions, what does the model predict the gross would be?
d) Is this likely to be a good prediction? Explain.

T 15. Police pay 2016, part 3. Using the regression table in Exercise 13, answer the following questions.

a) How was the *t*-ratio of 0.221 found for *Police Pay*? (Show what is computed using numbers from the table.)
b) How many states are used in this model. How do you know?
c) The *t*-ratio for *Graduation Rate* is negative. What does that mean?

T 16. Broadway shows, part 3. Using the regression table in Exercise 14, answer the following questions.

a) How was the *t*-ratio of 2.83 found for *Attendance*? (Show what is computed using numbers found in the table.)
b) How many seasons are included in this regression? How can you tell?
c) The *t*-ratio for the intercept is negative. What does that mean?

T 17. Police pay 2016, part 4. Consider the coefficient of *Police Pay* in the regression table of Exercise 13.

a) State the standard null and alternative hypotheses for the true coefficient of *Police Pay*.
b) Test the null hypothesis (at $\alpha = 0.05$) and state your conclusion.

T 18. Broadway shows, part 4. Consider the coefficient of *Playing Weeks* in the regression table of Exercise 14.

a) State the standard null and alternative hypotheses for the true coefficient of *Playing Weeks*.
b) Test the null hypothesis (at $\alpha = 0.05$) and state your conclusion.
c) A Broadway investor challenges your analysis. He points out that the scatterplot of *Gross* vs. *Playing Weeks* in Exercise 12 shows a strong relationship and claims that your result in part a can't be correct. Explain to him why this is not a contradiction.

T 19. Police pay 2016, part 5. A Police union leader accepts your analysis in Exercise 17 but claims that it proves that paying police more will reduce violent crime. Explain why this interpretation is not a valid use of this regression model. Offer some alternative explanations.

T 20. Broadway shows, part 5. The investor in Exercise 18 now accepts your analysis but claims that it demonstrates that it doesn't matter how many weeks a show plays on Broadway; receipts will be essentially the same. Explain why this interpretation is not a valid use of this regression model. Be specific.

T 21. Police pay 2016, part 6. Here are some plots of residuals for the regression of Exercise 13.

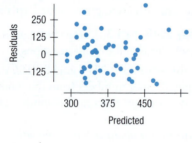

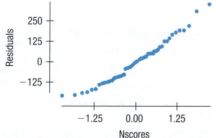

Which of the regression conditions can you check with these plots?

Do you find that those conditions are met?

T 22. Broadway shows, part 6. We really should have examined the residuals. Here is a scatterplot of the residuals from the regression of Exercise 14.

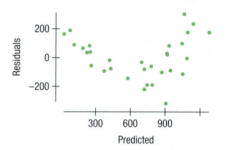

a) Which assumptions and conditions for regression can you check with this plot? What do you conclude?

Perhaps we should re-express *Gross* revenue. Here is a new regression and residual plot using the logarithm of *Gross*:

```
Response variable is: LogGross
R squared = 96.0%  R squared (adjusted) = 95.6%
s = 0.0571 with 33 − 4 = 29 degrees of freedom
```

Variable	Coefficient	SE(Coeff)	t-ratio	P-value
Intercept	1.28979	0.1092	11.8	<0.0001
Attendance	0.154219	0.0225	6.85	<0.0001
Playing Weeks	−3.75769e−4	0.0002	−1.81	0.0807
New Productions	9.70391e−3	0.0026	3.72	0.0009

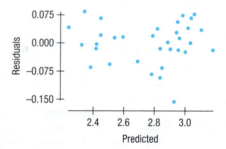

b) Would you prefer the second (re-expressed) regression model to the first? Explain all the reasons you reach this conclusion.
c) If you wished to predict Gross revenues for a year with larger attendance than has been seen thus far, which model would you choose? Why?

23. Real estate prices. A regression was performed to predict selling *Price* of houses in dollars from their *Area* in square feet, *Lotsize* in square feet, and *Age* in years. The R^2 is 92%. The equation from this regression is given here.

$$Price = 169,328 + 35.3\ Area + 0.718\ Lotsize − 6543\ Age$$

One of the following interpretations is correct. Which is it? Explain what's wrong with the others.

a) Each year a house ages, it is worth $6543 less.
b) Every extra square foot of area is associated with an additional $35.50 in average price, for houses with a given lot size and age.
c) Every additional dollar in price means lot size increases 0.718 square feet.
d) This model fits 92% of the data points exactly.

24. Wine prices. Many factors affect the price of wine, including such qualitative characteristics as the variety of grape, location of winery, and label. Researchers developed a regression model considering two quantitative variables: the tasting score of the wine and the age of the wine (in years) when released to market. They found the following regression equation, with an R^2 of 65%, to predict the price (in dollars) of a bottle of wine.

$$Price = 6.25 + 1.22\ Tasting\ Score + 0.55\ Age$$

One of the following interpretations is correct. Which is it? Explain what's wrong with the others.

a) Each year a bottle of wine ages, its price increases about $.55.
b) This model fits 65% of the points exactly.
c) For a unit increase in tasting score, the price of a bottle of wine increases about $1.22.
d) After allowing for the age of a bottle of wine, a wine with a one unit higher tasting score can be expected to cost about $1.22 more.

25. Appliance sales. A household appliance manufacturer wants to analyze the relationship between total sales and the company's three primary means of advertising (television, magazines, and radio). All values were in millions of dollars. They found the following regression equation.

$$Sales = 250 + 6.75\ TV + 3.5\ Radio + 2.3\ Magazine$$

One of the following interpretations is correct. Which is it? Explain what's wrong with the others.

a) If they did no advertising, their income would be $250 million.
b) Every million dollars spent on radio makes sales increase $3.5 million, all other things being equal.
c) Every million dollars spent on magazines increases TV spending $2.3 million.
d) Sales increase on average about $6.75 million for each million spent on TV, after allowing for the effects of the other kinds of advertising.

26. Wine prices, part 2. Here are some more interpretations of the regression model to predict the price of wine developed in Exercise 24. One of these interpretations is correct. Which is it? Explain what is wrong with the others.

a) The minimum price for a bottle of wine that has not aged is $6.25.
b) The price for a bottle of wine increases on average about $.55 for each year it ages, after allowing for the effects of tasting score.
c) Each year a bottle of wine ages, its tasting score increases by 1.22.
d) Each dollar increase in the price of wine increases its tasting score by 1.22.

27. Cost of pollution. What is the financial impact of pollution abatement on small firms? The U.S. government's Small Business Administration studied this and reported the following model.

$$Pollution\ abatement/employee = -2.494 - 0.431$$
$$\ln(Number\ of\ Employees) + 0.698\ \ln(Sales)$$

Pollution abatement is in dollars per employee.

a) The coefficient of ln(*Number of Employees*) is negative. What does that mean in the context of this model? What does it mean that the coefficient of ln(*Sales*) is positive?
b) The model uses the (natural) logarithms of the two predictors. What does the use of this transformation say about their effects on pollution abatement costs?

Ⓣ 28. OECD economic regulations. A study by the U.S. Small Business Administration used historical data to model the GDP per capita of 24 of the countries in the Organization for Economic Cooperation and Development (OECD) (Crain, M. W., *The Impact of Regulatory Costs on Small Firms*, available at www.sba.gov/advocacy/7540/49291). One analysis estimated the effect on GDP of economic regulations, using an index of the degree of OECD economic regulation and other variables. They found the following regression model.

$$\overline{GDP/Capita(1998-2002)} = 10487 - 1343\ OECD$$

$Economic\ Regulation\ Index + 1.078\ GDP/Capita(1988)$

$- 69.99\ Ethno\text{-}linguistic\ Diversity\ Index$

$+ 44.71\ Trade\ as\ share\ of\ GDP\ (1998-2002)$

$- 58.4\ Primary\ Education(\%Eligible\ Population)$

All *t*-statistics on the individual coefficients have P-values <0.05, except the coefficient of *Primary Education*.

a) The researchers hoped to show that more regulation leads to lower GDP/Capita. Does the coefficient of the OECD Economic Regulation Index demonstrate that? Explain.
b) The F-statistic for this model is 129.61 (5, 17 df). What do you conclude about the model?
c) If *GDP/Capita (1988)* is removed as a predictor, then the F-statistic drops to 0.694 and none of the *t*-statistics is significant (all P-values > 0.22). Reconsider your interpretation in part a.

29. Home prices. Many variables have an impact on determining the price of a house. A few of these are size of the house (square feet), lot size, and number of bathrooms. Information for a random sample of homes for sale in the Statesboro, Georgia, area was obtained from the Internet. Regression output modeling the asking price with square footage and number of bathrooms gave the following result.

```
Dependent Variable is: Asking Price
s = 67013   R-Sq = 71.1%   R-Sq(adj) = 64.6%
```

Predictor	Coeff	SE(Coeff)	t-ratio	P-value
Intercept	−152037	85619	−1.78	0.110
Baths	9530	40826	0.23	0.821
Area	139.87	46.67	3.00	0.015

Analysis of Variance

Source	DF	SS	MS	F	P-value
Regression	2	99303550067	49651775033	11.06	0.004
Residual	9	40416679100	4490742122		
Total	11	1.39720E+11			

a) Write the regression equation.
b) How much of the variation in home asking prices is accounted for by the model?
c) Explain in context what the coefficient of *Area* means.
d) The owner of a construction firm, upon seeing this model, objects because the model says that the number of bathrooms has no effect on the price of the home. He says that when *he* adds another bathroom, it increases the value. Is it true that the number of bathrooms is unrelated to house price? (*Hint:* Do you think bigger houses have more bathrooms?)

30. Home prices, part 2. Here are some diagnostic plots for the home prices data from Exercise 29. These were generated by a computer package and may look different from the plots generated by the packages you use. (In particular, note that the axes of the Normal probability plot are swapped relative to the plots we've made in the text. We only care about the pattern of this plot, so it shouldn't affect your interpretation.) Examine these plots and discuss whether the assumptions and conditions for the multiple regression seem reasonable.

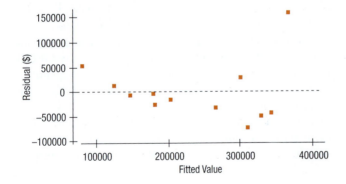

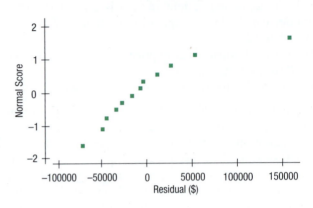

Normal Probability Plot

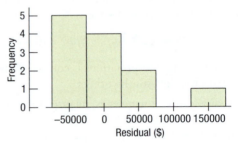

31. Secretary performance. The AFL-CIO has undertaken a study of 30 secretaries' yearly salaries (in thousands of dollars). The organization wants to predict salaries from several other variables. The variables to be considered potential predictors of salary are:

$X1$ = months of service

$X2$ = years of education

$X3$ = score on standardized test

$X4$ = words per minute (wpm) typing speed

$X5$ = ability to take dictation in words per minute

A multiple regression model with all five variables was run on a computer package, resulting in the following output.

Variable	Coeff	Std. Error	t-value
Intercept	9.788	0.377	25.960
X1	0.110	0.019	5.178
X2	0.053	0.038	1.369
X3	0.071	0.064	1.119
X4	0.004	0.0307	0.013
X5	0.065	0.038	1.734

$s = 0.430$ $R\text{-sq} = 0.863$

Assume that the residual plots show no violations of the conditions for using a linear regression model.

a) What is the regression equation?
b) From this model, what is the predicted salary (in thousands of dollars) of a secretary with 10 years (120 months) of experience, 9th grade education (9 years of education), 50 on the standardized test, 60 wpm typing speed, and the ability to take 30 wpm dictation?

c) Test whether the coefficient for words per minute of typing speed (X4) is significantly different from zero at $\alpha = 0.05$.

d) How might this model be improved?

e) A correlation of age with salary finds $r = 0.682$, and the scatterplot shows a moderately strong positive linear association. However, if X6 = Age is added to the multiple regression, the estimated coefficient of age turns out to be $b_6 = -0.154$. Explain some possible causes for this apparent change of direction in the relationship between age and salary.

32. Walmart revenue. Here's a regression of monthly revenue of Walmart Corp, during 2004–2006 relating that revenue to the Total U.S. Retail Sales, the Personal Consumption Index, and the Consumer Price Index.

```
Dependent variable is: Walmart_Revenue
R squared = 66.7%  R squared (adjusted) = 63.8%
s = 2.327 with 39 - 4 = 35 degrees of freedom
```

Source	Sum of Squares	df	Mean Square	F-ratio
Regression	378.749	3	126.250	23.3
Residual	189.474	35	5.41354	

Variable	Coeff	SE(Coeff)	t-ratio	P-value
Intercept	87.0089	33.60	2.59	0.0139
Retail Sales	0.000103	0.000015	6.67	<0.0001
Persnl Consmp	0.00001108	0.000004	2.52	0.0165
CPI	-0.344795	0.1203	-2.87	0.0070

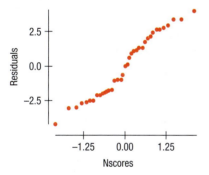

a) Write the regression model.

b) Interpret the coefficient of the Consumer Price Index (CPI). Does it surprise you that the sign of this coefficient is negative? Explain.

c) Test the standard null hypothesis for the coefficient of CPI and state your conclusions.

33. Gross domestic product. The gross domestic product (GDP) is an important measure of the overall economic strength of a country. GDP per capita makes comparisons between different size countries more meaningful. A researcher looking at GDP, fit the following model based on an educational variable, *Primary School Completion Rate (%)*, and finds:

```
Dependent variable is: GDP per Capita
R squared = 3.44%
s = 15945.46 with 96 - 1 = 95 df
```

Term	Estimate	Std Error	t-Ratio	P-value
Intercept	1935.5693	5987.938	0.320	0.7472
Primary Completion Rate	122.3288	66.8131	1.830	0.0703

a) Explain to the researcher why, on the basis of the regression summary, she might want to consider other predictor variables in the model.

b) Explain why you are not surprised that the sign of the slope is positive.

The researcher adds two variables to the regression and finds:

```
Dependent variable is: GDP per Capita
R squared = 80.00%
s = 7327.65 with 96 - 4 = 92 df
```

Term	Estimate	SE(Coeff)	t-Ratio	P-value
Intercept	2775.98251	2803.32606	0.99	0.3247
Cell phones/ 100 people	92.84968	37.38697	2.48	0.0148
Internet users per 100 people (2004)	480.49061	54.04020	8.89	<0.0001
Primary completion rate	-63.28454	32.25614	-1.96	0.0528

c) Explain how the slope of *Primary Completion Rate* can now be negative.

34. Lobsters 2016, revisited. In Chapter 17, Exercise 53 predicted the annual value of the Maine lobster industry catch from the number of licensed lobster fishers. The lobster industry is an important one in Maine, with annual landings worth more than $500,000,000 and employment consequences that extend throughout the state's economy. We saw in Chapter 17 that it was best to transform Value by logarithms. Here's a more sophisticated multiple regression to predict the logValue from other variables published by the Maine Department of Marine Resources (maine .gov/dmr/commercial-fishing/landings/documents/lobster .table.pdf). The predictors are number of *Traps* (millions), number of licensed *Fishers*, and *Pounds/Trap* during the years 1950 to 2016. (If you wish to replicate this regression in your statistics package, you have to compute Pounds(M)/ Traps(M) as the third predictor variable.)

```
Response variable is: LogValue
R squared = 96.9% R squared (adjusted) = 96.8%
s = 0.1036 with 67 - 4 = 63 degrees of freedom
```

Variable	Coefficient	SE(Coeff)	t-ratio	P-value
Intercept	6.73738	0.1057	63.7	<0.0001
Traps(M)	0.607250	0.0138	43.9	<0.0001
License holders	-0.000042	0.0000	-3.47	0.0010
Pounds/Trap	0.000474	0.0013	3.64	0.0006

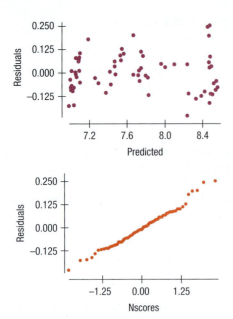

a) Write the regression model.
b) Are the assumptions and conditions met?
c) Interpret the coefficient of *License Holders*. Would you expect that restricting the number of lobstering licenses to even fewer fishers would increase the value of the harvest?
d) State and test the standard null hypothesis for the coefficient of *Pounds/Trap*. Scientists claim that this is an important predictor of the harvest. Do you agree?

T 35. Lobsters 2016, revisited, part 2. In Chapter 17, Exercise 54 predicted the price ($/lb) of lobster harvested in the Maine lobster fishing industry. Here's a multiple regression to predict the *Price* from the number of *Traps* (millions), the number of *License Holders*, and *Pounds/Trap* during the years 1950 to 2016.

```
Response variable is: Price/lb
R squared = 94.1%  R squared (adjusted) = 93.8%
s = 0.3127 with 67 − 4 = 63 degrees of freedom
```

Variable	Coefficient	SE(Coeff)	t-ratio	P-value
Intercept	0.729693	0.3191	2.29	0.0256
Traps(M)	1.26703	0.0417	30.4	<0.0001
License holders	−0.000134	0.0000	−3.66	0.0005
Pounds/Trap	−0.006075	0.0039	−1.54	0.1276

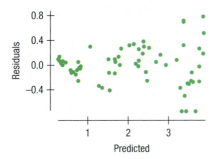

a) Write the regression model.
b) Are the assumptions and conditions met?

Here is an alternative regression model predicting the logarithm of Price/lb:

```
Response variable is: Log(Price/lb)
R squared = 95.1%  R squared (adjusted) = 94.8%
s = 0.0810 with 67 − 4 = 63 degrees of freedom
```

Variable	Coefficient	SE(Coeff)	t-ratio	P-value
Intercept	−0.049433	0.0826	−0.598	0.5518
Traps(M)	0.328341	0.0108	30.4	<0.0001
License holders	−0.0000276	0.0000	−2.91	0.0050
Pounds/Trap	−0.0077	0.0010	−7.60	<0.0001

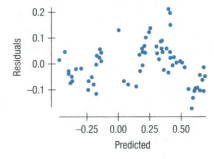

c) Which regression model would you prefer? Why?
d) State and test the standard null hypothesis for the coefficient of *License Holders* in the second model.
e) Does the coefficient of *Pounds/Trap* mean that when more lobsters are landed per trap the price of lobsters will decrease?

T 36. HDI 2016. In 1990, the United Nations created a single statistic, the Human Development Index or HDI, to summarize the health, education, and economic status of countries. Here is a multiple regression model trying to predict *HDI*.

```
Response variable is: HDI
R squared = 99.9%  R squared (adjusted) = 99.9%
s = 0.0050 with 188 − 5 = 183 degrees of freedom
```

Variable	Coefficient	SE(Coeff)	t-ratio	P-value
Intercept	−0.337578	0.0042	−80.1	<0.0001
Life expectancy	0.00463	0.0001	57.2	<0.0001
Expected Schooling	0.010581	0.0003	39.6	<0.0001
Mean yrs of school	0.012389	0.0002	54.1	<0.0001
Log(GNI/cap)	0.116918	0.0014	85.5	<0.0001

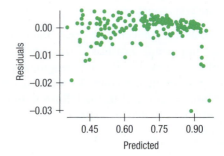

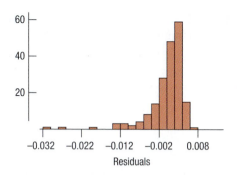

a) Write the regression model.

b) Are the assumptions and conditions met?

c) State and test the standard null hypothesis for the coefficient of *Expected Years of Schooling*. Use the standard-level of $\alpha = 0.05$ and state your conclusion.

d) What effects do your observation in response to part b have on your test in part c?

e*) If you have a statistics program, open the data file **HDI 2016**. Look at plots of individual variables and pairs of variables from this analysis to see if you can find the outliers. What do you conclude about these outliers?

T 37. Walmart revenue, part 2. Walmart is the second largest retailer in the world. The data file on the disk holds monthly data on Walmart's revenue, along with several possibly related economic variables.

a) Using computer software, find the regression equation predicting Walmart revenues from the *Retail Index*, the Consumer Price index (*CPI*), and *Personal Consumption*.

b) Does it seem that Walmart's revenue is closely related to the general state of the economy?

T 38. Walmart revenue, part 3. Consider the model you fit in Exercise 37 to predict Walmart's revenue from the Retail Index, CPI, and Personal Consumption index.

a) Plot the residuals against the predicted values and comment on what you see.

b) Identify and remove the four cases corresponding to December revenue and find the regression with December results removed.

c) Does it seem that Walmart's revenue is closely related to the general state of the economy?

*39. Clinical trials. An important challenge in clinical trials is patients who drop out before the trial is completed. This can cost pharmaceutical companies millions of dollars because patients who have received a tested treatment for months must be combined with those who received it for a much shorter time. Can we predict who will drop out of a study early? We have data for 428 patients from a clinical trial of depression. We have data on their *Age*, and their *Hamilton Rating Depression Scale* (*HRDS*) and whether or not they completed the study (*Drop 1 = Yes*; *0 = No. Completed the study*).

Here is the output from a logistic regression model of *Drop* on *HRDS* and *Age*.

Term	Estimate	Std Error	z	P-Value
Intercept	0.441972938	0.488270354	0.9055	0.3654
AGE	0.037904831	0.011511729	3.292	0.001
HDRS	−0.046817607	0.015903137	2.944	0.0032

a) Write out the estimated regression equation.

b) What is the predicted log odds (logit) of the probability that a 30-year-old patient with an HDRS score of 30 will drop out of the study?

c) What is the predicted dropout probability of that patient?

d) What is the predicted log odds (logit) of the probability that a 60-year-old patient with an HDRS score of 8 will drop out of the study?

e) What is the associated predicted probability?

*40. Cost of higher education. Are there fundamental differences between liberal arts colleges and universities? In this case, we have information on the top 25 liberal arts colleges and the top 25 universities in the United States. We will consider the type of school as our response variable and will use the percent of students who were in the top 10% of their high school class and the amount of money spent per student by the college or university as our explanatory variables. The output from this logistic regression is given here.

Logistic Regression Table

Predictor	Coeff	SE(Coeff)	z	P
Intercept	−13.1461	3.98629	−3.30	0.001
Top 10%	0.0845469	0.0396345	2.13	0.033
$/Student	0.0002594	0.0000860	3.02	0.003

a) Write out the estimated regression equation.

b) Is the percent of students in the top 10% of their high school class statistically significant in predicting whether or not the school is a university? Explain.

c) Is the amount of money spent per student statistically significant in predicting whether or not the school is a university? Explain.

T 41. Dirt bikes 2014. More than one million motorcycles are sold annually (www.webbikeworld.com). Off-road motorcycles (often called "dirt bikes") are a market segment (about 18%) that is highly specialized and offers great variation in features. This makes it a good segment to study to learn about which features account for the cost (manufacturer's suggested retail price, MSRP) of a dirt bike. Researchers collected data on dirt bikes. Their original goal was to study market differentiation among brands (Jiang Lu, Joseph B. Kadane, and Peter Boatwright, *The Dirt on Bikes: An Illustration of CART Models for Brand Differentiation*). We have updated the data and can use it to predict msrp from other variables.

Here are scatterplots of three potential predictors, *Wheelbase (in)*, *Displacement (cu in)*, and *Bore (in)*.

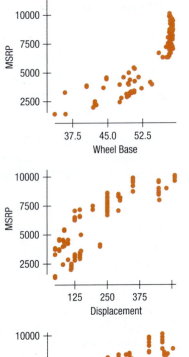

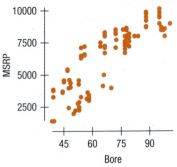

Comment on the appropriateness of using these variables as predictors on the basis of the scatterplots.

T 42. Dirt bikes 2014, part 2. In Exercise 41, we saw data on off-road motorcycles and examined scatterplots. Review those scatterplots. Here's a regression of *MSRP* on both *Displacement* and *Bore*. Both of the predictors are measures of the size of the engine. The displacement is the total volume of air and fuel mixture that an engine can draw in during one cycle. The bore is the diameter of the cylinders.

Response variable is: MSRP
R squared = 72.2% R squared (adjusted) = 71.7%
s = 1299 with 114 − 3 = 111 degrees of freedom

Variable	Coefficient	SE(Coeff)	t-ratio	P-value
Intercept	−323.299	1197	−0.270	0.7875
Displacement	4.38220	4.108	1.07	0.2884
Bore	82.9084	30.54	2.71	0.0077

a) State and test the standard null hypothesis for the coefficient of *Displacement*.
b) Both of these predictors seem to be linearly related to *MSRP*. Explain what your result in part a means.

T 43. Dirt bikes 2014, part 3. Here's another model for the *MSRP* of off-road motorcycles.

Response variable is: MSRP
R squared = 88.9% R squared (adjusted) = 88.6%
s = 828.3 with 112 − 4 = 108 degrees of freedom

Variable	Coefficient	SE(Coeff)	t-ratio	P-value
Intercept	−9561.50	716.8	−13.3	<0.0001
Bore	79.9424	7.498	10.7	<0.0001
Weight	−17.8908	3.110	−5.75	<0.0001
Wheel Base	260.399	20.31	12.8	<0.0001

a) Would this be a good model to use to predict the price of an off-road motorcycle if you knew its bore, clearance, and engine strokes? Explain.
b) The Honda CRF450X has an MSRP of $8440, a wheel base of 58.3, and a bore of 96. Can you use this model to estimate its *Weight*? Explain.

T 44. Demographics. The dataset holds various measures of the 50 United States. The *Murder* rate is per 100,000, *HS Graduation* rate is in %, *Income* is per capita income in dollars, *Illiteracy* rate is per 1000, and *Life Expectancy* is in years. Find a regression model for *Life Expectancy* with three predictor variables by trying all four of the possible models.

a) Which model appears to do the best?
b) Would you leave all three predictors in this model?
c) Does this model mean that by changing the levels of the predictors in this equation, we could affect life expectancy in that state? Explain.
d) Be sure to check the conditions for multiple regression. What do you conclude?

T 45. Burger King items. Like many fast-food restaurant chains, Burger King (BK) provides data on the nutrition content of its menu items on its website. Here's a multiple regression predicting calories for Burger King foods from *Protein* content (g), *Total Fat* (g), *Carbohydrate* (g), and *Sodium* (mg) per serving.

Response variable is: Calories R squared = 99.9%
R squared (adjusted) = 99.9%
s = 8.752 with 122 − 4 = 118 degrees of freedom

Source	Sum of Squares	df	Mean Square	F-ratio
Regression	6434653	3	2144884	28002
Residual	9038.61	118	76.5984	

Variable	Coefficient	SE(Coeff)	t-ratio	P-value
Intercept	1.55770	1.965	0.793	0.4296
Protein(g)	3.86017	0.0952	40.6	<0.0001
Fat(g)	9.22763	0.0863	107	<0.0001
Carbs(g)	3.87753	0.0467	83.1	<0.0001

a) Do you think this model would do a good job of predicting calories for a new BK menu item? Why or why not?
b) The mean of *Calories* is 452.1 with a standard deviation of 230.8. Discuss what the value of *s* in the regression means about how well the model fits the data.

c) Does the R^2 value of 99.9% mean that the residuals are all actually equal to zero?

46. Health expenditures. Can the amount of money that a country spends on health (as % of GDP) be predicted by other economic indicators? Here's a regression predicting *Expenditures on Public Health (as % of GDP)* from *Expected Years of Schooling* and *Internet Users (per 100 people):*

```
Dependent variable is: Expenditures on Public Health
R squared = 55.17%
s = 1.710 with 96 − 3 = 93
```

Term	Estimate	Std Error	t-Ratio	P-value
Intercept	0.19941	0.95009	0.21	0.8342
Expected Years of Schooling (of children) (years)	0.23244	0.08259	2.81	0.006
Internet Users Per 100 People (2004)	0.05142	0.01031	4.99	<0.0001

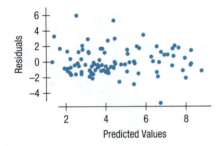

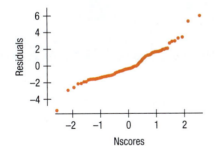

a) Write the regression model.

b) Are the assumptions and conditions met?

c) State and test the standard null hypothesis for the coefficient of *Expected Years of Schooling*. Use the standard α-level of $\alpha = 0.05$ and state your conclusion.

d) Does the coefficient of *Internet Users/100 people* mean that when Internet use increases, the expenditures on public health will increase as well?

JUST CHECKING ANSWERS

1 58.4% of the variation in *Percent Body Fat* can be accounted for by the multiple regression model using *Height*, *Age*, and *Weight* as predictors.

2 For a given *Height* and *Weight*, an increase of one year in *Age* is associated with an increase of 0.137% in *Body Fat* on average.

3 The multiple regression coefficient is interpreted for *given* values of the other variables. That is, for people of the *same Weight* and *Age*, those who are one inch taller on average have 1.2764% less *Body Fat*.

4 Histograms are used to examine the shapes of distributions of individual variables. We check especially for multiple modes, outliers, and skewness. They are also used to check the shape of the distribution of the residuals for the Nearly Normal Condition.

5 Scatterplots are used to check the Linearity Condition in plots of *y* vs. any of the *x*'s. They are used to check plots of the residuals or Studentized residuals against the predicted values, against any of the predictors, or against Time to check for patterns.

6 The Normal model is needed only when we use inference; it isn't needed for computing a regression model. We check the Nearly Normal Condition on the residuals.

Bolliger and Mabillard

The story is told that when John Wardley, the award-winning concept designer of theme parks and roller coasters, including *Nitro* and *Oblivion*, was about to test the roller coaster *Nemesis* for the first time, he asked Walter Bolliger, the president of the coaster's manufacturer, B&M, "What if the coaster stalls? How will we get the trains back to the station?" Bolliger replied, "Our coasters never stall. They always work perfectly the first time." And, it did work perfectly.

Roller coaster connoisseurs know that Bolliger & Mabillard Consulting Engineers, Inc. (B&M) is responsible for some of the most innovative roller coasters in the business. The company was founded in the late 1980s when Walter Bolliger and Claude Mabillard left Intamin AG, where they had designed the company's first stand-up coaster. B&M has built its reputation on innovation. They developed the first "inverted" roller coaster in which the train runs under the track with the seats attached to the wheel carriage and pioneered "diving machines," which feature a vertical drop, introduced first with *Oblivion*.

B&M coasters are famous among enthusiasts for particularly smooth rides and for their reliability, easy maintainability, and excellent safety record. Unlike some other manufacturers, B&M does not use powered launches, preferring,

as do many coaster connoisseurs, gravity-powered coasters. B&M is an international leader in the roller coaster design field, having designed 24 of the top 50 steel roller coasters on the 2009 Golden Ticket Awards list and 3 of the top 10 in the 2013 Awards.

WHO	Roller coasters
WHAT	See Table 19.1 for the variables and their units.
WHERE	Worldwide
WHEN	All were in operation in 2018.
WHY	To understand characteristics that affect speed and duration

Theme parks are big business. In the United States alone, there are nearly 500 theme and amusement parks that generate over $10 billion a year in revenue. The U.S. industry is fairly mature, but parks in the rest of the world are still growing. Europe now generates more than $1 billion a year from their theme parks, and Asia's industry is growing fast. Although theme parks have started to diversify to include water parks and zoos, rides are still the main attraction at most parks, and at the center of the rides is the roller coaster. Engineers and designers compete to make them bigger and faster. For a two-minute ride on the fastest and best roller coasters, fans will wait for hours.

Can we learn what makes a roller coaster fast? What are the most important design considerations in getting the fastest coaster? Here are data on some typical coasters. (Data in **Coasters 2015**)

TABLE 19.1 Facts about some roller coasters. (Source: The Roller Coaster Database at www.rcdb.com.)

Name	Park	Track	Duration (sec)	Speed (mph)	Height (ft)	Drop (ft)	Length (ft)	Inversions
Mind Eraser	Six Flags America	Steel	125	55	115	95	2170	1
Silver Bullet	Frontier City	Steel	75	55	83	75	1942	1
Starliner	Miracle Strip Park	Wood		55	70	76	2640	0
T2	Six Flags Kentucky	Steel	125	55	115	95	2170	1
Thunderbolt	Kennywood Park	Wood	90	55	70	95	2887	0
Timber Wolf	Worlds of Fun	Wood	133	53	100	95	4230	0

A small selection of coasters from the larger dataset **Coasters 2015**.

- *Track* indicates what kind of track the roller coaster has. The possible values are "Wood" and "Steel."
- *Duration* is the duration of the ride in seconds.
- *Speed* is top speed in miles per hour.
- *Height* is maximum height above ground level in feet.
- *Drop* is greatest drop in feet.
- *Length* is total length of the track in feet.
- *Inversions* reports whether riders are turned upside down during the ride. It has the values 1 (yes) and 0 (no). Some coasters have multiple inversions.

Coaster fans want their ride to be fast and to last. How are these two properties related? Figure 19.1 shows a scatterplot of the relationship.

FIGURE 19.1 The *Duration* and *Speed* of coasters are related.

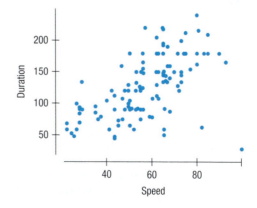

Two coasters stick out in the scatterplot. One is the *Tower of Terror*, a ride at several Disney parks that tells a story and drops vertically at faster than the acceleration of gravity. It is clearly not a "roller coaster" in the traditional sense of the term, and probably doesn't belong with the others. We will set it aside. The other is the *Xcelerator*, which is a hydraulically launched ride that does not depend on gravity for its speed. We can set this one aside as well.

The regression model for the remaining coasters is in Table 19.2.

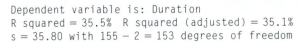

```
Dependent variable is: Duration
R squared = 35.5%  R squared (adjusted) = 35.1%
s = 35.80 with 155 - 2 = 153 degrees of freedom
```

Source	Sum of Squares	df	Mean Square	F-ratio
Regression	108135	1	108135	84.4
Residual	196085	153	1281.60	

Variable	Coefficient	SE(Coeff)	t-ratio	P-value
Intercept	23.1193	11.36	2.04	0.0435
Speed	1.80344	0.1963	9.19	<0.0001

TABLE 19.2 A regression model after setting aside two outlying coasters.

Starting from an intercept of 23.12 seconds, coaster rides tend to last 1.8 seconds more per one mile per hour of speed. The R^2 says that 35.5% of the variation in *Duration* is accounted for by this regression model.

The residual plot (Figure 19.2) suggests that the regression assumptions are satisfied.

FIGURE 19.2 Residuals vs. predicted values for the regression of Table 19.2.

19.1 Indicator (or Dummy) Variables

Of course, there's more to these data. One interesting variable is the kind of track the coasters run on. Traditional coasters run on wood and have impressive wooden structures and a classical "rumble" to the ride. Many modern coasters run on steel tracks and can perform tricks such as inversions, where the riders are turned upside down. Does the kind of track affect the speed, duration, or the relationship between these variables? Figure 19.4 uses color and plot symbol to show the two kinds of track.

Until now, all our predictor variables have been quantitative. The kind of track a coaster has is a categorical variable ("wood" or "steel"). In Figure 19.3, steel track coasters are plotted with blue dots and wood track coasters are plotted with red x's. The figure also shows a separate regression line for each group.

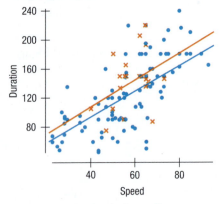

FIGURE 19.3 Figure 19.2 repeated with track type indicated by color and symbol. Wood track is plotted with red x's, steel track with blue dots. Regression lines are shown for each group.

It's easy to see that, for a given speed, the roller coasters on wood tracks have rides that take a bit longer and that for each type of track, the slopes of the relationship between duration and speed are almost equal. If we split the data into two groups and compute the regression for each group, the output looks like this:

```
Dependent variable is: Duration
cases selected according to Wood
R squared = 16.1%  R squared (adjusted) = 12.1%
s = 34.60 with 23 - 2 = 21 degrees of freedom
```

Variable	Coefficient	SE(Coeff)	t-ratio	P-value
Intercept	33.2167	54.31	0.612	0.5474
Speed	1.85997	0.9252	2.01	0.0574

```
Response variable is: Duration
cases selected according to Steel
R squared = 37.6%  R squared (adjusted) = 37.1%
s = 35.74 with 132 - 2 = 130 degrees of freedom
```

Variable	Coefficient	SE(Coeff)	t-ratio	P-value
Intercept	22.3380	11.58	1.93	0.0559
Speed	1.77552	0.2007	8.85	<0.0001

TABLE 19.3 The regressions computed separately for the two types of roller coasters show similar slopes but different intercepts.

As the scatterplot showed, the slopes are very similar, but the intercepts are different. When we have a situation like this with roughly parallel regressions for each group,[1] there's an easy way to add the group information to a single regression model. We create a new variable that *indicates* what type of roller coaster we have, giving it the value 1 for roller coasters that have steel tracks and the value 0 for those that have wood tracks. (We could have reversed the coding; it's an arbitrary choice.[2]) Such variables are called **indicator variables** or *indicators* because they indicate which category each case is in. They are also often called **dummy variables**. When we add our new indicator, *Track* to the regression model as a second variable, the multiple regression model looks like this.

```
Response variable is: Duration
R squared = 37.1%  R squared (adjusted) = 36.3%
s = 35.47 with 155 - 3 = 152 degrees of freedom
```

> *Track* = 1 if a coaster has a steel track.
> *Track* = 0 if the track is wood.

Variable	Coefficient	SE(Coeff)	t-ratio	P-value
Intercept	37.9228	13.54	2.80	0.0058
Speed	1.77909	0.1949	9.13	<0.0001
Track	-15.7830	8.031	-1.97	0.0512

TABLE 19.4 The regression model with a dummy, or indicator, variable for Track type.

This looks like a better model than the simple regression for all the data. The R^2 is larger, the *t*-ratios of both coefficients are large, and now we can understand the effect of Track type with a single model without having to compare two regressions. (The residuals look reasonable as well.) But what does the coefficient for *Track* mean? Let's see how an indicator variable works when we calculate predicted values for two of the roller coasters listed in Table 19.1.

Name	Park	Type	Duration	Speed	Height	Drop	Length	Inversion?
Mind Eraser	Six Flags America	Steel	125	55	115	95	2170	1
Timber Wolf	Worlds of Fun	Wood	133	53	100	95	4230	0

---

[1] The fact that the individual regression lines are nearly parallel is a part of the Linearity Condition. You should check that the lines are nearly parallel before using this method or read on to see what to do if they are not parallel enough.

[2] Some implementations of indicator variables use 1 and −1 for the levels of the categories.

Ignoring the variable *Track* for the moment, the model (in Table 19.4) says that for all coasters, the predicted *Duration* is:

$$37.92 + 1.78 \ Speed - 15.78 \ Track.$$

Now remember that for this indicator variable, the value 1 means that a coaster has a steel track, and a 0 means it has a wooden track. For *Timber Wolf*, on a wooden track, the value of *Track* is 0, so the coefficient of *Track* doesn't affect the prediction at all. With a speed of 53 mph, we predict its duration as:[3]

$$37.92 + 1.78 \times 53 - 15.78 \times 0 = 132.26 \ \text{seconds},$$

which is close to its actual duration of 133 seconds. The *Mind Eraser* has a steel track, and so the model predicts an "adjustment" of 15.78 seconds for its duration:

$$37.92 + 1.78 \times 55 - 15.78 \times 1 = 120.04 \ \text{seconds}.$$

That compares well with the actual duration of 125 seconds.

Notice how the indicator works in the model. When there is a steel track (as in *Mind Eraser*), the value 1 for the indicator causes the amount of the indicator's coefficient, 15.78, to be subtracted from the prediction. When there is a wooden track (as in *Timber Wolf*), the indicator is 0, so nothing is subtracted. Looking back at the scatterplot, we can see that this is exactly what we need. The difference between the two lines is a vertical shift of about 16 seconds. This may seem a bit confusing at first because we usually think of the coefficients in a multiple regression as slopes. For indicator variables, however, they act differently. They're vertical shifts that keep the slopes for the other variables apart.

An indicator variable that is 0 or 1 can only shift the line up and down. It can't change the slope, so it works only when we have lines with the same slope and different intercepts.

Indicators for Three or More Categories

Business and economic variables such as *Month* or *Socioeconomic Class* may have several levels, not just two. You can construct indicators for a categorical variable with several levels by constructing a separate indicator for each of these levels. There's just one thing to keep in mind. If a variable has *k* levels, you can create only *k* − 1 indicators. You have to choose one of the *k* categories as a "baseline" and *leave out* its indicator. Then the coefficients of the other indicators can be interpreted as the amount by which their categories differ from the baseline, after allowing for the linear effects of the other variables in the model. (There are ways to code the variables so that each is compared to the overall mean. See the comment in Footnote 2.)

For the two-category variable *Track*, we used "Wood" as the baseline, and coasters with steel tracks got a 1. We needed only one variable for two levels. If we wished to represent *Month* with indicators, we would need 11 of them. We might, for example, define *January* as the baseline and make indicators for *February*, *March*, . . . , *November*, and *December*. Each of these indicators would be 0 for all cases except for the ones that had that value for the variable *Month*.

Why couldn't we use a single variable with "1" for *January*, "2" for *February*, and so on? That would require the pretty strict assumption that the responses to the months are linear and equally spaced—that is, that the change in our response variable from January to February is the same in both direction and amount as the

---

[3]We round coefficient values when we write the model and sometimes, as here, when we show calculations in the text. But, in general, we recommend calculating with full precision, rounding only at the end of the calculation.

change from July to August. That's a pretty severe restriction and usually isn't true. Using 11 indicators releases the model from that restriction even though it adds complexity to the model.

Once you've created multiple indicator variables (up to $k - 1$) for a categorical variable with k levels, it often helps to combine levels with similar characteristics and with similar relationships with the response. This can help keep the number of variables in a multiple regression from exploding.

IN PRACTICE 19.1   Building better models by using indicator variables

In Chapter 17 we looked at data on the prices of diamonds (see page 568). Although, in general, higher carat weight means higher cost, *Carat Weight* is not the only factor that determines a diamond's price. A typical diamond is pale yellow. The less color a diamond has, the higher its color grade and—generally—its price. We want to build a model that incorporates both *Carat Weight* and *Color* to predict a diamond's price. The data here are a collection of 749 diamonds: *Weight* is between 0.3 and 1.4 carats; color grades are D (highest possible), G (medium), and K (fairly low). We'll use $Log_{10}Price$ as the response to make the relationship more linear. Here are scatterplots of *Price* and $Log_{10}Price$ versus *Carat Weight* for these diamonds:

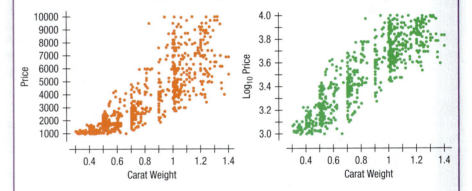

A linear model for $Log_{10}Price$ on *Carat Weight* alone finds:

```
Response Variable: Log₁₀Price
R² = 77.39%  Adjusted R² = 77.36%
s = 0.1364 with 749 - 2 = 747 degrees of freedom
```

Variable	Coeff	SE(Coeff)	t-ratio	P-value
Intercept	2.76325	0.01532	180.42	<0.0001
Carat.Weight	0.90020	0.01780	50.56	<0.0001

Here is a scatterplot of $Log_{10}Price$ vs. *Carat Weight* showing the three different color grades (D, G, and K):

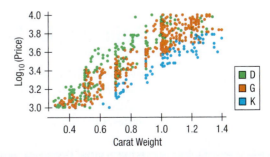

(continued)

To account for the differences, two indicator variables were created:

$$Color\ D = 1\ \text{if } Color = D \text{ and } 0 \text{ otherwise}$$
$$Color\ G = 1\ \text{if } Color = G \text{ and } 0 \text{ otherwise}$$

A multiple regression of $Log_{10}Price$ was run with three predictors: *Carat Weight*, *Color D*, and *Color G*.

Here is the output:

```
Response Variable: Log₁₀Price
R² = 85.66%  Adjusted R² = 85.61%
s = 0.1088 with 749 − 4 = 745 degrees of freedom
```

Variable	Coeff	SE(Coeff)	t-ratio	P-value
Intercept	2.43978	0.01981	123.14	<0.0001
Carat.Weight	1.02865	0.01589	64.75	<0.0001
ColorD	0.29405	0.01424	20.65	<0.0001
ColorG	0.21883	0.01278	17.12	<0.0001

MANAGER Of course, I understand the four C's of diamond pricing. I think I understand your model for predicting price (or log price) for each color diamond. Why did you put indicator variables for *Color* in the model with *Carat Weight*, and why are there only two even though there are three different colors that we considered?

CONSULTANT We could build a separate model for each of the three colors, but by using indicators we can borrow strength from the entire dataset. The interpretation is the same, although by using only indicators as we have, we have restricted the slopes to be the same and are only changing the intercepts. I can add interaction (discussed in the next section) to estimate different slopes for each color as well. The indicator variable adjusts the intercept value for the two color levels, D and G. Since diamonds of color K have both dummy variables set to 0, the equation for diamonds with *Color K* is simply:

$$\widehat{Log_{10}Price} = 2.440 + 1.029\ Carat\ Weight$$

For diamonds with *Color G*, we add 0.219 to the intercept, so:

$$\widehat{Log_{10}Price} = (2.440 + 0.219) + 1.029\ Carat\ Weight = 2.659 + 1.029\ Carat\ Weight$$

Similarly for diamonds with *Color D*, we add 0.294 to the intercept, so:

$$\widehat{Log_{10}Price} = (2.440 + 0.294) + 1.029\ Carat\ Weight = 2.734 + 1.029\ Carat\ Weight$$

Both indicator variables are highly significant, which means that the differences in intercept are large enough to justify the addition of the variables.

With 3 levels of color, we need only 2 indicator variables. (In general k levels require $k − 1$ indicators.)

19.2 Adjusting for Different Slopes—Interaction Terms

WHO	Burger King menu items
WHAT	Calories, Carbohydrates, Protein, Type of item
WHEN	Current
WHERE	Posted in stores and online
WHY	Informing customers

Even consumers of fast food are increasingly concerned with nutrition. So, like many restaurant chains, Burger King publishes the nutrition details of its menu items on its website (www.bk.com). Many customers count calories or carbohydrates. Of course, these are likely to be related to each other. We can examine that relationship in Burger King foods by looking at a scatterplot. (Data in **Burger King items**. Breakfast items omitted here.)

FIGURE 19.4 *Calories* of Burger King food plotted against *Carbs* seems to fan out.

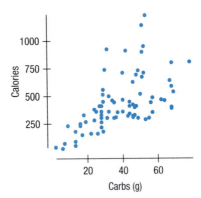

It's not surprising to see that an increase in *Carbs* is associated with more *Calories*, but the plot seems to thicken as we move from left to right. Could there be something else going on?

We can divide Burger King foods into two groups, coloring those with meat (including chicken and fish) with red x's and those without meat with blue dots. Looking at the regression lines for each group (Figure 19.5), we see a different picture:

FIGURE 19.5 Plotting the meat-based and nonmeat items separately, we see two distinct linear patterns.

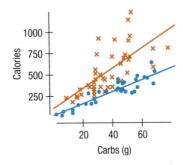

> ### Burger King
>
> James McLamore and David Edgerton, graduates of the Cornell University School of Hotel Administration, opened their first Burger King (BK) restaurant in 1954. McLamore had been impressed with the assembly-line–based production innovated by Dick and Mac MacDonald. BK grew in the Miami area and then expanded nationally through franchising. Pillsbury acquired BK in 1967 and expanded it internationally. After a number of owners, BK was purchased by private investors and taken public. The initial public offering (IPO) in 2006 generated $425 million in revenue—the largest IPO of a U.S.-based restaurant chain on record.

Clearly, meat-based items contribute more calories from their carbohydrate content than do other Burger King foods. But unlike Figure 19.3, when the lines were parallel, we can't account for the kind of difference we see here by just including a dummy variable in a regression. It isn't just the intercepts of the lines that are different; they have entirely different slopes.

We'll start, as before, by constructing the indicator for the two groups, *Meat*, which is 1 for foods that contain meat and 0 for the others. The variable *Meat* can adjust the intercepts of the two lines. To adjust the slopes, we have to construct another variable—the *product* of *Meat* and the predictor variable *Carbs*. The coefficient of this **interaction term** in a multiple regression gives an adjustment to the slope for the cases in the indicated group. The resulting variable *Carbs*Meat* has the value of *Carbs* for foods containing meat (those coded 1 in the *Meat* indicator) and the value 0 for the others. By including this interaction variable in the model, we can adjust the slope of the line fit to the meat-containing foods. Here's the resulting analysis:

TABLE 19.5 The regression model with both an indicator variable and an interaction term.

```
Response variable is: Calories
R squared = 65.5%  R squared (adjusted) = 64.1%
s = 146.6 with 77 - 4 = 73 degrees of freedom
```

Source	Sum of Squares	df	Mean Square	F-ratio
Regression	2976010	3	992003	46.2
Residual	1568378	73	21484.6	

Variable	Coefficient	SE(Coeff)	t-ratio	P-value
Intercept	20.2727	58.96	0.344	0.7319
Carbs(g)	6.99260	1.306	5.35	<0.0001
Meat	83.3843	83.70	0.996	0.3224
Carbs*Meat	4.78831	1.984	2.41	0.0183

What does the coefficient for the indicator *Meat* do? It provides a different intercept to separate the meat and nonmeat items at the origin (where *Carbs* = 0). Each group has its own slope, but the two lines nearly meet at the origin, so there seems to be no need for an additional intercept adjustment. That's why the coefficient for the indicator variable *Meat* has a small *t*-ratio (−0.996).

By contrast, the coefficient of the interaction term, *Carbs*Meat*, says that the slope relating calories to carbohydrates is steeper by 4.79 calories per carbohydrate gram for meat-containing foods than for meat-free foods. Its small P-value suggests that this difference is real. Overall, the regression model predicts calories to be:

$$20.27 + 6.99\ Carbs + 83.38\ Meat + 4.79\ Carbs*Meat.$$

Let's see how these adjustments work. A BK Whopper with cheese has 52 grams of carbohydrates and is a meat dish. The model predicts its *Calories* as:

$$20.27 + 6.99 \times 52 + 83.38 \times 1 + 4.79 \times (52 \times 1) = 716.21\ calories,$$

not far from the measured calorie count of 710. By contrast, the Veggie Burger, with 43 grams of carbohydrates, has value 0 for *Meat* and so has a value of 0 for *Carbs*Meat* as well. Those indicators contribute nothing to its predicted calories:

$$20.27 + 6.99 \times 44 + 83.38 \times 0 + 4.79 \times 0 = 327.83\ calories.$$

IN PRACTICE 19.2 Changing slopes by adding interaction terms

After adding the indicator variables for *Color*, which showed different intercepts for the three different color levels, the consultant wonders if the slopes for the three color levels might be different as well, so she adds two more predictors, *ColorD*Carat Weight* and *ColorG*Carat Weight*, to the model (see page 653). The regression output shows:

```
Response Variable: Log10Price
R-squared = 85.77%  Adjusted R-squared = 85.67%
s = 0.1085 with 749 - 6 = 743 degrees of freedom
```

Variable	Coeff	SE(Coeff)	t-ratio	P-value
Intercept	2.54151	0.06000	42.361	<0.0001
Carat.Weight	0.92968	0.05734	16.212	<0.0001
ColorD	0.16466	0.06302	2.613	0.00916
ColorG	0.12656	0.06287	2.013	0.04448
Carat.Weight*ColorD	0.14076	0.06356	2.215	0.02709
Carat.Weight*ColorG	0.08809	0.06095	1.445	0.14877

> **MANAGER** What did you discover about the model for price when you added the interaction terms?
>
> **CONSULTANT** The only significant interaction term is the one for *ColorD* by *Carat Weight*, so we probably don't need different slopes for levels *G* and *K*. We should refit the regression without the interaction term *ColorG*Carat Weight*. When we do, we find that the term for *Carat Weight*ColorD* is marginally significant. The decision whether to include it is a judgment call. To make a final decision, we should also consider residual analysis and diagnostics. For the sake of simplicity we will proceed with the simpler model with only the indicator variables and not the interaction (the model fit in the previous example).
>
> In summary, the intercepts are different for each color and Color D has a different slope than G and K.

JUST CHECKING

A researcher in the Human Resource department wants to study the relationships among *Salary, Years Experience, Education,* and *Gender*. For *Education*, there are 3 levels: high school or some college (*HS*), college grad (*BA*), and post graduate (*PG*).

1 If she wants to account for differences in the relationship between *Salary* and *Years Experience* for men and women, what terms should she enter in the regression?

2 If she wants to study the differences in the relationship between *Salary* and *Years Experience* for different *Education* levels, how many indicator variables will she need for *Education*?

19.3 Multiple Regression Diagnostics

We often use regression analyses to make important business decisions. By working with the data and creating models, we can learn a great deal about the relationships among variables. As we saw with simple regression, sometimes we can learn as much from the cases that *don't* fit the model as from the bulk of cases that do. Extraordinary cases often tell us more just by the ways in which they fail to conform and the reasons we can discover for those deviations. If a case doesn't conform to the others, we should identify it and, if possible, understand why it is different. In simple regression, a case can be extraordinary by standing away from the model in the *y* direction or by having unusual values in an *x*-variable. In multiple regression, it can also be extraordinary by having an unusual *combination* of values in the *x*-variables. Just as in simple regression, large deviations in the *y* direction show up in the residuals as outliers. Deviations in the *x*'s show up as *leverage*.

Leverage

In a regression of a single predictor and a response, it's easy to see if a value has high leverage, because it's far from the mean of the *x*-values in a scatterplot. In a multiple regression with *k* predictor variables, things are more complicated. A point might actually not be far from any of the *x* means and yet still exert large leverage because it has an unusual *combination* of predictor values. Even a graphics program designed to display points in high dimensional spaces may not make it obvious. Fortunately, we can calculate leverage values for each case. These are standard for most multiple regression programs.

The **leverage** of a case is easy to understand. For any case, add 1 to its *y*-value. Recompute the regression, and see how much the *predicted* value of the case changes. The amount of the change is the leverage. It can never be greater than 1 or less than 0. A point with zero leverage has no effect at all on the regression slope, although it does participate in the calculations of the intercept, R^2, *s*, and the *F*- and *t*-statistics. The leverage of the *i*th point in a dataset is often denoted by h_i.

Standard Error

In some software regression tables, the standard deviation of the residuals, which we denote s_e, is called a "standard error." In this text, "standard error" refers to the estimated standard deviation of a statistic, and we denote it SE(statistic). The standard deviation of the residuals is not a standard error. Although it is a data-based estimate of a standard deviation, it is not the standard deviation of an estimated statistic. Other statistics programs call this value the residual standard error or root mean square error. Remember that it's the estimated standard deviation of the residuals, not a summary.

A point with high leverage may not actually influence the regression coefficients if it follows the pattern of the model set by the other points, but it's worth examining simply because of its *potential* to do so. Looking at leverage values can be an effective way to discover cases that are extraordinary on a combination of *x*-variables. In business, such cases often deserve special attention.

There are no tests for whether the leverage of a case is too large. The average leverage value among all cases in a regression is $1/n$, but that doesn't give us much of a guide. Some packages use rules of thumb to indicate high leverage values.[4] Another common approach is to just make a histogram of the leverages. Any case whose leverage stands out in a histogram of leverages probably deserves special attention. You may decide to leave the case in the regression or to see how the regression model changes when you delete the case, but you should be aware of its potential to influence the regression.

We've already seen that the *Duration* of a roller coaster ride depends linearly on its *Speed*. But even more than speed, roller coaster customers like that stomach-kicking drop that gives the coaster its initial speed. So, rather than predict the duration of a roller coaster ride, let's build a model for how fast it travels. A multiple regression with two predictors shows that both the total *Height* and the *Drop* (the maximum distance from the top to the bottom of the largest drop in the ride) are important factors as you can see in Table 19.6:[5]

```
Response variable is: Speed
R squared = 89.6%  R squared (adjusted) = 89.4%
s = 4.746 with 118 − 3 = 115 degrees of freedom
```

Source	Sum of Squares	df	Mean Square	F-ratio
Regression	22325.8	2	11162.9	496
Residual	2590.37	115	22.5250	

Variable	Coefficient	SE(Coeff)	t-ratio	P-value
Intercept	34.5913	1.053	32.8	<0.0001
Height	0.037202	0.0164	2.27	0.0253
Drop	0.163203	0.0171	9.52	<0.0001

```
The estimated regression equation is
```
$$\widehat{Speed} = 34.59 + 0.037\,Height + 0.163\,Drop$$

TABLE 19.6 A multiple regression of *Speed* on *Height* and *Drop*. Both coefficients are significant.

The regression certainly seems reasonable.

The histogram of the leverage values in Figure 19.6, however, shows something interesting:

FIGURE 19.6 The distribution of leverage values shows a few high values and one extraordinarily high-leverage point.

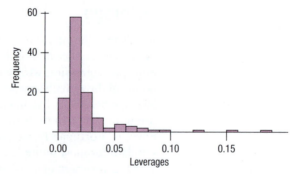

---

[4]One common rule for determining when a leverage is large is to indicate any leverage value greater than $3(k + 1)/n$, where k is the number of predictors.

[5]This analysis works with the entire dataset to make it easier for you to replicate if you wish. Adding back in the two coasters does not change the model in any important way.

The case with the highest leverage is a coaster called *Oblivion*, a steel roller coaster in England that opened as the world's first "vertical drop coaster" in 1998. What's unusual about *Oblivion* is that its *Height* is only about 65 feet above ground (placing it below the median), and yet it drops 180 feet to achieve a top speed of 68 mph. The unique feature of *Oblivion* is that it plunges *underground* nearly 120 feet. So when considered together, its height and drop are a very unusual combination.

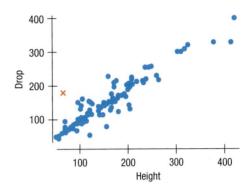

FIGURE 19.7 A plot of the two predictors shows why *Oblivion* has high leverage.

Leverage points can affect not only the coefficients of the model, but also our choice of whether to include a predictor in a regression model as well. The more complex the regression model, the more important it is to look at high-leverage values and their effects.

Residuals and Standardized Residuals

Residuals are not all alike. Consider a point with leverage 1.0. That's the highest a leverage can be, and it means that the line follows the point perfectly. So, a point like that must have a zero residual. And since we know the residual exactly, that residual has zero standard deviation. This tendency is true in general: The larger the leverage, the smaller the standard deviation of its residual. When we want to compare values that have differing standard deviations, it's a good idea to standardize them. We can do that with the regression residuals, dividing each one by an estimate of its own standard deviation. Such standardized residuals are called **studentized residuals**.[6] In a simple regression, it makes little difference, but for a multiple regression, it's a good idea to examine studentized residuals rather than the simple residuals to check the Nearly Normal Condition and the Equal Spread Condition. Any studentized residual that stands out from the others deserves your attention.

It may occur to you that we've always plotted the *unstandardized* residuals when we made regression models. We treated them as if they all had the same standard deviation when we checked the Nearly Normal Condition. It turns out that this was a simplification. It didn't matter much for simple regression, but for multiple regression models, it's a better idea to use the studentized residuals when checking the Nearly Normal Condition and when making scatterplots of residuals against predicted values.

[6]There's more than one way to studentize residuals according to how you estimate the standard deviation of the residuals. You may find statistics packages referring to *externally studentized residuals* and *internally studentized residuals*. The *externally studentized* version follows a *t*-distribution, so those are the ones we recommend.

Influence Measures

A case that has *both* high leverage and a large studentized residual may have changed the regression model substantially all by itself. Such a case is said to be **influential**. An influential case cries out for special attention because removing it is likely to give a different regression model. The surest way to tell whether a case is influential is to try leaving it out[7] and see how much the regression model changes. You should call a case "influential" if omitting it changes the regression model by enough to matter for *your* purposes.

To identify possibly influential cases, check the leverage and studentized residuals. Two statistics that combine leverage and studentized residuals into a single measure of influence, **Cook's Distance** (Cook's D) and **DFFITS**, are offered by many statistics programs. You should examine a histogram of these measures and pay special attention to any case with an extraordinarily large value because it may be exerting a lot of influence on your regression model.

A histogram of the Cook's Distances from the model in Table 19.6 shows two influential values:

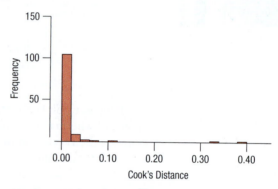

Here are the details on those two influential points.

TABLE 19.7   Coasters with high Cook's D.

Cook	Name	Speed	Height	Drop	Length	Inversions
0.38069253	Xcelerator	82	205	130	2202	0
0.33260326	Volcano, The Blast Coaster	70	155	80	2757	1

A little research finds that these coasters *are* different as well. They have something extra—a hydraulic catapult that accelerates the coasters more than gravity alone. In fact, the *Xcelerator* reaches 82 mph in 2.3 seconds. Removing those two coasters from the model has a striking effect as Table 19.8 shows:

TABLE 19.8   Removing the two influential blast coasters has made *Height* no longer important to the model. A simple regression model, such as in Table 19.9, may be a more effective summary than the model with two predictor variables.

```
Response variable is: Speed
R squared = 92.4%   R squared (adjusted) = 92.2%
s = 4.074 with 116 − 3 = 113 degrees of freedom
```

Source	Sum of Squares	df	Mean Square	F-ratio
Regression	22704.0	2	11352.0	684
Residual	1875.57	113	16.5979	

Variable	Coefficient	SE(Coeff)	t-ratio	P-value
Intercept	34.1329	0.9080	37.6	<0.0001
Height	0.0043	0.0150	0.288	0.7738
Drop	0.1982	0.0157	12.7	<0.0001

---

[7]Or, equivalently, include an indicator variable that selects only for that case. See the discussion in the next section.

The *Height* of the coaster is no longer a statistically significant predictor, so we might choose to omit that variable. Notice that the adjusted R^2 actually increases slightly, reflecting that we have a simpler model with an equivalently good fit. (See Table 19.9)

```
Response variable is: Speed
R squared = 92.4%  R squared (adjusted) = 92.3%
s = 4.058 with 116 - 2 = 114 degrees of freedom
```

Source	Sum of Squares	df	Mean Square	F-ratio
Regression	22702.6	1	22702.6	1379
Residual	1876.94	114	16.4644	

Variable	Coefficient	SE(Coeff)	t-ratio	P-value
Intercept	34.1659	0.8971	38.1	<0.0001
Drop	0.202411	0.0055	37.1	<0.0001

TABLE 19.9 A simple linear regression model without the three blast coasters and with *Height* deleted.

Indicators for Influence

One good way to examine the effect of an extraordinary case on a regression is to construct a special indicator variable that is zero for all cases *except* the one we want to isolate. Including such an indicator in the regression model has the same effect as removing the case from the data, but it has two special advantages. First, it makes it clear to anyone looking at the regression model that we have treated that case specially. Second, the *t*-statistic for the indicator variable's coefficient can be used as a test of whether the case is influential. If the P-value is small, then that case really didn't fit well with the rest of the data. Typically, we name such an indicator with the identifier of the case we want to remove. Table 19.10 shows the last roller coaster model in which we have removed the influence of the three blast coasters by constructing indicators for them instead of by removing them from the data. Notice that the coefficient for drop is just the same as the ones we found by omitting the cases.

```
Response variable is: Speed
R squared = 92.5%  R squared (adjusted) =  92.3%
s = 4.058 with 118 - 4 = 114 degrees of freedom
```

Source	Sum of Squares	df	Mean Square	F-ratio
Regression	23039.2	3	7679.74	466
Residual	1876.94	114	16.4644	

Variable	Coefficient	SE(Coeff)	t-ratio	P-value
Intercept	34.1659	0.8971	38.1	<0.0001
Drop	0.202411	0.0055	37.1	<0.0001
Xcelerator	21.5206	4.076	5.28	<0.0001
Volcano, Blast	19.6412	4.093	4.80	<0.0001

TABLE 19.10 The two indicator variables effectively remove the coasters they target from the regression. Their P-values confirm that each of these roller coasters doesn't fit with the others.

Diagnosis Wrapup

What have we learned from diagnosing the regression? We've discovered three roller coasters that may be influencing the model. And for each of them, we've been able to understand why and how it differed from the others. The oddness of

Oblivion plunging into a hole in the ground may have caused us to value *Drop* as a predictor of *Speed* more than *Height*. The two influential cases with high Cook's D values are "blast coasters" that don't rely only on gravity for their acceleration. Although we can't count on always discovering why influential cases are special, diagnosing influential cases raises the question of what about them might be different and can help us understand our model better. In business decisions, it is essential to recognize and identify influential cases to avoid making decisions that are driven by only one or two observations.

When a regression analysis has cases that have both high leverage and large studentized residuals, it would be irresponsible to report only the regression on all the data. You should also compute and discuss the regression found with such cases removed, and discuss the extraordinary cases individually if they offer additional insight. If your interest is to make a sound business decision, the extraordinary cases may tell you more than the rest of the model. If your only interest is in the model (for example, because you hope to use it for prediction), then you'll want to be certain that the model wasn't determined by only a few influential cases, but instead was built on the broader base of the body of your data.

IN PRACTICE 19.3 Going further with regression diagnostics

Two other measures of quality of a diamond (see page 653) are its *Table* size and *Depth*; both are expressed as percentages. *Table* size is the ratio of the flat top part (the table) diameter to the diameter of the stone. *Depth* is the ratio of the distance from table to bottom (culet) to the diameter. The output of the regression of $Log_{10}Price$ on *Carat Weight*, *Color D*, *Color G*, *Table*, and *Depth* shows:

```
Response Variable: Log10Price
R-squared = 85.92%  Adjusted R-squared = 85.82%
s = 0.1080 with 749 − 6 = 743 degrees of freedom
```

Variable	Coeff	SE(Coeff)	t-ratio	P-value
Intercept	3.464326	0.322336	10.748	<0.0001
Carat.Size	1.031627	0.015799	65.295	<0.0001
ColorD	0.291119	0.014214	20.481	<0.0001
ColorG	0.213842	0.012760	16.759	<0.0001
Table	−0.008497	0.002345	−3.623	0.000311
Depth	−0.008638	0.003765	−2.294	0.022043

Influence measures can be adversely affected by indicator variables, so studentized residuals, Cook's Distance, and leverage were all calculated on this model without the indicator variables for *Color*.

Here are the histograms and boxplots for these three measures. Several points have unusually high values on one or more measures.

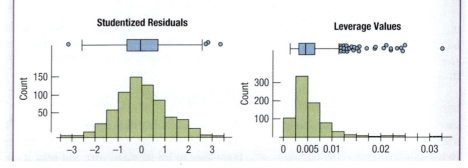

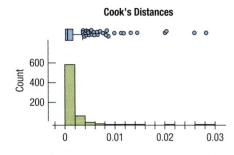

Cook's Distances

The analyst identified 5 diamonds that had high leverage (1) or Cook's Distance (4). Two of these also had large studentized residuals. Indicator variables were created for these 5 points and a regression was run with these new variables:

Variable	Coeff	SE(Coeff)	t-ratio	P-value
Intercept	4.5658	0.3972	11.49	<0.0001
Carat Size	0.9125	0.0177	51.54	<0.0001
Depth	−0.0190	0.0047	−4.04	<0.0001
Table	−0.0111	0.0029	−3.84	0.0001
Diamond 1	0.0478	0.1343	0.36	0.7221
Diamond 2	0.0837	0.1344	0.62	0.5336
Diamond 3	−0.1332	0.1361	−0.98	0.3283
Diamond 4	−0.3205	0.1346	−2.38	0.0176
Diamond 5	−0.4284	0.1346	−3.18	0.0015

MANAGER I know you've found several diamonds that don't fit the model. How will you change the model now?

CONSULTANT The indicator variables indicated that of the 5 suspected high influence points, only Diamonds 4 and 5 actually influence the regression. I'll run the regression again without these two points to see what coefficients change. If there is anything identifiably different about these two diamonds, I'll set them aside or create a new variable for the newly identified characteristic (if possible) that distinguishes these diamonds.

19.4 Building Regression Models

When many possible predictors are available, we will naturally want to select only a few of them for a regression model. But which ones? The first and most important thing to realize is that often there is no such thing as the "best" regression model. In fact, no regression model is "right." Often, several alternative models may be useful or insightful. The "best" for one purpose may not be best for another, and the one with the highest R^2 may not be best for many purposes.

Multiple regressions are subtle. The coefficients often don't mean what they may appear to mean at first. The choice of which predictors to use determines almost everything about the regression. Predictors interact with each other, which complicates interpretation and understanding. So it is usually best to build a parsimonious model, using as few predictors as you can. On the other hand, we don't want to leave out predictors that are theoretically or practically important. Making this trade-off is the heart of the challenge of selecting a good model.[8]

---

[8]This trade-off is sometimes referred to as Occam's Razor after the medieval philosopher William of Occam.

The best regression models, in addition to satisfying the assumptions and conditions of multiple regression, have:

- Relatively few predictors, to keep the model simple.
- A relatively high R^2, indicating that much of the variability in y is accounted for by the regression model.
- A relatively small value of s_e, the standard deviation of the residuals, indicating that the magnitude of the errors is small.
- Relatively small P-values for the F- and t-statistics, showing that the overall model is better than a simple summary with the mean and that the individual coefficients are reliably different from zero.
- No cases with extraordinarily high leverage that might dominate and alter the model.
- No cases with extraordinarily large residuals, and studentized residuals that appear to be nearly Normal. Outliers can alter the model and certainly weaken the power of any test statistics, and the Nearly Normal Condition is required for inference.
- Predictors that are reliably measured and relatively unrelated to each other.

The term "relatively" in this list is meant to suggest that you should favor models with these attributes over others that satisfy them less, but of course, there are many trade-offs and no absolute rules. In addition to favoring predictors that can be measured reliably, you may want to favor those that are less expensive to measure, especially if your model is intended for prediction with values not yet measured.

It should be clear from this discussion that the selection of a regression model calls for judgment. This is yet another of those decisions in statistics that just can't be made automatically. Indeed, it is one that we shouldn't want to make automatically; there are so many aspects of what makes a model useful that human judgment is necessary to make a final choice. Nevertheless, there are tools that can help by identifying potentially interesting models.

Best Subsets and Stepwise Regression

How can we find the best multiple regression model? The list of desirable features we just looked at should make it clear that there is no simple definition of the "best" model. The choice of a multiple regression model always requires judgment to choose among potential models. Sometimes it can help to look at models that are "good" in some arbitrary sense to understand some possibilities, but such models should never be accepted blindly.

If we choose a single criterion such as finding a model with the highest adjusted R^2, then, for modest size datasets and a modest number of potential predictors, it is actually possible for computers to search through *all* possible models. The method is called a **best subsets regression**. Often the computer reports a collection of "best" models: the best with three predictors, the best with four, and so on.[9] Of course, as you add predictors, the R^2 can never decrease, but the improvement may not justify the added complexity of the additional predictors. One criterion that might help is to use adjusted R^2. Best subsets regression programs usually offer a choice of criteria, and of course, different criteria usually lead to different "best" models.

---

[9]Best subsets regressions don't actually compute every regression. Instead, they cleverly exclude models they know to be worse than some they've already examined. Even so, there are limits to the size of the data and number of variables they can deal with comfortably.

Although best subsets programs are quite clever about computing far fewer than all the possible alternative models, they can become overwhelmed by more than a few dozen possible predictors or very many cases. So, unfortunately, they aren't useful in many data mining applications. (We'll discuss those more in Chapter 21.)

Another alternative is to have the computer build a regression "stepwise." In a **stepwise regression**, at each step, a predictor is either added to or removed from the model. The predictor chosen to add is the one whose addition increases the adjusted R^2 the most (or similarly improves some other measure such as an F-statistic). The predictor chosen to remove is the one whose removal reduces the adjusted R^2 least (or similarly loses the least on some other measure). The hope is that by following this path, the computer can settle on a good model. The model will gain or lose a predictor only if that change in the model makes a big enough change in the performance measure. The changes stop when no more changes pass the criterion.

Best subsets and stepwise methods offer both a final model and information about the paths they followed. The intermediate stage models can raise interesting questions about the data and suggest relationships that you might not have thought about. Some programs offer the chance for you to make choices as the process progresses. By interacting with the process at each decision stage, you can exclude a variable that you judge inappropriate for the model (even if including it would help the statistic being optimized) or include a variable that wasn't the top choice at the next step, if you think it is important for your purposes. Don't let a variable that doesn't make sense enter the model just because it has a high correlation, but at the same time, don't exclude a predictor just because you didn't initially think it was important. (That would be a good way to make sure that you never learn anything new.) Finding the balance between these two choices underlies the art of successful model building and makes it challenging.

Unlike best subset methods, stepwise methods can work even when the number of potential predictors is so large that you can't examine them individually. In such cases, using a stepwise method can help you identify potentially interesting predictors, especially when you use it sequentially.

Both methods are powerful. But as with many powerful tools, they require care when you use them. You should be aware of what the automated methods *fail* to do: They don't check the assumptions and conditions. Some, such as the independence of the cases, you can check before performing the analyses. Others, such as the Linearity Condition and concerns over outliers and influential cases, must be checked for each model. There's a risk that automated methods will be influenced by non-linearities, by outliers, by high leverage points, by clusters, and by the need for constructed dummy variables to account for subgroups.[10] And these influences affect not just the coefficients in the final model, but the *selection* of the predictors themselves. If there is a case that is influential for even one possible multiple regression model, a best subsets search is guaranteed to consider that model (because it considers *all* possible models) and have its decision influenced by that one case.

	HP	Disp	Wt
Horsepower	1.000		
Displacement	0.872	1.000	
Weight	0.917	0.951	1.000

- **Choosing the Wrong "Best" Model.** Here's a simple example of how stepwise and best subsets regressions can go astray. We might want to find a regression to model *Horsepower* in a sample of cars from the car's engine size (*Displacement*) and its *Weight*. The simple correlations are in the table at left.

---

[10]This risk grows dramatically with larger and more complex datasets—just the kind of data for which these methods can be most helpful.

Because *Weight* has a slightly higher correlation with *Horsepower*, stepwise regression will choose it first. Then, because *Weight* and engine size (*Displacement*) are so highly correlated, once *Weight* is in the model, *Displacement* won't be added to the model. And a best subsets regression will prefer the regression on *Weight* because it has a higher R^2 and adjusted R^2. But *Weight* is, at best, a lurking variable leading to both the need for more horsepower and a larger engine. Don't try to tell an engineer that the best way to increase horsepower is to add weight to the car and that the engine size isn't important! From an engineering standpoint, *Displacement* is a far more appropriate predictor of *Horsepower*, but stepwise regression can't find that model.

Challenges in Building Regression Models

The dataset used to construct the regression in the Guided Example of Chapter 18 originally contained more than 100 variables on more than 10,000 houses in the upstate New York area. Part of the challenge in constructing models is simply preparing the data for analysis. A simple scatterplot can often reveal a data value mistakenly coded, but with hundreds of potential variables, the task of checking the data for accuracy, missing values, consistency, and reasonableness can become the major part of the effort. We will return to this issue when we discuss data mining in Chapter 21.

Another challenge in building large models is Type I error. Although we've warned against using 0.05 as an unquestioned guide to statistical significance, we have to start somewhere, and this critical value is often used to test whether a variable can enter (or leave) a regression model. Of course, using 0.05 means that about 1 in 20 times, a variable whose contribution to the model may be negligible will appear as significant. Using something more stringent than 0.05 means that potentially valuable variables may be overlooked. Whenever we use automatic methods (stepwise, best subsets, or others), the actual number of different models considered becomes huge, and the probability of a Type I error grows with it. There is no easy remedy for this problem. Building a model that includes predictors that actually contribute to reducing the variation of the response and avoiding predictors that simply add noise to the predictions is the challenge of modern model building. Much current research is devoted to criteria and automatic methods to make this search easier and more reliable, but for the foreseeable future, you will need to use your own judgment and wisdom in addition to your statistical knowledge to build sensible useful regressions.

IN PRACTICE 19.4 Choosing models via stepwise regression

In addition to the predictor variables from the last In Practice (pages 662–663) we also have information on the quality of the *Cut* (4 grades: *Good, Very Good, Excellent,* and *Ideal*) and the quality of the *Clarity* (7 grades: *VVS2, VVS1, VS2, VS1, SI2, SI1,* and *IF*). A model was fit to predict $Log_{10}Price$ from all the predictors we have available: *Carat Weight, Color, Cut, Clarity, Depth,* and *Table* on all 749 diamonds. A backward elimination of terms was performed, and the following model was selected:

```
Response Variable: Log10Price
R-squared = 94.46%  Adjusted R-squared = 94.37%
s = 0.06806 with 749 - 13 = 736 degrees of freedom
```

Variable	Coeff	SE(Coeff)	t-ratio	P-value
Intercept	2.437903	0.014834	164.349	<0.0001
Carat.Weight	1.200301	0.011365	105.611	<0.0001
ColorD	0.342888	0.009107	37.649	<0.0001
ColorG	0.254024	0.008159	31.135	<0.0001
CutGood	−0.028884	0.011133	−2.594	0.00966
CutVeryGood	−0.015374	0.005503	−2.793	0.00535
CutIdeal	0.012127	0.010022	1.210	0.22662
ClaritySI1	−0.237850	0.011736	−20.267	<0.0001
ClaritySI2	−0.312076	0.012454	−25.058	<0.0001
ClarityVS1	−0.130431	0.012118	−10.764	<0.0001
ClarityVS2	−0.178439	0.011684	−15.273	<0.0001
ClarityVVS1	−0.064518	0.012445	−5.184	<0.0001
ClarityVVS2	−0.076747	0.011878	−6.461	<0.0001

MANAGER As I've told you, I've always believed in the four C's. Your previous model considered only *Carat Weight* and *Color*. What have you learned by adding *Cut* and *Clarity*?

CONSULTANT This new model has several advantages over the simpler model. First, the residual standard error is now 0.068 $\log_{10}$ dollars, a decrease from 0.109 $\log_{10}$ dollars. (We can transform that back to dollars as $10^{0.068} = \$1.17$—quite a small standard deviation.)

Correspondingly, the R^2 is now 94.46% compared to 85.66%. Nearly all the terms are highly statistically significant. The one exception is the indicator for the *Ideal* level of *Cut*. We could consider omitting this indicator (which would then combine the levels *Excellent* and *Ideal*), but for simplicity we will leave it as is. Before deploying this model, however, we should look at all the assumptions and conditions, which we will do in the final example of this chapter, but it certainly looks that as though your intuition is right. All four variables are important!

GUIDED EXAMPLE Housing Prices

Let's return to the upstate New York dataset to predict house prices, this time using a sample of 1734 houses and 16 variables. (Data in **Housing prices GE19**)

The variables available include:

Price	The price of the house as sold in 2002
Lot Size	The size of the land in *acres*
Waterfront	An indicator variable coded as 1 if the property contains waterfront, 0 otherwise
Age	The age of the house in *years*
Land Value	The assessed value of the property without the structures
New Construct	An indicator variable coded as 1 if the house is new construction, 0 otherwise
Central Air	An indicator variable coded as 1 if the house has central air conditioning, 0 otherwise

(continued)

Fuel Type	A categorical variable describing the main type of fuel used to heat the house
Heat Type	A categorical variable describing the heating system of the house
Sewer Type	A categorical variable describing the sewer system of the house
Living Area	The size of the living area of the house in *square feet*
Pct College	The percent of the residents of the ZIP code that attended four-year college (from the U.S. Census Bureau)
Bathrooms	The *number* of bathrooms
Bedrooms	The *number* of bedrooms
Fireplaces	The *number* of fireplaces

PLAN **Define** the problem. State the objective of the study.

Identify the variables.

Model Think about the assumptions and check the conditions. A scatterplot matrix is a good way to examine the relationships for the quantitative variables.

We want to build a model to predict house prices for a region in upstate New York. We have data on *Price* ($), and 15 potential predictor variables selected from a much larger list.

✔ **Linearity Condition.** To fit a regression model, we first require linearity. (Scatterplots of *Price* against *Living Area*, *Age*, *Bedrooms*, *Bathrooms*, and *Fireplaces* are similar to the plots shown in the regression of Chapter 18 and are not shown here.)

✔ **Independence Assumption.** We can regard the errors as being independent of one another since the houses themselves were a random sample.

✔ **Randomization Condition.** These 1734 houses are a random sample of a much larger set. That supports the idea that the errors are independent.

To check equal variance and Normality, we usually find a regression and examine the residuals. Linearity is all we need for that.

Remarks

Examination of *Fuel Type* showed that there were only 6 houses that did not have categories 2, 3, or 4.

Because there are 7 levels of *Fuel Type*, we expect to need 6 indicator variables. We can use *None* as the baseline. *Fuel2* has the value 1 for Gas and 0 for all other types; *Fuel3* has value 1 for Electric and 0 for all other types. As the bar chart shows, only 6 houses have values other than 2, 3, and 4. So we can omit those cases and use just 2 indicators, *Fuel2* and *Fuel3*, indicating Gas and Electric, respectively, leaving Oil as the baseline. The 6 houses (out of over 1700) set aside have a very small impact on the model.

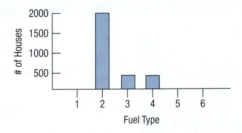

All six of those also had *Heat Type* 1. We decided to set these 6 houses aside, leaving three categories of each variable. So we can use two dummy variables for each. We now have 17 potential predictor variables.

We started by fitting a model to all of them.

```
Dependent variable is: Price
R-squared = 65.1%  R-squared (adjusted) = 64.8%
s = 58408 with 1728 − 18 = 1710 degrees of freedom
```

Variable	Coeff	SE(Coeff)	t-ratio	P-value
Intercept	18794.0	23333	0.805	0.4207
Lot.Size	7774.34	2246	3.46	0.0006
Waterfront	119046	15577	7.64	<0.0001
Age	−131.642	58.54	−2.25	0.0246
Land.Value	0.9258	0.048	19.4	<0.0001
New.Construct	−45234.8	7326	−6.17	<0.0001
Central.Air	9864.30	3487	2.83	0.0047
Fuel Type[Gas]	4225.35	5027	0.840	0.4008
Fuel Type[Electric]	−8148.11	12906	−0.631	0.5279
Heat Type[Hot Air]	−1185.54	12345	−0.096	0.9235
Heat Type[Hot Water]	−11974.4	12866	−0.931	0.3521
Sewer Type[Private]	4051.84	17110	0.237	0.8128
Sewer Type[Public]	5571.89	17165	0.325	0.7455
Living.Area	75.769	4.24	17.9	<0.0001
Pct.College	−112.405	151.9	0.740	0.4593
Bedrooms	−4963.36	2405	2.06	0.0392
Fireplaces	768.058	2992	0.257	0.7975
Bathrooms	23077.4	3378	6.83	<0.0001

✔ **Equal Spread Condition.** A scatterplot of the studentized residuals against predicted values shows no thickening or other patterns. There is a group of homes whose residuals are larger (both negative and positive) than the vast majority, whose studentized residual values are larger than 3 or 4 in absolute value. We'll revisit them after we've selected our model.

We need the Nearly Normal Condition only if we want to do inference and the sample size is not large. If the sample size is large, we need the distribution to be Normal only if we plan to produce prediction intervals.

✔ **Nearly Normal Condition, Outlier Condition.** The histogram of residuals is unimodal and symmetric, but slightly long tailed.

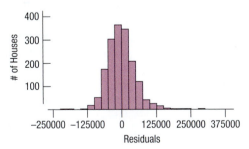

Under these conditions, we can proceed to search for a suitable multiple regression model using a subset of the predictors. We will return to some of our concerns in the discussion.

(continued)

DO

Mechanics We first let the stepwise program proceed backward from the full model on all 17 predictors.

Here is the computer output for the multiple regression, starting with all 17 predictor variables and proceeding backward until no more candidates were nominated for exclusion.

```
Dependent variable is: Price
R-squared = 65.1%  R-squared (adjusted) = 64.9%
s = 58345 with 1728 - 12 = 1716 degrees of freedom
```

Variable	Coeff	SE(Coeff)	t-ratio	P-value
Intercept	9643.14	6546	1.47	0.1409
Lot.Size	7580.42	2049	3.70	0.0002
Waterfront	119372	15365	7.77	<0.0001
Age	−139.704	57.18	−2.44	0.0147
Land.Value	0.921838	0.0463	19.9	<0.0001
New.Construct	−44172.8	7159	−6.17	<0.0001
Central.Air	9501.81	3402	2.79	0.0053
Heat Type[Hot Air]	10099.9	4048	2.50	0.0127
Heat Type[Hot Water]	−791.243	5215	−0.152	0.8794
Living.Area	75.9000	4.124	18.4	<0.0001
Bedrooms	−4843.89	2387	−2.03	0.0426
Bathrooms	23041.0	3333	6.91	<0.0001

The estimated equation is:

$$Price = 9643.14 + 7580.42 LotSize$$
$$+ 119{,}372 Waterfront - 139.70 Age$$
$$+ 0.922 LandValue$$
$$- 44{,}172.8 NewConstuction$$
$$+ 9501.81 CentralAir$$
$$+ 10099.9 Heat\ Type{:}Hot\ Air$$
$$- 791.24 Heat\ Type{:}Hot\ Water$$
$$+ 75.90 Living\ Area$$
$$- 4843.89 Bedrooms$$
$$+ 23041 Bathrooms$$

Nearly all of the P-values are small, which indicates that even with 11 predictors in the model, most are contributing. The exception is the indicator for Heat Type *Hot Water*, which is included to provide a complete set of indicators for Heat Type. We could consider dropping this indicator and combining those houses with those that have levels *None* and *Electric*. However, for simplicity we have left the model as the stepwise search found it. The R^2 value of 65.1% indicates that more than 65% of the overall variation in house prices has been accounted for by this model, and the fact that the adjusted R^2 has actually increased suggests that we haven't removed any important predictors from the model. The residual standard error of $58,345 gives us a rough indication that we can predict the price of a home to within about $2 \times \$58{,}345 = \$116{,}690$. If that's close enough to be useful, then our model is potentially useful as a price guide.

Remarks

We also tried running the stepwise regression program forward and obtained the same model. There are some houses that have large studentized residual values and some that have somewhat large leverage, but omitting them from the model did not significantly change the coefficients. We can use this model as a starting basis for pricing homes in the area.

REPORT **Summarize and present** your conclusions. Summarize your results and state any limitations of your model in the context of your original objectives.

MEMO

Re: Regression analysis of home price predictions

A regression model of *Price* on 11 predictors accounts for about 65% of the variation in the price of homes in these data from upstate New York. Tests of each coefficient show that each of these variables appears to be an aspect of the price of a house.

This model reflects the common wisdom in real estate about the importance of various aspects of a home. An important variable not included is the location, which every real estate agent knows is crucial to pricing a house. This is ameliorated by the fact that all these houses are in the same general area. However, knowing more specific information about where they are located would probably improve the model. The price found from this model can be used as a starting point for comparing a home with comparable homes in the area.

As with all multiple regression coefficients, when we interpret the effect of a predictor, we must take account of all the other predictors and be careful not to suggest a causal relationship between the predictor and the response variable. Here are some interesting features of the model. It appears that among houses with the same values of the other variables, those with waterfront access are worth on average about $119,000 more. Among houses with the same values of the other variables, those with more bedrooms have lower sale prices by, on average, $4800 for each bedroom, while among those with the same values of the other variables, those with more bathrooms have higher prices by, on average, $23,000 per bathroom. Not surprisingly, the value of the land is positively associated with the sale price, accounting for, on average, about $0.92 of the sale price for each $1 of assessed land value among houses that are otherwise alike on the other variables.

This model reflects the prices of 1728 homes in a random sample of homes taken in this area.

Model Selection: Training the Model

When we fit a multiple regression model to data, using stepwise or any other model building strategy, we use various criteria like R^2, adjusted R^2, t-statistics, and F-statistics to decide which predictor variables to include. All of these measures (and many others that we didn't discuss) are based on the assumption that the errors are Normally distributed. The reason we don't keep adding variables to a regression model is the possibility that we will fit the data too well. That sounds like a good thing, but with too many variables we run into the danger of fitting the noise in the data as well as the signal that we're trying to see. The result is that the R^2 for the data we used to fit the model will be very high, but when we fit the model to new data, it will drop significantly. This is called **overfitting** the data. We'd like to find a model that works reasonably well for the data we use to fit and also predicts well in new situations.

Rather than wait for new data, we can simulate how well the model works on new data by splitting the data we have randomly into two, using one part for fitting the data and the other part for testing. The first dataset is called the **training set** and the other is called the **test set**. The test set is always left alone and is never used for fitting the model. This strategy of using random sets to select and test the model is called **cross-validation**.

The simplest way to construct the datasets is to choose percentages of the original dataset you want to denote as training, tuning, and test and then randomly select cases according to the percentages. There is no good rule of thumb for knowing what percentages to use, but typically, the majority of the data goes into training. Choices like 75% training, 10% tuning, and 15% test are not uncommon. When datasets are very small, other strategies are needed.

The R^2 on the test set is a more realistic measure of how the model will perform on new datasets, although it's important to remember that future datasets may be more different from the training data than a test dataset that is randomly chosen from the data at hand. Models don't last forever. Environments change, and even if a model predicts well for customers today, there is no guarantee that it will work as well in a week, a month or a year from now.

IN PRACTICE 19.5 Testing models via cross-validation

The 1734 houses in the Guided Example (data in **Housing Prices GE19**) have been randomly split into training (75%) and test (25%) sets (variable *Test* indicates which set 0 = Training; 1 = Test).

Fitting a backward stepwise regression as in the Guided Example, but using only the training set to fit the model we find a slightly different model than before:

```
Dependent variable is: Price
Residual standard error: 57310 on 1286 degrees of freedom
Multiple R-squared: 0.6415, Adjusted R-squared: 0.6379
F-statistic: 177 on 13 and 1286 DF, p-value: <2.2e-16
```

Variable	Coeff	SE(Coeff)	t-ratio	P-value
(Intercept)	15336.35162	7417.83528	2.067	0.03889
Lot.Size	9006.49503	2268.90735	3.970	<0.0001
Waterfront	122813.58703	16889.04096	7.272	<0.0001
Age	−103.30694	63.66455	−1.623	0.10490
Land.Value	0.91266	0.05115	17.843	<0.0001
New.Construct	−42108.97379	8256.90838	−5.100	<0.0001
Central.Air	7660.87262	3863.24541	1.983	0.04758
Heat.TypeHot Air	11320.31927	4590.29594	2.466	0.01379
Heat.TypeHot Water	1491.63083	5894.94368	0.253	0.80028
Heat.TypeNone	−36639.82313	26829.68817	−1.366	0.17229
Living.Area	68.66405	5.13703	13.366	<0.0001
Bedrooms	−8751.92800	2845.88809	−3.075	0.00215
Bathrooms	23297.21628	3737.59847	6.233	<0.0001
Rooms	2177.68054	1083.02504	2.011	0.04456

The estimated equation is:

$Price = 15336.35 + 9006.50 LotSize$
$\qquad + 122{,}814 Waterfront - 103.31 Age$
$\qquad + 0.913 LandValue$
$\qquad - 42{,}108.97 NewConstuction$
$\qquad + 7660.87 CentralAir$
$\qquad + 11320.32 Heat\,Type{:}Hot\,Air$
$\qquad + 1491.63 Heat\,Type{:}Hot\,Water$
$\qquad - 36639.82 Heat\,Type{:}None$
$\qquad + 68.66 Living\,Area$
$\qquad - 8751.93 Bedrooms$
$\qquad + 23297.22 Bathrooms$
$\qquad + 2177.68 Rooms$

Model Summary:
Training set: R-squared: 0.6415
Test set: R-squared: 0.6922

> **MANAGER** You built a model for house prices by using all the data. Now you've split the data into two sets and used only the 75% training set to build the model. What did you learn? Are the models different?
>
> **CONSULTANT** The models are very similar both in the variables they selected and in their predictive performance. I was worried about overfitting in the Guided Example model. The R^2 for that model (see page 670) was 65.1% using all 1728 houses. I thought that perhaps that would go down when the model was applied to a new dataset. So, I refit the stepwise procedure on only the 1300 houses in the training set. The R^2 value did drop slightly to 64.2%. However, when I used this model to predict prices on the 434 houses in the test set, the R^2 did not suffer (in fact, it actually increased slightly to 69.2%). The bottom line here is that the model we built (either one) is a reasonably good way to predict the price of a house in this area, with the caveat that the standard error is more than $50,000. So the model is unlikely to be able to capture the price to more accuracy than about $+/-\$100,000$. Moreover, we should diagnose the model to make sure that our assumptions and conditions are reasonably met.

An even more thorough way to evaluate models is to split the dataset randomly into training and test repeatedly, cross-validating more than once. Typically 90% of the data are used to fit and 10% used to evaluate in each iteration. When repeated test sets are used, they are often called **hold out samples** or simply **hold outs**. The model fitting is repeated on all the training sets, computing the sum of squared errors (SSE) on each hold out. The total SSE on all the hold out sets will be the final measure of how well the model fits.

Choosing a model always requires judgment. It's good to remember George Box's warning that "All models are wrong, but some are useful." Choosing a model based on any one criterion is dangerous. Domain knowledge (one aspect of which is called common sense), performance, and appropriateness (assumptions and conditions) are all-important when choosing a model.

19.5   Collinearity

Anyone who has shopped for a home knows that houses with more rooms generally cost more than houses with fewer rooms. A simple regression of *Price* on *Rooms* for the New York houses looks like this: (Data in **Housing prices GE19**)

Variable	Coefficient	SE(Coeff)	t-ratio	P-value
Intercept	52091.0	6399	8.14	<0.0001
Rooms	22674.5	864.2	26.2	<0.0001

An additional room seems to be "worth" about $22,600 on average to these homes. We can also see that the *Living Area* of a house is an important predictor. Each square foot is worth about $113:

Variable	Coefficient	SE(Coeff)	t-ratio	P-value
Intercept	12844.2	4973	2.58	0.0099
Living.Area	113.373	2.675	42.4	<0.0001

Finally, the *Price* increases with the number of *Bedrooms*, with each *Bedroom* worth, on average, $48,504:

Variable	Coefficient	SE(Coeff)	t-ratio	P-value
Intercept	58673.9	8631	6.80	<0.0001
Bedrooms	48504.8	2651	18.3	<0.0001

But, when we put more than one of these variables into a regression equation simultaneously, things can change. Here's a regression with both *Living Area* and *Bedrooms*:

Variable	Coefficient	SE(Coeff)	t-ratio	P-value
Intercept	35878.3	6586	5.45	<0.0001
Living.Area	125.602	3.523	35.7	<0.0001
Bedrooms	−14109.3	2672	−5.28	<0.0001

Now, it appears that each bedroom is associated with a *lower* sale *Price*.

This type of coefficient change often happens in multiple regression and can seem counterintuitive. When two predictor variables are correlated, their coefficients in a multiple regression (with both of them present) can be quite different from their simple regression slopes. In fact, the coefficient can change from being significantly positive to significantly negative with the inclusion of one correlated predictor, as is the case here with *Bedrooms* and *Living Area*. The problem arises when one of the predictor variables can be predicted well from the others. This phenomenon is called **collinearity**.[11]

Collinearity in the predictors can have other consequences in a multiple regression. If instead of adding *Bedrooms* to the model, we add *Rooms*, we see a different outcome:

Variable	Coefficient	SE(Coeff)	t-ratio	P-value
Intercept	10985.7	5498	2.00	0.0459
Living.Area	111.073	3.944	28.2	<0.0001
Rooms	837.476	1055	0.794	0.4276

The coefficient for *Living Area* has hardly changed at all. It still shows that a house costs about $111 per square foot, but now the P-value of the coefficient for *Rooms* says that it is indistinguishable from 0. With the addition of *Living Area* to the model the coefficient for *Rooms* changed from having a *t*-statistic over 25, with a very small P-value (in the simple regression), to having a P-value of 0.4276. Notice also that the standard errors of the coefficients have increased. The standard error of *Living Area* increased from 2.68 to 3.94. That may not seem like much, but it's an increase of nearly 50%.

This variance inflation of the coefficients is another consequence of collinearity. The stronger the correlation between predictors, the more the variance of their coefficients increases when both are included in the model. Sometimes this effect can change a coefficient from statistically significant to indistinguishable from zero.

Datasets in business often have related predictor variables. General economic variables, such as interest rates, unemployment rates, GDP, and other productivity measures, are highly correlated. The choice of which predictors to include in the model can significantly change the coefficients, their standard errors, and their P-values, making both selecting regression models and interpreting them difficult.

How can we detect and deal with collinearity? Let's look at a regression among just the predictor variables. If we regress *Rooms* on *Bedrooms* and *Living Area* we find:

```
Response variable is: Rooms
R squared = 60.4%   R squared (adjusted) = 60.3%
s = 1.460 with 1734 − 3 = 1731 degrees of freedom
```

Variable	Coefficient	SE(Coeff)	t-ratio	P-value
Intercept	0.669966	0.1403	4.77	<0.0001
Bedrooms	0.948919	0.0569	16.7	<0.0001
Living.Area	0.00192	0.0001	25.6	<0.0001

> **What the Coefficients Tell Us When Predictors Are Correlated**
>
> Sometimes we can understand what the coefficients are telling us even in such paradoxical situations. Here, it seems that a house that allocates more of its living area to bedrooms (and correspondingly less to other areas) will be worth less.
>
> In the second example, we see that more rooms don't make a house worth more if they just carve up the existing living area. The value of more rooms we saw before was probably because houses with more rooms tend to have more living area as well.

---

[11]You may see also this problem called "multicollinearity."

Look at the R^2 for that regression. What does it tell us? Since R^2 is the fraction of variability accounted for by the regression, in this case, that's the fraction of the variability in *Rooms* accounted for by the other two predictors.

Now we can be precise about collinearity. If that R^2 were 100%, we'd have perfect collinearity. *Rooms* would then be perfectly predictable from the other two predictors and so could tell us nothing new about *Price* because it didn't vary in any way not already accounted for by the predictors already in the model. In fact, we couldn't even perform the calculation. Its coefficient would be indeterminate, and its standard error would be infinite. (Statistics packages usually print warnings when this happens.[12]) Conversely, if the R^2 were 0%, then *Rooms* would bring entirely new information to the model, and we'd have no collinearity at all.

Clearly, there's a range of possible collinearities for each predictor. The statistic that measures the degree of collinearity of the jth predictor with the others is called the **Variance Inflation Factor (VIF)** and is found as:

$$VIF_j = \frac{1}{1 - R_j^2}.$$

The R_j^2 here shows how well the jth predictor can be predicted by the other predictors. The $1 - R_j^2$ term measures what that predictor has left to bring to the regression model. If R_j^2 is high, then not only is that predictor superfluous, but it can damage the regression model. The VIF tells how much the variance of the coefficient has been inflated due to collinearity. The higher the VIF, the higher the standard error of its coefficient and the less it can contribute to the regression model. Since R_j^2 can't be less than zero, the minimum value of the VIF is 1.0. The VIF takes into account the influence of all the other predictors—and that's important. You can't judge whether you have a collinearity problem simply by looking at the correlations among the predictors because those only consider each "pair" of predictors.

As a final blow, when a predictor is collinear with the other predictors, it's often difficult to figure out what its coefficient means in the multiple regression. We've blithely talked about "removing the effects of the other predictors," but now when we do that, there may not be much left. What is left is not likely to be about the original predictor, but more about the fractional part of that predictor not associated with the others. In a regression of *Horsepower* on *Weight* and *Engine Size*, once we've removed the effect of *Weight* on *Horsepower*, *Engine Size* doesn't tell us anything *more* about *Horsepower*. That's certainly not the same as saying that *Engine Size* doesn't tell us anything at all about *Horsepower*. It's just that most cars with big engines also weigh a lot. So *Engine Size* may be telling us mostly about sporty cars that have larger engines than expected for their weight.

To summarize, when a predictor is collinear with the other predictors in the model, two things can happen:

1. Its coefficient can be surprising, taking on an unanticipated sign or being unexpectedly large or small.
2. The standard error of its coefficient can be large, leading to a smaller t-statistic and correspondingly large P-value.

One telltale sign of collinearity is the paradoxical situation in which the overall F-test for the multiple regression model is significant, showing that at least one of the coefficients is significantly different from zero, and yet all of the individual coefficients have small t-values, each in effect denying that *it* is the significant one.

---

[12]Excel does not. It gives 0 as the estimate of most values and a NUM! warning for the standard error of the coefficient.

What should you do about a collinear regression model? The simplest cure is to remove some of the predictors. That both simplifies the model and generally improves the *t*-statistics. If several predictors give pretty much the same information, removing some of them won't hurt the model's ability to describe the response variable. Which should you remove? Keep the predictors that are most reliably measured, least expensive to find, or even those that are politically important. Another alternative that may make sense is to construct a new predictor by combining variables. For example, several different measures of a product's durability (perhaps for different parts of it) could be added together to create a single durability measure.

Facts About Collinearity

- The collinearity of any predictor with the others in the model can be measured with its Variance Inflation Factor.
- High collinearity leads to the coefficient being poorly estimated and having a large standard error (and correspondingly low *t*-statistic). The coefficient may seem to be the wrong size or even the wrong sign.
- Consequently, if a multiple regression model has a high R^2 and large F, but the individual *t*-statistics are not significant, you should suspect collinearity.
- Collinearity is measured in terms of the R_j^2 between a predictor and *all* of the other predictors in the model. It is not measured in terms of the correlation between any two predictors. Of course, if two predictors are highly correlated, then the R_j^2 with even more predictors must be at least that large and will usually be even higher.

JUST CHECKING

> **3** In a study of *Salary*, a regression on several variables shows high collinearity of *Age* and *Years Experience*. Explain why this might be and what you would do about it.

19.6   Quadratic Terms

WHO	Downhill racers in the 2002 Winter Olympics
WHAT	Time, Starting Position
WHEN	2002
WHERE	Salt Lake City

After the women's downhill ski racing event at the Winter Olympic Games in Salt Lake City, Picabo Street of the U.S. team was disappointed with her 16th place finish after she'd posted the fastest practice time. Changing snow conditions can affect finish times, and in fact, the top seeds can choose their starting positions and try to guess when the conditions will be best. But how much impact was there? On the day of the women's downhill race, it was unusually sunny. Skiers expect conditions to improve and then, as the day wears on, to deteriorate, so they try to pick the optimum time. But their calculations were upset by a two-hour delay. Picabo Street chose to race in 26th position. By then conditions had turned around, and the slopes had begun to deteriorate. Was that the reason for her disappointing finish?

The regression in Table 19.11 seems to support her point. Times did get slower as the day wore on.

```
Dependent variable is: Time
R-squared = 37.9%   R-squared (adjusted) = 36.0%
s = 1.577 with 35 − 2 = 33 degrees of freedom
```

Variable	Coeff	SE(Coeff)	t-ratio	P-value
Intercept	100.069	0.5597	179	<0.0001
StartOrder	0.108563	0.0242	4.49	<0.0001

TABLE 19.11   Time to ski the women's downhill event at the 2002 Winter Olympics depended on starting position.

But a plot of the residuals warns us that the Linearity Assumption isn't met.

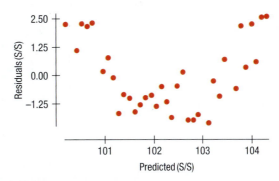

FIGURE 19.8 The residuals reveal a bend.

If we plot the data, we can see that re-expression can't help us because as the skiers expected, the times first trended down and then turned around and increased.

FIGURE 19.9 The original data trend down and then up. That kind of bend can't be improved with re-expression.

How can we use regression here? We can introduce a squared term to the model:

$$\widehat{Time} = b_0 + b_1 startorder + b_2 startorder^2.$$

The fitted function is a *quadratic*, which can follow bends like the one in these data. Table 19.12 has the regression table.

```
Dependent variable is: Time
R-squared = 83.3%  R-squared (adjusted) = 82.3%
s = 0.8300 with 35 − 3 = 32 degrees of freedom
```

Source	Sum of Squares	df	Mean Square	F-ratio
Regression	110.139	2	55.0694	79.9
Residual	22.0439	32	0.688871	

Variable	Coeff	SE(Coeff)	t-ratio	P-value
Intercept	103.547	0.4749	218	<0.0001
StartOrder	−0.367408	0.0525	−6.99	<0.0001
StartOrder^2	0.011592	0.0012	9.34	<0.0001

TABLE 19.12 A regression model with a quadratic term fits these data better.

This model fits the data better. Adjusted R^2 is 82.3%, up from 36.0% for the linear version. And the residuals look generally unstructured, as Figure 19.10 shows.

FIGURE 19.10 The residuals from the quadratic model show no structure.

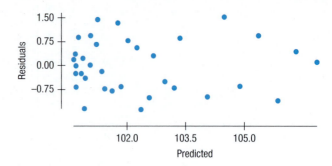

However, one problem remains. In the new model, the coefficient of *Start Order* has changed from significant and positive to significant and negative. As we've just seen, that's a signal of possible collinearity. Quadratic models often have collinearity problems because for many variables, x and x^2 are highly correlated. In these data, *Start Order* and *Start Order*^{2} have a correlation of 0.97.

There's a simple fix for this problem. Instead of using *Start Order*^{2}, we can use $(Start\ Order - \overline{Start\ Order})^2$. The form with the mean subtracted has a *zero* correlation with the linear term. Table 19.13 shows the resulting regression. (Writing *Start Order* as *SO* for brevity.)

```
Dependent variable is: Time
R-squared = 83.3%  R-squared (adjusted) = 82.3%
s = 0.8300 with 35 - 3 = 32 degrees of freedom
```

Source	Sum of Squares	df	Mean Square	F-ratio
Regression	110.139	2	55.0694	79.9
Residual	22.0439	32	0.688871	

Variable	Coeff	SE(Coeff)	t-ratio	P-value
Intercept	98.7493	0.3267	302	<0.0001
StartOrder	0.104239	0.0127	8.18	<0.0001
(SO-mean)^2	0.011592	0.0012	9.34	<0.0001

TABLE 19.13 Using a centered quadratic term alleviates the collinearity.

The predicted values and residuals are the same for these two models,[13] but the coefficients of the second one are easier to interpret.

So, did Picabo Street have a valid complaint? Well, times did increase with start order, but (from the quadratic term), they decreased before they turned around and increased. Picabo's start order of 26 has a predicted time of 101.83 seconds. Her performance at 101.17 was better than predicted, but her residual of −0.66 is not large in magnitude compared to that for some of the other skiers. Skiers who had much later starting positions *were* disadvantaged, but Picabo's start position was only slightly later than the best possible one (about 16th according to this model), and her performance was not extraordinary by Olympic standards.

One final note: Quadratic models can do an excellent job of fitting curved patterns such as this one. But they are particularly dangerous to use for extrapolating beyond the range of the x-values. So you should use them with care.

---

[13]This can be shown algebraically for any quadratic model with a centered squared term.

IN PRACTICE 19.6 Adding quadratic terms

We have fit a model of *Log₁₀ Price* to *Carat Weight, Color, Cut,* and *Clarity.* (See pages 666–667.) The R^2 is an impressive 94.46%. The 749 diamonds are a random sample of diamonds of three *Color* levels and of *Weight* between 0.3 and 1.5 carats. We transformed *Price* using the log (base 10) to linearize the relationship with *Carat Weight*. However, a plot of residuals vs. predicted values reveals:

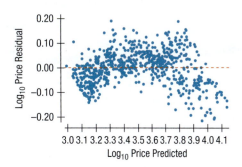

There appears to be a curved relationship between residuals and predicted values. What happens if we add (*Carat Weight*)² as a predictor?

Here's the regression output:

```
Response Variable: Log10Price
R-squared = 97.31%  Adjusted R-squared = 97.27%
s = 0.04741 with 749 − 14 = 735 degrees of freedom
```

Variable	Coeff	SE(Coeff)	t-ratio	P-value
Intercept	2.040547	0.017570	116.138	<0.0001
Carat.Weight	2.365036	0.042400	55.780	<0.0001
Carat.Weight²	−0.699846	0.025028	−27.962	<0.0001
ColorD	0.347479	0.006346	54.755	<0.0001
ColorG	0.252336	0.005683	44.398	<0.0001
CutGood	−0.038896	0.007763	−5.010	<0.0001
CutIdeal	0.016165	0.006982	2.315	0.020877
CutVery Good	−0.014988	0.003834	−3.910	0.000101
ClaritySI1	−0.286641	0.008359	−34.292	<0.0001
ClaritySI2	−0.353371	0.008800	−40.155	<0.0001
ClarityVS1	−0.161288	0.008513	−18.947	<0.0001
ClarityVS2	−0.215559	0.008246	−26.141	<0.0001
ClarityVVS1	−0.077703	0.008682	−8.950	<0.0001
ClarityVVS2	−0.103078	0.008327	−12.378	<0.0001

The plot of residuals against predicted values shows:

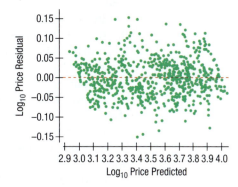

(continued)

A histogram, boxplot, and Normal probability plot of the residuals show:

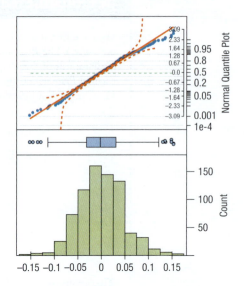

MANAGER Your last model contained all the variables, and seemed quite strong, but you mentioned that you needed to check some assumptions, especially about linearity. What have you found?

CONSULTANT My previous model had only linear terms. I added quadratic terms for *Carat Weight*. This model is based on *Carat Weight, Carat Weight², Color (3 levels), Cut (4 levels),* and *Clarity (7 levels).* The R^2 for this model is 97.31% (97.27% adjusted), and the residual standard deviation is only 0.047 (in $Log_{10}Price$). Every term included in the model is statistically significant. The assumptions and conditions of multiple regression are all met. The residuals appear to be symmetric and roughly Normal. The inclusion of the squared term for *Carat Weight* has eliminated the pattern in the plot of residuals vs. predicted values. This model seems appropriate to use for other diamonds in this range of *Carat Weight*s.

Regression Roles

We build regression models for a number of reasons. One reason is to model how variables are related to each other in the hope of understanding the relationships. Another is to build a model that might be used to predict values for a response variable when given values for the predictor variables. When we hope to understand, we are often particularly interested in simple, straightforward models in which predictors are as unrelated to each other as possible. We are especially happy when the *t*-statistics are large, indicating that the predictors each contribute to the model.

By contrast, when prediction is our goal, we are more likely to care about the overall R^2. Good prediction occurs when much of the variability in *y* is accounted for by the model. We might be willing to keep variables in our model that have relatively small *t*-statistics simply for the stability that having several predictors can provide. We care less whether the predictors are related to each other because we don't intend to interpret the coefficients anyway, so collinearity is less of a concern.

In both roles, we may include some predictors to "get them out of the way." Regression offers a way to approximately control for factors when we have observational data because each coefficient estimates a relationship *after removing the effects of the other predictors*. Of course, it would be better to control for factors in a randomized experiment, but in the real world of business that's often just not possible.

⊘ WHAT CAN GO WRONG?

- **Be alert for collinearity when you set aside an influential point.** Removing a high influence point may have surprising consequences. Sometimes variables are collinear *except* when the point is there, so removing it actually introduces collinearity. In this case, you should consider removing one of the variables from the model. On the other hand, sometimes variables are collinear only because of one outlying point, so removing it removes the collinearity—and probably results in a more useful regression model.

- **Beware missing data.** Values may be missing or unavailable for any case in any variable. In simple regression, when the cases are missing for reasons that are unrelated to the variable we're trying to predict, that's not a problem. We just analyze the cases for which we have data. But when several variables participate in a multiple regression, any case with data missing on any of the variables will be omitted from the analysis. You can unexpectedly find yourself with a much smaller set of data than you started with. Be especially careful, when comparing regression models with different predictors, that the cases participating in the models are the same.

- **Don't forget linearity.** The **Linearity Assumption** requires linear relationships among the variables in a regression model. As you build and compare regression models, be sure to plot the data to check that it is straight. Violations of this assumption make everything else about a regression model invalid.

- **Check for parallel regression lines.** When you introduce an indicator variable for a category, check the underlying assumption that the other coefficients in the model are essentially the same for both groups. If not, consider adding an interaction term.

ETHICS IN ACTION

Fred Barolo heads a travel company that offers, among other services, customized travel packages. These packages provide a relatively high profit margin for his company, but Fred worries that a weakened economic outlook will adversely affect this segment of his business.

He read in a recent Travel Industry Association report that there is increasing interest among U.S. leisure travelers in trips focused on a unique culinary and wine-related experience. To gain an understanding of travel trends in this niche market, he seeks advice from a market analyst, Smith Nebbiolo, whose firm also handles promotional campaigns. Smith has access to several databases, some through membership with the Travel Industry Association and others through the U.S. Census Bureau and Bureau of Economic Analysis.

Smith suggests developing a model to predict demand for culinary wine-related travel, and Fred agrees. As the dependent variable, Smith uses the monthly dollar amount spent on travel packages advertised as culinary wine experiences. He considers a number of monthly economic indicators such as gross domestic product (GDP) and personal consumption expenditures (PCE); variables related to the travel industry (e.g., the American Consumer Satisfaction Index (ACSI) for airlines and hotels, etc.); and factors specific to culinary and wine travel experiences such as advertising expenditure and price. With so many variables, Smith uses an automatic stepwise procedure to select among them.

The final model Smith presents to Fred does not include any monthly economic indicators; ACSI for airlines and hotels are included as was advertising expenditure for these types of trips. Fred and Smith discuss how it appears that the economy has little effect on this niche travel market and how Fred should start thinking of how he will promote his new culinary wine-related travel packages.

- **Identify the ethical dilemma in this scenario.**

- **What are the undesirable consequences?**

- **Propose an ethical solution that considers the welfare of all stakeholders.**

FROM LEARNING TO EARNING

**LEARNING
OBJECTIVES**

Use indicator (dummy) variables intelligently.

- An indicator variable that is 1 for a group and 0 for others is appropriate when the slope for that group is the same as for the others, but the intercept may be different.

- If the slope for the indicated group is different, then it may be appropriate to include an interaction term in the regression model.

- When there are three or more categories, use a separate indicator variable for each, but leave one out to avoid collinearity.

Diagnose multiple regressions to expose any undue influence of individual cases.

- Leverage measures how far a case is from the mean of all cases when measured on the x-variables.

- The leverage of a case tells how much the predicted value of that case would change if the y-value of that case were changed by adding 1 and nothing else in the regression changed.

- Studentized residuals are residuals divided by their individual standard errors. Externally studentized residuals follow a t-distribution when the regression assumptions are satisfied.

- A case is influential if it has both sufficient leverage and a large enough residual. Removing an influential case from the data will change the model in ways that matter to your interpretation or intended use. Measures such as *Cook's D* and *DFFITS* combine leverage and studentized residuals into a single measure of influence.

- By assigning an indicator variable to a single influential case, we can remove its influence from the model and test (using the P-value of its coefficient) whether it is in fact influential.

Build multiple regression models when many predictors are available.

- Seek models with few predictors, a relatively high R^2, a relatively small residual standard deviation, relatively small P-values for the coefficients, no cases that are unduly influential, and predictors that are reliably measured and relatively unrelated to each other.

- Automated methods for seeking regression models include best subsets and stepwise regression. Neither one should be used without carefully diagnosing the resulting model.

Recognize collinearity and deal with it to improve your regression model. Collinearity occurs when one predictor can be well predicted from the others.

- The R^2 of the regression of one predictor on the others is a suitable measure. Alternatively, the *Variance Inflation Factor*, which is based on this R^2, is often reported by statistics programs.

- Collinearity can have the effect of making the P-values for the coefficients large (not significant) even though the overall regression fits the data well.

- Removing some predictors from the model or making combinations of those that are collinear can reduce this problem.

**Consider fitting quadratic terms in your regression model when the residuals show a bend.
Re-expressing y is another option, unless the bent relationship between y and the x's is not monotonic.**

Recognize why a particular regression model is fit.

- We may want to understand some of the individual coefficients.

- We may simply be interested in prediction and not be concerned about the coefficients themselves.

TERMS

Best subsets regression	A regression method that checks all possible combinations of the available predictors to identify the combination that optimizes an arbitrary measure of regression success.
Collinearity	When one (or more) of the predictors can be fit closely by a regression on the other predictors, we have collinearity. When collinear predictors are in a regression model, they may have unexpected coefficients and often have inflated standard errors (and correspondingly small t-statistics).
Cook's Distance	A measure of the influence of a single case on the coefficients in a multiple regression.
Cross validation	A method of evaluating the performance of a model. In one round of cross-validation the model is fit on the training set and evaluated on the hold out (or test) set.
DFFITS	A measure of the influence of a single case on a multiple regression model.
Indicator variable (dummy variable)	A variable constructed to indicate for each case whether it is in a designated group or not. Usually the values are 0 and 1, where 1 indicates group membership.
Influential case	A case is *influential* on a multiple regression model if, when it is omitted, the model changes by enough to matter for your purposes. (There is no specific amount of change defined to declare a case influential.) Cases with high leverage and large studentized residual are likely to be influential.
Interaction term	A variable constructed by multiplying a predictor variable by an indicator variable. An interaction term adjusts the slope of that predictor for the cases identified by the indicator.
Leverage	A measure of the amount of influence an individual case has on the regression. Moving a case in the y direction by 1 unit (while changing nothing else) will move its predicted value by the leverage. The leverage of the ith case is denoted h_i.
Overfitting	The problem of fitting a model typically using all the data (instead of using a hold out set), in which the model fits the training data very well, but predicts poorly on data it hasn't used.
Stepwise regression	An automated method of building regression models in which predictors are added to or removed from the model one at a time in an attempt to optimize a measure of the success of the regression. Stepwise methods rarely find the best model and are easily affected by influential cases, but they can be valuable in winnowing down a large collection of candidate predictors.
Studentized residual	When a residual is divided by an estimate of its standard deviation, the result is a studentized residual. The type of studentized residual that has a t-distribution is an *externally studentized residual*.
Test (or hold out) set	The dataset used in a supervised classification or regression problem not used to build the predictive model. The test set is withheld (held out) from the model building stage of the process, and the model's predictions on the test set are used to evaluate the model performance.
Training set	The dataset used in a supervised classification or regression problem to build the predictive model.
Variance Inflation Factor (VIF)	A measure of the degree to which a predictor in a multiple regression model is collinear with other predictors. It is based on the R^2 of the regression of that predictor on all the other predictors in the model: $$VIF_j = \frac{1}{1 - R_j^2}$$

TECH SUPPORT Building Multiple Regression Models

Statistics packages differ in how much information they provide to diagnose a multiple regression. Most packages provide leverage values. Many provide far more, including statistics that we have not discussed. But for all, the principle is the same. We hope to discover any cases that don't behave like the others in the context of the regression model and then to understand why they are special.

Many of the ideas in this chapter rely on the concept of examining a regression model and then finding a new one based on your growing understanding of the model and the data. Regression diagnosis is meant to provide steps along that road. A thorough regression analysis may involve finding and diagnosing several models.

Statistics software will omit from a regression analysis any case that is missing a value on any variable in the model. As a result, when variables are added to or removed from a model, the cases in that model may change in subtle ways.

EXCEL

Excel and XLStat do not offer diagnostic statistics with its regression function.

COMMENTS

Although the dialog offers a Normal probability plot of the residuals, the data analysis add-in does not make a correct probability plot, so don't use this option. The "standardized residuals" are just the residuals divided by their standard deviation (with the wrong df), so they too should be ignored.

XLSTAT

XLStat can handle both qualitative (indicator) and quantitative explanatory variables. To use stepwise regression:

- Choose **Modeling data**.
- Select all desired explanatory variables in the dialog box for **Linear regression**.
- On the **Options** tab, XLStat gives you options for building a **Best model** using various criteria, or building a model based on significance in a **stepwise** or **forward** or **backward** direction.

JMP

- From the **Analyze** menu select **Fit Model**.
- Specify the response, Y. Assign the predictors, X, in the **Construct Model Effects** dialog box.
- Click on **Run Model**.
- Click on the red triangle in the title of the Model output to find a variety of plots and diagnostics available.

COMMENTS

JMP chooses a regression analysis when the response variable is "Continuous."

In JMP, stepwise regression is a *Personality* of the **Model Fitting** platform; it is found in the upper right of the **Model Specification** dialog. Stepwise provides several options including forward, backward, and mixed selection and can find best subsets with an **All Possible Models** command, accessible from the red triangle drop-down menu on the stepwise control panel after you've selected a stepwise regression analysis.

MINITAB

- Choose **Regression** from the **Stat** menu.
- Choose **Fit Regression Model** from the **Regression** submenu.
- In the Regression dialog, assign the Y-variable to the Response box and assign the X-variables to the Continuous and Categorical Predictors boxes.
- In the Regression **Storage** dialog, you can select a variety of diagnostic statistics. They will be stored in the columns of your worksheet.
- Click the **OK** button to return to the Regression dialog.
- To specify displays, click **Graphs**, and check the displays you want.

- Click the **OK** button to return to the Regression dialog.
- Click the **OK** button to compute the regression.

COMMENTS

You will probably want to make displays of the stored diagnostic statistics. Use the usual Minitab methods for creating displays.

Minitab also offers both stepwise and best subsets regression from the **Regression** dialog. Indicate the response variable, the predictors eligible for inclusion, and any predictors that you wish to force into the model.

R

Suppose the response variable *y* and predictor variables *x1*, . . . , *xk* are in a data frame called mydata. After fitting a multiple regression of *y* on *x1* and *x2* via:

- mylm = lm(y~x1+x2,data=mydata).
- summary(mylm) # gives the details of the fit, including the ANOVA table.
- plot(mylm) # gives a variety of plots.
- lm.influence(mylm) # gives a variety of regression diagnostic values.
- To get partial regression plots (called Added Variable plots in **R**), you need the library car:
- library(car).
- Then to get the partial regression plots:
- avPlots(mylm) # one plot for each predictor variable–interactions not permitted.
- Stepwise regression is available using the step() function on an existing model.

STATCRUNCH

To perform a multiple regression:
- Click on **Stat**.
- Choose **Regression > Multiple Linear**.
- Choose the **Y variable** and the **X variables** (interactions can be added optionally).
- There are **All subsets** and **Stepwise** options

To get plots (actual vs. predicted, partial regression plots and residuals vs. predicted).
- Choose **Graphs** and select desired graphs.
- Click on **Compute!**

COMMENTS

Residuals, studentized residuals, predicted values, confidence intervals, prediction intervals, and a variety of diagnostics can be saved by
- Choose **Save**:
- Select the options you want.

SPSS

- Choose **Regression** from the **Analyze** menu.
- Choose **Linear** from the **Regression** submenu.

- When the Linear Regression dialog appears, select the Y-variable and move it to the dependent target. Then move the X-variables to the independent target.
- Click the **Save** button.
- In the Linear Regression Save dialog, choose diagnostic statistics. These will be saved in your worksheet along with your data.
- Click the **Continue** button to return to the Linear Regression dialog.
- Click the **OK** button to compute the regression.

COMMENTS

SPSS offers stepwise methods (use the **Method** drop-down menu), but not best subsets (in the student version). Click on the **Statistics** button to find collinearity diagnostics and on the **Save** button for influential point diagnostics. (The residuals SPSS calls "Studentized deleted" are the externally studentized residuals that we've recommended in this chapter.) You may want to plot the saved diagnostics using SPSS's standard graphics methods.

BRIEF CASE

Building Models

The Paralyzed Veterans of America (PVA) is a philanthropic organization sanctioned by the U.S. government to represent the interests of those veterans who are disabled. (For more information on the PVA see the opening of Chapter 21.) To generate donations, the PVA sends out greeting cards and mailing address labels periodically with their requests for donations. To increase their efficiency, they would like to be able to model the amount of donations based on past giving and demographic variables on their donors. The dataset **PVA** contains data on 3648 donors who gave to a recent solicitation. There are 26 predictor variables and 1 response variable. The response variable (GIFTAMNT) is the amount of money donated by the donor to the last solicitation. Find a model from the 26 predictor variables using any model selection procedure you like to predict this amount. The variables include:

Variables based on the donor's ZIP code

> MALEVET (% Male veterans)
> VIETVETS (% Vietnam Veterans)
> WWIIVETS (% WWII veterans)
> LOCALGOV (% Employed by local government)
> STATEGOV (% Employed by state government)
> FEDGOV (% Employed by federal government)

Variables specific to the individual donor

> HOMEOWNER (N = No; Y = Yes)
> HIT (Number of times donor has responded to mail order offers other than PVA's)
> CARDPROM (Number of card promotions received lifetime)
> MAXADATE (Date of most recent promotion received in YYMM Year Month format)
> NUMPROM (Number of promotions received lifetime)
> CARDPRM12 (Number of card promotions received in last 12 months)
> NUMPRM12 (Number of promotions received in last 12 months)
> NGIFTALL (Number of gifts given lifetime to date)
> CARDGIFT (Number of gifts to card promotions given lifetime to date)

(continued)

BRIEF CASE   *(continued)*

MINRAMNT (Amount of smallest gift to date in $)

MINRDATE (Date associated with the smallest gift to date—YYMM format)

MAXRAMNT (Amount of largest gift to date in $)

MAXRDATE (Date associated with the largest gift to date—YYMM format)

LASTGIFT (Amount of most recent gift in $)

AVGGIFT (Average amount of gifts to date in $)

CONTROLN (Control number—unique record identifier)

HPHONE_D (Indicator variable for presence of a published home phone number: 1 = Yes; 0 = No)

CLUSTER2 (Marketing Cluster Code—nominal field)

CHILDREN (Number of children living at home)

Response variable

GIFTAMNT (Response variable—amount of last gift in $)

Be sure to include exploratory data analysis and evaluate the relationship among these variables using graphical and correlation analysis to guide you in building your regression models. Write a report summarizing your analysis.

CHAPTER 19 EXERCISES

SECTION 19.1

1. For each of the following, show how you would code dummy (or indicator) variables to include in a regression model.

a) Company unionization status (Unionized, No Union)
b) Gender (Female, Male)
c) Account Status (Paid on time, Past Due)
d) Political party affiliation (Democrat, Republican, Other)

2. A marketing manager has developed a regression model to predict quarterly sales of his company's down jackets based on price and amount spent on advertising. An intern suggests that he include an indicator (dummy) variable for the Fall quarter.

a) How would you code such a variable? (What values would it have for each quarter?)
b) Why does the intern's suggestion make sense?
c) Do you think a regression with the indicator variable for Fall would model down jacket sales better than one without that predictor?

3. Do movies of different types have different rates of return on their budgets? Here's a scatterplot of Gross Revenue in US ($M) vs. Budget ($M) for recent movies whose MPAA Rating is either PG (blue) or R (red):

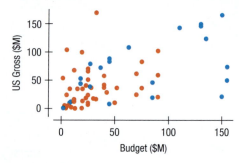

a) Why might a researcher want to use an indicator variable for the MPAA Rating?
b) What would the data values in such an indicator variable be?

4. Here is the regression for Exercise 3 with an indicator variable:

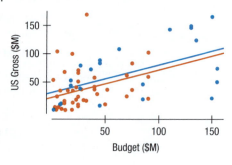

```
Dependent variable is: USGross($M)
R-squared = 0.193, Adjusted R-squared: 0.166
s = 37.01 with 62 - 3 = 59 degrees of freedom
```

Variable	Coefficient	SE(Coeff)	t-ratio	P-value
Intercept	49.2642	12.5736	3.918	0.000235
Budget	0.3292	0.1264	2.605	0.011612
R Rating	-12.4871	11.2145	-1.113	0.270018

a) Write out the regression model.

b) In this regression, the variable *R Rating* is an indicator variable that is 1 for movies that have an R rating. How would you interpret the coefficient of *R Rating*?

c) What null hypothesis can we test with the *t*-ratio for *R Rating*?

d) Can you reject the null hypothesis of part c? Explain.

5. For each of the following, show how you would code dummy (indicator) variables to include in a regression model.

a) Type of residence (Apartment, Condominium, Townhouse, Single family home)

b) Employment status (Full-time, Part-time, Unemployed)

6. A marketing manager has developed a regression model to predict quarterly sales of his company's mid-weight microfiber jackets based on price and amount spent on advertising. An intern suggests that he include indicator (dummy) variables for each quarter.

a) How would you code the variables? (How many dummy variables do you need? What values would they have?)

b) Why does the intern's suggestion make sense?

c) Do you think a regression with the indicator variables would model jacket sales better than one without those predictors?

SECTION 19.2

7. Are R rated movies as profitable as those rated PG-13? Here's scatterplot of USGross ($M) vs. Budget ($M) for PG-13 (green) and R (purple) rated movies

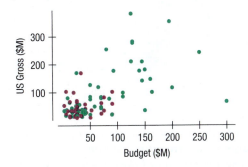

a) How would you code the indicator variable? (Use PG-13 as the base level.)

b) How would you construct the interaction term variable?

8. Here is the scatterplot of the variables in Exercise 7 with regression lines added for each kind of movie:

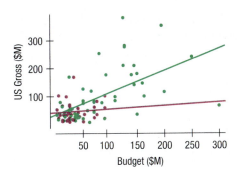

The regression model is:

```
Dependent variable is: USGross($M)
R-squared = 0.3674, Adjusted R-squared: 0.3491
s = 58.24 with 107 - 3 = 104 degrees of freedom
```

Variable	Coefficient	SE(Coeff)	t-ratio	P-value
Intercept	34.0262	10.6595	3.192	0.00187
Budget	0.7902	0.1143	6.912	<0.0001
R Rating	9.9217	18.8666	0.526	0.60009
Budget*R Rating	-0.6679	0.3798	-1.758	0.08163

a) Write out the regression model.

b) In this regression, the variable *Budget*R Rating* is an interaction term. How would you interpret its coefficient?

c) What null hypothesis can we test with the *t*-ratio for *Budget*R Rating*?

d) Would you reject that hypothesis at 0.05? What do you conclude?

SECTION 19.3

9. For the regression model in Exercise 8, the leverage values look like this:

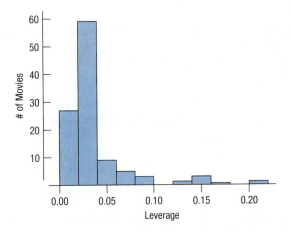

The movie with the highest leverage of 0.219 is Walt Disney's *John Carter*, which grossed $66M but had a budget of $300M.

If the budget for *John Carter* had been $1M higher than it was (and everything else remained the same), how much would the model's prediction of *John Carter*'s U.S. gross revenue change?

10. For the same regression as in Exercise 9, the Cook's Distances look like this:

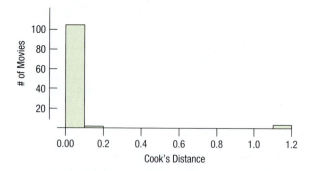

The outlier, once again, is *John Carter*, whose budget was more than $200M more than its gross revenue in the U.S. Setting this movie aside and rerunning the regression from Exercise 8, we find:

```
Dependent variable is: USGross($M)
R-squared = 0.4635, Adjusted R-squared: 0.4478
s = 53.89 with 106 – 3 = 103 degrees of freedom
```

Variable	Coefficient	SE(Coeff)	t-ratio	P-value
Intercept	21.6562	10.2755	2.108	0.0375
Budget	1.0224	0.1188	8.607	<0.0001
R Rating	22.2916	17.6941	1.260	0.2106
Budget*R Rating	−0.9001	0.3556	−2.531	0.0129

a) What are the main differences between this model with *John Carter* removed and the model from Exercise 7 with it included?
b) Which model do you prefer? Explain briefly.

SECTION 19.4

11. An analyst wants to build a regression model to predict spending from the following four predictor variables: *Past Spending, Income, Net Worth,* and *Age*. A correlation matrix of the four predictors shows:

	Income	Net Worth	Age
Past Spending	0.442	0.433	0.446
Income		0.968	0.992
Net Worth			0.976

Why might a stepwise regression search not find the same model as an "all subsets" regression?

12. The analyst in Exercise 11 fits the model with the four predictor variables. The regression output shows:

```
Response Variable: Spending
R² = 84.92%  Adjusted R² = 84.85%
s = 48.45 with 908 – 5 = 903 degrees of freedom
```

Variable	Coeff	SE(Coeff)	t-ratio	P-value
Intercept	−3.738e + 00	1.564e + 01	−0.239	0.811
Past Spending	1.063e − 01	4.203e − 03	25.292	<0.0001
Income	1.902e − 03	3.392e − 04	5.606	<0.0001
Networth	2.900e − 05	3.815e − 05	0.760	0.447
Age	6.065e − 01	7.631e − 01	0.795	0.427

a) How many observations were used in the regression?
b) What might you do next?
c) Is it clear that *Income* is more important to predicting *Spending* than *Networth*? Explain.

SECTION 19.5

13. The analyst from Exercise 11, worried about collinearity, regresses *Age* against *Past Spending, Income,* and *Networth*. The output shows:

```
Response Variable: Age
R² = 98.75%  Adjusted R² = 98.74%
s = 2.112 with 908 – 4 = 904 degrees of freedom
```

Variable	Coeff	SE(Coeff)	t-ratio	P-value
(Intercept)	2.000e + 01	1.490e − 01	134.234	<0.0001
Past Spending	3.339e − 04	1.828e − 04	1.826	0.0681
Income	3.811e − 04	7.610e − 06	50.079	<0.0001
Networth	2.420e − 05	1.455e − 06	16.628	<0.0001

What is the VIF for *Age*?

14. If the VIF for *Networth* in the regression of Exercise 11 was 20.83, what would the R^2 be from the regression of *Networth* on *Age, Income,* and *Past Spending*?

SECTION 19.6

15. A collection of houses in a neighborhood of Boston shows the following relationship between *Price* and *Age* of the house:

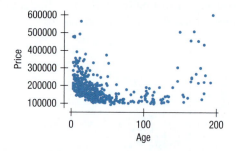

a) Describe the relationship between *Price* and *Age*. Explain what this says in terms of house prices.
b) A linear regression of *Price* on *Age* shows that the slope for *Age* is not statistically significant. Is *Price* unrelated to *Age*? Explain.
c) What might you do instead?

16. A regression model from the collection of houses in Exercise 15 shows the following:

Variable	Coeff	SE(Coeff)	t-ratio	P-value
Intercept	217854.85	4197.417	51.90	<0.0001
Age	−1754.254	127.3356	−13.78	<0.0001
(Age-38.5122)^2	20.401223	1.327713	15.37	<0.0001

a) The slope of *Age* is negative. Does this indicate that older houses cost less, on average? Explain.
b) Why did the model subtract 38.5122 from *Age* in the quadratic term?

CHAPTER EXERCISES

T **17. Pizza ratings.** Manufacturers of frozen foods often reformulate their products to maintain and increase customer satisfaction and sales. So they pay particular attention to evaluations of their products in comparison to their competitors' products. Frozen pizzas are a major sector of the frozen food market, accounting for an average of $3.1 billion in sales in the five-year period from 2008 to 2012 (www.companiesandmarkets.com). The prestigious Consumer's Union rated frozen pizzas for flavor and quality, assigning an overall score to each brand tested. A regression model to predict the Consumer's Union score from Calories, Type (1 = cheese, 0 = pepperoni), and Fat content gives the following result:

```
Dependent variable is: Score
R-squared = 28.7%  R-squared (adjusted) = 20.2%
s = 19.79 with 29 − 4 = 25 degrees of freedom
```

Source	Sum of Squares	df	Mean Square	F-ratio
Regression	3947.34	3	1315.78	3.36
Residual	9791.35	25	391.654	

Variable	Coeff	SE(Coeff)	t-ratio	P-value
Intercept	−148.817	77.99	−1.91	0.0679
Calories	0.743023	0.3066	2.42	0.0229
Type	15.6344	8.103	1.93	0.0651
Fat	−3.89135	2.138	−1.82	0.0807

a) What is the interpretation of the coefficient of *Type* in this regression? According to these results, what type would you expect to sell better—cheese or pepperoni?
b) What displays would you like to see to check assumptions and conditions for this model?

18. Traffic delays. The Texas Transportation Institute (tti.tamu.edu) studies traffic delays. They estimate that in 2014 the average commuter lost 42 hours in traffic congestion, compared to 18 hours in 1982, and wasted 19 gallons of fuel. Total costs of congestion reached $160B in lost productivity and fuel costs, or nearly 1% of US GDP, about 4 times the 1982 level. A large study was completed in 2015, but a 2001 study included physical variables like speed on the highway. Those data included measurements on the *Total Delay per Person* (hours per year spent delayed by traffic), the *Average Arterial Road Speed* (mph), the *Average Highway Road Speed* (mph), and the *Size* of the city (small, medium, large, very large). The regression model based on these variables looks like this. The variables *Small*, *Large*, and *Very Large* are indicators constructed to be 1 for cities of the named size and 0 otherwise.

```
Dependent variable is: Delay/person
R-squared = 79.1%  R-squared (adjusted) = 77.4%
s = 6.474 with 68 − 6 = 62 degrees of freedom
```

Source	Sum of Squares	df	Mean Square	F-ratio
Regression	9808.23	5	1961.65	46.8
Residual	2598.64	62	41.9135	

Variable	Coeff	SE(Coeff)	t-ratio	P-value
Intercept	139.104	16.69	8.33	<0.0001
HiWay MPH	−1.07347	0.2474	−4.34	<0.0001
Arterial MPH	−2.04836	0.6672	−3.07	0.0032
Small	−3.58970	2.953	−1.22	0.2287
Large	5.00967	2.104	2.38	0.0203
Very Large	3.41058	3.230	1.06	0.2951

a) Why is there no coefficient for *Medium*?
b) Explain how the coefficients of *Small*, *Large*, and *Very Large* account for the size of the city in this model.

T **19. Pizza ratings, part 2.** Here's a scatterplot of the residuals against predicted values for the regression model found in Exercise 17.

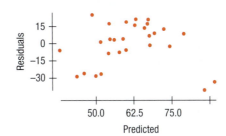

a) The two extraordinary points in the lower right are *Reggio's* and *Michelina's*, two gourmet brands. Interpret these points.
b) Do you think these two pizzas are likely to be influential in the regression. Would setting them aside be likely to change the coefficients? What other statistics might help you decide?

20. Traffic delays, part 2. Here's a scatterplot of the residuals from the regression in Exercise 18 plotted against mean *Highway mph*.

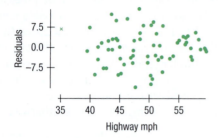

a) The point plotted with an x is Los Angeles. Read the graph and explain what it says about traffic delays in Los Angeles and about the regression model.
b) Is Los Angeles likely to be an influential point in this regression?

T **21. Walmart revenue.** Each week about 100 million customers—nearly one-third of the U.S. population—visit one of Walmart's U.S. stores. How does Walmart's revenue relate to the state of the economy in general? Before the financial crisis of 2009, Walmart reported sales each month, but since then it has switched to quarters. Here's a regression table predicting Walmart's monthly revenue ($Billion) from the end of 2003 through the start of 2007 from the Consumer Price Index (*CPI*), and a scatterplot of the relationship.

```
Dependent variable is: WM_Revenue
R-squared = 11.4%  R-squared (adjusted) = 9.0%
s = 3.689 with 39 − 2 = 37 degrees of freedom
```

Variable	Coeff	SE(Coeff)	t-ratio	P-value
Intercept	−24.4085	19.25	−1.27	0.2127
CPI	0.071792	0.0330	2.18	0.0358

A scatterplot can give us some clues as to why they turned away from monthly reporting.

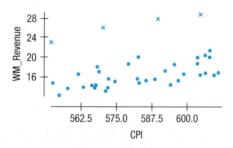

a) The points plotted with x are the December values. We can construct a variable that is "1" for those four values and "0" otherwise. What is such a variable called?

Here's the resulting regression.

```
Dependent variable is: WM_Revenue
R-squared = 80.3%  R-squared (adjusted) = 79.2%
s = 1.762 with 39 − 3 = 36 degrees of freedom
```

Variable	Coeff	SE(Coeff)	t-ratio	P-value
Intercept	−34.7755	9.238	−3.76	0.0006
CPI	0.087707	0.0158	5.55	<0.0001
December	10.4905	0.9337	11.2	<0.0001

b) What is the interpretation of the coefficient of the constructed variable *December*?
c) What additional assumption is required to include the variable *December* in this model? Is there reason to believe that it is satisfied?

T **22. Baseball attendance.** Pedro Martinez, who retired from Major League Baseball in 2012, had a stellar career, helping the Boston Red Sox to their first World Series title in 86 years in 2004. The next year he became a free agent and the New York Mets picked him up for $53 million for 4 years. Even after the move to New York, Martinez had his own fans. Possibly, he attracted more fans to the ballpark when he pitched at home, helping to justify his multi-million dollar contract. Was there really a "Pedro effect" in attendance? We have data for the Mets home games of the 2005 season. The regression has the following predictors:

Weekend	1 if game is on a weekend day or night, 0 otherwise
Yankees	1 if game is against the Yankees (a hometown rivalry), 0 otherwise
Rain Delay	1 if the game was delayed by rain (which might have depressed attendance), 0 otherwise
Opening Day	1 for opening day, 0 for the others
Pedro Start	1 if Pedro was the starting pitcher, 0 otherwise

Here's the regression.

```
Dependent variable is: Attendance
R-squared = 53.9%  R-squared (adjusted) = 50.8%
s = 6998 with 80 − 6 = 74 degrees of freedom
```

Variable	Coeff	SE(Coeff)	t-ratio	P-value
Intercept	28896.9	1161	24.9	<0.0001
Weekend	9960.50	1620	6.15	<0.0001
Yankees	15164.3	4218	3.59	0.0006
Rain Delay	−17427.9	7277	−2.39	0.0192
Opening Day	24766.1	7093	3.49	0.0008
Pedro Start	5428.02	2017	2.69	0.0088

a) All of these predictors are of a special kind. What are they called?
b) What is the interpretation of the coefficient for *Pedro Start*?
c) If we're primarily interested in Pedro's effect on attendance, why is it important to have the other variables in the model?
d) Could Pedro's agent claim, based on this regression, that his man attracts more fans to the ballpark? What statistics should he cite?

23. Pizza ratings, part 3. In Exercise 19, we raised questions about two gourmet pizzas. After removing them, the resulting regression looks like this.

```
Dependent variable is: Score
R-squared = 64.4%  R-squared (adjusted) = 59.8%
s = 14.41 with 27 − 4 = 23 degrees of freedom
```

Source	Sum of Squares	df	Mean Square	F-ratio
Regression	8649.29	3	2883.10	13.9
Residual	4774.56	23	207.590	

Variable	Coeff	SE(Coeff)	t-ratio	P-value
Intercept	−363.109	72.15	−5.03	<0.0001
Calories	1.56772	0.2824	5.55	<0.0001
Type	25.1540	6.214	4.05	0.0005
Fat	−8.82748	1.887	−4.68	0.0001

A plot of the residuals against the predicted values for this regression looks like this. It has been colored according to the *Type* of pizza.

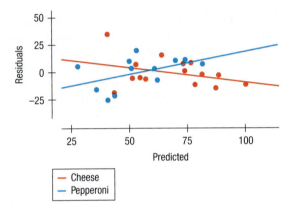

— Cheese
— Pepperoni

a) What does this plot say about how the regression model deals with these two types of pizza?

We constructed another variable consisting of the indicator variable *Type* multiplied by *Calories*. Here's the resulting regression.

```
Dependent variable is: Score
R-squared = 73.1%  R-squared (adjusted) = 68.2%
s = 12.82 with 27 − 5 = 22 degrees of freedom
```

Source	Sum of Squares	df	Mean Square	F-ratio
Regression	9806.53	4	2451.63	14.9
Residual	3617.32	22	164.424	

Variable	Coeff	SE(Coeff)	t-ratio	P-value
Intercept	−464.498	74.73	−6.22	<0.0001
Calories	1.92005	0.2842	6.76	<0.0001
Type	183.634	59.99	3.06	0.0057
Fat	−10.3847	1.779	−5.84	<0.0001
Type*Cals	−0.461496	0.1740	−2.65	0.0145

b) Interpret the coefficient of *Type*Cals* in this regression model.

c) Is this a better regression model than the one in Exercises 17 and 19?

24. Traffic delays, part 3. Here's a plot of the studentized residuals from the regression model of Exercise 18 plotted against *ArterialMPH*. The plot is colored according to *City Size* (Small, Medium, Large, and Very Large), and regression lines are fit for each city size.

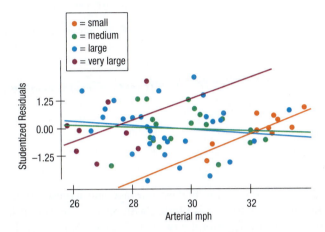

a) The model in Exercise 18 includes indicators for city size. Considering this display, have these indicator variables accomplished what is needed for the regression model? Explain.

Here is another model that adds two new constructed variables to the model in Exercise 18. They are the product of *ArterialMPH* and *Small* and the product of *ArterialMPH* and *VeryLarge*.

```
Dependent variable is: Delay/person
R-squared = 80.7%  R-squared (adjusted) = 78.5%
s = 6.316 with 68 − 8 = 60 degrees of freedom
```

Source	Sum of Squares	df	Mean Square	F-ratio
Regression	10013.0	7	1430.44	35.9
Residual	2393.82	60	39.8970	

Variable	Coeff	SE(Coeff)	t-ratio	P-value
Intercept	153.110	17.42	8.79	<0.0001
HiWayMPH	−1.02104	0.2426	−4.21	<0.0001
ArterialMPH	−2.60848	0.6967	−3.74	0.0004
Small	−125.979	66.92	−1.88	0.0646
Large	4.89837	2.053	2.39	0.0202
VeryLarge	−89.4993	63.25	−1.41	0.1623
AM*Sml	3.81461	2.077	1.84	0.0712
AM*VLg	3.38139	2.314	1.46	0.1491

b) What does the predictor *AM*Sml* (*ArterialMPH* by *Small*) do in this model? Interpret the coefficient.
c) Does this model improve on the model in Exercise 18? Explain.

25. Insurance (life expectancy). Insurance companies base their premiums on many factors, but basically all the factors are variables that predict life expectancy. Life expectancy varies from state to state. Here's a regression that models *Life Expectancy* in terms of other demographic variables.

The variables are *Murder* rate per 100,000, *HighSchool Graduation* rate in %, *Income* per capita in dollars, *Illiteracy* rate per 1000, and *Life Expectancy* in years.

Dependent variable is: Life exp
R-squared = 67.0% R-squared (adjusted) = 64.0%
s = 0.8049 with 50 − 5 = 45 degrees of freedom

Source	Sum of Squares	df	Mean Square	F-ratio
Regression	59.1430	4	14.7858	22.8
Residual	29.1560	45	0.647910	

Variable	Coeff	SE(Coeff)	t-ratio	P-value
Intercept	69.4833	1.325	52.4	<0.0001
Murder	−0.261940	0.0445	−5.89	<0.0001
HSGrad	0.046144	0.0218	2.11	0.0403
Income	1.24948e − 4	0.0002	0.516	0.6084
Illiteracy	0.276077	0.3105	0.889	0.3787

a) The state with the highest leverage and largest Cook's Distance is Alaska. It is plotted with an **x** in the residuals plot. Here are a scatterplot of the residuals, a Normal probability plot of the leverage values, and a histogram of Cook's Distance values. What evidence do you have from these diagnostic plots that Alaska might be an influential point?

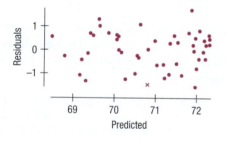

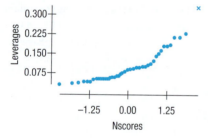

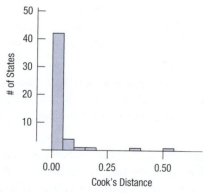

Here's another regression with a dummy variable for Alaska added to the regression model.

Dependent variable is: Life exp
R-squared = 70.8% R-squared (adjusted) = 67.4%
s = 0.7660 with 50 − 6 = 44 degrees of freedom

Source	Sum of Squares	df	Mean Square	F-ratio
Regression	62.4797	5	12.4959	21.3
Residual	25.8193	44	0.586802	

Variable	Coeff	SE(Coeff)	t-ratio	P-value
Intercept	67.6377	1.480	45.7	<0.0001
Murder	−0.250395	0.0426	−5.88	<0.0001
HSGrad	0.055792	0.0212	2.63	0.0116
Illiteracy	0.458607	0.3053	1.50	0.1401
Income	3.68218e − 4	0.0003	1.46	0.1511
Alaska	−2.23284	0.9364	−2.38	0.0215

b) What does the coefficient for the dummy variable for Alaska mean? Is there evidence that Alaska is an outlier in this model?

c) Which model would you prefer for understanding or predicting *Life Expectancy*? Explain.

T 26. Cereals. Breakfast cereal manufacturers publish nutrition information on each box of their product. As we saw in Chapter 17, there is a long history of cereals being associated with nutrition. Here's a regression to predict the number of *Calories* in breakfast cereals from their *Sodium*, *Potassium*, and *Sugar* content, and some diagnostic plots.

Dependent variable is: Calories
R-squared = 38.4% R-squared (adjusted) = 35.9%
s = 15.60 with 77 − 4 = 73 degrees of freedom

Variable	Coeff	SE(Coeff)	t-ratio	P-value
Intercept	83.0469	5.198	16.0	<0.0001
Sodium	0.057211	0.0215	2.67	0.0094
Potassium	−0.019328	0.0251	−0.769	0.4441
Sugar	2.38757	0.4066	5.87	<0.0001

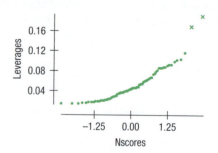

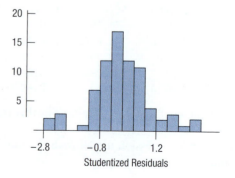

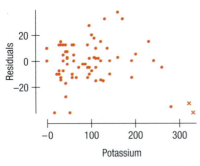

Potassium

The shaded part of the histogram corresponds to the two cereals plotted with x's in the Normal probability plot of the leverages and the residuals plot. These are *All-Bran with Extra Fiber* and *All-Bran*.

a) What do the displays say about the influence of these two cereals on this regression? (The histogram is of the studentized residuals.)

Here's another regression with dummy variables defined for each of the two bran cereals.

```
Dependent variable is: Calories
R-squared = 50.7%  R-squared (adjusted) = 47.3%
s = 14.15 with 77 − 6 = 71 degrees of freedom
```

Variable	Coeff	SE(Coeff)	t-ratio	P-value
Intercept	79.0874	4.839	16.3	<0.0001
Sodium	0.068341	0.0198	3.46	0.0009
Potassium	0.043063	0.0272	1.58	0.1177
Sugar	2.03202	0.3795	5.35	<0.0001
All-Bran	−50.7963	15.84	−3.21	0.0020
All-Bran Extra	−52.8659	16.03	−3.30	0.0015

b) Explain what the coefficients of the bran cereal dummy variables mean.

c) Which regression would you select for understanding the interplay of these nutrition components. Explain. (Note: Both are defensible.)

d) As you can see from the scatterplot, there's another cereal with high potassium. Not too surprisingly, it is *100% Bran*. But it does not have leverage as high as the other two bran cereals. Do you think it should be treated like them (i.e., removed from the model, fit with its own dummy, or left in the model with no special attention, depending on your answer to part c)? Explain.

T 27. Cost of Living 2017. The Brief Case in Chapter 4 introduced the Cost of Living dataset that contains an estimate of the cost of living for 511 cities worldwide in 2017. In addition to the overall *Cost of Living Index* are: the *Rent Index*, *Groceries Index*, *Restaurant Index*, and the *Local Purchasing Power Index*, which measures the relative purchasing power of buying goods and services in a city compared to the average wage in that city. Can we reconstruct the overall *Cost of Living Index* from the four component indices? Here is some multiple regression output:

```
Response variable is: CLI
R squared = 97.8%  R squared (adjusted) =  97.8%
s = 3.317 with 511 − 5 = 506 degrees of freedom
```

Variable	Coefficient	SE(Coeff)	t-ratio	P-value
Intercept	10.6639	0.4530	23.5	<0.0001
Rent Index	0.026108	0.0137	1.90	0.0581
Groceries Index	0.479399	0.0126	38.2	<0.0001
Restaurant indx	0.432446	0.0112	38.6	<0.0001
Local Purchas indx	−0.026215	0.0059	−4.42	<0.0001

Assuming that the assumptions and conditions for this model are satisfied,

a) What might you recommend as a next step for developing a regression model? Why?

The researcher looking at this problem has proposed the following model:

```
Response variable is: CLI
R squared = 97.8%  R squared (adjusted) =  97.8%
s = 3.326 with 511 − 4 = 507 degrees of freedom
```

Variable	Coefficient	SE(Coeff)	t-ratio	P-value
Intercept	10.4024	0.4327	24.0	<0.0001
Groceries Index	0.487257	0.0119	41.0	<0.0001
Restaurant Indx	0.437897	0.0108	40.4	<0.0001
Local Purchas indx	−0.024461	0.0059	−4.16	<0.0001

b) What are the advantages of this model compared to the previous model with four predictors?

c) Why did the researcher remove the *Rent Index* from the model?

d) Do you think the model with three predictors is better? Explain briefly.

T 28. Cost of Living 2017, revisited. For the first model considered in Exercise 27, with all four predictors in the model, a plot of Leverage values shows the two largest values are San Francisco, USA (0.094), and Hamilton, Bermuda (0.077).

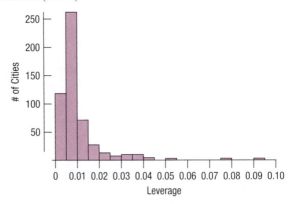

a) By examining the values of their predictor variables find out why these two cities might be such high leverage points.

b) Why don't these cities show up as influential points in the diagnostics of the 3 predictor model?

T 29. Health expenditures revisited. In Chapter 18, Exercise 46 we found a model for national *Health Expenditures* from an economic variable, *Internet Users/100 people*, and *Primary Completion Rate*. A look at leverage values and Cook's Distances identifies several countries as possible high influence points. Here are the values for those countries:

	Lesotho	Djibouti	Singapore	Cuba	Eritrea
Expenditures on Public Health	8.50	4.70	1.40	9.70	1.30
Internet Users/100 people	2.18	0.78	61.90	8.41	1.16
Expected Years of Schooling	9.60	5.10	14.40	16.20	4.60

a) From the data, find the distribution of each variable and explain why each country was identified as a possible high influence point.
b) Find the regression model as in Chapter 18, Exercise 46 without these points and discuss briefly the difference in the two models. Should you report the model with or without these points?

T 30. Dirt bikes 2014, revisited. Off-road motorcycles (often called "dirt bikes") are a segment (about 18%) of the growing motorcycle market. Because dirt bikes offer great variation in features, they are a good market segment to study to learn about which features account for the cost (manufacturer's suggested retail price, *MSRP*) of a bike. Researchers collected data on 2005-model dirt bikes (lib.stat.cmu.edu/datasets/dirtbike_aug.csv). Their original goal was to study market differentiation among brands (Jiang Lu, Joseph B. Kadane, and Peter Boatwright, *The Dirt on Bikes: An Illustration of CART Models for Brand Differentiation*). We've updated their data to 2014-model bikes. In Chapter 18, Exercises 41, 42, and 43 dealt with these data.
    Here's a regression model and some associated graphs.

```
Response variable is: MSRP
R squared = 95.9%  R squared (adjusted) =  95.6%
s = 550.0 with 57 − 5 = 52 degrees of freedom
```

Source	Sum of Squares	df	Mean Square	F-ratio
Regression	365430120	4	91357530	302
Residual	15730703	52	302514	

Variable	Coefficient	SE(Coeff)	t-ratio	P-value
Intercept	−10417.0	681.6	−15.3	<0.0001
Weight	−22.1163	5.939	−3.72	0.0005
Wheel Base	265.191	28.18	9.41	<0.0001
Rake	28.0126	4.813	5.82	<0.0001
Bore	85.2723	7.742	11.0	<0.0001

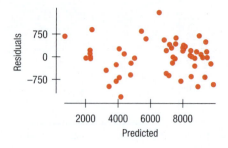

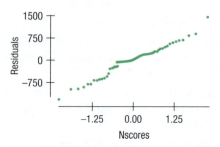

a) List aspects of this regression model that lead to the conclusion that it is likely to be a useful model.
b) What aspects of the displays indicate that the model is a good one?

31. Movie revenue, revisited. In Exercise 8 we found a model for the gross revenue from U.S. movie theatres for 106 recent movies that were rated either R or PG-13. A plot of residuals against predicted revenue shows:

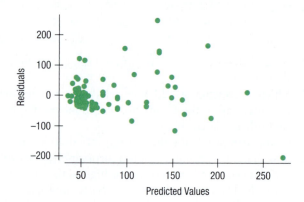

A histogram of the *y*-variable, *US Gross*, shows:

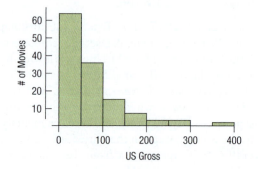

a) What assumptions and/or conditions are violated by this model?

b) What would you recommend doing next to help improve the model?

T 32. Dirt bikes 2014, revisited. The model in Exercise 30 is missing one predictor that we might have expected to see. *Engine Displacement* is highly correlated ($r = 0.783$) with *MSRP*, but that variable has not entered the model (and, indeed, would have a P-value of 0.54 if it were added to the model). Here is some evidence to explain why that may be. (*Hint:* Notice that *Displacement* is the response variable in this regression.)

```
Response variable is: Displacement
R squared = 95.7%  R squared (adjusted) = 95.5%
s = 29.88 with 59 − 4 = 55 degrees of freedom
```

Variable	Coefficient	SE(Coeff)	t-ratio	P-value
Intercept	−228.722	34.65	−6.60	<0.0001
Rake	0.500980	0.2286	2.19	0.0326
Wheel Base	−1.74909	0.9312	−1.88	0.0656
Bore	7.77225	0.3180	24.4	<0.0001

a) What term describes the reason *Displacement* doesn't contribute to the regression model for *MSRP*?

b) Find the value of the Variance Inflation Factor for *Displacement* in the regression on *MSRP*.

T 33. Gross domestic product (diagnostics). In Chapter 18, Exercise 33 we found a model for *GDP per Capita* from three country characteristics: *Cell phones/100 people*, *Internet Users/100 people*, and *Primary Completion Rate*. A look at leverage values and Cook's Distance identifies three countries with high leverage (above 0.10) as Bahrain, Burkina Faso, and Israel and one country, Luxembourg, that stands as an outlier in Cook's Distance.

Below are summary statistics for each variable in the model and the rows for those four countries.

	Minimum	Median	Mean	Maximum	Std Dev	IQR
GDP Per Capita	128	3925	12486.271	74389	16141.658	21078.25
Cell phones/100 people	0.214	36.483	44.818	111.601	35.763	72.74
Internet Users/100 people	0.031	11.08	22.908	84.147	24.929	32.963
Primary Completion Rate	−3.255	89.624	86.249	135.988	24.486	30.593

	Bahrain	Burkina Faso	Israel	Luxembourg
GDP Per Capita	16726	351	18589	74389
Cell phones/100 people	96.7256163	2.87125874	111.60086	104.238747
Internet Users/100 people	21.4586805	0.40029529	21.6409437	64.84354
Primary Completion Rate	25.8616547	−3.2553808	88.5975782	73.0649076

a) Explain why each country was identified as a possible high influence point.

b) What might you consider doing next?

T 34. Gross domestic product diagnostics revisited. In Exercise 33 we saw that there were several potential high influence points. After a researcher set aside those four countries, she refit the model in Exercise 33. A plot of residuals vs. predicted values showed:

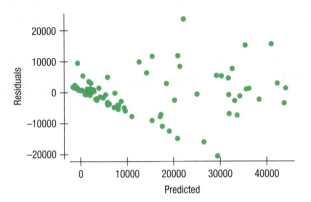

a) What assumption and/or condition does the model violate?

A histogram of *GDP per capita* shows:

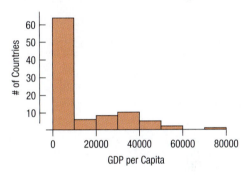

b) Why might this be problematic? What might you suggest to the researcher before proceeding?

T **35.** **HDI 2016, diagnostics.** In Chapter 18, Exercise 36 we found a model for *HDI* (the UN's Human Development Index) from *Life expectancy*, *schooling*, *mean years of school*, and *log(GNI/capita)* for 188 countries. Using software that provides regression diagnostics (leverage values, Cook's Distance, studentized residuals), find three countries that have potentially large influence and discuss briefly what is unusual about these countries.

T **36.** **HDI 2016, model comparison.** In Exercise 35 you identified several countries that had potentially large influence on the model in Chapter 18, Exercise 36, predicting HDI. Set those countries aside and rerun the model. Write up a few sentences on the impact that leaving these countries out has on the regression and give your recommendation on which model you would prefer.

JUST CHECKING ANSWERS

1 The predictors would be *Years Experience + Gender + Years Experience * Gender*. The last term will account for possible different slopes.

2 There would need to be two *Education* indicator variables to account for the three levels.

3 It is not surprising that *Age* and *Years Experience* are correlated, leading to the collinearity. One of them should be removed, or they should somehow be combined into one variable.

CHAPTER 20

Time Series Analysis

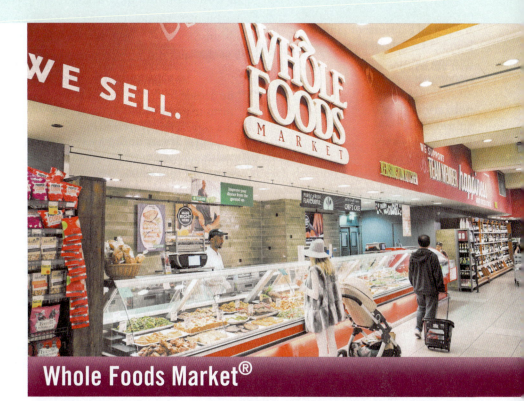

Whole Foods Market®

In 1978, twenty-five-year-old John Mackey and twenty-one-year-old Rene Lawson Hardy borrowed $45,000 from family and friends to open the doors of a small natural foods store they named SaferWay in Austin, Texas. Two years later, they joined forces with Clarksville Natural Grocery to open the first Whole Foods Market. With 10,500 square feet of floor space and a staff of 19, their store was large in comparison to other health food stores of the time.

During the next 15 years, Whole Foods Market grew rapidly, in part due to several mergers and acquisitions. Among the stores they acquired were Wellspring Grocery, Bread & Circus, Mrs. Gooch's Natural Foods, and Fresh Fields Markets. Since 2000, Whole Foods has expanded outside of North America with the purchase of seven Fresh & Wild stores in the United Kingdom. In 2007, they merged with Wild Oats of Boulder, Colorado. The firm has continued to grow both by opening new stores and by acquiring related firms, and by 2017 had nearly 91,000 employees in 473 locations.

In spite of its wholesome image, the company has not been without controversy. It has been threatened from time to time with national boycotts for issues as varied as opinions by its CEO on health care, business practices, labor issues, treatment of animals, and most recently, suspension of employees, allegedly for speaking Spanish.

Criticized for selling genetically modified (GMO) foods, Whole Foods announced in March 2013, "that by 2018, all products in our U.S. and Canadian stores must be labeled to indicate whether they contain genetically modified organisms (GMOs)."[1]

In August 2017, Whole Foods was acquired by Amazon, the giant Internet retailer. Amazon promptly began making changes to the traditional Whole Foods business model. However, one of the most interesting parts of Whole Foods' history was during the years leading up to the merger. We'll take a look at the sales during that period.

The decade of the 1990s was a period of growth for most companies, but unlike firms in many other industries, Whole Foods Market continued to grow. Here is a time series plot showing the quarterly *Sales* ($M) plotted by quarter from 1995 to 2016. If you were asked to summarize the trend in *Sales* over this decade what would you say?

FIGURE 20.1   Quarterly Sales (in $M) for Whole Foods from 1995 to 2016. (Data in **Whole Foods 2016**)

WHAT	Quarterly Sales
UNITS	Millions of U.S. dollars
WHEN	1995–2016
WHERE	United States, Canada, and United Kingdom
WHY	To forecast sales for Whole Foods Market

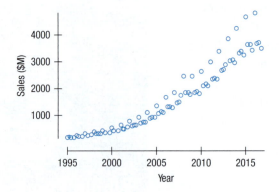

Clearly, sales at Whole Foods Market, Inc., grew between 1995 and 2016, starting at below $250 million and reaching more than $3 billion per quarter. But we'd like to be able to say something more than that, and ultimately, we'd like to *model* the growth. Time series models are primarily built for predicting into the near future. Some also offer interpretable coefficients.

Corporations often look at time series plots to examine prior patterns in the data and to forecast future values. The executives at Whole Foods Market, Inc., might have been interested in understanding patterns in *Sales* so that they could:

- Plan inventory and distribution of goods
- Schedule hiring and staffing
- Understand the impact of seasons, or time of the year, on sales
- Develop advertising campaigns
- Forecast profits and plan corporate strategy

Suppose that you were an analyst at Amazon Inc., in 2016 and you were asked to forecast Whole Food's *Sales* for the next four quarters. How can you analyze the time series to produce accurate forecasts of *Sales*? How can you measure accuracy and compare your different forecasting models?

---

[1]Source: Official Whole Foods Market website: www.wholefoodsmarket.com.

20.1 What Is a Time Series?

The Whole Foods sales are recorded each financial quarter, and we're interested in the growth of sales over time. Whenever we have data recorded sequentially over time, and we consider *Time* to be an important aspect of the data, we have a **time series**.[2] Most time series are equally spaced at roughly regular intervals, such as monthly, quarterly, or annually.[3] The Whole Foods sales data in Figure 20.1 are a time series measured quarterly. The fiscal year at Whole Foods Market, Inc., starts on or near September 30, so, unlike many companies, the first fiscal quarter reports sales for the end of the calendar year.

Because a time series is likely to be revealed to us sequentially and only up to the present, most time series methods use prior values of a series to predict future values. Some methods describe the overall pattern in the series and predict that it will continue, at least for a short while. Other methods estimate *time series models* that identify structured components like trends and seasonal fluctuation in the series and model those. Some introduce external variables to help predict the response, as in regression, while others simply look at the prior values in the series to try to discern patterns.[4] The objective of most time series analyses is to provide **forecasts** of future values of the time series. Predicting the future is valuable to business decision makers, so time series methods are widely used.

Time series analysis is a rich and sophisticated topic. This chapter can do little more than survey the field and give you a taste of how time series are special. If you want to understand time series in depth, we recommend taking a course devoted to the topic.

20.2 Components of a Time Series

When we examine the distribution of a single variable, we look at its shape, center, and spread. When we look at scatterplots of two variables, we ask about the direction, form, and strength. For a time series, we look for the trend, seasonal patterns, and long-term cycles. Some time series exhibit some of these components, some show all of them, and others have no particular large-scale structure at all.

The Trend Component

Look at the time series plot of the Whole Foods *Sales* data in Figure 20.1. What overall pattern are the *Sales* following? Not only have sales at Whole Foods Market been increasing, but they seem to be accelerating. Of course, there are fluctuations around this pattern, but viewed over more than a decade, the overall trend is clear. We'd describe the direction as positive, and the shape as curving upwards. This overall pattern is the **trend component** of the time series. This is often the most interesting aspect of a time series. For example, it is what an investor would want to know about.

Most series have an increasing or decreasing trend with other fluctuations around the trend. Some, however, just fluctuate randomly, much like residual plots from a successful regression. If a series shows no particular trend over time and has a relatively consistent mean, it is said to be **stationary in the mean**.

---

[2]Actually, the methods of this chapter can be applied to any values that are ordered.

[3]Some series, such as those recording values for trading days or on the first day of each month, are not exactly equally spaced. If there are actual gaps in a time series, researchers use a variety of methods to fill in the missing observations before analyzing the data.

[4]Advanced models, such as dynamic regression models or distributed lag models, are outside the scope of this text.

If the trend grows roughly linearly, we can use the linear regression methods of Chapters 4 and 16 to estimate the linear component. We'll do that later in this chapter. (You may wonder if we can use regression for data in which successive errors are not likely to be independent. But if we don't plan to test the coefficients against the standard regression null hypothesis, we don't need any regression assumptions other than linearity.)

The Seasonal Component

Many time series fluctuate regularly. Sales of skis, for example, are always higher in the fall and lower in the spring. Sales of swimsuits peak in the summer. The **seasonal component** of a time series is the part of the variation in a time series that fluctuates in a way that is roughly stable over time with respect to timing, direction, and magnitude. In Figure 20.1, you can easily find that kind of consistent pattern around the general trend. In particular, the first quarter of every fiscal year records more sales than the adjacent quarters, but these fluctuations are relatively small compared to the overall trend. Because seasonal components are usually related to external patterns they are generally stable and predictable. For example, a retail outlet can forecast sales for the next holiday season from information about the previous holiday season and the overall trend. Even though the retail environment may change, they know that this year's holiday season will look more like last year's holiday season than like last April's sales. Typically seasonal components repeat annually, but patterns that repeat more frequently (for example, hourly energy use by a company during a 24-hour period) are still called seasonal components and are modeled with the same methods. A **deseasonalized**, or seasonally adjusted, series is one from which the seasonal component has been removed.

The time between peaks of a seasonal component is referred to as the **period**. The period is independent of the actual timing of peaks and valleys. For example, many retail companies' sales spike during the holiday season in December, and sales of water skis peak in early summer, but both have a seasonal period of one year.

Cyclic Component

Regular cycles in the data with periods longer than one year are referred to as **cyclic components**. Economic and business cycles can sometimes be modeled, but often we do little more than describe them. If a cyclic component can be related to a predictable phenomenon, then it can be modeled based on some regular behavior or by introducing a variable that represents that predictable phenomenon, and adding it to whatever model we are building for the time series.

Irregular Component

We will see a number of ways to model time series. Just as we did with linear models and regression in Chapter 4, in this chapter we'll find that the residuals—the part of the data *not* fit by the model—can be informative. In time series modeling, these residuals are called the **irregular component**. As with regression residuals, it's a good idea to plot the irregular component to look for extraordinary cases or other unexpected patterns. Often our interest in the irregular component is in how variable it is, whether that variability changes over time, and whether there are any outliers or spikes that may deserve special attention. A time series that has a relatively constant variance is said to be **stationary in the variance**.

To summarize, we identify four *components* of a time series:

1. Trend component (T)
2. Seasonal component (S)
3. Cyclic component (C)
4. Irregular component (I)

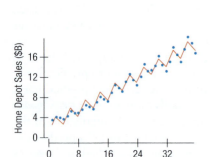

Quarterly data often show a seasonal component that repeats every 4 points. The red trace exhibits such a seasonal fluctuation overlaying a linear trend.

Component	Description	Rationale	Period Length
Trend	Positive and nonlinear	Overall increase in sales, with a change in the rate of increase of sales in the last 22 years	
Seasonal	Peaks every first quarter in 1995 through 2016	Larger sales in first quarter; reason unknown at present	4 quarters—yearly
Cyclic	No evidence of cycle, although some impact of the economic downturn in 2008 and divestment of Wild Oats	Could be due to economic cycles and factors, such as inflation, interest rates, and employment that might impact consumer spending	No expected period length
Irregular	Random fluctuations in data	Due to irregular or unpredictable events, such as mergers and acquisitions of other companies, or natural disasters, such as floods	No regular repeating pattern; no period

TABLE 20.1   Time series components terms applied to the series *Sales* for Whole Foods Market, Inc., from 1995 to 2016.

Table 20.1 provides a summary of the components as applied to the Whole Foods *Sales* data.

Even though some time series exhibit only two or one of these components, or even none, an understanding of them can help us structure our understanding of a time series. Just as we look at the direction, form, and strength of a scatterplot, remembering to think about the trend, seasonal, and cyclic parts of a time series can clarify our view of a time series.

Modeling Time Series

> I have seen the future and it is just like the present, only longer.
>
> —Kehlog Albran, "The Profit"

Methods for forecasting a time series fall into two general classes. Smoothing methods work from the bottom up. They try to "smooth out" the irregular component so any underlying patterns will be easier to see. They have the advantage that they don't assume that there is a trend or seasonal component—and indeed, they'll work even when no seasonal component is present and the trend is complex. For example, we can use smoothing methods on a time series that has only a general cyclic component but no clear trend or seasonal fluctuations to model. The disadvantage of smoothing methods is that they can forecast only the immediate future. Lacking a model of behaviors that can be trusted to continue (such as a seasonal component based on calendar shopping patterns or temperature variation over the year), smoothing models don't have a basis for long-term forecasting. Instead, they rely on the assumption that most time series show patterns that vary more slowly than each successive observation, so the next value in the future will resemble the most recent ones.

When we can discern a trend or both a trend and seasonal component, we'll often prefer regression-based modeling methods. These use the methods of multiple regression we've learned in Chapters 18 and 19 to estimate each component's contribution to the time series and to build a model for the time series. As with any regression-based model, models of this kind can be used to forecast for any value of *Time* and thus can generate forecasts further into the future than one time period. However, as always, we'll need to be cautious with such extrapolations.

The next sections discuss several kinds of smoothing methods, followed by a discussion of regression-based models. Although the smoothing methods don't explicitly use the time series components, it is a good idea to keep them in mind. The regression models explicitly estimate the components as a basis for building the models.

IN PRACTICE 20.1   Truck border crossings in Alaska

TRANSPORTATION MANAGER   It is important for our company to be able to forecast commercial traffic, particularly to and from Alaska, where we do significant business. I have a dataset from the U.S. Department of Transportation that includes records of border crossings into each state on the U.S. border. Here are the border crossings by trucks for Alaska, recorded each month from 1999 through 2017. Can you help me make sense of this dataset? (Data in **Trucks**)

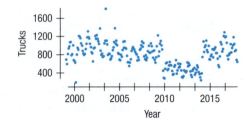

ANALYST   Yes, I can help you to understand the data. Because time is the independent variable, we have a time series. To characterize a time series, we break it into four components, which I describe below:

Trend: Generally constant; there was a slight downward trend from 2002 through 2014, but it reversed after 2014, and has been relatively constant since.

Seasonal: Strong seasonal component each 12 months, possibly reflecting the difficulty of driving in Alaska in the winter.

Cyclic: Not enough data to see any long-term cycles; trucking reflects long-term cycles, and the financial crisis of 2008 seems to have decreased truck traffic substantially for a few years.

Irregular: There is clearly some random fluctuation around the seasonal and trend patterns. There are also a few outlying points that may be worth investigating.

20.3   Smoothing Methods

Most time series contain some random fluctuations that vary up and down rapidly—often for consecutive observations. But, precisely because they are random, these fluctuations provide no help in forecasting. Even if we believe that a time series will continue to fluctuate randomly, we can't predict *how* it will do so. The only aspects of a time series that we have any hope of predicting are those that vary either regularly or slowly. One way to identify these aspects is to smooth away the rapid random fluctuations.[5] To forecast the value of a time series in the future, we want to identify the underlying, consistent behavior of the series. In many time series, these slower changes have a kind of inertia. They change and fluctuate, but recent behavior is often a good indication of behavior in the near future. Smoothing methods damp down random fluctuations and try to reveal the underlying behavior so we can use it to forecast values in the immediate future.

The time series for the daily value of the Dow Jones Industrial Average in 2012 (Figure 20.2) provides an excellent example with which to demonstrate techniques for time series analysis. It shows no regular repeating patterns and no evidence of a regular seasonal effect. But it does show rapid fluctuations and some evidence of longer-term movements. (Data extracted from **DJIA 2017**)

---

[5]To an engineer, this would be separating the signal from the rapidly varying noise.

FIGURE 20.2   Daily closing value of the DJIA in 2012 shows no seasonal pattern.

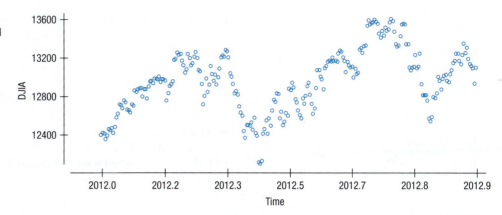

Methods for smoothing out the apparently random fluctuations generally work by averaging adjacent values in the series. We know from the Central Limit Theorem that means vary less than the underlying data. We can use that principle to find values that are typical of the local value of the series while varying less than the original data.

Simple Moving Average Methods

The most commonly used smoothing method is the method of **moving averages**. A moving average replaces each value in a time series by an average of the adjacent values. The number of values we use to construct the averages is called the *length* of the moving average (L). Almost every stock tracking service on the Internet offers a variety of moving averages (often with 50-, 100-, and 200-day lengths) to help track stock movements.

A moving average simply uses the mean of the previous L values as the fitted value at each time. Because it focuses on only the recent values, a moving average with a short length can respond to rapid changes in a time series. A moving average with a longer length will respond more slowly. The general form of a moving average is:

$$\tilde{y}_t = \frac{\displaystyle\sum_{i=t-L+1}^{t} y_i}{L}$$

The length, L, of a moving average is a subjective choice, but it must be specified when discussing a moving average. We write MA(L) for a moving average of length L, indicate the range of values involved in the sum with subscripts below and above the summation sign, and use the tilde to denote a moving average calculated from a sequence of data values.

Let's begin by using a moving average of length of 5 on the DJIA series to illustrate the calculation. The data are in Table 20.2 and the formulas to calculate the smoothed stock price for the fifth and sixth day in the series are:

$$\widetilde{\text{Price}}_5 = \frac{\displaystyle\sum_{1}^{5}\text{Price}_t}{5} = \frac{12397.38 + 12418.42 + \cdots + 12392.69}{5} = 12396.82$$

and

$$\widetilde{\text{Price}}_6 = \frac{\displaystyle\sum_{2}^{6}\text{Price}_t}{5} = \frac{12418.42 + 12415.70 + \cdots + 12462.47}{5} = 12409.84$$

Summarizing and Predicting

If we just want to summarize the patterns in a time series, a centered moving average will usually be a better choice. A centered moving average summarizes each value in a time series with the mean of the $L/2$ values on either side. A centered MA will track a time series with a strong trend better than one that uses only previous values, but it can't provide a forecast because it would need the $L/2$ values in the future to provide a smooth value for the most recent observation.

Differing Answers

The smoother-based analyses in this chapter were calculated in Excel 2016. Similar analyses calculated in other packages may differ due to different assumptions about starting and ending values.

Dow	MA5	MA15
12397.38		
12418.42		
12415.70		
12359.92		
12392.69	12396.82	
12462.47	12409.84	
12449.45	12416.05	
12471.02	12427.11	
12422.06	12439.54	
12482.07	12457.41	
12578.95	12480.71	
12623.98	12515.62	
12720.48	12565.51	
12708.82	12622.86	
12675.75	12661.60	12505.28
12756.96	12697.20	12529.25
12734.63	12719.33	12550.33
12660.46	12707.32	12566.65
12653.72	12696.30	12586.23
12632.91	12687.74	12602.25
12716.46	12679.64	12619.18
12705.41	12673.79	12636.25
12862.23	12714.15	12662.33
12845.13	12752.43	12690.53
12878.20	12801.49	12716.94
12883.95	12834.98	12737.27
12890.46	12871.99	12755.04
12801.23	12859.79	12760.42
12874.04	12865.58	12771.44
12878.28	12865.59	12784.94

TABLE 20.2 Moving averages for $L = 5$, or MA(5), and $L = 15$, or MA(15), for the closing DJIA values for the first 30 trading days of 2012.

The MA(5) smoothed stock price for each day in the series in 2012 is computed from that day's closing price and the preceding four daily closing prices using similar formulas. If we instead select $L = 15$ for our moving averages, then the calculations will average the 15 previous closing prices (including today's price). Table 20.2 shows the computed values for the two moving averages using $L = 5$ and $L = 15$ and the actual closing price of the DJIA for the first 30 days when the market was open in 2012.

There are no moving averages for the first $(L - 1)$ days in the series for each moving average model. What happens to the moving average as the length, L, increases? Of the two smoothed series produced by computing moving averages for the daily DJIA value using $L = 5$ and $L = 15$, Figure 20.3 shows that the moving average series with the greater length is smoother. That should be what you expected. Of course, a smoother series is not necessarily a better model for the data because it has a hard time following the series when it changes rapidly. Look, for example, at the two times during the year the DJIA fell rapidly, but the MA(15) smooth changed too slowly, running above the data for several weeks before it "caught up."

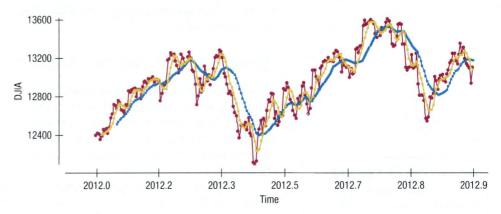

FIGURE 20.3 A time series plot of the daily Dow Jones Industrial Average closing values in 2012 (in red) with MA(5) (in yellow) and MA(15) (in blue) forecasts superimposed. The moving average with the smaller length, $L = 5$, follows the data more closely while the moving average with the longer length is smoother.

Smoothed Values and Forecast Values

To model the smooth pattern that we think might underlie a time series, it makes sense to include the observed value at time t in calculating the smooth value we'll plot at that time point. There's little sense in ignoring information that we have.

When we forecast the next value, that most recent smoothed value is a good choice, since it is recent and incorporates information from several recent time periods, damping out the short-term fluctuations.

We use a tilde to denote the smoothed values. We follow the convention from regression of using a hat to denote a predicted value.

To obtain a forecast for a new time point, analysts use the last average in the series:

$$\hat{y}_{t+1} = \widetilde{y}_t$$

This is the **simple moving average forecast**. Of course, this method can forecast only one time period into the future, for $Time = t + 1$. (You can repeat that value as a forecast beyond period $t + 1$, but unless the time series is essentially unstructured and horizontal, it won't be a very good forecast.) If the length of the moving average is 1 ($L = 1$), then the forecast is simply that the next value will be the same as the previous one, $\hat{y}_{t+1} = y_t$. As the simplest forecast, this is called the **naïve forecast**.

Often, moving averages are used primarily as summaries of how a time series is changing. The length selected depends on the purpose of the analysis. If the focus is on long-term behavior, a longer moving average is appropriate. But an analyst interested in shorter-term changes would choose a shorter length. Sometimes (as you can see in the sidebar) analysts compare a shorter-length moving average and one with a longer length, hoping to learn something from how they compare.

One potential problem with a moving average is that, as we know from Chapter 3, means can be affected by outliers. An outlier in a time series would be a spike in the series far from the adjacent values. Such a spike will contaminate all of the averages in which it participates, spreading its influence over a number of values.

Weighted Moving Averages

In a simple moving average, we just average the most recent L values. But we can benefit from a more sophisticated averaging scheme. We can assign a *weight* to each value according to how far it is before the current value. The result is a *weighted* average. In a weighted average, each value is multiplied by a *weight* before they are added up, and the total is divided by the sum of the weights:

$$\widetilde{y}_t = \frac{\sum w_i y_{t-i}}{\sum w_i}$$

The weights might be specified, or they might be found as part of the smoothing process.

Weighted moving averages form a very general class of smoothers.[6] We will consider two types of weighted moving average smoothers that are commonly used on time series data, exponential smoothers and autoregressive moving averages.

> ### Bull Markets and Bear Markets
>
> Moving averages are widely used in so-called technical analyses of the stock market. Many investors believe that the movement of a short-term (such as a 15- or 50-day) moving average compared to a long-term (typically the 100- or 200-day) moving average measures the "momentum" of the price and provides guidance as to whether to buy or sell the stock or mutual fund. Because averages with more observations vary less than those with fewer observations, many analysts believe that the longer-term average should carry more weight in the analysis. So, when a short-term moving average falls below, or "crosses over," the long-term moving average, it's a bearish (sell) signal called a "death cross." On the other hand, when the short-term moving average breaks above the long-term, it's a bullish (buy) signal called a "golden cross." Note, however, that neither of these signals has ever been proven to provide reliable information about the future performance of a stock or mutual fund.

IN PRACTICE 20.2   The value of the euro

MANAGER The euro is the second-most traded currency (after the dollar). Because we are an international company, the value of the euro relative to the dollar is of great interest to us. One euro was equal to one U.S. dollar when the new European currency was launched on January 1, 1999. Since that time the value has fluctuated. On October 26, 2000, the euro was at its lowest point, $0.8252. But on July 15, 2008, it reached a maximum of $1.5990. I obtained the data for the weekly price of the euro for all of 2017, and I plotted it in a graph, below. I also summarized some of the data as a table. Could you use it to predict the euro for the first week of 2018? (Data in **Euro dollar**)

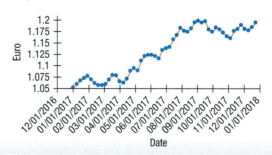

(continued)

---

[6] In this general form, these smoothers are known as *linear smoothers*. They are important in engineering and finance.

Here are some of those euro values in dollars for the weeks of July and August 2012.

Date	Value ($)
11/6/17–11/12/17	1.160
11/13/17–11/19/17	1.176
11/20/17–11/26/17	1.180
11/27/17–12/3/17	1.189
12/4/17–12/10/17	1.180
12/11/17–12/17/17	1.177
12/18/17–12/24/17	1.184
12/25/17–12/30/17	1.194

ANALYST Yes. As the time series plot of 50 weekly euro/dollar values between January 2, 2017, and December 31, 2017 shows, recent fluctuations show little pattern, so smoothing methods may be the best approach to short-term prediction of euro values.

I decided to use a 3-term moving average for these data to predict the value for the next week.

Date	Value ($)	MA(3)
11/6/17–11/12/17	1.160	
11/13/17–11/19/17	1.176	
11/20/17–11/26/17	1.180	1.172
11/27/17–12/3/17	1.189	1.182
12/4/17–12/10/17	1.180	1.183
12/11/17–12/17/17	1.177	1.182
12/18/17–12/24/17	1.184	1.180
12/25/17–12/30/17	1.194	1.185

My prediction is $1.185.

Exponential Smoothing Methods

Smoothing methods summarize each value of a time series with an average of recent values. In many time series, recent values of the series are more relevant for modeling than older ones. So a weighted moving average that weights the more recent values more heavily than the older ones makes sense. Exponential smoothing does just that. **Exponential smoothing** is a weighted moving average with weights that decline exponentially into the past. The most recent data are weighted the most and the most distant data are weighted the least. This model is the **single-exponential smoothing (SES) model**:

$$\widetilde{y}_t = \alpha y_t + (1 - \alpha)\widetilde{y}_{t-1}$$

The choice of the weight α is up to the data analyst, although it is usually restricted to $0 < \alpha < 1$. When $\alpha = 0.50$, the current data point and the entire set of historical data (all points before the current one) are weighted equally. If $\alpha = 0.75$, then historical data are weighted only 25% and the current value has more weight at 75%. If the objective is to produce forecasts that are stable and smoother, then choose a smoothing coefficient closer to zero. If, however, the objective is to react to volatile events rapidly, then choose a smoothing coefficient close to one.[7]

Unlike a simple moving average, exponential smoothing uses *all* previous values, although distant ones typically get very small weight. If we expand the calculation, we can see that the smoothed value at time t is a *weighted* average of the current value and all the previous values, with the weights depending on a smoothing coefficient, α:

$$\tilde{y}_t = \alpha y_t + \alpha(1 - \alpha)y_{t-1} + \alpha(1 - \alpha)^2 y_{t-2} + \alpha(1 - \alpha)^3 y_{t-3} + \cdots.$$

As with the moving average model, we use $\tilde{y}_t$ as our prediction for time $t + 1$.

Figure 20.4 shows the DJIA values again, this time with exponentially smoothed values using $\alpha = 0.75$ and $\alpha = 0.10$. You can see that the curve computed using the larger α follows the original series closely. By contrast, the curve computed using the smaller α is smoother, but doesn't follow rapid changes in the series such as the sharp price drop in June.

FIGURE 20.4 The DJIA with exponential smoothing models ($\alpha = 0.75$ in purple, $\alpha = 0.10$ in yellow). The model with the larger alpha follows the data more closely, and the model with the smaller alpha is smoother.

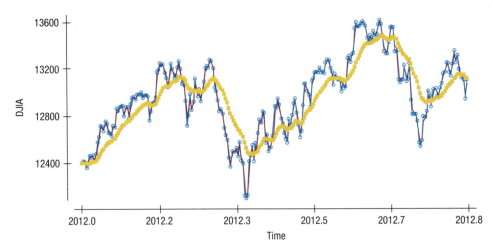

20.4 Summarizing Forecast Error

Whenever we model a time series, it is natural to ask how closely the model fits the series. A closely related question is how well the model *forecasts* the series. For smoothing models, we use the most recent model value as the forecast for the next time period. When we make a plot of the data and the smoothed series, we usually plot the smoothed value $\tilde{y}_t$ at time t. But if we are interested in the error the model makes when trying to forecast each value, we must compare the data value y_t not to $\tilde{y}_t$, but rather to $\hat{y}_t$, which is actually equal to $\tilde{y}_{t-1}$. We can find a **forecast error** for each time in the series for which we have such a forecast:

$$e_t = (y_t - \hat{y}_t)$$

When there is a particular forecast of interest, it makes sense to look at the forecast error, e_t. More often, we ask about the overall success of a model at forecasting for a time series. That calls for a summary of the forecast errors and, as often happens in statistics, we have several summaries to choose among.

---

[7]The initial smoothed value to get the algorithm started is either the initial observed value ($\tilde{y}_1 = y_1$) or the average of some of the initial values. In Minitab, for example, the initial smoothed value is equal to the average of the first six observations. We have used the initial value for the examples here.

In Chapter 18, we found the **mean squared error (MSE)** to summarize the magnitude of the errors. We can use a similar calculation for the forecast errors:

$$MSE = \frac{1}{n}\Sigma(y_t - \hat{y}_t)^2$$

The MSE penalizes large forecast errors because the errors are squared. It also has the problem that it is not in the same units as the data, but rather in the square of those units. We can, of course, take the square root of the MSE, the root MSE, or the **root mean square error (RMSE)**. Another approach to address both of these problems is to sum the *absolute values* of the errors. That gives the **mean absolute deviation (MAD)**:

$$MAD = \frac{1}{n}\Sigma|y_t - \hat{y}_t|$$

The most common approach to measuring forecast error compares the absolute errors to the magnitude of the estimated quantities and sums up the *proportions* of the values that are in error. Multiplying the proportions by 100 gives the **absolute percentage error (APE)**. If we average the APE for all the forecasts, we have the **mean absolute percentage error (MAPE)**:

$$MAPE = 100 \times \frac{1}{n}\Sigma\frac{|y_t - \hat{y}_t|}{|y_t|}$$

The MAPE is expressed in percent, so it doesn't depend on the units of the *y*-variable. If you choose to rescale *y*, both the MSE and MAD will change, but the MAPE will remain the same.

In summary, MSE resembles the error measures we've used for regression models, but it isn't in the same units as the data. MAD is in the same units as the data, but that means that it will be rescaled if the measurements are rescaled. MAPE is a percentage relating the size of the errors to the magnitudes of the data values.

Date	DJIA	SES(.10)	Forecast(.10)	Error(.10)	SES(.75)	Forecast(.75)	Error(.75)	AbsErr(.10)	AbsErr(.75)
Monday, February 11, 2013	13971.24	13823.37	13806.94	164.29	13974.18	13982.99	−11.75	164.29	11.74
Tuesday, February 12, 2013	14018.70	13842.91	13823.37	195.32	14007.57	13974.18	44.52	195.32	44.52
Wednesday, February 13, 2013	13982.91	13856.91	13842.91	139.99	13989.07	14007.57	−24.66	139.99	24.65
Thursday, February 14, 2013	13973.39	13868.55	13856.91	116.47	13977.31	13989.07	−15.68	116.47	15.68
Friday, February 15, 2013	13981.76	13879.87	13868.55	113.20	13980.65	13977.31	4.45	113.20	4.44
Tuesday, February 19, 2013	14035.67	13895.45	13879.87	155.79	14021.91	13980.65	55.02	155.79	55.02
Wednesday, February 20, 2013	13927.54	13898.66	13895.45	32.08	13951.13	14021.91	−94.37	32.08	94.37
Thursday, February 21, 2013	13880.62	13896.86	13898.66	−18.04	13898.25	13951.13	−70.51	18.04	70.51
Friday, February 22, 2013	14000.57	13907.23	13896.86	103.70	13974.99	13898.25	102.32	103.70	102.32
Monday, February 25, 2013	13784.17	13894.92	13907.23	−123.06	13831.87	13974.99	−190.82	123.06	190.81
				$\alpha = 0.1$		$\alpha = 0.75$			
			MAD	206.806		89.8830937			
			MSE	64973.88		15049.0208			
			MAPE	1.955		0.84277661			

TABLE 20.3 The initial DJIA values in the series along with smoothed values reported as forecasts one period ahead for two models. For this series, the single-exponential smoothing (SES) model with the larger coefficient ($\alpha = 0.75$) has a larger forecast error.

Table 20.3 shows forecast error for two different single-exponential smoothing (SES) models over the final 10 days of the DJIA values along with the MAD, MSE, and MAPE computed for the entire time series from 2002 to 2013.

IN PRACTICE 20.3   Forecast errors

MANAGER   How good were our forecasts of the euro prices?

ANALYST   Below, I have displayed the forecast values, the errors, and the measures of forecast error.

Date	Value ($)	MA(3)	Forecast	Error
11/20/17–11/26/17	1.180	1.172		
11/27/17–12/3/17	1.189	1.182	1.172	0.02
12/4/17–12/10/17	1.180	1.183	1.182	(0.00)
12/11/17–12/17/17	1.177	1.182	1.183	(0.01)
12/18/17–12/24/17	1.184	1.180	1.182	0.00
12/25/17–12/30/17	1.194	1.185	1.180	0.01
1/2/18–1/9/18	1.2050		1.185	0.02
	MSE	0.0002		
	MAD	0.0100		
	MAPE	0.8412		

The MAD and MAPE are the most interpretable. The MAD of 0.01 implies that, on average, our forecasts were off by about 1 cent, and the MAPE implies that this amount was slightly under a 1% deviation from the true value.

20.5   Autoregressive Models

Simple moving averages and exponential smoothing methods are good choices for time series with no regular long-term patterns. But if some patterns are present—even if they don't rise to the level of a well-structured seasonal fluctuation—we may want to choose weights that facilitate modeling that structure—something that exponential smoothing can find difficult to do. Such weights might even be negative. (Imagine a series with values that alternated up and down for successive times. A good weighted average would give a negative weight to the most recent value and a positive weight to the one before that.)

But how can we find appropriate weights and how can we choose among the huge number of possible weights? It turns out that we can use the methods of multiple regression we saw in Chapters 18 and 19, along with the fact that the data come to us in time sequence order, to discover weights for a weighted moving average smoother. We shift the data by a time period or a few time periods. This shift is known as *lagging*, and the resulting variables are called *lagged variables*. For example, Table 20.4 shows the first 15 values of the daily DJIA values in 2012 along with the lagged values for lags of one, two, three, and four days.

If we fit a regression to predict a time series from its lag1 and lag2 versions,

$$\hat{y} = b_0 + b_1 y_{lag1} + b_2 y_{lag2},$$

each predicted value, $\hat{y}_t$, is just a sum of the two previous values, y_{lag1} and y_{lag2} (plus a constant), weighted by the fitted coefficients b_1 and b_2. That's just a weighted moving average with weights found by the regression.

But wait. Regression methods assume that the errors are mutually independent. And this method works only if recent values can help predict current ones, which makes it likely that recent errors will be like the current one. Isn't this a violation

TABLE 20.4 The lagged values for the first 15 days in the DJIA 2012 time series for one, two, three, and four days.

DJIA	DJIA$_{lag1}$	DJIA$_{lag2}$	DJIA$_{lag3}$	DJIA$_{lag4}$
12397.38	*	*	*	*
12418.42	12397.38	*	*	*
12415.70	12418.42	12397.38	*	*
12359.92	12415.70	12418.42	12397.38	*
12392.69	12359.92	12415.70	12418.42	12397.38
12462.47	12392.69	12359.92	12415.70	12418.42
12449.45	12462.47	12392.69	12359.92	12415.70
12471.02	12449.45	12462.47	12392.69	12359.92
12422.06	12471.02	12449.45	12462.47	12392.69
12482.07	12422.06	12471.02	12449.45	12462.47
12578.95	12482.07	12422.06	12471.02	12449.45
12623.98	12578.95	12482.07	12422.06	12471.02
12720.48	12623.98	12578.95	12482.07	12422.06
12708.82	12720.48	12623.98	12578.95	12482.07

of the regression model? Well, yes and no. The Independence Assumption is certainly required for inference on the coefficients, for example, to test the standard null hypothesis that the true coefficient is zero. But we're not doing inference here; we're just building a model. And for that purpose, the failure of independence is really more an opportunity than a problem.

In fact, we can specifically account for the association of cases with previous ones. The correlation between a series and a **lagged** version of the same series that is offset by a fixed number of time periods is called **autocorrelation**.[8] Table 20.5 shows some autocorrelations for the DJIA series.

	DJIA	Lag1	Lag2	Lag3	Lag4
DJIA	1.000				
Lag1	0.956	1.000			
Lag2	0.910	0.956	1.000		
Lag3	0.862	0.910	0.957	1.000	
Lag4	0.815	0.862	0.911	0.957	1.000

TABLE 20.5 Autocorrelations of the DJIA daily values for all of 2012 for lags 1, 2, 3, and 4.

A regression model that is based on an average of prior values in the series weighted according to a regression on lagged versions of the series, is called an **autoregressive model**. A model based on only the first lagged variable is called a *first-order* autoregressive model, often abbreviated as AR(1). As you may be able to guess, models can include more than one lagged version of the response variable, and we name these models based on how many lags are included. So, a model that includes two lags is a second-order autoregressive model, abbreviated AR(2).

A *p*th-order autoregressive model has the form:

$$\hat{y} = b_0 + b_1 y_{lag1} + \cdots + b_p y_{lag\,p}.$$

For the DJIA series, we find the coefficients for a fourth-order autoregressive model from a multiple regression of the series on its first four lagged values, as shown in Table 20.6.

---

[8]Recall that we evaluated the presence of lag-1 autocorrelation using the Durbin-Watson statistic in Chapter 17.

TABLE 20.6 A fourth-order autoregressive model for the DJIA series. Note that there are 249 values in the series but, because lagged variables have missing values at the beginning of the series, there are only 245 complete cases.

```
Dependent variable is: DJIA
249 total cases of which 4 are missing
R squared = 91.0%  R squared (adjusted) = 90.9%
s = 94.96 with 245 − 5 = 240 degrees of freedom
```

Variable	Coefficient	SE(Coeff)	t-ratio	P-value
Intercept	733.345	256.1	2.86	0.0046
Lag1	0.978554	0.0649	15.1	<0.0001
Lag2	0.008051	0.0916	0.088	0.9300
Lag3	−0.042241	0.0918	−0.460	0.6457
Lag4	−0.000682	0.0648	−0.011	0.9916

The resulting fourth-order autoregressive model is

$$\hat{y}_t = 733.345 + 0.978554 y_{lag1} + 0.008051 y_{lag2} - 0.042241 y_{lag3} - 0.000682 y_{lag4}$$

Looking at the coefficients, we can see that the model puts most of its weight on the data value just preceding the one we're estimating (the lag 1 value). Figure 20.5 shows how well the model fits the data.

FIGURE 20.5 The DJIA series with an AR(4) model.

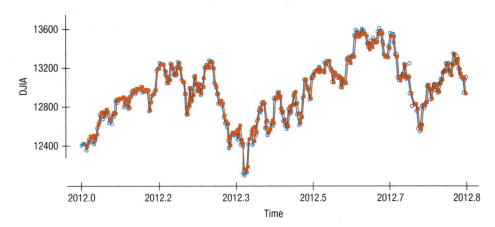

We can use an autoregressive model to predict the next value in a time series, but, to predict further into the future, we must substitute predicted values in the lag variables, which of course is likely to make our errors larger.

IN PRACTICE 20.4 An autoregressive model for the euro

MANAGER Is there an alternative way to model the euro prices?

ANALYST Yes, instead of a smoothing model, I could fit an autoregressive model.

```
Dependent variable is: Value($)
50 total cases
R squared = 97.2%
s = 0.0086 with 50 − 3 = 47 degrees of freedom
```

Variable	Coefficient	SE(Coeff)	t-ratio	P-value
Intercept	0.0260	0.0276	0.94	0.3522
Lag1	1.2002	0.1434	8.37	<0.0001
Lag2	−0.2213	0.1417	−1.56	0.125

The Lag 1 term is significant, suggesting that changes in the value of the euro show short-term serial correlation; today's value is much like yesterday's.

Unlike simple moving average models and single exponential smoothing models, AR models can follow time series that have seasonal fluctuations. The AR method will assign a larger weight to lags that correspond to the period of the fluctuation. For example, AR models will tend to predict quarterly sales that show a seasonal cycle by assigning a large weight to the lag4 version of the series, so sales in the same quarter of the previous year are counted heavily.

Of course, because AR models are regression models, you should plot the residuals. For time series, residuals are usually plotted against time rather than against predicted values.

JUST CHECKING

J. Crew is a clothing company known for its preppy fashions, including jeans, khakis, and other basic items sold to young professionals through its catalogs, websites, and some 260 retail and outlet stores in the United States. (Michelle Obama shops there.) We have their reported quarterly revenue from Q1 2003 through the first quarter of 2013. Here's a time series plot: (Data in JCrew)

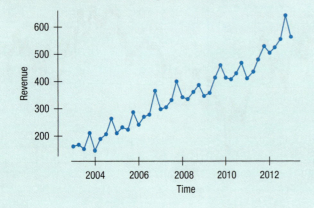

1 Which time series components do you see in this plot?
2 The final four values for 2012 are

Q1 2012	503.5
Q2 2012	525.5
Q3 2012	555.8
Q4 2012	642.9

Given these four values, where on the graph would the final value of a 4-point simple moving average be? Do you think it would be a good prediction for Q1 of 2013?

3 If the exponential smooth value for Q3 of 2012 is 550, what is the exponential smooth value of Q4 when an α of 0.5 is used?

4 If you wished to fit an autoregressive model, how many terms should you include? Why?

Random Walks

All moving average models include the special naïve model that predicts that the next value will be the same as the current one. For an autoregressive model, when the coefficient of y_{lag1} is close to one and the estimated intercept is close to zero, the first-order autoregressive model is approximately

$$\hat{y}_{t+1} = y_t$$

The naïve forecast model is the best we can do when the underlying time series has no other structure. A series with no other structure can be described as just adding a random kick to the previous value:

$$y_{t+1} = y_t + e_t$$

where the "e" are independent random values with some distribution. The "e" are sometimes referred to as "white noise." This kind of time series is called a **random walk** because each new value can be thought of as a random step away from the previous value.

Time series that are modeled by a random walk can have rapid and sudden changes in direction, but they also may have long periods of runs up or down that can be mistaken for cycles.[9] Random walks include series such as the assets of a gambler over time, the location of a molecule in a gas, and the path taken by a foraging animal. The random walk hypothesis in finance predicts that in an efficient market, stock prices should follow a random walk.[10,11] There is a large literature dealing with random walks. They show up in mathematics, economics, finance, and physics, as well as other fields.

GUIDED EXAMPLE   Comparing Time Series Methods

The Home Depot chain of home improvement stores grew in the 1980s and 1990s faster than any other retailer in history. By 2005, it was the second largest retailer in the United States. But its extraordinary record of growth was slowed by the financial crisis of 2008. How do different methods of modeling time series compare for understanding these data?

PLAN **Define** the problem—state your objective. Identify the quantitative variables you wish to examine. Report the time frame over which the data have been collected and define each variable.	We want to build time series models for quarterly sales at The Home Depot from 1995 through 2012. We have quarterly sales ($Billion).
Plot Plot the time series and clearly label the axes to identify the scale and units.	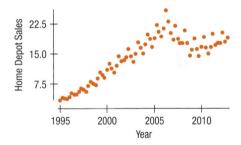
Model Think about the assumptions and check the conditions.	These are quantitative data measured over time at consistent intervals. So it is appropriate to use time series methods. There was a consistent increasing trend until the end of 2006. After that, sales fell sharply. They appear to have been recovering. Throughout this period, however, there are fluctuations around the trend that appear to be seasonal because they repeat every four quarters. Some smoothing methods may have difficulty with the seasonal fluctuations, but they are likely to be successful at following the sudden change in fortunes following 2006.

(continued)

---

[9]This is one reason we recommended that the identification of cycles be based on theory, on established patterns, or on other variables.
[10]The fact that only the first term in the AR(4) model on page 711 was significant supports the random walk theory for stock prices.
[11]Princeton economist Burton Malkiel made the random walk theory of the stock market famous in his book *A Random Walk Down Wall Street: The Time-Tested Strategy for Successful Investing*, first published in 1973. The theory originated in the 1950s with Sir Maurice Kendall, a prominent British statistician.

DO **Mechanics, Part 1** Try a moving average. For data with a strong seasonal component, such as these, a moving average length that is a multiple of the period is a good idea. But series with a strong trend, such as this one, won't be fit well by an uncentered moving average.

Here is a simple moving average of length 4:

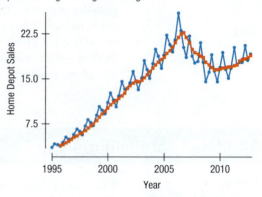

Evaluate how well this method fits the series.

We can also calculate

MAD = 1.134
MSE = 2.209
MAPE = 7.756

Make a forecast for Q1 2013.

The program offers a forecast of 18.908 $B for the first quarter of 2013.

Mechanics, Part 2 Exponential smoothing can be a good compromise between a simple moving average smoother and a fit with a seasonal component.

In series with a strong trend such as this one, exponential smooths will inevitably lag behind the data.

Let's try an exponential smooth. Now we have to choose a smoothing weight. We'll use $\alpha = 0.5$, which weights the current data value equally with all the rest in the past. Here's the result from a computer-generated smooth:

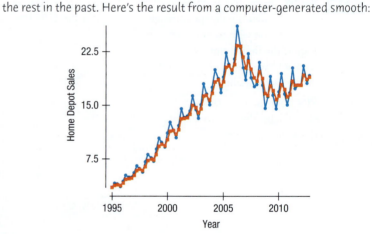

Evaluate how well this model fits.

MAD = 0.7277
MSE = 0.8677
MAPE = 5.043

Forecast sales for Q1 2013.

The smoother generates a prediction of 18.8928 $B for the first quarter of 2013.

Mechanics, Part 3 An autoregressive model is a multiple regression on the series itself lagged, or offset, by 1, 2, or more time periods. When we know that there is a seasonal component, it is important to include the corresponding lag—here lag4. This model has terms for each lag.

Now let's fit an autoregressive model. Because we know that the seasonal pattern is 4 quarters long, we'll fit four terms, using multiple regression to find the smoothing weights:

```
Dependent variable is: HDSales
72 total cases of which 4 are missing
R squared = 94.2%  R squared (adjusted) = 93.8%
s = 1.319 with 68 − 5 = 63 degrees of freedom
```

Variable	Coefficient	SE(Coeff)	t-ratio	P-value
Intercept	1.6943	0.4721	3.59	0.006
Lag1	0.4695	0.1124	4.18	<0.0001
Lag2	−0.2551	0.1245	−2.05	0.0446
Lag3	0.2233	0.1284	1.74	0.0869
Lag4	0.4871	0.1123	4.34	<0.0001

Plot the fit.

The AR(4) model is

$$\hat{y}_t = 1.694 + 0.4695y_{t-1} - 0.255y_{t-2} + 0.223y_{t-3} + 0.487y_{t-4}$$

Plot the residuals.

The forecast errors show some disturbance around the time of the financial crisis. Because sales at that time stopped resembling previous behavior with respect to growth, lagged versions of the series were less successful predictors.

Calculate fit measures and a prediction.

MAD = 0.952
MSE = 1.1612
MAPE = 6.517

A predicted value for the first quarter of 2013 is:

$$1.694 + 0.4695 \times 17.61$$
$$- 0.225 \times 19.226 + 0.2233$$
$$\times 19.237 + 0.487 \times 18.348 = 19.317$$

REPORT **Conclusion** Compare the advantages and disadvantages of the time series methods. Be sure to state your interpretations in the proper context.

MEMO

Re: Time series analyses of The Home Depot quarterly sales

We compared several time series methods to fit quarterly data on sales at The Home Depot for the period from 1995 through 2012. The actual sales in Q1 of 2013 were $19.124B.

The different methods had differing strengths and weaknesses. The moving average method smooths out most of the seasonal effects and, because it lags behind the series, has trouble modeling the sudden change in 2007, but it provides a good description of the trend.

The exponential smoothing method follows the seasonal pattern more closely, and has the best average error.

The autoregressive method seems to have the greatest difficulty following the sudden adjustment in 2007. It appears to be getting back on track as growth resumed in the most recent years.

Each of these methods is within about 1% in its prediction for the first quarter of 2013.

20.6 Multiple Regression–Based Models

We noted earlier that some time series have identifiable components: a trend, a seasonal component, and possibly a cyclic component. Simple moving average models work best on time series that lack any consistent structures like these. Exponential smoothing models don't usually follow a seasonal component well either. Autoregressive moving averages can follow all of these components provided the length of the smoother is at least as long as the period of the seasonal or cyclic component.

When some or all of these components are present, we can gain two distinct advantages by modeling them directly. First, we may be able to forecast beyond the immediate next time period—something the smoothing models can't do easily. Second, we may be able to understand the components themselves and reach a deeper understanding of the time series itself.

Modeling the Trend Component When a time series has a **linear trend**, the natural thing to do is to model it with a regression. If the trend is linear, a linear regression of y_t on *Time* can model the trend. The residuals would then be a *detrended* version of the time series.

During its period of record growth until about 2006, The Home Depot sales seem to have a roughly linear trend. We can't fit a linear model to the entire series, but we can model that period of initial growth. The regression to estimate the trend for 1995 to the end of 2005 is in Table 20.7.

TABLE 20.7 Estimating the trend component in the sales data for The Home Depot by regression for the period of record growth up to 2006.

```
Dependent variable is: HDSales
R squared = 95.5%  R squared (adjusted) = 95.4%
s = 1.044 with 40 - 2 = 38 degrees of freedom

Variable    Coeff      SE(Coeff)   t-ratio   P-value
Intercept   2.67102    0.3241      8.24      <0.0001
Time        0.405707   0.0143      28.4      <0.0001
```

One attractive feature of a regression-based model is that the coefficient of *Time* can be interpreted directly as the change in *y* (here, Home Depot Sales) *per* time unit (here, quarters). The trend in Home Depot sales was that they increased by 0.405 billion dollars per quarter.

By contrast, we saw in Figure 20.1 that the Whole Foods sales data *don't* have a linear trend. As we learned in Chapter 17, we can often improve the linearity of a relationship with a re-expression. The re-expression that most often works for time series is the logarithm. That's because many time series grow or shrink exponentially. Typically, the bigger you are, the larger the absolute increment in your profits. Growth by a consistent percentage is *exponential growth*. For example, if sales each year are 5% higher than the previous year, then the overall growth will be exponential. And the logarithm makes exponential growth linear. Figure 20.6 shows the result of taking logs in the Whole Foods data.

FIGURE 20.6 The logarithm of Whole Foods quarterly sales is linear over time.

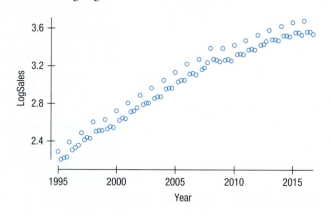

Which Log?

Financial models that talk about exponential growth usually describe them using the constant $e = 2.71828$, and its corresponding inverse function is the *natural* logarithm, written *ln*. When we re-express data to improve linearity, we usually prefer the base-10 logarithm, written *log* or log_{10}, because it is a bit easier to interpret. Which should you use? In fact, it doesn't matter at all. For all values, $ln(y) = log(y) \times ln(10)$, so the two functions differ only by a scale factor—a constant that doesn't affect our analyses. For consistency with our earlier analyses, we'll use base-10 logarithm here.

Recording *Time*

The Whole Foods Market sales are reported quarterly, but the time variable here is *Year*. The time variable in a time series often is just a count of the number of time periods (weeks, months, quarters, etc.) since the series began. So, the periods are often recorded as 1, 2, 3, . . . as we did for the sales data from The Home Depot. If we want to use the actual date as the predictor variable and we have quarterly data, we need to express each time period as a fractional year, such as 1995.0, 1995.25, 1995.5, ... The only difference this will make is in interpreting the coefficients. Moving average methods take no note of how time is recorded, but when you use a regression-based model, you must be aware of that so you can interpret the *Time* coefficient correctly.

For example, if we had used a time variable that counted 1, 2, 3, . . . in the regression instead of fractional year, the slope coefficient would have been 1/4 of the one we found and it would have estimated the *quarterly* growth in log sales rather than the annual growth.

The corresponding model for the trend is

```
Response variable is: LogSales
R squared = 96.3%  R squared (adjusted) = 96.2%
s = 0.0824 with 88 − 2 = 86 degrees of freedom

Variable     Coefficient    SE(Coeff)    t-ratio    P-value
Intercept    −128.056       2.776        −46.1      <0.0001
Year         0.06535        0.0014       47.2       <0.0001
```

TABLE 20.8 A regression model for the trend in LogSales of Whole Foods. Taking logs has made the relationship more nearly linear.

Now the interpretation of the trend coefficient is different. Adding 0.06535 to the logarithm of sales each year is the same as multiplying sales by $10^{0.06535} \approx 1.16$. And that's an increase of 16 percent. So we can say that Whole Foods Market's sales were increasing by 16 percent per year.[12]

Re-expressing the Whole Foods quarterly sales data by logarithms reveals a second advantage of the re-expression. The seasonal fluctuations evident in Figure 20.1 grew in magnitude as the sales themselves grew. But in Figure 20.6, those fluctuations are nearly constant in size. That will make them much easier to model. And, although it is visible in Figure 20.1, the "adjustment" in sales growth due to the financial crisis of 2008 is much easier to see in Figure 20.6. We can also see that after the crisis, sales growth was slower than it had been before 2008.

Modeling the Seasonal Component Figure 20.6 shows that the Whole Foods data have a strong seasonal component. Every fourth quarter there's a spike. That's not unusual in time series related to retail sales. The simplest version of a seasonal component is one that adds a different value to the series (in addition to the trend) for each season. We can see that this is a good description of the Whole Foods data; the first fiscal quarter is above the overall trend by roughly the same amount each year. Figure 20.7 shows the pattern.

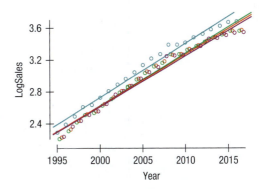

FIGURE 20.7 The logarithm of Whole Foods quarterly sales. Each quarter is displayed in its own color and has a regression line fit to it. The lines differ almost exclusively by a shift up or down. The change in growth due to the financial crisis is evident. We'll want to take note of that in our analyses.

[12]Of course, if you use natural logarithms rather than base-10 logarithms, the function that returns to the original units is e^b where *b* is the trend coefficient. But the interpretation of the result (and, allowing for rounding error, the value itself) will be the same.

As we learned in Chapter 19, a pattern such as the one shown in Figure 20.7 can be modeled by introducing an indicator or dummy variable for each season. For example, we can define our indicator variables to be:

$Q_1 = 1$ in quarter 1 and 0, otherwise

$Q_2 = 1$ in quarter 2 and 0, otherwise, and

$Q_3 = 1$ in quarter 3 and 0, otherwise.

Recall from Chapter 19 that for a categorical variable with k levels to enter a regression model we use $k - 1$ indicator variables. We can't use all k because that would create a collinearity. So we leave out one of them. It doesn't really matter which one we choose to leave out, but because the omitted one becomes the standard of comparison, we often choose the one that is the most typical. The intercept coefficient will estimate a level for the period "left out," and the coefficient of each indicator variable estimates the shift up or down in the series relative to that base level. With four quarters, we use three indicator variables. For this example, we'll arbitrarily choose to leave out the indicator for Q4. Then cases in Q4 will have the value zero for all three of our indicator variables (Q_1, Q_2, and Q_3) and the mean adjustment relative to the trend will be estimated by the intercept (b_0). In any other quarter, the adjustment relative to Q4 will be the coefficient for that quarter's indicator variable.

IN PRACTICE 20.5   A regression model for truck border crossings

MANAGER Is there an alternative model for the border crossing data from our previous In Practice? (The data are in the file **Trucks**.)

ANALYST Yes, it makes sense to construct a regression-based model of these data.

The model is:

```
Dependent variable is: Trucks
R squared = 34.1%
s = 218 with 228 - 12 = 215 degrees of freedom
```

Variable	Coefficient	SE(Coeff)	t-Ratio	p-value
Intercept	27771.6	5295	5.24	<0.0001
Year	-13.517	2.637	-5.13	<0.0001
Feb	72.442	70.75	1.02	0.3070
March	204.832	70.75	2.90	0.0042
April	171.800	70.75	2.43	0.0160
May	238.927	70.76	3.38	0.0009
June	393.264	70.76	5.56	<0.0001
July	346.969	70.76	4.90	<0.0001
Aug	277.780	70.77	3.93	0.0001
Sept	201.433	70.77	2.85	0.0049
Oct	156.349	70.78	2.21	0.0282
Nov	7.633	70.79	0.108	0.9142
Dec	-46.504	70.79	-0.657	0.5120

The model shows that the trend is declining over time, but only by about 13 trucks per month per year. (The units of the series are "Trucks per month.") The coefficient of the trend indicates that 13 fewer trucks cross the border each month than in the previous year, after allowing for the (very substantial) seasonal pattern. The model estimates a strong seasonal pattern with crossings low in winter months (November to February) and high in the summer (May to August)—not a surprising pattern for Alaska.

Additive and Multiplicative Models

Adding indicator variables to the regression of a time series on *Time* turns what was a simple one-predictor regression, such as we dealt with in Chapter 4, into a multiple regression, such as those we learned about in Chapter 18. If we model the original values, we have added the seasonal component (in the form of dummy variables) to the trend component (in the form of an intercept coefficient and a regression with the *Time* variable as a predictor). We can write $\hat{y}_t = T + S$.

This is an **additive model** because the components are added up in the model. For example, we've seen that Sales from The Home Depot seem to grow linearly during its period of record growth between 1995 and the end of 2005. And we've noted a seasonal pattern. Table 20.9 shows the regression that models those sales in terms of a trend component and three quarterly dummy variables.

```
Dependent variable is: HDSales
R squared = 98.7%  R squared(adjusted) = 98.5%
s = 0.5915 with 40 − 5 = 35 degrees of freedom
```

Variable	Coeff	SE(Coeff)	t-ratio	P-value
Intercept	1.38314	0.2534	5.46	<0.0001
Time	0.410336	0.0081	50.4	<0.0001
Q1	1.22191	0.2657	4.60	<0.0001
Q2	2.41907	0.2650	9.13	<0.0001
Q3	1.14944	0.2647	4.34	<0.0001

TABLE 20.9 A regression to model Home Depot sales with a trend component and three dummy variables representing a seasonal component in an additive model.

The model contains a trend component that predicts growth at about \$0.41B per quarter with adjustments for each quarter that are consistent over the entire time period. For example, because Q4 is the quarter without a dummy variable, sales in Q4 are predicted to be on average $1.38 + 0.41\,Time$ billion dollars. The seasonal dummy variable coefficients adjust the predictions for each quarter by adding the value of their coefficients to the intercept. For example, sales in Q1 are predicted to be $1.38 + 0.41\,Time + 1.22 = \$2.60B + 0.41\,Time$ (see Figure 20.8). But you can see from Figure 20.8 that the seasonal fluctuations are small early in the series and grow larger later in the series—a pattern this model doesn't fit.

FIGURE 20.8 Sales at The Home Depot with predictions from the additive model. The model predicts a consistent seasonal component although the seasonal component of the data varies.

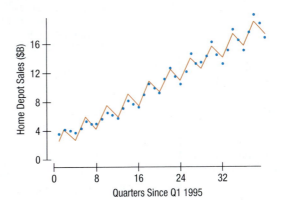

When we examined the Whole Foods sales data, we saw that we could straighten the trend and make the seasonal fluctuations more nearly the same size by finding the *logarithm*. We can still find a multiple regression, using the re-expressed response variable. The model is in Table 20.10.

```
Response variable is: LogSales
R squared = 98.0%  R squared (adjusted) = 97.9%
s = 0.0615 with 88 − 5 = 83 degrees of freedom
```

Source	Sum of Squares	df	Mean Square	F-ratio
Regression	15.4276	4	3.85690	1020
Residual	0.313998	83	0.00378	

Variable	Coefficient	SE(Coeff)	t-ratio	P-value
Intercept	−128.760	2.073	−62.1	<0.0001
Year	0.065681	0.0010	63.6	<0.0001
Q1	0.139587	0.0186	7.52	<0.0001
Q2	0.021852	0.0186	1.18	0.2422
Q3	0.016555	0.0185	0.893	0.3747

TABLE 20.10 A regression model for the logarithm of the Whole Foods quarterly Sales data with trend and seasonal components.

However, the residuals from this regression (Figure 20.9) sound a warning.

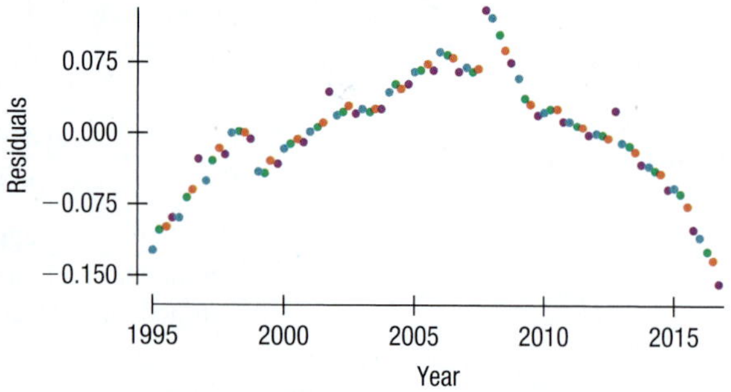

FIGURE 20.9 The residuals from the regression model of Table 20.10. Colored by quarter as in Figure 20.7.

After 2007, sales leveled off. They then resumed their growth, but at a less rapid pace, never recovering the pre-crash growth rate. In recent years, sales may even be tapering off more.

To predict future sales, we must recognize that the regression model's assumption of linearity has been violated. If we wish to use regression models, we'd do better to fit one to the pre-2008 data and another to the more recent data.

Here's the fit to the data from the third quarter of 2007 through 2016:

```
Response variable is: LogSales
cases selected according to years 2007.75-2016
R squared = 97.6%  R squared (adjusted) = 97.3%
s = 0.0206 with 37 − 5 = 32 degrees of freedom
```

Variable	Coefficient	SE(Coeff)	t-ratio	P-value
Intercept	−80.2780	2.560	−31.4	<0.0001
Year	0.041583	0.0013	32.7	<0.0001
Q1	0.143358	0.0095	15.1	<0.0001
Q2	0.023473	0.0095	2.48	0.0186
Q3	0.017445	0.0095	1.84	0.0749

TABLE 20.11 A regression model for the logarithm of the final years of the Whole Foods quarterly Sales data with trend and seasonal components.

Now, however, there's a difference in the model. Because we are modeling the logarithm of sales, when we think in terms of the sales themselves, the model components are multiplied rather than added, so we have a **multiplicative model**,

$$\hat{y} = T \times S.$$

Logarithms Reminder

Logarithms have the special property that they turn multiplication into addition. Before technology, that made them a workhorse tool. To understand why a model for the logarithm of a series is a *multiplicative* model, recall that

If

$$y = T \times S$$

then

$$\log(y) = \log(T) + \log(S)$$

The terms **exponential model** and *multiplicative model* are equivalent for these models and can be used interchangeably.

Although we acknowledge that the terms in a multiplicative model are multiplied, we always fit the multiplicative model by taking logs, changing the form to an additive model that can be fit by multiple regression.

As we observed earlier, seasonal fluctuations are often proportional to the overall level of the values in the series. The largest coefficient is for Q1. The Q1 lift in sales in a multiplicative model is a *proportion* of overall sales, not a fixed additive increment. Specifically, it is $10^{0.1434} \approx 1.39$—about 39% higher than the sales at that time. Because the sales themselves were growing (at $10^{0.04158} = 1.10$ or 10% per year), this 39% lift grew as well, in dollar terms. But after taking logs, it is a constant lift, and easier to model.

Look back at the Whole Foods sales in Figure 20.1 on page 698. You can see this growth in the size of the seasonal component in the plot as well as in the trend. Taking logs not only turns exponential growth into linear growth, but it also tends to stabilize the size of the seasonal fluctuations.

Cyclic and Irregular Components

Many time series are more complex than the trend and seasonal components can model. The Dow Jones series of Figure 20.2 on page 703 is one example. Models of time series components are usually said to include two additional components, a cyclic component and an irregular component. Consistent with their form for the trend and seasonal components, we write for additive models:

$$\hat{y}_t = T + S + C + I,$$

and for multiplicative models:

$$\hat{y}_t = T \times S \times C \times I.$$

The Cyclic Component Long-term business cycles may influence economic and financial time series. Other time series may be influenced by other long-term fluctuations. Whenever there is a business, economic, or physical cycle whose cause is understood and can be relied on, we should look for an external or **exogenous** variable to model the cycle. The regression models we've been considering can accommodate such additional predictors naturally.

Just calling a long-term fluctuation in the data that isn't fit by the trend or seasonal component a "cyclic component" doesn't add much to our understanding. Cyclic patterns may not be immediately evident in the data, so it is wise to compute and plot the residuals, known for time series models as the irregular component.

Irregular Components The irregular components are the residuals—what's left over after we fit all the other components. We should examine them to check any assumptions and also to see if there might be other patterns apparent in the residuals that we might model. For multiple regression, most statistics programs plot the residuals against the predicted values, but for time series models, it is essential to plot them against *Time*. Figure 20.10 shows the residuals of the initial years of the Whole Foods data plotted against year. Two quarters stand out. Both extraordinary quarters are fourth quarters of their years, which suggests that our seasonal model may need to be improved.[13] We also see a possible cyclic pattern with a period of about 4 years. This might be something worth investigating to see if we can add a component to our model.

---

[13]It's possible to include an indicator (dummy) variable to model a specific event in time. Doing so is known as intervention analysis.

FIGURE 20.10 The irregular component, or residuals, of the multiplicative model for the Whole Foods sales. In the beginning years, growth was apparently faster than after 1999 or so. There are also a couple of quarters that deserve attention: Q4 of 2001 and Q4 of 2007, which were underestimated.

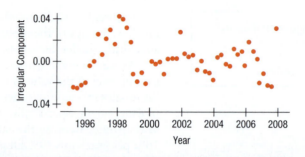

IN PRACTICE 20.6 Additive and multiplicative models

MANAGER I'm confused. Is the model for Alaska truck border crossings that you put together before (see page 718) an additive or a multiplicative model? Can you explain the model to me more clearly?

ANALYST This is an additive model. There is an overall negative trend of -13.52 truck crossings per month per year. There is a strong seasonal pattern, fit by the indicator variables for month. December was left out. One month had to be left out to avoid collinearity among the indicator variables.[14] There are generally fewer border crossings between October and March and more between April and September—probably due to the difficulty of driving in the winter in Alaska.

The residuals show no cyclic pattern. The irregular component shown in the residuals has a few outlying months that may deserve looking into. (For example, January of 2000 was a month with particularly heavy snows in Alaska.)

JUST CHECKING

Continuing our analysis of the J. Crew revenue data from the previous Just Checking (page 712), here is a regression fitting a linear model to predict *Revenue* ($M):

```
Dependent variable is: Revenue
R squared = 97.2%  R squared (adjusted) = 96.9%
s = 21.75 with 40 − 5 = 35 degrees of freedom
```

Variable	Coefficient	SE(Coeff)	t-ratio	P-value
Intercept	191.904	9.316	20.6	<0.0001
Q#since 2003	10.0017	0.2993	33.4	<0.0001
Q1	−65.1649	9.766	−6.67	<0.0001
Q2	−59.5866	9.744	−6.12	<0.0001
Q3	−48.8483	9.730	−5.02	<0.0001

5 Locate and interpret the trend coefficient.

6 Why is there no term for Q4?

7 Is the average value for Q4 higher or lower than the other three quarters? Why?

Forecasting with Regression-Based Models

Regression models are easy to use for forecasting because they give us a formula. It is easy to substitute future values for *Time*, for the appropriate dummy variables, and for any exogenous variables and calculate a predicted value. Unlike smoothing

---

[14]December was selected by the software because it was the "last" month. That's not a particularly good reason. You should be alert for arbitrary decisions made by your analysis software.

models, regression-based models can forecast beyond the next time period. But any kind of forecast is uncertain, and the uncertainty grows the further we extrapolate, so it's wise to limit forecasts to the near term. The forecast error measures we discussed in Section 20.4 apply equally well to regression models and are computed from the residuals (or irregular component).

We can make a prediction from the Whole Foods regression model. Because of the non-linearity we noticed, we'll use just the post-crash model in Table 20.11. We'll predict the final quarter of sales for the pre-Amazon merger with Whole Foods. That is the third quarter of 2017. The model is

$$\widehat{\text{logsales}} = -80.278 + 0.04158 \times 2017.75 + 0.017445$$

The final term is the coefficient of the Q3 indicator in the model. That comes to 3.644, so the model predicts sales as $10^{3.644} = 4.407$ billion dollars. In fact, Whole Foods reported third quarter sales of only 3.725B. Looking back at Figure 20.7, we can see the turn-down in sales. Was this a good time to sell Whole Foods? To purchase it? Amazon seems to think that Whole Foods prices have been too high and has been cutting them. It will be interesting to watch sales as Amazon takes over.

The most reliable part of a regression time series model may be the seasonal component—especially when it is driven by fairly regular economic or environmental phenomena. We can reasonably expect those patterns to continue into the future, so we can feel comfortable basing longer-term forecasts on them. A company that sees large fourth-quarter holiday season sales can probably count on higher fourth-quarter sales even several years in the future.

The trend component is less reliable. As much as we might like to think that a growing company will continue to grow, it should be clear that no company can grow forever and that the economy may experience sudden shocks that change the business climate. Exponential growth is even harder to maintain. Changes in the trend can be quite sudden. The business news is filled with stories of companies whose growth "suddenly" stopped or slowed, of products whose sales unexpectedly shot up and then, just as unexpectedly fell back, and of economic predictions by experts that, in retrospect, look ill-informed. While long-term government forecasts can be found for such reliable indicators as the Gross Domestic Product (GDP) and Disposable Income (DI), long-term forecasts should be made with great care. Changes in the economy or the market cannot be anticipated by the trend component, and can change a company's business quite suddenly.

The reliability of cyclic components for forecasting is something you must simply judge for yourself based on your knowledge and understanding of the underlying economic cycles. An empirical cycle that is not understood makes a risky basis for prediction. A cycle that is understood and is due to underlying phenomena that are stable over time would be a more reliable component of a forecast.

GUIDED EXAMPLE   Comparing Time Series Methods, Part 2

In 2010, the People's Republic of China became the world's second largest economy. China is the largest foreign holder of U.S. public debt. Trade between the two largest economies of the world is an important factor in the global economy. Forecasting U.S. imports from China is important because it is a key factor in the health of the U.S. economy. We have quarterly data starting in 1995. Let's try the regression models to see how well they do.

(continued)

PLAN **Define** the problem—state your objective. Identify the quantitative variables you wish to examine. Report the time frame over which the data have been collected and define each variable.

We want to build regression-based time series models for the logarithm of U.S. imports from China. Because we have already concluded that the exponential growth in imports calls for taking logarithms, we will fit a multiplicative model.

Plot Plot the time series and clearly label the axes to identify the scale and units.

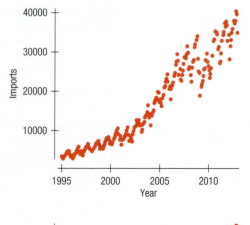

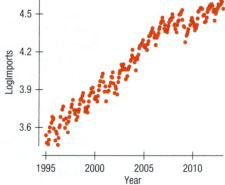

Model Think about the assumptions and check the conditions.

This is a time series recording quantitative values.

There is a consistent, increasing trend and fluctuations around it that may be seasonal. However, it is clearly growing exponentially. The logarithm is much more nearly linear. So we should take logs and fit a multiplicative model.

DO **Mechanics** Fit a multiplicative model with trend and seasonal terms.

```
Dependent variable is: LogImports
R squared = 96.6%  R squared (adjusted) = 96.4%
s = 0.0625 with 216 − 13 = 203 degrees of freedom
```

Variable	Coefficient	SE(Coeff)	t-ratio	P-value
Intercept	−118.340	1.641	−72.1	<0.0001
Year	0.061102	0.0008	74.6	<0.0001
Feb	−0.061534	0.0208	−2.96	0.0035
March	−0.062441	0.0208	−3.00	0.0030
April	−0.025918	0.0208	−1.24	0.2146
May	6.30778e-4	0.0208	0.030	0.9759
June	0.026409	0.0208	1.27	0.2061
July	0.049512	0.0208	2.38	0.0183
Aug	0.069299	0.0208	3.33	0.0010
Sep	0.072621	0.0208	3.49	0.0006
Oct	0.085385	0.0208	4.10	<0.0001
Nov	0.037045	0.0208	1.78	0.0768
Dec	−0.022210	0.0208	−1.07	0.2877

Plot the fit vs. the data (here on the log scale) and the residuals.

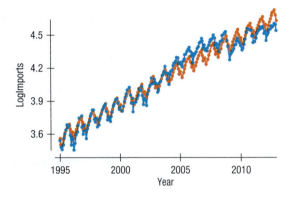

The data are the blue series and the model is the more regular red pattern.

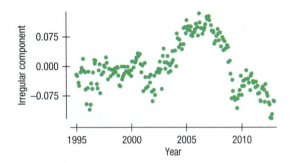

The irregular component shows that the growth in imports slowed during the financial crisis of 2008.

MAD = 0.049
MSE = 0.0391
MAPE = 1.1614

To make a prediction with a multiplicative model, we use the inverse function of the logarithm.

Forecast for January 2013 is easy to find because January is the indicator that was left out. We calculate $2013 \times 0.061102 - 118.340 = 4.6583$ corresponding to $10^{4.6583} = \$45,533M$.

REPORT

Conclusion Compare the advantages and disadvantages of the time series models. Be sure to state your interpretations in the proper context.

MEMO

Re: Time series analyses of U.S. imports from China

A multiplicative regression model fit to the monthly data on U.S. imports from China for the period from 1995 through 2012 provides a reasonable fit. However, its greatest value is to highlight the fact that the nature of the series changed with the financial crisis of 2008. Models that expect a consistent pattern, such as the regression models, can't follow sudden changes as well as smoothers.

The actual imports in January 2013 were $37,172M.

To obtain a better prediction, it might be better to model only the years since 2011; however, such a short series might not have sufficient data for reliable model-fitting.

20.7 Choosing a Time Series Forecasting Method

We've considered several methods for modeling and forecasting time series. How can you choose from among them the ones that fit your needs? Your choice depends both on the nature of your data and on what you hope to learn from the data.

Simple moving averages demand the least of the data. You can apply them to almost any time series. However:

- They can forecast well only for the next time period. Longer forecasts just repeat the single forecast value.
- They are sensitive to spikes or outliers in the series, and can smear the shock of a spike across several adjacent time periods.
- They don't do well on series that have a strong trend, tending to lag behind the trend.

Exponential smoothing methods also make few assumptions about the data. They have the advantage of controlling the importance of recent values relative to older ones, and do a good job of following the movement of a time series. However:

- They can forecast well only for the next time period. Longer forecasts just repeat the single forecast value.
- They are sensitive to spikes or outliers in the series.
- They don't do well on series that have a strong trend, tending to lag behind the trend.

Autoregressive models use automatically determined weights to allow them to follow time series that may have regular fluctuations, such as a seasonal component, or series with a consistent trend. However:

- They can forecast for a limited span before they must "recycle" forecast values to use them to make more distant forecasts.
- They are sensitive to spikes or outliers in two different ways. Those outliers will influence the regression that determines the smoothing weights. And then again, when the smoothing is done, the effect of spikes in the series can be spread out, contaminating several points.

Regression-based models estimate the trend and seasonal components by regression against *Time* and using dummy variables to represent the seasonal period. They can incorporate exogenous variables to help model business cycles and other phenomena. And, unlike moving average models, they can forecast into the future. However:

- You must decide whether to fit an additive model to the time series (if the trend is linear and the seasonal fluctuations have a consistent size) or to re-express the series by logarithms and fit the resulting multiplicative model.
- Because they are based on regression, these models are sensitive to outliers and failures of linearity. Because they use dummy variables to estimate the seasonal effects, those effects must be consistent in magnitude during the time covered by the data.
- Forecasts depend on the continuation of the trend and seasonal patterns. Although seasonal patterns may be reliable, trends are difficult to forecast and hazardous to assume beyond the near future. Cycles are best forecast when they are based on some identifiable (and predictable) phenomenon.

20.8 Interpreting Time Series Models: The Whole Foods Data Revisited

When you use a time series model based on moving averages, you can (and should) summarize the patterns seen in the series and any patterns noticed in the residuals around the smooth trend. But time series models based on regression encourage us to interpret the coefficients.

Many time series of retail sales have a strong seasonal component. We've seen some in this chapter. But one of those, the quarterly sales at Whole Foods, is problematic. No, there's no problem with the models we've fit. But there is a problem if we interpret them without thinking.

Why should there be a seasonal spike in Whole Foods' sales? Food isn't a seasonal item. To be honest, it took the authors a while before we asked this question. That sent us back to the original source—the quarterly reports posted online by Whole Foods Market. Now that we were looking for it, we realized that Whole Foods Market divides its financial year into three quarters of 12 weeks and one of 16 weeks. The spike is entirely due to this bookkeeping anomaly. You can check for yourself; the seasonal peaks are close to $16/12 = 1.33$ times as big as the other quarters—just about what the multiplicative model estimated them to be.

That doesn't invalidate any of our models. We'd still have to allow for the seasonal peak to model Whole Foods sales. But it is a cautionary tale that warns us not to jump to conclusions when interpreting our models.

⊘ WHAT CAN GO WRONG?

- **Don't use a linear trend model to describe a nonlinear trend.** Be sure to examine the scatter of the observations around the linear trend line to determine if there is a pattern. A curved pattern may indicate a need to transform the series. Plot the residuals. Variation in the residuals that increases when the central value is higher is a sign of a need to take logarithms. Series that grow or shrink by a constant percentage each time period are exponential and should be transformed before fitting a model.

- **Don't use a trend model for short-term forecasting.** Trend models are most effective for long-term forecasting and are rarely the best models to forecast one or two time periods ahead. Be aware that forecast errors are greater for long-term forecasting.

- **Don't use a moving average or an exponential model for long-term forecasting.** Smoothing models are most effective for short-term forecasting because they require continuous updating as new values in the time series are observed. However, it is less important to transform an exponentially trending series for these models because they base their predictions on recent values.

- **Don't ignore autocorrelation if it is present.** Look at correlations among the lagged versions of the time series. Compute the Durbin-Watson statistic, and make residual plots to identify autocorrelation but don't limit your attention to lag1 autocorrelation (as Durbin-Watson does). If present, then try using lagged variables to model the time series.

ETHICS IN ACTION

GoLearn is a new social networking site designed mainly for college students who have an interest in study abroad. Students from both within and outside the United States are beginning to join, although the majority of users are from the United States. U.S. students are typically interested in short-term semester or summer programs, while those who come to the United States from other countries tend to stay long-term and pursue degrees. GoLearn provides its users a place to "gather" around this common interest and share experiences, information, photos, and advice. It also hopes to attract others to the site, including organizations that sponsor international study (e.g., host universities, consortiums), families who serve as hosts for exchange students, and agencies that provide financial support (e.g., aid and grants).

GoLearn was the brainchild of Charlie Gavigan, president and CEO, who credits his own study abroad experience for changing his life. He founded GoLearn nearly three years ago starting with investments from the "3 Fs" (Family, Friends, and Fools). With a small staff of programmers, graphic designers, and marketing people, the start-up launched the site, initiated a pilot program with students from 20 regional colleges, and created some buzz through local interviews and blogs. The site is periodically updated with new features, and the number of users has been climbing steadily.

Having just concluded a round with angel investors, Charlie knows that it is time to pursue venture capitalists to get the investments needed to take GoLearn to the next level. One area in which progress has been lackluster is attracting advertisers to the site. If GoLearn wants to increase its chances for securing venture capitalist funds, Charlie and his team will need to have more advertisers on board. So Charlie and Pat Conrad, the head of marketing and sales, sit down to discuss some strategies for increasing advertisers on the site. A common concern expressed by many of the potential advertisers Pat had visited was simply the number of users on the site. They believe that GoLearn is too narrow in scope and will not grow at a rate comparable to other popular social networks.

Since the number of GoLearn users had been increasing over time, Charlie asked Pat to fit a trend line to these data. Charlie thought it would be a good idea to have such a model available to show advertisers the projected growth in users. Pat did just that, using the monthly number of users since GoLearn went live. He then checked the residuals and noticed a curvature. So he transformed the data by logs and got a better fitting model. However, when he used each model to project the future growth in GoLearn users, the linear trend provided higher numbers. He thought it best not to apply the log transformation. After all, this would be more difficult to explain to prospective advertisers.

- **Identify the ethical dilemma in this scenario.**
- **What are the undesirable consequences?**
- **Propose an ethical solution that considers the welfare of all stakeholders.**

CHAPTER
20 FROM LEARNING TO EARNING

LEARNING OBJECTIVES

Be able to recognize when data are in a time series.

- A *time series* consists of data recorded sequentially over time, usually at equally spaced intervals.
- Time series analyses often attempt to provide forecasts of future values of the series.

Recognize the four components of a time series.

- The trend component measures the overall tendency of the series to increase or decrease. It is ordinarily estimated as the slope of a regression against *Time*.
- The seasonal component measures regular, repeating fluctuations. Often these are due to seasons of the year, but the term applies to any such regular fluctuation. Seasonal components are often estimated by introducing indicator (dummy) variables in a regression model.
- The Cyclic component accounts for such things as long-term business cycles.
- The irregular component is the random fluctuation around the time series model. It corresponds to the residuals from a time series model.

Use smoothing methods to see past random fluctuations (noise) in a time series to detect an underlying smoother pattern (signal).

- Simple moving average methods average a relatively small number of adjacent values to obtain a smooth value for each time period.
- Weighted moving average methods introduce weights. Because the weights can determine the behavior of the smoother, these are a very general class of time series methods.
- Exponential smoothing methods are weighted moving averages with weights that decline exponentially into the past.
- Autoregressive models use regression methods, predicting the time series from versions of the same series offset, or *lagged*, in time. The result is a weighted moving average method in which the weights are estimated from the data.

Estimate and report forecast error with statistics such as MSE, MAD, and MAPE.

Use multiple regression methods to model a structured time series, using *Time*, indicator variables for the seasonal component, and exogenous variables that might account for the Cyclic component.

- Multiple regression models have the advantage that they can provide forecasts further into the future.
- *Additive mode*ls estimate the components using multiple regression methods to find a model in which the estimates are added to yield the predicted values.
- Multiplicative models for a time series model the series as a product of its components.
- Multiplicative models are ordinarily estimated by taking the logarithm of the time series values and then using multiple regression as for additive models.

TERMS

Absolute percentage error (APE)

A measure of the error of a forecast:

$$APE = \frac{|y_t - \hat{y}_t|}{|y_t|}$$

Additive model

A model for a time series that models the series with a sum of all or some of the following terms: a trend, a seasonal pattern, and a cyclic pattern.

Autocorrelation

The correlation between a data sequence, such as a time series, and that same sequence offset (or lagged) by one or more positions. Autocorrelation is one measure of association over time among the individual cases.

Autoregressive model

A pth-order autoregressive model has the form:

$$\hat{y} = b_0 + b_1 y_{lag1} + \cdots + b_p y_{lag\,p}.$$

Cyclic component

The part of a model for a time series that describes regular repeating fluctuations with a period longer than a year (or whatever the base period for the seasonal component is).

Deseasonalized

A time series that has had a seasonal component estimated and subtracted.

Exogenous

Variables that are not part of a time series but nevertheless might be helpful in modeling it.

Exponential model

A model for a time series that grows exponentially. It is estimated by transforming the response variable by the logarithm:

$$\widehat{log(y)} = b_0 + b_1 Time + other\ terms.$$

Exponential smoothing, Single exponential smoothing (SES model)

An exponential smoother has the form

$$\tilde{y}_t = \alpha y_t + (1 - \alpha)\tilde{y}_{t-1}$$

or equivalently,

$$\tilde{y}_t = \alpha y_t + \alpha(1 - \alpha)y_{t-1} + \alpha(1 - \alpha)^2 y_{t-2} + \alpha(1 - \alpha)^3 y_{t-3}\ldots$$

The parameter α determines how the smoother behaves. Larger values of α give more weight to recent values of the series. Smaller values give more weight to more distant values.

Forecast	Many analyses of time series attempt to forecast future values. We denote a forecast value $\hat{y}_t$.
Forecast error	The difference between the observed value and the forecasted value for a particular time in a time series: $$e_t = y_t - \hat{y}_t.$$
Irregular component	The part of a time series model that describes random, or unpredictable, behavior; the residuals.
Lagged series	A time series shifted in time by one or more time units.
Linear trend model	A time series model that assumes a constant rate of increase (or decrease) over time: $$\hat{y} = b_0 + b_1 t.$$
Mean absolute deviation (MAD)	A measure of forecast error of the form: $$MAD = \frac{1}{n}\Sigma|y_t - \hat{y}_t|.$$
Mean absolute percentage error (MAPE)	A measure of forecast error of the form: $$MAPE = 100 \times \frac{1}{n}\Sigma\frac{|y_t - \hat{y}_t|}{|y_t|}.$$
Mean squared error (MSE)	A measure of forecast error of the form: $$MSE = \frac{1}{n}\Sigma(y_t - \hat{y}_t)^2.$$
Moving average	An estimate that uses the arithmetic average of the prior L values in a time series to forecast the next value $$\tilde{y}_t = \frac{\displaystyle\sum_{i=t-L+1}^{t} y_i}{L}.$$
Multiplicative model	A classical time series model consisting of four components, $$\hat{y} = T \times S \times C \times I,$$ where T is the trend component, S is the seasonal component, C is the cyclic component, and I is the irregular component.
Naïve forecast	Forecasting that the next value in a time series will be equal to the current one: $$\hat{y}_{t+1} = y_t.$$
Period	The time between peaks of a regular oscillation in a time series.
Random walk	A time series that exhibits random periods of upturns and downturns and is best modeled using a naïve forecast.
Root mean square error (RMSE)	A measure of forecast error that is the square root of the MSE.
Seasonal component	The part of a model for a time series that fits a regular pattern that has a period of less than or equal to 12 months.
Simple moving average forecast	A simple moving average averages L consecutive values of a time series, where L is the length of the moving average. When the final L values have been averaged, the resulting smooth value for time t can be used to forecast the series for time $t + 1$. (See Moving average.)
Single exponential smoothing (SES) model	(See Exponential smoothing.)
Stationary in the mean	A time series that has a relatively constant mean value over the time frame of the series is said to be stationary in the mean.
Stationary in the variance	A time series that has a relatively constant variance is said to be stationary in the variance. This is equivalent to the Equal Spread Condition. (If a time series is simply said to be stationary, most often what is meant is that it has stationary variance.)
Time series	A time series is data recorded sequentially over time at roughly equally spaced intervals.
Trend component	The part of a model for a time series that fits long-term changes in the mean of the series.

TECH SUPPORT   Time Series

EXCEL

Excel offers some, but not all, the time series methods in this chapter. Others are easy to compute with basic Excel functions. For example, to find a moving average of length 4, type = Average( ) in the cell next to the fourth cell of your series and indicate the first four cells of your series as the arguments inside the parentheses. Then fill down.

Exponential smoothing:

- Choose **Data > Data Analysis > Exponential Smoothing**.
- Enter the input and output range and the smoothing coefficient (Damping factor in Excel).

Moving Averages:

- Choose **Data > Data Analysis > Moving Average**.
- Enter the input and output range and the Length (Interval in Excel).

XLSTAT

To construct an autoregressive moving average (ARMA(p,q)) model:

- Select **Modeling data**, then select **ARMA**.
- Enter the cell range of the data under **Time series**.
- Note that you can center the data by selecting the appropriate box.
- XLStat requires input of parameters of the model such that $p + q > 0$.

JMP

- From the **Analyze** menu choose **Specialized Modeling > Time Series**.
- Put the data series in **Y**. The data must be in time order and equally spaced.
- JMP will display a time series plot and report the Autocorrelation.
- Commands for analyzing the series are under the red triangle.

MINITAB

The time series commands are in the **Time Series** submenu of the **Stat** menu. They are generally self-explanatory. Most commands open a dialog in which you specify the series to analyze, specify parameters (e.g., for smoothers), and request predictions.

SPSS

SPSS 20 and higher offers an add-on Forecasting Module, which can be purchased as an addition to the SPSS Statistics Core System. All forecasting analyses discussed in this chapter can be done using this module.

R

The ts() command defines a time series object:

A variety of functions operate on its objects, including

- stl(), which fits an additive model with seasonal and irregular components.
- ets(), which fits exponential models.
- arima(), which fits autoregressive moving average models.

STATCRUNCH

The **Stat > Time Series** menu has commands for smoothing, for trend analysis based on regression, for checking autocorrelation with graphical methods, and for lagging a variable. The Graph menu offers an index time plot.

BRIEF CASE

U.S. Trade with the European Union

How has trade between the United States and the European Union developed? The file **EU Imports** contains U.S. imports($M) from the European Union countries from 1997 to 2012. (Source: Download from the bottom of www.census.gov/foreign-trade/balance/c5700.htm)

Plot the data and describe what you see. Fit a regression on time (use the variable *Year*). Plot the residuals vs. time (or predicted) and comment on the patterns you see.

Include indicator variables for the months and refit the model. Compare this to the original model. Which do you prefer and why?

(continued)

BRIEF CASE *(continued)*

Consider breaking the dataset up into three different time periods. Where would you choose the breaks, and why? Fit each of these time periods separately and comment on the differences.

Forecast the imports for January of 2013, and compare to the actual value of 28,883.8.

Tiffany & Co.

Tiffany was founded in 1837, when Charles Lewis Tiffany opened his first store in downtown Manhattan. Tiffany retails and distributes a selection of Tiffany & Co. brand jewelry at a range of prices. Today, more than 150 Tiffany & Co. stores sell to customers in U.S. and international markets. In addition to jewelry, it sells Tiffany & Co. brand merchandise in the following categories: timepieces and clocks; sterling silver merchandise; stainless steel flatware; crystal, glassware, china, and other tableware; custom engraved stationery; writing instruments; and fashion accessories. Fragrance products are sold under the trademarks Tiffany, Pure Tiffany, and Tiffany for Men. Tiffany also sells other brands of timepieces and tableware in its U.S. stores.

Tiffany's quarterly sales from 2005 to the middle of 2017 are in the file **Tiffany 2017**. They are shown here.

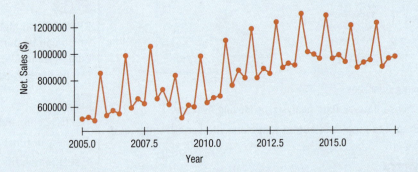

Build alternative time series models for Tiffany's sales and forecast future sales. In addition, find supportive economic data, such as gross domestic product (GDP), consumer price index (CPI), disposable income, unemployment, and interest rates over this same time period, and try using them in a regression model. For any model be sure to plot residuals over time and interpret what you see. Comment on any trends in the recent growth of Tiffany's sales. Compare your models and recommend a model for the executives at Tiffany to use for forecasting their quarterly sales.

CHAPTER 20 EXERCISES

SECTION 20.1

1. Are the following data time series? If not, explain why.

a) Quarterly earnings of Microsoft Corp.
b) Unemployment in August 2010 by Education level.
c) Time spent in training by workers in NewCo.
d) Numbers of e-mails sent by employees of SynCo each hour in a single day.

2. Are the following data time series? If not, explain why.

a) Reports from the Bureau of Labor Statistics on the number of U.S. adults who are employed full-time in each major sector of the economy.
b) The quarterly Gross Domestic Product (GDP) of France from 1980 to the present.

c) The dates on which a particular employee was absent from work due to illness over the past two years.

d) The number of cases of flu reported by the CDC each week during a flu season.

SECTION 20.2

T 3. Here is a table of values from the U.S. Bureau of Labor Statistics: (Data in **BLS output**)

Year	Output/hr Labor (2005 = 100)	Output/unit Capital (2005 = 100)
1993	73.407	86.944
1994	74.049	90.416
1995	74.086	92.913
1996	76.248	94.391
1997	77.577	97.576
1998	79.879	99.502
1999	82.692	101.488
2000	85.553	102.534
2001	88.146	100.316
2002	92.081	97.905
2003	95.623	97.247
2004	98.279	98.417
2005	100	100
2006	100.945	102.071
2007	102.407	102.617
2008	103.111	100.573
2009	106.251	93.383
2010	109.484	93.309
2011	109.852	95.200
2012	110.554	97.273

For the series of Output per hour of labor:

a) Make a time series plot.

b) Describe the trend component. (Remember: Direction, Form, and Strength.)

c) Is there evidence of a seasonal component?

T 4. For the series of Output per unit of capital:

a) Make a time series plot.

b) Describe the trend component.

c) Is there evidence of a seasonal component?

d) Is there evidence of a cyclic component?

SECTION 20.3

Here are data on the monthly price of Delicious apples and gas, which are both components of the Consumer

Price Index.[15] The timeplot shows the years 2006–2009 for apples; the data table shows just 2006, for both.

Month	Apples	Gas
Jan	0.963	2.359
Feb	0.977	2.354
Mar	0.935	2.444
Apr	0.958	2.801
May	1.021	2.993
Jun	1.053	2.963
Jul	1.146	3.046
Aug	1.235	3.033
Sep	1.256	2.637
Oct	1.138	2.319
Nov	1.089	2.287
Dec	1.027	2.380

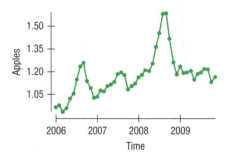

T 5. For the Apple prices: (Data in **Apples and gas**)

a) Find a 2-point moving average of the first year (2006).

b) Use it to predict the value for January 2007.

T 6. For the Gas prices: (Data in **Apples and gas**)

a) Find a 2-point moving average of the first year.

b) Use it to predict the value for January 2007.

SECTION 20.4

T 7. For the Apple prices smoothed in Exercise 5, the actual value for January 2007 was 1.034. Find the absolute percentage error of your forecast.

T 8. For the Gas prices of Exercise 6, the actual value for January 2007 was 2.321. Find the absolute percentage error of your forecast.

---

[15]The Consumer Price Index (CPI) represents changes in prices of all goods and services purchased for consumption by urban households. User fees (such as water and sewer service) and sales and excise taxes paid by the consumer are also included. Income taxes and investment items (such as stocks, bonds, and life insurance) are not included. Most of the specific CPI indexes have a 1982–1984 reference base. That is, the average index level (representing the average price level) is set with the 36-month period covering the years 1982, 1983, and 1984 equal to 100 and then measures changes in relation to that figure. An index of 110, for example, means there has been a 10-percent increase in price since the reference period. See www.bls.gov/cpi for more information.

SECTION 20.5

🅣 9. For the Apple prices of Exercise 5, find the lag1 version of the prices.

🅣 10. For the Gas prices of Exercise 6, find the lag2 version of the prices.

11. A second-order autoregressive model for the apple prices (for all 4 years of data) is

```
Dependent variable is: Apples
R squared = 78.1%  R squared (adjusted) = 71.9%
s = 0.0574 with 10 - 3 = 7 degrees of freedom
```

Variable	Coefficient	SE(Coeff)	t-ratio	P-value
Intercept	0.327717	0.1881	1.74	0.1250
Lag1(Apples)	1.32814	0.3114	4.27	0.0037
Lag2(Apples)	-0.634127	0.2959	-2.14	0.0693

Using the values from the table, what is the predicted value for January 2007 (the value just past those given in the table)?

12. A second-order autoregressive model for the gas prices is:

```
Dependent variable is: Gas
R squared = 82.2%  R squared (adjusted) = 77.1%
s = 0.1498 with 10 - 3 = 7 degrees of freedom
```

Variable	Coefficient	SE(Coeff)	t-ratio	P-value
Intercept	1.28207	0.4644	2.76	0.0281
Lag1(Gas)	1.31432	0.2383	5.51	0.0009
Lag2(Gas)	-0.788250	0.2457	-3.21	0.0149

Using values from the table, what is the predicted value for January 2007 (the value just past those given in the table)?

SECTION 20.6

13. An additive regression model for the Apple prices is:

```
Dependent variable is: Apples
R squared = 51.9%  R squared (adjusted) = 34.9%
s = 0.1108 with 47 - 13 = 34 degrees of freedom
```

Variable	Coefficient	SE(Coeff)	t-ratio	P-value
Intercept	-114.825	29.46	-3.90	0.0004
Time	0.057746	0.0147	3.94	0.0004
Jan	-0.001438	0.0783	-0.018	0.9855
Feb	-0.007062	0.0783	-0.090	0.9287
Mar	0.003626	0.0784	0.046	0.9634
Apr	0.015064	0.0784	0.192	0.8488
May	0.058751	0.0785	0.749	0.4592
Jun	0.115689	0.0786	1.47	0.1501
Jul	0.173627	0.0787	2.21	0.0342
Aug	0.169815	0.0788	2.16	0.0383
Sep	0.049253	0.0789	0.624	0.5368
Oct	0.006191	0.0791	0.078	0.9381
Nov	-0.014249	0.0847	-0.168	0.8675

a) What is the name for the kind of variable called *Jan* in this model?
b) Why is there no predictor variable for December?

14. An additive model for the Gas prices is:

```
Dependent variable is: Gas
R squared = 28.6%  R squared (adjusted) = 3.3%
s = 0.5524 with 47 - 13 = 34 degrees of freedom
```

Variable	Coefficient	SE(Coeff)	t-ratio	P-value
Intercept	66.3101	146.9	0.451	0.6546
Time	-0.031816	0.0732	-0.435	0.6664
Jan	-0.036401	0.3907	-0.093	0.9263
Feb	0.162901	0.3907	0.417	0.6793
Mar	0.395053	0.3908	1.01	0.3192
Apr	0.644704	0.3910	1.65	0.1084
May	0.788105	0.3914	2.01	0.0520
Jun	0.774757	0.3918	1.98	0.0562
Jul	0.673908	0.3923	1.72	0.0949
Aug	0.544059	0.3929	1.38	0.1752
Sep	0.333961	0.3937	0.848	0.4022
Oct	0.167112	0.3945	0.424	0.6745
Nov	-0.029645	0.4226	-0.070	0.9445

a) What is the value predicted by this model for January 2010 (Time = 2010)?
b) Do you think the predictions from this model are likely to be accurate? Explain.

CHAPTER EXERCISES

15. Concepts.

a) Which will be smoother, a 50-day or a 200-day moving average?
b) Which will be smoother, a single exponential smoothing (SES) model using $\alpha = 0.10$ or a model using $\alpha = 0.80$?
c) What is the difference in how historical data are used when the smoothing coefficient in a single exponential smoothing (SES) model is raised from 0.10 to 0.80?

16. Concepts, again. We are trying to forecast monthly sales for a company that sells ski equipment and clothing. Assume that the company's sales peak each December and that the monthly sales have been growing at the rate of 1% each month. Answer the following questions.

a) Based on the description of these data, what time series components can you identify?
b) If you identified a seasonal component, what is the period?
c) If you use seasonal dummy variables, specify the dummy variables you would use.
d) After examining the residuals and using the information provided, you decide to transform the sales data. What transformation are you likely to suggest? Why?

17. More concepts. For each of the following time series, suggest an appropriate model:

a) Weekly stock prices that reveal erratic periods of up and down swings.

b) Annual sales that reveal a consistent percentage annual increase.

c) Quarterly sales for a bicycle shop that reveal a seasonal pattern where sales peak in Q2 of each year.

18. Final concepts. For each of the following time series, suggest an appropriate model:

a) Daily stock prices that reveal erratic periods of up and down swings.

b) Monthly sales that reveal a consistent percentage increase from month to month.

c) Quarterly sales for a woman's clothing company that reveal an annual peak each December.

19. Liquid assets. The Bank of New York Company was founded by Alexander Hamilton in 1784 and was a major commercial bank until its merger with the Mellon Financial Corporation in 2007. Their year-end financial reports for the final five years of independent operation give the following values for their liquid assets (Source: *The Financial Times*).

Year	Liquid Assets ($M)
2002	18,546
2003	22,364
2004	22,413
2005	19,881
2006	26,670

a) Use a 3-year moving average to predict what liquid assets would have been in 2007.

b) Predict the value for 2007 using a single exponential smooth with smoothing parameter $\alpha = 0.2$.

20. Baking profits. Sara Lee Corp., maker of food, beverage, and household products, is known especially for its baked products, marketed under its corporate name. For the five years ending July 1 of each year from 2002 to 2006, their bakery division reported the following profits.

Fiscal Year	Profits ($M)
2002	97
2003	98
2004	156
2005	−4
2006	−197

a) Use a 4-year moving average to predict profits for 2007.

b) Predict the profits for 2007 using a single exponential smooth with smoothing parameter $\alpha = 0.5$.

c) Think about the exponential smoother. If the parameter were 0.8 would you expect the prediction to be higher or lower? What if it were 0.2? Explain.

21. Banana prices. The price of bananas fluctuates on the world market. Here are the prices ($/tonne) for the years 2000–2004 (Source: *Holy See Country Review*, 2008).

2000	2001	2002	2003	2004
422.27	584.70	527.61	375.19	524.84

a) Find a 3-year moving average prediction for the price in 2005.

b) Find a prediction for 2005 with an exponential smoothing model with $\alpha = 0.4$.

c) The actual price of bananas in 2005 was 577 $/tonne (you can find current prices at www.imf.org/external/np/res/commod/table3.pdf.) Compute the absolute percentage error for each prediction.

22. Target earnings. Target Corp. operates "big box" stores that sell everyday essentials and fashionable differentiated merchandise. It also operates an online business at target.com. Target's reported gross earnings per share for the years 2003–2006 are given here.

2003	2004	2005	2006
$1.82	2.02	2.17	2.73

a) Find a prediction for 2007 based on a 3-year moving average and one for a 4-year moving average.

b) Find a prediction for 2007 based on an exponential smoothing model with $\alpha = 0.8$.

c) Earnings per share in 2007 were, in fact, $3.18. Compute the absolute percentage error for each prediction.

T **23. Toyota stock prices 2013.** The following time series graph shows daily closing stock prices for Toyota Motor Manufacturing from April 1, 2008, through June 21, 2013 (Source: Yahoo! Finance).

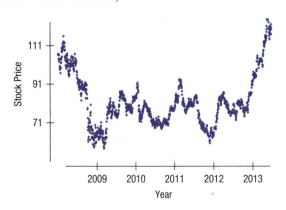

a) Which time series components seem to be present?

The method of moving averages was applied to these data. Here are time series graphs showing moving average results using two different lengths.

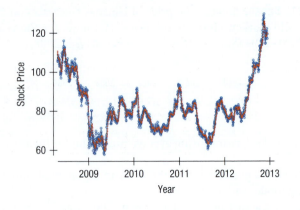

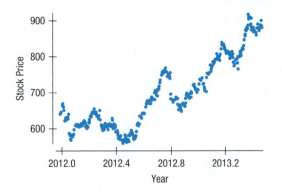

b) In which application is a larger length used?

T 24. Google stock price. The following time series graph shows daily closing stock prices (adjusted for splits and dividends) for Google, Inc., from January 1, 2008, through June 21, 2013 (Source: Yahoo! Finance).

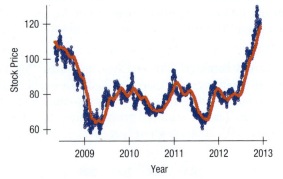

a) Which time series components are evident?

Single exponential smoothing (SES) models were found for these data. Examine the following time series graphs showing two different smoothing coefficients values ($\alpha = 0.2$ and $\alpha = 0.8$).

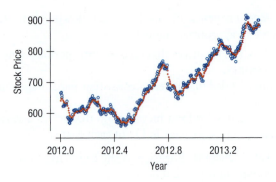

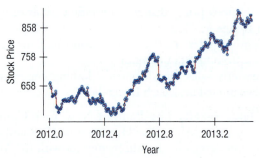

b) In which graph is a larger value of α used?

T 25. Men's weekly earnings 2013. This graph shows the quarterly median weekly earnings from the first quarter of 2003 through the first quarter of 2013 for men, 25 years of age or older, in the United States (U.S. Bureau of Labor Statistics; www.bls.gov).

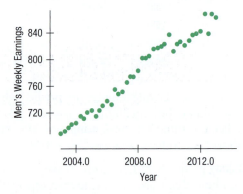

Here are time series plots showing a 2-quarter moving average and an 8-quarter moving average.

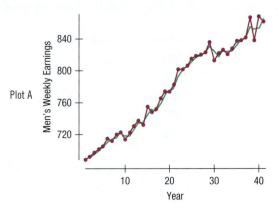

Plot A

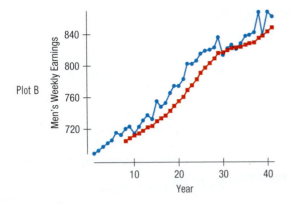

Identify which plot is the 2-quarter moving average and which is the 8-quarter moving average. Explain why the better-fitting model fits better.

T 26. Women's weekly earnings 2013. The following graph shows the quarterly median weekly earnings for U.S. women 25 years of age or older (U.S. Bureau of Labor Statistics; www.bls.gov). Data are provided from the first quarter of 2003 through the first quarter of 2013.

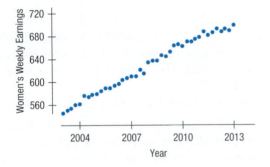

Here is single exponential smoothing model to these data using $\alpha = 0.2$.

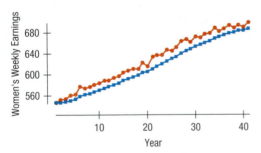

Here is the exponential smoothing model using $\alpha = 0.8$:

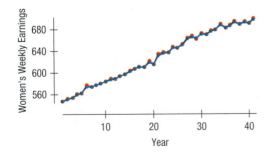

Why does the exponential smoother with the higher coefficient fit the series better? What about this series is important for this result? What does this suggest about using exponential smoothers on such time series?

27. Autoregressive model. Suppose an autoregressive model is used for data in which quarterly sales in 2013 were: 1.9, 1.7, 2.2, and 2.3 ($Billion).

a) If a first-order autoregressive model is developed with estimated parameters of $b_0 = 0.100$ and $b_1 = 1.12$, compute the forecast for Q1 of 2014.
b) Compare this forecast to the actual value ($2.9B) by computing the absolute percentage error (APE). Did you over-forecast or under-forecast?
c) Assuming these quarterly sales have a seasonal component of length 4, use the following model to compute a forecast for Q4 of 2014: $y_t = 0.410 + 1.35\,y_{t-4}$. In fact, Q4 sales were $3.4B. Compare the APE for this forecast to that in part a. Compare the appropriateness of the different models.

28. Another autoregressive model. Suppose an autoregressive model is used to model sales for a company that peaks twice per year (in June and December).

a) What lagged variables would you try in a regression to forecast sales? Explain.
b) How would you determine which of your lagged variables should remain in the model? Explain.

T 29. Coffee prices 2017. Coffee is the world's second largest legal export commodity (after oil) and is the second largest source of foreign exchange for developing nations. The United States consumes about one-fifth of the world's coffee. The International Coffee Organization (ICO) computes a coffee price index using Colombian, Brazilian, and a mixture of other coffee data. Data are provided for the monthly average ICO price index (in $US) from January 1990 to December 2017.

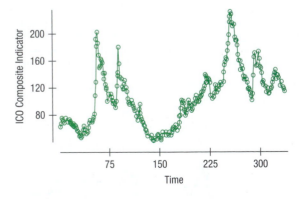

Here's an autoregressive model for the composite prices.

```
Response variable is: ICO Composite indicator
R squared = 96.4%  R squared (adjusted) = 96.4%
s = 7.980 with 334 - 4 = 330 degrees of freedom
```

Variable	Coefficient	SE(Coeff)	t-ratio	P-value
Intercept	2.33255	1.202	1.94	0.0531
t	0.00533	0.0052	1.02	0.3098
Lag1	1.18576	0.0538	22.1	<0.0001
Lag2	-0.215672	0.0538	-4.01	<0.0001

a) Here are the last several values of the series: 128.24, 124.46, 120.01, 117.26, and 114.00. What price does this model predict for the next value in the series ($t = 337$)?
b) Find a prediction based on a 2-point moving average.

T 30. Gas prices 2016. We have data on the weekly average retail price (cents per gallon) of regular gas nationwide. We'll extract the data from 2011 through June 2013. Here's a time series plot.

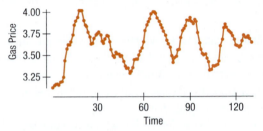

Here are a 4-point moving average and a 3-term autoregressive model fit to these data.

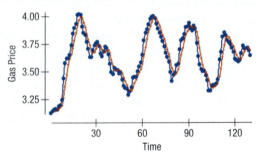

```
Dependent variable is: gas
130 total cases of which 3 are missing
R squared = 95.5%  R squared (adjusted) = 95.4%
s = 0.0440 with 127 - 4 = 123 degrees of freedom
```

Variable	Coefficient	SE(Coeff)	t-ratio	P-value
Intercept	0.258788	0.0703	3.68	0.0003
Lag1	1.55336	0.0901	17.2	<0.0001
Lag2	-0.610098	0.1568	-3.89	0.0002
Lag3	-0.014045	0.0882	-0.159	0.8738

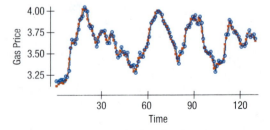

Which model is the better fit for the data?

31. Gallup Poll. The Gallup organization periodically asks the following question:

If your party nominated a generally well-qualified person for president who happened to be a woman, would you vote for that person?

Here is a time series plot of the percentage answering "yes" versus the year of the (20th) century. The least squares trend line is given by: $\hat{y}_t = 5.58 + 0.999 Year$, where $Year = 37, 45, \ldots 99$ to represent the years during which the survey was given.

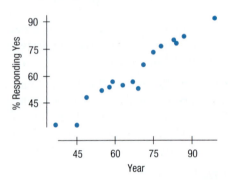

a) The R^2 for this trend line is 94%. A student decided to use this linear model to obtain a forecast for the percent who would respond "yes" in 2012. What value should the student use for *Year*?
b) Find the predicted value for the year 2012. Is it realistic?

T 32. CPI 2017. The most common use of the Consumer Price Index (CPI) is as an economic indicator to forecast inflation and evaluate the effectiveness of government policies. Following is the time series plot for the monthly CPI (not seasonally adjusted) from January 2007 to December 2017. The linear trend line is: $CPI = 207.2 + 0.304\,t$, where $t = 0, 1, \ldots 131$ to represent the months in the series.

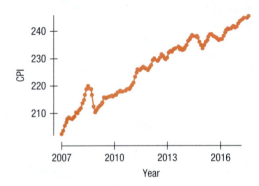

a) What does the intercept 207 represent in this trend line? What does the slope represent?
b) Is this model appropriate for this series? Explain.
c) A regression model fit to the same data from 2009 on has the equation of $207.3 + 0.305t$. Which model would you prefer to use to predict the CPI for June 2018? Explain.

T **33. Gas prices 2016, part 2.** In Exercise 30 we looked at the weekly average retail price (cents per gallon) of regular gas nationwide from 2011 through June 2013. Here's the time series plot again:

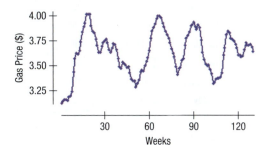

a) What components can you see in this plot?

Here's an AR(14) model fit to these data.

```
Dependent variable is: Gas Price
130 total cases of which 14 are missing
R squared = 31.0%  R squared (adjusted) = 30.4%
s = 0.1587 with 116 - 2 = 114 degrees of freedom
```

Variable	Coefficient	SE(Coeff)	t-ratio	P-value
Intercept	5.34842	0.2354	22.7	<0.0001
Lag14	−0.463680	0.0647	−7.16	<0.0001

Here's a time series plot of the model.

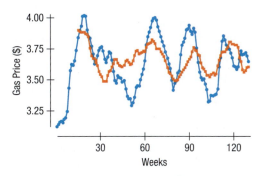

b) Does this model show that there is a (possibly unsuspected) 14-week seasonal cycle in gas prices? Explain.
c) Would you use this model to predict future gas prices? Explain.

T **34. Interest rates 2009.** Average annual interest rates (banks prime lending) in the United States from 1966 through 2009 are shown in the following time series graph.

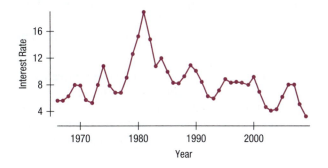

a) What components do you see in this series?

Here's an autoregressive model with a 13-week lag fit to these data.

```
Dependent variable is: Rate
44 total cases of which 13 are missing
R squared = 17.2%  R squared (adjusted) = 14.4%
s = 3.164 with 31 - 2 = 29 degrees of freedom
```

Variable	Coefficient	SE(Coeff)	t-ratio	P-value
Intercept	12.8110	1.755	7.30	<0.0001
Lag13	−0.451563	0.1838	−2.46	0.0203

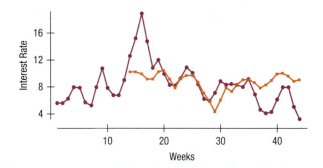

b) Does this model show that there is a (possibly unsuspected) 13-week seasonal cycle in interest rates? Explain.
c) Would you use this model to predict future gas prices? Explain.

35. Seasonal model. Use the following model to forecast quarterly sales ($Million) for a company (where time is rescaled to begin at zero and Q_2, Q_3, and Q_4 are dummy variables for the indicated quarters), and answer the following questions.

$$\hat{y} = 1.1 + 0.2\,t - 0.1\,Q_2 - 0.5\,Q_3 + 0.5\,Q_4$$

a) For the first quarter of the time series, what are the sales?
b) What is the quarter that on average has the lowest level of sales over the time frame of the series?
c) What is the quarter that on average has the highest level of sales over the time frame of the series?
d) Interpret the coefficient of the dummy variable named Q_4.

36. Another seasonal model. Use the following model to forecast quarterly sales ($000) for a start-up (where time is rescaled to begin at zero and Q_2, Q_3, and Q_4 are dummy variables for the indicated quarters), and answer the following questions.

$$\hat{y} = 15.1 + 10.5\,t - 5.0\,Q_2 - 7.2\,Q_3 + 7.5\,Q_4$$

a) For the first quarter of the time series, what are the sales?
b) What is the quarter that on average has the lowest level of sales over the time frame of the series?
c) What is the quarter that on average has the highest level of sales over the time frame of the series?
d) Interpret the coefficient of the dummy variable named Q_4.

37. Walmart revenue. Walmart grew rapidly in the years leading up to the financial crisis. Here is the monthly revenue ($Billion) for Walmart from November 2003 to January 2007.

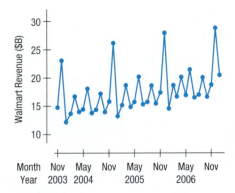

a) What components of a time series do you see in this timeplot?

Here's a regression model fit using dummy variables for months and a *Time* variable that counts from 1 for the first data value in the series.

```
Dependent variable is: WM Rev
R squared = 94.3%  R squared (adjusted) = 91.6%
s = 1.121 with 39 − 13 = 26 degrees of freedom
```

Variable	Coeff	SE(Coeff)	t-ratio	P-value
Intercept	12.0322	0.6562	18.3	<0.0001
Time	0.145241	0.0163	8.93	<0.0001
Feb	1.46096	0.8599	1.70	0.1013
Mar	2.84671	0.8585	3.32	0.0027
Apr	1.67981	0.8574	1.96	0.0609
May	0.870232	0.8567	1.02	0.3191
Jun	4.99999	0.8562	5.84	<0.0001
Jul	0.106417	0.8560	0.124	0.9020
Aug	0.434176	0.8562	0.507	0.6164
Sep	3.25327	0.8567	3.80	0.0008
Oct	−0.219640	0.8574	−0.256	0.7998
Nov	1.87023	0.7932	2.36	0.0262
Dec	11.5625	0.7927	14.6	<0.0001

b) Interpret the coefficient of *Time*.
c) Interpret the coefficient of *Dec*.
d) What revenue would you predict for Walmart in February 2007 (the 40th month in this series)?
e) What does it mean that the coefficient for *Oct* is the only negative coefficient in the model?

38. Harry Potter revenue. The movie *Harry Potter and the Sorcerer's Stone* opened as a great success. But every movie sees declining revenue over time. Here are the daily revenues for the movie during its first 17 days.

Day	Date	Earnings ($M)
Friday	11/16/01	35
Saturday	11/17/01	30
Sunday	11/18/01	25
Monday	11/19/01	9
Tuesday	11/20/01	10
Wednesday	11/21/01	10
Thursday	11/22/01	10
Friday	11/23/01	22
Saturday	11/24/01	23
Sunday	11/25/01	13
Monday	11/26/01	3
Tuesday	11/27/01	3
Wednesday	11/28/01	3
Thursday	11/29/01	2
Friday	11/30/01	9
Saturday	12/1/01	9
Sunday	12/2/01	6

a) Without plotting the data, what components can you see in this series? Be specific.

For some series, a "seasonal" effect repeats weekly rather than annually. Here's a regression model fit to these data with dummy variables for days of the week. (*Day#* counts days starting at 1.)

```
Dependent variable is: Earnings
R squared = 96.9%  R squared (adjusted) = 94.6%
s = 2.365 with 17 − 8 = 9 degrees of freedom
```

Variable	Coeff	SE(Coeff)	t-ratio	P-value
Intercept	21.0000	2.090	10.0	<0.0001
Day#	−1.42857	0.1194	−12.0	<0.0001
Friday	12.4286	2.179	5.70	0.0003
Saturday	12.5238	2.166	5.78	0.0003
Sunday	7.95238	2.160	3.68	0.0051
Monday	−4.28571	2.392	−1.79	0.1068
Tuesday	−2.35714	2.377	−0.992	0.3473
Wednesday	−0.928571	2.368	−0.392	0.7041

b) Interpret the coefficient of *Day#*.
c) Interpret the coefficient of *Saturday* in this model.
d) Predict what earnings probably were for Monday 12/3/01. What does this say about the model?
e) What probably happened to earnings after the initial 17 days?

39. Hawaii tourism. Much of the public and private industry in Hawaii depends on tourism. The following time series plot shows the number of domestic visitors to Hawaii by air from the rest of the United States per month from January 2002 through December 2006 before the financial crisis of 2008.

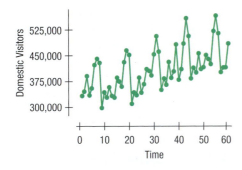

Here is a regression model fit to these data with dummy variables for months and a *Time* variable that starts at 0 and counts months:

```
Response variable is: Domestic
R squared = 95.5%  R squared (adjusted) = 94.4%
s = 14336 with 60 − 13 = 47 degrees of freedom
```

Variable	Coefficient	SE(Coeff)	t-ratio	P-value
Intercept	312312	6925	45.1	<0.0001
Time	2016.84	109.1	18.5	<0.0001
Feb	8924.36	9068	0.984	0.3301
Mar	58693.7	9070	6.47	<0.0001
Apr	20035.3	9073	2.21	0.0321
May	19501.0	9078	2.15	0.0369
Jun	90440.8	9084	9.96	<0.0001
Jul	132893	9091	14.6	<0.0001
Aug	96037.3	9099	10.6	<0.0001
Sep	−27919.7	9109	−3.07	0.0036
Oct	1244.42	9120	0.136	0.8921
Nov	−12181.4	9133	−1.33	0.1887
Dec	39201.9	9146	4.29	<0.0001

a) Interpret the P-value for the trend coefficient.
b) You are planning to visit Hawaii and hope to avoid the crowds. A friend says that September and November have the fewest average visitors. Why might that not be correct?
c) Do you find evidence of a seasonal effect? Explain.
d) How many tourists would you predict for Hawaii in April 2007 (month 63 of this series)?

T 40. Hawaii tourism, part 2. In Exercise 39 we examined domestic tourists who visit Hawaii. Now, let's consider international tourism. Here's a time series plot of international visitors for the same time period.

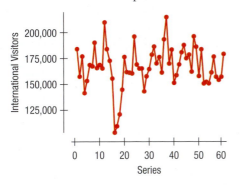

Here's the linear trend model with dummy variables for months.

```
Response variable is: International
R squared = 62.9%  R squared (adjusted) = 53.4%
s = 13684 with 60 − 13 = 47 degrees of freedom
```

Variable	Coefficient	SE(Coeff)	t-ratio	P-value
Intercept	185963	6610	28.1	<0.0001
Time	73.1937	104.1	0.703	0.4854
Feb	−231348	8655	−2.67	0.0103
Mar	−14961.8	8657	−1.73	0.0905
Apr	−50026.4	8660	−5.78	<0.0001
May	−41912.4	8664	−4.84	<0.0001
Jun	−33370.4	8670	−3.85	0.0004
Jul	−21521.2	8677	−2.48	0.0168
Aug	−5021.56	8685	−0.578	0.5659
Sep	−22294.3	8694	−2.56	0.0136
Oct	−20751.5	8705	−2.38	0.0212
Nov	−27338.9	8717	−3.14	0.0029
Dec	6075.27	8730	0.696	0.4899

a) Interpret the P-value for the *Time* coefficient.
b) The R^2 for this model is lower than for the model fit to domestic visitors in Exercise 39. Does that mean that an exponential trend model would do better?
c) International tourists often visit Hawaii in January. How can you tell that from this model?
d) Even though the R^2 for this model is lower than the corresponding R^2 for the model fit in Exercise 39 to domestic tourist visits, you might feel more comfortable predicting the number of international visitors for April 2007 with this model than you did predicting the number of domestic visitors with the previous model. Explain why.

T 41. Oakland passengers 2016. The Port of Oakland airport reports the number of passengers passing through each month. The time series plot shows fluctuations that may relate to the economy. By recognizing the series as a time series, we may learn more.

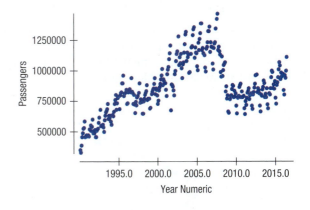

Here is an additive model that accounts for seasonal effects.

```
Response variable is: Passengers
R squared = 34.3%  R squared (adjusted) = 31.7%
s = 184109 with 318 - 13 = 305 degrees of freedom
```

Variable	Coefficient	SE(Coeff)	t-ratio	P-value
Intercept	570293	39539	14.4	<0.0001
Year since...	13810.7	1350	10.2	<0.0001
Feb	−28890.4	50108	−0.577	0.5647
Mar	94215.6	50109	1.88	0.0610
Apr	97451.7	50109	1.94	0.0527
May	133434	50110	2.66	0.0082
Jun	180677	50111	3.61	0.0004
Jul	213821	50588	4.23	<0.0001
Aug	249728	50588	4.94	<0.0001
Sep	76468.0	50588	1.51	0.1317
Oct	118654	50589	2.35	0.0196
Nov	91900.7	50590	1.82	0.0703
Dec	104326	50591	2.06	0.0400

a) Interpret the slope.

b) Interpret the intercept.

c) Which months have the lowest traffic at Oakland airport? (Hint: Consider all 12 months.)

Here's a plot of the residuals from the model fit to the Oakland airport passengers:

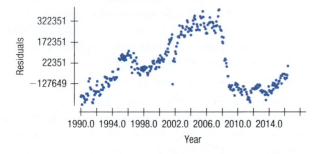

d) What components would you now say are in this series?

T **42. Gas prices monthly.** We have seen that gas prices can fluctuate. But during some periods they have moved consistently. Here are the data extracted for one week of each month from January 2002 to May 2007.

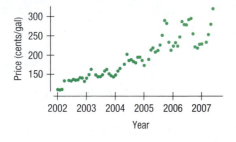

The bend in the plot and the increasing variation suggest a multiplicative model. Here is a multiplicative model with seasonal dummy variables for months.

```
Dependent variable is: Log price
R squared = 92.0%  R squared (adjusted) = 90.2%
s = 0.0377 with 66 - 13 = 53 degrees of freedom
```

Variable	Coeff	SE(Coeff)	t-ratio	P-value
Intercept	2.04566	0.0164	125	<0.0001
Year since 2002	0.071754	0.0030	24.2	<0.0001
Feb	0.002682	0.0210	0.128	0.8988
Mar	0.030088	0.0210	1.43	0.1574
Apr	0.053455	0.0210	2.55	0.0138
May	0.058316	0.0210	2.78	0.0075
Jun	0.044912	0.0221	2.03	0.0471
Jul	0.055008	0.0221	2.49	0.0159
Aug	0.061186	0.0221	2.77	0.0077
Sep	0.057329	0.0221	2.60	0.0122
Oct	0.039903	0.0221	1.81	0.0764
Nov	0.012609	0.0221	0.571	0.5704
Dec	−0.085243	0.0221	−0.386	0.7011

a) Interpret the slope.

b) Interpret the intercept.

c) In what month of the year are gas prices highest?

43. Oakland outlier. The plot of residuals in Exercise 41 shows large fluctuations starting in 2006 and an earlier outlier that wasn't as evident in the data. The outlier is September 2001. This wasn't a typical month for air travel because of the 9/11 attacks. Here are three models fit to the series up through 2006; a single exponential smooth, a 12-point moving average, and the fitted values from a seasonal regression model. Discuss how each deals with the outlier.

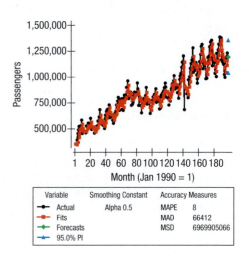

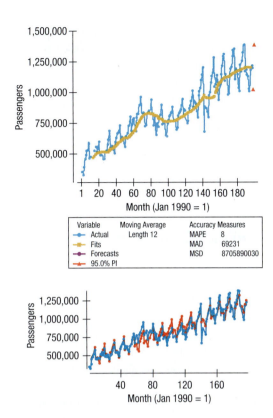

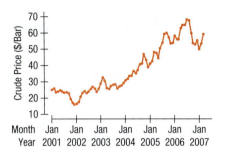

The remaining exercises require the use of statistics software. Statistics packages vary in their capabilities and in the default decisions that some make. As a result, depending upon which package you choose, your answers may differ from those in the back of the book.

T **44. E-commerce.** Quarterly e-commerce retail sales (in millions of dollars) in the United States are provided. (Source: U.S. Census Bureau; www.census.gov.) Use this time series to answer the following questions.

a) Fit a linear trend model to this series but do not use the last two quarters (Q4 2007 and Q1 2008).
b) Fit an exponential trend model to this series but do not use the last two quarters.
c) Use both models to forecast the quarterly values for Q4 2007 and Q1 2008. Which model produces better forecasts?
d) What other time series components (besides trend) are likely present in this series?

T **45. E-commerce, part 2.**

a) Fit a linear trend model with dummy variables for the seasonal effect to the e-commerce data in Exercise 44.
b) Fit an exponential trend (multiplicative) model with dummy variables to these data.
c) Which model fits better?

T **46. Gas prices monthly, part 2.** Using the data from Exercise 42, develop and compare the following models.

a) Fit an appropriate autoregressive model by testing for the significance of each autoregressive term.

b) Obtain a forecast for the week of May 28, 2007.
c) Compare your forecast to the actual value (by computing APE).
d) Do you think this is an appropriate model for forecasting this time series?

T **47. Oil prices monthly.** A time series plot of monthly crude oil price ($/barrel) from January 2001 to March 2007 is shown here.

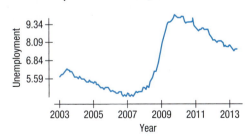

Using these data,

a) Fit a first-order autoregressive model.
b) Obtain a forecast for March 2007.

T **48. Oil prices monthly, again.** Return to the oil price data of Exercise 47.

a) Find a linear model for this series.
b) Find an exponential (multiplicative) model for this series.
c) For the model of Exercise 47 and the models of parts a and b, compute the MAPE. Which model did best? Given the plot in Exercise 47, explain why.
d) Use these methods to forecast the crude oil price for April 2007. The April price was $60.48. Which forecast was closest? Does that mean it's the best model?

T **49. U.S. unemployment 2017.** The following time series plot shows the data for the monthly U.S. *Unemployment rate* (%) from January 2003 to June 2013. These data have been seasonally adjusted (meaning that the seasonal component has already been removed).

a) What time series components do you observe in this series?
b) Develop a 6-month and 12-month moving average model for this series.
c) Fit a single exponential smoothing model ($\alpha = 0.7$) to this series.
d) Comment on how these models do with these data.

T **50. U.S. unemployment 2017, part 2.** Using the data from Exercise 49 develop and compare the following models:

a) Fit a regression model with just Year as the predictor.
b) Add a lag1 component to the model of part a. How does it change the coefficient of Year?
c) Add lag2 and lag3 components to the model. How do the coefficients change?
d) Can you account for these changes? (Hint: Find the correlations among the Rate and lagged versions of the Rate.)

T **51. Hawaii tourism, part 3.** In Exercise 39, we fit a linear regression for the number of monthly domestic visitors to Hawaii (for the years 2002 through 2006) using *Time* and dummy variables for the months as predictors. The R^2 value was 96.6% and a residual plot against *Time* would show no discernible pattern. The dataset for this exercise contains the same data for the period January 2000 through May 2013.

a) Fit the linear model from Exercise 39 to this entire time period.
b) Would you use this model? Explain.
c) The impact of what two major events can you see in the plot of residuals against *Time*?

52. Hawaii tourism, part 4. In Exercise 40, we fit a linear regression for the number of monthly international visitors to Hawaii (for the years 2002 through 2006) using *Time* and dummy variables for the months as predictors.

The R^2 value was 59.9% and a residual plot against *Time* would show a few low outliers, but no discernible pattern. The dataset for this exercise contains the same data for the period January 2000 through May 2013.

a) Fit the linear model from Exercise 40 to this entire time period.
b) Is the trend term statistically significant?
c) Would you use this model? Explain.
d) Why does the no trend model from Exercise 40 no longer work?

JUST CHECKING ANSWERS

1 Trend and seasonal.

2 The value is the mean of the final 4 values, about 557. It might be a bit low as a prediction.

3 $(550 + 642.9)/2 = 596.45$.

4 Four terms because there is a strong seasonal component with period 4.

5 10.0017. Revenue grew at about 10 million dollars per quarter.

6 Dummy variables require that we leave one out.

7 Higher. The four quarterly effects have to sum to zero and the others are all negative.

Health Care Costs

Heart disease is the leading cause of death for both men and women. According to the Centers for Disease Control and Prevention, as of 2013, about 715,000 heart attacks occur in the United States each year.[1] The cost of cardiovascular diseases in the United States, including health care expenditures and lost productivity from deaths and disability, is estimated to be more than $444 billion each year.

Many businesses have seen their cost for health insurance grow beyond bounds. Negotiations with insurance companies can depend, in part, on the demographics of a company's workforce. To understand the relationship between costs and other variables, companies must understand how factors such as age and sex can help predict health costs. Because diseases and therapies vary greatly, it is best to build a separate model for each disease group. And, of course, heart disease is near the top of the list as an important condition to predict.

Models for health care costs can help in predicting and controlling costs. The data file **Heart attack charges** holds records for 12,844 patients admitted to hospitals in the Northeast United States with a diagnosis of acute myocardial infarction (heart attack; AMI). The data are available from Medicare records for public use. These data provide a good example of the kinds of models we can build to understand and predict health care expenses.

The variables available in this dataset are:

Charges: the total hospital charges in dollars.

Age: in years.

Sex: coded M for males, F for females.

DRG: the Diagnosis Related Group, which groups together patients with similar management. In this dataset there are three different DRGs.

> 121: patients with AMIs and cardiovascular complications who did not die.

> 122: patients with AMIs without cardiovascular complications who did not die.

> 123: patients with AMIs who died.

LOS: hospital length of stay in days.

Died: 1 for patients who died in hospital and a 0 otherwise.

Build a model to predict *Charges*. Here are some things to consider in building the model:

1. Should *Charges* be re-expressed? Examine displays and find a suitable re-expression.
2. Should *LOS* be re-expressed? Are there unusual features of the distribution that may deserve special attention?
3. Some of these records may hold errors or otherwise be extraordinary. Make appropriate displays and set aside records that may not be reliable.
4. How do men and women differ? Consider, for example, the distribution of *Age* for male and female patients. Should you introduce *Sex* as a variable in your model? How will you do that?
5. Can you use *DRG* in your regression model as it is presented here, or should it be recoded in some way? *Diagnosis* raises similar questions. If our purpose is to predict costs based on demographic information, should these variables be predictors in our model?
6. Ultimately, how well can you predict *Charges*? Consider not just the R^2, but also the s_e. (Be sure to transform the s_e back to dollars if you are working with a transformed version of *Cost*.) Discuss how well your model predicts health care costs due to heart attack.

---

[1] www.cdc.gov/chronicdisease/resources/publications/AAG/dhdsp.htm

Introduction to Big Data and Data Mining

Paralyzed Veterans of America

The Paralyzed Veterans of America (PVA) is a philanthropic and service organization chartered by the U.S. government to serve the needs of U.S. veterans who suffer from spinal cord injury or disease. Since 1946, PVA has raised money to support a variety of activities, including advocacy for veterans' health care, research and education in spinal cord injury and disease, and support for veterans' benefits and rights.

PVA raises money in a variety of ways, but the majority of their fund-raising comes from direct mail campaigns. They send free address labels or greeting cards to potential donors on their mailing list and request a donation for receiving these gifts.

PVA sends out regular solicitations to a list of more than four million donors. In 2016, PVA received about $100 million in donations, but the effort cost them over $40 million in postage, administrative, and gift expenses. Much of that money was spent on mailings to people who never responded. In fact, in any one solicitation, groups like PVA are lucky to get responses from more than a few percent of the people they contact. Response rates for commercial companies such as large credit card banks are so low that they often measure responses not in percentage points, but in basis points—hundredths of a percent.

If the PVA could avoid mailing to just half of the people who won't respond, they could save $20 million a year and produce only half as much wasted paper. Can statistical and data mining methods help them decide who should get what mail?

21.1 Data Mining and the Big Data Revolution

You learned about Big Data in Chapter 1, and you hear about it on the news almost every day. The technological advances of the past few decades have enabled us to capture information virtually everywhere and automatically. When you visit a social networking site, data about you, your likes, your photos, your friends, and your habits are uploaded to servers, waiting for analysis. Your smartphone sends information about the calls you make, the texts you send, and even your location to central servers. Whether this information is being used in a prudent way by the government and industry is the subject of recent news and citizen concerns,[1] but the collection of data by business, science, and government is exploding and will continue to explode into the foreseeable future. And these data will be used to solve problems using techniques that are based on methods similar to those you've learned to master in this course.

Terms like *data mining*, *data science*, and *analytics* are all used to describe different parts of the process of curating data and applying statistical methods to large datasets. In particular **Data science** has come to mean the entire field of collecting, managing, curating, and analyzing data and then communicating the results. In Chapter 1, we defined **data mining** as the process that uses a variety of data analysis tools to discover patterns and relationships in data to help build useful models and make predictions. The more general term **business analytics** (or sometimes simply *analytics*) describes any use of statistical analysis to drive business decisions from data, whether the purpose is predictive or simply descriptive. **Big data** is a term for datasets so large and complex that it becomes difficult to use traditional methods to capture, store, visualize, and analyze them (see sidebar). But the definition of how "big" the database should be to qualify keeps changing with advancing computer speeds and storage capabilities.

What can companies hope to learn from all these data, and how do they analyze them? With information about the transactions you make, the websites you visit, and the social media you interact with, retailers can customize offers to you and predict when and how to deliver those offers to maximize the chance that you will purchase. Advertisers can place their message in specific channels to maximize the impact for the group of consumers they are targeting.

The Obama presidential campaign used analytics rather than conventional wisdom to determine when and where to place ads during the fall of 2012. As part of their sophisticated targeting operations, they bought "detailed data on TV viewing by millions of cable subscribers, showing which channels they were watching, sometimes on a second-by-second basis."[2] The campaign then "used a third-party company to match viewing data to its own internal list of voters and poll responses," helping to make the most out of their advertising budget during the final weeks of the 2012 campaign. The *New York Times* reported that the system "allowed Mr. Obama's team to direct advertising with a previously unheard-of level of efficiency,"[3] with some analysts crediting this data mining with Obama's victory.

---

[1]"Momentum Builds Against N.S.A. Surveillance," *New York Times*, July 28, 2013.
[2]"Obama Campaign Took Unorthodox Approach to Ad Buying," *Washington Post*, November 14, 2012.
[3]"Secret of the Obama Victory? Rerun Watchers, for One Thing," *New York Times*, November 12, 2012.

Most of the models used in analytics and data mining are based on the regression ideas that you've studied in previous chapters. But because data mining has benefited from work in other fields as well, it has a much richer set of tools. Some of the techniques enable more automatic re-expressions and more flexible fitting than the multiple regression and time series methods you saw in Chapters 18, 19, and 20, but they are based on the same ideas. The skills you've acquired by learning to fit models, diagnose them, and assess their limitations already prepare you to start entering the world of big data. The collection of models used is sometimes referred to as **machine learning algorithms** because of the role computers have in fitting these models (adding even more hype to a collection of models).

The Goals of Data Mining

The broad purpose of data mining is to extract useful information hidden in large databases. With a database as large as a typical data warehouse (see Chapter 1), that search can be like looking for a needle in a digital haystack. How can analysts hope to find what they're looking for? They may start their search by using a sequence of queries to deduce facts about customer behavior, asking specific questions based on the data. Guided by their knowledge of the specific business, they may try a query-driven approach, asking a series of specific questions to deduce patterns. Such an approach is **online analytical processing** or **OLAP**. Analysts in sales, marketing, budgeting, inventory, and finance often use OLAP to answer specific questions involving many variables. An OLAP question for the PVA might be: "What percentage of potential donors under the age of 65 with incomes between $40,000 and $60,000 in the Western region who have not donated in the previous two years gave more than $25 to the most recent solicitation?" Although OLAP is efficient in answering such multivariable queries, it is question-specific. OLAP produces answers for specific queries, but does not build a predictive model, and so it is not possible to generalize using OLAP.

Data mining can address different types of problems, some of which we have already encountered. When the goal is to predict a quantitative response variable, the problem is generically called a **regression problem**, regardless of whether linear regression is used (or even considered) as one of the models. When the response variable is categorical, the problem is referred to as a **classification problem** because the model will either guess the most likely category for each or assign a probability to each class for that code. For example, for the classification problem of predicting *whether or not* a particular donor will give to the next campaign, a model will produce either the most probable class (*donate or not*) or the probabilities of each of these. Predicting the *amount* of money a donor will donate is a regression problem.

In contrast to an OLAP query, the outcome of a data mining analysis is a **predictive model**—a model that uses predictor variables to predict a response. For a quantitative response variable (as in linear regression), the model will predict the *value* of the response, whereas for a categorical response, the model estimates the most probable category of the response, often with the probability that the response variable is in that class (as in logistic regression). Both linear and logistic multiple regressions are common tools of a data miner. Query-based methods like OLAP are restricted only to the data at hand. But data mining models, like all statistical models, are predictive and can be used to make decisions about future situations.

For example, an analyst using an OLAP query might find that customers in a certain age group responded to a recent product promotion. But without building a model, the analyst can't understand the relationship between the customer's age and the success of the promotion, and thus may be unable to predict how the product will do in a more general setting. The goal of a data mining project is to

Data Mining—Some History

In the 1980s, credit card companies realized that with the incredible amount of data they routinely had to collect, there might be some extra value in the data, other than simply recording all their transactions. They knew that customers had different "profiles." For example, some customers used their cards primarily for travel, while others used them for everyday purchases. This market segmentation was enabled by analyzing the transactional data.

By putting customers into different groups, credit card companies could more effectively choose the offers each group would receive.

increase business understanding and knowledge by building a model to answer a specific set of questions raised at the beginning of the project that can generalize to future situations.

Both regression and classification problems are referred to as **supervised problems** because for the data on which the model is based, the response variable's outcome is known. For example, for the PVA data we encounter, we *know* for at least one group of donors the values of the responses *TARGET-B* (did you give?) and *TARGET-D* (how much did you give?). We use these values to construct the model. All the models you've seen so far in the text have been for supervised problems.

By contrast, there are problems for which there is no variable that measures what we are trying to predict. For example, a company may want to cluster their customers into groups with similar buying behaviors and tastes. That's a fine goal, but, unfortunately, customers are not labeled this way. In this case, there is no response variable—we just want to group together similar customers. Whether the grouping we find is "correct" is impossible to determine. Whether it is useful has to be determined by the person who will actually use the results. Problems like these are known as **unsupervised problems** because there is no actual response variable.

Cluster analysis, grouping similar objects together, is the most common type of unsupervised problem. Many different algorithms are available to find clusters, but they all rely on a measure of how similar (or, equivalently, how distant) the objects are to each other. For example, when clustering bank customers, we might base the distance between them on the sum of the total (absolute) differences that they spend in different categories. If customer A spent $100 on travel and $300 on restaurants last month and customer B spent $200 on travel and $200 on restaurants, a possible distance between them might be $|100 - 200| + |300 - 200| = 200$. Customers who spend most similarly would be the first to be put into the same spending group (see sidebar). (Further discussion of clustering and other unsupervised methods is beyond the scope of this text.)

Data Mining and Statistics

Data mining is similar to traditional statistical analysis in that it involves exploratory data analysis and modeling. However, several aspects of data mining distinguish it from more traditional statistical analysis. Although there is no consensus on exactly what data mining is and how it differs from statistics, some of the most important differences include:

- **The size of the databases.** Although no particular size is required for an analysis to be considered data mining, an analysis involving only a few hundred cases or only a handful of variables would not usually be considered data mining.
- **The exploratory nature of data mining.** Unlike a statistical analysis that might test a hypothesis or produce a confidence interval, the outcome of a data mining effort is typically a model used for prediction. Usually, the data miner is not interested in the values of the parameters of a specific model or in testing hypotheses. A classic example is predicting ZIP codes from hand-written envelopes. The manager of the New York Post Office is unlikely to care what variables were included in the algorithm that reads the correct ZIP code automatically with a high level of accuracy.
- **The data are "happenstance."** In contrast to data arising from a designed experiment or survey, the typical data on which data mining is performed have not been collected in a systematic way. This is an important difference, often overlooked in business. Warnings not to confuse association with causation are especially pertinent for data mining. In addition, the sheer number of variables involved makes any search for relationships among variables prone to

Type I errors. Humans love to see signals and relationships among variables even when none exists. Resist the temptation to believe too strongly in these models. Although they can be useful to generate hypotheses to be tested, they are, by nature, exploratory. Be especially careful to check the "pedigree" of the data. The phrase "Garbage in, garbage out" was never more true than when applied to data mining.

- **The results of a data mining effort are "actionable."** For business applications, there should be a consensus of what the problem of interest is and how the model will help solve the problem. There should be an action plan in place for a variety of possible outcomes of the model. Exploring large databases out of curiosity or just to see what they contain is not likely to be productive.

- **The modeling choices are automatic.** Typically the data miner will try several different types of models to see what each has to say, but doesn't want to spend a lot of time choosing which variables to include in the model or being careful in the kinds of choices he or she might make in a more traditional statistical analysis. Unlike the analyst who wants to understand the terms in a stepwise regression, the data miner is more concerned with the predictive ability of the model. As long as the resulting model can help make decisions about who should receive the next offer, who is best suited for an online coupon, or who is most likely to switch cable providers next month, the data miner is likely to be satisfied.

Data Mining Myths

Data mining software usually contains a variety of exploratory and model-building tools and a graphical user interface designed to guide the user through the data mining process. Some people buy data mining software in the hope that the tools will find information in their databases and write reports that spew knowledge with little or no effort or input from the user. Software vendors often capitalize on this hope by exaggerating the capabilities and the automatic nature of data mining to increase sales of their software. Data mining can often *assist* the analyst to find meaningful patterns and help predict future customer behavior, but the more the analyst knows about his or her business, the more likely he or she will be successful using data mining. Data mining is not a magic wand that can overcome poor data quality or collection. A product may have tools for detecting outliers and may be able to impute (assign a value for) missing data values, but all the issues you learned about good statistical analysis are still relevant for data mining.

Here are some of the more common myths about what data mining can do.

- **Myth 1:** Find answers to unasked questions.

    Even though data mining can build a model to help answer a specific question, it does not have the ability to answer questions that haven't been asked. In fact, formulating a precise question is a key first step in any data mining project.

- **Myth 2:** Automatically monitor a database for interesting patterns.

    Data mining techniques build predictive models and can answer queries, but do not find interesting patterns on their own any more than regression models do.

- **Myth 3:** Eliminate the need to understand the business.

    In fact, the more an analyst understands his or her business, the more effective the data mining effort will be.

- **Myth 4:** Eliminate the need to collect good data.

    Good data are as important for a data mining model as for any other statistical model that you've encountered. While some data mining software contains tools to help with missing data and data transformations, there is no substitute for quality data.

- **Myth 5:** Eliminate the need for good data analysis skills.

  The better the data analysis skills of the miner—the skills you've learned in every chapter of this text—the better the analysis will be when using data mining tools. Data mining tools are more powerful and flexible than a statistical tool like regression but are similar in the way they work and in how they're implemented.

- **Myth 6:** Machine learning algorithms think like humans.

  Some of the hype about data mining and machine learning revolves around the belief that these algorithms, or models, think and learn. In fact, they "learn" about the relationship between the predictors (x) and response (y) no more, and no less, than linear regression learned about it. They simply fit a model to the data. Some do it in an automatic way, which may lead one to think they are actually learning, but this is simply a human interpretation of a powerful algorithm.

JUST CHECKING

A bank vice president brings in her analytic team to talk about several things she wants to know about a recent offer the bank mailed out to open an IRA (individual retirement account). For each of the following, identify if it's an appropriate data mining problem. If so, is it a supervised or an unsupervised problem? If supervised, is it a regression or a classification problem?

1 Why did some people not respond to the offer?

2 What percentage of those under 65 who have been bank customers for more than 5 years responded to the offer?

3 Using the bank products that customers currently use and other demographic information, group customers into different segments for the purposes of sending different retirement offers.

4 On the basis of past data, what is the chance that a given customer will accept a new offer that the bank sends out?

5 How many transactions is a given customer likely to make next month based on their past behavior and other demographics?

21.2 The Data Mining Process

Data mining projects require a number of different skills. For that reason, a data mining project should be a team effort. No one person is likely to have the business knowledge, computer and database management skills, software expertise, and statistical training needed for all the steps in the process. Because data mining projects tend to be complex, it's useful to map out the steps for a successful project. A group of data mining experts have shared their combined expertise in a project called the Cross Industry Standard Process for Data Mining (CRISP-DM).[4] A CRISP-DM schematic of the data mining cycle appears in Figure 21.1.

Let's use PVA as an example and follow the data mining cycle from beginning to end. The process starts with the *business understanding* phase, in which the problem to be addressed is carefully articulated. For any data exploration, it is best to have a specific problem before starting, but for data mining, with potentially very large databases, this is absolutely crucial. For PVA, the goal of "understanding how to best manage donors" might sound like a good idea, but is not precise enough for a data mining project. A better, more specific question might be to build a model to

---

[4]In 2015, IBM announced an updated version of CRISP-DM called ASUM-DM, which stands for Analytics Solutions Unified Method for Data Mining/Predictive Analytics, but the basic principles remain the same.

FIGURE 21.1 A picture of the CRISP-DM data mining process.

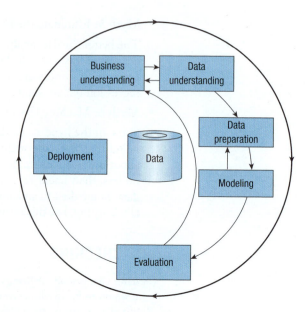

discover which donors are most likely to give enough in the next solicitation to justify sending them a free gift. It's important to have all the members of the data mining team involved at this stage, and the team should be representative of all parts of the business that may be affected by the resulting decisions. If key constituents aren't represented, the model is in danger of not answering the right question. It can't be overemphasized how important it is to have consensus on a precise, correctly formulated problem to be addressed before continuing with the data mining effort.

The next phase of *data understanding* is central to the entire data mining project. If you want to know which donors are likely to participate in the next mailing, you have to have data that can actually answer that question. This is where many data mining projects fail. A traditional statistics approach might be to survey donors before the next mailing, but, typically, a data mining project uses only data the company has already collected. Much of that data is **transactional data**—data that simply record a transaction between the customer and the company. This could be a purchase, a donation, or any other transaction, even a phone call to an 800 number or a web query. Other data are **demographic**—information about the customer that might include the customer's income, number of children, education, and other customer-specific information. This information may have been supplied by the customer or may be purchased from other companies. Still other data are **historical** based on past history between the customer and the company. These data sources are typically stored on different computers or servers, which means that they need to be merged before the analyst can access them. Usually, someone well versed in database architecture and data storage is needed to extract the relevant information in different databases and to merge them into a form that is useful for analysis. This requires teamwork and communication skills. And, unfortunately, all of this means that the answer to a specific question may not be found in these data, even when using a very powerful algorithm designed to search for it.

Customer-specific data can also be purchased from a variety of commercial organizations. For example, a credit card company may want to send out an offer of free flight insurance to customers who travel frequently. To help know which customers those are, the company may buy information about customers' magazine subscriptions to identify customers who subscribe to travel or leisure magazines. The sharing and selling of individual information is controversial and raises privacy concerns, especially when the purchased data involve health records and personal information. In fact, concerns over the sharing of health data in the United States led to a set of strict guidelines known as HIPAA (Health Insurance

Portability and Accountability Act) regulations. Restrictions on the collection and sharing of information about customers vary widely from country to country.

The PVA customer database[5] is a typical mix of variables. It contains 481 demographic and historical variables on each of nearly 100,000 donors. There are 479 potential predictor variables and two responses: *TARGET_B*, a 0/1 variable that indicates whether the donor contributed to the most recent campaign, and *TARGET_D*, that gives the dollar amount of the contribution. The demographic variables are both donor specific (e.g., age, income, number of children) and ZIP code specific (e.g., percent with college education, average income, percent minority). Both types of variables can be collected by the company itself or purchased from other organizations, both private and governmental (the U.S. Census Bureau is a source of information at various levels). About 10% of the PVA variables describe past giving behavior collected by the PVA itself. More than half of the variables are regional data based on ZIP codes, most likely purchased from the Census Bureau. The rest of the variables are donor specific, either gathered by the PVA or purchased from other organizations. The historical data pertain to the past behavior of the donor and include whether and how much the individual donated to various campaigns in the past. Table 21.1 shows the first 18 records for a subset of the 481 variables found in the PVA data. We can guess what some of the variables mean from their names, but others are more mysterious.

Becoming familiar with a complex dataset can take many months. Information about the variables, including their definitions, how they are collected, the date of collection, and so forth, is collectively called **metadata**. The variables in the PVA dataset shown in Table 21.1 are typical of the types of data found in the customer records of many companies. We shouldn't be surprised to find out that *AGE* is the donor's age measured in years and that *ZIP* is the donor's postal ZIP code. But without the metadata, it would be hard to know that *TCODE* is the code used before the title on the address label (0 = blank, 1 = Mr., 2 = Mrs., 28 = Ms., and so on) or that *RFA_2A* is a summary of past giving.

The choice of the variables to explore depends on the business knowledge of the team. As is clear from the PVA data, it is probably inefficient to spend a lot of time exploring each variable. This is one of the great challenges of a data mining project. At the beginning of the project, it's best to include as many variables as possible that might be useful, but keep in mind that having *too* many variables can make the model selection phase more difficult.

Once the variables have been selected and the response variable(s) agreed upon, it's time to begin the *data preparation* phase for modeling. As mentioned earlier, this can be a time-consuming part of the process and is also likely to be a team effort (see sidebar). Investigating missing values, correcting wrong and inconsistent entries, reconciling data definitions, and merging data sources are all challenging issues. Some of these can be handled automatically, while others require painstaking, detailed analysis. The team will have to decide how much effort is reasonable to make the dataset as complete and reliable as possible, given the time and resource constraints of the project.

Part of the data preparation phase involves both transforming predictor variables (as we did in Chapter 17) and creating new variables from combinations of them. This is often referred to as **feature creation**. A new feature (variable) can be created *a priori* from the analyst's domain knowledge or sometimes more

---

What Does a Data Scientist Do?

In response to this question on Quora (quora.com), James Madison (data scientist) answered:

1. Clean data.
2. Clean data.
3–12. Clean data.
13. Do some math.
14. Try to get everyone to understand my findings.
15–25. Try to get everyone to understand my findings.
26. Repeat.

---

[5] The PVA made some of their data available for the 1998 Knowledge Discovery and Data Mining (KDD) contest. The object of the contest was to build a model to predict which donors should receive the next solicitation based on demographic and past giving information. The results were presented at the KDD conference (www.kdnuggets.com). The variables discussed in this chapter are some of the ones that PVA made available. We have used various subsets of the PVA dataset in previous chapters, sometimes changing the variable names for clarity. The entire dataset can be found at the University of California at Irvine Data Repository: kdd.ics.uci.edu/databases/kddcup98/kddcup98.html.

ODATEDW	OSOURCE	TCODE	STATE	ZIP	DOB	RFA_2A	AGE	OWN	INC	SEX	WEALTH	AVGGIFT	TARGET_B	TARGET_D
9401	L16	2	GA	30738	6501	F	33	U	5	F	2	11.66667	0	0
9001	L01	1	MI	49028	2201	F	76	H	1	M	2	8.777778	0	0
8601	DNA	1	TN	37079	0	E		U	1	M		8.619048	1	10
8601	AMB	1	WI	53719	3902	G	59			M		16.27273	0	0
8601	EPL	2	TX	79925	1705	E	81	H	2	F	6	10.15789	0	0
8701	LIS	1	IN	46771	0	F				M		8.871333	0	0
9201	GRI	1	IL	60016	1807	F	79	H	4	M	6	13.8	0	0
9401	HOS	0	KS	67218	5001	G	48	U	7	F	7	18.33333	0	0
8901	DUR	0	MI	48304	1402	F	84	H	7	M	9	12.90909	0	0
8601	AMB	0	FL	34746	1412	F	83	H	2	F	3	9.090909	0	0
9501	CWR	2	LA	70582	0	D		U	5	F		5.8	0	0
9501	ARG	0	MI	48312-	4401	E	54			F		8	0	0
8601	ASC	0	TX	75644	2401	G	74	U	7	F		13.20833	0	0
9501	DNA	28	CA	90059	2001	E	78	H	1	F		10	0	0
9201	SYN	0	FL	33167	1906	F	79	U	2	M	3	10.09091	0	0
9401	MBC	2	MO	63084	3201	F	66	H	5	F		10	0	0
9401	HHH	28	WI	54235	0	F		H	7	F		20	0	0
9101	L02	28	AL	36108	4006	F	58	H	5	F		10.66667	0	0

TABLE 21.1 Part of the customer records from the PVA dataset. Shown here are 15 of the 481 variables and 18 of the nearly 100,000 customer records used in the 1998 KDD (Knowledge Discovery and Data Mining) data mining competition.[6] The actual PVA customer database contains several million customer records.

automatically by the data mining algorithms themselves. For example, a banker trying to model the chance of customer bankruptcy might see that customer *debt* and *income* have been measured and, from his or her experience, decide to create the *debt/income* ratio. For the Paralyzed Veteran's data, the numerous past giving variables were combined into three new variables that summarized when the donor last contributed (called *recency*), how often the donor gives (*frequency*), and how much the donor gives (*monetary*). This type of RFM (recency, frequency, monetary) analysis is widely used in marketing science.

Once the data have been prepared, the analysts begin the *modeling* phase by exploring and developing models. If the number of variables is very large, a preliminary, exploratory model (such as a decision tree, described in a later section) might be a good way to narrow the candidate predictor variables down to a reasonable number. However, if the number of predictors is reasonably small, modelers can use traditional graphical displays (histograms, bar charts) to explore each variable and then investigate the relationship between each predictor and the response with displays such as scatterplots, boxplots, or segmented bar charts. The more knowledge of the data and the variables that go into the model, the higher the chance of success for the project.

Once the collection of variables has been determined, the analysts typically fit several models for the response variable. At this point the *evaluation* phase can begin. Looking at the structure of each model, including which predictors are important for each model, should give the analysts information about the relationship between the predictors and the response that each model is built on. In the *evaluation* phase, the candidate models are tested by predicting the response values

[6]The KDD Cup is the leading data mining competition in the world and is organized by the SIGKDD interest group of the ACM (Association for Computing Machinery).

Why Not Just Report the Total Error Rate When Judging Models?

Fraud detection is a huge problem in the credit card industry and costs billions of dollars a year. Fortunately, it is fairly rare, affecting less than 1% of all transactions (wallethub.com/edu/credit-debit-cardfraud-statistics/25725/). So, simply reporting all transactions as fraud-free will result in an overall error rate of less than 1%. An accuracy rate of greater than 99% may sound good, but it's much better to look at the two types of errors (that we learned about in Chapter 13), separately, even weighing the different costs of each mistake.

on the test set as we discussed in Chapter 19, Section 4. Various criteria are used to judge the models, depending on the type of problem. For example, for a regression problem with a quantitative response, the sum of squares of the residuals (or a version of R^2—discussed in the next section) on the test set might be compared across models. For a problem predicting a two-level categorical variable (with levels NO and YES), the two types of errors that arise (predicting YES when the true response is NO and vice versa) can be balanced in different ways. Placing different costs on the two types of errors might be warranted, and the total cost of misclassification should reflect that (see sidebar).

At this point, the business question that motivated the project should be revisited. Does the model help to answer the question? If not, it might be necessary to go back to one of the previous steps to investigate why that happened. This kind of cycling through the various steps of the process is not uncommon. The reason that so many phases of the CRISP-DM diagram (Figure 21.1) have arrows both to and from them is that this process is not a straightforward movement through the phases—it is an iterative and interconnected process.

If a particular model (or average of several models) seems to give insight into the business problem and predicts well enough to be useful, then it's time for the *deployment* phase. Usually, that means using the model to predict an outcome on a larger dataset than the original, or on more recent data than were used to build the model. Knowledge gained at any phase may trigger a reexamination of an earlier phase. Even the "final" phase, deployment, is not really final. In many business situations, the environment changes rapidly, so models can become stale quickly. Although a data mining project is complex and involves the efforts of many people, mapping out the different phases can help ensure that the project is as successful and reproducible as possible.

Successful Data Mining

The size of a typical data warehouse makes any analysis challenging. The ability to store data is growing faster than the ability to use it effectively. Commercial data warehouses often contain terabytes (TB)—more than 1,000,000,000,000 (1 trillion) bytes—of data (1 TB is equivalent to about 260,000 digitized songs), and warehouses containing petabytes (PB—1 PB = 1000 TB) are now common. According to *Gizmodo* magazine[7], about 300 million photos and 500 TB of data are uploaded to Facebook every day. All the U.S. Census data from 1790 to 2000 would take about 600 TB. Data miners hope to uncover some important strategic information lying hidden within these massive collections of data.

As we have seen, to have a successful data mining outcome, the first step is to have a well-defined business problem. With 500 variables, there are over 100,000 possible two-way relationships between pairs of variables. The number of pairs that will be related just by chance is likely to be large. And it's human nature to find many of these relationships interesting and even to posit plausible reasons why two variables might be associated. Some of these variables may appear to provide a useful predictive model, when in fact they do not. A well-defined business objective can help avoid going down a lot of blind paths.

As in painting a house, much of the effort of a data mining project lies in preparation and cleaning. And just as a painter would much rather get right to the more enjoyable part of painting, unless enough time is spent prepping the wood, all that effort will ultimately be wasted. It is estimated that for any data mining project, 65% to 90% of the total project time is spent in such data preparation—investigating missing values, correcting wrong and inconsistent

---

[7]gizmodo.com/5937143/what-facebook-deals-with-everyday-27-billion-likes-300-million-photos-uploaded-and-500-terabytes-of-data

entries, reconciling data definitions, and possibly creating new variables from the original ones. The data may need to be extracted from several databases and combined. Errors must be corrected or eliminated, and outliers must be identified.

So, a successful data mining effort often requires a substantial amount of time devoted to basic preparation of the data before any modeling is performed. It will have a clear objective, agreed to by a team of people who will share the work and the responsibility of the data mining. It will have an action plan once the results of the data mining are known, whether those results are what the team expected or desired. Finally, the data mining should be accompanied by as much knowledge about both the data and the business question as possible. Blind searches for patterns in large databases are rarely fruitful and will waste valuable analytic resources.

IN PRACTICE 21.1   Data preparation

MANAGER I've started looking at our (Paralyzed Veterans of America) database to try to understand who our current donors are. Just looking at the variable *AGE*, can we use it to predict who is most likely to give to our next campaign? What corrections or adjustments would be appropriate?

ANALYST Here are a histogram and boxplot for the variable *AGE* for all 94,649 records of the PVA dataset.

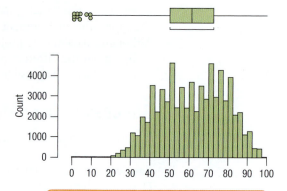

	Quantiles	
100.0%	maximum	98.000
99.5%		95.000
97.5%		90.000
90.0%		83.000
75.0%	quartile	75.000
50.0%	median	62.000
25.0%	quartile	48.000
10.0%		39.000
2.5%		31.000
0.5%		26.000
0.0%	minimum	1.000

Mean	61.598019
Std Dev	16.666865
Std Err Mean	0.0624749
upper 95% Mean	61.720469
lower 95% Mean	61.475568
N	71170

There is a group of cases with ages below 20 that should immediately draw our attention. Are people that young likely to be donors? A closer examination reveals that there are even a handful of cases whose ages are below 15, of whom 17 are younger than 5 years old and 9 are 1 year old. There are also 23,479 missing values for the variable *AGE*. From what I know about our database, ages below 20 (and certainly those below 10) are likely to be errors. I could go back and investigate those individually, but I think given how few there are, simply deleting the values below 21 is probably the wisest course of action for now.[8]

JUST CHECKING

The bank vice president from the previous Just Checking wants to know some things about the data and the data mining process. Respond briefly to her assumptions and questions to a data mining consultant.

6 To me, it seems best and most efficient to build the team from one department, like my information technology group, rather than make a cross-disciplinary team for the project. What do you think?

7 I assume that once we identify the data sources we'll use, we can get right into modeling the issue, correct?

8 These data mining techniques are so powerful that I'm virtually guaranteed the predictions will be accurate, right?

9 Rather than look at one small problem, I think it might be a good idea to just explore the database and see what's in there. What do you think?

10 Once we test the model and it seems to work well, we'll be able to use it for the next few years at least.

21.3 Data Mining Algorithms: A Sample

Data mining models are often referred to as **algorithms**, a term that describes a sequence of programming steps with a specific purpose. You may hear a method (even one like linear regression) referred to as a model, an algorithm, a tool, or generically as a method. The terms seem to be used interchangeably. Technically, the algorithm is the set of rules that the computer uses to compute the value of the model. The algorithm then uses the data to find the optimal values of the parameters, to fit the data most closely. As with linear regression, by most closely we typically mean minimizing the sum of squares of the differences between the data and the predicted values.

This section touches on only a few of the models used in data mining. Some of the most common models used for prediction are decision trees, neural networks and random forests (discussed below), and the regression methods discussed in Chapters 18 and 19. It's a lively research field and new algorithms are appearing all the time.

Model Selection: Training the Model

Data mining algorithms are powerful. That's great, but with that power comes the ability to fit every pattern in the data, including noise. As mentioned in Chapter 19, to avoid overfitting, the data are typically split randomly into training and test data.

---

[8]Further analysis revealed that age was calculated from date of birth by a computer algorithm, but only the last two digits of the date of birth year were used. So, some people (perhaps no longer living) who were in the database had ages 100 years too young.

The training data are used to fit (or train) the model. Then the model predicts the response of the test data. The test set has not been used to choose the parameters or the variables in the model. We use this cross-validation to see how well the model predicts on data that it has never seen.

What Is a Data Mining Algorithm?

"A data mining algorithm is a well-defined* procedure that takes data as input and produces output in the form of models or patterns."

Principles of Data Mining, **Hand, Mannila, and Smyth**

**Well-defined* means it can be encoded into a set of commands into a computer.

A more thorough way to evaluate models is to split the dataset randomly into training and test repeatedly, cross-validating more than once. Typically, 90% of the data are used to fit and 10% used to evaluate in each iteration. When repeated test sets are used, they are often called **hold outs**. The model fitting is repeated on all the training sets, computing a performance measure on each hold out. The average performance on all the hold out sets will be the final measure of how well the model fits.

What do we mean by predicting well? For a continuous predictor, we might use the sum of squares of the deviations on the test set, or the R^2 on the test set defined as:

$$R^2 = 1 - \text{SSE/SST}.$$

This is the same definition we used for multiple regression, but for the new data, R^2 can actually go negative if the predictions for the test are farther away from the actual response than they are from their mean.

For categorical data there are a variety of performance measures all based on the number of misclassified cases in the test set. The simplest is to count up all the misclassifications. However, it's often more serious to misclassify one of the levels of the response than another, so weighting the misclassifications is also popular.

For example, it is far worse to miss finding cancer than it is to tell someone that he or she may have cancer, and then to discover that it is not there. Similarly, it may well be much worse to permit credit card fraud than to inconvenience people with a false alarm (when the company says that a transaction may be fraud, but, in fact, it was not).

Fortunately, many algorithms do some sort of cross-validation automatically and report back the best model. We'll see how this works in practice in the following examples.

Tree Models

Trees are simple models used for both classification and regression problems. To illustrate how a tree works, imagine that we want to predict whether someone will default on a mortgage. To build the tree, we use past data from a group of customers on whom we have measured some predictor variables and for whom we know whether they defaulted or not. (So, this is a supervised classification problem.) For this simplified example, let's assume we'll predict *Default* only from the following variables:

- *Age* (years)
- *Household Income* ($)
- *On the Job* (years)
- *Debt* ($)
- *Homeowner* (Yes/No)

Perhaps the easiest way to understand what a tree is doing is to look at its output. Figure 21.2 shows a tree fit to our hypothetical default example. At each level of the tree, data are split into two parts based on the values of a predictor variable. The first split is on *Household Income* at the value $40,000. Those whose incomes are > $40,000 (indicated by "Yes") are on the right. Following down the tree, the tree next splits that group on household *Debt*. For people who have both *Income* > $40,000 and *Debt* > $10,000, the tree estimates a 0.05 probability of *Default*. For those with *Income* > $40,000 but *Debt* not > $10,000, the probability is only 0.01. Going back up to the top, for the left branch of the first split, the tree splits on years *On the Job* (and not *Debt*). For the customers with *Income* not >$40,000 and more than 5 years *On the Job*, the *Default* probability is estimated to be 0.06, and for those with *Income* not >$40,000 and 5 years or less *On the Job*, the probability is highest—at 0.11.

FIGURE 21.2 Part of a tree model on a hypothetical examination of mortgage default. The tree selects *Household Income* as the most important variable to split on and selects $40,000 as the split point. For those customers whose *Income* is more than $40,000, *Debt* is the next most important variable, while for those whose income is less than $40,000, how long they've been *On* their current *Job* is more important. For each of the four groups, the estimated probability of *Default* is shown at the bottom at the terminal nodes.

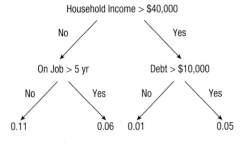

One of the benefits of the tree is how simple it is to interpret. But how does the tree choose the variables and the values to split on? The answer might be surprising. The tree essentially does it by brute force, trying every possible predictor variable and split point to see which combination produces the largest *difference* in default rates.[9]

The tree starts by considering all the data, and tries splitting the data into two groups based on each predictor variable, looking at the impact that makes on the response variable. It searches for that combination of variable and split that produces the largest difference in the response.[10] For a nonordered categorical predictor, the model considers every possible way of splitting the categories into two groups. For an ordered categorical variable, the modeler may choose to respect the order and restrict the possible splits (see sidebar). For a quantitative variable, the possible splits are at every possible value the variable can take (other then the min and the max).

After the algorithm finds the first split, it continues searching again on the two resulting groups, finding the next best variable and split point (possibly using the same variable as the previous split again). It continues in this way until one of several criteria is met (for example, number of customers is too small, not a large enough difference in rates is found) and then stops at what are called **terminal nodes**, where the model produces a prediction. The predictions at the terminal nodes are simply the average (if the response is quantitative) or the proportions of each category (for a classification problem) of the cases at that node.

Tree models are very easy to implement and, in principle, are easy to interpret. They have the advantage of showing their logic clearly and are easy to explain to people who don't have a deep background in statistics. Even when they aren't used as a final model in a data mining project, they can be very useful for selecting a smaller subset of variables on which to do further analysis.

Splitting a Categorical Variable

If our categorical predictor is *Region (East, North, South, West)*, there are 7 possible splits:

East—North, South, West
North—East, South, West
South—East, North, West
West—East, North, South
East, North—South, West
East, South—North, West
East, West—North, South

If the categorical variable is ordered and the modeler wants to keep that order, then the splits are restricted. For example, if the variable is *Age (Child, Young Adult, Adult, Senior)*, then the only possible splits are:

Child—Young Adult, Adult, Senior
Child, Young Adult—Adult, Senior
Child, Young Adult, Adult—Senior

---

[9]This is a simplification. Tree algorithms have shortcuts so they don't have to try every possible combination. In fact, they are computationally very efficient. Readers who want to know the details can read more advanced books on data mining or decision trees.

[10]There are several different criteria for measuring the difference in the response on the two sides of the split.

Unlike many other data mining algorithms, a tree can handle a great number of potential predictor variables, both categorical and quantitative. This makes it a great model for starting a data mining project. It also handles outliers and high influence values in the predictors well because it simply splits the predictor into two groups. Once the tree model is fit, the analyst can then choose whether to use this model as a final model for predicting the response, or simply to use the variables suggested by the tree as inputs to other models that are more computationally intensive and less able to handle very large numbers of predictors.

IN PRACTICE 21.2   Gaining insights from a tree model

MANAGER Can you help me understand who responded to our most recent solicitation?

ANALYST I think that a tree model would be appropriate here. The tree model starts at the root node with all 94,649 donors (listed under Count in the top box of the figure).

The first split of the tree is on the variable *RFA_4*, a variable that summarizes past giving. This is one of the RFM variables that marketing created to summarize past giving. The fact that the tree chose it first is a great credit to their efforts! The algorithm identifies this as the best single predictor of *TARGET_B*, splitting the levels of that variable into two groups, with 29,050 customers split to the left and the remaining 65,599 customers to the right. The variable *RFA_4* comprises codes that contain information on how recently the last gift solicitation was received, how frequently the donor has given, and how large the last gift was. (Examples of these codes are A3C, S4B, and so on, seen in parentheses after the variable name in the output display.) The percentages next to the levels 0 and 1 indicate the proportion of those who donated or not (*TARGET_B 1 or 0*, respectively) in each node. Notice that 7.34% of those in the left node contributed, which was almost twice the 4.06% in the right node who contributed.

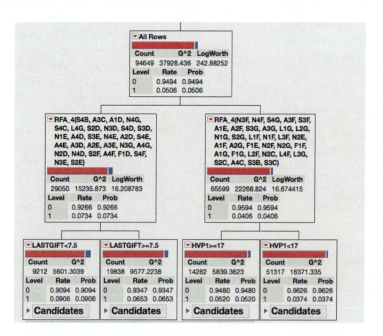

FIGURE 21.3 Part of a tree model run on the PVA data using JMP® software. (Source: Created with JMP® 13 Pro software. Copyright 2016, SAS Institute, Cary, NC, USA. All Rights Reserved. Reproduced with permission of SAS Institute, Inc, Cary, NC.)

The tree continues to split each subpopulation. Notice that the variable chosen to split the left branch of the tree (*LASTGIFT*) is not the same as the variable chosen to split the right branch (*HVP1*). The terminal nodes are found in the bottom row. The terminal node at the bottom left of the figure shows that 9.06% of the 9212 potential donors in this subgroup donated, a substantial improvement over the average of all potential donors (5.06%) shown in the root node at the top. Even at this stage of the analysis, if directed our solicitations to names on our list that satisfied the conditions found in the path through the tree to this node, we might reduce our costs and increase our yield substantially.

It's interesting to see that of the 479 potential predictor variables, 2 of the top 3 variables selected by the decision tree algorithm involve past giving history rather than demographics. *RFA_4* is a summary of past giving and *LASTGIFT* measures the amount of the last gift. *HVP1* is a demographic variable, measuring the percentage of residents in the donor's ZIP code whose homes are worth at least $200,000. By letting the tree grow further, I've increased the list of potential predictors to the top 20 (see Figure 21.4). Notice that most of the important variables involve past giving of the donors and a few key demographic variables about the donor's neighborhood. I suggest we look at the data only for those 20 variables and spend some time visualizing these variables and assessing data quality and dealing with missing data issues before proceeding with more model building.

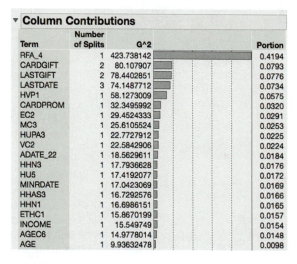

▼ Column Contributions

Term	Number of Splits	G^2		Portion
RFA_4	1	423.738142		0.4194
CARDGIFT	2	80.107907		0.0793
LASTGIFT	2	78.4402851		0.0776
LASTDATE	3	74.1487712		0.0734
HVP1	1	58.1273009		0.0575
CARDPROM	1	32.3495992		0.0320
EC2	1	29.4524333		0.0291
MC3	1	25.6105524		0.0253
HUPA3	1	22.7727912		0.0225
VC2	1	22.5842906		0.0224
ADATE_22	1	18.5629611		0.0184
HHN3	1	17.7936628		0.0176
HU5	1	17.4192077		0.0172
MINRDATE	1	17.0423069		0.0169
HHAS3	1	16.7292576		0.0166
HHN1	1	16.6986151		0.0165
ETHC1	1	15.8670199		0.0157
INCOME	1	15.549749		0.0154
AGEC6	1	14.9778014		0.0148
AGE	1	9.93632478		0.0098

FIGURE 21.4   The 20 most important predictor variables from a large tree model. Notice that the top 4 account for nearly two thirds of the total variable importance and all involve past donor giving.

*How Big (or Deep) Should the Tree Be?

If we continue to split the data enough times, eventually each data point will be in its own cell and the tree will fit the data "perfectly," a classic example of overfitting. Splitting only once is likely to underfit the data. So, what's the right compromise? Although there are some theoretical criteria that attempt (like adjusted R^2) to choose the right size, cross-validation is usually a good way, in practice, to answer the question. Here's an example using 30% of the data as a hold out on the PVA data:

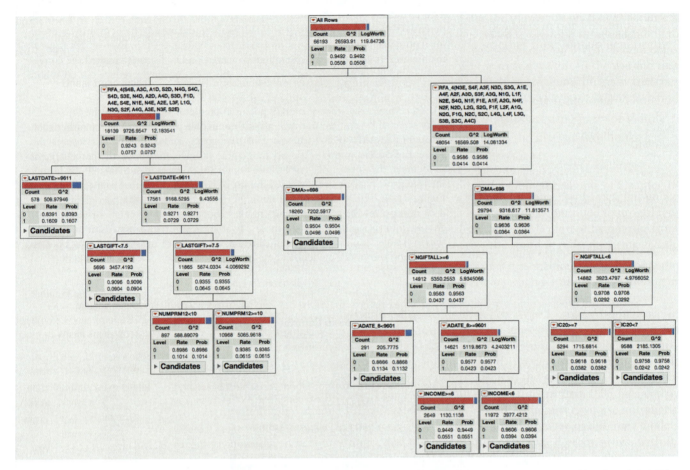

FIGURE 21.5   With a random 30% of the data as hold out, the tree algorithm found that this size tree, using 70% of the data as training to fit the model, had the best performance on the remaining 30% test set. The criterion used was based on the number of misclassifications—predicting that someone would respond to the solicitation when they didn't and vice versa. (Source: Created with JMP® 13 Pro software. Copyright 2016, SAS Institute, Cary, NC, USA. All Rights Reserved. Reproduced with permission of SAS Institute, Inc, Cary, NC.)

Exploring the tree by splitting by hand (as the analyst did in the In Practice 21.2) can be a useful way to *explore* the data, but some sort of cross-validation should always be used to avoid overfitting.

JUST CHECKING

The vice president is interested in using a tree model to predict the likelihood that a customer will sign up for the IRA offer recently sent out by the bank. She has a few questions.

11 When we run the tree model, will it automatically find the best combination of variables to predict the sign-up probability?

12 Last year we used a logistic regression to predict a similar sign-up probability. Will the tree perform better?

13 We have a few customers with very high incomes that proved to be a problem for logistic regression because of their high impact. We had to take them out of the model and treat them separately. How will the tree deal with them?

Neural Networks

Another popular data mining tool is the multilayer perceptron or (artificial) **neural network**. This algorithm sounds more impressive than it really is. Although it was inspired by models that tried to mimic the function of the brain, it's really just an automatic, flexible, non-linear regression model. The neural network, like multiple regression, models the response variable with a function of the predictor variables but, unlike multiple regression, the functions are not linear. They are more closely related to the smoothing functions you saw back in Chapter 20. And unlike stepwise regression, the neural network retains all the predictors, even if some of them have little effect on the response.

Because the "network" is made up by adding together many small non-linear functions, the equation that predicts the response is uninterpretable and results in what's called a **black box** model. That's a major disadvantage for many applications. In multiple regression, the fitted model shows how each predictor influences the response. In a tree, the splits show the role of each predictor as you move down the tree. Sometimes, however, a black box model is acceptable. For example, if the neural network can correctly distinguish the digits of a hand-written ZIP code on a random letter with high accuracy, the US Postal Service might not really care how it's doing it. But, if a neural network determined that you are not qualified for a student loan, you'd probably want to know why—something that would be hard to tell from a black box model!

The basic idea of a neural network is to first create new functions (called **nodes** or **features**) from the original predictors. These nodes are just linear combinations (weighted averages) of the original predictors. The weights used are similar to coefficients in a linear regression. The collection of these new functions is called the **hidden layer**. The reason they are called hidden is that the response, *y*, is not used directly to estimate the weights. The fitting is done by a computationally intensive method, the most common of which is called **back propagation**. The hidden functions are then transformed by an S-shaped curve (like the one you saw in logistic regression) and are given the colorful name **sigmoidal activation functions** (which really just means S-shaped curve!). Finally, the response is fit by a regression on these transformed functions. If the response is quantitative, the regression is linear. If it's categorical, then another sigmoid is applied to model the probability of belonging to each class. The fact that the nodes are transformed using a non-linear function gives the model its flexibility—and the ability to approximate a wide variety of phenomena.

FIGURE 21.6 A neural network to predict *Shirt Size* from various other body measurements. The network has 3 nodes in the hidden layer. The S symbol indicates that the network is using sigmoidal activation functions.

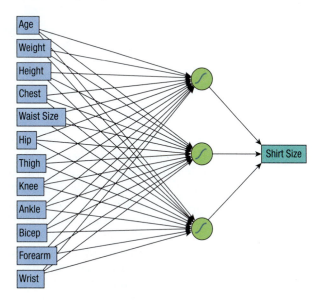

A diagram of such a network with three nodes in the hidden layer is shown in Figure 21.6. In this example, a shirt manufacturer wants to predict a man's shirt size (to the nearest half inch) from his other measurements (data in **Shirt sizes full**). Various methods are employed to ensure that the model doesn't overfit the data, and the final model is chosen by cross-validation.

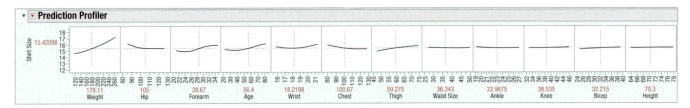

FIGURE 21.7 The profiler in JMP® shows the influence of each predictor variable on *Shirt Size*. The neural network model is nearly linear in *Weight*, and somewhat curved in the next few variables. The last few have relatively little effect on the response. (Source: Created with JMP® 13 Pro software. Copyright 2016, SAS Institute, Cary, NC, USA. All Rights Reserved. Reproduced with permission of SAS Institute, Inc, Cary, NC.)

Although the model is, in general, uninterpretable, there are some implementations of neural networks that provide insight into the effect of the predictors by profiling the effect of each predictor using sensitivity curves and measuring the importance of the predictors. Figure 21.7 shows the profile of predictor influences on *Shirt Size* (measured in inches), with a listing of variable importance as produced by JMP® (Table 21.2).

TABLE 21.2 The Summary Report shows numerical values for the relative importance of each predictor. *Weight* is by far the most important predictor of *Shirt Size*, accounting for more than half of the predictive power of the model. The model reports an R^2 of 0.69 on the training set and higher on the test set. (This increase is probably just an anomaly, but it at least indicates that the model is not overfit.)

Summary Report

Column	Main Effect	Total Effect	.2 .4 .6 .8
Weight	0.432	0.557	
Hip	0.069	0.187	
Forearm	0.049	0.157	
Age	0.019	0.151	
Wrist	0.033	0.132	
Chest	0.011	0.086	
Thigh	0.029	0.069	
Waist Size	0.012	0.051	
Ankle	0.013	0.043	
Knee	0.008	0.03	
Bicep	0.008	0.022	
Height	0.003	0.01	

Crossvalidation

Source	RSquare	RASE	Freq
Training Set	0.6911	0.48978	186
Validation Set	0.7641	0.50461	37
Test Set	0.8702	0.30148	25

This model was fit using 75% of the data for training and 10% for testing (out of 250 cases). Another 15% was set aside as a "tuning set." We specified 3 hidden nodes and used the tuning set to select the best model. Table 21.2 shows the performance on each set. On the training data, the model reports an R^2 of 0.69, and the model actually fit the test set best, but this is probably an anomaly.

When the R^2 on the test set is much lower than the R^2 on the training set, this usually indicates overfitting. When the performance is approximately the same, it doesn't necessarily indicate a powerful model, but at least it's evidence that the model is not overfitting. When the model actually performs best on the test set (data that it hasn't seen) it's probably just random noise. Models in general perform best on the data on which they are fit (or trained).

The language used to describe neural network models and the method of estimating their parameters is colorful and designed to make you think of the way the human brain works. Don't be fooled. The model is really just a flexible function fitter and the network doesn't "learn" any more (or less) than any other statistical model. If you applied these terms to multiple regression, the intercept and slopes would be called weights. The act of fitting the regression to a set of training data would be called training the network, or "learning." The resulting predictions would be called knowledge. A glossary of terms is given in Table 21.3.

Glossary	
Neural network	A non-linear regression model using transformed linear combinations of the predictors to predict the response
Weight	A coefficient in the neural network model
Back propagation	A computational method for estimating all the weights in the model
Hidden node	A linear combination of the original predictor variables
Sigmoidal activation function	An S-shaped curve used to transform the hidden "nodes"
Training and learning	Colorful names for the process of estimating the coefficients of the model from a set of training data
Knowledge	The output from the model—really just the predictions
Deep learning	A neural network with more than one hidden layer

TABLE 21.3 A glossary of some of the most common terms used in neural networks.

In the 1980s some mathematical theorems were proved that showed that neural networks can approximate nearly any function (with enough data). They also showed that one hidden layer (with enough nodes) is all that is needed. In spite of this, some researchers have put a lot of effort into studying multi-layer networks. One of these research groups won an image recognition contest in 2012 with an algorithm that was twice as accurate as the runner-up. These multi-layer networks now go by the name **deep learning**, continuing the trend in making fanciful names that sound like they are doing more than they are.

JUST CHECKING

Our vice president is back with a couple of questions.

14 Because the neural network thinks like a human, it will be the best model that we can run, correct?

15 A customer who had a very high probability of taking our offer, as predicted by the neural network, didn't. Can the neural network tell us why?

21.4 Models Built from Combining Other Models

Many other algorithms besides trees and neural networks are used by data miners, and new ones are being developed all the time. Typically, a data miner will build several different models, test them in various ways, and then simply select one to use based on a combination of the best performance and other criteria like interpretability. Or, the data miner might decide to average several models. For a classification problem, the "average" prediction for a case might actually be the "mode"—the class that's predicted most often by all the models under consideration. For a regression problem, the prediction might be the average or a weighted average of the predictions of all the models. Averaging models provides protection against choosing the "wrong" model, but usually at a cost of not being able to interpret the resulting predictions. Finding the best ways to combine many different models is an active and exciting area of current research in data mining. We'll discuss a few of these ideas in this section.

In recent years, research has focused on combining many versions of similar models. Imagine you're a CEO or president who needs to make a decision. You assemble your advisors, listen to each, and then combine their opinions in some way to make a final choice. The most common methods of combining models are called **bagging** and **boosting**. Each of these methods creates "committees" of models. In bagging (short for **b**ootstrap **agg**regat**ing**), you fit a model (say, a tree) to the training data. Then you take a bootstrap sample of the data (see Chapter 11) and fit another tree. Repeat this a large number of times (say, 1000). Now use the average prediction (or most frequent class) as the prediction for each case in the test set. Boosting is more technical, but one way to think about it for classification is to fit a small model (for example, a tree with just 2 or 3 splits) to the training data. Now, give more weight to the cases that were misclassified, and create another tree. Repeat this over and over, each time giving more weight to the misclassified cases. The later trees will fit the harder cases better (and the easier cases perhaps less well). Now average all the trees by their overall performance. In principle, you can use bagging and boosting for nearly any model, but commonly trees are used.

Random Forests

Perhaps the most common version of bagged trees is the **random forest**. The random forest creates trees on many bootstrapped samples of the training data and then averages them, but with one important wrinkle. Every time each tree looks for a split, it does so on only a small random sample of the predictors (often 10%). This seems counterintuitive. For example, suppose that only 10 or so of the nearly 500 predictors in the PVA data are important. If we restrict each split to only 50 randomly chosen predictors each time, there's a good chance that none of those 10 will be in the sample and the tree will make a uninformative split. But it turns out that that doesn't really hurt performance. In fact, it provides a richer set of trees that seem to find more signal in the data than simply bagging lots of trees.

Continuing our *Shirt Size* example, here is the output of a random forest of 100 trees fit to the training data (Table 21.4) and the profiler, showing the effect of the predictors (Figure 21.8).

TABLE 21.4 The Column Contributions show the relative importance of each predictor. The order is quite different than the order produced by the neural network, although both models claim to fit the test set fairly well.

▼ Column Contributions

Term	Number of Splits	SS		Portion
Chest	32	16.2302808		0.2282
Forearm	31	11.4753715		0.1613
Weight	29	10.4729397		0.1472
Wrist	31	7.70337005		0.1083
Waist Size	28	6.04566438		0.0850
Hip	25	5.81539012		0.0818
Bicep	26	5.36643865		0.0754
Knee	29	2.7386453		0.0385
Thigh	18	2.02304012		0.0284
Ankle	27	1.42607054		0.0200
Age	26	1.27974214		0.0180
Height	16	0.55646824		0.0078

	RSquare	RMSE	N
Training	0.811	0.3835496	186
Validation	0.686	0.5820115	37
Test	0.773	0.3985855	25

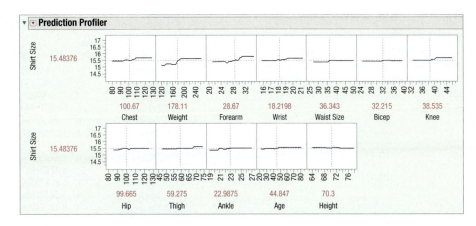

FIGURE 21.8 The profiler for the random forest shows a typical pattern for tree-based models, with sharp step-like increases for *Shirt Size* at various levels of the predictors. (Source: Created with JMP® 13 Pro software. Copyright 2016, SAS Institute, Cary, NC, USA. All Rights Reserved. Reproduced with permission of SAS Institute, Inc, Cary, NC.)

The random forest fit an R^2 of 0.811 on the training set and then slightly lower (0.773) on the test set (Table 21.4). Although it is a somewhat automatic method, performance can often be improved by optimizing some of the parameters (number of trees fit, percentage of predictors chosen at each split, size of each tree, and so on). Notice also that the random forest used the predictors quite differently than the neural network did, placing more importance on *Chest* and *Forearm* size and less on *Waist Size*. It's important to remember that these models are sensitive to the training data that were selected as well as some random aspects of their fitting. Large differences between data mining models can provide insights into the phenomenon being studied, or they can be an indication that the models are fitting noise as well as signal. It is always wise to be cautious in putting too much faith in a model that is automatically fit, especially on a "found" set of data.

Boosted Trees

Trees can also be boosted, and the resulting ensemble (set) of trees is usually a more powerful predictor than a single tree. Of course, like any ensemble, it's much less interpretable, especially compared to the simple structure of a tree. The random forest creates an ensemble by fitting trees on different bootstrap samples of the dataset. The boosted tree does not resample the data, but fits a *sequence* of trees on the original sample. However, after the first tree, it gives more importance (weight) to the cases that were predicted badly. So the next tree focuses more on the hard-to-predict cases. At each stage, the misclassified cases are upweighted so that later trees focus on repeatedly misclassified cases. These later trees may not do as well overall on classifying the data, but they may perform better on the hard-to-predict cases. The final model averages the predictions from all the trees, with more weight given to the trees that do best overall. Boosting can be applied to a variety of models, and the resulting ensemble often outperforms a single model.

The boosted tree on the *Shirt Size* data gave the summary in Table 21.5 and the profiler in Figure 21.9. The model produces the typical step functions of a tree, as one can see in the profiler. In contrast to the random forest, however, the importance it gives to the variables is similar to that given by the neural network. Its performance on the test set ($R^2 = 0.792$) falls between the two previous models.

TABLE 21.5 The Column Contributions show that the boosted tree agrees with the neural network that *Weight* is the most important predictor. Its performance is quite consistent with an R^2 on the test set of 0.792, close to the training set R^2 of 0.834.

▼ **Column Contributions**

Term	Number of Splits	SS		Portion
Weight	23	315.348009		0.4973
Wrist	19	79.3915553		0.1252
Waist Size	15	77.6304535		0.1224
Forearm	26	61.5933939		0.0971
Chest	16	47.27591		0.0746
Bicep	4	13.0290865		0.0205
Ankle	12	11.016775		0.0174
Thigh	9	7.89480506		0.0124
Age	10	6.37984947		0.0101
Hip	7	5.90129527		0.0093
Height	4	4.94421839		0.0078
Knee	5	3.73171268		0.0059

▼ **Overall Statistics**

	RSquare	RMSE	N
Training	0.834	0.3589126	186
Validation	0.717	0.5529333	37
Test	0.792	0.3814433	25

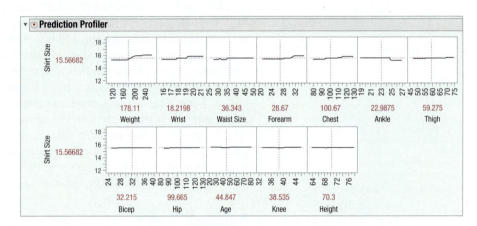

FIGURE 21.9 The profiler for the boosted tree shows the same typical pattern for tree-based models with sharp step-like increases for *Shirt Size* at various levels of the predictors. (Source: Created with JMP® 13 Pro software. Copyright 2016, SAS Institute, Cary, NC, USA. All Rights Reserved. Reproduced with permission of SAS Institute, Inc, Cary, NC.)

JUST CHECKING

And . . .

16 Which of the 1000 trees that the Random Forest uses is the best? Can we look at it?

17 When we classified people into "Likely to buy" and "Not likely to buy," using a Boosted Tree we got a 20% error rate on the training set, but a 50% error on the test set. What's the likely cause of that?

21.5 Comparing Models

Usually there is no way of knowing which of many models will predict best on future data. Choosing a model (or models) requires judgment. If several models perform about equally well, one might be preferred on the basis of scientific or other domain knowledge. Performance measures for quantitative responses include

R^2 on the test set (defined earlier) and the **RASE or RMSE (square root of averaged squared prediction error or root mean squared error)** on the test set, which is the same as the residual standard deviation that we saw in multiple regression (except that it's evaluated on the test set).

For categorical responses, there is always a trade-off between Type I and Type II errors. A graphical display called an ROC curve[11] can often help compare models over a range of choices. This display shows the trade-off between Power and Type I error over a range of possible error rates.

These measures (in addition to business knowledge) can help guide researchers in choosing the "best" model. Sometimes, however, there is no reason to prefer one over another and the analyst might be just as happy to average the predictions from all of them. This average can be a simple arithmetic average of each prediction, or a weighted average, or the predictions from various models can even be used as inputs to another neural network, which will then optimize a function of them based on other training data. In the next Guided Example, we will display all the models we have just discussed for *Shirt Size* and compare them to a simple multiple regression.

GUIDED EXAMPLE   Model Comparisons

Let's return to the problem of estimating a man's shirt size (inches around the neck to the nearest half inch) from other body measurements.

PLAN	**Define** the problem—state the objective of the study. Identify the variables. If reasonable, plot the variables and look for relationships among the variables, outliers and other interesting features.	We want to build and compare several models to predict *Shirt Size* from other body measurements. The available variables on men from a scientific study include:

Age	(yr)
Weight	(lb)
Height	(in.)
Chest	(cm)
Waist	(in.)
Hip	(cm)
Thigh	(cm)
Knee	(cm)
Ankle	(cm)
Bicep	(cm)
Forearm	(cm)
Wrist	(cm)
Shirt Size	(nearest half in.)

(continued)

---

[11]Originally called receiver operating characteristic (ROC) curves, they plot the true positive rate (TPR) against the false positive rate (FPR) for all values between 0 and 1. The TPR is equivalent to the Power (the probability of correctly classifying a positive) and the FRP is the probability of a Type I error (probability of misclassifying a negative).

If there are too many variables to display, running an exploratory model such as a tree can help select the most important variables, which can then be displayed.

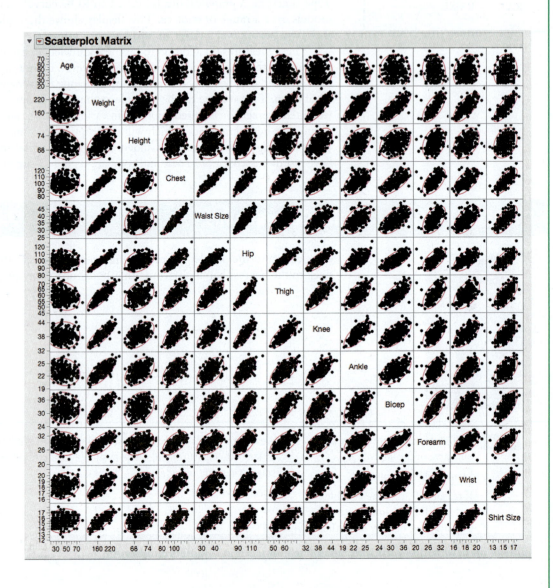

There are many strong, nearly linear relationships among the variables. In particular, most of the measurements (except *Age*) seem to have a positive linear relationship with *Shirt Size*, which makes sense. Men who are larger, heavier, and taller tend to have larger shirt sizes. There are no obvious outliers.

DO   **Mechanics** Fit a stepwise multiple regression model, starting with all the predictors and their interactions.

Here is the computer output for the stepwise multiple regression, starting with all 13 predictor variables and their interactions, and proceeding forward until no more candidates were nominated for exclusion.

```
Dependent variable is: Shirt Size
R-squared = 69.1%  R-squared (adjusted) = 68.1%
s = 0.499 with 186 − 7 = 179 degrees of freedom
```

Term	Estimate	Std Error	t-Ratio	Prob > |t|
Intercept	13.34017106	2.02415021	6.59	<0.0001
Weight	0.032632385	0.005077533	6.43	<0.0001
Height	−0.04587073	0.017441901	−2.63	0.0093
Hip	−0.044188241	0.016614473	−2.66	0.0085
Ankle	−0.109697048	0.041553449	−2.64	0.009
Forearm	0.047588487	0.024155895	1.97	0.0504
Wrist	0.278018404	0.063206759	4.4	<0.0001

The estimated equation is:

$Shirt\ Size = 13.34 + 0.033\ Weight − 0.046\ Height − 0.044\ Hip − 0.110\ Ankle + 0.048\ Forearm + 0.278\ Wrist$

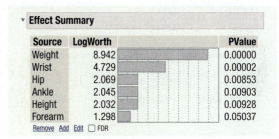

Effect Summary

Source	LogWorth		PValue
Weight	8.942		0.00000
Wrist	4.729		0.00002
Hip	2.069		0.00853
Ankle	2.045		0.00903
Height	2.032		0.00928
Forearm	1.298		0.05037

Remove Add Edit ☐ FDR

Crossvalidation

Source	RSquare	RASE	Freq
Training Set	0.6911	0.48978	186
Validation Set	0.7641	0.50461	37
Test Set	0.8702	0.30148	25

Variable importance shows that *Weight* and *Wrist* size are the most important predictors. The model gets an R^2 of 0.691 on the training set and a surprisingly high 0.870 on the test set.

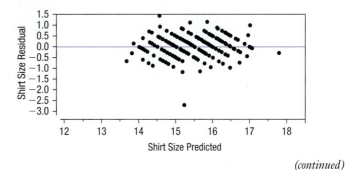

(continued)

The residual plot shows one case with a low residual, but without large influence on the model. Other than the striped pattern because the shirt sizes are discrete (every half inch), the plot is patternless.

Fit a tree, neural network, random forest, and boosted tree.

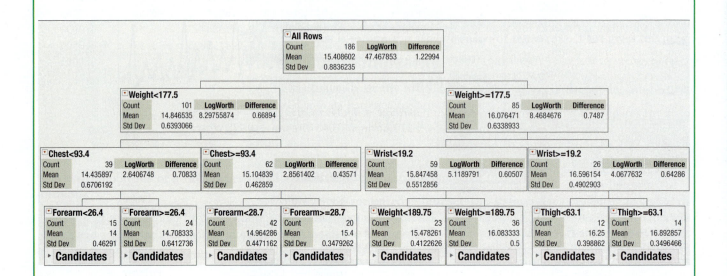

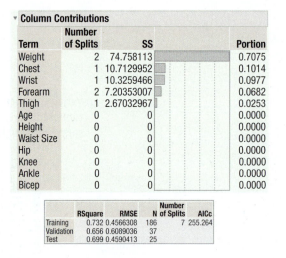

The tree fits less well on the test set than the multiple regression, with an R^2 of 0.699 on the test set. The most important variable is *Weight*, followed by *Chest* size. *Wrist*, second in the multiple regression, is third here.

Results for the neural network, random forest, and boosted tree are found in the previous section. Here is a summary of all 5 models and their performance on the test set:

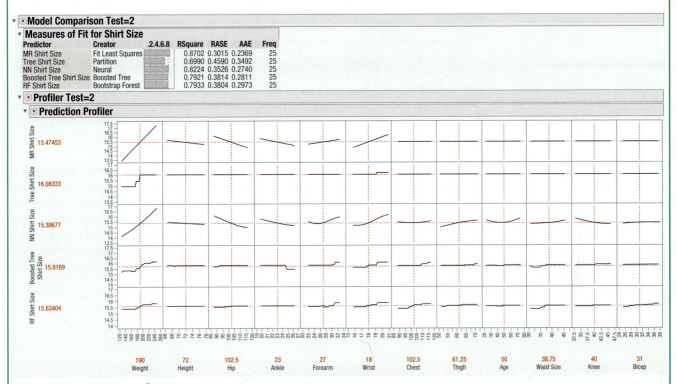

Model Comparison Test=2						
Measures of Fit for Shirt Size						
Predictor	Creator	.2.4.6.8	RSquare	RASE	AAE	Freq
MR Shirt Size	Fit Least Squares		0.8702	0.3015	0.2369	25
Tree Shirt Size	Partition		0.6990	0.4590	0.3492	25
NN Shirt Size	Neural		0.8224	0.3526	0.2740	25
Boosted Tree Shirt Size	Boosted Tree		0.7921	0.3814	0.2811	25
RF Shirt Size	Bootstrap Forest		0.7933	0.3804	0.2973	25

Source: Created with JMP® 13 Pro software. Copyright 2016, SAS Institute, Cary, NC, USA. All Rights Reserved. Reproduced with permission of SAS Institute, Inc, Cary, NC.

REPORT **Summary and present** your conclusions.

Summarize your results and state any limitations of your model in the context of your original objectives.

MEMO

Re: Models for shirt size prediction

Five models for *shirt size* were fit to a training set and predicted on a small test set of 25 randomly chosen cases. The models included multiple regression, a decision tree, a neural network, a random forest, and a boosted tree.

The models were similar in finding that *Weight* and *Wrist* size are important predictors. *Chest*, *Hip*, and *Forearm* size also appeared important in some models to a lesser degree. *Weight* and *Waist* size are positively related to *Shirt Size*, but because of collinearity with those variables in the model, *Hip* size is negatively related. Most of the predictors are roughly linear with *Shirt Size*, which helps to explain why a multiple linear regression was competitive with more flexible models.

All of the models gave R^2 values on the test set between 0.70 and 0.87, with the multiple regression highest and the tree lowest. The RASE averaged about 0.38 inch, which means that, roughly, we can predict a typical men's shirt size to within about 0.75 inch (2*0.38), which is about a size and a half. This may not be accurate enough for remote fitting. We recommend that the man try on the shirt for best fit.

21.6   Summary

There are many similarities between the modeling process of data mining and the basic approach to modeling that you've been learning throughout this text. What makes data mining different really has to do with the large number of algorithms and types of models available to the data miner and with the size and complexity of the datasets. But most of what makes a data mining project successful would make any statistical analysis successful. The same principles of understanding and exploring variables and their relationships are key to both processes. A famous statistician, Jerry Friedman, was once asked if there was a difference between statistics and data mining. Before answering, he asked if the questioner wanted the long answer or the short answer. Because the response was "the short answer," Jerry said simply, "No." We never got to hear the long answer, but we suspect it may have contained some of the differences discussed in this chapter.

Having a good set of statistical and data analysis tools is a great beginning to becoming a successful data miner. Being willing to learn new techniques, whether they come from statistics, computer science, machine learning, or other disciplines, is essential. Learning to work with other people whose skills complement yours not only will make the task more pleasant but also is key to a successful data mining project. The need to understand the information contained in large databases will increase in the years ahead, so it will continue to be important to know about this rapidly growing field.

⊘ WHAT CAN GO WRONG?

- **Be sure that the question to be answered is specific.** Make sure that the business question to be addressed is specific enough so that a model can help to answer it. A goal as vague as "improving the business" is not likely to lead to a successful data mining project.

- **Be sure that the data have the potential to answer the question.** Check the variables to see whether a model can reasonably be built to predict the response. For example, if you want to know which type of customers are going to a particular web page, make sure that data are being collected that link the web page to the customer visiting the site.

- **Beware of overfitting to the data.** Because data mining tools are powerful and because the datasets used to train them are usually large, it is easy to think you're fitting the data well. Make sure you validate the model on a test set—a dataset not used to fit the model.

- **Make sure that the data are ready to use in the data mining model.** Typically, data warehouses contain data from several different sources. It's important to confirm that variables with the same name actually measure the same thing in two different databases. Missing values, incorrect entries, and different time scales are all challenges to be overcome before the data can be used in the model-building phase.

- **Don't try it alone.** Data mining projects require a variety of skills and a lot of work. Assembling the right team of people to carry out the effort is crucial.

ETHICS IN ACTION

With U.S. consumers becoming more environmentally conscious, there has been an explosion of eco-friendly products on the market. One notable entry has been the gas-electric hybrid car.

A large nonprofit environmental group would like to target customers likely to purchase hybrid cars in the future with a message expressing the urgency to do so sooner rather than later. They understand that direct mailings are very effective in this regard, but staying true to their environmental concerns, they want to avoid doing a nontargeted mass mailing.

The executive team met to discuss the possibility of using data mining to help identify their target audience. The initial discussion revolved around data sources. Although they have several databases on demographics and transactional information for consumers who have purchased green products and donated to organizations that promote sustainability, someone suggested that they get data on contributions to political parties. After all, there was a Green Party, and Democrats tend to be more concerned about environmental issues than Republicans. Another member of the team was genuinely surprised that this was even possible. She wondered how ethical it is to use information about individuals that they may assume is being kept confidential.

- **Identify the ethical dilemma in this scenario.**
- **What are the undesirable consequences?**
- **Propose an ethical solution that considers the welfare of all stakeholders.**

CHAPTER

21 FROM LEARNING TO EARNING

LEARNING OBJECTIVES

Understand the uses and value of data mining in business.

Recognize data mining approaches.

- OLAP approaches answer specific questions about data in a database that may involve many variables.
- Predictive model approaches build complex models that attempt to predict a response.

Be aware that data preparation is essential to sound data mining.

- Data must be cleaned of errors and impossible or implausible values.
- Missing values may be a serious issue.
- Data preparation may take the majority of time and effort devoted to a data mining project.

Be able to articulate the goal of a data mining project and understand that data mining efforts differ according to the kind of dependent variable.

- When the goal is to predict a quantitative response, the problem is called a regression problem.
- When the goal is to classify individuals according to a categorical variable, the problem is called a classification problem.

Be aware of the variety of models and algorithms that are used to build predictive models.

- Tree models build interpretable models that select predictor variables and split points to best predict the response in either a regression or classification problem.
- Neural networks build black box models that use all the predictor variables for both regression and classification problems.
- Many other data mining algorithms such as random forests, boosting and ensemble methods that combine models are used as well, and new competitors are continually being developed.

Understand that successful data mining is a team effort that requires a variety of skills.

- Defining the problem and objective of interest is crucial for success.
- The CRISP data mining process provides a good outline for a data mining project.

TERMS

Algorithm	A set of instructions used for calculation and data processing. The algorithm specifies how the model is built from the data.
Back propogation	A computational method for estimating the weights in the neural network model.
Bagging	Abbreviation for B(ootstrap) agg(regat)ing a model. For any model, take a bootstrap sample and refit the model. Repeat this many times and use the average of all the models as the prediction.
Big Data	The collection and analysis of datasets so large and complex that traditional methods typically brought to bear on the problem would be overwhelmed.
Black box	A model whose equation is either hidden or so complicated that it is impossible to interpret. Examples include neural networks and random forests.
Boosting	A process of taking a simple model, fitting it to a set of data, and then using the results of that model to build a new model, putting more emphasis on the values that were predicted poorly.
Business analytics (or analytics or predictive analytics)	The process of using statistical analysis and modeling to make predictions and drive business decisions.
Classification problem	A prediction problem that involves a categorical response variable. (See also regression problem.)
Cluster analysis	A task of grouping similar objects (rows) based on their values of a set of variables.
Data mining	A process that uses a variety of data analysis tools to discover patterns and relationships in data that are useful for making predictions.
Data preparation	The process of cleaning data and checking its accuracy prior to modeling. Data preparation includes investigating missing values, correcting wrong and inconsistent entries, and reconciling data definitions.
Data warehouse	A digital repository for several large databases.
Decision tree (data mining version)	A model that predicts either a categorical or quantitative response in which the branches represent variable splits and the terminal nodes provide the predicted value.
Deep learning	A term often used to describe a neural network with more than one hidden layer.
Demographic variable	A variable containing information about a customer's personal characteristics or the characteristics of the region in which the customer lives. Commonly used demographics include age, income, race, and education.
Feature (and feature creation)	A variable in a machine learning model. Feature creation implies that a new variable has been created.
Hidden node (hidden layer)	A linear combination of the original predictor variables used to predict the response (sometimes called a latent feature or variable). The ensemble of hidden nodes is called the hidden layer.
Hold out (or test) set	The dataset used in a supervised classification or regression problem not used to build the predictive model. This datset is withheld (held out) from the model building stage of the process, and the model's predictions on the test set are used to evaluate the model performance.
Knowledge	The insights gained from the model and its predictions.
Learning	The process of estimating the parameters of the model.
Machine learning	The name given to a collection of models that are heavily computational and often black box models. Neural networks and random forests are common machine learning algorithms or models.
Metadata	Information about the data including when and where the data were collected.
Neural network	A model based on analogies with human brain processing that uses combinations of predictor variables and non-linear regression to predict either a categorical or quantitative response variable.
Node	The variables in a neural network model, including the variables in the "hidden" layer are referred to as nodes. The variables in the first hidden layer are linear combinations of the original variables.
Online analytical processing (OLAP)	An approach for providing answers to queries that typically involve many variables simultaneously.

Predictive model	A model that provides predictions for the response variable.
Random forest	A model built by bagging a set of trees, with the added restriction that only a small random subset of predictors are used at each split of each tree.
Regression problem	A prediction problem that has a quantitative response variable. (See classification problem.)
Sigmoidal activation function	An S-shaped curve used to transform the hidden "nodes." The logistic function from logistic regression is one of the most common activation functions.
Supervised problem	A classification or regression problem in which the analyst is given a set of data for which the response is known to use to build a model.
Terminal node	The final leaves of a decision tree where the predictions for the response variable are found.
Test set	The dataset used in a supervised classification or regression problem *not used* to build the predictive model. The test set is withheld from the model-building stage of the process, and the model's predictions on the test set are used to evaluate the model performance.
Training	Fitting a model, usually from a training set.
Training set	The dataset used in a supervised classification or regression problem to build the predictive model.
Transactional data	Data describing an event involving a transaction, usually an exchange of money for goods or services.
Unsupervised problem	A problem, unlike classification or regression problems, with no response variable. The goal of an unsupervised problem is typically to put similar cases together into homogeneous groups or clusters.
Weight	A coefficient in the neural network model (a parameter of the model).

CHAPTER

21   EXERCISES

SECTION 21.1

1. Your manager is confused by Big Data. Explain what makes "big data" different than "data."

2. Your manager learned all about databases, and frequently makes queries such as: "What fraction of our customers who bought a product in the last six months are female and live within 5 miles of the store?" He says that he is data mining. Is he right? Explain.

SECTION 21.2

3. Your manager has read a couple of articles about data mining and artificial intelligence. He wants to use data mining to find the best customers. What would you suggest to structure this problem?

4. Is any one portion of the CRISP-DM more important than the others? Why?

SECTION 21.3

5. What are the advantages and disadvantages of using tree vs. neural network models?

6. Your manager wants to use the total accurate classification rate (percent of all cases properly classified) as the metric to evaluate the division's models. Is this a good idea? Why or why not?

SECTION 21.4

7. What are the pros and cons of combining multiple models to produce a prediction? Should we always combine models?

8. Your manager wants to just find and use "the best" model, but you have found that a combined model (boosting) is better. Explain why boosting might help, and why it may be better than trying to find "the best."

SECTION 21.5

9. Your manager asked you to fit many models to predict which customers will buy this holiday season. The firm is going to pick only one. What criteria would you recommend that the firm use to evaluate the various models and to compare them?

JUST CHECKING ANSWERS

1 Not a data mining problem. Too vague.

2 Not data mining. OLAP / Database query.

3 Data mining, unsupervised clustering.

4 Data mining, supervised, classification because Accept is dichotomous.

5 Yes, supervised regression.

6 Bad idea to have everyone from one department. Good solutions need people with business knowledge, too.

7 No. Need cleaning.

8 No. Need good data, and data mining is not magic.

9 Bad idea. First, problem is too vague. Second, even if the problem were exploratory, there are too many relationships, and some will look significant, even if they are not.

10 Depends on the business environment. Probably not.

11 Ambiguous. Some software will cross-validate by default.

12 Maybe.

13 Tree will handle with aplomb, because it essentially functions like a median, splitting in two parts.

14 Neural nets do not "think" at all, nor do they "think" like humans. They may or may not be a good choice of model.

15 No, in general, neural networks are "black boxes" and do not provide information about the basis of classification or prediction.

16 Not really.

17 Tree is overfitting, and fitting the noise is not helpful.

Answers

CHAPTER 1
SECTION EXERCISE ANSWERS

1. a) Each row represents a different house. It is a case.
   b) There are 7 variables including the house identifier.

3. a) House_ID is an identifier (categorical, not ordinal). Neighborhood is categorical (nominal). Mail_ZIP is categorical (nominal – ordinal in a sense, but only on a national level). Acres is quantitative (units – acres). Yr_Built is quantitative (units – year). Full_Market_Value is quantitative (units – dollars). Size is quantitative (units – square feet).
   b) These data are cross-sectional. All variables were measured at about the same time.

5. It is not clear if the data were obtained from a survey. They are certainly not from an experiment. Most likely they are just a collection of recent sales. We don't know if those sales are representative of all sales, so we should be cautious in drawing conclusions from these data about the housing market in general.

CHAPTER EXERCISE ANSWERS

7. Answers will vary.

9. *Who*—college students; *What*—2025 opinion and whether they'd purchase an electric vehicle; *When*—current; *Where*—your location; *Why*—Automobile manufacturer wants college student opinions; *How*—survey; *Variables*—There are 2 categorical variables. "Whether they'd purchase" is ordinal. The data are cross-sectional.

11. Answers will vary.

13. *Who*—MBA applicants at school in northeast U.S.; *What*—sex, age, whether or not they accepted, whether or not they attended, and the reasons; *When*—not specified; *Where*—school in the northeastern United States; *Why*—The researchers wanted to investigate any patterns in female acceptance and attendance; *How*—data obtained internally from admissions office; *Variables*—There are 5 variables. Sex, whether or not applicant accepted, whether or not applicant attended, and the reasons are all categorical variables; only age (years) of applicant is quantitative. The data are a cross-section.

15. *Who*—experiment volunteers; *What*—herbal cold remedy or sugar solution, and cold severity; *When*—not specified; *Where*—major pharmaceutical firm; *Why*—Scientists were testing the efficacy of a herbal compound on the severity of the common cold; *How*—The scientists set up an experiment; *Variables*—There are 2 variables. Type of treatment (herbal or sugar solution) is categorical, and severity rating is quantitative; *Concerns*—The severity of a cold seems subjective and difficult to quantify. Also, the scientists may feel pressure to report negative findings about the herbal product. The data are cross-sectional and from a designed experiment.

17. *Who*—vineyards; *What*—size of vineyard (possibly in acres), number of years in existence, state, varieties of grapes grown, average case price (probably in dollars), gross sales (probably in dollars), and percent profit; *When*—not specified; *Where*—not specified; *Why*—Business analysts hoped to provide information that would be helpful to producers of U.S. wines; *How*—not specified; *Variables*—There are 5 quantitative variables and 2 categorical variables. Size of vineyard, number of years in existence, average case price, gross sales, and percent profit are quantitative variables. State and variety of grapes grown are categorical variables. The data are a cross-section collected in a designed survey.

19. *Who*—every model of automobile in the United States; *What*—vehicle manufacturer, vehicle type, weight (probably in pounds), horsepower (in horsepower), and gas mileage (in miles per gallon) for city and highway driving; *When*—This information is collected currently; *Where*—United States; *Why*—The Environmental Protection Agency uses the information to track fuel economy of vehicles; *How*—The data are collected from the manufacturer of each model; *Variables*—There are 6 variables. City mileage, highway mileage, weight, and horsepower are quantitative variables. Manufacturer and type of car are categorical variables. The data are a cross-section.

21. *Who*—restaurants; *What*—% of customers liking restaurant, average meal cost ($), food rating (0–30), decor rating (0–30), service rating (0–30). *When*—current; *Where*—United States; *Why*—service to provide information for consumers; *How*—not specified; *Variables*—There are 5 variables. % liking and average cost are quantitative. Ratings (food, decor, and service) are ordered categories. The data are a cross-section.

23. *Who*—students in an MBA statistics class; *What*—total personal investment in stock market ($), number of different stocks held, total invested in mutual funds ($), and name of each mutual fund; *When*—not specified; *Where*—school in the northeastern United States; *Why*—The information was collected for use in classroom illustrations; *How*—An online survey was conducted. Presumably, participation was required for all

members of the class; *Variables*—There are 4 variables. Name of mutual fund is a categorical variable. Number of stocks held, total amount invested in market ($), and in mutual funds ($) are quantitative variables. The data are a cross-section.

25. *Who*—taxi rides in NYC; *What*—vendor ID, pickup time, dropoff time; number of passengers, trip distance, pickup longitude and latitude, dropoff longitude and latitude, fare amount, tip amount, toll amount, total amount; *Why*—It is interesting to look at the behavior of taxi riders; *How*—The New York City Taxi and Limousine Commission records the trips; *Variables*—There are 13 variables. Number of passengers, trip distance, pickup and dropoff longitude and latitude, fare amount, tip amount, toll amount, total amount, and the date and time of pickup are quantitative (but the dates could also be considered categorical).

27. Each row should be a single mortgage loan. Columns hold the Loan number (which identifies the rows), last 4 of SSN, borrower name, and amount.

29. Each row is a week. Columns hold week number (to identify the row), sales prediction, sales, and difference.

31. Cross-sectional.

33. Time series.

CHAPTER 2
SECTION EXERCISE ANSWERS

1. a) Frequency table:

None	AA	BA	MA	PhD
164	42	225	52	29

b) Relative frequency table (divide each number by 512 and multiply by 100):

None	AA	BA	MA	PhD
32.03%	8.20%	43.95%	10.16%	5.66%

3. a)

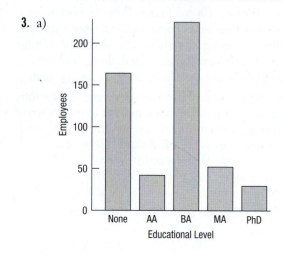

b)

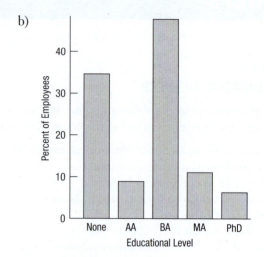

c)

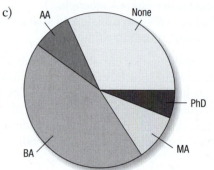

5. a) The vast majority of employees have either no college degree or a bachelor's degree (32% and 44%, respectively). About 10% have master's degrees, 8% have associate's degrees, and nearly 6% have PhDs.

b) I would not be comfortable generalizing this to any other division or company. These data were collected only from my division. Other companies might have vastly different educational distributions.

7. a)

	Totals
<1 Year	95
1–5 Years	205
More Than 5 Years	212

b) Yes

None	AA	BA	MA	PhD
164	42	225	52	29

9. a)

Percent	None	AA	BA	MA	PhD
<1 Year	6.1	7.1	22.2	38.5	41.4
1–5 Years	25.6	21.4	49.8	51.9	51.7
More Than 5 Years	68.3	71.4	28.0	9.6	6.9

b) No. The distributions look quite different. More than $2/3$ of those with no college degree have been with the company longer than 5 years, but almost none of the PhDs (less than 7%) have been there that long.

c)

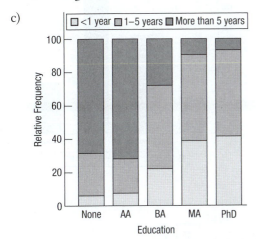

d) It's possible to see it in the table, but the stacked bar chart makes the differences much clearer.

e) A mosaic plot would display the different counts for each degree type. Areas of the plot representing each cell would then reflect the cell counts accurately.

CHAPTER EXERCISE ANSWERS

11. Answers will vary.

13. Answers will vary.

15. a) Yes, the categories divide a whole.
    b) Coca-Cola.

17. a) The pie chart does a better job of showing portions of a whole.
    b) There is no bar for "Other."

19. a) Yes, it is reasonable to assume that heart and respiratory disease caused approximately 38% of U.S. deaths in this year, since there is no possibility for overlap. Each person could only have one cause of death.
    b) Since the percentages listed add up to 73.7%, other causes must account for 26.3% of U.S. deaths.
    c) A bar graph or pie chart would be appropriate if a category for Other with 26.3% were added.

21. Cisco and Polycom are battling for first place in the Netherlands, and the remainder of the market is fragmented. A pie chart or bar chart would be appropriate.

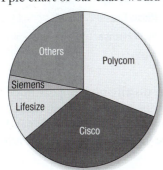

23. a) They don't total 100%. Others must have refused to answer or didn't know.
    b)

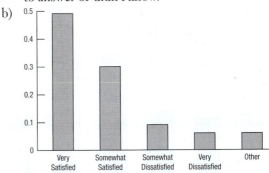

    c) Only if the "other" category were added.

25. The bar chart shows that Grounding and Collisions are the most common causes of oil spillage. It is possible to rank order the other causes as well. The pie chart is also acceptable as a display. The pie chart makes it easier to see that Grounding and Collisions make up around 60% of the total causes of spillage, but it is more difficult to figure out the relative size of various causes that are close, for example, Grounding vs. Collisions or Hull Failure vs. Fire/Explosion. To make comparisons of counts easy, use the bar chart; to showcase the causes of large oil spills as a fraction of all oil spills, use the pie chart.

27. a) 31%
    b) Because the bars do not start at zero, it looks like India's percentage is about 6 times as big, but in fact, it's not even twice as big.
    c) Start the percentages at 0% on the vertical axis, not 40%.
    d)

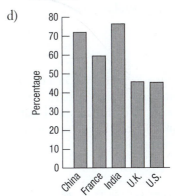

    e) The percentage of people who say that wealth is important to them is highest in China and India (around 70%), followed by France (around 60%) and then the United States and United Kingdom where the percentage was only about 45%.

29. a) They must be column percentages because the sums do not equal 100% across the rows and all the columns add to 100%.

b)
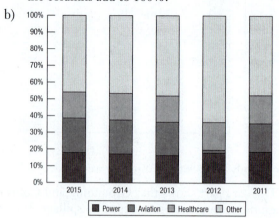

c) Over 50% of GE's revenue comes from the Power, Aviation, and Healthcare divisions, except in 2012, which seems to have had a massive collapse of revenue in Aviation. Other sources of revenue account for the balance of around 45% of revenue in a typical year.

31. a) 45.1%
b) 34.9%
c) 5.3%
d) 59.8%
e) 41.3%
f) 65.8%
g) Companies that reported a positive change on October 24 were more likely to report a negative change for the year than companies who reported a negative change on October 24.

33. a) 10%
b) 33.4%
c) 12.5%
d) Overall, the change was −71.0%. On a compound annual growth rate basis, this is −26.6% per year.
e) Answers may vary. Two things stand out—the numbers are rounded for 2012 and two numbers in 2014 and 2015 are identical.

35.

	R or NC-17	PG-13	PG	G
(a) Conditional on Action	44.1%	52.9%	2.9%	0.0%
(b) Conditional on PG-13	15.1%	21.8%	51.3%	11.8%

c) Depending on what you want to emphasize, either graph below is appropriate. Placing Genre on the x-axis emphasizes that Dramas are the most commonly made film. Placing MPAA Rating on the x-axis shows that R (or NC-17) movies are the most commonly made.

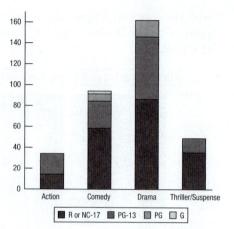

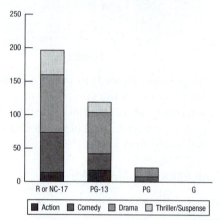

d) Genre and rating don't look independent. It appears that it is much more likely for a Drama or a Comedy to be rated PG than Action or Thriller. Similarly, Thriller/Suspense movies are more likely to be rated R.

37. a) 62.7%
b) 62.8%
c) 62.5%
d) 23.9% from Asia, 1.9% Europe, 7.8% Latin America, 3.7% Middle East, and 62.7% North America.
e) The column percentages are given in the table.

		MBA Program		
		Two-Yr	Evening	Total
	Asia	18.90	31.73	23.88
	Europe	3.05	0.00	1.87
Origin	**Latin America**	12.20	0.96	7.84
	Middle East	3.05	4.81	3.73
	North America	62.80	62.50	62.69
	Total	100.00	100.00	100.00

f) No. The distributions appear to be different. For example, the percentage from Latin America among those in Two-Year programs is nearly 12.2% while for those in Evening programs it is less than 1%.

39. a) 2.0%
    b) 2.5%
    c) 1.2%
    d) 20.0%
    e) 54.5%
    f) Here are row percentages:

		MPAA				
Row %	NC-17	R	PG-13	PG	G	Not Rated
Time Range 2006–2010	0.15	33.11	20.80	9.87	2.13	33.94
2011–2016	0.16	30.36	19.64	8.40	1.81	39.63

More movies were unrated in the later time period than earlier. However, of movies that were rated, the distributions are quite similar. There are slightly more R rated movies in the earlier time period, but this may be because makers of R rated movies choose instead to release them unrated in more recent times.

41. The study by the University of Texas Southwestern Medical Center provides evidence of an association between having a tattoo and contracting hepatitis C. Around 33% of the subjects who were tattooed in a commercial parlor had hepatitis C, compared with 13% of those tattooed elsewhere, and only 3.5% of those with no tattoo. If having a tattoo and having hepatitis C were independent, we would have expected these percentages to be roughly the same.

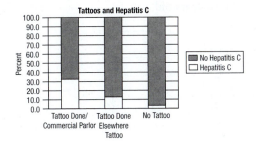

43. a) 51%
    b) Men are slightly higher, 54%.
    c) The distributions are similar, but slightly more men say that a high-paying job is "very" important, and slightly more women say that a high-paying job is "somewhat" important.

45. a)

	Caucasian	Hispanic	African-American	Other
Population	66.0%	16.0%	12.0%	6.0%
Moviegoers	63.0%	19.0%	12.0%	6.0%
Tickets	56.0%	26.0%	11.0%	7.0%

    b) The distributions of moviegoers are quite similar to the population as a whole, but Hispanics seem to buy proportionally more tickets and Caucasians fewer. Hispanics appear to go to the movies more often, on average, than Caucasians.

47. a) 53.0%
    b) 44.7%

49. a) The marginal totals have been added to the table:

	Hospital Size		
	Large	Small	Total
Procedure Major Surgery	120 of 800	10 of 50	130 of 850
Minor Surgery	10 of 200	20 of 250	30 of 450
Total	130 of 1000	30 of 300	160 of 1300

160 of 1300, or about 12.3% of the patients had a delayed discharge.

    b) Major surgery patients were delayed 15.3% of the time.
Minor surgery patients were delayed 6.7% of the time.

    c) Large hospital had a delay rate of 13%.
Small hospital had a delay rate of 10%.
The small hospital has the lower overall rate of delayed discharge.

    d) Large hospital: major surgery 15% and minor surgery 5%.
Small hospital: major surgery 20% and minor surgery 8%.
Even though the small hospital had the lower overall rate of delayed discharge, the large hospital had a lower rate of delayed discharge for each type of surgery.

    e) Yes. While the overall rate of delayed discharge is lower for the small hospital, the large hospital did better with *both* major surgery and minor surgery.

    f) The small hospital performs a higher percentage of minor surgeries than major surgeries. 250 of 300 surgeries at the small hospital were minor (83%). Only 200 of the large hospital's 1000 surgeries were minor (20%). Minor surgery had a lower delay rate than major surgery (6.7 to 15.3%), so the small hospital's overall rate was artificially inflated. The larger hospital is the better hospital when comparing discharge delay rates.

51. a) 1284 applicants were admitted out of a total of 3014 applicants. 1284/3014 = 42.6%

b) 1022 of 2165 (47.2%) of males were admitted. 262 of 849 (30.9%) of females were admitted.

		Males Accepted (of Applicants)	Females Accepted (of Applicants)	Total
Program	1	511 of 825	89 of 108	600 of 933
	2	352 of 560	17 of 25	369 of 585
	3	137 of 407	132 of 375	269 of 782
	4	22 of 373	24 of 341	46 of 714
	Total	1022 of 2165	262 of 849	1284 of 3014

c) Since there are four comparisons to make, the table shown below organizes the percentages of males and females accepted in each program. Females are accepted at a higher rate in every program.

Program	Males	Females
1	61.9%	82.4%
2	62.9%	68.0%
3	33.7%	35.2%
4	5.9%	7.0%

d) The comparison of acceptance rate within each program is most valid. The overall percentage is an unfair average. It fails to take the different numbers of applicants and different acceptance rates of each program. Women tended to apply to the programs in which gaining acceptance was difficult for everyone. This is an example of Simpson's Paradox.

CHAPTER 3
SECTION EXERCISE ANSWERS

1. a)
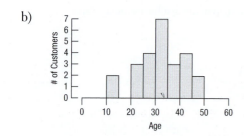

b)

c)
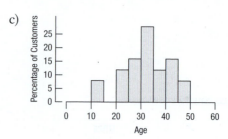

3. a) Unimodal
b) Around 35 years old
c) Fairly symmetric
c) No outliers

5. a) About the same. The distribution is fairly symmetric.
b) 31.84 years
c) 32 years

7. a) Q1 = 26; Q3 = 38 (Answers may vary slightly.)
b) Q1 = 25.5; Q3 = 40
c) IQR = 12 years
d) SD = 9.84 years

9. a) The distribution is skewed to the right. There are a few negative values. The range is about $6000. Center around $2000; IQR around $2000.
b) The mean will be larger because the distribution is right skewed.
c) Because of the skewness, the median is a better summary.

11. a) 11 has a z-score of −2.12; 48 has a z-score of +1.64.
b) The min, 11, is more extreme.
c) 61.36 years old

13. a)
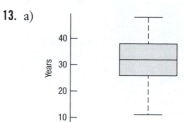

b) No.
c) 38 + 1.5*12 = 56 years old

15. a) Skewed to the right, since the mean is much greater than the median.
b) Yes, at least one high outlier, since 250 is far greater than Q3 + 1.5 IQRs.
c) We don't know how far the high whisker should go because we don't know the largest value inside the fence, or where other possible outliers might be.

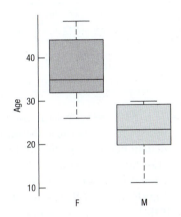

17. The ages of the women are generally higher than those of the men by about 10 years. As the boxplot shows, more than 3/4 of the women are older than all the men.

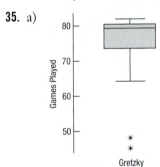

19. Sales in Location #1 were higher than sales in Location #2 in nearly every week. The company might want to compare other stores in locations like these to see if this phenomenon holds true for other locations.

21. The upper outlier limit is
$121.5 + 1.5*(121.5 − 34.3) = 252.3$.
The lower outlier limit is
$34.3 − 1.5*(121.5 − 34.3) = −96.5 < 0$.
Yes, the maximum value is an outlier. We should look at a boxplot to know how to proceed.

23. a) Yes.
b) No—data are from a single time point.
c) No—response is "time" but measured at only one time point.
d) Yes.

25. A logarithmic transformation might make the distribution of revenues more symmetric.

CHAPTER EXERCISE ANSWERS

27. Answers will vary.

29. a) It is symmetric, with a center between 14.5 and 15 inches. *Size* varies from 12.5 inches to 17.5 inches and has no outliers.
b) The bin from 14.5 to 15 and the bin from 15 to 15.5

c) Men in the bin from 14.5 to 15 would need a 15.5 inch shirt. Those in the 15 to 15.5 bin would need a 16 inch shirt. So, 15.5 and 16 inches.

31. a) The distribution is unimodal and skewed to the right. The median return appears to be around 8% (actually 6.4%).
b) About 75% of the funds returned less than the 12.5% return of the S&P index.

33. a)

Min.	1st Qu.	Median	3rd Qu.	Max.
−2.59	2.39	6.43	12.27	28.72

b) Median is 6.43%; IQR is 9.88%.
c)

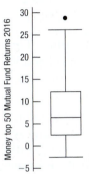

d) The histogram (not shown here) shows the asymmetry of the distribution better than the boxplot.

35. a)

b) The distribution of the number of games played per season by Wayne Gretzky is skewed to the low end and has low outliers. The median is 79, and the range is 37 games.
c) There are two outlier seasons with 45 and 48 games. He may have been injured. The season with 64 games is also separated by a gap.

37. a) The median because the distribution is skewed.
b) Lower, because the distribution is skewed toward the low end.
c) That display is not a histogram. It's a time series plot using bars to represent each point. The histogram should split up the number of games played into bins, not display the number of games played over time.

39. a) Descriptive Statistics: Price ($)

Minimum	Q1	Median	Q3	Maximum
2.21	2.51	2.61	2.72	3.05

b) Range = max − min = 3.05 − 2.21 = $0.84; IQR = Q3 − Q1 = 2.72 − 2.51 = $0.21

c)

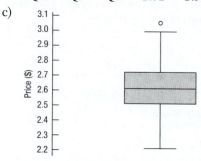

d) Symmetric with one high outlier. The mean is $2.62, with a standard deviation of $0.156.

e) There is one unusually high price that is greater than $3.00 per frozen pizza.

41. As we can see from the graph and boxplot, the main part of the distribution is unimodal and symmetric, but there are three high outlier states (North Dakota, Alaska, and Wyoming). The median consumption is 87M BTU/person in transportation. Fifty percent of states have per capita consumption in the range of 74.5M to 101.7M BTU/capita.

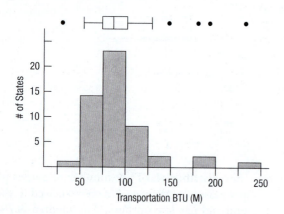

43. a) 1611 yards

b) Between Quartile 1 = 5585.75 yards, and Quartile 3 = 6131 yards.

c) The distribution of golf course lengths appears roughly symmetric, so the mean and the standard deviation are appropriate.

d) The distribution of the lengths of all the golf courses in Vermont is roughly unimodal and symmetric. The mean length of the golf courses is approximately 5900 yards and the standard deviation is 386.6 yards.

45. a) A boxplot is shown. A histogram would also be appropriate.

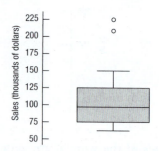

b) Descriptive Statistics: Sales ($) (Different statistics software may yield slightly different results.)

Variable	N	Mean	SE Mean	StDev	Minimum
Sales ($)	18	107845	11069	46962	62006

Q1	Median	Q3	Maximum
73422.5	95975	112330.0	224504

The mean sale is $107,845, and the median is $95,975. The mean is higher because the outliers pull it up.

c) The median because the distribution has outliers.

d) The standard deviation of the distribution is $46,962 and the IQR is $38,907.50. (Answers may vary slightly due to different quartile algorithms.)

e) The IQR because the outliers inflate the standard deviation.

f) The mean would decrease. The standard deviation would decrease. The median and IQR would be less affected.

47. A histogram shows that the distribution is unimodal and skewed to the left. There do not appear to be any outliers. The median failure rate for these 17 models is 16.2%. The middle 50% of the models have failure rates between 10.87% and 21.2%. The best rate is 3.17% for the 60GB Video model, and the worst is the 40GB Click Wheel at 29.85%.

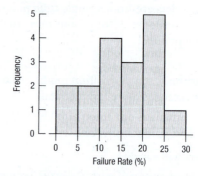

49. a) Gas prices generally increased over the nine-year period except for the dip in 2009. The distribution of prices in 2003 appears symmetric with a relatively small spread. Median prices rose in 2006, fell slightly by 2009, and then increased to new highs in 2012. There are low outliers in 2009 and 2012, but they appear to be quite near the lower fences.

   b) The distribution of gas prices in 2003 were most stable because it has the smallest IQR. Prices in 2006 and 2009 were least stable.

51. a) There is one wine in Seneca more expensive than any other.

   b) Both Cayuga and Seneca produce cheaper wines than Keuka, but Seneca has several high outliers.

   c) Keuka Lake.

   d) Cayuga Lake vineyards and Seneca Lake vineyards have approximately the same average price of about $15 a bottle, while a typical Keuka Lake vineyard has a price near $22. Keuka Lake vineyards have consistently high prices between about $18 and $26 a bottle. Cayuga Lake vineyards have prices from $13 to $19, and Seneca Lake vineyards have highly variable prices from about $12 to over $30.

53. a) The median speed is the speed at which 50% of the winning horses ran slower. Find 50% on the left, move straight over to the graph and down to a speed of about 36 mph.

   b) Q1 = 35 mph; Q3 = 37 mph (answers may vary slightly)

   c) Range = 7 mph
     IQR = 2 mph

   d)

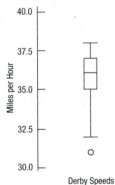

   e) The distribution of winning speeds in the Kentucky Derby is skewed to the left. The lowest winning speed is around 31 mph, and the fastest speed is nearly 38 mph. The median speed is approximately 36 mph, and 50% of the winning speeds are between 35 and 37 mph. Speeds below 32 mph would be considered low outliers.

55. a) Class 3.

   b) Class 3.

   c) Class 3 because it is the most highly skewed. Median is higher.

   d) Class 1.

   e) Probably Class 1. But without the actual scores, it is impossible to calculate the exact IQRs.

57. There is an extreme outlier for the slow-speed drilling. One hole was drilled almost an inch away from the center of the target! If that distance is correct, the engineers at the computer production plant should investigate the slow-speed drilling process closely. It may be plagued by extreme, intermittent inaccuracy. The outlier in the slow-speed drilling process is so extreme that no graphical display can display the distribution in a meaningful way while including that outlier. That distance should be removed before looking at a plot of the drilling distances.

   With the outlier removed, we can see that the slow drilling process is more accurate. The greatest distance from the target for the slow drilling process, 0.000098 inches, is still more accurate than the smallest distance for the fast drilling process, 0.000100 inches.

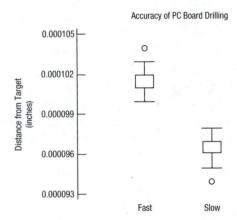

59. a) The mean of 54.41 is meaningless. These are categorical values.

   b) Typically, the mean and standard deviation are influenced by outliers and skewness.

   c) No. Summary statistics are only appropriate for quantitative data.

61. Although the numbers are not large, it appears that Bond funds performed worse, and more consistently than the other funds. The Domestic Equity funds appear to have performed best except for one low outlier. The lower quartile of the Domestic Equity funds are higher than the medians of the other types of funds.

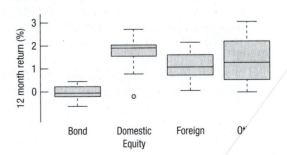

63. a) Even though MLS ID numbers are categorical identifiers, they are assigned sequentially, so this graph has some information. Most of the houses listed long ago have sold and are no longer listed.

b) A histogram is generally not an appropriate display for categorical data.

65. a) The histogram is unimodal and slightly skewed to the right. There is one large outlier (2005).

b) The time series plot clearly supports increasing numbers of storms.

c) The time series plot reveals a clear upward trend with respect to time, and it also shows that there has been substantial variation around that trend. There are also several points—bivariate outliers—that are not apparent in the histogram.

67. What is the *x*-axis? If it is time, what are the units? Months? Years? Decades? How is "productivity" measured?

69. The house that sells for $400,000 has a *z*-score of $(400,000 - 167,900)/77,158 = 3.01$, but the house with 4000 sq. ft. of living space has a *z*-score of $(4000 - 1819)/663 = 3.29$. So it's even more unusual.

71. U.S. *z*-scores are -0.04 and 1.63, total $= 1.59$. Ireland *z*-scores are 0.25 and 2.77, total 3.02. So Ireland "wins" the consumption battle.

73. a) The histogram shows a bimodal distribution, with a larger peak around $3.60 and a broad, flat peak around $2.25 to $2.90. The distribution is not symmetric.

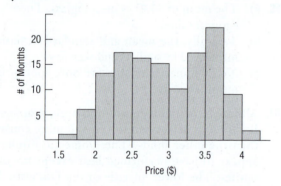

b) Prices show considerable variation. From 2007 to 2008, prices were rising, peaking at more than $4.00. After the financial crisis of 2008, prices dropped precipitously before increasing again until mid 2011. From that point until 2014, prices were relatively stable, moving between $3.25 and $3.75. After 2014, prices dropped precipitously again, stabilizing around $2.25 from late 2016 to 2017.

c) The time series plot is more informative because the prices have changed so much over time.

75. a) The bimodality of the distribution.

b) The trend over time.

c) The time series plot because it reveals much more of the structure of the data. The rates are not stationary.

d) Unemployment appears cyclical, with decreasing rates followed by rapidly increasing rates and then a long decline to lower unemployment again. From 2003 to 2007 it decreased from around 6% to 4%. During the recession of 2008, it increased and peaked at 10%. Since 2010, the unemployment rate has been decreasing, and is just above 4% in 2017.

77. a) The distribution is skewed. That makes it difficult to estimate anything meaningful from the graph.

b) Transform these data using either square roots or logs.

CHAPTER 4
SECTION EXERCISE ANSWERS

1. a)

b) Positive.

c) Linear.

d) Strong.

e) No.

3. a) Years of experience.
   b) Salary.
   c) Salary.

5. a) True.
   b) False. It will not change the correlation.
   c) False. Correlation has no units.

7. Correlation does not demonstrate causation. The analyst's argument is that sales staff cause sales. However, the data may reflect the store hiring more people as sales increase, so any causation would run the other way.

9. a) False. The line usually touches none of the points. We minimize the sum of the squared errors.
   b) True.
   c) False. It is the sum of the squares of all the residuals that is minimized.

11. a) $2 \times 0.965 = 1.93$ SDs
    b) $17.6 + 1.93 \times 5.34 = 27.906$ or \$27,906
    c) 0.965 SDs below the mean
    d) \$12,447

13. a) $b_1 = 0.914$ if found by hand. $b_1 = 0.913$ if found by technology. (Difference is due to rounding error.)
    b) It means that an additional 0.914 (\$1000) or \$914 of sales is associated with each additional sales person working.
    c) $b_0 = 8.10$
    d) It would mean that, on average, we expect sales of 8.10 (\$1000) or \$8100 with 0 sales people working. Doesn't really make sense in this context.
    e) $\widehat{Sales} = 8.10 + 0.914\,Number\ of\ Sales\ People\ Working$
    f) \$24.55 (\$1000) or \$24,550. (24,540 if using the technology solution.)
    g) 0.45 (\$1000) or \$450. (\$460 with technology.)
    h) Underestimated.

15. The winners may be suffering from regression to the mean. Perhaps they weren't really better than other rookie executives, but just happened to have a lucky year.

17. a) Thousands of dollars.
    b) 2.77 (the largest residual in magnitude).
    c) 0.07 (the smallest residual in magnitude).

19. $R^2 = 93.12\%$. About 93% of the variance in *Sales* can be accounted for by the regression of *Sales* on *Number of Sales Workers*.

21. 16, 16, 36, 49, 49, 64, 100. They are skewed to the high end.

CHAPTER EXERCISE ANSWERS

23. a) Number of text messages: explanatory; cost: response. To predict cost from number of text messages. Positive direction. Linear shape. Possibly an outlier for contracts with fixed cost for texting.
    b) Fuel efficiency: explanatory; sales volume: response. To predict sales from fuel efficiency. There may be no association between mpg and sales volume. Environmentalists hope that a higher mpg will encourage higher sales, which would be a positive association. We have no information about the shape of the relationship.
    c) Neither variable is explanatory. Both are responses to the lurking variable of temperature.
    d) Price: explanatory variable; demand: response variable. To predict demand from price. Negative direction. Linear shape in a narrow range, but curved over a larger range of prices.

25. a) None.
    b) 3 and 4
    c) 2, 3, and 4
    d) 2 and 4
    e) 3 and 1

27. a)

    b) Unimodal, skewed to the right. The skewness.
    c) The positive, somewhat linear relation between batch number and broken pieces.

29. a) 0.006
    b) 0.777
    c) −0.923
    d) −0.487

31. a) *Price.*
    b) *Sales.*
    c) Sales decrease by 24,369.49 pounds for every additional dollar charged.
    d) It is just a base value. It means nothing because stores won't set their price to \$0.
    e) 56,572.32 pounds
    f) 3427.69 pounds

33. a) *Salary.*
b) *Wins.*
c) On average, teams who spend $1M more in salary win 0.099 games more.
d) Number of wins predicted for a team that spends $0 on salaries. This is not meaningful here.
e) 0.99 games more
f) Much better. They were predicted to win 7.2 games.
g) 5.8 games
h) Not very useful. The residual standard deviation says that we cannot predict better than about $+/-6$ games. For a prediction of 8 games won, that's 2 to 14 games. All but the Cleveland Browns who won 1 game were already in that range.

35. About 47,084 pounds

37. "Packaging" isn't a variable. At best, it is a category. There's no basis for computing a correlation.

39. The model is meaningless because the variable Region is not quantitative. The slope makes no sense because Region has no units. The boxplot comparisons are useful but the regression is meaningless.

41. a) There is a strong negative linear association between Carbon Footprint and Highway mpg.
b) Quantitative variables. The hybrid cars appear to be essentially different from the others, so it is probably not appropriate to report a correlation for all the data; we have two different kinds of vehicles combined together.
c) $r = -0.931$. Removing the hybrids leaves a more consistent collection of cars, which are more linearly associated.

43. a) Positive association.
b) Plot is not linear, violating the linearity condition. There may be an outlier at 17 rooms.

45. a) The variables are both quantitative (with units % of GDP), and the plot is reasonably straight, but without much pattern. There is an outlier with a very low Euro GDP, but the pattern is not improved after setting it aside. The spread is roughly constant (although the spread is large). We should be cautious in interpreting the model too strictly.
b) Almost none (less than 1%) the variation in the growth rates of developing countries is accounted for by the growth rates of Euro Area.
c) The years 1983–2016

47. a) $\widehat{Growth\,(Least\ Developed\ Countries)} = 4.34 - 0.066$ $Growth\,(Euro\ Area)$
b) It's the predicted growth of the least developed countries in years of 0% growth in the Euro Zone. Yes, this makes sense.
c) On average, GDP in the least developed countries decreased -0.066% for every 1% increase in growth in the Euro zone.

d) 4.076%
e) More; we would predict 4.14%.
f) 5.27%

49. a) Yes, although the association is weak, the form does seem to be somewhat linear.
b) As the number of runs increases, the attendance also increases.
c) There is a slight positive association, but even if it were stronger it does not *prove* that more fans would come if the number of runs increased. Association does not indicate causality.

51. a) The predicted value of the money *Flow* if the *Return* was 0%.
b) An increase of 1% in mutual fund return was associated with an increase of $771 million in money flowing into mutual funds.
c) $9747 million
d) $-$4747 million; overestimated.

53. a) Model seems appropriate. Residual plot looks fine.
b) Model not appropriate. Relationship is nonlinear.
c) Model not appropriate. Spread is increasing.

55. There are two outliers that inflate the R^2 value and affect the slope and intercept. Without those two points, the R^2 drops from 79% to about 31%. The analyst should set aside those two customers and refit the model.

57. 0.03. For every $1000 increase in ad expenditure, sales are most likely to increase by $30,000.

59. a) R^2 is an indication of the strength of the model, not the appropriateness of the model.
b) The agent should have said, "The model predicts that annual sales will be $10 million when $1.5 million is spent on advertising."

61. a) Quantitative variable condition: Both variables are quantitative (*GPA* and *Starting Salary*).
b) Linearity condition: Examine a scatterplot of *Starting Salary* by *GPA*.
c) Outlier condition: Examine the scatterplot.
d) Equal spread condition: Plot the regression residuals versus predicted values.

63. a)
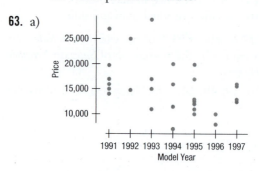

b) There is a weak negative association between *Price* and *Model Year* of used BMW 8's.
c) Yes, but the relationship is not very strong.

d) -0.415

e) 17.2% of the variability in *Price* of a used BMW 8 series can be accounted for by the year the car was made.

f) The relationship is not perfect. Other factors, such as options, condition, and mileage, may account for some of the variability in price.

65. a) The association between cost of living in 2017 and 2009 is positive and quite strong. There are no apparent outliers. The scatterplot indicates that the linear model is appropriate.

b) 73.2% of the variability in cost of living in 2017 can be accounted for by the cost of living in 2009.

c) 0.86

d) $\widehat{Index\ 2017} = 9.42 + 0.695\ \widehat{Index\ 2009}$

e) Paris is predicted to have a cost of living in 2017 of 98.24. Its actual 2017 value is 89.98, so its residual is $89.98 - 98.24 = -8.26\%$.

67. a) The association is positive, moderately strong, and roughly straight, with several states whose HCI seems high for their median income and one state whose HCI appears low given its median income.

b) The correlation would still be 0.65.

c) The correlation wouldn't change.

d) DC would be a moderate outlier whose HCI is high for its median income. It would lower the correlation slightly.

e) No. We can only say that higher median incomes are associated with higher housing costs, but we don't know why. There may be other economic variables at work.

69. a)

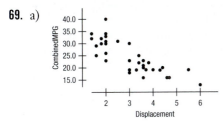

b) Negative, linear, strong

c) -0.797

d) There is a strong negative relationship between engine size and gas mileage. Lower fuel efficiency is generally associated with larger engines.

CHAPTER 5
SECTION EXERCISE ANSWERS

1. a) Independent (unless a large group of one gender comes to the ATM machine together).

b) Independent. The last digit of one student's SS number provides no information about another.

c) Not independent. How you perform on one test provides information about other tests.

3. a) Won't work, but won't hurt. Each number drawn is equally likely and independent of the others, so this set of numbers is just as likely as any other in the next drawing.

b) Won't work, but won't hurt. Each number drawn is equally likely and independent of the others and of previous drawings, so the previous winners are just as likely as any other in the next drawing.

5. a) 0.40

b) 0.60

c) $0.60^2 = 0.36$

d) $0.60 + 0.60 - (0.36) = 0.84$ or $1 - (0.4^2) = 0.84$

7. a) $755/1200 = 0.629$

b) Marginal.

c) $210/1200 = 0.175$

d) Joint.

9. a) $210/500 = 0.42$

b) $210/755 = 0.278$

c) $415/500 = 0.83$

11. a) $100\% - 30\% = 70\%$

b) Joint.

c)

		Online Banking		
		Yes	**No**	
Age	**Under 50**	0.25	0.15	0.40
	50 or Older	0.05	0.55	0.60
		0.30	0.70	1.00

d) $0.25/0.40 = 0.625$

e) No, because the conditional probability of banking online for those under 50 is 0.625. The probability of banking online is 0.30, which is not the same.

13. a)

Instant Discount 0.20	Purchase 0.06	0.012
	No Purchase 0.94	0.188
Free Shipping 0.30	Purchase 0.05	0.015
	No Purchase 0.95	0.285
No Offer 0.50	Purchase 0.02	0.01
	No Purchase 0.98	0.49

b) 3.7%

c) 0.405

15. a) White: 0.68, Black: 0.11, Hispanic/Latino/Other: 0.21; White Male: 0.54, White Female: 0.46; Black Male: 0.52, Black Female: 0.48; Hispanic/Latino/Other Male: 0.58, Hispanic/Latino/Other Female: 0.42.
   b) 0.0528
   c) 0.46
   d) 0.6893

CHAPTER EXERCISE ANSWERS

17. a) Individual outcomes can't be predicted, although in the long run the relative frequencies may be known (and for a roulette wheel should be equal).
   b) This is likely a personal probability expressing his degree of belief that there will be a new high.

19. a) There is no such thing as the "law of averages." The overall probability of an airplane crash does not change due to recent crashes.
   b) There is no such thing as the "law of averages." The overall probability of an airplane crash does not change due to a period in which there were no crashes.

21. a) It would be foolish to insure your neighbor's house for $300. Although you would probably simply collect $300, there is a chance you could end up paying much more than $300. That risk is not worth the $300.
   b) The insurance company insures many people. The overwhelming majority of customers pay and never have a claim. The few customers who do have a claim are offset by the many who simply send their premiums without a claim. The relative risk to the insurance company is low.

23. a) Yes.
   b) Yes.
   c) No, probabilities sum to more than 1.
   d) Yes.
   e) No, sum isn't 1 and one value is negative.

25. 0.078

27. The events are disjoint. Use the Addition Rule.
   a) 0.72
   b) 0.89
   c) 0.28

29. a) 0.5184
   b) 0.0784
   c) 0.4816

31. a) The repair needs for the two cars must be independent of one another.
   b) This may not be reasonable. An owner may treat the two cars similarly, taking good (or poor) care of both. This may decrease (or increase) the likelihood that each needs to be repaired.

33. a) 0.68
   b) 0.32
   c) 0.04

35. a) The events are disjoint (an M&M can't be two colors at once), so use the Addition Rule where applicable.
      i) 0.30
      ii) 0.30
      iii) 0.90
      iv) 0
   b) The events are independent (picking out one M&M doesn't affect the outcome of the next pick), so use the Multiplication Rule.
      i) 0.027
      ii) 0.128
      iii) 0.512
      iv) 0.271

37. a) Disjoint.
   b) Independent.
   c) No. Once you know that one of a pair of disjoint events has occurred, the other one cannot occur, so its probability has become zero.

39. a) 0.125
   b) 0.125
   c) 0.875
   d) Independence.

41. a) 0.0225
   b) 0.092
   c) 0.00008
   d) 0.556

43. a) Your thinking is correct. There are 47 cards left in the deck, 26 black and only 21 red.
   b) This is not an example of the Law of Large Numbers. The card draws are not independent.

45. a) 0.21
   b) 0.66

47. a) 0.642
   b) 0.035
   c) $1 - (410 + 815)/1270$

49. a)

   b) 0.16
   c) 0.667

51. a) 0.244
b) 0.10
c) 0.101
d) 0.434

53. a) 0.10
b) 0.17
c) 0.026
d) 0.24

55. a) 0.1062
b) 0.4469
c) 0.0785

57. a) 0.11
b) 0.27
c) 0.407
d) 0.344

59. No. 28.8% of men with OK blood pressure have high cholesterol, but 40.7% of men with high blood pressure have high cholesterol.

61. a) 0.026
b) 0.84
c) 0.20
d) 0.053
e) 0.554
f) $P(\text{more time} \mid <25 \text{ years}) = 0.158$. $P(\text{more time}) = 0.10$. These probabilities are not equal, so the events are not independent.

63. a) 0.47
b) 0.266
c) $P(\text{pool}) = 0.21$, $P(\text{pool} \mid \text{garage}) = 0.266$. Having a garage and a pool are not independent events.
d) $P(\text{pool and garage}) = 0.17$. Having a garage and a pool are not disjoint events.

65. a) 0.71
b) $P(<500K \mid 3 \text{ Br}) = 0$. $P(<500K) = 0.71$. Since not equal, they are not independent.

67. a) 15.4%
b) 11.4%
c) 73.9%
d) 18.5%

*69. a)

```
                    Require Service
                          0.15 ──────── 0.084
         Laptop
          0.56      Don't Require Service
                          0.85 ──────── 0.476

                    Require Service
                          0.05 ──────── 0.022
        Desktop
          0.44      Don't Require Service
                          0.95 ──────── 0.418
```

b) 10.6%
c) 0.792

CHAPTER 6
SECTION EXERCISE ANSWERS

1. a) Discrete.
b) Yes/no.

3. 0.7

5. 0.781

7. a) $19
b) $7

9. a) $\mu = 30$; $\sigma = 6$
b) $\mu = 26$; $\sigma = 5$
c) $\mu = 30$; $\sigma = 5.39$
d) $\mu = -10$; $\sigma = 5.39$

11. a) 110 and 12.
b) 450 and 40.
c) 190 and 14.422.
d) X and Y are independent for the SD calculation, but not necessarily for the sum.

13. a) Yes. Outcomes are independent with probability $p = 1/6$. The outcomes are {getting a 6} and {not getting a 6}.
b) No. More than two outcomes are possible.
c) No. The chance of a woman (or man) changes depending on who has already been picked.
d) Yes, assuming responses (and cheating) are independent among the students.

15. Yes.

17. Geometric: $p = 0.358$, and the expected number of calls before the first success $= 1/0.358 = 2.79$ calls.

19. a) 0.5488
b) 0.4512

CHAPTER EXERCISE ANSWERS

21. a) $1, 2, \ldots, n$
b) Discrete.

23. a) 1.7
b) 0.9

25. a) 2.25 lights
b) 1.26 lights

27. a) No, the probability he wins the second changes depending on whether he won the first.
b) 0.42
c) 0.08
d)

X	0	1	2
$P(X = x)$	0.42	0.50	0.08

e) $E(X) = 0.66$ tournaments; $\sigma = 0.62$ tournaments.

29. a) No, the probability of one battery being dead will depend on the state of the other one since there are only 10 batteries.

b)

Number Good	0	1	2
P(number good)	$\left(\frac{3}{10}\right)\left(\frac{2}{9}\right) = \frac{6}{90}$	$\left(\frac{3}{10}\right)\left(\frac{7}{9}\right) + \left(\frac{7}{10}\right)\left(\frac{3}{9}\right) = \frac{42}{90}$	$\left(\frac{7}{10}\right)\left(\frac{6}{9}\right) = \frac{42}{90}$

  c) $\mu = 1.4$ batteries
  d) $\sigma = 0.61$ batteries

31. $\mu = E$ (total wait time) $= 74.0$ seconds
$\sigma = SD$ (total wait time) ≈ 20.57 seconds
(Answers to standard deviation may vary slightly due to rounding of the standard deviation of the number of red lights each day.) The standard deviation may be calculated only if the stoplights are independent of each other. This seems reasonable.

33. a) $\mu = 13.6, \sigma = 2.55$
  b) Assuming the hours are independent of each other.
  c) A typical 8-hour day will have about 11 to 16 repair calls.
  d) 19 or more repair calls would be a lot! That's more than two standard deviations above average.

35. a) $B =$ number basic; $D =$ number deluxe; Net Profit $= 120B + 150D - 200$
  b) $928.00
  c) $187.45
  d) Mean—no; SD—yes (sales are independent).

37. a) $50
  b) $100

39. a) Let $X_i =$ price of ith Hulk figure sold; $Y_i =$ price of ith Iron Man figure sold; Insertion Fee $= \$0.55$; $T =$ Closing Fee $= 0.0875(X_1 + X_2 + \cdots + X_{19} + Y_1 + \cdots + Y_{13})$; Net Income $= (X_1 + X_2 + \cdots + X_{19} + Y_1 + \cdots + Y_{13}) - 32(0.55) - 0.0875(X_1 + X_2 + \cdots + X_{19} + Y_1 + \cdots + Y_{13})$
  b) $\mu = E$ (net income) $= \$313.24$
  c) $\sigma = SD$ (net income) $= \$6.625$
  d) Yes, to compute the standard deviation.

41. a) No, these are not Bernoulli trials. The possible outcomes are 1, 2, 3, 4, 5, and 6. There are more than two possible outcomes.
  b) Yes, these may be considered Bernoulli trials. There are only two possible outcomes: Type A and not Type A. Assuming the 120 donors are representative of the population, the probability of having Type A blood is 43%. The trials are not independent because the population is finite, but the 120 donors represent less than 10% of all possible donors.

  c) No, these are not Bernoulli trials. The probability of choosing a man changes after each promotion and the 10% condition is violated.
  d) No, these are not Bernoulli trials. We are sampling without replacement, so the trials are not independent. Samples without replacement may be considered Bernoulli trials if the sample size is less than 10% of the population, but 500 is more than 10% of 3000.
  e) Yes, these may be considered Bernoulli trials. There are only two possible outcomes: sealed properly and not sealed properly. The probability that a package is unsealed is constant at about 10%, as long as the packages checked are a representative sample of all.

43. a) 0.0819
  b) 0.0064
  c) 0.16
  d) 0.992

45. $E(X) = 14.29$, so 15 patients

47. a) 0.078 pixels
  b) 0.280 pixels
  c) 0.374
  d) 0.012

49. Using the Poisson model, the mean rate of occurrence is 29 hurricanes/18 years $= 1.611$ hurricanes/year.
  a) $p(X = 0) = 0.20$
  b) $p(X = 1) = 0.32$
  c) $p(X \geq 2) = 1 - (0.20 + 0.32) = 0.48$

51. a) 0.0745
  b) 0.502
  c) 0.211
  d) 0.0166
  e) 0.0179
  f) 0.9987

53. a) A uniform; all numbers should be equally likely to be selected.
  b) 0.5
  c) 0.001

55. a) The Poisson model.
  b) 0.9502
  c) 0.0025

57. a) 0.65
  b) 0.75
  c) 7.69 picks

59. a) $\mu = 10.44, \sigma = 1.16$
  b) 0.812
  c) 0.475
  d) 0.00193
  e) 0.998

61. Use the Binomial model. $N = 120$ trials (people walking into the showroom), $p = 0.35$.

  a) $P(\text{bonus}) = P(\text{at least 50 sales}) = 1 - P(49 \text{ or fewer sales}) = 1 - \text{Binom}(49, 120, 0.35, \text{Cumulative} = \text{True}) = 0.077$
  b) 0.628
  c) Increasing $P(\text{success})$ to 0.40 makes his probability of making his bonus $= 0.388$
      Increasing N from 120 to 140 makes $P(\text{bonus}) = 0.461$
      Therefore, increasing N is better than increasing $P(\text{success})$ in this case by 0.073 in the probability of getting the bonus.
  d) Yes, he should accept the offer. Using the result from part c, we find that $P(\text{bonus} \mid p = 0.35, N = 140) = 0.461$. From part a we found that the baseline $P(\text{bonus}) = 0.077$. There is an increase of $0.461 - 0.073 = 0.388$ in the probability of getting the $100,000 bonus. The expected value of the increase $= 0.388 \times \$100,000 = \$38,800$. Since $15,000 is less than the expected value of increasing the number of people, it is worth it.
  e) $38,800 is the maximum value that a risk-neutral decision maker should pay.
  f) Use the Binomial model with $n = 10$, $p = 0.2$, and calculate $P(\text{no Big Spender})$. Then find the complement: 0.893

CHAPTER 7
SECTION EXERCISE ANSWERS

1. In economics she scored 1.25 standard deviations above the mean. On the math exam she scored 1.50 standard deviations above the mean, so she did "better" on the math exam.

3. You scored 2.2 standard deviations above the mean.

5. a) According to the 68–95–99.7 Rule, only 5% of the distribution is beyond 2 standard deviations from the mean, so only 2.5% is more than 2 standard deviations above the mean. So less than 3% of the distribution is above a z-score of 2.20. You qualify.
  b) You need to assume that the distribution is unimodal and symmetric for the 68–95–99.7 Rule to apply.

7. a)

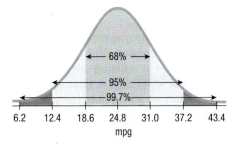

  b) 18.6 to 31.0 mpg
  c) 16%
  d) 13.5%
  e) less than 12.4 mpg

9. a) 6.68%
  b) 98.78%
  c) 71.63%
  d) 61.71%

11. a) 0.842
  b) -0.675
  c) -1.881
  d) -1.645 to 1.645

13. Yes. The histogram is unimodal and symmetric and the Normal probability plot is straight.

15. a) $\mu = E(\text{miles remaining}) = 164 \text{ miles}$
      $\sigma = SD(\text{miles remaining}) \approx 19.80 \text{ miles}$
  b) 0.580

17. a) 0.141 (0.175 with continuity correction)
  b) Answers may vary. That's a fairly high proportion, but the decision depends on the relative costs of not selling seats and bumping passengers.

19. a) A uniform; all numbers should be equally likely to be selected.
  b) 0.02
  c) 0.10

21. a) $\lambda = 1/3$.
  b) 0.811

CHAPTER EXERCISE ANSWERS

23. a) 16%
  b) 50%
  c) 95%
  d) 0.15%

25. a) 6.2%
  b) 8.0%
  c) 2.6%
  d) $4.4\% < x < 8.0\%$

27. a) 50%
  b) 16%
  c) 2.5%
  d) More than 1.40 is more unusual.

29. a) $x > 1.33$
b) $x < 1.24$
c) $1.07 < x < 1.41$
d) $x < 1.07$

31. a) 36.9% (using technology).
b) 78.1%
c) 99.8%
d) 0.003%

33. a) $x > 8.51\%$
b) $x < 4.69\%$
c) $5.26\% < x < 7.14\%$
d) $x > 4.69\%$

35. a) 5.74%
b) 10.39%
c) 2.43%

37. a) 79.58
b) 18.50
c) 95.79
d) −2.79

39. $z_{SAT} = 1.30$; $z_{ACT} = 2$. The ACT score is the better score because it is farther above the mean in standard deviation units than the SAT score.

41. Any Job Satisfaction score more than 2 standard deviations below the mean or less than $100 - 2(12) = 76$ might be considered unusually low. We would expect to find someone with a Job Satisfaction score less than $100 - 3(12) = 64$ very rarely.

43. a) About 16%
b) One standard deviation below the mean is −1.27 hours, which is impossible.
c) Because the standard deviation is larger than the mean, the distribution is strongly skewed to the right, not symmetric.

45. a)

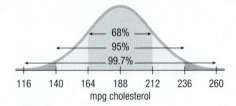

b) 30.85%
c) 17.00%
d) $IQR = Q3 - Q1 = 32.38$
e) Above 212.87 points.

47. a) To know about their consistency and how long they might last. Standard deviation measures variability, which translates to consistency in everyday use. A type of battery with a small standard deviation would be more likely to have life spans close to their mean life span than a type of battery with a larger standard deviation.

b) The second company's batteries have a higher mean life span, but a larger standard deviation, so they have more variability. The decision is not clear-cut. The first company's batteries are not likely to fail in less than 21 months, but that wouldn't be surprising for the second company. But the second company's batteries could easily last longer than 39 months—a span very unlikely for the first company.

49. CEOs can have between 0 and maybe 40 (or possibly 50) year's experience. A standard deviation of 1/2 year is impossible because many CEOs would be 10 or 20 SDs away from the mean, whatever it is. An SD of 16 years would mean that 2 SDs on either side of the mean is plus or minus 32, for a range of 64 years. That's too high. So, the SD must be 6 years.

51. a) 1 oz
b) 0.5 oz
c) 0.023
d) $\mu = 4$ oz, $\sigma = 0.5$ oz
e) 0.159
f) $\mu = 12.3$ oz, $\sigma = 0.54$ oz

53. a) 12.2 oz
b) 0.51 oz
c) 0.058

55. a) $\mu = 37.6$ min, $\sigma = 3.7$ min
b) No, 30 min is more than 2 SDs below the mean.

57. a) $\mu = 1920$, $\sigma = 48.99$; $P(T > 2000) = 0.051$
b) $\mu = \$220$, $\sigma = 11.09$; No—$300 is more than 7 SDs above the mean.
c) $P(D - \frac{1}{2}C > 0) \approx 0.26$

59. 0.053 or 0.066 using continuity correction

61. 0.025 or 0.0296 using continuity correction

63. a) 0.5
b) 0.25

65. a) The Poisson model
b) The exponential model
c) 1/3 minutes
d) 0.0473

CHAPTER 8
SECTION EXERCISE ANSWERS

1. a) retrospective
b) prospective

3. a) False. Sampling error cannot be avoided, even with unbiased samples.
b) True.
c) True.
d) False. Randomization will match the characteristics in a way that is unbiased. We can't possibly

think of all the characteristics that might be important or match our sample to the population on all of them.

5. a) Organic farmers in the northeast United States.
   b) NOFA membership listing.
   c) Proportion who think global climate change is affecting crop yield.

7. a) No. It would be nearly impossible to get exactly 500 males and 500 females by random chance.
   b) Stratified sample, stratified by whether the respondent is male or female.

9. Systematic sample.

11. a) Population—Human resources directors of *Fortune* 500 companies.
   b) Parameter—Proportion who don't feel surveys intruded on their workday.
   c) Sampling Frame—List of HR directors at *Fortune* 500 companies.
   d) Sample—23% who responded.
   e) Bias—Hard to generalize because who responds is related to the question itself (nonresponse bias).

13. a) Organic farmers in the Northeast.
   b) The members who attended the recent symposium.
   c) The sampling frame is not necessarily representative of the entire group of farmers. Those who attended the symposium may have different opinions from those who didn't. His sample isn't random and may be biased toward those most interested in the topic. Finally, the script is biased and may lead to an estimate of a higher proportion who think government should be doing more to fight global warming than is true within the population.

15. a) Answers will vary. Question 1 seems appropriate. Question 2 predisposes the participant to agree that $50 is a reasonable price, and does not seem appropriate.
   b) Question 1 is the more neutrally worded. Question 2 is biased in its wording.

17. a) True.
   b) False. Often parts of the population are not sampled.
   c) False. Measurement error refers to inaccurate responses. Sampling error refers to sample-to-sample variability.
   d) True.

19. a) This is a multistage design, with a cluster sample at the first stage and a simple random sample for each cluster.

   b) If any of the three churches you pick at random is not representative of all churches then you'll introduce sampling error by the choice of that church.

CHAPTER EXERCISE ANSWERS

21. a) Voluntary response.
   b) We have no confidence at all in estimates from such studies.

23. a) The population of interest is all adults in the United States.
   b) The sampling frame is U.S. adults with telephones. Because they use computers to generate random numbers from all possible numbers this seems representative.

25. a) Population—U.S. teens.
   b) Parameter—Proportion who have access to computers and proportion who generally access the Internet by cell phone.
   c) Sampling Frame—not specified.
   d) Sample—802 teens and parents.
   e) Method—Not specified. Probably a random digit dialed survey.
   f) Bias—If teens were interviewed in front of their parents, it might have biased their responses.

27. a) Population—Adults.
   b) Parameter—Proportion who think drinking and driving is a serious problem.
   c) Sampling Frame—Bar patrons.
   d) Sample—Every 10th person leaving the bar.
   e) Method—Systematic sampling.
   f) Bias—Those interviewed had just left a bar. They probably think drinking and driving is less of a problem than do adults in general.

29. a) Population—Soil around a former waste dump.
   b) Parameter—Concentrations of toxic chemicals.
   c) Sampling Frame—Accessible soil around the dump.
   d) Sample—16 soil samples.
   e) Method—Not clear.
   f) Bias—Don't know if soil samples were randomly chosen. If not, may be biased toward more or less polluted soil.

31. a) Population—Snack food bags.
   b) Parameter—Weight of bags, proportion passing inspection.
   c) Sampling Frame—All bags produced each day.
   d) Sample—10 randomly selected cases, 1 bag from each case for inspection.
   e) Method—Multistage sampling.
   f) Bias—Should be unbiased.

33. Bias. Only people watching the news will respond, and their preference may differ from that of other voters. The sampling method may systematically produce samples that don't represent the population of interest.

35. a) Voluntary response. Only those who both see the ad *and* feel strongly enough will respond.
   b) Cluster sampling. One town may not be typical of all.
   c) Attempted census. Will have nonresponse bias.
   d) Stratified sampling with follow-up. Should be unbiased.

37. a) This is a systematic sample.
   b) It is likely to be representative of those waiting for the roller coaster. Indeed, it may do quite well if those at the front of the line respond differently (after their long wait) than those at the back of the line.
   c) The sampling frame is patrons willing to wait for the roller coaster on that day at that time. It should be representative of the people in line, but not of all people at the amusement park.

39. Only those who think it worth the wait are likely to be in line. Those who don't like roller coasters are unlikely to be in the sampling frame, so the poll won't get a fair picture of whether park patrons overall would favor still more roller coasters.

41. a) Biased toward yes because of "pollute." "Should companies be responsible for any costs of environmental cleanup?"
   b) Biased toward no because of "enforce" and "strict." "Should companies have dress codes?"

43. a) Not everyone has an equal chance. People with unlisted numbers, people without phones, and those at work cannot be reached. There may be a slight bias against people from large households.
   b) Generate random numbers and call at random times.
   c) Under the original plan, those families in which one person stays home are more likely to be included. Under the second plan, many more are included. People without phones are still excluded.
   d) It improves the chance of selected households being included.
   e) This takes care of phone numbers. Time of day may be an issue. People without phones are still excluded.

45. a) Answers will vary.
   b) The amount of change you typically carry. Parameter is the true mean amount of change. Population is the amount on each day around noon.
   c) Population is now the amount of change carried by your friends. The average estimates the mean of these amounts.

   d) Possibly for your class. Probably not for larger groups. Your friends are likely to have similar needs for change during the day.

47. a) Assign numbers 001 to 120 to each order. Use random numbers to select 10 transactions to examine.
   b) Sample proportionately within each type. (Do a stratified random sample.)

49. a) Select three cases at random; then select one jar randomly from each case.
   b) Use random numbers to choose three cases from numbers 61 through 80; then use random numbers between 1 and 12 to select the jar from each case.
   c) No. Multistage sampling.

51. a) Depends on the Yellow Pages listings used. If from regular (line) listings, this is fair if all doctors are listed. If from ads, probably not, as those doctors may not be typical.
   b) Not appropriate. This cluster sample will probably contain listings for only one or two business types.

CHAPTER 9

SECTION EXERCISE ANSWERS

1. Experimental units: Cookies
   Treatments: Chocolate chip choice (milk, dark, semi-sweet)
   Response: Rating by trained testers
   Randomization: Random presentation to the tasters

3. Control: All other aspects of the recipes were kept the same
   Randomization: Cookies presented to tasters in random order
   Replication: 10 tasters did the rating

5.
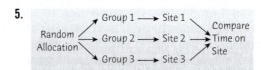

7. Single-blind. Customers were blind to treatments, but the kitchen staff knew.

9. There is not enough information in the experiment to say whether it was blinded or not, but it can be made double-blind by making sure that neither the servers nor the tasters know which chips were used in each cookie batch. Randomization should still be used.

11. a) Chips (milk, dark, semi) and Oil (butter, margarine)
   b) 6 treatments: milk/butter, dark/butter, semi/butter, milk/margarine, dark/margarine, semi/margarine
   c) It would mean that the effect of the oil (butter vs. margarine) on ratings was not the same for the different chocolate types (or vice versa).

CHAPTER EXERCISE ANSWERS

13. a) Temperature, Washing time, Detergent
b) Temperature (Hot, Cold), Washing time (Short, Long), Detergent (Standard, New).
c) Whiteness as measured by an optical scanner

15. a) Both detergents should be tested under the same conditions to ensure that the results are comparable.
b) It will be impossible to generalize to cold water washing.
c) Treatments should be run in random order to ensure that no other unforeseen influences could affect the response in a systematic way.

17. a) The differences among the Mozart and quiet groups were more than would have been expected from ordinary sampling variation.
b)

c) The Mozart group seems to have the smallest median difference and thus the *least* improvement, but there does not appear to be a significant difference.
d) No, the difference does not seem significant compared with the usual variation.

19. a) Observational; randomly select a group of children, ages 10 to 13, have them taste the cereal, and ask if they like the cereal.
b) Answers may vary. Get volunteers ages 10 to 13. Each volunteer will taste one cereal, randomizing the assignment. Compare the percentage of favorable ratings for each cereal.

c) Answers may vary. From the volunteers, identify the children who watch Frump and identify the children who do not watch Frump. Use a blocked design to reduce variation in cereal preference that may be associated with watching the Frump cartoon.

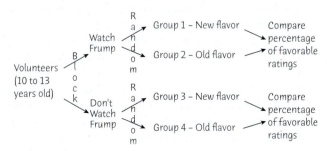

21. a) The students were not randomly assigned. Those who signed up for the prep course may be a special group whose scores would have improved anyway.
b) Answers may vary. Find a group of volunteers who are willing to participate. Give all volunteers the SAT exam. Randomly assign the subjects to the review or no review group. Give the tutoring to one group. After a reasonable time, retest both groups. Check to see that the tutored group had a significant improvement in scores when compared with the no review group.
c) After the volunteers have taken the first SAT exam, separate the volunteers into blocks of low, average, and high SAT exam score performance. Now assign half of each block to the review and half to the no review groups. Give the tutoring. Now retest all groups. Compare the differences between treatments for each block.

23. a) No, because nothing was manipulated.
b) Yes.

25. a) The design is not blinded. The shoes should be dyed/modified so that there are no distinguishing marks on them, and so that neither the athletes nor the observers (those doing the timing or starting) can tell which is which. Also, each athlete should run multiple times with each shoe.
b) Olympic athletes may be different from regular runners in many ways, and their footwear needs may be different. What improves an Olympic athlete's results may not improve an average runner's time.

27. a) Having a parachute or not.
b) Volunteer skydivers (the dimwitted ones).
c) A parachute that looks real but doesn't work.
d) A good parachute and a placebo parachute.
e) Whether parachutist survives the jump (or extent of injuries).
f) All should jump from the same altitude in similar weather conditions and land on similar surfaces.
g) Randomly assign people the parachutes.
h) The skydivers (and the people involved in distributing the parachute packs) shouldn't know who got a working chute. And the people evaluating the subjects after the jumps should not be told who had a real parachute either!

29. a) No.
b) Female heads of household spend more, on average, than male heads of household. Coupons increase expenditures for both groups by about $20 per family per week.
c) The experiment is partially blinded, because those people who get a coupon will know that they got one, but it is unlikely that those not receiving a coupon would know that they didn't get one (and others did). In this case, it would be almost impossible to fully blind the experiment.

31. a) There is no evidence that the changes in swelling were different among the three treatments. Contrast baths, with or without exercise, did not appear to reduce swelling any more than exercise alone.

b) Patients were assigned to treatments at random. The exercise treatment was the control group.

c) If exercise is the standard treatment, then using it as a control seems appropriate.

33. a) The difference in the depression rates for the two groups is greater than would be expected by natural sampling variation.

b) Observational study. There was no experimental treatment.

c) The difference could be explained by lurking variables. Perhaps swimmers are more affluent (can afford a membership at the Y or have access to a pool), or perhaps depressed people tend to swim less.

d) Answers may vary. Give the subjects a test to measure depression. Then randomly assign the 120 subjects to one of three groups: the control group (no exercise program), the anaerobic exercise group, and the aerobic exercise group. Monitor subjects' exercise (have them report to a particular gym or pool). At the end of 12 weeks, administer the depression test again. Compare the post- and pre-exercise depression scores.

35. a) Multi-factor design (specifically, a 2 factor randomized design)

b) Yes. Although it was replicated over many people, it was also only conducted at a single grocery store in Philadelphia.

c) As long as we only want to generalize to the one store, yes.

d) The analyst is wrong. A plot (on the next page) shows why. Although it is true that, on average, day of week does not matter, there is an interaction between day of week and coupon type, such that $.50 off coupons are better on Fridays (and worse on Wednesdays). Buy-one-get-one free coupons are better on Wednesdays and worse on Fridays. Yes, it helps to create the interaction plot and to visualize the results.

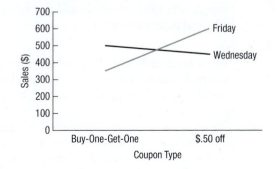

37. a) Randomized block design

b)

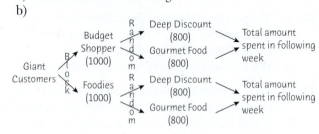

c) Yes. The implication is that both the Deep Discount and the Gourmet Food circulars are new marketing techniques that are being tested. If this is true, there is no control group.

d) The analyst has overstepped the data. Given the lack of control group, we cannot conclude that "Foodies are wealthier and spend more on food in general." Although this is a plausible claim, supporting it would require data from a control group of Foodies and Budget shoppers who received neither circular. Because of this error, the analyst also has made the remainder of her claims tenuous. A neutral interpretation would be: It appears that Budget shoppers spend about the same amount per week regardless of which circular they receive, but Foodies spend more when sent the Gourmet Food circular than the Deep Discount circular. Without a control group, we cannot say whether this is because the Deep Discount circular causes a decrease in spending, the Gourmet Food circular causes an increase in spending, or a combination of the two effects occurs.

39. Answers may vary. Randomly select half of the patients who agree to the study to get large doses of vitamin E after surgery. Give the other half a similar-looking placebo pill. Monitor their progress, recording the time until they have reached an easily agreed upon level of healing. Have the evaluating doctor blinded to whether the patient received the placebo or not. Compare the number of days until recovery of the two groups.

41.

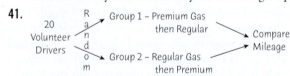

Answers may vary. This experiment has 1 factor (type of gasoline), at 2 levels (premium and regular), resulting in 2 treatments. The response variable is gas mileage. An experiment diagram for a matched design appears above. Have each of the volunteers use each kind of gas for a month. Randomly assign 10 of them to use regular first, the other 10 to use premium first. Ask them to keep driving logs (the number of miles driven and the gallons of gasoline) for each month. Compare the differences in the fuel economy for the two kinds of gasoline.

43. a) Answers may vary. Randomly assign the eight patients to either the current medication or the new medication. Have nurses assess the degree of shingles involvement for the patient. Ask patients to rate their pain levels. Administer the medications for a prescribed time. Have nurses reassess the degree of shingles involvement. Ask patients to rate their pain levels post-medication. Compare the improvement levels.

b) Let A = 1, B = 2 . . . H = 8.
Assign the first four randomly selected to the first group, the remainder to the second. So Group 1 is D, A, H, C, and Group 2 is B, E, F, G.

c) Assuming that the ointments look alike, it would be possible to blind the experiment for the subject and for the administrator of the treatment.

d) A block design with factors for gender and for ointment would be appropriate. Subjects would be randomly assigned to each treatment group in the blocked design.

45. a) The students were not randomly assigned. Those who signed up for the prep course may be a special group whose scores would have improved anyway.

b) Answers may vary. Find a group of volunteers who are willing to participate. Give all volunteers the SAT. Randomly assign the subjects to the review or no review group. Give the tutoring to the one group. After a reasonable time, retest both groups. See if the tutored group had a significant improvement in scores when compared with the no-review group.

c) After the volunteers have taken the first SAT, separate the volunteers into blocks of low, average, and high SAT score performance. Now assign half of each block to the review and half to the no-review groups. Give the tutoring. Now retest all groups. Compare the differences between treatments for each block.

47. Answers may vary. There are two factors: temperature of the water and wash cycle. Since each factor has 2 levels, there are 4 treatment groups (hot-reg., cold-reg., hot-del., cold-del.). It would be nice to have 32 shirts, but having equal numbers of shirts in each group is not necessary. Randomly assign shirts to each of the 4 treatment groups. Rate the level of cleaning for the grass-stained shirts. Compare the 4 groups and determine the best use of the product.

CHAPTER 10
SECTION EXERCISE ANSWERS

1. a) Normal.
   b) 0.36
   c) They wouldn't change. The shape is still approximately Normal and the mean is still the true proportion.

3. a) 0.0339
   b) 0.5
   c) 0.842 (0.843 using a rounded answer from part a)
   d) 0.01
   e) 0.039

5. Yes. Assuming the survey is random, they should be independent. We don't know the true proportion, so we can't check np and nq, but we have observed 10 successes and 30 failures, which is sufficient.

7. a) 0.0357
   b) 400

9. a) p is the proportion of all backpacks entering the stadium which contain alcoholic beverages; $\hat{p}$ is the proportion in the sample $\hat{p} = 17/130 = 13.08\%$. Yes. This seems to be a random sample.
   b) p is the proportion of all visitors to the website who approve of recent bossnapping. $\hat{p}$ is the proportion in the sample $\hat{p} = 49.2\%$. No. This is a volunteer sample and may be biased.
   c) This question is about the mean weight, not a proportion. The methods of this chapter are not appropriate.

11. a) 0.35
    b) 0.034
    c) (0.283, 0.417)

13. a) False. Doesn't make sense. Workers are not proportions.
    b) True.
    c) False. Our best guess is 0.48 not 0.95.
    d) False. Our best guess is 0.48, but we're not sure that's correct.
    e) False. The statement should be about the true proportion, not future samples.

15. a) Narrower. (0.295, 0.405) (using 1.645 standard errors on each side)
    b) Narrower. (0.296, 0.404)
    c) Wider. (0.263, 0.437) (using 2.576 standard errors on each side)
    d) 4 times as large : 800 students.

17. a) About 2401 (using 1.96 standard errors)
    b) About 4148 (using 2.576 standard errors)
    c) About 385 (using 1.96 standard errors)

19. a) 141
    b) 318
    c) 564

CHAPTER EXERCISE ANSWERS

21. All the histograms are centered near 0.05. As n gets larger, the histograms approach the Normal shape, and the variability in the sample proportions decreases.

23. a)

n	Observed mean	Theoretical mean	Observed st. dev.	Theoretical st. dev.
20	0.0497	0.05	0.0479	0.0487
50	0.0516	0.05	0.0309	0.0308
100	0.0497	0.05	0.0215	0.0218
200	0.0501	0.05	0.0152	0.0154

b) They are all quite close to what we expect from the theory.

c) The histogram is unimodal and symmetric for $n = 200$.

d) The Success/Failure Condition says that np and nq should both be at least 10, which is not satisfied until $n = 200$ for $p = 0.05$. The theory predicted my choice.

25. a) Symmetric, because probabilities of success and failure are equal.

b) 0.5

c) Standard deviation would be 0.125.

d) $np = 8 < 10$

27. a) About 68% should have proportions between 0.4 and 0.6, about 95% between 0.3 and 0.7, and about 99.7% between 0.2 and 0.8.

b) $np = 12.5, nq = 12.5$; both are ≥ 10.

c)

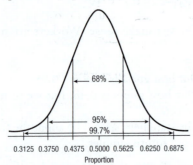

0.3125 0.3750 0.4375 0.5000 0.5625 0.6250 0.6875
Proportion

$np = nq = 32$; both are ≥ 10. Samples are random, but stock movements might not be independent.

d) Becomes narrower (less spread around 0.5).

29. a) This is a fairly unusual result: about 2.28 SDs above the mean.

b) The probability of that is about 0.012. So, in a class of 100 it is certainly reasonable that one person would do this well.

31. a)

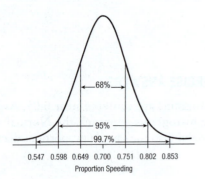

0.547 0.598 0.649 0.700 0.751 0.802 0.853
Proportion Speeding

b) Both $np = 56$ and $nq = 24 \geq 10$. Drivers *may* be independent of each other, but if flow of traffic is very fast, they may not be. Or weather conditions may affect all drivers. In these cases they may get more or fewer speeders than they expect.

33. a) Assume that these children are typical of the population. They can be considered a random sample that represents fewer than 10% of all children. We expect 20.4 nearsighted and 149.6 not; both are at least 10.

b)

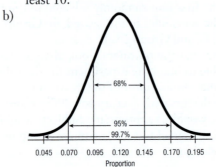

0.045 0.070 0.095 0.120 0.145 0.170 0.195
Proportion

c) Probably between 12 and 29.

35. a) $\mu = 7\%, \sigma = 1.8\%$

b) Assume that clients pay independently of each other, that we have a random sample of all possible clients, and that these represent less than 10% of all possible clients. $np = 14$ and $nq = 186$ are both at least 10.

c) 0.048

37.

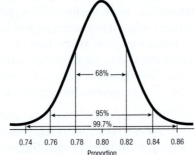

0.74 0.76 0.78 0.80 0.82 0.84 0.86
Proportion

These are not random samples, and not all colleges may be typical (representative). $np = 320, nq = 80$ are large enough.

39. Yes; if their students were typical, a retention rate of $551/603 = 91.4\%$ would be 7 standard deviations above the expected rate of 80%.

41. 0.212. Reasonable that those polled are independent of each other and represent less than 10% of all potential voters. We assume the sample was selected at random. Success/Failure Condition met: $np = 208, nq = 192$. Both ≥ 10.

43. 0.088 using $N(0.08, 0.022)$ model.

45. a) Not correct. This implies certainty.
   b) Not correct. Different samples will give different results. Most likely, none of the samples will have *exactly* 88% on-time orders.
   c) Not correct. A confidence interval says something about the unknown population proportion, not the sample proportion in different samples.
   d) Not correct. In this sample, we *know* that 88% arrived on time.
   e) Not correct. The interval is about the parameter, not about the days.

47. a) False.
   b) True.
   c) True.
   d) False.

49. We are 90% confident that between 29.9% and 47.0% of U.S. cars are made in Japan.

51. a) 0.025 or 2.5%
   b) The pollsters are 90% confident that the true proportion of adults who do not use e-mail is within 2.5% of the estimated 38%.
   c) A 99% confidence interval requires a larger margin of error. In order to increase confidence, the interval must be wider.
   d) 0.039 or 3.9%.
   e) Smaller margins of error will give us less confidence in the interval.

53. a) (12.7%, 18.6%)
   b) We are 95% confident that between 12.7% and 18.6% of all accidents involve teenage drivers.
   c) About 95% of all random samples of size 582 will produce intervals that contain the true proportion of accidents involving teenage drivers.
   d) Contradicts—the interval is completely below 20%.

55. Probably nothing. Those who bothered to fill out the survey are a voluntary response sample, which may be biased.

57. This was a random sample of less than 10% of all Internet users; there were $703 \times 0.18 = 127$ successes and 576 failures, both at least 10. We are 95% confident that between 15.2% and 20.8% of Internet users have downloaded music from a site that was not authorized. (Answer could be 15.2% to 20.9% if $n = 127$ is used instead of 0.18).

59. a) $385/550 = 0.70$; 70% of U.S. chemical companies in the sample are certified.
   b) This was a random sample, but we don't know if it is less than 10% of all U.S. chemical companies; there were $550(0.70) = 385$ successes and 165

failures, both at least 10. We are 95% confident that between 66.2% and 73.8% of the chemical companies in the United States are certified. It appears that the proportion of companies certified in the United States is less than in Canada.

61. a) There may be response bias based on the wording of the question.
   b) (45.5%, 51.5%)
   c) The margin of error based on the pooled sample is smaller, since the sample size is larger.

63. a) This was a random sample of less than 10% of all English children; there were $2700(0.20) = 540$ successes and 2160 failures, both at least 10; (18.2%, 21.8%).
   b) We are 98% confident that between 18.2% and 21.8% of English children are deficient in vitamin D.
   c) About 98% of random samples of size 2700 will produce confidence intervals that contain the true proportion of English children that are deficient in vitamin D.
   d) No. The interval says nothing about causation.

65. a) This was a random sample of less than 10% of all companies in Vermont; there were 12 successes and 0 failures, which is not greater than 10, so the sample is not large enough.
   b) Sample is not large enough to compute CI.

67. a) This was a random sample of less than 10% of all self-employed taxpayers; there were 20 successes and 206 failures, both at least 10.
   b) (5.1%, 12.6%)
   c) We are 95% confident that between 5.1% and 12.6% of all self-employed individuals had their tax returns audited in the past year.
   d) If we were to select repeated samples of 226 individuals, we'd expect about 95% of the confidence intervals we created to contain the true proportion of all self-employed individuals who were audited.

69. a) The 95% confidence interval for the true proportion of all 18- to 29-year-olds who believe the United States is ready for a woman president will be about twice as wide as the confidence interval for the true proportion of all U.S. adults, since it is based on a sample about one-fourth as large. (Assuming approximately equal proportions.)
   b) This was a random sample of less than 10% of all U.S. 15- to 29-year-old-adults; there were $250 \times 0.62 = 155$ successes and 95 failures, both at least 10. We are 95% confident that between 56.0% and 68.0% of 18- to 29-year-olds believe the United States is ready for a woman president.

71. a) This was a random sample of less than 10% of all Internet users; there were $703(0.64) = 450$ successes and 253 failures, both at least 10. We are 90% confident that between 61.0% and 67.0% of Internet users would still buy a CD.

b) In order to cut the margin of error in half, they must sample 4 times as many users; $4 \times 703 = 2812$ users.

73. 1801

75. 384 total, using $p = 0.15$

77. Since $z^* \approx 1.634$, which is close to 1.645, the pollsters were probably using 90% confidence.

79. This was a random sample of less than 10% of all customers; there were 67 successes and 433 failures, both at least 10. From the data set, $\hat{p} = 67/500 = 0.134$. We are 95% confident that the true proportion of customers who spend $1000 per month or more is between 10.4% and 16.4%.

CHAPTER 11

SECTION EXERCISE ANSWERS

1. a) Prices cannot be less than 0, but there is nothing to prevent some from being expensive, so they are likely to be skewed to the high end.

b) It should resemble the population distribution and be skewed to the right.

c) Nearly Normal. The Central Limit Theorem tells us this.

3. a) Normal.

b) 215 mg/dL

c) 4.63 mg/dL

d) Only c would change, to 3.0 mg/dL.

5. a) One would expect many small fish and a few large ones.

b) We don't know the exact distribution, but we know it is skewed, so it can't be Normal.

c) Probably not. With a skewed distribution, a sample of size 5 is not large enough to use the Central Limit Theorem.

d) The standard deviation is 0.30.

e) 4.5 pounds is more than 3 standard deviations above the mean, so by the 68--95--99.7 Rule, it would happen less than 0.15% of the time.

7. a) 1.968 years

b) 0.984 year (half as large)

9. a) 24

b) 99

11. a) 2.064

b) 1.984

13. a) (27.78, 35.90) years

b) 4.06 years

c) (27.92, 35.76) years. Slightly narrower.

15. Independence: The data were from a random survey and should be independent.
Randomization: the data were selected randomly.
10% Condition: These customers are fewer than 10% of the customer population.
Nearly Normal: The histogram is unimodal and symmetric, which is sufficient.

17. a) (232.434, 237.13)

b) We are 95% confident that the true mean cholesterol level is between 232.4 and 237.1 mg/dL.

c) That the individual values in the sample were independent. For example, it helps if the sample was random.

CHAPTER EXERCISE ANSWERS

19. a) 1.74

b) 2.37

21. As the variability of a sample increases, the width of a 95% confidence interval increases, assuming that the sample size remains the same.

23. a) ($4.382, $4.598)

b) ($4.400, $4.580)

c) ($4.415, $4.565)

25. a) Not correct. A confidence interval is for the mean weight gain of the population of all cows. It says nothing about individual cows.

b) Not correct. A confidence interval is for the mean weight gain of the population of all cows, not individual cows.

c) Not correct. We don't need a confidence interval about the average weight gain for cows in this study. We are certain that the mean weight gain of the cows in this study is 56 pounds.

d) Not correct. This statement implies that the average weight gain varies. It doesn't.

e) Not correct. This statement implies that there is something special about our interval, when this interval is actually one of many that could have been generated, depending on the cows that were chosen for the sample.

27. The assumptions and conditions for a t-interval are not met. With a sample size of only 20, the distribution is too skewed. There is also a large outlier that is pulling the mean higher.

29. a) The data are a random sample of all days; the distribution is unimodal and symmetric with no outliers.

b) ($122.20, $129.80)

c) We are 90% confident that the interval $122.20 to $129.80 contains the true mean daily income of the parking garage.

d) 90% of all random samples of size 44 will produce intervals that contain the true mean daily income of the parking garage.

e) $128 is a plausible value.

31. a) We can be more confident that our interval contains the mean parking revenue.

b) Wider (and less precise) interval.

c) By collecting a larger sample, they could create a more precise interval without sacrificing confidence.

33. a) (2230.4, 2469.6)

b) The assumptions and conditions that must be satisfied are:
1 Independence: probably OK.
2 Nearly Normal Condition: can't tell.
3 Sample size of 51 is large enough.

c) We are 95% confident the interval $2230.4 to $2469.6 contains the true mean increase in sales tax revenue.
Examples of what the interval *does not* mean: The mean increase in sales tax revenue is $2350 95% of the time. 95% of all increases in sales tax revenue increases will be between $2230.4 and $2469.6. There's 95% confidence the next small retailer will have an increase in sales tax revenue between $2230.4 and $2469.6.

35. a) Given no time trend, the monthly on-time departure rates should be independent. Though not a random sample, these months should be representative, and they're fewer than 10% of all months. The histogram looks unimodal, but slightly left-skewed; not a concern with this large sample.

b) (80.25, 81.18)

c) We can be 90% confident that the interval from 80.25 to 81.18 holds the true mean monthly percentage of on-time flight departures.

37. a) The histogram of the lab fees shows 2 extreme outliers, so with the outliers included, the conditions for inference are violated.

b) With the outliers left in, the 95% confidence interval is (44.9, 81.6) minutes. If we remove the two extreme outliers, it is (54.6, 68.4).
In either case, we would be reluctant to conclude that the mean is above 55 minutes. The sample size is small and the presence of two large outliers advises us to be cautious about conclusions from this sample.

39. a) The assumptions and conditions that must be satisfied are:
The data come from a nearly Normal distribution. The air samples were selected randomly, and there is no bias present in the sample.

b) The histogram of air samples is not nearly Normal, but the sample size is large, so inference is OK.

41. a) $14.90 - 11.6$ or ± 3.3 miles per hour

b) We can find the needed sample size from: $1.96 \times 8/2 = \sqrt{n}$. $(7.84)^2 = n = 61.46$ use 62.

43. a) Interval: $653 to $707

b) The confidence interval suggests the mean audit cost is now greater than $650.

45. a) The timeplot shows no pattern, so it seems that the measurements are independent. Although this is not a random sample, an entire year is measured, so it is likely that we have representative values. We certainly have fewer than 10% of all possible wind readings. The histogram appears nearly Normal.

b) A 95% confidence interval for the true mean speed is (7.795, 8.243) mph. Because there are many plausible values below 8 mph, we cannot be confident that the true mean is at least 8 mph. We would not recommend that the turbine be placed here.

47. a) Random sample. Nearly Normal Condition is reasonable by examining a Normal probability plot. The histogram is roughly unimodal (although somewhat uniform) and symmetric with no outliers. (Show your plot.)

b) (114.9, 148.8) calories

c) The mean number of calories in a serving of vanilla yogurt is between 115 and 149, with 95% confidence. We conclude that the diet guide's claim of 120 calories is toward the lower end, but is reasonable.

CHAPTER 12

1. The new drug is not more effective than aspirin, or H_0: $p = 0.44$, where p = rate of reduction in heart attacks.

3. a) Let p = probability of winning on the slot machine. H_0: $p = 0.01$ vs. H_A: $p \neq 0.01$

b) Let μ = mean spending per customer this year. H_0: $\mu = \$35.32$ vs. H_A: $\mu \neq \$35.32$

c) Let p = proportion of patients cured by the new drug. H_0: $p = 0.3$ vs. H_A: $p \neq 0.3$

d) Let p = proportion of clients now using the website. H_0: $p = 0.4$ vs. H_A: $p \neq 0.4$

5. a) One-sided. They are interested in discovering only if their drug is more effective than aspirin, not if it is less effective than aspirin.

b) There is convincing evidence to conclude that the new drug is better than aspirin.

c) There is not convincing evidence that the new drug is more effective than aspirin.

7. a) H_0: The proportion, p, of people in the county that are of Hispanic or Latino origin is $p = 0.16$.

$$H_a: p \neq 0.16$$

b) This is a one-proportion z-test. The 437 residents were a random sample from the county of interest. 437 is almost certainly less than 10% of the population of a county. We expect $np_0 = 69.9$ successes and $nq_0 = 367.1$ failures, which are both more than 10. The conditions are satisfied, so it's okay to use a Normal model and perform a one-proportion z-test.

c) $\hat{p} = \dfrac{44}{437} = 0.101$;

$$SD(\hat{p}) = \sqrt{\dfrac{p_0 q_0}{n}} = \sqrt{\dfrac{0.16 \times 0.84}{437}} = 0.0175;$$

$$z = \dfrac{\hat{p} - p_0}{SD(\hat{p})} = \dfrac{0.101 - 0.16}{0.0175} = -3.37;$$

P-value $= 2 \cdot P(z < -3.37) < 0.001$

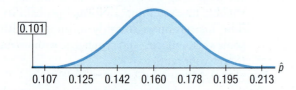

| 0.101 |

0.107   0.125   0.142   0.160   0.178   0.195   0.213 $\hat{p}$

d) Because the P-value is so low, there is evidence that the Hispanic/Latino population in this county differs from that of the nation as a whole.

9. a) An increase in the mean score would mean that the mean difference (After – Before) is positive. So $H_0: \mu_{diff} = 0$, $H_A: \mu_{diff} > 0$.

b) Because the P-value is large, there is not convincing evidence that the course works.

c) Because the P-value is greater than 0.5 and the alternative is one-sided (>0), we can conclude that the actual difference was less than 0. (If it had been positive, the probability to the right of that value would have to be less than 0.5.)

11. If, in fact, the mean cholesterol level of pizza eaters does not indicate a health risk, then only 7 of every 100 people sampled, on average, would have a mean cholesterol level as high as (or higher than) was observed in this sample.

13. a) The drug may not be approved for use. Then people will miss out on a beneficial product and the company will miss out on potential sales.

b) The drug will go into production and people will suffer the side effect.

15. a) $H_0: p = 0.30$; $H_A: p < 0.30$

b) $H_0: p = 0.50$; $H_A: p \neq 0.50$

c) $H_0: p = 0.20$; $H_A: p > 0.20$

17. Statement d is correct. It talks about the probability of seeing the data, not the probability of the hypotheses.

19. No. We can say only that there is a 27% chance of seeing the observed effectiveness just from natural sampling variation. There is insufficient evidence that the new formula is more effective, but we can't conclude that they are equally effective.

21. a) No. There's a 25% chance of losing twice in a row. That's not unusual.

b) 0.125

c) No. We expect that to happen 1 time in 8.

d) Answers may vary. The chance of 5 losses in a row is only 1 in 32, which seems unusual. On the other hand, I'm very skeptical of the claim and will need extraordinary evidence to be convinced (and to verify that he's not cheating!).

23. 1) Use p, not $\hat{p}$, in hypotheses.

2) The question was about failing to meet the goal, so H_A should be $p < 0.96$.

3) Did not check $0.04(200) = 8$. Since $nq < 10$, the Success/Failure Condition is violated. Didn't check 10% Condition.

4) $188/200 = 0.94$; $SD(\hat{p}) = \sqrt{\dfrac{(0.96)(0.04)}{200}} = 0.014$

5) z is incorrect; should be $z = \dfrac{0.94 - 0.96}{0.014} = -1.43$.

6) $P = P(z < -1.43) = 0.076$

7) There is only weak evidence that the new instructions do not work.

25. a) $H_0: p = 0.30$; $H_A: p > 0.30$

b) Possibly an SRS; we don't know if the sample is less than 10% of his customers, but it could be viewed as less than 10% of all possible customers; $(0.3)(80) \geq 10$ and $(0.7)(80) \geq 10$. Wells are independent only if customers don't have farms on the same underground springs.

c) $z = 0.73$; P-value $= 0.232$

d) If his dowsing is no different from standard methods, there is more than a 23% chance of seeing results as good as those of the dowser's, or better, by natural sampling variation.

e) These data provide insufficient evidence that the dowser's chance of finding water is any better than normal drilling.

27. a) $H_0: p_{2000} = 0.34$; $H_A: p_{2000} \neq 0.34$
   b) Students were randomly sampled and should be independent. 34% and 66% of 8302 are greater than 10. 8302 students is less than 10% of the entire student population of the United States.
   c) $P = 0.054$ or 0.055 using tables
   d) The P-value provides weak evidence against the null hypothesis.
   e) No. A difference this small, even if statistically significant, is probably not meaningful. We might look at new data in a few years.

29. a) $H_0: p = 0.05$ vs. $H_A: p < 0.05$
   b) We assume the whole mailing list has over 1,000,000 names. This is a random sample, and we expect 5000 successes and 95,000 failures.
   c) $z = -3.178$; P-value $= 0.00074$, so we reject H_0; there is strong evidence that the donation rate would be below 5%.

31. $H_0: p = 0.20$; $H_A: p > 0.20$. SRS (not clear from information provided); 22 is more than 10% of the population of 150; $(0.20)(22) < 10$. Do not proceed with a test.

33. $H_0: p = 0.03$; $p \neq 0.03$. $\hat{p} = 0.015$. One mother having twins will not affect another, so observations are independent; not an SRS; sample is less than 10% of all births. However, the mothers at this hospital may not be representative of all teenagers; $(0.03)(469) = 14.07 \geq 10$; $(0.97)(469) \geq 10$. $z = -1.92$; P-value $= 0.055$. These data show some (although weak) evidence that the rate of twins born to teenage girls at this hospital may be less than the national rate of 3%. It is not clear whether this can be generalized to all teenagers.

35. $H_0: p = 0.25$; $H_A: p > 0.25$. SRS; sample is less than 10% of all potential subscribers; $(0.25)(500) \geq 10$; $(0.75)(500) \geq 10$. $z = 1.24$; P-value $= 0.1075$. The P-value is high, so do not reject H_0. These data do not provide sufficient evidence that more than 25% of current readers would subscribe; the company should not go ahead with the WebZine solely on the basis of these data.

37. $H_0: p = 0.40$; $H_A: p < 0.40$. Data are for all executives in this company and may not be able to be generalized to all companies; $(0.40)(43) \geq 10$; $(0.60)(43) \geq 10$. $z = -1.31$; P-value $= 0.096$. Because the P-value is high, we fail to reject H_0. These data do not show that the proportion of women executives is less than the 40% of women in the company in general.

39. $H_0: p = 0.059$; $H_A: p > 0.059$. $\hat{p} = 0.060$; $z = 0.179$; P-value $= 0.429$. Because the P-value is not very low, we fail to reject H_0. These data do not provide convincing evidence that the dropout rate has increased.

41. $H_0: p = 0.90$; $H_A: p < 0.90$. $\hat{p} = 0.844$; $z = -2.05$; P-value $= 0.020$. Because the P-value is so low, we reject H_0. There is strong evidence that the actual rate at which passengers with lost luggage are reunited with it within 24 hours is less than the 90% claimed by the airline.

43. a) Yes. Assuming this sample to be a typical group of people, P-value $= 0.0008$. This cancer rate is very unusual.
   b) No, this group of people may be atypical for reasons that have nothing to do with the radiation.

45. a) Interval: $649.35 to $710.64
   b) The confidence interval suggests the mean audit cost is not greater than $650.

47. If the mean cholesterol level really does not exceed the value considered to indicate a health risk, there is a 4% probability that a random sample of this size would have a mean as high as (or higher than) that in this sample.

49. a) Probably a representative sample; the Nearly Normal Condition seems reasonable. (Show a Normal probability plot or histogram.) The histogram is nearly uniform, with no outliers or skewness.
   b) $\bar{y} = 28.78$, $s = 0.40$
   c) $t = 2.94$, $df = 5$, P-value $= 0.032$. Because the P-value is low, we reject H_0. We have convincing evidence that the mean weight of bags of Ruffles potato chips is not 28.3 grams.

51. Yes. These are a random sample of bags and the Nearly Normal Condition is met. (Show a Normal probability plot or histogram.) $t = -2.51$ with 7 df for a one-sided P-value of 0.0203.

53. a) Random sample; the Nearly Normal Condition seems reasonable from a Normal probability plot. The histogram is roughly unimodal and symmetric with no outliers. This is definitely less than 10% of all bags of Chips Ahoy!
   b) $H_0: \mu = 1000$, $H_A: \mu > 1000$, where μ is the mean number of chips per bag; $\bar{y} = 1238.2$, $s = 94.3$, $t = 10.1$, $df = 15$, P-value < 0.0001. Because the P-value is so low, we reject the null hypothesis. We have convincing evidence that the mean number of chips per bag is greater than 1000. However, their statement isn't about the mean. They claim that *all* bags have at least 1000 chips. So this test doesn't really answer the question.

55. a) The Normal probability plot is relatively straight, with one outlier at 93.8 sec. Without the outlier, the conditions seem to be met. The histogram is roughly unimodal and symmetric with no other outliers. (Show your plot.)

b) Because the question asks for "at most one minute," $H_0: \mu = 60$, $H_A: \mu < 60$, where μ is the mean number of seconds to complete the maze. With the outlier, $\bar{y} = 52.2$, $s = 13.6$, $t = -2.63$, $df = 20$, P-value $= 0.008$. Without the outlier, the evidence for the alternative hypothesis should be even stronger because the mean will be lower, as will the standard deviation. The numbers without the outlier are $\bar{y} = 50.13$, $s = 9.9$, $t = -4.46$, $df = 20$, P-value $= 0.0001$. Because the P-value is low both with and without the outlier, we reject the null hypothesis. We have convincing evidence that the mean number of seconds to complete the maze is less than 60. It appears that, even with the occasional slow mouse, this maze meets the requirement that the time be at most one minute. However, if the researcher wants the mean time to be one minute, we have evidence that this requirement is not met.

57. a) $(45.271, 59.939)$

b) Because of the outlier at 93.8 seconds.

c) It makes the interval not symmetric around the sample mean.

d) Because 60 seconds is not in the interval, it is not plausible that the mean time is 60 seconds. The mean time appears to be less than 60 seconds.

e) We want the proportion of cases farther than 7.79 seconds from 60 seconds. On the left, that is fewer than 0.05% of cases. On the right, it is fewer than 0.5% of cases. We might estimate the P-value at about 0.004.

CHAPTER 13
SECTION EXERCISE ANSWERS

1. a) False. It provides evidence against it but does not show it is false.

b) False. The P-value is not the probability that the null hypothesis is true.

c) True

d) False. Whether a P-value provides enough evidence to reject the null hypothesis depends on the risk of a Type I error that one is willing to assume (the α-level).

3. a) True.

b) False. The alpha level is set independently and does not depend on the sample size.

c) False. The P-value would have to be less than 0.01 to reject the null hypothesis.

d) False. It simply means we do not have enough evidence at that alpha level to reject the null hypothesis.

5. a) $z = \pm 1.96$

b) $z = 1.645$

c) $t = \pm 2.03$

d) $z = 2.33$; n is not relevant for critical values for z.

e) $z = -2.33$

7. a) $(0.196, 0.304)$

b) No, because 0.20 is a plausible value.

c) The SE is based on $\hat{p}$, so:
$$SE(\hat{p}) = \sqrt{\frac{\hat{p}\hat{q}}{n}} = \sqrt{\frac{(0.25)(0.75)}{250}} = 0.0274.$$
The SD is based on the hypothesized value 0.20, so
$$SD(\hat{p}) = \sqrt{\frac{p_0 q_0}{n}} = \sqrt{\frac{(0.20)(0.80)}{250}} = 0.0253.$$

d) The SE, since it is sample based.

9. a) $SE = \dfrac{s}{\sqrt{n}} = \dfrac{2.0}{\sqrt{25}} = 0.4$

b) t^* with 24 df for a 90% confidence interval is 1.711.

c) $(15.82, 17.18)$

d) No, we fail to reject H_0 (one-sided) at $\alpha = 0.05$ because 16.0 is in the corresponding two-sided 90% confidence interval.

11. a) Type I error. The actual value is not greater than 0.3 but they rejected the null hypothesis.

b) No error. The actual value is 0.50, which was not rejected.

c) Type II error. The actual value was 55.3 points, which is greater than 52.5.

d) Type II error. The null hypothesis was not rejected, but it was false. The true relief rate was greater than 0.25.

13. a) All other things being equal, the power is reduced when trying to detect a smaller effect size.

b) She should use a larger sample size to keep the power the same.

15. At $\alpha = 0.10$ he would have made the same decision because the P-value was < 0.05 (and so < 0.10). But if $\alpha = 0.01$ he will reach the same decision only if the P-value is also < 0.01.

17. a) There is basically zero chance of seeing a sample proportion as low as 97.4% vaccinated by natural sampling variation if 98% have really been vaccinated.

b) We conclude that p is below 0.98, but a 95% confidence interval would suggest that the true proportion is between $(0.971, 0.977)$. Most likely, a decrease from 98% to 97.6% would not be considered important. On the other hand, with 1,000,000 children a year vaccinated, even 0.1% represents about 1000 kids—so this may very well be important.

19. a) No mention of an SRS or randomization, so proceed with caution; successes and failures both >10; $(0.486, 0.534)$.

   b) Because 45% is not in the interval we have strong evidence that more than 45% of men identify themselves as the primary grocery shopper.

   c) $\alpha = 0.01$; it's an upper-tail test based on a 98% confidence interval.

21. a) Less likely

   b) Alpha levels must be chosen *before* examining the data. Otherwise the alpha level could always be selected to reject the null hypothesis.

23. a) The mean download time is 15 standard errors below the hypothesized mean.

   b) $t_{19,.001} = -3.5794$. Since $-15 < -3.5794$, we can reject H_0 at $\alpha < 0.001$.

   c) We know that 15 standard errors is very unlikely no matter how many degrees of freedom there are.

25. a) The value 0.98 lies above the interval, which leaves 1% of the plausible values on that side. So she can reject the null hypothesis that $p = 0.98$.

   b) The true value may be as high as 97.73%. She would need to do a cost analysis to see what the cost of an extra 0.27% measles cases would mean to her company.

27. a) Type II error.

   b) Type I error.

   c) By making it easier to get the loan, the bank has reduced the alpha level.

   d) The risk of a Type I error is decreased and the risk of a Type II error is increased.

29. a) Power is the probability that the bank denies a loan that would not have been repaid.

   b) Raise the cutoff score.

   c) A larger number of trustworthy people would be denied credit, and the bank would miss the opportunity to collect interest on those loans.

31. a) The null is that the level of home ownership remains the same. The alternative is that it rises.

   b) The city concludes that home ownership is on the rise, but in fact the tax breaks don't help.

   c) The city abandons the tax breaks, but home ownership is actually increasing.

   d) A Type I error causes the city to forego tax revenue, while a Type II error withdraws help from those who might have otherwise been able to buy a home.

   e) The power of the test is the city's ability to detect an actual increase in home ownership.

33. a) It is decided that the shop is not meeting standards when it is.

   b) The shop is certified as meeting standards when it is not.

   c) Type I.

   d) Type II.

35. a) The probability of detecting a shop that is not meeting standards.

   b) 40 cars. Larger n.

   c) 10%. More chance to reject H_0.

   d) A lot. Larger differences are easier to detect.

37. a) One-tailed. The company wouldn't be sued if "too many" minorities were hired.

   b) Deciding the company is discriminating when it is not.

   c) Deciding the company is not discriminating when it is.

   d) The probability of correctly detecting actual discrimination.

   e) Increases power.

   f) Lower, since n is smaller.

39. a) One-tailed. The software is supposed to increase the final exam scores.

   b) $H_0: \mu = 105$; $H_A: \mu > 105$

   c) He buys the software when it doesn't help students.

   d) He doesn't buy the software when it does help students.

   e) The probability of correctly deciding the software is helpful.

41. Given this confidence interval, we cannot reject the null hypothesis of a mean $200 collection using $\alpha = 0.05$. However, the confidence interval suggests that there may be a large upside potential. The collection agency may be collecting as much as $250 per customer on average, or as little as $190 on average. If the possibility of collecting $250 on average is of interest to them, they may want to collect more data.

43. a) Upper-tail. We want to show it will hold 500 pounds (or more) easily.

   b) They will decide the stands are safe when they're not.

   c) They will decide the stands are unsafe when they are in fact safe.

45. a) Decrease α. This means a smaller chance of declaring the stands safe if they are not.

   b) The probability of correctly detecting that the stands are capable of holding more than 500 pounds.

   c) Decrease the standard deviation—probably costly. Increase the sample size—takes more time for testing and is costly. Increase α—more Type I errors. Increase the "design load" to be well above 500 pounds—again, costly.

47. a) H_A: The coin is the 30% heads coin.
b) Reject the null hypothesis if the coin comes up tails—otherwise fail to reject.
c) $P(\text{tails given the null hypothesis}) = 0.1 = \alpha$
d) $P(\text{tails given the alternative hypothesis}) = \text{power} = 0.70$
e) Spin the coin more than once and base the decision on the sample proportion of heads.

49. Yes, there is a large ($50) upside potential. The larger trial will likely narrow the confidence interval and make the decision clearer.

51. a) H_0: $\mu = 55$; H_A: $\mu < 55$; Independence Assumption: Since the times are not randomly selected, we will assume that the times are independent and representative of all the champion's times. Nearly Normal Condition: The histogram of the times is unimodal and roughly symmetric; P-value = 0.235; fail to reject H_0. There is insufficient evidence to conclude the mean time is less than 55 seconds. They should not market the new ski wax.
b) Type II error. They won't market a competitive wax and thus lose the potential profit from having done so.

CHAPTER 14
SECTION EXERCISE ANSWERS

1. a) $\bar{y}_1 = 58.0$ years; $\bar{y}_2 = 47.0$ years
b) 11 years
c) $s_1^2 = 50$; $s_2^2 = 54$
d) $s_1 = 7.07$ years; $s_2 = 7.35$ years
e) 4.16 years

3. a) 9.6 years
b) 1.91 years
c) 5.03

5. a) 2.64
b) 9.985
c) 5
d) 0.0247
e) 0.0459
f) For either method of calculating df, there is reasonably strong evidence to suggest that we reject the null hypothesis and conclude that the mean age of houses is not the same in the two neighborhoods.

7. a) <0.001
b) <0.001
c) In both cases, reject H_0. There is very strong evidence to suggest that there is a difference in the mean ages of houses in the two neighborhoods.

9. a) (1.72, 20.28) years
b) No.
c) It suggests that we should reject H_0, since 0 is not a plausible value for the true mean difference.

11. a) (5.77, 13.43) years
b) The sample sizes are larger.
c) No.
d) It suggests that we should reject H_0, since 0 is not a plausible value for the true mean difference.

13. a) $t = 2.642$; P-value = 0.0246. Reject H_0 and conclude that there is sufficient evidence to suggest that the true means are different.
b) (1.72, 20.28) years
c) Not really. Because the standard deviations are fairly close, the two methods will result in essentially the same confidence intervals and hypothesis tests.

15. a) $t = 5.01$; P-value < 0.001. Reject H_0. There is strong evidence to reject the hypothesis that the means are equal.
b) (5.77, 13.43) years
c) Very close to previous results because the standard deviations are fairly close. In such a case, the two methods will result in essentially the same confidence intervals and hypothesis tests.

17. a) Paired. Each pair consists of a volunteer using each chair.
b) Not paired. The samples are random within each neighborhood.
c) Paired. Each pair consists of an hour in which the productivity of the two workers is compared.

19. a) Yes, each pair is a store in which the customers with and without the program are compared.
b) 3 customers
c) 4.52 customers
d) 1.43 customers
e) 2.098
f) 9
g) One-sided. They want to know if traffic increased.
h) 0.0327
i) We can reject the null hypothesis. There is evidence of an increase in traffic.

21. (0.379, 5.621) customers

CHAPTER EXERCISE ANSWERS

23. The P-value is too high to reject H_0 at any reasonable α-level.

25. a) 2.927 points
b) Larger.
c) We are 95% confident that the mean score for the CPMP math students will be between 5.573 and 11.427 points higher on this assessment than the mean score of the traditional students.
d) Since the entire interval is above 0, there is strong evidence that students who learn with CPMP will have higher mean scores in applied algebra than those in traditional programs.

27. a) $H_0: \mu_C - \mu_T = 0$; $H_A: \mu_C - \mu_T \neq 0$

b) If the mean scores for the CPMP and traditional students are really equal, there is less than a 1 in 10,000 chance of seeing a difference as large or larger than the observed difference of 9.4 points just from natural sampling variation.

c) There is strong evidence that the CPMP students have a different mean score than the traditional students. The evidence suggests that the CPMP students have a lower mean score.

29. $H_0: \mu_C - \mu_T = 0$; $H_A: \mu_C - \mu_T \neq 0$
$P = 0.1602$; fail to reject H_0. There is no evidence that the CPMP students have a different mean score on the word problems test than the traditional students.

31. a) $(1.36, 4.64)$; df $= 33.1$

b) Since the CI does not contain 0, there is evidence that Route A is faster on average.

33. a) $H_0: \mu_C - \mu_A = 0$; $H_A: \mu_C - \mu_A \neq 0$

b) Independent Groups Assumption: The percentage of sugar in the children's cereals is unrelated to the percentage of sugar in adult cereals. Randomization Condition: It is reasonable to assume that the cereals are representative of all children's cereals and adult cereals, in regard to sugar content. Nearly Normal Condition: The histogram of adult cereal sugar content is skewed to the right, but the sample sizes are reasonably large. The Central Limit Theorem allows us to proceed.

c) $(32.49, 40.80)\%$

d) Since the 95% confidence interval does not contain 0, we can conclude that the mean sugar content for the two cereals is significantly different at the 5% level of significance.

35. a) $H_0: \mu_{\text{Taxable}} - \mu_{\text{Municipal}} = 0$
$H_A: \mu_{\text{Taxable}} - \mu_{\text{Municipal}} \neq 0$

b) Distributions are symmetric. Funds are independent. Outliers in boxplot not severe enough to cause concern.

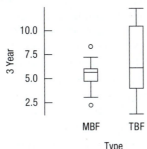

c) Difference Between Means $= 1.055$ t-Statistic $= 1.020$ w/16.54 df $P = 0.3225$

d) There does not appear to be a significant difference between these types of funds.

37. $H_0: \mu_N - \mu_C = 0$; $H_A: \mu_N - \mu_C > 0$. Independent Groups Assumption: Student scores in one group

should not have an impact on the scores of students in the other group. Randomization Condition: Students were randomly assigned to classes. Nearly Normal Condition: The histograms of the scores are unimodal and symmetric. $P = 0.017$; reject H_0. There is evidence that the students taught using the new activities have a higher mean score on the reading comprehension test than the students taught using traditional methods.

39. a) $H_0: \mu_{1997-2006} - \mu_{2007-2017} = 0$
$H_A: \mu_{1997-2006} - \mu_{2007-2017} \neq 0$

b) Both time periods have values that show as possible outliers in boxplots, but neither one seems particularly extreme. The two time periods are plausibly independent.

c) Performing a two-sample t-test, $t = 0.551$ with 14.65 df, $P = 0.59$. Fail to reject H_0.

41. a) If the mean memory scores for people taking ginkgo biloba and people not taking it are the same, there is a 93.74% chance of seeing a difference in mean memory score this large or larger simply from natural sampling variability.

b) Since the P-value is so high, there is no evidence that the mean memory test score for ginkgo biloba users is higher than the mean memory test score for non-users.

c) Type II.

43. a) Males: $(18.67, 20.11)$ pegs; females: $(16.95, 18.87)$ pegs

b) It may appear to suggest that there is no difference in the mean number of pegs placed by males and females, but a two-sample t-interval should be constructed to assess the difference in mean number of pegs placed.

c) $(0.29, 2.67)$ pegs

d) We are 95% confident that the mean number of pegs placed by males is between 0.29 and 2.67 pegs higher than the mean number of pegs placed by females.

e) Two-sample t-interval.

f) If you attempt to use two confidence intervals to assess a difference in means, you are actually adding standard deviations. But it's the variances that add, not the standard deviations. The two-sample difference of means procedure takes this into account.

45. a) $H_0: \mu_N - \mu_S = 0$; $H_A: \mu_N - \mu_S \neq 0$
$t = 6.47$, df $= 53.49$, $P < 0.001$
Since the P-value is low, we reject H_0. There is strong evidence that the mean mortality rate is different for towns north and south of Derby. There is evidence that the mortality rate north of Derby is higher.

b) The possible outlier slightly raised the mean and inflated the variance for North Derby. The t-statistic is large and the outlier not particularly extreme, so omitting that point would likely make little difference in our conclusion.

47. a) Paired Data Assumption: The data are before and after job satisfaction rating for the same workers. Randomization Condition: The workers were randomly selected to participate. Nearly Normal Condition: A histogram of differences between before and after job satisfaction ratings is roughly unimodal and symmetric.

b) $H_0: \mu_d = 0$; $H_A: \mu_d > 0$; $t = 3.60$; df $= 9$; P-value $= 0.0029$; reject H_0. There is evidence that the mean job satisfaction rating has increased since the implementation of the exercise program.

49. Independent Groups Assumption: Assume that orders in June are independent of orders in August. Independence Assumption: Orders were a random sample. Nearly Normal Condition: Hard to check with small sample, but no outliers. $H_0: \mu_J - \mu_A = 0$; $H_A: \mu_J - \mu_A > 0$; $t = -1.17$; $P = 0.136$; fail to reject H_0. Thus, although the mean delivery time during August is higher, the difference in delivery time from June is not significant. A larger sample may produce a different statistical result, but the size of the difference may not be important from a business standpoint.

51. a) We are 95% confident that the mean number of brand names remembered by viewers of shows with violent content will be between 1.6 and 0.6 lower than the mean number of brand names remembered by viewers of shows with neutral content.

b) If they want viewers to remember their brand names, they should consider advertising on shows with neutral content, as opposed to shows with violent content.

53. a) She might attempt to conclude that the mean number of brand names recalled is greater after 24 hours.

b) The groups are not independent. They are the same people, asked at two different time periods.

c) A person with high recall right after the show might tend to have high recall 24 hours later as well. Also, the first interview may have helped the people to remember the brand names for a longer period of time than they would have otherwise.

d) Randomly assign half of the group watching that type of content to be interviewed immediately after watching, and assign the other half to be interviewed 24 hours later.

55. a) The differences that were observed between the group of students with Internet access and those without were too great to be attributed to natural sampling variation.

b) Type I.

c) No. There may be many other factors.

d) It might be used to market computer services to parents.

57. a) 8759 pounds

b) Independent Groups Assumption: Sales in different seasons should be independent. Randomization Condition: Not a random sample of weeks, but it is of stores. Nearly Normal Condition: Can't verify, but we will proceed cautiously. We are 95% confident that the interval 3630.54 to 13,887.39 pounds contains the true difference in mean sales between winter and summer.

c) Weather and sporting events may impact pizza sales.

59. Because runners are assigned to heats at random, we expect there to be no statistically significant difference between the heats.

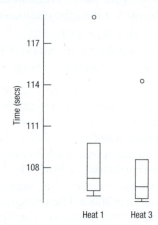

Boxplots show only a small difference in medians. But both heats had a high outlier time, making a formal test problematic.

61. $H_0: \mu_S - \mu_R = 0$; $H_A: \mu_S - \mu_R > 0$. Assuming the conditions are satisfied, it is appropriate to model the sampling distribution of the difference in means with a Student's t-model, with 7.03 degrees of freedom (from the approximation formula). $t = 4.57$; $P = 0.0013$; reject H_0. There is strong evidence that the mean ball velocity for Stinger tees is higher than the mean velocity for regular tees.

63. a) $H_0: \mu_M - \mu_R = 0$; $H_A: \mu_M - \mu_R > 0$. Independent Groups Assumption: The groups are not related in regards to memory score. Randomization Condition: Subjects were randomly assigned to groups. Nearly Normal Condition: We don't have the actual data. We will assume that the distributions of the populations of memory test scores are Normal. $t = -0.70$; df $= 45.88$; $P = 0.7563$; fail to reject H_0. There is no evidence that the mean number of objects remembered by those who listen to Mozart is higher than the mean number of objects remembered by those who listen to rap music.

b) We are 90% confident that the mean number of objects remembered by those who listen to Mozart is between 0.19 and 5.35 objects lower than the mean of those who listened to no music.

65. a) Paired Data Assumption: These data are paired, as they are the 1- and 5-year returns of the same mutual funds. Randomization Condition: random sample of funds. Nearly Normal Condition: Histogram of differences is skewed left, but we will proceed with caution.
b) $H_0: \mu_{5yr} - \mu_{1yr} = 0$; $H_A: \mu_{5yr} - \mu_{1yr} > 0$
c) In fact the mean paired difference is -2.40, so the P-value will be higher than 0.50. (The actual one-sided P-value is nearly 1.0.)
d) $(-3.50, -1.29)$

67. a) Independent Groups Assumption: The attendance numbers in different leagues are independent. Randomization Condition: Not a random sample, but we will assume it's representative. Nearly Normal Condition: Both histograms are reasonably unimodal and symmetric with no outliers.
b) $H_0: \mu_{AL} - \mu_{NL} = 0$; $H_A: \mu_{AL} - \mu_{NL} < 0$
c) $t = 2.448$; $P = 0.0105$
d) We can conclude that the mean attendance at road games is higher, on average, in the National League. We reject the null hypothesis.
e) $t = 2.448$; $P = 0.0104$. Same conclusion as in part d.

69. Adding variances requires that the variables be independent. These price quotes are for the same cars, so they are paired. Drivers quoted high insurance premiums by the local company will be likely to get a high rate from the online company, too.

71. a) The histogram—we care about differences in price.
b) Insurance cost is based on risk, so drivers are likely to see similar quotes from each company, making the differences relatively smaller.
c) The price quotes are paired; they were for a random sample of fewer than 10% of the agent's customers; the histogram of differences looks approximately Normal.

73. $H_0: \mu_{Local-Online} = 0$; $H_A: \mu_{Local-Online} > 0$; $t = 0.826$ with 9 df. With a P-value of 0.215, we cannot reject the null hypothesis. These data don't provide evidence that online premiums are lower, on average.

75. a) $H_0: \mu_d = 0$; $H_A: \mu_d \neq 0$
b) $t_{144} = 2.406$; 2-sided $P = 0.017$
We are able to reject the null hypothesis (with a P-value of 0.017) and conclude that mean number of keystrokes per hour has changed.
c) 95% CI for mean keystrokes per hour $22.7 \pm t_{0.025, 144} s/\sqrt{n} = (4.05, 41.35)$

77. a) Paired Data Assumption: The data are paired by type of exercise machine. Randomization Condition: Assume that the men and women participating are representative of all men and women in terms of number of minutes of exercise required to burn 200 calories. Nearly Normal Condition:

The histogram of differences between women's and men's times is roughly unimodal and symmetric. We are 95% confident that women take an average of 4.8 to 15.2 minutes longer to burn 200 calories than men when exercising at a light exertion rate.
b) Nearly Normal Condition: There is no reason to think that this histogram does not represent differences drawn from a Normal population. We are 95% confident that women exercising with light exertion take an average of 4.9 to 20.4 minutes longer to burn 200 calories than women exercising with hard exertion.
c) Since these data are averages, we expect the individual times to be more variable. Our standard error would be larger, resulting in a larger margin of error.

79. a) Randomization Condition: These stops are probably representative of all such stops for this type of car, but not for all cars. Nearly Normal Condition: A histogram of the stopping distances is roughly unimodal and symmetric. We are 95% confident that the mean dry pavement stopping distance for this type of car is between 133.6 and 145.2 feet.
b) Independent Groups Assumption: The wet pavement stops and dry pavement stops were made under different conditions and not paired in any way. Randomization Condition: These stops are probably representative of all such stops for this type of car, but not for all cars. Nearly Normal Condition: The histogram of wet pavement stopping distances is more uniform than unimodal, but no outliers. We are 95% confident that the mean stopping distance on wet pavement is between 50.4 and 75.6 feet longer than the mean stopping distance on dry pavement.

81. a) The data are paired. They are for the same airlines in two different years and our concern is about whether the involuntary DB rate has changed. We would measure improvement for each airline.
b) Boxplots are *not* the appropriate display because the data are paired. Here is a histogram of the pairwise differences.

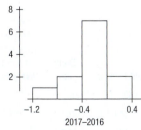

A paired *t*-test finds a mean of paired differences (2017−2016) of -0.0226. The corresponding *t*-statistic is -2.596 with 11 df. That gives a P-value of 0.0249, which is small enough to conclude that there is a real change.

CHAPTER 15
SECTION EXERCISE ANSWERS

1. a) (30, 30, 30, 30), 30 for each season
   b) 1.933
   c) 3

3. a) 3
   b) No, it's smaller than the mean.
   c) It would say that there is no evidence to reject the null hypothesis that births are distributed uniformly across the seasons.
   d) 7.815
   e) Do not reject the null hypothesis. As in part c, there is no evidence to suggest that births are not distributed uniformly across the seasons.

5. a) $(-0.913, 0.913, 0.365, -0.365)$
   b) No, they are quite small for z-values.
   c) Because we did not reject the null hypothesis, we shouldn't expect any of the standardized residuals to be large.

7. a) The age distributions of customers at the two branches are the same.
   b) Chi-square test of homogeneity.
   c)

	Age			
	Less Than 30	30–55	56 or Older	Total
In-Town Branch	25	45	30	100
Mall Branch	25	45	30	100
Total	50	90	60	200

   d) 9.778
   e) 2
   f) 5.991
   g) Reject H_0 and conclude that the age distributions at the two branches are not the same.

9. a) Men 62%, women 71%
   b) Difference = 9%
   c) SE = 0.022
   d) (0.046, 0.133) or 4.6% to 13.3%

11. a)

Household Income	Every day	At least once a day but not every day	Once a week or less	Totals
Less than $25,000	140.8	24.5	9.6	175
$25,000 to $49,000	164.2	28.6	11.2	204
$50,000 to $84,999	204.4	35.6	14.0	254
$85,000 to $124,999	196.4	34.2	13.4	244
$125,000 or more	143.2	25.0	9.8	178
Totals	849	148	58	1055

   b) 78.9
   c) 8
   d) We reject the null hypothesis that household income and Internet use are independent.

CHAPTER EXERCISE ANSWERS

13. a) Chi-square test of independence; One sample, two variables. We want to see if the variable *Account type* is independent of the variable *Trade type*.
    b) Some other statistical test; the variable *Account size* is quantitative, not counts.
    c) Chi-square test of homogeneity; we have two samples and one variable, *Courses*. We want to see if the distribution of *Courses* is the same for the two groups.

15. a) 10
    b) Goodness-of-fit.
    c) H_0: The die is fair. (All faces have $p = 1/6$.)
       H_A: The die is not fair. (Some faces are more or less likely to come up than others.)
    d) Count data; rolls are random and independent of each other; expected frequencies are all greater than 5.
    e) 5
    f) $\chi^2 = 5.600$; $P = 0.3471$
    g) Since $P = 0.3471$ is high, fail to reject H_0. There is not enough evidence to conclude that the die is unfair.

17. a) Weights are quantitative, not counts.
    b) Count the number of each type of nut, assuming the company's percentages are based on counts rather than weights (which is not clear).

19. a) Goodness-of-fit.
    b) Count data; assume the lottery mechanism uses randomization and guarantees independence; expected frequencies are all greater than 5.
    c) H_0: Likelihood of drawing each numeral is equal.
       H_A: Likelihood of drawing each numeral is *not* equal.
    d) $\chi^2 = 6.46$; df = 9; $P = 0.693$; fail to reject H_0.
    e) The P-value says that if the drawings were in fact fair, an observed chi-square value of 6.46 or higher would occur about 69% of the time. This is not unusual at all, so we won't reject the null hypothesis that the values are uniformly distributed. The variation that we observed seems typical of that expected if the digits were drawn equally likely.

21. a) 40.2%
    b) 8.1%
    c) 62.2%
    d) 285.48
    e) Chi-square test of independence. H_0: Survival was independent of status on the ship. H_A: Survival was not independent of the status.

f) 3

g) We reject the null hypothesis. Survival depended on status. We can see that first-class passengers were more likely to survive than passengers of any other class.

23. a) Independence.

b) H_0: College choice is independent of birth order.
H_A: There is an association between college choice and birth order.

c) Count data; not a random sample of students, but assume that it is representative; expected counts are low for both the Social Science and Professional Colleges for both third and fourth or higher birth order. We'll keep an eye on these when we calculate the standardized residuals.

d) 9

e) With a P-value this low, we reject the null hypothesis. There is some evidence of an association between birth order and college enrollment.

f) None are particularly large, but 4 cells have expected counts less than 5, so we should be cautious in making conclusions. Perhaps we should group 3 with 4 or more and redo the analysis. Unfortunately, 3 of the 4 largest standardized residuals are in cells with expected counts less than 5. We should be very wary of drawing conclusions from this test.

25. a) Chi-square test for homogeneity.

b) Count data; assume random assignment to treatments (although not stated); expected counts are all greater than 5.

c) H_0: The proportion of infection is the same for each group.
H_A: The proportion of infection is different among the groups.

d) $\chi^2 = 7.776$; df = 2; $P = 0.02$; reject H_0

e) Since the P-value is low, we reject the null hypothesis. There is strong evidence of difference in the proportion of urinary tract infections for cranberry juice drinkers, lactobacillus drinkers, and women that drink neither of the two beverages.

f) The standardized residuals are:

	Cranberry	Lactobacillus	Control
Infection	−1.87276	1.191759	0.681005
No infection	1.245505	−0.79259	−0.45291

The significant difference appears to be primarily due to the success of cranberry juice.

27. a) $P = 0.3766$. With a P-value this high, we fail to reject. There is not enough evidence to conclude that either men or women are more likely to make online purchases of books.

b) Type II.

c) (−4.09%, 10.86%)

29. a) $P < 0.001$. There is strong evidence that the proportions of the two groups are not equal.

b) (0.096, 0.210) (proportion of old − proportion of young)

31. a) The standard error of the difference in proportions is 0.0094, but the difference in proportions is 0.009, which is about one standard error. That is not a statistically significant difference.

b) A 90% CI is 0.009 ± 0.0155.

33. a) Observational prospective study; Swedish men were selected and then followed for 30 years.

b) Independence.

c) H_0: Prostate cancer and fish consumption are independent.
H_A: There is an association between prostate cancer and fish consumption.
Count data; assume that these men are representative of all men; expected counts are all greater than 5. $\chi^2 = 3.677$; df = 3; $P = 0.2985$; fail to reject H_0. There is not enough evidence to conclude that there is an association between prostate cancer and fish consumption.

d) No, it only fails to show an association. We cannot prove that one does not exist.

35. a) Chi-square test for homogeneity.

b) Count data; adult respondents were surveyed randomly; expected counts are all greater than 5.

c) H_0: The distribution of attitudes about the importance of financial success was the same for men and women 18 to 34 years old.
H_A: The distribution of attitudes was not the same.

d) $\chi^2 = 17.43$; df = 3; $P = 0.0006$

e) The P-value is small so we reject the null hypothesis and conclude that men and women in this age group have different attitudes about the importance of this type of success.

37. a) A test of independence would be appropriate.

b) The data are counts; no cells are too small.

c) $\chi^2 = 14.43$ with 2 df; $P = 0.0007$

d)

	No	Yes
Yes	−1.22856	1.53931
No	2.01107	−2.51975
Retired	0.250431	−0.313775

e) Those who are employed are more likely to own stock than either those who are not employed or those who are retired.

39. a)

	Men	Women
Excellent	6.667	5.333
Good	12.778	10.222
Average	12.222	9.778
Below Average	8.333	6.667

Count data; assume that these executives are representative of all executives that have ever completed the program; expected counts are all greater than 5.

b) Decreased from 4 to 3.

c) $\chi^2 = 9.306$; $P = 0.0255$. Since the P-value is low, we reject the null hypothesis. There is evidence that the distributions of responses about the value of the program for men and women executives are different.

41. H_0: There is no association between race and the section of the apartment complex in which people live. H_A: There is an association between race and the section of the apartment complex in which people live. Count data; assume that the recently rented apartments are representative of all apartments in the complex; expected counts are all greater than 5. $\chi^2 = 14.058$; df = 1; $P < 0.001$. Since the P-value is low, we reject the null hypothesis. There is strong evidence of an association between race and the section of the apartment complex in which people live. An examination of the components shows us that blacks are less likely to rent in Section A (component = 6.2215) and that blacks are more likely to rent in Section B (component = 5.0517).

43. $\hat{p}_B - \hat{p}_A = 0.206$
95% CI = $(0.107, 0.306)$

45. a) Chi-square test for independence.
b) Count data; assume that the sample was taken randomly; expected counts are all greater than 5.
c) H_0: Outsourcing is independent of industry sector. H_A: There is an association between outsourcing and industry sector.
d) $\chi^2 = 2815.968$; df = 9; P-value is essentially 0.
e) Since the P-value is so low, we reject the null hypothesis. There is strong evidence of an association between outsourcing and industry sector.

47. a) Chi-square test for homogeneity. (Could be independence if the categories are considered exhaustive.)
b) Count data; assume that the sample was taken randomly; expected counts are all greater than 5.
c) H_0: The distribution of employee job satisfaction level attained is the same for different management styles. H_A: The distribution of employee job satisfaction level attained is different for different management styles.
d) $\chi^2 = 178.453$; df = 12; P-value is essentially 0.

e) Since the P-value is so low, we reject the null hypothesis. There is strong evidence that the distribution of employee job satisfaction level attained is different across management styles. Generally, exploitative authoritarian management is more likely to have lower levels of employee job satisfaction than consultative or participative styles.

49. Assumptions and conditions for test of independence satisfied. H_0: Reading online journals or blogs is independent of generation. H_A: There is an association between reading online journals or blogs and generation. $\chi^2 = 48.408$; df = 8; $P < 0.001$. We reject the null hypothesis and conclude that reading online journals or blogs is not independent of generational age.

51. Chi-square test of homogeneity (unless these two types of firms are considered the only two types, in which case it's a test of independence).
Count data; assume that the sample was random; expected counts are all greater than 5.
H_0: Systems used have same distribution for both types of industry.
H_A: Distributions of type of system differ in the two industries.
$\chi^2 = 157.256$; df = 3; P-value is essentially 0.
Since the P-value is low, we can reject the null hypothesis and conclude that the type of ERP system used differs across industry type. Those in manufacturing appear to use more of the inventory management and ROI systems.

53. Chi-square test of independence.
Count data; we assume that this time period is representative; expected counts are less than 5 in three cells, but very close.
H_0: GDP % change is independent of Region of the United States.
H_A: GDP % change is not independent of Region of the United States.
$\chi^2 = 19.0724$; df = 3; $P < 0.001$.
The P-value is low so we reject the null hypothesis and conclude that GDP % change and Region are not independent. The result seems clear enough even though the expected counts of 3 cells were slightly below 5.

CHAPTER 16
SECTION EXERCISE ANSWERS

1. a) 9.8, 8.5, 5.9, 2.0, 8.5, 11.1
b) −0.8, −0.5, −1.9, 1.0, 1.5, 0.9
c) 1.46

3. $s_x = 12.5167$, $s_e = 1.46$, $n = 6$, $SE(b_1) = 0.052$

5. a) 5.837
b) 3
c) 0.01
d) Yes, the P-value is smaller than 0.05.

7. a) Linearity: the plot appears linear.

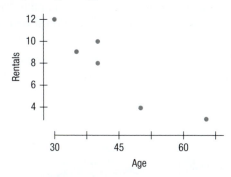

b) Independence: It is likely that the customers are independent. It is likely that errors made by the regression will be independent.

c) Equal Spread: the plot appears to have a consistent spread.

d) Normality: We can't tell from what we know.

9. a) 19.06 ($1000)

b) $19.06 \pm 1.12 = (17.94, 20.19)$ in $1000's

c) $19.06 \pm 3.59 = (15.47, 22.65)$ in $1000's

11. a) 95% of potential customers in the community from households that have annual incomes of $80,000 can be expected to spend between $35.60 and $55.60 eating out each week. Pricing an individual meal in this range might attract that demographic.

b) We can be 95% confident that the mean amount spent weekly by individuals whose household incomes are $80,000 is between $40.60 and $50.60. The mean is a summary for this demographic.

c) We can estimate means more accurately than we can estimate values for individuals. That's why the confidence interval for the mean is narrower than the corresponding interval for an individual.

13. a) 464.8 ($000)

b) $464.8 \pm 97.52 = (366.2, 563.4)$ in $1000

c) No. Extrapolating what their sales might be with 500 employees based on data with between 2 and 20 employees working is likely to be very wrong.

CHAPTER EXERCISE ANSWERS

15. a)

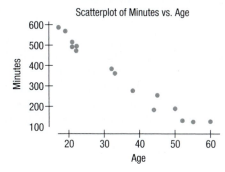

b) This scatterplot appears to have curvature at both ends of the age distribution so a linear regression may not be completely appropriate.

c) The regression equation is
$\widehat{Minutes} = 750 - 11.5\,Age$.

d) The residual plots are:

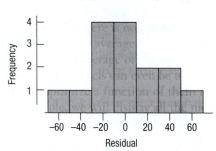

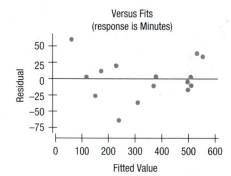

The Nearly Normal Condition is satisfied. There may be some curvature to the residual plot.

17. a) $\widehat{Budget} = -31.39 + 0.71\,Run\;Time$. The model suggests that movies cost about $710,000 per minute to make.

b) A negative starting value makes no sense, but the P-value of 0.07 indicates that we can't discern a difference between our estimated value and zero. The statement that a movie of zero length should cost $0 makes sense.

c) Amounts by which movie costs differ from predictions made by this model vary, with a standard deviation of about $33 million.

d) 0.15$M/min

e) If we constructed other models based on different samples of movies, we'd expect the slopes of the regression lines to vary, with a standard deviation of about $150,000 per minute.

19. a) The scatterplot looks straight enough, the residuals look random and roughly Normal, and the residuals don't display any clear change in variability although there may be some increasing spread.

b) I'm 95% confident that the cost of making longer movies increases at a rate of between 0.41 and 1.01 million dollars per minute. (CI is 0.41 to 1.02 using raw data.)

21. a) H_0: There is no linear relationship between calcium concentration in water and mortality rates for males. ($\beta_1 = 0$) H_A: There is a linear relationship between calcium concentration in water and mortality rates for males. ($\beta_1 \neq 0$)

b) $t = -6.65, P < 0.0001$; reject the null hypothesis. There is strong evidence of a linear relationship between calcium concentration and mortality. Towns with higher calcium concentrations tend to have lower mortality rates.

c) For 95% confidence, use $t^*_{59} \approx 2.001$, or estimate from the table $t^*_{50} \approx 2.009$; $(-4.20, -2.26)$.

d) We are 95% confident that the average mortality rate decreases by between 2.26 and 4.20 deaths per 100,000 for each additional part per million of calcium in drinking water.

23. a) $\widehat{2010Index} = 33.187 + 0.6869 \times 2007Index$

b) The plot tends to thicken, but the regression is otherwise OK.

c) The P-value for the slope is 0.0025. That is small enough to be confident that the true slope is not zero.

d) $R^2 = 21.2\%$

25. a)

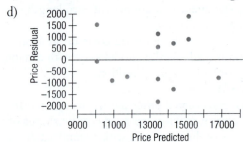

Price vs. Age

b) Yes, the plot seems linear.

c) $\widehat{Advertised\ Price} = 17674 - 844 \times Age$

d)

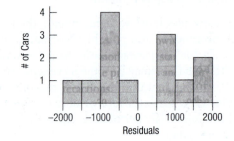

The residual plot does not look Normal, but a Q-Q plot shows that it is acceptably Normal. With only 13 data points, we should be careful about using the model.

27. Based on these data, we are 95% confident that a used car's *Price* decreases between $523 and $1166 per year.

29. a)

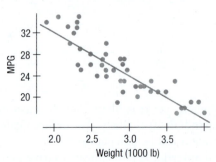

$\widehat{mpg} = 48.7393 - 8.21362\,(weight)$

b) Yes, the conditions seem satisfied. Histogram of residuals is unimodal and symmetric; residual plot looks okay, but some "thickening" of the plot with increasing values. There may be one possible outlier.

c) H_0: There is no linear relationship between the weight of a car and its fuel efficiency. ($\beta_1 = 0$) H_A: There is a linear relationship between the weight of a car and its mileage. ($\beta_1 \neq 0$)

d) $t = -12.2$, df $= 48$, $P < 0.0001$; reject the null hypothesis. There is strong evidence of a linear relationship between weight of a car and its mileage. Cars that weigh more tend to have lower gas mileage.

31. a) H_0: There is no linear relationship between SAT Verbal and Math scores. ($\beta_1 = 0$) H_A: There is a linear relationship between SAT Verbal and Math scores. ($\beta_1 \neq 0$)

b) Assumptions seem reasonable, since conditions are satisfied. Residual plot shows no patterns (one outlier); histogram is unimodal and roughly symmetric.

c) $t = 11.9$, df $= 160$, $P < 0.0001$; reject the null hypothesis. There is strong evidence of a linear relationship between SAT Verbal and Math scores. Students with higher SAT Verbal scores tend to have higher SAT Math scores.

33. a) H_0: $\beta_1 = 0$ vs. H_A: $\beta_1 \neq 0$

b) The P-value of 0.03 provides some evidence to reject the null hypothesis. It seems that higher salaries are associated with more wins.

c) However, there are two teams with low salaries and only 1 or 2 wins. Without those teams, the P-value is 0.67, and would lead us not to reject the null hypothesis. It seems that there is little relationship between salary and wins excluding those two teams.

35. a) $(-9.57, -6.86)$ mpg per 1000 pounds

b) We are 95% confident that the mean mileage of cars decreases by between 6.86 and 9.57 miles per gallon for each additional 1000 pounds of weight.

37. a) H_0: No linear relationship between *Population* and *Ozone*, $\beta_1 = 0$.
H_A: *Ozone* increases with *Population*, $\beta_1 > 0$. $t = 3.48$; P-value = 0.0018. With a P-value so low, we reject H_0. These data show evidence that *Ozone* increases with *Population*.

b) Yes. *Population* accounts for 84% of the variability in *Ozone* level, and s is just over 5 parts per million.

39. a) Based on this regression, each additional million residents corresponds to an increase in average ozone level of between 3.29 and 10.01 ppm, with 90% confidence.

b) The mean *Ozone* level for cities with 600,000 people is between 18.47 and 27.29 ppm, with 90% confidence.

41. a) 34 tablets.

b) Yes. The scatterplot is roughly linear with lots of scatter; plot of residuals vs. predicted values shows no overt patterns; Normal probability plot of residuals is reasonably straight.

c) H_0: No linear relationship between *Battery Life* and *Screen Brightness*, $\beta_1 = 0$. H_A: *Battery Life* is associated with *Screen Brightness*, $\beta_1 \neq 0$. $t = 2.02$; P-value = 0.052. There is a slight *positive* association between *Screen Brightness* and *Battery Life*. The CI just barely includes zero, with a P-value right at 0.05. There is about a 5% chance of seeing a slope of this size by chance alone, even if there were no relationship between brightness and battery life.

d) Not particularly. $R^2 = 11\%$ and $s = 2.13$ hours. Since the range of battery life is only about 9 hours, an s of 2.13 is quite large.

e) *Hours* = 5.39 + 0.009 *Screen Brightness*

f) $(-0.0001, 0.0182)$ hours per cd/m^2 units

g) *Battery life* increases, on average, between -0.0001 and 0.0182 *hours* per one cd/m^2 units, with 95% confidence.

43. a) H_0: $\beta_1 = 0$ (There is no linear relationship between the Total Cost of Living Index and the Grocery Index.) vs. H_A: $\beta_1 \neq 0$ (There is a linear relationship.)

b) The P-value is very small, so we can reject the null hypothesis and conclude that cities in which groceries are expensive are also expensive in general.

c) 91% of the variation in Total Cost of Living can be accounted for by the Grocery Index.

d) No, we cannot interpret the regression in this causal manner. It may be that grocery cost is a component of total cost, or it may be that a third factor (a lurking variable) causes both groceries and all other costs to be higher in some cities.

45. a) For a one-unit increase in the Restaurant Index, the Total Cost of Living Index increases by 0.80. Assuming that regression assumptions are met, the CI does not contain zero, and the P-value is very small, indicating that we reject the null hypothesis that there is no relationship between Restaurant costs and total cost of living.

b) It is possible because the two variables are likely to be correlated, or caused by the same (unobserved or unmodeled) factor. If we ran a multiple regression with both variables included, we would find that the R^2 does not exceed 1, as this is impossible.

47. a)

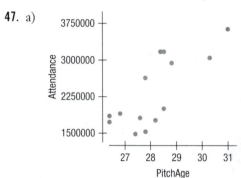

b) Yes, there appears to be a linear association.

c)
```
Dependent variable is: Attend/G
R-squared = 59.3% R-squared (adjusted) = 55.9%
s = 6025 with 14 − 2 = 12 degrees of freedom
```

Variable	Coeff	SE(Coeff)	t-Ratio	P-Value
Intercept	−120463	35750	−3.37	0.0056
PitchAge	5305.56	1269	4.18	0.0013

Teams with pitchers who are a year older tend to have about 5305 more fans on average at each game.

49. a) We are 95% confident that the mean fuel efficiency of cars that weigh 2500 pounds is between 27.34 and 29.07 miles per gallon.

b) We are 95% confident that a car weighing 3450 pounds will have fuel efficiency between 15.44 and 25.36 miles per gallon.

51. a) $(-4.99, 5.29)$

b) Yes, it will probably be accurate, but not very useful, since most of the pitchers fall into this range.

53. a) We'd like to know if there is a linear association between *Price* and *Highway MPG* in cars. We have data on 2012 model-year cars giving their highway mpg and retail price. H_0: $\beta_1 = 0$ (no linear relationship between *Price* and *Highway MPG*); H_A: $\beta_1 \neq 0$.

b) The scatterplot shows that the Straight Enough Condition is reasonably satisfied. The residual plots show no particular pattern, so we can continue.

c) We find a moderately strong, negative linear relationship between efficiency and price. An increase in price of $1000 is associated, on average, with a decrease of 0.42 highway mpg.

55. a) The 95% prediction interval shows the interval of uncertainty for a single country's predicted male unemployment rate, given its female unemployment rate.

b) The 95% confidence interval shows the interval of uncertainty for the mean male unemployment rate given a sample of female unemployment rates. Because this is an interval for an average, the variation or uncertainty is less, so the interval is narrower.

c) There are no obvious outliers, but Greece, Spain, and Italy are high leverage. They are not high influence, however, and there does not appear to be cause for alarm.

57. a) The 95% prediction interval shows the interval of uncertainty for the predicted energy use in 2010 based on energy use in 2006 for a single country.

b) The 95% confidence interval shows the interval of uncertainty for the mean energy use in 2010 based on the same energy use in 2006 for a sample of countries. Because this is an interval for an average, the variation or uncertainty is less, so the interval is narrower.

c) The outlier is Iceland. It does impact the regression. After removing it, the slope is lowered to 0.922 (SE 0.06) and the intercept becomes 5.744 (SE 9.06). The R^2 is lowered to 88.6% from 91.3%. The standard deviation of the residuals is now 13.10, which is much smaller than the original 22.53. This will make the intervals narrower and our predictions more precise.

59. a) $\widehat{Jan} = 120.73 + 0.6995\ Dec$. We are told this is an SRS. One cardholder's spending should not affect another's. These are quantitative data with no apparent bend in the scatterplot. The residual plot shows some increased spread for larger values of January charges. A histogram of residuals is unimodal and slightly skewed to the right with several high outliers. We will proceed cautiously.

b) $1519.73

c) ($1330.24, $1709.24)

d) ($290.76, $669.76)

e) The residuals show increasing spread, so the confidence intervals may not be valid. I would be skeptical of interpreting them too literally.

CHAPTER 17

SECTION EXERCISE ANSWERS

1. The different cardholder segments are not scattered at random throughout the scatterplot. Each segment may have a different relationship.

3. Yes, it is clear that the relationship between January and December spending is not the same for all five segments. Using one overall model to predict January spending would be very misleading.

5. a) 464.6 ($000)

b) No. Extrapolating what their sales might be with 500 employees based on data with between 2 and 20 employees working is likely to be very wrong.

7. a) $354,472

b) An extrapolation this far from the data is unreliable.

9. a) $\widehat{Sales} = 14.32 + 0.297\ Number\ of\ Sales\ People\ Working$

b) The intercept is higher and the slope is much lower.

c) High leverage and influential.

d) Not really. The line is so influenced by the new point that it passes close to it.

11. a)

Quarter	Sales ($M)	Predicted	Residual
1	12	19.02	−7.02
2	41	23.89	17.11
3	15	28.76	−13.76
4	48	33.63	14.37
5	25	38.5	−13.5
6	55	43.37	11.63
7	23	48.24	−25.24
8	69	53.11	15.89
9	51	57.98	−6.98
10	80	62.85	17.15
11	54	67.72	−13.72
12	87	72.59	14.41
13	64	77.46	−13.46
14	94	82.33	11.67
15	62	87.2	−25.2
16	108	92.07	15.93

b)

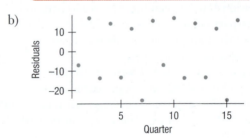

c) $D = 3.62$

d) 1.10, 1.37

e) No. $D > 1.37$

f) Yes. $D > 4 - 1.10$

13. a) $d_L = 1.48$, $d_U = 1.57$. The observed value is less than d_L so we can reject the null hypothesis of no autocorrelation.

b) The statistic tests for time-related correlation. We can conclude that there is evidence of positive autocorrelation.

15. No. The scatterplot shows a linear relationship and the residual plot has no obvious pattern. No transformation is suggested.

17. A re-expression is called for. Taking the log or reciprocal of *Cost per Unit* would probably improve the linearity.

19. a) Log
    b) 0

21. a) The trend appears to be somewhat linear and declining until about 1940, but from 1940 to about 1970 the pattern is horizontal with some bend. From 1975 on, the trend is roughly linear.
    b) Relatively strong for certain periods.
    c) No, as a whole the graph is clearly nonlinear. Within certain periods (1975 to the present) the correlation is high.
    d) Overall, no. You could fit a linear model to the period from 1975 to the present, but it wouldn't be safe to extrapolate very far.

23. a) The relationship is not straight.
    b) It will be curved downward.
    c) No. The relationship will still be curved.

25. a) No. We need to see the scatterplot first to see if the conditions are satisfied.
    b) No. In spite of the high R^2, the linear model might still be inappropriate.

27. a) Millions of dollars per minute of run time.
    b) Budgets for dramas depend on the duration of the film in the same way as other movies.
    c) At any run time, dramas cost less by about $30 million.

29. a) The use of Oakland airport has been growing at about 46,000 passengers/year, starting from about 456,000 in 1990.
    b) 85.2% of the variation in number of passengers is accounted for by this model.
    c) Errors in predictions based on this model have a standard deviation of 100,359 passengers.
    d) No, that would extrapolate too far from the years we've observed, and the series is autocorrelated.

31. a) 1) High leverage, small residual.
       2) No, not influential for the slope.
       3) Correlation would decrease because outlier has large z_x and z_y, increasing correlation.
       4) Slope wouldn't change much because the outlier is in line with other points.
    b) 1) High leverage, probably small residual.
       2) Yes, influential.
       3) Correlation would weaken and become less negative because scatter would increase.
       4) Slope would increase toward 0, since outlier makes it negative.
    c) 1) Some leverage, large residual.
       2) Yes, somewhat influential.
       3) Correlation would strengthen, since scatter would decrease.
       4) Slope would increase slightly.

    d) 1) Little leverage, large residual.
       2) No, not influential.
       3) Correlation would become stronger and become more negative because scatter would decrease.
       4) Slope would change very little.

33. 1) e   2) d   3) c   4) b   5) a

35. Perhaps high blood pressure causes high body fat, high body fat causes high blood pressure, or both could be caused by a lurking variable such as a genetic or lifestyle issue.

37. a) *Cost* decreases by $2.13 per degree of average daily *Temp*. So warmer temperatures indicate lower costs.
    b) For an avg. monthly temperature of 0°F, the cost is predicted to be $133.
    c) Too high; the residuals (observed − predicted) around 32°F are negative, showing that the model overestimates the costs.
    d) $111.7
    e) About $105.7
    f) No, the residuals show a definite curved pattern. The data are probably not linear.
    g) No, there would be no difference. The relationship does not depend on the units.

39. a) 0.88
    b) Interest rates during this period grew at about 0.25% per year, starting from an interest rate of about 0.64%.
    c) Substituting 50 in the model yields a predicted value of about 13%.
    d) Not really. Extrapolating 20 years beyond the end of these data would be dangerous and unlikely to be accurate. Errors are autocorrelated as well.

41. a) The two models both fit well, but they have very different slopes and intercepts.
    b) This model predicts the interest rate in 2000 to be 3.76%, lower than the other model predicts.
    c) We can trust the new predicted value because it is in the middle of the data used for the regression.
    d) The best answer is "I can't predict that."

43. *Sex* and *Colorblindness* are both categorical variables, not quantitative. Correlation is meaningless for them, but we can say that the variables are associated.

45. a) No re-expression needed.
    b) Re-express to straighten the relationship.
    c) Re-express to equalize spread.

47. a) There's a pattern during the year, so the residuals cycle up and down.
    b) No, this kind of pattern can't be helped by re-expression.

49. a) 2.8   b) 16.44   c) 7.84   d) 0.36   e) 2.09

51. a) 3.842   b) 501.187   c) 4.0

53. a) Linearity Condition violated. Possibly increased variation at higher values. Independence may be in doubt since this is a time series.

  b) This plot looks both straighter and more consistent in variation.

  c) The residuals show a pattern, but it tracks up and down and could not be improved by an alternative transformation.

55. a) The DJIA increases with the GDP at the rate of 0.839 dollar per billion GDP dollar.

  b) 72.5% of the variation in DJIA is accounted for by this regression.

57. a) Although 98% of the variation in GDP can be accounted for by this model, we should examine a scatterplot of the residuals to see if it's appropriate.

  b) No. The residuals show clear curvature.

59. a)

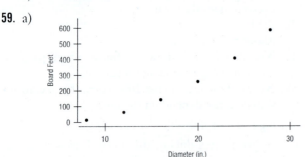

$$\widehat{\sqrt{Bdft}} = -4 + diam$$

The model is exact.

  b) 36 board feet.

  c) 1024 board feet.

61.
```
Dependent variable is: 1998 GDP/Cap
R-squared = 94.2%  R-squared (adjusted) = 93.9%
s = 2803 with 24 − 2 = 22 degrees of freedom
```

Source	Sum of Squares	df	Mean Square	F-ratio
Regression	2800375675	1	2800375675	356
Residual	172861656	22	7857348	

Variable	Coeff	SE(Coeff)	t-ratio	P-value
Intercept	3295.80	1307	2.52	0.0194
88 GDP CAP	1.090	0.058	18.9	<0.0001

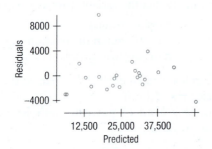

The regression has a high R^2 but the residuals show two influential points, Ireland with the largest positive residual and Switzerland with the largest negative residual. Assuming the data for these countries are correct, they should be set aside from the analysis and further work done to understand why each is unusual. Reports both with and without the outliers should be compared.

CHAPTER 18
SECTION EXERCISE ANSWERS

1. a) $99,859.89

  b) $35,140.11

  c) The house sold for about $35,100 more than our estimate.

3. a) $\widehat{USGross} = -22.9898 + 1.13442\,Budget + 24.9724\,Stars - 0.403296\,RunTime$

  b) After allowing for the effects of *RunTime* and *Stars*, each million dollars spent making a film yields about 1.13 million dollars in gross revenue.

5. a) Linearity: The plot is reasonably linear with no bends.

  b) Equal spread: The plot fails the Equal Spread Condition. It is much more spread out to the right than on the left.

  c) Normality: A scatterplot of two of the variables doesn't tell us anything about the distribution of the residuals.

7. a) $H_0: \beta_{Stars} = 0$

  b) $t = 4.24$

  c) $P \le 0.0001$

  d) Reject the null hypothesis and conclude that the coefficient of *Stars* is not zero.

9. a) $R^2 = 0.474$ or 47.4%
      About 47.4% of the variation in *USGross* is accounted for by the least squares regression on *Budget*, *RunTime*, and *Stars*.

  b) Adjusted R^2 accounts for the number of predictors, so it differs from R^2, which does not.

CHAPTER EXERCISE ANSWERS

11. a) Linearity: The scatterplots show little pattern, but are not non-linear.
      Independence: States are not a random sample, but for these variables, they may be independent of each other.
      Equal Variance: The scatterplots do not appear to have a changing spread.
      Normality: To check the Nearly Normal Condition, we'll need to look at the residuals; we can't check it with these plots.

  b) 14.0%

13. a) $\widehat{Violent\ Crime} = 1305.51 - 0.347\ Police\ Pay - 1097.36\ Graduation\ Rate$

b) After allowing for the effects of graduation rate (or, alternatively, among states with similar graduation rates), states with higher police officer wages have slightly lower violent crime rates that are lower by 0.00035 crime per 100,000 for each dollar per hour of average wage.

c) 410.259 crimes per 100,000

d) Not very good; R^2 is only 15.1% and $s = 137.3$.

15. a) $-0.205 = \dfrac{-0.3472}{1.690}$

b) 49 states. There are 46 degrees of freedom and that's equal to $n - k - 1$. With two predictors, $49 - 2 - 1 = 46$.

c) The t-ratio is negative because the coefficient is negative.

17. a) $H_0: \beta_{Police\ Pay} = 0$ $H_A: \beta_{Police\ Pay} \neq 0$

b) $P = 0.8381$ that's not small enough to reject the null hypothesis at $\alpha = 0.05$ and conclude that the coefficient is discernibly different from zero.

19. This is a causal interpretation, which is not supported by regression. For example, among states with high graduation rates, it may be that those with lower violent crime rates choose to spend more to hire police officers, or that states with higher costs of living must pay more to attract qualified police officers but also have lower crime rates. Moreover, the coefficient of *Police Pay* cannot be distinguished from 0.

21. Equal Spread Condition: may be met by the residuals vs. predicted plot (but some may judge otherwise). Nearly Normal Condition: met by the Normal probability plot

23. a) Doesn't mention other predictors; suggests direct relationship

b) Correct

c) Can't predict x from y

d) Incorrect interpretation of R^2

25. a) Extrapolates far from the data

b) Suggests a perfect relationship

c) Can't predict one explanatory variable from another

d) Correct

27. a) The sign of the coefficient for ln(*number of employees*) is negative. This means that for businesses that have the same amount of sales, those with more employees spend less per employee on pollution abatement on average. The sign of the coefficient for ln(*sales*) is positive. This means that for businesses with the same number of employees, those with larger sales spend more on pollution abatement on average.

b) The logarithms mean that the effects become less severe (in dollar terms) as companies get larger either in sales or in number of employees.

29. a) $\widehat{Price} = -152{,}037 + 9530\ Baths + 139.87\ Area$

b) $R^2 = 71.1\%$

c) For houses with the same number of bathrooms, each square foot of area is associated with an increase of $139.87 in the price of the house, on average.

d) The regression model says that for houses of the same size, those with more bathrooms are not priced higher. It says nothing about what would happen if a bathroom were added to a house. That would be a predictive interpretation, which is not supported by regression.

31. a) The regression equation is: $\widehat{Salary} = 9.788 + 0.110\ Service + 0.053\ Education + 0.071\ Test\ Score + 0.004\ Typing\ wpm + 0.065\ Dictation\ wpm$

b) $Salary = 29.205$ or $29,205

c) The t-value is 0.013 with 24 df. P-value = 0.9897, which is not significant at $\alpha = 0.05$.

d) Take out the explanatory variable for typing speed, since it is not significant.

e) *Age* is likely to be collinear with several of the other predictors already in the model. For example, secretaries with longer terms of *Service* will probably also be older.

33. a) This model explains less than 4% of the variation in *GDP per Capita*. The P-value is not particularly low.

b) Because more education is generally associated with a higher standard of living, it is not surprising that the simple association between *Primary Completion Rate* and GDP is positive

c) The coefficient now is measuring the association between *GDP/Capita* and *Primary Completion Rate* after accounting for the two other predictors.

35. a) $\widehat{Price} = 0.7297 + 1.267\ Traps\ (M) - 0.000134\ License\ Holders - 0.006075\ Pounds/Trap$

b) The residuals show greater spread on the right. We might wonder whether values from year to year are mutually independent. We should interpret the model with caution.

c) The second (Log(Price/lb)) regression model seems to satisfy the regression assumptions better.

d) $H_0: \beta_{License\ Holders} = 0$, $H_A: \beta_{License\ Holders} \neq 0$; the P-value is 0.0050. It appears that *License Holders* does contribute to the model.

e) Although such a relationship makes sense because in a controlled fishery, a larger harvest can depress prices, this regression cannot be used to demonstrate a causal relationship. We don't know from this analysis how things would change if one (or more) of the predictors were changed.

37. a)
```
R squared = 66.7%  R squared (adjusted) = 63.8%
s = 2.327 with 39 - 4 = 35 degrees of freedom
```

Variable	Coeff	SE(Coeff)	t-ratio	P-value
Intercept	87.0089	33.60	2.59	0.0139
CPI	-0.344795	0.1203	-2.87	0.0070
Personal Consumption	1.10842e-5	4.403e-6	2.52	0.0165
Retail Sales	1.03152e-4	1.545e-5	6.67	<0.0001

$$\widehat{Revenue} = 87.0 - 0.344\ CPI + 0.000011$$
Personal Consumption $+ 0.0001$ *Retail Sales*

b) R^2 is 66.7%, and all *t*-ratios are significant. It looks like these variables can account for much of the variation in Walmart revenue.

39. a) $\widehat{Logit(Drop)} = 0.4419 + 0.0379\ Age - 0.0468$ *HDRS*
   b) 0.1749
   c) 0.544
   d) 2.342
   e) 0.912

41. *Displacement* and *Bore* would be good predictors. Relationship with *Wheelbase* isn't linear.

43. a) Yes, R^2 of 88.9% says that most of the variability of *MSRP* is accounted for by this model. However, the residuals suggest there might be two or more groups of bikes. (Consider engine cooling, for example.)
   b) No, a regression model may not be inverted in this way.

45. a) Yes, R^2 is very large.
   b) The value of *s*, 8.752 calories, is very small compared with the initial standard deviation of *Calories*. This indicates that the model fits the data quite well, leaving very little variation unaccounted for.
   c) A true value of 100% would indicate zero residuals, but with real data such as these, it is likely that the computed value of 99.9% leaves room for some residuals that are not zero.

CHAPTER 19
SECTION EXERCISE ANSWERS

1. a) Unionized = 1, No Union = 0 (or the reverse)
   b) Female = 1, Male = 0 (or the reverse)
   c) Paid on time = 1, Past Due = 0 (or the reverse)
   d) Two variables. One variable could have Democrat = 1, 0 otherwise and another Republican = 1 and 0 otherwise.

3. a) To make two different intercepts for the two types of movie.
   b) If R then 1; If PG then 0

5. (One possible answer for each: other equivalent codings are possible.)

a) Three variables: One variable that is 1 for Apartment, 0 for others. One that is 1 for Condo, 0 for others. One that is 1 for Townhouse, 0 for others.
b) Two variables: One that is 1 for Full-time, 0 for others. One that is 1 for Part-time, 0 for others.

7. a) If *PG-13* then 0; If *R* then 1.
   b) The interaction term is the product of the indicator variable and the Budget variable.

9. A bit more than $0.2M (actually, $0.219M). This is a fundamental property of leverage.

11. Because of the high correlation between several of the predictor variables, a stepwise search might find a very different model from the best of the all subsets model.

13. 80.00

15. a) It is curved upward at both extremes of *Age*. It says that the most expensive homes are either quite new or very old.
   b) No. Although the relationship is not linear in *Age*, it is probably quadratic.
   c) Add a quadratic term in (Age^2).

17. a) Cheese pizzas (*Type* 1) scored about 15.6 points higher, after allowing for the effects of calories and fat. Cheese pizzas can be expected to sell better than pepperoni pizzas based on these results.
   b) Scatterplots of the data and of residuals to check linearity and constant variance; a histogram or probability plot of residuals to check Normality.

19. a) Both pizzas are predicted to have high scores. But both have scores more than 30 points lower than predicted.
   b) Yes, their unusually large predicted values indicate that they must be different from the other pizzas in some ways, and their large (negative) residuals indicate that they would pull on the regression. It might be helpful to see leverage values or Cook's Distance values for these points.

21. a) An indicator or "dummy" variable
   b) Sales are about 10.5 billion dollars higher in December, after accounting for the *CPI*.
   c) Must assume that the slope is the same for the December points as for the others. That appears to be true in the scatterplot.

23. a) There are different slopes for the two types.
   b) This is an interaction term. It says that cheese pizzas (*Type* 1) have scores that grow less rapidly with *Calories* (a slope 0.46 smaller) than do pepperoni pizzas.
   c) The adjusted R^2 for this model is higher than the adjusted R^2 for the previous model. Also, the *t*-ratios are larger. Overall, this looks like a more successful regression model.

25. a) Large Cook's Distance suggests that Alaska is influential. Its leverage is high, and its residual is one of the largest in magnitude (very negative).

b) After allowing for the other predictors, Alaska's life expectancy is 2.23 years lower than the model predicts from the other states. The P-value of 0.02 says that Alaska is an outlier because the coefficient of the dummy variable is significantly not zero.

c) The model is better (higher adjusted R^2, smaller standard deviation of residuals) when Alaska is removed from the model with a dummy variable.

27. a) Because the P-value for *Rent Index* is not significant at $\alpha = 0.05$, we could consider dropping it from the model.

b) The adjusted R^2 value is the same and it has fewer predictors. All predictors have P-values below 0.05.

c) Because the P-value for *Rent Index* was not statistically significant.

d) The 3 variable model has the same adjusted R^2 with one less predictor variable. However, there is, in fact, very little difference between the models. They make roughly the same predictions and have very similar coefficients.

29. a) Lesotho has an unusually high level of public health expenditures. Djibouti has a very low number of Internet users and low expected years of schooling. Singapore has a low expenditure for health given the predictor values. Cuba has an extraordinarily high public health expenditure for its predictor variables and Eritrea is low on all three variables.

b) Answers may vary. The coefficients don't change a great deal, but the R^2 increases from 55.17% to 69.80%. It's a more accurate model without these points, but there may be no justification for just deleting them. It's best to report both models.

31. a) The Equal Spread Condition shows that the Equal Variance Assumption is violated.

b) Try a re-expression of *US Gross*, perhaps log.

33. a) Bahrain has a relatively high number of *Cell phones/100* people, but a very low *Primary Completion Rate*. Burkina Faso has the lowest (negative?) *Primary Completion Rate* and low *Internet Users/100 people*. Israel has the highest number of *Cell phones/100 people* and Luxembourg has the highest *GDP per Capita* and high *Cell phones/100 people*.

b) Consider verifying the data (especially the negative *Primary Completion Rate)* and running a new model without these points to see the impact they make on the model selection and the coefficients.

35. Qatar, Niger, and Australia all have large studentized residuals and Cook's Distance. Australia has the second highest HDI, while Niger is tied for lowest HDI. Qatar, due to oil revenue, has an extremely high GNI/capita.

CHAPTER 20
SECTION EXERCISE ANSWERS

1. a) Yes
b) No, not vs. time
c) No, for each worker, not over time
d) Yes

3. a)

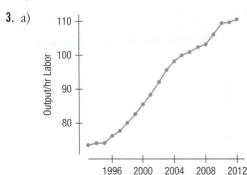

b) Trend: positive, slightly curved, strong.
c) No evidence of a seasonal component.

5. a)

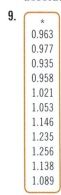

*
0.9700
0.9560
0.9465
0.9895
1.0370
1.0995
1.1905
1.2455
1.1970
1.1135
1.0580

b) 1.058

7. 2.32% (If your value was negative, you forgot the absolute value.)

9.

*
0.963
0.977
0.935
0.958
1.021
1.053
1.146
1.235
1.256
1.138
1.089

11. 1.0012

13. a) Dummy or indicator variable.
b) A set of indicator variables must omit one to avoid collinearity.

15. a) The 200-day moving average will be smoother.
b) The SES model using $\alpha = 0.10$ is smoother.
c) When the α is raised from 0.10 to 0.80, the most recent data point is weighted more heavily, so the model responds more quickly and is not as smooth.

17. a) Random walk, so use AR(1) or naïve forecast.
b) Exponential model
c) Seasonal dummy variable model, or AR model that uses sales from the same quarter in prior years (lag4).

19. a) 22,988 $M
b) 21,270 $M

21. a) 475.88 $/tonne
b) 481.20 $/tonne
c) 17.53%, 16.60%

23. a) Irregular
b) Second graph

25. The 2-quarter moving average is shown in A and fits better. This series has a strong, consistent trend component, so a longer-span moving average is dragged down below the series.

27. a) $2.676B
b) APE = 7.7% (underforecast)
c) Forecast is $3.515B; APE = 3.34% (overforecast).

29. a) 114.016
b) 115.63

31. a) 112
b) The forecast will be over 100%, which is not possible.

33. a) Irregular components and possible cycles.
b) No. This could be a local artifact. We would want some independent reason to believe in a 14-week cycle.
c) It wouldn't be wise to use this model for prediction unless we had some reason to believe in the 14-week cycle.

35. a) $1.1 million
b) Q3
c) Q4
d) Sales on average are $0.5 million greater in Q4 than in Q1.

37. a) A positive trend component and a seasonal component
b) Walmart revenues have been increasing at about $0.145 billion per month.
c) Revenues in December tend to be about $11.56 billion more than in January (the base month).
d) $19.3028 billion

e) October is the only month in which Walmart revenues are typically lower than they are in January, after allowing for the overall growth trend in revenue.

39. a) The P-value indicates that the slope of the time trend is significantly different from zero.
b) The coefficient for November is not significantly different from zero, so it should not be interpreted.
c) Yes. Many of the month indicators are highly significant.
d) 459,408

41. a) Traffic through the airport grew at about 13,800 passengers per month.
b) In January 1990 there were about 570,000 passengers.
c) January and February; we can tell that January is low because it is the base for the dummy variables and the other coefficients are positive.
d) Trend and seasonal.

43. The single exponential smooth is pulled down by the outlier. The moving average spreads out the effect of the outlier across several months. The seasonal regression is not noticeably affected. (The September dummy coefficient absorbs the effect and spreads it out over other Septembers, but that isn't evident in the plot.)

45. a) Dependent variable is: E-Commerce Sales (Millions $)
R squared = 96.9%   R squared (adjusted) = 96.4%
s = 1740 with 34 − 5 = 29 degrees of freedom

Variable	Coeff	SE(Coeff)	t-ratio	P-value
Intercept	2022.8	777.4	2.60	0.014
Time	900.138	30.45	29.6	<0.0001
Q2	−486.223	845.9	−0.575	0.5699
Q3	−709.611	845.4	0.839	0.4081
Q4	3288.03	820.7	4.01	0.0004

Note: Choosing a different quarter as the base quarter will yield a different model, but one with the same R^2.

b) Dependent variable is: logE-commerce Sales
R squared = 98.7%   R squared (adjusted) = 98.5%
s = 0.0297 with 34 − 5 = 29 degrees of freedom

Variable	Coeff	SE(Coeff)	t-ratio	P-value
Intercept	3.73222	0.0136	274	<0.0001
Time	0.024502	0.0005	47.1	<0.0001
Q2	−2.63785e-3	0.0145	−0.182	0.8566
Q3	−5.43049e-3	0.0145	−0.376	0.7099
Q4	0.072158	0.0140	5.14	<0.0001

c) The multiplicative model fits better judging from R^2 or adjusted R^2.

47. a) The regression equation is $\widehat{\text{Crude Price } (\$/\text{Bar})}$ = 0.809 + 0.991 lag1.
b) Forecast is 53.26.

49. a) Irregular and cyclic; note that since these are deseasonalized data, we are unable to observe the seasonal component.

b) Check on graph below

c) Key:

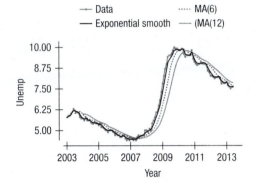

d) The exponential smooth fits the data most closely. The moving average smoothers lag behind the large movements in the unemployment rate.

51. a) R squared = 69.5%   R squared (adjusted) = 67.0%
s = 34260 with 161 − 13 = 148 degrees of freedom

Variable	Coefficient	SE(Coeff)	t-ratio	P-value
Intercept	331767.84	10243.52	32.388	<0.0001
Time	531.37	58.14	9.140	<0.0001
Feb	10513.49	12948.92	0.812	0.418142
Mar	64524.62	12949.31	4.983	<0.0001
Apr	29200.97	12949.97	2.255	0.025606
May	26785.10	12950.88	2.068	0.040361
Jun	88457.52	13195.59	6.704	<0.0001
Jul	120284.30	13195.46	9.116	<0.0001
Aug	92049.70	13195.59	6.976	<0.0001
Sep	−29294.74	13195.97	−2.220	0.027941
Oct	3442.89	13196.61	0.261	0.794538
Nov	−5470.94	13197.51	−0.415	0.679076
Dec	46271.85	13198.66	3.506	0.000603

b) No. The time plot shows that the trend is not a simple linear one. The residual plot shows major changes in the behavior of the time series. A simple linear model is no longer adequate.

c) You can see both 9/11 (Sept 2001) and the impact of the 2008 financial crisis on the number of visitors.

CHAPTER 21

1. Big data is differentiated by the fact that the datasets are too large to be processed on standard computing systems or databases. It is also characterized by the "4 V's": Volume, Velocity, Variety, and Veracity (although some of those V's apply to smaller datasets as well).

3. The problem is too vague, and the criterion for what constitutes the "best" customer needs to be defined more clearly. After defining the problem more clearly, the approach should be structured using CRISP-DM, so that a logical and orderly set of steps are followed to define the problem, find and clean the data, generate candidate models, evaluate the models, and deploy the models across the organization.

5. Tree models make the "logic" of predictions clear and easy to see (for simple trees—boosted and more complex tree models may not share this characteristic), whereas neural networks are "black boxes" whose logic cannot really be understood. Both will run quickly once trained. Neural networks tend to require more data and time to train.

7. Combining models frequently results in greater overall accuracy because the combination process ameliorates idiosyncratic model overfitting, creates multiple models that can deal with easy vs. more difficult cases, and may result in more stable model predictions.

9. This is a classification problem. We should look at classification accuracy on a test dataset that is different from the training dataset. The primary way to do this is to split the dataset into two parts, and to use one part for training and the second for test. In evaluating classification performance, both "true positive" (predict that the person will buy, and he or she did buy) and "false positive" (predict that the person will buy, but he or she did not). ROC curves provide a graphical approach to examining classification accuracy. Sophisticated companies use multiple splits of the data, with multiple training and test sets to increase robustness (i.e., k-fold cross-validation).

CHAPTER 22
SECTION EXERCISE ANSWERS

1. a)

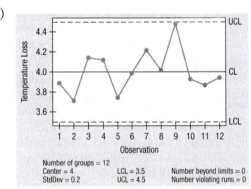

b) Yes, but one container was quite close to the upper limit.

c) 0.833

d) They need to decrease the process standard deviation. There is too great a chance that a container will fall outside the specification limits.

3. a)

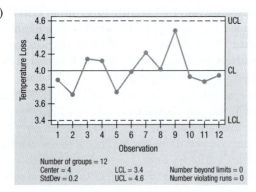

b) No.
c) No.
d) No.
e) No.
f) No.
g) No.
h) The process seems to be in control.

5. a) 0.00447 m (or 0.447 cm)
b) Outside (91.387, 91.413) m
c) $SD(\overline{X}) = 0.00316$ m; Outside (91.391, 91.409) m

7. a) 0.0198
b) (0, 0.0794)
c) 4 (round up 3.97)

9. These would be control limits because they are based on the process itself and not on external criteria.

11. These are lower specification limits set by the NHSF below which no pad should fall.

13. This is an upper specification limit set by Gemini.

15. This is common-cause variation based on random fluctuations.

17. 0.0027 based on the observations being Normal.

19. a) and b)

$$\overline{\overline{X}} = 8.05; \quad \overline{R} = 0.65 \Rightarrow \hat{\sigma} = \frac{\overline{R}}{d_2} = \frac{0.65}{2.059} = 0.316$$

$\overline{X}$ chart: LCL: $8.05 - 3\left(\dfrac{0.316}{\sqrt{4}}\right) = 7.576$

UCL: $8.05 + 3\left(\dfrac{0.316}{\sqrt{4}}\right) = 8.524$

R chart: $LCL = 0(0.65) = 0$
$UCL = 2.282(0.65) = 1.483$

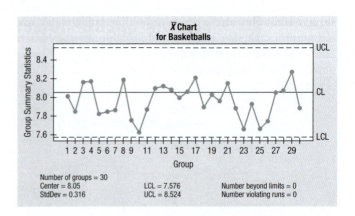

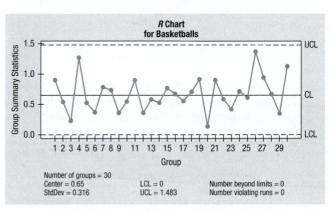

c) Both charts indicate that the process is in control as defined by the calibration period.

21. a) and b)

$$\mu = 21.2; \sigma = 0.29 \Rightarrow \sigma_R = d_3\sigma = 0.888 \times 0.29 = 0.258$$

$\overline{X}$ chart: $LCL = \mu - 3\dfrac{\sigma}{\sqrt{n}} = 21.2 - 3\dfrac{0.29}{\sqrt{3}} = 20.70$

$UCL = \mu + 3\dfrac{\sigma}{\sqrt{n}} = 21.2 + 3\dfrac{0.29}{\sqrt{3}} = 21.70$

Center line: $\overline{R} = d_2\sigma = 1.693 \times 0.29 = 0.491$

R chart: $LCL = D_3\overline{R} = 0$
$UCL = D_4\overline{R} = 2.574(0.491) = 1.264$

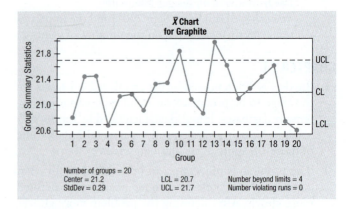

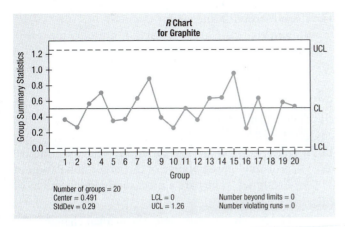

c) The process is out of control. Although the *R* chart appears to be in control, the $\bar{X}$ chart shows numerous samples outside the 3σ limits.

d)

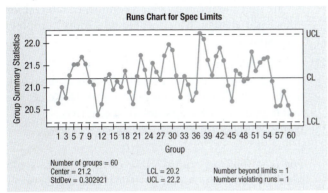

All but one of the samples meets the specification limits.

23. a) 0.0616
b) 0.1072
c) 0.0160
d) See the following chart.
e) The process seems to be in control.

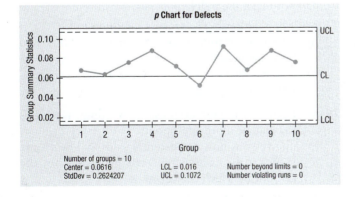

25. a) See the following chart.

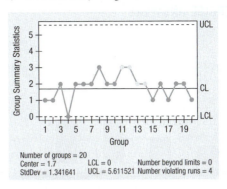

b) Although no day exceeds the upper control limit, there are more than 9 days on the same side of the desired center line. The process appears to be out of control.

27. a) 4.57
b) 10.99
c) 0
d) See the following chart.
e) The process is not in control on day 5.

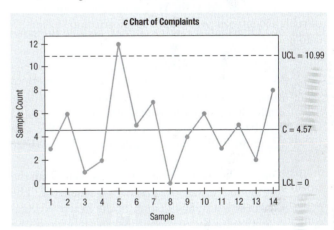

29. a)

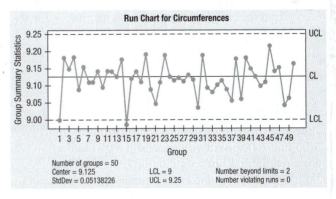

b) No, there are two balls that are too small.
c) Two.
d) Right away. The first ball produced was too small.

CHAPTER 23
SECTION EXERCISE ANSWERS

1. a) Ranks
   b) Ranks
   c) Not ranks—units are points earned on the exam.

3. b

5. d

7. a

9. c (possibly e)

11. e (possibly c)

13. a) The assumptions and conditions are met. The experiment was randomized, so the groups are independent and the individual participants are independent. From technology we find that P = 0.01, which is small enough to reject the null hypothesis.
   b) It would be better to design this as a before/after study, testing the children at the start of the teaching period, then randomly assigning them to treatment groups, and finally testing them again and comparing their results. An appropriate nonparametric method would be the Wilcoxon signed-rank test.

15. a) H_0: Distributions of sugar content have the same center.
   H_A: They have different centers.
   b) We don't know whether these cereals are a random sample from any particular population, but they are likely to be mutually independent.
   c) $P < 0.001$ (according to technology). We can reject the null hypothesis and conclude that there is a difference in sugar content.
   d) The distribution for Adults' cereals is skewed but the distribution for Children's cereals is symmetric. The skewness is a mild violation of the nearly Normal condition for the t-test, but we can't re-express one without re-expressing the other the same way, and that would make the currently symmetric distribution skewed. The nonparametric method is a better choice.

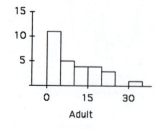

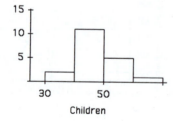

17. Use a Mann-Whitney test

Variable	n	median
size19th	5	27.00
size20th	9	15.50

W = 54.5

Test of medians equal vs medians not equal is significant at 0.0856
Reject the null at $\alpha = 0.10$

19. a) The subjects are not randomly selected, but are probably representative of the larger population of Freshmen. They are almost surely independent of each other.

   H_0: No change over time; the median change is 0.
   H_A: Change over time.
   $P < 0.001$.

   b) The *paired t-test* is probably more appropriate here because all assumptions and conditions it requires are met and it can provide a confidence interval for weight change, which would be a more complete response.

21. $n = 8$, n for test = 7.
   $T = 2.5$. From Table, one sided 0.05 critical value is 4, so $P < 0.05$ (from technology $P = 0.031$). Reject the null hypothesis. ERP appears to be effective.

23. Wilcoxon signed-rank test
   $n = 5$; $T^+ = 15$; $T^- = 0$: $T = 0$
   For $\alpha = 0.05$ no critical value exists (sample is too small). From technology, $P = 0.0625$. So, do not reject the null hypothesis.

25.
species	N	Median	Ave Rank	Z
Robin	16	22.55	19.2	−1.46
Sparrow	14	23.05	26.7	1.26
Wagtail	15	23.05	23.7	0.24
Overall	44		23.0	

H = 2.51 DF = 2 P = 0.285
H = 2.55 DF = 2 P = 0.279 (adjusted for ties)

Do not reject the null hypothesis.

27. a) The relationship is strongly monotonic.
   b) There is a strong association between GDP and Crowdedness.
   c) The association is not linear, so Pearson correlation is not appropriate.

29. a) Because the plot shows some bending, Kendall's tau may be more appropriate.
   b) Tau tells us how consistently sales at The Home Depot grow as housing starts grow, but not the amount by which they grow.

31. Kendall's tau tells us that there is a fairly consistent positive association between the housing cost index and median family income. But it does not allow any conclusions about causation.

CHAPTER 24
SECTION EXERCISE ANSWERS

1. a) State of Nature
   b) Action
   c) Action

3.

Action	State	Outcome
Out-source	Recession	220
	Stable	350
	Expansion	300
In-House	Recession	150
	Stable	240
	Expansion	390

5. a) Out-source
   b) In-house

7. a) $EV(\text{Out-source}) = 294$, $EV(\text{In-house}) = 312$
   b) Out-source

9. $SD(\text{Out-source}) = 41.76$, $CV(\text{Out-source}) = 0.14$, $SD(\text{In-house}) = 99.68$, $CV(\text{In-house}) = 0.32$

11.

	Stay for Interview	
Action	**No**	**Yes**
Fully Changeable Fare	$750	$750
Nonrefundable Fare	$650	$800

13.

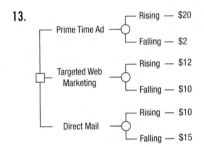

15.

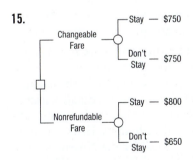

17. $EV(\text{Fully Changeable Fare}) = \$750$
$EV(\text{Nonrefundable Fare}) = \$695$
Choose the nonrefundable fare because we want to minimize the expected cost.

19. $EV(\text{Fully Changeable Fare}) = \$750$, $EV(\text{not changeable})$ is now $755, so the changeable fare is a better choice.

21. a) If $P(\text{rising confidence}) = 0.70$, $EV(\text{Prime Time}) = \$14.60$. $EV(\text{Targeted Web Marketing}) = \$11.40$; $EV(\text{Direct Mail}) = \$11.50$
Choose Prime Time, since expected payoff is highest.
   b) If $P(\text{rising confidence}) = 0.40$, $EV(\text{Prime Time}) = \$9.20$; $EV(\text{Targeted Web Marketing}) = \$10.80$; $EV(\text{Direct Mail}) = \$13$.
Choose Direct Mail in this case, since expected payoff is highest.

23. a) $3.90
   b) $4.00

25. a)

```
                                                    .7 × $20
                                     Prime Time —○           $14.60
                                                    .3 × $2
                                                    .7 × $12
                    P(rising) =.70 —□   Web     —○           $11.40
                                                    .3 × $10
                                                    .7 × $10
                                     Direct Mail —○          $11.50
                                                    .3 × $15
    Hire Consultant —○
                                                    .4 × $20
                                     Prime Time —○           $9.20
                                                    .6 × $2
                                                    .4 × $12
                    P(rising) =.40 —□   Web     —○           $10.80
                                                    .6 × $10
                                                    .4 × $10
                                     Direct Mail —○          $13.00
                                                    .6 × $15
□
                                                    .5 × $20
                                     Prime Time —○           $11.00
                                                    .5 × $2
                                                    .5 × $12
    Don't Hire Consultant —————————□    Web     —○           $11.00
                                                    .5 × $10
                                                    .5 × $10
                                     Direct Mail —○          $12.50
                                                    .5 × $15
```

   b) Yes, both alternatives with information have a better return.
   c) $1.30

27.

		Growing Season	
		Good	**Bad**
Purchase Decision	2 Tractors	$27,400	$2400
	3 Mowers	$8575	$3575
	No Purchase	$0	−$1000

29. Shawn favors Tractors, with an upside gain of $27,400. Lance prefers the Mowers, whose worst result is $3575.

31. a) and b)

Purchase Decision		EV	SD	RRR
	2 Tractors	$19,900.00	11,456.44	1.737
	3 Mowers	$7075.00	2291.28	3.088
	No Purchase	−$300.00	458.26	−0.655

c) Purchasing Mowers has the highest RRR, which is preferred.

33. a)

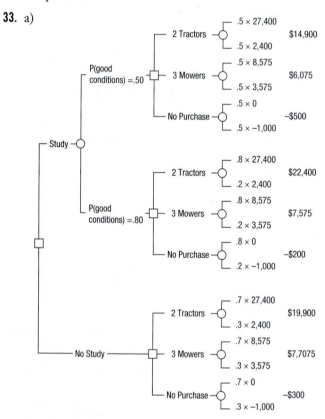

b) $17,900

c) No. In all scenarios, the Tractors investment seems the best course to take.

35. a) EV(Stock A) = $800; EV(Stock B) = $2300
b) SD(Stock A) = $2749.55;
SD(Stock B) = $1833.03
c) CV(Stock A) = 3.437; CV(Stock B) = 0.797;
RRR(Stock A) = 0.291; RRR(Stock B) = 1.255
d) Stock B; it has a higher expected value and a lower SD. Its RRR is much higher, which shows it has a better reward to risk ratio.

37. a) EV(High-End Bike) = $4465; EV(Moderately Priced Bike) = $2650
b) SD(High-End Bike) = $1995.00;
SD(Moderately Priced Bike) = $1050.00
c) CV(High-End Bike) = 0.447; CV(Moderately Priced Bike) = 0.396; RRR(High-End Bike) = 2.238; RRR (Moderately Priced Bike) = 2.524

d) Answers may vary. The high-end bike has a much higher EV, but also a higher SD. Its RRR is lower but is very close to the moderately priced bike. The decision will depend on the store owner's appetite for risk.

CHAPTER 25
SECTION EXERCISE ANSWERS

1. a) 3, 36, and 39
b) 321.90
c) 285.36
d) 8.94

3. a) H_0: Mean cell phone adoption rates are equal in the three regions.
H_A: Mean cell phone adoption rates are not all equal in the three regions.
b) Countries were selected randomly from the three regions, so the Randomization Condition is met. However, boxplots suggest the spreads may differ, and show several outliers, which may require attention. Other plots should be used to check the Nearly Normal Condition.

CHAPTER EXERCISE ANSWERS

5. a) $H_0: \mu_1 = \mu_2 = \mu_3 = \mu_4$ vs. the alternative that not all means are equal. Here, μ_k refers to the mean activation time using recipe k.
b) The data provide strong evidence with a P-value <0.0001 to reject the null hypothesis and conclude that the means are not all equal. This experiment provides strong evidence that the mean activation times differ among the recipes.
c) Yes. Because we have rejected the null hypothesis, we can proceed with a multiple comparisons method to compare all the groups.

7. No. This is an observational study. There may be other factors (such as age) that are influencing the response.

9. a) Observational study; the factors are not deliberately manipulated to specify treatments.
b) Boxplots of the hourly wages by both manager type and region indicate that the Equal Variance Assumption is reasonable. Also, the boxplots indicate fairly symmetric distributions. However, other plots should be used to check the Nearly Normal Condition once the model has been fit. The states were randomly selected from the three regions, so the Randomization Condition is satisfied.
c) Based on the P-values, we can conclude that there is no significant interaction effect. There is no evidence that the mean hourly wages are different across the three regions but are different for sales and advertising managers.
d) Yes, because the interaction effect is not significant.

11. a) The null hypothesis is that the mean *Mileage* for all cylinder levels is the same. The alternative is that not all means are equal.

b) Randomization not specified, so inference is not clear. The spreads of the four groups look very different. The response variable probably should be re-expressed before proceeding with an analysis of variance. Consider omitting the single 5-cylinder car from the study, since it is the only one in its group. Boxplots appear symmetric, but other plots should be used to check the Nearly Normal Condition.

13. a) $H_0: \mu_1 = \mu_2 = \mu_3 = \mu_4 = \mu_5 = \mu_6$ (That is, each of the tellers takes, on average, the same amount of time to serve a customer.) vs. the alternative that not all means are equal. Here μ_k refers to the mean *Time* it takes *Teller k* to serve a customer.

b) With a P-value of 0.19, we can't reject the null hypothesis.

c) No, because we do not reject the null hypothesis, we cannot perform multiple comparisons.

15. a) Observational; the factor was not deliberately manipulated.

b) Retrospective; using previously collected data.

c) H_0: Mean responses to the e-security questions are all equal for the three types of community.
H_A: Mean responses to the e-security questions are not all equal for the three types of community.

d) $F = 6.24$

e) With such a small P-value, we can reject the null hypothesis and conclude that mean responses to the e-security question are not all equal for the three types of community. A causal link cannot be established because this is an observational study.

17. a) Experimental

b) Drug

c) Reported pain level (1 to 10)

d)

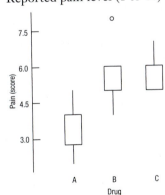

Drug

Analysis of Variance

Source	DF	Sum of Squares	Mean Square	F-ratio	P-value
Drug	2	28.2222	14.1111	11.9062	0.0003
Error	24	28.4444	1.1852		
Total	26	56.6666			

19. a) Experiment; the factors are deliberately manipulated to specify treatments, and the subjects are assigned to the treatments randomly.

b) Website trustworthiness measured on a 10-point scale.

c) There are two factors: (1) website configuration with respect to assurance and (2) type of product purchased.

d) There are nine treatments.

e) H_0: The mean *trustworthiness ratings* of websites are the same for those *with a third-party assurance seal, a self-proclaimed assurance displayed,* and *no assurance seal.*
H_0: The mean *trustworthiness* of websites is the same for online purchases of *books, cameras,* and *insurance.*
H_0: There is no interaction effect. (The effect of each factor is the same at all levels of the other factor.)

21. a) Observational study.

b) The mean DJIA closing is roughly the same each day of the week. The mean DJIA closing is roughly the same each month. Differences in days are no different from month to month.

c) There is no apparent difference in DJIA according to day of the week.

d) There does appear to be a difference from month to month.

e) There is no interaction between day of the week and month.

23. a) Experiment; the machine setting factor was deliberately manipulated. Shift is a blocking factor.

b) Size error of the part is the response variable.

c) There are nine treatments.

d) There is no significant interaction effect so we can conclude that both the Shift and the Machine Setting appear to have a significant effect. However, from this table alone, we cannot determine which of these effects is more important.

25. a) MST = 8.65; MSE = 0.0767

b) $F = 112.78$

c) The data provide very strong evidence that the means are not equal.

d) We have assumed that the experimental runs were performed in random order, that the variances of the treatment groups are similar, and that the residuals are nearly Normal.

e) A boxplot of the *Scores* by *Method*, a plot of residuals vs. predicted values, a Normal probability plot, and a histogram of the residuals.

f) $s_p = \sqrt{0.0767} = 0.277$ point

27. a) An observational study

b) The null hypothesis is that the mean *Sugar Content* is the same for the cereals on each *Shelf*. The alternative is that not all the means are equal.

c) The P-value of 0.0012 provides strong evidence that the mean *Sugar Content* is not the same for each *Shelf*.

d) We cannot conclude that cereals on *Shelf* 2 have a different mean *Sugar Content* than cereals on *Shelf* 3 or that cereals on *Shelf* 2 have a different mean *Sugar Content* than cereals on *Shelf* 1. We can conclude only that the means are not all equal.

e) The Bonferroni test shows that at $\alpha = 0.05$ the shelves are different, except for Shelf 1 and Shelf 3, which are not discernibly different. Now we can conclude that the mean *Sugar Content* of cereals on *Shelf* 2 is *not* equal to the mean *Sugar Content* on *Shelf* 1 and *Shelf* 3. In other words, we can conclude from this test what we wanted to conclude in part d.

29. a) H_0: Head injuries are, on average, about the same regardless of the size of the car
H_0: Which seat you sit in doesn't affect the degree of head injury.

b) The conditions appear to be met. We assume the data were collected independently, the boxplots show that the variance is roughly constant, and there are no patterns in the scatterplot of residuals vs. predicted values.

c) There is no significant interaction. The P-values for both *Seat* and *Size* are <0.0001. Thus, we reject both the null hypotheses and conclude that both the *Seat* and the *Size* of car affect the severity of head injury.

Appendix B Tables and Selected Formulas

TABLE D Critical Values d_L and d_U of the Durbin-Watson Statistic (Critical Values are One-Sided)[a]

$\alpha = 0.05$

	k = 1		k = 2		k = 3		k = 4		k = 5	
n	d_L	d_U	d_L	d_U	d_L	d_U	d_L	d_U	d_L	d_U
15	1.08	1.36	.95	1.54	.82	1.75	.69	1.97	.56	2.21
16	1.10	1.37	.98	1.54	.86	1.73	.74	1.93	.62	2.15
17	1.13	1.38	1.02	1.54	.90	1.71	.78	1.90	.67	2.10
18	1.16	1.39	1.05	1.53	.93	1.69	.82	1.87	.71	2.06
19	1.18	1.40	1.08	1.53	.97	1.68	.86	1.85	.75	2.02
20	1.20	1.41	1.10	1.54	1.00	1.68	.90	1.83	.79	1.99
21	1.22	1.42	1.13	1.54	1.03	1.67	.93	1.81	.83	1.96
22	1.24	1.43	1.15	1.54	1.05	1.66	.96	1.80	.86	1.94
23	1.26	1.44	1.17	1.54	1.08	1.66	.99	1.79	.90	1.92
24	1.27	1.45	1.19	1.55	1.10	1.66	1.01	1.78	.93	1.90
25	1.29	1.45	1.21	1.55	1.12	1.66	1.04	1.77	.95	1.89
26	1.30	1.46	1.22	1.55	1.14	1.65	1.06	1.76	.98	1.88
27	1.32	1.47	1.24	1.56	1.16	1.65	1.08	1.76	1.01	1.86
28	1.33	1.48	1.26	1.56	1.18	1.65	1.10	1.75	1.03	1.85
29	1.34	1.48	1.27	1.56	1.20	1.65	1.12	1.74	1.05	1.84
30	1.35	1.49	1.28	1.57	1.21	1.65	1.14	1.74	1.07	1.83
31	1.36	1.50	1.30	1.57	1.23	1.65	1.16	1.74	1.09	1.83
32	1.37	1.50	1.31	1.57	1.24	1.65	1.18	1.73	1.11	1.82
33	1.38	1.51	1.32	1.58	1.26	1.65	1.19	1.73	1.13	1.81
34	1.39	1.51	1.33	1.58	1.27	1.65	1.21	1.73	1.15	1.81
35	1.40	1.52	1.34	1.58	1.28	1.65	1.22	1.73	1.16	1.80
36	1.41	1.52	1.35	1.59	1.29	1.65	1.24	1.73	1.18	1.80
37	1.42	1.53	1.36	1.59	1.31	1.66	1.25	1.72	1.19	1.80
38	1.43	1.54	1.37	1.59	1.32	1.66	1.26	1.72	1.21	1.79
39	1.43	1.54	1.38	1.60	1.33	1.66	1.27	1.72	1.22	1.79
40	1.44	1.54	1.39	1.60	1.34	1.66	1.29	1.72	1.23	1.79
45	1.48	1.57	1.43	1.62	1.38	1.67	1.34	1.72	1.29	1.78
50	1.50	1.59	1.46	1.63	1.42	1.67	1.38	1.72	1.34	1.77
55	1.53	1.60	1.49	1.64	1.45	1.68	1.41	1.72	1.38	1.77
60	1.55	1.62	1.51	1.65	1.48	1.69	1.44	1.73	1.41	1.77
65	1.57	1.63	1.54	1.66	1.50	1.70	1.47	1.73	1.44	1.77
70	1.58	1.64	1.55	1.67	1.52	1.70	1.49	1.74	1.46	1.77
75	1.60	1.65	1.57	1.68	1.54	1.71	1.51	1.74	1.49	1.77
80	1.61	1.66	1.59	1.69	1.56	1.72	1.53	1.74	1.51	1.77
85	1.62	1.67	1.60	1.70	1.57	1.72	1.55	1.75	1.52	1.77
90	1.63	1.68	1.61	1.70	1.59	1.73	1.57	1.75	1.54	1.78
95	1.64	1.69	1.62	1.71	1.60	1.73	1.58	1.75	1.56	1.78
100	1.65	1.69	1.63	1.72	1.61	1.74	1.59	1.76	1.57	1.78

$\alpha = 0.01$

	k = 1		k = 2		k = 3		k = 4		k = 5	
n	d_L	d_U	d_L	d_U	d_L	d_U	d_L	d_U	d_L	d_U
15	.81	1.07	.70	1.25	.59	1.46	.49	1.70	.39	1.96
16	.84	1.09	.74	1.25	.63	1.44	.53	1.66	.44	1.90
17	.87	1.10	.77	1.25	.67	1.43	.57	1.63	.48	1.85
18	.90	1.12	.80	1.26	.71	1.42	.61	1.60	.52	1.80
19	.93	1.13	.83	1.26	.74	1.41	.65	1.58	.56	1.77
20	.95	1.15	.86	1.27	.77	1.41	.68	1.57	.60	1.74
21	.97	1.16	.89	1.27	.80	1.41	.72	1.55	.63	1.71
22	1.00	1.17	.91	1.28	.83	1.40	.75	1.54	.66	1.69
23	1.02	1.19	.94	1.29	.86	1.40	.77	1.53	.70	1.67
24	1.04	1.20	.96	1.30	.88	1.41	.80	1.53	.72	1.66
25	1.05	1.21	.98	1.30	.90	1.41	.83	1.52	.75	1.65
26	1.07	1.22	1.00	1.31	.93	1.41	.85	1.52	.78	1.64
27	1.09	1.23	1.02	1.32	.95	1.41	.88	1.51	.81	1.63
28	1.10	1.24	1.04	1.32	.97	1.41	.90	1.51	.83	1.62
29	1.12	1.25	1.05	1.33	.99	1.42	.92	1.51	.85	1.61
30	1.13	1.26	1.07	1.34	1.01	1.42	.94	1.51	.88	1.61
31	1.15	1.27	1.08	1.34	1.02	1.42	.96	1.51	.90	1.60
32	1.16	1.28	1.10	1.35	1.04	1.43	.98	1.51	.92	1.60
33	1.17	1.29	1.11	1.36	1.05	1.43	1.00	1.51	.94	1.59
34	1.18	1.30	1.13	1.36	1.07	1.43	1.01	1.51	.95	1.59
35	1.19	1.31	1.14	1.37	1.08	1.44	1.03	1.51	.97	1.59
36	1.21	1.32	1.15	1.38	1.10	1.44	1.04	1.51	.99	1.59
37	1.22	1.32	1.16	1.38	1.11	1.45	1.06	1.51	1.00	1.59
38	1.23	1.33	1.18	1.39	1.12	1.45	1.07	1.52	1.02	1.58
39	1.24	1.34	1.19	1.39	1.14	1.45	1.09	1.52	1.03	1.58
40	1.25	1.34	1.20	1.40	1.15	1.46	1.10	1.52	1.05	1.58
45	1.29	1.38	1.24	1.42	1.20	1.48	1.16	1.53	1.11	1.58
50	1.32	1.40	1.28	1.45	1.24	1.49	1.20	1.54	1.16	1.59
55	1.36	1.43	1.32	1.47	1.28	1.51	1.25	1.55	1.21	1.59
60	1.38	1.45	1.35	1.48	1.32	1.52	1.28	1.56	1.25	1.60
65	1.41	1.47	1.38	1.50	1.35	1.53	1.31	1.57	1.28	1.61
70	1.43	1.49	1.40	1.52	1.37	1.55	1.34	1.58	1.31	1.61
75	1.45	1.50	1.42	1.53	1.39	1.56	1.37	1.59	1.34	1.62
80	1.47	1.52	1.44	1.54	1.42	1.57	1.39	1.60	1.36	1.62
85	1.48	1.53	1.46	1.55	1.43	1.58	1.41	1.60	1.39	1.63
90	1.50	1.54	1.47	1.56	1.45	1.59	1.43	1.61	1.41	1.64
95	1.51	1.55	1.49	1.57	1.47	1.60	1.45	1.62	1.42	1.64
100	1.52	1.56	1.50	1.58	1.48	1.60	1.46	1.63	1.44	1.65

[a]n = number of observations; k = number of independent variables.

Source: This table is reproduced from *Biometrika*, 41 (1951): 173 and 175, with the permission of the *Biometrika* Trustees.

TABLE F

Numerator df

$\alpha = .01$	1	2	3	4	5	6	7	8	9	10	11	12	13	14	15	16	17	18	19	20	21	22
1	4052.2	4999.3	5403.5	5624.3	5764.0	5859.0	5928.3	5981.0	6022.4	6055.9	6083.4	6106.7	6125.8	6143.0	6157.0	6170.0	6181.2	6191.4	6200.7	6208.7	6216.1	6223.1
2	98.50	99.00	99.16	99.25	99.30	99.33	99.36	99.38	99.39	99.40	99.41	99.42	99.42	99.43	99.43	99.44	99.44	99.44	99.45	99.45	99.45	99.46
3	34.12	30.82	29.46	28.71	28.24	27.91	27.67	27.49	27.34	27.23	27.13	27.05	26.98	26.92	26.87	26.83	26.79	26.75	26.72	26.69	26.66	26.64
4	21.20	18.00	16.69	15.98	15.52	15.21	14.98	14.80	14.66	14.55	14.45	14.37	14.31	14.25	14.20	14.15	14.11	14.08	14.05	14.02	13.99	13.97
5	16.26	13.27	12.06	11.39	10.97	10.67	10.46	10.29	10.16	10.05	9.96	9.89	9.82	9.77	9.72	9.68	9.64	9.61	9.58	9.55	9.53	9.51
6	13.75	10.92	9.78	9.15	8.75	8.47	8.26	8.10	7.98	7.87	7.79	7.72	7.66	7.60	7.56	7.52	7.48	7.45	7.42	7.40	7.37	7.35
7	12.25	9.55	8.45	7.85	7.46	7.19	6.99	6.84	6.72	6.62	6.54	6.47	6.41	6.36	6.31	6.28	6.24	6.21	6.18	6.16	6.13	6.11
8	11.26	8.65	7.59	7.01	6.63	6.37	6.18	6.03	5.91	5.81	5.73	5.67	5.61	5.56	5.52	5.48	5.44	5.41	5.38	5.36	5.34	5.32
9	10.56	8.02	6.99	6.42	6.06	5.80	5.61	5.47	5.35	5.26	5.18	5.11	5.05	5.01	4.96	4.92	4.89	4.86	4.83	4.81	4.79	4.77
10	10.04	7.56	6.55	5.99	5.64	5.39	5.20	5.06	4.94	4.85	4.77	4.71	4.65	4.60	4.56	4.52	4.49	4.46	4.43	4.41	4.38	4.36
11	9.65	7.21	6.22	5.67	5.32	5.07	4.89	4.74	4.63	4.54	4.46	4.40	4.34	4.29	4.25	4.21	4.18	4.15	4.12	4.10	4.08	4.06
12	9.33	6.93	5.95	5.41	5.06	4.82	4.64	4.50	4.39	4.30	4.22	4.16	4.10	4.05	4.01	3.97	3.94	3.91	3.88	3.86	3.84	3.82
13	9.07	6.70	5.74	5.21	4.86	4.62	4.44	4.30	4.19	4.10	4.02	3.96	3.91	3.86	3.82	3.78	3.75	3.72	3.69	3.66	3.64	3.62
14	8.86	6.51	5.56	5.04	4.69	4.46	4.28	4.14	4.03	3.94	3.86	3.80	3.75	3.70	3.66	3.62	3.59	3.56	3.53	3.51	3.48	3.46
15	8.68	6.36	5.42	4.89	4.56	4.32	4.14	4.00	3.89	3.80	3.73	3.67	3.61	3.56	3.52	3.49	3.45	3.42	3.40	3.37	3.35	3.33
16	8.53	6.23	5.29	4.77	4.44	4.20	4.03	3.89	3.78	3.69	3.62	3.55	3.50	3.45	3.41	3.37	3.34	3.31	3.28	3.26	3.24	3.22
17	8.40	6.11	5.19	4.67	4.34	4.10	3.93	3.79	3.68	3.59	3.52	3.46	3.40	3.35	3.31	3.27	3.24	3.21	3.19	3.16	3.14	3.12
18	8.29	6.01	5.09	4.58	4.25	4.01	3.84	3.71	3.60	3.51	3.43	3.37	3.32	3.27	3.23	3.19	3.16	3.13	3.10	3.08	3.05	3.03
19	8.18	5.93	5.01	4.50	4.17	3.94	3.77	3.63	3.52	3.43	3.36	3.30	3.24	3.19	3.15	3.12	3.08	3.05	3.03	3.00	2.98	2.96
20	8.10	5.85	4.94	4.43	4.10	3.87	3.70	3.56	3.46	3.37	3.29	3.23	3.18	3.13	3.09	3.05	3.02	2.99	2.96	2.94	2.92	2.90
21	8.02	5.78	4.87	4.37	4.04	3.81	3.64	3.51	3.40	3.31	3.24	3.17	3.12	3.07	3.03	2.99	2.96	2.93	2.90	2.88	2.86	2.84
22	7.95	5.72	4.82	4.31	3.99	3.76	3.59	3.45	3.35	3.26	3.18	3.12	3.07	3.02	2.98	2.94	2.91	2.88	2.85	2.83	2.81	2.78
23	7.88	5.66	4.76	4.26	3.94	3.71	3.54	3.41	3.30	3.21	3.14	3.07	3.02	2.97	2.93	2.89	2.86	2.83	2.80	2.78	2.76	2.74
24	7.82	5.61	4.72	4.22	3.90	3.67	3.50	3.36	3.26	3.17	3.09	3.03	2.98	2.93	2.89	2.85	2.82	2.79	2.76	2.74	2.72	2.70
25	7.77	5.57	4.68	4.18	3.85	3.63	3.46	3.32	3.22	3.13	3.06	2.99	2.94	2.89	2.85	2.81	2.78	2.75	2.72	2.70	2.68	2.66
26	7.72	5.53	4.64	4.14	3.82	3.59	3.42	3.29	3.18	3.09	3.02	2.96	2.90	2.86	2.81	2.78	2.75	2.72	2.69	2.66	2.64	2.62
27	7.68	5.49	4.60	4.11	3.78	3.56	3.39	3.26	3.15	3.06	2.99	2.93	2.87	2.82	2.78	2.75	2.71	2.68	2.66	2.63	2.61	2.59
28	7.64	5.45	4.57	4.07	3.75	3.53	3.36	3.23	3.12	3.03	2.96	2.90	2.84	2.79	2.75	2.72	2.68	2.65	2.63	2.60	2.58	2.56
29	7.60	5.42	4.54	4.04	3.73	3.50	3.33	3.20	3.09	3.00	2.93	2.87	2.81	2.77	2.73	2.69	2.66	2.63	2.60	2.57	2.55	2.53
30	7.56	5.39	4.51	4.02	3.70	3.47	3.30	3.17	3.07	2.98	2.91	2.84	2.79	2.74	2.70	2.66	2.63	2.60	2.57	2.55	2.53	2.51
32	7.50	5.34	4.46	3.97	3.65	3.43	3.26	3.13	3.02	2.93	2.86	2.80	2.74	2.70	2.65	2.62	2.58	2.55	2.53	2.50	2.48	2.46
35	7.42	5.27	4.40	3.91	3.59	3.37	3.20	3.07	2.96	2.88	2.80	2.74	2.69	2.64	2.60	2.56	2.53	2.50	2.47	2.44	2.42	2.40
40	7.31	5.18	4.31	3.83	3.51	3.29	3.12	2.99	2.89	2.80	2.73	2.66	2.61	2.56	2.52	2.48	2.45	2.42	2.39	2.37	2.35	2.33
45	7.23	5.11	4.25	3.77	3.45	3.23	3.07	2.94	2.83	2.74	2.67	2.61	2.55	2.51	2.46	2.43	2.39	2.36	2.34	2.31	2.29	2.27
50	7.17.	5.06	4.20	3.72	3.41	3.19	3.02	2.89	2.78	2.70	2.63	2.56	2.51	2.46	2.42	2.38	2.35	2.32	2.29	2.27	2.24	2.22
60	7.08	4.98	4.13	3.65	3.34	3.12	2.95	2.82	2.72	2.63	2.56	2.50	2.44	2.39	2.35	2.31	2.28	2.25	2.22	2.20	2.17	2.15
75	6.99	4.90	4.05	3.58	3.27	3.05	2.89	2.76	2.65	2.57	2.49	2.43	2.38	2.33	2.29	2.25	2.22	2.18	2.16	2.13	2.11	2.09
100	6.90	4.82	3.98	3.51	3.21	2.99	2.82	2.69	2.59	2.50	2.43	2.37	2.31	2.27	2.22	2.19	2.15	2.12	2.09	2.07	2.04	2.02
120	6.85	4.79	3.95	3.48	3.17	2.96	2.79	2.66	2.56	2.47	2.40	2.34	2.28	2.23	2.19	2.15	2.12	2.09	2.06	2.03	2.01	1.99
140	6.82	4.76	3.92	3.46	3.15	2.93	2.77	2.64	2.54	2.45	2.38	2.31	2.26	2.21	2.17	2.13	2.10	2.07	2.04	2.01	1.99	1.97
180	6.78	4.73	3.89	3.43	3.12	2.90	2.74	2.61	2.51	2.42	2.35	2.28	2.23	2.18	2.14	2.10	2.07	2.04	2.01	1.98	1.96	1.94
250	6.74	4.69	3.86	3.40	3.09	2.87	2.71	2.58	2.48	2.39	2.32	2.26	2.20	2.15	2.11	2.07	2.04	2.01	1.98	1.95	1.93	1.91
400	6.70	4.66	3.83	3.37	3.06	2.85	2.68	2.56	2.45	2.37	2.29	2.23	2.17	2.13	2.08	2.05	2.01	1.98	1.95	1.92	1.90	1.88
1000	6.66	4.63	3.80	3.34	3.04	2.82	2.66	2.53	2.43	2.34	2.27	2.20	2.15	2.10	2.06	2.02	1.98	1.95	1.92	1.90	1.87	1.85

Denominator df

TABLE F (CONT.)

Numerator df

$\alpha = .01$	23	24	25	26	27	28	29	30	32	35	40	45	50	60	75	100	120	140	180	250	400	1000
1	6228.7	6234.3	6239.9	6244.5	6249.2	6252.9	6257.1	6260.4	6266.9	6275.3	6286.4	6295.7	6302.3	6313.0	6323.7	6333.9	6339.5	6343.2	6347.9	6353.5	6358.1	6362.8
2	99.46	99.46	99.46	99.46	99.46	99.46	99.46	99.47	99.47	99.47	99.48	99.48	99.48	99.48	99.48	99.49	99.49	99.49	99.49	99.50	99.50	99.50
3	26.62	26.60	26.58	26.56	26.55	26.53	26.52	26.50	26.48	26.45	26.41	26.38	26.35	26.32	26.28	26.24	26.22	26.21	26.19	26.17	26.15	26.14
4	13.95	13.93	13.91	13.89	13.88	13.86	13.85	13.84	13.81	13.79	13.75	13.71	13.69	13.65	13.61	13.58	13.56	13.54	13.53	13.51	13.49	13.47
5	9.49	9.47	9.45	9.43	9.42	9.40	9.39	9.38	9.36	9.33	9.29	9.26	9.24	9.20	9.17	9.13	9.11	9.10	9.08	9.06	9.05	9.03
6	7.33	7.31	7.30	7.28	7.27	7.25	7.24	7.23	7.21	7.18	7.14	7.11	7.09	7.06	7.02	6.99	6.97	6.96	6.94	6.92	6.91	6.89
7	6.09	6.07	6.06	6.04	6.03	6.02	6.00	5.99	5.97	5.94	5.91	5.88	5.86	5.82	5.79	5.75	5.74	5.72	5.71	5.69	5.68	5.66
8	5.30	5.28	5.26	5.25	5.23	5.22	5.21	5.20	5.18	5.15	5.12	5.09	5.07	5.03	5.00	4.96	4.95	4.93	4.92	4.90	4.89	4.87
9	4.75	4.73	4.71	4.70	4.68	4.67	4.66	4.65	4.63	4.60	4.57	4.54	4.52	4.48	4.45	4.41	4.40	4.39	4.37	4.35	4.34	4.32
10	4.34	4.33	4.31	4.30	4.28	4.27	4.26	4.25	4.23	4.20	4.17	4.14	4.12	4.08	4.05	4.01	4.00	3.98	3.97	3.95	3.94	3.92
11	4.04	4.02	4.01	3.99	3.98	3.96	3.95	3.94	3.92	3.89	3.86	3.83	3.81	3.78	3.74	3.71	3.69	3.68	3.66	3.64	3.63	3.61
12	3.80	3.78	3.76	3.75	3.74	3.72	3.71	3.70	3.68	3.65	3.62	3.59	3.57	3.54	3.50	3.47	3.45	3.44	3.42	3.40	3.39	3.37
13	3.60	3.59	3.57	3.56	3.54	3.53	3.52	3.51	3.49	3.46	3.43	3.40	3.38	3.34	3.31	3.27	3.25	3.24	3.23	3.21	3.19	3.18
14	3.44	3.43	3.41	3.40	3.38	3.37	3.36	3.35	3.33	3.30	3.27	3.24	3.22	3.18	3.15	3.11	3.09	3.08	3.06	3.05	3.03	3.02
15	3.31	3.29	3.28	3.26	3.25	3.24	3.23	3.21	3.19	3.17	3.13	3.10	3.08	3.05	3.01	2.98	2.96	2.95	2.93	2.91	2.90	2.88
16	3.20	3.18	3.16	3.15	3.14	3.12	3.11	3.10	3.08	3.05	3.02	2.99	2.97	2.93	2.90	2.86	2.84	2.83	2.81	2.80	2.78	2.76
17	3.10	3.08	3.07	3.05	3.04	3.03	3.01	3.00	2.98	2.96	2.92	2.89	2.87	2.83	2.80	2.76	2.75	2.73	2.72	2.70	2.68	2.66
18	3.02	3.00	2.98	2.97	2.95	2.94	2.93	2.92	2.90	2.87	2.84	2.81	2.78	2.75	2.71	2.68	2.66	2.65	2.63	2.61	2.59	2.58
19	2.94	2.92	2.91	2.89	2.88	2.87	2.86	2.84	2.82	2.80	2.76	2.73	2.71	2.67	2.64	2.60	2.58	2.57	2.55	2.54	2.52	2.50
20	2.88	2.86	2.84	2.83	2.81	2.80	2.79	2.78	2.76	2.73	2.69	2.67	2.64	2.61	2.57	2.54	2.52	2.50	2.49	2.47	2.45	2.43
21	2.82	2.80	2.79	2.77	2.76	2.74	2.73	2.72	2.70	2.67	2.64	2.61	2.58	2.55	2.51	2.48	2.46	2.44	2.43	2.41	2.39	2.37
22	2.77	2.75	2.73	2.72	2.70	2.69	2.68	2.67	2.65	2.62	2.58	2.55	2.53	2.50	2.46	2.42	2.40	2.39	2.37	2.35	2.34	2.32
23	2.72	2.70	2.69	2.67	2.66	2.64	2.63	2.62	2.60	2.57	2.54	2.51	2.48	2.45	2.41	2.37	2.35	2.34	2.32	2.30	2.29	2.27
24	2.68	2.66	2.64	2.63	2.61	2.60	2.59	2.58	2.56	2.53	2.49	2.46	2.44	2.40	2.37	2.33	2.31	2.30	2.28	2.26	2.24	2.22
25	2.64	2.62	2.60	2.59	2.58	2.56	2.55	2.54	2.52	2.49	2.45	2.42	2.40	2.36	2.33	2.29	2.27	2.26	2.24	2.22	2.20	2.18
26	2.60	2.58	2.57	2.55	2.54	2.53	2.51	2.50	2.48	2.45	2.42	2.39	2.36	2.33	2.29	2.25	2.23	2.22	2.20	2.18	2.16	2.14
27	2.57	2.55	2.54	2.52	2.51	2.49	2.48	2.47	2.45	2.42	2.38	2.35	2.33	2.29	2.26	2.22	2.20	2.18	2.17	2.15	2.13	2.11
28	2.54	2.52	2.51	2.49	2.48	2.46	2.45	2.44	2.42	2.39	2.35	2.32	2.30	2.26	2.23	2.19	2.17	2.15	2.13	2.11	2.10	2.08
29	2.51	2.49	2.48	2.46	2.45	2.44	2.42	2.41	2.39	2.36	2.33	2.30	2.27	2.23	2.20	2.16	2.14	2.12	2.10	2.08	2.07	2.05
30	2.49	2.47	2.45	2.44	2.42	2.41	2.40	2.39	2.36	2.34	2.30	2.27	2.25	2.21	2.17	2.13	2.11	2.10	2.08	2.06	2.04	2.02
32	2.44	2.42	2.41	2.39	2.38	2.36	2.35	2.34	2.32	2.29	2.25	2.22	2.20	2.16	2.12	2.08	2.06	2.05	2.03	2.01	1.99	1.97
35	2.38	2.36	2.35	2.33	2.32	2.30	2.29	2.28	2.26	2.23	2.19	2.16	2.14	2.10	2.06	2.02	2.00	1.98	1.96	1.94	1.92	1.90
40	2.31	2.29	2.27	2.26	2.24	2.23	2.22	2.20	2.18	2.15	2.11	2.08	2.06	2.02	1.98	1.94	1.92	1.90	1.88	1.86	1.84	1.82
45	2.25	2.23	2.21	2.20	2.18	2.17	2.16	2.14	2.12	2.09	2.05	2.02	2.00	1.96	1.92	1.88	1.85	1.84	1.82	1.79	1.77	1.75
50	2.20	2.18	2.17	2.15	2.14	2.12	2.11	2.10	2.08	2.05	2.01	1.97	1.95	1.91	1.87	1.82	1.80	1.79	1.76	1.74	1.72	1.70
60	2.13	2.12	2.10	2.08	2.07	2.05	2.04	2.03	2.01	1.98	1.94	1.90	1.88	1.84	1.79	1.75	1.73	1.71	1.69	1.66	1.64	1.62
75	2.07	2.05	2.03	2.02	2.00	1.99	1.97	1.96	1.94	1.91	1.87	1.83	1.81	1.76	1.72	1.67	1.65	1.63	1.61	1.58	1.56	1.53
100	2.00	1.98	1.97	1.95	1.93	1.92	1.91	1.89	1.87	1.84	1.80	1.76	1.74	1.69	1.65	1.60	1.57	1.55	1.53	1.50	1.47	1.45
120	1.97	1.95	1.93	1.92	1.90	1.89	1.87	1.86	1.84	1.81	1.76	1.73	1.70	1.66	1.61	1.56	1.53	1.51	1.49	1.46	1.43	1.40
140	1.95	1.93	1.91	1.89	1.88	1.86	1.85	1.84	1.81	1.78	1.74	1.70	1.67	1.63	1.58	1.53	1.50	1.48	1.46	1.43	1.40	1.37
180	1.92	1.90	1.88	1.86	1.85	1.83	1.82	1.81	1.78	1.75	1.71	1.67	1.64	1.60	1.55	1.49	1.47	1.45	1.42	1.39	1.35	1.32
250	1.89	1.87	1.85	1.83	1.82	1.80	1.79	1.77	1.75	1.72	1.67	1.64	1.61	1.56	1.51	1.46	1.43	1.41	1.38	1.34	1.31	1.27
400	1.86	1.84	1.82	1.80	1.79	1.77	1.76	1.75	1.72	1.69	1.64	1.61	1.58	1.53	1.48	1.42	1.39	1.37	1.33	1.30	1.26	1.22
1000	1.83	1.81	1.79	1.77	1.76	1.74	1.73	1.72	1.69	1.66	1.61	1.58	1.54	1.50	1.44	1.38	1.35	1.33	1.29	1.25	1.21	1.16

Denominator df

TABLE F (CONT.)

$\alpha = .05$

Numerator df

Denominator df	1	2	3	4	5	6	7	8	9	10	11	12	13	14	15	16	17	18	19	20	21	22
1	161.4	199.5	215.7	224.6	230.2	234.0	236.8	238.9	240.5	241.9	243.0	243.9	244.7	245.4	245.9	246.5	246.9	247.3	247.7	248.0	248.3	248.6
2	18.51	19.00	19.16	19.25	19.30	19.33	19.35	19.37	19.38	19.40	19.40	19.41	19.42	19.42	19.43	19.43	19.44	19.44	19.44	19.45	19.45	19.45
3	10.13	9.55	9.28	9.12	9.01	8.94	8.89	8.85	8.81	8.79	8.76	8.74	8.73	8.71	8.70	8.69	8.68	8.67	8.67	8.66	8.65	8.65
4	7.71	6.94	6.59	6.39	6.26	6.16	6.09	6.04	6.00	5.96	5.94	5.91	5.89	5.87	5.86	5.84	5.83	5.82	5.81	5.80	5.79	5.79
5	6.61	5.79	5.41	5.19	5.05	4.95	4.88	4.82	4.77	4.74	4.70	4.68	4.66	4.64	4.62	4.60	4.59	4.58	4.57	4.56	4.55	4.54
6	5.99	5.14	4.76	4.53	4.39	4.28	4.21	4.15	4.10	4.06	4.03	4.00	3.98	3.96	3.94	3.92	3.91	3.90	3.88	3.87	3.86	3.86
7	5.59	4.74	4.35	4.12	3.97	3.87	3.79	3.73	3.68	3.64	3.60	3.57	3.55	3.53	3.51	3.49	3.48	3.47	3.46	3.44	3.43	3.43
8	5.32	4.46	4.07	3.84	3.69	3.58	3.50	3.44	3.39	3.35	3.31	3.28	3.26	3.24	3.22	3.20	3.19	3.17	3.16	3.15	3.14	3.13
9	5.12	4.26	3.86	3.63	3.48	3.37	3.29	3.23	3.18	3.14	3.10	3.07	3.05	3.03	3.01	2.99	2.97	2.96	2.95	2.94	2.93	2.92
10	4.96	4.10	3.71	3.48	3.33	3.22	3.14	3.07	3.02	2.98	2.94	2.91	2.89	2.86	2.85	2.83	2.81	2.80	2.79	2.77	2.76	2.75
11	4.84	3.98	3.59	3.36	3.20	3.09	3.01	2.95	2.90	2.85	2.82	2.79	2.76	2.74	2.72	2.70	2.69	2.67	2.66	2.65	2.64	2.63
12	4.75	3.89	3.49	3.26	3.11	3.00	2.91	2.85	2.80	2.75	2.72	2.69	2.66	2.64	2.62	2.60	2.58	2.57	2.56	2.54	2.53	2.52
13	4.67	3.81	3.41	3.18	3.03	2.92	2.83	2.77	2.71	2.67	2.63	2.60	2.58	2.55	2.53	2.51	2.50	2.48	2.47	2.46	2.45	2.44
14	4.60	3.74	3.34	3.11	2.96	2.85	2.76	2.70	2.65	2.60	2.57	2.53	2.51	2.48	2.46	2.44	2.43	2.41	2.40	2.39	2.38	2.37
15	4.54	3.68	3.29	3.06	2.90	2.79	2.71	2.64	2.59	2.54	2.51	2.48	2.45	2.42	2.40	2.38	2.37	2.35	2.34	2.33	2.32	2.31
16	4.49	3.63	3.24	3.01	2.85	2.74	2.66	2.59	2.54	2.49	2.46	2.42	2.40	2.37	2.35	2.33	2.32	2.30	2.29	2.28	2.26	2.25
17	4.45	3.59	3.20	2.96	2.81	2.70	2.61	2.55	2.49	2.45	2.41	2.38	2.35	2.33	2.31	2.29	2.27	2.26	2.24	2.23	2.22	2.21
18	4.41	3.55	3.16	2.93	2.77	2.66	2.58	2.51	2.46	2.41	2.37	2.34	2.31	2.29	2.27	2.25	2.23	2.22	2.20	2.19	2.18	2.17
19	4.38	3.52	3.13	2.90	2.74	2.63	2.54	2.48	2.42	2.38	2.34	2.31	2.28	2.26	2.23	2.21	2.20	2.18	2.17	2.16	2.14	2.13
20	4.35	3.49	3.10	2.87	2.71	2.60	2.51	2.45	2.39	2.35	2.31	2.28	2.25	2.22	2.20	2.18	2.17	2.15	2.14	2.12	2.11	2.10
21	4.32	3.47	3.07	2.84	2.68	2.57	2.49	2.42	2.37	2.32	2.28	2.25	2.22	2.20	2.18	2.16	2.14	2.12	2.11	2.10	2.08	2.07
22	4.30	3.44	3.05	2.82	2.66	2.55	2.46	2.40	2.34	2.30	2.26	2.23	2.20	2.17	2.15	2.13	2.11	2.10	2.08	2.07	2.06	2.05
23	4.28	3.42	3.03	2.80	2.64	2.53	2.44	2.37	2.32	2.27	2.24	2.20	2.18	2.15	2.13	2.11	2.09	2.08	2.06	2.05	2.04	2.02
24	4.26	3.40	3.01	2.78	2.62	2.51	2.42	2.36	2.30	2.25	2.22	2.18	2.15	2.13	2.11	2.09	2.07	2.05	2.04	2.03	2.01	2.00
25	4.24	3.39	2.99	2.76	2.60	2.49	2.40	2.34	2.28	2.24	2.20	2.16	2.14	2.11	2.09	2.07	2.05	2.04	2.02	2.01	2.00	1.98
26	4.23	3.37	2.98	2.74	2.59	2.47	2.39	2.32	2.27	2.22	2.18	2.15	2.12	2.09	2.07	2.05	2.03	2.02	2.00	1.99	1.98	1.97
27	4.21	3.35	2.96	2.73	2.57	2.46	2.37	2.31	2.25	2.20	2.17	2.13	2.10	2.08	2.06	2.04	2.02	2.00	1.99	1.97	1.96	1.95
28	4.20	3.34	2.95	2.71	2.56	2.45	2.36	2.29	2.24	2.19	2.15	2.12	2.09	2.06	2.04	2.02	2.00	1.99	1.97	1.96	1.95	1.93
29	4.18	3.33	2.93	2.70	2.55	2.43	2.35	2.28	2.22	2.18	2.14	2.10	2.08	2.05	2.03	2.01	1.99	1.97	1.96	1.94	1.93	1.92
30	4.17	3.32	2.92	2.69	2.53	2.42	2.33	2.27	2.21	2.16	2.13	2.09	2.06	2.04	2.01	1.99	1.98	1.96	1.95	1.93	1.92	1.91
32	4.15	3.29	2.90	2.67	2.51	2.40	2.31	2.24	2.19	2.14	2.10	2.07	2.04	2.01	1.99	1.97	1.95	1.94	1.92	1.91	1.90	1.88
35	4.12	3.27	2.87	2.64	2.49	2.37	2.29	2.22	2.16	2.11	2.07	2.04	2.01	1.99	1.96	1.94	1.92	1.91	1.89	1.88	1.87	1.85
40	4.08	3.23	2.84	2.61	2.45	2.34	2.25	2.18	2.12	2.08	2.04	2.00	1.97	1.95	1.92	1.90	1.89	1.87	1.85	1.84	1.83	1.81
45	4.06	3.20	2.81	2.58	2.42	2.31	2.22	2.15	2.10	2.05	2.01	1.97	1.94	1.92	1.89	1.87	1.86	1.84	1.82	1.81	1.80	1.78
50	4.03	3.18	2.79	2.56	2.40	2.29	2.20	2.13	2.07	2.03	1.99	1.95	1.92	1.89	1.87	1.85	1.83	1.81	1.80	1.78	1.77	1.76
60	4.00	3.15	2.76	2.53	2.37	2.25	2.17	2.10	2.04	1.99	1.95	1.92	1.89	1.86	1.84	1.82	1.80	1.78	1.76	1.75	1.73	1.72
75	3.97	3.12	2.73	2.49	2.34	2.22	2.13	2.06	2.01	1.96	1.92	1.88	1.85	1.83	1.80	1.78	1.76	1.74	1.73	1.71	1.70	1.69
100	3.94	3.09	2.70	2.46	2.31	2.19	2.10	2.03	1.97	1.93	1.89	1.85	1.82	1.79	1.77	1.75	1.73	1.71	1.69	1.68	1.66	1.65
120	3.92	3.07	2.68	2.45	2.29	2.18	2.09	2.02	1.96	1.91	1.87	1.83	1.80	1.78	1.75	1.73	1.71	1.69	1.67	1.66	1.64	1.63
140	3.91	3.06	2.67	2.44	2.28	2.16	2.08	2.01	1.95	1.90	1.86	1.82	1.79	1.76	1.74	1.72	1.70	1.68	1.66	1.65	1.63	1.62
180	3.89	3.05	2.65	2.42	2.26	2.15	2.06	1.99	1.93	1.88	1.84	1.81	1.77	1.75	1.72	1.70	1.68	1.66	1.64	1.63	1.61	1.60
250	3.88	3.03	2.64	2.41	2.25	2.13	2.05	1.98	1.92	1.87	1.83	1.79	1.76	1.73	1.71	1.68	1.66	1.65	1.63	1.61	1.60	1.58
400	3.86	3.02	2.63	2.39	2.24	2.12	2.03	1.96	1.90	1.85	1.81	1.78	1.74	1.72	1.69	1.67	1.65	1.63	1.61	1.60	1.58	1.57
1000	3.85	3.00	2.61	2.38	2.22	2.11	2.02	1.95	1.89	1.84	1.80	1.76	1.73	1.70	1.68	1.65	1.63	1.61	1.60	1.58	1.57	1.55

TABLE F (CONT.)

Numerator df

$\alpha = .05$	23	24	25	26	27	28	29	30	32	35	40	45	50	60	75	100	120	140	180	250	400	1000
1	248.8	249.1	249.3	249.5	249.6	249.8	250.0	250.1	250.4	250.7	251.1	251.5	251.8	252.2	252.6	253.0	253.3	253.4	253.6	253.8	254.0	254.2
2	19.45	19.45	19.46	19.46	19.46	19.46	19.46	19.46	19.46	19.47	19.47	19.47	19.48	19.48	19.48	19.49	19.49	19.49	19.49	19.49	19.49	19.49
3	8.64	8.64	8.63	8.63	8.63	8.62	8.62	8.62	8.61	8.60	8.59	8.59	8.58	8.57	8.56	8.55	8.55	8.55	8.54	8.54	8.53	8.53
4	5.78	5.77	5.77	5.76	5.76	5.75	5.75	5.75	5.74	5.73	5.72	5.71	5.70	5.69	5.68	5.66	5.66	5.65	5.65	5.64	5.64	5.63
5	4.53	4.53	4.52	4.52	4.51	4.50	4.50	4.50	4.49	4.48	4.46	4.45	4.44	4.43	4.42	4.41	4.40	4.39	4.39	4.38	4.38	4.37
6	3.85	3.84	3.83	3.83	3.82	3.82	3.81	3.81	3.80	3.79	3.77	3.76	3.75	3.74	3.73	3.71	3.70	3.70	3.69	3.69	3.68	3.67
7	3.42	3.41	3.40	3.40	3.39	3.39	3.38	3.38	3.37	3.36	3.34	3.33	3.32	3.30	3.29	3.27	3.27	3.26	3.25	3.25	3.24	3.23
8	3.12	3.12	3.11	3.10	3.10	3.09	3.08	3.08	3.07	3.06	3.04	3.03	3.02	3.01	2.99	2.97	2.97	2.96	2.95	2.95	2.94	2.93
9	2.91	2.90	2.89	2.89	2.88	2.87	2.87	2.86	2.85	2.84	2.83	2.81	2.80	2.79	2.77	2.76	2.75	2.74	2.73	2.73	2.72	2.71
10	2.75	2.74	2.73	2.72	2.72	2.71	2.70	2.70	2.69	2.68	2.66	2.65	2.64	2.62	2.60	2.59	2.58	2.57	2.57	2.56	2.55	2.54
11	2.62	2.61	2.60	2.59	2.59	2.58	2.58	2.57	2.56	2.55	2.53	2.52	2.51	2.49	2.47	2.46	2.45	2.44	2.43	2.43	2.42	2.41
12	2.51	2.51	2.50	2.49	2.48	2.48	2.47	2.47	2.46	2.44	2.43	2.41	2.40	2.38	2.37	2.35	2.34	2.33	2.33	2.32	2.31	2.30
13	2.43	2.42	2.41	2.41	2.40	2.39	2.39	2.38	2.37	2.36	2.34	2.33	2.31	2.30	2.28	2.26	2.25	2.25	2.24	2.23	2.22	2.21
14	2.36	2.35	2.34	2.33	2.33	2.32	2.31	2.31	2.30	2.28	2.27	2.25	2.24	2.22	2.21	2.19	2.18	2.17	2.16	2.15	2.15	2.14
15	2.30	2.29	2.28	2.27	2.27	2.26	2.25	2.25	2.24	2.22	2.20	2.19	2.18	2.16	2.14	2.12	2.11	2.11	2.10	2.09	2.08	2.07
16	2.24	2.24	2.23	2.22	2.21	2.21	2.20	2.19	2.18	2.17	2.15	2.14	2.12	2.11	2.09	2.07	2.06	2.05	2.04	2.03	2.02	2.02
17	2.20	2.19	2.18	2.17	2.17	2.16	2.15	2.15	2.14	2.12	2.10	2.09	2.08	2.06	2.04	2.02	2.01	2.00	1.99	1.98	1.98	1.97
18	2.16	2.15	2.14	2.13	2.13	2.12	2.11	2.11	2.10	2.08	2.06	2.05	2.04	2.02	2.00	1.98	1.97	1.96	1.95	1.94	1.93	1.92
19	2.12	2.11	2.11	2.10	2.09	2.08	2.08	2.07	2.06	2.05	2.03	2.01	2.00	1.98	1.96	1.94	1.93	1.92	1.91	1.90	1.89	1.88
20	2.09	2.08	2.07	2.07	2.06	2.05	2.05	2.04	2.03	2.01	1.99	1.98	1.97	1.95	1.93	1.91	1.90	1.89	1.88	1.87	1.86	1.85
21	2.06	2.05	2.05	2.04	2.03	2.02	2.02	2.01	2.00	1.98	1.96	1.95	1.94	1.92	1.90	1.88	1.87	1.86	1.85	1.84	1.83	1.82
22	2.04	2.03	2.02	2.01	2.00	2.00	1.99	1.98	1.97	1.96	1.94	1.92	1.91	1.89	1.87	1.85	1.84	1.83	1.82	1.81	1.80	1.79
23	2.01	2.01	2.00	1.99	1.98	1.97	1.97	1.96	1.95	1.93	1.91	1.90	1.88	1.86	1.84	1.82	1.81	1.81	1.79	1.78	1.77	1.76
24	1.99	1.98	1.97	1.97	1.96	1.95	1.95	1.94	1.93	1.91	1.89	1.88	1.86	1.84	1.82	1.80	1.79	1.78	1.77	1.76	1.75	1.74
25	1.97	1.96	1.96	1.95	1.94	1.93	1.93	1.92	1.91	1.89	1.87	1.86	1.84	1.82	1.80	1.78	1.77	1.76	1.75	1.74	1.73	1.72
26	1.96	1.95	1.94	1.93	1.92	1.91	1.91	1.90	1.89	1.87	1.85	1.84	1.82	1.80	1.78	1.76	1.75	1.75	1.73	1.72	1.71	1.70
27	1.94	1.93	1.92	1.91	1.90	1.90	1.89	1.88	1.87	1.86	1.84	1.82	1.81	1.79	1.76	1.74	1.73	1.73	1.71	1.70	1.69	1.68
28	1.92	1.91	1.91	1.90	1.89	1.88	1.88	1.87	1.86	1.84	1.82	1.80	1.79	1.77	1.75	1.73	1.71	1.71	1.69	1.68	1.67	1.66
29	1.91	1.90	1.89	1.88	1.88	1.87	1.86	1.85	1.85	1.83	1.81	1.79	1.77	1.75	1.73	1.71	1.70	1.69	1.68	1.67	1.66	1.65
30	1.90	1.89	1.88	1.87	1.86	1.85	1.85	1.84	1.84	1.81	1.79	1.77	1.76	1.74	1.72	1.70	1.68	1.68	1.66	1.65	1.64	1.63
32	1.87	1.86	1.85	1.85	1.84	1.83	1.82	1.82	1.80	1.79	1.77	1.75	1.74	1.71	1.69	1.67	1.66	1.65	1.64	1.63	1.61	1.60
35	1.84	1.83	1.82	1.82	1.81	1.80	1.79	1.79	1.77	1.76	1.74	1.72	1.70	1.68	1.66	1.63	1.62	1.61	1.60	1.59	1.58	1.57
40	1.80	1.79	1.78	1.77	1.77	1.76	1.75	1.74	1.73	1.72	1.69	1.67	1.66	1.64	1.61	1.59	1.58	1.57	1.55	1.54	1.53	1.52
45	1.77	1.76	1.75	1.74	1.73	1.73	1.72	1.71	1.70	1.68	1.66	1.64	1.63	1.60	1.58	1.55	1.54	1.53	1.52	1.51	1.49	1.48
50	1.75	1.74	1.73	1.72	1.71	1.70	1.69	1.69	1.67	1.66	1.63	1.61	1.60	1.58	1.55	1.52	1.51	1.50	1.49	1.47	1.46	1.45
60	1.71	1.70	1.69	1.68	1.67	1.66	1.66	1.65	1.64	1.62	1.59	1.57	1.56	1.53	1.51	1.48	1.47	1.46	1.44	1.43	1.41	1.40
75	1.67	1.66	1.65	1.64	1.63	1.63	1.62	1.61	1.60	1.58	1.55	1.53	1.52	1.49	1.47	1.44	1.42	1.41	1.40	1.38	1.37	1.35
100	1.64	1.63	1.62	1.61	1.60	1.59	1.58	1.57	1.56	1.54	1.52	1.49	1.48	1.45	1.42	1.39	1.38	1.36	1.35	1.33	1.31	1.30
120	1.62	1.61	1.60	1.59	1.58	1.57	1.56	1.55	1.54	1.52	1.50	1.47	1.46	1.43	1.40	1.37	1.35	1.34	1.32	1.30	1.29	1.27
140	1.61	1.60	1.58	1.57	1.57	1.56	1.55	1.54	1.53	1.51	1.48	1.46	1.44	1.41	1.38	1.35	1.33	1.32	1.30	1.29	1.27	1.25
180	1.59	1.58	1.57	1.56	1.55	1.54	1.53	1.52	1.51	1.49	1.46	1.44	1.42	1.39	1.36	1.33	1.31	1.30	1.28	1.26	1.24	1.22
250	1.57	1.56	1.55	1.54	1.53	1.52	1.51	1.50	1.49	1.47	1.44	1.42	1.40	1.37	1.34	1.31	1.29	1.27	1.25	1.23	1.21	1.18
400	1.56	1.54	1.53	1.52	1.51	1.50	1.50	1.49	1.47	1.45	1.42	1.40	1.38	1.35	1.32	1.28	1.26	1.25	1.23	1.20	1.18	1.15
1000	1.54	1.53	1.52	1.51	1.50	1.49	1.48	1.47	1.46	1.43	1.41	1.38	1.36	1.33	1.30	1.26	1.24	1.22	1.20	1.17	1.14	1.11

Denominator df

TABLE F (CONT.)

Numerator df

α = .1	1	2	3	4	5	6	7	8	9	10	11	12	13	14	15	16	17	18	19	20	21	22
1	39.9	49.5	53.6	55.8	57.2	58.2	58.9	59.4	59.9	60.2	60.5	60.7	60.9	61.1	61.2	61.3	61.5	61.6	61.7	61.7	61.8	61.9
2	8.53	9.00	9.16	9.24	9.29	9.33	9.35	9.37	9.38	9.39	9.40	9.41	9.41	9.42	9.42	9.43	9.43	9.44	9.44	9.44	9.44	9.45
3	5.54	5.46	5.39	5.34	5.31	5.28	5.27	5.25	5.24	5.23	5.22	5.22	5.21	5.20	5.20	5.20	5.19	5.19	5.19	5.18	5.18	5.18
4	4.54	4.32	4.19	4.11	4.05	4.01	3.98	3.95	3.94	3.92	3.91	3.90	3.89	3.88	3.87	3.86	3.86	3.85	3.85	3.84	3.84	3.84
5	4.06	3.78	3.62	3.52	3.45	3.40	3.37	3.34	3.32	3.30	3.28	3.27	3.26	3.25	3.24	3.23	3.22	3.22	3.21	3.21	3.20	3.20
6	3.78	3.46	3.29	3.18	3.11	3.05	3.01	2.98	2.96	2.94	2.92	2.90	2.89	2.88	2.87	2.86	2.85	2.85	2.84	2.84	2.83	2.83
7	3.59	3.26	3.07	2.96	2.88	2.83	2.78	2.75	2.72	2.70	2.68	2.67	2.65	2.64	2.63	2.62	2.61	2.61	2.60	2.59	2.59	2.58
8	3.46	3.11	2.92	2.81	2.73	2.67	2.62	2.59	2.56	2.54	2.52	2.50	2.49	2.48	2.46	2.45	2.45	2.44	2.43	2.42	2.42	2.41
9	3.36	3.01	2.81	2.69	2.61	2.55	2.51	2.47	2.44	2.42	2.40	2.38	2.36	2.35	2.34	2.33	2.32	2.31	2.30	2.30	2.29	2.29
10	3.29	2.92	2.73	2.61	2.52	2.46	2.41	2.38	2.35	2.32	2.30	2.28	2.27	2.26	2.24	2.23	2.22	2.22	2.21	2.20	2.19	2.19
11	3.23	2.86	2.66	2.54	2.45	2.39	2.34	2.30	2.27	2.25	2.23	2.21	2.19	2.18	2.17	2.16	2.15	2.14	2.13	2.12	2.12	2.11
12	3.18	2.81	2.61	2.48	2.39	2.33	2.28	2.24	2.21	2.19	2.17	2.15	2.13	2.12	2.10	2.09	2.08	2.08	2.07	2.06	2.05	2.05
13	3.14	2.76	2.56	2.43	2.35	2.28	2.23	2.20	2.16	2.14	2.12	2.10	2.08	2.07	2.05	2.04	2.03	2.02	2.01	2.01	2.00	1.99
14	3.10	2.73	2.52	2.39	2.31	2.24	2.19	2.15	2.12	2.10	2.07	2.05	2.04	2.02	2.01	2.00	1.99	1.98	1.97	1.96	1.96	1.95
15	3.07	2.70	2.49	2.36	2.27	2.21	2.16	2.12	2.09	2.06	2.04	2.02	2.00	1.99	1.97	1.96	1.95	1.94	1.93	1.92	1.92	1.91
16	3.05	2.67	2.46	2.33	2.24	2.18	2.13	2.09	2.06	2.03	2.01	1.99	1.97	1.95	1.94	1.93	1.92	1.91	1.90	1.89	1.88	1.88
17	3.03	2.64	2.44	2.31	2.22	2.15	2.10	2.06	2.03	2.00	1.98	1.96	1.94	1.93	1.91	1.90	1.89	1.88	1.87	1.86	1.86	1.85
18	3.01	2.62	2.42	2.29	2.20	2.13	2.08	2.04	2.00	1.98	1.95	1.93	1.92	1.90	1.89	1.87	1.86	1.85	1.84	1.84	1.83	1.82
19	2.99	2.61	2.40	2.27	2.18	2.11	2.06	2.02	1.98	1.96	1.93	1.91	1.89	1.88	1.86	1.85	1.84	1.83	1.82	1.81	1.81	1.80
20	2.97	2.59	2.38	2.25	2.16	2.09	2.04	2.00	1.96	1.94	1.91	1.89	1.87	1.86	1.84	1.83	1.82	1.81	1.80	1.79	1.79	1.78
21	2.96	2.57	2.36	2.23	2.14	2.08	2.02	1.98	1.95	1.92	1.90	1.87	1.86	1.84	1.83	1.81	1.80	1.79	1.78	1.78	1.77	1.76
22	2.95	2.56	2.35	2.22	2.13	2.06	2.01	1.97	1.93	1.90	1.88	1.86	1.84	1.83	1.81	1.80	1.79	1.78	1.77	1.76	1.75	1.74
23	2.94	2.55	2.34	2.21	2.11	2.05	1.99	1.95	1.92	1.89	1.87	1.84	1.83	1.81	1.80	1.78	1.77	1.76	1.75	1.74	1.74	1.73
24	2.93	2.54	2.33	2.19	2.10	2.04	1.98	1.94	1.91	1.88	1.85	1.83	1.81	1.80	1.78	1.77	1.76	1.75	1.74	1.73	1.72	1.71
25	2.92	2.53	2.32	2.18	2.09	2.02	1.97	1.93	1.89	1.87	1.84	1.82	1.80	1.79	1.77	1.76	1.75	1.74	1.73	1.72	1.71	1.70
26	2.91	2.52	2.31	2.17	2.08	2.01	1.96	1.92	1.88	1.86	1.83	1.81	1.79	1.77	1.76	1.75	1.73	1.72	1.71	1.71	1.70	1.69
27	2.90	2.51	2.30	2.17	2.07	2.00	1.95	1.91	1.87	1.85	1.82	1.80	1.78	1.76	1.75	1.74	1.72	1.71	1.70	1.70	1.69	1.68
28	2.89	2.50	2.29	2.16	2.06	2.00	1.94	1.90	1.87	1.84	1.81	1.79	1.77	1.75	1.74	1.73	1.71	1.70	1.69	1.69	1.68	1.67
29	2.89	2.50	2.28	2.15	2.06	1.99	1.93	1.89	1.86	1.83	1.80	1.78	1.76	1.75	1.73	1.72	1.71	1.69	1.68	1.68	1.67	1.66
30	2.88	2.49	2.28	2.14	2.05	1.98	1.93	1.88	1.85	1.82	1.79	1.77	1.75	1.74	1.72	1.71	1.70	1.69	1.68	1.67	1.66	1.65
32	2.87	2.48	2.26	2.13	2.04	1.97	1.91	1.87	1.83	1.81	1.78	1.76	1.74	1.72	1.71	1.69	1.68	1.67	1.66	1.65	1.64	1.64
35	2.85	2.46	2.25	2.11	2.02	1.95	1.90	1.85	1.82	1.79	1.76	1.74	1.72	1.70	1.69	1.67	1.66	1.65	1.64	1.63	1.62	1.62
40	2.84	2.44	2.23	2.09	2.00	1.93	1.87	1.83	1.79	1.76	1.74	1.71	1.70	1.68	1.66	1.65	1.64	1.62	1.61	1.61	1.60	1.59
45	2.82	2.42	2.21	2.07	1.98	1.91	1.85	1.81	1.77	1.74	1.72	1.70	1.68	1.66	1.64	1.63	1.62	1.60	1.59	1.58	1.58	1.57
50	2.81	2.41	2.20	2.06	1.97	1.90	1.84	1.80	1.76	1.73	1.70	1.68	1.66	1.64	1.63	1.61	1.60	1.59	1.58	1.57	1.56	1.55
60	2.79	2.39	2.18	2.04	1.95	1.87	1.82	1.77	1.74	1.71	1.68	1.66	1.64	1.62	1.60	1.59	1.58	1.56	1.55	1.54	1.53	1.53
75	2.77	2.37	2.16	2.02	1.93	1.85	1.80	1.75	1.72	1.69	1.66	1.63	1.61	1.60	1.58	1.57	1.55	1.54	1.53	1.52	1.51	1.50
100	2.76	2.36	2.14	2.00	1.91	1.83	1.78	1.73	1.69	1.66	1.64	1.61	1.59	1.57	1.56	1.54	1.53	1.52	1.50	1.49	1.48	1.48
120	2.75	2.35	2.13	1.99	1.90	1.82	1.77	1.72	1.68	1.65	1.63	1.60	1.58	1.56	1.55	1.53	1.52	1.50	1.49	1.48	1.47	1.46
140	2.74	2.34	2.12	1.99	1.89	1.82	1.76	1.71	1.68	1.64	1.62	1.59	1.57	1.55	1.54	1.52	1.51	1.50	1.48	1.47	1.46	1.45
180	2.73	2.33	2.11	1.98	1.88	1.81	1.75	1.70	1.66	1.63	1.61	1.58	1.56	1.54	1.53	1.51	1.50	1.48	1.47	1.46	1.45	1.45
250	2.73	2.32	2.11	1.97	1.87	1.80	1.74	1.69	1.65	1.62	1.60	1.57	1.55	1.53	1.51	1.50	1.49	1.47	1.46	1.45	1.44	1.44
400	2.72	2.32	2.10	1.96	1.86	1.79	1.73	1.69	1.65	1.61	1.59	1.56	1.54	1.52	1.50	1.49	1.47	1.46	1.45	1.44	1.43	1.42
1000	2.71	2.31	2.09	1.95	1.85	1.78	1.72	1.68	1.64	1.61	1.58	1.55	1.53	1.51	1.49	1.48	1.46	1.45	1.44	1.43	1.42	1.41

Denominator df

TABLE F (CONT.)

Numerator df

$\alpha = .1$	23	24	25	26	27	28	29	30	32	35	40	45	50	60	75	100	120	140	180	250	400	1000
1	61.9	62.0	62.1	62.1	62.1	62.2	62.2	62.3	62.3	62.4	62.5	62.6	62.7	62.8	62.9	63.0	63.1	63.1	63.1	63.2	63.2	63.3
2	9.45	9.45	9.45	9.45	9.45	9.46	9.46	9.46	9.46	9.46	9.47	9.47	9.47	9.47	9.48	9.48	9.48	9.48	9.49	9.49	9.49	9.49
3	5.18	5.18	5.17	5.17	5.17	5.17	5.17	5.17	5.17	5.16	5.16	5.16	5.15	5.15	5.15	5.14	5.14	5.14	5.14	5.14	5.14	5.1
4	3.83	3.83	3.83	3.83	3.82	3.82	3.82	3.82	3.81	3.81	3.80	3.80	3.80	3.79	3.78	3.78	3.78	3.77	3.77	3.77	3.77	3.76
5	3.19	3.19	3.19	3.18	3.18	3.18	3.18	3.17	3.17	3.16	3.16	3.15	3.15	3.14	3.13	3.13	3.12	3.12	3.12	3.11	3.11	3.11
6	2.82	2.82	2.81	2.81	2.81	2.81	2.80	2.80	2.80	2.79	2.78	2.77	2.77	2.76	2.75	2.75	2.74	2.74	2.74	2.73	2.73	2.72
7	2.58	2.58	2.57	2.57	2.56	2.56	2.56	2.56	2.55	2.54	2.54	2.53	2.52	2.51	2.51	2.50	2.49	2.49	2.49	2.48	2.48	2.47
8	2.41	2.40	2.40	2.40	2.39	2.39	2.39	2.38	2.38	2.37	2.36	2.35	2.35	2.34	2.33	2.32	2.32	2.31	2.31	2.30	2.30	2.30
9	2.28	2.28	2.27	2.27	2.26	2.26	2.26	2.25	2.25	2.24	2.23	2.22	2.22	2.21	2.20	2.19	2.18	2.18	2.18	2.17	2.17	2.16
10	2.18	2.18	2.17	2.17	2.17	2.16	2.16	2.16	2.15	2.14	2.13	2.12	2.12	2.11	2.10	2.09	2.08	2.08	2.07	2.07	2.06	2.06
11	2.11	2.10	2.10	2.09	2.09	2.08	2.08	2.08	2.07	2.06	2.05	2.04	2.04	2.03	2.02	2.01	2.00	2.00	1.99	1.99	1.98	1.98
12	2.04	2.04	2.03	2.03	2.02	2.02	2.01	2.01	2.01	2.00	1.99	1.98	1.97	1.96	1.95	1.94	1.93	1.93	1.92	1.92	1.91	1.91
13	1.99	1.98	1.98	1.97	1.97	1.96	1.96	1.96	1.95	1.94	1.93	1.92	1.92	1.90	1.89	1.88	1.88	1.87	1.87	1.86	1.86	1.85
14	1.94	1.94	1.93	1.93	1.92	1.92	1.92	1.91	1.91	1.90	1.89	1.88	1.87	1.86	1.85	1.83	1.83	1.82	1.82	1.81	1.81	1.80
15	1.90	1.90	1.89	1.89	1.88	1.88	1.88	1.87	1.87	1.86	1.85	1.84	1.83	1.82	1.80	1.79	1.79	1.78	1.78	1.77	1.76	1.76
16	1.87	1.87	1.86	1.86	1.85	1.85	1.84	1.84	1.83	1.82	1.81	1.80	1.79	1.78	1.77	1.76	1.75	1.75	1.74	1.73	1.73	1.72
17	1.84	1.84	1.83	1.83	1.82	1.82	1.81	1.81	1.80	1.79	1.78	1.77	1.76	1.75	1.74	1.73	1.72	1.71	1.71	1.70	1.70	1.69
18	1.82	1.81	1.80	1.80	1.80	1.79	1.79	1.78	1.78	1.77	1.75	1.74	1.74	1.72	1.71	1.70	1.69	1.69	1.68	1.67	1.67	1.66
19	1.79	1.79	1.78	1.78	1.77	1.77	1.76	1.76	1.75	1.74	1.73	1.72	1.71	1.70	1.69	1.67	1.67	1.66	1.65	1.65	1.64	1.64
20	1.77	1.77	1.76	1.76	1.75	1.75	1.74	1.74	1.73	1.72	1.71	1.70	1.69	1.68	1.66	1.65	1.64	1.64	1.63	1.62	1.62	1.61
21	1.75	1.75	1.74	1.74	1.73	1.73	1.72	1.72	1.71	1.70	1.69	1.68	1.67	1.66	1.64	1.63	1.62	1.62	1.61	1.60	1.60	1.59
22	1.74	1.73	1.73	1.72	1.72	1.71	1.71	1.70	1.69	1.68	1.67	1.66	1.65	1.64	1.63	1.61	1.60	1.60	1.59	1.59	1.58	1.57
23	1.72	1.72	1.71	1.70	1.70	1.69	1.69	1.69	1.68	1.67	1.66	1.64	1.64	1.62	1.61	1.59	1.59	1.58	1.57	1.57	1.56	1.55
24	1.71	1.70	1.70	1.69	1.69	1.68	1.68	1.67	1.66	1.65	1.64	1.63	1.62	1.61	1.59	1.58	1.57	1.57	1.56	1.55	1.54	1.54
25	1.70	1.69	1.68	1.68	1.67	1.67	1.66	1.66	1.65	1.64	1.63	1.62	1.61	1.59	1.58	1.56	1.56	1.55	1.54	1.54	1.53	1.52
26	1.68	1.68	1.67	1.67	1.66	1.66	1.65	1.65	1.64	1.63	1.61	1.60	1.59	1.58	1.57	1.55	1.54	1.54	1.53	1.52	1.52	1.51
27	1.67	1.67	1.66	1.65	1.65	1.64	1.64	1.64	1.63	1.62	1.60	1.59	1.58	1.57	1.55	1.54	1.53	1.53	1.52	1.51	1.50	1.50
28	1.66	1.66	1.65	1.64	1.64	1.63	1.63	1.63	1.62	1.61	1.59	1.58	1.57	1.56	1.54	1.53	1.52	1.51	1.51	1.50	1.49	1.48
29	1.65	1.65	1.64	1.63	1.63	1.62	1.62	1.62	1.61	1.60	1.58	1.57	1.56	1.55	1.53	1.52	1.51	1.50	1.50	1.49	1.48	1.47
30	1.64	1.64	1.63	1.63	1.62	1.62	1.61	1.61	1.60	1.59	1.57	1.56	1.55	1.54	1.52	1.51	1.50	1.49	1.49	1.48	1.47	1.46
32	1.63	1.62	1.62	1.61	1.60	1.60	1.59	1.59	1.58	1.57	1.56	1.54	1.53	1.52	1.50	1.49	1.48	1.47	1.47	1.46	1.45	1.44
35	1.61	1.60	1.60	1.59	1.58	1.58	1.57	1.57	1.56	1.55	1.53	1.52	1.51	1.50	1.48	1.47	1.46	1.45	1.44	1.43	1.43	1.42
40	1.58	1.57	1.57	1.56	1.56	1.55	1.55	1.54	1.53	1.52	1.51	1.49	1.48	1.47	1.45	1.43	1.42	1.42	1.41	1.40	1.39	1.38
45	1.56	1.55	1.55	1.54	1.53	1.53	1.52	1.52	1.51	1.50	1.48	1.47	1.46	1.44	1.43	1.41	1.40	1.39	1.38	1.37	1.37	1.36
50	1.54	1.54	1.53	1.52	1.52	1.51	1.51	1.50	1.49	1.48	1.46	1.45	1.44	1.42	1.41	1.39	1.38	1.37	1.36	1.35	1.34	1.33
60	1.52	1.51	1.50	1.50	1.49	1.49	1.48	1.48	1.47	1.45	1.44	1.42	1.41	1.40	1.38	1.36	1.35	1.34	1.33	1.32	1.31	1.30
75	1.49	1.49	1.48	1.47	1.47	1.46	1.45	1.45	1.44	1.43	1.41	1.40	1.38	1.37	1.35	1.33	1.32	1.31	1.30	1.29	1.27	1.26
100	1.47	1.46	1.45	1.45	1.44	1.43	1.43	1.42	1.41	1.40	1.38	1.37	1.35	1.34	1.32	1.29	1.28	1.27	1.26	1.25	1.24	1.22
120	1.46	1.45	1.44	1.43	1.43	1.42	1.41	1.41	1.40	1.39	1.37	1.35	1.34	1.32	1.30	1.28	1.26	1.26	1.24	1.23	1.22	1.20
140	1.45	1.44	1.43	1.42	1.42	1.41	1.41	1.40	1.39	1.38	1.36	1.34	1.33	1.31	1.29	1.26	1.25	1.24	1.23	1.22	1.20	1.19
180	1.43	1.43	1.42	1.41	1.40	1.40	1.39	1.39	1.38	1.36	1.34	1.33	1.32	1.29	1.27	1.25	1.23	1.22	1.21	1.20	1.18	1.16
250	1.42	1.41	1.41	1.40	1.39	1.39	1.38	1.37	1.36	1.35	1.33	1.31	1.30	1.28	1.26	1.23	1.22	1.21	1.19	1.18	1.16	1.14
400	1.41	1.40	1.39	1.39	1.38	1.37	1.37	1.36	1.35	1.34	1.32	1.30	1.29	1.26	1.24	1.21	1.20	1.19	1.17	1.16	1.14	1.12
1000	1.40	1.39	1.38	1.38	1.37	1.36	1.36	1.35	1.34	1.32	1.30	1.29	1.27	1.25	1.23	1.20	1.18	1.17	1.15	1.13	1.11	1.08

Denominator df

TABLE R

n	d_2	d_3	D_3	D_4
2	1.128	0.852	0	3.267
3	1.693	0.888	0	2.574
4	2.059	0.880	0	2.282
5	2.326	0.864	0	2.114
6	2.534	0.848	0	2.004
7	2.704	0.833	0.076	1.924
8	2.847	0.820	0.136	1.864
9	2.970	0.808	0.184	1.816
10	3.078	0.797	0.223	1.777
11	3.173	0.787	0.256	1.744
12	3.258	0.779	0.283	1.717
13	3.336	0.771	0.307	1.693
14	3.407	0.763	0.328	1.672
15	3.472	0.756	0.347	1.653
16	3.532	0.750	0.363	1.637
17	3.588	0.744	0.378	1.622
18	3.640	0.738	0.391	1.608
19	3.689	0.734	0.403	1.597
20	3.735	0.728	0.415	1.585
21	3.778	0.724	0.425	1.575
22	3.819	0.721	0.434	1.566
23	3.858	0.716	0.443	1.557
24	3.895	0.711	0.451	1.548
25	3.931	0.709	0.459	1.541

Two-tail probability One-tail probability	0.20 0.10	0.10 0.05	0.05 0.025	0.02 0.01	0.01 0.005	
df						**df**

TABLE T

Values of t_α

Two tails

One tail

df	0.20 / 0.10	0.10 / 0.05	0.05 / 0.025	0.02 / 0.01	0.01 / 0.005	df
1	3.078	6.314	12.706	31.821	63.657	1
2	1.886	2.920	4.303	6.965	9.925	2
3	1.638	2.353	3.182	4.541	5.841	3
4	1.533	2.132	2.776	3.747	4.604	4
5	1.476	2.015	2.571	3.365	4.032	5
6	1.440	1.943	2.447	3.143	3.707	6
7	1.415	1.895	2.365	2.998	3.499	7
8	1.397	1.860	2.306	2.896	3.355	8
9	1.383	1.833	2.262	2.821	3.250	9
10	1.372	1.812	2.228	2.764	3.169	10
11	1.363	1.796	2.201	2.718	3.106	11
12	1.356	1.782	2.179	2.681	3.055	12
13	1.350	1.771	2.160	2.650	3.012	13
14	1.345	1.761	2.145	2.624	2.977	14
15	1.341	1.753	2.131	2.602	2.947	15
16	1.337	1.746	2.120	2.583	2.921	16
17	1.333	1.740	2.110	2.567	2.898	17
18	1.330	1.734	2.101	2.552	2.878	18
19	1.328	1.729	2.093	2.539	2.861	19
20	1.325	1.725	2.086	2.528	2.845	20
21	1.323	1.721	2.080	2.518	2.831	21
22	1.321	1.717	2.074	2.508	2.819	22
23	1.319	1.714	2.069	2.500	2.807	23
24	1.318	1.711	2.064	2.492	2.797	24
25	1.316	1.708	2.060	2.485	2.787	25
26	1.315	1.706	2.056	2.479	2.779	26
27	1.314	1.703	2.052	2.473	2.771	27
28	1.313	1.701	2.048	2.467	2.763	28
29	1.311	1.699	2.045	2.462	2.756	29
30	1.310	1.697	2.042	2.457	2.750	30
32	1.309	1.694	2.037	2.449	2.738	32
35	1.306	1.690	2.030	2.438	2.725	35
40	1.303	1.684	2.021	2.423	2.704	40
45	1.301	1.679	2.014	2.412	2.690	45
50	1.299	1.676	2.009	2.403	2.678	50
60	1.296	1.671	2.000	2.390	2.660	60
75	1.293	1.665	1.992	2.377	2.643	75
100	1.290	1.660	1.984	2.364	2.626	100
120	1.289	1.658	1.980	2.358	2.617	120
140	1.288	1.656	1.977	2.353	2.611	140
180	1.286	1.653	1.973	2.347	2.603	180
250	1.285	1.651	1.969	2.341	2.596	250
400	1.284	1.649	1.966	2.336	2.588	400
1000	1.282	1.646	1.962	2.330	2.581	1000
∞	1.282	1.645	1.960	2.326	2.576	∞
Confidence levels	80%	90%	95%	98%	99%	

TABLE W1 Critical Values of T_L and T_U for the Wilcoxon Rank Sum Test: Independent Samples

Test statistic is the rank sum associated with the smaller sample (if equal sample sizes, either rank sum can be used). Reject the null hypothesis at the indicated α level if the test statistic falls below the lower bound, T_L, or above the upper bound, T_U. For groups larger than 10, use the Normal approximation given in the text.

a. α = .025 one-tailed; α = .05 two-tailed

n_1 \ n_2	3 T_L	3 T_U	4 T_L	4 T_U	5 T_L	5 T_U	6 T_L	6 T_U	7 T_L	7 T_U	8 T_L	8 T_U	9 T_L	9 T_U	10 T_L	10 T_U
3	5	16	6	18	6	21	7	23	7	26	8	28	8	31	9	33
4	6	18	11	25	12	28	12	32	13	35	14	38	15	41	16	44
5	6	21	12	28	18	37	19	41	20	45	21	49	22	53	24	56
6	7	23	12	32	19	41	26	52	28	56	29	61	31	65	32	70
7	7	26	13	35	20	45	28	56	37	68	39	73	41	78	43	83
8	8	28	14	38	21	49	29	61	39	73	49	87	51	93	54	98
9	8	31	15	41	22	53	31	65	41	78	51	93	63	108	66	114
10	9	33	16	44	24	56	32	70	43	83	54	98	66	114	79	131

a. α = .05 one-tailed; α = .10 two-tailed

n_2 \ n_1	3 T_L	3 T_U	4 T_L	4 T_U	5 T_L	5 T_U	6 T_L	6 T_U	7 T_L	7 T_U	8 T_L	8 T_U	9 T_L	9 T_U	10 T_L	10 T_U
3	6	15	7	17	7	20	8	22	9	24	9	27	10	29	11	31
4	7	17	12	24	13	27	14	30	15	33	16	36	17	39	18	42
5	7	20	13	27	19	36	20	40	22	43	24	46	25	50	26	54
6	8	22	14	30	20	40	28	50	30	54	32	58	33	63	35	67
7	9	24	15	33	22	43	30	54	39	66	41	71	43	76	46	80
8	9	27	16	36	24	46	32	58	41	71	52	84	54	90	57	95
9	10	29	17	39	25	50	33	63	43	76	54	90	66	105	69	111
10	11	31	18	42	26	54	35	67	46	80	57	95	69	111	83	127

Source: From F. Wilcoxon and R. A. Wilcox, "Some Rapid Approximate Statistical Procedures," 1964. Copyright © 1964 by BASF Corporation.

TABLE W2   Critical Values of T in the Wilcoxon Paired Difference Signed-Rank Test. Reject the null hypothesis at the indicated α levels if the test statistic is smaller than the corresponding critical value.

One-Tailed	Two-Tailed	n = 5	n = 6	n = 7	n = 8	n = 9	n = 10
$\alpha = .05$	$\alpha = .10$	1	2	4	6	8	11
$\alpha = .025$	$\alpha = .05$		1	2	4	6	8
$\alpha = .01$	$\alpha = .02$			0	2	3	5
$\alpha = .005$	$\alpha = .01$				0	2	3
		n = 11	n = 12	n = 13	n = 14	n = 15	n = 16
$\alpha = .05$	$\alpha = .10$	14	17	21	26	30	36
$\alpha = .025$	$\alpha = .05$	11	14	17	21	25	30
$\alpha = .01$	$\alpha = .02$	7	10	13	16	20	24
$\alpha = .005$	$\alpha = .01$	5	7	10	13	16	19
		n = 17	n = 18	n = 19	n = 20	n = 21	n = 22
$\alpha = .05$	$\alpha = .10$	41	47	54	60	68	75
$\alpha = .025$	$\alpha = .05$	35	40	46	52	59	66
$\alpha = .01$	$\alpha = .02$	28	33	38	43	49	56
$\alpha = .005$	$\alpha = .01$	23	28	32	37	43	49
		n = 23	n = 24	n = 25	n = 26	n = 27	n = 28
$\alpha = .05$	$\alpha = .10$	83	92	101	110	120	130
$\alpha = .025$	$\alpha = .05$	73	81	90	98	107	117
$\alpha = .01$	$\alpha = .02$	62	69	77	85	93	102
$\alpha = .005$	$\alpha = .01$	55	61	68	76	84	92
		n = 29	n = 30	n = 31	n = 32	n = 33	n = 34
$\alpha = .05$	$\alpha = .10$	141	152	163	175	188	201
$\alpha = .025$	$\alpha = .05$	127	137	148	159	171	183
$\alpha = .01$	$\alpha = .02$	111	120	130	141	151	162
$\alpha = .005$	$\alpha = .01$	100	109	118	128	138	149
		n = 35	n = 36	n = 37	n = 38	n = 39	
$\alpha = .05$	$\alpha = .10$	214	228	242	256	271	
$\alpha = .025$	$\alpha = .05$	195	208	222	235	250	
$\alpha = .01$	$\alpha = .02$	174	186	198	211	224	
$\alpha = .005$	$\alpha = .01$	160	171	183	195	208	
		n = 40	n = 41	n = 42	n = 43	n = 44	n = 45
$\alpha = .05$	$\alpha = .10$	287	303	319	336	353	371
$\alpha = .025$	$\alpha = .05$	264	279	295	311	327	344
$\alpha = .01$	$\alpha = .02$	238	252	267	281	297	313
$\alpha = .005$	$\alpha = .01$	221	234	248	262	277	292
		n = 46	n = 47	n = 48	n = 49	n = 50	
$\alpha = .05$	$\alpha = .10$	389	408	427	446	466	
$\alpha = .025$	$\alpha = .05$	361	379	397	415	434	
$\alpha = .01$	$\alpha = .02$	329	345	362	380	398	
$\alpha = .005$	$\alpha = .01$	307	323	339	356	373	

Source: From F. Wilcoxon and R. A. Wilcox, "Some Rapid Approximate Statistical Procedures," 1964. Copyright © 1964 by BASF Corporation.

Right-tail probability		0.10	0.05	0.025	0.01	0.005
TABLE X	df					
Values of χ^2_α	1	2.706	3.841	5.024	6.635	7.879
	2	4.605	5.991	7.378	9.210	10.597
	3	6.251	7.815	9.348	11.345	12.838
	4	7.779	9.488	11.143	13.277	14.860
	5	9.236	11.070	12.833	15.086	16.750
	6	10.645	12.592	14.449	16.812	18.548
	7	12.017	14.067	16.013	18.475	20.278
	8	13.362	15.507	17.535	20.090	21.955
	9	14.684	16.919	19.023	21.666	23.589
	10	15.987	18.307	20.483	23.209	25.188
	11	17.275	19.675	21.920	24.725	26.757
	12	18.549	21.026	23.337	26.217	28.300
	13	19.812	22.362	24.736	27.688	29.819
	14	21.064	23.685	26.119	29.141	31.319
	15	22.307	24.996	27.488	30.578	32.801
	16	23.542	26.296	28.845	32.000	34.267
	17	24.769	27.587	30.191	33.409	35.718
	18	25.989	28.869	31.526	34.805	37.156
	19	27.204	30.143	32.852	36.191	38.582
	20	28.412	31.410	34.170	37.566	39.997
	21	29.615	32.671	35.479	38.932	41.401
	22	30.813	33.924	36.781	40.290	42.796
	23	32.007	35.172	38.076	41.638	44.181
	24	33.196	36.415	39.364	42.980	45.559
	25	34.382	37.653	40.647	44.314	46.928
	26	35.563	38.885	41.923	45.642	48.290
	27	36.741	40.113	43.195	46.963	49.645
	28	37.916	41.337	44.461	48.278	50.994
	29	39.087	42.557	45.722	59.588	52.336
	30	40.256	43.773	46.979	50.892	53.672
	40	51.805	55.759	59.342	63.691	66.767
	50	63.167	67.505	71.420	76.154	79.490
	60	74.397	79.082	83.298	88.381	91.955
	70	85.527	90.531	95.023	100.424	104.213
	80	96.578	101.879	106.628	112.328	116.320
	90	107.565	113.145	118.135	124.115	128.296
	100	118.499	124.343	129.563	135.811	140.177

TABLE Z	Second Decimal Place in Z										
Areas under the standard Normal curve	0.09	0.08	0.07	0.06	0.05	0.04	0.03	0.02	0.01	0.00	z
										0.0000[†]	−3.9
	0.0001	0.0001	0.0001	0.0001	0.0001	0.0001	0.0001	0.0001	0.0001	0.0001	−3.8
	0.0001	0.0001	0.0001	0.0001	0.0001	0.0001	0.0001	0.0001	0.0001	0.0001	−3.7
	0.0001	0.0001	0.0001	0.0001	0.0001	0.0001	0.0001	0.0001	0.0002	0.0002	−3.6
	0.0002	0.0002	0.0002	0.0002	0.0002	0.0002	0.0002	0.0002	0.0002	0.0002	−3.5
	0.0002	0.0003	0.0003	0.0003	0.0003	0.0003	0.0003	0.0003	0.0003	0.0003	−3.4
	0.0003	0.0004	0.0004	0.0004	0.0004	0.0004	0.0004	0.0005	0.0005	0.0005	−3.3
	0.0005	0.0005	0.0005	0.0006	0.0006	0.0006	0.0006	0.0006	0.0007	0.0007	−3.2
	0.0007	0.0007	0.0008	0.0008	0.0008	0.0008	0.0009	0.0009	0.0009	0.0010	−3.1
	0.0010	0.0010	0.0011	0.0011	0.0011	0.0012	0.0012	0.0013	0.0013	0.0013	−3.0
	0.0014	0.0014	0.0015	0.0015	0.0016	0.0016	0.0017	0.0018	0.0018	0.0019	−2.9
	0.0019	0.0020	0.0021	0.0021	0.0022	0.0023	0.0023	0.0024	0.0025	0.0026	−2.8
	0.0026	0.0027	0.0028	0.0029	0.0030	0.0031	0.0032	0.0033	0.0034	0.0035	−2.7
	0.0036	0.0037	0.0038	0.0039	0.0040	0.0041	0.0043	0.0044	0.0045	0.0047	−2.6
	0.0048	0.0049	0.0051	0.0052	0.0054	0.0055	0.0057	0.0059	0.0060	0.0062	−2.5
	0.0064	0.0066	0.0068	0.0069	0.0071	0.0073	0.0075	0.0078	0.0080	0.0082	−2.4
	0.0084	0.0087	0.0089	0.0091	0.0094	0.0096	0.0099	0.0102	0.0104	0.0107	−2.3
	0.0110	0.0113	0.0116	0.0119	0.0122	0.0125	0.0129	0.0132	0.0136	0.0139	−2.2
	0.0143	0.0146	0.0150	0.0154	0.0158	0.0162	0.0166	0.0170	0.0174	0.0179	−2.1
	0.0183	0.0188	0.0192	0.0197	0.0202	0.0207	0.0212	0.0217	0.0222	0.0228	−2.0
	0.0233	0.0239	0.0244	0.0250	0.0256	0.0262	0.0268	0.0274	0.0281	0.0287	−1.9
	0.0294	0.0301	0.0307	0.0314	0.0322	0.0329	0.0336	0.0344	0.0351	0.0359	−1.8
	0.0367	0.0375	0.0384	0.0392	0.0401	0.0409	0.0418	0.0427	0.0436	0.0446	−1.7
	0.0455	0.0465	0.0475	0.0485	0.0495	0.0505	0.0516	0.0526	0.0537	0.0548	−1.6
	0.0559	0.0571	0.0582	0.0594	0.0606	0.0618	0.0630	0.0643	0.0655	0.0668	−1.5
	0.0681	0.0694	0.0708	0.0721	0.0735	0.0749	0.0764	0.0778	0.0793	0.0808	−1.4
	0.0823	0.0838	0.0853	0.0869	0.0885	0.0901	0.0918	0.0934	0.0951	0.0968	−1.3
	0.0985	0.1003	0.1020	0.1038	0.1056	0.1075	0.1093	0.1112	0.1131	0.1151	−1.2
	0.1170	0.1190	0.1210	0.1230	0.1251	0.1271	0.1292	0.1314	0.1335	0.1357	−1.1
	0.1379	0.1401	0.1423	0.1446	0.1469	0.1492	0.1515	0.1539	0.1562	0.1587	−1.0
	0.1611	0.1635	0.1660	0.1685	0.1711	0.1736	0.1762	0.1788	0.1814	0.1841	−0.9
	0.1867	0.1894	0.1922	0.1949	0.1977	0.2005	0.2033	0.2061	0.2090	0.2119	−0.8
	0.2148	0.2177	0.2206	0.2236	0.2266	0.2296	0.2327	0.2358	0.2389	0.2420	−0.7
	0.2451	0.2483	0.2514	0.2546	0.2578	0.2611	0.2643	0.2676	0.2709	0.2743	−0.6
	0.2776	0.2810	0.2843	0.2877	0.2912	0.2946	0.2981	0.3015	0.3050	0.3085	−0.5
	0.3121	0.3156	0.3192	0.3228	0.3264	0.3300	0.3336	0.3372	0.3409	0.3446	−0.4
	0.3483	0.3520	0.3557	0.3594	0.3632	0.3669	0.3707	0.3745	0.3783	0.3821	−0.3
	0.3859	0.3897	0.3936	0.3974	0.4013	0.4052	0.4090	0.4129	0.4168	0.4207	−0.2
	0.4247	0.4286	0.4325	0.4364	0.4404	0.4443	0.4483	0.4522	0.4562	0.4602	−0.1
	0.4641	0.4681	0.4721	0.4761	0.4801	0.4840	0.4880	0.4920	0.4960	0.5000	−0.0

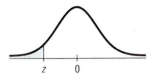

[†]For $z \leq -3.90$ the areas are 0.0000 to four decimal places.

TABLE Z (CONT.)

Areas under the standard
Normal curve

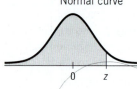

z	0.00	0.01	0.02	0.03	0.04	0.05	0.06	0.07	0.08	0.09
0.0	0.5000	0.5040	0.5080	0.5120	0.5160	0.5199	0.5239	0.5279	0.5319	0.5359
0.1	0.5398	0.5438	0.5478	0.5517	0.5557	0.5596	0.5636	0.5675	0.5714	0.5753
0.2	0.5793	0.5832	0.5871	0.5910	0.5948	0.5987	0.6026	0.6064	0.6103	0.6141
0.3	0.6179	0.6217	0.6255	0.6293	0.6331	0.6368	0.6406	0.6443	0.6480	0.6517
0.4	0.6554	0.6591	0.6628	0.6664	0.6700	0.6736	0.6772	0.6808	0.6844	0.6879
0.5	0.6915	0.6950	0.6985	0.7019	0.7054	0.7088	0.7123	0.7157	0.7190	0.7224
0.6	0.7257	0.7291	0.7324	0.7357	0.7389	0.7422	0.7454	0.7486	0.7517	0.7549
0.7	0.7580	0.7611	0.7642	0.7673	0.7704	0.7734	0.7764	0.7794	0.7823	0.7852
0.8	0.7881	0.7910	0.7939	0.7967	0.7995	0.8023	0.8051	0.8078	0.8106	0.8133
0.9	0.8159	0.8186	0.8212	0.8238	0.8264	0.8289	0.8315	0.8340	0.8365	0.8389
1.0	0.8413	0.8438	0.8461	0.8485	0.8508	0.8531	0.8554	0.8577	0.8599	0.8621
1.1	0.8643	0.8665	0.8686	0.8708	0.8729	0.8749	0.8770	0.8790	0.8810	0.8830
1.2	0.8849	0.8869	0.8888	0.8907	0.8925	0.8944	0.8962	0.8980	0.8997	0.9015
1.3	0.9032	0.9049	0.9066	0.9082	0.9099	0.9115	0.9131	0.9147	0.9162	0.9177
1.4	0.9192	0.9207	0.9222	0.9236	0.9251	0.9265	0.9279	0.9292	0.9306	0.9319
1.5	0.9332	0.9345	0.9357	0.9370	0.9382	0.9394	0.9406	0.9418	0.9429	0.9441
1.6	0.9452	0.9463	0.9474	0.9484	0.9495	0.9505	0.9515	0.9525	0.9535	0.9545
1.7	0.9554	0.9564	0.9573	0.9582	0.9591	0.9599	0.9608	0.9616	0.9625	0.9633
1.8	0.9641	0.9649	0.9656	0.9664	0.9671	0.9678	0.9686	0.9693	0.9699	0.9706
1.9	0.9713	0.9719	0.9726	0.9732	0.9738	0.9744	0.9750	0.9756	0.9761	0.9767
2.0	0.9772	0.9778	0.9783	0.9788	0.9793	0.9798	0.9803	0.9808	0.9812	0.9817
2.1	0.9821	0.9826	0.9830	0.9834	0.9838	0.9842	0.9846	0.9850	0.9854	0.9857
2.2	0.9861	0.9864	0.9868	0.9871	0.9875	0.9878	0.9881	0.9884	0.9887	0.9890
2.3	0.9893	0.9896	0.9898	0.9901	0.9904	0.9906	0.9909	0.9911	0.9913	0.9916
2.4	0.9918	0.9920	0.9922	0.9925	0.9927	0.9929	0.9931	0.9932	0.9934	0.9936
2.5	0.9938	0.9940	0.9941	0.9943	0.9945	0.9946	0.9948	0.9949	0.9951	0.9952
2.6	0.9953	0.9955	0.9956	0.9957	0.9959	0.9960	0.9961	0.9962	0.9963	0.9964
2.7	0.9965	0.9966	0.9967	0.9968	0.9969	0.9970	0.9971	0.9972	0.9973	0.9974
2.8	0.9974	0.9975	0.9976	0.9977	0.9977	0.9978	0.9979	0.9979	0.9980	0.9981
2.9	0.9981	0.9982	0.9982	0.9983	0.9984	0.9984	0.9985	0.9985	0.9986	0.9986
3.0	0.9987	0.9987	0.9987	0.9988	0.9988	0.9989	0.9989	0.9989	0.9990	0.9990
3.1	0.9990	0.9991	0.9991	0.9991	0.9992	0.9992	0.9992	0.9992	0.9993	0.9993
3.2	0.9993	0.9993	0.9994	0.9994	0.9994	0.9994	0.9994	0.9995	0.9995	0.9995
3.3	0.9995	0.9995	0.9995	0.9996	0.9996	0.9996	0.9996	0.9996	0.9996	0.9997
3.4	0.9997	0.9997	0.9997	0.9997	0.9997	0.9997	0.9997	0.9997	0.9997	0.9998
3.5	0.9998	0.9998	0.9998	0.9998	0.9998	0.9998	0.9998	0.9998	0.9998	0.9998
3.6	0.9998	0.9998	0.9999	0.9999	0.9999	0.9999	0.9999	0.9999	0.9999	0.9999
3.7	0.9999	0.9999	0.9999	0.9999	0.9999	0.9999	0.9999	0.9999	0.9999	0.9999
3.8	0.9999	0.9999	0.9999	0.9999	0.9999	0.9999	0.9999	0.9999	0.9999	0.9999
3.9	1.0000[†]									

[†]For $z \geq 3.90$, the areas are 1.0000 to four decimal places.

Row					Table of Random Digits					
1	96299	07196	98642	20639	23185	56282	69929	14125	38872	94168
2	71622	35940	81807	59225	18192	08710	80777	84395	69563	86280
3	03272	41230	81739	74797	70406	18564	69273	72532	78340	36699
4	46376	58596	14365	63685	56555	42974	72944	96463	63533	24152
5	47352	42853	42903	97504	56655	70355	88606	61406	38757	70657
6	20064	04266	74017	79319	70170	96572	08523	56025	89077	57678
7	73184	95907	05179	51002	83374	52297	07769	99792	78365	93487
8	72753	36216	07230	35793	71907	65571	66784	25548	91861	15725
9	03939	30763	06138	80062	02537	23561	93136	61260	77935	93159
10	75998	37203	07959	38264	78120	77525	86481	54986	33042	70648
11	94435	97441	90998	25104	49761	14967	70724	67030	53887	81293
12	04362	40989	69167	38894	00172	02999	97377	33305	60782	29810
13	89059	43528	10547	40115	82234	86902	04121	83889	76208	31076
14	87736	04666	75145	49175	76754	07884	92564	80793	22573	67902
15	76488	88899	15860	07370	13431	84041	69202	18912	83173	11983
16	36460	53772	66634	25045	79007	78518	73580	14191	50353	32064
17	13205	69237	21820	20952	16635	58867	97650	82983	64865	93298
18	51242	12215	90739	36812	00436	31609	80333	96606	30430	31803
19	67819	00354	91439	91073	49258	15992	41277	75111	67496	68430
20	09875	08990	27656	15871	23637	00952	97818	64234	50199	05715
21	18192	95308	72975	01191	29958	09275	89141	19558	50524	32041
22	02763	33701	66188	50226	35813	72951	11638	01876	93664	37001
23	13349	46328	01856	29935	80563	03742	49470	67749	08578	21956
24	69238	92878	80067	80807	45096	22936	64325	19265	37755	69794
25	92207	63527	59398	29818	24789	94309	88380	57000	50171	17891
26	66679	99100	37072	30593	29665	84286	44458	60180	81451	58273
27	31087	42430	60322	34765	15757	53300	97392	98035	05228	68970
28	84432	04916	52949	78533	31666	62350	20584	56367	19701	60584
29	72042	12287	21081	48426	44321	58765	41760	43304	13399	02043
30	94534	73559	82135	70260	87936	85162	11937	18263	54138	69564
31	63971	97198	40974	45301	60177	35604	21580	68107	25184	42810
32	11227	58474	17272	37619	69517	62964	67962	34510	12607	52255
33	28541	02029	08068	96656	17795	21484	57722	76511	27849	61738
34	11282	43632	49531	78981	81980	08530	08629	32279	29478	50228
35	42907	15137	21918	13248	39129	49559	94540	24070	88151	36782
36	47119	76651	21732	32364	58545	50277	57558	30390	18771	72703
37	11232	99884	05087	76839	65142	19994	91397	29350	83852	04905
38	64725	06719	86262	53356	57999	50193	79936	97230	52073	94467
39	77007	26962	55466	12521	48125	12280	54985	26239	76044	54398
40	18375	19310	59796	89832	59417	18553	17238	05474	33259	50595

Selected Formulas

$Range = Max - Min$

$IQR = Q3 - Q1$

Outlier Rule-of-Thumb: $y < Q1 - 1.5 \times IQR$ or $y > Q3 + 1.5 \times IQR$

$$\bar{y} = \frac{\sum y}{n}$$

$$s = \sqrt{\frac{\sum (y - \bar{y})^2}{n - 1}}$$

$$z = \frac{y - \mu}{\sigma} \text{ (model based)} \qquad z = \frac{y - \bar{y}}{s} \text{ (data based)}$$

$$r = \frac{\sum z_x z_y}{n - 1}$$

$$\hat{y} = b_0 + b_1 x \qquad \text{where } b_1 = r \frac{s_y}{s_x} \text{ and } b_0 = \bar{y} - b_1 \bar{x}$$

$P(\mathbf{A}) = 1 - P(\mathbf{A}^C)$

$P(\mathbf{A} \text{ or } \mathbf{B}) = P(\mathbf{A}) + P(\mathbf{B}) - P(\mathbf{A} \text{ and } \mathbf{B})$

$P(\mathbf{A} \text{ and } \mathbf{B}) = P(\mathbf{A}) \times P(\mathbf{B}|\mathbf{A})$

$$P(\mathbf{B}|\mathbf{A}) = \frac{P(\mathbf{A} \text{ and } \mathbf{B})}{P(\mathbf{A})}$$

If $\mathbf{A}$ and $\mathbf{B}$ are independent, $P(\mathbf{B}|\mathbf{A}) = P(\mathbf{B})$

$$E(X) = \mu = \sum x \cdot P(x) \qquad Var(X) = \sigma^2 = \sum (x - \mu)^2 P(x)$$

$$E(X \pm c) = E(X) \pm c \qquad Var(X \pm c) = Var(X)$$

$$E(aX) = aE(X) \qquad Var(aX) = a^2 Var(X)$$

$$E(X \pm Y) = E(X) \pm E(Y) \qquad Var(X \pm Y) = Var(X) + Var(Y)$$

$$\text{if } X \text{ and } Y \text{ are independent}$$

Geometric: $\qquad P(x) = q^{x-1} p \qquad \mu = \dfrac{1}{p} \qquad \sigma = \sqrt{\dfrac{q}{p^2}}$

Binomial: $\qquad P(x) = {}_n C_x p^x q^{n-x} \qquad \mu = np \qquad \sigma = \sqrt{npq}$

$$\hat{p} = \frac{x}{n} \qquad \mu(\hat{p}) = p \qquad SD(\hat{p}) = \sqrt{\frac{pq}{n}}$$

Poisson probability model for successes: Poisson (λ)

λ = mean number of successes.

X = number of successes.

$$P(X = x) = \frac{e^{-\lambda} \lambda^x}{x!}$$

$$\text{Expected value:} \qquad E(X) = \lambda$$

$$\text{Standard deviation:} \qquad SD(X) = \sqrt{\lambda}$$

Sampling distribution of $\bar{y}$:

(CLT) As n grows, the sampling distribution approaches the Normal model with

$$\mu(\bar{y}) = \mu_y \qquad SD(\bar{y}) = \frac{\sigma}{\sqrt{n}}$$

Inference:

Confidence interval for parameter = **statistic ± critical value × SE(statistic)**

$$\text{Test statistic} = \frac{statistic - parameter}{SD(statistic)}$$

Parameter	Statistic	SD (statistic)	SE (statistic)
p	$\hat{p}$	$\sqrt{\dfrac{pq}{n}}$	$\sqrt{\dfrac{\hat{p}\hat{q}}{n}}$
μ	$\bar{y}$	$\dfrac{\sigma}{\sqrt{n}}$	$\dfrac{s}{\sqrt{n}}$
$\mu_1 - \mu_2$	$\bar{y}_1 - \bar{y}_2$	$\sqrt{\dfrac{\sigma_1^2}{n_1} + \dfrac{\sigma_2^2}{n_2}}$	$\sqrt{\dfrac{s_1^2}{n_1} + \dfrac{s_2^2}{n_2}}$
μ_d	$\bar{d}$	$\dfrac{\sigma_d}{\sqrt{n}}$	$\dfrac{s_d}{\sqrt{n}}$
σ_ε	$s_e = \sqrt{\dfrac{\sum (y - \hat{y})^2}{n - 2}}$	(divide by $n - k - 1$ in multiple regression)	
β_1	b_1	(in simple regression)	$\dfrac{s_e}{s_x \sqrt{n - 1}}$
μ_ν	$\hat{y}_\nu$	(in simple regression)	$\sqrt{SE^2(b_1) \cdot (x_\nu - \bar{x})^2 + \dfrac{s_e^2}{n}}$
y_ν	$\hat{y}_\nu$	(in simple regression)	$\sqrt{SE^2(b_1) \cdot (x_\nu - \bar{x})^2 + \dfrac{s_e^2}{n} + s_e^2}$

Pooling: For testing difference between proportions: $\hat{p}_{pooled} = \dfrac{y_1 + y_2}{n_1 + n_2}$

For testing difference between means: $s_p = \sqrt{\dfrac{(n_1 - 1)s_1^2 + (n_2 - 1)s_2^2}{n_1 + n_2 - 2}}$

Substitute these pooled estimates in the respective SE formulas for both groups when assumptions and conditions are met.

Chi-square: $\chi^2 = \sum \dfrac{(Obs - Exp)^2}{Exp}$

Assumptions for Inference	And the Conditions That Support or Override Them

Proportions (z)

- **One sample**
  1. Individuals are independent.
  2. Sample is sufficiently large.

1. SRS and $n < 10\%$ of the population.
2. Successes and failures each ≥ 10.

Means (t)

- **One Sample** (df $= n - 1$)
  1. Individuals are independent.
  2. Population has a Normal model.

1. SRS and $n < 10\%$ of the population.
2. Histogram is unimodal and symmetric.*

- **Matched pairs** (df $= n - 1$)
  1. Data are matched.
  2. Individuals are independent.
  3. Population of differences is Normal.

1. (Think about the design.)
2. SRS and $n < 10\%$ OR random allocation.
3. Histogram of differences is unimodal and symmetric.*

- **Two independent samples** (df from technology)
  1. Groups are independent.
  2. Data in each group are independent.
  3. Both populations are Normal.

1. (Think about the design.)
2. SRSs and $n < 10\%$ OR random allocation.
3. Both histograms are unimodal and symmetric.*

Distributions/Association (χ^2)

- **Goodness of fit** (df $=$ # of cells $- 1$; one variable, one sample compared with population model)
  1. Data are counts.
  2. Data in sample are independent.
  3. Sample is sufficiently large.

1. (Are they?)
2. SRS and $n < 10\%$ of the population.
3. All expected counts ≥ 5.

- **Homogeneity** [df $= (r - 1)(c - 1)$; many groups compared on one variable]
  1. Data are counts.
  2. Data in groups are independent.
  3. Groups are sufficiently large.

1. (Are they?)
2. SRSs and $n < 10\%$ OR random allocation.
3. All expected counts ≥ 5.

- **Independence** [df $= (r - 1)(c - 1)$; sample from one population classified on two variables]
  1. Data are counts.
  2. Data are independent.
  3. Sample is sufficiently large.

1. (Are they?)
2. SRSs and $n < 10\%$ of the population.
3. All expected counts ≥ 5.

Regression with k predictors (t, df $= n - k - 1$)

- **Association** of each quantitative predictor with the response variable
  1. Form of relationship is linear.

  2. Errors are independent.

  3. Variability of errors is constant.

  4. Errors follow a Normal model.

1. Scatterplots of y against each x are straight enough. Scatterplot of residuals against predicted values shows no special structure.
2. No apparent pattern in plot of residuals against predicted values.
3. Plot of residuals against predicted values has constant spread, doesn't "thicken."
4. Histogram of residuals is approximately unimodal and symmetric, or Normal probability plot is reasonably straight.*

Analysis of Variance (F, df dependent on number of factors and number of levels in each)

- **Equality** of the mean response across levels of categorical predictors
  1. Additive Model (if there are 2 factors with no interaction term).
  2. Independent errors.
  3. Equal variance across treatment levels.

  4. Errors follow a Normal model.

1. Interaction plot shows parallel lines (otherwise include an interaction term if possible).
2. Randomized experiment or other suitable randomization.
3. Plot of residuals against predicted values has constant spread. Boxplots (partial boxplots for 2 factors) show similar spreads.
4. Histogram of residuals is unimodal and symmetric, or Normal probability plot is reasonably straight.

*Less critical as n increases

Quick Guide to Inference

Plan			Do				Report
Inference about?	One group or two?	Procedure	Model	Parameter	Estimate	SE	Chapter
Proportions	One sample	1-Proportion z-Interval	z	p	$\hat{p}$	$\sqrt{\dfrac{\hat{p}\hat{q}}{n}}$	10
		1-Proportion z-Test				$\sqrt{\dfrac{p_0 q_0}{n}}$	12
Means	One sample	t-Interval t-Test	t $\mathrm{df} = n - 1$	μ	$\bar{y}$	$\dfrac{s}{\sqrt{n}}$	12
	Two independent groups	2-Sample t-Test 2-Sample t-Interval	t df from technology	$\mu_1 - \mu_2$	$\bar{y}_1 - \bar{y}_2$	$\sqrt{\dfrac{s_1^2}{n_1} + \dfrac{s_2^2}{n_2}}$	13
	Matched pairs	Paired t-Test Paired t-Interval	t $\mathrm{df} = n - 1$	μ_d	$\bar{d}$	$\dfrac{s_d}{\sqrt{n}}$	14
Distributions (one categorical variable)	One Sample	Goodness-of-Fit	χ^2 $\mathrm{df} = cells - 1$				
	Many independent groups	Homogeneity χ^2 Test	χ^2 $\mathrm{df} = (r-1)(c-1)$			$\displaystyle\sum \dfrac{(Obs - Exp)^2}{Exp}$	15
Independence (two categorical variables)	One sample	Independence χ^2 Test					
Association (two quantitative variables)	One sample	Linear Regression t-Test or Confidence Interval for β	t $\mathrm{df} = n - 2$	β_1	b_1	$\dfrac{s_e}{s_x \sqrt{n-1}}$ (compute with technology)	16
		*Confidence Interval for μ_ν		μ_ν	$\hat{y}_\nu$	$\sqrt{SE^2(b_1) \cdot (x_\nu - \bar{x})^2 + \dfrac{s_e^2}{n}}$	
		*Prediction Interval for y_ν		y_ν	$\hat{y}_\nu$	$\sqrt{SE^2(b_1) \cdot (x_\nu - \bar{x})^2 + \dfrac{s_e^2}{n} + s_e^2}$	
Association (one quantitative and two or more categorical variables)	One sample	Multiple Regression t-test or Confidence interval for each β_j	t $df = n - (k+1)$	β_j	b_j	(from technology)	18, 19
		F test for regression model	F $df = k$ and $n - (k+1)$			MST/MSE	18, 19
Association (one quantitative and two or more categorical variables)	Two or more	ANOVA	F $df = k - 1$ and $N - k$			MST/MSE	25

Appendix C Photo Acknowledgments

Meet the Authors

v: (Norean R. Sharpe): Courtesy of Robert A. Mangione/ St. John's University; (Richard D. De Veaux): Courtesy of Richard D. De Veaux; (Paul F. Velleman): Photo by Susan Michlovitz; **vi:** Courtesy of Eric M. Eisenstein

Chapter 1

1: Stefano Ember/Shutterstock; **9:** (top) Margo Harrison/ Shutterstock; (bottom): Pearson Education, Inc.; **16:** Lightpoet/Fotolia

Chapter 2

21: Dalia Research; **22:** Dalia Research; **25:** (top) 4kclips/ Shutterstock; (top middle): Rawpixel.com/Shutterstock; (middle, bottom middle): Maksim Toome/Shutterstock; (bottom): Axyse/Shutterstock; **35:** 1000 Words/ Shutterstock; **46:** Feng Yu/Shutterstock

Chapter 3

56: David Parker/Alamy Stock Photo; **69:** Lindasj22/ Shutterstock; **71:** Pressmaster/Shutterstock; **73:** Africa Studio/Fotolia; **83:** Ithaca Times; **90:** Artazum/Shutterstock

Chapter 4

105: Plattform/Getty Images; **109:** Library of Congress Prints and Photographs Division [LC USZ62 61365]; **111:** Hurst Photo/Shutterstock; **115:** Crystal Kirk/ Shutterstock; **119:** Arena Creative/Shutterstock; **120:** Pearson Education, Inc.; **121:** Pearson Education, Inc.; **126:** Boryana Manzurova/Shutterstock; **133** (left): Pics721/Shutterstock; (right): RSnapshotPhotos/ Shutterstock; **136:** Ufulum/Shutterstock; **142:** Michael Shake/Fotolia; **155:** Daniel Wallace/Tampa Bay Times/ ZUMA Press Inc./Alamy Stock Photo

Chapter 5

157: Comstock Images/Stockbyte/Getty Images; **160:** Interfoto/Alamy Stock Photo; **161** (left): Rex Argent/ Alamy Stock Photo; (right): PhotoEdit; **166:** AvigoPhotos/ Fotolia; **172:** Artazum/Shutterstock; **173:** Kim Steele/ Photodisc/Getty Images; **180:** Yummy pic/Shutterstock

Chapter 6

190: Maksym Topchii/123RF; **195:** Marcin Balcerzak/ Shutterstock; **202:** Pearson Education, Inc.; **205:** Cathy Yeulet/123RF; **212:** Elena Elisseeva/Shutterstock

Chapter 7

220: Paul Hakimata/Alamy Stock Photo; **227:** David Buffington/Blend Images/Getty Images; **232:** Cathy Yeulet/123RF; **244:** Scanrail/iStock/Getty Images

Chapter 8

252: CSU Archives/Everett Collection/Alamy Stock Photo; **256:** Michael Lamotte/Cole Group/Photodisc/ Getty Images; **262:** Digital Vision/Getty Images; **263:** Tatiana Popova/Shutterstock; **269:** Creators Syndicate; **273:** Goodluz/Shutterstock

Chapter 9

280: Dean Bertoncelj/Shutterstock; **289:** Victorburnside/ iStock/Getty Images; **295:** Dmitriy K/Fotolia; **302:** Aleksey Stemmer/Fotolia

Chapter 10

310: Oleksiy Mark/Shutterstock; **315:** Galina Barskaya/ Shutterstock; **322:** Pearson Education, Inc.; **323:** Nicolas Maeterlinck/ZUMA Press/Newscom; **327:** Peter Alvey/ Alamy Stock Photo; **343:** RsnapshotPhotos/Shutterstock

Chapter 11

344: Anton_Ivanov/Shutterstock; **347:** Photo12/Elk Opid/Alamy Stock Photo; **352:** International Statistical Institute; **359:** Sapsiwai/Shutterstock; **366:** Planet Observer/UIG/Universal Images Group North America LLC/Alamy Stock Photo; **371:** Pastorscott/E+/Getty Images

Chapter 12

381: Avatar_023/Shutterstock; **388:** © 2013 Randall Munroe. Reprinted with permission. All rights reserved; **391:** Lotus_studio/Shutterstock; **394:** Jim Lopes/ Shutterstock; **398:** Photo Researchers/Science History Images/Alamy Stock Photo; **401:** Tim Sharp/Reuters/ Alamy Stock Photo; **405:** © 2013 Randall Munroe. Reprinted with permission. All rights reserved; **411:** Pastorscott/E+/Getty Images

Chapter 13

419: Niday Picture Library/Alamy Stock Photo; **422:** AlcelVision/Fotolia; **424:** Pearson Education, Inc.; **426:** Pearson Education, Inc.; **430:** Lotus_studio/ Shutterstock; **439:** LM Otero/AP Images

Chapter 14

447: Anton Ivanov/Shutterstock; **449:** Peter Cade/ Photodisc/Getty Images; **453:** Beth Anderson/Pearson Education, Inc.; **454:** Jupiterimages/Stockbyte/Getty Images; **457:** larry1235/Shutterstock; **458:** Lenaer/ Shutterstock; **460:** Monkey Business Images/iStock/Getty Images; **465:** Ariel Skelley/DigitalVision/Getty Images; **476:** Eric Vega/E+/Getty Images

Chapter 15
493: Philip Sayer/Alamy Stock Photo; **498:** Tischenko Irina/Shutterstock; **508:** Minerva Studio/Fotolia; **518:** Jakub Jirsák/Fotolia; **530:** WavebreakmediaMicro/Fotolia

Chapter 16
531: Levente Imre Takacs/Shutterstock; **538:** Gurineb/iStock/Getty Images; **547:** Peter Teller/Photodisc/Getty Images; **551** (top): Joe Gough/Shutterstock; (bottom): Pearson Education, Inc.

Chapter 17
565: Vaclav Volrab/123RF; **571** (top): Heather A. Craig/Shutterstock; (bottom): Romantic Jewels in the Regalia, worn in the royal crowns at the coronation of King George VI (1895–1952) and Queen Elizabeth (1900–2002) on 12th May 1937 (colour litho), English School, (20th century)/Private Collection/Bridgeman Images; **572:** World History Archive/Alamy Stock Photo; **575:** Michael Betts/DigitalVision/Getty Images; **580:** Bryn Lennon/Getty Images; **584:** Pete Spiro/Shutterstock; **592:** Tentacle/Fotolia

Chapter 18
607: Nycshooter/E+/Getty Images; **611:** Monkey Business/Fotolia; **617:** Rob Marmion/Shutterstock; **626:** Yamini Chao/DigitalVision/GettyImages; **628:** Brian A Jackson/Shutterstock; **636:** Djtaylor/Fotolia

Chapter 19
648: Rafael Ben Ari/Alamy Stock Photo; **649:** Zanariah Salam/Shutterstock; **650:** Minoru Kuriyama/EyeEm/Getty Images; **655:** Joao Virissimo/Shutterstock; **659:** Andrew Fox/Alamy Stock Photo; **667:** Deatonphotos/Fotolia; **676:** Scott Markewitz/Photographer's Choice RF/Getty Images; **685:** Anke van Wyk/Shutterstock

Chapter 20
697: Alex Segre/Shutterstock; **706:** Dambuster/Fotolia; **713:** Mariusz Prusaczyk/123RF; **723:** Alan Novelli/Alamy Stock Photo; **727:** Trong Nguyen/Shutterstock; **731:** Petrovich9/iStock/Getty Images; **745:** Stephan Morrosch/Fotolia

Chapter 21
746: Robert Carner/123RF; **748:** ProStockStudio/Shutterstock; **769:** Cemark/Shutterstock

Subject Index

Note: Page numbers in **boldface** indicate chapter-level topics; page numbers followed by n indicate footnotes.

Assumptions for Inference	And the Conditions That Support or Override Them

Proportions (z)

- **One sample**
  1. Individuals are independent.
  2. Sample is sufficiently large.

1. SRS and $n < 10\%$ of the population.
2. Successes and failures each ≥ 10.

Means (t)

- **One Sample** (df = $n - 1$)
  1. Individuals are independent.
  2. Population has a Normal model.

1. SRS and $n < 10\%$ of the population.
2. Histogram is unimodal and symmetric.*

- **Matched pairs** (df = $n - 1$)
  1. Data are matched.
  2. Individuals are independent.
  3. Population of differences is Normal.

1. (Think about the design.)
2. SRS and $n < 10\%$ OR random allocation.
3. Histogram of differences is unimodal and symmetric.*

- **Two independent samples** (df from technology)
  1. Groups are independent.
  2. Data in each group are independent.
  3. Both populations are Normal.

1. (Think about the design.)
2. SRSs and $n < 10\%$ OR random allocation.
3. Both histograms are unimodal and symmetric.*

Distributions/Association (χ^2)

- **Goodness of fit** (df = # of cells $- 1$; one variable, one sample compared with population model)
  1. Data are counts.
  2. Data in sample are independent.
  3. Sample is sufficiently large.

1. (Are they?)
2. SRS and $n < 10\%$ of the population.
3. All expected counts ≥ 5.

- **Homogeneity** [df = $(r - 1)(c - 1)$; many groups compared on one variable]
  1. Data are counts.
  2. Data in groups are independent.
  3. Groups are sufficiently large.

1. (Are they?)
2. SRSs and $n < 10\%$ OR random allocation.
3. All expected counts ≥ 5.

- **Independence** [df = $(r - 1)(c - 1)$; sample from one population classified on two variables]
  1. Data are counts.
  2. Data are independent.
  3. Sample is sufficiently large.

1. (Are they?)
2. SRSs and $n < 10\%$ of the population.
3. All expected counts ≥ 5.

Regression with k predictors (t, df = $n - k - 1$)

- **Association** of each quantitative predictor with the response variable
  1. Form of relationship is linear.

  2. Errors are independent.

  3. Variability of errors is constant.

  4. Errors follow a Normal model.

1. Scatterplots of y against each x are straight enough. Scatterplot of residuals against predicted values shows no special structure.
2. No apparent pattern in plot of residuals against predicted values.
3. Plot of residuals against predicted values has constant spread, doesn't "thicken."
4. Histogram of residuals is approximately unimodal and symmetric, or Normal probability plot is reasonably straight.*

Analysis of Variance (F, df dependent on number of factors and number of levels in each)

- **Equality** of the mean response across levels of categorical predictors
  1. Additive Model (if there are 2 factors with no interaction term).
  2. Independent errors.
  3. Equal variance across treatment levels.

  4. Errors follow a Normal model.

1. Interaction plot shows parallel lines (otherwise include an interaction term if possible).
2. Randomized experiment or other suitable randomization.
3. Plot of residuals against predicted values has constant spread. Boxplots (partial boxplots for 2 factors) show similar spreads.
4. Histogram of residuals is unimodal and symmetric, or Normal probability plot is reasonably straight.

*Less critical as n increases